LATIN AMERICAN
POLITICS

Clio Bibliography Series No. 16

Gail A. Schlachter, Editor
Pamela R. Byrne, Executive Editor

LATIN AMERICAN
POLITICS

A Historical Bibliography

ABC-CLIO

Santa Barbara, California
Oxford, England

Library of Congress Cataloging in Publication Data
Main entry under title:

Latin American politics.

(Clio bibliography series; no. 16)
Includes index.
1. Latin America—Politics and government—
1948-   —Periodicals—Indexes. I. ABC-Clio
Information Services. II. Series.
Z1609.P64L39 1984 [F1414.2] 016.98 83-27156
ISBN 0-87436-377-2

10   9   8   7   6   5   4   3   2

ABC-Clio, Inc.
2040 Alameda Padre Serra
P.O. Box 4397
Santa Barbara, CA 93140-4397

Clio Press Ltd.
55 St. Thomas St.
Oxford OX1 1JG, England

Printed and bound in the United States of America

Design and graphics by Lance J. Klass

TABLE OF CONTENTS

PREFACE

Few have expressed the continuing plight, the complexities, and the drama of the Latin American political reality as sensitively and as perceptively as author Gabriel García Márquez who, on accepting the 1982 Nobel Prize for Literature, spoke eloquently of both "the immeasurable violence and pain of our history . . . the result of age-old inequities and untold bitterness," and the region's "quest for independence and originality." Mexican novelist and social critic Carlos Fuentes recently echoed García Márquez's description of the solitude and uniqueness of the Latin American political reality in a commencement address at Harvard University. To Fuentes, the basic issues in understanding Latin American politics revolve around "the traditions of paternalistic surrender to the caudillo, the profound faith in ideas over facts, the strength of elitism and personalism and the weakness of the civil societies—with the struggles between theocracy and political institutions, and between centralism and local government." Clearly, the Cold War view of Latin America as an ideological battleground between East and West is increasingly put into question by a diverse political and cultural tradition that denies the appropriateness of extra-hemispheric political or military intervention in the continuing Latin American struggles between democratic populism and right-wing authoritarianism, elite hegemony and economic pluralism, and Iberian Catholicism's dogma and hierarchy and revolutionary morality.

The continuing enigma of Latin American politics has stimulated a prolific body of international scholarship designed to analyze, it would seem, every facet and detail of the political and social environment of each country, as well as the complex international relations between hemispheric states and with major world powers and international organizations. This immense body of scholarship has now been made accessible in a one-volume bibliography containing abstracts that summarize a decade of journal literature on modern Latin American and Caribbean politics since 1914. Its entries are drawn from the vast history data base of ABC-Clio Information Services, covering more than 2,000 periodicals published in almost 90 countries. In order to create this unique bibliographic volume, the editors reviewed the many thousands of abstracts of

articles published during 1973-1982 and selected every abstract that related to Latin American politics. Thus, this volume offers an in-depth representation of the scholarship published in the world's periodical literature on this subject and far exceeds what one could expect to find through an online search of the data base or even through a manual search of the subject index for the ABC-Clio Information Services' history data base as a whole.

The general organization of the volume is by geographical area, preceded by chapters which include studies dealing with more than one nation. These multi-country studies, when taken together, put Latin American politics into historical perspective by analyzing the international relations, economic and development policies, political ideologies and movements, military development, and efforts at regional or continental integration of the many diverse states that form this complex and dynamic region. The specific country studies provide an in-depth look at the political dynamics of each nation. The variance in the size of the chapters represents not any predisposition on the part of the editors, but rather the amount of scholarship on each topic that was published in the journal literature during the decade covered by this volume.

Latin American Politics utilizes ABC-SPIndex, one of the most advanced and comprehensive indexing systems yet developed. ABC-SPIndex allows fast, analytical, and pinpoint access by linking the key subject terms and historical period of each abstract to form a composite index entry that provides a profile of the journal article. Each set of index terms is then rotated so that the complete profile appears in the index under each of the subject terms. Thus, the number of access points is increased severalfold over conventional hierarchical indexes, and irrelevant material can be eliminated early in the search process. The explanatory note at the beginning of the subject index provides more information about ABC-SPIndex.

Care has been taken to eliminate inconsistencies that might have appeared in the subject index as a result of combining a decade of data base material. The subject profile index thus reflects a highly labor-intensive effort, the product of many hours of editing and reediting, and allows easy access to the material included in this volume. Additional cross-references have been included to ensure fast and accurate searching. The result is a bibliography that is extremely thorough in its treatment of the recent periodical literature on the political history of Latin America and the Caribbean.

This volume represents the collaboration of a skilled and diverse group. Pamela R. Byrne, Executive Editor of the Clio Bibliography Series, directed the project from the initial planning stage through the complex editorial processes of the computer-assisted indexing system and machine-readable data base, to the final design and production of the book. Distinguished Latin American scholar and historian David Bushnell of the University of Florida provided essential direction and advice in the formative stages of this volume. Assistant Editors Lance J. Klass and Susan K. Kinnell selected, organized, and indexed the entries that comprise this volume. At critical points in the editorial process they were assisted by other ABC-Clio Information Services editors and staff, among them Roger W. Davis, Suzanne Robitaille Ontiveros, Jeffery B. Serena, and Kerry McCoy Andrade.

The Data Processing Services Department, under the supervision of Ken Baser, Director, and Deborah Looker, Production Supervisor, ably manipulated the data base to fit the editorial specifications of this bibliography. Most especially, appreciation is extended to the world-wide community of scholars who provided the abstracts that form this volume and without whose work this contribution to Latin American scholarship and research would not have been possible.

1. LATIN AMERICAN POLITICS IN HISTORICAL PERSPECTIVE

General

1. Alschuler, Lawrence R. SATELLIZATION AND STAGNATION IN LATIN AMERICA. *Int. Studies Q. 1976 20(1): 39-82.* Establishes a causal connection between Latin American underdevelopment and the international system, especially its institutions of aid, multinational corporations, and clientele classes, based on data from the 1960's.

2. Alvarez, Orieta and Yero, Elsa. EL MOVIMIENTO ESTUDIANTIL UNIVERSITARIO EN AMERICA LATINA ENTRE 1917-1930 [The university student movements in Latin America, 1917-30]. *Santiago [Cuba] 1982 (45): 33-62.* The movements for university reform that began in 1918 in Latin America, especially in Argentina, Peru, and Mexico, reflected the growth of the petty bourgeoisie and its interests. Although the educational reform went beyond faculty changes and led to the creation of popular universities, it was unable to transform the university itself, and did not represent a qualitative change in the society. Many of the reform leaders ended up occupying bureaucratic posts. In some countries the reform had an anticlerical aspect and ecclesiastical forces opposed it. Although the reform had continental dimensions, it was in Argentina that it had the greatest success. 47 notes.
J. V. Coutinho

3. Antoine, Charles. APRÈS PUEBLA: SATISFACTION MODÉRÉE [After Puebla: moderate satisfaction]. *Études [France] 1979 350: 549-556.* The January-February 1979 meeting of the bishops of the Roman Catholic Church of Latin America in Puebla, Mexico, opened by Pope John Paul II, sought to reconcile the role of the Church as a religious institution with the new theology of liberation which has stressed participation in revolutionary movements in the 1970's.

4. Aviel, JoAnn Fagot. POLITICAL PARTICIPATION OF WOMEN IN LATIN AMERICA. *Western Pol. Q. 1981 34(1): 156-173.* Examines education and economic status as factors contributing to the amount and type of political participation by women in Latin America, 1960-79. Women's role in the family, although typically perceived as an obstacle to participation, also serve as a rationalization for leadership as well as a catalyst for mobilization against the regime. Mainly secondary sources; 2 tables, 82 notes.
J. Powell

5. Barcia Trelles, Camilo. EL COMPLEJO TRANCE DEL MUNDO AMERICANO [The complex situation of the American world]. *Rev. de Política Int. [Spain] 1973 (127): 13-36.* Surveys the international history of Latin America from the 1880's to 1973 emphasizing the various attempts at regional development and integration, and United States involvement, particularly on the issue of the Panama Canal.

6. Basadre, Jorge. LOS CONFLICTOS DE PASIONES Y DE INTERESES IN TACNA Y ARICA (1922-1929) [Conflicts of passions and of interests in Tacna and Arica, 1922-29]. *Hist. y Cultura [Peru] 1974 8: 5-68.* Discusses the struggle between Peru and Chile for possession of the Peruvian provinces occupied by Chile after the War of the Pacific (1879-83). The author focuses on his personal experiences while serving with the Peruvian boundary delegation in the 1920's, the abortive attempts by generals John J. Pershing and William Lassiter to arrange a plebiscite, and the pro-Chilean good offices of Secretary of State Frank B. Kellogg. The common people of Tacna and Arica were the real heroes in this struggle. Based on US and British diplomatic correspondence, materials from Peruvian archives, published documents, and secondary sources; 88 notes, appendixes.
D. P. Werlich

7. Bath, Richard. LATIN AMERICAN CLAIMS ON LIVING RESOURCES OF THE SEA. *Inter-Am. Econ. Affairs 1974 27(4): 59-85.* Examines Latin American claims on marine resources, especially fishing rights controversies.
S

8. Bellini, Giusseppe. *EL SEÑOR PRESIDENTE* Y LA TEMATICA DE LA DICTADURA EN LA NUEVA NOVELA HISPANOAMERICANA [*Lord President* and the theme of dictatorship in the New Hispanic American novel]. *Anuario de Estudios Centroamericanos [Costa Rica] 1977 3: 27-51.* Preoccupation with the dignity of man and his liberty is a common theme of Latin American writers dating back to Garcilaso de la Vega's (1503-36) *El Inca.* It also is evident in the 19th-century writings of José Joaquín Fernández de Lizardi and José Julian Martí. Pablo Neruda and Miguel Angel Asturias (b. 1899) of Guatemala are the best expressions of the theme in the 20th century. The latter in his *El señor Presidente* denounced dictatorship and provided a model for Latin American novelists, such as Alejo Carpentier, Gabriel García Márquez, Demetrio Aguilera Malta, and Augusto Roa Bastos. Primary sources, 82 notes.
H. J. Miller

9. Bender, Lynn-Darrell. POLITICAL FORCES IN LATIN AMERICA. *Problems of Communism 1980 29(5): 65-67.* A review of Brian Loveman and Thomas M. Davies, Jr., ed., *The Politics of Antipolitics: The Military in Latin America* (Lincoln: U. of Nebraska Pr., 1978); Luis E. Aguilar, ed., *Marxism in Latin America* (Philadelphia: Temple U. Pr., 1978); Robert D. Bond, ed., *Contemporary Venezuela and Its Role in International Affairs* (New York: New York U. Pr. for the Council on Foreign Relations, 1977); and John A. Booth and Mitchell A. Seligson, ed., *Political Participation in Latin America,* 2 vol. (New York: Holmes and Meier Publishers, 1978 and 1979). Most Latin American countries—democratic Venezuela being the most notable exception—are ruled by authoritarian regimes in which the masses exert little political influence beyond the local level. The challenge to such regimes now comes less from old-line Marxist parties than from radical nationalists pledged to revolutionary change.
J. M. Lauber

10. Benedetti, Annibale. AMERICA DEL SUD E LATINITÀ [South America and latinism]. *Civitas [Italy] 1973 24(6): 13-22.* "Latin America is going through a very hard trial. The contradictions of development, the tendencies to unity, are fighting against a series of difficulties which can be overcome, in the future, by the explosive strength of the natural and human wealth of the American 'undercontinent.' "
J

11. Benedetti, Mario. EL ESCRITOR LATINOAMERICANO Y LA REVOLUCIÓN POSIBLE [The Latin American author and the possible revolution]. *Rev. Mexicana de Ciencia Pol. [Mexico] 1974 20(77): 17-26.* Discusses the literary and journalistic activities of Latin American activists prior to the realization of their revolutionary careers.

12. Berrocal, Luciano. EL DIALOGO EURO-LATINOAMERICANO: MAS ALLÁ DE UN NEOCOLONIALISMO LARVADO? [The Euro-Latin American dialogue: beyond a concealed neocolonialism?]. *Rev. de Inst. Europeas [Spain] 1980 7(3): 947-967.* While the European Economic Community (EEC) is increasing trade with other developing nations, Latin America is an ever more marginal partner. Latin American integration efforts and mistrust of multinational corporations and of European intentions have been problems.

13. Biggs, Gonzalo. EXPLOTACIÓN MINERA DE LOS OCEANOS: IMPACTO SOBRE AMÉRICA LATINA Y URGENCIA DE UNA POLÍTICA REGIONAL [Mineral exploitation of the oceans: impact on Latin America and the urgency of a regional policy]. *Foro Int. [Mexico] 1976 16(3): 287-312.* Speculates on the effect of the exploitation of mineral resources in the oceans of Latin American countries; discusses the UN's initiatives to regulate exploitation and US actions in fostering exploitation to the detriment of developing nations. Concludes by suggesting that Latin America organize to meet "a new era in its economic development." Primary and secondary sources; 8 tables, 63 notes.
D. A. Franz

14. Bonfil Batalla, Guillermo. LA NUEVA PRESENCIA POLÍTICA DE LOS INDIOS: UN RETO A LA CREATIVIDAD LATINOAMERICANA [The new political presence of the Indians: a challenge to Latin American creativity]. *Anuario Indigenista [Mexico] 1980 40: 165-191.* Recent Latin American Indian political thought has centered on rejection of Western culture, Pan-Indianism, the rewriting of history from an Indian perspective, recognition of the worth of Indian culture, and criticism of colonial domination and its components—capitalism, imperialism, and racism. There is an obvious need for organized Indian political projects to carry on the struggle for reforms demanded by Indians in four major areas: land reform, recognition of Indian linguistic and cultural rights, political and legal equality, and an end to repression and violence. Based on documents produced by Latin American and other international Indian political organizations and works of Indian political writers and intellectuals; 6 notes.   G.-A. Patzwald

15. Bravo Lira, Bernardino. ETAPAS HISTÓRICAS DEL ESTADO CONSTITUCIONAL EN LOS PAÍSES DE HABLA CASTELLANA Y PORTUGUESA (1811-1980) [Historical stages of the constitutional state in Spanish- and Portuguese-speaking countries, 1811-1980]. *Rev. de Estudios Histórico-Jurídicos [Chile] 1980 5: 35-84.* Over 200 constitutions were sanctioned during the period 1811-1980 in the 21 countries encompassed by this study, but the examples of consolidated constitutional states is much smaller (not quite half a dozen), mostly due to practical difficulties in maintaining a separation of powers. The number of parliament closings shows that only a few constitutions were respected for 50 years or longer, as exemplified by Brazil, Chile, and Argentina, none of which is still a constitutional state.

16. Britton, John A. CARLETON BEALS ON THE AMBIGUITIES OF REVOLUTIONARY CHANGE IN MEXICO AND PERU. *West Georgia Coll. Studies in the Social Sci. 1978 17: 89-98.* Reviews the interwar journalism of Carleton Beals, an avowed anti-imperialist and supporter of revolutionary movements, particularly his accounts of the negative effects of revolutionary change in Mexico and Peru.

17. Brunet, Yves. URBANISATION CIRCUM-CARAÏBÉENNE: ANTÉCÉDENT HISTORIQUE ET TENDANCES ACTUELLES [Circum-Caribbean urbanization: historical background and present trends]. *Cahiers de Géographie du Québec [Canada] 1979 23(60): 399-417.* An analysis of urbanization in Central America, the Antilles, Venezuela, and Colombia. Comments on changes in urban structures through time and space, as related to various factors, including number of cities, political or historical conditions, the impact of international function, and the influence of the physical environment.

18. Burton, Julianne. THE CAMERA AS "GUN": TWO DECADES OF CULTURE AND RESISTANCE IN LATIN AMERICA. *Latin Am. Perspectives 1978 5(1): 49-76.* Examines the militant film movement in Latin America, beginning with Brazil's Cinema Novo movement in the late 1950's.

19. Buşe, Constantin and Vianu, Alexandru. DIN ISTORIA RELAŢIILOR DINTRE S.U.A. ŞI AMERICA LATINĂ [The history of US-Latin American relations]. *Analele U. Bucureşti: Istorie [Rumania] 1977 26: 57-71.* Traces the rapid expansion of US commercial involvement in Latin America and especially political involvement in the Caribbean from the late 19th century until the world economic crisis of 1929, noting the emergence of anti-imperialist policies in Latin American states.

20. Calamai, Marco. LA SITUAZIONE DELL'AMERICA LATINA [The situation of Latin America]. *Problemi di Ulisse [Italy] 1978 14(86): 35-42.* The terrorism of revolutionary groups in Latin America, both of the Left and Right, has often been matched by brutal political repression by area governments, in many cases dominated by the military.

21. Calvo, Roberto. THE CHURCH AND THE DOCTRINE OF NATIONAL SECURITY. *J. of Interamerican Studies and World Affairs 1979 21(1): 69-88.* In the name of national security military governments have risen to power over more than half the Latin American population during the 1960's and 1970's. The tension that developed between the Catholic Church and the military state pervades Latin America. The total security logic of the national security argument has expanded to proscribe almost all groups, even the Church, as potential

threats. The national security regime thus has marginalized the majority of society. The Brazilian bishops have protested this war upon those who do not agree with the authoritarian vision. 16 notes, ref.
T. D. Schoonover

22. Castellanos, Jorge and Martínez, Miguel A. EL DICTADOR HISPANOAMERICANO COMO PERSONAJE LITERARIO [The Hispanic American dictator as literary subject]. *Latin Am. Res. Rev. 1981 16(2): 79-105.* Novels dealing with dictators have been of two types. The traditional *novela de la dictadura,* with its prototype in Mármol's *Amalia,* is primarily sociological and political in orientation and aims to denounce dictatorship. With the publication of novels of Alejo Carpentier, Augusto Roa Bastos, Gabriel García Márquez, and Arturo Uslar Pietri, 1974-76, the *novela de dictatores* emerged. These new works provide a careful study of the personality and psychology of dictators. Based on Latin American novels on dictatorship; 20 notes.
J. K. Pfabe

23. Cerutti-Gulberg, Horacio V. LA MANIFESTACIÓN MAS RECIENTE DEL PENSAMIENTO LATINOAMERICANO [The most recent manifestation of Latin American thought]. *Cuadernos Hispanoamericanos [Spain] 1982 127(379): 61-85.* The philosophy of liberation is the latest manifestation of Latin American thought. The article describes its antecedents, the variety of its manifestations, distinguishing four types, and its problems. Recent work in this field emphasizes methodological, epistemological, and historical problems and a critical examination of its relations with Marxism and with the Third World. 29 notes.
J. V. Coutinho

24. Chalmers, Douglas A. PARTIDOS POLÍTICOS Y SOCIEDAD EN AMÉRICA LATINA [Political parties and society in Latin America]. *Estudios Andinos 1974-75 4(1): 39-83.* The role of political parties in Latin America reveals a sociopolitical structure common to Latin American countries. This structure exhibits four characteristics: 1) social status and alliances are vertically structured, yet diffused; 2) political rank conforms to social status; 3) alliances among elites are fluid but tend toward confrontation; and 4) technical experts play a large role in decisionmaking. Within this sociopolitical framework, political parties represent status groups rather than specific interests. Parties, moreover, fail to represent all groups in the status hierarchy. Political parties do not deal directly with the masses, but act through power brokers. In total decision-making the role of political parties is small. The most important function of political parties in Latin America is to bring new interest groups into the political process. Secondary sources; 29 notes.   J. L. White

25. Chinchilla, Norma Stoltz. MOBILIZING WOMEN: REVOLUTION IN THE REVOLUTION. *Latin Am. Perspectives 1977 4(4): 83-102.* General overview of the possibilities for women's movements within socialist revolutions in Latin America.

26. Corradi, Juan Eugenio. THE POLITICS OF SILENCE: DISCOURSE, TEXT, AND SOCIAL CONFLICT IN SOUTH AMERICA. *Radical Hist. Rev. 1978 (18): 38-57.* Examines culture and politics in the dependent societies of the South American countries in the past two decades.

27. Cueva, Agustín et al. EL ESTADO EN AMÉRICA LATINA (MESA REDONDA) [The state in Latin America (round table)]. *Rev. Mexicana de Ciencias Pol. y Soc. [Mexico] 1975 21(82): 9-48.* A round table on Latin America described it for the most part as capitalistic and governed by the interests of the middle classes.

28. Czajowski, Jacek. PARTIE POLITYCZNE W REALIACH SPOŁECZNO-POLITYCZNYCH AMERYKI ŁACIŃSKIEJ [Political parties in the social and political reality of Latin America]. *Studia Nauk Politycznych [Poland] 1979 (3): 89-109.* Latin American political parties are characterized by personalism, instability of party structures, exclusiveness, and "aggressive intolerance" in relations between parties.   J/S

29. Debuyst, Frédéric. SÉCURITÉ ET DÉVELOPPEMENT EN AMÉRIQUE LATINE: DE L'ALLIANCE POUR LE PROGRÈS À LA "DÉMOCRATIE VIABLE" [Security and development in Latin America: from the Alliance for Progress to viable democracy]. *Cultures*

et Développement [Belgium] 1980 12(3-4): 387-440. Analyzes the political evolution of Latin American countries since 1960, particularly the relation between national security and economic development, depending largely on US initiatives and policies.

30. Dessau, Adalbert. LOS ESTUDIOS LATINOAMERICANOS EN LA REPÚBLICA DEMOCRÁTICA ALEMANA Y LA REVOLUCIÓN CUBANA [Latin American studies in the German Democratic Republic and the Cuban revolution]. *Casa de las Américas [Cuba] 1979 19(112): 69-72.* Interest in Latin American studies in East Germany dates back to Alexander von Humboldt (1769-1859). Since the 1950's, there has been a Latin American studies revival as is evidenced at the universities of Karl Marx, Leipzig, Humboldt, Wilhelm Pieck, and Rostock. The themes of the studies embrace economic, political, social, scientific, and cultural analyses. Leading scholars include Johann-Lorenz Schmidt, Traugott Böhme, and Walter Markov. The most popular study is Cuba and its revolution. H. J. Miller

31. Díaz de Arce, Omar. CONTRADICCIONES INTERIMPERIALISTAS EN AMÉRICA LATINA ENTRE LAS DOS GUERRAS MUNDIALES [Interimperialist contradictions in Latin America between the wars]. *Santiago [Cuba] 1979 (33): 23-86.* Describes the competition and rivalry of Great Britain, Germany, and the United States for the control of Latin America's resources and markets. Britain has been largely replaced by the United States and Germany was only temporarily displaced. The article studies the economic policies of the various powers, the development of their investment structure, and the politico-military system of the regime. 107 notes. J. V. Coutinho

32. Díaz Muller, Luis. EL SISTEMA ECONOMICO LATINOAMERICANO EN LA POLITICA INTERNACIONAL DE PAX FRIA [The Latin American Economic System (SELA) in the international politics of the cold peace]. *Estudios Sociales Centroamericanos [Costa Rica] 1981 10(30): 9-32.* Describes the world system as one of "cold peace," and discusses factors that have impeded progress toward regional integration in Latin America, and finally proposes the Latin American Economic System (SELA) as a mechanism of regional political-economic cooperation capable of moving Latin America toward autonomy. Based on printed primary and secondary sources; 23 notes. T. D. Schoonover

33. Dickson, Thomas. AN ECONOMIC OUTPUT AND IMPACT ANALYSIS OF CIVILIAN AND MILITARY REGIMES IN LATIN SOUTH AMERICA. *Development and Change [Netherlands] 1977 8(3): 325-345.* Preliminary conclusions on a comparison of civilian and military regimes in 10 Latin American countries between 1961 and 1970 indicate that military regimes appear to have been more conservative in fiscal matters than civilian regimes, and civilian regimes appear to have been more developmentally oriented than military ones.

34. Dix, Robert H. NON-URBAN OPPOSITIONS IN LATIN AMERICA. *Inter-Am. Econ. Affairs 1977 31(3): 75-91.* Examines the theory that urban centers have been the principal seats of political opposition to ruling parties in Latin America, 1945-77. The urban center opposition theory should not preclude an examination of regional, radical, historical, and traditional forms of opposition or be allowed to obscure geographical and historical factors affecting opposition. Secondary sources; 30 notes. D. A. Franz

35. Drake, Paul W. POPULISM IN SOUTH AMERICA. *Latin Am. Res. Rev. 1982 17(1): 190-199.* Reviews the following works: Candido Mendes' *Beyond Populism* (1977), Christopher Mitchell's *The Legacy of Populism in Bolivia: From the MNR to Military Rule* (1977), Rafael Quintero L.'s *El mito del populismo en el Ecuador: Análisis de los fundamentos socio-económicos del surgimiento del "velasquismo": 1895-1934* (1980), Richard E. Sharpless's *Gaitán of Colombia: A Political Biography* (1978), and Steve Stein's *Populism in Peru: The Emergence of the Masses and the Politics of Social Control* (1980). As an analytical concept, populism holds promise if it can integrate socioeconomic and structural features and variables. Relating political history to social and economic history will make populism a more effective tool for analysis. Biblio. J. K. Pfabe

36. Duport, Claudie. CATALOGUE DES THÈSES ET MÉMOIRES, SUR L'AMÉRIQUE LATINE SOUTENUES EN FRANCE ENTRE 1975 ET 1978 [Catalog of theses and memoirs on Latin America sustained in France between 1975 and 1978]. *Cahiers des Amériques Latines [France] 1979 19: 5-78.* Works are cataloged under the topical headings general bibliographies, law, history, literature-philology, economic problems, political problems, social problems; and by country. D. R. Stevenson

37. Dzidzienyo, Anani. ACTIVITY AND INACTIVITY IN THE POLITICS OF AFRO-LATIN AMERICA. *Secolas Ann. 1978 9: 48-61.* At the moment, there is little Afro-American political activity in Latin America; yet there seems to be some prospect that there will be more in the future to protest racism in many Latin American countries. Secondary sources; 38 notes. J. A. Lewis

38. Eckstein, Susan. DESPUÉS DE LA REVOLUCIÓN: UNA COMPARACIÓN DE MÉXICO Y BOLIVIA [After the revolution: a comparison between Mexico and Bolivia]. *Estudios Andinos 1974-75 4(1): 5-38.* Compares the long-term effects of the Mexican Revolution of 1910-17 with those of the Bolivian revolutionary movements of 1952 and 1964. Mexico and Bolivia remain widely separated in terms of economic development. The Bolivian economy, based on tin mining, is dependent on foreign markets and US aid. Mexico has nationalized its economy more completely and has more capital investment. Dominant political parties have emerged in both countries. Thus no two postrevolutionary countries develop along identical lines, even when both revolutions take place within the context of capitalism. Secondary sources; 12 notes. J. L. White

39. Eckstein, Susan. HOW ECONOMICALLY CONSEQUENTIAL ARE REVOLUTIONS? A COMPARISON OF MEXICO AND BOLIVIA. *Studies in Comparative Int. Development 1975 10(3): 48-62.* Social revolutions in agrarian Bolivia and in Mexico have produced varying consequences. Bolivia received more American support than any other Latin American country from 1952 to 1964 but did not generate a domestic capitalist class. In Mexico a productive industrial and agricultural economy has appeared. Although neither country is following the development pattern of capitalist countries, their experiences indicate that economic growth depends on how the powers of the state are used; 6 notes. D. Balmuth

40. Edmonds, David C. THE 200-MILES FISHING RIGHTS CONTROVERSY: ECOLOGY OR HIGH TARIFFS? *Inter-Am. Econ. Affairs 1973 26(4): 3-18.* The 200-mile jurisdictional claim in waters off Chile, Ecuador, and Peru "hinges in large part on fears that foreign flag vessels will sweep the coastal regions clean of commercial fish." S

41. Elizondo, J. Rodríguez. EMERGENCIA Y DESARROLLO CONTROLADO DEL REVOLUCIONARISMO PEQUEÑO BURGUÉS EN AMÉRICA LATINA COMO FACTOR DE LA ESTRATEGIA POLÍTICO-MILITAR DE LOS ESTADOS UNIDOS EN LA DÉCADA DEL 60 [The emergence and controlled development of revolutionism by the petit bourgeoisie in Latin America as a factor in the politicomilitary strategy of the United States in the 1960's]. *Lateinamerika [East Germany] 1977 (Spr): 35-47.* Argues that American foreign policy in Latin America involves the use of regional armed forces against the "enemy inside" that is leftist radicals.

42. English, Adrian J. THE CHACO WAR. *Army Q. and Defence J. [Great Britain] 1979 109(3): 350-358.* Discusses the background and campaigns of the Chaco War between Bolivia and Paraguay over the Chaco Boreal, 100,000 square miles of desert and thicket, 1911-38.

43. Epstein, Edward C. UNION ELECTION DATA AS A POLITICAL INDICATOR. *Latin Am. Res. Rev. 1976 11(2): 160-167.* Cites the risks involved in using statistics in the study of Latin America, in this case: trade union electoral statistics as quantitative indicators of social, political, and economic phenomena.

44. Erickson, Kenneth Paul and Peppe, Patrick V. DEPENDENT CAPITALIST DEVELOPMENT, U.S. FOREIGN POLICY, AND REPRESSION OF THE WORKING CLASS IN CHILE AND BRAZIL. *Latin Am. Perspectives 1976 3(1): 19-44.* Dependent capitalist

development in Chile and Brazil has not expanded the industrial labor force in proportion to growth in economic output. Patterns of production stemming from the dependent development supported by US foreign policy have increased income inequality and worker exploitation. In light of increased exploitation, the authors advance a hypothesis for understanding the rise of repressive state regimes.   J. L. Dietz

45. Erickson, Kenneth Paul; Peppe, Patrick V.; and Spalding, Hobart A., Jr. RESEARCH ON THE URBAN WORKING CLASS AND ORGANIZED LABOR IN ARGENTINA, BRAZIL, AND CHILE: WHAT IS LEFT TO BE DONE? *Latin Am. Research Rev. 1974 9(2): 115-142.* Examines the issue in three parts: 1) labor movement, political parties, and ideologies; 2) relations between elites and workers, including populism, socioeconomic development, and labor legislation; and 3) the application of theories and techniques of outside studies and the connections between the world economy and Latin America as they affect the working class, 1960-74.

46. Fernández Jilberto, Alex. AMERICA LATINA: RESTRUCTURACION DEL CAPITALISMO PERIFERICO Y MILITARIZACION DEL SUBDESARROLLO [Latin America: restructuring peripheral capitalism and the militarization of underdevelopment]. *Bol. de Estudios Latinoamericanos y del Caribe [Netherlands] 1981 (30): 21-47.* Notes the growth of capitalism and the increasing tendency toward military dictatorships in many Latin American countries. These dictatorships have been intimately linked with a general process of restructuring the capitalism of this peripheral region to conform to the industrial-capitalist core of North America and western Europe. The authoritarian governments promote the expansion of industries that are subordinate to foreign capitalist interests, and in the process they are creating fascist states. Chile is offered as a specific example. Based principally on secondary sources; 2 tables, 56 notes.   R. L. Woodward, Jr.

47. Figueroa, Teresa Orrego de. YOUTH IN LATIN AMERICA: REALITIES AND EXPECTATIONS. *Américas (Organization of American States) 1974 26(1): S1-S16.* A special supplement on the social, political, and economic role of youth in Latin America.   S

48. Fix-Zamudio, Héctor. EL JUICIO DE AMPARO EN LATINOAMÉRICA [The writ of amparo in Latin America]. *Memoria del Colegio Nac. [Mexico] 1978 8(4): 101-138.* The writ of amparo is a means whereby persons harmed by the action of government may claim redress. The author traces the history of such laws and compares their use in various Latin American countries. Primary and secondary sources; 104 notes.   J. D. Barnard

49. Flora, Cornelia B. WOMEN IN LATIN AMERICA: A FORCE FOR TRADITION OR CHANGE? *Secolas Ann. 1976 7: 68-78.* Tradition has provided Latin American females with power in the home. They will not willingly give up this power for a change unless alternative forms of feminine power seem possible. Secondary sources; 42 notes.
                      J. A. Lewis

50. Francis, Michael J. STUDYING LATIN AMERICAN POLITICS: METHODS OR FADS. *Rev. of Pol. 1980 42(1): 35-55.* Scholarly examination of Latin American politics has been characterized by "faddishness" and the "frequent rediscovery of the same concepts." Latin American scholars have concentrated too much on the study of a particular country or emphasized theoretical approaches. What is needed is a return to basic research. 76 notes.   L. E. Ziewacz

51. Galeano, Eduardo. OPEN VEINS OF LATIN AMERICA: SEVEN YEARS AFTER. *Monthly Rev. 1978 30(7): 12-35.* An introduction to Eduardo Galeano's *Open Veins of Latin America* (Monthly Rev. Pr.), which discusses the impact of imperialism on Latin America during the past seven years.

52. Galeano, Eduardo. OPEN VEINS OF LATIN AMERICA. *Monthly R. 1973 25(4): 28-36.* Considers the past four and a half centuries of social and economic exploitation in Latin America by Western nations.   S

53. Galich, Manuel. MAPA HABLADO DE LA AMÉRICA LATINA EN EL AÑO DEL MONCADA [Political map of Latin America

in the year of Moncada]. *Casa de las Américas [Cuba] 1973 14(79): 9-40.* Gives a political map of Latin America in 1953, stressing the influence and interventions by big business and by the US government in the internal affairs of Latin American nations. Article to be continued.

54. Galich, Manuel. MAPA HABLADO DE LA AMÉRICA LATINA EN LA AÑO DEL MONCADA [Political map of Latin America in the year of Moncada]. *Casa de las Américas [Cuba] 1973 14(80): 4-46.* Continued from a previous article (see preceding abstract). Discusses the Latin American political map in the year 1953, including relations between the Latin American countries and the United States.

55. Gallagher, Mary A. Y. LATIN AMERICA: INTERACTIONS. *Trends in Hist. 1979 1(1): 153-164.* Review essay of recent periodical literature (1977-78) on Latin America from preconquest to the 1970's, focusing on Latin America's "continued need to reach outside itself to obtain essential ingredients of its existence," including recent work on the dependency theory.

56. García Herrera, Alvaro. ALGUNAS CONTROVERSIAS SOBRE LIMITES DE COLOMBIA [Some controversies about the boundaries of Colombia]. *Boletín de Hist. y Antigüedades [Colombia] 1974 61(705): 317-334.* The peaceful settlement of Colombia's frontier dispute with Peru was the subject of negotiations during 1920-22, in which Foreign Minister Laureano García Ortiz provided leadership for the Colombian side. The resulting treaty faced objections both in Peru and from the government of Brazil, but the Brazilian objections were overcome through the good offices of the United States and the negotiation of a Brazil-Colombia border treaty that was signed by García Ortiz as plenipotentiary and finally ratified in 1930. Inaugural address to the Colombian Academy of History.   D. Bushnell

57. Garcia-Amador, F. V. THE LATIN AMERICAN CONTRIBUTION TO THE DEVELOPMENT OF THE LAW OF THE SEA. *Am. J. of Internat. Law 1974 68(1): 33-50.*

58. Germain, Louis. L'IMPORTANCE STRATÉGIQUE DE L'AMÉRIQUE LATINE POUR LES ÉTATS-UNIS [The strategic importance of Latin America for the United States]. *Défense Natl. [France] 1975 31(1): 88-104.* Examines US interest in Latin America from the point of view of security and economics, and discusses its strategic importance.

59. Gibson, Charles. LATIN AMERICA AND THE AMERICAS. Kammen, Michael, ed. *The Past Before Us: Contemporary Historical Writing in the United States* (Ithaca, N.Y.: Cornell U. Pr., 1980): 187-202. There is a long tradition of US historiography on Latin America, beginning with William H. Prescott's studies on the Spanish Conquest of Mexico and Peru. The trend since World War II has been toward social history and away from laws and institutions. The "Berkeley school" began extensive studies on Indians using new techniques of social and economic history. The "forgotten" 17th century is now being examined as a period in its own right and in relation to decline in Spain and Portugal. Slavery continues to draw attention. Politics dominate 19th-and 20th-century historiography, but Latin America as part of the Third World has attracted economic historians, particularly concerning dependency theory. New methodologies of quantitative methods and prosopography (collective biography) are used by younger scholars. The chauvinism of a century ago has been replaced by sympathy and understanding. 30 notes.   S

60. Gilbert, Guy J. SOCIALISM AND DEPENDENCY. *Latin Am. Perspectives 1974 1(1): 107-123.* The main thrust of the criticism of dependency theory has focused on the hypothesis that dependency is a universal phenomenon making any alternative for Latin American development impossible. Neither the Soviet Union nor China penetrate and exploit other socialist countries through the vehicle of ownership of foreign capital, nor have they attempted to maintain weaker countries as suppliers of cheap raw materials. The political elites of the Latin American socialist countries are to varying degrees subservient to the Soviet Union or China, but this is based not on the wealth of these two powers nor on their penetration in the economic and social life of these countries of Latin America. Instead influence is through common ideological and practical considerations and/or party bureaucracy. Thus, in the socialist

sphere we do not find the functional equivalent of the dependence relation found within the capitalist sphere. **A**

61. Gomez, José Maria. POUR UNE APPROCHE CRITIQUE DU POPULISME EN AMÉRIQUE LATINE [A critical approach to populism in Latin America]. *Cultures et Développement. Rev. Int. des Sci. du Développement [Belgium] 1979 11(4): 617-664.* Populism in Latin America since 1930, its characteristics, and various interpretations.

62. Goncarova, T. V. DIE IDEOLOGIE DER "DRITTEN WELT" UND DIE ENTWICKLUNG DES REVOLUTIONÄREN PROZESSES IN LATEINAMERIKA [The ideology of the Third World and the development of the revolutionary process in Latin America]. *Lateinamerika [East Germany] 1977 (Spr): 49-56.* Asserts that in the 1970's the basic concept of developing nations has had a strong impact on the masses in Latin America, especially on the nationalistic youth. 46 notes.

63. Góngora, Mario. CENTENARIO DE SPENGLER [Spengler's centenary]. *Historia [Chile] 1981 16: 335-341.* Oswald Spengler (1880-1936), the controversial German historian and author of the *The Decline of the West,* continues to be studied despite official and academic opposition to some of his theories because of his profound analyses of the style of various civilizations. He was an acute observer of the trend of the times and made some very accurate forecasts about historical developments of the present century. The reading of his works was one of the most profound intellectual experiences of the educated Latin American public of the 1930's and 1940's and continues to be thought-provoking.
J. V. Coutinho

64. González Echevarría, Roberto. THE DICTATORSHIP OF RHETORIC/THE RHETORIC OF DICTATORSHIP: CARPENTIER, GARCÍA MÁRQUEZ, AND ROA BASTOS. *Latin Am. Res. Rev. 1980 15(3): 205-228.* Reviews three 1974 dictator novels: Alejo Carpentier's *El recurso del método,* Gabriel García Márquez's *El otoño del patriarca,* and Augusto Roa Bastos's *Yo el Supremo.* These novels analyze the cancellation of a central authority in society, showing that dictators are not powerful telluric forces, but phantoms created by the real powers in today's world. 27 notes.
J. K. Pfabe

65. González Faus, José I. LA TEOLOGÍA LATINOAMERICANA DE LA LIBERACIÓN [The Latin American theology of liberation]. *Actualidad Bibliográfica de Filosofía y Teología [Spain] 1973 (20): 359-448.* An appraisal of the theological theses characteristic of and recurring in the contemporary South American liberationist ideology of José Porfirio Miranda, *Marx y la Biblia* [Marx and the Bible]; Rubem A. Alves, *Religión ?opio o instrumento de liberación?* [Religion: Opiate or instrument of liberation?]; Hugo Assman, *Opresión-liberación: desafío a los cristianos* [Oppression-liberation: challenge to Christians]; Gustavo Gutiérrez, *Teología de la liberación* [Theology of liberation]; and Paulo Freire, *Pedagogía del oprimido* [Pedagogy of the oppressed]. Other liberationist works (22 in all) are reviewed. Appendix.
J. B. R. (IHE 88968)

66. Gonzalo, Marisol de. RELACIONES ENTRE ESTADOS UNIDOS Y AMÉRICA LATINA A COMIENZOS DE LA PRIMERA GUERRA MUNDIAL: FORMULACIÓN DE UNA POLÍTICA COMERCIAL [Relations between the United States and Latin America at the beginning of World War I: the development of a commercial policy]. *Bol. Hist. [Venezuela] 1978 (47): 181-241.* Discusses factors contributing to the growth of the United States commercial and financial hegemony in Latin America, 1914-15. 108 notes, biblio.
D. A. Franz

67. Goodman, Margaret Ann. THE POLITICAL ROLE OF THE UNIVERSITY IN LATIN AMERICA. *Comparative Politics 1973 5(2): 279-292.* Contrary to the traditional view that Latin American universities suffer from being too political, in truth they are not political enough. Governments control the schools by means of fund allocations and the right to depose university administrative personnel. The schools seldom protest and students rarely riot. The universities are repositories of the bulk of Latin American social and technological expertise, but by not using this knowledge to improve society and to speed up the rate of social change, the universities are defeating their purpose in society. 21 notes.
V. L. Human

68. Gordon, Dennis R. THE QUESTION OF THE PACIFIC: CURRENT PERSPECTIVES ON A LONG-STANDING DISPUTE. *World Affairs 1979 141(4): 321-335.* Discusses the conflict in the 1970's among the South American nations of Peru, Chile, and Bolivia, an outgrowth of the 1879-83 War of the Pacific in which Chile took possession of valuable Peruvian nitrate regions and Bolivia's outlet to the sea; describes diplomatic activity, 1975-76.

69. Graham, Richard. POPULAR CHALLENGES AND ELITE RESPONSES: AN INTRODUCTION. Bernhard, Virginia, ed. *Elites, Masses, and Modernization in Latin America, 1850-1930* (Austin: U. of Texas Pr., 1979): 3-10. Introduces and compares E. Bradford Burns's article in this volume "Cultures in Conflict: The Implication of Modernization in Nineteenth-Century Latin America" and Thomas E. Skidmore's "Workers and Soldiers: Urban Labor Movements and Elite Responses in Twentieth-Century Latin America." Burns interprets 19th-century Latin American culture as a conflict between the modernizing, European-oriented elite and the traditional, racially mixed masses. According to Skidmore the emerging field of labor history in Latin America reveals the historical roots of the present tensions, which are compounded by the secular struggle of army against workers. 6 notes. **S**

70. Grant, Frances. LATIN AMERICA. *Freedom at Issue 1976 (34): 27-29.* Human rights fared poorly in Latin America in 1975, notably in Chile where the military junta has failed to return the country to constitutional status.

71. Grenier, Richard. THE CURIOUS CAREER OF COSTA-GAVRAS. *Commentary 1982 73(4): 61-71.* Discusses the anti-Americanism and pro-Communism of Greek-born French filmmaker Constantin Costa-Gavras since 1964, noting his inability to separate fact from fantasy in dealing with the US role in Latin America.

72. Grieb, Kenneth J. CARIBBEAN DICTATORSHIPS AND REVISIONISM. *Rev. Interamericana [Puerto Rico] 1977 7(3): 524-528.* Dogmatic ideological parties, personal feuds, fragmented political circles, general instability (which tended to inhibit positive social changes and economic growth), and mass popularity characterize Latin American dictatorships of the 20th century. Further study of the evolution of Latin American dictatorships is necessary in order to better comprehend reformist aspects which aimed at economic development and social justice.
G. A. Hewlett

73. Grieb, Kenneth J. HISTORY'S CONTRIBUTION TO THE STUDY OF SOCIAL REVOLUTION IN LATIN AMERICA. *Centennial Rev. 1976 20(4): 378-384.* History plays an important role in the study of social revolution. The assessment of a revolution must be based on its results and is a function of time. Perspective, history's principal contribution, is also essential "during the Revolutionary process, to enable comparison of the movement with its predecessors and the introduction of long-range projection into the assessment and planning of current policies." History allows a better understanding of social revolution by both scholars and revolutionaries, during the initial as well as later phases.
T. L. Powers

74. Griffith, William J. SOME LATIN AMERICAN BIBLIOGRAPHIES. *Latin Am. Res. Rev. 1980 15(1): 256-261.* Reviews the following works: *Latin America and Japan: A Bibliography* (Los Angeles: Latin American Studies Center, California State U., 1975), *Central America: A Bibliography* (Los Angeles: Latin American Studies Center, California State U., 1976), and Sidney David Markman's *Colonial Central America: A Bibliography* (Tempe: Center for Latin American Studies, Arizona State U., 1977). The first two items are not trustworthy guides, but Markman's is a valuable research tool.
J. K. Pfabe

75. Hanson, Mark. ORGANIZATIONAL BUREAUCRACY IN LATIN AMERICA AND THE LEGACY OF SPANISH COLONIALISM. *J. of Inter-American Studies and World Affairs 1974 16(2): 199-219.* Bureaucracy in Latin America often has been incapable of supporting rapid modernization. The organizational and administrative mechanisms of social and institutional governance have been unable to depart from Spanish colonial practices. For example, the administrative model used in Venezuela in the modern era is basically the same as that dictated by the Spanish monarchy in the colonial age. Consequently, to

understand today's organizational model it is necessary to examine the traditional model of administration. This is true not only in Venezuela but in all Spanish-American nations. Based on state documents, primary and secondary sources; biblio.   J. R. Thomas

76. Harrison, John P. MASS, STATUS, AND NATIONAL DEVELOPMENT IN LATIN AMERICAN UNIVERSITIES. *Secolas Ann. 1975 (6): 10-23.* The rapid growth and politicization of the national universities in Latin America during the 20th century has produced graduates who are badly prepared to aid the modernizing private sector. In order to obtain qualified graduates, government and business have created a host of small specialized universities throughout the continent. The elitist education of the colonial period has not disappeared but simply assumed a different form. Primary and secondary sources; 16 notes.
J. Lewis

77. Hayes, Margaret Daly. DER SÜDATLANTIK: INTERESSEN DER GROSSMÄCHTE UND DER ANLIEGER [The South Atlantic: the interests of the superpowers and the adjoining states]. *Europa Archiv [West Germany] 1978 33(18): 589-598.* Since the beginning of the 1960's Argentina, Brazil, and South Africa tried to establish a South Atlantic Ocean alliance to safeguard the vulnerable route around the southern end of Africa, given the growing maritime power of the USSR.

78. Hill, Kim Quaile and Hurley, Patricia A. FREEDOM OF THE PRESS IN LATIN AMERICA: A THIRTY-YEAR SURVEY. *Latin Am. Res. Rev. 1980 15(2): 212-218.* An analysis of indices at five-year intervals from 1945 to 1975 shows that most Latin American nations have experienced declines in press freedom, nine nations have shown stable conditions, and the eleven unstable nations show little likelihood of permanent increase in freedom of the press. Based on surveys taken by Russell Fitzgibbon and Kenneth Johnson; table, 11 notes.
J. K. Pfabe

79. Hough, Jerry F. THE EVOLVING SOVIET DEBATE ON LATIN AMERICA. *Latin Am. Res. Rev. 1981 16(1): 124-143.* By the early 1970's, three major views had emerged among Soviet Latin Americanists. Most widely held was the view that stressed the dependent situation in Latin America and that local Communists should cooperate with the bourgeoisie. The second stance was more prorevolution, seeing little prospect for development under capitalism. The third position argued that Latin American countries were moving toward more advanced states of capitalism and that governments were defending local capitalism from foreign monopolies. This view was more cautious about the prospects of a socialist revolution. 55 notes.   J. K. Pfabe

80. Huizer, Gerritt. ROL VAN VAKBONDEN (VOORAL BOEREN-ORGANISATIES) IN LATIJNS-AMERIKA [The role of trade unions (especially peasant organizations) in Latin America], *Annalen van het Thijmgenootschap [Netherlands] 1974 62(2): 49-59, 135.* Discusses the peasants' need to organize to protect their land from large landowners who, with the support of the military and government, harshly suppress the beginnings of unionization. This leads to greater peasant radicalization and rebellions under strong leadership. They are sometimes successful, though always at great cost of life and usually to the profit of landlords, governments, and multinational organizations. Documentary and secondary sources; biblio.   G. Herritt

81. Huneeus, Carlos. ELECCIONES NO-COMPETITIVAS EN LAS DICTADURAS BUROCRÁTICO-AUTORITARIAS EN AMÉRICA LATINA [Noncompetitive elections in Latin America's bureaucratic-authoritarian dictatorships]. *Rev. Española de Investigaciones Sociológicas [Spain] 1981 (13): 101-138.* Discusses the bureaucratic-authoritarian systems appearing in Latin America, from Brazil in 1964 to Argentina in 1976, to study changes in the relationship between state and society. Examines noncompetitive elections, using Chile's Augusto Pinochet as an example of a dictator who employs them.

82. Hurwitz, Edith F. MEXICO AND THE CARIBBEAN. *Trends in Hist. 1979 1(1): 165-170.* Review essay of recent periodical literature on various areas of Mexican history during the republic and modern periods, and the history of the Caribbean region from the 17th century to the 1970's focusing on sugar planting, slavery and race relations, and foreign relations during World War II.

83. Iqbal, Mehrunnisa. PAKISTAN'S RELATIONS WITH AFRICA AND LATIN AMERICA. *Pakistan Horizon [Pakistan] 1974 27(2): 57-61.* Pakistan shares a common background with Africa; both are developing nations whose aim is economic independence. Pakistan has supported Africa's efforts to end colonialism and racism. Economic cooperation has developed between them. Pakistan's relations with Latin America are friendly but not close. 15 notes.   H. M. Evans

84. James, Ariel. LA UNITED FRUIT COMPANY Y LA PENETRACIÓN IMPERIALISTA EN EL ÁREA DEL CARIBE [The United Fruit Company and imperialism in the Caribbean]. *Santiago [Cuba] 1974 (15): 69-80.* Examines the origins of large-scale banana commerce in the United States in the 1870's; the establishment of the United Fruit Company's monopoly, 1899; its neocolonial domination of Central America; and its exploitation and development of Cuban markets; 8 notes.   P. J. Taylorson

85. Jaquette, Jane S. FEMALE POLITICAL PARTICIPATION IN LATIN AMERICA. Iglitzin, Lynne B. and Ross, Ruth, eds. *Women in the World* (Santa Barbara, Calif.: Clio Books, 1976): 55-74. Women have the vote in all Latin American countries, but registration of eligible women voters is generally lower than that of men. While more women vote in urban areas, the majority of people in all areas and classes believe politics is for men. Economic inequalities and class exploitation concern women more than political issues or sexual inequalities. It is easier for middle- and upper-class women to enter politics because servants are able to take care of their families. Moreover, there is "no stigma attached to a professional career for the woman." Women in politics tend to concentrate on such "feminine" issues as education, health, and social welfare. Elimination of sex role differences could cause women to lose political power since the "mother-role" in Latin American politics is a strong force. Secondary sources; 45 notes.   J. Holzinger

86. Jarpa Gerhard, Sergio. LAS FRONTERAS DE AMÉRICA [Borders in the Americas]. *Rev. de Marina [Chile] 1981 98(1): 92-113.* Follows changes of boundaries in the New World from the Treaty of Tordesillas through independence and the settlement of final borders.

87. Johnson, Allen. ESSAYS AND POLEMICS: LATIN AMERICAN SOCIETY FROM DIVERSE PERSPECTIVES. A REVIEW ARTICLE. *Comparative Studies in Soc. and Hist. [Great Britain] 1980 22(3): 478-484.* Reviews six works on Latin American society, including the role of peasants, women, and work.

88. Johnson, Peter T. ACADEMIC PRESS CENSORSHIP UNDER MILITARY AND CIVILIAN REGIMES: THE ARGENTINE AND BRASILIAN CASES, 1964-1975. *Luso-Brazilian Rev. 1978 15(1): 3-25.* While government efforts to control academic publishing have varied in Argentina and Brazil, 1964-75, publishers in both nations have been forced to exercise self-censorship. The Brazilian Constitution of 1967 institutionalized censorship. New technocratic orientation and the purging of faculty members in universities was reflected in the publishing shift away from contemporary history and the social sciences. The control of creative writing hindered the development of a national literature and contributed to the foreign dominance of domestic book markets. Subjective censorship and government subsidization further encouraged self-censorship. Despite the lack of legal restrictions on Argentinian freedom of the press, a highly unstable political situation has resulted in government pressure, inconsistently and often indirectly applied, but always threatening. Government support for academic research for the publication of the work of national authors has been lacking. Based on legal reference works, newspapers and periodicals, and 75 anonymous interviews; 38 notes.   J. M. Walsh

89. Johnson, Peter T. SPECIALIZED LATIN AMERICAN BIBLIOGRAPHIES. *Latin Am. Res. Rev. 1980 15(1): 241-248.* Reviews the following works: Juan R. Freudenthal and Patricia M. Freudenthal's *Index to Anthologies of Latin American Literature in English Translation* (Boston: G. K. Hall, 1977); Meri Knaster's *Women in Spanish America: An Annotated Bibliography from Pre-Conquest to Contemporary Times* (Boston: G. K. Hall, 1977); and John V. Lombardi, German Carrera Damas, Roberta E. Adams, et al's *Venezuelan History: A Comprehensive Working Bibliography* (Boston: G. K. Hall, 1977). Freudenthal and Knaster are important contributions, but *Venezuelan History* presents some problems due to its organization. 12 notes.
J. K. Pfabe

90. Jordan, David C. PERON'S RETURN, ALLENDE'S FALL AND COMMUNISM IN LATIN AMERICA. *Orbis 1973 17(3): 1025-1052.* Discusses Latin American politics concerning Juan Peron and Argentina, Salvador Allende and Chile, and communism in the 1970's. S

91. Jorge, Antonio. IDEOLOGIA, MODERNIZACIÓN Y DESARROLLO [Ideology, modernization, and development]. *Estudios Sociales Centroamericanos [Costa Rica] 1980 9(26): 187-194.* In order to explore some ideas and relationships about whether a "Latin American way" exists for social transformation, any elite or social group looking to achieve social, economic, or political objectives must pass through certain levels of thought and action which are 1) philosophical, anthropological, and cultural considerations; 2) world view; 3) ideology; 4) motivations, attitudes, and incentives; 5) institutions, organizations, and structure; and 6) praxeology. T. D. Schoonover

92. Kahl, Joseph A. LATIN AMERICANS TURN AGAIN. *Worldview 1974 17(3): 36-42.* Pablo Gonzáles Casanova of Mexico and Fernando Henrique Cardoso of Brazil are developing a sociology to study industrialization and imperialism in Latin America since the 1930's.

93. Kaplan, Stephen S. THE DISTRIBUTION OF AID TO LATIN AMERICA: A CROSS-NATIONAL AGGREGATE DATA AND TIME SERIES ANALYSIS. *J. of Developing Areas 1975 10(1): 37-60.* An assessment of the criteria in giving economic and military aid to 20 Latin American nations, 1946-73, for the purpose of explaining its unequal distribution. The high degree of continuity in patterns of aid distribution results from distribution of aid as a function of relative population size, basically a nonchanging factor. Aid was related to the recipient nation's balance of payments position (more important during the Kennedy administration than before), the absolute value of military expenditures, and to trade with the United States—all of which are functions of population size. Of less significance for distribution of aid were infant mortality rates and the political structure of the regime. Little or no relationship was found between aid and per capita GNP, energy consumption per capita, US direct investment, change in US direct investment, military expenditure as a percentage of government revenue or military expenditure as a percentage of GNP. F ratios, correlations, and regression formulas were used to develop the analysis. 9 tables, 47 notes. O. W. Eads, Jr.

94. Kirichenko, V. JAPAN-LATIN AMERICA: ZAIBATSU ON THE OFFENSIVE. *Far Eastern Affairs [USSR] 1980 (2): 72-80.* Rapid growth combined with the lack of domestic raw materials and difficulties in selling of industrial products impelled Japan into Latin America, formerly a US preserve. Imperialist industrialization is aimed at preserving Latin America as a dependent part of the world capitalist system.

95. Knaster, Meri. WOMEN IN LATIN AMERICA: THE STATE OF RESEARCH, 1975. *Latin Am. Res. Rev. 1976 11(1): 3-74.* Lists and assesses the various research activities, with an emphasis on publications after 1970, in the field of women in Latin America and includes a substantial bibliography of women in Latin America.

96. Knudsen, Jerry W. WHATEVER BECAME OF "THE PURSUIT OF HAPPINESS"? THE U.S. PRESS AND SOCIAL REVOLUTION IN LATIN AMERICA. *Gazette [Netherlands] 1974 20(4): 201-214.* The hostility of the American press toward Latin American revolutions—Mexico in 1910, Cuba in 1959, and Chile 1970-73—stems from the belief in the inseparability of representative democracy from private ownership, a belief which does not correspond to Latin ideals of social change.

97. König, Hans Joachim. LIBERACION NACIONAL Y CAMBIO SOCIAL [National liberation and social change]. *Bol. Hist. [Venezuela] 1977 (45): 285-314.* The War of Venezuelan Independence in the 19th century was only able to break the link with Spain, and colonial society was not fundamentally changed as it was dominated by the white élite born in America. Latin America gained its political independence but not economic independence and it is now controlled by the industrial powers. Although there were several attempts in different countries to rearrange the old social order, and redistribute property and political power only three revolutions were successful in this connection: Mexico in 1910,

Bolivia in 1952 and Cuba in 1959. An analysis of these cases shows the importance of agrarian reform as a basis for further developments. 65 notes. L. Makin

98. Korableva, L. Iu. CHAKSKAIA VOINA V OSVESHCHENII AMERIKANSKIKH ISTORIKOV [The Chaco War as seen by American historians]. *Amerikanskii Ezhegodnik [USSR] 1980: 196-215.* A historiographical article. US historiographic interest in the Bolivian-Paraguayan war for the Chaco region during 1932-35 and for Latin American diplomatic history, in general, began in the 1960's and early 1970's. These studies reflect a bourgeois bias affecting correct evaluation of causative factors, military affairs, and political events. They disclaim any link between the State Department's Latin American policy and monopolistic interests of US oil companies and ascribe US participation in the resolution of the Chaco War to impartial pacifist and humanitarian motives. 102 notes. N. Frenkley

99. Lamadrid, Sergio Araoz de. GUERRILLA ENVIRONMENT. *Marine Corps Gazette 1974 58(10): 25-30.* "The 'indirect strategy' espoused by Mao Tse-tung continues to be employed by subversive forces in Latin America." S

100. Lanning, Eldon. A TYPOLOGY OF LATIN AMERICAN POLITICAL SYSTEMS. *Comparative Pol. 1974 6(3): 367-394.*

101. Laport, Hugo Murialdo. EL CONCEPTO MARXISTA DE IDEOLOGÍA Y SU APLICACIÓN AL FENÓMENO CINEMATOGRÁFICO LATINOAMERICANO [The Marxist conception of ideology and its application in Latin American films]. *Rev. Mexicana de Ciencia Pol. [Mexico] 1975 21(79): 27-35.* Examines the relationship between sociopolitical processes and the cultural expression of those processes in the cinema of Cuba, Brazil, and Allende's Chile, especially the Marxist concept of the ideological nature of art from the 19th to the 20th century.

102. Leffall, Dolores C. THE BLACK EXPERIENCE IN AFRICA, LATIN AMERICA, AND THE CARIBBEAN: A SELECTED BIBLIOGRAPHY OF ARTICLES APPEARING IN PERIODICALS 1973-1974. *J. of Negro Hist. 1974 59(4): 352-395.*

103. LeoGrande, William M. CUBA AND NICARAGUA: FROM THE SOMOZAS TO THE SANDINISTAS. *Caribbean Rev. 1980 9(1): 11-14.* Analyzes Nicaragua's relations with Cuba, particularly since 1959, indicating that Cuba's role in the Nicaraguan revolution was minor.

104. Lerner, Natan. NATIONALISM AND MINORITIES IN LATIN AMERICA. *Patterns of Prejudice [Great Britain] 1977 11(1): 17-22.* Examines the attitudes of Latin American nationalist movements toward religious, ethnic, and cultural minorities and discusses their impact upon the development of nationalism since the 19th century.

105. Lernoux, Penny. THE LATIN AMERICAN CHURCH. *Latin Am. Res. Rev. 1980 15(2): 201-211.* Being in a state of political flux, the Roman Catholic Church in Latin America deserves close watching. Need exists for empirical data on *comunidades de base,* the use of popular religiosity as an educative tool, and social commitment of priests and nuns. One useful source is Catholic periodicals, which reveal a growing agreement on the need to defend human rights and on commitment to the poor. Based on Catholic periodicals; 5 notes, biblio., appendix. J. K. Pfabe

106. Levine, Daniel H. AUTHORITY IN CHURCH AND SOCIETY: LATIN AMERICAN MODELS. *Comparative Studies in Soc. and Hist. [Great Britain] 1978 20(4): 517-544.* Examines the development of central religious concepts, their changing expression in organizational structures and patterns of behavior, and the evolution of the Church's role in Latin American society and politics, 1940's-70's.

107. Levine, Daniel H. REVIEW ESSAY: RELIGION AND POLITICS, RECENT WORKS. *J. of Inter-Am. Studies and World Affairs 1974 16(4): 497-507.* A number of recent books on the relationship of politics and religion in Latin America conclude that individual Christians cannot avoid involvement in the political activities of their countries. Consequently, many difficult questions have arisen such as the relation-

ship of Catholic lay groups to the institutionalized church and the relation of Catholics to Marxism. Further, Catholics are confronted with the dilemma of whether to use force and violence to attain political objectives. Based on the five books reviewed and secondary works; 11 notes, biblio.

J. R. Thomas

108. Levine, Daniel Henry. RELIGION AND POLITICS, POLITICS AND RELIGION: AN INTRODUCTION. *J. of Interamerican Studies and World Affairs 1979 21(1): 5-29.* While the Catholic Church has historically reinforced the existing social relationships in Latin America, this is not a necessary relationship. Still religion and politics are analytically and empirically inseparable, hence Catholicism can be harnessed for a good social and political order and since the 1960's this has occurred. Both politics and religion are concerned with the values, organizing principles, and symbols of the entire society, thus not surprisingly both are "problems" for each other. 16 notes, ref.

T. D. Schoonover

109. Levy, Daniel. STUDENT POLITICS IN CONTEMPORARY LATIN AMERICA. *Can. J. of Pol. Sci. [Canada] 1981 14(2): 353-376.* Examines and compares Latin American student political activity in the 1970's in four categories of political regimes: traditional, oligarchical, reconciliation, and modern authoritarian. The type of political regime and the distinction between public and private universities are major determinants of student activism. The growth of authoritarian regimes and of private sectors in higher education largely account for the decline of highly politicized student activity in the 1970's. Table, 44 notes.

K. E. Miller

110. Maidanik, K. SOTSIAL'NO-POLITICHESKIĬ KRIZIS V LATINSKOĬ AMERIKE I PERSPEKTIVY EGO PREODOLENIÎA [The sociopolitical crisis in Latin America and future prospects for overcoming it]. *Mirovaia Ekonomika i Mezhdunarodnye Otnosheniia [USSR] 1974 (7): 50-62.* Analyzes the reasons for the sociopolitical crisis in Latin America by discussing the experience of different countries and proposing revolutionary solutions to their problems.

111. Martins, Antonio J. ÉTAT ET SOCIÉTÉ EN AMÉRIQUE LATINE: ÉLÉMENTS DE BIBLIOGRAPHIE [State and society in Latin America: elements of a bibliography]. *Rev. de l'Inst. de Sociologie [Belgium] 1981 (1-2): 397-426.* A bibliography of the evolution of the relations between the state and society in Latin America, classified according to populist relations, authoritative relations, and becoming a state and state bureaucracy. Part of a special issue on state and society in Belgium.

112. Martins, Luciano. LES CAPITAUX ÉTRANGERS EN AMÉRIQUE LATINE: LES RAISONS DES NOUVELLES RÉGLES DU JEU [Foreign capital in Latin America: reasons for the new rules of the game]. *Problèmes d'Amérique Latine [France] 1981 (61): 8-17.* An analysis of the new attitude of Latin American countries toward foreign investments, which over the last twenty years have tended to permit Latin American countries greater power in negotiations while maintaining their structural dependency.

113. Martz, Mary Jeanne Reid. STUDYING LATIN AMERICAN POLITICAL PARTIES: DIMENSIONS PAST AND PRESENT. *J. of Latin Am. Studies [Great Britain] 1980 12(1): 139-167.* Political scientists' interest in Latin America dates largely from World War II. Geographical studies and comparative political studies made noted strides, but early concepts such as a dichotomy between Western and non-Western influences have given way to concepts of political culture, political development, and, more recently, to dependency and corporatism and noncorporatism. The study of political parties, although of some interest in the 1960's and early 1970's, has never been firmly anchored. More field research on actual party activities is needed to avoid the narrowness of exclusivity of previous studies. Secondary sources; 96 notes.

M. A. Burkholder

114. M'Bow, Amadou-Mahtar. LATIN AMERICA AND THE CARIBBEAN: CULTURAL DIMENSION OF THE DEVELOPMENT. *Cultures [France] 1978 5(3): 11-18.* Speculates on the preservation of linguistic, social, cultural, and moral traditions in Latin America and the West Indies in the face of modern technological, educational, and political development, 1960's-70's.,

115. McGrath, Marcos G. ARIEL OR CALIBAN? *Foreign Affairs 1973 52(1): 75-95.* Latin America must correct existing injustice, but is hindered by inbuilt colonial injustice in which, from its poverty, it pays tribute to and supports the economy of the richer nations to the north. Without equal rights for all nations, there can be no true progress for the peoples of the world.

R. Riles

116. McGreevey, William Paul. RECENT MATERIALS AND OPPORTUNITIES FOR QUANTITATIVE RESEARCH IN LATIN AMERICAN HISTORY: NINETEENTH AND TWENTIETH CENTURIES. *Latin Am. Research Rev. 1974 9(2): 73-82.* Examines works published 1960-74 on 19th- and 20th-century Latin America, classified under the headings bibliography and general works, demographic and urban studies, industrial development, export economics, mining, agriculture, slavery, politics, and transportation.

117. McNamara, Patrick H. CONSCIENCE, CATHOLICISM, AND SOCIAL CHANGE IN LATIN AMERICA. *Social Res. 1979 46(2): 329-349.* Surveys Catholic Latin American social thought on human rights, 1961-79.

118. Menges, Constantine C. COPING WITH RADICAL DESTABILIZATION IN THE MIDDLE EAST AND CENTRAL AMERICA/MEXICO: TRENDS, CAUSES, AND ALTERNATIVES. *Conflict 1981 3(1): 1-31.* Describes the causes of and future potential for radical destabilization in the Persian Gulf and Central America and Mexico from the perspective of events during the last two years of the Carter Administration, 1978-80, and the appeal of the USSR's anticapitalist propaganda for developing countries, which fail to recognize the Soviet threat to their independence.

119. Milenky, Edward S. LATEINAMERIKA UND DIE DRITTE WELT [Latin America and the Third World]. *Europa-Archiv [West Germany] 1977 32(14): 441-452.* Latin America has drawn further than ever away from the developing nations of Africa and Asia in recent years. Traditional ties as well as conservative regimes and social structures hinder relations with radical regimes in Africa and Asia and bind the continent to Europe.

120. Millett, Richard. A CHURCH IN FERMENT: THREE STUDIES OF ROMAN CATHOLICISM IN TODAY'S LATIN AMERICA. *Fides et Hist. 1974 6(2): 48-54.* Review article on Frederic C. Turner *Catholicism and Political Development in Latin America* (U. of North Carolina Press, 1971), David E. Mutchler, *The Church as a Political Factor in Latin America with Particular Reference to Colombia and Chile* (Praeger, 1971), and Jose de Broucker, *Dom Helder Camara: The Violence of a Peace Maker* (Maryknoll, N.Y.: Orbis Books, 1970). Discusses the Roman Catholic Church's ability to overcome its own heritage of oppression in Latin America and become a factor in social change. Turner and Mutchler focus specifically on the institution; the former is methodologically weak, while the latter "is must reading" in the field. De Broucker analyzes the famous leftist Brazilian Archbishop, Dom Helder, whose political and economic positions have their roots in Christian ethics and faith.

R. Butchart

121. Millett, Richard. THE PROTESTANT ROLE IN TWENTIETH CENTURY LATIN AMERICAN CHURCH-STATE RELATIONS. *J. of Church and State 1973 15(3): 367-380.*

122. Milne, R. S. POLITICS, ETHNICITY AND CLASS IN GUYANA AND MALAYSIA. *Social and Econ. Studies [Jamaica] 1977 26(1): 18-37.* Compares and contrasts politics in two ethnically divided countries. After an initial period with ethnic based political parties, Guyana is now attempting to deemphasize ethnic differences and appeal to class differences. In Malaysia ethnicity is still the basis of political parties but the government functions as a result of the union of several ethnic parties. 33 notes, 70 refs.

E. S. Johnson

123. Min, Man-Shik. KOREAN-LATIN AMERICAN RELATIONSHIPS: POLITICAL AND ECONOMIC ASPECTS. *Korea & World Affairs [South Korea] 1980 4(2): 322-334.* Examines relations between South Korea and Latin America since 1950 as political considerations have been replaced by economic ones.

124. Müller, Ronald. POVERTY IS THE PRODUCT. *Foreign Policy 1973/74 (13): 71-103.* Discusses the effects of multinational corporations on Latin America.   S

125. Nadra, F. THE REVOLUTIONARY AWAKENING IN LATIN AMERICA. *Int. Affairs [USSR] 1977 (12): 49-56.* Traces the growth of revolutionary movements in Latin America and particularly in Argentina. The Mexican revolution of 1910-17 was the most important event on the continent after the wars for independence, but it failed. Communist parties appeared in Latin America under the impact of the October Revolution in Russia and class struggle intensified. The Cuban revolution opened a new phase in the struggle and dispelled the myth of geographical fatalism. Cuba was host for the significant Conference of Latin American Communist Parties in 1975. The conference's final document proves the validity of proletarian internationalism.
W. R. Hively

126. Needler, Martin C. THE CLOSENESS OF ELECTIONS IN LATIN AMERICA. *Latin Am. Res. Rev. 1977 12(1): 115-122.* Recent presidential elections in Latin America reveal smaller winning margins than were found around 1950. Several possible reasons are: 1) alienation of marginal supporters by incumbent parties; 2) the building of "minimum winning coalitions"; 3) secular trends of increased support for opposition parties; 4) minimal fraud used by the party in power. Elections are closer because Latin America has developed politically. In certain nations close elections appear to stimulate increased dissidence and to weaken a government's legitimacy. Based on secondary sources; 4 tables, 5 notes.
J. K. Pfabe

127. Needler, Martin C. DETENTE: IMPETUS FOR CHANGE IN LATIN AMERICA? *J. of Internat. Affairs 1974 28(2): 219-228.* The question of direct action vs. legalism and intransigence vs. collaboration and their relations to other leftist groups have caught Latin American Communists between the authoritarian right and the insurrectionary left. Older leaders work within their systems while younger members fail at urban and rural guerrilla war. Cuba is honored, as Chile once was, for its independence of the United States, but internal movements in each nation overshadow international events such as detente.
R. D. Frederick

128. Newton, Ronald C. NATURAL CORPORATISM AND THE PASSING OF POPULISM IN SPANISH AMERICA. *R. of Pol. 1974 36(1): 34-51.*

129. Nguyen, Ngoc Mao and Han, Van Tam. VAI NET VE CUOC DAU TRANH CHONG SU NO DICH VE KINH TE CUA DE QUOC MY O CHAU MY LA TINH TU SAU CACH MANG CUBA [Some features of the struggle against the economic subjection to US imperialism in Latin America since the Cuban revolution]. *Nghien Cuu Lich Su [Vietnam] 1981 (1): 77-84.* Examines US maneuvers for the economic subjection of Latin America and the struggle of the people of Latin America against US imperialism and foreign capitalists since the victory of the Cuban revolution in 1959.   J/S

130. Nichols, Glenn. VENTURAS E DESVENTURAS NO ESTUDO DA POLÍTICA NA AMÉRICA LATINA [Fortune and misfortune in the study of politics in Latin America]. *Rev. Brasileira de Estudos Pol. [Brazil] 1979 (48): 47-83.* Studies historic and theoretical reasons for general failure of democratic institutions and marginality of political parties in modern Latin America. Marxist, pluralist, and other theories fail to adequately cover observed facts. Analyzes postwar Brazil and its parties and classes. The peculiarity of Latin American politics is due in part to a very fragmented society, which leads to a "corporative" structure of politics and, too frequently, to a military seizure of power. Constructs an index of fragmentation for Latin American states and compares the facts of unrest and coups to expectation, demonstrating the explanatory power of social fragmentation. 59 notes, 3 tables, graph.
R. Garfield

131. Nin de Cardona, José María. LAS TENSIONES SOCIOPOLÍTICAS HISPANOAMERICANAS DEL SIGLO XX [Hispanic American sociopolitical tensions in the 20th century]. *Rev. de Pol. Int. [Spain] 1975 (141): 65-111.* Discusses sociopolitical tensions in Hispanic America in the 20th century, focusing on the region as a whole and then analyzing the Cuban and Mexican revolutions, offering a prognosis for the future of all Hispanic American people.

132. O'Donnell, Guillermo. REFLECTIONS ON THE PATTERNS OF CHANGE IN THE BUREAUCRATIC-AUTHORITARIAN STATE. *Latin Am. Res. Rev. 1978 13(1): 3-38.* The emergence, impact, and dynamics of bureaucratic-authoritarian domination patterns must be studied in close relation with changes in a specific type of capitalism. Relationships are complex, not a result of a single factor. The bureaucratic-authoritarian state emerged during the 1960's in Latin America, first in Brazil and Argentina, largely in reaction to the political activation of the popular sector and to economic crisis. The exclusion of the popular sector was deemed necessary for social order, economic stability, and attraction of large quantities of foreign capital. With time, the state became less orthodox and more nationalistic, and it made greater appeals to the national bourgeoisie. Secondary sources; 2 graphs, 72 notes.
J. K. Pfabe

133. Orfila, Alejandro. HUMAN RIGHTS IN THE AMERICAS. *Américas (Organization of American States) 1977 29(5): 18-20.* General overview of the state of human rights in the western hemisphere, 19th-20th centuries, including discussions of Latin American revolutionary movements and contemporary efforts through the Organization of American States.

134. Oszlak, Oscar. THE HISTORICAL FORMATION OF THE STATE IN LATIN AMERICA: SOME THEORETICAL AND METHODOLOGICAL GUIDELINES FOR ITS STUDY. *Latin Am. Res. Rev. 1981 16(2): 3-32.* The struggle for independence was an inadequate basis for a nation. The material foundation for the new nation developed when local economies were integrated into the world capitalist system and power was consolidated in a dominant class. This economic system required control of a political organization to maintain and expand it. The issues of "order" and "progress" dominated the attention of political leaders and defined areas of state action to control their destabilizing consequences. 45 notes.
J. K. Pfabe

135. Pearson, Neale J. SOME VIEWS OF LATIN AMERICAN POLITICS. *Social Sci. J. 1981 18(1): 121-124.* According to *The Politics of Antipolitics: The Military in Latin America* (1978), edited by Brian Loveman and Thomas M. Davies, Jr., Latin American military leaders in the 1960's desired to abolish civilian politics in order to modernize and stabilize their countries; the papers in *Political Participation in Latin America,* Vol. I, *Citizen and State* (1978), edited by John A. Booth and Mitchell A. Seligson suggest that there was broad citizen participation in the economic and political development sought by the military leaders.

136. Petras, James. SOCIAL DEMOCRACY IN LATIN AMERICA. *Can. Dimension [Canada] 1981 15-16(8-1): 15-18.* Examines the development of Social Democratic parties in Latin America during the 1970's, their relationships to the regimes in power, and the support they have received from European Social Democratic parties.

137. Petrov, M. DENUCLEARISED ZONE IN LATIN AMERICA. *Int. Affairs [USSR] 1974 (8): 43-51.* Discusses the USSR's role in establishing a denuclearized zone in Latin America, 1962-73, in an effort to limit the arms race, emphasizing aspects of international law.

138. Pico Estrada, Luis. LATIN AMERICAN HISTORICAL FILMS: THE EPIC OF THE UNDERDOGS. *Cultures [France] 1974 2(1): 169-198.* Through an examination of Latin American historical films, provides a framework for understanding politics and social conditions in Latin American countries, as well as an understanding of the tendency to portray humiliation, injustice, and defeat rather than unrealistic images.

139. Pinto, Luis A. Costa. POPULISM IN LATIN AMERICA. *Studies in Comparative Internat. Development 1973 8(2): 208-212.* Patterns of correlations between social change, resistance to change, and politics of populism.   S

140. Poblete, Renato. FROM MEDELLÍN TO PUEBLA: NOTES FOR REFLECTION. *J. of Interamerican Studies and World Affairs*

1979 21(1): 31-44. The 1968 Medellín conference influenced the formation of socioeconomic and political issues in Latin America. Medellín and Puebla manifest the Church's process of doctrinal clarification and renewed commitments. The widely circulated Puebla preconference document addresses doctrinal matters and sociopolitical matters such as Marxism, national security theory, goals of a new society, and division of social power. Puebla will be a step forward from Medellín. Printed documents; 3 notes, ref.   T. D. Schoonover

141. Pollock, John Crothers.   AN ANTHROPOLOGICAL APPROACH TO MASS COMMUNICATION RESEARCH: THE U.S. PRESS AND POLITICAL CHANGE IN LATIN AMERICA. *Latin Am. Res. Rev. 1978 13(1): 158-172.* An anthropological analysis of political reporters and reporting in historical and comparative context, of news production rather than consumption, and of communications as a complex, interactive process provides insight into underlying reasons for the nature of US reporting. It allows the examination of journalism as a profession functioning to maintain a society and focusing on shared beliefs. Secondary sources; 5 notes, biblio.   J. K. Pfabe

142. Prieto, Alberto.   LA BURGUESÍA LATINOAMERICANA EN EL SIGLO XX   [The Latin American middle class in the 20th century]. *Santiago [Cuba] 1979 (34): 9-54, (35): 37-108.* Part I. Traces the development of the Latin American industrial middle classes and their transformations due, on the one hand, to the penetration of foreign capital and imperialism and, on the other, the socialist revolution in Russia and the general crisis of capitalism. Studies industrial growth as well as dependency on foreign capital, nationalism and reform, and the tendency to authoritarianism. Part II. Focuses on the growth of US hegemony in the continent, the transformation of the national bourgeoisie in certain countries into monopolistic classes, the political evolution of Mexico, Brazil, Argentina, Guatemala, and Bolivia, and the impact of the Cuban revolution. 151 notes.   J. V. Coutinho

143. Prymatov, V. V.   PRO SUCHASNYI ROSVYTOK REVOLIUTSIINOHO PROTSESU V KRAINAKH LATYNS'KOI AMERYKY   [The contemporary development of the revolutionary process in the countries of Latin America]. *Ukrains'kyi Istorychnyi Zhurnal [USSR] 1974 6: 31-39.* Describes the growing struggle against US imperialism in Latin American countries since the 1950's and the growing influence of communist parties and the working class in these countries.

144. Puccini, Dario.   AMERICA LATINA: IL PREZZO DELL'AUTOCOSCIENZA   [Latin America: the price of self-awareness]. *Quaderni Storici [Italy] 1977 12(1): 79-98.* Briefly describes the situation of Latin America in the 1930's: the expansionism of financial capital from the United States, which resorted to subtler techniques to assert its political dominance; and the rise of progressive governments committed to a policy of national resistance against imperialism. The author brings into focus the origin of a Latin American ideal, parallel to the anti-imperialist ideal, and its literary expressions; the effects of the Spanish civil war and of antifascism on Latin American cultural life, the main representatives of which are engaged in the elaboration of a political and literary avant-garde; and the controversy between dependence and autonomy, as it emerges both from the Pen Clubs Congress held in Buenos Aires in 1937, and from the rejection of exoticism by a sector of Latin American literary production.   J

145. Quester, George H.   NUCLEAR PROLIFERATION IN LATIN AMERICA. *Current Hist. 1982 81(472): 52-55.* Discusses the special regime governing the expansion of nuclear weapons capabilities as well as international relations in Latin America and the pressures on countries there to adopt the less pacific ways of the rest of the world and the lessons the Latin American pattern might provide for others.

146. Rachum, Ilan.   THE LATIN AMERICAN REVOLUTIONS OF 1930: A NON-ECONOMIC INTERPRETATION. *Am. Latina [Brazil] 1976 17: 3-17.* Study of political and social events in Peru, Brazil, Argentina, and Cuba in the 1920's, to substantiate the view that the revolutions of 1930 in these countries (1933 in Cuba) were not primarily a result of the Depression. With Bernard Haring, the author contends that the Depression was a contributing cause, but the economic factor was secondary to long-standing political and social problems. 32 notes.
                                              C. B. Fitzgerald

147. Ramos, Dionisio Bejarano and Soler, Miguel Angel.   BUILDING UP STRENGTH. *World Marxist R. [Canada] 1973 16(3): 95-100.* Discussion between the general secretaries of the Communist parties of Paraguay and Honduras on socialism in Latin America.   S

148. Randall, Margaret.   LA PENETRACIÓN IMPERIALISTA Y SUS CONSECUENCIAS PARA LA MUJER LATINOAMERICANA   [Imperialism and its effects on the Latin American woman]. *Santiago [Cuba] 1974 (15): 227-247.* The influence of US ideology in Latin America has particularly affected women through the mass media. The latter has been used to promote antifeminism and the values of consumer society. Birth control programs are instruments of capitalistic power in developing nations designed to maintain the economic and social status quo.
                                          P. J. Taylorson/S

149. Rangel, Carlos.   LE FORME DEL POTERE POLITICO IN AMERICA LATINA   [The forms of political power in Latin America]. *Comunità [Italy] 1978 32(180): 67-138.* Surveys the differing forms of political power in Latin America from traditional *caudillismo* to the new *caudillos* of the Left, such as Fidel Castro, and the Right, such as Augusto Pinochet, from Mexico's one party but constitutional state to the multiparty democracies, such as Chile under Salvador Allende, which failed, and Venezuela, which succeeded.

150. Ranis, Peter.   POST POPULIST MODELS OF THE LATIN AMERICAN POLITY. *Polity 1980 13(1): 126-133.* The liberal prescriptions of the early 1960's gave way to economic structuralist and neo-Marxist analyses of Latin American polity which, in turn, have helped shape the works under review: Ernest Halperin, in *Terrorism in Latin America* (Beverly Hills: Sage Publ., 1976), Robert R. Kaufman, in *Transition to Stable Authoritarian-Corporate Regimes: The Chilean Case?* (Beverly Hills: Sage Professional Papers in Comparative Politics, 1976), Gustavo Lagos and Horacio H. Godoy, in *Revolution of Being: A Latin American View of the Future* (New York: Free Pr., 1977), and Candido Mendes, in *Beyond Populism* (Albany: State U. of New York, 1977), having witnessed the failure of populist experiences in Chile, Argentina, Uruguay, and Brazil, see a consensual model of political development, based on a general will as opposed to the competing demands of a democratic-pluralist society, as leading to political and economic stability in Latin America.

151. Redclift, M. R.   SQUATTER SETTLEMENTS IN LATIN AMERICAN CITIES: THE RESPONSE FROM GOVERNMENT. *J. of Development Studies [Great Britain] 1973 10(1): 92-109.* Government response to Latin American urban squatters since the 1950's has been of little benefit to the communities involved.

152. Redclift, Michael.   PEASANTS AND REVOLUTIONARIES: SOME CRITICAL COMMENTS.   *J. of Latin Am. Studies [Great Britain] 1975 7(1): 135-144.* Review article of ten recent studies. David Ronfeldt's *Atencingo, the Politics of Agrarian Struggle in a Mexican Ejido* is the only substantive study of peasant rivalries vis-à-vis large landowners, state provincial and federal bureaucracies, and national party organizations. James Petras and Hugo Zemelman Merino, *Peasants in Revolt: A Chilean Case Study,* is doctrinaire in tone, incredibly naive in content, and methodologically incompetent. Gerrit Huizer's *Peasant Rebellion in Latin America* is a useful condensation of a vast amount of data; Orlando Fals Borda's *Cooperatives and Rural Development in Latin America* holds out little "hope for significant changes in rural society" from cooperatives. Sutti R. Ortiz, *Uncertainties in Peasant Farming, A Colombian Case,* Frank Cancian, *Change and Uncertainty in a Peasant Economy,* and Marlin D. Clausner, *Rural Santo Domingo: Settled, Unsettled and Resettled* exhibit ample evidence of peasant rationality which so surprised Petras and Zemelman. John Gerassi (ed.), *Camilo Torres: Revolutionary Priest,* M. Zeitlin (ed.), *Revolutionary Writings: Father Camilo Torres,* and Hugo Blanco, *Land or Death* offer little hope from such revolutionaries as Torres and Blanco. Based on secondary sources; 25 notes.   K. M. Bailor

153. Reich, Peter L.   QUANTITATIVE DEVELOPMENTS IN LATIN AMERICAN STUDIES: A REVIEW OF SOME RECENT LITERATURE. *Hist. Methods 1979 12(4): 169-176.* This essay reviews Ernest Duff and John McCamant's *Violence and Repression in Latin America: a Quantitative and Historical Analysis* (New York: Free Pr.,

1976); Peter H. Smith's *The Labyrinths of Power: Political Recruitment in Twentieth Century Mexico* (Princeton: Princeton U. Pr., 1979); and Billie R. DeWalt's *Modernization in a Mexican Ejido: a Study in Economic Adaptation* (New York: Cambridge U. Pr., 1979). While these works demonstrate a knowledge of quantitative methods, they suffer from an incompleteness in research and conceptualization. Nevertheless, they represent new and creative ways of dealing with the raw data of history. 60 notes.   D. K. Pickens

154. Remmer, Karen L.   ECONOMIC DEPENDENCE AND PO-LITICAL CONFLICT: CHILE AND ARGENTINA, 1900-1925. *Studies in Comparative Int. Development 1976 11(2): 3-24.* Concentrates on the relationship between external economic independence and patterns of elite dominance. Briefly discusses general patterns of modernization, examines tariff exchange and commercial policies, and surveys the socioeconomic structure of Argentina and Chile. Evidence indicates the monetary policies encouraged a coalition of native rural and urban elites at the expense of foreign capital and the working class. This coalition delayed industrial development. The existing literature has misrepresented the consequences of dependency for the structure of political conflict and for the relative political influence of foreign interests. Moreover, the resulting alliance closely resembles the coopted bourgeois modernization pattern of Mediterranean Europe. Based on primary and secondary sources; 3 tables, 14 notes, biblio.   S. A. Farmerie

155. Richardson, Neil R. and Kegley, Charles W., Jr.   TRADE DE-PENDENCE AND FOREIGN POLICY COMPLIANCE: A LON-GITUDINAL ANALYSIS. *Int. Studies Q. 1980 24(2): 191-222.* From 1950 to 1973, the United States was able to secure support for its position on Cold War issues in the UN General Assembly from a group of 25 countries, most of them in Latin America. Because all of these states were trade dependent on the United States, their foreign policy behavior may be viewed as partial payment in exchange for benefits derived from their economic ties with the dominant partner. 2 fig., 4 tables, 55 notes.
                                                             E. Palais

156. Roett, Riordan and Menéndez-Carrión, Amparo.   AUTORI-TÄRE REGIERUNGSSYSTEME IN LATEINAMERIKA. DIE VERÄNDERUNG DER PERSPEKTIVEN [Authoritarian systems of government in Latin America: the altering of the perspectives]. *Europa-Archiv [West Germany] 1978 33(9): 253-262.* In the 1950's and early 1960's, many thought Latin America would soon be dominated by liberal-democratic, socialist, or even communist regimes, but the opposite has happened: the continent has become the home of numerous right-wing military dictatorships and other authoritarian regimes.

157. Romero, José Luis.   TOWN AND COUNTRYSIDE: THE TENSIONS BETWEEN TWO IDEOLOGIES. *Cultures [France] 1978 5(3): 32-55.* Originating in the Spanish conquest of Latin America, tensions between modern and traditional, rural and urban ideologies, and nationalism and "national being" continue to plague Latin America, 16th-20th centuries.

158. Rosales, Juan.   REVOLUTION, SOCIALISM, THEOLOGY. *World Marxist R. [Canada] 1975 18(6): 80-90.* Discusses the role of the Catholic Church in Latin America and its attitude toward social progress.
                                                                  S

159. Ross, Stanley R.   RECENT UNITED STATES BIBLIO-GRAPHICAL CONTRIBUTIONS TO LATIN AMERICAN HIS-TORIOGRAPHY. *Rev. de Hist. de Am. [Mexico] 1974 (77/78): 207-218.* Surveys current US research and publication about Latin America. The standard references to special collections in this area are listed with brief comments on the nature of their coverage. Evaluates recent and extensive contributions to this field of research, especially the historiography of Mexico. A parallel but abbreviated report of this historiographical progress is given in Spanish.   T. B. Davis

160. Rowe, Edward Thomas.   NATIONAL ATTRIBUTES ASSO-CIATED WITH MULTILATERAL AND US BILATERAL AID TO LATIN AMERICA, 1960-1971. *Int. Organization 1978 32(2): 463-476.* Whatever the determinants behind decisions on the allocation of bilateral and multilateral aid, the same considerations with regard to the politics of potential recipients do not appear to be operating. All of this does not

mean that US interests are not being served by multilateral programs. They may be served in a variety of ways, and still be consistent with the results reported here.   J

161. Ruhl, J. Mark.   URBANIZATION AND POLITICAL DE-MAND MEASUREMENT IN LATIN AMERICA: THE PROBLEM OF LAG EFFECT. *Latin Am. Res. Rev. 1979 14(1): 145-149.* Urbanized nations become more socially mobilized, politically demanding, and volatile unless demands are satisfied. But simple percentages of urban population can be misleading where urban growth has been recent, because the first generation of migrants usually remains politically passive. Quantitative studies should allow for a lag effect of about 20 years when using percent urban as an indicator. Secondary sources; table, 3 notes, biblio.   J. K. Pfabe

162. Russell, Charles A.   LATIN AMERICA: REGIONAL RE-VIEW. *Terrorism 1980 4(1-4): 277-292.* A statistical survey of the incidents of terrorism in Latin America, 1970-78; Latin America with 24.5% is second only to Europe with 47.2% in worldwide terrorist activity.

163. Russell, Charles A.; Miller, James A.; and Hildner, Robert E. THE URBAN GUERRILLA IN LATIN AMERICA: A SELECT BIB-LIOGRAPHY. *Latin Am. Research Rev. 1974 9(1): 37-80.* Bibliography of works published 1962-72.

164. Salomon, Noël.   COSMOPOLITISM AND INTERNATION-ALISM IN THE HISTORY OF IDEAS IN LATIN AMERICA. *Cultures [France] 1979 6(1): 83-108.* Analyzes "cosmopolitanism," since the word appeared in the 16th century, noting its changing meaning and comparing it with "internationalism" in Latin American history. Presently cosmopolitanism has a negative connotation, while internationalism has become compatible with nationalism and has assumed a positive meaning.

165. Sanders, Thomas G.   THE POLITICS OF CATHOLICISM IN LATIN AMERICA. *J. of Interamerican Studies and World Affairs 1982 24(2): 241-248.* Recent studies by Thomas C. Bruneau, *The Church in Brazil: The Politics of Religion* (1982), Daniel N. Levine, *Religion and Politics in Latin America: The Catholic Church in Venezuela and Colombia* (1981), and Brian H. Smith, *The Church and Politics in Chile: Challenges to Modern Catholicism* (1982) all make important contributions to understanding the political role of Catholicism in Latin America. They also contribute to a broader understanding of Christianity's role in the modern world. They are weak however in integrating the discussion of national churches into the current "official" projection of the institutional church.   T. D. Schoonover

166. Saulniers, Alfred H.   PUBLIC ENTERPRISES IN LATIN AMERICA: AN ANNOTATED LIST OF RECENT RESEARCH PA-PERS. *J. of Interamerican Studies and World Affairs 1980 22(4): 463-470.* Lists and annotates 49 unpublished papers presented at five recent major conferences, overviews detailed studies, think pieces, and polemics.
                                                     T. D. Schoonover

167. Schaedel, Richard P.   PEASANT MOVEMENTS: CASE HIS-TORIES AND ANALYSIS. *J. of InterAm. Studies and World Affairs 1976 18(4): 505-515.* In the last decade many studies on peasant movements in Latin America have been carried out. These show the diversity of peasant groups and the different aspirations of their leaders. For example, freeholding peasants do not want the same things as usufruct or hacienda peasants. Surprisingly, peasant movements are more easily generated among the freeholders than among the more oppressed hacienda workers. This is because the hacienda peasants have already lost everything, while the freeholders are in the process of losing what they have gained and hope to keep their position through collective action. While past studies on peasants have been valuable, more research is needed to enable government leaders to establish policies that will advance the cause of the peasants. Based on four recent books on peasant movements along with secondary books and articles; biblio.   J. R. Thomas

168. Schiller, Herbert I.   DECOLONIZATION OF INFORMA-TION: EFFORTS TOWARD A NEW INTERNATIONAL ORDER. *Latin Am. Perspectives 1978 5(1): 35-48.* Discusses recent efforts to end

political colonialism in Latin America since the mid-1940's, particularly efforts to end cultural domination and free the flow of information and open communication channels in developing countries in the late 1960's.

169. Schmidt, Steffen W. POLITICAL PARTICIPATION AND DEVELOPMENT: THE ROLE OF WOMEN IN LATIN AMERICA. *J. of Int. Affairs 1976-77 30(2): 243-260.* To what extent the ideal type of women as wives and mothers has prevailed in Latin America is difficult to ascertain, though there is evidence that in the past some groups of women deviated from the ideal and participated in national development as part of the economically active population and in the political process, the crucial factor involved in the deviation being class. Graph, 3 tables, 56 notes.   V. Samaraweera

170. Shaw, Edward L. THE U.S. AND LATIN AMERICA IN CARTOONS. *Latin Am. Res. Rev. 1982 17(2): 277-280.* Reviews Ron Tyler, ed., *Posada's Mexico* (1979) and John J. Johnson's *Latin America in Caricature* (1980). Posada's work reveals how different the Mexican outlook on life and death is from the North American. Johnson's perceptive work shows the negative manner in which North American cartoonists have depicted Latin Americans, which weakens the possibilities for mutual respect.   J. K. Pfabe

171. Sigmund, Paul E. LATIN AMERICAN CATHOLICISM'S OPENING TO THE LEFT. *R. of Pol. 1973 35(1): 61-76.*

172. Siles Salinas, Luis Adolfo. AMÉRICA LATINA: TRAGEDIA Y PROMESA [Latin America: tragedy and promise]. *Cuadernos Hispanoamericanos [Spain] 1978 111(332): 181-205.* Discusses the process and consequences of social and economic disintegration in 20th-century Latin America, in particular the failure of the application of liberal, populist, and development models. Secondary sources; 13 notes.
                                                          P. J. Taylorson

173. Simian-Yofre, Horacio. DIE THEOLOGIE DER BEFREIUNG UND IHRE BIBELTHEOLOGISCHEN VORAUSSETZUNGEN [The theology of liberation and its biblical theological basis]. *Stimmen der Zeit [West Germany] 1978 196(12): 807-818.* Until 1965 the most frequent term in Latin American theology was development, a notion that changed radically into a theology of liberation, more in keeping with the social tendencies of explanation of the Bible and the confrontation with total exploitation.

174. Smith, Brian H. CHURCHES AND HUMAN RIGHTS IN LATIN AMERICA: RECENT TRENDS IN THE SUBCONTINENT. *J. of Interamerican Studies and World Affairs 1979 21(1): 89-127.* Using emotion laden symbols of anticommunism, nationalism, and the protection of private property, the armed forces have asserted control throughout South America except for Colombia and Venezuela during the 1970's. Military government's have violated many human rights in the process. Churches have become important institutions in opposing these violations. However, Latin American churches are generally underdeveloped institutions; they have not been strong defenders of rights. 29 notes, ref.
                                                      T. D. Schoonover

175. Soares, Glaúcio Ari Dillon. NOTAS METODOLÓGICAS SOBRE AS CONSEQÜÊNCIAS POLÍTICAS DA MIGRAÇÃO INTERNA [Methodological notes on the political consequences of internal migration]. *Rev. Brasileira de Estudos Pol. [Brazil] 1977 (45): 59-92.* Attempts to clarify some of the structural problems in the study of the political effects of urban migration in Latin America. Although many researchers have concluded that urban migration increases radical political behavior, in reality such studies often have been inadequately conceived, especially by failing to distinguish between various levels of analysis, the peoples affected, direct and indirect effects, and what does or does not constitute radicalism. 29 notes.   B. J. Chandler

176. Stoetzer, O. Carlos. POSITIVISM AND IDEALISM IN THE HISPANIC WORLD: THE POSITIVIST CASE OF BRAZIL AND KRAUSEAN INFLUENCE IN SPANISH AMERICA. *Revista/- Review Interamericana [Puerto Rico] 1979 9(2): 168-187.* European philosophical systems always crossed the Atlantic and frequently have played important roles in the New World. Positivism, for example, helped destroy the monarchy in Brazil in the 1880's. Krausism, to give a second

example, played an extremely important role in the political career of Hipólito Yrigoyen, president of Argentina from 1916 to 1922. Based on printed sources; 70 notes.   J. A. Lewis

177. Stoll, David. THE SUMMER INSTITUTE OF LINGUISTICS AND INDIGENOUS MOVEMENTS. *Latin Am. Perspectives 1982 9(2): 84-99.* Examines the political, or ideological, involvement of the Summer Institute of Linguistics (SIL), a companion unit of Wycliffe Bible Translators, in Guatemala, Mexico, Peru, and Brazil. Information is fragmentary and dubious; the SIL has protected its neutrality as much as it has lent credence to reports of cooperation with government and intelligence agencies. Often, charges against the SIL disguise the anti-indigenist policies of host governments. Ref.   J. F. Vivian

178. Stone, Carl. POLITICAL DETERMINANTS OF SOCIAL POLICY ALLOCATIONS IN LATIN AMERICA. *Comparative Studies in Soc. and Hist. [Great Britain] 1975 17(3): 286-308.* Examines political determination of social policy allocations in Latin America 1940-60, focusing on two conflicting theories of the responsiveness of liberal democracy.

179. Street, James H. POLITICAL INTERVENTION AND SCIENCE IN LATIN AMERICA. *Bull. of the Atomic Scientists 1981 37(2): 14-23.* Discusses political intervention in public universities and scientific institutes, in Argentina, Brazil, Chile, Uruguay, and Paraguay, which has resulted in the deterioration of scholarly work and scientific research since the 1940's.

180. Szymański, Edward. STARE I NOWE PROBLEMY AMERYKI ŁACIŃSKIEJ [The old and new problems of Latin America]. Szymański, Edward, ed. *Tradycja i Współczesność w Azji, Afryce i Ameryce Łacińskiej* (Warsaw: Polska Akademia Nauk Zakład Krajów Pozaeuropejskich, 1978): 347-362. Three centuries of colonial exploitation by Spain led to independence for the countries of Latin America, but independence did not change the existing social and economic order until modernization and national integration created new tensions for immature political systems: economic growth without social reform has led to revolution.

181. Terterián, Inna. LA CULTUROLOGÍA EXTRANJERA DEL SIGLO XX Y EL PENSAMIENTO LATINOAMERICANO [Twentieth-century foreign culturology and Latin American thought]. *Am. Latina [USSR] 1978 (2): 100-121, (3): 114-139.* Part I. Various European philosophies emphasizing the decadence of Western civilization were among the chief influences on early 20th-century Latin American thought. This was true even though the Europeans said little about the concrete problems of Latin America. Otto Spengler's *Decline of the West* made a real impact on Latin American intellectuals. José Ortega y Gasset was also very influential. The Russian Revolution ushered in a new era in Latin American thought. 24 notes. Part II. The ideas of Hermann Alexander Keyserling, akin to fascist ideas on blood, soil, and racism, enjoyed popularity in Latin America. Waldo Frank was also widely acclaimed, mainly because he criticized the imperialism of the United States, his native country. Arnold J. Toynbee's philosophy of history was widely interpreted to mean that Latin America was the civilization of the future. The spiritual philosophies which have influenced Latin America are now giving way to scientific ideas. 29 notes.   J. D. Barnard

182. Thompson, Lawrence S. LATIN AMERICANA AND RELATED MATERIAL IN MICROFORM. *Inter-Am. Rev. of Biblio. 1974 24(2): 162-166.* Early books about or printed in Latin America are scarce and widely scattered. Major projects to film these rare items are discussed. 4 notes.   B. D. Johnson

183. Tomassini, Luciano. LOS ESTUDIOS INTERNACIONALES EN AMÉRICA LATINA: ALGUNAS CONTRIBUCIONES [International studies in Latin America: some contributions]. *Estudios Int. [Chile] 1980 13(52): 545-552.* Cites the importance of international studies, which focus on the wider context of national development processes and efforts, and examines the progress made by the discipline during recent years, as seen in the work of contributors to the review *Estudios Internacionales.*

184. Torriente Brau, Pablo de la; Abad, Diana, introduction. CARLOS APONTE: PELEADOR SIN TREGUA [Carlos Aponte: a fighter who gave no quarter]. *Rev. de la Biblioteca Nac. José Martí [Cuba] 1980 22(2): 9-15.* Carlos Aponte Hernández, Venezuelan by birth, became a professional revolutionary during the 1930's, fighting against Juan Vicente Gómez in Venezuela, reaching the rank of colonel in Augusto César Sandino's army in Nicaragua, and dying in combat in Cuba in the mid-1930's. Reprint of a 1935 article.
J. A. Lewis

185. Trebat, Thomas J. and Wogart, Jan Peter. INTRODUCTION. *J. of Interamerican Studies and World Affairs 1980 22(4): 395-399.* Introduction to a special issue on government enterprise in Latin America. The postwar period has witnessed increasing government intervention in the economy throughout Latin America, and there have been important links between public firms and the development strategies of Latin American governments. As economic goals changed, these public enterprises emerged as flexible instruments of government policy. Secondary sources; 2 notes, ref.
T. D. Schoonover

186. Truitt, Rolland D. DEFINING LATIN AMERICAN SECURITY ISSUES. *Military Affairs 1976 40(4): 169-175.* Counters criticism of Latin American military spending by showing that the realities of the local political environment and the makeup of the national security problem are quite real to Latin American governments. There are a number of perceived security threats, not all of which are serious: extrahemispheric, Cuban, ideological contamination, Latin American nuclear, the United States, internal insurgency, and interstate. Interstate is the most important factor; the threat of large-scale conflict exists between Argentina and Brazil. Primary and secondary sources; 42 notes.
A. M. Osur

187. Tunnermann Berheim, Carlos. EL NUEVO CONCEPTO DE EXTENSIÓN UNIVERSITARIA Y DIFUSIÓN CULTURAL Y SU RELACIÓN CON LAS POLÍTICAS DE DESARROLLO CULTURAL EN AMERICA LATINA [The new concept of university extension and cultural diffusion and its relation to the policies of cultural development in Latin America]. *Anuario de Estudios Centroamericanos [Costa Rica] 1978 4: 73-126.* The colonial universities were elitist and served Church and state interests. The 1800's witnessed the development of professional schools to serve elite and state interests. The 1918 Cordova reform started a new era by opening the university to all students, calling for academic freedom, democratizing the university, and stressing a social mission. The contemporary trend toward a more effective social mission is in evidence through "concientización" that studies national reality and seeks to develop cultural identity. Based on proceedings of Latin American conferences and UNESCO; secondary sources; 29 notes.
H. J. Miller

188. Turner, Frederick C. CATHOLICISM AND NATIONALISM IN LATIN AMERICA. *Am. Behavioral Scientist 1974 17(6): 845-864.*

189. Vargas Llosa, Mario; Kemp, Lysander, transl. CENTRALISM AS PRAGMATIC TRADITION: A CRITIQUE. *J. of Interamerican Studies and World Affairs 1981 23(3): 345-351.* Review essay on Claudio Véliz's *The Centralist Tradition of Latin America* (1980). Véliz claims a deep and ancient centralist tradition in Latin America, but consciously refuses to define it clearly, insisting that it is pragmatic rather than ideological, which he downgrades. Véliz rejects organizational forms from Europe or the United States as inconsistent with Latin America's centralist nature. The force of any tradition could be overcome, however, even Vélez's centralism, by the desire to live in freedom.
T. D. Schoonover

190. Véliz, Claudio. LA TRADICIÓN CENTRALISTA EN AMÉRICA LATINA [The centralist tradition in Latin America]. *Estudios Int. [Chile] 1980 13(50): 151-162.* The centralist tradition in Latin America, invented by the Spanish court, proceeds as before with negative implications for industrialization, economic growth, and political decentralization.

191. Verner, Joel G. EDUCATIONAL BACKGROUNDS OF LATIN AMERICAN LEGISLATORS: A THREE-COUNTRY ANALYSIS. *Comparative Pol. 1974 6(4): 617-634.* Surveys Guatemala, Uruguay, and Brazil.
S

192. Verner, Joel G. LOS SISTEMAS DE SELECCIÓN DE PRESIDENTES EN AMÉRICA LATINA, 1930-1970 [The systems of presidential selection in Latin America, 1930-70]. *Foro Internacional [Mexico] 1973 13(52): 490-512.* Presents characteristics of a "typical" Latin American president based on a statistical analysis of the area's chief executives, 1930-70. Primary and secondary sources; 8 tables, 24 notes. (See also abstract 20B:2865).
D. A. Franz

193. Vieira, Gilberto. GENERAL AND PARTICULAR IN LIBERATION STRUGGLE. *World Marxist R. [Canada] 1973 16(10): 45-50.* The Colombian Party secretary-general discusses the progress of the anti-imperialist struggle in Latin America.
S

194. Villaverde, Juan. EDUCATION POLICY FOR DEVELOPMENT. *Américas (Organization of American States) 1973 25(8/9): 38-41.* Examines the goals of education policy for developing nations in Latin America.
S

195. Villegas, Osiris. AMÉRICA DO SUL: GEOPOLÍTICA DA INTEGRAÇÃO E DO DESENVOLVIMENTO [South America: the geopolitics of integration and development]. *Rev. Brasileira de Pol. Int. [Brazil] 1973 16(63-64): 23-34.* Considers the circumstances that have shaped long-term instability in South America and discusses regional and national integration as a means of overcoming problems of underdevelopment.
P. J. Taylorson

196. Waldmann, Peter. *CAUDILLISMO* ALS KONSTANTE DER POLITISCHEN KULTUR LATEINAMERIKAS? [Are caudillos a constant in the political culture of Latin Americas?]. *Jahrbuch für Geschichte von Staat, Wirtschaft und Gesellschaft Lateinamerikas [West Germany] 1978 15: 191-207.* Isolates social and political factors which contribute to reducing the value of the caudillo, the alleged constant in Latin America's political culture. As a dominating political force, dictatorship has occurred in those lands which most closely resemble the socioeconomic backwardness prevailing in 19th-century Latin America. These are normally the smaller lands such as Nicaragua, Haiti, the Dominican Republic, Cuba, and Paraguay. Secondary sources; 31 notes.
T. D. Schoonover

197. Walker, John. CONDEMNED TO CIVILIZATION. LATIN AMERICAN CULTURE: THE STRUGGLE FOR IDENTITY. *Humanities Assoc. Rev. [Canada] 1979 30(4): 302-321.* The struggle for Latin American identity, as reflected in its politics and literature, has been a struggle between an often decadent civilization, on the one hand, and an often brutal primitivism on the other. The conquest of the Indian in the 16th century, the winning of independence in the 19th (after which the triumphant Creoles identified with and idealized the Indian), the excesses of mestizo dictators, and the ensuing movement to re-Europeanize Latin America are giving way to universalism, which some feel amounts to North Americanization and a loss of identity, but which others feel will promote a less bitter and more successful struggle.

198. Weaver, Jerry L. THE POLITICS OF LATIN AMERICAN FAMILY-PLANNING POLICY. *J. of Developing Areas 1978 12(4): 415-437.* Delegates at the World Population Conference (1974) defined population rates as central in the struggle to redefine distribution of resources and power between industrial and Third World nations. They analyzed the influence of government, political parties, labor unions, mass media, Catholic Church, lower classes, and the UN on national population. The role of social norms including racism, and regime ideology such as nationalism were examined. Large families sometimes represented a conscious economic choice. Government intervention generally was opposed by the military, the Catholic hierarchy, leftists, students, Marxists, and Indian communities. Secondary sources; table, 104 notes.
O. W. Eads, Jr.

199. Weinert, Richard S. MULTINATIONALS IN LATIN AMERICA. *J. of InterAm. Studies and World Affairs 1976 18(2): 253-260.* The activities of multinational corporations in Latin American developing countries have led to the dependency theory of political science which condemns these corporations in two areas. First, they are charged with undermining sovereignty and, secondly, with distorting the development of the nation. Literature on the subject is divided into theories and case studies. Theorists and case study authors do not interact, with the result

that each group produces works that lack insights from the other. A balanced view of multinational corporations requires a linking of the theorists with the case study authors. Based on five recent books on multinational corporations.

J. R. Thomas

200. Wiarda, Howard J. DEMOCRACY AND HUMAN RIGHTS IN LATIN AMERICA: TOWARD A NEW CONCEPTUALIZATION. *Orbis 1978 22(1): 137-160.* The longtime US perception of Latin America as often violating norms for human rights and democracy is due in good part to cultural differences. Latins see the individual as an organic part of a society made up of institutions and corporatie entities, not as a distinct, isolated being in an atomized world. The individual therefore has constraints, limits, and protections that he lacks in English-speaking countries. Anglo-Saxons distrust the prominent role for the Church or the armed forces normal to the Latin. Latins should be judged by Latin rather than by American standards. 37 notes.

J. C. Billigmeier

201. Wiarda, Howard J. HACIA UN SISTEMA TEÓRICO PARA EL ESTUDIO DEL PROCESO DE CAMBIO SOCIO-POLÍTICO DENTRO DE LA TRADICIÓN IBERO-LATINA: EL MODELO CORPORATIVO [Toward a theoretical system for the study of the process of socio-political change within the Ibero-Latin tradition: the corporative model]. *Estudios Andinos 1974/75 4(1): 241-278.* A traditional, corporatist social order is part of the Latin American colonial heritage. Because the region therefore lacks a liberal tradition, liberal intellectuals have ignored the process of political change in Latin America. This process of change involves conserving as much of the traditional order as possible while meeting the demands of new interest groups in politics and society. In a context of corporatism the government initiates and orchestrates such change. Special imperatives in the Ibero-Latin tradition must thus be recognized to understand change and development in Latin American countries. Secondary sources; 29 notes.

J. L. White

202. Wilde, Alexander. TEN YEARS OF CHANGE IN THE CHURCH: PUEBLA AND THE FUTURE. *J. of Interamerican Studies and World Affairs 1979 21(3): 299-312.* The Puebla Conference in 1979 capped a decade of far-reaching change in the Catholic Church. With unprecedented regional integration, the Church's commitment to the poor has placed it in a confrontation with political authority unmatched since the 19th century in Latin America. 8 notes, ref.

T. D. Schoonover

203. Williams, Edward J. THE EMERGENCE OF THE SECULAR NATION-STATE AND LATIN AMERICAN CATHOLICISM. *Comparative Politics 1973 5(2): 261-277.* A review of the current position of the Catholic Church in Latin America. The Church originally shunned connection with the nation-state, but recent challenges from Protestants, Communists, and nationalists have forced it to change its policy. Now the Church is acting to support the state and even to legitimize its rule. Church-state hostility has almost disappeared. The remaining problems include determining the precise role of the Church, how far it should go, and how to circumvent arising internal problems. 36 notes.

V. L. Human

204. Williams, Edward J. SECULARIZATION, INTEGRATION AND RATIONALIZATION: SOME PERSPECTIVES FROM LATIN AMERICAN THOUGHT. *J. of Latin Am. Studies [Great Britain] 1973 5(2): 199-216.* Posits continuity in the evolution of Latin American thought. From Simón Bolívar to Che Guevara, Latin American *pensadores* have continuously anticipated and advocated the three major analyses and remedies prescribed by contemporary developmentalism. Sociocultural secularization, as a necessary precursor to growth, would be achieved by massive northern European and North American immigration, according to 19th-century thinkers, or in the 20th century by sending the young to Europe or North America for training or importing people with the necessary skills. Other thinkers in the 19th century designed educational programs to further secularization which continues to have 20th-century followers. The subject of much negative analysis in the 19th century, national integration has become the most important ideology as a result of the development of *hispanidad, modernismo,* and later *indigenismo.* Rationalizing the utilization of scarce resources was distinctively outlined in Spanish colonial mercantilism, deeply affected by 19th-century positivism, and reinforced and modified by socialist influences in the 20th century. Secondary sources; 30 notes.

K. M. Bailor

205. Wionczek, Miguel S. RULES FOR MULTINATIONALS: THE LATIN AMERICAN CONTEXT. *Worldview 1975 18(10): 27-33.* Presents the Latin America case for international regulation of multinational corporations. Discusses conflicts between the interests of multinational companies and those of the host countries.

M. L. Frey

206. Wolff, Thomas. MEXICAN-GUATEMALAN IMBROGLIO: FISHERY RIGHTS AND NATIONAL HONOR. *Americas (Acad. of Am. Franciscan Hist.) 1981 38(2): 235-248.* The attack by Guatemalan Air Force planes in December 1958 on Mexican vessels allegedly fishing in Guatemalan waters was the culmination of a period of worsening relations between the two countries. It led in turn to a rupture of diplomatic relations and outbursts of public protest in both. The dispute was formally ended the following September. 52 notes.

D. Bushnell

207. Zea, Leopoldo. LATINOAMÉRICA Y LA POLÍTICA DE LA CULTURA [Latin America and the politics of culture]. *Rev. Nac. de Cultura [Venezuela] 1976 34(224): 9-18.* The term politics of culture, coined by Umberto Campagnolo, denotes the intellectual's reasoned commitment to social reality transcending personal political stance. After World War II, totalitarian physical and moral violence was institutionalized against those defined as subversive to established interests. The politicized Latin American milieu has witnessed the dedication of the intellectual and the university student to the culture of liberation, a new awareness of humanity, the rejection of exclusivism, and the acceptance of concrete diversity.

G. Pizzimenti

208. Zea, Leopoldo. THE MEANING OF HISTORY: FROM DEPENDENCE TO SOLIDARITY. *Cultures [France] 1978 5(3): 111-128.* Chronicles the stages of history in Latin America from colonization to national servitude and cultural imperialism, to revolution and nationalism in the 19th century, and to Pan-Americanism in the 20th century.

209. Zubritski, Iu. A. MOTIVOS POLÍTICOS EN LA POESÍA QUECHUA [Political motifs in Quechuan poetry]. *Latin Am. Res. Rev. 1977 12(2): 161-170.* Political themes in Quechuan poetry first appeared in the works of Juan Hualparimachi Mayta (b. 1793). Following independence other Quechuan poets emerged. By the turn of the 20th century Luis Néstor Lizarasu was demanding social justice for his people. Luis Cordero (1833-1925) wrote of the suffering of his people and of hope for a better future. Distinguished in recent years is the poetry of Kilku Warak'a. Inspired by the Russian Revolution and Lenin, he introduced motifs of human desperation and struggle for a better future. Based on Quechuan poetry and secondary sources; 19 notes.

J. F. Pfabe

210. Zylberberg, Jacques. ETAT-CORPORATISME-POPULISME: CONTRIBUTION A UNE SOCIOLOGIE POLITIQUE DE L'AMERIQUE LATINE [State corporatism-populism: toward a policy sociology of South America]. *Études Int. [Canada] 1976 7(2): 215-251.* Discusses the various stages and types of state development which have recently appeared in Latin America, as well as 19th-century European and American models as historical antecedents. Relates the effect of this nation-state growth on society. Examines several forms of corporatism including political, military, and economic. Secondary sources; 67 notes.

J. F. Harrington, Jr.

211. Zylberberg, Jacques. MODÈLES D'ETAT, MODÈLES DE CROISSANCE: LE CAS LATINO-AMÉRICAIN [Types of states, types of growth: the case of Latin America]. *Civilizations [Belgium] 1980 30(1-2): 60-71.* Examines the stages in political and economic development in Latin America.

212. —. THE DECISIVE STRUGGLES LIE AHEAD. *World Marxist R. [Canada] 1974 17(6): 101-108.*
Jagan, Cheddi. FROM GUYANA TO CHILE, *pp. 101-104.* The Chilean coup d'etat was similar in spirit if not in precise form to the rightist takeover in Guyana in 1961, which was also initiated and supported by the forces of international imperialism.
Nina, Tadeo. FORMULAS FOR COUNTER-REVOLUTIONARY COUPS, *pp. 104-107.* US and Brazilian agents rehearsed their success in Chile with the overthrow of the progressive Torres regime in Bolivia.
Lara, O. WORDS OF WRATH, *pp. 107-108.* Reviews *Chile: Ein Schwartzbuch* [Chile: a black book] Hans Werber Bartsch et al., eds. (Köln: Paul Rugenstein Verlag, 1974).

S

213. —. DECLARACIÓN DE TLATELOLCO [Tlatelolco Declaration]. *Foro Internacional [Mexico] 1974 14(56): 618-625.* Presents background and conclusions of the Tlatelolco Conference held in Mexico City 18-24 February 1974 by Latin American foreign ministers and the US secretary of state on inter-American economic and foreign relations.
D. A. Franz

214. —. ECONOMIC DEVELOPMENT AND HUMAN RIGHTS: BRAZIL, CHILE, AND CUBA. *Am. J. of Internat. Law 1973 67(5): 198-227.*
Ferguson, Clarence Clyde, Jr., Chairman.
Trubek, David M. WHEN IS AN OMELET? WHAT IS AN EGG? SOME THOUGHTS ON ECONOMIC DEVELOPMENT AND HUMAN RIGHTS IN LATIN AMERICA, pp. 198-205.
Domínguez, Jorge I. THE PERFORMANCE OF THE CUBAN REVOLUTION: A PROVISIONAL ASSESSMENT, pp. 205-208.
Tyson, Brady. ECONOMIC GROWTH AND HUMAN RIGHTS IN BRAZIL: THE FIRST NINE YEARS OF MILITARY TUTELAGE, pp. 208-213.
Orrego-Vicuña, Francisco. ECONOMIC DEVELOPMENT, POLITICAL DEMOCRACY, AND EQUALITY: THE CHILEAN CASE, pp. 213-217.
Gordon, Lincoln. COMMENTS, pp. 217-221.
Wachtel, Howard M. THE EPOCH OF SOCIALISM AND THE INTEGRATION OF WORLD CAPITALISM, pp. 221-227. Panel discussion and comments from the floor at the 67th Annual Meeting, American Society of International Law, 12-14 April 1973.
S

215. —. EL MITO DE LOS PARTIDOS DOMINANTES EN LA CONSOLIDACIÓN DE REVOLUCIONES: UNA COMPARACIÓN ENTRE MÉXICO Y BOLIVIA [The myth of the role of dominant parties in the consolidation of revolutions: a comparison between Mexico and Bolivia]. *Rev. Mexicana de Ciencia Pol. [Mexico] 1975 21(80): 51-64.* Compares postrevolutionary developments of Mexico and Bolivia to demonstrate that the establishment of similar political institutions in dissimilar social environments does not necessarily produce the same results.

216. —. EL PROBLEMA DE LA DISCRIMINACIÓN RACIAL [The problem of racial discrimination]. *Anuario Indigenista [Mexico] 1975 35: 21-54.* Since its founding in 1940, the Instituto Indigenista Interamericano has devoted considerable effort to fighting the political, social, and economic discrimination against the native populations of the Americas. At its conferences the institute has promulgated resolutions favoring personal freedom, political equality, native participation in economic development, agrarian reform, improved public health services for Indians, an end to forced labor, recognition of the right to practice native customs, equal educational opportunity, equal protection under the law, and other rights for Indians. The organization has also published antiracist material in its two journals (*Anuario Indigenista* and *América Indígena*) and in two monograph series (*Ediciones Especiales* and *Antropología Social*) and has sponsored a seminar and courses on Indian rights. Based on publications of the Institute and secondary sources; table, diagram, 12 notes, biblio. and a list of Institute publications.
G.-A. Patzwald

217. —. [FRENCH PH.D. DISSERTATIONS, 1976-78]. *Cahiers du Monde Hispanique et Luso-Brésilien [France] 1980 (numero special): 11-130.*
LISTE ALPHABÉTIQUE DES THÈSES DE TROISIÈME CYCLE SOUTENUES EN FRANCE DE 1976 À 1978 [Alphabetical list of dissertations defended in France, 1976-78], pp. 11-19. Provides an alphabetical list by author of 112 dissertations defended in French universities, 1976-78, in all branches of Latin American studies, including title, supervisor, university, year, and category.
POSITIONS ET RÉSUMÉS CONCERNANT LES THÈSES DE TROISIÈME CYCLE SOUTENUES EN FRANCE (1976-1978) EN DROIT, HISTOIRE, LINGUISTIQUE, LITTÉRATURE, PHILOSOPHIE, PSYCHOLOGIE, SCIENCES DE L'EDUCATION, SOCIOLOGIE, POLITIQUE DE L'AMÉRIQUE LATINE [Arguments and summaries of dissertations defended in France, 1976-78, in Latin American law, history, linguistics, literature, philosophy, psychology, education, sociology, and politics], pp. 21-130. Contains 44 abstracts in French and Spanish.
P. J. Durell

218. —. LA INTERVENCIÓN DE MÉXICO EN NICARAGUA SEGÚN LA PRENSA NORTEAMERICANA [Mexican intervention in Nicaragua according to the US press]. *Bol. del Archivo General de la Nación [Mexico] 1980 4(1): 29-35.* Reprints nine documents concerning the portrayal of Mexican activities in Nicaragua by US newspapers. Taken from the papers of Presidents Obregón and Calles at the Archivo General de la Nación; 2 photos.
J. A. Lewis

219. —. LA POSICIÓN DEL GOBIERNO MEXICANO FRENTE A LA INTERVENCIÓN NORTEAMERICANA EN NICARAGUA Y LA PROPOSICIÓN SANDINISTA DE ALIANZA LATINOAMERICANA, 1926-1930 [The position of the Mexican government toward North American intervention in Nicaragua and toward the Sandinista proposal of a Latin American alliance, 1926-30]. *Bol. del Archivo General de la Nación [Mexico] 1980 4(1): 36-49.* Reprints 10 documents reflecting official Mexican reaction to American intervention in Nicaragua and to the idea of General Augusto César Sandino to unite Latin America against the United States. Taken from the papers of Presidents Obregón, Calles, and Portes Gil in the Archivo General de la Nación; 2 photos.
J. A. Lewis

220. —. LA RECHERCHE LATINO-AMÉRICANISTE EN FRANCE (1979) [Latin American research in France (1979)]. *Cahiers du Monde Hispanique et Luso-Brésilien [France] 1980 (35): 205-308.* An alphabetical list of dissertations defended in France in 1979.
D. R. Stevenson

221. —. THE LATIN AMERICAN CHURCH AS AN INFLUENCE FOR STRUCTURAL CHANGE AND AGRARIAN REFORM. *Civilisations [Belgium] 1973-1974 23-24(1-2): 2-29.* Documents issued following the Catholic Church episcopal conference in Medellin (1968), the Peruvian episcopate (1971), and a group of prelates in northeast Brazil (1973) show that agrarian reform and socialism in Latin America are necessary. A theology of liberation reflecting social change has come into being. The clergy have begun to protest against unjust governmental policies and growing social inequalities. 15 notes.
H. L. Calkin

222. —. [LITERATURE ON INTER-AMERICAN RELATIONS]. *Latin Am. Res. Rev. 1979 14(3): 235-237.*
Wood, Bryce. LITERATURE ON INTER-AMERICAN RELATIONS: COMMENT, pp. 235-236. Criticizes Jorge I. Domínguez's earlier article which ignored the "time factor" in historical studies as well as the impact of differing personalities and perceptions of leaders.
Domínguez, Jorge I. LITERATURE ON INTER-AMERICAN RELATIONS: REPLY, p. 237. Admits that his article ignored the "time factor," but recent political science literature has not ignored personalities and perceptions of leaders.
J. K. Pfabe

223. —. [THE PERFORMANCE OF SOUTH AMERICAN CIVILIAN AND MILITARY GOVERNMENTS FROM A SOCIOECONOMIC PERSPECTIVE]. *Development and Change [Netherlands] 1979 10(3): 461-487.*
Pluta, Joseph. THE PERFORMANCE OF SOUTH AMERICAN CIVILIAN AND MILITARY GOVERNMENTS FROM A SOCIOECONOMIC PERSPECTIVE, pp. 461-483. Methodology for evaluating the performance of military and civilian governments in Latin America in the 1970's.
Dickson, Thomas. COMMENT ON PLUTA'S ARTICLE, pp. 485-487.

International Relations

224. Băluţă-Kiss, Lucreţia. UN SIÈCLE DEPUIS L'ÉTABLISSE-MENT DES PREMIERS CONTACTS OFFICIELS ENTRE LE ROUMANIE ET DES ÉTATS DE L'AMÉRIQUE LATINE [The centennial of the first official contacts between Romania and some states of Latin America]. *Rev. Roumaine d'Études Int. [Romania] 1981 15(2): 179-182.* Reviews a symposium in Bucharest, initiated by the Association de Droit International et des Relations Internationales (ADIRI), on the history of Romania's relations with Latin America and the progress made in political, legal, economic, and cultural relations.　　　G. P. Cleyet

225. Barber, Willard F. FOREIGN POLICY INTERRELATION-SHIPS: A REVIEW ESSAY. *J. of Inter-Am. Studies and World Affairs 1974 16(2): 234-242.* Review essay on: G. Pope Atkins and Larman C. Wilson's *The United States and the Trujillo Regime* (Rutgers U. Press, 1972); Daniel A. Sharp's *Foreign Policy and Peru* (U. of Texas Press, 1972); and Miles D. Wolpin's *Cuban Foreign Policy and Chilean Politics* (Heath, 1971).　　　J. R. Thomas

226. Bitar, Sergio. AMÉRICA LATINA Y ESTADOS UNIDOS: RELACIONES ECONÓMICAS EN LOS AÑOS SETENTA [Latin America and the United States: economic relations in the 1970's]. *Estudios Int. [Chile] 1982 15(58): 205-224.* Concentrates on the asymmetry of US-Latin American economic relations and the relative interdependence of Latin America and the United States, especially during the 1970's.

227. Boardman, Thomas and Kelly, Philip. INTERVENTION AND THE CARIBBEAN: LATIN AMERICAN RESPONSES TOWARD UNITED NATIONS PEACEKEEPING. *Rev. Interamericana [Puerto Rico] 1976 6(3): 403-411.* Statistical analysis of UN voting patterns regarding international interventions in the Suez crisis of 1956 and the Congo crisis of 1960 shows that Latin American nations voted on these issues on the basis of their sensitivity to potential US intervention in the Western Hemisphere. The Caribbean and Central American countries consistently voted against UN intervention, and South American countries voted for such intervention. Based on primary sources; 2 tables, appendix, 10 notes.　　　J. A. Lewis

228. Bohne, Regina. DIE TRAGISCHE "SCHICKSALSGEMEIN-SCHAFT" ZWISCHEN DEN USA UND LATEINAMERIKA [The tragic "community of fate" between the United States and Latin America]. *Frankfurter Hefte [West Germany] 1982 37(5): 15-23.* The 1947 Rio Treaty strengthened the US supremacy in Latin America earlier established on the basis of the Monroe Doctrine, and like the earlier declaration combined political and strategic interests with economic.

229. Bologna, Alfredo Bruno. RUPTURA DEL SISTEMA IN-TERAMERICANO [Rupture of the inter-American system]. *Rev. de Pol. Int. [Spain] 1977 (151): 191-207.* Discusses the relationship between the United States and Latin America between 1969 and 1977 in the light of the latter's concern for independence.

230. Bueno, Salvador. LAS RELACIONES ENTRE HUNGRÍA Y AMÉRICA LATINA EN EL SIGLO XX (HASTA 1945) [Relations between Hungary and Latin America in the 20th century, to 1945]. *Rev. de la Biblioteca Nac. José Martí [Cuba] 1977 19(3): 41-51.* Massive Hungarian immigration to the New World began in 1877, but during 1919-23 and 1929-33, immigration to Latin America, especially Argentina and Brazil, increased significantly. In most Latin American countries Hungarians entered the middle class, but remained predominantly laborers in Argentina. Hungarian-language newspapers emerged in the 1930's. During the 1930's, leftists fled Hungary for France and Switzerland, immigrating to Latin America beginning in 1940. Strong antifascist organizations developed in Mexico and Cuba. Until the end of World War II, literature in Hungary tended to characterize Latin America as exotic and uncivilized. Excerpted from a forthcoming book.　　　R. D. Rodríguez

231. Carmagnani, Marcello. AMERICA LATINA E APOLITICITÀ NOSTRANA [Latin America and our nonpolicy]. *Belfagor [Italy] 1981 36(4): 443-452.* In the context of the internationaliza-tion of the struggle for democracy in Latin America, discusses European attitudes to Latin American problems and the absence of an Italian policy or initiative.

232. Cochrane, James D. REVIEW ESSAY: SOME PERSPEC-TIVES ON LATIN AMERICAN INTERNATIONAL RELATIONS. *J. of Inter-Am. Studies and World Affairs 1975 17(2): 225-236.* Reviews eight recently published books on Latin American international relations, focusing on Soviet and intra-Latin American relations and the role of Latin America in the UN.　　　J. R. Thomas

233. Connell-Smith, Gordon. LATIN AMERICA IN THE FOR-EIGN RELATIONS OF THE UNITED STATES: REVIEW ARTI-CLE. *J. of Latin Am. Studies [Great Britain] 1976 8(1): 137-150.* Federico G. Gil's *Latin American-United States Relations* (Harcourt Brace Jovanovich, 1971) is "a useful overview" for undergraduate courses; Joseph S. Tulchin's *The Aftermath of War: World War I and US Policy Toward Latin America* (New York U. Pr., 1971) argues that by 1925 the United States had achieved its major goals of expanding communications facilities under American control, winning control over foreign petroleum reserves, and replacing European with American bankers; Dana Munro's *The United States and the Caribbean Republics, 1921-1933* (Princeton U. Pr., 1974) concentrates on the gradual transition from intervention to nonintervention; F. Parkinson's *Latin America, The Cold War, and the World Powers, 1945-1973: A Study in Diplomatic History* (Beverly Hills and London: Sage, 1974) shows how the Cold War influenced intra-Latin American relations in ways which indicate that Latin American relations will increasingly resemble the 19th century; Jerome Levinson and Juan de Onis, *The Alliance that Lost Its Way: A Critical Report on the Alliance for Progress* (Chicago: Quadrangle Books, 1970), argue that "the democratic ideals of President Kennedy have been abandoned"; Richard B. Gray's *Latin America and the United States in the 1970's* (Itasca, Ill.: F. E. Peacock, 1971) is a collection of speeches and articles that show the low importance given Latin America during the early Nixon years; Julio Cotler's and Richard R. Fagen's anthology, *Latin America and the United States: The Changing Political Realities* (Stanford U. Pr., 1974), tends to reinforce the view that Latin America does not exist "except as defined by US interests and actions"; Frank D. McCann, Jr.'s *The Brazilian American Alliance, 1937-1945* (Princeton U. Pr., 1973) demonstrates the illusions of Brazil's leaders and how much more special the US-Brazil relationship was to Brazil than to the United States; Wayne A. Selcher's *The Afro-Asian Dimension of Brazilian Foreign Policy, 1956-1972* (U. of Florida Pr., 1974) argues that Brazil is the best-suited American nation to approach the nonwhite Third World, but that this has limited advantages to Brazil; and Karl M. Schmitt's *Mexico and the United States, 1821-1973: Conflict and Coexistence* (New York: John Wiley, 1974) provides "a useful new survey" of the power imbalance between these two countries.　　　K. M. Bailor

234. Dangond Uribe, Alberto. ANTONIO JOSE URIBE Y SU TIEMPO ¿POR QUE PERDIMOS A PANAMA? [Antonio José Uribe and his time: why did we lose Panama?]. *Bol. de Hist. y Antigüedades [Colombia] 1980 67(728): 87-114.* Antonio José Uribe, who served as Undersecretary of Foreign Relations during part of the US-Colombian canal negotiations and was Minister of Education during the debate on the resulting Hay-Herrán Treaty, correctly foresaw the consequences of a failure to reach agreement with the United States. He therefore defended the Hay-Herrán Treaty, and subsequently, as Minister of Foreign Relations, he supported the Urrutia-Thompson Treaty, 1922, which restored amicable relations between the two countries. The loss of Panama was, however, the fault of Colombians generally, not of any one faction or individual.　　　D. Bushnell

235. Díaz Albónico, Rodrigo. EL SISTEMA DE SEGURIDAD IN-TERAMERICANA Y SUS NUEVOS DESARROLLOS A TRAVÉS DEL TRATADO DE TLATELOLCO [New developments in the interamerican security system through the Treaty of Tlatelolco]. *Estudios Int. [Chile] 1980 13(51): 345-381.* The Treaty of Tlatelolco added a new dimension to interamerican peace and stability and helped to guarantee the peaceful uses of atomic energy in the region.

236. Drekonia Kornat, Gerhald. APROXIMACIONES A LA POLÍTICA EXTERIOR LATINOAMERICANA [Approaches to Latin American foreign policy]. *Estudios Int. [Chile] 1981 14(53): 89-104.*

In discussing the new foreign policy of the Latin American countries one must widen the concept to include not only autonomous initiatives with regard to other countries but also participation in the North-South dialogue, maintenance of the First-Third world equilibrium, and discussions within the ranks of the Group of 77 and UNCTAD.

237. Espiell, Hector Gros. U.S.A. E DENUCLEARIZZAZIONE NELL'AMERICA LATINA [The United States and denuclearization in Latin America]. *Riv. di Studi Pol. Int. [Italy] 1977 44(4): 565-578.* Examines the diplomatic background, 1973-77, to the signing by Jimmy Carter, 29 May 1977, of an additional protocol to the Treaty of Tlatelolco, prohibiting the development of nuclear arms in Latin America.

238. Francis, Michael J. THE UNITED STATES AT RIO, 1942: THE STRAINS OF PAN-AMERICANISM. *J. of Latin Am. Studies [Great Britain] 1974 6(1): 77-95.* Explains why at the Rio Conference (1942) a rupture of diplomatic relations with the Axis powers rather than a joint declaration of war or a unanimous termination of relations with the Axis was recommended. In explaining this outcome, the author focuses on the domestic and foreign policy considerations of representatives from Chile, Argentina, and Brazil. Different analyses of Latin American realities, plus sharp personal rivalry between US Under Secretary of State Sumner Welles and Secretary Cordell Hull added to the difficulties of the United States in obtaining the unanimous break which Hull thought more desirable. Based on the US National Archives, Department of State, and *Foreign Relations of the United States* and some secondary works; 95 notes.
K. M. Bailor

239. Fukumasu, Kunio. TANAKA SHUSHO NO LATEN AMERIKA HŌMON TO NIHON SHIHON NO NERAI [Premier Tanaka's visit to Latin America and the aim of Japanese capital]. *Ajia Afurika Kenkyū [Japan] 1974 14(10): 1-4.* Reviews points at issue surrounding Premier Kakuei Tanaka's visit to Mexico and Brazil in September 1974. The rapid export of Japanese capital was brought on by the economic, political, and industrial conditions of both Japan and the countries of Latin America. Questions whether the introduction of Japanese capital meets the interests of the developing countries.
H. Kawanami

240. Gannon, Francis X. LATIN AMERICA AND THE U.S.—THAT "SPECIAL RELATIONSHIP." *Worldview 1977 20(4): 34-41.* The Latin American policy of the United States since the late 1950's has vacillated between neglect and involvement.

241. Gay, Daniel. LA PRESSE D'EXPRESSION FRANÇAISE DU QUÉBEC ET L'AMÉRIQUE LATINE: INVENTAIRE D'EDITORIAUX ET DE PARA-EDITORIAUX, 1959-1973 [The French press of Quebec on Latin America: an inventory of editorials, 1959-73]. *Études Int. [Canada] 1976 7(3): 359-392.* This subject-author inventory of signed and unsigned editorials in *Action Catholique* and *Le Soleil* of Quebec, *Le Devoir* and *La Presse* of Montreal, 1959-73, facilitates the study of Canadian-Latin American and Quebec-Latin American relations. Secondary sources; 3 notes.
J. F. Harrington, Jr.

242. Gil, Federico G. THE FUTURE OF UNITED STATES-LATIN AMERICAN RELATIONS. *Secolas Ann. 1976 7: 5-19.* Brazil, Venezuela, Peru, and Cuba have emerged in the 1970's as leading countries in Latin America. In the future, Washington will have to conduct its relations with Latin America in the same fashion that diplomatic contact is maintained with Europe.
J. A. Lewis

243. Gil, Federico G. LAS RELACIONES ENTRE ESTADOS UNIDOS Y AMÉRICA LATINA EN LA DÉCADA DEL 70 [Relations between the United States and Latin America in the 1970's]. *Rev. Española de la Opinión Pública [Spain] 1976 (43): 320-332.* Reports on the deterioration in foreign relations between the United States and Latin America following World War II, and outlines the background to the situation in the early 1970's.

244. Glinkin, A. CHANGES IN LATIN AMERICA. *Int. Affairs [USSR] 1975 (1): 51-58.* Latin America is assuming a new and important role in world affairs, ending US domination of the continent, establishing sovereignty over domestic and foreign relations, and moving toward nonalignment and closer economic contact with socialist nations. 13 notes.
D. K. McQuilkin

245. Gómez, Mario Ojeda. THE UNITED STATES-LATIN AMERICAN RELATIONSHIP SINCE 1960. *World Today [Great Britain] 1974 30(12): 513-521.* "Last May participants from eleven countries in Western Europe and the Americas attended a Chatham House conference on 'Latin America in the international system,' organized as part of a study program supported by the Ford Foundation. Amongst the objectives of this conference was to ask what kind of world the Latin American countries must confront, particularly in the light of the great changes in the Northern Hemisphere since the mid-1960s, and what sort of actors they are themselves becoming on the international scene."
J

246. Grabendorff, Wolf. GEWALT UND AUSSENPOLITIK: ZUM KONFLIKTVERHALTEN LATEINAMERIKANISCHER STAATEN SEIT DEM ZWEITEN WELTKRIEG [Force and foreign policy: conflict behavior of Latin American states since World War II]. *Jahrbuch für Geschichte von Staat, Wirtschaft und Gesellschaft Lateinamerikas [West Germany] 1978 15: 397-424.* The traditional reasons for relative force-free foreign relations conduct in Latin America, such as a low level of armaments, internal stability, and a regional security system, have dissipated since World War II. Based upon printed secondary sources; 66 notes, 4 tables.
T. D. Schoonover

247. Grabendorff, Wolf. LATEINAMERIKA UND DIE VEREINIGTEN STAATEN [Latin America and the United States]. *Europa-Archiv [West Germany] 1977 32(14): 433-440.* Traces the course of US-Latin American foreign relations over the past 20 years, maintaining that the influence of the United States is progressively weakening.

248. Green, Rosario. LA IMPORTANCIA DEL ESTUDIO DE LAS RELACIONES INTERNACIONALES DE LOS PAÍSES LATINOAMERICANOS [The importance of the study of the international relations of Latin American countries]. *Estudios Int. [Chile] 1980 13(52): 527-544.* Given the insufficiency of the theory of imperialism to explain the phenomena of the periphery and the theoretical erosion of the dependency approach, the author argues for a systematic in-depth study of the external relations of the countries of Latin America.

249. Grieb, Kenneth J. AWAKENING GIANTS: LATIN AMERICA ENTERS THE WORLD ARENA. *North Dakota Q. 1977 45(2): 73-83.* Examines economic and social development in Latin American countries during the 20th century and the implications of this development for Latin American foreign policy and traditional US predominance in the Western hemisphere.

250. Grindle, Merilee. ARMED INTERVENTION AND U.S.-LATIN AMERICAN RELATIONS. *Latin Am. Res. Rev. 1981 16(1): 207-217.* Reviews seven works on US intervention in Latin America. Latin American elites have manipulated US involvement to serve their own purposes. In recent years, the decision to use troops has passed from State Department functionaries to higher level decisionmakers. Since World War II global issues have played a larger role than previously. US intervention has altered significantly the outcome of internal Latin American conflicts and the political and economic development of the area. 7 notes.
J. K. Pfabe

251. Grodona, Mariano. DIE AUSWIRKUNGEN DER ENTSPANNUNG AUF LATEINAMERIKA. EIN BEITRAG AUS LATEINAMERIKANISCHER SICHT [The impact of detente on Latin America: a contribution from the Latin American viewpoint]. *Europa Archiv [West Germany] 1977 32(5): 147-156.* Anti-Communist regimes in South America interpret detente as a disguise for penetration of their sociopolitical systems; the only positive effect is the possibility of trade relations with the Communist countries.

252. Haines, Gerald K. UNDER THE EAGLE'S WING: THE FRANKLIN ROOSEVELT ADMINISTRATION FORGES AN AMERICAN HEMISPHERE. *Diplomatic Hist. 1977 1(4): 373-388.* The Franklin D. Roosevelt administration evolved a comprehensive program for minimizing the influence of the Axis powers in Latin America. Secret police of friendly nations were trained by FBI agents, and Axis aid to local military forces was displaced by American aid. Newspapers, firms, and radio stations thought to be pro-Axis were blacklisted; for example, American firms were told to restrict their tax deductible Latin

American advertising to friendly newspapers and stations. Government censorship was encouraged, while the region was blanketed with pro-American propaganda. The US effort was coordinated by the Office of the Coordinator of Inter-American Affairs (OCIAA) beginning in 1940, headed by Nelson Rockefeller. Based on archival and secondary sources; 60 notes.   L. W. Van Wyk

253. Haley, P. Edward. COMPARATIVE INTERVENTION: MEXICO IN 1914 AND THE DOMINICAN REPUBLIC IN 1965. *Australian J. of Pol. and Hist. [Australia] 1974 20(1): 32-44.* Compares President Wilson's intervention in Mexico in 1914 with President Johnson's in the Dominican Republic in 1965 against a background of US military intervention in the 20th century. The characteristic American reaction to foreign revolution is neither defense of self-determination nor exploitation. Rather the United States has sought to devise and put into operation a liberal democratic alternative to radical social revolution. This predates the Cold War and great power status and is determined by the beliefs of American leaders, domestic political needs, the policymakers' comprehension of the situation, capability, and a favorable international situation. Based on monographs and memoirs.
                                                   W. D. McIntyre

254. Harbron, John. GROWING PRESSURES ON CANADA TO SEEK HEMISPHERIC IDENTITY. *Internat. Perspectives [Canada] 1974 (3): 31-35.* Discusses relations between Canada and Latin America in the 1970's.   S

255. Healy, David. ADMIRAL WILLIAM B. CAPERTON AND UNITED STATES NAVAL DIPLOMACY IN SOUTH AMERICA, 1917-1919. *J. of Latin Am. Studies [Great Britain] 1976 8(2): 297-323.* Caperton's (1855-1941) attempts to get Brazil, Uruguay, and Argentina into World War I against Germany were impressive but not successful; only Brazil eventually declared war on Germany, Uruguay was already pro-Allied, and Argentina stayed neutral and ambivalent. His use of his subsequent popularity and his fleet to replace British with American influence in these countries after the war was much more successful. Americans replaced the British as the principal suppliers and advisers to the Brazilian Navy, and by 1926 the United States had become the leading source of Brazil's imports. Caperton's superiors completely disagreed with his diplomatic interests once his initial contacts had apparently succeeded. Based primarily on Caperton's "History of US Naval Operations Under Command of Rear Admiral W. B. Caperton, USN Commencing January 5, 1915, ending April 30, 1919," US National Archives Record Group 45, and Naval Records Collection of the Office of Naval Records and Library, Subject File ZN (Personnel), 1911-27; 49 notes.
                                                    K. M. Bailor

256. Jaguaribe, Helio. EL INFORME LINOWITZ Y LAS RELACIONES ESTADOS UNIDOS-AMÉRICA [The Linowitz Report and US-Latin American relations]. *Estudios Int. [Chile] 1977 10(40): 47-59.* Evaluates favorably and places in historical perspective the recommendations of the second report of the US Commission on Relations between the United States and Latin America, under the direction of Sol M. Linowitz, 20 December 1976.

257. Jamison, Edward Alden. CUBA AND THE INTER-AMERICAN SYSTEM: EXCLUSION OF THE CASTRO REGIME FROM THE ORGANIZATION OF AMERICAN STATES. *Americas (Acad. of Am. Franciscan Hist.) 1980 36(3): 317-346.* After the failure of the Bay of Pigs invasion to overthrow the government of Fidel Castro, the United States renewed efforts to obtain inter-American action against Cuba. Colombia, while criticizing past unilateral US actions, took the initiative in working for OAS sanctions. Mexico was strongly opposed but adopted a less adamant position once Castro formally declared himself a "Marxist-Leninist." The culmination came at a meeting in Punta del Este in early 1962 that formally excluded Cuba from the Organization of American States. Based on personal recollections as well as published materials; 71 notes.   D. Bushnell

258. Kaufman, Aby and Shapira, Yoram. JEWS AND ARABS IN LATIN AMERICA. *Patterns of Prejudice [Great Britain] 1976 10(1): 15-26.* Jewish communities in Latin America have exerted political influence on their respective governments in support of Israel since 1948; the pressure of events since 1967 and increased efforts by Arab diplomats are leading to a similar pattern among Latin American Arabs.

259. Kelly, Philip L. THE PARTICIPATION OF THE LATIN AMERICAN STATES IN THE LEAGUE OF NATIONS. *R. Interamericana [Puerto Rico] 1973 2(4): 574-586.* All 20 Latin American republics eventually joined the League of Nations, but some took far more interest in the organization than did others. Many Latin American countries viewed the League as a possible counterweight to US influence in the hemisphere. Ultimately, the cost of membership and the interest of the League in European affairs caused most countries to curtail their League activities. Primary and secondary sources; table, 26 notes.
                                                       J. Lewis

260. Kessler, Francis P. KISSINGER'S LEGACY: A LATIN AMERICAN POLICY. *Current Hist. 1977 72(424): 76-78, 86-88.* Examines the evolution in US Latin American policy during the Nixon and Ford administrations while Henry A. Kissinger was Secretary of State. President Carter's administration is likely to follow a policy similar to that established by Kissinger.

261. Kevrov, A. I. NOVYE TENDENTSII VO VNESHNEI POLITIKE LATINOAMERIKANSKIKH STRAN [New trends in the foreign policy of Latin American countries]. *Novaia i Noveishaia Istoriia [USSR] 1977 (4): 68-82.* The recently intensified tendencies toward independent foreign policy in Latin America have led to the crisis of the bloc diplomacy in the Western hemisphere. The failure of the blockade against Cuba, the establishment of the Latin American economic system (without the USA), the decline of the influence of the OAS and the entire Pan-American system are vivid proof of this crisis. The author deals with all these aspects in polemics with bourgeois authors.   J

262. Khripunov, I. CANADA AND LATIN AMERICA. *Int. Affairs [USSR] 1976 (9): 110-114.* In an effort to diminish the influence which the United States holds politically and economically in the Western Hemisphere, Canada and several Latin American countries have established diplomatic relations, 1970-76.

263. Kirichenko, V. P. SSHA I REPRESSIVNYI APPARAT DIKTATORSKIKH REZHIMOV LATINSKOI AMERIKI [The United States and the repressive apparatus of Latin American dictatorial regimes]. *Sovetskoe Gosudarstvo i Pravo [USSR] 1980 (9): 102-104.* Although the Carter administration has declared itself the world's champion of human rights and has conducted under this banner an anti-Communist and anti-Soviet campaign against alleged human rights violations in socialist countries, the United States, through its treaties and agreements with the most repressive military regimes in Latin America, is itself a supporter of governments which systematically and harshly deny their citizens fundamental human rights. This is justified on the basis of a theory of "divided responsibility," according to which the security of the Western Hemisphere (and of the Latin American regimes) is guaranteed by US access to the natural, military, and manpower resources of Latin America. 18 notes.   S

264. Kirkpatrick, Jeane. U.S. SECURITY & LATIN AMERICA. *Commentary 1981 71(1): 29-40.* The ideology embodied in Zbigniew Brzezinski's *Between Two Ages*, the two Linowitz reports, and *The Southern Connection*, a report issued by the Institute for Policy Studies Ad Hoc Working Group on Latin America, all of which abandoned the Monroe Doctrine for a global, rather than hemispheric approach, determined the Carter administration's policy toward Latin America. The resulting commitment to "change" in Latin America has led to a Cuban-backed takeover in Nicaragua, the probability of another in El Salvador and, but for a military coup, the accession of the leftist Hernán Siles Zuazo in Bolivia.

265. Kramer-Kase, Liselotte. DIE BÜRGERLICHE HISTORIOGRAPHIE IN DEN USA ZUR ROLLE DES INTERAMERIKANISCHEN SYSTEMS BEI DER HERAUSBILDUNG DER GLOBALEN STRATEGIE DES KALTEN KRIEGES [Bourgeois historiography in the United States on the role of the Inter-American System in the development of the global strategy of the Cold War]. *Jahrbuch für Geschichte [East Germany] 1978 18: 253-294.* Sketches foreign relations between the United States and Latin America, 1945-50, and reviews the major trends in American historiography on the role of Latin America in US Cold War policy in the 1950's and 1960's. In the 1950's American historiography was dominated

by an orthodox conventional or semi-official government view, but important variants included right revisionist and liberal traditional interpretations. Under the changed international conditions of the 1960's, the semi-official government orthodox view split into realistic and strictly orthodox wings. The right revisionists played a minimal role in the 1960's, but a new leftist bourgeois view entered the debates. The author analyzes a few representatives of these views. 164 notes.   J. B. Street

266. Kudriavtsev, A. PEKING'S POLICY IN LATIN AMERICA. *Far Eastern Affairs [USSR] 1980 (2): 89-101.* Hegemonism, antisocialism and anti-Sovietism characterized China's policy in Latin America in the 1970's. Apart from purely political goals, China's main tasks were to gain access to modern Western technology and to penetrate the system of capitalist international economic relations.

267. Kyrychenko, V. P. FAL'SYFIKATSIIA AMERYKANS'-KOIU BURZHUAZNOIU ISTORIOHRAFIEIU POLITYKY SSHA V LATYNS'KIY AMERYTSI V 1939-1945 RR [The falsification of US policy in Latin America, 1939-45, by US bourgeois historiography]. *Ukrains'kyi Istorychnyi Zhurnal [USSR] 1975 (1): 134-138.* Comments on US foreign policy in Latin America, 1939-45, referring to the mutual treaties which when drawn up appeared to favor Latin America but which were also advantageous for the United States.

268. Lambert, Denis-Clair. UN PIEGE DES GLOBALISATIONS NORD-SUD: LE PLAFONNEMENT DES ECHANGES ENTRE L'EUROPE ET L'AMERIQUE LATINE [A trap of North-South globalizations: the limits of trade between Europe and Latin America]. *Problèmes d'Amérique Latine [France] 1982 (64): 35-78.* Examines the peculiar economic and political relations between Europe and Latin America, illustrating room for improvement and dispelling myths of harmony of interests and mutual needs of the countries concerned. Presents possible directions for improved and successful relations.

269. Lambrecht, Rainer. GRUNDZÜGE DER GENESIS UND EVOLUTION DES INTERAMERIKANISCHEN POLITISCH-MILITÄRISCHEN SYSTEMS [Main features of the genesis and evolution of the inter-American political-military system]. *Militärgeschichte [East Germany] 1980 19(1): 41-52.* Starting from the Monroe Doctrine, the author discusses the chief political and military aspects of American policy toward Latin America, particularly the inter-American political-military system, its components, and the stages of its development. This system dominated by the United States, is comparable to a military bloc. The author indicates the most important actions of the United States against Latin America since World War II. 2 tables, 39 notes.
J/T (H. D. Andrews)

270. LaOrden Miracle, Enrique. ESPAÑA ANTE IBEROAMÉRICA, HOY DÍA [Spain faced with contemporary Latin America]. *Rev. de Política Int. [Spain] 1978 (157): 11-39.* Describes the history of Latin America, 1492-1978, and stresses the importance of mutual cooperation with Spain.

271. Lebergott, Stanley. THE RETURNS TO U.S. IMPERIALISM, 1890-1929. *J. of Econ. Hist. 1980 40(2): 229-252.* Focuses on US foreign investment, noting its trivial impact on returns to US capital and its greater importance for five industry groups, reviewing the economic advantages accruing to US citizens from intervention in Panama and Cuba, and examining the impact of US foreign investment on Latin American factor returns. No evidence in the antiimperialist literature supports the assertions that such investment cut labor incomes or landowners' capital gains in these nations. The struggle between two groups of capitalists, native and foreign, was more central to the economic aspects of "imperialist" conflict.   J

272. Lima, M. Regina Soares de and Hirst, Mónica. ESTADOS UNIDOS Y AMERICA LATINA: CERRANDO UNA EPOCA EN DESCOMPOSICION [The United States and Latin America: closing an epoch of decay]. *Estudios Int. [Chile] 1981 14(56): 530-552.* Discusses the necessity of political and economic reorganization, both internally and externally, of the United States and Latin American countries, so that equitable bilateral relations will exist between all countries involved.

273. López Segrera, Francisco. LOS NO ALINEADOS Y LA AMÉRICA LATINA [The nonaligned nations and Latin America]. *Casa de las Américas [Cuba] 1979 20(115): 3-9.* Beginning with the summit conference of nonaligned nations in 1961, Cuba has played an important role in these meetings. At the Belgrade conference (1961) Cuba was the only Latin American participant. The number of Latin American participants and observers increased significantly in subsequent summits. At the meetings Cuba voiced strong opposition to imperialism, neocolonialism, and US military bases in Latin America. This strong voice helped make Cuba the site selected for the 1979 summit.   H. J. Miller

274. Lowenthal, Abraham. THE UNITED STATES AND LATIN AMERICA: ENDING THE HEGEMONIC PRESUMPTION. *Foreign Affairs 1976 55(1): 199-213.* US control of the Western Hemisphere can no longer be maintained. Past instances of US interference in the affairs of other American republics only serve to emphasize the emergence of a new relationship within the hemisphere. Traditional hemispheric policy is giving way to a global policy. Cuba's success in removing itself from US domination serves as a symbol to other Latin American countries. 8 notes.   R. Riles

275. Lowenthal, Abraham F. EL FIN DE LA PRESUNCIÓN HEGEMÓNICA [The end of the presumption of supremacy]. *Estudios Int. [Chile] 1977 10(37): 45-67.* Refers to US intervention in Latin America, notably Chile, and the gradual erosion of the concept of special relations which justified US hegemony in the past.

276. Mariscal, Karime L. de and Dorantes, Xóchitl P. de. ARTÍCULOS DE REVISTA RELACIONADOS CON LA ESTRATEGIA Y POLÍTICA INTERNACIONAL DE ESTADOS UNIDOS Y AMÉRICA LATINA [Review article on strategy and international policy of the United States and Latin America]. *Rev. Mexicana de Ciencias Pol. y Soc. [Mexico] 1975 21(81): 183-191.* Lists articles published 1973-75.

277. Meitín, Enrique A. MECANISMOS DE DOMINACIÓN DEL IMPERIALISMO EN EL MOVIMIENTO OBRERO LATINOAMERICANO (1945-1970) [Imperialist mechanisms of domination in the Latin American labor movement, 1945-70]. *Santiago [Cuba] 1981 (43): 9-49.* The Cold War ideology designed to contain the spread of socialism and the founding in 1945 of the World Federation of Trade Unions (WFTU), which brought together the world's most powerful trade union organizations with the exception of the American Federation of Labor, led the US State Department through the Central Intelligence Agency to infiltrate the Latin American labor movement to divide its ranks and to try to dominate its development. The article documents the activities of the AFL-CIO in this context. 40 notes, biblio.
J. V. Coutinho

278. Milenky, Edward S. LATIN AMERICA'S MULTILATERAL DIPLOMACY: INTEGRATION, DISINTEGRATION AND INTERDEPENDENCE. *Int. Affairs [Great Britain] 1977 53(1): 73-96.* Discusses the evolution since the 1960's of multilateral relations from the old regional organizations for economic integration to the new pattern of interdependence and the emergence of the Latin American Economic System (SELA). Although conflicts still occur among Latin American nations where international interests diverge, interdependence has increased. Inevitably "this new pattern of multilateral diplomacy will affect the collective and individual behaviour of Latin American nations." Based on Latin American press sources; 62 notes.   P. J. Beck/S

279. Moffitt, Michael. THE SECOND LINOWITZ COMMISSION REPORT. *Monthly Rev. 1978 29(9): 54-60.* The Linowitz Commission Report, *The United States and Latin America: Next Steps* (New York: Center of Inter-American Relations, 1976) on US-Latin American relations fails to address the major issues of poverty and deprivation in Latin America and retains a patronizing tone.

280. Needler, Martin C. THE INFLUENCE OF AMERICAN INSTITUTIONS IN LATIN AMERICA. *Ann. of the Am. Acad. of Pol. and Social Sci. 1976 (428): 43-51.* The US influence has had a major role in the formation of Latin American political institutions, especially with respect to the separation of powers, the two-chamber legislature, the central role of the president, and the requirement for periodic elections.

European influences have been more marked in administrative organization and the legal system, and there have been some attempts to institute cabinet responsibility to the legislature. However, both models have been adapted to the idiosyncracies of the political dynamics of the region, especially to the frequency of dictatorship, rebellions, and other emergencies.   J

281. Olsen, Edward A.   JAPAN AND LATIN AMERICA. *Asian Affairs: An Am. Rev. 1979 7(2): 117-128.* Discusses the mutually beneficial political and trade relationship between Latin America and Japan. Examines such aspects as investment, commodity power, foreign aid, future economic prospects, and influence. Focuses on relations with Panama, Cuba, and Brazil. Based on official documents and secondary sources; 2 tables, 2 notes.   R. B. Mendel

282. Orrego Vicuña, Francisco.   EUROPA Y AMÉRICA LATINA: HACIA UN ROL INTERNACIONAL COMPLEMENTARIO? [Europe and Latin America: toward a complementary international role?]. *Estudios Int. [Chile] 1981 14(53): 3-16.* Fallen from its former position of power and hampered by problems inherited from its more powerful past, Europe seems to be looking for a partnership with Latin America in dealing with the Third World. The article examines some of the conditions for such a special relationship.

283. Padula, Alfred.   THE CIA IN LATIN AMERICA. *Revista/Review Interamericana [Puerto Rico] 1979 9(2): 240-250.* A review essay on Philip Agee's *Inside the Company: CIA Diary* (1975); Bradley Earl Ayers's *The War That Never Was* (New York, 1976); Ray S. Cline, *Secrets, Spies and Scholars* (Washington, D.C., 1976); Howard Hunt's *Give Us This Day* (New Rochelle, 1973); David Atlee Phillips's *The Night Watch* (New York, 1977); Harry Rositzke's *The CIA's Secret Operations* (New York, 1977); and Joseph B. Smith's *Portrait of a Cold Warrior* (New York, 1976). The Central Intelligence Agency's activity in Latin America was typified by tactics that exaggerated the threat of subversion to the United States, the use of agents provocateurs, lies and deceptions, and the absence of ambassadorial control. Their operations were excessively expensive and often produced such a local reaction against their activities that they were in the end counterproductive.   J. A. Lewis

284. Parkinson, F.   LATIN AMERICAN FOREIGN POLICIES IN THE ERA OF DETENTE. *Internat. Affairs [Great Britain] 1974 50(3): 439-450.* Discusses the foreign policies of Latin American states and emphasizes the growing role of Brazil and the "low profile" policy assumed by the United States. Suggests future developments. Based on research in Latin America and Latin American sources; 37 notes.   P. J. Beck

285. Perez, Louis A., Jr.   INTERNATIONAL DIMENSIONS OF INTER-AMERICAN RELATIONS, 1944-1960. *Inter-Am. Econ. Affairs 1973 27(1): 47-68.*

286. Pérez Llana, Carlos.   ¿POTENCIAS INTERMEDIAS O PAÍSES MAYORES? LA POLÍTICA EXTERIOR DE ARGENTINA, BRASIL Y MÉXICO [Intermediate or great powers?: the foreign policy of Argentina, Brazil, and Mexico]. *Estudios Int. [Chile] 1975 8(29): 47-105.* Studies the effects of international conditions on intraregional relations in Latin America, ca. 1700-1975, as seen in the foreign policies of Argentina, Brazil, and Mexico.

287. Pike, Fredrick B.   CORPORATISM AND LATIN AMERICAN-UNITED STATES RELATIONS. *R. of Pol. 1974 36(1): 132-170.*

288. Pinto, Aníbal.   GUERRA FRÍA Y DISTENSIÓN EN AMÉRICA LATINA: A LA LUZ DE LOS ENSAYOS DE DON JOSÉ MEDINA ECHAVARRÍA [Cold War and détente in Latin America in the light of José Medina Echavarría's essays]. *Estudios Int. [Chile] 1981 14(54): 145-165.* Using José Medina Echavarría's views on the Cold War and détente as a frame of reference and stating that the special relationship existing between the United States and Latin America consists in the subordination of the latter to US foreign policy and the economic interests of multinational corporations in the area, finds that during the Cold War political relations were more restrictive for Latin America than they are now during détente.

289. Porzecanski, Arturo C.   A COMPARATIVE STUDY OF EXCHANGE RATE POLICY UNDER INFLATION. *J. of Developing Areas 1978 12(2): 133-152.* Compares exchange rate policies in Brazil, Argentina, Chile, and Uruguay, countries with rates of domestic inflation significantly and persistently above the world average. Exchange rate adjustments and price level movements have been intimately related. Because of internal political factors, a government may not always set a realistic exchange rate. Based on International Monetary Fund data; 6 tables, 15 notes.   O. W. Eads, Jr.

290. Rabe, Stephen G.   THE ELUSIVE CONFERENCE: UNITED STATES ECONOMIC RELATIONS WITH LATIN AMERICA, 1945-1952. *Diplomatic Hist. 1978 2(3): 279-294.* The idea of a hemispheric conference on postwar economic cooperation, mentioned in a resolution of the third meeting of foreign ministers held in Rio in 1942 was much discussed during the Truman administration, but no such meeting actually took place until 1954. Soon after the close of World War II hostilities, it became clear that the conference, if held, would in all likelihood become the scene of an embarrassing confrontation over a most fundamental issue. The question was whether economic liberalism or government planning should be the dominant feature of inter-American cooperation—whether, in other words, the US government should finance development in Latin America, or whether the region's governments should take steps to attract substantial private American capital. Primary sources; 36 notes.   L. Van Wyk

291. Rabkin, Rhoda Pearl.   U.S.-SOVIET RIVALRY IN CENTRAL AMERICA AND THE CARIBBEAN. *J. of Int. Affairs 1980-81 34(2): 329-351.* Appraises the causes and implications for US-USSR rivalry in Maurice Bishop's left-wing coup in Grenada, the Sandinista revolt in Nicaragua, and the civil war in El Salvador.

292. Raditsa, Leo.   INTELLIGENCE ABOUT SOUTH AMERICA. *Midstream 1979 25(7): 39-44.* Discusses Carlos Rangel's *The Latin Americans, Their Love-Hate Relationship with the United States* (New York: Harcourt Brace Jovanovich, 1977) which examines the political failure of Spanish-speaking America, contrasting it with the success of the United States and briefly outlining South America's political history since 1830.

293. Rogers, William D.   OF MISSIONARIES, FANATICS, AND LAWYERS: SOME THOUGHTS ON INVESTMENT DISPUTES IN THE AMERICAS. *Am. J. of Int. Law 1978 72(1): 1-16.* The Latin American position is that local law is the final arbiter for investment disputes involving foreign companies. This position was reaffirmed in the 1974 UN Charter of Economic Rights and Duties of States. The position of the United States is that international law should be the final arbiter. The formal positions of the Latin Americans and the United States were modified in the 1976 settlement of the Peruvian nationalization of the Marcona iron ore operations, in the settlement of the 1974 Venezuelan oil nationalization, and in the ongoing attempt to settle the Cuban dispute.   R. J. Jirran

294. Rommel, Waldemar.   POLAND AND LATIN AMERICA. *Studies on the Developing Countries [Poland] 1975 (7): 5-27.* Discusses foreign relations between Poland and Latin America in three phases: prior to 1918, 1918-39, and 1944-74.

295. Rosario Green, Maria del.   LAS RELACIONES DE ESTADOS UNIDOS Y AMÉRICA LATINA EN EL MARCO DE LA DEPENDENCIA [United States—Latin American relations within the model of dependence]. *Foro Internacional [Mexico] 1973 13(51): 327-347.* Surveys economic, military, and political relations between the United States and Latin America within the context of the dependence model of foreign relations. Primary and secondary sources; 30 notes.   D. A. Franz

296. Rubin, Barry.   LATIN AMERICA AND THE ARAB-ISRAELI CONFLICT. *Wiener Lib. Bull. [Great Britain] 1976 19(37-38): 30-39.* Analyzes the changing nature and composition of Latin American attitudes and reactions to the Arab-Israeli conflict from 1947. Ideology has had very little to do with the Middle East policies of the Latin American countries. While Arab oil and financial power has been a great factor in changing Latin American policies, the countries most responsive to Arab pressure have not been those most hurt by the higher price of oil,

but those with the greatest hopes and prospects of economic development if given Arab aid. Such aid has not been certain, even if the Arab cause has been supported. The author suggests several factors which have contributed to the unpredictability of Latin American responses to the Arab-Israeli conflict. Based on published sources. 32 notes.   J. P. Fox

297. Salisbury, Richard V. GOOD NEIGHBORS? THE UNITED STATES AND LATIN AMERICA IN THE TWENTIETH CENTURY. Haines, Gerald K. and Walker, J. Samuel, ed. *American Foreign Relations: A Historiographical Review* (Westport, Conn.: Greenwood Pr., 1981): 311-333. An assessment, through a review of recent scholarly publications, of the relationship between the United States and Latin America during the first half of the 20th century. By 1900 the United States had embarked on an imperial course in Latin America and in the next 50 years inter-American relationships varied from outright military intervention to the overt disavowal of such intervention in both the Good Neighbor policy and the spirit of hemispheric cooperation during World War II. New interpretations, perspectives, and schools of thought have emerged since 1950, challenging the assumptions held and the methodologies used by previous generations of diplomatic historians in their analyses of inter-American affairs. Secondary sources; 61 notes.   J. Powell

298. Schiff, Warren. GERMAN LATIN AMERICAN RELATIONS: THE FIRST HALF OF THE TWENTIETH CENTURY. *J. of Interamerican Studies and World Affairs 1980 22(1): 109-117*. Reviews T. Baecker's *Die Deutsche Mexikopolitik 1913-1914* (1971), G. Brunn's *Deutschland und Brasilien (1889-1914)* (1971), A. Ebel's *Das Dritte Reich und Argentinien* (1971), J. Schaefer's *Deutsche Militaerhilfe an Suedamerika* (1974), and K. Volland's *Das Dritte Reich und Mexiko* (1976), which provide an economic determinist analysis of Germany's relations with Latin America.   T. D. Schoonover/S

299. Schoultz, Lars. U.S. FOREIGN POLICY AND HUMAN RIGHTS VIOLATIONS IN LATIN AMERICA: A COMPARATIVE ANALYSIS OF FOREIGN AID DISTRIBUTIONS. *Comparative Pol. 1981 13(2): 149-170*. Discusses the implementation of the human rights policy formulated by the US government during the 1970's focusing on the relationship between US military and economic assistance to Latin America and the recipient governments' repression of basic human rights. A survey of human rights experts was undertaken and their composite judgment was used as an estimate of the degree of human rights violations in Latin America. A pattern of US aid to repressive governments during this period is seen as opposed to isolated incidents. Based on survey, newspapers, and hearings before US House and Senate Subcommittees; 4 tables, 3 fig., 36 notes.   M. A. Kascus

300. Schroeder, Hans-Juergen. HAUPTPROBLEME DER DEUTSCHEN LATEINAMERIKAPOLITIK, 1933-1941 [Central problems of Germany's Latin American policy, 1933-41]. *Jahrbuch für Geschichte von Staat, Wirtschaft und Gesellschaft Lateinamerikas [West Germany] 1975 12: 408-433*. Reviewing recent German and US scholarship reveals the key aspects of Germany's Latin American policy in the pre-World War II years. After 1933, Berlin considered German economic interests the determining factor in its Latin American policy. Washington saw in the growing German involvement a menace to North American interests and tried to limit or eliminate German influence in Latin America. Based on manuscript and printed sources; 77 notes.   T. D. Schoonover

301. Selivanov, Valentin. EL 200 ANIVERSARIO DE LOS EE.UU. Y SU EXPANSIÓN EN AMÉRICA LATINA [The 200th anniversary of the United States and its expansion in Latin America]. *Am. Latina [USSR] 1976 (3): 37-55*. The American Revolution was one of the great liberating revolutions in history but the capitalists dominated the country, and this led to an imperialist foreign policy. The democratic tradition did not completely die, and a few people opposed expansion, but the basic fact was expansion, especially against Latin America. The United States has not only taken land from Latin American countries and interfered militarily but has also exploited them economically. Secondary sources; 34 notes.   J. D. Barnard

302. Shapira, Yoram. ISRAEL'S INTERNATIONAL COOPERATION PROGRAM WITH LATIN AMERICA: THE POLITICAL

ANGLE. *Inter-Am. Econ. Affairs 1976 30(2): 3-31*. Assesses, from the Israeli viewpoint, the political aspects of Israeli technical assistance to Latin America. Although assistance was not politically motivated, it has had a positive political and economic impact obtained at slight cost. 4 tables, 55 notes.   D. A. Franz

303. Sharif, Regina. LATIN AMERICA AND THE ARAB-ISRAELI CONFLICT. *J. of Palestine Studies [Lebanon] 1977 7(1): 98-122*. Latin American policies towards the Middle East have changed from a noncommittal to a more serious approach since the Arab oil embargo and the increasing importance of the Palestinian problem in international forums since 1974. The author analyzes these policies in the light of bilateral relations and voting behavior in the UN. Based on UN documents and contemporary secondary sources; 5 tables, 77 ref.   A. Menicant

304. Sizonenko, A. I. ISTORIIA OTNOSHENII SSSR SO STRANAMI LATINSKOI AMERIKI V RABOTAKH LATINOAMERIKANSKIKH ISSLEDOVATELEI [The history of relations between the USSR and the countries of Latin America in the works of Latin American scholars]. *Istoriia SSSR [USSR] 1979 (5): 216-223*. Reviews works on Soviet-Latin American relations produced by Latin American scholars during the period 1950-79, excepting studies on Soviet-Cuban relations. Since 1945 there has been a marked increase in interest among Latin Americans in the study of relations with the USSR. In general, the works produced by recent Latin American scholars have been less anti-Soviet than those published in the bourgeois West and have reflected the conviction that the establishment of relations between the Soviet Union and the majority of the states of Latin America serves the vital interests of their peoples and the cause of world peace. 34 notes.   J. W. Long

305. Sizonenko, A. I. RAZVITIE SVIAZEI SSSR S LATINSKOI AMERIKOI V 30-E GODY [The development of relations between the USSR and Latin America in the 1930's]. *Voprosy Istorii [USSR] 1977 (6): 49-58*. Focuses on two questions of the utmost importance: the Soviet Union's contacts and cooperation with Latin American countries in international organizations, first and foremost in the League of Nations, and bilateral relations. The author comes to the conclusion that Soviet-Latin American relations in the period under review became more diversified and covered a wider range of problems than in the 1920's. It was precisely in the 1930's that a firm foundation was laid for the Soviet Union's relations with Latin American countries and the basic preconditions were created for the further development of their mutual relations.   J

306. Slater, Jerome. REVIEW ARTICLE: THE UNITED STATES AND LATIN AMERICA: THE NEW RADICAL ORTHODOXY. *Econ. Development and Cultural Change 1977 25(4): 747-761*. Reviews Julie Cotler and Richard R. Fagen, eds., *Latin America and the United States: The Changing Political Realities* (Stanford U. Pr., 1974), a collection of essays on US-Latin American relations. For every essay written by a North American, the editors chose two written by Latin Americans. Many of the selections were written by Marxists and most perceive the United States as an imperialist power whose intent is to keep Latin America in a dependent position. 11 notes.   J. W. Thacker, Jr.

307. Spalding, Hobart A., Jr. U.S. AND LATIN AMERICAN LABOR: THE DYNAMICS OF IMPERIALIST CONTROL. *Latin Am. Perspectives 1976 3(1): 45-69*. Analyzes the history of US labor's involvement in Latin American labor movements. Organized labor (first the AFL, then the AFL-CIO) has consistently supported US foreign policy in supporting unions which are procapitalist. The author emphasizes the role of the American Institute for Free Labor Development (AIFLD). Labor's role has been to hold back independent forces in Latin America and has facilitated its domination by foreign and domestic capital.   J. L. Dietz

308. Stemplowski, Ryszard. LATIN AMERICA, THE U.S., AND DIPLOMACY: NEW BOOKS, OLD PROBLEMS. *Latin Am. Res. Rev. 1980 15(1): 206-210*. Reviews the following works: Jorge Mañach's *Frontiers in the Americas: A Global Perspective*, Philip H. Phenix, transl. (New York: Teachers Coll. Pr., 1975); Annette Baker Fox's *The Politics of Attraction: Four Middle Powers and the United States* (New

York: Columbia U. Pr., 1977); Frederick B. Pike's *The United States and the Andean Republics: Peru, Bolivia, and Ecuador* (Cambridge: Harvard U. Pr., 1977); Harold F. Peterson's *Diplomat of the Americas: A Biography of William I. Buchanan, 1825-1909* (Albany: State U. of New York Pr., 1977); and Harold Eugene Davis, John J. Finan, and F. Taylor Peck's *Latin American Diplomatic History: An Introduction* (Baton Rouge: Louisiana State U. Pr., 1977). J. K. Pfabe

309. Szulc, Tad. L'EVOLUZIONE DELLE RELAZIONI IN-TERAMERICANE [The evolution of inter-American relations]. *Affari Esteri [Italy] 1975 7(28): 676-691.* The foreign relations between the United States and Latin America are better than at any time since President Kennedy launched the Alliance for Progress in 1961, but they are based now on a more realistic assessment by each of the position of the other.

310. Toinet, Marie-France. LE LOBBY LATINO-AMÉRICAIN À WASHINGTON [The Latin American lobby in Washington]. *Problèmes d'Amérique Latine [France] 1981 (60): 73-86.* Studies Washington lobbies and pressure groups that aim at influencing US foreign policy in Latin America.

311. Torshin, Mijail. RELACIONES INTERNACIONALES DE LOS TRABAJADORES DE LA URSS Y DE AMÉRICA LATINA [International relations between the workers of the USSR and Latin America]. *Am. Latina [USSR] 1978 (4): 138-149.* From the first days of the Soviet Union there have been strong ties of proletarian solidarity between the working class of the USSR and Latin America. The Organization of Aid to Revolutionaries (International Red Aid) was founded in 1922-23 to help proletarian movements around the world. It had a significant following in most of Latin America and helped strengthen the ties with the Soviet people. Secondary sources; 20 notes. J. D. Barnard

312. Trask, Roger R. THE IMPACT OF THE COLD WAR ON UNITED STATES-LATIN AMERICAN RELATIONS, 1945-1949. *Diplomatic Hist. 1977 1(3): 271-284.* Seeks to describe and determine the impact of the early years of the Cold War on US-Latin American relations. In 1945 the United States favored universal rather than regional organization, but by 1948, the charter of the Organization of American States (OAS) had been drawn up as a safeguard against Communist attempts at incursion into Latin America. The massive economic aid sought by Latin America was not forthcoming, however, perhaps altering the course of US-Latin American relations. 33 notes. J. Tull

313. Valdes S., Gabriel. REVIEW ESSAY: THE AMERICAS IN A CHANGING WORLD AS A RESPONSE TO THE CONSENSUS OF VIÑA DEL MAR. *J. of Inter-Am. Studies and World Affairs 1975 17(2): 207-216.* After World War II the United States aimed to include Latin America in its political-military sphere. Latin America sought economic assistance, but after Washington had concluded mutual assistance agreements and established the Alliance for Progress, it turned its attention to Europe and Asia. Since no threat appears to exist, the United States has shown little concern for Latin America. Should a threat from the Communist world arise, the United States would deal with the Soviet Union or China, not with Latin America. J. R. Thomas

314. Valenzuela-Fuenzalida, Juan J. INDIFERENCIA, ES-TEREOTIPO Y COOPERACION HORIZONTAL: OBSTACULOS PARA LA COOPERACION ENTRE AFRICA Y AMERICA LAT-INA [Indifference, stereotyping, and mutual cooperation: obstacles in the cooperation between Africa and Latin America]. *Estudios de Asia y Africa [Mexico] 1981 16(1): 124-160.* Describes Juan J. Valenzuela-Fuenzalida's Proyecto Gondwana, which was begun in 1974 at Ahmadu Bello University, Zaria, Nigeria to ascertain the African perception of Latin Americans. Results of a survey showed the lack of accurate knowledge regarding Latin America. These are obstacles in the Third World to mutual international cooperation and growth. Based on a work presented at the 1st meeting of the Latin American Association of Afro-Asian Studies, Mexico City, 16 July 1978; biblio., 2 appendixes, 27 notes, 7 charts. N. A. Newhouse

315. Varg, Paul A. THE ECONOMIC SIDE OF THE GOOD NEIGHBOR POLICY: THE RECIPROCAL TRADE PROGRAM

AND SOUTH AMERICA. *Pacific Hist. Rev. 1976 45(1): 47-71.* Only three of the ten South American republics entered into agreements with the United States under the Reciprocal Trade Agreement Act (1934) between 1934 and 1939, and at least two of those three (Brazil and Colombia) did so for political rather than economic reasons. The act failed because special interests with political clout in the United States blocked the granting of special concessions which South American countries needed and because the United States insisted that all forms of discrimination against American imports be removed before trade negotiations could begin. The removal of such discriminations would have forced cancellation of many bilateral South American-European trade pacts. South Americans were unwilling to do so because they would have to give up more than they would gain. Based on published primary sources, manuscripts in the National Archives, and secondary works; 79 notes. W. K. Hobson

316. Varromi, Joel and Feldman, Carlos. LATIN AMERICAN VOTING ON ISRAELI ISSUES IN THE U.N. GENERAL ASSEMBLY, 1947-1968. *Jewish Social Studies 1974 36(2): 142-165.* Analyzes the voting scores of Latin American nations at the UN from 1947 to 1968. Liberal Latin American regimes tended to be the most positive supporters of Israel. The presence of Jewish and Arab populations in several countries had no impact on the voting patterns. In recent years, despite declining support of Israel by the Latin American bloc in the UN, they accepted the existence of the state of Israel. Primary and secondary sources; 26 notes. P. E. Schoenberg

317. Vélez, Claudio. ERRORES Y OMISIONES: NOTAS SOBRE LA POLÍTICA EXTERIOR DE LOS PAÍSES DE AMÉRICA LAT-INA DURANTE LOS ÚLTIMOS DIEZ AÑOS [Errors and omissions: notes on the foreign policy of Latin American countries, 1967-77]. *Estudios Int. [Chile] 1977 10(40): 5-12.* The failure of Latin American countries, with the exception of Brazil and Cuba, to seize opportunities to enhance their influence in post-Cold War international affairs, 1967-77, is due to a lack of professionalism in the training, attitude, and conduct of Latin American diplomatic personnel.

318. Veliz, Claudio. REVIEW ESSAY: INTER-AMERICAN PERILS OF KNOWLEDGE-MAKING AND KNOWLEDGE-USING. *J. of Inter-Am. Studies and World Affairs 1975 17(2): 217-224.* According to one point of view the United States and Latin America should show greater interest in inter-American relations. Increased knowledge and the use of that knowledge would improve the relationship between the United States and Latin America and among the Latin American nations. However, this attitude places too much value on the US role in Latin America. Not all events in the area result from US activity even though many writers perpetuate this myth. Secondary sources. J. R. Thomas

319. Vinhosa, Francisco Luiz Teixeira. A DIPLOMACIA BRASILEIRA E A REVOLUÇÃO MEXICANA, 1913-1915 [Brazilian diplomacy and the Mexican revolution, 1913-15]. *Rev. do Inst. Hist. e Geog. Brasileiro [Brazil] 1980 (327): 19-81.* When the United States refused to recognize the Victoriano Huerta government in Mexico, diplomatic relations were severed between the two countries. The Brazilian embassy took charge of American affairs in Mexico and played an important part in the search for a solution of the Mexican-American crisis as well as in the reconciliation of the warring factions within Mexico. Based on documents in the archives of the Brazilian Foreign Ministry and the US Department of State; 121 notes, biblio. J. V. Coutinho

320. Vishnia, G. SSHA I LATINSKAIA AMERIKA: VZAIMO-OTNOSHENIIA V USLOVIIAKH RAZRIADKI [The United States and Latin America: their interrelations under the conditions of detente]. *Mirovaia Ekonomika i Mezhdunarodnye Otnosheniia [USSR] 1975 (8): 83-89.* Describes the attempts of the United States since 1969 to establish a new partnership with Latin America, the aim being considered in the context of the worldwide anti-imperialist movement.

321. Volgy, Thomas J. and Kenski, Henry. SYSTEMS THEORY AND FOREIGN POLICY RESTRUCTURING: DISTANCE CHANGE IN LATIN AMERICA, 1953-1970. *Int. Studies Q. 1982 26(3): 445-474.* Scholars of international politics have had little experience with systematically measuring, predicting, or accounting for the

occurrence of major changes between states. Systems theory can be profitably utilized as a starting point for this type of research. One application of this theory is the measurement of distance change, or the degree of congruence in the behavior of one state to the behavior of another. Between 1953 and 1970, there were 43 cases of distance change for the Latin American subsystem, slightly over half of which represented movement away from US leadership. 37 notes, 6 tables.   E. S. Palais

322. Volgy, Thomas J. and Kenski, Henry C. TOWARD AN EXPLORATION OF COMPARATIVE FOREIGN POLICY DISTANCE BETWEEN THE UNITED STATES AND LATIN AMERICA: A RESEARCH NOTE. *Int. Studies Q. 1976 20(1): 143-166*. Examines significant foreign policy changes between the United States and Latin America, based on changes in trade patterns, diplomatic contacts, UN voting, verbal exchanges, and conflict behavior, 1953-70.

323. Whitaker, Arthur P. THE NEW NATIONALISM IN LATIN AMERICA. *R. of Pol. 1973 35(1): 77-90*. A discussion of Latin American nationalism, often a reaction to US imperialism, and how it can be a factor in improved Latin American relations with the USSR.   S

324. Wood, Bryce. THE END OF THE GOOD NEIGHBOR POLICY: CHANGING PATTERNS OF US INFLUENCE. *Caribbean Rev. 1982 11(2): 24-27, 54*. Discusses the failure of the US Good Neighbor Policy toward Latin America, particularly the Caribbean, first announced in Franklin D. Roosevelt's inaugural address, in which he committed the United States to pursue a policy of nonintervention. Because of that and subsequent failures, the United States no longer labels its Latin American policy, choosing instead to deal with each country individually when problems arise.

325. ACCOMPLISHMENTS OF THE U.S. PUBLIC-SAFETY PROGRAM IN LATIN AMERICA. *Inter-Am. Econ. Affairs 1973 26(4): 83-90*. Government documents.   S

326. —. AUSTRALIA'S LINKS WITH LATIN AMERICA. *Australian Foreign Affairs Record [Australia] 1973 44(4): 232-241*. Describes the politics of Latin America and Australian diplomatic ties with that area since 1945. Australian exports have included wheat, wool, coke, rice, oats, milk products, steel, automotive parts, and agricultural machinery. Imports from Latin America include nuts, coffee, sulphates, fish meal, rum, and timber. The trade is mainly with Chile, Peru, Brazil, Mexico, Argentina, and Cuba. Common diplomatic interest centers on a nuclear test ban treaty and the law of the sea. 12 photos.   W. W. Elison

327. —. MÉXICO, ESTADOS UNIDOS Y LA GUERRA CONSTITUCIONALISTA DE NICARAGUA [Mexico, the United States, and the Constitutionalist War in Nicaragua]. *Bol. del Archivo General de la Nación [Mexico] 1980 4(1): 15-28*. Reprint of 28 documents concerning the differences between the United States and Mexico over the changing political situation in Nicaragua in the period of the US intervention in the 1920's and 1930's. Taken from the papers of Presidents Obregón, Calles, and Portes Gil in the Archivo General de la Nación; 3 photos.   J. A. Lewis

Economic and Development Policies

328. Ames, Barry. A NOTE ON THE POLITICAL EXPENDITURE CYCLE IN LATIN AMERICA. *Policy Studies J. 1980 9(1): 40-47*. Examines civilian and military executives in 18 countries, 1945-70, and concludes that they manipulate public expenditures to further their tenures in office.

329. Ames, Barry. THE POLITICS OF PUBLIC SPENDING IN LATIN AMERICA. *Am. J. of Pol. Sci. 1977 21(1): 149-175*. This paper proposes and evalutes a theory of public spending by the central governments of 17 Latin American countries between 1948 and 1970. The theory emphasizes both the need to build political support through government expenditures and the setting in which efforts to maximize sup-

port operate. Political support is increased through the effects of electoral and military cycles, responses to insecurity, and constituency preferences. Efforts to increase support operate in a framework of economic, bureaucratic, and ideological constraints. The results generally support the theory. While the most important influence on spending is the resource base, civilian governments respond to the political demands of the electoral cycle and to their constituencies. Military governments also follow a cyclical pattern, with spending decreasing after an initial spurt.   J

330. Arroyo, Gonzalo. MODELOS DE ACUMULACIÓN, CLASES SOCIALES Y AGRICULTURA [Models of accumulation, social classes, and agriculture]. *Estudios Sociales Centroamericanos [Costa Rica] 1979 8(22): 15-37*. In order to analyze the political potential of peasants and Indians in Latin America, it is necessary to examine the effect of political and economic imperialism upon agricultural and rural forms of accumulation, that is to examine agroindustry. Agroindustry is not an evil in itself, but it is important to know what type of agroindustry is being developed and who will benefit from its development in each case. Cuban agroindustry reveals broader-based distribution of benefits and fewer benefits to foreign capital and small national minorities.   T. D. Schoonover

331. Ayres, Robert L. DEVELOPMENT POLICY AND THE POSSIBILITY OF A "LIVABLE" FUTURE FOR LATIN AMERICA. *Am. Pol. Sci. R. 1975 69(2): 507-525*. The legacy of problems associated with Latin American development policy in the postwar era necessitates the asking of some fundamental questions about the future of development in that region. Economic growth rates have been insufficient, and the employment and distributional problems have been worsening. This situation is in large measure attributable to specific policies pursued by Latin American governments, especially the array of policies included under the rubric of "import-substituting industrialization." Such policies are critically analyzed as a prelude to the discussion of a suggested reorientation of Latin American development policy. The goal of such a redirected, poverty-oriented development policy is the creation of "livable" (if not "developed") societies. The effort to fashion development policies aiming at "livability" entails, at the most general level, distributional and short-run emphases. But it also involves the need for major innovations in such diverse areas as technological, agricultural, regional, and educational development. Reorientation of international development lending would also be required. The economic problems of the livability approach are formidable, but recent findings indicate that poverty-oriented development strategies may be economically viable. The political problems are equally if not more formidable, and it is likely that their confrontation will involve new ways of thinking about "political development" and about the relationship of political regime types to economic development.   J

332. Berberoglu, Berch. THE POLITICAL ECONOMY OF HISTORICAL AND CONTEMPORARY STRUCTURES OF UNDERDEVELOPMENT IN LATIN AMERICA. *Can. Rev. of Sociol. and Anthrop. [Canada] 1978 15(1): 76-92*. Examines the historical and contemporary dependency structures of Latin American underdevelopment since the 16th century from a political economy perspective. Colonial relations between Latin America and, at first, Spain, later Great Britain, and presently the United States have subjected Latin societies to dependent capitalist development that has brought polarization in the accumulation of capital and in inter- and intranational development levels. Metropolitan monopoly capitalist penetration of Latin American economies and the internal polarization of social classes have intensified since 1945. The inevitable outcome has been massive confrontations between the dominant and exploited classes, and the ascendance of military dictatorships throughout Latin America.   J

333. Boatler, Robert W. COMPARATIVE ADVANTAGE: A DIVISION AMONG DEVELOPING COUNTRIES. *Inter-Am. Econ. Affairs 1978 32(2): 59-66*. Examines the developing nations of Argentina, Brazil, and Mexico, which sought to export labor intensive products to increase foreign capital and relieve unemployment during 1953-70.

334. Bruce, David C. THE IMPACT OF THE UNITED NATIONS ECONOMIC COMMISSION FOR LATIN AMERICA: TECHNOCRATS AS CHANNELS OF INFLUENCE. *Inter-American Econ. Affairs 1980 33(4): 3-28*. Graduates of basic planning courses offered by

the UN Economic Commission for Latin America (ECLA) for national government technicians moved heavily into private business and international organizations after graduation and were less likely than has often been assumed to be carriers of ECLA doctrine in national economic planning efforts.

335. Cail-Coms, Michèle. L'ENCADREMENT DES POPULATIONS RURALES DES ZONES PIONNIÈRES DU BASSIN MOYEN DU PARANA: LES EXEMPLES DE L'OUEST DE L'ÉTAT DU PARANA (BRÉSIL) ET DU PARAGUAY ORIENTAL [The infrastructure of rural populations of the pioneer zones in Parana middle basin: the examples of western Parana, Brazil, and eastern Paraguay]. *Travaux & Mémoires de l'Inst. des Hautes Études de l'Amérique Latine [France] 1979 (32): 95-102.* Examines public and private infrastructural investments in agriculture in western Parana, Brazil, and the settlement of eastern Paraguay, presenting various phases from autarky to integration into the export economy, which benefits large enterprises and multinational corporations.

336. Caporaso, James A. DEPENDENCY THEORY: CONTINUITIES AND DISCONTINUITIES IN DEVELOPMENT STUDIES. *Int. Organization 1980 34(4): 605-628.* The mainstream development theories that emerged in the 1950's focused primarily on domestic causes of development whereas Latin American dependency theory has emphasized external factors. The recent publication in English of *Dependency and Development in Latin America* by Fernando Henrique Cardoso and Enzo Faletto, translated by Marjory Mattingly Urquidi (Berkeley: U. of California Pr., 1978), demonstrates the complex interactions of internal and external forces behind the dependency situation in Latin America. The nearly simultaneous publication of Peter Evans's *Dependent Development: The Alliance of Multinational, State and Local Capital In Brazil* (Princeton: Princeton U. Pr. 1979) offers a case in point. A sympathetic reading of the two books will depend in part, however, on an understanding of their authors' developmentalist, as opposed to formalist, view of history.

337. Cardoso, Fernando Henrique. THE CONSUMPTION OF DEPENDENCY THEORY IN THE UNITED STATES. *Latin Am. Res. Rev. 1977 12(3): 7-24.* Dependency theory became accepted and popular because it explained certain realities in Latin America better than other frameworks and revealed inadequacies in modernization theory. But widespread acceptance led to distortions, such as the assumption that dependency explained every social and ideological development, the absence of scientific neutrality, the belief that the dialectical process was the starting point for all analysis, and the ignoring of dynamic processes at work in Latin America. Future research must avoid simplistic reductionism and abstract formulas which pose as syntheses. Based on secondary sources; 16 notes.   J. K. Pfabe

338. Cavarozzi, Marcelo. EL "DESARROLLISMO" Y LAS RELACIONES ENTRE DEMOCRACIA Y CAPITALISMO DEPENDIENTE EN *DEPENDENCIA Y DESARROLLO EN AMÉRICA LATINA.* ["Developmentalism" and the relations between democracy and dependent capitalism in *Dependency and Development in Latin America*]. *Latin Am. Res. Rev. 1982 17(1): 152-165.* The line between populism and developmentalism is presented by Fernando Henrique Cardoso and Enzo Faletto in *Dependency and Development in Latin America* (1979) as a tension between contradictory elements known as "developmentalist populism." Commitments to populism seriously impeded developmentalist policies. Governments had to guarantee that they could restrict the demands of popular sectors. The antipopular component was necessary to maintain the support of bourgeois sectors. The absence of purely political means of bourgeois dominance in populist governments was supplanted by purely structural control by bourgeois groups in bureaucratic-authoritarian regimes. 17 notes, biblio.   J. K. Pfabe

339. Chafee, Wilbur A., Jr. ENTREPRENEURS AND ECONOMIC BEHAVIOR: A NEW APPROACH TO THE STUDY OF LATIN AMERICAN POLITICS. *Latin Am. Res. Rev. 1976 11(3): 55-68.* Reviews economic analyses of Latin American politics, and applies assumptions of human behavior drawn from microeconomic theory in explaining political competition and structures.

340. Correa, Hector. LA FUNCIÓN TÉCNICA EN LA PLANIFICACIÓN SOCIOECONÓMICA: COMENTARIO SOBRE LA TEORÍA Y LA PRÁCTICA EN LOS PAÍSES LATINOAMERICANOS [Technical aspects of socioeconomic planning: theory and practice in Latin America]. *Estudios Andinos 1973 3(7): 57-90.* The direction of national planning is frequently determined by central government officials, local public officials, "technical experts," private business interests, and foreign investors. The author outlines the methods used by the technical experts in predicting and implementing their national planning schemes; lists and introduces socioeconomic planning schemes in Bolivia, Brazil, Chile, Colombia, Ecuador, Paraguay, Peru, and Venezuela; describes several scientific and economic models used in Latin American national planning; and estimates the success of national planning in these eight countries. 9 tables.   R. Scott

341. Cueva, Agustín. EL ESTADO LATINOAMERICANO EN LA CRISIS DEL CAPITALISMO [The Latin American state and the crisis of capitalism]. *Investigación Econ. [Mexico] 1982 40(157): 257-271.* The most recent phase of the crisis of the Latin American state, especially in the 1970's, had its origin in an attempt to utilize economic surplus to correct social inequalities. The attempt came not from the almost nonexistent modernizing bourgeoisie but from popular forces in Chile, Uruguay, Argentina, Bolivia, and elsewhere. It marked the bankruptcy of earlier populist and reformist experiences and the state institutions to which they had given rise. 3 notes.   J. V. Coutinho

342. Diaz Alejandro, Carlos F. OPEN ECONOMY, CLOSED POLITY? *Millennium: J. of Int. Studies [Great Britain] 1981 10(3): 203-219.* Briefly traces 19th- and 20th-century Latin American economic history and reviews various hypotheses and conjectures which have been proposed concerning the apparent link between economic openness and political authoritarianism in most Latin American countries.

343. Falk, Pamela S. WHATEVER HAPPENED TO CANCUN? THE 600 BILLION DOLLAR QUESTION. *Caribbean Rev. 1982 11(3): 14-17, 45-47.* Discusses the 1981 conference attended by 22 heads of state from developed and developing nations at Cancún, Mexico to discuss economic assistance plans, particularly the US Caribbean Basin Initiative, which combines government incentives for private sector investing with public cushions for increased trade to help the southern countries become more economically and politically stable.

344. Felix, David. LATIN AMERICAN POWER: TAKEOFF OR PLUS C'EST LA MEME CHOSE? *Studies in Comparative Int. Development 1977 12(1): 59-85.* Examines recent uneven growth and change, analyzes major growth strategies, and offers some arguments from comparative history for questioning the general viability of the Latin American development approach. For any shifts in development strategy to succeed, dramatic political changes would be required. 9 tables, fig., 12 notes, 10 refs.   S. A. Farmerie

345. Ferrer, Aldo. LATIN AMERICA AND THE WORLD ECONOMY: SOME OBSERVATIONS ON EXTERNAL INDEBTEDNESS AND THE INTERNATIONAL MONETARY SYSTEM. *J. of Interamerican Studies and World Affairs 1978 20(3): 321-339.* Economic recession in the industrial countries and oil price increases have compelled the Latin American nations to regulate domestic demand, to advance import substitution, and to increase borrowing in the international capital markets, with consequent sharply increased external debt. Nevertheless, Latin American countries have increased potential for autonomy due to the dispersion of the world economy, the diminished importance of Latin America to the industrialized world, and its own development of capital accumulation and technological change. Based on printed secondary materials.   T. D. Schoonover

346. Finch, M. J. H. LATIN AMERICAN DEVELOPMENT: THE POLITICS OF THE ECONOMICS (REVIEW ARTICLE). *J. of Latin Am. Studies [Great Britain] 1973 5(2): 279-287.* Reviews 14 new books on Latin American economic development since 1948, noting the central themes which dominate this literature: reform dependence and economic independence. Based on secondary works and reports; 25 notes.   K. M. Bailor

347. Gereffi, Gary and Evans, Peter. TRANSNATIONAL CORPORATIONS, DEPENDENT DEVELOPMENT, AND STATE POLICY IN THE SEMIPERIPHERY: A COMPARISON OF BRAZIL AND MEXICO. *Latin Am. Res. Rev. 1981 16(3): 31-64.* Since 1955 Mexico and Brazil have undergone the transition from periphery to semiperiphery, with emphasis on expanded and diversified manufacturing, followed by diversified export production. Export promotion is not a victory over dependency. Even mildly nationalistic government policies result in reduced foreign investment. Favorable government policies have not ended unfavorable balances of trade. Multinational corporations still determine the export market and local production. Export production faces possible retaliation from home governments of the firms. 6 tables, 20 notes, biblio.
J. K. Pfabe

348. Gilbert, Alan. THE STATE AND REGIONAL INCOME DISPARITIES IN LATIN AMERICA. Robinson, David J., ed. *Studying Latin America: Essays in Honor of Preston E. James* (Ann Arbor: U. Microfilms Int. for Dept. of Geography, Syracuse U., 1980): 215-244. Regional equalization through effective government policies based on geographic, economic, and social research is needed to overcome income and development disparities in Latin America.

349. Girvan, Norman. THE DEVELOPMENT OF DEPENDENCY ECONOMICS IN THE CARIBBEAN AND LATIN AMERICA: REVIEW AND COMPARISON. *Social and Econ. Studies [Jamaica] 1973 22(1): 1-33.* Reviews two schools of economic theory regarding development in Latin America. The first argues for industrialization as the cure for underdevelopment. The second examines the area's economic status from a "historical/structural/institutional" approach, and concludes that dependent economies are merely subsystems of the larger economies, and consequently change occurs only with change in the entire system. 38 notes.
E. S. Johnson

350. Graciarena, Jorge. LA DINÁMICA DEL CAPITALISMO SUBDESARROLLADO EN AMÉRICA LATINA [The dynamics of underdeveloped capitalism in Latin America]. *Foro Internacional [Mexico] 1973 13(52): 427-441.* Analyzes the economic conditions of capitalist countries in Latin America and their possible future problems.
D. A. Franz

351. Grosfeld, Jan. AGRARIAN REFORM IN LATIN AMERICA. *Studies on the Developing Countries [Poland] 1979 (10): 97-120.* Examines the objectives and consequences of land reform in Latin America.

352. Gvozdev, Y. LATIN AMERICA: DEVELOPMENT MODELS. *Int. Affairs [USSR] 1976 23(2): 74-81.* Three models for socioeconomic development presently exist in Latin America: the socialist, the capitalist, and the patriotic-nationalist. Of the three, only the socialist or Cuban model guarantees the radical reorganization of Latin American society critical for the promotion of national independence and the end of monopoly and imperialist domination. Capitalism as illustrated by Brazilian developments since 1964 perpetuates such domination. The national-patriotic model as found in Peru, Ecuador, and Panama, though incomplete, represents a progressive effort to reduce dependence upon monopoly and imperialist forces and therefore deserves socialist support.
D. K. McQuilkin

353. Halperin-Donghi, Tulio. "DEPENDENCY THEORY" AND LATIN AMERICAN HISTORIOGRAPHY. *Latin Am. Res. Rev. 1982 17(1): 115-130.* Assesses the impact of dependency theory after a decade of heated debate. Fernando Henrique Cardoso and Enzo Faletto's *Dependencia y Desarrollo en América Latina* (1969) offered a counterview to the work of André Gunder Frank. Barbara and Stanley Stein appear to rely little on Frank and reject his static view of the Latin American situation. Dependency theory had a more varied reception among Latin American than among North American scholars. Many Latin Americans found it difficult to place colonial socioeconomic relations into a framework of either feudal or capitalist mode of production. Many Marxist scholars rejected Frank's work. 24 notes.
J. K. Pfabe

354. Hamilton, Nora. STATE AUTONOMY AND DEPENDENT CAPITALISM IN LATIN AMERICA. *British J. of Sociol. [Great Britain] 1981 32(3): 305-329.* Examines the importance of the state in promoting economic development in the dependent capitalist countries of Latin America between 1929 and 1979. There is no necessary connection between increased state control of economic resources and state autonomy. 40 notes.

355. Hampe, Alexander. EUROPA UND LATEINAMERIKA— EINE PARTNERSCHAFT, DIE SICH LOHNT? [Europe and Latin America: a profitable partnership?]. *Europa Archiv [West Germany] 1975 30(23): 741-750.* Latin America's rapid economic development especially in finished products and raw materials in the 1960's and early 1970's, has not overcome its economic underdevelopment but did interest the EEC in close trade links, intensified after 1971.
R. Wagnleitner

356. Hanson, Simon G. QUESTIONABLE PAYMENTS: NOTES ON BUSINESS PRACTICES IN LATIN AMERICA. *Inter-American Econ. Affairs 1977 31(2): 25-40.* Examines "questionable payments" —bribery, graft, and extortion—in business dealings with Latin America by American firms and argues that such payments can be ended only where host countries are willing to see them end. Secondary sources; 3 notes.
D. A. Franz

357. Harding, Timothy F. DEPENDENCY, NATIONALISM AND THE STATE IN LATIN AMERICA. *Latin Am. Perspectives 1976 3(4): 3-11.* Introduction to the articles in this issue on "Dependency Theory and Dimensions of Imperialism." Analyzes the trends within economic development theories associated with the ideas of dependency and the relationship of these ideas with Marxist theories. Explains the weaknesses of dependency theory in general and traces the debates about dependency that have appeared in the pages of *Latin American Perspectives.*
J. L. Dietz

358. Hellist, W. Ladd and Johnson, Thomas H. POLITICAL CONSEQUENCES OF INTERNATIONAL ECONOMIC RELATIONS: ALTERNATIVE EXPLANATIONS OF UNITED STATES/LATIN AMERICAN NONCOOPERATION. *J. of Pol. 1979 41(4): 1125-1155.* Examines economic exchanges and international cooperation between the United States and Brazil and Mexico, 1950-74. Unequal distribution of resources and assymetric exchanges were politically evaluated as noncooperative. Dependence (trade, investment, aid) is not useful in predicting international cooperation. 3 illus., 6 tables, 36 notes.
A. W. Novitsky

359. Henfrey, Colin. DEPENDENCY, MODES OF PRODUCTION, AND THE CLASS ANALYSIS OF LATIN AMERICA. *Latin Am. Perspectives 1981 8(3-4): 17-54.* Dependency theory served its original purpose, but has not proven so useful in understanding imperialism and the class struggle. More might be learned from examination of Latin American social formations. Biblio.
J. F. Vivian

360. Janvry, Allain de and Ground, Lynn. TYPES AND CONSEQUENCES OF LAND REFORM IN LATIN AMERICA. *Latin Am. Perspectives 1978 5(4): 90-112.* Analyzes the effectiveness of recent land reform efforts in Latin America and discusses the nature of Latin American capitalism. Not less than 17 forms of current land reform programs are listed. Notes the inherent contradictions of capitalism and the necessity of state intervention to counteract its consequences. The recognition of often ignored relevant factors will determine the success or failure of the programs. 2 tables, 12 notes, ref.
V. L. Human

361. Kearney, Michael. AGRIBUSINESS AND THE DEMISE OF THE RISE OF THE PEASANTRY. *Latin Am. Perspectives 1980 7(4): 115-124.* Reviews books by David Barkin, Roger Burbach and Patricia Flynn, Gustavo Esteva, and Stephen Gudeman dealing with peasants in Mexico and Latin America, concluding that the 20th-century Latin American peasantry conforms neither to traditional Marxist concepts nor to images perpetuated by bourgeois social sciences.
J. F. Vivian

362. Keilany, Ziad. STRUCTURALISM AND THE ECONOMIC DEVELOPMENT IN LATIN AMERICA. *Politico [Italy] 1974 39(1): 29-43.* Discusses the internal impediments and the inapplicability of the economic theories of the industrialized countries to the Latin American nations. The structuralists argue that "persistent poverty in Latin Amer-

ica is due to external relations as well as the internal patterns of economic, social and political organization. Until these relations are radically altered or modified, real improvement in the standard of living of people in Latin America is not likely to take place." Structuralism concerns itself with the political and social mechanism by which decisions are actively carried out or frustrated and emphasizes "the transference of larger private monopolies in the industrial sector to state direction, increased state involvement in agricultural production, and state control of financial enterprises." 39 notes.

D. D. Cameron

363. Kollár, Zoltán. KÜLFÖLDI TŐKE ÉS ELMARADOTTSÁG LATIN-AMERIKÁBAN [Foreign capital and backwardness in Latin America]. *Acta U. Szegediensis de Attila József Nominatae: Acta Hist. [Hungary] 1976 59: 43-55.* Argues that foreign investments in developing nations have made the latter dependent on the capitalist countries, and that the industrialization policy of foreign capitalist investors has prevented the healthy transformation of Latin American economies, 1961-72. Maintains that the views of the Peruvian writer José Carlos Mariátegui (1895-30) on this subject are still valid. 10 notes.

R. Hetzron

364. Kovalev, E. V. BOR'BA KREST'IANSTVA LATINSKOI AMERIKI ZA AGRARNUIU REFORMY [The peasants of Latin America fight for agrarian reform]. *Voprosy Istorii [USSR] 1979 (6): 60-77.* Characterizes the objective economic and social factors which, in the conditions obtaining today, tend to intensify the struggle waged by the peasants in the Latin American countries for an agrarian reform, as well as the chief forms and methods of this struggle. The author singles out the following principal forms of this struggle: petitions and resolutions; demonstrations and protest marches; strikes; seizure of land; armed struggle. The most important condition insuring the success of the peasant movement is for the rural laborers to unite and form independent class organizations. As far as the proletariat is concerned, the policy of winning over the peasantry—its natural ally—is closely linked with the struggle for the far-reaching agrarian reform, which constitutes an important element of the whole complex of socioeconomic transformations supported by the progressive forces of the continent.

J

365. Kovalev. E. V. GENEZIS, EVOLIUTSIIA I NEKOTORYE KHARAKTERNYE CHERTY AGRARNYKH OTNOSHENII V LATINSKOI AMERIKE [Genesis, evolution, and some specific features of Latin American agrarian relations]. *Voprosy Istorii [USSR] 1982 (1): 36-56.* Agrarian relations in Latin America have been formed under the impact of Spanish and Portuguese conquests, they were based on both preconquest type of relations and relations brought to the region by the Spaniards and Portuguese. Their most characteristic feature has become slave or serf dependence of the indigenous population, which has slackened capitalist development in agriculture, proceeding in a more or less "Prussian" way. Concentration of land in the hands of few big landowners leads to the situation when the bulk of the peasantry has little or no land, they fight for land and new forms of production and social organization in agriculture, against latifundism.

J

366. Kovalyov, Y. LATIN AMERICA: THE STRUGGLE FOR AGRARIAN REFORM. *Int. Affairs [USSR] 1974 (2): 60-64.* Discusses aspects of socialist and bourgeois land reforms in Peru, Chile, Bolivia, Colombia, Venezuela, Mexico and Cuba.

367. Kownacki, Piotr. POLITYCZNE UWARUNKOWANIA LATYNOAMERYKAŃSKIEJ INTEGRACJI GOSPODARCZEJ [Political aspects of Latin American economic integration]. *Studie Nauk Politycznych [Poland] 1979 4(40): 47-66.* Discusses the political aspects of economic integration in Latin America. Presents domestic and foreign policy factors influencing integration. Attempts at economic integration have strengthened movements to improve social and economic conditions in Latin America.

J/S

368. Laba, Roman. FISH, PEASANTS, AND STATE BUREAUCRACIES: THE DEVELOPMENT OF LAKE TITICACA. *Comparative Pol. Studies 1979 12(3): 335-361.* The governments of Peru, Bolivia, and the United States in the first international development project in Latin America sought to create a commercial fishery on Lake Titicaca, but the project failed, 1935-78.

369. Lagos, Ricardo. AMÉRICA LATINA: ALGUNOS HECHOS ECONÓMICOS RECIENTES Y SU PODER DE NEGOCIACIÓN [Latin America: some recent economic facts and its negotiating power]. *Estudios Int. [Chile] 1980 13(51): 291-308.* The economic position of Latin America in terms of the increase in intraregional trade, the flow of foreign capital, the defensive capacity of its economies, and other factors give it a strong position in international trade negotiations.

370. Lagos Escobar, Ricardo. LATIN AMERICA AND THE INTERNATIONAL ECONOMY: A REVIEW ARTICLE. *J. of Interam. Studies and World Affairs 1976 18(1): 100-114.* Reviews Grant L. Reuber, *Private Foreign Investment in Development* (Oxford U. Pr., 1973), Victor L. Urqidi and Rosemary Thorp, eds., *Latin America in the International Economy* (John Wiley and Sons, 1973), and Constantine V. Vaitsos, *Intercountry Income Distribution and Transnational Enterprises* (Oxford U. Pr., 1974). The author discusses private foreign investment, multinational corporations, import substitution, trade policy and exports, and technology in the developing nations of Latin America. None of the books reviewed touches on the very important consequences of the international monetary crisis or on the new power enjoyed by the weaker nations. Based on the books reviewed and other secondary sources; 6 notes, biblio.

J. R. Thomas

371. Lehman, David. GENERALIZING ABOUT PEASANT MOVEMENTS. *J. of Development Studies [Great Britain] 1973 9(2): 323-343.* Reviews Henry Landsberger, ed., *Latin American Peasant Movements* (Ithaca and London: Cornell U. Press, 1969), Rodolfo Stavenhagen, ed., *Agrarian Problems and Peasant Movements in Latin America* (New York and London: Doubleday-Anchor, 1970), Eric Wolf, *Peasant Wars of the Twentieth Century* (New York: Harper and Row, 1969, and London: Faber and Faber, 1971), and John Womack, *Zapata and the Mexican Revolution* (New York: Vintage Books, 1969, and London: Thames and Hudson, 1970), which discuss various land reform movements throughout history.

372. Lehman, David. MOVIMENTI CONTADINI NELL-'AMERICA LATINA [Peasant movements in Latin America]. *Riv. Storica Italiana [Italy] 1975 87(2): 298-310.* Reviews Henry Landsberger's *Peasant Movements* (Ithaca, 1969), Rodolfo Stavenhagen's *Agrarian Problems and Peasant Movements in Latin America* (New York, 1970) and *Peasant Wars of the Twentieth Century* (New York, 1969) and John Womack Jr.'s *Zapata and the Mexican Revolution* (New York, 1970). Uses a Marxist approach to discuss land reform movements in Chile, Mexico, Bolivia, and Peru, comparing their agricultural and social conditions with those of the USSR, China, and East Germany. 3 notes.

F. Pollaczek

373. Lichtensztejn, Samuel. UNA APROXIMACIÓN A CIERTAS EXPERIENCIAS DE POLITICA ECONÓMICA EN AMÉRICA LATINA [An approximation to certain economic policy experiences in Latin America]. *Investigación Econ. [Mexico] 1980 39(152): 81-98.* Economic policies adopted by countries such as Argentina, Brazil, Chile, Colombia, Mexico, and Uruguay after the 1930 crisis were not representative of the rest of Latin America, which in general remained in the classical primary export pattern. They were meant to facilitate continued capital accumulation by the upper, agricultural class and incidentally led to industrialization, aided by government control of finances and economy and the formation of public corporations. Soon industrialization-related balance-of-payments problems led to internationalization of capital and "stabilization" policies in the 1950's that increased both inflation and dependence on foreign capital and led to concentration of income and sociopolitical problems, especially in Argentina, Brazil, Chile, and Uruguay. Tighter control often came through reform movements, with government control of economic planning.

374. Lindqvist, Sven. JORD OCH MAKT I SYDAMERIKA [Land and power in South America]. *Internasjonal Politikk [Norway] 1974 (2): 361-376.* "Focuses on relations between the landowners and other elite groups. The author lists six main components regarding the landowners' power on the national scale and discusses their relative importance, as well as the relations between the various elite groups." From a recent book.

J

375. Long, Millard F. EXTERNAL DEBT AND THE TRADE IM-PERATIVE IN LATIN AMERICA. *Q. Rev. of Econ. and Business 1981 21(2): 280-301.* Since 1973 there have been repeated shocks of unprecedented magnitude in world trade. For many Latin American countries this has meant more costly imports, higher interests rates on external debt, and in some cases lower quantities of exports. Rather than adjust solely through reducing import quantities, the non-oil Latin American countries have borrowed extensively abroad. The first section of the paper attempts to assess by country how much the debt has increased in nominal terms, in real terms, and in net of increases in foreign asset holdings. The second contains an analysis of the changes that have taken place in each country's balance of payments, and the third section uses the material in the first two sections to consider what might happen to external debt in the future. J

376. Lupsha, Peter A. DRUG TRAFFICKING: MEXICO AND COLOMBIA IN COMPARATIVE PERSPECTIVE. *J. of Int. Affairs 1981 35(1): 95-115.* Compares the drug trade and control policy in Mexico and Colombia, and their impacts on these countries and the United States, points out deficiencies of the US policy approach and suggests alternatives to stop this form of economic subversion.

377. Mamalakis, Markos J. MINERALS, MULTINATIONALS, AND FOREIGN INVESTMENT IN LATIN AMERICA. *J. of Latin Am. Studies [Great Britain] 1977 9(2): 315-336.* A survey of recent books on the operations of multinational corporations in Latin America during the last 20 years shows that companies are often hampered by changing political fortunes in the host country. This has led some corporations to try to influence host country politics. Mining and mineral interests have been particularly hard-hit by shifting regimes. It is necessary now for more monographs to treat the effects of corporate investments on the surplus capital and free money supply in host countries. 8 notes.
J. W. Leedom

378. Mandle, Jay R. PROBLEMS OF THE NONCAPITALIST PATH OF DEVELOPMENT IN GUYANA AND JAMAICA. *Pol. and Soc. 1977 7(2): 189-197.* Traces the similarities and differences in the noncapitalist paths of economic development followed by the new socialist governments of Guyana and Jamaica in the 1970's, after the failure of the "industrialization through invitation" economic policy in both countries in the 1950's and 1960's. 15 notes.
D. G. Nielson

379. Mansilla, H. C. F. LATEINAMERIKA ZWISCHEN MOD-ELLPLURALISMUS UND STAATSAUSDEHNUNG [Latin America between model pluralism and the increasing power of the state]. *Schweizer Monatshefte [Switzerland] 1981 61(5): 413-422.* Since the late 1950's, private capitalist as well as radical socialist models of Latin American development have attempted to reach the same structural goals —economic growth, industrialization, urbanization—with basically the same means, the expansion of the influence of the central state.

380. Marini, Ruy Mauro. AMERICA LATINA ANTE LA CRISIS MUNDIAL [Latin America and the world crisis]. *Investigación Econ. [Mexico] 1982 40(157): 273-292.* The economy of Latin America faces the present crisis of capitalism in conditions quite different from those of the immediate postwar period. This period has seen a large growth of manufacturing industry, which has modified Latin America's role in the international division of labor but only incompletely. Problems have arisen as regards import policies and the movement of capital. The growth process was rudely interrupted by the recession of 1974-75. The world crisis has only accentuated the tendency to integrate Latin American production with international capitalism. The winds of redemocratization with which the military-bourgeois elites try to buttress their projects have both international and domestic motivations that are peculiar to the local oligarchies. Biblio.
J. V. Coutinho

381. Martinez-Alier, Juan. PEASANTS AND LABOURERS IN SOUTHERN SPAIN, CUBA and HIGHLAND PERU. *J. of Peasant Studies [Great Britain] 1974 1(2): 133-163.* Discusses some of the differences and similarities between a peasantry and an agricultural proletariat and considers the economic relations between peasants or laborers and landowners in the 20th century. The examples are drawn mainly from studies of Southern Spain, Cuba, and Peru. The paper deemphasizes the

specificity of "peasant society" as an object of study both from the economic and the sociopolitical point of view. 12 notes, biblio. J

382. Pastorino, Enrique. THE "SUPERNATIONAL" MASK OF MONOPOLY CAPITALISM. *World Marxist Rev. [Canada] 1976 19(12): 15-25.* In discussing the growth of multinational corporations in the developing nations of Latin America, 1945-76, examines the attempts of socialists to throw off the effects of imperialism in these countries.

383. Perlman, Janice E. RIO'S FAVELAS AND THE MYTH OF MARGINALITY. *Pol. and Soc. 1975 5(2): 131-160.* Evaluates the marginality theory as it applies to the *favelados*, or urban poor, of Rio de Janeiro, reviewing the roots of the concept in Latin America and its importance in shaping ideas about, and official policies toward, cityward migrants and the urban poor. Constructs an ideal type of favela group based on literature embodying the social, cultural, economic, and political themes of marginality. A comparison of the ideal with the realities of the favela show large discrepancies. These discrepancies exist throughout Latin America. The marginality thesis is based on myth. Favelados are integrated rather than marginal in Rio's urban society. They are exploited economically and repressed politically, but are not excluded in a sociocultural sense. Primary and secondary sources; table, 39 notes.
D. G. Nielson

384. Petras, James. LATIN AMERICA: CLASS CONFLICT AND CAPITALIST DEVELOPMENT. *Monthly Rev. 1981 33(7): 11-37.* Examines the patterns and tendencies of class struggle in Latin America, and attempts to establish its parameters and identify its underlying political-economic processes; notes the role of US foreign policy and investment.

385. Petras, James F. THE LATIN AMERICAN AGRO-TRANS-FORMATION FROM ABOVE AND OUTSIDE AND ITS SOCIAL AND POLITICAL IMPLICATIONS. *J. of the Hellenic Diaspora 1978 4(4): 29-48.* Provides agricultural production statistics for Latin American countries during 1967-73 and concludes that reformist ideas for improving agricultural organization in the area are inappropriate because they fail to realize that modern agriculture is but a step in the industrialization process; proletarianization and the resulting class struggle for socialism are the key processes underlying the creation of agrarian social movements, not dependence and agrarian reform.

386. Reynal, Susana Mallo. BIBLIOGRAFÍA SOBRE MOVI-MIENTO OBRERO LATINOAMERICANO [Bibliography of the Latin American labor movement]. *Rev. Mexicana de Ciencias Pol. y Sociales [Mexico] 1977 23(89): 223-233.* Presents a bibliography on the labor movement for each of 20 Latin American countries.

387. Roca, Sergio. IDEOLOGY AND DEVELOPMENT POLICY: A COMPARISON OF MEXICO AND CUBA. *Rev. Interamericana [Puerto Rico] 1977 7(2): 193-206.* The Mexican and Cuban Revolutions offer two alternate paths to economic development. The pragmatic approach of the Mexicans has permitted consistent growth of the economy, but at the price of persistent poverty among part of their population. The ideological path of the Cubans has helped equalize wealth, but at the cost of slow economic development. 35 notes.
J. A. Lewis

388. Sheahan, John. MARKET-ORIENTED ECONOMIC POLI-CIES AND POLITICAL REPRESSION IN LATIN AMERICA. *Econ. Development and Cultural Change 1980 28(2): 267-292.* Examines the relationship between the growth of market-oriented "orthodox" economic policies and the intensification of political repression in Latin America between 1955 and 1970. Provides both indexes of economic development and political repression, concluding that political repression is used by Latin American governments in order to increase economic efficiency. 4 tables, 22 notes.
J. W. Thacker, Jr.

389. Singelmann, Peter. CAMPESINO MOVEMENTS AND CLASS CONFLICT IN LATIN AMERICA: THE FUNCTIONS OF EXCHANGE AND POWER. *J. of Inter-Am. Studies and World Affairs 1974 16(1): 39-72.* Campesinos in Latin America have traditionally been dependent upon the landholders for whom they toiled, docilely accepting landholder demands because they were powerless in the confrontation between the classes. Dependence and scarcity led campesino

movements to dissipate their energies in internecine struggles while the landholders retained their power. As modernization came to rural life the campesino became less reliant on his patron, his bargaining power increased, and campesino unions emerged. Primary and secondary sources; 14 notes, biblio.   J. R. Thomas

390. Singelmann, Peter. LOS MOVIMIENTOS CAMPESINOS Y LA MODERNIZACIÓN POLÍTICA EN AMÉRICA LATINA: APUNTES CRÍTICOS [Peasant movements and political modernization in Latin America: critical notes]. *Bol. de Estudios Latinoamericanos y del Caribe [Netherlands] 1976 (20): 34-53.* Rebuts the conventional interpretation of modernization which argues that Latin American peasants are being integrated gradually into participatory politics. Disagrees with neo-Marxist scholars who reject the whole concept of modernization as necessarily involving exploitation of the peasantry and who set up a revolutionary ideology in opposition to it. Genuine modernization demands emancipation of the peasantry from exploitation, probably by revolution. Unless the peasants are thus liberated, they will continue to be controlled by the traditional landholding elites and their political surrogates, who are using ever more sophisticated techniques of manipulation and repression. Based on published sources in English and Spanish; 29 notes, biblio.   D. M. Cregier

391. Skidmore, Thomas E. THE ECONOMIC DIMENSIONS OF POPULISM IN ARGENTINA AND BRAZIL: A CASE STUDY IN COMPARATIVE PUBLIC POLICY. *New Scholar 1978 7(1-2): 129-166.* A comparative analysis of inflation in Argentina and Brazil during the presidencies of Juan Perón (1946-55) and Getúlio Vargas (1951-54). Considers how successfully both presidents faced up to the need to carry out unpopular measures and examines policy-making, export policies and the international market, attitudes toward state intervention in the economy and the use of foreign capital, the governments impact on labor and labor unions, and the influence of both leaders on their people. Secondary sources; 35 notes, 11 tables.   G. L. Neville

392. Skidmore, Thomas E. WORKERS AND SOLDIERS: URBAN LABOR MOVEMENTS AND ELITE RESPONSES IN TWENTIETH-CENTURY LATIN AMERICA. Bernhard, Virginia, ed. *Elites, Masses, and Modernization in Latin America, 1850-1930* (Austin: U. of Texas Pr., 1979): 79-126. Focuses on the period of Anarchist, Anarcho-Syndicalist, and Syndicalist influence on labor mobilization, 1914-27. Discusses recent trends in Latin American labor historiography, in particular the influence of the ruling elites' reaction to the challenge of the Anarchist-led urban labor movements in Argentina, Brazil, and Chile in the 1920's on contemporary relations. Originally delivered as part of the 1978 B. K. Smith Lectures in History at the University of St. Thomas; 80 notes.   S

393. Sloan, John W. DEPENDENCY THEORY AND LATIN AMERICAN DEVELOPMENT: ANOTHER KEY FAILS TO OPEN THE DOOR. *Inter-Am. Econ. Affairs 1977 30(3): 21-40.* Analyzes and critiques the economic dependency theory as applied to Latin America. The theory is not the key to understanding Latin American development. Secondary sources; 38 notes.   D. A. Franz

394. Soares, Glaucio Ary Dillon. LO STATO IN AMERICA LATINA [The state in Latin America]. *Riv. Italiana di Sci. Pol. [Italy] 1976 6(2): 331-351.* The state in Latin America has followed a historical path that is different from the pattern observed in the more advanced industrial capitalist societies. First, the share of public expenditure in the GDP in Latin America reached levels that in the more advanced countries were only reached when they were far more industrialized and urbanized. Second, the composition of these expenditures in Latin America is economic in essence, with little or no concern for social development. Thus, controlling for relative size, the state in Latin America is essentially developmentalist, contrasting with the social welfare state of the more advanced countries. Third, the extraordinary growth of public expenditure in Latin America was largely due to the multiplication and growth of public enterprises to a much greater extent than in the advanced capitalist societies. Fourth, this growth took place in a socioeconomic movement in which a substantial share of the population was rural, illiterate, and ununionized, suggesting that the burdens of growth were carried mainly by the poorer agricultural classes. These findings suggest a large degree of specificity in the Latin American states, which is not adequately explained by traditional, Eurocentric theories of the state.   J

395. Soto Godoy, Juan. L'ÉTAT ET LA TRANSFORMATION DES STRUCTURES AGRAIRES EN AMÉRIQUE LATINE [The state and the transformation of agrarian structures in Latin America]. *Rev. de l'Inst. de Sociologie [Belgium] 1981 (1-2): 305-318.* Discusses governments' important role in determining Latin American agrarian structures, factors that have impeded agrarian transformation, and the rural populations' hope for land reform projects that might resolve conflicts between popular preference and government objectives.

396. Stavenhagen, Rodolfo. THE FUTURE OF LATIN AMERICA: BETWEEN UNDERDEVELOPMENT AND REVOLUTION. *Latin Am. Perspectives 1974 1(1): 124-148.* Presents a general overview of recent social and economic trends in Latin America and discusses possible future alternatives in development. In terms of future needs, the economic performance of Latin America has been unsatisfactory. This is due in part to structural disequilibria in the agricultural sector where the latifundia-minifundia complex prevails and which has become increasingly polarized between rich and poor, despite a certain number of agrarian reforms. The process of urbanization and industrialization, in turn, has created problems of structural marginality of the population. The causes for these phenomena are to be found in dependent development and internal colonialism. The political expressions of these tendencies are discussed, such as the failure of liberal democracy, the populist movements, and the military regimes. Finally, the following alternative futures are considered: the continuation of dependent development, autonomous capitalist development, and revolutionary socialism.   A

397. Street, James H. LATIN AMERICAN ADJUSTMENTS TO THE OPEC CRISIS AND THE WORLD RECESSION. *Social Science Q. 1978 59(1): 60-76.* Describes the impact of the OPEC increase in petroleum prices on the 19 oil-importing countries of Latin America. Reviews the attendant adjustments made at the regional, national, and worldwide levels. The costs were borne chiefly by the poor and working classes within the region.   J

398. Sunkel, Osvaldo. TRANSNATIONAL CAPITALISM AND NATIONAL DISINTEGRATION IN LATIN AMERICA. *Social and Econ. Studies [Jamaica] 1973 22(1): 132-176.* Discusses five concepts (development, underdevelopment, dependence, marginality, and spatial imbalance) in the context of Latin America. In recent decades the growth of multinational corporations has resulted in the social, cultural, political and economic disintegration of underdeveloped countries. 6 tables, 7 figs., 7 notes.   E. S. Johnson

399. Thiesenhusen, William C. LAND REFORM IN LATIN AMERICA: SOME CURRENT LITERATURE. *Latin Am. Res. Rev. 1982 17(2): 199-211.* Reviews Marta Cehelsky's *Land Reform in Brazil: The Management of Social Change* (1979), Jeannine Swift's *Agrarian Reform in Chile: An Economic Study* (1979), Kyle Steenland's *Agrarian Reform Under Allende: Peasant Revolt in the South* (1977), Michael R. Redclift's *Agrarian Reform and Peasant Organization on the Ecuadorian Coast* (1978), and Mitchell A. Seligson's *Peasants of Costa Rica and the Development of Agrarian Capitalism* (1980). The books show the complexities of agrarian reform. Each, however, is somewhat deficient in using the multidisciplinary framework needed to analyze agrarian reform. 14 notes.   J. K. Pfabe

400. Trento, Angelo. FASI E CARATTERI DELL'INTERVENTO DEL CAPITALE STRANIERO IN AMERICA LATINA [The phases and character of the intervention of foreign capital in Latin America]. *Quaderni Storici [Italy] 1974 9(1): 9-45.* Traces the different forms of foreign capital penetration into Latin America and its role in the underdevelopment of that continent. Stresses, however, the need to consider the internal contradictions of each country in order to fully understand the process of underdevelopment. The author discusses the history of free trade among Latin America, Europe, and the United States in the 19th and 20th centuries, with specific emphasis on the 1870-1930 period. Primary and secondary sources; 76 notes.   M. T. Wilson

401. Vargas, Jorge A. THE LEGAL NATURE OF THE PATRIMONIAL SEA: A FIRST STEP TOWARDS THE DEFINITION OF THE EXCLUSIVE ECONOMIC ZONE. *German Y. of Int. Law [Germany] 1979 22: 142-177.* Emphasizes the development by Latin Americans of the patrimonial sea concept, which holds that nations with

coastlines have the exclusive right to exploit the resources of the sea adjacent to their shores to the geographical limits determined by "reasonable criteria."

402. Vilar, Pierre. MOUVEMENTS PAYSANS EN AMERIQUE LATINE [Peasant movements in Latin America]. *Cahiers Int. d'Hist. Écon. et Sociale [Italy] 1976 6: 61-77.* Synthesizes reports at the International Colloquium (Naples, 1969) on peasant movements in Latin America from the 18th to the 20th century. Regional variations are so immense that generalizations are risky, but synthesis is possible based on five themes: peasant movements against seigneurial power, peasant movements within the limits of traditional agriculture, the connections between peasant and national movements, problems of land acquisition, and movements seeking to adapt agriculture to the market economy or resulting from its integration into the industrial and commercial sector.

F. X. Hartigan

403. Vogel, Robert C. THE DYNAMICS OF INFLATION IN LATIN AMERICA, 1950-69. *Am. Econ. R. 1974 64(1): 102-114.* Investigates the monetary factors of inflation in 16 Latin American countries, using Harberger's model. Rates of inflation reflect differences in the behavior of the money supply; however, because of political considerations, Latin American nations cannot "afford" a period of austerity while inflation rates adjust to changes in the money supply. Documented.

D. K. Pickens

404. Weaver, Frederick Stirton. CAPITALIST DEVELOPMENT, EMPIRE, AND LATIN AMERICAN UNDERDEVELOPMENT: AN INTERPRETIVE ESSAY ON HISTORICAL CHANGE. *Latin Am. Perspectives 1976 3(4): 17-53.* Integrates an understanding of imperialism into theories of Latin American development and underdevelopment. The economic relations between European and North American imperial centers and the nations of Latin America dialectically reflected and conditioned the development of the forces of production in both sets of nations. The major effect of foreign economic penetration in inhibiting economic development in Latin America has been through the formation of domestic classes and class relationships inimical to economic growth. Historical analysis calls dependency analysis into question.

J. L. Dietz

405. Whitaker, Arthur P. THE AMERICAN IDEA AND THE WESTERN HEMISPHERE: YESTERDAY, TODAY, AND TOMORROW. *Orbis 1976 20(1): 161-178.* Following the independence of Latin America, there developed between the new countries and the United States the "Western Hemisphere idea"—an essentially political idea which held that "the United States and Latin America are bound together in a special relationship to the exclusion of the political and economic influence of Europe and the rest of the non-American world." The idea retained a degree of vitality until the beginning of World War I. Since then, though, "it has suffered a rapid and apparently irreversible decline in Latin America." In the future, "it will be hard to talk with a straight face about common political ideas and institutions as a bond of unity among the nations of the New World" while "the current disarray in hemispheric relations seems likely to continue for years to come." 9 notes.

A. N. Garland

406. Wilkins, Mira. MULTINATIONAL OIL COMPANIES IN SOUTH AMERICA IN THE 1920S. *Business Hist. R. 1974 48(3): 414-446.* Considers the nature of foreign oil development in South America during the decade following World War I. Fears of a coming world oil shortage stimulated exploration and development. Certain nations encouraged these activities, others discouraged them, and Chile banned them entirely. American, British, and Dutch firms dominated the activity. Governments involved did not act to protect the companies. The end of the decade brought general disillusionment—the road to multinationalism was rocky and the feared world oil shortage had turned into a surplus. 3 tables, 128 notes.

V. L. Human

407. Williamson, Robert B. THE ROLE OF EXPORTS AND FOREIGN CAPITAL IN LATIN AMERICAN ECONOMIC GROWTH. *Southern Econ. J. 1978 45(2): 410-420.* Provides statistical evidence of the relationships between economic growth and underlying investment levels on the one hand and exports and foreign investment on the other, 1960's-75.

408. —. [LATIN AMERICAN TRADE POLICIES IN THE 1970'S]. *Q. J. of Econ. 1975 89(3): 483-489.*
Balassa, Bela. LATIN AMERICAN TRADE POLICIES IN THE 1970'S: A COMMENT, *pp. 483-486.*
Schydlowsky, Daniel M. LATIN AMERICAN TRADE POLICIES IN THE 1970'S: REPLY, *pp. 487-489.* Discuss Schydlowsky's earlier "Latin American Trade Policies in the 1970's: A Prospective Appraisal," on using international competition as an index of national industrial efficiency in a system of multiple exchange rates.

S

409. —. LATIN AMERICAN INDUSTRY: ALIVE AND GROWING. *Américas (Organization of Am. States) 1976 28(9): 2-7.* Discusses industrialization in Latin America, 1960-75, and the role of the Inter-American Development Bank.

410. —. [LATIN AMERICAN LABOR HISTORY]. *Latin Am. Res. Rev. 1980 15(1): 167-182.*
Sofer, Eugene F. RECENT TRENDS IN LATIN AMERICAN LABOR HISTORIOGRAPHY, *pp. 167-176.* Reviews the following works: Alan Angell's *Politics and the Labour Movement in Chile* (London: Oxford U. Pr., 1972); "The Situation of the Working Class in Latin America," in LARU Studies 1976 (1); "Imperialism and the Working Class in Latin America," in *Latin American Perspectives* 1976 3(1); Hobart A. Spalding's *Organized Labor in Latin America, 1850-1960* (New York: New York U. Pr., 1977); and Richard J. Walter's *The Socialist Party of Argentina, 1890-1930* (Austin: Texas Pr. Services, 1977). Most of these works show little conceptual or methodological innovation. More work is needed on writing the history of the working class from the bottom up. 13 notes.
Erickson, Kenneth Paul; Peppe, Patrick V.; and Spalding, Hobart A., Jr. COMMENT, *pp. 177-181.* Agree with many points made by Sofer, but the international variable in the shaping of the working class needs greater emphasis than Sofer allows. Biblio.
Sofer, Eugene F. REPLY, *p. 182.* The results of debates will stimulate further study of the complexities of the working class.

J. K. Pfabe

411. —. OPERATING IN MORE THAN ONE JURISDICTION: THE CAPTAIN'S PARADISE? (A) BUSINESS; (B) LABOR. *Am. Soc. of Int. Law Pro. 1974 68: 250-265.*
Moorhead, Thomas B. REMARKS BY THE CHAIRMAN, *pp. 250-251.*
Vagts, Detlev. OPERATING IN MORE THAN ONE JURISDICTION—BUSINESS, *pp. 251-254.*
Johnson, Keith. A TRADE UNION POINT OF VIEW, *pp. 254-258.*
Wionczek, Miguel S. THE LATIN AMERICAN VIEW OF TRANSNATIONALS, *pp. 258-260.*
Schwartz, Louis B. COMMENTS, *pp. 261-262.*
Jager, Elizabeth. COMMENTS, *pp. 262-263.*
Olive, David Allen. DISCUSSION, *pp. 263-265.*
Considers the international legal problems in North America created by the divergent regulation of multinational corporations and international labor unions in the United States, Canada, and Mexico since 1937.

412. —. [POLICY RESPONSES TO EXTERNAL SHOCKS IN SELECTED LATIN AMERICAN COUNTRIES]. *Q. Rev. of Econ. and Business 1981 21(2): 131-167.*
Belassa, Bela. POLICY RESPONSES TO EXTERNAL SHOCKS IN SELECTED LATIN-AMERICAN COUNTRIES, *pp. 131-164.* Examines the economic effects and policy measures taken in response to external shocks in Brazil, Mexico, and Uruguay, 1973-78. Uruguay was able to surmount these shocks without increased external debt by turning toward greater outward orientation. Brazil promoted import substitution and substantially increased its external debt, with the proceeds used largely for consumption and for investments of often doubtful social profitability. With increased petroleum production, Mexico suffered less from external shocks but nevertheless increased reliance on foreign loans to finance its expansionary policies.
Longo, Carlos A. COMMENT ON "POLICY RESPONSES TO EXTERNAL SHOCKS IN SELECTED LATIN-AMERICAN COUNTRIES," *pp. 165-167.*

J/S

The Role of the Military

413. Allemann, Fritz René. DEMOKRATISIERUNG MIT FRAGEZEICHEN [Democratization with a question mark]. *Schweizer Monatshefte [Switzerland] 1980 60(4): 289-298.* Compares the domestic development of Latin American military governments between 1948 and 1970 with first signs of democratization in some states, e.g. Peru, since the beginning of the 1970's.

414. Avery, William P. DOMESTIC INFLUENCES ON LATIN AMERICAN IMPORTATION OF U.S. ARMAMENTS. *Int. Studies Q. 1978 22(1): 121-142.* Factors such as the size of the armed forces, defense expenditures, militarism, civil strife, political instability, or resource availability affect the level of Latin American purchase of arms from the United States. Statistical analysis indicates that the availability of Latin American economic resources (as measured by gross national product) is the primary factor, while political instability makes a sizable contribution. Surprisingly, military participation in government has no systematic effect on arms imports. Arms buildups in Latin America may result as countries with expanding economic resources spend more on arms. Based on government publications and secondary sources; 3 tables, 50 notes.   E. S. Palais

415. Barnhart, Harley E. NEW RELATIONS WITH THE "NEW MILITARY"? *Air U. R. 1974 25(5): 66-75.* Reviews Philippe C. Schmitter, ed., *Military Rule in Latin America: Function, Consequences and Perspectives* (Beverly Hills: Sage Publications, 1973), Miles D. Wolphin, *Military Aid and Counterrevolution in the Third World* (Lexington: Lexington Books, 1972) and Luigi Einaudi et al., *Beyond Cuba: Latin America Takes Charge of Its Future* (New York: Crane, Russak, 1973). Presents a composite picture of the political, social, economic and military aspects of Latin America. 15 notes.   J. W. Thacker, Jr.

416. Bozbag, Ali F. MILITÄRS UND POLITIK IN LATEINAMERIKA [The military and politics in Latin America]. *Schweizer Monatshefte [Switzerland] 1974 55(4): 232-236.* The military regimes of Brazil and Peru have moved in sharply different directions since 1964: in Brazil to the Right; in Peru, with programs of nationalization and land reform, to the Left.

417. Brogan, Christopher. MILITARY HIGHER EDUCATION AND THE EMERGENCE OF "NEW PROFESSIONALISM": SOME CONSEQUENCES FOR CIVIL-MILITARY RELATIONS IN LATIN AMERICA. *Army Q. and Defence J. [Great Britain] 1982 112(1): 20-30.* Discusses the emergence of new professional and developmentalist military officers in Latin America, focusing on Brazil and Peru in the early 1960's. Their rise supplements three other Latin American officer types: the classic professionalist, who is apolitical with allegiance to the government in power, the constitutionalist, who "regards military intervention as legitimate if the government indulges in unconstitutional acts," and the arbiter, who "places no fixed or well defined limits on military intervention."

418. Carrière, J. MILITAIREN IN DE POLITIEK [The military in politics]. *Spiegel Hist. [Netherlands] 1976 11(6): 332-337.* Because Latin America never had a West European social structure it was very difficult for the small middle class to promote capitalism and industrial development. The middle class is attempting to achieve its objectives through military dictatorships; those of present-day Brazil and Peru are specifically discussed. Illus., biblio.   G. D. Homan

419. Child, John. STRATEGIC CONCEPTS OF LATIN AMERICA: AN UPDATE. *Inter-American Econ. Affairs 1980 34(1): 61-82.* Reviews the main points of the author's article ("Latin America: Military-Strategic Concepts" *Air University Review* 1976 27(6): 27-42) and discusses the new strategic concepts which have emerged in response to trends since 1976.

420. Cochrane, James D. LATIN AMERICA AND ARMS, 1966-1975: NOTES ON ACQUISITION. *Revista/Review Interamericana [Puerto Rico] 1980 10(2): 156-172.* The United States did not and could not monopolize the sale of arms to Latin America in the decade from 1966 to 1975. Latin American nations believed that they needed arms and were willing to buy them from a variety of sources. Primary and secondary sources; 3 tables, 26 notes.   J. A. Lewis

421. Cochrane, James D. TENDENCIA DEL GASTO MILITAR Y DEL TAMAÑO DE LAS FUERZAS ARMADAS EN AMÉRICA LATINA (1961-1970) [Trend of military expenditure and the growth of Latin American armed forces, 1961-70]. *Foro Int. [Mexico] 1976 16(3): 380-400.* Analyzes the growth of the military in Latin America, 1961-70, to determine trends. Secondary sources; 4 tables, 17 notes.   D. A. Franz

422. Collier, David. INDUSTRIALIZATION AND AUTHORITARIANISM IN LATIN AMERICA. *Social Sci. Res. Council Items 1978 31-32(4-1): 5-13.* Military takeovers in Latin American countries, 1964-70's, which seem to affirm the desire for authoritarian rule within Latin American society, have inspired research by the Joint Committee on Latin American Studies which has reformulated its modernization theory.

423. Corbett, Charles D. POLITICS AND PROFESSIONALISM: THE SOUTH AMERICAN MILITARY. *Orbis 1973 16(4): 927-951.* Discusses the role of the military in Latin American government since the 1950's.   S

424. Fitch, John Samuel. HUMAN RIGHTS AND THE U.S. MILITARY TRAINING PROGRAM: ALTERNATIVES FOR LATIN AMERICA. *Human Rights Q. 1981 3(4): 65-80.* Discusses the impact in Latin America of the 1978 amendment to the Foreign Assistance Act of 1961, which provides human rights education to military officers of other nations being trained in the US International Military Education and Training Program.

425. Fitch, John Samuel. THE POLITICAL IMPACT OF U.S. MILITARY AID TO LATIN AMERICA: INSTITUTIONAL AND INDIVIDUAL EFFECTS. *Armed Forces and Soc. 1979 5(3): 360-386.* There is evidence on both sides about the "indoctrination effect" of US military aid to Latin America, but further statistical analysis suggests that military assistance has at least increased the level of professionalization of Latin American military forces. This increase in turn enhanced the military's role in politics, and moved in the direction of greater autonomy from the civilian leadership. Whatever the effects on political attitudes of individual officers, the professionalization has been more significant politically, contributing to the institutionalized coup d'etat. 3 tables, 48 notes.   R. V. Ritter

426. Fitch, John Samuel. POLITYCZNE SKUTKI POMOCY MILITARNEJ USA DLA KRAJÓW AMERYKI ŁACIŃSKIEJ [Political effects of US military assistance to the countries of Latin America]. *Studia Nauk Pol. [Poland] 1981 (1): 81-105.* Miltary aid programs have had both institutional and ideological effects on the military. By increasing the professionalization of the army in Latin America, the programs enforce the role the army plays in the policy of a given country, which results in the military coup d'état as a political process. The institutionalized coup d'état in turn causes a setback in the social, economic, and political development of the countries to which the military assistance is given.   J/S

427. González, Heliodoro. U.S. ARMS TRANSFER POLICY IN LATIN AMERICA: FAILURE OF A POLICY. *Inter-Am. Econ. Affairs 1978 32(2): 67-95.* Though the Carter Administration sought to curtail the arms trade with Latin America, by 1978 arms transfers and new arms orders were increasing. The percentage from the United States, however, decreased. 1976-78.

428. Horowitz, Irving Louis and Trimberger, Ellen Kay. STATE POWER AND MILITARY NATIONALISM IN LATIN AMERICA. *Comparative Pol. 1976 8(2): 223-244.* Analyzes the doctrines of exceptionalism affecting Latin America based on the assumption that its laws of development are different from the rest of the world, even other developing nations. The explanations include various concepts involved in the colonial era. The dependency theory involving the economic needs of the imperial powers should be discarded. The state must be developed so that it can become autonomous from class forces, as well as economic forces. The role of the military can be explained by the area's late economic

development. Three patterns of suspected late development which illustrate the potentials and problems are: state-initiated national capitalist development, state-initiated dependent capitalist development, and state-directed socialist development. Statism has developed at a later date in Latin America. The military has played different roles in the various states and has developed a new consciousness to reverse trends toward backwardness, to pay heavy costs of social change, and to meet heavier costs in political liberties. 32 notes. R. I. Vexler

429. Kaplan, Stephen S. U.S. ARMS TRANSFERS TO LATIN AMERICA, 1945-1974: RATIONAL STRATEGY, BUREAUCRATIC POLITICS, AND EXECUTIVE PARAMETERS. *Int. Studies Q. 1975 19(4): 399-431.* An attempt to explain US decisionmaking concerning arms transfers to Latin America, 1945-74, by interrelating the following modes of analysis: rational strategic theory, bureaucratic politics, and executive parameters. The author focuses on Brazil and the Dominican Republic. 12 notes. G. J. Boughton

430. Klette, Immanuel J. U.S. ASSISTANCE TO VENEZUELA AND CHILE IN COMBATTING INSURGENCY, 1963-1964: TWO CASES. *Conflict 1982 3(4): 227-244.* US military aid sent to Venezuela and Chile in 1963 and 1964 was intended to insure peaceful elections in Venezuela in light of the activities of Castroist Fuerzas Armadas de Liberacion Nacional (FALN) and to insure peaceful elections in Chile in 1964 in light of Fidel Castro's support of Salvador Allende, leader of the leftist Popular Action Front.

431. Koch, Eckhart. GEWALT UND MILITÄR. ÜBER DIE STAATLICHE REPRESSION IN DREI SÜDAMERIKANISCHEN MILITÄRREGIMEN [Force and the military: government repression in three South American military regimes]. *Jahrbuch für Geschichte von Staat, Wirtschaft und Gesellschaft Lateinamerikas [West Germany] 1978 15: 209-258.* The armed forces normally undertake to protect their nation from foreign attack. However, wars between Latin American states occur rarely. Latin American armed forces are often used against their own countrymen with the justification that the security of the country is in danger. Based upon printed primary and secondary sources; 2 tables, graph, 110 notes. T. D. Schoonover

432. Lowenthal, Abraham F. ARMIES AND POLITICS IN LATIN AMERICA. *World Pol. 1974 27(1): 107-130.* An extensive literature analyzes military participation in Latin American politics. Case studies and a few comparative works undermine the faith of a decade ago—that military involvement in Latin American politics would decline as a result of economic development, social modernization, military professionalization, and American influence. Attention has turned increasingly to the variety of military involvements: direct and indirect; personal; factional; and institutional; intermittent and long-term; reformist and regressive. Analyses stressing the confluence and interaction of macrosocial factors with those internal to the military institution seem most persuasive in explaining the diverse political roles played by Latin American officers. One central proposition which deserves further research is that the relation between the levels of military institutionalization and the institutionalization of civilian political procedures importantly affects these varying roles. J

433. Lowenthal, Abraham F. EJÉRCITOS Y POLÍTICA EN AMÉRICA LATINA [Armies and politics in Latin America]. *Estudios Int. [Chile] 1976 9(35): 38-64.* Considers publications on the relationship between the military and politics in Latin America, explaining the reasons for increasing military governmental control, and outlining the differences between military and civilian governments, 1930-76.

434. Mühlemann, Christoph. DIE MILITARISIERUNG DER SÜDAMERIKANISCHEN POLITIK [The militarization of South American politics]. *Schweizer Monatshefte [Switzerland] 1975 55(2): 113-127.* A new type of military government has replaced the older type of junta, as well as constitutional regimes, over much of Latin America; these newer regimes emphasize development and are technologically oriented, with wide-ranging programs of reform and industrialization.

435. Needler, Martin C. MILITARY MOTIVATION IN THE SEIZURE OF POWER. *Latin Am. Res. Rev. 1975 10(3): 63-80.* Provides criteria for the investigation of military takeovers in Latin America and

develops at length the motivations of the military officers who actually staged the takeovers, 1954-68.

436. Needler, Martin C. THE MILITARY WITHDRAWAL FROM POWER IN SOUTH AMERICA. *Armed Forces and Soc. 1980 6(4): 614-624.* During the 1970's the military regimes of Ecuador, Peru, Bolivia, Argentina, and Brazil relinquished or planned to relinquish their power to civilian governments. A study of these withdrawals from power suggests that they were the result of coups within the military itself, much like the initial coups that led to military power. 8 notes.
E. L. Keyser

437. Nunn, Frederick M. EUROPEAN MILITARY INFLUENCE IN SOUTH AMERICA: THE ORIGINS AND NATURE OF PROFESSIONAL MILITARISM IN ARGENTINA, BRAZIL, CHILE AND PERU, 1890-1940. *Jahrbuch für Geschichte von Staat, Wirtschaft und Gesellschaft Lateinamerikas [West Germany] 1975 12: 230-252.* The impact of European military influence upon the military elites of Argentina, Brazil, Chile, and Peru since 1890 went much farther than mere military training. This European military influence stimulated rather than dampened the political interest and motivation of the professional, elitist army officer corps, particularly when they became convinced that the civilians were incapable. The role of the European military influence should be studied as an integral element in the social, political, and economic development of Latin America. 38 notes.
T. D. Schoonover

438. Philip, George. THE MILITARY INSTITUTION REVISITED: SOME NOTES ON CORPORATISM AND MILITARY RULE IN LATIN AMERICA. *J. of Latin Am. Studies [Great Britain] 1980 12(2): 421-436.* In the late 1960's writings on the military were concerned with the consequence of political instability. Weaknesses in military rule were stressed as part of general weakness of political institutions in Latin America. In the 1970's writers focused on political effects of variables not in themselves directly political. The article examines P. Schmitter's and A. Stepan's work on corporatist politics. It argues that political terms not the concepts of corporatism better indicate the prospects for survival or downfall of regimes. Recent right-wing bureaucratic-authoritarian regimes have altered few underlying realities. 20 notes.
M. A. Burkholder

439. Rankin, Richard C. THE EXPANDING INSTITUTIONAL CONCERNS OF THE LATIN AMERICAN MILITARY ESTABLISHMENTS: A REVIEW ARTICLE. *Latin Am. Research Rev. 1974 9(1): 81-109.* Reviews various works, 1960-74, on the military and its importance in Latin America.

440. Revers, Jeanne. L'ARMÉE EN AMÉRIQUE LATINE [The army in Latin America]. *Défense Natl. [France] 1974 30(5): 85-94.* Studies the development of military government in Latin America in response to the threat of chaos.

441. Smith, Arthur K. CORPORATISM AND THE GARRISON-MANAGERIAL STATE. *Society 1975 12(4): 63-68.* Focuses on the civil-military relations in Latin American countries to explore direct military participation in politics, or the garrison-managerial state. S

442. Stemplowski, Ryszard. ENLISTMENT IN BRAZIL TO THE POLISH ARMED FORCES, 1940-1944. *Polish Western Affairs [Poland] 1976 17(1-2): 161-172.* The main factor determining World War II enlistment of Brazilian Poles was the peasants' attachment to their land. Comparison of the enlistment campaign in Brazil and Argentina indicates that the tendency to join the army was stronger for candidates whose economic-occupational position was less stable, or whose opinions were less socially radical. Based on documents in General Wladyslaw Sikorski's (1881-1943) staff archives. M. Swiecicka-Ziemianek

443. Tannahill, R. Neal. THE PERFORMANCE OF MILITARY GOVERNMENTS IN SOUTH AMERICA. *J. of Pol. and Military Sociol. 1976 4(2): 233-244.* Examines the comparative performance of military and civilian governments in South America from 1948 to 1967, finding little difference between civilian and military performance regarding economic growth although in such discrete areas of economic performance as industrial growth and currency stabilization, military regimes

are more successful than their civilian counterparts. The chief differences between military and civilian governments, however, are political. In this area, military regimes prove more repressive and more conservative than civilian governments.   J

444. Tarasov, K. THE PENTAGON VS. LATIN AMERICA. *Int. Affairs [USSR] 1973 (2): 37-41.* Discusses the US military aid to political and military counterinsurgency operations against national liberation movements in the Panama Canal Zone, Guatemala, Colombia, Brazil, Costa Rica, Argentina, and other Latin American nations, 1963-70's.

445. Thompson, William R. SYSTEMIC CHANGE AND THE LATIN AMERICAN MILITARY COUP. *Comparative Pol. Studies 1975 7(4): 441-459.*

446. Weaver, Jerry L. ARMS TRANSFERS TO LATIN AMERICA: A NOTE ON THE CONTAGION EFFECT. *J. of Peace Res. [Norway] 1974 11(3): 213-219.* Correlates air force budgets in six rival Latin American states (Argentina, Brazil, Chile, Peru, Colombia, and Venezuela) for 1960-70. "All six countries increased their dollar-expenditures for the armed forces during the 1960s, but increases in the percent of the GDP going to the military budgets were not, as often alleged, particularly associated with military governments." Suggests that "arms transfers to the region will have a selective, often profound, impact on the levels of military spending by other members of the inter-American community." Table, 2 figs., 13 notes.   D. D. Cameron

447. Wolpin, Miles D. MILITARY RADICALISM IN LATIN AMERICA. *J. of Interamerican Studies and World Affairs 1981 23(4): 395-428.* Rejects the thesis of Samuel Huntington and others that political conservatism is inherent in the military mind, ethos, or profession. Such conservatism is due to recruitment, socialization, and historical factors. The declining US role as world power and its diversion of essential resources to fund renewed militarization will increase the receptiveness of the military to assimilate economically nationalist and leftist ideas. The traditional tendency for the military to function as a Bonapartist trustee for a nonhegemonic elite may diminish appreciably. Secondary sources; 7 notes, 3 tables, ref.   T. Schoonover

448. —. THE MILITARY BALANCE 1974/75: LATIN AMERICA. *Air Force Mag. 1974 57(12): 82-86.* Discusses the defensive treaties made by the Latin American states and other powers from the Act of Havana in 1940 to 1975, and describes the strength and deployment of the military forces of each state.

Political Ideologies and Movements

449. Ameringer, Charles D. THE TRADITION OF DEMOCRACY IN THE CARIBBEAN: BETANCOURT, FIGUERES, MUÑOZ AND THE DEMOCRATIC LEFT. *Caribbean Rev. 1982 11(2): 28-31, 55-56.* Traces 30 years of democracy in Venezuela under Rómuio Betancourt, Costa Rica under José Figueres, and Puerto Rico under Luis Muñoz Marin, all followers of the philosophy of the Peruvian, Víctor Raúl Haya de la Torre, founder of the American Popular Revolutionary Alliance (APRA).

450. Anderle, Ádám. AZ APRA IDEOLÓGIAÁJÁNAK ALAP-VONÁSAI A PÁRTALAKULÁS IDŐSZAKÁBAN (1928-1932) [The basic characteristics of APRA'S ideology in the period of the creation of the party, 1928-32]. *Acta U. Szegediensis de Attila József Nominatae: Acta Hist. [Hungary] 1973 46: 19-43.* The American Popular Revolutionary Alliance (APRA) was founded in 1924 in Mexico by Peruvian students in exile, led by Víctor Raúl Haya de la Torre. Its program advocated opposition to American imperialism, the unity of Indian America, the nationalization of land and industry, the internationalization of the Panama Canal, and solidarity with oppressed nations. The author considers Haya de la Torre's concept of the state, 1928-31, views which were developed into an idea of 'functional democracy.' Contrary to the 'imported' theory of Marxism, APRA claims to have an original Latin American ideology. 98 notes.   R. Hetzron/S

451. Arismendi, Rodmy. EINIGE GEDANKEN ZUM FASCHIS-MUS IM HEUTIGEN LATEINAMERIKA [Some reflections on fascism in present-day Latin America]. *Einheit [East Germany] 1977 32(2): 211-219.* The cooperation of the local oligarchies of Chile, Guatemala, Brazil, Bolivia, and Uruguay with US military and economic interest groups in the 1960's and 1970's strengthened fascist tendencies in these societies. Action was taken against the national liberation movements of these countries, which combined socialist and liberal democratic elements.

452. Blanksten, George I. CUBA, CHILE, AND THE CRISIS OF DEMOCRACY. *Secolas Ann. 1973 4: 11-15.* Compares Cuba and Chile in the context of the decentralization of the Communist movement and the state of value analysis in political science. One of eight papers on Cuba and Chile read at the annual meeting of the Southeastern conference on Latin American Studies.   S

453. Bohning, Don; Tamayo, Juan O.; and Diederich, Bernard. THE SPRINGTIME OF ELECTIONS: THE STATUS OF DEMOCRACY IN THE CARIBBEAN. *Caribbean Rev. 1982 11(3): 4-7, 40-41.* Brief account of the elections in nine countries making up the Caribbean basin, 7 February-4 July 1982: Costa Rica, El Salvador, Mexico, Guatemala, the Dominican Republic, St. Lucia, the Bahamas, the Dutch Antilles, and Colombia, in which three countries elected parties more conservative than their predecessors, with the rest electing incumbent governments or those without much change in ideology, a trend that has been seen since 1980.

454. Bushuyev, V. REVOLUTION AND COUNTER-REVOLUTION IN LATIN AMERICA. *Int. Affairs [USSR] 1974 (5): 30-36.* Discusses measures by imperialist and counterrevolutionary forces in the repression of national liberation movements in Chile and other Latin American nations; considers the Cuban Revolution as an example of the proletariat's triumph over the upper and middle classes, 1960's-70's.

455. Caregorodcev, V. A. DIE LINKSRADIKALEN IN LATEINAMERIKA [Leftist radicals in Latin America]. *Lateinamerika [East Germany] 1977 (Spr): 25-33.* Discusses the damaging influence of leftist radicals on the main line of the revolutionary movement in Latin America, 1970-77. 12 notes.

456. Ciria, Alberto. IDEOLOGIES: ALIVE AND WELL IN LATIN AMERICA. *New Scholar 1978 7(1-2): 283-290.* Reviews and compares *Terms of Conflict: Ideology in Latin America Politics* Morris J. Blachman and Ronald G. Hallman, eds., Inter-American Politics Series, No. 1 (1977), and *Ideology and Social Change in Latin America.* June Nash and Hobart Spalding, Jr., eds. (1977). These works provide a useful starting point for the discussion of ideologies and their practical impact in Latin America today, and the reviewer elaborates on some controversial points raised in both books, such as parliamentary socialism in Chile. Secondary sources; 7 notes.   G. L. Neville

457. Crain, David A. GUATEMALAN REVOLUTIONARIES AND HAVANA'S IDEOLOGICAL OFFENSIVE OF 1966-1968. *J. of Inter-Am. Studies and World Affairs 1975 17(2): 175-205.* Following Cuba's successful revolution, Fidel Castro attempted to build a Latin American revolution, based on an independent Marxist approach. Castro supported armed intervention in other governments and actually intervened in the operations of Communist parties throughout Latin America. The Guatemalan Labor Party, a Communist organization whose Castroite faction inhibited the party's growth, became disturbed over Castro's activity. After the death of Che Guevara, however, Castro backtracked on the hemisphere-wide revolution and became more conciliatory toward America's Communist parties. Based on Cuban and Guatemalan documents and secondary sources; 24 notes, biblio.   J. R. Thomas

458. Davis, Harold Eugene. ELEMENTS OF TRADITIONALISM IN LATIN AMERICAN THOUGHT. *Humánitas [Mexico] 1979 20: 83-92.* The roots of Latin American autonomy were laid from independence on, as national units and identities emerged, based on a tradition part European and part local. The initially conservative-to-monarchical ideas following independence later moved to more liberal views, which predominated by the later 19th century. Traditionalism in the 20th century tends to be nationalist and liberal, producing such phenomena as the

Sinarquism in Mexico, the Integralism in Brazil, and Peronism in Argentina.

459. Dealy, Glen. LA TRADICIÓN DE LA DEMOCRACIA MONISTA EN AMÉRICA LATINA [The tradition of unitary democracy in Latin America]. *Estudios Andinos 1974/75 4(1): 159-201.* Democratic pluralism, a political norm in most Western countries, is notably absent in Latin America. Unitary or single-party democracy derives from a cultural, religious, and economic consensus. Roman Catholic, Thomistic philosophy stresses unity and the common good. Latin American constitutions define political rights and representation in Thomistic terms. Social justice, not political equality, is the aim. Unitary democracy is the result of 20th-century, conservative revolutions and the rise of the middle class in Latin America. Mexico and Cuba are typical examples. Primary and secondary sources; 55 notes.   J. L. White

460. Dealy, Glen. THE TRADITION OF MONISTIC DEMOCRACY IN LATIN AMERICA. *J. of the Hist. of Ideas 1974 35(4): 625-646.* Argues that Latin America is an exception to the general expectation that a rising middle class will foster pluralistic democracy. Latin American governments since 1945 have been increasingly dominated by middle class elements, and have been "moving from half-hearted imitations of pluralistic democracy toward the structuring of more monistic institutional arrangements." The commitment to monism, strong throughout Latin American history, is exemplified by the pronouncements of Simón Bolívar, set in the context of Catholic thought and compared with the Protestant and liberal ideas in which North American pluralism is rooted. Based on published primary and secondary sources; 60 notes.   D. B. Marti

461. Delgado, Alvaro. LATIN AMERICA'S PRIESTS IN REVOLT. *World Marxist R. [Canada] 1973 16(3): 68-75.* Catholic priests are beginning to aid the movement toward communism in Latin America.   S

462. Dix, Robert H. DEMOCRACY IN LATIN AMERICA. *Latin Am. Res. Rev. 1980 15(3): 240-245.* Reviews Juan J. Linz and Alfred Stepan, ed., *The Breakdown of Democratic Regimes* (Baltimore: Johns Hopkins U. Pr., 1978): Part I. Juan J. Linz, *Crisis, Breakdown, and Reequilibration;* Part II. Juan J. Linz and Alfred Stepan, ed., *Europe;* Part III. Juan J. Linz and Alfred Stepan, ed., *Latin America;* and Part IV. Arturo Valenzuela, *Chile.* Departing from traditional approaches to conditions that foster democracy, the work emphasizes the role of leadership and responses of parties and groups to change as important in the breakdown of democracy. Biblio.   J. K. Pfabe

463. Dodson, Michael. THE CHRISTIAN LEFT IN LATIN AMERICAN POLITICS. *J. of Interamerican Studies and World Affairs 1979 21(1): 45-68.* After long neglect, Latin American Catholicism's unimagined potential for social change brought it new attention. The trend has been to interpret the Catholic Church within the framework of development analysis, thus emphasizing the role of the progressives. The roles of the Right and Left have been neglected. Development theory does not explain the roles of the democratic left in Argentina or Chile, nor the clerical radicals' failure to demand that the laity defend the Church's corporate interests. 6 notes, ref.   T. D. Schoonover

464. Dodson, Michael. LIBERATION THEOLOGY AND CHRISTIAN RADICALISM IN CONTEMPORARY LATIN AMERICA. *J. of Latin Am. Studies [Great Britain] 1979 11(1): 203-222.* Liberation theology, no matter how empathetic, contains three flaws: the erroneous assumption of a "pan-Latin Americanism," the facile identification of poverty with indigenous political movements, and the imperfect application of Marxist tenets to national social structures and political groupings. Latin American liberation theology is inclined to romantic ideology; it would do better with pragmatic assessment. 28 notes.   J. F. Vivian

465. Domínguez, Jorge I. and Mitchell, Christopher N. THE ROADS NOT TAKEN: INSTITUTIONALIZATION AND POLITICAL PARTIES IN CUBA AND BOLIVIA. *Comparative Pol. 1977 9(2): 173-196.* Examines revolutionary political parties in Cuba, 1959-76, and Bolivia, 1952-64, in terms of the interplay of three important variables in the revolutionary process: mass political participation, structural and attitudinal social reorganization, and internal and external criticism.

466. Dumoulin, John. EL FASCISMO Y LAS CRISIS DE DESARROLLO CAPITALISTA [Fascism and the crises of capitalist development]. *Santiago [Cuba] 1979 (35): 9-36.* Analyzes the nature of fascism between the two world wars in Europe and presently in Latin America. Fascism represents a stage in the historical development of capitalism, viz. the crisis of capitalism of "middle development" faced with the threat of the socialist alternative and looking for a solution in State monopoly capitalism. Despite many differences the essential features of fascism are to be found both in Latin American and "classical" European fascist regimes. 9 notes.   J. V. Coutinho

467. Fernandez, Raúl A. and Ocampo, José F. THE LATIN AMERICAN REVOLUTION: A THEORY OF IMPERIALISM, NOT DEPENDENCE. *Latin Am. Perspectives 1974 1(1): 30-61.* The theory of dependence is a revision of Marxism which resurrects, in its application to Latin America, an ancient polemic among Marxists, and brings to the forefront the necessity for a theoretical basis of the Latin American revolution. The theory of dependence does not explain the nature and persistence of backwardness in Latin America; it ignores the theory of imperialism as a guide for revolution and leads to grave errors of strategy and tactics. The theory of imperialism and backwardness identifies the basic contradictions in Latin America as those between imperialism and the nations in Latin America and between backwardness and the great masses of the people. The "revolution of new democracy" is proposed as a solution to this double contradiction.   A

468. Gavrikov, Iu. P. KHOSE KARLOS MARIATEGI—BORETS ZA IDEI MARKSIZMA-LENINIZMA V LATINSKOI AMERIKE (1894-1930 GG.) [José Carlos Mariátegui (1894-1930), champion of Marxist-Leninist ideas in Latin America]. *Novaia i Noveishaia Istoriia [USSR] 1978 (4): 80-89.* Biography of the founder of the Communist Party of Peru. Describes his early journalistic career in Lima, covert persecution for support of the workers' movement, political exile (1919) in the guise of a three-year scholarship abroad, involvement in socialist and antifascist movements in France and Italy, friendship with the French writer Henri Barbusse (1873-1935) and Russian pro-Communist intellectuals, conversion to Marxism-Leninism and internationalism, and return to Peru in 1923. 32 notes.   N. Frenkley

469. Grigulevich, I. ARMIIA I REVOLIUTSIONNYI PROTSESS V LATINSKOI AMERIKE [The army and the revolutionary process in Latin America]. *Mirovaia Ekon.: Mezhdunarodnye Otnosheniia [USSR] 1973 (12): 40-55.* Describes the army's role in the history of Latin America. Patriots led Latin American armies during the war for independence and liberation, 1810-26. Later, army generals served the interests of the ruling oligarchy and often usurped power for themselves. After World War I, social reform and anti-imperialist forces penetrated Latin American armies. This worried the United States, which created local police corps headed by native agents in the countries they occupied. After US evacuation, these police corps were turned into armies and their commanders became presidents. After World War II, the armies underwent further differentiation and polarization. The author describes the crises of the traditional military dictatorships, and progressive and reactionary tendencies of contemporary Latin American military leaders and armies. Secondary sources; 15 notes.   L. Kalinowski

470. Herrick, Paul B., Jr., and Robins, Robert S. VARIETIES OF LATIN AMERICAN REVOLUTIONS AND REBELLIONS. *J. of Developing Areas 1976 10(3): 317-336.* A typology of revolution is presented based on four levels of change (total revolution, political revolution, policy rebellion, and palace rebellion) and four types of discontinuity (institutional, elite, policy, or value discontinuity). In Latin America major political change is frequently achieved by revolution, a concept referring to major and deep social, political, and ideological change. Revolution is a multidimensional phenomenon which may be analyzed in political, economic, or social terms. Latin American revolutions in Mexico (total revolution 1910-40), Brazil (political revolution 1964), Venezuela (policy rebellion 1948), and Bolivia (palace rebellion 1920) were studied. Table, 48 notes.   O. W. Eads, Jr.

471. Hübener, Karl-Ludolf. THE SOCIALIST INTERNATIONAL AND LATIN AMERICA: PROBLEMS AND POSSIBILITIES. *Caribbean Rev. 1982 11(2): 38-41.* Describes the Socialist International's influence in Latin America since the first conference of the Latin Ameri-

can Committee of the SI held in Santo Domingo in 1980, focusing on ideological disagreements in the movement's leadership and platform.

472. Israel, Ricardo. LA TEORÍA POLÍTICA Y EL ESTUDIO DEL FACISMO [Political theory and the study of fascism]. *Estudios Pol. [Mexico] 1979 4(13-14): 149-177.* A political essay on the nature of fascism, particularly in Latin America. Current theories of fascism are either subjective or objective: subjective theories stress moral, sociological, or philosophical relationships between fascism and the ascendency of the middle classes; objective theories view this movement as a product of capitalism's internal logic. These theories confuse fascism's outward symbols with its repressive reality. Rejecting these theories, he interprets fascism as an expression of monopoly capitalism, wielding the symbols of middle- and working-class nationalism to unite society to serve its interests. Secondary works; 51 notes.   F. J. Shaw, Jr.

473. Jungueira, José Cesar. THE RE-EMERGENCE OF THE CHRISTIAN LEFT IN LATIN AMERICA. *Can. Dimension [Canada] 1979 13(5): 46-49.* Discusses the emergence of the Christian Left in Latin America in the 1960's, as a result of the breakdown of liberal democracy.

474. Koval', B. I. VLIIANIE VELIKOGO OKTIABRIA NA LATINSKUIU AMERIKU [The influence of the Great October Revolution on Latin America]. *Novaia i Noveishaia Istoriia [USSR] 1977 (6): 27-43.* The triumph of the proletarian revolution in Russia accelerated the merger of Marxism with the working-class movement, which began in some countries of the continent in the previous decade and led to the establishment of Communist parties in Latin American countries. In each country this process was different.   J

475. Landry, David M. THE DECLINE OF LIBERALISM IN LATIN AMERICAN POLITICS. *Southern Q. 1976 14(2): 125-131.* Explains the effect of authoritarianism on Latin American politics and the failure of liberalism to gain acceptance there, 1930-73. 11 notes.   R. W. Dubay

476. Lloyd, Arthur S. LIBERATION AND THE CHURCH IN LATIN AMERICA. *J. of the Hellenic Diaspora 1975 2(3): 43-50.* Discusses liberation movements and the Catholic Church in Latin America, 1960's-70's.   S

477. López Vallecillos, Italo. AMÉRICA LATINA Y EL SOCIALISMO DEMOCRÁTICO [Latin America and Democratic Socialism]. *Estudios Centroamericanos [El Salvador] 1980 35(381-382): 685-696.* Latin American democratic socialism is distinct from European social democracy, especially in its emphasis on Latin America's need for independence from the world capitalist system. While tied to the Socialist International headquartered in London, it is more properly aligned with similar movements in Africa and Asia opposed to the capitalist-oriented Trilateral Commission. Based principally on secondary sources; table, biblio.   R. L. Woodward, Jr.

478. Mansilla, H. C. F. DIE LATEINAMERIKANISCHEN GUERILLAS: GEWALT UND SELBSTVERSTÄNDNIS [The Latin American guerrillas: force and self-understanding]. *Schweizer Monatshefte [Switzerland] 1982 62(1): 27-39.* Latin American guerrilla movements are only original in some elements of strategy and some secondary aspects of constitutional thought; otherwise they follow the models of already established state socialist societies, the use of physical force being a deeply rooted feature of the Iberian Catholic tradition.

479. Nálevka, Vladimír. VELKÁ ŘIJNOVÁ SOCIALISTICKÁ REVOLUCE A POČÁTKY KOMUNISTICKÉHO HNUTÍ V LATINSKÉ AMERICE [The Great October Socialist Revolution and the beginnings of the Communist movement in Latin America]. *Československý Časopis Hist. [Czechoslovakia] 1977 25(6): 839-857.* Surveys the rise of Communist parties in Latin America after World War I. Industrial expansion during the war had strengthened the labor movements, and the October Revolution brought on their greater internal differentiation. Since the revolutionary elites had come largely from Europe, they tended to apply European socialist standards to the less developed Latin American societies; they also had to overcome their anarcho-syndicalist tendencies and their sectarian refusals to cooperate

with poor peasants or anti-imperialist sections of the bourgeoisie. By 1934 Communist parties agreed on the pressing need for a broadly popular anti-imperialist front. Secondary sources; 79 notes.   R. E. Weltsch

480. Obyden, K. M. LATINSKAIA AMERIKA I RASPAD KOLONIAL'NOI SISTEMY IMPERIALIZMA [Latin America and the disintegration of imperialism's colonial system]. *Novaia i Noveishaia Istoriia [USSR] 1981 (1): 61-76.* Treats Lenin's approach to the typology of dependent countries in the epoch of imperialism. According to Lenin, there are, besides colonies, transitional types of dependent countries: semicolonies and countries independent politically but not financially, diplomatically, or militarily. Lenin did not include the transitional types of countries (Latin American, for instance) in imperialism's colonial system.   J

481. Orrillo, Winston. PRIMERAS HUELLAS DE MARIÁTEGUI EN CUBA [First traces of Mariátegui in Cuba]. *Casa de las Américas [Cuba] 1977 16(100): 178-181.* The first contact between the Peruvian Communist, José Mariátegui, and Julio Antonio Mella, the founder of the Cuban Communist party, occurred in 1924. Other contacts with Cuban Marxist intellectuals followed in 1927. The contacts led to the exchange of articles for publication. The influence of Mariátegui is very much in evidence in the thinking of later Cuban revolutionaries such as Osvaldo Dorticós, Carlos Rafael Rodríguez, Raúl Roa, and Juan Marinello. Excerpt from the author's forthcoming *Mariátegui y la Revolución Cubana.* Based on published primary sources and interviews; 14 notes.   H. J. Miller

482. Petras, James. POLITICAL CHANGE, CLASS CONFLICT, AND THE DECLINE OF LATIN AMERICAN FASCISM. *Monthly Rev. 1979 31(2): 26-37.* Discusses the trends for the 1980's among the popular opposition to rightist and fascist regimes in Latin America, and traces the rise of rightist regimes since the 1964 Brazilian coup.

483. Schöttlei, Urs. LIBERALISMUS IN LATEINAMERIKA [Liberalism in Latin America]. *Schweizer Monatshefte [Switzerland] 1980 60(4): 279-287.* The radical-liberal movements in Ecuador, Colombia, Argentina, Uruguay, Paraguay, and Peru show classic features of European liberal parties of the 19th century, especially in their policies favoring democratic and constitutional rights.

484. Soares, Jose. DOES FASCISM EXIST IN LATIN AMERICA? *World Marxist Rev. [Canada] 1976 19(12): 79-86.* Examines the political development of Latin America, 1945-76, and discusses whether the repressive regimes in Chile, Brazil, Uruguay, Guatemala, and Bolivia are truly fascist.

485. Teitelboim, Volodia. LA AMÉRICA LATINA Y LOS SESENTA AÑOS DE OCTUBRE [Latin America and the 60th anniversary of the October Revolution]. *Casa de las Américas [Cuba] 1977 18(105): 5-11.* Describes the Russian Revolution's impact on Latin America. V. I. Lenin was not a doctrinaire Marxist but one who felt the need for updating Marxism to meet changing conditions. His chief contribution was to develop a united party to make it truly representative of the proletariat. The Russian Revolution serves as a model for ending capitalist exploitation of Latin America as noted in the political thought of Emiliano Zapata, José Carlos Mariátegui, and in labor congresses, 1918-20. The resultant Cuban revolution was the first victory for socialism in Latin America.   H. J. Miller

486. Vendrell, Roberto. NATIONALISM AND REVOLUTIONARY TRENDS IN LATIN AMERICA. *Taamuli [Tanzania] 1978 8(1): 14-25.* From 1945 the increasing industrialization of Latin America and the growth of the working class led to a rise in nationalist sentiment. Successful socialist revolutions, like that of Agustino Sandino in Nicaragua, used the nationalists as the core of their revolution. Bolivia, Peru, Chile, and Argentina are all examples of countries where progressive regimes have failed to retain power. 41 notes.   D. S. Rockwood

487. Volksi, Victor. LA INFLUENCIA DE LA REVOLUCION DE OCTUBRE DE 1917 EN EL PROCESO LIBERADOR DE AMERICA LATINA [The influence of the October 1917 Revolution on the liberation process in Latin America]. *Am. Latina [USSR] 1978 1(17): 30-42.*

Asserts that the capitalist countries of Latin America were well-placed to repeat the Russian revolutionary experience and examines the revolutions in Cuba and Chile.

488. Walker, Thomas W. DIMENSIONS OF THE LEFT IN LATIN AMERICA. *Polity 1977 10(1): 111-120.* Reviews eight books on various segments of the Left in Latin America. Even if one simplifies matters considerably, one must still distinguish four general movements: traditional communism, the democratic Left, revolutionary Marxism, and the Catholic Left. The books reviewed provide some clues to the reasons why the Left has been active and vocal but not particularly effective in 20th-century Latin America. W. R. Hively

489. —. [FASCISM IN THE AMERICAS, PAST AND PRESENT]. *Explorations in Ethnic Studies 1982 5(1): 3-39.*
Forbes, Jack D. FASCISM: A REVIEW OF ITS HISTORY AND ITS PRESENT CULTURAL REALITY IN THE AMERICAS, *pp. 3-25.* Traces the origins of fascism to the Middle East before Christ, and traces its history in the Americas to Argentina during the 1830's under Juan Manuel de Rosas and to the American Confederacy during 1860-65, and discusses how fascism continues to exist in disguised form today.
Cavaioli, Frank J. CRITIQUE, *pp. 25-27.*
Binder, Wolfgang. CRITIQUE, *pp. 28-32.*
Johnson, David M. CRITIQUE, *pp. 32-35.*
Brown, Shirley Vining. CRITIQUE, *pp. 35-39.*

490. —. LATIN AMERICA: EXPERIENCE AND LESSONS OF REVOLUTIONARY STRUGGLE; INTERNATIONAL SEMINAR. *World Marxist R. [Canada] 1974 17(5): 95-109.* Reports on a 1974 seminar among Latin American Communists concerning the revolutionary movement in Latin America. S

Continental Integration and Cooperation

492. Aftalión, Marcelo E. PODER NEGOCIADOR LATINOAMERICANO [Latin American negotiating power]. *Foro Int. [Mexico] 1975 15(60): 536-562.* Discusses Latin American attempts at international economic negotiations with the European Common Market and the United States, 1960-75. Successes have been in name only, and the negotiating position of the Latin American states needs to be strengthened through closer ties among them. Reprinted modification of an article in *Revista de la Integración* [Argentina], (18). Primary and secondary sources; 53 notes. D. A. Franz

493. Alcalá Quintero, Francisco. MÉXICO Y SU RELACIÓN CON EL MERCADO COMÚN CENTROAMERICANO [Mexico and its relation with the Central American Common Market]. *Foro Internacional [Mexico] 1973 14(54): 175-203.* Discusses financial and commercial relations between Mexico and the Central American Common Market with trade statistics. Primary and secondary sources; 5 tables, 7 notes. D. A. Franz

494. Almeida, Rómulo. REFLEXIONES SOBRE LA INTEGRACIÓN LATINOAMERICANA [Reflections of Latin American integration]. *Estudios Int. [Chile] 1980 13(52): 417-459.* Reviews the background and present international context of Latin American integration and offers practical measures that could be taken toward an integrated plan of development to overcome current economic inequalities.

495. Arriola, Carlos. AL ACERCAMIENTO MEXICANO-CHILENO [Mexican-Chilean rapprochement]. *Foro Internacional [Mexico] 1974 14(56): 507-547.* Examines reasons behind the development of closer Mexican-Chilean ties since 1972, the objectives of rapprochement, its development, and its repercussions in Mexico. Based primarily on newspaper reports; 72 notes. D. A. Franz

496. Arriola, Carlos. EL PRESIDENTE ECHEVERRÍA EN LATINOAMÉRICA [President Echeverría in Latin America]. *Foro Internacional [Mexico] 1974 15(57): 103-115.* Discusses Mexican President

Luis Echeverría's July 1974 visit to South America, his attempt to gain support for a regional organization excluding the United States, and his policy of Latin American solidarity. Based primarily on newspaper reports; 18 notes. D. A. Franz

497. Axline, W. Andrew and Mytelka, Lynn K. SOCIÉTÉ MULTINATIONALE ET INTEGRATION REGIONALE DANS LE GROUPE ANDIN ET DANS LA COMMUNAUTÉ DES CARAIBES [The multinational corporation and regional integration in the Andean group and the Caribbean community]. *Études Int. [Canada] 1976 7(2): 163-192.* Discusses the effect of Resolution 24 on the various regional free trade associations in the Caribbean, including the Caribbean Community (CARICOM), the Caribbean Free Trade Association (CARIFTA), and the Latin American Free Trade Association (LAFTA). Examines the models these groups adopted to regulate foreign investment and to stimulate the development of native industrial technology in order to insure the future economic independence of the Caribbean. 49 notes.
J. F. Harrington, Jr.

498. Barcia Trelles, Camilo. PROLOGO, TRAMA Y EPILOGO EN LAS RELACIONES INTERAMERICANAS [Prologue, plot, and epilogue in interamerican relations]. *Rev. de Política Int. [Spain] 1975 (137): 19-46.* Examines relations among the South American states, US influence in Latin America from the end of European rule to the 1974 Quito Conference, and the decisions taken by many Latin American states to reestablish links with Cuba despite US disapproval.

499. Boersner, Demetrio. VENEZUELA AND THE CARIBBEAN. *Caribbean Rev. 1979 8(4): 8-11, 50-51.* Chronicles Venezuela's foreign relations with the Caribbean islands and Central America, 1936-78.

500. Bond, Robert D. VENEZUELA, BRAZIL AND THE AMAZON BASIN. *Orbis 1978 22(3): 635-650.* Discusses Brazilian and Venezuelan relations between 1960 and 1978, focusing on international agreements for the development of the Amazon Basin. Briefly describes conflicts over the importance of democracy and human rights, the supply and price of oil, and the New International Economic Order. Describes Latin American fears of Brazilian expansionism and outlines factors leading to the multilateral Amazon Pact signed by eight South American countries on 3 July 1978. Points to possible areas of future conflict and cooperation between Brazil and Venezuela. Based on interviews and published sources; 24 notes. J. D. Moore

501. Bond, Robert D. VENEZUELA, LA CUENCA DEL CARIBE Y LA CRISIS CENTROAMERICANA [Venezuela, the Caribbean basin, and the Central American crisis]. *Foro Int. [Mexico] 1981 22(2): 164-179.* Examines Venezuelan foreign policy in the Caribbean basin with emphasis on relations with Nicaragua and El Salvador. From a symposium 2-3 April 1981 at the Woodrow Wilson International Center for Scholars, Washington, D.C. Based on printed primary and secondary sources and interviews; 15 notes. D. A. Franz

502. Brandt, Niels. DIE TÄTIGKEIT DER ORGANISATION DER AMERIKANISCHEN STAATEN (OAS) IN DEN JAHREN 1970 UND 1971 [The activity of the Organization of American States (OAS), 1970-71]. *Jahrbuch für Int. Recht [West Germany] 1973 16: 475-494.* Covers the first two years of the Organization of American States under its reformed Charter of 27 February 1970; includes its resolutions and actions concerning terrorism, the El Salvador-Honduras war of 1969, and the problem of tariffs instituted by developed countries against imports from less developed countries.

503. Brock, Lothar. DIE FUNKTION DER OAS FÜR DIE RECHTFERTIGUNG DER LATEINAMERIKA-POLITIK DER USA [The role of the Organization of American States (OAS) in legitimizing US Latin American policy]. *Pol. Vierteljahresschrift [West Germany] 1978 19(1): 1-21.* Problems of legitimization are central to the functioning of international organizations, particularly in the case of developing nations seeking a new basis for economic agreement with industrial nations. Inter-American policy has been committed to the principle of nonintervention and the right of each country to its own resources. The organization of American States (OAS) was founded not to promote pan-Americanism, but to protect Latin American interests against outside incursions. Graph, 28 notes. S. Bonnycastle

504. Casanova, Manuel. LA PARTICIPACIÓN DE AMÉRICA LATINA EN LA SISTEMA ECONÓMICO INTERNACIONAL DE LA POSTGUERRA [Latin American participation in the postwar international economic system]. *Estudios Int. [Chile] 1979 12(46): 177-203.* Discusses the horizontal relationships among the various Latin American countries in the context of the international economic order which emerged from World War II, and especially the consolidation of an international economic philosophy destined to homogenize the foreign policies of the countries participating in that order.

505. Castro, Héctor David. EL PRINCIPIO DE NO INTERVENCIÓN Y LAS CONFERENCIAS DE LA HABANA Y MONTEVIDEO [The nonintervention principle and the conferences of Havana and Montevideo]. *Estudios Centro Americanos [El Salvador] 1973 28(296): 369-375.* Gives a detailed analysis of the arguments on the principle of nonintervention which took place at the 6th International Conference of the American States in Havana (1928) and at the 7th Conference in Montevideo (1933).

506. Child, John. PEACEKEEPING AND THE INTER-AMERICAN SYSTEM. *Military Rev. 1980 60(10): 40-54.* Examines the theory of peacekeeping and the role that Latin American countries have played in both UN and inter-American peacekeeping efforts since 1932. By creating an environment that is conducive to negotiation and resolution of actual or potential conflicts, peacekeeping forces play an integral role in maintaining world and hemispheric cooperation and peace. The Latin American countries have offered substantial contributions in this area, and there remains the potential for continuing aid from this source. 2 tables, 5 notes.   D. H. Cline

507. Cochrane, James D. and Sloan, John W. LAFTA AND THE CACM: A COMPARATIVE ANALYSIS OF INTEGRATION IN LATIN AMERICA. *J. of Developing Areas 1973 8(1): 13-38.* Compares the process of economic integration in the Latin American Free Trade Association (LAFTA) and the Central American Common Market (CACM), 1961-69.   S

508. Conroy, Michael E. REJECTION OF GROWTH CENTER STRATEGY IN LATIN AMERICAN REGIONAL DEVELOPMENT PLANNING. *Land Econ. 1973 49(4): 371-380.*

509. Davydov, V. BEZ"IADERNYE ZONY—VAZHNYI FAKTOR MEZHDUNARODNOI BEZOPASNOSTI [Nuclear-free zones: an important factor in international security]. *Mirovaia Ekonomika i Mezhdunarodnye Otnosheniia [USSR] 1981 (12): 30-41.* Examines the Treaty of Tlatelolco, which established the first nuclear-free zone in Latin America, and assesses the prospects for further development of such zones with the support and cooperation of the USSR opposing the negativism of the United States.

510. de Tella, Guido. REGIONAL COHESION AND INCOHERENCE IN LATIN AMERICA. *World Today [Great Britain] 1974 30(12): 522-528.*

511. Domínguez, Jorge I. CONSENSUS AND DIVERGENCE: THE STATE OF THE LITERATURE ON INTER-AMERICAN RELATIONS IN THE 1970'S. *Latin Am. Res. Rev. 1978 13(1): 87-126.* Examines areas of consensus in recent writings on inter-American relations in addition to eight divergent perspectives. The author proposes a hierarchy of approaches to the study of inter-American relations—at the top, using unorthodox dependency and strategic perspectives; at the middle, organizational ideology and presidential politics perspectives; and at the bottom, the political system perspective. Secondary sources; 2 tables, 103 notes, appendix.   J. K. Pfabe

512. Ducatenzeiler, Graciela and Fuente, Manuel de la. ACTEURS ET STRATÉGIES DANS LE PROCESSUS D'INTÉGRATION ÉCONOMIQUE EN AMÉRIQUE LATINE [Actors and strategies in the economic integration process in Latin America]. *Can J. of Pol. Sci. [Canada] 1979 12(4): 775-797.* Analyzes the process of economic integration in Latin America worked out mainly by the industrial bourgeoisie and the state through the action of the Latin America Free Trade Association (LAFTA), created in 1960, and the Andean Pact, concluded in 1969. LAFTA failed because the time was inappropriate for the industrial

bourgeoisie to achieve leadership. The Andean Pact has aimed at a renegotiation of dependency relationships among the states, the several national bourgeoisies, and the multinational corporations. 33 notes.
                                                              G. P. Cleyet

513. E. J. C. AMÉRICA LATINA: SU IMPORTANCIA EN LOS PAISES NO ALINEADOS [Latin America: its importance among the nonaligned nations]. *Estudios Centroamericanos [El Salvador] 1979 34(372-373): 990-994.* The movement of nonaligned nations may be said to have begun in 1955 at an Afro-Asian countries conference in Bandung, which called for the removal of foreign bases, opposition to all forms of discrimination, and development of a new international order. The movement has developed as a means of political expression for the Third World. Major concerns of the conference held in September 1979 in Cuba were the penetration of national economies by multinational corporations, the New International Economic Order, and a charter of rights and obligations of states, particularly in regard to the international monetary system. 2 notes.   P. J. Durell

514. Ferris, Elizabeth G. THE ANDEAN PACT AND THE AMAZON TREATY: REFLECTIONS OF CHANGING LATIN AMERICAN RELATIONS. *J. of Interamerican Studies and World Affairs 1981 23(2): 147-175.* The Andean Pact has changed from sectoral programming and trade liberalization to institutionalization of subregional cooperation. It has also emerged as an outspoken advocate of reformist solutions to Latin American problems, emphasizing human rights and democracy. If domestic economic adversity promotes increased regional cooperation, then Latin America may experience economic integration movements in the coming years. 6 notes, ref.
                                                              T. D. Schoonover

515. Flores Caballero, Romeo. MÉXICO Y EL PACTO ANDINO [Mexico and the Andean Pact]. *Foro Internacional [Mexico] 1974 14(56): 579-617.* Discusses the formation of the Andean Common Market and its relations with the Latin American Free Trade Association (LAFTA) and Mexico. Primary and secondary sources; 71 notes.
                                                              D. A. Franz

516. Furtak, Robert K. DES SISTEMA ECONÓMICO LATINOAMERICANO: KOOPERATION IM ZEICHEN KOLLEKTIVEN SELBSTVERTRAUENS [The Latin American Economic System: cooperation as a sign of collective self-confidence]. *Jahrbuch für Geschichte von Staat, Wirtschaft und Gesellschaft Lateinamerikas [West Germany] 1979 16: 407-435.* In 1975, urged by Mexican President Luis Echeverría, 25 Latin American nations founded the Latin American Economic System (SELA), not to integrate their economies in the sense of a common market, but rather to encourage regional cooperation via autonomous forces and mutual consultation to coordinate positions and strategies. The need to cooperate in the face of the large economic powers has given the SELA some success, but it remains uncertain if it will be able to lead to a stage of self-sustaining development among the SELA members. 38 notes.   T. D. Schoonover

517. Gilderhus, Mark T. PAN-AMERICAN INITIATIVES: THE WILSON PRESIDENCY AND REGIONAL INTEGRATION, 1914-1917. *Diplomatic Hist. 1980 4(4): 409-423.* President Woodrow Wilson in his first term of office, 1913-17, sought to institute a policy of Pan-American regional integration. He and his aides envisioned for the Americas a functioning network of trade and investment coordinated with a united resistance to potential European intervention. A related Pan-American treaty would provide for a multilateral police force to maintain order in the hemisphere. Although American trade within the hemisphere did grow, amateurish American diplomacy and Latin American fears of US domination doomed the completion of his vision. 43 notes.
                                                              T. L. Powers

518. González, Eduardo Reyes. A MULTINATIONAL SUCCESS. *Américas (Org. of Am. States) 1978 30(10): 2-6.* Created in 1890 as the International Union of American Republics, the Organization of American States since the mid-1960's has become a major force in the educational, scientific, and cultural development in the Americas.

519. Greño Velasco, José Enrique. LA CONTROVERSIA ARGENTINA-BRASILEÑA EN EL ALTO PARANÁ [The controversy be-

tween Argentina and Brazil on the Alto Paraná]. *Rev. de Política Int. [Spain] 1974 (133): 91-109.* Discusses the background to, and meaning of, the Treaty of Yacireta of 1973 between Argentina and Paraguay.

520. Herrera, Felipe. LA TAREA INCONCLUSA: AMERICA LATINA INTEGRADA [The incompleted task: Latin American integration]. *Internat. Development R. 1973 15(3): 2-6.* An economically integrated Latin America is a pervasive theme among intellectuals. Today, with increasing communications and mutual technical assistance, this long postponed dream may finally become a reality. While deep ideological divisions and internal economic problems pose possible obstacles, the increasing commonality of national economies transcends historical differences. To implement such a program, the unification of the Spanish-speaking countries of Latin America, a permanent organization of the highest governmental officials should be created.
S. F. Strausberg

521. Jacobini, H. B. LA CONTRIBUCION LATINOAMERICANA AL DERECHO DE LAS NACIONES Y AL "DERECHO INTERNACIONAL AMERICANO" [The Latin American contribution to the law of nations and "American International Law"]. *Foro Int. [Mexico] 1982 22(3): 304-319.* Examines the diversity of international law interests and the influence of Latin American states and addresses the concept of a body of American regional international law. 60 notes.
D. A. Franz

522. Kissinger, Henry A. "GOOD PARTNER" POLICY FOR THE AMERICAS. *Society 1974 11(6): 16-17, 18-22.* Calls for a cooperative effort toward the economic development of Latin America. Address to OAS General Assembly.
S

523. König, Wolfgang. MÉXICO FRENTE A LA ALALC Y LOS OTROS MECANISMOS LATINOAMERICANOS DE INTEGRACIÓN ECONÓMICA [Mexico and LAFTA and other Latin American mechanisms of economic integration]. *Foro Internacional [Mexico] 1974 14(56): 548-578.* Discusses Mexican relations with the Latin American Free Trade Association (LAFTA), Central American Common Market, Caribbean Free Trade Association (CARIFTA), and the Andean Pact. Primary and secondary sources; 64 notes.
D. A. Franz

524. Kosztirko, Rafał. INTEGRATION PROCESSES AND ECONOMIC GROWTH IN LATIN AMERICAN COUNTRIES. *Studies on the Developing Countries [Poland] 1977 (8): 130-152.* Since 1960 the Latin American Free Trade Association and the Central American Common Market have been trying to foster economic growth and mutual aid through liberalized trade and international economic planning among their member nations, with reasonable success in both cases, but especially in CACM.

525. Leeta, Francesco. IL SISTEMA DI SICUREZZA INTERAMERICANO NEL PROTOCOLLO DI EMENDAMENTO DEL TRATTATO DI RIO DE JANEIRO [The interamerican security system in the protocol of an amendment to the Treaty of Rio de Janiero]. *Comunità Int. [Italy] 1977 32(1): 26-56.* In seeking to amend the Interamerican Treaty of Mutual Assistance of 1947, the Conference of the Organization of American States meeting in San Jose, Costa Rica, July 1975, provided an opportunity to reconsider the interamerican system of security and allowed the American states to testify as to the feasibility and success of the already existing continental security system.

526. Martz, Mary Jeanne Reid. OAS REFORMS AND THE FUTURE OF PACIFIC SETTLEMENT. *Latin Am. Res. Rev. 1977 12(2): 176-186.* Recent changes in the Rio Treaty (1947) may influence the process of peaceful settlement of disputes between Western hemisphere states: Article 11 urges collective economic security to keep peace; Article 20 allows a majority to rescind collective measures; Article 5 will require an act of aggression or serious event for collective action; Article 6 restricts assistance if one party refuses it. The Organization of American States probably will act more cautiously, but pacific settlement will remain an important function. Based on OAS documents and secondary sources; 34 notes.
J. K. Pfabe

527. Medina Luna, Ramón. PROYECCIÓN DE MÉXICO SOBRE CENTROAMÉRICA [Mexico and Central America]. *Foro Internacional*

cional [Mexico] 1974 14(56): 438-473.* Examines the Mexican attempt to diversify markets by seeking closer ties with Central America and the obstacles to this attempt created by the development of the Central American Common Market. Primary and secondary sources; table, 93 notes.
D. A. Franz

528. Meek, George. U.S. INFLUENCE IN THE ORGANIZATION OF AMERICAN STATES. *J. of Inter-Am. Studies and World Affairs 1975 17(3): 311-325.* The degree of US influence in the Organization of American States is widely debated. Some argue that the United States dominates the organization while others insist that little influence is exerted from North America. An analysis of roll call votes since 1948 indicates that on issues relating to Communism and the Cold War the United States was quite influential, but since 1965 Latin American nations have become increasingly sensitive on interventionist issues, and the United States has not had as much success. In the future the United States will be able to prevent major action detrimental to its interests in the OAS, but it will not be able to use that organization to back up its unilateral actions as in the past. Based on OAS statistics and secondary books and articles; 4 tables, 5 notes.
J. R. Thomas

529. Molestina, Carlos J. THE INTER-AMERICAN INSTITUTE OF AGRICULTURAL SCIENCES. *Américas (Organization of American States) 1973 25(4): S1-S16.* Chronicles agriculture from prehistory to the present in Latin America with special emphasis on the operations of the Inter-American Institute of Agricultural Sciences.

530. Moneta, Carlos J. AMÉRICA LATINA Y EL SISTEMA INTERNACIONAL EN LA DÉCADA DEL OCHENTA: ¿HACIA UN NUEVO ORDEN ANTÁRTICO? [Latin America and the international system in the eighties: toward a new Antarctic order?]. *Estudios Int. [Chile] 1980 13(52): 481-526.* Given the importance of the Antarctic region in the search for important raw materials and the state of fluidity of the present international system, examines the possibilities and conditions of a new agreement among the interested countries.

531. Ojeda Gómez, Mario. LAS RELACIONES DE MÉXICO CON EL RÉGIMEN REVOLUCIONARIO CUBANO [Mexican relations with the Cuban revolutionary regime]. *Foro Internacional [Mexico] 1974 14(56): 474-506.* Mexican-Cuban relations fall in four periods: sympathy and cordiality (1959-61), coldness and reserve (1962-67), deterioration of relations (1968-70), and thaw to rapprochement (1971-73). Based primarily on newspaper reports; table, 62 notes.
D. A. Franz

532. Ojeda Gómez, Mario. PRESENTACIÓN: LE NUEVA POLÍTICA DE MÉXICO HACIA AMÉRICA LATINA [Introduction: The new policy of Mexico toward Latin America]. *Foro Internacional [Mexico] 1974 14(56): 433-437.* Surveys reasons for Mexican neglect of Latin America and summarizes the main points of each of the five articles in this issue, which deal with Mexico's Latin American policies area by area.
D. A. Franz

533. Orrego Vicuña, Francisco. HACIA NUEVA FORMAS DE INTEGRACION ECONOMICA EN AMERICA LATINA: LECCIONES DE UNA EXPERIENCIA [Toward new forms of economic integration in Latin America: lessons from an experience]. *Estudios Int. [Chile] 1981 14(56): 568-577.* With the failure of Latin America's several economic integration schemes, describes the political and institutional crises in the region and the need for balanced, pragmatic, and pluralist context for integration.

534. Pellicer de Brody, Olga. COMENTARIO SOBRE LA CONFERENCIA DE CANCILLERES AMERICANOS Y LA POLÍTICA DE MÉXICO HACIA LA AMÉRICA LATINA [Commentary on the American ministerial conference and Mexican policy toward Latin America]. *Foro Internacional [Mexico] 1974 14(56): 626-630.* Analyzes the Declaration of Tlatelolco and discusses Mexico's Latin American policy of spearheading Latin American unity and solidarity.
D. A. Franz

535. Peña, Félix. TENDENCIAS Y PERSPECTIVAS DE LA INTEGRACIÓN ECONÓMICA EN AMÉRICA LATINA [Trends and prospects of economic integration in Latin America]. *Estudios Int. [Chile] 1975 8(29): 137-152.* Discusses Latin American economic integra-

tion, the balance between regionalization and overall integration, and the problem of maintaining independence simultaneously with effective regional solidarity, 1950's-75.

536. Petković, Ranko. ŠESTA KONFERENCIJA NESVRSTANIH ZEMALJA U HAVANI [The 6th Conference of nonaligned nations in Havana]. *Medjunarodni Problemi [Yugoslavia] 1979 31(4): 9-25.* The sixth summit in Havana dealt with the future position, role, and activities of the nonaligned movement, the main principles being nonalignment as a political doctrine, international movement, and Third World national policy. The Havana Conference reaffirmed the concept of nonalignment as a global and independent factor in international relations.

537. Plaza, Galo. TRENDS AND PROSPECTS IN LATIN AMERICA. *Secolas Ann. 1975 (6): 5-9.* The OAS secretary general believes that Latin America is still committed to democracy as the ideal form of government, and he foresees greater economic cooperation among all Latin American countries. Speech to the Latin American Historians Luncheon, Southern Historical Association, Atlanta, 9 November 1973.
J. Lewis

538. Prats, Raymond. INTÉGRATION PHYSIQUE ET AMÉNAGEMENT DU TERRITOIRE DANS LE BASSIN DE LA PLATA [Physical integration and national development in the Río de la Plata basin]. *Travaux & Mémoires de l'Inst. des Hautes Études de l'Amérique Latine [France] 1980 33: 143-173.* Examines the problems of planning and international cooperation in the integrated utilization of the waters of four rivers of the Río de la Plata basin involving Brazil, Argentina, Paraguay, Uruguay, and Bolivia.

539. Quintana, Lucio M. Moreno. AMERICAN INTERNATIONAL LAW. *Int. J. of Pol. 1976 6(1-2): 128-132.* Discusses the evolution of international law in Latin American countries, 1883-1945.

540. Redick, John R. REGIONAL NUCLEAR ARMS CONTROL IN LATIN AMERICA. *Int. Organization 1975 29(2): 415-445.* The Treaty for the Prohibition of Nuclear Weapons in Latin America (Treaty of Tlatelolco) was signed in 1967 and is now in force for eighteen Latin American nations (the important exceptions being Argentina and Brazil). Under the terms of the treaty the Organization for the Prohibition of Nuclear Weapons in Latin America (OPANAL) was established in 1969. With headquarters in Mexico City, OPANAL is a sophisticated control mechanism composed of three principal organs: a General Conference, Council and Secretariat. This article examines the effort to establish a regional nuclear weapons free zone in Latin America and analyzes the ability of the Tlatelolco Treaty to provide the legal and political framework for containment of the growing military potential of Latin American nuclear energy programs. Particular attention is given to the positions of key Latin American nations within the region, nuclear weapons states, and those nations retaining territorial interest within the nuclear weapons free zone. In addition several policy options are advanced which could facilitate the more complete implementation of regional nuclear arms control in Latin America. Evidence is presented in this study that technical developments in Argentina, Brazil and Mexico (primarily a byproduct of ongoing nuclear power programs) are yielding the aforementioned nations a growing military potential. While such a development has serious implications for regional and global peace and security, there are definitely less stable areas containing far more likely examples of "nth" countries. However, Latin America presents a unique opportunity, due to historic and strategic factors, for legal and political norms to manage and control an accelerating technological momentum. Finally it is suggested that the Latin American nuclear weapons free zone is a model which may stimulate duplication in other regions, and can be an important step toward general and complete disarmament.　　J

541. Redick, John R. REGIONAL RESTRAINT: U.S. NUCLEAR POLICY AND LATIN AMERICA. *Orbis 1978 22(1): 161-200.* The Treaty of Tlatelolco (1967), currently in force for 21 Latin American states established Latin America as the first inhabited continent free of nuclear arms. Four militarily significant countries—Argentina, Brazil, Chile, and Cuba—are not full parties to the treaty. Both signatory and nonsignatory states are among those in Latin America with active nuclear energy programs. Worries in the United States about the possibility of these states developing nuclear weapons has led to American efforts to block export of nuclear technology and equipment to them, most notably in the case of Brazil's acquisition of hardware and technology from West Germany. This led to bitter recriminations between the United States and Brazil. An answer may lie in directly involving nations with accelerating nuclear programs, like Argentina and Brazil, in the search for a solution to the problems of nuclear proliferation. 73 notes.
J. C. Billigmeier

542. Redick, John R. THE TLATELOLCO REGIME AND NON-PROLIFERATION IN LATIN AMERICA. *Int. Organization 1981 35(1): 103-134.* The nuclear free zone established by the Treaty of Tlatelolco was fostered by careful preparations and negotiations, individual leadership, the existence of certain shared cultural and legal traditions of Latin American countries, and the temporary stimulus of the Cuban missile crisis. Lack of overt superpower pressure on Latin America, has permitted continued progress toward full realization of the zone, Tlatelolco's negotiating process, as well as the substance of the Treaty, deserve careful consideration relative to other areas.　　J/S

543. Ropp, Steve C. CUBA AND PANAMA: SIGNALING LEFT AND GOING RIGHT? *Caribbean Rev. 1980 9(1): 15-20.* The warmth of Panama's relations with Cuba has been based on the degree to which both countries' interests converged or diverged.

544. Sánchez, Walter. THIRD WORLD PERSPECTIVES ON REGIONAL ARRANGEMENTS FOR PEACE AND SECURITY: THE LATIN AMERICAN CASE. *Jerusalem J. of Int. Relations [Israel] 1981 5(2): 1-15.* Analyzes the structures and processes involved in Latin American regional arrangements for peace and security, examining the legal, military, and political issues connected with the politics of such arrangements in the 1970's. Discusses their impact on Soviet-American rivalry in the Third World.

545. Shiffer, Jeannette. HEALTH: A RIGHT. *Américas (Organization of American States) 1973 25(5): S1-S16.* Overview of the operations of the Pan-American Health Organization, 1909-73, and its work throughout Latin America.

546. Siebenmann, Gustav. LATEINAMERIKAS IDENTITÄT [The identity of Latin America]. *Schweizer Monatshefte [Switzerland] 1976 56(8): 699-710.* The ethnic mixture and national development of the South American states prevented the growth of a South American identity after 19th-century decolonization.

547. Soares, Álvaro Teixeira. ALFREDO VALLADÃO E A OBRA "BRASIL E CHILE NA ÉPOCA DO IMPÉRIO" [Alfredo Valladão and the work *Brazil and Chile in the Imperial Era*]. *Rev. do Inst. Hist. e Geográfico Brasileiro [Brazil] 1974 (302): 179-199.* A review article of Valladão's *Brazil and Chile in the Imperial Era* (1959). Discusses diplomatic relations between the two countries in the later colonial and independence era and argues that imperial diplomacy suceeded in establishing a profound understanding between Santiago and Rio de Janeiro. Also considers events during the Spanish Civil War, when the Chilean embassy in Madrid gave asylum to Spaniards, and the Brazilian Ambassador obtained both the renewal of relations and the expulsion of those who had sought asylum.
K. A. Ross

548. Stansifer, Charles L. LA APLICACIÓN DE LA DOCTRINA TOBAR A CENTROAMÉRICA [The application of the Tobar Doctrine to Central America]. *Rev. del Pensamiento Centroamericano [Nicaragua] 1977 32(154): 45-57.* Reviews Carlos Tobar's doctrine of nonrecognition of governments that gained power by unconstitutional means and the attempts to apply it to Central America in the early 20th century. The United States and Mexico sponsored efforts to end the instability on the isthmus, and the Tobar Doctrine became the basis for agreement at the Central American Peace Conference in Washington in 1907. Subsequent agreements reflected Central American acceptance of the doctrine and by the second Central American Conference in 1923 it had been applied in several cases. The doctrine of nonrecognition was reiterated in the treaty of 1923, yet by 1930 there was considerable doubt in both Central America and the United States of the value of the doctrine. Nonrecognition had failed to stop revolution and ceased to be adhered to after 1930. Primary and secondary sources; 66 biblio. notes.
R. L. Woodward, Jr.

549. Sutton, Paul K. PATTERNS OF FOREIGN POLICY AMONG THE INDEPENDENT STATES OF CENTRAL AMERICA AND THE CARIBBEAN 1948-1964: A QUANTITATIVE APPROACH. *Social and Econ. Studies [Jamaica] 1977 26(2): 121-145.* Uses small group theory to explain the increased political interaction of these states, especially after the 1959 conflict. Geography has had a significant influence on the pattern of interaction. 5 tables, 12 notes, 23 references, appendix.   E. S. Johnson

550. Tomassini, Luciano. TENDENCIAS FAVORABLES O ADVERSAS EN LA FORMACIÓN DE UN SISTEMA REGIONAL LATINOAMERICANO [Favorable or adverse trends in the formation of a regional system in Latin America]. *Estudios Int. [Chile] 1975 8(29): 3-46.* Discusses Latin American international relations before and after 1970, the region's increasing awareness of its identity, and coordination of the foreign policies of the various countries of South America.

551. Tomassini, Luciano. TENDENCIAS FAVORABLES Y ADVERSAS A LA FORMACIÓN DE UN SUBSISTEMA REGIONAL LATINOAMERICANO [Favorable and adverse tendencies toward the formation of a Latin American regional subsystem]. *Foro Int. [Mexico] 1975 15(60): 563-606.* Discusses Latin America's self-image, the coherence and coordination of Latin American foreign policies, and reciprocal relations among the Latin American states since 1970. Originally presented at a Round Table on the Latin American Subsystem and its Participation in the International System held in Buenos Aires, 3-5 July 1974. Primary and secondary sources; 39 notes.   D. A. Franz

552. Toth, Charles. BULWARK FOR FREEDOM: SAMUEL GOMPERS' PAN AMERICAN FEDERATION OF LABOR. *Revista/Review Interamericana [Puerto Rico] 1979 9(3): 455-491.* Samuel Gompers's Pan-American Federation of Labor was formed to promote trade unionism in Latin America. Its success was limited, partly because the organization faced difficult political issues. It tried to curtail German influence in Latin America during World War I and stop the tide of revolutionary socialism in the New World. It opposed US intervention in Latin American political affairs. 116 notes, biblio.
                                                    J. A. Lewis

553. Woods, Randall B. DECISION-MAKING IN DIPLOMACY: THE RIO CONFERENCE OF 1942. *Social Sci. Q. 1975 55(4): 901-918.* In formulating policy, diplomats respond not only to a concept of national interest, but to the needs of a particular governmental organization, and the demands of a political or bureaucratic career as well. This hypothesis is used to examine the evolution of Argentine-American policy in regard to the Inter-American Conference held in Rio de Janeiro. The article uses the construct to shed new light on this very important meeting called by the United States in the wake of Pearl Harbor to commit the Western Hemisphere to the forthcoming struggle against the Axis. The historical situation is also examined to test the validity of the construct.
                                                                J

554. Zacklin, Ralph. LATIN AMERICA AND THE DEVELOPMENT OF THE LAW OF THE SEA. *Ann. d'Études Int. [Switzerland] 1973 4: 31-54.* Identifies and clarifies from the politico-economic perspective the positions of the Latin American states on renovating the international law of the sea, ca. 1945-73.

555. Zéndegui, Guillermo de. OAS TWENTY-FIFTH ANNIVERSARY. *Américas (Organization of American States) 1973 25(3): S1-S16.* History of the Organization of American States and the preliminary conferences which preceded its establishment, 1910-73.

556. —. REFERENCIAS EN TORNO A LA POLÍTICA DE MÉXICO HACIA CENTROAMÉRICA, 1923-1937 [References to the general policy of Mexico toward Central America, 1923-37]. *Bol. del Archivo General de la Nación [Mexico] 1980 4(1): 4-14.* Reprint of five documents concerning Mexican foreign policy in Central America. Taken from the papers of Presidents Obregón, Calles, and Cárdenas in the Archivo General de la Nación; 3 photos.   J. A. Lewis

2. MEXICO

General

557. Camp, Roderic Ai. MEXICAN GOVERNORS SINCE CARDENAS: EDUCATION AND CAREER CONTACTS. *J. of Inter-Am. Studies and World Affairs 1974 16(4): 454-481.* An examination of all Mexican governors who held office between 1935 and 1973 reveals that these men were a part of the federal bureaucracy before becoming governors. Consequently, they knew less about state problems than one would expect. In addition, they had no competition from other parties. The only opposition came from within the PRI; nomination by the party was tantamount to election. Finally, governors usually came from the middle class; no workers or peasants were elected state governors in the period under study. Based on newspapers, reports, and secondary works; 9 tables, 16 notes, biblio.   J. R. Thomas

558. Alisky, Marvin. MEXICO VERSUS MALTHUS: NATIONAL TRENDS. *Current Hist. 1974 66(393): 200-203, 227-230.* Discusses various social and economic problems caused by the population explosion and mentions party and government social policies.   S

559. Allen, Elisabeth A. INFRASTRUCTURAL INVESTMENT AND NEW SETTLEMENT: THE PAPALOAPAN BASIN, MEXICO. *Travaux & Mémoires de l'Inst. des Hautes Études de l'Amérique Latine [France] 1979 (32): 29-36.* An analysis of the infrastructural investment and the process of development in the Papaloapan basin, Mexico, by the Comisión del Papaloapan, a regional agency concerned with the integration of this peripheral region of settlement into the national economy.

560. Angelier, Jean-Pierre. LE SECTEUR DE L'ÉNERGIE AU MEXIQUE [The energy sector in Mexico]. *Problèmes d'Amérique Latine [France] 1979 (52): 105-145.* Analyzes the evolution of Mexican energy policy until 1973 and its important development since 1974, emphasizing the agreements with the United States and with France in 1979, which allowed the possibility of Mexico's export of oil and production of nuclear power.

561. Astiz, Carlos A. MEXICO'S FOREIGN POLICY: DISGUISED DEPENDENCY. *Current Hist. 1974 66(393): 220-223, 225.* Reviews Mexico's middle-of-the-road foreign policy and its relations with Cuba and the United States in particular.   S

562. Ayala, José. LA EMPRESA PÚBLICA Y SU INCIDENCIA EN LA ACUMULACIÓN DE CAPITAL EN MEXICO DURANTE LOS AÑOS SETENTA [Government enterprises and their contribution to capital accumulation in Mexico during the 1970's]. *Investigación Econ. [Mexico] 1979 38(150): 401-430.* The prime function of state enterprises in Mexico was, in the period 1934-45, to supplement private investment; in the period 1945-60, it was to support private capital accumulation; and after 1960, it was to initiate diversification and favor high technology investments, bringing in foreign capital. But by 1975, half of Mexico's public expenditures and much of its new external debt were absorbed by the public corporations, forcing a slow-down.

563. Baena Paz, Guillermina and Monroy Arenas, Luis. CIRO MENDOZA Y EDUARDO ARELLANO: DOS LÍDERES TEXTILES CEGETISTAS [Ciro Mendoza and Edward Arellano: two textile union leaders]. *Estudios Pol. [Mexico] 1978 4(16): 63-71.* Workers from the textile industry formed the backbone of the General Confederation of Labor (CGT), a labor union seeking independence from government control during the 1920's and 1930's. The careers of Ciro Mendoza and Edward Arellano, two union leaders, illustrate the Confederation's diversity. Born in poverty, Ciro Mendoza was an incorruptible founder of the confederation. Avoiding ideological issues, Mendoza devoted himself to practical matters such as teaching workers how to interpret their contracts. Arellano, in contrast, was an anarchist ideologist, arguing against worker participation in politics while demanding government recognition of their rights. Secondary works; 7 notes.   F. J. Shaw, Jr.

564. Barcia Trelles, Camilo. EL PETRÓLEO, GRAN PROTAGONISTA [Oil, the great protagonist]. *Rev. de Política Int. [Spain] 1973 (130): 11-28.* Examines the use of oil as a weapon in international politics, in war and peace. Relations between the United States and Mexico show that foreign control of such a valuable economic resource can prevent political peace and economic development.

565. Barkin, David and Esteva, Gustavo. SOCIAL CONFLICT AND INFLATION IN MEXICO. *Latin Am. Perspectives 1982 9(1): 48-64.* Mexican government policy may not be able to forestall violent social conflict. Transnational investments and resulting growth and jobs have offset deficit financing, inflation, and devaluation, yet without achieving price stability or equalizing earning power. Primary and secondary sources; 7 notes, biblio.   J. F. Vivian

566. Bartra, Roger. MODES OF PRODUCTION AND AGRARIAN IMBALANCES. *Int. Social Sci. J. [France] 1979 31(2): 226-236.* In the light of the Marxist theory of modes of production, which is also the Marxist theory of social class structure, the author analyzes the evolution of the modes of production and characteristics of social classes in rural Mexico.

567. Basurto, Jorge. OLIGARQUÍA, NACIONALISMO Y ALIANZA DE CLASES EN MÉXICO [Oligarchy, nationalism, and class alliances in Mexico]. *Rev. Mexicana de Ciencia Pol. [Mexico] 1975 21(80): 43-50.* Compares the relationship between the landowners and the oligarchy in early 20th-century Mexico to the current relationship between the middle class and the Mexican government, showing that the same elements which made Porfirio Díaz's dictatorship insupportable are present to an even greater degree in the political scene of today.

568. Bath, C. Richard. RESOLVING WATER DISPUTES. *Pro. of the Acad. of Pol. Sci. 1981 34(1): 181-188.* Reviews important past water disputes and discusses actual and potential conflict over water resources, particularly the legal, administrative, and political context for the resolution of water issues between Mexico and the United States. Successful resolution of the water issues facing Mexico and the United States will require a great deal of patience, time, and will. 2 notes.   T. P. Richardson

569. Benjamin, Thomas. EL TRABAJO EN LAS MONTERIAS DE CHIAPAS Y TABASCO—1870-1946 [Mahogany cutting in Chiapas and Tabasco: 1870-1946]. *Hist. Mexicana [Mexico] 1981 30(4): 506-529.* The *monterias,* mahogany lumber camps, were veritable prisons and graveyards of the Indian laborers employed in them from the time of Porfirio Díaz to that of Lázaro Cárdenas. Indebted men were condemned to work in them, the conditions were surrounded by secrecy, and government efforts to improve the situation were minimal and usually indirect through unions. The writer B. Traven was the first to expose the truth about the inhuman conditions. Based on primary material in Mexican and US archives; biblio., 61 notes.   J. V. Coutinho

570. Bennett, Douglas and Sharpe, Kenneth. EL ESTADO COMO BANQUERO Y EMPRESARIO: EL CARÁCTER DE ÚLTIMA INSTANCIA DE LA INTERVENCIÓN ECONÓMICA DEL ESTADO MEXICANO, 1917-1970 [The state as banker and entrepreneur: the last resort character of Mexican state economic intervention, 1917-70]. *Foro Int. [Mexico] 1979 20(1): 29-72.* The Mexican government became involved in the nation's economy as a last resort in areas where private enterprise failed to act. 73 notes.   D. A. Franz

571. Bennett, Douglas and Sharpe, Kenneth. THE STATE AS BANKER AND ENTREPRENEUR: THE LAST-RESORT CHARACTER OF THE MEXICAN STATE'S ECONOMIC INTERVENTION, 1917-76. *Comparative Pol. 1980 12(2): 165-189.* Discusses the emergence of the state as the major banker and entrepreneur in Mexico. Develops Alexander Gerschenkron's thesis that the industrialization process in less developed countries requires institutions without counterpart in industrialized countries, focusing on the Mexican state's own needs to intervene in the economy, in the period of the constitution of the state, 1914-40, in reaction to subsequent crises, and in response to changes in government personnel. An institution of last resort, the state's intervention is evidenced by the 10% of 1974 gross domestic product attributable to state enterprises. Based on confidential interviews and official documents; 42 notes.   M. A. Kascus

572. Britton, John A. TEACHER UNIONIZATION AND THE CORPORATE STATE IN MEXICO, 1931-1945. *Hispanic Am. Hist. Rev. 1979 59(4): 674-690.* By 1930 a number of teachers' unions had developed in Mexico in an effort to cope with poor and erratic salaries and job insecurity. The government promoted unification of these unions and tried to avoid Communist Party control of them. In 1943 the new national union, Sindicato Nacional de Trabajadores de la Educación was formed. This union worked with the government and was more interested in education than in ideology. The roles of Ministers of Education Narciso Bassols, Gonazlo Vázquez Vela, and Octavio Vejar Vázquez and union leaders David Vilchis, Lino Santacruz, and Vicente Lombardo Toledano are discussed. 83 notes.   B. D. Johnson

573. Brown, Lyle C. POLITICAL AND MILITARY HISTORY OF THE STATE OF MICHOACÁN, 1910-1940. Frost, Elsa Cecilia; Meyer, Michael C.; and Zoraida Vázquez, Josefina, ed. *El Trabajo y los Trabajadores en la Historia de México* (Mexico City: Colegio de México, 1979): 801-805. Bibliographical essay on the historiography of the Mexican state of Michoacán. Secondary sources; 43 notes.
                                                            J. P. H. Myers

574. Brownell, Herbert and Eaton, Samuel D. THE COLORADO RIVER SALINITY PROBLEM WITH MEXICO. *Am. J. of Internat. Law 1975 69(2): 255-271.* Public Law 93-320, signed on 24 June 1974, provides for construction of the world's largest desalting plant in Arizona. A 1944 treaty assured Mexico a specific quantity of water from the Colorado River. From 1962 to 1972 Mexico argued that the Colorado River water entering Mexico was too salty, but the Basin States were suspicious of any agreement between Washington and Mexico City. Nevertheless, negotiations launched in 1972 led to the 1974 resolution of the problem. Based on published government documents and secondary sources; 35 notes.   M. I. Elzy

575. Buve, Raymond. PEASANT MOBILISATION AND REFORM INTERMEDIARIES DURING THE NINETEEN THIRTIES: THE DEVELOPMENT OF A PEASANT CLIENTELE AROUND THE ISSUES OF LAND AND LABOR IN A CENTRAL MEXICAN HIGHLAND MUNICIPIO: HUAMANTLA, TLAXCALA. *Jahrbuch für Geschichte von Staat, Wirtschaft und Gesellschaft Lateinamerikas [West Germany] 1980 17: 355-393.* Rubén C. Carrizosa built a large peasant following in the village of Huamantla and regionally in Tlaxcala without alienating his landed friends. Local political leaders like Carrizosa could create peasant clients by actually or apparently intervening on their behalf for land and by keeping competing mobilizers out of their domain. Thus, although the federal government oversaw the land distribution, these leaders could take credit for the distribution. The peasants also had to avoid alienating the leader. Displeasing the leader could produce the loss of the peasant's acquired land. Thus, those hoping for land and those fearing its loss could become clients. Based on Archivo Secretaría de Reforma Agraria, the Collection Rubén C. Carrizosa (Huamantla), interviews with Carrizosa, and printed primary materials; 2 maps, 82 notes.   T. D. Schoonover

576. Buve, Raymond and Holthus, Cunera. A SURVEY OF MEXICAN MATERIALS AT THE INTERNATIONAL INSTITUUT VOOR SOCIALE GESCHIEDENIS IN AMSTERDAM. *Latin Am. Res. Rev. 1975 10(1): 155-192.* A bibliography of Mexican materials at the International Institute of Social History, including periodicals, daily newspapers, pamphlets, and books for the period 1880-1940.

577. Cabrera Ipina, Octaviano. EL HOMBRE EN SAN LUIS POTOSÍ [Man in San Luis Potosí]. *Humánitas [Mexico] 1978 19: 341-360.* Describes the social, economic, and political development of the mining center of San Luis Potosí, Mexico, from the earliest times to the present day.

578. Cádenas, Arturo and Hernández, Eulalio. PROBLEMAS DEL DESARROLLO REGIONAL EN MÉXICO [Problems of regional development in Mexico]. *Investigación Econ. [Mexico] 1973 32(127): 499-517.* The problems associated with regional development in Mexico are seen as the result of the country's geographical features and economic policies at national level, especially since 1940.

579. Camacho, Manuel. LOS NUDOS HISTÓRICOS DEL SISTEMA POLÍTICO MEXICANO [The historical knots of the Mexican political system]. *Foro Int. [Mexico] 1977 17(4): 587-651.* Surveys theories regarding the growth of political systems and examines the political growth of Mexico and suggests possible future paths of political development. 5 graphs, 76 notes.   D. A. Franz

580. Camp, Roderic Ai. THE ELITE LORE OF MEXICO'S REVOLUTIONARY FAMILY. *J. of Latin Am. Lore 1978 4(2): 149-182.* Examines the cultural attitudes of the postwar political elite in Mexico, known as the Revolutionary Family.

581. Camp, Roderic Ai. THE NATIONAL SCHOOL OF ECONOMICS AND PUBLIC LIFE IN MEXICO. *Latin Am. Res. Rev. 1975 10(3): 137-154.* Examines data on the careers of graduates of the National School of Economics of the National Autonomous University of Mexico to determine its socializing power on public officials, the influence of particular faculty members, and the school's role in the recruitment of public officials, 1929-52.

582. Camp, Roderic Ai. QUIENES ALCANZAN LA CUMBRE: LA ÉLITE POLÍTICA MEXICANA [Those who reach the top: the Mexican political elite]. *Foro Int. [Mexico] 1978 19(1): 24-61.* An analysis of Mexico's political elite based on social, educational, and career characteristics. Based on statistical analysis and secondary sources; 16 tables, 22 notes.   D. A. Franz

583. Camp, Roderic Ai. A REEXAMINATION OF POLITICAL LEADERSHIP AND ALLOCATION OF FEDERAL REVENUES IN MEXICO, 1932-1973. *J. of Developing Areas 1976 10(2): 193-212.* An explanation is sought for the uneven development between states and regions of Mexico. The "favorite son" explanation does not hold. There was no conclusive relationship between a high percentage of national leadership from a state and federal spending in that state. There is, however, a relationship between lack of representation and lack of federal funds. The "president's home state" explanation does not hold over time, though home states have been politically overrepresented in the president's own administration and that following. No significant changes were found in patterns of socioeconomic development. Analysis of the "party vote" hypothesis did find a relationship between low federal investment in a state and low PRI votes. The "experience of the governor" argument found support in those states where the governor was appointed by the president at the time he took office. In those states revenue surpluses consistently occurred. The federal government contribution to regional development in Mexico is slanted in favor of the already developed states. 4 tables, 36 notes.   O. W. Eads, Jr.

584. Camp, Roderic Ai. UNIVERSITY ENVIRONMENT AND SOCIALIZATION: THE CASE OF MEXICAN POLITICIANS. *Hist. of Educ. Q. 1980 20(3): 313-335.* Examines the social environment of Mexican universities and its effect on those generations of leaders who guided Mexico's development from 1946 to 1970. Overwhelmingly these leaders studied at the university from 1920 to 1940. Students are exposed to considerable ideological diversity. Because of exposure to and participation in intellectual and political activities, and because of the encouragement of many professors, there seemed to be an emphasis on public careers going beyond the typical personal desires of some individuals to make politics their profession, or because public life was the only concrete professional alternative. Most of these leaders felt a sense of unity through identification as part of a special generation. Based on secondary sources; 79 notes.   J. Powell

585. Camp, Roderic Ai. WOMEN AND POLITICAL LEADERSHIP IN MEXICO: A COMPARATIVE STUDY OF FEMALE AND MALE POLITICAL ELITES. *J. of Pol. 1979 41(2): 417-441.* As a result of the 1910 revolution, women in the Yucatán received the right to vote in local elections in 1922, and Chiapas granted women political

equality in 1925. While women's groups had been organized in the 1920's, and expanded in subsequent decades, women were not granted the right to vote in municipal elections throughout Mexico until 1946 and in off-year elections for national deputies in 1955. Women have consistently scored lower than men in political knowledge and interest, but discrepancies have decreased as education increased. Politically, women have been most successful as candidates for the Chamber of Deputies and Senate, but have received few administrative posts and play a very small role among the political elite. Female political leaders are no younger than men, come from middle and upper-class families and are frequently natives of urban areas which provide greater educational opportunities. 6 tables, 43 notes.   A. W. Novitsky

586. Cañedo, Patricia Salcido and Weiss, David Arriaga. EL MOVIMIENTO OBRERO EN EL SEXENIO DE CÁRDENAS Y EN LA CRISIS DE 1958-1959 (HEMEROGRAFÍA) [The labor movement under Cárdenas and in the crises of 1958-59: references]. *Rev. Mexicana de Ciencias Pol. y Sociales [Mexico] 1977 23(89): 211-221.* Lists works concerning the labor movement during the presidency of Lázaro Cárdenas (1895-1970) and during the 1958-59 labor strife.

587. Carpizo, Jorge. NOTAS SOBRE EL PRESIDENCIALISMO MEXICANO [Notes on Mexican presidentialism]. *Rev. de Estudios Pol. [Spain] 1978 (3): 19-36.* Describes the executive office in Mexico to indicate the sources and powers of the presidency, and enumerates these powers to indicate presidential dominance of the nation and the manner in which all political life centers on that office. In Mexico executive power predominates despite several constitutional and political limits which include: the six-year, one-term limit on presidential service; the strength of an independent federal judiciary; pressure groups; and the labor organizations and their international ties. 17 notes.
                                                       N. A. Rosenblatt

588. Carrillo Flores, Antonio. EL CONTROL DE LA CONSTITUCIONALIDAD DE LAS LEYES Y ACTOS DE AUTORIDAD EN MÉXICO [The control of the constitutionality of the laws and acts of Mexican authority]. *Rev. de la Facultad de Derecho de México [Mexico] 1976 26(103-104): 133-148.* Describes the legal processes and acts which have established the constitutional norms, fundamental rights, and democratic nature of the Mexican republic.

589. Carrillo Flores, Antonio. LA EDUCACIÓN Y LA POLÍTICA [Education and politics]. *Memoria del Colegio Nac. [Mexico] 1979 9(2): 153-168.* Surveys the growth of the Mexican educational system through federal government action and discusses the autonomy of Mexican universities. Reprint of a speech presented at the Universidad Pedagógica Mexicana.   D. A. Franz

590. Carrillo Flores, Antonio. LA SUPREMA CORTE DE JUSTICIA COMO TRIBUNAL FEDERAL DE ULTIMA INSTANCIA. UN TESTIMONIO DE ANTONIO CARRILLO FLORES [The Supreme Court of Justice as a federal court of final appeal: testimony of Antonio Carrillo Flores]. *Memoria del Colegio Nac. [Mexico] 1978 8(4): 75-99.* The Supreme Court of Mexico hears cases involving disputes between states, between lower federal tribunals, and between state and federal courts and cases concerning diplomatic personnel, cases concerned with maritime law, cases between a state and residents of another state, and controversies over people claiming damages due to the application of federal laws. These powers are commonly thought to have originated mainly since 1930, but in actuality they were in use before then. Based on primary and secondary sources; 6 notes, appendix.
                                                       J. D. Barnard

591. Cleaves, Peter S. MEXICAN POLITICS: AN END TO THE CRISIS? *Latin Am. Res. Rev. 1981 16(2): 191-202.* A review article based on six books which fall into three categories: general historical surveys, scholarly monographs, and works which suggest solutions for Mexican problems. Petroleum income has stabilized the Mexican system. Thus, the long-term patterns described in these books probably will be the soundest predictors for the future. 6 notes.   J. K. Pfabe

592. Cochrane, James D. EMBAJADORES NORTEAMERICANOS EN MÉXICO Y EMBAJADORES MEXICANOS EN ESTADOS UNIDOS: CARACTERÍSTICAS DE SUS CARR-

ERAS Y EXPERIENCIA PROFESIONAL [US ambassadors in Mexico and Mexican ambassadors in the United States: career characteristics and professional experience]. *Foro Int. [Mexico] 1981 22(1): 90-105.* Examines career characteristics and professional diplomatic experience of eight Mexican ambassadors to the United States and 11 US ambassadors to Mexico who served during the period 1935 to 1979. Secondary sources; 18 notes.   D. A. Franz

593. Cole, Richard R. THE MEXICAN PRESS SYSTEM: ASPECTS OF GROWTH, CONTROL AND OWNERSHIP. *Gazette [Netherlands] 1975 21(2): 65-81.* Discusses the growth of the press in Mexico, 1960's-74, the exercise of social and governmental controls, and patterns of private and corporate ownership since 1917.

594. Coleman, Kenneth M. and Wanat, John. ON MEASURING MEXICAN PRESIDENTIAL IDEOLOGY THROUGH BUDGETS: A REAPPRAISAL OF THE WILKIE APPROACH. *Latin Am. Res. Rev. 1975 10(1): 77-88.* Examines those areas where executive impact on budgetary policy can be clearly isolated in order to develop James W. Wilkie's thesis concerning the impact of who governs upon how people are governed.

595. Conklin, John G. ELITE STUDIES: THE CASE OF THE MEXICAN PRESIDENCY. *J. of Latin Am. Studies [Great Britain] 1973 5(2): 247-269.* Delineates the characteristics of men who have become president of Mexico in the 19th and 20th centuries in terms of birthplace, education, occupation, and age when assuming the presidency. As a group they are quite heterogeneous and represent political modernization. Methodologically, the author's positional approaches greatly reduce the problem of elite identification, lend themselves to comparative analysis, and are relatively easy to design. However, not all data are suitable for quantitative methods, although quantification does bring "a semblance of order to a large number of observations." Secondary sources; 13 tables, 30 notes, 4 appendixes.   K. M. Bailor

596. Cordera Campos, Rolando and Ruiz Durán, Clemente. ESQUEMA DE PERIODIZACIÓN DEL DESARROLLO CAPITALISTA EN MÉXICO: NOTAS [Notes for a periodization scheme for capitalist development in Mexico]. *Investigación Econ. [Mexico] 1980 39(153): 13-62.* Significant stages in Mexico's late and thus dependent capitalism have been industrial accumulation, 1940-54, with dropping real wages and low external deficit; transition, 1955-61, with growing internationalization of capital; and oligopolist development, 1962-77, with rapid growth initially and industrialization toward durable consumer goods and a downward crisis starting in 1971, accompanied by monetary and financial chaos and social and political instability.

597. Crespi, Roberto Simón. JOSÉ REVUELTAS (1914-1976): A POLITICAL BIOGRAPHY. *Latin Am. Perspectives 1979 6(3): 93-113.* José Revueltas (1914-76) devoted 40 years to creating an independent Marxist alternative in Mexico, through novels, newspaper columns, speeches, and social and political activism. He alternately joined and quit the Communist Party, supported and condemned Vicente Lombardo Toledano, and tried and deplored forming a movement of his own. He may be best remembered for *México: una democracia bárbara* (1958), an incisive critique of Octavio Paz's *Labyrinth of Solitude,* and his arrest and trial as the author of the Tlatelolco crisis, 1968. 12 notes, biblio.
                                                       J. F. Vivian

598. Daus, Ronald. DIE ROLLE DER GEWALT IM MEXIKANISCHEN REVOLUTIONSROMAN [The role of violence in Mexican revolution novels]. *Jahrbuch für Geschichte von Staat, Wirtschaft und Gesellschaft Lateinamerikas [West Germany] 1978 15: 103-122.* An attempt to establish relationships between literary works and certain contemporary social phenomena. To study violence should not mean just to treat its existence, but to describe how individuals, groups, and people perceive it. The rather high value accorded to violence in Latin America makes it an especially suitable area for investigating such problems. Based upon printed primary and secondary sources; 25 notes.
                                                       T. D. Schoonover

599. Davis, Charles L. and Coleman, Kenneth M. POLITICAL SYMBOLS, POLITICAL EFFICACY AND DIFFUSE SUPPORT FOR THE MEXICAN POLITICAL SYSTEM. *J. of Pol. & Military Sociol. 1975 3(1): 27-42.*

600. DelaPeña, Sergio. PROLETARIAN POWER AND STATE MONOPOLY CAPITALISM IN MEXICO. *Latin Am. Perspectives 1982 9(1): 20-35.* Mexico's oligopolistic economic structure will require proletarian consideration of interclass alliances, socialization of labor unions, cooperatives and communes, and more direct involvement in electoral politics. Secondary sources; 2 notes, biblio.
                                                          J. F. Vivian

601. Delarbe, Raúl Trejo. THE MEXICAN LABOR MOVEMENT: 1917-1975. *Latin Am. Perspectives 1976 3(1): 133-153.* A history of the labor movement in Mexico. Considers the important role of the state and its impact on organized labor. The state-party-union formula has been fundamental to the Mexican system and is basic to an understanding of the Mexican labor movement.   J. L. Dietz

602. Fernandez, Raul A. THE BORDER INDUSTRIAL PROGRAM ON THE UNITED STATES-MEXICO BORDER. *R. of Radical Pol. Econ. 1973 5(1): 37-52.* Examines the economic impact of multinational corporations on the US-Mexico border region, 1940-70.
                                                          S

603. Flores Zavala, Ernesto. TRAYECTORÍA DEL IMPUESTO SOBRE LA RENTA EN MÉXICO [The development of the income taxes in Mexico]. *Rev. de la Facultad de Derecho de México [Mexico] 1975 25(99-100): 627-662.* Systematically reviews and interprets the 11 Mexican laws governing property and income tax, passed between 20 July 1920 and 30 December 1964, with some comparison with taxation systems in England, France, and the United States.

604. Florescano, Enrique et al. MOUVEMENT PAYSANS ET PROBLÈMES AGRAIRES AU MEXIQUE DE 1770 À NOS JOURS [Peasant movements and agrarian problems in Mexico from 1770 to the present]. *Cahiers Int. d'Hist. Écon. et Sociale [Italy] 1978 8: 220-281.* Part I. Studies peasant conditions, 1770-1810, emphasizing the cultivation of grain. Peasant problems created an atmosphere conducive to the popular revolution led by Miguel Hidalgo y Costilla (1753-1811) in 1810. Part II. Studies peasant problems, 1810-1978. There were 26 important rebellions, 1821-61. The history of the peasant movements in the revolutionary period, 1910-40 remains to be considered. The institutionalization of the revolution since 1940 has affected peasant movements. Part III. Studies peasant movements in Tlaxcala and their role in incipient agrarian reform. Part IV. Discusses agrarian reform in the postrevolutionary period. 78 notes.   F. X. Hartigan

605. Folbre, Nancy. POPULATION GROWTH AND CAPITALIST DEVELOPMENT IN ZONGOLICA, VERACRUZ. *Latin Am. Perspectives 1977 4(4): 41-55.* Describes the effects which capitalist development in Zongolica, Veracruz, Mexico, had on population growth, 1900-72, and the effects which that growth had on the political economy and land distribution.

606. Friedlander, Judith. THE SECULARIZATION OF THE CARGO SYSTEM: AN EXAMPLE FROM POSTREVOLUTIONARY CENTRAL MEXICO. *Latin Am. Res. Rev. 1981 16(2): 132-143.* The cargo system, a series of ranked offices in indigenous communities, has been adapted to serve the interests of non-Indian Mexico. The government uses this traditional structure to develop loyalty to the national system. Political celebrations organized through the cargo system have taken their place alongside standard religious festivals. 9 notes, biblio.
                                                          J. K. Pfabe

607. Gallaga, Roberto. LA HISTORIA DEL TRABAJO DE LOS CAMPESINOS CAÑEROS EN EL SIGLO XX [Sugar plantation workers in the 20th century]. Frost, Elsa Cecilia; Meyer, Michael C.; and Zoraida Vázquez, Josefina, ed. *El Trabajo y los Trabajadores en la Historia de México* (Mexico City: Colegio de México, 1979): 565-598. The sugar industry (the first to be organized in Mexico after the Conquest) survived the destructive years of revolution, and, fully modernized, flourished until the world crisis of 1929. The various financial and political restructurings, 1920-75, have not bridged the gap between the peasants on the plantations and the men running the refineries. There has been little improvement in the position of the peasants and there is little prospect of any. Commentaries, pp. 99-601. Secondary sources; 102 notes.
                                                          J. P. H. Myers

608. Gereffi, Gary. LOS OLIGOPOLIOS INTERNACIONALES, EL ESTADO Y EL DESARROLLO INDUSTRIAL EN MÉXICO: EL CASO DE LA INDUSTRIA DE HORMONAS ESTEROIDES [International oligopolies, the state, and industrial development in Mexico: the case of the hormonal steroid industry]. *Foro Int. [Mexico] 1977 17(4): 490-541.* Examines the development of the hormonal steroid industry in Mexico, government policies in regard to it, and the influence of multinational corporations on the industry. 4 tables, 103 notes, appendix.
                                                          D. A. Franz

609. Gerhard, Peter. CONTINUITY AND CHANGE IN MORELOS, MEXICO. *Geographical R. 1975 65(3): 335-352.* Postulates of political and demographic change in Mexico since the Spanish Conquest are examined in a small region of the central highlands, the present state of Morelos. Here, a basic unit of pre-Columbian social and territorial organization, the *señorío,* survived as the colonial *pueblo* and in some cases retains approximate boundaries and certain political institutions to the present. Settlement patterns and land use were radically altered after the great epidemic of 1545-1548, however, when the scattered peasant survivors were moved into compact villages and much subsistence farm land was left unused or was converted to pasture or sugarcane. Despite urban growth in recent decades, an almost static number of peasants exploits only a fraction of the land cultivated at the time of the first European contact.   J

610. Glade, William P. ENTREPRENEURSHIP IN THE STATE SECTOR: CONASUPO OF MEXICO. Greenfield, Sidney M.; Strickon, Arnold; and Aubey, Robert T., ed. *Entrepreneurs in Cultural Context* (Albuquerque: U. of New Mexico Pr., 1979): 199-222. The government of Mexico became involved with agricultural and trade financing with the establishment of the Compañía Exportadora e Importadora Mexican, S. A. (CEIMSA), in effect a department of the Foreign Trade Bank, in 1937. Attracting considerable criticism for lack of orientation, CEIMSA was reorganized as Compañía Nacional de Subsistencias Populares, S. A. (CONASUPO) in 1961. Operating essentially as a state-owned holding company, CONASUPO is an entrepreneurially directed state firm that has been successful in operating a complex marketing system. Table, 16 notes.   S

611. Goldman, Shifra M. MEXICAN MURALISM: ITS SOCIAL-EDUCATIVE ROLES IN LATIN AMERICA AND THE UNITED STATES. *Aztlán 1982 13(1-2): 111-133.* Traces the development of Mexican mural art and its influence on Chicano artists in the 1960's and 1970's. The first great muralists—Rivera, Orozco, and Siqueiros—drew on indigenous themes in the 1920's; they and other artists also paid homage to the mestizo in Mexican history and the important figures of the 1910 Revolution. Their work influenced mural artists in many Latin American countries. Since the 1960's, Chicanos have done more than 1,000 murals in California alone, varying greatly in style but united in theme through the common experiences of living in the United States. The murals have promoted political action, taught the history of the Mexican heritage, and played an important social role in modern Mexico and in the US Southwest. Biblio.   A. Hoffman

612. González, Eduardo. POLÍTICA ECONÓMICA Y ACUMULACIÓN DE CAPITAL EN MÉXICO DE 1920 A 1955 [Economic policy and capital accumulation in Mexico from 1920 to 1955]. *Investigación Econ. [Mexico] 1980 39(153): 113-142.* Studies the pattern of capital accumulation in Mexico before the era of "stabilizing development." Early foreign investments centered on mining, communications, and railroads. Local investment was in land and agriculture, in which production was becoming capitalist. Postrevolutionary reconstruction based on private property was followed by heavy public investment in agriculture under Lázaro Cárdenas (1934-40) and in industrialization, both infrastructure and production, thereafter. With imports increasing generally and exports only in agriculture, the peso was devalued. Foreign investment in industry increased sevenfold, 1946-55.

613. González Navarro, Moisés. LAS TIERRAS OCIOSAS [The idle lands]. *Hist. Mexicana [Mexico] 1977 26(4): 503-539.* Examines 32 laws passed in Mexico, 1914-64, which encouraged the cultivation of idle land. Plans to ensure cultivation were prominent in all land reform, but faced many problems. Based on parliamentary debates, the press, and published reports; 87 notes.   S. P. Carr/S

614. Goodman, Margaret. DOES POLITICAL CORRUPTION REALLY HELP ECONOMIC DEVELOPMENT?: YUCATAN, MEXICO. *Polity 1974 7(2): 143-162.* Analyzes the new look at corruption, which views corruption amorally and functionally, on the premise that it is a transitional phenomenon occurring in a competitive political-economic system. Examines the effects of corruption in modernizing, authoritarian regimes, with the hypotheses that corruption inhibits evolution toward universalistic norms and protects incompetence rather than rewarding the efficient producer. The state of Yucatan, Mexico, nicely uncompetitive and corrupt, is used to test the hypotheses. In Yucatan, "the persistence of political corruption reinforces the unequal distribution of political and economic power within the society." Corruption in Mexico serves those who already have; it is not a dynamic, humane, or democratic force.   J

615. Grabendorff, Wolf. MEXICO'S FOREIGN POLICY—INDEED A FOREIGN POLICY? *J. of Interamerican Studies and World Affairs 1978 20(1): 85-92.* A review article of recent studies by Mexican foreign policy advisers and critics. Mexico has been more concerned with its domestic political system and related problems than with conceptualizing and creating an international role for itself. Secondary studies; ref.
T. D. Schoonover

616. Grayson, George W. THE MAPLE LEAF, THE CACTUS, AND THE EAGLE: ENERGY TRILATERALISM. *Inter-American Econ. Affairs 1981 34(4): 49-75.* Discusses the potential for the formation of an energy common market comprising Canada, Mexico, and the United States. Describes hydrocarbon reserves in Canada and Mexico from 1930 to 1980, analyzes North American reaction to the proposal for an energy union, and focuses on differences in the three nations' political systems which complicate the acceptance of such a plan.

617. Grayson, George W. MEXICO AND THE UNITED STATES: THE NATURAL GAS CONTROVERSY. *Inter-American Econ. Affairs 1978 32(3): 3-27.* Reviews the history of the Mexican petroleum industry from 1901 to the present, stressing American negotiations for Mexican natural gas.

618. Grigulevich, I. R. DAVID AL'FARO SIKEIROS: SOLDAT, KHUDOZHNIK, KOMMUNIST [David Alfaro Siqueiros: soldier, artist, communist]. *Novaia i Noveishaia Istoriia [USSR] 1980 (1): 92-106.* Continued from an earlier article (see abstract 914). Siqueiros's life from his imprisonment and trial in 1962 through the award of Mexico's National Arts Prize in 1966 to his 1973 visit to the USSR. Based on published works in Russian and Spanish; 19 notes.
D. N. Collins

619. Hall, Linda B. MEXICAN PRESIDENTIALISM FROM DÍAZ TO ECHEVERRÍA: AN INTERPRETIVE STUDY. *Social Sci. J. 1980 17(1): 41-52.* Analyzes the character of the Mexican presidency, emphasizing its role in providing continuity and stability.

620. Hellman, Judith Adler. MEXICO IN THE AGE OF PETRO-PESOS. *Queen's Q. [Canada] 1980 87(2): 234-247.* Consistent patterns of Mexican industrialization over the past 50 years show that it would require a major feat of economic and political engineering to spread Mexico's recent petroleum profits more equitably through Mexican society. The troubled presidency of Luis Echeverria, 1970-76, illustrated the futility of Mexican reform capitalism. The agrarian policies of the incumbent Jose Lopez Portillo guarantee that few of the new petroleum pesos will "trickle down" to the vast majority of the poorly organized and politically inarticulate masses, and Mexico will parallel Venezuela's oil history. 10 notes.   L. V. Eid

621. Hellman, Judith Adler. SOCIAL CONTROL IN MEXICO. *Comparative Pol. 1980 12(2): 225-242.* Review article based on 11 works that discuss how the political elite in power in Mexico since the revolution of 1910-17 managed to retain control of a country that experienced a popular armed revolution. 79 notes.   M. A. Kascus

622. Herner, Irene. LA CENSURA [Censorship]. *Rev. Mexicana de Ciencias Pol. y Soc. [Mexico] 1976-77 (86-87): 183-197.* An example of institutions that censor the media in Mexico, the Censorship Commission of Publications and Illustrated Magazines, which oversees the *fotonovela;* includes the articles of its code and a list of publications it has censored, 1970's.

623. Jimeno Salvatierra, Pilar. CUAJINICUILAPA: SOBRE LOS ANTECEDENTES DE LA POBLACIÓN NEGRA EN MÉJICO [Cuajinicuilapa: on the background of the black population in Mexico]. *Cuadernos Hispanoamericanos [Spain] 1976 103(309): 385-389.* Reviews Gonzalo Aquirre Beltrán's *Cuijla. Esbozo etnográfico de un pueblo negro* (Mexico: FCE, 1974), a sociological and historical study of a Mexican town. Focuses on the acculturation process involving the native, Spanish, and African population groups and their influence on the town's development. Considers the contemporary composition of the population, demographic statistics, and the continuing influence of African culture on social customs, building techniques, family relationships, religious practice, superstitions, taboos, land ownership, agriculture, and local government.   P. J. Taylorson

624. Jordan, David Herrera. THE UNITED STATES-MEXICAN INTERNATIONAL BOUNDARY AND WATER COMMISSION, *Am. Soc. of Int. Law Pro. 1974 68: 226-229.* Discusses the use of international judicial organizations and bilateral commissions for solving disputes between the US and Mexico from the 19th century through 1974.

625. Joseph, Gilbert M. MEXICO'S "POPULAR REVOLUTION": MOBILIZATION AND MYTH IN YUCATAN, 1910-1940. *Latin Am. Perspectives 1979 6(3): 46-65.* Felipe Carrillo Puerto (d. 1924), head of Yucatan's Partido Socialista del Sureste (PSS), failed to effect a radical agrarian reform in henequen districts. Presidents Obregón and Calles forestalled it and Cárdenas imposed an ejidal distribution—the largest ever attempted in Mexico—that satisfied few. The Yucatecan 20th-century experience demonstrates the myth of Mexico's "popular" revolution and the reality of its "institutional" revolution. 14 notes, biblio.
J. F. Vivian

626. Kane, N. Stephen. BANKERS AND DIPLOMATS: THE DIPLOMACY OF THE DOLLAR IN MEXICO, 1921-1924. *Business Hist. R. 1973 47(3): 335-352.* Examines the cooperative relations between American investment bankers, the US State Department, and Mexico, illustrating the interdependency of the dollar and diplomacy in the 1920's. Secretary of State Charles Evans Hughes used conditional recognition and financial pressure in the form of loan bans and closed markets to force Mexico to come to terms with the United States both politically and economically. The International Committee of Bankers on Mexico representing holders of defaulted securities and working closely with the diplomats achieved their goals of a settlement with Mexico wherein the debt would be paid. Diplomatic recognition came later. Mexican political instability hindered financial relations and eventually the Lamont-de la Huerta Agreement (1922) was suspended by Mexico. Dollar diplomacy achieved immediate American ends, but later proved self-defeating. Based on US Government documents, bankers' committee papers, contemporary newspaper reports, and other primary and secondary sources; 55 notes.   N. J. Street

627. Katz, Bernard S. MEXICO'S IMPORT LICENSING STRATEGY FOR PROTECTING IMPORT REPLACEMENTS. *Am. J. of Econ. and Sociol. 1974 33(4): 381-392.* Discusses Mexico's import control since 1930 through tariffs, import licenses, and official prices. Secondary sources; table, 22 notes.   W. L. Marr

628. Katz, Bernard S. MEXICO'S TARIFF POLICY: A STUDY IN ALTERNATIVES. *Am. J. of Econ. and Sociol. 1976 35(3): 235-250.* Tariffs may normally be justified to improve a nation's terms of trade, revenue, or balance of payments. In Mexico, 1930-65, except for isolated instances, tariffs were protectionist, implemented to achieve industrial development.   J/S

629. Kiran, Ketil. INDIANERKULTURENES SKJEBNE [The fate of Indian culture]. *Samtiden [Norway] 1977 86(3): 183-189.* Outlines Indian culture and society in Mexico in the pre-Conquistador era and Spanish annihilation of Indian traditions, arguing that Indians today continue to be oppressed socially, politically, and culturally.

630. Koppes, Clayton R. THE GOOD NEIGHBOR POLICY AND THE NATIONALIZATION OF MEXICAN OIL: A REINTERPRE-

TATION. *J. of Am. Hist. 1982 69(1): 62-81.* Mexico's nationalization of foreign oil companies in 1938 was a demonstration of economic self-determination that brought Mexico and the United States to the brink of diplomatic rupture. The Cooke-Zevada agreement of 1942 addressed only the issue of expropriation, leaving the main issue of nationalization for later resolution. The United States, however, did not accept the principle of nationalization in Mexico and tried consistently to reverse the decision of 1938. The US government supported the claims of American oil firms and of capitalism in general at the expense of Mexico's economic aspirations. Based on State Department records, the Roosevelt Papers, and the Harold Ickes Papers; 47 notes.   T. P. Linkfield

631. Leal, Juan Felipe. THE MEXICAN STATE: 1915-1973. A HISTORICAL INTERPRETATION. *Latin Am. Perspectives 1975 2(2): 48-63.* Analyzes the development of Mexico during 1915-73, including the growth of bureaucracy, unity between military and political groups, corporatism, social change, political stability, capitalism, and imperialism. The Mexican state promotes capitalism within the confines of US imperialism.

632. León Torres, Gerardo de. TRES BENÍTEZ GOBERNADORES DE NUEVO LEÓN [Three Benítez governors of Nuevo León]. *Humánitas [Mexico] 1974 15: 491-510.* Gives a history of the life and career of each of three governors of Nuevo León from the Benítez family: Don Jesús María Benítez y Pinillos (1828-99), Pedro Benítez Leal (1861-1945), and José Benítez (1891-1954).

633. Lerner, Victoria. HISTORIA DE LA REFORMA EDUCATIVA—1933-1945 [History of educational reform, 1933-45]. *Hist. Mexicana [Mexico] 1979 28(1): 91-132.* Between 1933 and 1945, political and ideological rather than educational forces impelled educational reforms in Mexico. Groups supporting reform—workers, peasants, teachers, and public employees' organizations—always possessed a semi-official character. Their zeal, however, was directly proportional to that of the President, the official party, and a few powerful congressional deputies. This observation leads to the suspicion that revolutionary education has been a weapon the state wielded to obtain consensus and legitimacy. Based on archives located in the Archivo General de la Nación in Mexico City; 104 notes.   F. J. Shaw, Jr.

634. Levine, Robert M. THE MEXICAN REVOLUTION: A RETROSPECTIVE VIEW. *Current Hist. 1974 66(393): 195-199, 231.* Attempts to determine the influence of the Mexican Revolution on today's Mexico.   S

635. Levy, Daniel. UNIVERSITY AUTONOMY IN MEXICO: IMPLICATIONS FOR REGIME AUTHORITARIANISM. *Latin Am. Res. Rev. 1979 14(3): 129-152.* The National University of Mexico has maintained a considerable degree of autonomy, despite governmental pressures. Student admissions and career choice, selection of rectors, and maintenance of government financing demonstrate the relative weakness of outside control. These findings raise questions about widely accepted conclusions that the Mexican government is an authoritarian system. Based on Mexican government statistics, interviews with university leaders, and other documentary sources; 2 tables, fig., 67 notes.   J. K. Pfabe

636. Llaca, Edmundo González. EL PRESIDENCIALISMO O LA PERSONALIZACIÓN DEL PODER [Presidentialism or the personalization of power]. *Rev. Mexicana de Ciencia Pol. [Mexico] 1975 21(80): 35-42.* Explores presidentialism, or the concentration of power in a single person, in the context of 20th-century Mexican politics, as determined by both internal and external factors, and as representative of a larger, international phenomenon.

637. Loeffler, William. MEXICO: REVOLUTION AND THE STATE. *Monthly Rev. 1981 33(5): 59-62.* Reviews Donald Hodges and Ross Gandy's *Mexico 1910-1979: Reform or Revolution?* (1979) and James Cockcroft's, *Imperialismo, la lucha de clases y el Estado en México* (1980), the first of which provides a history of the Mexican Revolution since 1910, a review of Marxist and non-Marxist views of the Revolution, and its effect on Latin America, and the second of which is a Marxist interpretation of Mexican history.

638. Ludlow, Leonor. LA UNIÓN NACIONAL SINARQUISTA (MAYO DE 1937-MARZO DE 1944) [The Unión Nacional Sinarquista, May 1937-March 1944]. *Hist. Mexicana [Mexico] 1977 3(10): 77-98.* Traces development of Sinarquismo from May 1937 to March 1944. Founded by lower-middle class Catholics seeking a moral and religious alternative to the anticlerical radicalism of Lázaro Cárdenas in the 1930's, the union spent its first three years gathering a constituency from among the rural peasantry of Guanajuato. From 1940 to 1942, Salvador de Abascal, the union's leader, organized his following of 300,-000 into a disciplined paramilitary heirarchy and attempted to establish the colony of María Auxiliadora in Lower California. Inhabitants of this colony resented its rigid discipline and system of communal property. Ridden with dissension, the colony failed in 1944 when the union's high command yielded to pressure from the Vatican, the United States, and Mexico, and withdrew financial support. Based on writings of Sinarquista leaders, newspaper articles, and secondary sources; 81 notes.   F. J. Shaw, Jr.

639. Mabry, Donald J. and Camp, Roderic Ai. MEXICAN POLITICAL ELITES 1935-1973: A COMPARATIVE STUDY. *Americas (Acad. of Am. Franciscan Hist.) 1975 31(4): 452-469.* Analysis of Mexican political elites shows them to be self-perpetuating, predominantly university-educated, with a high percentage of rural origin despite geographic overrepresentation of the Federal District itself. There is little difference between figures associated with the ruling Partido Revolucionario Institucional and leaders of the opposition Partido Acción except that more of the latter are of urban origin or from west-central Mexico. Mexican federal deputies, of whom a special study was made, were found generally similar to those of Brazil, Guatemala, and Uruguay. 22 notes.   D. Bushnell

640. Mabry, Donald J. MEXICO'S PARTY DEPUTY SYSTEM: THE FIRST DECADE. *J. of Inter-American Studies and World Affairs 1974 16(2): 221-233.* Since 1929 the PRI party has dominated Mexican politics. The opposition that did exist could be found mainly in the Chamber of Deputies. But even there only three to five per cent of the seats have been held at any one time by members of opposition parties. In 1963 the government guaranteed opposition parties seats in the Chamber through the so-called party deputy system. But the intricate system actually hindered opposition and aided the PRI to continue its dominance of the legislature, while giving the appearance of greater opposition activity in government. Based on political parties' records, government documents, and secondary sources; 3 tables, 5 notes, biblio.   J. R. Thomas

641. Macklin, Barbara Jane and Crumrine, N. Ross. THREE NORTH MEXICAN FOLK SAINT MOVEMENTS. *Comparative Studies in Soc. and Hist. [Great Britain] 1973 15(1): 89-105.* Compares the careers of three folk saints and curers: Santa Teresa of Sonora, El Niño Santo Fidencio of Nuevo León, and San Damian of Sonora; and finds a common four-stage transformational process in operation. The first step involves a 'call' and initiates the folk saint's career. The saint then attracts a group of adherents followed by the development of an ideology with social, political, and religious ramifications. The final stage begins with the application of political pressure by the traditional power structure and the saint must then relinquish secular power and return to a career of curer. Based on the authors' field research, oral data, and primary and secondary written material; 16 notes.   M. M. McCarthy

642. Magaña-Esquivel, Antonio. LA POLÍTICA EN EL TEATRO MEXICANO [Politics in Mexican theater]. *Inter-American Rev. of Biblio. 1977 27(2): 125-134.* Politics has been a continuing theme in Mexican drama since 1810. The author discusses dramatists and their plays as they reflect the Mexican political situation.   B. D. Johnson

643. Matesanz, José Antonio. DE CÁRDENAS A LÓPEZ PORTILLO: MÉXICO ANTE LA REPÚBLICA ESPAÑOLA, 1936-1977 [From Cardenas to Lopez Portillo: Mexico's relations with the Spanish Republic, 1936-77]. *Estudios de Hist. Moderna y Contemporánea de México [Mexico] 1980 8: 179-231.* From 1939 to 1976 seven Mexican presidents refused to establish diplomatic relations with the government of general Francisco Franco. During the same period human, cultural, and economic exchanges continued. This ambivalent attitude toward

Spain is explained by the Mexican government's need to project a certain leftist image as well as other factors, both internal and external. The complex motivation of this attitude is what gave it permanence and constitutes its historical importance. 54 notes. J. V. Coutinho

644. Mathes, W. Michael. THE ARCHIVO HISTÓRICO DE BAJA CALIFORNIA SUR PABLO L. MARTÍNEZ, LA PAZ, BAJA CALIFORNIA SUR. *Americas (Acad. of Am. Franciscan Hist.) 1979 36(1): 116-120.* Describes the history, resources, and services of this major repository for history of Baja California, 1744-1950, and of Upper California up to 1848. 7 notes. D. Bushnell

645. Mendieta y Núñez, Luis. INFLUENCIA DE LA POLÍTICA SOBRE LA LEGISLACIÓN AGRARIA [Political influence on agrarian legislation]. *Humánitas [Mexico] 1977 18: 531-545.* Traces the political motivation behind agrarian reforms, with special reference to Mexico from the Spanish Conquest.

646. Meyer, Jean. LOS INTELECTUALES Y EL ESTADO EN MÉXICO EN EL SIGLO XX [Intellectuals and the state in 20th-century Mexico]. Frost, Elsa Cecilia; Meyer, Michael C.; and Zoraida Vázquez, Josefina, ed. *El Trabajo y los Trabajadores en la Historia de México* (Mexico City: Colegio de México, 1979): 890-893. The role of the state in intellectual and artistic matters in the 20th century. Examines the power of the state since colonial times, state control of education, the role of the Church in education, and dissident movements.
J. P. H. Myers

647. Meyer, Jean A. CROISSANCE ET DÉVELOPPEMENT AU MEXIQUE [Growth and development in Mexico]. *Annales: Économies, Sociétés, Civilisations [France] 1974 29(2): 498-503.* Analysis of recent work on economic growth and development in Mexico in the late 19th and 20th centuries. Economic growth poses political problems since it has set the stage for broader social participation in the political process. 27 notes. R. Howell

648. Meyer, Lorenzo. CONTINUIDADES E INNOVACIONES EN LA VIDA POLÍTICA MEXICANA DEL SIGLO XX. EL ANTIGUO Y EL NUEVO RÉGIMEN [Continuities and innovations in 20th-century Mexican political life: the old and the new regime]. *Foro Int. [Mexico] 1975 16(1): 37-63.* Discusses the political nature of Mexico during the Porfiriato, 1877-1911, compares it to political conditions since the revolution, and speculates on the political future of the country. Indicates that the political nature of Mexico has remained about the same despite the revolution. Primary and secondary sources; 35 notes.
D. A. Franz

649. Meyer, Lorenzo. LA ETAPA FORMATIVA DEL ESTADO MEXICANO CONTEMPORÁNEO (1928-1940) [The formative period of the contemporary Mexican state, 1928-40]. *Foro Int. [Mexico] 1977 17(4): 453-476.* Discusses the establishment of a one-party political system in Mexico through absorption, cooptation, and purges. The roles of Plutarco Elías Calles and Lázaro Cárdenas are stressed. 21 notes.
D. A. Franz

650. Miller, Richard U. AMERICAN RAILROAD UNIONS AND THE NATIONAL RAILWAYS OF MEXICO: AN EXERCISE IN NINETEENTH-CENTURY PROLETARIAN MANIFEST DESTINY. *Labor Hist. 1974 15(2): 239-260.* Analyzes the effects of the involvement of the American Railroad Brotherhoods in Mexico 1880-1912. American unions provided the model for Mexican railway unions from 1912 to 1933. The strike of 1912 was the final blow, but the existence of American unions in Mexico promoted the development of railroads, affected the Mexican labor movement, and fostered the adoption of "business unionism" until 1933, and may have lengthened the Mexican Revolution by increasing tension between Mexico and the US. Based on the *Mexican Herald,* labor publications, and Mexican sources. 3 tables, 57 notes. L. L. Athey

651. Molina Piñeiro, Luis. MADURACION IDEOLOGICA DE LA INSTITUCIONALIZACION REVOLUCIONARIA EN MEXICO Y ALGUNAS REGLAS DEL JUEGO DE SU SISTEMA POLITICO [Ideological wisdom of revolutionary institutionalization in Mexico and some rules of the game of its political system]. *Rev. de la Facultad de*

Derecho de Mexico [Mexico] 1980 30(115): 161-167. Discusses the various theories underlying the formulation of Mexican ideology and presents seven theses pertaining to Mexican social structure and politics.

652. Moliner, José Maria. RAÍCES DE LA PINTURA EXPRESIONISTA MEJICANA [Roots of Mexican expressionist painting]. *Cuadernos Hispanoamericanos [Spain] 1982 127(379): 130-140.* Defines expressionist painting as that which expresses depressive and obsessive states of mind caused by the sight of social injustice and spiritual problems. Nordic and Germanic ideas, influences from Aztec art and European painters and an oppressive political situation explain the art of the group that included Diego Rivera, Jose Orozco, and Alfaro Siqueiros.
J. V. Coutinho

653. Mumme, Stephen P. MEXICAN POLITICS AND THE PROSPECTS FOR EMIGRATION POLICY: A POLICY PERSPECTIVE. *Inter-American Econ. Affairs 1978 32(1): 67-94.* Reviews the Mexican government's perception of labor emigration to the United States since the 1920's, and examines the political environment in which emigration policy evolves and the policymaking capabilities of the Mexican government. 43 notes. D. A. Franz

654. Muriá, José María. SUGERENCIAS PARA DOTAR DE NUEVAS PERSPECTIVAS A LA HISTORIOGRAFÍA REGIONAL [Suggestions for a new outlook for regional historiography]. *Humánitas [Mexico] 1977 18: 375-385.* The Mexican Association of Regional History and the six regional centers created by the National Institute of Anthropology and History are important in providing guidelines and coordinating the work of historians on Mexican regional history.

655. Nahmad, Salomon. MEXICAN COLONIALISM? *Society 1981 19(1): 51-58.* Describes how Mexico has tried to amalgamate its so-called non-Spanish-speaking Indian inhabitants into the national mainstream since 1910 via bilingual education and land distribution. Often inefficient and poorly funded educational methods have meant that the Indians are forced to remain a marginal, monolingual population, subject to further exploitation and oppression.

656. Paoli Bolio, Francisco José. PETROLEUM AND POLITICAL CHANGE IN MEXICO. *Latin Am. Perspectives 1982 9(1): 65-77.* Following devaluation of the Mexican peso in 1976, the national executive and Pemex oil monopoly were forced to concede public accountability for their policy actions. Results by 1980 indicated official sensitivity, and public criticism had produced wider media coverage and unusual discussions. Mexican oil policy may engender "unified action" among the "broad left" for popular political reform. Biblio. J. F. Vivian

657. Paré, Louise. CACIQUISME ET STRUCTURE DU POUVOIR DANS LE MEXIQUE RURAL [*Caciquismo* and the power structure in rural Mexico]. *Can. R. of Sociol. and Anthrop. 1973 10(1): 20-43.* "The author tries to demonstrate how the political phenomenon known to Mexican historians as *caciquismo* (absolute control over local political power by a holder of economic power) is not a part of the pre-revolutionary past in rural Mexico. By using data collected in Eastern Mexico she shows that *cacisquismo,* under a modified form, is still the focus of political life. She stresses the links between this phenomenon and the much studied factionalism: far from being exclusive of each other as might seem at first sight, both are concurrent devices which aim at strengthening the control of the upper class—here, landowners and merchants—over the proletarians. Except in periods of transition (the power passing over from one *cacique* to another) the factions, in which the middle classes (here: teachers, shop-keepers) play an active part, remain subordinate to the *cacique,* merely fighting for his support. They therefore serve, in this context, both as an adaptive mechanism of the *cacique* to rapidly changing conditions and as a way of manipulating the middle classes whose alliance with the proletarians could constitute a threat to what is in fact an archaic form of capitalist domination." J

658. Paz, Octavio. THE PHILANTHROPIC OGRE. *Dissent 1979 26(1): 43-52.* Describes the modernization of Mexico since the dictatorship of Porfirio Diaz being carried out by the revolutionary state and discusses the often difficult interaction of bodies within the state; the patrimonialist administration and the Partido Revolucionario Institucional, Mexico's official party since 1929, and the other dominant forces in the country: private capitalism and working-class bureaucracies.

659. Perissinotto, Giorgio. EDUCATIONAL REFORM AND GOVERNMENT INTERVENTION IN MEXICO. *Current Hist. 1974 66(393): 208-211, 226.* Studies the Mexican concept of centralized control of education as a means of molding national character. S

660. Plana, Manuel. LA CLASSE OPERAIA NELLA STORIA DEL MESSICO [The working class in the history of Mexico]. *Movimento Operaio e Socialista [Italy] 1981 4(4): 507-520.* Reviews a 17-volume collective work, *La Clase Obrera en la Historia de Mexico,* of which seven volumes have so far appeared. Under the general editorship of Pablo González Casanova, the authors attempt to give an up-to-date view of the development of the Mexican working class and a critical reevaluation of the political development of the labor movement since the 1910 revolution. The work goes beyond militant history and synthesizes recent monographs in order to reflect on the role of the workers' movement in contemporary Mexican society. 34 notes.
J. V. Coutinho

661. Poitras, Guy E. WELFARE BUREAUCRACY AND CLIENTELE POLITICS IN MEXICO. *Administrative Sci. Q. 1973 18(1): 18-26.* By denying effective representation to all but elite members of clientele groups, the IMSS has failed to aid those most in need. S

662. Pomerleau, Claude. THE CHANGING CHURCH IN MEXICO AND ITS CHALLENGE TO THE STATE. *Rev. of Pol. 1981 43(4): 540-559.* Pomerleau examines the history of Church-state relations in Mexico in the 19th and 20th centuries. Mexican independence placed the Church in a defensive position; its alliance with conservative elements put it at odds with liberal governments. Compromises were struck but fell through, and by 1940, the Church had fewer priests than in 1810. Although dioceses and priests have increased since 1940, the relations between Church and state have been in a delicate equilibrium between interests that will never completely coincide. Discusses the internal transformation of the Church that resulted from Vatican II and the Second Latin American Episcopal Conference (Puebla, 1979). Secondary sources; 45 notes.
D. F. Ring

663. Pompa y Pompa, Antonio. EVOLUCION DE LA REVOLUCION [Evolution of the revolution]. *Humanitas [Mexico] 1981 22: 303-310.* Discusses various political and philosophical concepts of evolution and revolution, and their relevance to the history and evolution of Mexico and Mexican society.

664. Purcell, Susan Kaufman. BUSINESS-GOVERNMENT RELATIONS IN MEXICO: THE CASE OF THE SUGAR INDUSTRY. *Comparative Pol. 1981 13(2): 211-233.* Discusses Mexico's ability to avoid the chronic political instability characteristic of many developing countries, focusing on the relationship between business and government as a partial explanation of this ability. The Mexican political leadership has been both willing and able to give precedence to political over economic considerations in any situation that threatened the political order by increasing their regulation of economic activity. The sugar industry is used as a case study to demonstrate the relationship between politics and the market in Mexico, beginning with the impact of the Mexican Revolution of 1910. 54 notes.
M. A. Kascus

665. Purcell, Susan Kaufman and Purcell, John F. H. STATE AND SOCIETY IN MEXICO: MUST A STABLE POLITY BE INSTITUTIONALIZED? *World Pol. 1980 32(2): 194-227.* The Mexican state is based on a constantly renewed bargain among several ruling groups and interests representing a broad range of ideological tendencies and social bases. Mexican political stability rests primarily not upon formal institutions, but upon the interaction of principles of political discipline closely linked to the concept of authoritarianism and political negotiation associated with the concept of protodemocracy. The combination of repression and co-optation with just the right mix of responsiveness and compromise produces: elites that are both linked to, and insulated from, their potential constituencies; a pattern of political and administrative decisionmaking called "policy incoherence"; and avoidance of the crystallization of factional alliances, and their opposition to one another. 39 notes.
J

666. Raat, W. Dirk. SYNTHESIZING THE MEXICAN EXPERIENCE. *Latin Am. Res. Rev. 1980 15(3): 266-272.* Reviews Michael C. Meyer and William L. Sherman's *The Course of Mexican History* (New York: Oxford U. Pr., 1979), Samuel H. Mayo's *A History of Mexico: From Pre-Columbia to Present* (Englewood Cliffs, N.J.: Prentice-Hall, Inc., 1978), and Jan Bazant's *A Concise History of Mexico: From Hidalgo to Cárdenas, 1805-1940* (New York: Cambridge U. Pr., 1977). These books provide an impressive treatment of Mexico's history, but all show the need for more systematic research for more substantial syntheses. 10 notes.
J. K. Pfabe

667. Reich, Peter L. ALGUNOS ARCHIVOS PARA EL ESTUDIO DE LA HISTORIA ECLESIÁSTICA MEXICANA EN EL SIGLO XX [Some archives for the study of 20th-century Mexican ecclesiastical history]. *Hist. Mexicana [Mexico] 1980 30(1): 126-133.* Studies of 20th-century church-state relations in Mexico have emphasized conflict at the expense of significant cooperation. This distortion is partially due to ignorance of archival sources. The Library of the Conciliar Seminary in Tlalpán, D. F., contains the largest collection of primary documents and secondary literature on church history during the independence period. The Archive of the Mexican Social Secretariat, San Jerónimo, D. F., is a repository for all sources published by Catholic institutions and unpublished documents of the Secretariat. The Plutarco Elías Calles Archive, Colonia Roma, Mexico City, contains Calles's uncatalogued political correspondence. The center for Historical Studies of Mexico, CONDUMEX, Chumalistac, D. F., contains 615 documents relating to religious conflict between 1910 and 1937. Based on original research and secondary sources.
F. J. Shaw, Jr.

668. Riddell, Adaljiza Sosa. FEMALE POLITICAL ELITES IN MEXICO: 1974. Iglitzin, Lynne B. and Ross, Ruth, eds. *Women in the World* (Santa Barbara, Calif.: Clio Books, 1976): 257-267. The small female political elite in Mexico represents neither women in general nor anyone of the lower social strata. From 1910, the feminist movement in Mexico aimed toward suffrage rights, which were granted in 1953. The movement then died out before raising other issues. *Machismo,* an attitude of male dominance, permeates society, affecting women particularly in the lower classes. Very few women are politically active at any level. In 1974 only 20 women were serving as deputies or senators in national government. These women constitute an elite, highly educated and influenced by US styles and standards. European in descent, they adhere to the male-dominated status quo, perpetuating an attitude of colonial condescension over the Mexican population. Secondary sources; 12 notes.
N. Barron

669. Rodriguez, Erwin. LAS PROYECCIONES MEXICANAS DE LA CRISIS GENERAL DEL CAPITALISMO (ELEMENTOS PARA SU ESTUDIO) [Mexican manifestations of the general crisis of capitalism: elements for its study]. *Estudios Pol. [Mexico] 1976 2(8): 5-14* An examination of the relationship between the general crisis of world capitalism and the Mexican economy (1929-76). The general crisis of capitalism is caused by the lack of international solvency, which causes "stagflation" in the highly industrialized economies of Western Europe and the United States. The inflationary component of this malaise has been exported to Mexico through the sale of capital goods at inflated prices. At the same time, recession in the United States has caused that nation to reduce its imports of Mexican primary products. The combination of inflation and falling exports in Mexico weakened demand for domestic manufactured goods, causing recession in the industrialized sector. This recession reduced the tax base of the Mexican government, impeding its public sector spending to stimulate the economy. Based on economic studies and the statistics of private and governmental institutions; 68 notes.
F. J. Shaw

670. Rosa, Martin de la. INTRODUCTION AU MEXIQUE CONTEMPORAIN [Introduction to contemporary Mexico]. *Études [France] 1978 349(4): 309-322.* The history of Mexico, 19th-20th centuries.

671. Rosenberg, Emily S. MEXICAN OIL AND UNITED STATES POLICY. *Latin Am. Res. Rev. 1980 15(3): 281-286.* Reviews Lorenzo Meyer's *Mexico and the United States in the Oil Controversy, 1917-1942,* translated by Muriel Vasconcellos (Austin: U. of Texas Pr., 1977), and Mark T. Gilderhus's *Diplomacy and Revolution: U.S.-Mexican Relations under Wilson and Carranza* (Tucson: U. of Arizona Pr., 1977). Both books show that during and after World War I, both theorists and politi-

cians in Mexico supported the idea of nationally directed oil development. 7 notes.   J. K. Pfabe

672. Ross, Stanley R. LA PROTESTA DE LOS INTELLEC-TUALES ANTE MÉXICO Y SU REVOLUCÍON [The protest of the intellectuals before Mexico and its revolution]. *Hist. Mexicana [Mexico] 1977 26(3): 396-437.* Discusses the development of intellectual protest against the dictatorship of Porfirio Díaz after 1900 when societies began to be organized, the response of the intellectuals to the revolution, and the evolution of intellectual protest until the student movements of the early 1970's. Based on the press and secondary sources; 75 notes.
S. P. Carr

673. Sabloff, Paula L. W. EL CACIQUISMO EN EL EJIDO POST REVOLUCIONARIO [Political bossism and the postrevolutionary ejido]. *Am. Indígena [Mexico] 1977 37(4): 851-881.* Caciquismo, or political bossism, is a type of autocratic political organization which has been found on the local level (village, hamlet, municipality) of many complex societies and which has been prevalent in rural agrarian Mexico for over 400 years. It has been especially noted in Mexican communities which have had corporate landholding, i.e., where title to the agricultural, pasture, and woodlands has been held by the community and usufruct rights to these lands have been granted to community members. Caciquismo exists in this type of community when one individual, with the help of a small group of followers, controls the economic, political, and sometimes even the social activity of the members of that community. He gains and maintains control through various means, patronage, coercion, cooptation, or violence. Tracts have been written explaining why communities with this form of land tenure arrangement have been prey to autocratic or cacique rule in previous centuries (e.g., Gibson 1964, Silva Herzog 1959, Tannenbaum 1929). It is not so clear, however, why many post-Revolution communities in which the majority of land is under ejido grant are still under cacique rule, for many parts of the 1917 Constitution and subsequent laws purposefully built a democratic form into the government of these communities.   J

674. Saldaña, José P. APUNTES POLÍTICOS Y SOCIO-ECONÓMICOS DE MONTERREY [Political and socioeconomic notes on Monterrey]. *Humánitas [Mexico] 1974 15: 447-490.* Brief notes on the political and socioeconomic conditions of Monterrey from 1810 to the present, divided into seven chronological steps of development.

675. Salovesh, Michael. POLÍTICA EN UNA COMUNIDAD MAYA [Politics in a Mayan community]. *Am. Indígena [Mexico] 1975 35(1): 39-48.* Discusses theory and empirical data to analyze a nonformal political system present in the Tzotzil community of San Bartolomé in Chiapas, Mexico. Defines politics and studies groups which conform to the political system, mainly its roles and the influence of its members in decision making. Among these are residentiary kindred groups, territorial working, ceremonial and community groups like the Agrarian Section and Common Goods. Devotes special attention to family groups as they constitute the basic unit in political participation and analyzes the political interaction within and among all the groups. Suggests a radical model where the groups for the local feast (belonging to ceremonial groups), appear as organizing center of the political system.   J/S

676. Sandos, James A. INTERNATIONAL WATER CONTROL IN THE LOWER RIO GRANDE BASIN, 1900-1920. *Agric. Hist. 1980 54(4): 490-501.* A joint International Boundary Commission, created in 1894 and consisting of a commissioner, engineer, and secretary, one each from the United States and Mexico, determined that since 1900, and especially during the Mexican Revolution period (1910-20), Texans were taking more than 70% of the mean annual river flow of the Rio Grande. It was further determined that some 70% of the water in the river originated within Mexico. As a result, by the late 1920's Texans were irrigating 338,000 acres, but in the corresponding area of Tamaulipas, Mexico, fewer than 20,000 acres were under irrigation. Based on Department of State records, RG-95, in the National Archives; map, table, 34 notes.   R. T. Fulton

677. Schone, V. ZUM CHARAKTER DES GEGENWÄRTIGEN MEXIKANISCHEN STAATES [A characterization of the present Mexican state]. *Lateinamerika [East Germany] 1977 (Aut): 69-100.* Mexico's economic development since 1917 can be characterized as changing from monopolistic capitalism to state capitalism. The Mexican economy is still integrated into the world capitalist system because it is dependent on foreign investment. Based on government and company production reports and secondary sources; 11 tables, 50 notes, 3 appendixes.
D. R. Stevenson

678. Sizonenko, A. I. U ISTOKOV SOVETSKO-MEKSIKAN-SKIKH OTNOSHENII [At the sources of Soviet-Mexican relations]. *Novaia i Noveishaia Istoriia [USSR] 1980 (5): 136-143.* An investigation of the course of Soviet-Mexican relations from the Bolshevik Revolution in 1917 to the official recognition of the USSR by the Mexican government in 1924, the first country in the Western hemisphere to do so. Until the early 1970's it was thought that there were no bilateral links before 1923, but this is not so. Lenin himself took a personal interest in the matter, and asked that Mikhail Borodin (Mikhail Markovich Grusenberg) be appointed consul general to Mexico. Based on the Archivo de la Relaciones Exteriores de México 1/131/303, the Soviet Archive of Foreign Affairs (fond 110), and published works; 46 notes.
D. N. Collins

679. Smith, Peter H. THE WOUNDS OF HISTORY. *Wilson Q. 1979 3(3): 130-141.* Chronicles the social problems that have faced Mexico since the Spanish conquest, stressing issues of political leadership and economic development in the 20th century.

680. Smith, Robert Freeman. WHO'S AFRAID OF SONJ? ENERGY AND NATIONALISM IN INTERNATIONAL RELATIONS. *Rev. in Am. Hist. 1978 6(3): 394-399.* Review essay of Lorenzo Meyer's *Mexico and the United States in the Oil Controversy, 1917-1942* translated by Muriel Vasconcellos (Austin: U. of Texas Pr., 1972, 1977).

681. Stavenhagen, Rodolfo. CAPITALISM AND THE PEASANTRY IN MEXICO. *Latin Am. Perspectives 1978 5(3): 27-37.* Studies the economic relationships between peasants and capitalists in Mexico. The traditional transition from peasant subsistence farming to capitalist production has not been followed. Capitalism simply has not been able to absorb the vast labor supply, which costs it nothing, that pours in from rural areas. The birthrate is too high and capitalistic development too slow. The government has been forced to maintain the peasantry by breaking up large landholdings and redistributing them in the form of small plots. 3 notes, ref.   V. L. Human

682. Stavenhagen, Rodolfo. COLLECTIVE AGRICULTURE AND CAPITALISM IN MEXICO: A WAY OUT OR A DEAD END. *Latin Am. Perspectives 1975 2(2): 146-163.* Analyzes *ejidos*, landholding units which sponsor cooperative farming enterprises under government auspices in Mexico, 1925-75. The institution is not really a viable one due to the basically capitalist nature of the Mexican economy.

683. Stevens, Evelyn P. PROTEST MOVEMENT IN AN AUTHORITARIAN REGIME: THE MEXICAN CASE. *Comparative Pol. 1975 7(3): 361-382.* Compares Spain and Mexico since the 1950's.
S

684. Story, Dale. THE PRIVATE SECTOR AND POLICY-MAKING IN MEXICO. *Secolas Ann. 1981 12: 78-88.* Examines the formal and informal relations between the private sector and the state in Mexico as well as the impact of organized business groups and individual business leaders on government policy, especially during the Echeverría and López Portillo administrations.

685. Suárez-Iñiguez, Enrique. LOS INTELECTUALES EN MÉXICO: LOS GRUPOS GENERACIONALES [Intellectuals in Mexico: the generation groups]. *Rev. Mexicana de Ciencias Pol. y Sociales [Mexico] 1979 25(95-96): 185-201.* Groups are formed as different generations react to their environment; some were only literary and cultural, such as the Ateneo, 1907-14, the Contemporáneos, 1928-30, and El Hiperión, 1946-50. Others, such as El Espectador, 1959-61, were politically oriented and attempted to organize the democratic left in Mexico, but did not get involved itself. Finally, groups such as Los Siete Sabios (The Seven Wise Men), 1916-22, an organization for debate of social and political themes, became involved in the revolution, participating in the government at various levels. The Movimiento de Liberación Nacional (MLN), 1961-64, was the only time the democratic left acted together, not as a party but

as a pressure group; the 1964 election divided it so badly that it did not survive.

686. Tardanico, Richard. PERSPECTIVES ON REVOLUTIONARY MEXICO: THE REGIMES OF OBREGÓN AND CALLES. Rubinson, Richard, ed. *Dynamics of World Development* (Beverly Hills, Calif.: Sage, 1981): 69-88. Focuses on the crucial state-making activities of the regimes of Álvaro Obregón (1920-24) and Plutarco Elías Calles (1924-28). Mexico was peripheralized during the expansion of the European world-economy in the 16th century. During the 20th century, Mexico has shifted its position to that of a semiperipheral state. The Mexican Revolution was crucial in creating a significantly stronger state apparatus, allowing Mexico to take advantage of economic shifts in the world economy to gain a larger share of the world economic surplus for itself and to outstrip other peripheral areas. But while the revolution allowed Mexico to shift upward in the world economy, it did not produce a situation of autonomous development. Rather, the economic consequences of the revolution were to reorganize its economic activities to simultaneously increase its advantages over other peripheral areas in Latin America and strengthen its dependence on the United States, the emerging hegemonic power in the world economy. Secondary sources; 12 notes.   J. Powell

687. Terán Mata, Juan Manuel. EVOLUCIÓN POLÍTICA DE LA DOCTRINA SOCIAL MEXICANA [Political evolution of Mexican social doctrine]. *Rev. de la Facultad de Derecho de México [Mexico] 1974 24(95-96): 637-645*. Discusses the political evolution of Mexican social policy as exemplified by Social Security, tracing its growth from 1900 to the present.

688. Trejo Delarbre, Raúl. NOTAS SOBRE LA INSURGENCIA OBRERA Y LA BUROCRACIA SINDICAL [Notes on workers' rebellions and labor union bureaucracy]. *Estudios Pol. [Mexico] 1978 4(16): 73-95*. Rebellion against the bureaucracy of the Mexican labor movement is a longstanding tradition. Owing to its role in economic development, the Mexican government became the sponsor of labor unionism. Although state sponsorship benefited the working class, it also reduced the ideological and political independence of the labor movement, making occasional rebellions inevitable. Where recent rebellions have confronted the state, they have been crushed. Where they have avoided confrontation, they have been assimilated into the official structure.
F. J. Shaw, Jr./S

689. Tribukait, Albrecht. EL DESARROLLO POLÍTICO DE MÉXICO CONTEMPORÁNEO [The political development of contemporary Mexico]. *Rev. Mexicana de Ciencia Pol. [Mexico] 1974 20(75): 85-103*. Describes socioeconomic and political change in 20th-century Mexico, examining the external and internal circumstances that have made such changes possible, in order to arrive at a viable theory of Mexican politics.

690. Valadés, Diego. EL PODER LEGISLATIVO MEXICANO [The power of the Mexican legislature]. *Rev. de Estudios Pol. [Spain] 1978 (4): 33-56*. A background on the power of the Mexican legislature granted by the constitutions of 1824, 1857, and 1917, and modified in 1963 and 1977.

691. Vaughan, Mary Kay. EDUCATION AND CLASS STRUGGLE IN THE MEXICAN REVOLUTION. *Latin Am. Perspectives 1975 2(2): 17-33*. Chronicles elementary educational policy in Mexico, 1890-1930. Programs were designed primarily to mold a labor force equipped with skills and social attitudes appropriate to the modernization process and with values which legitimized bourgeois rule.

692. Vazquez, M. Seara. THE SUBJECTS OF INTERNATIONAL LAW. *Int. J. of Pol. 1976 6(1-2): 133-137*. Discusses various doctrines of American international law as they related to or emanated from Mexico, including the Tobar Doctrine (1907), the Estrada Doctrine (1930), and the Díaz Ordaz Doctrine (1969).

693. Venegas Trejo, Francisco. LA DEMOCRACIA COMO AMBICIÓN POLÍTICA DE LOS PUEBLOS [Democracy as the political ambition of the people]. *Rev. de la Facultad de Derecho de México [Mexico] 1976 26(103-104): 341-355*. Democracy is the form of government that all people and all nations aspire to. The author presents constants and variations in Mexican democracy with which Mexico's people are dissatisfied.

694. Vigil, Ralph H. THE LORDS OF NEW SPAIN AND MEXICO. *Rocky Mountain Social Sci. J. 1974 11(2): 103-112*. Reviews 12 studies of Mexican social structure and political power.   S

695. Villoro Toranzo, Miguel. DERECHO PÚBLICO Y DERECHO PRIVADO [Public and private law]. *Rev. de la Facultad de Derecho de México [Mexico] 1975 25(99-100): 901-924*. Defines the distinction between public and private law in Mexico and their applications toward the formation of a unitarian system of government based on the Enlightenment principles of self-government and free will, ca. 1798-1974.

696. Walker, William O., III. CONTROL ACROSS THE BORDER: THE UNITED STATES, MEXICO, AND NARCOTICS POLICY, 1936-1940. *Pacific Hist. Rev. 1978 47(1): 91-106*. Between 1936 and 1940 US narcotic diplomacy transformed Mexican drug policy. The United States defined as illegal all nonmedical and nonscientific use of narcotics and made little distinction between users and peddlers. Although Mexico formally agreed to these policies in agreements signed in 1930 and 1932, its enforcement efforts did not gain American approval. In 1938, Leopold Salazar Viniegra became head of Mexico's Federal Narcotics Service. He did not believe in a punitive drug control program; instead he favored channeling the flow of illegal drugs through government controlled distribution centers. American diplomatic pressure led to Salazar's removal in August 1939 and to a more vigorous Mexican law enforcement policy. Based on documents in the National Archives, the Bureau of Narcotics Library, and Mexican newspapers; 51 notes.
W. K. Hobson

697. Wasserstrom, Robert. LA EVOLUCIÓN DE LA ECONOMÍA REGIONAL EN CHIAPAS: 1528-1975 [The evolution of the regional economy in Chiapas: 1528-1975]. *Am. Indígena [Mexico] 1976 36(3): 479-498*. Examines those forces which, since the 16th century, have transformed the social, economic, and political situation of the indigenous groups from the central part of the Chiapas Highlands, with special attention to the way commercial agriculture transformed indigenous life. Far from allowing the isolation of the indigenous communities, the development of commercial agriculture rearranged their economic life. Given the low productivity of corn, beans, chile, coffee, and others, many Indians had to migrate seasonally in search of additional income; others were forced to expand their agricultural lands by renting. Based on historical documents and oral tradition in the Tzotzil municipality of Zinacantan.
J/S

698. Weeks, Charles A. USES OF A JUÁREZ MYTH IN MEXICAN POLITICS. *Politico [Italy] 1974 39(2): 210-232*. The Mexicans have transformed the historical figure of Benito Juárez into the protagonist of their greatest national myth. The author shows how, from the era in which Juárez lived to the centennial of his death in 1972, Mexicans used the Juárez myth to serve various political causes in the search for a national identity.
J/S

699. Weeks, Charles A. USES OF A JUÁREZ MYTH IN MEXICAN POLITICS. *Politico [Italy] 1974 39(2): 210-233*. The mythology surrounding Benito Juárez is one of the most potent forces in Mexico's political life, and is used today, as it has been for a century, by politicians of all shades.

700. Weinert, Richard S. FOREIGN CAPITAL IN MEXICO. *Pro. of the Acad. of Pol. Sci. 1981 34(1): 115-124*. Examines Mexico's policies toward foreign investments and considers some outstanding policy issues for Mexico-United States relations. US private interests are strong allies of Mexico, and are eager to expand their relationship. Foreign capital and Mexico are likely to continue a strong complementary relationship, and pose few challenges to US-Mexican relations.
T. P. Richardson

701. Williams, Edward J. THE TRADITIONS OF REVOLUTION: MEXICAN PATHOLOGY, PERSISTENCE AND PARADOX. *Secolas Ann. 1976 7: 34-43*. Mexico's dedication to industrialization has brought unexpected and difficult problems. Primary and secondary sources; 17 notes.
J. A. Lewis

702. Wionczek, Miguel. THE ROOTS OF THE MEXICAN AGRI-CULTURAL CRISIS: WATER RESOURCES DEVELOPMENT POLICIES (1920-1970). *Development and Change [Netherlands] 1982 13(3): 365-399.* A survey of water development policies with the view that the policy of maintaining the big haciendas and of leaving control of the land to a chosen few was more decisive in effecting agricultural development than the actual building of waterworks, and that the current crisis in agriculture in Mexico is not related to past water resources development practices.

703. Woldemberg, José. CARACTERÍSTICAS DE LOS ESTUDIOS SOBRE CLASE Y MOVIMIENTO OBREROS EN MÉXICO [Studies on class and labor movements in Mexico]. *Estudios Pol. [Mexico] 1978 4(16): 131-183.* Examines recent literature on Mexican labor and social classes published, 1970-78 in Mexico. Most of this literature deals with the post-1940 period. The two most popular themes are state-working class relations and labor conflicts. Secondary sources; 8 notes, biblio.
F. J. Shaw, Jr.

704. Wolf, Donna M. WOMEN IN MODERN MEXICO. *Studies in Hist. and Society 1976 1(1): 28-53.* Discusses the woman suffrage movement in Mexico, 1916-53, and related political events. Reviews 19th-century laws on women's relationship to the family, and the important changes made after the revolution of 1910, principally the Civil Code of 1928. The Mexican Revolutionary Party resisted full suffrage in the 1920's-30's because of the strong influence of the Church, and hence the Right, on women. *Machismo,* as shown by the increasing divorce rate, has been on the decline, while women's role in the work force has expanded along with their educational achievements. Despite modernization the socially ingrained role of subservience in women has continued to be the norm. 15 tables, 84 notes, appendixes.
S

705. —. ASUNTOS DE POLÍTICA INTERNACIONAL, 1926-1934 [International relations, 1926-34]. *Bol. del Archivo General de la Nación [Mexico] 1979 3(4): 50-55.* Reprint of eight documents concerning Mexico's reaction to events in Nicaragua and Great Britain from 1926 to 1934. Taken from the Archivo Plutarco Elías Calles at the National Archives of Mexico.
J. A. Lewis

706. —. DOCUMENTOS DEL PERIODO DEL MAXIMATO, 1929-1936 [Documents from the Maximato period, 1929-1936]. *Bol. del Archivo General de la Nación [Mexico] 1979 3(4): 77-86.* Eleven documents from the period when ex-President Plutarco Elías Calles ruled Mexico from behind the scenes. Several of these documents illustrate the relationship between Calles and Lázaro Cárdenas, president of Mexico from 1934 to 1940. Taken from the Archivo Plutarco Elías Calles at the National Archives of Mexico; 4 photos.
J. A. Lewis

707. —. LA DINÁMICA DEL SECTOR MINERO EN MÉXICO, 1877-1970 (CON PROYECCIONES A 1980) [The dynamics of the mining sector in Mexico, 1877-1970, with projections to 1980]. *Investigación Econ. [Mexico] 1973 32 (126): 377-439.* Considers the socioeconomic and political history of mining in Mexico, focusing on the period 1920-70.

708. —. LAND AND POLITICS IN MEXICO. *Can. J. of Pol. Sci. 1975 8(2): 299-307.*
Adie, Robert F. LAND AND POLITICS IN MEXICO, pp. 299-305. The *ejidos* (village communal lands) have served the important political function of maintaining stability in the Mexican countryside. 46 notes.
Hellman, Judith Adler and North, Liisa. A REJOINDER TO ROBERT ADIE'S "LAND AND POLITICS IN MEXICO," pp. 305-307. Agree with Adie's conclusion but disagree with the arguments by which he arrived at it. 7 notes.
R. V. Kubicek

Revolution and Reconstruction, 1914-1934

709. Adleson, S. Lief; Meyer, Jean and Matute, Álvaro, commentaries. COYUNTURA Y CONCIENCIA: FACTORES CONVERGENTE EN LA FUNDACIÓN DE LOS SINDICATOS PETROLEROS DE TAMPICO DURANTE LA DÉCADA DE 1920 [Opportunity and consciousness: factors leading to the founding of oil workers' unions in Tampico in the 1920's]. Frost, Elsa Cecilia; Meyer, Michael C.; and Zoraida Vázquez, Josefina, ed. *El Trabajo y los Trabajadores en la Historia de México* (Mexico City: Colegio de México, 1979): 632-661. This description of the successful strikes of 1923-24 is part of a wider study of Tampico, which in 1921 numbered 100,000 people and depended almost entirely on oil. There had been strikes of varying degrees of success in Tampico since 1911, but in combination with the electrical workers the carefully planned campaign in the El Águila refinery ended in complete success in June 1924, thereby laying the base for a rapid extension of union activities in other refineries. Some of the success was due to local government support. Commentaries, archival and secondary sources; 110 notes.
J. P. H. Myers

710. Andino, Alberto. LOS JUEGOS POLÍTICOS, CLASISTAS Y ÉTNICOS EN LAS NOVELAS DE MARIANO AZUELA SOBRE LA REVOLUCIÓN MEXICANA [The political, class, and ethnic games in the novels of Mariano Azuela on the Mexican revolution]. *Cuadernos Hispanoamericanos [Spain] 1981 123(370): 144-150.* Mariano Azuela (1873-1952), pioneer writer of the Mexican revolution, chronicled the course of the revolution in novels that present a panorama of contemporary social and political conditions. Azuela uses the technique of presenting the masses as protagonist, showing the Mexican people as the victims of various political, class, and ethnic ploys and strategies that debased the revolutionary process. Though firmly opposed to the old order, Azuela expresses criticism of the barbarous aspects of the revolution. Novels examined are *Mala Yerba, María Luisa, Andrés Pérez, Maderista, Los Caciques, Las Moscas,* and *Los de Abajo.* Based mainly on the novels of Azuela; biblio.
P. J. Durell

711. Aoki, Yoshio. CHOBATSU ENSEITAI (1916-17)—MEKI-SHIKO KAKUMEI TO AMERIKA [The Mexican revolution and the American punitive expedition]. *Shirin [Japan] 1977 60(4): 533-562.* Locates the negotiations during World War I between the United States and Mexico on the withdrawal of the punitive expedition which the United States had sent to Mexico. Before the 1910 Mexican revolution Mexico had been subordinate to the US economy. The author discusses the economic policy of the Carranza government, which aimed at freedom from economic subordination. Based on the memoirs of Woodrow Wilson and Venustiano Carranza and documents; 129 notes.
Y. Aoki

712. Arriola, Enrique. LOS INTERESES PETROLEROS, CALLES Y LOS CONFLICTOS DE 1924 [The oil interests, Calles, and the conflict of 1924]. *Bol. del Archivo General de la Nación [Mexico] 1977 1(1): 26-30.* Reprints four letters between American businessmen Vernon J. Rose and Arthur C. Rath on the attitude of US corporations toward the Mexican oil policies of President Plutarco Elías Calles, 1924-28. Based on documents in the Archivo General de la Nacion; illus.
J. A. Lewis

713. Avrich, Paul. PRISON LETTERS OF RICARDO FLORES MAGON TO LILLY SARNOFF. *Int. Rev. of Social Hist. [Netherlands] 1977 22(3): 379-422.* Ricardo Flores Magón (1874-1922), the foremost Mexican anarchist of the 20th century, spent the last 19 years of his life in the United States. During half of that time he was imprisoned, and he died at Leavenworth penitentiary. While there he began his long correspondence with Lilly Sarnoff, a young New York anarchist and member of the defense committee working for his release. From the files of the International Institute of Social History in Amsterdam, 21 letters of Magón to Sarnoff, covering the period from October 1920 to November 1922, are reprinted here in their original form. Written in English, these letters reveal the horrors of prison life, Magón's attitudes toward the Bolshevik Revolution, and a florid style characteristic of an age of romantic revolutionism.
G. P. Blum

714. Baena Paz, Guillermina. LA CONFEDERACIÓN GENERAL DE TRABAJADORES (1921-1931) [The General Confederation of Labor (CGT), 1921-31]. *Rev. Mexicana de Ciencias Pol. y Soc. [Mexico] 1976 21(83): 113-186.* A history of this Mexican labor confederation when its orientation was radical and anarcho-syndicalist; includes a list of its organizations and policies.

715. Bailey, David C. REVISIONISM AND THE RECENT HISTORIOGRAPHY OF THE MEXICAN REVOLUTION. *Hispanic Am. Hist. Rev. 1978 58(1): 62-79.* Increased access to archival sources, new bibliographical tools, and improved oral history techniques have changed scholarship on the Mexican revolution since the mid-1960's. Revisionist historians today are questioning the success of the revolution. The author discusses Marxist historians and other revisionists. 78 notes.
B. D. Johnson

716. Bellingeri, Marco. L'ECONOMIA DEL LATIFONDO IN MESSICO. L'HACIENDA SAN ANTONIO TOCHATLACO DAL 1880 AL 1920 [The latifundium economy in Mexico: the hacienda San Antonio Tochatlaco, 1880-1920]. *Ann. della Fondazione Luigi Einaudi [Italy] 1976 10: 287-428.* Examines production and labor organization on Mexican haciendas, and considers the penetration of foreign capital in agriculture under Porfirio Díaz, as well as the consequences of railroad extension into central Mexico. Also considers the state of Hidalgo and the hacienda San Antonio Tochatlaco, specifying four different periods in the rise and the evolution of new internal and external contradictions in the traditional system of agricultural production. The Mexican revolution laid the bases for the definitive overthrow of this system through land redistribution. Based on official sources, reviews, and publications; 27 statistical tables, 3 graphs, l06 notes, biblio., appendix.
M. de Leonardis

717. Britton, John A. IN DEFENSE OF REVOLUTION: AMERICAN JOURNALISTS IN MEXICO, 1920-1929. *Journalism Hist. 1978-79 5(4): 124-130, 136.* Analyzes the works of Carleton Beals, Ernest Gruening, and Frank Tannenbaum whose pro-Mexican revolution writings of 1920-29 were in opposition to the American State Department's position.

718. Brown, Jerry B. OIL ON THE PERIPHERY: THE HISTORY OF THE MEXICAN OIL EXPROPRIATION. *Caribbean Rev. 1981 10(3): 12-15, 39-41.* Presents the background to the 18 March 1938 expropriation of 17 foreign oil companies' lands in Mexico by President Lázaro Cárdenas. Triggered by a labor dispute, the problem originated with the 19th-century introduction of foreign capital in Latin America in amounts and ways that resulted in the development of unstable one- or two-product economies with high import coefficients. Many Latin American countries began to reconquer the lands they sold as they achieved some economic stability at the beginning of the 20th century.

719. Burke, Michael E. THE UNIVERSITY OF MEXICO AND THE REVOLUTION, 1910-1940. *Americas (Acad. of Am. Franciscan Hist.) 1977 34(2): 252-273.* The relationship between the National University of Mexico and the Mexican Revolution was marked by continual tensions between humanistic and strictly professional orientations on the one hand, and revolutionary goals and political involvement on the other. Student activism served frequently contradictory purposes, and university autonomy was seen by the government as a convenient way to dissociate itself from university problems. Nevertheless, the university "was an effective partner" of the revolution. 65 notes.
D. Bushnell

720. Buse, Constantin. REVOLUŢIA MEXICANĂ (1910-1917), ÎNCEPUTUL LUPTEI PENTRU CEA DE-A DOUA INDEPENDENŢĂ A AMERICII LATINE [The Mexican Revolution, 1910-17: the beginning of the struggle for the second independence of Latin America]. *Rev. de Istorie [Romania] 1980 33(1): 117-146.* Describes the events of the Mexican Revolution, stressing its profound implications for Mexico and the world at large. Examines the causes of the revolution, the reaction of the Great Powers to the liberal constitutional regime of Francisco Madero, the causes and implications of military intervention by the United States, and especially the significance of the 1917 constitution. Concludes that the Mexican Revolution began the Latin American struggle for economic independence. Based on French diplomatic correspondence in official Latin American archives; 281 notes. French summary.
R. O. Khan

721. Buve, Raymond Th. J.; Salamini, Heather Fowler and Warman, Arturo, commentaries. MOVILIZACIÓN CAMPESINA Y REFORMA AGRARIA EN LOS VALLES DE NATÍVITAS, TLAXCALA (1917-1923): ESTUDIO DE UN CASO DE LUCHA POR RECUPERAR TIERRAS HABIDAS DURANTE LA REVOLUCIÓN ARMADA [Peasant mobilization and agrarian reform in the valleys of Natívitas, Tlaxcala (1917-23): the study of a struggle to recover land seized during the armed revolution]. Frost, Elsa Cecilia; Meyer, Michael C.; and Zoraida Vázquez, Josefina, ed. *El Trabajo y los Trabajadores en la Historia de México* (Mexico City: Colegio de México, 1979): 533-564. An examination of landholding, 1917-23, in the Natívitas valley, a prosperous farming zone politically transitional between the Zapatistas and the Constitutionalists. Both parties had had to accept peasant seizures of land after the Revolution in 1910: the problem for the peasants, recounted here in detail for two large haciendas, was to retain it. The former owners, if weak politically, were strong financially; the peasants were well mobilized but needed government support to operate a complicated system to insure their rights; and the government, subject to varying pressure, was weak but accepted seizure as the only road to pacification. Commentaries, pp. 599-601; 70 notes.
J. P. H. Myers

722. Buve, Raymond Th. J. PEASANT MOVEMENTS, CAUDILLOS AND LAND REFORM DURING THE REVOLUTION (1910-1917) IN TLAXCALA, MEXICO. *Bol. de Estudios Latinoamericanos y del Caribe [Netherlands] 1975 (18): 112-152.* A study of the changing social conditions in Tlaxcala, Mexico, 1910-17, demonstrates that the peasants of Tlaxcala were in a "takeoff position," in the process of becoming a modern, industrial society.
J. B. Reed

723. Camp, Roderic Ai. LA CAMPAÑA PRESIDENCIAL DE 1929 Y EL LIDERAZGO POLÍTICO EN MÉXICO [The presidential campaign of 1929 and political leadership in Mexico]. *Hist. Mexicana [Mexico] 1977 27(2): 231-259.* The presidential campaign of 1929 in which José Vasconcelos, former Secretary of Public Education, unsuccessfully challenged Pascual Ortiz Rubio, the candidate of the National Revolutionary Party, profoundly influenced Mexican political life. Loyalties formed while campaigning for Vasconcelos catalyzed a generation of political activists and linked future presidents Miguel Alemán and Adolfo López Mateos to their supporters. The victory of the official National Revolutionary Party over its first serious opposition permitted it to establish the precedent of rapidly reintegrating talented opponents into its own ranks. Finally, the failure of Vasconcelos's hastily organized opposition movement convinced his most obstinate backers to establish postrevolutionary Mexico's first permanent opposition parties. Based on memoirs, biographies, and secondary sources; 32 notes.
F. J. Shaw

724. Cardoso, Lawrence A. LA REPATRIACÍON DE BRACEROS EN ÉPOCA DE OBREGÓN—1920-1923 [The repatriation of laborers in the epoch of Obregón, 1920-23]. *Hist. Mexicana [Mexico] 1977 26(4); 576-595.* A grave problem was faced by the Alvaro Obregón administration when 100,000 Mexicans lost their jobs in the United States during the depression following World War I. The government attempted to help and to avoid a similar event by discouraging emigration, but the events of the 1930's highlighted the failure of these plans. Based on Obregón's presidential papers, and American and Mexican archives; 39 notes.
S. P. Carr

725. Cardoso, Lawrence A. LABOR EMIGRATION TO THE SOUTHWEST, 1916 TO 1920: MEXICAN ATTITUDES AND POLICY. *Southwestern Hist. Q. 1976 79(4): 400-416.* The Mexican government of Venustiano Carranza tried in vain to slow or at least regulate the flow of laborers to the US, 1916-20. Terrible economic conditions in Mexico and the need for labor in the Southwest kept the emigration going. With the support of most Mexicans, the Carranza government used propaganda and administrative controls to discourage the labor flow, and also tried to protect Mexican workers from mistreatment in the US. They had little success with any of these policies. Based on primary sources; 35 notes.
J. H. Broussard

726. Cardoso, Lawrence A. PROTESTANT MISSIONARIES AND THE MEXICAN: AN ENVIRONMENTALIST IMAGE OF CULTURAL DIFFERENCES. *New Scholar 1978 7(1-2): 223-236.* Examines the position of Protestant missionaries in Mexico and the southwestern United States, 1867-1930, and considers their belief that

Anglo Saxon Americans had nothing to fear from Mexicans, and that Mexicans could become upstanding citizens of the United States. They hoped that Mexico's evolution would benefit greatly from the contact brought about by northward immigration. Also analyzes the aftermath of the 1910 Mexican revolution, such as the strong impetus given to morality and justice, the flight of Mexico's lower classes to the United States, 1914-30, and female emancipation in 1917. Secondary sources; 27 notes.

G. L. Neville

727. Carr, Barry; Meyer, Jean; and Matute, Álvaro, commentaries. THE *CASA DEL OBRERO MUNDIAL*, CONSTITUTIONALISM AND THE PACT OF FEBRUARY 1915. Frost, Elsa Cecilia; Meyer, Michael C.; and Zoraida Vázquez, Josefina, ed. *El Trabajo y los Trabajadores en la Historia de México* (Mexico City: Colegio de México, 1979): 603-632. The Casa del Obrero Mundial began after the 1910 Revolution as an organization chiefly belonging to the skilled workers in Mexico City. Its aims were to propagate advanced ideas and replace the Mexican mutualist tradition with aggressive trade unions. Its leaders were divided over coming to terms with whichever government was in power, and it was finally crushed in the 1916 strike, having failed to recognize the dominant role the state intended to play and to attract support from unskilled workers or, more important, the peasants. Commentaries and notes, pp. 661-666. 83 notes.   J. P. H. Myers

728. Carr, Barry. LAS PECULIARIDADES DEL NORTE DEL MEXICO, 1880-1937: ENSAYO DE INTERPRETACIÓN [The peculiarities of northern Mexico, 1880-1937: an interpretative essay]. *Hist. Mexicana [Mexico] 1973 22(3): 320-346.* By the end of the 19th century the north had become one of the most politically important regions. It was the birthplace of Benito Pablo Juarez and Porfirio Díaz, and between 1913 and 1934 provided most of the revolutionary leaders. Places these leaders in the social, economic, and political context of the north. 47 notes.   S. P. Carr

729. Carr, Barry. RECENT REGIONAL STUDIES OF THE MEXICAN REVOLUTION. *Latin Am. Res. Rev. 1980 15(1): 3-14.* Regional studies help to disaggregate general truths and to show how political styles and policies developed. Recent studies reveal little change in resource distribution, the hegemony of the bourgeois in most revolutionary coalitions, and the maintenance of traditional forms of local control. Needs in future research include the economic level of human activity, study of how regions actually are defined, and a synthesis of regional and national levels within the perspective of the expansion of capitalism. 33 notes.   J. K. Pfabe

730. Castro, José Rivera. LE SYNDICALISME OFFICIEL ET LE SYNDICALISME RÉVOLUTIONNAIRE AU MEXIQUE DANS LES ANNÉES 1920 [Official trade unionism and revolutionary syndicalism in Mexico in the 1920's]. *Mouvement Social [France] 1978 103: 31-52.* Reflects on the two rival labor movements in Mexico in the 1920's. The Action group established a labor movement called the Confederación Regional Obrera Mexicana (CROM) and its political arm, the Labor Party. CROM and the army were the two pillars of the state. Simultaneously, anarcho-syndicalists and Communists organized an independent labor movement, the General Confederation of Labor (CGT). Though soon in conflict, they both found themselves in conflict with the state. Revolutionary and official unions struggles over the control of industrial disputes, especially in the petroleum, transport, and textile industries. The CGT stimulated strikes, whereas CROM tried to break them.   J/S

731. Clements, Kendrick A. EMISSARY FROM A REVOLUTION: LUIS CABRERA AND WOODROW WILSON. *Américas (Acad. of Am. Franciscan Hist.) 1979 35(3): 353-371.* Though Woodrow Wilson preferred Venustiano Carranza and the Constitutionalists in their struggle against the regime of Victoriano Huerta in Mexico, Carranza rejected his demand for guarantees of good behavior as a form of intervention. By sending the able Luis Cabrera to Washington as special agent, Carranza helped induce Wilson to relax the arms embargo on Mexico and otherwise favor the Constitutionalists without explicit concessions in return. On two subsequent occasions Cabrera served Mexico well as a representative in the United States. Based on American and British diplomatic records and Mexican published sources; 51 notes.   D. Bushnell

732. Córdova, Arnaldo de. EL MOVIMIENTO OBRERO MEXICANO EN LOS ALBORES DE LA CRISIS DE 1929 [The Mexican labor movement on the eve of the crisis of 1929]. *Estudios Pol. [Mexico] 1979 4(13-14): 69-96.* A description of the crisis experienced by the Mexican labor movement during the administration of President Emilio Portes Gil, 1928-30. Although Portes Gil was not hostile to organized labor, he desired unions firmly under state control. Attributing unruly labor relations to the absence of appropriate federal legislation, he attempted in 1928 to establish a labor code mandating compulsory arbitration in disputes. His initiative brought turmoil to the labor scene. Already in decline before 1928, the Confederación Regional Obrera Mexicana (CROM) found itself shattered by factionalism. Unable to prevent the armed rebellion of affiliate peasant organizations, the Communist Party earned the enmity of the government. Although the Confederación General de Trabajadores (CGT) benefited from the misfortunes of its rivals, it lacked the leadership and ideology to take advantage of the situation. Based on government reports, newspaper articles, and secondary sources; 72 notes.   F. J. Shaw, Jr.

733. Cox, Dwayne. RICHARD HENRY TIERNEY AND THE MEXICAN REVOLUTION, 1914-1917. *Mid-America 1977 59(2): 93-101.* Editor of the Jesuit weekly *America* from March 1914 to February 1925, Richard Henry Tierney campaigned against the anti-Catholic stance of the Mexican revolution during his first three years at this post. He especially opposed the leadership of Venustiano Carranza whom he saw as a threat to Catholicism everywhere. His crusade was carried out through editorials and speeches until the spring of 1917 when American entry into World War I became the major issue. Although he toiled actively on behalf of the Catholic Church in denouncing governmental practices in Mexico, he did little to influence American foreign policy in this direction. Based on archival and secondary material; 27 notes.
J. M. Lee

734. DeBaca, Vincent C. THE PEASANT MYSTIQUE OF THE MEXICAN REVOLUTION. *Aztlán 1981 12(2): 193-209.* Assesses the influence of the agrarian question on the Mexican Revolution of 1910. Earlier writers viewed the issues of land and labor as central to the revolution, but recent scholars have contended that no simple explanations suffice. As a highly regional country, Mexico experienced a revolution based on a multiplicity of factors. Subsequent agricultural policies have not solved Mexico's agrarian problems and have cast doubt on whether the revolution was fought by and for Mexico's peasants. Many Chicanos view the revolution of 1910 as a peasant revolution without examining all of the issues affecting Mexico in this period. Contemporary and secondary published works; 42 notes.   A. Hoffman

735. Deeds, Susan M. JOSE MARIA MAYTORENA AND THE MEXICAN REVOLUTION IN SONORA. *Arizona and the West 1976 18(2): 125-148.* Continued from a previous article. Counterrevolution in 1913 toppled the Madero government in Mexico. By 1915, Sonora governor José María Maytorena had suffered so many frustrations and losses of power that he resigned and went into exile. His moderate reforms had been nullified. Sonora was worse off economically than before his tenure in office. His long-range contribution, made unwittingly, was to the erosion of the privileges of the aristocracy. 7 illus., map, 54 notes.
D. L. Smith

736. Dennis, Philip A. THE ANTI-CHINESE CAMPAIGNS IN SONORA, MEXICO. *Ethnohistory 1979 26(1): 65-80.* Summarizes the history of the Chinese in Sonora, Mexico and describes the anti-Chinese campaigns and propaganda leading to their expulsion in 1931. While Chinese racial and cultural differences became focal symbols for hostility, this interethnic conflict masked an underlying class conflict. Anti-Chinese political propaganda intensified after many Mexicans returned to Mexico from the United States unable to acquire jobs there because of the Great Depression. In Sonora they discovered that the Chinese controlled jobs and wealth that they wanted. Discriminatory laws were passed, and in 1931 the Chinese were forced to liquidate their holdings and leave. It is easier to generate class conflict when cultural and racial differences separate the groups involved.   J

737. England, Juliet Kibbey, ed. EL ALAMO PREPARES FOR A SIEGE: THE DIARY OF W.[ILLIAM] BECKFORD KIBBEY, APRIL 15-MAY 4, 1929. *J. of Arizona Hist. 1979 20(1): 121-138.* An

excerpt from a diary by William Beckford Kibbey in which he sets forth his reactions and preparations against Mexican rebel forces led by General José Gonzalo Topete and Governor Fausto Topete of Sonora. Kibbey made his home near Magdalena, Sonora—El Alamo—into a minor fortress with fortified inner and outer gun placements. Employees were restricted in their movements. He was able to receive cattle and scout some rebel movements in the area. In the end, no one came, and his intricate plans for defense were never put to the test. 4 photos, notes.

K. E. Gilmont

738. Fleischmann, Ulrich. DER INTELLEKTUELLE UND DIE MEXIKANISCHE REVOLUTION-ÜBERLEGUNGEN ZUM ROMANWERK VON MARIANO AZUELA [The intellectual and reflections on the Mexican revolution in Mariano Azuela's novels]. *Jahrbuch für Geschichte von Staat, Wirtschaft und Gesellschaft Lateinamerikas [West Germany] 1978 15: 123-124.* From the literature of the 1930's, a national understanding developed of the events of the revolution. 30 notes.

T. D. Schoonover

739. Forster, Merlin H. US INTERVENTION IN MEXICO: THE 1914 OCCUPATION OF VERACRUZ. *Military Rev. 1977 57(8): 88-96.* Narrates the US military occupation of Veracruz, showing its successes and failures. The action was carried out with very few casualties and the occupation administration was extremely efficient. However, the disappointment of the high moral principles that sent Americans into Mexico should have prevented American military involvement in other areas. 4 illus., 18 notes.

D. J. Kommer

740. Fuentes Mares, José. LOS DIPLOMÁTICOS ESPAÑOLES ENTRE OBREGÓN Y EL MAXIMATO [Spanish diplomats between Obregón and the Maximato]. *Hist. Mexicana [Mexico] 1974 24(2): 206-229.* Spanish diplomats in the 1920's maneuvered to protect the interests of Spanish landowners faced with expropriation by Mexican agrarian reforms. They moved also to protect Spanish clergymen determined to maintain influence in the Mexican Church despite the revolution. The author describes diplomatic analysis of Mexican politics and gives a detailed account of Álvaro Obregón's (1880-1928) reelection, his political opposition, and the consequences of his assassination while president-elect. Gives accounts of anti-Spanish public opinion in Mexico and analyzes the position of the United States during the same period. 60 notes.

J. Perez

741. Furman, Necah S. VIDA NUEVA: A REFLECTION OF VILLISTA DIPLOMACY, 1914-1915. *New Mexico Hist. Rev. 1978 53(2): 171-192.* Traces the change from pro-American, anti-Carranza propaganda of Pancho Villa's newspaper, *Vida Nueva,* to its anti-American position of November 1915, a process reflecting Villa's rise and fall, 1914-15. In spite of the Tampico and Veracruz incidents, Villa and his newspaper voiced no criticism to the US occupation of Veracruz and opposed Venustiano Carranza's treatment of Americans as interventionists. Diplomatically weakened by military defeats, Villa and *Vida Nueva* attributed raids on the US southern borders to Carranza's forces, said to be seeking US recognition. Carranza won that recognition in October 1915, as well as an embargo on arms and munitions to Villa. A disillusioned Villa, who had respected and protected American interests and espoused American ideals, correctly predicted the revolution's continuance "according to . . . the bandido tactics of an earlier day." Based on memoirs, published American documents, *Vida Nueva,* and secondary sources; 68 notes.

S

742. Gilderhus, Mark T. DIPLOMATIC PERSPECTIVES: MEXICO, AN EARLY VOICE FROM THE THIRD WORLD. *Social Sci. J. 1978 15(2): 123-130.* Mexico's foreign policy in the period 1910-30's presaged current Third World distrust of great powers.

743. Gilderhus, Mark T. HENRY P. FLETCHER IN MEXICO, 1917-1920: AN AMBASSADOR'S RESPONSE TO REVOLUTION. *Rocky Mountain Social Sci. J. 1973 10(3): 61-70.*

744. Hall, Linda B. ÁLVARO OBREGÓN Y EL PARTIDO ÚNICO MEXICANO [Álvaro Obregón and the Mexican single party]. *Hist. Mexicana [Mexico] 1980 29(4): 602-622.* Although Álvaro Obregón was one of Venustiano Carranza's leading generals in the struggle against Victoriano Huerta, he found himself a powerless bystander in the struggle

between the Villa-Zapata and Carranza factions during the 1914 Convention of Aguascalientes. Lacking a political organization of his own, he created one that attracted both workers and peasants, who also filled the ranks of his army. At the same time he created a formal organization within which his lieutenants could determine policy for postrevolutionary reconstruction. The two structures, the mass political party and the elite policymaking apparatus, formed the original structure of modern Mexico's single political party, the Institutional Revolutionary Party. Based on primary sources located in the Archivo de Amado Aguire and the Archivo del Departamento de Telégrafos in Mexico City and secondary works; 53 notes.

F. J. Shaw, Jr.

745. Hall, Linda B. ALVARO OBREGÓN AND THE POLITICS OF MEXICAN LAND REFORM, 1920-1924. *Hispanic Am. Hist. Rev. 1980 60(2): 213-238.* Álvaro Obregón was known as an agrarian reformer before becoming president of Mexico in December 1920. During the next four years, he brought land distribution largely under his control, using it partly to reward or to gain political supporters. Land was taken from large landholders, including some companies with US investors, such as the Corralitos Company. The patterns of land distribution in Durango, Chihuahua, and Puebla are discussed. Based on records of the Comisión Nacional Agraria, Archivo de la Secretaría de la Reforma Agraria; US Department of State Archives, Internal Affairs of Mexico; letters in the Archivo General de la Nación, México; and other primary sources; 4 tables, 53 notes.

B. D. Johnson

746. Hall, Linda B. THE MEXICAN REVOLUTION AND THE CRISIS IN NACO: 1914-1915. *J. of the West 1977 16(4): 27-35.* There was much fighting between the Villista and the Maytorena forces for the control of Naco, Sonora. Citizens of Naco, Arizona were outraged over the effects of this fighting on the US side of the border. Several Americans were killed by stray bullets and there was much property damage. President Wilson tried to avoid intervention. José María Maytorena and the Villistas were finally driven from Sonora by Alvaro Obregón in 1915.

R. Alvis

747. Hansis, Randall. THE POLITICAL STRATEGY OF MILITARY REFORM: ALVARO OBREGON AND REVOLUTIONARY MEXICO, 1920-1924. *Americas (Acad. of Am. Franciscan Hist.) 1979 36(2): 199-233.* As president of Mexico, 1920-24, Alvaro Obregón gave special attention to reorganizing the Mexican military. Technical modernization and professionalization were important parts of his program. However, in promoting reform of the officer corps, Obregón did not hesitate to sanction controlled graft as a means of assuring loyalty. He also shifted commands and employed continual vigilance to make sure that uprisings, when they occurred, were efficiently suppressed. By purging or executing many who did rebel he delivered to his successors a less troublesome military establishment. Based on US military and State Department records, presidential papers in the Archivo General de la Nación; 112 notes.

D. Bushnell

748. Harper, James W. THE EL PASO-JUÁREZ CONFERENCE OF 1916. *Arizona and the West 1978 20(3): 231-244.* Pancho Villa violated American territory and took American lives during his raid on Columbus, New Mexico, 9 March 1916. General John J. Pershing invaded Mexico several days later to capture the guerrilla leader. Public opinion on both sides of the border polarized and seriously restricted the diplomatic flexibility of the two governments. Although the May 1916 El Paso-Juárez Conference failed to resolve the questions raised by the invasions, it temporarily reduced border tension and gave the United States time to deal with a crisis that had developed with Germany over submarine warfare. 4 illus., 36 notes.

D. L. Smith

749. Harper, James W. HUGH LENOX SCOTT Y LA DIPLOMACIA DE LOS ESTADOS UNIDOS HACIA LA REVOLUCIÓN MEXICANA [Hugh Lenox Scott and the foreign policy of the United States toward the Mexican revolution]. *Hist. Mexicana [Mexico] 1978 27(3): 427-445.* The response of Woodrow Wilson to the Mexican revolution was the first chapter in the response of North American diplomacy to the nationalist revolutions of the 20th century. Through Hugh Lenox Scott, Wilson rejected full-scale direct intervention and sought to establish a reasonably efficient and friendly government in Mexico through support of Pancho Villa and his partisans. This objective was frustrated by Carranza's victory over Villa in central Mexico in 1915.

Recognizing the failure of indirect intervention, Scott still maintained a moderate position and opposed military intervention. Scott's rejection of military intervention in Mexican affairs belies usual claims that Wilson engaged in "idealistic imperialism."   F. J. Shaw, Jr.

750. Harris, Charles H., III and Sadler, Louis R. THE PLAN OF SAN DIEGO AND THE MEXICAN-UNITED STATES WAR CRISIS OF 1916: A REEXAMINATION. *Hispanic Am. Hist. Rev. 1978 58(3): 381-408.* The Plan of San Diego called for a Mexican-American rebellion and the establishment of an independent republic in the Southwest. Guerrilla raids on Anglos in South Texas followed, February 1915-July 1916. These were fomented by Mexican leader Venustiano Carranza (1859-1920) in a move first to force US recognition of his government and later to force the removal of American troops which had pursued raiders into Mexico. There is no solid evidence of German involvement in the plan. The plan resulted in a legacy of racial tension in South Texas. 100 notes.   B. D. Johnson

751. Harris, Charles I., III and Sadler, Louis R. WITZKE AFFAIR: GERMAN INTRIGUE ON THE MEXICAN BORDER, 1917-1918. *Military Rev. 1979 59(2): 36-50.* Relates the attempt of German intelligence agents to infiltrate the United States from Mexico in 1917. The attempt failed because two of the three agents actually worked for the Allies. Throughout the remainder of the war German agents in Mexico were too busy avoiding Allied counterintelligence operatives to contemplate penetrating the United States again. 41 notes.
E. C. Hopkins

752. Harrison, Benjamin T. CHANDLER ANDERSON AND BUSINESS INTERESTS IN MEXICO: 1913-1920: WHEN ECONOMIC INTERESTS FAILED TO ALTER U.S. FOREIGN POLICY. *Inter-American Econ. Affairs 1979 33(3): 3-23.* Chandler Anderson was an international attorney who represented business interests in Mexico during Wilson's presidency; Chandler failed to win Wilson's support in protecting American commercial interests 1913-20.

753. Hart, John M. THE URBAN WORKING CLASS AND THE MEXICAN REVOLUTION: THE CASE OF CASA DEL OBRERO MUNDIAL. *Hispanic Am. Hist. Rev. 1978 58 (1): 1-20.* The Mexican workers' organization Casa del Obrero Mundial grew to predominance, 1909-14, when it led a number of strikes. A brief alliance with the Constitutionalists against the Villistas and the Zapatistas ended by mid-1915. The general strike of 31 July-2 August 1916 was crushed by the Constitutionalist government, and the Casa was outlawed. 43 notes.
B. D. Johnson

754. Hernández Chávez, Alicia. LA DEFENSA DE LOS FINQUEROS EN CHIAPAS, 1914-1920 [The landowners' rising in Chiapas, 1914-20]. *Hist. Mexicana [Mexico] 1979 28(3): 335-369.* Describes the failure of the Mexican revolutionary government to suppress a landowners' rebellion in Chiapas between 1914 and 1920. Native Chiapans, regardless of economic and social class, viewed the revolutionary government and army, composed mainly of northerners, as foreign. Agrarian reform laws threatened economic well-being of migratory Indian laborers as well as landowners. Revolutionary anticlerical legislation offended all segments of a population that was devoutly Catholic. Formal resistance to government lasted until 1920, when Álvaro Obregón drove Venustiano Carranza from power. Adapting his pacification policy to regional needs, Obregón restored peace in Chiapas by guaranteeing the rights of property. Based on documents located in the Archivo de la Secretaría de Defensa Nacional in Mexico City and the National Archives in Washington, D.C., government reports, and secondary works; map, 5 tables, 59 notes.
F. J. Shaw

755. Herzog, Bodo. DIE ROLLE DES KLEINEN KREUZERS "DRESDEN" IN DEN MEXIKANISCHER WIRREN 1914 [The role of the light cruiser *Dresden* in the Mexican fracas, 1914]. *Marine Rundschau [West Germany] 1976 73(2): 75-85.* The Mexican revolution of 1913 found the *Dresden* refitting in Germany. Ordered to the Caribbean, it took part in the international action at Tampico and Veracruz, evacuating German and American civilians in face of Mexican mob action. The *Dresden* took the deposed dictator Victoriano Huerta (1854-1916) to Jamaica at the end of the operation. Primary and secondary sources; 4 illus., 37 notes.   K. W. Estes

756. Hindeman, E. James. ¿CONFUSIÓN O CONSPIRACIÓN? ESTADOS UNIDOS FRENTE A OBREGÓN [Confusion or conspiracy? The United States and Obregón]. *Hist. Mexicana [Mexico] 1975 25(2): 271-301.* Analyzes the conflicts, 1913-23, between Álvaro Obregón (1880-1928) and the United States. As an officer in the Mexican army and later president of the republic, Obregón met preconceived US ideas about his revolutionary past. Because these prejudices guided its policy, the United States failed to understand the Mexican revolution and refused to accept it. Based on Mexican department of state records relating to internal affairs; 79 notes.   S. P. Carr/S

757. Horn, James J. MEXICAN OIL DIPLOMACY AND THE LEGACY OF TEAPOT DOME. *West Georgia Coll. Studies in the Social Sci. 1978 17: 99-112.* Threats of military intervention in Mexico over enactment of legal provisions forbidding foreign ownership of lands, particularly oil land, died when public disclosure of the Teapot Dome Scandal made headlines, 1926-27.

758. Horn, James J. U. S. DIPLOMACY AND THE "SPECTER OF BOLSHEVISM" IN MEXICO (1924-1927). *Americas: A Q. Rev. of Inter-Am. Cultural Hist. (Acad. of Am. Franciscan Hist.) 1975 32(1): 31-45.* Discusses the US fear of Mexican Bolshevism, a manifestation of a strong "Mexico for Mexicans" movement which incorporated nationalism and a particular sovereignty consciousness, and contributed to the deterioration of diplomatic relations between Mexico and the United States.

759. Houston, Donald E. THE OKLAHOMA NATIONAL GUARD ON THE MEXICAN BORDER, 1916. *Chronicles of Oklahoma 1975-76 53(4): 447-462.* On 18 June 1916, President Woodrow Wilson ordered the entire National Guard to the Mexican border while General John Pershing pursued Pancho Villa deep inside Mexico. Oklahoma responded with enthusiasm as civic leaders and veterans offered their services. Oklahoma units served in south Texas and underwent training exercises, but saw only limited action against bandits. Withdrawn from border duty only a short time before US entry into World War I, the guardsmen had gained valuable experience which would aid them on the battlefields of Europe. Primary sources; 3 photos, map, 28 notes.
M. L. Tate

760. Hu-DeHart, Evelyn. IMMIGRANTS TO A DEVELOPING SOCIETY: THE CHINESE IN NORTHERN MEXICO, 1875-1932. *J. of Arizona Hist. 1980 21(3): 275-312.* Summarizes the success of Chinese immigrants to Northern Mexico, who came to dominate the intermediary farming and mercantile sections of the economy while generating virulent anti-Chinese legislation and riots among the resentful, nationalistic Mexican population. The Chinese were expelled in 1931. Based on Mexican and US primary and secondary sources; 9 illus., 54 notes.   G. O. Gagnon

761. Jacques, Leo M. HAVE QUICK MORE MONEY THAN MANDARINS: THE CHINESE IN SONORA. *J. of Arizona Hist. 1976 17(2): 201-218.* In its efforts to bring rapid economic development of the country in the 1890's, Mexico gave official encouragement to Chinese immigration in order to build up the labor force. In Sonora especially, contrary to Mexican expectations, the Chinese went into business, soon became prosperous, and gradually came to dominate small-scale mercantile activities. With their increase in numbers and growing influence in the state's economy, public opposition intensified, with anti-Chinese arguments stemming largely from racial and cultural antagonisms. They suffered violence during the revolution and increasing legal harassment. The antiforeign provisions of the constitution of 1917 encouraged intensification of the anti-Chinese campaign which soon spread to all Mexico, especially while the "Sonoran Dynasty" governed the country. The 1931 decree which expelled most of the Chinese from Sonora shook the state's already weakened economic structure. 4 illus., 35 notes.   D. L. Smith

762. Johnson, William Weber. MODERN MEXICO WAS FORMED IN THE CRUCIBLE OF REVOLUTION. *Smithsonian 1980 11(4): 31-41.* Relates the story of the Mexican Revolution and its main figures, Porfirio Díaz, Francisco Madero, Victoriano Huerta, Venustiano Carranza, Alvaro Obregón, Emiliano Zapata, and Pancho Villa. The fall of Díaz in 1911 led to nine years of fighting and bloody

scrambling for freedom and power. But the Constitution of 1917 was achieved, and led to the nationalization of oil in 1938 as well as an unorthodox brand of democracy in which the president personally chooses his successor.   D. J. Valiulis

763. Joseph, Gilbert M. THE FRAGILE REVOLUTION: CACIQUE POLITICS AND REVOLUTIONARY PROCESS IN YUCATÁN. *Latin Am. Res. Rev. 1980 15(1): 41-64.* An analysis of the rise and decline of Felipe Carrillo Puerto's socialist regime in Yucatán, 1922-24, must take into account the system of caciquism. Carrillo made agreements with many local bosses and used various forms of patronage to maintain their support for his government. In turn, local bosses performed numerous services for Carrillo. His precipitous fall from power was, in part, due to this structure because the caciques preferred to avoid using the popularly-based *ligas de resistencia.* Based on documents in the archives of the State of Yucatán, of Mexico, the U.S. National Archives, and local newspapers; table, 69 notes.   J. K. Pfabe

764. Katz, Friedrich. INNEN- UND AUSSENPOLITISCHE UR-SACHEN DES MEXIKANISCHEN REVOLUTIONSVERLAUFS [Domestic and foreign policy impact on the course of the Mexican revolution]. *Jahrbuch für Geschichte von Staat, Wirtschaft und Gesellschaft Lateinamerikas [West Germany] 1978 15: 95-101.* Despite the destruction of the Federal Army during the Mexican revolution, few social changes occurred, 1910-20. Nonetheless, the events of these years did influence the ultimate social revolution accomplished during the administration of Lázaro Cárdenas.   T. D. Schoonover/S

765. Katz, Friedrich. PANCHO VILLA AND THE ATTACK ON COLUMBUS, NEW MEXICO. *Am. Hist. Rev. 1978 83(1): 101-130.* Describes and analyzes the main causes for Pancho Villa's attack on Columbus, New Mexico in March 1916. Villa believed that a secret pact had been signed between Venustiano Carranza and Woodrow Wilson that would have converted Mexico into a US protectorate. While there is no evidence or probability that such a pact had been agreed upon, Villa's suspicions are not entirely groundless. A secret pact of this type had in fact been elaborated by the head of the Mexican Division of the US State Department, Leon Canova (acting without the knowledge or approval of the administration in Washington), US business interests, and Mexican conservatives, whose spokesman was Eduardo Iturbide, chief of police of Mexico City under Victoriano Huerta. Villa, hearing of this pact, assumed that it constituted official US policy and that Carranza had signed such a pact in return for US recognition. His attack on Columbus was aimed at breaking the de facto protectorate he believed the United States was exercising in Mexico. Based on US, Mexican, and European primary sources, including the recently declassified State Department papers.   A

766. Knight, Alan. THE MEXICAN REVOLUTION. *Hist. Today [Great Britain] 1980 30(May): 28-34.* Discusses the revolution in Mexico which began when the middle class, led by Francisco Madero, revolted against dictator Porfirio Diaz (1876-1911), and traces events related to the revolution until 1938.

767. Kunimoto, Iyo. MEKISHIKO KAKUMEI TO NIHON, 1916-1917-KARANSA SEIKEN NO TAINICHI SEISAKU [The Mexican Revolution and Japan, 1916-17: the Carranza government's policy toward Japan]. *Rekishigaku Kenkyū [Japan] 1978 (455): 15-27.* In view of worsening relations with the United States during the Mexican Revolution, the government of Venustiano Carranza sought Japan's friendship in order to obtain munitions and to check US intervention. Although the Japanese navy and private enterprise were in favor of this proposal, the Ministry of Foreign Affairs remained indifferent. Meanwhile, in the spring of 1917, relations between Mexico and the United States improved. 65 notes.   Y. Aoki/S

768. Lempérière, Annick. PANCHO VILLA, RÉVOLUTION-NAIRE OU BANDIT? [Pancho Villa, revolutionary or bandit?]. *Histoire [France] 1981 (34): 84-86.* Discusses how an ignorant peasant became a great revolutionary chief in Mexico.

769. Lerner, Victoria. LOS FUNDAMENTOS SOCIOECONÓM-ICOS DEL CACICAZGO EN EL MÉXICO POSTREOVOLU-CIONARIO: EL CASO DE SATURNINO CEDILLO

[Socioeconomic fundamentals of "Cacicazgo" in postrevolutionary Mexico: the case of Saturnino Cedillo]. *Hist. Mexicana [Mexico] 1980 29(3): 375-446.* Like many other revolutionary caciques Saturnino Cedillo, the cacique of San Luis Potosí, rose to power on a wave of widespread economic unrest. His nucleus of support, however, remained the poorer peasants, who were the first to join and the last to desert him. After 1920 Cedillo acted as an agent of modernization, rebuilding the local economy, constructing highways, putting down banditry, and reforming agriculture. As industry replaced agriculture as the dominant economic activity, the power of the central government grew, encroaching on Cedillo's authority. Based on documents in the Archivo General de la Nación, the Archivo de la Secretaría de Gobernación, the Archivo Histórico de la Secretaría de la Defensa Nacional, Archivo de la Secretaría de Reforma Agraria, and Archivo de Venustiano Carranza, all in Mexico City; 18 tables, 21 notes.   F. J. Shaw, Jr.

770. Mabry, Donald J. MEXICAN ANTICLERICS, BISHOPS, *CRISTEROS,* AND THE DEVOUT DURING THE 1920'S: A SCHOLARLY DEBATE. *J. of Church and State 1978 20(1): 81-92.* Examines Robert E. Quirk's "The Mexican Revolution and the Catholic Church, 1910-1929: An Ideological Study," (1950), Nicolás Larin's *Borba tzerkvi s gosudarstvom u Meksike* (1965), Alicia Olivera Sedano's *Aspectos del conflicto religioso de 1926 a 1929: sus antecedentes y consecuencias* (1966), David C. Bailey's *!Viva Cristo Rey! The Cristero Rebellion and the Church-State Conflict in Mexico* (1974), and Jean Meyer's three-volume study, *La Cristiada,* (1973-74) to determine the influence of nationality on the authors' perceptions of the 1917-29 conflict between the revolutionary government of Mexico and the Catholic Church. 16 notes.   E. E. Eminhizer

771. Machado, Manuel A., Jr. THE MEXICAN REVOLUTION AND THE DESTRUCTION OF THE MEXICAN CATTLE INDUS-TRY. *Southwestern Hist. Q. 1975 79(1): 120.* An analysis of the effects of the Mexican Revolution on the Mexican cattle industry. The assorted revolutionary groups perceived that cattle would serve both as food and as an exchange medium for acquiring weapons. The US government confused the situation further by regulating beef imports so as to favor one or another group. The Mexican government attempted to prevent shipments, for they served to arm its enemies. By 1923, the once-flourishing industry was in tatters. 61 notes.   V. L. Human

772. Macías, Anna. FELIPE CARRILLO PUERTO AND WOM-EN'S LIBERATION IN MEXICO. Lavrin, Asunción, ed. *Latin American Women* (London: Greenwood Press, 1978): 286-301. Felipe Carrillo Puerto, socialist governor of Yucatan, 1922-24, was the center of the Mexican women's liberation movement. His predecessor, Salvador Alvarado, had been a feminist advocate, implementing significant reforms in jobs, education, and political participation. Although not close friends, the two shared similar ideas on social and economic issues. Carrillo Puerto consolidated his predecessor's reforms and sought to free women from the Church, interest them in political affairs, and liberate them from their exclusive concern with domestic life. His radical views on marriage, divorce, and birth control, however, convinced conservatives that feminism was dangerous, causing Mexican feminists to disassociate themselves from him in 1923. Newspaper articles, other primary, and secondary sources; 73 notes.   S. Tomlinson-Brown

773. Macias, Anna. WOMEN AND THE MEXICAN REVOLU-TION, 1910-1920. *Americas (Acad. of Am. Franciscan Hist.) 1980 37(1): 53-82.* In the Mexican Revolution a significant number of women —especially schoolteachers—made their mark as precursors, propagandists, or other activists. President Venustiano Carranza's collaborator Hermila Galindo was just one of those who combined service to the revolutionary cause with campaigning for women's rights that brought few immediate accomplishments but catalyzed further efforts. Many more women served as *soldaderas* or "soldiers' women"; some were female soldiers. Also important was the role of women in opposition to the revolution, particularly its anticlerical aspects. Based on contemporary press accounts, oral history, and secondary sources; 134 notes.   D. Bushnell

774. McCright, Grady E. PERSHING'S AIRWAR IN MEXICO. *Aviation Q. 1979 5(4): 348-357.* The first US test of military aviation against a foreign power was with the use of eight fragile Jennys of the First

Aero Squadron in the punitive expedition led by General John J. Pershing against Pancho Villa of Mexico in 1916.

775. Meyer, Jean. GRANDES COMPAÑÍAS, EJÉRCITOS POPULARES, Y EL EJÉRCITO ESTATAL EN LA REVOLUCIÓN MEXICANA (1910-1930) [Big companies, popular armies, and the regular army in the Mexican revolution, 1910-30]. *Anuario de Estudios Americanos [Spain] 1974 31: 1005-1030.* The regular Mexican army of 1910 resembled that of the 19th century with enforced enlistment, archaic maneuvers, and widespread graft. Its real purpose was domestic control. With the outbreak of the revolution, this organization disintegrated; and with victory for the revolution assured, civilian soldiers of the people's armies disbanded while professional soldiers continued their service. Today, as under Díaz, the army guards the civilian populace. Its volunteers indicate reluctance to enter the service, and officers continue to find irregular profits. 28 notes.   T. B. Davis

776. Meyer, Jean; Meyran, Daniel; and Panabière, Louis. LES ACCULTUREURS: ANTIALCOOLISME, DEFANATISATION ET THEATRE AU MEXIQUE (1929-1930) [The culture makers: temperance, antifanaticism, and the theater in Mexico, 1929-30]. *Cahiers du Monde Hispanique et Luso-Brésilien [France] 1977 (28): 259-274.* From a 1930 theater review by George Cuesta, the authors recall the Mexican government's policy of using art, especially theater, to fight alcoholism and religious "fanaticism" among peasants and workers and instill in them the ideals of the revolution. On the other hand, they document the strong opposition of a group of intellectuals known as the *contemporaneos* to what they considered a belittling of art and of the Mexican people. That conflict between power and knowledge may have been, they feel, at the root of the estrangement between the Mexican government and the intellectual community. 39 notes.   L. Garon

777. Millard, George A. US ARMY LOGISTICS DURING THE MEXICAN PUNITIVE EXPEDITION OF 1916. *Military Rev. 1980 60(10): 58-68.* Describes the problems and experiences of the logistical support for the Mexican Punitive Expedition of 1916. Faced with the problems of long lines of support across foreign territory, the Quartermaster Corps learned of the advantages of trucks and planes over horses and mules and other lessons that would prove beneficial in the world war a year later. Based on reports by expedition leaders and secondary sources; 7 illus., map, 44 notes.   D. H. Cline

778. Mols, Manfred and Tobler, Hans Werner. MEXIKO: BILANZ EINER REVOLUTION. REVOLUTION UND NACHREVOLUTIONÄRE ENTWICKLUNG IM LICHTE DER HISTORISCHEN UND SOZIALWISSENSCHAFTLICHEN FORSCHUNG [Mexico: the balance-sheet of a revolution. Revolution and postrevolutionary development in light of historical and social science research]. *Jahrbuch für Geschichte von Staat, Wirtschaft und Gesellschaft Lateinamerikas [West Germany] 1975 12: 284-392.* Recently there has been an increasingly strong tendency to revise the traditional views of the Mexican revolution and postrevolutionary development. This trend has been reflected in the historical and social science fields. The need is for an extensive historiographical review which aims less at being a detailed survey of the scholarly literature than a discussion of the trends and directions of scholarly interest and research. Based on secondary sources; 288 notes.
T. D. Schoonover

779. Moreno, Daniel. NUESTRA TRADICIÓN JURÍDICA: EL PROGRAMA DEL PARTIDO LIBERAL Y LA CONSTITUCIÓN DE 1917 [Our juridical tradition: the program of the Liberal Party and the Constitution of 1917]. *Rev. de la Facultad de Derecho de México [Mexico] 1975 25(97-98): 273-276.* Discusses the influence of the Liberal Party program of 1906, and especially the influence of Ricardo Flores Magón, on the Mexican Constitution of 1917.

780. Moseley, Edward H. MYTH AND REALITY IN THE NOVEL OF THE MEXICAN REVOLUTION: A TOOL FOR THE HISTORIAN. *Secolas Ann. 1975 (6): 24-41.* Historians ought not to ignore novels dealing with the Mexican Revolution. Although they must be used with care, novels offer insights that cannot be obtained elsewhere. Primary and secondary sources; 84 notes.   J. Lewis

781. Mumme, Stephen P. THE BATTLE OF NACO: FACTIONALISM AND CONFLICT ON SONORA, 1914-15. *Arizona and the West 1979 21(2): 157-186.* In the fall of 1914, Sonora Governor José Maria Maytorena attacked revolutionist armies at Naco on the Arizona-Sonora border who were conspiring to unseat him. As hostilities developed into "an extended siege," American troops moved to the area to protect American citizens. An American mediator arranged a treaty to end the conflict which had stretched into 1915 and had become the longest battle of the Mexican Revolution. The treaty, however, only briefly postponed the use of force in Sonora, which finally decided the outcome of the revolution. 9 illus., map, 59 notes.   D. L. Smith

782. Muriá, José María. JOSÉ VASCONCELOS Y LA REVOLUCIÓN MEXICANA [José Vasconcelos and the Mexican revolution]. *Bol. Hist. [Venezuela] 1974 (35): 238-255.* The Mexican historian José Vasconcelos Calderón, noted particularly for *La raza cósmica* (1925) and *Breve historia de México* (1940), is a controversial figure in Mexico's history. Although his inconsistent attitudes and biased perspectives weaken the effectiveness of his writings, Vasconcelos's thought is typical of that of the first half of the 20th century. He charged the United States with attempting to obliterate all traces of Spain's influence in Spanish America. Exiled four times by the leaders of the Mexican revolution, all of whom he opposed except for Francisco Madero, Vasconcelos criticized their rigidity, persecution of the Church, and land reform. 51 notes.
G. Pizzimenti

783. Naylor, Thomas H. MASSACRE AT SAN PEDRO DE LA CUEVA: THE SIGNIFICANCE OF PANCHO VILLA'S SONORA CAMPAIGN. *Western Hist. Q. 1977 8(2): 124-150.* Francisco (Pancho) Villa attempted to reverse his sagging fortunes in late 1915 by invading Sonora, Mexico. During his retreat from the desertion-plagued Sonora campaign, he personally directed and carried out a massacre at the village of San Pedro de la Cueva. Villa's calamitous campaign made him more desperate and depraved. This helps to explain and understand his shooting of 17 American mining engineers at Santa Isabel, Chihuahua, and his surprise raid on Columbus, New Mexico, both in early 1916. 2 maps, 105 notes.   D. L. Smith

784. Nieto, Rafael. [DOCUMENTOS] [Documents]. *Bol. del Archivo General de la Nación [Mexico] 1981 5(3): 4-50.* Reprints nine documents by Mexican diplomat Rafael Nieto regarding the League of Nations, peace in Europe, the rise of Fascism in Italy, and the participation of Latin America in world affairs. Based on documents in the Archivo General de la Nación, Fondo Alvaro Obregón-Plutarco Elías Calles.   J. A. Lewis/S

785. Palacios, Guillermo. CALLES Y LA IDEA OFICIAL DE LA REVOLUCIÓN MEXICANA [Calles and the official idea of the Mexican Revolution]. *Hist. Mexicana [Mexico] 1973 22(3): 261-278.* One of the most notable themes of the constitutional period of Plutarco Elías Calles's (1877-1945) presidency was that the ideal of the will of the people to justify political actions fell into disuse and was replaced by the idea of revolution as the legitimizer of power. The revolution thereby became increasingly institutionalized within the ideological framework of Mexican politics. Based on speeches, reports, and programs of Mexican presidents, 1910-30.   S. P. Carr

786. Prévôt-Schapira, Marie-France. TRAVAILLEURS DU PÉTROLE ET POUVOIR SYNDICAL AU MEXIQUE [Oil workers and labor union power in Mexico]. *Cahiers des Amériques Latines [France] 1979 20: 65-94.* A study of labor union power in the Mexican economy and politics since 1935, centering on activities of local branches of the Oil Workers Union (STPRM) in the Coatzacoalcos-Minatitlán oil production zone. Examines the union's cooperation with the government's oil production company, Petróleos Mexicanos (Pemex) and its role in the hiring of workers, marshalling the Pemex labor force, and organizing its social and political control of Mexican oil production centers. Based in part on interviews with oil workers and Pemex staff; biblio., 2 appendixes, 70 notes.   G. P. Cleyet

787. Raby, David L. LOS PRINCIPIOS DE LA EDUCACÍON RURAL EN MÉXICO: EL CASO DE MICHOACÁN, 1915-1929 [The beginnings of rural education in Mexico: the case of Michoacán, 1915-29]. *Hist. Mexicana [Mexico] 1973 22(4): 553-581.* Before the Revo-

lution of 1910 and the creation of the secretariat of public education in 1921, there was a lack of education for the vast majority in rural Mexico. The author examines the impact of educational reform in Michoacán, and asserts that, despite the resistance of the clergy and the landlords, rural education became a powerful instrument of social and political change. Based on documents in the archive of the secretariat; 73 notes.

S. P. Carr

788. Redclift, Michael. AGRARIAN POPULISM IN MEXICO: THE "VIA CAMPESINA". *J. of Peasant Studies [Great Britain] 1980 7(4): 492-502.* Examines the main components of Mexican agrarian populism *(campesinismo)* and its attractions in the light of difficulties in Mexican agriculture since 1950. The *campesinistas* have incorporated aspects of Marxist analysis, but claim that peasant economy can be used as a basis for development and can coexist with capitalism for a protracted period. They look to the peasantry as a vehicle for rural development and claim that a proper understanding of peasant production will facilitate alternatives to present policies. There are various weaknesses in their analyses and the present government favors using oil money to finance food imports, leaving the peasant sector to stagnate. Based on populist writings; 2 notes.

D. J. Nicholls

789. Richardson, William. MAIAKOVSKII EN MÉXICO [Maiakovski in Mexico]. *Hist. Mexicana [Mexico] 1980 29(4): 623-639.* Visits to Mexico and the United States in 1925 left Soviet poet Vladimir Maiakovski with paradoxical impressions. Revolutionary Mexico, he believed, was a sham, hiding corruption, violent anarchy, and thieves posing as reformers. He admired the capitalist Unites States for its vigor, innovation, and commitment to industrialization. Based on Maiakovski's poetry, and secondary works; 48 notes.

F. J. Shaw, Jr.

790. Richmond, Douglas W. EL NACIONALISMO DE CARRANZA Y LOS CAMBIOS SOCIOECONÓMICOS—1915-1920 [Carranza's nationalism and socioeconomic changes: 1915-20]. *Hist. Mexicana [Mexico] 1976 26(1): 107-129.* Venustiano Carranza's power base was built on the urban workers and the progressive bourgeoisie. To maintain his position Carranza had to maintain good relations with these groups; so he laid the foundations for land reform, exercised strict central control on the banks, and attempted to control the national economy by reducing overseas interference. Carranza enjoyed a degree of support rare in Mexican history. 81 notes.

S. P. Carr

791. Richmond, Douglas W. FACTIONAL POLITICAL STRIFE IN COAHUILA, 1910-1920. *Hispanic Am. Hist. Rev. 1980 60(1): 49-68.* As governor of the northern Mexico state of Coahuila 1911-13, Venustiano Carranza effected political, fiscal, educational, and modest land reforms and expanded health services. Victoriano Huerta forced him from office. Huerta-appointed governors alienated all economic classes with tax centralization and educational policies. Pancho Villa succeeded Huerta, but the Villistas in Coahuila were plagued by inflation, currency problems, and a lack of food as a result of warfare. When Carranza assumed national power in September 1915, he appointed Gustavo Espinosa Mireles governor of Coahuila. Espinosa Mireles returned to Carranza's successful reform policies of 1911-13. Based partly on materials at the Archivo General del Estado de Coahuila, Saltillo, Mexico; 60 notes.

B. D. Johnson

792. Richmond, Douglas W. LA GUERRA DE TEXAS SE RENOVA: MEXICAN INSURRECTION AND CARRANCISTA AMBITIONS, 1900-1920. *Aztlán 1980 11(1): 1-32.* Traces efforts by the Mexican government, under the leadership of President Venustiano Carranza, to foment revolt among the Mexicans living in Texas. Since 1848 Mexicans, numerically the vast majority of the population of south Texas, had endured discrimination and exploitation. Prompted by American reluctance to give legitimacy to his movement and by anger over Anglo mistreatment of Texas Mexicans, Carranza supported the Plan of San Diego in 1915, an effort designed to recapture Texas for Mexico through a coalition of Mexicans, Negroes, and Indians. The scheme failed to attract widespread support, but for over a year Mexican raids over the border resulted in numerous outbreaks of violence and created political turmoil in south Texas. Tensions between Mexico and the United States increased with the Pershing Expedition to chase Pancho Villa in Mexico in 1916, and a point short of war was reached in 1919 as Texas conservatives advocated armed intervention in Mexico. As long as Carranza re-

mained in power, he continued to support revolutionary agitation in Texas. 94 notes.

A. Hoffman

793. Richmond, Douglas W. REGIONAL ASPECTS OF THE MEXICAN REVOLUTION. *New Scholar 1978 7(1-2): 297-304.* Reviews Héctor Aguilar Camín's *La Frontera Nómada: Sonora y la Revolución Mexicana* (1977), which considers Sonora and the Mexican Revolution, 1910-20. The book outlines the major events and discusses the leaders of the Mexican Revolution in Sonora. The work also examines the social structure, land ownership, urbanization, and the situation of the Indians, and relates these topics to political changes. The author criticizes Aguilar Camín for a short bibliography, weak organization of introductory and concluding chapters, and a lack of economic data, and also presents a general survey of Mexican local studies, 1969-78.

G. L. Neville

794. Rodríguez, Miguel. LOS TRANVIARIOS EN LOS AÑOS VEINTE: SUS LUCHAS E INCORPORACIÓN AL APARATO ESTATAL [The streetcar workers of the 1920's: their struggle and incorporation in the state apparatus]. *Estudios de Hist. Moderna y Contemporánea de México [Mexico] 1980 8: 127-178.* The streetcar workers of Mexico City, in spite of their small numbers, were able to play an important role in the nation's labor history because they were organized. In fact, their struggle during the 1920's illustrates certain characteristics of the labor movement of the time, the relations between workers and labor leaders, between labor unions, and between government, capital, and labor. The 1920's saw the first attempts to insert the working class into the state apparatus. Based on primary material in the State Archives of Mexico; 167 notes.

J. V. Coutinho

795. Roman, Richard. CHURCH-STATE RELATIONS AND THE MEXICAN CONSTITUTIONAL CONGRESS, 1916-1917. *J. of Church and State 1978 20(1): 73-88.* Considers the concern of the Constitutional Congress of 1916-17 with relations between church and state, and traces the roots of extreme and bitter anticlericalism in Mexico with emphasis on the period between 1910 and 1916. 21 notes.

E. E. Eminhizer

796. Roman, Richard. POLITICAL DEMOCRACY AND THE MEXICAN CONSTITUTIONALISTS: A RE-EXAMINATION. *Americas (Acad. of Am. Franciscan Hist.) 1977 34(1): 81-89.* Examination of the proceedings of the Mexican constitutional congress of 1916-17 reveals on the part of the Venustiano Carranza administration and many congressmen an elitist fear of "mass participation," although the constitutional text finally adopted did not include certain proposals that were advanced to lessen its democratic content. Published sources; 22 notes.

D. Bushnell

797. Rosas, Javier. UN ESTADO EN TRANSICION: EL CASO MEXICANO, 1905-1928 [A state in transition: the Mexican case, 1905-28]. *Estudios Pol. [Mexico] 1977 3(12): 61-74.* The Mexican Revolution did not destroy a conservative, capitalist state and replace it with a revolutionary one dominated by popular elements. Rather, it replaced a politically inflexible system with one that guaranteed political mobility through mandatory single-term presidencies. As a result, the revolution promoted the fundamental goals of the Diáz regime: upper middle-class political domination and a capitalistic economic system.

F. J. Shaw, Jr.

798. Ross, Stanley R. CHRONOLOGY AND PERIODIZATION OF THE MEXICAN REVOLUTION. *Texas Q. 1973 16(2): 7-21.* Reviews the periodization of Mexican history which facilitates management of data and provides hypotheses for interpreting the Mexican Revolution. Since divisions are artificial, one learns to study transitional periods which furnished watersheds for Mexico's self reorientation as during Manuel Avila Camacho's administration, 1940-46, when he linked Cardenas's agrarian revolution with the industrial revolution of Miguel Alemán. Secondary sources; 17 notes.

R. H. Tomlinson

799. Ross, Steve. ZAPATA AND THE REVOLT OF THE MORELOS "INDIANS." *Mankind 1975 5(1): 28-37.* Emiliano Zapata (1877?-1919) shared the views of his fellow Indian peasants in southern Mexico regarding the necessity for shared democratic civilian rule. His example fostered in the Mexican people a sense of pride and a desire to fulfill the

egalitarian aims of the Mexican Revolution. His own authority originated in a village council and he remained true to the aims of the people's revolution for land and bread in southern Mexico.   N. Lederer

800. Sanchez Noriaga, Maria de los Angeles. REFLEXIONES SOBRE EL MOVIMIENTO CRISTERO [Reflections on the Cristero Movement]. *Estudios Pol. [Mexico] 1977 3(12): 47-60.* The Cristero Movement, 1926-29, was a fundamental political crisis in the development of the Mexican capitalist state, during which the government redefined its interests and placed tight controls on the Catholic Church. At the end of the crisis, however, both church and state accepted a capitalist economic system that was the best guarantee of each other's existence. 38 notes.   F. J. Shaw, Jr.

801. Sandos, James A. PANCHO VILLA AND AMERICAN SECURITY: WOODROW WILSON'S MEXICAN DIPLOMACY RECONSIDERED. *J. of Latin Am. Studies [Great Britain] 1981 13(2): 293-311.* Against a background of border disturbances for which the US government considered Venustiano Carranza ultimately responsible, Pancho Villa raided New Mexico in early 1916. Woodrow Wilson sent John J. Pershing with troops to break up and disperse Villa's bands (accomplished by June 1916) and, indirectly, to force Carranza to secure the border. Carranza, under serious internal pressure from dissidents taxing his resources, managed to cope with Villa and secure the border by early 1917. As a result, Wilson ordered Pershing to withdraw. By allowing Carranza to arouse nationalism against the invasion, the punitive expedition had politically helped him, ultimately influencing 20th-century Mexican government. US and Mexican archives; 89 notes.   M. A. Burkholder

802. Sandos, James A. PROSTITUTION AND DRUGS: THE UNITED STATES ARMY ON THE MEXICAN-AMERICAN BORDER, 1916-1917. *Pacific Hist. Rev. 1980 49(4): 621-645.* General John J. Pershing, commander of the American Punitive Expedition into Mexico, reduced the number of venereal disease cases among his men at Columbus, New Mexico and in Mexico by regulating prostitution so as to maintain troop morale and prevent infection. The venereal disease rate in his command was lower than elsewhere in the army, where War Department policy of abolishing prostitution in the vicinity of army camps was practiced. The ban on drugs worked better in Pershing's command than elsewhere, because Pershing isolated his men from towns and civilians, provided other diversions, and regulated prostitution. Based on the John J. Pershing Papers, reports of the Punitive Expedition in the National Archives, and other primary sources; 103 notes.   R. N. Lokken

803. Schneiderová, Jindra. MEXICKÁ REVOLUCE 1910-1917 A JEJÍ VLIV NA SPOLEČENSKÉ A STÁTNÍ ZŘÍZENÍ V MEXIKU [The Mexican Revolution 1910-17 and its influence on social and state establishment in Mexico]. *Právněhistorické Studie [Czechoslovakia] 1981 24: 191-203.* The Mexican Revolution was basically socialist in nature, followed by land redistribution and attempts at breaking old feudal patterns of Mexican society. But the Mexican governments were unable to withstand the pressure from the United States to revert to strictly capitalist policies, which they resumed in the 1940's and 1950's. Only in the 1970's has there been an attempt at independent policy by Presidents Echeverria and López Portillo. 14 notes.   B. Reinfeld

804. Silva Herzog, Jesús. DURANTE LA PRESIDENCIA DEL GENERAL PLUTARCO ELIAS CALLES. SUCESOS QUE ES MENESTAR RECORDAR [During the presidency of Plutarco Elias Calles: events that need to be recorded]. *Memoria del Colegio Nac. [Mexico] 1978 8(4): 45-72.* Presents a number of events during the presidency of Calles in Mexico, 1924-28. Some of the topics covered include the creation of a national party, attempts to separate the military from politics, the separation of Church and state, relations with the United States, relations with other foreign countries, Calles and labor, Calles and the foreign oil interests, and the internal policies of Calles on various fronts.   J. D. Barnard

805. Smith, Peter H. LA POLÍTICA DENTRO DE LA REVOLUCIÓN: EL CONGRESO CONSTITUYENTE DE 1916-1917 [Politics inside the revolution: the constitutional convention, 1916-17]. *Hist. Mexicana [Mexico] 1973 22(3): 363-395.* Examines the social origins and the divisions separating the delegates to the constitutional convention, 1916-17. The convention was dominated by a well-educated social elite, the members of which were young and middle class. Political divisions between the moderates and the Jacobins conformed to regional demarcations with little relationship to social status. Map, 5 tables, graph, diagram, 2 appendixes, 39 notes.   S. P. Carr

806. Smith, Peter H. THE MEXICAN REVOLUTION AND THE TRANSFORMATION OF POLITICAL ELITES. *Bol. de Estudios Latinoamericanos y del Caribe [Netherlands] 1978 (25): 3-20.* After Mexico's violent mass revolution, 1910-20, its privileged middle class remained preeminent in national politics. Contrary to the official version of the revolution, lower-class political power increased relatively little. The most dynamic results of Mexico's mass revolution may have been a rapid transfer of power to a younger generation, a reduced upper-class political involvement, and a downward redistribution of power within the middle class. However, these political changes parallel similar trends in other capitalist countries and are partly attributable to such general economic developments as industrialization. Based on Mexican official statistics and secondary sources; 5 tables, 30 notes.   D. M. Cregier

807. Stein, Harry H. LINCOLN STEFFENS AND THE MEXICAN REVOLUTION. *Am. J. of Econ. and Sociol. 1975 34(2): 197-212.* Discusses the involvement of Lincoln Steffens (1866-1936) in Mexico's revolution and in Mexican-American relations, 1913-27, estimating the consequences of his journalism. Primary and secondary sources; 25 notes.   W. L. Marr

808. Su, Margo. EL TEATRO DE REVISTA [Revue theater]. *Rev. Mexicana de Ciencias Pol. y Sociales [Mexico] 1979 25(95-96): 123-133.* The stage review in Mexico is a form of social and political criticism that started with the revolution around 1910, when it became impossible to continue bringing in principally Spanish companies and there were few Mexican authors or plays to present. The need for entertainment was filled by review theater, where the role of the show and the comic became one of molding public opinion. With the appearance of the more respectable sound film and radio, theaters turned to Hollywood-style musical productions, seeking the approval of the middle class.

809. Tardanico, Richard. REVOLUTIONARY NATIONALISM AND STATE BUILDING IN MEXICO, 1917-1924. *Pol. & Soc. 1980 10(1): 59-86.* Examines the regimes of Venustiano Carranza and Álvaro Obregón using world system theory of state-making in peripheral countries. Both leaders were hampered by the legacies of Porfirio Díaz. Unlike Carranza, however, Obregón made some progress in building an independent national economy by opting for a short-term clientelistic strategy to attract necessary external capital. 95 notes.   D. G. Nielson

810. Tate, Michael L. PERSHING'S PUNITIVE EXPEDITION: PURSUER OF BANDITS OR PRESIDENTIAL PANACEA? *Americas: A Q. Rev. of Inter-Am. Cultural Hist. (Acad. of Am. Franciscan Hist.) 1975 32(1): 46-71.* Discusses Woodrow Wilson's decision for intervention in Mexico, 1916, as a reflection of his general foreign relations attitude toward all of Latin America and evaluates the resultant animosity between Mexico and the United States which sped nationalization of foreign petroleum interests in Mexico.

811. Taylor, William B. REVOLUTION AND TRADITION IN RURAL MEXICO. *Peasant Studies Newsletter 1976 5(4): 31-37.* Discusses recent historiography dealing with social organization of rural Mexico in the 20th century, emphasizing peasants' attitudes toward social change.

812. Tobler, Hans Werner EINIGE ASPEKTE DER GEWALT IN DER MEXIKANISCHEN REVOLUTION [Aspects of violence in the Mexican revolution]. *Jahrbuch für Geschichte von Staat, Wirtschaft und Gesellschaft Lateinamerikas [West Germany] 1978 15: 83-94.* The violence of Mexico's revolution destroyed the possibility of a return to Diaz's system, thereby permitting the division of governing power and of the social and economic structure. No fundamental change in the ruling and social structure occurred, however. Only Lázaro Cárdenas's rise to power prompted such changes. 21 notes.   T. D. Schoonover

813. Unc, Gheorghe. 1910-1917 MEXICUL ÎN REVOLUȚIE [Mexico in revolution, 1910-17]. *Magazin Istoric [Romania] 1976 10(4): 39-41.* Describes events in Mexico after the overthrow of the dictator Porfirio Díaz (1830-1915) especially as reflected in the Romanian press, up to the end of the civil war in 1917.

814. Vigil, Ralph H. REVOLUTION AND CONFUSION: THE PECULIAR CASE OF JOSÉ INÉS SALAZAR. *New Mexico Hist. Rev. 1978 53(2): 145-170.* Recounts the changeable political and military career of José Inés Salazar, a notorious figure in US-Mexican borderlands history during the course of the Mexican Revolution, 1910-17. Illus., 57 notes.

815. Werner, Joseph Richard. ESTÉBAN CANTÚ Y LA SOBERANÍA MEXICANA EN BAJA CALIFORNIA [Estéban Cantú and Mexican sovereignty in Baja California]. *Hist. Mexicana [Mexico] 1980 30(1): 1-32.* Estéban Cantú, military strongman of Baja California, 1914-20, did not betray Mexican sovereignty by his refusal to resist Pershing's 1915 invasion of Mexico. Isolated from central Mexico during the civil war, Cantú realized that resistance to Pershing might serve the United States as an excuse for Baja California's annexation. His much criticized involvement in prostitution and gambling provided his treasury with revenues to maintain an army and operate public services. Based on documents located in the National Archives in Washington, D.C. and secondary works; 117 notes. F. J. Shaw, Jr.

816. White, E. Bruce. THE MUDDIED WATERS OF COLUMBUS, NEW MEXICO. *Americas: A Q. Rev. of Inter-Am. Cultural Hist. (Acad. of Am. Franciscan Hist.) 1975 32(1): 72-98.* Discusses the events, 1913-16, leading up to Pancho Villa's attack on Columbus, New Mexico, 9 March 1916.

817. Womack, John Jr. THE MEXICAN ECONOMY DURING THE REVOLUTION, 1910-1920: HISTORIOGRAPHY AND ANALYSIS. *Marxist Perspectives 1978 1(4): 80-123.* Provides economic answers, as opposed to positivistic interpretations, for the meaning and success of the Mexican Revolution, 1910-20.

818. Zilinskas, Raymond. JAPANESE AT TURTLE BAY, LOWER CALIFORNIA, 1915. *Southern California Q. 1978 60(1): 45-58.* Analyzes the reasons for the Japanese naval presence at Turtle Bay, Baja California (400 miles south of San Diego), in 1915. Stories circulated, especially by the Los Angeles *Times,* to the effect that Japan was forming an alliance with Mexico and that Turtle Bay was being occupied and colonized as part of a grand Japanese military-political strategy. The ostensible reason for Japan's presence at the bay was the salvaging of the cruiser *Asama,* which had run aground. War scare stories notwithstanding, the *Asama* did need extensive repairs requiring the assistance of other vessels and many men. Primary and secondary sources; diagram, 30 notes. A. Hoffman

819. —. ASUNTOS DE POLÍTICA INTERNA, 1923-1930 [Domestic policy, 1923-30]. *Bol. del Archivo General de la Nación [Mexico] 1979 3(4): 36-49.* A series of 10 documents concerning Mexico's internal affairs from 1923 to 1930. Taken from the Archivo Plutarco Elías Calles at the National Archives of Mexico; 4 photos. J. A. Lewis

820. —. CANDIDATURA PRESIDENCIAL, 1923 [Presidential candidacy, 1923]. *Bol. del Archivo General de la Nación [Mexico] 1979 3(4): 32-35.* Reprint of eight documents concerning Plutarco Elías Calles's candidacy for the presidency of Mexico in 1924. Taken from the Archivo Plutarco Elías Calles at the National Archives of Mexico; photo. J. A. Lewis

821. —. CHURCH AND STATE RELATIONS IN MEXICO. *Pro. of South Carolina Hist. Assoc. 1981: 79-97.*
Ferrell, William R., III CHURCH AND STATE RELATIONS IN MEXICO FROM 1910 TO 1940, *pp. 79-95.* Analyzes the relationship between the Catholic Church and the Mexican government between 1910 and 1940. Overestimating its influence, the Church formed a Catholic Party to protect its interests in 1910, which forced the Mexican government to take action against the Church and eliminate religious education in the public and even private schools. "Learning a painful lesson, therefore, the church began to march in unison with the government. That sharing of common goals with the church in a conspicuously subordinate role to the government has been one of the lasting legacies of the turbulent years from 1910 to 1940." Primarily secondary sources; 37 notes.
Harris, William L. COMMENTARY, *pp. 96-97.* Criticizes the above article and suggests that a broader perspective and consideration of liberalism, anticlericalism, and positivism would have improved it. J. W. Thackery, Jr.

822. —. DOCUMENTOS SOBRE LA CUESTIÓN PETROLERA, 1919-1933 [Documents on the oil problem, 1919-33]. *Bol. del Archivo General de la Nación [Mexico] 1979 3(4): 60-66.* Seven documents concerning the ownership of oil in Mexico from 1919 to 1933. Taken from the Archivo Plutarco Elías Calles at the National Archives of Mexico. J. A. Lewis

823. —. EL PACTO DE LA CASA DEL OBRERO MUNDIAL [The agreement with the Casa del Obrero Mundial]. *Bol. del Archivo General de la Nación [Mexico] 1981 5(1): 9-12.* Reprints eight documents concerning the agreement signed between the Casa del Obrero Mundial and Venustiano Carranza's government in 1915. Documents located in the Archivo General de la Nación; 2 photos. J. A. Lewis

824. —. INSTITUCIONES, 1929-1933 [Institutions, 1929-33]. *Bol. del Archivo General de la Nación [Mexico] 1979 3(4): 67-72.* Six documents concerning domestic organizations such as the Regional Confederation of Mexican Labor (CROM), the national labor union, and the National Revolutionary Party (PNR), the political party of the revolution. Taken from the Archivo Plutarco Elías Calles at the National Archives of Mexico; photo, foldout. J. A. Lewis

825. —. LA CASA DEL OBRERO MUNDIAL, LOS SINDICATOS Y EL DEPARTAMENTO DEL TRABAJO [The Casa del Obrero Mundial, the unions, and the Department of Labor]. *Bol. del Archivo General de la Nación [Mexico] 1981 5(1): 46-49.* Reprints five documents showing the occasional cooperation between the Mexican Department of Labor and the Casa del Obrero Mundial in spite of the latter's anarchosyndicalist ideology. From the Fondo Departamento del Trabajo at the Archivo General de la Nación; photo. J. A. Lewis

826. —. LA CASA DEL OBRERO MUNDIAL Y LAS AGRUPACIONES DE RESISTENCIA [The Casa del Obrero Mundial and resistance organizations]. *Bol. del Archivo General de la Nación [Mexico] 1981 5(1): 26-27.* Reprints three documents showing the hostility between the anarchosyndicalist Casa del Obrero Mundial and their labor opponents organized by the government of Mexico. Based on material in the Fondo Departamento del Trabajo in the Archivo General de la Nación. J. A. Lewis

827. —. LA CASA DEL OBRERO MUNDIAL Y El MOVIMIENTO ZAPATISTA [The Casa del Obrero Mundial and the Zapatista movement]. *Bol. del Archivo General de la Nación [Mexico] 1981 5(1): 7-8.* Reprints three letters to and from Emiliano Zapata demonstrating the connection between the Casa del Obrero Mundial and the Zapatista movement in Mexico. Based on material in the Fondo Correspondencia Emiliano Zapata at the Archivo General de la Nación; photo. J. A. Lewis

828. —. LAS AGRUPACIONES DE RESISTENCIA Y EL DEPARTAMENTO DEL TRABAJO [Resistance groups and the Department of Labor]. *Bol. del Archivo General de la Nación [Mexico] 1981 5(1): 19-25.* Reprints 10 documents concerning union groups organized by the government to resist the efforts of the Casa del Obrero Mundial. Documents from the Fondo Departamento del Trabajo at the Archivo General de la Nación; photo. J. A. Lewis

829. —. PLUTARCO ELÍAS CALLES DATOS PERSONALES [Plutarco Elías Calles: personal information]. *Bol. del Archivo General de la Nación [Mexico] 1979 3(4): 4-8.* Reprint of three documents concerning the life of Plutarco Elías Calles, president of Mexico from 1924 to 1928. From the Archivo Plutarco Elías Calles at the National Archives of Mexico; 4 photos. J. A. Lewis

830. —. SOBRE LA REBELIÓN ESCOBARISTA, EL EJÉRCITO Y LA SITUACIÓN POLÍTICA DEL PAIS [Concerning the Escobarista Rebellion, the Army, and the political situation of the country]. *Bol. del Archivo General de la Nación [Mexico] 1979 3(4): 73-76.* A report by General Plutarco Elías Calles after the Escobarista Rebellion of March 1929. Taken from the Archivo Plutarco Elías Calles at the National Archives of Mexico; 2 photos. J. A. Lewis

831. —. SOBRE LA REBELIÓN DELAHUERTISTA, 1923-1926 [Concerning Adolfo de la Huerta's rebellion, 1923-26]. *Bol. del Archivo General de la Nación [Mexico] 1979 3(5): 9-31.* A series of 14 documents concerning the uprising of Adolfo de la Huerta in Mexico in 1923-24. From the Archivo Plutarco Elías Calles at the National Archives of Mexico; 8 photos. J. A. Lewis

The Cárdenas Era, 1934-1940

832. Aoki, Yoshio. MEKISHIKO NO JŪZOKUTEKI KŌGYŌKA TO KARUDENASU [Lázaro Cárdenas and dependent industrialization in Mexico]. *Rekishigaku Kenkyū [Japan] 1979 (466): 23-31.* Analyzes Cárdenas's failure to achieve endogenous industrialization in Mexico through nationalization of the oil industry and redistributions of agricultural land and describes Mexico's consequent dependence on US industry since 1950. Examines early business difficulties of Petróleos Mexicanos (PEMEX), established in 1938, the retreat on land reform due to the diplomatic concern and financial deadlock, and cooperation with the United States in World War II. Based on primary sources including the diplomatic papers of the US Department of State, letters of Cárdenas; 69 notes. Y. Aoki

833. Britton, John A. URBAN EDUCATION AND SOCIAL CHANGE IN THE MEXICAN REVOLUTION, 1931-40. *J. of Latin Am. Studies [Great Britain] 1973 5(2): 233-245.* Illustrates the shift in the Mexican revolution from the *campo* to the city and industrialization in the activities of the Ministry of Education. Four successive ministers and their associates challenged the National University, the Catholic school system, and public secondary schools. They suggested that public institutions should no longer copy the traditional liberal arts curriculum. They created a three-stage technical school system, culminating in the university level *Instituto Politécnico Nacional.* They increased the number of public and urban secondary schools and gradually assumed control over many private secondary schools. Finally, they attempted but failed to create a complete and separate system of education for urban working-class children. Marxism was the intellectual rationalization for all four ministers, who "wanted to use urban education to improve the condition of the lower classes and, at the same time, counter the influence" of traditional, elitist, conservative values. Based on ministers' *Memorias* in the Secretaría de Educación Pública, newspapers, and secondary works; 42 notes. K. M. Bailor

834. Buve, Raymond. POLITICAS LOCALES: EL CASA DE TLAXCALA [Local politics: the case of Tlaxcala]. *Rev. Française d'Hist. d'Outre-mer [France] 1979 66(3-4): 357-375.* A case study of a central Mexican state, showing how a group of local politicians came to control the electoral power and the organization of the landless peasants who had benefited from agrarian reform in the 1930's. Condenses a larger study published in English in the *Jahrbuch für die Geschichte von Staat, Wirtschaft und Gesellschaft Lateinamerikas* 1980. Biblio. D. G. Law

835. Falcón, Romana. EL SURGIMIENTO DEL AGRARISMO CARDENISTA—UNA REVISIÓN DE LAS TESIS POPULISTAS [The rise of Cardenas agrarianism: a revision of the populist thesis]. *Hist. Mexicana [Mexico] 1978 27(3): 333-386.* Challenges the traditional thesis that the agrarian populism of President Lázaro Cárdenas (1936-1940) represented an abrupt break with the policy of preceding regimes. Prior to the Cardenas administration, the National Peasants Confederation, an organ of the official National Revolutionary Party, adopted a policy of moderate agrarianism and abolished laws limiting redistribution of land. Cardenas's own agrarianism was a far more moderate version of that practiced in the states of Veracruz, Morelos, and Michoacan, 1928-32. Working within existing institutions and the law, this moderate agrarian-

ism became Cardenas's weapon to wrest control of the official party from followers of Plutarco Elias Calles. Reflecting a power struggle within the established political elite, this agrarianism never threatened existing political institutions. Based on secondary sources and documents in the Historical Archive of the Secretary of National Defense and the Archive of the Secretary of Agrarian Reform in Mexico, the National Archives, Washington, and the Public Records Office, London; 94 notes. F. J. Shaw, Jr.

836. Hamilton, Nora. MEXICO: THE LIMITS OF STATE AUTONOMY. *Latin Am. Perspectives 1975 2(2): 81-108.* Analyzes attempts by the Lázaro Cárdenas administration, 1934-40, to implement revolutionary concepts of the autonomous state. Irreconcilable contradictions within the theory resulted in changes in class-state relations and ended by favoring the dominant social classes.

837. Horváth, Gyula. A MEXIKÓI MUNKÁSMOZGALOM ÉS A NÉPFRONTPOLITIKA (1935-1938) [The Mexican labor movement and popular front policies, 1935-38]. *Párttörténeti Közlemények [Hungary] 1981 27(4): 117-154.* The Communist Party of Mexico was founded in 1919 and outlawed between 1929 and 1935. Its membership was 1,010 in 1933. Inspired by the Comintern and misunderstanding the Mexican political situation, the Party aimed at the establishment of a Soviet Mexico. From 1935 the Communists worked for a popular front against fascism and imperialism. Noncommunist left-wing elements formed their own popular front. The Communist Party attempted to penetrate this organization, but sectarian struggle within Communist ranks greatly hindered labor unity and Communist influence within the popular front. Based on secondary sources; 106 notes. Russian and French summaries. P. I. Hidas

838. León, Samuel. ALIANZA DE CLASE Y CÁRDENISMO (JUNIO DE 1935-FEBRERO DE 1936) [Class alliance and Cárdenism, June 1935-February 1936]. *Rev. Mexicana de Ciencias Pol. y Sociales [Mexico] 1977 23(89): 25-76.* Examines the unification of the Mexican working class and its alliance with the Cárdenist faction. Also analyzes the principals of Cárdenism and the implementation of Cárdenist policies.

839. Lerner, Victoria. EL REFORMISMO DE LA DÉCADA DE 1930 EN MÉXICO [Reformism in the 1930's in Mexico]. *Hist. Mexicana [Mexico] 1976 26(2): 188-215.* The reformism of the 1930's reflects the growing importance of the middle and petite bourgeoisie who confronted the bigger national and international capitalists. As they acquired economic preeminence they also obtained political importance by pursuing economic reform. They were opposed by strong groups and hampered by the 1937 crisis of inflation and strikes. 2 tables, 45 notes. S. P. Carr

840. Levenstein, Harvey. LENINISTS UNDONE BY LENINISM: COMMUNISM AND UNIONISM IN THE UNITED STATES AND MEXICO, 1935-1939. *Labor Hist. 1981 22(2): 237-261.* The Communist Party in the United States and Mexico during the Popular Front period (1935-39) encouraged its members to cooperate with other leftists and moderates in the organizing of workers in the two countries. The Party's leadership, however, actively discouraged Communists from gaining and maintaining powerful positions in such United States unions as the United Steelworkers and United Auto Workers and the Confederación de Trabajadores Mexicanos in Mexico. The restraint preached by the Party leadership so weakened the Party's position in union activities as to facilitate a purge of all Communists from these unions in the 1940's. Based on the Earl Browder Papers and other primary sources; 44 notes. L. F. Velicer

841. Marván, Ignacio. EL FRENTE POPULAR EN MÉXICO DURANTE EL CARDENISMO [The Popular Front in Mexico during the Cardenist period]. *Rev. Mexicana de Ciencias Pol. y Sociales [Mexico] 1977 23(89): 9-23.* Analyzes the politics of the Popular Front and the progressive integration of the interests of the government and the government party.

842. Mújica Vélez, Rubén. CAPITALISMO Y REFORMA AGRARIA: LA COMARCA LAGUNERA [Capitalism and agricultural reform: the Laguna region]. *Investigación Econ. [Mexico] 1973 32(128): 763-773.* Refers to the 1936 reapportionment of a vast agricul-

tural area of the Laguna district by Lázaro Cárdenas and highlights the relationships between the natural, historical, social, and economic factors that shaped the economic development of the region.

843. Raby, David and North, Lisa. LA DINÁMICA DE LA REVOLUCIÓN Y LA CONTRARREVOLUCIÓN: MÉXICO BAJO CÁRDENAS, 1934-1940 [The dynamic of revolution and counterrevolution: Mexico under Lázaro Cárdenas, 1934-40]. *Estudios Pol. [Mexico] 1978 4(16): 9-61.* Challenges standard liberal and Marxist interpretations of the Cárdenas regime in Mexico, 1934-40. The middle-class leadership of the Cárdenista movement did not manipulate its working-class membership. Mexico under Cárdenas struggled to achieve economic independence, and Cárdenas launched a series of radical reforms which established the basis of modern Mexican capitalism, but institutionalized the political power of the urban laborer and peasant. Although a new hierarchy of inequalities existed by 1940, Cárdenas's reforms had achieved a profound transformation of Mexican society. Secondary sources; 116 notes, biblio.   F. J. Shaw, Jr./S

844. Roman, Richard. RAILROAD NATIONALIZATION AND THE FORMATION OF ADMINISTRACION OBRERA IN MEXICO, 1937-1938. *Inter-American Econ. Affairs 1981 35(3): 3-22.* Discusses the nationalization of the railroads of Mexico and the creation of a workers' administration to run them, as part of the efforts of President Lázaro Cárdenas to foster national capital development and to ameliorate the conditions of the working class and peasantry during the Depression.

845. Ross, Delmer G. THE WORKERS' ADMINISTRATION OF THE NATIONAL RAILWAYS OF MEXICO. *R. Interamericana [Puerto Rico] 1973 2(4): 587-596.* Because of labor support for his government, President Lázaro Cárdenas turned over control of the nationalized railroads to their employees in 1938. By 1940 worker administration had proven inefficient and responsible for numerous accidents. As a result, the government assumed direct control of the industry. The experience with the railroads influenced the government not to try worker administration of other nationalized industries. Based on primary and secondary works; 23 notes.   J. Lewis

846. Rühle-Gerstel, Alice; Underwood, J. A., transl. NO VERSES FOR TROTSKY: A DIARY IN MEXICO (1937). *Encounter [Great Britain] 1982 58(4): 26-41.* A 1937 memoir relating the relationship between Alice Rühle-Gerstel and her husband Otto, who had taken refuge in Mexico in the 1930's, and Leon Trotsky, who was granted asylum in Mexico in 1936 by the Cárdenas government and who became their friend and comrade.

847. Williman, John B. ADALBERTO TEJEDA AND THE THIRD PHASE OF THE ANTI-CLERICAL CONFLICT IN TWENTIETH CENTURY MEXICO. *J. of Church and State 1973 15(3): 437-454.* Discusses the conflict between church and state in the 1930's and Governor Adalberto Tejeda's law limiting the number of Catholic priests.   S

848. Zavala Echavarría, Iván. EL ESTADO Y EL MOVIMIENTO OBRERO MEXICANO DURANTE EL CARDENISMO [The state and the Mexican labor movement during the Cardenas era]. *Estudios Pol. [Mexico] 1978 3(9): 5-19.* A systematic model of the relationship between the Mexican government and the labor movement during the administration of Lázaro Cárdenas, 1936-40. Contrary to traditional interpretation, Cárdenas was neither an unequivocal foe of the Regional Confederation of Mexican Labor (CROM) nor an ardent ally of the Marxist Confederation of Mexican Workers (CTM). Presidential policy aimed at the creation of a strong centralized labor union and avoided direct confrontation with the CROM. The Cárdenas administration even sided with CROM during intraunion disputes with the larger CTM. Because of CROM's past political affiliations, conservative ideology, and notorious corruption, however, Cárdenas relegated it to second place in the Mexican labor movement. CROM wavered between conditional support and reserved criticism of the president. Cárdenas, on the other hand, favored the CTM because its Marxist ideology supported his economic nationalism and regulation of private enterprise. He limited its influence, however, by forbidding it to organize the peasantry or the bureaucracy and denying it direct access to government policymaking. Based on published government and union records, memoirs, and secondary sources; 160 notes.   F. J. Shaw

849. —. LA CASA DEL OBRERO MUNDIAL Y EL PRESIDENTE LÁZARO CÁRDENAS [The Casa del Obrero Mundial and President Lázaro Cárdenas]. *Bol. del Archivo General de la Nación [Mexico] 1981 5(1): 53.* Reprints a document showing the loyalty of surviving members of the anarchosyndicalist Casa del Obrero Mundial in the 1930's to Lázaro Cárdenas as president of Mexico. Based on material in the Fondo Lázaro Cárdenas in the Mexican National Archive.
                                                                         J. A. Lewis

The Institutional Revolution since 1940

850. Acevedo de Silva, María Guadalupe. CRISIS DEL DESARROLLISMO Y TRANSFORMACIÓN DEL APARATO ESTATAL: MÉXICO 1970-1975 [Crisis of development and transformation of the apparatus of state: Mexico, 1970-75]. *Rev. Mexicana de Ciencias Pol. y Soc. [Mexico] 1975 21(82): 133-163.* Examines the theory of economic growth and political stability and the growing congestion of government bureaucracies that have taken on a life of their own, 1970-75.

851. Alisky, Marvin. CONASUPO: A MEXICAN AGENCY WHICH MAKES LOW-INCOME WORKERS FEEL THEIR GOVERNMENT CARES. *Inter-Am. Econ. Affairs 1973 27(3): 47-59.*

852. Alvarez, Alejandro. DESARROLLO RECIENTE DEL MOVIMIENTO OBRERO EN MÉXICO [Recent development of the labor movement in Mexico]. *Investigación Econ. [Mexico] 1979 38(150): 321-357.* The 1976 devaluation of the Mexican peso was followed by economic stagnation, unemployment, inflation, and a growing external debt. The agreement with the International Monetary Fund promised strict control on government spending and wage increases, of the advantage to the dominant class. Real income for labor dropped nearly 40%, 1977-79. Strike movements were broken by force and political dismissals, and even assassinations occurred.

853. Alvarez Uriarte, Miguel. LA POLITICA ECONOMICA Y LA ECONOMIA POLITIZADA DE MEXICO [The economic policy and the politicized economy of Mexico]. *Foro Int. [Mexico] 1982 22(3): 247-267.* Examines official economic policy and the economy of Mexico during each presidential period from 1959 to 1976. Provides insight into the state of the Mexican economy by the end of 1976. 4 notes.
                                                                         D. A. Franz

854. Ángeles Sánchez N., Maria de los. EL ESTADO Y LA BURGUESÍA NORTEÑA [The state and the northern bourgeoisie]. *Estudios Pol. [Mexico] 1978 3(9): 55-68.* Analysis of economic, political, and social relationships that led to the 1976 expropriation of privately held agricultural land in Northern Mexico. Expropriation was a remedy for an agricultural crisis resulting from the clash between highly productive capitalist agriculture and precapitalist subsistence agriculture. Seizure of highly improved farmlands permitted continuation of state-sponsored agricultural production without unduly large federal expenditures. Distribution of land to the most advanced cooperatives was designed to draw displaced or economically marginal peasants into productive agricultural sectors. By limiting land expropriation to a relatively few wealthy families, government has weakened a powerful political faction that had obstinately resisted expansion of state power. Since the private sector still controls industry, banking, and commerce, its political and economic power remains strong. Expropriations, nonetheless, insured state control of agricultural production and distribution, consolidating its economic and political control of the region. Based on published official statistics, government reports, and secondary sources; 6 tables, 18 notes.
                                                                         F. J. Shaw

855. Arriola, Carlos. LA CRISIS DEL PARTIDO ACCIÓN NACIONAL (1975-1976) [The crisis of the National Action Party, 1975-76]. *Foro Int. [Mexico] 1977 17(4): 542-556.* Discusses the failure of the National Action Party (PAN) to run a presidential candidate in the 1976 Mexican elections because of ideological and personality conflicts within the party. 24 notes.   D. A. Franz

856. Arroyo, Luis Leobardo. CHANGES IN THE NON-AGRICULTURAL EMPLOYMENT STRUCTURE OF MÉXICO, 1950-1970. *Aztlán 1975 6(3): 409-432.* A comparison of the 1950, 1960, and 1970 Mexican population censuses reveals a shift from agricultural employment to manufacturing. The growth in manufacturing occupations has been more than the combined employment gains in services and commerce. Decreasing opportunities in agriculture and a slowing in the growth of manufacturing has created social and political pressures. Based on Mexican census schedules and secondary works; 47 notes, biblio.
R. Griswold del Castillo

857. Baerresen, Donald W. UNEMPLOYMENT AND MEXICO'S BORDER INDUSTRIALIZATION PROGRAM. *Inter-Am. Econ. Affairs 1975 29(2): 79-90.* Discusses factors affecting Mexico's program of stimulating employment by assembling US components for reexport. The program is in the interest of both countries. Primary and secondary sources; table, 17 notes.
D. A. Franz

858. Bailey, John J. PRESIDENCY, BUREAUCRACY, AND ADMINISTRATIVE REFORM IN MEXICO: THE SECRETARIAT OF PROGRAMMING AND BUDGET. *Inter-American Econ. Affairs 1980 34(1): 27-59.* Assesses the administrative reform in the late 1970's and argues that congruence between planning-budgeting arrangements, political institutions, and the substance of public policy is the key factor in the fate of the Secretariat of Programming and Budget.

859. Barkin, David. MEXICO'S ALBATROSS: THE U.S. ECONOMY. *Latin Am. Perspectives 1975 2(2): 64-80.* There is an intricate relationship between Mexico's social and economic problems and the manner in which US imperialism has shaped Mexico's economic structure. Capitalist development within Mexico has occurred only as far as American imperialism has allowed, 1950-70.

860. Barnett, Alan W. THE RESURGENCE OF POLITICAL ART IN MEXICO? *San José Studies 1976 2(2): 4-30.* Traces the struggle of political artists in Mexico during the 1950's and 1960's. The author also discusses the art of political protest which has reappeared in Mexico since 1975 and considers its origins in the dream of a democratic and egalitarian society fostered by the revolution of 1910.

861. Bartra, Armando. EL PANORAMA AGRARIO EN LOS 70 [The agriculture panorama in the 1970's]. *Investigación Econ. [Mexico] 1979 38(150): 179-235.* Agriculture-based capitalism in Mexico changed from its function through the 1960's of financing the import of capital goods to the transfer of added-value capital to industry and the reproduction and maintenance of part of the labor force consumed by capital. After 1965, growth stopped, and subsequent economic problems created enormous social and political pressures and turned Mexico into a net importer of foodstuffs. Unrest, though repressed by national and private armed forces, continues in the form of land seizures. President Lopez Portillo's announcement of the end of 60 years of land reform undercut the legitimacy of the government in peasants' eyes and created further revolutionary pressure.

862. Bartra, Roger. CAPITALISM AND THE PEASANTRY IN MEXICO. *Latin Am. Perspectives 1982 9(1): 36-47.* The revolutionary potential of Mexico's peasants has been exhausted. Its proletarian potential is emerging, brought on by economic realities and the "development of modern forms in agriculture." Primary and secondary sources; 2 tables, biblio.
J. F. Vivian

863. Bataillon, Claude. LA SOCIÉTÉ MEXICAINE 1977-1979: LES NOUVELLES ORIENTATIONS [Mexican society, 1977-79: new orientations]. *Problèmes d'Amérique Latine [France] 1980 57(4579-4580): 29-46.* Examines Mexican society since 1977 under José López Portillo's government and his reforms in the organization of the administration and in education, control of public enterprises, fight against corruption, creation of a new demographic policy and urban development; notes an increase in labor disputes and acts of violence.

864. Benneth, Douglas and Sharpe, Kenneth. EL CONTROL SOBRE LAS MULTINACIONALES, LAS CONTRADICCIONES DE LA MEXICANIZACION [Control of the multinationals: the contradictions of Mexicanization]. *Foro Int. [Mexico] 1981 21(4): 388-429.*

Examines the validity of stated reasons for the post-1973 "Mexicanization" of multinational corporations and suggests that the program has benefitted small cliques without meeting stated goals. Based on interviews, newspaper reports, and secondary sources; 54 notes, appendix, biblio.
D. A. Franz

865. Bennett, Douglas C. and Sharpe, Kenneth E. TRANSNATIONAL CORPORATIONS AND THE POLITICAL ECONOMY OF EXPORT PROMOTION: THE CASE OF THE MEXICAN AUTOMOBILE INDUSTRY. *Int. Organization 1979 33(2): 177-201.* Export promotion has replaced import substitution as the orthodox strategy for economic development. In sectors dominated by transnational corporations, however, such a strategy may run afoul of difficulties not immediately apparent from the neoclassical comparative-advantage perspective that has provided its principal theoretical support. Evidence from the Mexican automobile industry shows that an export promotion policy may face problems of a) demand rigidities in TNC intracompany transfers, b) decision dependency, c) difficulties in enforcing sanctions in cases of recalcitrance, and d) an unequal distribution of benefits between foreign-owned and domestically-owned firms.
J

866. Bennett, Douglas C. and Sharpe, Kenneth E. AGENDA SETTING AND BARGAINING POWER: THE MEXICAN STATE VERSUS TRANSNATIONAL AUTOMOBILE CORPORATIONS. *World Pol. 1979 32(1): 57-89.* Explores the often conflictual bargaining relations between transnational corporations and host governments of less developed countries. They focus particular attention on the conflict that surrounded the creation of the Mexican automobile industry (1960-64), criticizing and reformulating a current approach to these issues. The argument proceeds in two parts—agenda setting and bargaining power. Each part is organized around a central criticism of the bargaining power approach and provides an alternative formulation which is then applied to an analysis of the bargaining relationship between the Mexican Government and the transnational automobile corporations. Mainly secondary sources; chart, 53 notes.
J

867. Bizarro, Salvatore. MEXICO UNDER ECHEVERRÍA. *Current Hist. 1974 66(393): 212-216, 224.*

868. Blanco, José. GÉNESIS Y DESARROLLO DE LA CRISIS EN MÉXICO, 1962-79 [Genesis and development of the crisis in Mexico, 1962-79]. *Investigación Econ. [Mexico] 1979 38(150): 21-88.* Mexico's economy followed the general capitalist trend of stability in the 1960's and stagnation and inflation in the 1970's. Income concentration led to decay in the gross internal product from 1974 on, with the concomitant lack of internal investment. Describes changes in productive structure 1962-70, capital formation, and the penetration of foreign capital and their effect on the balance of payments and income distribution. Traces the 1970-77 "stagflation," its causes, and government economic policies. The creation of a privileged caste and an under-consuming general population led to an impossible situation for the government, forced to attend to the demands of both, requiring contradictory measures.

869. Blank, David Eugene. THE POLITICS OF NEW TOWN PLANNING: THE CASE OF LAZARO CARDENAS CITY, MEXICO. *Secolas Ann. 1979 10: 109-124.* In order to broaden economic development possibilities and to dilute the constant influx of people to already overcrowded metropolitan areas the Lázaro Cárdenas City project sought to build an industrial center in a previously uninhabited area in the state of Michoacan, Mexico, 1970-78.

870. Brannon, Jeffery and Baklanoff, Eric N. GOAL AMBIVALENCE OF A SEMI-AUTONOMOUS PUBLIC ENTERPRISE: CORDEMEX. *Secolas Ann. 1981 12: 39-53.* Evaluates the nationalization of the state of Yucatán's fiber-using cordage mills through the establishment of Cordemex.

871. Cabrera A., Gustavo. MEXICO: POLITICA DEMOGRAFICA SOBRE MIGRACION INTERNA (1978-1982) [Mexico: demographic policy on internal migration, 1978-82]. *Demografía y Econ. [Mexico] 1982 16(3): 439-448.* Discusses the policies of the Consejo Nacional de Población de Mexico regarding domestic distribution and redistribution of the Mexican population.

872. Calkin, G. A. THE DEVELOPMENT OF RELATIONS BE-TWEEN CANADA AND MEXICO. *Internat. Perspectives [Canada] 1973 (3): 55-58.* Discusses the evolution and importance of Canada's relations with Mexico since 1944.   L. S. Frey

873. Camp, Roderic Ai. EDUCATION AND POLITICAL RE-CRUITMENT IN MEXICO: THE ALEMÁN GENERATION. *J. of Interam. Studies and World Affairs 1976 18(3): 295-322.* At least since the administration of President Miguel Alemán (1946-52) student contact has been a major form of political recruitment. Analyzes the "Alemán generation" at the University of Mexico and its law school (1925-29) to demonstrate how this occurs. Presidents select their cabinet members from among friends made at these educational institutions. Faculty members encountered in these schools are also brought into government. This suggests that the universities, and not the bureaucracy or party membership, are major stepping stones to important political jobs. Based on Mexican educational reports and secondary sources; 6 tables, 17 notes, biblio.   J. R. Thomas/S

874. Camp, Roderic Ai. RECLUTAMIENTO POLÍTICO Y CAMBIO EN EL MÉXICO DE LOS SETENTAS [Political recruit-ment and change in the Mexico of the 70's]. *Foro Int. [Mexico] 1980 20(3): 463-483.* Discusses institutional and social factors in the recruit-ment of Mexican political leaders (1976-79) and the relationship between recruitment and political change. 2 tables, 71 notes.
D. A. Franz

875. Campos Icardo, Salvador. PROGRESS IN BILATERAL RE-LATIONS. *Pro. of the Acad. of Pol. Sci. 1981 34(1): 28-31.* Discusses four major topics of US-Mexican relations that have emerged in recent years: energy, trade, migration, and problems in the border area. A frame-work to deal with these topics was created by President Jimmy Carter and President José López Portillo, which resulted in a consultative mecha-nism. The consultative mechanism itself is not a guarantee that bilateral relations will be free of conflict, but it enhances the possibility of resolving issues between the two countries.   T. P. Richardson

876. Castell Cancino, Jorge. RELATORÍA DEL SIMPOSIO MÉX-ICO DE LOS 70 [Report on the symposium Mexico in the 1970's]. *Investigación Econ. [Mexico] 1979 38(150): 13-19.* The general trend in the Mexican economy of the 1970's was production stagnation, with inflation, rising external debt, which tied Mexico to international finan-cial orthodoxy, declining real wages, increased unemployment, and in-creased income from capital—because of price increases not productivity gains. These changes widened existing social and class differences, and relative recovery based on increased oil exports has not solved the prob-lem, which would require increased industrialization and government action to modify the current pattern of accumulation. Introduction to a special issue devoted to symposium papers.

877. Castro, Alejandro Carrillo. RECENT MOVEMENTS TO-WARD DECENTRALIZATION IN MEXICO. *Am. Soc. of Int. Law Pro. 1974 68: 190-192.* Discusses Mexico's recent efforts to decentralize its federal government.

878. Clement, Norris and Green, Louis. THE POLITICAL ECON-OMY OF DEVALUATION IN MEXICO. *Inter-American Econ. Af-fairs 1978 32(3): 47-75.* Reviews the Mexican economy from 1950 to the present, covering the "economic miracle" of the years 1950-73, and con-cluding with the devaluation of the peso in 1976.

879. Comacho, Manuel. LA HUELGA DE SALTILLO, UN IN-TENTO DE REGENERACIÓN OBRERA [The Saltillo Strike: a de-sign of worker regeneration]. *Foro Int. [Mexico] 1975 15(59): 414-451.* Discusses the Saltillo Industrial Group and provides political analysis of the atypical strike at Saltillo, Mexico, 16 April-3 June 1974. Based on interviews; 4 graphs, 5 notes.   D. A. Franz

880. Cordera C., Rolando. CRISIS NACIONAL Y POLÍTICA ECONÓMICA [National crisis and economic policy]. *Rev. Mexicana de Ciencia Pol. [Mexico] 1975 21(80): 27-33.* Identifies the basic eco-nomic contradictions inherent in the Mexican political system of the 1970's, which necessitates a revision of governmental attitudes toward national development.

881. Cordero, Salvador and Gómez Tagle, Silvia. ESTADO Y TRABAJADORES DE LAS EMPRESAS ESTATALES EN MÉXICO [The state and workers in Mexican public enterprises]. *Estudios Pol. [Mexico] 1978 4(16): 97-130.* Recently labor unions in government oper-ated enterprises have demanded radical social, political, and economic reforms. These radicals, however, have always maintained their loyalty to the ruling party and its ideological goals. Since this party is an organ of state capitalism, the radical unionists have found themselves frustrated and confused. Secondary sources; 8 tables, 48 notes.
F. J. Shaw, Jr.

882. Córdoba, José and Ortiz, Guillermo. ASPECTOS DEFLACIO-NARIOS DE LA DEVALUACIÓN DEL PESO MEXICANO DE 1976 [Anti-inflationary aspects of the devaluation of the Mexican peso in 1976]. *Demografía y Econ. [Mexico] 1980 14(3): 291-324.* In the context of a wider study on the causes and consequences of the devaluation of the peso in 1976, studies its inflation-curbing effects as a result of the reduc-tion in private investment.

883. Craig, Richard. OPERATION CONDOR: MEXICO'S ANTI-DRUG CAMPAIGN ENTERS A NEW ERA. *J. of Interamerican Studies and World Affairs 1980 22(3): 345-363.* In late 1976 Mexico finally decided to use chemical defoliants to reduce its illegal drug produc-tion. While its international image, its domestic drug problem, and diplo-matic pressure played roles in persuading Mexico to use defoliation, the dominant reasons relate to the drug wealth dominating local politics and economies, and the growing violence in the Sierras. Mexico's only party, the Partido Revolutionario Institucional, is made uneasy by the wealth and activity forming in the former rural guerrilla areas and is determined to crack down hard and permanently. Based on interviews with US and Mexican officials and US newspaper and journal sources; 8 notes, ref.
T. D. Schoonover

884. Craig, Richard B. HUMAN RIGHTS AND MEXICO'S ANTI-DRUG CAMPAIGN. *Social Sci. Q. 1980 60(4): 691-701.* Discusses the Mexican government's antidrug policy, focusing on four areas of human rights violations: 1) the use of dangerous herbicides, 2) the failure or inability to protect those who attack drug-related corruption, 3) the abuse of fundamental rights during arrest, detention, and imprisonment for narcotics violations, and 4) the disregard of campesino rights during drug-related maneuvers in the countryside. Based on interviews and newspaper reports; 22 notes, biblio.   L. F. Velicer

885. Craig, Richard B. LA CAMPAÑA PERMANENTE: MEXI-CO'S ANTIDRUG CAMPAIGN. *J. of Interamerican Studies and World Affairs 1978 20(2): 107-131.* Mexico has served as a source for most marijuana, heroin, and cocaine entering the US market since the late 1940's. Thus the narcotics traffic has become a crucial aspect of contem-porary US-Mexican relations, ranking with trade and illegal migration. Mexico's campaign against drug traffic and use dates back to 19th-cen-tury efforts to suppress opium use by the Chinese of Mexico City. Charges of corruption, mistreatment, dual standards, and confused and inconsis-tent policy formation have been leveled during the recent cooperative period in the antidrug campaign. Based on secondary sources and inter-views; 7 notes, ref.   T. D. Schoonover

886. Craig, Richard B. OPERATION INTERCEPT: THE INTER-NATIONAL POLITICS OF PRESSURE. *Rev. of Pol. 1980 42(4): 556-580.* Operation Intercept was an American plan to halt or slow the flow of drugs across the Mexican-United States border. Adopted by the Nixon administration in 1969, it was poorly planned and administered and lacked coordination with the Mexican government. It angered busi-nessmen on both sides of the border, antagonized the Mexican govern-ment, and disrupted the flow of traffic between the countries. The operation was ended after pressure from border state congressmen. Resid-ual benefits, however, included a greater awareness by the Mexican gov-ernment of its growing drug problem. Letters, interviews, minutes, reports, hearings, and secondary sources; 52 notes.   D. F. Ring

887. Dehouve, Danièle. L'INTERVENTION DE L'ÉTAT DANS LE DÉVELOPPEMENT DU CAPITALISME: LA SIERRA MADRE DE L'ÉTAT DE GUERRERO (MEXIQUE) DE 1964 À 1976 [Government intervention in the development of capitalism: the Sierra Madre in Guerrero, Mexico, 1964-76]. *Travaux & Mémoires de l'Inst. des*

Hautes Études de l'Amérique Latine [France] 1979 (32): 49-54. A study of the intervention of the state in the development of the Sierra Madre region in Guerrero, Mexico.

888. DeLaTorre Villar, Ernesto. LOS ESTADOS UNIDOS DE NORTEAMÉRICA Y SU INFLUENCIA IDEOLÓGICA EN MEXICO [The ideological influence of the United States on Mexico]. *Humánitas [Mexico] 1977 18: 439-474.* The ideological influence the US exerted on Mexico was similar to that of an older brother, a mature country whose friendship, help, and protection Mexico sought, the relationship evolving from admiration, followed by imitation, and finally by fear and mistrust.

889. Drysdale, Robert S. WHAT MEXICO'S PRESIDENT INHERITED. *Worldview 1977 20(11): 36-42.* Describes the problems José López Portillo faced when he took office in 1976 following the inept administration of Luis Echeverría who governed from 1970-76.

890. Edelman, Marc. AGRICULTURAL MODERNIZATION IN SMALLHOLDING AREAS OF MEXICO: A CASE STUDY IN THE SIERRA NORTE DE PUEBLA. *Latin Am. Perspectives 1980 7(4): 29-49.* Examination of three Mexican "little green revolutions"—Plan Puebla, Plan Zacapoaxtla, and Programa de Inversiones Públicas para el Desarrollo Rural (PIDER) programs—yields disappointing contradictions, mostly attributable to the political basis of decisionmaking. Economic and commercial considerations remain secondary, so that the rural population is neither benefited nor advantaged. 12 notes, biblio.
J. F. Vivian

891. Engel, Bernard F. SO CLOSE TO THE UNITED STATES. *Colorado Q. 1974 23(1): 111-119.* Examines Mexican journalists' criticism of the US role in Mexico's economic stagnation. S

892. Felix, David. INCOME INEQUALITY IN MEXICO. *Current Hist. 1977 72(425): 111-114, 136.* Chronicles income inequalities in Mexico, 1930-76, concentrating on the policies of President Luis Echeverría, 1970-76, and the drop in private investment due to tax reforms and the exchange rate collapse brought about primarily through foreign credit financing of physical and social investment programs.

893. Fernández Christlieb, Fatima. LOS MEDIOS DE INFORMACIÓN MASIVA Y LA REFORMA ADMINISTRATIVA DE JOSÉ LÓPEZ PORTILLO [Mass media and the administrative reform of José López Portillo]. *Rev. Mexicana de Ciencias Pol. y Soc. [Mexico] 1976-77 (86-87): 199-212.* Discusses the state of the mass media—radio, television, and newspapers—in the liberal atmosphere of the government of José López Portillo, and compares it to the stagnation of previous years, 1970's.

894. FitzGerald, E. V. K. A NOTE ON CAPITAL ACCUMULATION IN MEXICO: THE BUDGET DEFICIT AND INVESTMENT FINANCE. *Development and Change [Netherlands] 1980 11(3): 391-417.* Proposes an alternative to the orthodox model relating public budgets and private investment in Mexico, where from 1925 to the 1950's the political economy of industrialization allowed the satisfaction of both fiscal deficit and private investment out of the manipulation of consumption.

895. Fitzgerald, E. V. K. THE STATE AND CAPITAL ACCUMULATION IN MEXICO. *J. of Latin Am. Studies [Great Britain] 1978 10(2): 263-282.* Analyzes the objects and results of state capital accumulation in Mexico in the 1940's and its uses to monitor capitalist expansion and industrialization, mainly in the private sector.

896. Flores, Heriberto. L'ÉVOLUTION DU RÉGIME MEXICAIN: DE L'OUVERTURE DÉMOCRATIQUE À LA RÉFORME POLITIQUE [The evolution of the Mexican regime: from democratic opening to political reform]. *Problèmes d'Amérique Latine [France] 1980 57(4579-4580): 47-71.* Examines the background of the Mexican political system, already open to democracy under former President Luis Echeverría, and analyzes the reforms initiated in 1977 by President José López Portillo, including plural political parties and a new system of elections. The 1979 July elections revealed, in spite of the success of the Institutional Revolutionary Party (PRI), a strong abstention in voting.

897. Fort, Odile. NOTES SUR LES STRUCTURES AGRAIRES ET ENCADREMENTS DES PAYSANS DANS LES SECTEURS DE COLONISATION DE L'ÉTAT DU QUINTANA ROO [Notes on the agrarian structures and infrastructural investments of the peasantry in sectors of settlement of Quintana Roo, Mexico]. *Travaux & Mémoires de l'Inst. des Hautes Études de l'Amérique Latine [France] 1979 (32): 103-106.* A study of rural settlements in Quintana Roo, presenting two types: one thoroughly supported by the government, the other almost autarkic.

898. Gamboa Villafranca, Xavier. LA "DESCAMPESINIZACIÓN: META ESTATAL EN EL AGRO (1970-1976) ["Depeasantization": state objective in agriculture, 1970-76]. *Estudios Pol. [Mexico] 1977 3(10): 99-132.* Analysis of the Mexican government's encouragement of capitalistic agriculture at the expense of ejidal agriculture, 1970-76. Although the state formally retains its traditional ideological commitment to communal agriculture, it has rejected it as stagnant and unproductive. To produce more food, provide rural employment, and alleviate the pressure of rural migration on urban areas, the government is encouraging the growth of large-scale capitalistic agriculture which will transform the rural peasantry into an agrarian proletariat. Through State Production Committees which allocate credit and irrigation water to productive private enterprise, government has created a mechanism to achieve this goal. In line with the shift to agrarian capitalism, propaganda now stresses alliance between city and countryside, the need to raise production, and educational and health benefits for the rural populace. Based on government reports and secondary sources; 168 notes.
F. J. Shaw, Jr.

899. Gamboa Villafranca, Xavier. LOS DETERMINANTES DE LOS CAMBIOS EN LOS APARATOS DE PODER DEL ESTADO NACIONAL MEXICANO Y SU REFLEJO EN LA ESTRATEGÍA DE IRRIGACIÓN VIGENTE DE 1970-1976 [Determinants of changes in the power mechanisms of the Mexican national state and its reflection in irrigation strategy, 1970-76]. *Estudios Pol. [Mexico] 1978 3(9): 27-53.* Depicts post-1970 Mexican irrigation policy as a state effort to restore political and social stability to rural areas while expanding its own strength and capitalist market agriculture. Prior to 1970, policymakers perceived of irrigation simply as a method of increasing agricultural production. In the wake of the recent economic crisis, irrigation policy now serves a multitude of goals. Investment accompanying extension of irrigation generates employent in economically depressed areas. Employment on irrigation projects diverts marginal peasantry from flight to cities and trains them for future work in productive agricultural sectors. Completed irrigation projects advance capitalist agriculture and integrate rural areas into modern sectors of the economy. Modernization also eliminates social and political groups existing beyond government control. Since projects are federally sponsored and supervised, the government also consolidates its political power and control in rural areas. Based on recent sociological, economic, and political studies; 182 notes.
F. J. Shaw

900. Gamboa Villafranca, Xavier. 1977, AÑO DE LA RECONSTRUCCIÓN: REFORMA POLÍTICA Y ALIANZA PARA LA PRODUCCIÓN EN EL AGRO MEXICANO [1977, year of reconstruction: political reform and alliance for production in Mexican agriculture]. *Estudios Pol. [Mexico] 1979 4(13-14): 97-142.* An explanation of the political reform that has accompanied Mexico's recent efforts to expand agricultural production and escape the stagflation that has afflicted the economy since the early 1970's. The Alliance for Agricultural Production favored large-scale capitalist agricultural enterprises at the expense of Mexico's numerically large but relatively unproductive peasantry.
F. J. Shaw, Jr.

901. Garza, Rudolph O. de la. LA FUNCIÓN RECLUTADORA DE LA CÁMARA DE DIPUTADOS [The function of the House of Deputies as a recruitment center]. *Rev. Mexicana de Ciencia Pol. [Mexico] 1975 21(80): 65-74.* Examines the role of the Mexican House of Deputies as a training ground and recruitment center for aspirants to the Mexican political elite, utilizing data from 1940 to 1973.

902. Gereffi, Gary. DRUG FIRMS AND DEPENDENCY IN MEXICO: THE CASE OF THE STEROID HORMONE INDUSTRY. *Int. Organization 1978 32(1): 237-286.* The relationship between foreign control and national development is a central concern of the Latin Ameri-

can "dependency school" of analysis, which focuses on the impact of investment by multinational corporations (MNC's) in the Third World. In the MNC-dominated steroid hormone industry in Mexico, foreign control has led to two major consequences which characterize it as "dependent": there has been an unequal distribution of benefits from its growth, favoring the central capitalist economies and the MNC's more than Mexico; and at the level of domestic policy formulation, there has been a restriction of choice among local development options, since these conflicted with "global" priorities implied by the dependent situation. As an alternative to MNC's, national firms in Mexico would very likely have performed better in terms of Mexican national welfare (defined as local industry growth) and global consumer welfare (defined as identical products at lower prices). The attempt made by the Mexican State during the last two years of the Echeverría administration (1975-76) to increase its automony vis-à-vis the MNC's by restructuring the industry with a new state-owned firm met with only limited success. Reasons for this include Mexico's declining prominence in the world industry due to the availability of substitutes for its raw material, and the ability of the MNC's to build a strong defense using local political allies. Yet despite the difficulties, Third World countries will need to develop strong states which can deal effectively with multinational corporations if they are to successfully establish their own development priorities.   J

903.   Godoy, Ricardo, and Tiedemann, R. G.   ANTONIO GARCIA: A MEXICAN PEASANT, POET AND REVOLUTIONARY. *J. of Peasant Studies [Great Britain] 1982 9(2): 241-251.* Reproduces a letter and poems written by Antonio Garcia Gonzales, Mexican peasant from Ixtlan. The letter was written in October 1971, shortly after his arrest for involvement in revolutionary activities in Mexico City, and the poems are from the early years of his imprisonment, between 1971 and 1973. An introduction gives some biographical remarks and a commentary sketches in the background of revolutionary organizations in Mexico, 1968-73. 6 notes.   D. J. Nicholls

904.   Gomezjara, Francisco A.   EL PROCESO POLÍTICO DE JENARO VÁZQUEZ HACIA LA GUERRILLA CAMPESINA [The political progress of Jenaro Vázquez toward the peasant war]. *Rev. Mexicana de Ciencias Pol. y Sociales [Mexico] 1977 23(88): 87-126.* Recounts the political writings and nonviolent activities of Jenaro Vázquez in support of the peasant movements in the state of Guerrero, 1960-66.

905.   González, Eduardo.   EMPRESARIOS Y OBREROS: DOS GRUPOS DE PODER FRENTE A LA CRISIS Y LA POLÍTICA ECONÓMICA DE LOS SETENTA [Industrialists and workers: two power groups facing the crisis and the economic policy of the 1970's]. *Investigación Econ. [Mexico] 1979 38(150): 289-319.* Mexico's industrial growth during the 1960's was financed by agricultural surplus, with state support. The contraction at the end of the 1960's, increased external debt and social unrest, and the 1973 oil crisis led to the 1976 devaluation and stabilization plan, which limited public spending and wage increases. Increased oil exports financed the deficits but did not remove the causes, or effects, of social unrest in the crisis facing business, labor, and the state.

906.   González-Souza, Luis F.   LA POLÍTICA EXTERIOR DE MÉXICO ANTE LA PROTECCIÓN INTERNACIONAL DE LOS DERECHOS HUMANOS [Mexican foreign policy and the international protection of human rights]. *Foro Int. [Mexico] 1977 18(1): 108-138.* Discusses Mexican foreign political and economic policy in support of human rights and the rationale behind Mexico's failure to sign international pacts relating to human rights. 5 tables, 113 notes.
                                                                     D. A. Franz

907.   Granados Chapa, Miguel Ángel.   NAYARIT: CONSOLIDACIÓN DEL MONOPARTIDO [Nayarit: one-party consolidation]. *Foro Int. [Mexico] 1976 16(4): 429-448.* Discusses strongly contested state elections in Mexico since 1959 and examines in detail the 1975 election in Nayarit. Quotes from an opposition petition to void the Nayarit election and Congressional denial of the request. Primary and secondary sources; 9 notes.   D. A. Franz

908.   Grayson, George W.   THE MAKING OF A MEXICAN PRESIDENT, 1976.   *Current Hist. 1976 70(413): 49-52, 83-84.* Describes the selection of Mexican president-designate José López Portillo and evaluates current president Luis Echeverría, a man of radical words and conservative action.

909.   Grayson, George W.   OIL AND POLITICS IN MEXICO. *Current Hist. 1980 78(454): 53-56, 83.* Against a backdrop of corruption and party politics discusses Mexico's efforts to escape underdevelopment by selling its oil and natural gas, 1970's.

910.   Grayson, George W.   OIL AND POLITICS IN MEXICO. *Current Hist. 1981 80(469): 379-383, 393.* Discusses the negative impact of petroleum production on the political environment of Mexico.

911.   Grayson, George W.   THE U.S.-MEXICAN NATURAL GAS DEAL AND WHAT WE CAN LEARN FROM IT.   *Orbis 1980 24(3): 573-607.* A detailed discussion of the complex negotiations between the United States and Mexico for the purchase of natural gas between 1977 and 1980. The failure of the negotiations was a result of misunderstandings on both sides and a lack of concerted action on the part of the US State Department. Concludes that the Mexican price was too high and that Energy Secretary James R. Schlesinger was right to veto the deal. Based on newspapers, government documents, and other published sources; map, table, 100 notes.   J. W. Thacker, Jr.

912.   Green, Maria del Rosario.   MEXICO'S ECONOMIC DEPENDENCE.   *Pro. of the Acad. of Pol. Sci. 1981 34(1): 104-114.* Places US loans to Mexico in the broad context of the country's public external debt. More attention should be given to the international strategies of the banks, regardless of national origin, and preference given to banks with important and long tradition in Third World countries. These banks will probably be more willing to do business with Mexico and consequently allow more flexibility for the expression of Mexican interests. Note.
                                                                 T. P. Richardson

913.   Green, Rosario.   DEUDA EXTERNA Y POLÍTICA EXTERIOR: LA VUELTA A LA BILATERALIDAD EN LAS RELACIONES INTERNACIONALES DE MÉXICO [External debt and foreign policy: The return to bilateralism in Mexican international relations]. *Foro Int. [Mexico] 1977 18(1): 54-80.* Discusses foreign policy implications for Mexico of large public and private debt increases and what is needed to reduce it, possibly including using oil export revenues to reduce debt. 5 tables, 36 notes.   D. A. Franz

914.   Grigulevich, I. R.   DAVID AL'FARO SIKEIROS: SOLDAT, KHUDOZHNIK, KOMMUNIST: STRANITSY ZHIZNI [David Alfaro Siqueiros: soldier, artist, and Communist: pages from his life]. *Novaia i Noveishaia Istoriia [USSR] 1979 (5): 99-119, (6): 93-111.* Part I. Describes the life of the Mexican painter and revolutionary David Alfaro Siqueiros (1896-1974) up to his departure from Europe in 1938. Siqueiros fought in the Mexican revolution (1913-17), joined the Mexican Communist Party in 1924 and took part in the Spanish Civil War in 1937. Part II. Follows Siqueiros from his return to America in 1939 up to 1961. Siqueiros worked as an artist in Mexico and Chile, specializing in murals for public buildings, but also continued his political activity. Links with Cuban Communists led to his arrest and imprisonment in Mexico in 1960. Based on Siqueiros's memoirs and other primary sources; 5 photos; 53 notes. Article to be continued (see abstract 618).   R. J. Ware

915.   Grindle, Merilee S.   PATRONS AND CLIENTS IN THE BUREAUCRACY: CAREER NETWORKS IN MEXICO.   *Latin Am. Res. Rev. 1977 12(1): 37-66.* A case study of CONASUPO, a federal agricultural agency. Bureaucratic careers are based on cultivating and preserving personal and political alliances, not upon party or ideology. The common tools used are *confianza* (trust), *palanca* (lever), *equipo* (team), and *camarilla* (clique). A form of the patron-client model exists among elites for the purpose of career advancement. Based on interviews with bureaucrats and secondary works; 2 tables, 6 figs., 12 notes, biblio.
                                                                     J. K. Pfabe

916.   Grindle, Merilee S.   POLICY CHANGE IN AN AUTHORITARIAN REGIME: MEXICO UNDER ECHEVERRÍA.   *J. of Interam. Studies and World Affairs 1977 19(4): 523-555.* Discusses policy change in Mexico under President Luis Echeverría, which is often dependent upon access to the president due to the lack of public debate or deliberation in the decisionmaking process. Change only occurs when it is clear that the president initiated or supports the proposal. This closed political system does not assure the president of correct or adequate information, but it is not rigid and unresponsive to policy change, merely

dependent upon the sensitivity and astuteness of the president and his advisers. 9 tables, 12 notes, biblio. T. D. Schoonover

917. Hamilton, William H. MEXICO'S "NEW" FOREIGN POLICY: A REEXAMINATION. *Inter-Am. Econ. Affairs 1975 29(3): 51-58.* Comments and elaborates on recent articles discussing Mexican foreign policy by Guy E. Poitras (see abstract 962) and Harvey J. Kaye (see abstract 929). Secondary sources; 14 notes. D. A. Franz

918. Handelman, Howard. THE POLITICS OF LABOR PROTEST IN MEXICO: TWO CASE STUDIES. *J. of Interam. Studies and World Affairs 1976 18(3): 267-294.* The failed strike movement of insurgent railroad workers in 1958-59 and the successful—and peaceful—campaign of independent electrical workers for government recognition in 1971-72 established the limits to which the Mexican government is prepared to go in permitting independence to labor unions. S

919. Harris, Richard L. A CRITIQUE OF NORTH AMERICAN LEFTIST ANALYSES OF MEXICO. *Latin Am. Perspectives 1982 9(1): 106-110.* Reviews James Cockcroft's *El imperialismo, la lucha de Clases y el Estado en Mexico* (1979) and Donald Hodges and Ross Handy's *Mexico, 1910-1976* (1979). Both books are found wanting in class analysis and bibliographic sources. J. F. Vivian

920. Harris, Richard L. THE POLITICAL ECONOMY OF MEXICO IN THE EIGHTIES. *Latin Am. Perspectives 1982 9(1): 2-19.* Concludes that Mexico is at a crossroads. Capitalist development is hard pressed to meet mass needs, while "popular forces" lack only organization to effect basic changes. Secondary sources; 2 tables, biblio. J. F. Vivian

921. Hernandez, Salvador and Delarbe, Raul Trejo. TRANSNACIONALES Y DEPENDENCIA EN MÉXICO (1940-1970) [Transnational corporations and dependence in Mexico (1940-70)]. *Rev. Mexicana de Ciencia Pol. [Mexico] 1975 21(80): 75-89.* Maintains that multinational corporations, as promoters of imperialist goals, are largely responsible for the continuing economic, technological, and cultural dependence of 20th-century Mexico, and studies their impact on the world economy in general.

922. Hernández Rodríguez, Rogelio. EL PROBLEMA DE LOS BRACEROS EN EL PERÍODO DE 1942 A 1946 [The Bracero problem from 1942 to 1946]. *Bol. del Archivo General de la Nacion [Mexico] 1980 4(4): 3-4.* There were two types of Mexican immigration into the United States during the war years of 1942-46, the traditional illegal immigration and that under the bracero program. The second type grew out of official agreements reached between the governments of the United States and Mexico. Secondary sources; note. J. A. Lewis

923. Hilger, Marye Tharp. DECISION-MAKING IN A PUBLIC MARKETING ENTERPRISE: CONASUPO IN MEXICO. *J. of Interamerican Studies and World Affairs 1980 22(4): 471-494.* The Compañía Nacional de Subsistencias Populares (CONASUPO) is an autonomous public enterprise which competes with private sector producers, wholesalers, and retailers in addition to its role in economic development. Its marketing operations are impinged upon by political factors. While private sector firms also operate with political influences, the relationship of politics to CONASUPO is considerably different. Based on unpublished CONASUPO materials and Marye Hilger's and G. E. Bigler's unpublished dissertations; 2 tables, fig., ref. T. D. Schoonover

924. Huerta, Arturo. EL PROCESO DE ACUMULACIÓN DE CAPITAL EN LA INDUSTRIA DE TRANSFORMACIÓN: EL CASO DE MÉXICO EN LAS DÉCADAS DE LOS SESENTA Y SETENTA [The capital accumulation process in the transformation industries: the case of Mexico in the 1960's and 1970's]. *Investigación Econ. [Mexico] 1979 38(150): 255-288.* During the 1960's Mexican economic growth allowed capital accumulation out of increases in productivity based on imported technology associated with multinational corporations' investments. The concentration of income stimulated growth of durable goods, reinforcing the cycle by capital transfer from agriculture. The 1970's saw stagnation, food imports, credit contraction, and reduced consumer spending. Profit margins were maintained by increasing work intensity and declining real wages. Resulting social unrest provoked the National Industrial Plan, which, however, favors only developed nations, while oil exports finance continuing trade deficits.

925. Jacobson, Peter. OPPOSITION AND POLITICAL REFORM IN MEXICO: AN ASSESSMENT OF THE PARTIDO ACCIÓN NACIONAL AND THE "APERTURA DEMOCRA1TICA." *New Scholar 1975 5(1): 19-30.* Studies current political practices in Mexico. The Partido Acción Nacional (PAN) is the major opposition to the ruling Partido Revolucionario Institucional (PRI) which operates more as a bureaucratic structure than as a political party. The series of reforms instituted by President Luis Echeverria in the early 1970's and known as the *Apertura democrática* might be more wish than reality. But their effect has been great, and the PRI authoritarian structure is eroding. PAN has a particularly important opportunity to help lead Mexico toward democracy with stability. 25 notes. D. K. Pickens/S

926. Jones, Errol D. and Lafrance, David. MEXICO'S FOREIGN AFFAIRS UNDER PRESIDENT ECHEVERRÍA: THE SPECIAL CASE OF CHILE. *Inter-Am. Econ. Affairs 1976 30(1): 45-78.* Explores the close connection between Mexico's overall foreign policy, domestic policy, and relations with Chile during the presidency of Luis Echeverría. Based on periodical literature and other secondary sources; 51 notes. D. A. Franz

927. Kane, N. Stephen. CORPORATE POWER AND FOREIGN POLICY: EFFORTS OF AMERICAN OIL COMPANIES TO INFLUENCE UNITED STATES RELATIONS WITH MEXICO, 1921-1928. *Diplomatic Hist. 1977 1(2): 170-198.* Two case studies of the interaction between American oil companies and the US Department of State indicate that the companies failed to exert effective influence on foreign policy in their efforts to protect their investments in Mexico. The State Department's position concerning Mexico's petroleum legislation was actually based on "the Department's longstanding commitment to the concept of fair treatment of United States citizens and their capital abroad in the fields of trade and investment within the framework of generally accepted principles of international law." Based on primary and secondary sources; 89 notes. G. H. Curtis

928. Kane, N. Stephen. THE UNITED STATES AND THE DEVELOPMENT OF THE MEXICAN PETROLEUM INDUSTRY, 1945-1950: A LOST OPPORTUNITY. *Inter-American Econ. Affairs 1981 35(1): 45-72.* Focuses on the United States and Mexico vis-à-vis the Mexican petroleum industry, 1945-50, a transitional period after the 1938 break in friendly relations instigated when President Lazaro Cardenas nationalized the industry and expropriated properties held by foreign oil companies.

929. Kaye, Harvey J. HOW "NEW" IS MEXICO'S FOREIGN POLICY? *Inter-Am. Econ. Affairs 1975 28(4): 87-92.* Reply to Guy E. Poitras's earlier article, "Mexico's 'New' Foreign Policy" (see abstract 917). Mexico's "new" foreign policy grew out of actions taken during Adolfo López Mateos' presidency, 1958-64. Based on newspaper reports and secondary sources; 13 notes. D. A. Franz

930. Leich, John Foster. REFORMA POLÍTICA IN MEXICO. *Current Hist. 1981 80(469): 361-364, 392-393.* The 1979 electoral reform was modeled on the West German parliamentary system, and it will not significantly change the control function of the Partido Revolucionario Institucional (PRI).

931. Lempérière, Annick. LE SECRET DE LA STABILITÉ MEXICAINE [The secret of Mexican stability]. *Histoire [France] 1982 (43): 100-102.* Analyzes the main features of Mexican government and gives the elements of an explanation for Mexico's remarkable political stability.

932. Loaeza, Soledad. LA POLÍTICA DEL RUMOR: MÉXICO, NOVIEMBRE-DICIEMBRE DE 1976 [The politics of rumor: Mexico, November-December 1976]. *Foro Int. [Mexico] 1977 17(4): 557-586.* Examines the political atmosphere in Mexico surrounding transfers of presidential power in 1970 and 1976 together with the growth of political and economic rumors during these periods. Based mainly on newspaper reports; 58 notes. D. A. Franz

933. Loyo, Aurora and Pozas H., Ricardo. LA CRISIS POLÍTICA DE 1958 (NOTAS EN TORNO A LOS MECANISMOS DE CONTROL EJERCIDOS POR EL ESTADO MEXICANO SOBRE LA CLASE OBRERA ORGANIZADA) [The political crisis of 1958: notes on the mechanisms of control over organized labor used by the Mexican state]. *Rev. Mexicana de Ciencias Pol. y Sociales [Mexico] 1977 23(89): 77-118.* The failure of government-dictated leadership in the labor movement resulted in illegal labor organizations and corresponding legal, physical, and economic pressures from the government to regain control.

934. Mabry, Donald J. CHANGING MODELS OF MEXICAN POLITICS: A REVIEW ESSAY. *New Scholar 1975 5(1): 31-37.* Review article on Evelyn P. Stevens's *Protest and Response in Mexico* (MIT Pr., 1974) as representative of an ongoing revolution in the historiography of the Mexican revolution and interpretation of Mexican politics. Where scholars (and Mexican politicians) once viewed Mexican politics according to a liberal model moving, however slowly, toward democracy, Stevens (with other modern commentators) asserts that Mexico is authoritarian and controls political mobilization to prevent change in present political arrangements or economic policies. 21 notes.   S

935. Manger, Annette and Mols, Manfred. REFORMA POLÍTICA UND OPPOSITION IN MEXIKO [Reforma política and opposition in Mexico]. *Jahrbuch für Geschichte von Staat, Wirtschaft und Gesellschaft Lateinamerikas [West Germany] 1980 17: 395-429.* Postrevolutionary Mexican politics are most often judged stable, but the permanence of the structural identity of the system should be doubted. President José López Portillo has recently attempted to establish the Institutional Mexican Revolution upon basically altered conditions. He has not tried to transform the social economy of the country, but to renew the legitimacy of the state by creating a release for the most salient discontent within the society while at the same time maintaining the system of domination. Based on newspapers, magazines, journals and other printed primary materials; 131 notes.   T. D. Schoonover

936. Mares, David R. ARTICULACIÓN NACIONAL—LOCAL EN EL DESARROLLO RURAL: LA IRRIGACIÓN [National-local articulation in rural development: irrigation]. *Am. Indígena [Mexico] 1980 40(3): 471-497.* Examines the institutional and social aspects of water distribution in Mexico. Interactions between government agency and large private farmers are found to be quite competitive, although they work toward a common goal. *Ejidatarios* are insured some influence through the workings of a clientelist system. Examines the consequences of the process of decisionmaking and water allocation: increased production and decreased social justice.   J

937. Mares, David R. MÉXICO Y ESTADOS UNIDOS: EL VÍNCULO ENTRE EL COMERCIO AGRÍCOLA Y LA NUEVA RELACIÓN ENERGÉTICA [Mexico and the United States: the link between agricultural trade and the new energy relationship]. *Foro Int. [Mexico] 1981 22(1): 1-69.* Examines the impact of US energy-related foreign policy on the sale of Mexican tomatoes in the United States. Table, 34 notes.   D. A. Franz

938. Marín Bosch, Miguel. MÉXICO Y EL DESARME [Mexico and disarmament]. *Foro Int. [Mexico] 1977 18(1): 139-154.* Summarizes Mexican activity in the UN and bilaterally to stimulate disarmament and reduce world armaments. 24 notes.   D. A. Franz

939. Márquez Ayala, David. EL TIPO DE CAMBIO COMO INSTRUMENTO DE POLÍTICA EN LOS 70 [Foreign exchange level as a political instrument in the 1970's]. *Investigación Econ. [Mexico] 1979 38(150): 391-400.* Mexico's nearly 100% devaluation in 1976 almost broke the economy and delivered the economy into foreign hands, represented by the International Monetary Fund.

940. Matamoro, Blas. OCTAVIO PAZ: DEL ARQUETIPO A LA HISTORIA [Octavio Paz: from the archetype to history]. *Cuadernos Hispanoamericanos [Spain] 1981 (367-368): 273-286.* Reviews *El Ogro Filantrópico* (1979) by Octavio Paz. The book is a sequel to *El laberinto de la soledad* (1950) and *Posdata* (1970). It marks the evolution of his thought from historicist and archetypal positions to dialectical and properly historical ones. From an impressionistic phenomenology of the Mexican "national character" Paz has come to reflect on worldwide

phenomena such as bureaucracy and to consider the concrete political and social processes of Mexico and other Latin American countries.
          J. V. Coutinho

941. Medina, Luis. ORIGEN Y CIRCUNSTANCIA DE LA IDEA DE UNIDAD NACIONAL [The origin and state of the idea of national unity]. *Foro Int. [Mexico] 1974 14(3): 265-290.* Analyzes the rise of national unity in Mexico, 1940-70, particularly as an instrument for peace in Mexican politics.

942. Mendirichaga Cueva, Tomás. LA SEGUNDA UNIVERSIDAD DE NUEVO LEON (AÑO LECTIVO 1947-1948) [The second University of Nuevo León, lecture year 1947-48]. *Humanitas [Mexico] 1981 22: 219-237.* Discusses the political, academic, and economic problems relating to the expansion and continuation of the University of Nuevo León.

943. Meyer, Lorenzo. PERMANENCIA Y CAMBIO SOCIAL EN EL MÉXICO CONTEMPORÁNEO [Social permanence and change in contemporary Mexico]. *Foro Int. [Mexico] 1980 21(2): 119-148.* Examines social change and political stability in Mexico after 1940 and relates social change to international and internal economic developments. 3 tables.   D. A. Franz

944. Middlebrook, Kevin J. POLITICAL CHANGE IN MEXICO. *Pro. of the Acad. of Pol. Sci. 1981 34(1): 43-54.* An examination of the 1977 political reform in the historical context of political change in Mexico. Analyzes the reform's origins, scope, and consequences, and evaluates the implications that contemporary political change in Mexico may have for US-Mexican relations.   T. P. Richardson

945. Mixon, J. Wilson; Poulson, Barry W.; and Wallace, Myles S. THE POLITICAL ECONOMY OF DEVALUATION IN MEXICO: SOME NEW EVIDENCE. *Inter-American Econ. Affairs 1979 33(2): 71-85.* Examines both fixed and flexible exchange rate systems in Mexico, 1955-77, focusing on the effect of each on monetary control and income.

946. Molina, Sylvia. OBSERVACIONES SOBRE PROBLEMAS UNIVERSITARIOS [Observations on university problems]. *Rev. Mexicana de Ciencia Pol. [Mexico] 1973 19(73): 27-35.* Examines problems of colleges and universities, focusing generally on Latin American universities and specifically on the National Autonomous University of Mexico, 1966-72. Conflicts arose because social criticism by members of the increasingly radical university community threatened the government.

947. Mols, Manfred. DER MEXIKANISCHE PRÄSIDENTSCHAFTSWAHLKAMPF 1969/70 [The Mexican presidential campaign, 1969-70]. *Jahrbuch für Gesch. von Staat, Wirtschaft und Gesellschaft Lateinamerikas [West Germany] 1981 18: 329-386.* The Partido Revolucionario Institucional (PRI) conducted a ritual-filled campaign in an electoral process that really did not allow any political alternative. The government unscrupulously suppressed the political opposition. Yet the National Action Party lost for reasons in addition to the political suppression. The problems evident in the 1969-70 campaign remain the current problems of Mexico's politics in the 1980's. Based on Mexican newspapers, interviews, Mexican government publications, and secondary sources; 87 notes, 6 fig.   T. Schoonover

948. Mumme, Stephen P. U.S.-MEXICAN GROUNDWATER PROBLEMS: BILATERAL PROSPECTS AND IMPLICATIONS. *J. of Interamerican Studies and World Affairs 1980 22(1): 31-55.* The United States and Mexico have a controversy over groundwater underlying the border areas. While this important issue will most likely exacerbate relations in the short run, it probably will not cause a major change in existing patterns of US-Mexican relations. Mexico and the United States will follow the traditional pattern of resolution by diplomatic means. Secondary sources; 12 notes, ref.   T. D. Schoonover

949. Navarro de Castro, Maria Ester. LAS ORGANIZACIONES CAMPESINAS OFICIALES [Official peasant organizations]. *Estudios Pol. [Mexico] 1979 4(15): 103-108.* Brief description of three important peasants' organizations with formal ties to official Institutional Revolutionary Party. Founded in 1938, the Central Campesina Nacional has become the largest peasants' organization in Mexico. With a membership consisting largely of small landowners, it refrains from radical acts, pre-

ferring to act through legal channels. Founded in 1949, the Unión General de Obreros y Campesinos de Mexico (UGOCM) opposed close government control of the labor movement. Noted for its support of peasant invasions of private land holdings, it has split into three factions. Founded in 1970, the Consejo Agrarista Mexicana draws its membership from peasants near Mexico City. It is notorious for its role in government-supported land seizures.   F. J. Shaw, Jr.

950. Needler, Martin C. DANIEL COSIO VILLEGAS AND THE INTERPRETATION OF MEXICO'S POLITICAL SYSTEM. *J. of InterAm. Studies and World Affairs 1976 18(2): 245-252.* The Mexican political system is so complex that it is difficult for Mexicans and non-Mexicans alike to understand it. The view of Mexico in the United States is that the government is a democracy in which there is no competition between parties, but among sectors of the official party. This view tends to ignore the real abuses of power such as the Tlatelolco Massacre of 1968. The Mexican view of their government is not very analytical. Daniel Cosío Villegas has moved in the direction of analysis but as an historian and not as a social scientist. While his approach has some shortcomings his work has been generally praiseworthy. Based on three recently published books by Daniel Cosío Villegas. Note, biblio.
J. R. Thomas

951. Nguyen, D. T. and Martinez Saldivar, M. L. THE EFFECTS OF LAND REFORM ON AGRICULTURAL PRODUCTION, EMPLOYMENT AND INCOME DISTRIBUTION: A STATISTICAL STUDY OF MEXICAN STATES, 1959-69. *Econ. J. [Great Britain] 1979 89(355): 624-635.* Tests a number of contentions concerning the economic effects of land reform statistically for the years 1959 and 1969. The land reform sector performed at least as well as the private sector in terms of growth rates of crop output and even better in terms of growth rates of output per unit of "total measured inputs," but this was partly due to transfer of land between private and land reform sectors. While crop yield was found to be lower in the land reform sector in both years, both average and marginal returns to expenditure on farm inputs were found to be considerably higher. Based on census data on 32 Mexican states, 1959 and 1969; 2 tables, 6 notes, appendix.
D. J. Nicholls

952. Niblo, Stephen R. PROGRESS AND THE STANDARD OF LIVING IN CONTEMPORARY MEXICO. *Latin Am. Perspectives 1975 2(2): 109-124.* Examines Mexico's attempts at modernization since 1940.

953. Ojeda, Mario. EL PODER NEGOCIADOR DEL PETRÓLEO: EL CASO DE MÉXICO [Petroleum's negotiating power: the Mexican case]. *Foro Int. [Mexico] 1980 21(1): 44-64.* Discusses the nature and limitations of internal and international economic power provided by oil exports, using Mexican-Israeli relations since 1975 and Mexican domestic politics since 1976 as examples. 2 tables, 27 notes.   D. A. Franz

954. Ojeda, Mario. MÉXICO ANTE LOS ESTADOS UNIDOS EN LA COYUNTURA ACTUAL [Current Mexican-United States relations]. *Foro Int. [Mexico] 1977 18(1): 32-53.* Examines US-Mexican relations since 1970, emphasizing Mexico's poor bargaining position because of its weak economy. 5 tables, 19 notes.   D. A. Franz

955. Ortiz Mendoza, Ángeles. LA CCI: HISTORIA DE UNA LUCHA (ANTECEDENTES DE LA CIOAC) [The CCI: history of a struggle: antecedents of the CIOAC]. *Estudios Pol. [Mexico] 1979 4(15): 109-140.* Founded in 1962, in reaction to the docility of the official National Peasants' Federation in Mexico, the Central Campesina Independiente (CCI) soon split into two groups. Led by Alonzo Garzón Santibáñez, the first group gained admission into the official revolutionary party, gaining its members access to state dispensed credit, fertilizer, and technical assistance. The second group, led by Ramón Danzós and Arturo Orona, forsook official status to lead landless rural workers in land seizures and militant agitation, and form the Central Independiente de Obreros Agrícolas y Campesinos (CIOAC). Secondary sources.
F. J. Shaw, Jr.

956. Paz, Octavio. THINKING BACK TO THE STUDENT REVOLT. *Dissent 1975 22(2): 148-153.* Discusses the Mexican student movement of 1968.   S

957. Pellicer de Brody, Olga. LA OPOSICIÓN EN MÉXICO: EL CASO DEL HENRIQUISMO [The opposition in Mexico: the case of Henriquismo]. *Foro Int. [Mexico] 1977 17(4): 477-489.* Examines the rise and fall of the Federation of Parties of the People (Federación de Partidos del Pueblo) which supported General Miguel Henríquez Guzman in the Mexican presidential elections of 1952. The piece provides a case study of how political opposition in Mexico is coopted, combated, and eliminated. 26 notes.   D. A. Franz

958. Pellicer de Brody, Olga. A MEXICAN PERSPECTIVE. *Pro. of the Acad. of Pol. Sci. 1981 34(1): 4-12.* Examines the penetration of US interests into the Mexican economy since 1977 and the presence of conflict in political relations unknown since the early 1940's. The two nations have common interests, but they are the product of differing histories, values, and needs, which lead them to view political and economic problems differently. Understanding these different perspectives is the best way to foster the mutual respect that should characterize the future of the bilateral relationship. Secondary sources; 2 notes.
T. P. Richardson

959. Pellicer de Brody, Olga. VEINTE AÑOS DE POLÍTICA EXTERIOR MEXICANA: 1960-1980 [Twenty years of Mexican foreign policy, 1960-80]. *Foro Int. [Mexico] 1980 21(2): 149-160.* Examines the impact of oil exports on Mexico's foreign relations, the treatment of foreign revolutionary regimes by Mexico, and some ambiguities in Mexican foreign policy. Secondary sources; 5 notes.   D. A. Franz

960. Peñaloza, Tomás. MECANISMOS DE LA DEPENDENCIA: EL CASO DE MÉXICO (1970-75) [Dependence mechanisms: the case of Mexico, 1970-75]. *Foro Int. [Mexico] 1976 17(2): 10-36.* Analyzes balance of payments components (imports, exports, services, and capital) between the United States and Mexico to gain insight into the mechanisms of economic dependence. Primary and secondary sources; 10 tables, 22 notes.   D. A. Franz

961. Peschard, Jacqueline. LA DINASTÍA REVOLUCIONARIA: PERSONIFICACIÓN DE LA AUTORIDAD MONÁRQUICO-REPUBLICANA [The revolutionary dynasty: personification of monarchical-republican authority]. *Estudios Pol. [Mexico] 1978 3(9): 123-137.* Disputes the traditional interpretation that postrevolutionary Mexican governments represent an abrupt break with the regime of Porfirio Díaz; in fact, they are its heirs. The Díaz regime imposed federal political authority throughout Mexico through a network of personal bonds connecting the dictator with regional caudillos. Although governing by extraconstitutional means, Díaz scrupulously respected constitutional norms. His only major political failure was his inability to provide for the peaceful and orderly transition of power. After the fall of Díaz, the Constitution of 1917 established centralized government which permitted participation of new social forces in national politics. The paramount problem of post-1917 regimes was to convert personal bonds uniting its leaders into institutional means of transferring and exercising power. This was done through the creation of a single political party, uniting all political factions in support of the revolutionary leadership. Secondary sources; 26 notes.   F. J. Shaw

962. Poitras, Guy E. MEXICO'S "NEW" FOREIGN POLICY. *Inter-Am. Econ. Affairs 1974 28(3): 59-77.* Discusses Mexico's "new" active foreign policy aimed at uniting Latin American states. Suggests that the policy is an attempt to renegotiate the terms of dependence and "increase the economic advantage of Mexico in relation to the United States." Primary and secondary sources; 2 tables, 28 notes.
D. A. Franz

963. Port-Levet, Frédérick. LA SELVA LACANDONA, CHIAPAS, MEXIQUE: CONTRÔLE DE L'ESPACE ET DES PRODUCTIONS, ET ENCADREMENT DE LA PAYSANNERIE INDIGÈNE [The Selva Lacandona in Chiapas, Mexico: control of space and production and the infrastructure of the native peasantry]. *Travaux & Mémoires de l'Inst. des Hautes Études de l'Amérique Latine [France] 1979 (32): 67-81.* An analysis of the processes of settlement and of the attempts by several Mexican government organizations in the development of the Selva Lacandona, in the eastern part of the state of Chiapas, Mexico.

964. Price, Thomas J. INTERNATIONAL TRANSPORTATION AND INTEGRATION: EVIDENCE FROM THE EL PASO/-JUAREZ MICROCOSM. *Int. Studies Notes 1979 6(1): 18-21.* Discusses the endeavors of El Paso, Texas and Juarez, Chihuahua to facilitate public and private transportation between the two cities from the 1950's to the 1970's.

965. Puente Leyva, Jesús. THE NATURAL GAS CONTROVERSY. *Pro. of the Acad. of Pol. Sci. 1981 34(1): 158-167.* On 21 September 1979, Mexico signed an agreement to export natural gas to the United States, thus ending a two-year public debate over its national oil development strategy. Mexico's decisions regarding natural gas represented the triumph of Lázaro Cárdenas's nationalist principles. Mexico would not produce oil in response to international pressures for higher consumption, but instead would limit its production to amounts that were in keeping with its overall economic development. 10 notes.

T. P. Richardson

966. Purcell, John F. H. MEXICAN SOCIAL ISSUES. *Pro. of the Acad. of Pol. Sci. 1981 34(1): 43-54.* Illustrates how Mexican social issues interact with US social issues in unexpected ways that affect the political relationship between the two countries. A major step forward in the relationship between the two countries can be made when North Americans involved with Mexico realize that Mexicans have a better framework for thinking about Mexican social issues than they do.

T. P. Richardson

967. Purcell, Susan Kaufman. DECISION-MAKING IN AN AUTHORITARIAN REGIME: THEORETICAL IMPLICATIONS FROM A MEXICAN CASE STUDY. *World Pol. 1973 26(1): 28-54.* An authoritarian regime is defined in terms of variables that facilitate comparison with other types of regimes. The framework is applied to the authoritarian regime of Mexico. The defining variables are then used to elaborate generalizations regarding the decisionmaking process in authoritarian regimes in general, and in Mexico in particular. The generalizations are tested against information obtained from the study of one major decision—that of Mexican President Adolfo López Mateos (1958-64) to implement the provisions of the Constitution of 1917 that provide for the distribution of a portion of industry's profits among the workers. Finally, a model of the decisionmaking process and its relation to current socioeconomic and political trends in Mexico are analyzed.

J

968. Rello, Fernando. SISTEMAS AGROINDUSTRIALES, TRANSNACIONALES Y ESTADO EN MEXICO [Agroindustrial systems, transnationals, and the state in Mexico]. *Investigación Econ. [Mexico] 1979 38(150): 153-177.* The vertical integration in the food industry of Mexico started in the 1960's, with the entrance of multinational corporations into agribusiness, seeking to control the entire process from raw materials to consumer in dairy products, meats, soy, and breakfast cereals. The state has taken on the role of regulator and mediator, facilitating profits to the transnationals by absorbing part of the costs, instead of helping national industries. The result has been the creation of consumer markets for processed foods with high profit yields.

969. Revel-Mouroz, Jean. AU MEXIQUE: DÉVELOPPEMENT AGRICOLE ET CRISE AGRAIRE AU TERME DE LA PRESIDENCE ECHEVERRÍA [Mexico: agricultural development and agrarian crisis at the end of the Echeverria presidency]. *Cahiers du Monde Hispanique et Luso-Brésilien [France] 1977 (28): 245-258.* After the agricultural boom of the 1940's and 1950's, Mexico suffered a production collapse during the sixties. To overcome the crisis, the Echeverria administration took several measures aimed at modernizing the small-farm economy, the ejido in particular, and transforming land reform from land distribution to the organization of collective production. Those reforms were however compromised by the devaluation of the peso and growing uneasiness about the government's capacity to maintain the industrialization program of the preceding two decades. Based on official publications, secondary works; tables, 11 notes.

L. Garon

970. Revel-Mouroz, Jean. LA POLITIQUE ÉCONOMIQUE MEXICAINE: 1976-1980 [Mexican economic policy: 1976-80]. *Problèmes d'Amérique Latine [France] 1980 57(4579-4580): 73-126.* Studies the economic policy of President José López Portillo of Mexico in 1979, when signs of recovery were visible, despite continued inflation, unemployment, and financial instability.

971. Reyna, Jose Luis. EL MOVIMIENTO OBRERO EN UNA SITUACIÓN DE CRISIS: MÉXICO 1976-1978 [The labor movement in a crisis situation: Mexico, 1976-78]. *Foro Int. [Mexico] 1979 19(3): 390-401.* Discusses the political reaction of organized labor to economic malaise in Mexico following the devaluation of the peso in 1976. 3 tables, 23 notes.

D. A. Franz

972. Rigg, Howard V. THE *MAQUILA* PROGRAM. *Revista/-Review Interamericana [Puerto Rico] 1980 10(1): 83-93.* Despite problems, Mexico's Border Industrialization Program has generally been successful for Mexico, the United States, and the companies involved. This success will continue in the future, however, only if all the participants benefit from the arrangement. 17 notes.

J. A. Lewis

973. Rivera, Julius and Goodman, Paul W. SYSTEM-ENVIRONMENT ADAPTATIONS: CORPORATIONS IN A U.S.-MEXICO BORDER METROPOLIS. *Studies in Comparative Int. Development 1981 16(2): 24-46.* Examines the *maquila,* or twin plant, system of industrialization on the US-Mexican border as a set of mutually adaptive relationships among large corporations, governments, and labor. Examines the demography and geography of the border community. Describes the Mexican Border Industrialization Program and its interrelationships with the two federal governments, customs officials, labor, and the border community, the system as it has developed since the 1960's. Compares multinational and international *maquilas*. The *maquila* system is functioning well, but this is only true because of the organizational weaknesses of labor. Primary sources; note, 4 ref., 2 tables.

S. A. Farmerie

974. Ross, Stanley R. THE ADMINISTRATION OF LUIS ECHEVERRIA A. *Texas Q. 1973 16(2): 45-61.* After Luis Echeverria became president of Mexico in 1970, government was more open to criticism and instituted redistributive tax reform to the benefit of lower income brackets and rural areas. The country is left, however, with problems of exchange, trade imbalances, and inflation. Primary sources; 25 notes.

R. H. Tomlinson

975. Rothstein, Frances. THE CLASS BASIS OF PATRON-CLIENT RELATIONS. *Latin Am. Perspectives 1979 6(2): 25-35.* Examination of the socioeconomic conditions in San Cosme, between Mexico City and Puebla, demonstrates the prevalence of patron-client relationships that yield the working class selected benefits of industrialization, while enabling capitalists to extend the benefits in return for cooperative political support. Based on field work and secondary sources; table, 14 notes.

J. F. Vivian

976. Ruiz Nápoles, Pablo. DESEQUILIBRIO EXTERNO Y POLÍTICA ECONÓMICA EN LOS SETENTA [External disequilibrium and economic policy in the 1970's]. *Investigación Econ. [Mexico] 1979 38(150): 359-389.* The burden of servicing Mexico's external debt was compounded by decreasing agricultural exports and the international recession of 1973-74. Devaluation (1976), IMF-forced stabilization, and oil exports softened but did not structurally alter the crisis situation. Excluding oil, the balance of payments deficit grew 67% from 1977 to 1978, and total external debt service required nine billion dollars in 1978, on a debt itself equivalent to 36% of of 1977 GNP. The 1976 devaluation became one more source of destabilization, affecting both the economy and the political situation.

977. Sanderson, Steven E. FLORIDA TOMATOES, U.S.-MEXICAN RELATIONS, AND THE INTERNATIONAL DIVISION OF LABOR. *Inter-American Econ. Affairs 1981 35(3): 23-52.* Discusses the Florida tomato war of the 1970's and its significance for economic and political relations between the United States and Mexico, concluding that the competition between Mexico and Florida in marketing winter tomatoes can only be understood in terms of international trade variables and the changing international division of labor.

978. Sandoval, Luis. LA CRISIS MONETARIA CAPITALISTA Y SUS REPERCUSIONES EN MÉXICO [The capitalist monetary crisis and its repercussions in Mexico]. *Investigación Econ. [Mexico] 1973 32(126): 251-268.* Examines the rise of the post-1945 capitalist monetary system based on gold and the dollar, and discusses contradictions within the system that have caused economic problems in Mexico in the 1970's.

979. Schmidt, Henry C. THE MEXICAN INTELLECTUAL AS POLITICAL PUNDIT, 1968-1976: THE CASE OF DANIEL COSIO VILLEGAS. *J. of Interamerican Studies and World Affairs 1982 24(1): 81-103.* Daniel Cosío Villegas's life's work spanned a wide variety of activity, from founding the Fonda de Cultura Economica, El Colegio de México and editing the multivolume *História Moderna de México* to public speaking, popular writing, journalism in *Excelsior,* and television script-writing. He played a key role in opening the debate on fundamental political issues and personalities in modern Mexico, but one should not overemphasize his independence. He retained close links to the elite and served in government posts for much of his life. Based on the printed works of Cosío Villegas, his associates and contemporary intellectuals; 10 notes, ref.　　　　　　　　　　　　　　　　T. D. Schoonover

980. Segovia, Rafael. LA REFORMA POLÍTICA: EL EJECUTIVO FEDERAL, EL P.R.I. Y LAS ELECCIONES DE 1973 [The political reform: the federal executive, the PRI and the elections of 1973]. *Foro Int. [Mexico] 1974 14(3): 305-330.* Analyzes the rising number of votes in the elections of 1967, 1970, and 1973 cast for the ruling Partido Revolucionario Institucional (PRI) and the Partido Accion Nacional (PAN).

981. Shapira, Yoram. LA POLÍTICA EXTERIOR DE MÉXICO BAJO EL RÉGIMEN DE ECHEVERRÍA: RETROSPECTIVA [Mexican foreign policy under the Echeverria regime: in retrospect]. *Foro Int. [Mexico] 1978 19(1): 62-91.* Examines the foreign policy of Luis Echeverría's government in terms of its relation to Mexican internal affairs. Primary and secondary sources; 51 notes.　　　　D. A. Franz

982. Shapira, Yoram. MEXICO: THE IMPACT OF THE 1968 STUDENT PROTEST ON ECHEVERRÍA'S REFORMISM. *J. of Interam. Studies and World Affairs 1977 19(4): 557-580.* The 1968 political protests by students in Mexico did not focus on professional or sectorial interests, but embraced a broad spectrum of social, economic, and political issues. President Luis Echeverría sought to develop a progressive liberal image to eliminate the reputation he acquired from his role in suppressing the 1968 student strike. The fact that Echeverría tried to influence the reform program beyond his six-year term by hand-picking his successor suggests his reform efforts were not just stylish. 14 notes.　　　　　　　　　　　　　　　　T. D. Schoonover

983. Shapira, Yoram. MEXICO'S FOREIGN POLICY UNDER ECHEVERRÍA: A RETROSPECT. *Inter-American Econ. Affairs 1978 31(4): 29-61.* Examines the foreign policy of Mexican President Luis Echeverría as a function of the economic and regime legitimizing goals of the government. 51 notes.　　　　　　　　　　D. A. Franz

984. Smith, Peter H. LA MOVILIDAD POLÍTICA EN EL MÉXICO CONTEMPORÁNEO [Political mobility in contemporary Mexico]. *Foro Int. [Mexico] 1975 15(59): 379-413.* Examines patterns of interpositional political mobility, relations between politicians and their social backgrounds, and the impact of the political recruitment process on the stability and capacity of the political system, based on a statistical analysis of the Mexican political elite. Revised version of a paper presented at the 1974 meeting of the American Political Science Association in Chicago. Primary and secondary sources; 6 tables, 2 graphs, 44 notes, appendix.　　　　　　　　　　　　　　　　D. A. Franz

985. Spalding, Rose J. STATE POWER AND ITS LIMITS: CORPORATISM IN MEXICO. *Comparative Pol. Studies 1981 14(2): 139-161.* Analyzes both the extent and the limitation of state power in Mexico, focusing on the development of the rural social security system during the administration of President Luis Echeverría (1970-76).

986. Story, Dale. TRADE POLITICS IN THE THIRD WORLD: A CASE STUDY OF THE MEXICAN GATT DECISION. *Int. Organization 1982 36(4): 767-794.* In 1980 Mexico decided not to join the General Agreement on Tariffs and Trade (GATT). Certain objective conditions formed a positive environment for Mexican adherence, but President López Portillo postponed Mexican entry indefinitely. This critical decision is examined from two perspectives: a left-leaning foreign policy, and domestic constraints in the Mexican political system. Major foreign policy factors were a growing resentment of US dominance combined with a preference for conducting relations with the United States on a bilateral basis. Internal political pressures reflected the continued

reform of the Mexican political system at the upper levels and the relative autonomy of some elite groups from the state. López Portillo's decision did not constitute an outright rejection of trade liberalization. However, the decision could have international repercussions in "politicizing" US-Mexican trade relations, in slowing trends toward freer trade (especially in Latin America), and in strengthening multilateral organizations like UNCTAD in which Third World countries exercise considerable power.　　　　　　　　　　　　　　　　　　　　　　　　　　　　J

987. Urquidi, Victor L. NOT BY OIL ALONE: THE OUTLOOK FOR MEXICO. *Current Hist. 1982 81(472): 78-81, 90.* Regarding Mexico's prospects in connection with its current oil boom, many Mexican social scientists believe that the next twenty years represent Mexico's last chance to create a more just, equal, flexible, and pluralistic society within a democratic system. Questions this exaggeration as well as optimistic rhetoric in the light of Mexico's gross problems: lack of food production, high inflation, and huge population increases.

988. Valdés, Luz María. ENSAYO SOBRE POLÍTICA DE POBLACIÓN 1970-1980 (PLANIFICACIÓN FAMILIAR) [An essay on population policy 1970-80: family planning]. *Demografía y Econ. [Mexico] 1980 14(4): 467-480.* Examines political measures that produced demographic changes in Mexico between 1970 and 1980 and how the public actions have been implemented in practice at the administrative level.

989. Velasco Fernández, Ciro. EL GASTO PÚBLICO DE LOS SETENTA [Public expenditures in the 1970's]. *Investigación Econ. [Mexico] 1979 38(150): 431-447.* A decade of growth and stability in Mexico in the 1960's was followed by a decade of instability and crisis. In the 1970's, growth nearly stopped, inflation was rampant, the balance of payments became acutely negative, and after the devaluation (1976), unemployment, shortages, and low wages coexisted with capital flight, dollarization, hoarding, and speculation. Public spending went from 26% in 1970 to over 44% of the GNP in 1979, accompanied by contradictory policies.

990. Villar, Samuel I. del. ESTADO Y PETRÓLEO EN MEXICO: EXPERIENCIAS Y PERSPECTIVAS [State and petroleum in Mexico: experiences and perspectives]. *Foro Int. [Mexico] 1979 20(1): 118-158.* Discusses development of petroleum production and policy in Mexico, operations of Petróleos Mexicanos (PEMEX), Mexican-US relations concerning oil, and the impact of oil policy and production on other sectors of the Mexican economy. 102 notes.　　　　D. A. Franz

991. Ward, Peter. POLITICAL PRESSURE FOR URBAN SERVICES: THE RESPONSE OF TWO MEXICO CITY ADMINISTRATIONS. *Development and Change [Netherlands] 1981 12(3): 379-407.* Compares the methods established by the Mexican administrations of Luis Echeverría, 1971-76, and José López Portillo, 1976- , for controlling the system of community participation in the allocation of urban services and the improvement of impoverished residential areas of Mexico City, focusing on the growing importance of the Juntas de Vecinos (neighborhood associations).

992. Wionczek, Miguel S. ECHEVERRIA'S VIEW OF MEXICO IN THE POST COLD WAR WORLD. *Int. Perspectives [Canada] 1973 (9-10): 35-41.* Reviews Mexican international relations, 1867-1940's and Mexico-US relations, 1940-70, detailing the diplomatic tour of state visits which Mexico's president Luis Echeverría took in 1973 in order to secure stronger economic relations between Mexico and other world powers and lessen Mexico's dependence on US economic policy.

993. Wolf, Eric. LA CRISIS DE LA SOCIEDAD CAMPESINA [The crisis of peasant society]. *Rev. Mexicana de Ciencia Pol. [Mexico] 1973 19(73): 97-100.* Maintains that modern-day Mexican peasant society, which represents peasant societies in general, is undergoing an ecological, political, and intellectual crisis caused by the poverty of the soil and the peasants' increasing dependence on an external socioeconomic system.

994. —. MEXICO: A REVOLUTIONARY DIARY. *Progressive Labor 1973 9(3): 69-79.* Reviews strikes, student unrest, and attempted intimidation of workers and socialists by authorities in Mexico from 5 January to 25 October 1972.

3. CENTRAL AMERICA

Regional Studies

995. Aleixo, José Carlos Brandi. O CONFLITO EL SALVADOR-HONDURAS E A INTEGRAÇÃO CENTRO-AMERICANA [The El Salvador-Honduras conflict and Central American integration]. *Rev. de Ciência Política [Brazil] 1977 20(2): 23-78, 20(3): 17-75.* Part I. Examines the 1969 war between El Salvador and Honduras, tracing its causes to a complex of economic, political, historic, juridical, military, demographic, and cultural factors. Pays particular attention to the conflicting positions adopted by the two countries because of their need to foster economic integration. Part II. Analyzes the opposing views of the protagonists, the military operations, the role of other countries, and the postwar development of both nations. Stresses the importance of the Central American Common Market and the overall implications of the war for Central American integration.

996. Ameringer, Charles D. THE THIRTY YEARS WAR BETWEEN FIGUERES AND THE SOMOZAS: INTERNATIONAL INTRIGUE IN COSTA RICA AND NICARAGUA. *Caribbean Rev. 1979 8(4): 4-7, 40-41.* Charts relations between Nicaragua and Costa Rica, which were particularly bitter during the 1940's-50's when President Anastasio Somoza García of Nicaragua attempted to prevent José Figueres from assuming the presidency of Costa Rica and then tried to overthrow his government while Figueres tried to destabilize Somoza's regime.

997. Anderson, Thomas P. THE AMBIGUITIES OF POLITICAL TERRORISM IN CENTRAL AMERICA. *Terrorism 1980 4(1-4): 267-276.* Considers the difficulty of labeling Central American terrorism as either right or left, a situation complicated by international factors such as connections with the Palestine Liberation Organization or Cuban exile groups.

998. Berryman, Phillip. CENTRAL AMERICA'S NEWS VS. U.S. VIEWS. *Freedomways 1981 21(3): 161-170.* Compares socioeconomic realities in Central America with the two approaches to the region's problems adopted by the United States: President Jimmy Carter's view that unresolved social problems in Central America make political change inevitable and must be countered by supporting moderates in the area's nations, and President Ronald Reagan's view that considers the region as an arena of US-Soviet confrontation. Both stances fail to consider the needs and hopes of the general population.

999. Bologna, Alfredo Bruno. CONSEQÜÊNCIAS DO CONFLITO ENTRE HONDURAS E EL SALVADOR [Consequences of the conflict between Honduras and El Salvador]. *Rev. de Ciência Pol. [Brazil] 1979 22(4): 127-141.* Describes the 1969 war between Honduras and El Salvador and lists a number of possible reasons for the conflict. Since 1969 diplomatic efforts to resolve the conflict have been stalled. In 1975 the president of El Salvador said he hoped 1976 would be a year of peace, but hostilities broke out again in July. Further diplomatic efforts and a professed desire to negotiate have created a truce. 49 notes.
J. V. Coutinho

1000. Bonpane, Blase. THE CHURCH AND REVOLUTIONARY STRUGGLE IN CENTRAL AMERICA. *Latin Am. Perspectives 1980 7(2-3): 178-189.* Reviews the active role of churchmen in 19th-century Central American independence movements and their acquiescence in the rise of Anastasio Somoza in the 1930's. Describes how the Cursillos de Capacitación Social, an originally anticommunist seminar-retreat movement sponsored by Jesuit and Maryknoll fathers, was transformed in Nicaragua into a Christian-Marxist dialogue on the needs of the nation and the people.
J. F. Vivian

1001. Burbach, Roger. CENTRAL AMERICA: THE END OF U.S. HEGEMONY? *Monthly Rev. 1981 33(8): 1-18.* Analyzes the strengths and weaknesses of the US position in Central America. The United States could unleash its great military power, but naked US aggression in Cen-

tral America might meet defeat since the world has changed dramatically in the past two decades. Analyzes counterinsurgency war as a US tactic in El Salvador, Guatemala, and Nicaragua.

1002. Bye, Vegard. USA OG MELLOM-AMERIKA: AVGJØRENDE PRØVE PÅ ET IMPERIUMS FRAMTID [The United States and Central America: a decisive test for the future of an empire]. *Internasjonal Politikk [Norway] 1980 (4): 783-820.* Analyzes main trends in recent US policy toward Central America, detailing the US involvement in Nicaragua and its failure to avoid a Sandinista victory, typical of the political helplessness of US policy in the region, confirmed by later events in El Salvador. The great danger is that this political weakness will provoke military reactions with far-reaching and tragic consequences. Offers two theses concerning US policy in the region, one describing the internal contradictions in US policymaking and the other suggesting that US options are acceptance of radical popular revolutions or open military intervention.
J

1003. Cabarrús, Carlos Rafael. LA ESTRATIFICACIÓN, PISTA PARA LA INTELECCIÓN DE LOS GRUPOS ÉTNICOS [Stratification, a route for intellectualizing the ethnic groups]. *Estudios Centroamericanos [El Salvador] 1979 34(363-364): 27-46.* Social stratification among the indigenous population of Panama and Guatemala has served capitalist purposes in providing economic benefits. The process has been applied in education, folklore, work, trade, and politics to divide and exploit the Indian population. However, social stratification has caused the most advanced individuals to question the system and strive for change and ethnic rights. 8 illus., table, biblio.
P. J. Durell

1004. Cabrera, Herman Hooker. EL BANCO CENTROAMERICANO DE INTEGRACIÓN ECONÓMICA [The Central American Bank of Economic Integration]. *Foro Internacional [Mexico] 1973 13(52): 469-489.* Discusses the Central American Bank of Economic Integration, its relations with the Central American Common Market, and its possible role in the economic future of Central America. Primary and secondary sources; 7 tables, 39 notes.
D. A. Franz

1005. Calvert, Peter. GUATEMALA AND BELIZE. *Contemporary Rev. [Great Britain] 1976 228(1320): 7-12.* Discusses the history of Guatemala's claim to Belize, 1839-1975.

1006. Cazali Avila, Augusto. LA AUTONOMIA UNIVERSITARIA EN CENTROAMERICA [University autonomy in Central America]. *Anuario de Estudios Centroamericanos [Costa Rica] 1977 3: 9-25.* A review of the development of Central American universities indicates that true autonomy did not arrive until 1944. Colonial and 19th-century university independence was limited either by the Church or the state. The impact of the movement to gain autonomy organized by Córdova University in Argentina in 1918 was a factor in the overthrow of Maximiliano Hernández Martínez in El Salvador and Jorge Ubico Castañeda in Guatemala in 1944. In both cases university students played a key role in pushing for university autonomy throughout Central America. Primary sources; 11 notes.
H. J. Miller

1007. Chinchilla, Norma Stoltz. CLASS STRUGGLE IN CENTRAL AMERICA: BACKGROUND AND OVERVIEW. *Latin Am. Perspectives 1980 7(2-3): 2-23.* Introduction to a special combined issue on Central America in light of the revolutionary victory in Nicaragua and the continuing struggle in El Salvador. The unifying theme is capitalism and its contradictions as seen in the creation of the Central American Common Market and the labor movement it spawned. Secondary sources; note, biblio.
J. F. Vivian

1008. Christou, G. and Wilford, W. T. TRADE INTENSIFICATION IN THE CENTRAL AMERICAN COMMON MARKET. *J. of Interam. Studies and World Affairs 1973 15(2): 249-264.* Five nations banded together in 1961 to form the Central American Common Market. Trade among these nations intensified in the 1960-68 period, but trade with nonmember nations decreased in the same period. Based on regional statistical data, primary and secondary books and articles. 7 tables, 4 notes, biblio.   J. R. Thomas

1009. Deere, Carmen Diana. A COMPARATIVE ANALYSIS OF AGRARIAN REFORM IN EL SALVADOR AND NICARAGUA 1979-81. *Development and Change [Netherlands] 1982 13(1): 1-41.* Examines the demand for land reform in El Salvador and Nicaragua, the relation between reform and politics in each country, and the scope of the reforms, and summarizes US financial assistance to the reforms under the Carter and Reagan administrations during the years 1979-81.

1010. Dorner, Peter and Quiros, Rodolfo. INSTITUTIONAL DUALISM IN CENTRAL AMERICA'S AGRICULTURAL DEVELOPMENT. *J. of Latin Am. Studies [Great Britain] 1973 5(2): 217-232.* The economic successes of the Central American Common Market contributed to the economic, social, and political isolation of the rural population in the 1960's because of the continuing dichotomy between the few large farms producing mainly for export and the many small farms for domestic consumption. This dichotomy included the transformation of a permanent farm labor force into a largely seasonal labor pool, resulting in some cases in regional labor shortages amidst widespread (national) unemployment and underemployment, reduced incomes and employment security for farm workers, massive displacement of small farmers, major declines in domestic food crops, and a concentration of credit and governmental services for the benefit of the export producers. "In this setting, serious doubts arise about the net benefits of export-led economic growth when its total benefits are weighted against the less obvious but allpervasive social costs." Based on government reports and secondary works; 4 tables, 23 notes.   K. M. Bailor

1011. Ebel, Roland H. POLITICAL INSTABILITY IN CENTRAL AMERICA. *Current Hist. 1982 81(472): 56-59, 86.* Central America's urban elites are now a beleaguered minority besieged by increasingly well-organized and well-armed lower-class groups demanding substantial changes in national economic, political, and social structures. Explores how far the United States is prepared to go to attempt to reverse these trends.

1012. Ellis, Frank. LA VALORACIÓN DE EXPORTACIONES Y LAS TRANSFERENCIAS ENTRE COMPAÑÍAS DEDICADAS A LA INDUSTRIA DE EXPORTACIÓN DEL BANANO EN CENTROAMÉRICA [Export evaluation and intercompany transfers among Central American banana export companies]. *Estudios Sociales Centroamericanos [Costa Rica] 1979 8(22): 227-247.* Since the turn of the century, Costa Rica, Guatemala, Honduras, and Panama have been the principal center of banana production, exporting to the developed countries without preferential treatment. Although the imposition of an export tax has augmented government revenues, it has not produced change in the relationship between production and marketing of the bananas. The exporters continued to receive only that proportion of the total value of banana sales which are consistent with the traditional objectives of the multinational corporations. Based on printed primary and secondary sources; 22 notes, 13 tables, map.   T. D. Schoonover

1013. Feinberg, Richard E. BACKGROUND TO CRISIS: U.S. POLICIES TOWARD CENTRAL AMERICA IN THE 1970S. *Towson State J. of Int. Affairs 1981 16(1): 29-40.* Discusses the origins of the crisis of the late 1970's in Central America, especially the failure of the United States to make a timely response, with special attention to the policies of the Carter Administration and its globalist human rights foreign policy.

1014. Fischer, Alfred Joachim. AGRARIAN POLICY IN CENTRAL AMERICA. *Contemporary Rev. [Great Britain] 1974 224(1299): 182-188.* Discusses the failure of land reform in Mexico, and its absence in Guatemala and El Salvador from 1910 to the present day.

1015. Flores Macal, Mario. DEPENDENCIA Y INTEGRACIÓN EN CENTROAMÉRICA [Dependency and integration in Central America]. *Anuario de Estudios Centroamericanos [Costa Rica] 1978 4: 67-78.* The history of Central America is one of economic dependency: Spain in the colonial era, England in the 19th century, and the United States in the 20th century. England opposed unionism because it ran

counter to its economic interests but the United States supported 19thcentury union movements. When the United States began to dominate the economic life of Central America at the end of the 19th century, it opposed unionism. Due to the ascendency of populism, the United States supported economic integration from the 1950's. The result was a Central American Common Market dominated by native and US interests. The failure of the market is due to the neglect of populist sectors. 9 notes.
                                                                                      H. J. Miller

1016. Flores Pinel, Fernando. EL CONVENIO DE MEDIACIÓN HONDURAS-EL SALVADOR O PACTO BORGONOVO-PALMA [The Honduras-El Salvador mediation agreement or the Borgonovo-Palma Pact]. *Estudios Centro Americanos [El Salvador] 1977 32(350): 920-923.* The signing of the treaty in October 1976 and its ratification by the El Salvador legislature in September 1977 signaled the end of a typical international conflict best resolved by international law. Of interest are the political, economic, and social conditions which permitted the signing of the pact. The historic ties among the Central American people make political conflict similar to civil war. In 1969 the success of the Central American Common Market was threatened as a result of the war. However, the processes of inflation and recession have since encouraged bilateral and multilateral cooperation.   J. M. Walsh

1017. Flores Pinel, Fernando. ENTRE LA GUERRA Y LA PAZ: EL CONFLICTO HONDURO-SALVADOREÑO 1969-1979 [Between war and peace: the conflict between Honduras and El Salvador 1969-79]. *Estudios Centroamericanos [El Salvador] 1979 34(369-370): 675-698.* Aims to explain the rationale behind the conduct of diplomacy and negotiations, the causes and results of the conflict between Honduras and El Salvador, and the effects of the crisis in Nicaragua. Lack of employment in El Salvador's agricultural sector caused mass migration to Honduras; the government of El Salvador has failed to improve conditions or prevent emigration, resulting in economic, demographic, and territorial repercussions for El Salvador. Discusses frontier negotiations, 1861-1968, including negotiators and topics of discussions, interregional trade in Central America, 1960-77, border incidents since 1969, and advances in and obstacles to mediation. Based mainly on periodical sources; 5 illus., 3 maps, 4 tables, 72 notes.   P. J. Durell

1018. Gleijeses, Piero. THE ELUSIVE CENTER IN CENTRAL AMERICA. *Working Papers Mag. 1981 8(6): 30-37.* Traces political events in Central America since the Alliance for Progress promoted political and social reforms to prevent a Communist takeover; focuses on criticisms of President Jimmy Carter's Central American policy by President Reagan's Republican supporters, some of whom believe that the Carter administration's naivete resulted in increased Communist presence in Nicaragua, Guatemala, and El Salvador, while others believe that Carter's leftist supporters worked to get the left wing in power.

1019. Gorguette, Jean. DÉFENSE DANS LE MONDE: L'ENJEU DE L'AMÉRIQUE CENTRALE [Defense policy throughout the world: the stakes in Central America]. *Défense Natl. [France] 1977 33(1): 143-148.* Discusses the strategic importance of the Central American countries in the international political spectrum of the 1970's.

1020. Grieb, Kenneth J. THE MYTH OF A CENTRAL AMERICAN DICTATORS' LEAGUE. *J. of Latin Am. Studies [Great Britain] 1978 10(2): 329-345.* Utilizes recently available records to unveil the origins of rumors of a mutual assistance pact between the military dictatorships of Central America, and the discrepancies between these rumors and the actual interaction between the states, 1934-45.

1021. Heath, Dwight B. CURRENT TRENDS IN CENTRAL AMERICA. *Current Hist. 1975 68(401): 29-35, 41-42.* Gives political profiles of Guatemala, El Salvador, Honduras, Nicaragua, Costa Rica, Belize, and Panama to show that regional integration is remote.   S

1022. Holly, Daniel. LE CONFLIT DU HONDURAS ET DU SALVADOR DE 1969 [The 1969 Honduras-El Salvador conflict]. *Études Int. [Canada] 1979 10(1): 19-52.* Examines this 1969 conflict, noting its causes, which evolved principally from migratory and national issues, and the role of the Organization of American States. Believes that Honduras emerged stronger from the encounter. Chart, 197 notes.
                                                                                      J. F. Harrington

1023. Jamail, Milton H. THE STRONGMEN ARE SHAKING. *Latin Am. Perspectives 1980 7(2-3): 190-200.* Reviews and lists numerous studies of Central America, including four recent publications by London's Latin American Bureau on Nicaragua, El Salvador, Guatemala, and Belize. Secondary sources; biblio.   J. F. Vivian

1024. Landry, David M. U.S. POLICY AND LESSONS LEARNED FROM THE CENTRAL AMERICAN ECONOMIC INTEGRATION EXPERIENCE. *Southern Q. 1973 11(4): 297-308.* Surveys recent inter-American economic developments. Describes the positions of Presidents Lyndon Johnson and Richard Nixon concerning a Latin American common market. Latin American economic integration should be encouraged, but the barriers raised in each country by special pressure groups impedes cooperation. 16 notes.   R. W. Dubay

1025. Lascaris, Constantino. LA DEPENDENCIA EN CENTRO AMERICA [Dependence in Central America]. *Rev. del Pensamiento Centroamericano [Nicaragua] 1976 31(153): 20-30.* Defines dependence and reviews ways in which Central America has been dependent on Spain in the colonial period, on Britain in the early 19th century, and progressively on the United States since 1850. Economic and cultural dependence has followed political dependence. Economically, Central America is dependent on the export of desserts—coffee, bananas, pineapples, chocolate, sugar, and coconuts—to the industrialized nations. Moreover, its population is dependent on unskilled labor. Central America's continued dependence is not lack of capital, however, but lack of technology and modern educational advancement. In addition to better pedagogy, ambition and motivation must be a part of Central America's educational systems.   R. L. Woodward, Jr.

1026. Levi, Darrell E. NATIONALISM IN CENTRAL AMERICA, PANAMA, AND BELIZE: SOME VIEWS OF THE 1970'S. *Can. Rev. of Studies in Nationalism [Canada] 1980 7(biblio): 70-81.* Annotated bibliography of works on Guatemala, Honduras, El Salvador, Nicaragua, Costa Rica, Panama, and Belize since 1970.   R. Aldrich

1027. Menges, Constantine C. CENTRAL AMERICA AND THE UNITED STATES. *SAIS Rev. 1981 (2): 13-33.* Examines the historical background of the current situations in El Salvador and Nicaragua (including US involvement) to illuminate the need for greater understanding of the political purposes, structures, and actions of three competing forces: the reformist moderates, the Communist Party, and the extreme right.

1028. Menon, P. K. THE ANGLO-GUATEMALAN TERRITORIAL DISPUTE OVER THE COLONY OF BELIZE (BRITISH HONDURAS). *J. of Latin Am. Studies [Great Britain] 1979 11(2): 343-371.* The Anglo-Guatemalan controversy over Belize arose out of the 1859 treaty. After abortive attempts to settle the issue, at times involving attempts at enlisting other powers' support, it reemerged in 1968 when a draft treaty was drawn up that tied Belize closely with Guatemala. The treaty, although making Belize nominally independent, tied it so closely to Guatemala as to make it less than fully sovereign. The plan was rejected by all parties after rioting in Belize. But Guatemala still lays claim to Belize, whose government rejects the claim. Based on UN records, Guatemalan government papers, and material in the British Public Record Office; 107 notes.   E. J. Adams

1029. Millett, Richard L. THE POLITICS OF VIOLENCE: GUATEMALA AND EL SALVADOR. *Current Hist. 1981 80(463): 70-74, 88.* Traces the causes of past and present political violence in El Salvador and Guatemala, and analyzes the politics of the successive governments in the 1970's in their attempts to alleviate economic and social problems, commenting also on US involvement in these countries.

1030. Molina Chocano, Guillermo. CRISIS, CAPITALISMO, INFLACIÓN Y PAPEL ECONÓMICO DEL ESTADO [Crisis, capitalism, inflation and the economic role of the state]. *Estudios Sociales Centroamericanos [Costa Rica] 1981 10(28): 9-41.* The increasing participation of the Central American state in the accumulation of capital is associated with the process of capital accumulation within the context of a world crisis and the economic recuperation of the agricultural export sector. State activity feeds on the process of the increasing internal state debt which makes capital more expensive just as the system demands

more capital and hence facilitates tightening the hold on the dependent economies. Based upon published primary and secondary sources; 12 tables, 37 notes.   T. D. Schoonover

1031. Opazo Bernales, Andrés. CRISIS DEL SOCIAL-CRISTIANISMO Y NUEVAS PRÁCTICAS POLÍTICAS DE LOS CRISTIANOS [Crisis of social Christianity and the new political practices of Christians]. *Estudios Sociales Centroamericanos [Costa Rica] 1981 10(28): 43-68.* Social Christianity in Central America has tended to surge during periods of bourgeois reform but often remains in the hands of the dominant classes. 32 notes.   T. D. Schoonover

1032. Palma, Diego. EL ESTADO CONTEMPORÁNEO EN CENTRO AMÉRICA [The contemporary state in Central America]. *Anuario de Estudios Centroamericanos [Costa Rica] 1979 5: 9-26.* While there are differences among Central American countries, they share common traits, such as neocolonialism and single-product agricultural export. The analysis focuses on the liberal oligarchical domination and its antecedents, the revamping of oligarchical rule in the 1930's, economic tendencies after World War II, classes, alliances, and the type of bourgeois domination that has become prominent in each country. Based on government statistical reports and secondary sources; 10 tables, 42 notes.   H. J. Miller

1033. Real Espinales, Blas A. and Ucles, Mario Lunge. LA PROBLEMÁTICA REGIONAL EN CENTROAMÉRICA [The regional problem in Central America]. *Estudios Sociales Centroamericanos [Costa Rica] 1979 8(23): 9-33.* The problem of regionalization in Central America is shaped by the fact that the development of capitalism required conformity and the integration of its diverse regions. Regionalization should be a function of the social division of labor rather than the territorial defect encountered in the technical division of labor. The regional structuralization of Central America leads historically to the disintegration of political federation and to repressive economic federation. Based on printed materials; 3 maps, 2 tables, 7 notes.   T. D. Schoonover

1034. Richter, Ernesto. SOCIAL CLASSES, ACCUMULATION, AND THE CRISIS OF "OVERPOPULATION" IN EL SALVADOR. *Latin Am. Perspectives 1980 7(2-3): 114-135.* Both Honduras and El Salvador used the so-called Soccer War of 1969 to influence domestic difficulties that still trouble the two societies. For Honduras, the war stemmed from poor integration into the Central American Common Market, and strengthened the existing order. For El Salvador, the war obscured the problem of population growth and was used to justify militarily repressive control measures. US interests were not adversely affected. Table, 3 notes, biblio.   J. F. Vivian

1035. Saez, Manuel Alcantara. DIEZ AÑOS DE CONFLICTO ARMADO ENTRE EL SALVADOR Y HONDURAS [Ten years of armed conflict between El Salvador and Honduras]. *Rev. de Estudios Int. [Spain] 1980 1(3): 725-740.* In spite of their common colonial heritage, the countries of Central America do not have a common ground. The creation in 1960 of the Central American Common Market, though a successful instrument in developing and expanding intraregional trade, failed to solve the basic problems of integration of the region. This failure was epitomized by the growing tension between El Salvador and Honduras, which exploded into the "one hundred hours" or "football" war of June 1969. Analyzes the development and consequences of the crisis with attention given to the role of the Organization of American States and of the United States. 15 notes.   D. Ardia

1036. Salisbury, Richard V. COSTA RICA Y LA CRISIS NICARAGÜENSE DE 1925-1926 [Costa Rica and the Nicaraguan crisis of 1925-26]. *Rev. del Pensamiento Centroamericano [Nicaragua] 1975 30(147): 9-18.* Although Costa Rica made a genuine effort at isolation from the other Central American republics during the late 19th and early 20th centuries, it could not do so completely, as was seen in the Nicaraguan crisis of 1925-26. The author details the crisis and Costa Rica's concern over foreign intervention in Central America. President Ricardo Jiménez' government opposed radical Mexican involvement in Central America, yet it consistently refused to recognize the Conservative government of Adolfo Díaz, which had been installed in Nicaragua with backing. Based on diplomatic correspondence. 68 notes.   R. L. Woodward, Jr.

1037. Salisbury, Richard V. COSTA RICA Y LA CRISIS HONDUREÑA DE 1924 [Costa Rica and the 1924 Honduras crisis]. *Rev. de Hist. [Costa Rica] 1978 3(6): 43-68.* Examines Costa Rican attempts, together with those of El Salvador, Guatemala, and the United States, to resolve the 1924 civil war in Honduras which followed the presidential elections there in 1923; also describes the internal repercussions in Costa Rica.

1038. Salisbury, Richard V. UNITED STATES INTERVENTION IN NICARAGUA: THE COSTA RICAN ROLE. *Prologue 1977 9(4): 209-217.* President Ricardo Jiménez of Costa Rica secretly supported the intervention of the United States in Central American affairs through his pro-interventionist stance during the Nicaraguan crises of 1912 and 1927. This fact was not even revealed to the Costa Rican establishment whom other presidents had closely consulted before action. Jiménez took the position that the United States should either keep entirely out of Central American affairs, or, what was most likely given the American-felt need to protect the Panama Canal, that the United States guarantee peace and stability in the isthmus in no uncertain manner. These views as expressed privately to American diplomats encouraged the interventionist thrust of the American government, leading to the stationing of US troops in Nicaragua. Primary sources. N. Lederer

1039. Sancho, José. ANTECEDENTES Y PERSPECTIVAS DE LA POLÍTICA CONSTITUCIONAL DE LA INTEGRACIÓN CENTROAMERICANA [Antecedents and perspectives of the constitutional policy of Central American integration]. *Anuario de Estudios Centroamericanos [Costa Rica] 1978 4: 23-37.* Investigates the possibilities of economic, political, social, and cultural integration. The 19th century witnessed political integration attempts. Economic integration started in the 1950's with the Central American Common Market. The obstacles faced included national interests, lack of financing and technology, and elite economic interests. The Normalizing Commission of the 1970's, attempted to resolve the problems by setting up informal procedures for input by diverse interests and a mechanism for a common law to prevail over national laws, thereby making the common good mutually beneficial for all the republics. H. J. Miller

1040. Seckinger, Ron. THE CENTRAL AMERICAN MILITARIES: A SURVEY OF THE LITERATURE. *Latin Am. Res. Rev. 1981 16(2): 246-258.* Provides a guide to published materials and dissertations on Central American militaries. Except for Guatemala, extant research is sparse, but it provides a much-needed foundation. 4 notes, biblio. J. K. Pfabe

1041. Stone, Samuel. PRODUCCIÓN Y POLÍTICA EN CENTROAMÉRICA [Production and politics in Central America]. *Cahiers du Monde Hispanique et Luso-Brésilien [France] 1981 (36): 5-21.* Economic production is dependent on political systems even more than on the economic resources. Central American governments since independence, have not for the most part encouraged economic production, even as they have promised and pressed for wider distribution of products. Secondary sources; 2 tables, 29 notes, biblio. D. R. Stevenson

1042. Teillac, Jean. L'AMÉRIQUE DU CENTRE [Central America]. *Défense Natl. [France] 1975 31(6): 90-98.* Compares and contrasts the demography, economies, and political history of the six central American states.

1043. Torres-Rivas, Edelberto. THE CENTRAL AMERICAN MODEL OF GROWTH: CRISIS FOR WHOM? *Latin Am. Perspectives 1980 7(2-3): 24-44.* The Central American Common Market, created in 1960, has thus far favored Guatemala and El Salvador, whose economies produce goods of wider demand in the midst of larger national populations. Yet, paradoxically, Nicaragua and Costa Rica grew more rapidly and enjoy higher levels of worker productivity. The market must, therefore, contemplate political solutions that will broaden its social as well as economic boundaries. 6 tables, 5 notes, biblio.
J. F. Vivian

1044. Valenta, Jiri. THE USSR, CUBA, AND THE CRISIS IN CENTRAL AMERICA. *Orbis 1981 25(3): 715-746.* Analyzes Cuban and Soviet perceptions of and strategies toward Central America and the Caribbean, emphasizing the specific tactics employed in Nicaragua and

El Salvador from 1973 to 1981. Compares the conditions and the nature of the revolutions in Nicaragua and El Salvador and suggests that the revolution in Nicaragua was genuine but the one in El Salvador is not. Based on published sources; 42 notes. J. W. Thacker, Jr.

1045. Walker, Thomas W. THE US AND CENTRAL AMERICA. *Caribbean Rev. 1979 8(3): 18-23.* Since the founding of the Alliance for Progress nearly two decades ago, the United States has maintained an unimaginative, unproductive, and ineffective policy of preserving the status quo in Central America, relying on aid to capitalist enterprises to trickle down to the masses. But the political, social, and economic situations in Central America have deteriorated rather than improved.

1046. Wilford, W. T. and Christou, G. C. INTRA-AREA TRADE AND URBANIZATION IN THE CENTRAL AMERICAN COMMON MARKET, 1960-1971. *Secolas Ann. 1974 5: 122-137.*

1047. Williams, Robert G. "THE CENTRAL AMERICAN COMMON MARKET: A CASE STUDY OF THE STATE AND PERIPHERAL CAPITALISM." *Secolas Ann. 1982 13: 71-82.* Discusses the Central American Common Market (CACM), promoted by the United States to provide "encouragement to fledgling industrialists through subsidized finance, infrastructure expenditures favorable to their interests, fiscal incentives, and protective tariffs," originally just in Guatemala but by 1959 in all the Central American countries, which did not "provide a stable alternative to revolution in the region," but rather "set up the preconditions for the market's fragmentation later on."

1048. —. AT THE WALLS OF THE CITADEL. *World Marxist R. [Canada] 1973 16(8): 80-88.*
Mora Valverde, Eduardo. "NO" TO A PUPPET, pp. 81-83.
Duch, Roberto. A SUCCESSION OF CRIMES, pp. 83-86.
Tamayo, Juan Miguel. STOLEN FREEDOM, pp. 86-87.
Describes need for anti-imperialist groups in Costa Rica, Nicaragua and Puerto Rico to overcome U.S. domination. Continuing series on "Political Portrait of Latin America." S

1049. —. LOS PAISES DEL M.C.C.A. ANTE LA CRISIS [The Central American Common Market in crisis]. *Anuario de Estudios Centroamericanos [Costa Rica] 1979 5: 103-109.* Since the colonial epoch Central America has been a single-product exporter at the mercy of the world market. In the 20th century, US monopolies set up banana enclaves accompanied by military intervention. Unsuccessful attempts to break dependency occurred in El Salvador and Guatemala. The Central American Common Market failed, but it encouraged rural and urban proletariats that demanded a voice in government. Central America faces the crisis of an oligarchical and despotic state incapable of providing democracy. Secondary sources; table, 16 notes. H. J. Miller

Belize

1050. Aguilera Peralta, Gabriel. DEPENDENCIA POLÍTICA Y COLONIALISMO IDEOLOGÍA INDEPENDENISTA Y LUCHA DE CLASES EN BELICE [Political dependence colonialism, independent ideology and the struggle of the classes in Belize]. *Anuario de Estudios Centroamericanos [Costa Rica] 1977 3: 81-95.* From the 17th to the 20th century a dominant white class developed in Belize with ties with Britain, the United States, and Canada. The working class consisted of black slaves until replaced by a salaried peon class in the 19th century. By the 1950's a small bourgeoisie with independence aspirations gained control of the colony. Its ties were to US corporate interests. At the bottom of the social pyramid there was an indigenous and black labor class. Secondary sources; 4 charts, 28 notes. H. J. Miller

1051. Ashdown, Peter. ANTONIO SOBERANIS AND THE 1934-35 DISTURBANCES IN BELIZE. *Belizean Studies [Belize] 1978 6(2): 12-19, 6(3): 7-12, 6(4): 8-15.* Part III. Disturbances among the labor organizations in Belize, specifically the Labor and Unemployment Association, included rioting and strikes prior to and following the incarceration of labor leader Antonio Soberanis, 1934-35. Part IV. Examines the importance of the Labor and Unemployment Association, led by Antonio Soberanis, in Belize's labor history. Part V. Internal divisiveness, lack of adequate leadership on the part of Antonio Soberanis, lack of middle-class support, and economic conditions combined to defeat the ends of the labor movement in Belize, 1934-35, which sought to attain working class representation in the legislature, implement constitutional change, and repeal repressive labor laws.

1052. Ashdown, Peter. MARCUS GARVEY, THE UNIA AND THE BLACK CAUSE IN BRITISH HONDURAS, 1914-1949. *J. of Caribbean Hist. [Barbados] 1981 15: 41-55.* After 1914, owing in part to the influence of Marcus Garvey, race consciousness, especially on the part of black creoles, increased in British Honduras, now Belize. His Universal Negro Improvement Association (UNIA) Party was an important anti-British force in the colony in the 1920's. Eventually, however, it lost importance to the more popular multiethnic Peoples United Party (PUP). Primary sources; 80 notes.   R. L. Woodward, Jr.

1053. Aznar Sánchez, Juan. LA SITUACIÓN INTERNACIONAL DE BELICE [The international situation of Belize]. *Rev. de Política Int. [Spain] 1974 (133): 67-90.* Examines the history of Belize, 1662-1972, and discusses the possible ways in which Great Britain could dispose of it.

1054. Bradley, Leo H. BARRIER REEF COUNTRY: ITS ADMINISTRATIVE CENTERS. *Belizean Studies [Belize] 1978 6(4): 1-7.* Brief overview of various government centers from which British Honduras was governed, 1638-1926, including St. Georges Cay, the courthouse at the mouth of the Belize River, Fort George, Convention Town, Belize City, and Belmopan.

1055. Hamill, Don. COLONIALISM AND THE EMERGENCE OF TRADE UNIONS IN BELIZE. *J. of Belizean Affairs [Belize] 1978 (7): 3-20.* Labor revolts and strikes of the 1930's were a result of anti-colonial sentiment toward Great Britain which continued into the 1950's-60's concomitant with the growth of nationalism, which sought independence for Belize as well as social justice for the working classes.

1056. Hanson, David. POLITICS, PARTISANSHIP, AND SOCIAL POSITION IN BELIZE. *J. of Inter-Am. Studies and World Affairs 1974 16(4): 409-435.* Belize student attitudes reflected little sympathy for political opposition, minimal ethnic prejudice, and little fear of an invasion from Guatemala. Based on a 1970 questionnaire, government reports, census data, and secondary works; 13 tables, note, biblio.
                                                          J. R. Thomas

1057. Harrington, Richard. BELIZE: EX-COLONY, NEW NATION. *Canadian Geographical J. 1975 90(2): 14-21.* Pictorial essay and background of Belize (formerly British Honduras).   S

1058. Herman, Paula. BRITISH HONDURAS: A QUESTION OF VIABILITY. *World Affairs 1975 138(1): 60-68.* Belize (British Honduras), with no industry or mineral resources, poor farming, and Guatemala claiming its entire territory, has poor chances of viable independent existence in 1975.

1059. Herrmann, Eleanor Krohn. BLACK CROSS NURSING IN BELIZE: A LABOUR OF LOVE. *Belizean Studies [Belize] 1980 8(2): 1-9.* Traces the development and projects of the Black Cross Nurses Association in Belize, which developed under the auspices of Marcus Garvey's Universal Negro Improvement Association with the purpose of improving the health of Negroes so that they could effectively form a united front.

1060. Nunes, Frederick E. ADMINISTRATION AND CULTURE: SUBSISTENCE AND MODERNIZATION IN CRIQUE SARCO, BELIZE. *Caribbean Q. [Jamaica] 1977 23(4): 17-46.* Details the process and results of the British colonial advisory effort in the Kekchi Indian community of Crique Sarco, Belize, 1953-62. A Maya liaison officer arrived there in 1953 to advise the Kekchi on hygiene, welfare, commercial, and agricultural matters. Under his tutelage considerable economic and demographic growth took place during the next six years. Yet when the liaison officer was transferred in 1959, all he had achieved quickly began to crumble, and by 1962 the population had greatly declined and heavy vegetation had overgrown most of the major buildings. Cultural factors, as well as political and economic, were highly important in the course of events there. 2 maps, 42 notes, biblio.
                                                          R. L. Woodward, Jr.

1061. Spinner, Thomas J., Jr. BELIZE, GUATEMALA AND THE BRITISH EMPIRE. *Rev. Interamericana [Puerto Rico] 1976 6(2): 282-290.* The Guatemalan threat to Belize's territory has prevented Belize's independence. Independence, however, is inevitable, as is Belize's future separate from Guatemala.   J. A. Lewis

1062. Wyeth, John. BELIZEAN ECONOMIC HISTORY: A HISTORY OF THE BELIZE BOARD OF COMMISSIONERS OF CURRENCY (1894 TO 1976). *J. of Belizean Affairs [Belize] 1979 (8): 3-60.* The Belizean Board of Commissioners of Currency worked quite well, in a passive way, to effect smooth currency exchanges, investment, and mercantile transactions between Belize and Great Britain, although the British pound devaluation in 1949 caused some problems because the Belizean dollar was by that time pegged to the US dollar, and trade between Belize and the United States had outstripped trade between Belize and England. Necessary adjustments were made (not without hardship to the Belizean economy) to establish a local currency, to insure the continuing convertibility of sterling, and to allow the seigniorage of the currency to accrue to the colonial government.

1063. —. [COMMENTS ON CAIGER'S *BRITISH HONDURAS PAST AND PRESENT*].
Ashdown, Peter. THE PERVERSION OF HISTORY: A CRITIQUE OF STEPHEN L. CAIGER'S *BRITISH HONDURAS PAST AND PRESENT*. *J.of Belizean Affairs [Belize] 1978 (6): 37-50.* Critiques Stephen Langrish Caiger's *British Honduras Past and Present*. A British Anglican priest, Caiger produced a history of the British Empire in Belize, 18th-20th centuries, that is, an example of imperialist rhetoric and misrepresentation of historical events.
Sanchez, I. E. COMMENT ON PETER ASHDOWN'S ARTICLE ON JOBA 6. *J. of Belizean Affairs [Belize] 1978 (7): 54-56.* A response to Peter Ashdown's critique of Caiger's book.

1064. —. ON THE SETTLEMENT OF THE DISPUTE OVER BELIZE. *Inter-American Econ. Affairs 1981 34(4): 91-94.* Reprints the 1981 statement of British Foreign Secretary Lord Carrington on the settlement of the dispute between Guatemala and Great Britain over Belize and the responses of other officials.

Costa Rica

1065. Barahona Riera, Francisco. REFORMA AGRARIA Y ORGANIZACIÓN CAMPESINA [Agrarian reform and peasant organization]. *Estudios Sociales Centroamericanos [Costa Rica] 1979 8(22): 207-226.* In Costa Rica some pilot experiments are being conducted with peasant community businesses. Laboring under the propaganda of the liberal capitalist system however, the Costa Rican peasant believes in his personal capacity to succeed in his titanic struggle to leave better conditions for his children. Perhaps some positive factors will aid in the construction of a peasant organization under a newly proposed law. Based upon printed primary and secondary sources; 26 notes.
                                                          T. D. Schoonover

1066. Bell, John Patrick. POLITICAL POWER IN CONTEMPORARY COSTA RICA. *J. of Interamerican Studies and World Affairs 1978 20(4): 443-454.* Review article on books by Oscar Arias Sanchez, Rodolfo Cerdas Cruz, or Samuel Stone Zemurray, none of which alone offers a full explanation of contemporary Costa Rica.
                                                          T. D. Schoonover

1067. Booth, John A. and Seligson, Mitchell A. PEASANTS AS ACTIVISTS: A REEVALUATION OF POLITICAL PARTICIPATION IN THE COUNTRYSIDE. *Comparative Pol. Studies 1979 12(1): 29-59.* Examines peasant political activism in Costa Rica from 1972 to 1976, concluding that peasant political participation is multidimensional. Landed peasants were significantly more active than landless ones within the system while landless peasants were more active outside it. The modes of activism were largely the same for peasants and city dwellers.

1068. Bozzoli de Wille, María E. LA FRONTERA AGRICOLA DE COSTA RICA Y SU RELACIÓN CON EL PROBLEMA AGRARIO EN ZONAS INDIGENAS [The agricultural frontier of Costa Rica and its relation with the agrarian problem in Indian zones]. *Anuario de Estudios Centroamericanos [Costa Rica] 1977 3: 225-234.* During the colonial era the plentiful supply of land and a sparse population in Costa Rica helped popularize the notion of an agricultural frontier. The clearing of forest lands started in the center and spread outward, including Indian areas. Depletion of soil caused small farmers to sell land to large land owners such as ranchers who produced for the export market. The result was less employment and reduced agricultural production. The government with its frontier mentality pushed immigration and failed to protect forests. Not until 1973 did it see a nation with limited land resources. Secondary sources; 16 notes. H. J. Miller/S

1069. Casey Gaspar, Jeffrey. LIMON: 1880-1940. UN ESTUDIO DE LA INDUSTRIA BANANERA EN COSTA RICA [Limón: 1880-1940. A study of the banana industry in Costa Rica]. *Estudios Sociales Centroamericanos [Costa Rica] 1979 8(23): 245-279.* Studies the impact of the banana industry in Costa Rica's Puerto Limón region. Racial and nationalist conflict stem from the use of imported labor at the beginning in an enclave dedicated to exports. The Limón population movement was tied to the banana industry cycle, and the national government was impotent in the banana enclave area. Based upon printed primary and secondary materials; 18 notes. T. D. Schoonover

1070. Cazanga Moncada, Osvaldo. EL PARTIDO SOCIALDEMO-CRATA DE COSTA RICA: UNA EXPERIENCIA POLÍTICA [The Social Democratic Party of Costa Rica: a political experience]. *Rev. de Filosofía de la U. de Costa Rica [Costa Rica] 1979 17(46): 173-184.* Social democracy represented upper-class economic and professional interests and not working-class interests as was the case in Europe. Included in the rise of the Social Democratic Party (1946-49) were opposition to communism, influence of *Rerum Novarum,* New Deal, allied antidictatorship propaganda of World War II and opposition to *caudillismo.* It was also influenced by ideas from Chile and Colombia. It was a broad-based ideological party whose major traits were anticommunism, rational and ethical humanism, and nationalism. Based on interviews, contemporary periodicals, and Constituent Assembly records of 1949; 16 notes. H. J. Miller

1071. Cerdas Cruz, Rodolfo. DEL ESTADO INTERVEN-CIONISTA AL ESTADO EMPRESARIO (NOTAS PARA EL ESTUDIO DEL ESTADO EN COSTA RICA) [From the interventionist state to the managerial state: notes for the study of the state in Costa Rica]. *Anuario de Estudios Centroamericanos [Costa Rica] 1979 5: 81-100.* Emerging from the colonial period, Costa Rica had an agricultural exporting economy dependent on Spain and a concomitant socioeconomic organization. This became more pronounced in the 19th century with coffee production and dependence on England. With banana production, dependence switched to the United States. The middle sectors gained little and the Revolution of 1948 supported an interventionist state, which later became a managerial state, most clearly illustrated in the formation of the Costa Rican Corporation of Development. Secondary sources; table, 2 graphs, chart, 21 notes. H. J. Miller

1072. Cruz, Vladimir de la. EL PRIMER CONGRESO DEL PARTIDO COMUNISTA DE COSTA RICA [The first congress of the Costa Rican Communist Party]. *Estudios Sociales Centroamericanos [Costa Rica] 1980 9(27): 25-63.* Examines the roots of worker and Communist activity in Costa Rica, the 1931 founding of the Communist Party, and its growth and spread. Based upon newspapers and secondary sources; 60 notes. T. D. Schoonover

1073. Gutierrez Espeleta, Nelson. NOTAS SOBRE LA EVOLUCIÓN DEL ESTADO COSTARRICENSE, 1821-1978 [Notes on the evolution of the Costa Rican state, 1821-1978]. *Estudios Sociales Centroamericanos [Costa Rica] 1981 10(28): 69-86.* Reviews the progress of bourgeois political arrangements in Costa Rica in light of the Nicaraguan revolution. 37 notes. T. D. Schoonover

1074. Høivik, Tord and Aas, Solveig. DEMILITARIZATION IN COSTA RICA: A FAREWELL TO ARMS? *J. of Peace Res. [Norway] 1981 18(4): 333-351.* Costa Rica is an apparent exception to the trend toward military regimes, violent changes of power, and local wars in Third World countries. In this Central American republic with about 2 million inhabitants, the armed forces were disbanded in 1948. For over 30 years Costa Rica, surrounded by dictatorships, has maintained a stable civilian government without a regular army. The abolition of the Costa Rican army, the country's handling of external and internal conflicts since 1948, the growth of its paramilitary forces, and the reality of its public policy of demilitarization are discussed. Costa Rican demilitarization was a response to an internal conflict rather than a deliberate international policy. The country has actually built up police forces that are used against labor and peasant unrest, but it is also the case that demilitarization has been stressed so consistently in policy declarations that regular military buildup has been inhibited. Costa Rica is partly demilitarized, but may become more or less so in the future. J

1075. Leonard, Thomas M. THE UNITED STATES AND COSTA RICA, 1944-1949: PERCEPTIONS OF POLITICAL DYNAMICS. *Secolas Ann. 1982 13: 17-31.* Examines US perceptions of Costa Rica's Communist Party in terms of the United States's early Cold War policy, and gives a background to Costa Rica's social, economic, and political order from the 1920's.

1076. Rosenberg, Mark B. REFORMA SOCIAL Y CONFLICTO POLÍTICO: LA HUELGA MÉDICA COMO PRELUDIO A LA GUERRA CIVIL COSTARRICENSE DE 1948 [Social reform and political conflict: the medical strike as a prelude to the Costa Rican civil war, 1948]. *Rev. de Hist. [Costa Rica] 1977 3(5): 149-170.*

1077. Rosenberg, Mark B. SOCIAL REFORM IN COSTA RICA: SOCIAL SECURITY AND THE PRESIDENCY OF RAFAEL ÁNGEL CALDERÓN. *Hispanic Am. Hist. Rev. 1981 61(2): 278-296.* Rafael Ángel Calderón Guardia, president of Costa Rica, 1940-44, had been influenced by the Catholic social reform doctrine. As president he introduced measures for social security, social guarantees, and labor legislation. Social security legislation, written largely by Guillermo Padilla Castro, passed in Congress, with modifications, in November 1941. Former president Julio Acosta was named director-general of the social security administration and Padilla his assistant. Support came from Archbishop Victor Sanabria. Priority was given to lower-income workers, and aid was limited. This program laid the basis for the later reforms of President José Figueres. Based on contemporary Costa Rican newspapers, interviews, and materials in the Archivo de la Junta Directiva de la Caja Costarricense de Seguro Social and Archivo Nacional de Costa Rica (San José); 67 notes. B. D. Johnson

1078. Rosenberg, Mark B. SOCIAL SECURITY POLICYMAKING IN COSTA RICA: A RESEARCH REPORT. *Latin Am. Res. Rev. 1979 14(1): 116-133.* The Costa Rican social security program developed in four stages, from a limited workmen's compensation law (1924-25) to a universal program begun in 1961 and more fully implemented in the 1970's. Pressure groups had little role in policymaking. Important factors in the evolution of the program have been the social insurance bureaucracy, progressive political leadership, and the International Labor Organization. Based on interviews, government statistics, and secondary sources; 2 tables, 15 notes, biblio. J. K. Pfabe

1079. Rosenberg, Mark B. STATE INTERVENTION AND PRESIDENTIAL CONTROL IN COSTA RICA: THE ROLE OF THE PARTIDO LIBERACIÓN NACIONAL. *Secolas Ann. 1979 10: 95-108.* Maintains that expansion of presidential power in Costa Rica is a result of attempts by the Partido Liberación Nacional to gain effective organizational control of state apparatus in order to implement its programs and maintain its power position, 1940-78.

1080. Salisbury, Richard V. THE ANTI-IMPERIALIST CAREER OF ALEJANDRO ALVARADO QUIRÓS. *Hispanic Am. Hist. Rev. 1977 57(4): 587-612.* Alejandro Alvarado Quirós (1876-1945) urged his anti-imperialist views as Costa Rica's representative at inter-American conferences 1920-23, including the Santiago conference of 1923. In the Costa Rican Congress he opposed a Central Union Trust Company loan and a United Fruit Company contract due to his fear of US domination. He advocated isthmian union as a force against US interference. 82 notes. B. D. Johnson

1081. Salisbury, Richard V. COSTA RICA AND THE 1920-1921 UNION MOVEMENT: A REASSESSMENT. *J. of Interam. Studies and World Affairs 1977 19(3): 393-418.* The dream of union has been a constant, if difficult to analyze, factor in Central American history. Costa Rica usually has played a negative role in union schemes, allegedly due to its isolationist tradition. The 1920-21 movement for union seemed promising, but even a pro-union campaign in Costa Rica led by President Julio Acosta could not prevent its failure. While Acosta favored the union plan as a means of protecting Costa Rica's rights in the Nicaraguan canal project, he, like other Costa Ricans, continued to perceive union as subordinate to national policy objectives. Based on manuscript, printed primary, and secondary sources; 7 notes, biblio.   T. D. Schoonover

1082. Salisbury, Richard V.   DOMESTIC POLITICS AND FOREIGN POLICY: COSTA RICA'S STAND ON RECOGNITION, 1923-1924.   *Hispanic Am. Hist. R. 1974 54(3): 453-478.* Examines Costa Rica's innovative and independent relationship with the United States in the 1920's and 1930's, and analyzes its policymaking role for recognition of Central America. Reviews the historical decisions and maneuvers of Costa Rican leaders on isthmian recognition policies, focusing on the opposing policies of Julio Acosta and Ricardo Jimenez. Costa Rican policy decisions were based on protecting its national interests, not on acting in concert with or in fear of the United States. Based on contemporary newspaper reports, Costa Rican and Guatemalan government documents, primary and secondary sources; 75 notes.   N. J. Street

1083. Salisbury, Richard V.   POLÍTICA INTERNA Y DOCTRINA DE RELACIONES INTERNACIONALES: LA POSTURA DE COSTA RICA EN EL RECONOCIMIENTO 1923-1934   [Internal politics and the doctrine of international relations: the stand of Costa Rica regarding recognition, 1923-34].   *Anuario de Estudios Centroamericanos [Costa Rica] 1977 3: 267-293.* Inter-American studies tend to focus on US relations with Latin America. The author stresses Costa Rica's relations with her isthmian neighbors. The Washington Conference of 1922-23 provided the basis for the republic's actions in the recognition crises of Honduras, Nicaragua, and El Salvador. In the case of the latter, the recognition of Maximiliano Hernández Martínez was a departure from the Conference agreement and took place because of the pressure of internal politics in Costa Rica. The actions of the republic show a policy independent of the United States. Based mainly on diplomatic correspondence; 75 notes.   H. J. Miller

1084. Seligson, Mitchell A.   AGRARIAN POLICIES IN DEPENDENT SOCIETIES: COSTA RICA.   *J. of Interam. Studies and World Affairs 1977 19(2): 201-232.* The present social and economic structure and development of Costa Rica can be traced to its shifting agrarian policies and its economic dependence. During the colonial period the external control of agricultural policy stifled production, but independence led to an independent policy directed toward the stimulation of coffee production and export. This successful coffee export policy produced a number of results detrimental to Costa Rica's development: foreign control of coffee financing, diminished food crop production, concentration of land, uncontrolled inflation, and an export-crop oriented transportation system. Recent efforts to rectify these problems offer little hope for optimism about the future. Based on secondary materials; 3 notes, biblio.   T. D. Schoonover

1085. Seligson, Mitchell A.   THE IMPACT OF AGRARIAN REFORM: A STUDY OF COSTA RICA.   *J. of Developing Areas 1979 13(2): 161-174.* Costa Rica's first effort at agrarian reform began in 1942 with an Office of Colonization and Distribution of State Lands to administer state forest preserves; very little was accomplished. An agrarian reform law passed in 1961 emphasized respect for private property to discourage massive squatting, and provided for full prior compensation for expropriated land. Tied to the financial ability of the state, this program was limited, but in 1962 a Land and Colonization Institute was created to settle landless peasants on virgin land and to help land users get titles. Several communes were established. Major problems were lack of roads, houses, and water systems. During the 1970's, individual parcel and communal enterprise programs were promoted. Attitudinal surveys were made of two groups: landless peasants, and other peasants who had received land. Those who had land were more trusting of government, more positive about the future, more efficacious than those who had not received land. 4 tables, charts, 18 notes.   O. W. Eads, Jr.

1086. Stone, Samuel.   COSTA RICA'S POLITICAL TURMOIL.   *Caribbean Rev. 1981 10(1): 42-46.* Examines the reasons for conservative

Costa Rica's support of the Sandinista rebels in Nicaragua and explores possible future political trends in Costa Rica paying special attention to the need to increase production and to develop a balanced wealth redistribution program.

El Salvador

1087. Bourdillat, Nicole.   DICTATURE ET OPPOSITION AU SALVADOR (25 JANVIER 1961-15 OCTOBRE 1979)   [Dictatorship and opposition in El Salvador: 25 January 1961-15 October 1979].   *Problèmes d'Amérique Latine [France] 1980 57(4579-4580): 7-28.* Discusses the context and phases of the political situation in El Salvador which have led to the present civil war: the establishment of a military regime in 1961, the victory of the opposition in legislative elections in 1972, and the military's use of violence which has increased since the last military coup in 1979.

1088. Brodersohn, Victor.   ESTRUCTURA Y DESARROLLO SOCIAL EN EL SALVADOR   [Social structure and development in El Salvador].   *Estudios Sociales Centroamericanos [Costa Rica] 1981 10(29): 37-53.* El Salvador's government has not developed as broad an entrepreneurial function in the productive system as most other Latin American states. Its role in those areas where it does seek to have impact has not sufficed to allow it to redefine the distribution of national revenues nor to transform the social and economic structure. A more integrated economy and greater social equilibrium will require the strengthening of the state. Based upon Salvadoran official publications, censuses, and secondary sources; 26 notes, 7 tables.   T. D. Schoonover

1089. Brodersohn, Víctor.   ESTRUCTURA Y DESARROLLO SOCIAL EN EL SALVADOR   [Structure and social development in El Salvador].   *Desarrollo Econ. [Argentina] 1980 20(77): 121-134.* Attempts to present the relationship between the social and economic structures of El Salvador over the past 15 years, focusing on the role of the state and its structural determinants. Differing development systems have been adopted in El Salvador, all of them based on production for export, thus, international trade has always been important. The resulting agrarian and industrial conformations have marginalized the popular sector, caused the unequal distribution of income, determined economic concentration, and established links between local and foreign capital. The state is seen as carrying out a passive role, not altering social and economic trends. 7 notes, 7 tables.   G. Makin

1090. Cáceres Prendes, Jorge Rafael.   CONSIDERACIONES SOBRE EL DISCURSO POLÍTICO DE LA REVOLUCIÓN DE 1948 EN EL SALVADOR   [Thoughts on the political discourse of the Revolution of 1948 in El Salvador].   *Anuario de Estudios Centroamericanos [Costa Rica] 1979 5: 33-52.* Since 1900 El Salvador has had a dependent capitalist society and a liberal authoritarian state. The crisis of the 1920's paved the way for the paternalistic militaristic regime of Maximiliano Hernández Martínez in the 1930's. The rise of an intellectual urban sector led to his overthrow in 1944 and initiated a transition to more democracy with socialist undertones. By 1950 the moderates under Oscar Osorio were in control but true democracy and socioeconomic reforms remained yet to be achieved. Based on government documents and secondary sources; 57 notes.   H. J. Miller

1091. Davis, L. Harlan.   FOREIGN AID TO THE SMALL FARMER: THE EL SALVADOR EXPERIENCE.   *Inter-Am. Econ. Affairs 1975 29(1): 81-91.* Discusses the experience of El Salvador in stimulating economic growth through foreign aid to the small farmer. Based on personal experience, primary and secondary sources; 12 notes.   D. A. Franz

1092. Gerlach, Allen.   EL SALVADOR: BACKGROUND TO THE VIOLENCE.   *Contemporary Rev. [Great Britain] 1981 239(1386): 1-7.* Discusses the socioeconomic problems which are the underlying causes of the political violence in El Salvador in 1980.

1093. Gordon, Sara.   EL SALVADOR: CRISIS POLÍTICA Y MOVIMIENTO POPULAR   [El Salvador: political crisis and popular movement].   *Estudios Sociales Centroamericanos [Costa Rica] 1980 9(27):*

207-216. In El Salvador, a spontaneous movement has generated autonomous power distinct from that of the governing class. Popular mobilization and political organization in El Salvador raise various pressing questions for Latin America regarding social transformation, such as the concepts of fascism which shape the tactics, strategy, and character of the alliances, and the type of popular front required to confront the state and to construct a political party. T. D. Schoonover

1094. Handal, Shafik Jorge. EL SALVADOR: A PRECARIOUS BALANCE. *World Marxist R. [Canada] 1973 16(6): 46-50.* An overview of political parties in El Salvador, their role in the elections of 1972, and the Communist Party's stress on unity of anti-imperialist groups within the country. Continuing series on "Political Portrait of Latin America." S

1095. Jacir Siman, Ana Evelyn. EL SALVADOR, ACUMULACION DE CAPITAL Y PROCESO REVOLUCIONARIO (1932-1981) [Capital accumulation and revolutionary process in El Salvador, 1932-81]. *Investigación Econ. [Mexico] 1982 40(157): 293-309.* El Salvador entered the world market in the last third of the last century with the export of raw materials. By 1932 a new phase had begun with the expansion of the control of banking by the bourgeoisie and the introduction of cotton as a new export item. The state became the chief promoter of industrialization. With the triumph of the Cuban revolution, the bourgeoisie allied itself with imperialism. The Central American Common Market failed because it went against the interests of the middle classes. The present (1981) Christian Democrat military junta is unable to solve the structural problems of the country because it is not based on the people and is incapable of orienting the development process by the criterion of social gain rather than private profit. J. V. Coutinho

1096. Karush, Gerald. TIERRA, POBLACIÓN Y POBREZA: LAS RAÍCES DE LA CRISIS DEMOGRÁFICA EN EL SALVADOR [Land, population, and poverty: the roots of the demographic crisis in El Salvador]. *Estudios Centro Americanos [El Salvador] 1977 32(350): 893-910.* Most studies of population problems in Latin America tend to focus on statistics and neglect socioeconomic conditions. The current demographic crisis in El Salvador is linked to general poverty which in turn is a function of the type of economic underdevelopment encountered in Latin America. Rural poverty and a high birth rate are inherent in the plantation economy. Government policy has focused on family planning but only institutional reforms and the creation of development opportunities can eliminate poverty. 12 tables, 20 notes, 3 appendixes. J. M. Walsh

1097. Kruger, Alexander. EL SALVADOR'S MARXIST REVOLUTION. *J. of Social, Pol. and Econ. Studies 1981 6(2): 119-139.* The Salvadorean guerrilla organizations that make up the leadership of El Salvador's revolutionary movement came into being through various subdivisions within the Communist Party during the last decade. Although invited to participate in the elections, the guerrillas refused because their popular support has fallen.

1098. LeoGrande, William M. and Robbins, Carla Anne. OLIGARCHS AND OFFICERS: THE CRISIS IN EL SALVADOR. *Foreign Affairs 1980 58(5): 1084-1103.* El Salvador's problems stem from social and economic imbalances. After the war with Honduras in 1969, El Salvador's economy deteriorated, leading to increased political tensions in the 1970's. Successive military governments did not institute major reforms, owing to opposition from the oligarchy of influential families. A new military junta assumed control in January 1980 and encouraged reform while repressing Leftists. The junta ought to permit Leftist participation in government so as to avert a civil war. 5 notes. A. A. Englard

1099. LeoGrande, William M. A SPLENDID LITTLE WAR: DRAWING THE LINE IN EL SALVADOR. *Int. Security 1981 6(1): 27-52.* Examines the importance of the conflict in El Salvador for the developing foreign policy of the Reagan Administration, focusing on Reagan's use of the situation to provide a concrete example of his stance toward the USSR. Compares Reagan's approach with that of former President Carter.

1100. Levenstein, Harvey. CANADA AND THE SUPPRESSION OF THE SALVADOREAN REVOLUTION OF 1932. *Can. Hist. Rev. [Canada] 1981 62(4): 451-469.* A study of the little-known intervention of Royal Canadian Navy destroyers in the Salvadorean Revolution of 1932, often called the first Communist revolution in the hemisphere. The intervention and the favorable response it elicited in Canada indicate that Canada's non-interventionist reputation in the Third World is the product, not of any historical differences in attitudes between it and the major imperial powers, but of its economic and military weakness. Based on archival sources in Ottawa, London, and Washington. A

1101. López Vallecillos, Italo. FUERZAS SOCIALES Y CAMBIO SOCIAL EN EL SALVADOR [Social forces and social change in El Salvador]. *Estudios Centroamericanos [El Salvador] 1979 34(369-370): 557-590.* Discusses the exercise of political and economic power by the dominant classes and the position of the lower classes since 1948. Examines divisions within the upper classes and the struggle for hegemony; the historical, economic, and political roots of conflict; the economic cycles, 1948-60 and 1962-75; the increase in state bureaucracy; number of fatalities caused by government repression and guerrilla action; ideological forces in the political process; political and social forces opposed to change; role of the army; and the achievements of workers' organizations and unions. Based mainly on government statistics; 11 illus., 11 tables. P. J. Durell

1102. López Vallecillos, Italo and Orellana, Víctor Antonio. LA UNIDAD POPULAR Y EL SURGIMIENTO DEL FRENTE DEMOCRÁTICO REVOLUCIONARIO [Popular unity and the emergence of the Revolutionary Democratic Front]. *Estudios Centroamericanos [El Salvador] 1980 35(377-378): 183-206.* During the 1970's several types of popular unity movements emerged in El Salvador against the oligarchy's economic, political, and military dictatorship. These included mass organizations, labor unions, and armed resistance, which have been united in the Revolutionary Democratic Front (FDR). The authors analyze these developments in detail and the role of the FDR in the contemporary Salvadoran struggle. 19 notes. R. L. Woodward, Jr.

1103. López Vallecillos, Italo. RASGOS SOCIALES Y TENDENCIAS POLÍTICAS EN EL SALVADOR (1969-1979) [Social characteristics and political trends in El Salvador, 1969-79]. *Estudios Centroamericanos [El Salvador] 1979 34(372-373): 863-884.* The structural weakness of the system allied with the control of the state and its governmental apparatus has resulted in a sharp deterioration in social relations and a clear confrontation between the dominant and dominated classes. The pattern of repression and subversion demonstrates the escalation of the conflict. The military coup of 15 October 1979 and its consequences could be regarded either as a means of strengthening the process of democratization or as the last attempt by the armed forces to avoid civil war. 5 illus. P. J. Durell

1104. López Vallecillos, Italo. REFLEXIONES SOBRE LA VIOLENCIA EN EL SALVADOR [Reflections on violence in El Salvador]. *Estudios Centro Americanos [El Salvador] 1976 31(327-328): 9-30.* Gives social, political, and economic antecedents to institutional violence in El Salvador since 1900, focusing particularly on government violence since the 1930's.

1105. Mariscal, Nicolás. REGIMENES POLÍTICOS EN EL SALVADOR [Political regimes in El Salvador]. *Estudios Centroamericanos [El Salvador] 1979 34(365): 139-152.* Categorizes the political regimes of El Salvador since independence in 1821: 1) anarchic caciquism 1821-39, 2) coffee industry caciquism 1839-1930, 3) conservative military-coffee industry dictatorship 1930-48, 4) military-bureaucratic authoritarianism with modernizing structural reform 1948-76, and 5) from 1976, military-oligarchic bourgeois authoritarianism with modernizing structural conservatism. Focuses on the relation between sociopolitical forces and government in formulating a hypothesis on future regimes. 5 illus., 2 tables, 41 notes. P. J. Durell

1106. Marroquin, Alejandro D. ESTUDIO SOBRE LA CRISIS DE LOS AÑOS TREINTA EN EL SALVADOR [The study of the 1930's crisis in El Salvador]. *Anuario de Estudios Centroamericanos [Costa Rica] 1977 3: 115-160.* The economic crisis, 1929-35, caused a drop in coffee prices. In El Salvador this resulted in a loss of national revenue, lower wages, unemployment, an unfavorable balance of trade, high internal and external debts, lower cereal prices, and deflation. Classical economics failed to resolve the problems and reforms by President Arturo Araujo in 1931 proved ineffective. Fear of Communism aided the coming to power of General Hernández Martínez, helped by the local oligarchy and the United States. The result was a 13-year dictatorship. Based mainly on government treasury reports; 25 charts, 49 notes.

H. J. Miller

1107. Martín-Baró, Ignacio. EL LIDERAZGO DE MONSEÑOR ROMERO (UN ANÁLISIS PSICO-SOCIAL) [The leadership of Monsignor Romero: a psychosocial analysis]. *Estudios Centroamericanos [El Salvador] 1981 36(389): 151-172.* Neither his personality nor his previous experience as a priest and bishop adequately explain the extraordinary leadership of Archbishop Oscar Romero of San Salvador. Confrontation with historic events and demands brought out his distinctive characteristics. In the face of public disunity engendered by the authorities, Romero served as a social unifier at both the spiritual and political levels. Opposing oppression, Romero became a revolutionary symbol, challenging the dominant ideology and, by his example and words, promoting radical social changes. His assassination assured his influence, which continues to animate the struggle of the Salvadoran people for liberty and justice. Biblio.

R. L. Woodward, Jr.

1108. Martín-Baró, Ignacio. LA GUERRA CIVIL EN EL SALVADOR [The civil war in El Salvador]. *Estudios Centroamericanos [El Salvador] 1981 36(387-388): 17-32.* The maturity of the Farabundo Martí National Liberation Front (FMLN) and international assistance to the Revolutionary Democratic Front (FDR) on the one hand and the narrowing of political maneuvering space for the government junta on the other led to the formal beginning of the civil war in El Salvador on 10 January 1981. The simultaneous attack of the insurgent forces surprised the armed forces and achieved significant gains in several areas. On the other hand, the FDR's call for a general strike failed because of logistical errors and a rapid government response. Faced with possible insurgent victory, the United States restored its military aid and assumed the burden of a counteroffensive on three fronts: military, propaganda, and diplomatic. These factors, especially the US intervention, resulted in stalemate by the end of February and point toward a bloody prolongation and Vietnamization of the Salvadoran conflict. Primary sources; map, 2 tables, 4 illus., biblio.

R. L. Woodward, Jr.

1109. Montes, Segundo. POLÍTICAS DE PLANIFICACIÓN FAMILIAR EN EL SALVADOR [Politics of family planning in El Salvador]. *Estudios Centro Americanos [El Salvador] 1974 29(310-311): 494-542.* Analyzes political implications of contemporary birth control policies in urban and rural El Salvador, focusing on factors such as educational level, rural/urban differences, and educational campaigns to provide various regions of the country with birth control information.

1110. Nadezhdin, E. M. KOMMUNISTICHESKAIA PARTIIA SAL'VADORA: PIAT'DESIAT LET BOR'BY [The Communist Party of El Salvador: 50 years of struggle]. *Voprosy Istorii KPSS [USSR] 1980 (3): 119-122.* The short-lived Arturo Araújo government in El Salvador fell to Maximiliano Hernández Martínez in 1931 and junta rule began, vigorously suppressing left-wing revolt. The Third Communist Party Congress in 1948 adopted the National Unity Program, and mass activization followed, boosted in 1959 by Cuba's victory. The National Opposition Union (UNO) coalition (1971), a Communist Party initiative, included the National Democratic Union, the Christian Democratic Party, and the National Revolution Movement. Despite UNO advances in the 1972 presidential elections, Colonel Molina of the Partido de Conciliación Nacional achieved power. In 1964 and 1975 the Communist Party participated in the international conferences of Latin American and Caribbean countries.

M. R. Colenso

1111. Navarro, Vicente. GENOCIDE IN EL SALVADOR. *Monthly Rev. 1981 32(11): 1-16.* Describes the reign of terror being carried on by the current military junta in El Salvador, including widespread murder and torture of citizens and agrarian reforms designed to control the peasantry, the US role in providing military and economic aid to the terrorists, and the efforts of armed struggles of liberation in El Salvador since the early 1970's.

1112. Péronne, Louis-P. EL SALVADOR: QUI ASSASSINE? [El Salvador: who is assassinating?]. *Études [France] 1981 354(5): 607-619.* Discusses the political crisis in El Salvador, the injustices it is suffering, the violence of the Junta, US involvement in the right-wing government's attempt to thwart the efforts of the militant left.

1113. Prosterman, Roy L.; Riedinger, Jeffrey M.; and Temple, Mary. LAND REFORM IN EL SALVADOR: THE DEMOCRATIC ALTERNATIVE. *World Affairs 1981 144(1): 36-54.* The 1980 land reform in El Salvador increased prospects for a moderate democratic outcome there.

1114. Schall, James V. CENTRAL AMERICA AND POLITICIZED RELIGION. *World Affairs 1981 144(2): 126-149.* Analyzes the role of the Roman Catholic clergy, the Jesuits in particular, in contemporary El Salvador, and the degree to which they support, or are perceived to support, the leftist cause.

1115. Sebastián, Luis de. FORMULACIÓN DE POLÍTICAS NACIONALES DE VIVIENDA [Formulation of national housing policies]. *Estudios Centro Americanos [El Salvador] 1975 30(318): 189-200.* Discusses the stages of planning housing policy in El Salvador, including the determination that housing policy must be national, and stressing both the housing and the urban development aspects of the problem.

1116. Sebastián, Luis de. LA ECONOMÍA NACIONAL, UN AÑO DESPUÉS DEL 15 DE OCTUBRE DE 1979 [The national economy, one year after 15 October 1979]. *Estudios Centroamericanos [El Salvador] 1980 35(384-385): 953-970.* An analysis of the Salvadoran economy in the year following the coup d'état of 15 October 1979. All indicators reflect a general decline and progressive deterioration of economic conditions, which the agrarian, banking, and foreign trade reforms of the past year have failed to arrest. Based on official statistics, government and private sector publications, and newspapers; 6 illus., 17 tables, 17 notes.

R. L. Woodward, Jr.

1117. Sebastián, Luis de. LAS CRISIS ECONÓMICAS MUNDIALES Y SU REPERCUSIÓN EN EL SALVADOR [World economic crises and their repercussion in El Salvador]. *Estudios Centro Americanos [El Salvador] 1974 29(307): 235-254.* Discusses worldwide economic problems since the 1950's, especially those of the United States, and shows how they affect the "open" economy of El Salvador in terms of food shortages, unemployment, and lack of monetary stability.

1118. Stein, Eduardo. EL MITO DE LA LIBERTAD DE PRENSA EN EL SALVADOR [The myth of freedom of the press in El Salvador]. *Estudios Centro Americanos [El Salvador] 1975 30(316-317): 151-155.* Replies to the naming of El Salvador as a country with freedom of the press by the InterAmerican Press Society, examining the newspaper industry of the country to support his argument that this freedom is a myth.

1119. Ungo, Guillermo Manuel. LA SUSPENSIÓN DE GARANTÍAS CONSTITUCIONALES EN EL SALVADOR [The suspension of constitutional guarantees in El Salvador]. *Estudios Centroamericanos [El Salvador] 1977 32(344): 359-366.* The suspension of certain constitutional guarantees in El Salvador has remained a juridical function established in the 19th century and strongly influenced by liberal thought. The Constitution of 1883 was the first in which guarantees were regulated; that of 1886 specified various restrictions. By 1939, suspensions were identified with the state of emergency concept. In mid-20th century, however, the 19th-century criteria of constitutional laws were rejected. In 1950 and 1962, guarantees were incorporated directly into the text of the constitutions of those years. Laws regulating states of emergency or martial law, however, are not formalized. Based on secondary sources; illus., 5 notes.

J. M. Walsh

1120. Vejar, Rafael Guidos. LA CRISIS POLÍTICA EN EL SALVADOR (1976-1979) [The political crisis in El Salvador, 1976-79]. *Estudios Centroamericanos [El Salvador] 1979 34(369-370): 507-526.* Analyzes development of the current crisis of authority in El Salvador, 1976-79. Crucial factors include the schisms among the dominant sectors, the balance of compromise in a situation of shared economic power, and new dimensions of the popular struggle. Discusses the part played by the Catholic Church, unions, political parties, peasants, students, and professors; the effects of economic conditions, the historical background, strikes, demonstrations, and government repression; and social conditions since 1976. 6 illus., 12 notes. P. J. Durell

1121. Zaid, Gabriel. ENEMY COLLEAGUES: A READING OF THE SALVADORAN TRAGEDY. *Dissent 1982 29(1): 13-40.* A comprehensive portrait of the inner workings of Salvadoran politics; warns against widening the war in El Salvador and military intervention.

1122. Zaid, Gabriel. UNE GUERRE DE CHEFS. LECTURE DE LA TRAGÉDIE SALVADORIENNE [A war among leaders: the tragedy of El Salvador]. *Esprit [France] 1981 (12): 26-38.* An account of political events in El Salvador since 1972, centering on the evolution of the civil war, which is actually a personal war among the country's leadership. The author recommends a cessation of violence and a withdrawal of US interference. A partial translation of an article in *Vuelta* [Mexico] 1981.

1123. Zéndegui, Guillermo de. IMAGE OF EL SALVADOR. *Américas (Organization of American States) 1973 25(2): S1-S24.* Overview of El Salvador covering geography, population, history, political development and organization, culture, and economic and social development, prehistory to 1973.

1124. Zwiefelhofer, Hans. KIRCHE IN EL SALVADOR [Church in El Salvador]. *Stimmen der Zeit [West Germany] 1979 197(2): 86-98.* The initiative of Catholic priests and nuns for the establishment of agricultural cooperatives for the rural population of El Salvador in the 1960's and 1970's has caused a growth of repressive measures by the military dictatorship against priests, nuns, and peasants, including terror attacks, punishments, imprisonment, and murder.

1125. —. MILITARY EXCESS AND DEMOCRATIC HOPES: AN INFLAMMATORY MIX. *Center Mag. 1982 15(1): 37-59.* Roundtable discussion among Raymond Bonner, Arnold Ramos, John A. Bushnell and Murat Williams dealing with the El Salvadoran military, land reform, press coverage of the civil war in El Salvador, and the US role in seeking a negotiated peace. Third in a series of articles on El Salvador and US policy there.

Guatemala

1126. Aguilera, P. Gabriel; Belfrage, Cedric, transl. THE MASSACRE AT PANZOS AND CAPITALIST DEVELOPMENT IN GUATEMALA. *Monthly Rev. 1979 31(7): 13-23.* The massacre of over 100 Indian peasants at Panzós, Guatemala in May 1978 was in defense of the interests of the Guatemalan state and of international capital in the modern industrial development in the country's so-called Northern Transverse Strip.

1127. Aguilera P., Gabriel. EL ESTADO, LA LUCHA DE CLASES Y LA VIOLENCIA EN GUATEMALA [The state, class struggle and violence in Guatemala]. *Estudios Centroamericanos [El Salvador] 1978 33(356-357): 378-397.* Traces violence in Guatemala in the War of Independence in 1812, the consolidation of power, and the reaction against it in the liberal revolution of 1871. Defines current worldwide terrorist violence; in Guatemala violence is an expression of the class struggle in its most advanced form, the armed confrontation. 14 illus., 3 tables, 27 notes. K. A. Talley

1128. Aguilera Peralta, Gabriel. EFECTOS CUANTITATIVOS DE LA POLÍTICA DEL TERROR DEL ESTADO GUATEMALTECO EN RELACIÓN AL MOVIMIENTO POPULAR [Quantitative effects of state political terror in Guatemala in relation to the popular movement]. *Estudios Sociales Centroamericanos [Costa Rica] 1980 9(27): 217-249.* Violence in Guatemala is related to the matter of state political terror as a means of social control. Especially since 1966, this violence is linked to the lack of legitimacy which the elite requires to conserve itself. This tactic of very violent repression via institutional mechanisms has taken on the permanent stamp of counterinsurgency. Political violence is exercised principally against the popular sectors of the population. Based on Guatemalan newspapers, other primary and secondary printed sources; 11 tables, 31 notes. T. D. Schoonover

1129. Aguilera Peralta, Gabriel. TERROR AND VIOLENCE AS WEAPONS OF COUNTERINSURGENCY IN GUATEMALA. *Latin Am. Perspectives 1980 7(2-3): 91-113.* Examination of Guatemalan conditions during the past 20 years indicates a change in guerrilla and counterinsurgency violence. Locally focused *(foquista)* guerrilla violence in the 1960's failed to develop mass organization, so struggle in the 1970's was based on economic and ideological opposition. Counterinsurgency violence from 1966 has been abetted by the state apparatus supported by the financial and industrial sector with connections to foreign capital. 6 notes, biblio. J. F. Vivian

1130. Albizurez, Miguel Angel. STRUGGLES AND EXPERIENCES OF THE GUATEMALAN TRADE-UNION MOVEMENT, 1976-JUNE 1978. *Latin Am. Perspectives 1980 7(2-3): 145-159.* Founder's account of the organization of the Comité Nacional de Unidad Sindical (CNUS) in 1976, government intimidation of it in 1977, and the 1978 strike against a hydroelectric plant being constructed by Mexican engineers. J. F. Vivian

1131. Baltodano, Emilio; LaCerda, Alfonso de; and Falla, Ricardo. RENOVACIÓN CRISTIANA DE LA COSTUMBRES INDÍGENAS DEL QUICHÉ [Christian reform of the native customs of Quiché]. *Estudios Centro Americanos [El Salvador] 1970 25(260-261): 286-300.* Continued from a previous article. Discusses the religious evolution of the Indians of Quiché, Guatemala. Provides details of Indian religious life, in the 1940's and 1950's, marriage ceremonies, finding a spouse, and the relationship between religion and politics. Based on the diary of a Chilean merchant who lived in the area for 22 years.

1132. Batz, Manuel Ajquij. LE RÉVEIL DES INDIENS DU GUATEMALA [The awakening of Guatemala Indians]. *Études [France] 1981 354(1): 7-18.* Analyzes the situation of the Guatemalan Indian population which is struggling against the ruling classes' violent repression and war of harassment, particularly since 1954.

1133. Bauer Paiz, Alfonso. LA REVOLUCIÓN GUATEMALTECA DE 20 DE OCTUBRE DE 1944 Y SUS PROYECCIONES ECONÓMICO-SOCIALES [The Guatemalan revolution of 20 October 1944 and its economic-social projections]. *Casa de las Américas [Cuba] 1974 14(84): 77-89.* Gives economic and social implications of the Guatemalan revolution of 20 October 1944, detailing an analysis of the political economy of revolution, including land reform.

1134. Booth, John A. A GUATEMALAN NIGHTMARE: LEVELS OF POLITICAL VIOLENCE, 1966-1972. *J. of Interamerican Studies and World Affairs 1980 22(2): 195-225.* By 1971 perhaps 50 persons per month were meeting violent politically related deaths in Guatemala, perhaps the peak in a long, continuing nightmare of political violence. Areas of Guatemala which seem to have balanced left- and right-wing political factions have experienced the highest levels of violence. Social change as measured did not contribute in a major way to the level of violence. Until competing elites develop institutional solutions for conflict, which seems unlikely, peace will probably elude Guatemala. Based on newspapers, magazines, and US State Department documents; 5 tables, 2 fig., 12 notes, ref. T. D. Schoonover

1135. Bulmer-Thomas, Victor. POLICY FOR LAND REFORM IN GUATEMALA. *Civilisations [Belgium] 1978 28(1-2): 76-87.* The issue of land reform has always been politically important in Guatemala: reform began in the largely rural population during the administration of Jacobo Arbenz (1951-54) and has proceeded at an uneven pace ever since.

1136. Cambranes, Julio C. ESTADO NACIONAL DE GUATEMALA [The national state of Guatemala]. *Anuario de Estudios Centroamericanos [Costa Rica] 1979 5: 27-31.* A Marxist analysis of Guatemalan revolutions during the national period. The independence struggles of 1821-23 were political. The first bourgeois liberal revolution, 1828-39, proved unsuccessful when the conservatives under Rafael Carrera gained control. The second bourgeois liberal revolution came in 1871 under Justo Rufino Barrios, who effected radical economic and political changes. The democratic bourgeois revolution arrived in 1944. Although defeated in 1954, it prepared the way for the coming revolution of the working class. Based on author's doctoral dissertation at the University of Leipzig. H. J. Miller

1137. Cardona, Rokael. LA LEGISLACIÓN AGRARIA Y EL PROBLEMA DE LA TIERRA EN GUATEMALA [Agrarian legislation and the land problem in Guatemala]. *Estudios Sociales Centroamericanos [Costa Rica] 1980 9(25): 319-353.* The Guatemalan counterrevolution did not prevent the modernization of Guatemalan agriculture. American capital has intervened in Guatemala agriculture not only through the private sector, but through state agencies. However, Guatemalan agrarian policies have always left intact the problems of land distribution and the expropriation of surplus production. Thus, despite modest reform efforts, Guatemala follows the agro-export model with all of its weaknesses and contradictions. 14 tables.

T. D. Schoonover

1138. Castro Torres, Carlos Felipe. CRECIMIENTO DE LAS LUCHAS CAMPESINAS EN GUATEMALA FEBRERO: 1976-MAYO 1978 [Growth of the peasants' struggle in Guatemala: February 1976-May 1978]. *Estudios Centroamericanos [El Salvador] 1978 33(356-357): 462-477.* The earthquake of 4 February 1976 was a catalyst in the repression of the peasants' struggle in Guatemala. Analyzes the causes and modes of struggle and the organizations involved. The National Committee for Labor Unity (CNUS) has been leading the peasants and denouncing repression, particularly following the Panzós massacre of 29 May 1977, when more than 100 peasants were killed by the army. 5 illus.

K. A. Talley

1139. Chapin, Jorge. ECOLOGÍA Y SOCIEDAD EN GUATEMALA [Ecology and society in Guatemala]. *Estudios Centro Americanos [El Salvador] 1975 30(316-317): 145-150.* Utilizing data from the 1973 census, examines the demographic and ecological problems of Guatemala, showing an interrelation between population pressure, land use, and institutionalized violence.

1140. Demyck, Michel. LA COLONISATION DANS LE NORD GUATÉMALTÈQUE [Settlement in northern Guatemala]. *Travaux & Mémoires de l'Inst. des Hautes Études de l'Amérique Latine [France] 1979 (32): 129-132.* History of the settlement in northern Guatemala, centering on the study of various government organizations and their neglect of the peasants' welfare.

1141. Diener, Paul. THE TEARS OF ST. ANTHONY: RITUAL AND REVOLUTION IN EASTERN GUATEMALA. *Latin Am. Perspectives 1978 5(3): 92-116.* A review of the relationship between ritual and revolution among the Chorti Indians of eastern Guatemala. This rural community is subservient to the more powerful towns, which are controlled by non-Indians. Rituals which make use of a saint, to which homage and sacrifices are due, are readily equated with the powerful non-Indian landlord to whom rents must be paid. Contrary to common conception, such rituals are not Christian efforts to take over resistant native belief, but rather are capitalist rituals deliberately implanted and manipulated to keep the Indian in his place. 11 notes, ref.

V. L. Human

1142. Dow, Leslie M., Jr. ETHNIC POLICY AND *INDIGENISMO* IN GUATEMALA. *Ethnic and Racial Studies [Great Britain] 1982 5(2): 140-155.* Examines the assumptions and impact of state ethnic policy and attitudes on interethnic relations in Guatemala from the nation's independence in 1822 to the 20th century, focusing on the concept of indigenismo (which views some Indian cultural values as obstacles to progress) and its sometimes negative role in relations between Guatemala's two major ethnic groups, the Indians and the Ladinos.

1143. Falla, Ricardo. EL MOVIMIENTO INDÍGENA [The Indian movement]. *Estudios Centroamericanos [El Salvador] 1978 33(356-357): 437-461.* Before establishing a policy for native Guatemalans in the 1970's, terms must be defined, a difficult task because the nationalities are no longer disparate. Concludes that there is only one Guatemalan nationality, and that there can only be one political system for all citizens, native and ladino. These must fight their common oppressors. 9 illus., 2 charts, 8 notes.

K. A. Talley

1144. Falla, Ricardo. PODER, PUEBLO Y FÉ EN LA GUATEMALA INDÍGENA: UNA VISIÓN ANTROPOLÓGICA [Power, people, and faith in indigenous Guatemala: an anthropological vision]. *Estudios Centro Americanos [El Salvador] 1974 29(312): 679-*

686. Discusses the impact of social change in Guatemala on the indigenous population since 1964, showing the evolution of responding political movements and religious conversion.

1145. Galich, Manuel. DIEZ AÑOS DE PRIMAVERA (1944-54) EN EL PAÍS DE LA ETERNA TIRANÍA (1838-1974) [Ten years of spring (1944-54) in the country of eternal tyranny (1838-1974)]. *Casa de las Américas [Cuba] 1974 14(84): 53-76.* Discusses the political history of Guatemala since 1838, focusing on the decade 1944-54 when Juan José Arévalo and Gustavo Árbenz Guzmán governed Guatemala in the country's own interests, rather than in the interests of the United Fruit Company or the United States.

1146. Grieb, Kenneth J. THE GUATEMALAN MILITARY AND THE REVOLUTION OF 1944. *Americas (Acad. of Am. Franciscan Hist.) 1976 32(4): 524-543.* The movement that in 1944 launched the era of social reform in Guatemala involved two separate revolutions. A protest of students and other civilian middle-class elements against the military dictatorship of Jorge Ubico obtained the dictator's resignation but left control in the hands of the military and members of the traditional ruling elite. A second coup d'etat, in October 1944, brought a more fundamental change. Carried out by junior military officers who were alienated from their military superiors and sympathized with civilian reformers, it placed a military-civilian junta temporarily in control and paved the way for election of a civilian, Juan José Arévalo, as president. But ultimate control still rested with the military. Based on US diplomatic dispatches, printed sources, and interviews; 69 notes.

D. Bushnell

1147. Grieb, Kenneth J. JORGE UBICO AND THE BELICE BOUNDARY DISPUTE. *Americas (Acad. of Am. Franciscan Hist.) 1974 30(4): 448-474.* Guatemalan claims to Belice or British Honduras had long been stalemated when "British desire to mark the boundary provided the regime of General Jorge Ubico with an opportunity to reassert" those claims in 1933. Though discussions with the British got nowhere, Ubico played up to the United States to enlist its good offices, and "launched a full scale propaganda campaign" on the issue for both domestic and foreign consumption. After the outbreak of World War II, the British made a formal proposal to settle the dispute, but on unacceptable terms. Nevertheless, the Ubico regime showed "considerable diplomatic skill" in handling the controversy. Its success in involving the United States did not produce a settlement, but the issue was used to cement the regime's internal position and hemispheric image while laying possible groundwork for later campaigns. Based on Guatemalan press and printed documents and US diplomatic dispatches; 94 notes.

D. Bushnell

1148. Grieb, Kenneth J. and Rivas, P. Geoffroy, transl. LOS ESTADOS UNIDOS Y LA PERMANENCIA DEL GENERAL UBICO EN EL PODER [The United States and the continuance in power of General Ubico]. *Estudios Centro Americano [El Salvador] 1974 29(305-306): 189-200.* Describes general Jorge Ubico Castañeda's rise to power as president of Guatemala, 1931-44, and discusses the influence of his pro-American policy on his continuance in power.

L. Russell

1149. Immerman, Richard H. GUATEMALA AS COLD WAR HISTORY. *Pol. Sci. Q. 1980-81 95(4): 629-653.* Analyzes US intervention in Guatemala in 1954. Argues that misperceptions led to that intervention and that those misperceptions later contributed to the Bay of Pigs fiasco.

J

1150. Jenkins, Brian and Sereseres, Caesar D. U.S. MILITARY ASSISTANCE AND THE GUATEMALAN ARMED FORCES. *Armed Forces and Soc. 1977 3(4): 575-595.* The United States provided Guatemala with military assistance loans and direct aid grants, 1953-73. Local guerrillas were the reason for the aid, but it produced a modernized and professionalized army that became politicized. Protection of the army as an institution was the motive behind several recent seizures of the government. Traditionally, army generals have controlled Guatemala for a variety of reasons; today they run the nation for the benefit of the army. Based on interviews, secondary literature, and periodicals; 15 notes.

J. P. Harahan

1151. Johnson, Kenneth F. ON THE GUATEMALAN POLITI-CAL VIOLENCE. *Pol. and Soc. 1973 4(1): 55-82.* A case study that explores the variables in the relationship between land tenure and political violence in Guatemala. The elite's assumption of an "amoral" position in asserting their right to use violence to suppress all challenges to their regime and control of the land evoked terrorist tactics by the challengers. Both sides have accepted violence as a way of life. The role of the United States in the institutionalization of violence in Guatemala and its psychological effects upon its citizens also is examined. Primary and secondary sources; 61 notes, appendix.   D. G. Nielson

1152. Kubyshkin, A. I. AMERIKANSKAIA BURZHUAZNAIIA ISTORIOGRAFIIA OB INTERVENTSII SSHA PROTIV REVOLI-UTSIONNOI GVATEMALY V 1954 G [American bourgeois historiography concerning US intervention in the Guatemala revolution of 1954]. *Vestnik Leningradskogo U.: Seriia Istorii, Iazyka i Literatury [USSR] 1978 (3): 48-53.* American interpretations of US intervention in Guatemala range from direct support for the intervention to outright criticism for the imperialistic methods employed, but they all reflect anti-Communist tendencies. 25 notes.   G. F. Jewsbury

1154. LeBot, Yvon. LE POUVOIR DE L'EGLISE EN PAYS QUICHE [Church power in Quiché country]. *Cahiers du Monde Hispanique et Luso-Brésilien [France] 1977 (28): 225-243.* Analyzes the restoration of church power in the Quiché region of Guatemala's western highlands after the fall of the Arbenz regime. After describing how it came about, the author argues that this restoration was part of an imperialist strategy devised by the United States, the Vatican, and the Guatemalan government to break up the opposition to progress among the most conservative elements of society and establish a strong rampart against the claims of popular movements. Based on field research and secondary works; 4 notes, biblio.   L. Garon

1155. Lujan, Herman D. THE STRUCTURE OF POLITICAL SUPPORT: A STUDY OF GUATEMALA. *Am. J. of Pol. Sci. 1974 18(1): 23-44.* "Applies concepts from the growing theory of political support to the analysis of citizen support for the political system in Guatemala. Using aggregated data from 375 interviews in seven municipalities, measures of the environment, the political community, the regime and the authorities are related to support for the system. Applying path analysis, the study concludes that the political community has major direct effects on the level of support. The environment has only indirect effects. The regime and authorities depend on these prior variables for their effects on support."   J

1157. Payne, Walter A. THE GUATEMALAN REVOLUTION 1944-1954. *Pacific Hist. 1973 17(1): Insert 1-32.*

1158. Peckenham, Nancy. LAND SETTLEMENT IN THE PETÉN. *Latin Am. Perspectives 1980 7(2-3): 169-177.* The government-sponsored colonization program in Petén, Guatemala, dating from 1966, does not appear viable. Ranching latifundia are advantaged, the Fomento y Desarrollo Económico del Petén (FYDEP), the supervising agency, is ineffective and increasingly influenced by the military, and multinational oil companies have acquired nearly preemptive privileges. Dependent capitalism does not promote land reform. Biblio.   J. F. Vivian

1159. Porras Castejón, Gustavo. GUATEMALA: LA PROFUNDA-ZIÓN DE LAS RELACIONES CAPITALISTAS [Guatemala: the deepening of capitalist relations]. *Estudios Centroamericanos [El Salvador] 1978 33(356-357): 368-377.* The Guatemalan rural economy is a contradiction, showing feudal elements in its system of large fincas and incorporating the latest in technical advances. Traces the history of the rural economy from the Jacobo Arbenz agrarian reform in 1953 through the formation and development of the Central American Common Market. In 1976 Guatemala underwent a period of economic growth due to the rise in the price of coffee in the world market. 5 illus., 2 tables, 8 notes.   K. A. Talley

1160. Premo, Daniel L. POLITICAL ASSASSINATION IN GUATEMALA: A CASE OF INSTITUTIONALIZED TERROR. *J. of Interamerican Studies and World Affairs 1981 23(4): 429-456.* Guatemalan terror is related in part to the general uncertainty in Central America. Guatemalan officials believe their country to be the target of an international Communist conspiracy. The government's creation of a climate of terror is aimed at paralyzing mass activity. Public assassinations are intended to show the state's vulnerability and its inability or unwillingness to guarantee personal safety. In few countries in the world is it as dangerous to struggle for individual self-improvement or democratic rights as in Guatemala. The rules of the game have changed drastically in Guatemalan politics in recent decades. Based on Guatemalan newspapers, Amnesty International reports, and other printed primary and secondary sources; 12 notes, table, ref.   T. Schoonover

1161. Reid, John T. FOLKLORIC SYMBOLS OF NATIONHOOD IN GUATEMALA. *Southern Folklore Q. 1974 38(2): 135-153.*

1162. Rivas, José M. ELECCIONES PRESIDENCIALES EN GUATEMALA: 1966-78: ILEGITIMIDAD PROGRESIVA DEL GOBIERNO [Guatemalan presidential elections: 1966-78: progressive illegitimacy of the government]. *Estudios Centroamericanos [El Salvador] 1978 33(356-357): 429-436.* Gives figures on voting behavior in Guatemala, showing discrepancies in the number of voters and final official counts of votes. The author concludes that it is difficult to take official voting data seriously. 4 illus., 4 tables.   K. A. Talley

1163. Rodriguez, Miguel. TWENTY-FIVE TRYING YEARS. *World Marxist R. [Canada] 1974 17(9): 25-33.* Traces the revolutionary struggle of Guatemala's Communist Party, the Party of Labor, 1944-74.   S

1164. Sarti Castañeda, Carlos A. LA REVOLUCIÓN GUATEMALTECA DE 1944-1954 Y SU PROYECCIÓN ACTUAL [The Guatemalan revolution of 1944-54 and its projection into the present]. *Estudios Sociales Centroamericanos [Costa Rica] 1980 9(27): 65-78.* The 1944-54 revolutionary period in Guatemala merely represented the passing of power from the landlords to the bourgeoisie and the reconstruction of a political alliance between them. 12 notes.   T. D. Schoonover

1165. Shapira, Yoram. THE 1954 GUATEMALA CRISIS. *Jerusalem J. of Int. Relations [Israel] 1978 3(2-3): 81-116.* Outlines the development of the Guatemalan crisis of 1954. US involvement limited the options of its adversary, the National Democratic Front under the leadership of Jacobo Arbenz, and prolonged the crisis.

1166. Torres, Pedro Gonzales. DICTATOR VERSUS PEOPLE. *World Marxist R. [Canada] 1973 16(4): 68-73.* The working class struggle goes on against the dictatorship of Araña Osorio of Guatemala. Part of the continuing series, "Political Portrait of Latin America."   S

1167. Tortolani, Paul. POLITICAL PARTICIPATION OF NATIVE AND FOREIGN CATHOLIC CLERGY IN GUATEMALA. *J. of Church and State 1973 15(3): 407-418.*

1168. Wasserstrom, Robert. REVOLUTION IN GUATEMALA: PEASANTS AND POLITICS UNDER THE ARBENZ GOVERNMENT. *Comparative Studies in Soc. and Hist. [Great Britain] 1975 17(4): 443-478.* Discusses the political and social pressures resulting in enactment of the land and labor reforms of the governments of Juan José Arévalo Bermejo (1904-) and Jacobo Arbenz (1914-) and the internal structure of Indian communities and local politics relative to the Guatemalan revolution of 1944-54.

1169. —. EL ESTADO, LA LUCHA DE CLASES Y LA VIOLENCIA EN GUATEMALA [The state, class struggle, and violence in Guatemala]. *Estudios Sociales Centroamericanos [Costa Rica] 1979*

8(23): 49-83. Evidence supports the hypothesis that the underpublicized violence in Guatemala during the past decades is class conflict conducted on an elevated level to prevent the developing revolutionary process. Although used primarily against the dominated classes—poor peasants and urban workers—the terror has in fact contributed toward weakening the dominant ideology and the legitimacy of the state, without halting the revolutionary process. 3 tables, 27 notes. T. D. Schoonover

1170. —. LOS PARTIDOS POLÍTICOS Y EL ESTADO GUATEMALTECO DESDE 1944 HASTA NUESTROS DÍAS [Political parties and the Guatemalan state from 1944 to the present]. *Estudios Centroamericanos [El Salvador] 1978 33(356-357): 418-438.* A collective study of political power in Guatemala, based on Antonio Gramsci's statement that in a class society, the state is an expression of the party in power. Divides bourgeois domination of Guatemala into three periods: 1944-54 was a period of capitalist development. During 1954-63, after the agrarian reform of Jacobo Arbenz, the party in power was characterized by a union of the landed oligarchy with imperialist interests. The years 1963-78 were a period of transition, with the army in power and a concurrent rise in counterinsurgency. Prepared by the Instituto de Investigaciones Políticas y Sociales. 6 illus., 2 tables. K. A. Talley

1171. —. TESIS ESQUEMÁTICAS SOBRE EL BALANCE DE PODER EN GUATEMALA FRENTE AL NUEVO PERÍODO PRESIDENCIAL [Schematic theses on the balance of power in Guatemala on the eve of the new presidential period]. *Estudios Centroamericanos [El Salvador] 1978 33(356-357): 398-413.* Develops themes on the basis for and balance of power in Guatemala. The formation of agroexporting capitalism based on the export of coffee placed potential power in the land and in the strength of human labor. The incoming administration must allow for broader participation from all parts of the population. Prepared by the Seminario Permanente de Análisis de la Realidad Guatemalteca. 5 illus. K. A. Talley

Honduras

1172. Bejarano, Dionisio Ramos. SOMETHING NEW IN HONDURAS? *World Marxist R. [Canada] 1973 16(5): 67-71.* Honduras' Communist Party analyzes the achievements of the military regime in social reform and economic development. S

1173. Morris, James A. and Ropp, Steve C.. CORPORATISM AND DEPENDENT DEVELOPMENT: A HONDURAN CASE STUDY. *Latin Am. Rcs. Rcv. 1977 12(2): 27-68.* The thesis that corporatism results from "delayed dependent development" does not apply to Honduras. Numerous interest groups compete for influence. The state has limited control over leaders and demands of these groups. Despite a military government, few corporatist tendencies have emerged. Factors contributing to the absence of corporatism are the strong external influence on structural differentiation in society and rapid growth of relatively independent groups and structures. It is unclear whether corporatism in Latin America is an effort to break dependency or a reflexive response to weakened dependency. Based on governmental legislation and secondary sources; table, 81 notes, biblio. J. K. Pfabe

1174. Morris, James A. HONDURAS: AN OASIS OF PEACE? *Caribbean Rev. 1981 10(1): 38-41.* The attention the United States has recently begun to focus on Honduras stems from a desire to regain influence in Central America and control of leftward change, to be accomplished by returning Honduras to constitutional rule via elections and progressive government, demonstrating an alternative approach to reforms in Central America.

1175. Padilla, Rigoberto. THE COLLAPSE OF BOURGEOIS REFORMISM AND THE COMMUNIST ALTERNATIVE: ON THE RESULTS OF THE THIRD CONGRESS OF THE COMMUNIST PARTY OF HONDURAS. *World Marxist Rev. 1977 20(11): 62-67.* Traces the battle waged by the Communist Party of Honduras between 1972 and 1977 against the political and economic tyranny of the reformist, bourgeois-reformist, ultra-rightist, and oligarchic elements seeking to gain hegemony in the national government.

1176. Paredes, Milton Rene. THE PARTY BEGINS WITH ITS BASIC UNIT, THE NUCLEUS. *World Marxist R. [Canada] 1975 18(4): 78-84.* Discusses the Communist Party in Honduras, 1954-75. S

1177. Posas, Mario. EVOLUCIÓN DEL SECTOR PÚBLICO EN HONDURAS (1866-1948) [Evolution of the public sector in Honduras 1866-1948]. *Anuario de Estudios Centroamericanos [Costa Rica] 1979 5: 53-64.* Traces the growth of government from José Maria Medina's administration, 1863-72, to the end of the Tiburcio Carías Andino regime in 1948. The state promoted education, railroads, agriculture, mining, law reform, the establishment of a rural police force, and more efficient public administration. After 1900 bananas became the principal export and the United Fruit Company exercised much political power. The major trait of the government during the period was centralization of power. Based on government publications and secondary sources; table, 31 notes. H. J. Miller

1178. Posas, Mario. HONDURAS AT THE CROSSROADS. *Latin Am. Perspectives 1980 7(2-3): 45-56.* A sociological analysis of Honduran national elections scheduled for April 1980. Neither a conservative military coup nor a revolutionary confrontation as in El Salvador need be anticipated. A moderate reformist victory is expected, based on short-term political stability. J. F. Vivian

1179. Posas, Mario. POLÍTICA ESTATAL Y ESTRUCTURA AGRARIA EN HONDURAS (1950-1978) [State policy and agrarian structure in Honduras, 1950-78]. *Estudios Sociales Centroamericanos [Costa Rica] 1979 8(24): 37-116.* The expression of and result of class conflict, Honduran state agricultural policy indicates the relationship of conflicting social forces. Agricultural reform introduced to produce exportable agroindustrial items and state aid to the cattle industry have placed Honduras within the international division of labor dominated by monopolistic international capital. This policy not only assured agricultural development but also the market for the transfer of technology and an increase in the level of capital accumulation. 4 tables, 172 notes. T. D. Schoonover

1180. Ropp, Steve C. THE HONDURAN ARMY IN THE SOCIOPOLITICAL EVOLUTION OF THE HONDURAN STATE. *Americas (Acad. of Am. Franciscan Hist.) 1974 30(4): 504-528.* The military in Honduras constitutes "an exceedingly new institution operating in a context of rapid soial change." From independence to the early 20th century, the armed forces were highly politicized and structurally incoherent. Professionalization began with U.S. assistance after World War I, receiving particular impetus in the regime of Tiburcio Carías Andino (1933-49); by-products of the process were greater centralized control of military institutions and growing influence of the urban lower-middle class. Military modernization alongside decline of traditional political parties favored autonomous armed forces, for which the military coup of 1957 was a major turning point. But military hegemony has not followed, despite an obvious increase in the military's political role. 58 notes. D. Bushnell

1181. Salinas-Paguada, Manuel. BREVE RESEÑA DEL CUENTO MODERNO HONDUREÑO [Brief review of the modern Honduran story]. *Cahiers du Monde Hispanique et Luso-Brésilien [France] 1981 (36): 63-74.* Decade-by-decade survey of the political and literary environment of Honduran authors and the development and modernization of the writing of short stories from the group surrounding Froylán Turcios in the 1920's to Oscar Acosta in the 1950's and the more recent work of Eduardo Bahr, Julio Escoto, Roberto Castillo, and others. D. R. Stevenson

1182. —. ENTREVISTA A RIGOBERTO PADILLA, VICESECRETARIO GENERAL DEL PARTIDO COMUNISTA DE HONDURAS [Interview with Rigoberto Padilla, General Vicesecretary of the Communist Party of the Honduras]. *Am. Latina [USSR] 1978 (4): 71-87.* Born in 1929 Padilla became a revolutionary in 1948 or 1949. For a time he toyed with the reformist ideas of various liberal groups but he soon became disillusioned with them and turned into a dedicated Communist. He saw that communism was the only solution for the problems of his country and the whole region. In spite of severe and prolonged persecution, the Honduran Communist Party has survived and will eventually triumph. J. D. Barnard

Nicaragua

1183. Adams, Richard N. THE SANDINISTAS AND THE INDIANS: THE "PROBLEM" OF THE INDIAN IN NICARAGUA. *Caribbean Rev. 1981 10(1): 22-25, 55-56.* Contrasts the differing cultural development of the Indians in Guatemala and Nicaragua and studies the way their differing cultural patterns caused them to respond to conquest and colonization dissimilarly. The least advanced aboriginal populations best survived these ordeals.

1184. Arellano, Jorge Eduardo. LA SITUACIÓN ANTROPOLÓGICA Y ARQUEOLÓGICA EN NICARAGUA [The anthropological and archaeological situation in Nicaragua]. *Am. Indígena [Mexico] 1980 40(2): 399-403.* Highlights two events since the triumph of the Sandinista Revolution. The first was a general assembly of the Indian groups of the Atlantic Coast, attended by Miskito, Sumo, and Rama ethnic groups. At this assembly the Indianist policies to be incorporated into the Nicaraguan revolutionary process were proposed by the Indian groups. The 700 delegates elected their representatives who are participating in the reconstruction of their nation. The second event concerns the massive recovery by the state, of archaeological pieces that were in private hands. These will form the basis of a new and authentic national museum.   J/S

1185. Arenal, Electa. TWO POETS OF THE SANDINISTA STRUGGLE. *Feminist Studies 1981 7(1): 19-27.* Poetic volumes *Sobrevivo* [I Survive] by Claribel Alegría and *Linea de fuego* [Firing Line] by Gioconda Belli, which recaptured elements of the people's war against Somozas' dictatorship, received the 1978 poetry prize of the prestigious Casa de las Americas in Havana. Alegría and Belli filled the role of "spokespoet" for a period of revolution and reconstruction, a role few women poets have fulfilled. Alegría's volume is characterized by a distilled and abstracted simplicity which interweaves complex historical and personal themes. Belli's volume expresses the fragility and fleetingness of life, woman's erotic sensuality amidst strife, and the ongoing resistance of a united people. 7 notes.   P. D. Hinnebusch

1186. Arismendi, Rodnei. NARODNAIA VESNA V NIKARAGUA [The People's Spring in Nicaragua]. *Voprosy Istorii KPSS [USSR] 1980 (2): 41-58.* Compares revolutionary events in Iran and Portugal with the overthrow of Somoza's regime in Nicaragua. Summarizes democratic achievements in Chile, Uruguay, Ecuador, Brazil, Peru, Panama, Jamaica, Venezuela, Mexico, and Costa Rica.
M. R. Colenso

1187. Bacevich, Andrew J., Jr. THE AMERICAN ELECTORAL MISSION IN NICARAGUA, 1927-1928. *Diplomatic Hist. 1980 4(3): 241-261.* In 1927, Brigadier General Frank R. McCoy was dispatched to Nicaragua to organize and conduct a free and honest election and to terminate "with honor" an increasingly embarrassing American military occupation. His strong-arm measures produced an admired election, but his failure to eliminate the anti-American opposition, led by Augusto César Sandino, doomed his mission. America neither established its authority nor withdrew its troops. True to pattern, the United States had intervened in the domestic affairs of a Caribbean nation for the purpose of securing a stability deemed vital to American interests, only to create greater instability and anti-Americanism in the process. 61 notes.
T. L. Powers

1188. Barahona Portocarrero, Amaru. ESTUDIO SOBRE LA HISTORIA CONTEMPORÁNEA DE NICARAGUA [A study of the contemporary history of Nicaragua]. *Rev. del Pensamiento Centroamericano [Nicaragua] 1977 32(157): 32-49.* Surveys the history of Nicaragua since about 1870 with particular reference to economic activity and the relationship of economic interests to political parties and the United States. US interventions, 1909-33, resulted in the formation of the National Guard and the Somoza dictatorship as well as Augusto Sandino's guerrilla uprising, 1928-34. Somoza built his power on US support, control of the military and state bureaucracy, and alliance with the dominant economic class, principally the Liberal Party coffee planters. By 1960 cotton had surpassed coffee, and three new economic power groups had emerged, centered around the Banco Nicaragüense, the Banco de América, and the Banco Nacional, all to some degree dependent on the

Somoza family, which has maintained a monopoly on political power. The clandestine Sandinista group has grown steadily since the 1960's. Based on primary and secondary sources; 54 notes.
R. L. Woodward, Jr.

1189. Belli, Humberto. UN ENSAYO DE INTERPRETACIÓN SOBRE LAS LUCHAS POLÍTICAS NICARAGÜENSES (DE LA INDEPENDENCIA HASTA LA REVOLUCIÓN CUBANA) [An interpretive essay on Nicaraguan political struggles: from independence to the Cuban revolution]. *Rev. del Pensamiento Centroamericano [Nicaragua] 1977 32(157): 50-59.* Surveys the political history of Nicaragua from 1824 to 1960. Political arguments were less important than struggles among economic interests. The Conservative-Liberal struggle went on throughout the 19th and well into the 20th century until the creation of the professional National Guard by the United States (1927). The guard altered the balance of power between the two political factions and made possible the long-term dictatorship of the Somoza family. There was a substantial increase in economic activity of the state since 1945. Tables.
R. L. Woodward, Jr.

1190. Booth, John A. CELEBRATING THE DEMISE OF *SOMOCISMO:* FIFTY RECENT SPANISH SOURCES ON THE NICARAGUAN REVOLUTION. *Latin Am. Res. Rev. 1982 17(1): 173-189.* Describes over fifty Spanish titles dealing with various phases of the Nicaraguan revolution. 4 notes, biblio.
J. K. Pfabe

1191. Bourgois, Philippe. CLASS, ETHNICITY, AND THE STATE AMONG THE MISKITO AMERINDIANS OF NORTHEASTERN NICARAGUA. *Latin Am. Perspectives 1981 8(2): 22-39.* The 60,000 Miskito peoples of Zelaya province, Nicaragua, must identify with the Sandinista revolution if they are to achieve cultural and ethnic affirmation against foreign exploitation and Ladino discrimination. The Sandinista leadership, for its part, must be prepared to concede, if necessary, regional autonomy in order to integrate indigenous groups into the reformist framework. Based on nine-month residence in Nicaragua and secondary sources; 14 notes, map, ref.
J. F. Vivian

1192. Bulychev, I. NIKARAGUA: NA PUTIAKH STROITEL'STVA NOVOI ZHIZNI [Nicaragua: on the way to constructing a new life]. *Mirovaia Ekonomika i Mezhdunarodnye Otnosheniia [USSR] 1980 (12): 80-94.* The anti-imperialist victory of the Sandinista National Liberation Front has created the real possibility of building a society of social justice, free from exploitation, with equality for all citizens by eradicating former political structures, forming new authorities, and reconstructing the national economy.

1193. Burbach, Roger. NICARAGUA: THE COURSE OF THE REVOLUTION. *Monthly Rev. 1980 31(9): 28-39.* Briefly discusses the inner workings of the Sandinista Front and describes its role in leading Nicaragua to socialism.

1194. Burstein, John N. ETHNIC MINORITIES AND THE SANDINIST GOVERNMENT. *J. of Int. Affairs 1982 36(1): 155-161.* Discusses the relationship between the ethnic minorities of Nicaragua and that nation's Sandinista government in the 1980's, focusing on the development of a Sandinista policy toward the nation's indigenous peoples and on guidelines for the future.

1195. Buşe, Constantin. MIŞCAREA DE ELIBERARE SOCIALĂ ŞI NAŢIONALĂ DIN NICARAGUA (1904-1934) [Nicaragua's national and social liberation movement]. *Rev. de Istorie [Rumania] 1978 31(12): 2259-2284.* Describes the military intervention by the United States in Nicaragua in 1919 and the subsequent movement against the American presence, tracing the activities of its leader, 1927-33, Augusto César Sandino, who succeeded in controlling part of the country. Considers him responsible for the reintroduction of constitutional democracy in 1932 and the withdrawal of US troops in 1933. However, he was assassinated in 1934 and a reactionary dictatorship took power in 1936. 218 notes.
R. O. Khan

1196. Buşe, Constantin. NICARAGUA 1909-1934: GENERALUL MUNCITOR REFUZĂ SĂ SE PREDEA [Nicaragua, 1909-34: the worker general will not surrender]. *Magazin Istoric [Romania] 1979 13(9): 28-31.* Describes the political struggles and US interventions in

Nicaragua after 1909, resulting in a brief success for the tenacious left-wing leader Augusto César Sandino.

1197. Cardenal, Fernando and Miller, Valerie. NICARAGUA 1980: BATTLE OF THE ABC'S. *Harvard Educ. Rev. 1981 51(1): 1-26.* Presents a first-hand account of the National Literacy Crusade's fight for literacy in Nicaragua in 1980.

1198. Casaus, Víctor. EL TESTIMONIO SOBRE LA MARCHA [Witness to the march]. *Casa de las Américas [Cuba] 1982 22(131): 164-169.* Reviews *Corresponsales de Guerra* (1981) by Fernando Pérez, on the Sandinista struggle for the liberation of Nicaragua. The book belongs to a new literary form which emerged during the Cuban revolutionary war, the genre of "testimony." In a direct and active communication with his public, Pérez describes the process of the awakening of the revolutionary consciousness of five Latin American youths and their gradual transformation by life, by the struggle, and by history. 3 notes.
J. V. Coutinho

1199. Castañeda, Jorge G. NICARAGUA: CONTRADICCIONES EN LA REVOLUCIÓN [Nicaragua: contradictions in the revolution]. *Investigación Econ. [Mexico] 1980 39(154): 85-88.* The fundamental characteristic and originality of the Nicaraguan revolution consists in its novel strategy based on armed mass struggle combined with a political alliance with a sector of the middle classes. This alliance is a constant of the Sandinista revolution and not a merely tactical move. It is also a contribution to Latin American revolutionary strategy. The author also discusses the anomalous behavior of the government of the United States vis-à-vis the Nicaraguan revolution; instead of frontal opposition, it has chosen the indirect route. This implies not a change in essence but only of method in its stance to anti-imperialist revolutions. Based on press reports.
J. V. Coutinho

1200. Castilla Urbina, Miguel de. LA EDUCACION COMO PODER, CRISIS SIN SOLUCION EN LA TRANSICION REVOLUCIONARIA: EL CASO DE NICARAGUA 1978-1981 [Education as power, a crisis without solution in the revolutionary transition: the case of Nicaragua, 1978-81]. *Estudios Sociales Centroamericanos [Costa Rica] 1982 11(31): 43-79.* Calls attention to a contradiction in Nicaraguan education—the conflict between scholarly education and nonscholarly education. This problem relates to the nature of the teaching force, that is the training and background of the educators. Proposes a study committee to create a new Nicaraguan education linked to groups like the National Crusade for Literacy, and a global plan and strategy for forming and qualifying for a national teacher-instructor body. Based on printed Nicaraguan government sources; 26 notes.
T. D. Schoonover

1201. Castillo, Oscar Mauricio. LAS ORGANIZACIONES POPULARES EN LA NUEVA NICARAGUA [Popular organizations in the new Nicaragua]. *Estudios Centroamericanos [El Salvador] 1980 35(381-382): 669-684.* Traces the establishment and organizational experience of popular organizations in Nicaragua and their major role in the overthrow of the Somoza dictatorship. At present these organizations participate together with government entities and other institutions in the construction of a new social order, in the literacy program, in economic reconstruction, and in several other areas which the Nicaraguan government has undertaken. These organizations are analyzed in terms of their problems, most of which date from the Somoza regime's policies. These organizations are contributing to the creation of a popular, participatory democracy.
R. L. Woodward, Jr.

1202. Cid, Luis Eduardo del. ¿POR QUÉ CAYÓ LA DINASTÍA SOMOCISTA? [Why did the Somoza dynasty fall?]. *Estudios Centroamericanos [El Salvador] 1979 34(369-370): 699-708.* Discusses the significance for Central America of the fall of the Somoza dictatorship, which for more than 40 years dominated Nicaragua and influenced Honduras, El Salvador, and Guatemala. Examines the intrinsic relation between the state and the formation of the Somoza group in order to explain its strong resistance to change in the power structure. Through control of the National Guard and state bureaucracy, the Somozas were able to manipulate the state apparatus and thus to exploit the economic and human resources of the country. Major factors in the Somoza downfall were longstanding bourgeois opposition and alliance with the Sandinistas and mass insurrection in response to the assassination of P. J. Chamorro in 1977. 4 illus.
P. J. Durell

1203. Corbi, Gustavo Daniel. LE NICARAGUA DANS LA LIGNE DI MIRE DE FIDEL CASTRO [Nicaragua in Fidel Castro's line of sight]. *Écrits de Paris [France] 1978 (386): 33-37.* Discusses the formation of and activities of the Sandinista Liberation Front of Nicaragua, focusing on its support from Cuba, 1959-74.

1204. Cruz Alfaro, Ernesto. EL PENSAMIENTO POLÍTICO DE CÉSAR A. SANDINO [The political thought of Augusto César Sandino]. *Estudios Centro Americanos [El Salvador] 1975 30(316-317): 95-114.* Discusses the nationalist and anti-imperialist political thought of General Augusto César Sandino (1883-1934), part two of a work by the author which also includes Sandino's role against US intervention in Nicaragua (1909-33) and his social thought.

1205. Cuzán, Alfred G. and Heggen, Richard J. A MICRO-POLITICAL EXPLANATION OF THE 1979 NICARAGUAN REVOLUTION. *Latin Am. Res. Rev. 1982 17(2): 156-170.* Anastasio Somoza De Bayle lost power when he attempted to expand the scope of the state and national resources without having the requisite abilities to persuade and coerce the population. A decline in the ratio of National Guard to population from 1965 to 1975, the declining legitimacy of the government due to such activities as profiteering from earthquake relief supplies, and the expanded scope of the state in the 1970's created an untenable position for Somoza. Table, 4 fig., 25 notes.
J. K. Pfabe

1206. Debray, Regis. NICARAGUA AÑO CERO [Nicaragua in the year zero]. *Casa de las Américas [Cuba] 1979 20(117): 79-90.* A study of the Sandinista Liberation Front with a focus on the factors that contributed to its success. Although youthful, the Sandinista struggle had started with Augusto César Sandino in 1927. It was both a national liberation and cultural rebirth movement that was converted into a political and military force. The three major factors that accounted for its success were mass support, arming the people, and unification of diverse factions. The unity is still evident in the collective leadership governing the nation. Based on journal articles; 2 notes.
H. J. Miller

1207. Dennis, Philip A. THE COSTEÑOS AND THE REVOLUTION IN NICARAGUA. *J. of Interamerican Studies and World Affairs 1981 23(3): 271-296.* The Miskito Indians have traditionally been unfriendly toward "Spaniards" (Spanish-speaking Nicaraguans) and friendly toward English-speaking foreigners. Relations with Somoza, given his many personal and political links to the United States, were good. The Miskitos fought with Somoza. Relations with the Sandinistas remain tense, but have not erupted into conflict yet. There is hope for gradually improving relations. The Sandinistas claim to support general access to education and more local participation in economic decisions, two matters which the Miskitos have long sought. Secondary sources; ref.
T. D. Schoonover

1208. Diederich, Bernard. DID HUMAN RIGHTS KILL ANASTASIO SOMOZA? AN EXCERPT FROM A RECENT BIOGRAPHY. *Caribbean Rev. 1981 10(4): 4-7, 41-43.* Jimmy Carter's human rights policy in 1976 may have indirectly led to Anastasio Somoza's assassination, since human rights became a major issue then between Nicaragua and the United States. Although Somoza still had many influential American friends in business and Congress, many others were calling for a halt in aid for Nicaragua until human rights would be respected.

1209. Dodd, Thomas J. A DOCUMENT: MILITARY FEATURES OF PUERTO CABEZAS AREA, NICARAGUA, 1928. *Rev. Interamericana [Puerto Rico] 1975 5(2): 225-235.* During the second military occupation of Nicaragua, 1927-33, Captain Matthew B. Ridgway wrote a report arguing for the strategic importance of Puerto Cabezas to the United States. As a result, this Atlantic seaport became a center for American armed forces in Nicaragua during this period. 2 illus., 7 notes.
J. A. Lewis

1210. Dodd, Thomas J. LOS ESTADOS UNIDOS EN LA POLITICA NICARAGUENSE: ELECCIONES SUPERVISADAS, 1928-1932 [The United States in Nicaraguan politics: supervised elections, 1928-32]. *Rev. del Pensamiento Centroamericano [Nicaragua] 1975 30(148): 5-102.* Details US involvement in Nicaragua, 1927-32, focusing on supervision of elections during the period, including presidential elections of 1928 and 1932, legislative elections of 1930, and municipal elections of 1931. While US financial intervention (1912-27) had been highly successful, political stability had not been achieved, owing to the clear US preference for Conservatives before 1927. Henry Stimson attempted to solve this problem by providing free elections with participation of the Liberals, who assumed power following the election of 1928. But the United States also worked subtly to prevent Liberal José M. Moncada from continuing in power beyond 1932. The election of Juan B. Sacasa was seen favorably in Washington for it achieved that goal, enabling the US to withdraw gracefully and to reach an agreement with Augusto Sandino to end his guerrilla warfare. The primary US motive was to maintain stability in Nicaragua, but the supervision of elections caused a change in the US *modus operandi* to support "popular will" and the Liberals. Stimson's efforts to make Nicaragua a "North America in miniature" were not successful, but they served US interests. Based on the author's dissertation, extensive primary and secondary sources; 465 notes, biblio.   R. L. Woodward

1211. Eeuwen, Daniel Van. DU SOMOZISME AU SANDINISME [From Somozism to Sandinism]. *Cultures et Développement [Belgium] 1980 12(3-4): 507-537.* Analyzes the events that led to dictator Somoza's fall in Nicaragua in 1979 and the rise to power of Sandinista Liberation Front.

1212. Fagen, Richard R. DATELINE NICARAGUA: THE END OF THE AFFAIR. *Foreign Policy 1979 (36): 178-191.* The Carter Administration's reactions to the collapse of the regime of Anastasio Somoza Debayle in Nicaragua revealed the persistence of Washington's inability to comprehend "the nature and implications of a popular insurrection against tyranny." Seeing only opportunities for Communist gain in a victory for the anti-Somoza Sandinista National Liberation Front, the administration continued to support Somoza almost until the bitter end, and then attempted vainly to insure the succession of a non-Sandinista government. The result was the further degrading of America's already low reputation in Latin America.   T. L. Powers

1213. Falla, Ricardo. EL PROBLEMA DE LOS MISKITOS EN NICARAGUA [The problem of the Miskitos in Nicaragua]. *Estudios Centroamericanos [El Salvador] 1982 37(401): 193-200.* The Miskitos are a racial and cultural minority who have not been assimilated into the mainstream of Nicaraguan life, concentrated on the Pacific watershed. There has been a growing sentiment toward incorporating the Miskitos into the Nicaraguan "nation" and under the Sandinista Revolution this will include participation in power as well. The Mosquitia question has also been manipulated by counterrevolutionary forces. Appendixes include testimony of persons who have visited the Miskito refugee camps and declarations of indigenous Latin American organizations rejecting the US intervention in Nicaraguan internal affairs.
R. L. Woodward, Jr.

1214. Fonseca, Carlos. CRÓNICA SECRETA: AUGUSTO CÉSAR SANDINO ANTE SUS VERDUGOS [Secret chronicle: Augusto César Sandino before his executioners]. *Casa de las Américas [Cuba] 1974 15(86): 4-15.* Discusses the last writings of Nicaraguan hero Augusto César Sandino in 1933-34, showing his writings as influencing later Latin American revolutionary writers.

1215. Galich, Manuel. NICARAGUA 1933-1936: GESTACIÓN Y NACIMIENTO DE LA DINASTÍA [Nicaragua 1933-36: gestation and birth of the dynasty]. *Casa de las Américas [Cuba] 1979 20(117): 65-75.* A study of Anastasio Somoza's rise to power from the death of Augusto César Sandino to his occupation of the presidency. Key factors in his rise to power were the control of the National Guard, trained by US marines; US-supervised elections in 1928 and 1932, and the assassination of Sandino. By means of instigated internal disorders, Somoza and his National Guard removed Juan Bautista Sacasa in 1936 and took over the presidency on 1 January 1937. Based on writings of Juan Bautista Sacasa, Anastasio Somoza, and contemporary journal articles; 6 notes.
H. J. Miller

1216. Gilly, Adolfo. ESTADO Y LUCHA DE CLASES EN LA REVOLUCIÓN NICARAGÜENSE [State and class struggle in the Nicaraguan revolution]. *Investigación Econ. [Mexico] 1980 39(154): 93-106.* In terms of classical definitions, the new Nicaraguan state cannot be called a socialist state nor the revolution a proletarian revolution. It is an atypical bourgeois state because the middle class has lost control of the coercive apparatus. Its future remains undetermined, given the absence of workers' hegemony, and it can equally evolve in a "Cuban" and in a "Bolivian" direction. The public sector is not predominant; this, together with the political influence of the bourgeoisie, inserts the public sector into the logic of capitalist accumulation. Despite petit bourgeois participation in power, the regime has not yet become a mass movement with proletarian predominance. The ambiguity of the class character of the state is reflected in the priorities of the economic policy and more concretely in the conflict between the social priorities of the plan and the demands of private accumulation. 7 notes.   J. V. Coutinho

1217. Godoy B., Julio César. NOTAS SOBRE EL ESTADO DEMOCRÁTICO REVOLUCIONARIO EN NICARAGUA [Notes on the democratic revolutionary state in Nicaragua]. *Estudios Sociales Centroamericanos [Costa Rica] 1981 10(28): 109-115.* Examines why the revolutionary democratic dictatorship is so important for "the decisive victory of the revolution" and why workers, peasants, and their organized vanguard possess so much coercive authority and the consent of such a large majority of the population. Secondary sources; 2 notes, biblio.
T. D. Schoonover

1218. Godoy R., Virgilio. INCIDENCIAS DE LA INTEGRACIÓN ECONÓMICA CENTROAMERICANA EN EL PROCESO POLÍTICO DE NICARAGUA [Effects of Central American economic integration on the political process in Nicaragua]. *Rev. del Pensamiento Centroamericano [Nicaragua] 1977 32(157): 77-99.* Reviews Nicaraguan political history since 1821 and argues that Central American economic integration has increased the power of the Somoza family, especially since 1960, by making the power structure more rigid, thereby concentrating real power at the top. Based principally on secondary sources; 4 tables, 36 notes.   R. L. Woodward, Jr.

1219. Goninski, S. A. DINASTIIA TIRANOV SOMOSA [The dynasty of the Somoza tyrants]. *Novaia i Noveishaia Istoriia [USSR] 1973 (1): 136-145, (2): 128-137.* The Somoza family has exercized great political power in Nicaragua since the late 19th century, and became closely linked to the United States from 1912 onwards. Their grip was shaken by Augusto César Sandino and his movement in the early 1930's, but this political opposition was destroyed in 1934. The Somoza rule grew increasingly repressive during the 1950's. In 1966 the current president, Anastasio Somoza, took office and since 1970 he has faced a growing popular opposition, led particularly by the Communists, to the repression and poverty which have characterized Nicaragua under Somoza rule. 51 notes.   A. J. Evans/S

1220. Gorman, Stephen M. POWER AND CONSOLIDATION IN THE NICARAGUAN REVOLUTION. *J. of Latin Am. Studies [Great Britain] 1981 13(1): 133-149.* By the end of the first year of the Nicaraguan revolution, the National Directorate (DNC) of the Sandinista National Liberation Front had consolidated both military and political power and political support. The disappearance of factional identification in the FSLN and lack of visible conflicts in the DNC aided the DNC's effectiveness. Use of bourgeois political parties, the delay in the creation of the Council of State, the absence of elections, the replacement of the National Guard with the Popular Sandinista Army, and the use of popular militias, police, and security forces also aided in the consolidation of power. Based on interviews and printed primary sources; 18 notes, 2 charts, 2 fig.   M. A. Burkholder

1221. Gorman, Stephen M. SANDINISTA CHESS: HOW THE LEFT TOOK CONTROL. *Caribbean Rev. 1981 10(1): 14-17.* Points out that the Sandinista National Directorate (DNC) which came into existence in 1979 has successfully dictated the institutional structure of the new Nicaraguan government and has dominated the political process by 1) retaining exclusive control of all military and police forces, 2) preventing moderates and conservatives from using their governmental positions to preempt leftist leadership of the popular organizations that grew out of the insurrection, and 3) forging an effective political alliance with small groups of so-called moderate members included in the new regime.

1222. Gutiérrez Mayorga, Gustavo. EL REFORMISMO ARTESA-NAL EN EL MOVIMIENTO OBRERO NICARGÜENSE (1931-1960) [Artisan reformism in the Nicaraguan labor movement, 1931-60]. *Rev. del Pensamiento Centroamericano [Nicaragua] 1978 33(159): 2-21.* Organized urban labor in Nicaragua during the period 1931-60 progressed from mutual aid societies to trade unionism. Two Marxist political parties, the Nicaraguan Labor Party (PTN) and the Nicaraguan Socialist Party (PSN) were important in helping urban workers organize, although their efforts were limited by the artisan nature of production and by state repression. Fascist labor ideology was also important during the Somoza dynasty, especially promoted by a group known as the Blue Shirts. Based on published materials and on personal interviews; 50 notes.
R. L. Woodward, Jr.

1223. Guy, James. THE AGONY OF NICARAGUA. *Int. Perspectives [Canada] 1979 (Sept-Dec): 25-29.* Unlike most coups and barracks revolts in Latin America, Nicaragua's 1979 upheaval bears all the signs of a real revolution. The victory of the Sandinistas over Anastasio Somoza Debayle, whose family maintained control for more than four decades, has irrevocably altered the political, social, and economic fabric of society. Nicaragua must now attempt to recover from the loss of 15,000 people, the destruction of villages and towns, and the ruin of many businesses. The absence of a charismatic leader like Cuba's Castro suggests uncertainty as to what institutions will emerge to fill the political vacuum. 2 photos.
E. S. Palais

1224. Herrera Zúniga, René. NICARAGUA: EL DESARROLLO CAPITALISTA DEPENDIENTE Y LA CRISIS DE LA DOMINA-CIÓN BURGUESA, 1950-1980 [Nicaragua: dependent capitalist development and the crisis of bourgeois dominance, 1950-80]. *Foro Int. [Mexico] 1980 20(4): 612-645.* Examines Nicaraguan political, economic, and social change from 1950 that led up to Sandinista revolutionary success and speculates on the nature of future development. 6 tables, 48 notes.
D. A. Franz

1225. Jara Holliday, Oscar. LA HEROICA MARCHA DEL PUE-BLO DE SANDINO [The heroic march of the people of Sandino]. *Estudios Sociales Centroamericanos [Costa Rica] 1980 9(25): 403-422.* Constructs a political interpretive periodization for the Nicaraguan revolutionary struggle. Presents a class basis for the diverse stages of historical development of the current revolutionary movement. Portrays the accumulation of popular forces, the relationships within the class structure, the relationship between masses and vanguard, and the role of American domination of Nicaragua. Chronological-periodization table.
T. D. Schoonover

1226. Karnes, Thomas L. LA STANDARD FRUIT Y LA STEAM-SHIP COMPANY EN NICARAGUA (LOS PRIMEROS ANOS) [The Standard Fruit and Steamship Company: the first years]. *Anuario de Estudios Centroamericanos [Costa Rica] 1977 3: 175-213.* The Standard Fruit Company started lumber and banana operations in Honduras in 1899. In 1921 it expanded operations into Nicaragua and it was here that the enterprise proved to be unprofitable during the 1920's and 1930's due to labor recruitment difficulties, inadequate supplies for workers, poor soil, banana diseases, economic instability, and civil wars, including the destruction of property by Augusto César Sandino's (1893-1934) forces. It was not until the 1970's that the firm, now called United Brands, showed signs of profitability. Based mainly on archives of the Standard Fruit Company; 31 notes.
H. J. Miller/S

1227. Knudson, Jerry W. THE NICARAGUAN PRESS AND THE SANDINISTA REVOLUTION. *Gazette [Netherlands] 1981 27(3): 163-179.* Postulates that the assassination of Pedro Joaquín Chamorro (1924-78), editor of the opposition newspaper *La Prensa* "touched off the spiral that ultimately dumped Somoza." Long opposed to the Somoza's family rule, *La Prensa* frequently suffered from government threats and censorship before the revolution. Burned in 1978, the paper resumed publication in 1980 after the Sandinistas had overthrown the government. Since the revolution, *Barricada* has emerged as the official organ of the new government, while *La Prensa* has slipped back into the role of government critic. Based on press reports, interviews, and secondary sources; 62 notes.
J. S. Coleman

1228. Millet, Richard. ANASTASIO SOMOZA GARCÍA, FUN-DADOR DE LA DINASTÍA SOMOZA EN NICARAGUA [Anastasio Somoza García, founder of the Somoza dynasty in Nicaragua]. *Estudios Centro Americanos [El Salvador] 1975 30(326): 725-741.* Discusses the influence in Nicaragua of the dynasty founded by Anastasio Somoza García (1896-1956), showing that the political power of the Somoza family did not end with the assassination of Anastasio Somoza García in 1956.

1229. Millett, Richard. ANASTASIO SOMOZA GARCÍA: A BRIEF HISTORY OF NICARAGUA'S "ENDURING" DICTATOR. *Rev. Interamericana [Puerto Rico] 1977 7(3): 486-508.* Anastasio Somoza's rise to power in the 1930's was in the caudillo tradition, but his ability to remain in power until 1956 rested on the balance between military and political powers. He established and strengthened the National Guard as well as the Liberal Nationalist Party, which maintained a base of rural support. He used his own wealth for political ends. He was able to take over the military and establish a political dynasty based on a system of economic and political corruption that permeated all aspects of Nicaraguan life.
G. A. Hewlett

1230. Montgomery, Robin Navarro. THE FALL OF SOMOZA: ANATOMY OF A REVOLUTION. *Parameters 1980 10(1): 47-57.* Reviews the history of the Somoza dynasty in Nicaragua from 1909 to 1979, the rise to power of the Sandinistas, and the overthrow of Somoza in 1979. The Sandinistas succeeded because Somoza had alienated many Nicaraguans through his corruption. This allowed the revolutionary movement to harness opposition which eventually led to the overthrow of the government. The role of the government of the United States, though well intentioned, was a major factor in the success of the Sandinistas. Primary sources; 53 notes.
J. Powell

1231. Pearson, Neale J. NICARAGUA IN CRISIS. *Current Hist. 1979 76(444): 78-80, 84.* Discusses the background to the successes of the Sandinista Front in 1978, beginning with the election of Anastasio Somoza García in 1936 and the administration of his son Anastasio Somoza Debayle, elected in 1967.

1232. Peña, Sergio de la. NICARAGUA: UNA REVOLUCIÓN AN-DANDO [Nicaragua: an on-going revolution]. *Investigación Econ. [Mexico] 1980 39(154): 89-92.* In Nicaragua the revolutionary process escaped the control of the anti-Somoza middle class and was determined by political factors rather than by property relations. In spite of middle-class participation in power the revolution cannot be called bourgeois; the ideological bases of the bourgeoisie have been eroded, and organs of popular power are being created. The Sandinista movement is becoming a dominant proletarian force, the masses are being politicized and mobilized, and the advance toward socialism appears irreversible.
J. V. Coutinho

1233. Petras, James. WHITHER THE NICARAGUAN REVOLU-TION? *Monthly Rev. 1979 31(5): 1-22.* Discusses the historical background of the Nicaraguan revolution and the nature and evolution of the Sandinista Front.

1234. Ramirez, Sergio. BREVE HISTORIA CONTEMPORÁNEA DE NICARAGUA [Brief contemporary history of Nicaragua]. *Casa de las Américas [Cuba] 1979 20(117): 17-39.* Analysis of Nicaraguan national history. The 19th century witnessed US and British interventions due to canal interests. Liberal and conservative struggles aided interventions, including those of William Walker and Cornelius Vanderbilt. The regime of José Zelaya (1893-1909) opposed the United States and set the stage for US military intervention (1912-). Augusto César Sandino subsequently headed a national liberation movement, 1926-34, and fought the US Marines and the National Guard headed by Anastasio Somoza. The revival of the Sandinistas in the 1950's led eventually to the overthrow of the Somoza dynasty in 1979.
H. J. Miller

1235. Ramírez, Sergio. WHAT THE SANDINISTAS WANT: NOT A NEW CUBA, BUT A NEW NICARAGUA. *Caribbean Rev. 1979 8(3): 24-27, 49-52.* The Nicaraguan people have struggled against US imperialism and imposition of puppet rulers since the mid-19th century, and now the Sandinista Front is demanding—from a position of strength and unity—dignified relations with the more powerful nations, relations based on mutual respect, without paternalism and debasing forms of interventionism and servility.

1236. René Vargas, Oscar. LA CRISIS DEL SOMOCISMO Y EL MOVIMIENTO OBRERO NICARAGÜENSE [The crisis of Somozaism and the Nicaraguan workers' movement]. *Estudios Centroamericanos [El Salvador] 1978 33(354): 205-216.* After the institution of martial law in 1977 the Sandinista Front for National Liberation began guerrilla warfare in parts of Nicaragua. Most of the troubles originated in the Anastasio Somoza regime's inability to solve the economic crisis which began with the 1967-71 worldwide recession and escalated. Because of underdevelopment the class struggle was late in coming to Nicaragua. 8 illus., 21 notes. K. A. Talley

1237. Sacasa, Juan B. COMO Y POR QUE CAÍ DEL PODER [How and why I fell from power]. *Rev. del Pensamiento Centroamericano [Nicaragua] 1978 33(161): 1-138.* Facsimile reprint of Juan Bautista Sacasa's *Como y por que caí del poder* (2d ed., León, Nicaragua, 1946). Sacasa was president of Nicaragua from 1933 to 1936, when he was replaced by Anastasio Somoza. Sacasa explains how Somoza, with his control of the National Guard, was able to gain power. The remainder of this memoir contains documents from the period. The documentary appendixes and explanatory notes were not included in the first (1936) edition. R. L. Woodward, Jr.

1238. Sereseres, Caesar D. U.S. MILITARY AID, AUTHORITARIAN RULE AND MILITARY POLICIES IN CENTRAL AMERICA. *Armed Forces and Soc. 1979 5(2): 329-334.* An essay review on Richard Millett's *Guardians of the Dynasty: A History of the U.S. Created Guardia Nacional de Nicaragua and the Somoza Family* (Maryknoll, N.Y.: Orbis, 1977), and Don L. Etchison's *The United States and Militarism in Central America* (New York: Praeger, 1975). The two books complement each other, the latter giving a broad historical and comparative analysis of US military assistance policies to several Central American countries, the former concentrating on Nicaragua, the Somoza family, the Guardia Nacional and US policies, especially the way in which the military modifies the relationship between state and society. R. V. Ritter

1239. Skinner, Joseph K. SOMOCISTAS ON TRIAL. *Monthly Rev. 1982 33(10): 49-59.* Offers case histories of the trials of some of the 4,500 civilian and military collaborators of the Somoza regime who were tried between December 1979 and February 1981 at the Tribunales Especiales in the Colonia Altamira, Nicaragua.

1240. Soustelle, Jacques. AU NICARAGUA: UN GENOCIDE BIEN TRANQUILLE [In Nicaragua: a well-silenced genocide]. *Rev. des Deux Mondes [France] 1982 (10): 16-22.* Although the Miskito and Sumo Indians have traditionally been given special and exempt status, this status deteriorated during the period 1979-81, with the fall of the Somoza government and the creation of the new Sandinista government; Cuban and East German influence is responsible for the many executions and deaths among Nicaragua's Indian population.

1241. Talavera S., José León. NICARAGUA: CRISIS DE LA DICTATURA MILITAR: 1967-1978 [Nicaragua: crisis of the military dictatorship, 1967-78]. *Estudios Sociales Centroamericanos [Costa Rica] 1979 8(23): 213-244.* Determining elements in the progressive crisis of Anastasio Somoza's military dictatorship include the failure of the political reform movement which was promoted on the international level by North American imperialism, the frustration of Central America integration, the presence of a timid but progressive revolutionary movement, worsening repressive activity, the desperate attempt of Somoza to strengthen his dictatorship via concession to Fernando Agüero's faction of the Conservative Party which tended to polarize other opposition factions, and the obstacle that capitalist development itself generated by provoking the disadvantaged. T. D. Schoonover

1242. Torres-Rivas, Edelberto. EL ESTADO CONTRA LA SOCIEDAD: LAS RAÍCES DE LA REVOLUCIÓN NICARAGÜENSE [The state against society: the roots of the Nicaraguan revolution]. *Estudios Sociales Centroamericanos [Costa Rica] 1980 9(27): 79-96.* The Somoza regime was not a bourgeois state. While the economy and the Somoza group were certainly capitalist, the Somoza dynasty exaggerated

and personalized centralized state power. The Nicaraguan state at the end, then, represented neither the nation nor the people. One must carefully avoid the word dictatorship since Somoza could not run the state alone, but used the army and the party in a combination of terror and corruption. Secondary sources; 9 notes. T. D. Schoonover

1243. Valle, Maria Esperanza. UDEL: LA EXPRESIÓN POLÍTICA DE UNA ALIANZA DE CLASE EN NICARAGUA, 1974-1978 [UDEL: the political expression of a class alliance in Nicaragua, 1974-78]. *Estudios Sociales Centroamericanos [Costa Rica] 1979 8(24): 387-395.* The Nicaraguan bourgeoisie asserted its domination of Nicaraguan society through a military dictatorship, consolidated under the Somoza family from 1933 until 1967. The refusal to carry out the Poder Electoral program and the self-interested move of the Somoza family to centralize all power in its hands rather than share it with the middle classes after 1967 led to increased opposition. Factions of the bourgeoisie united with workers' centrals to form the Union Demócratica de Liberación [Democratic Union of Liberation] which called and directed the national strike of 1978. T. D. Schoonover

1244. Vanden, Harry E. THE IDEOLOGY OF THE NICARAGUAN REVOLUTION. *Monthly Rev. 1982 34(2): 25-41.* Traces the socioeconomic roots and major themes of the ideology of the Nicaraguan leftist revolution from the 19th century to 1982, focusing on the history of the Sandinista National Liberation Front from its founding in 1961 to 1979, when it emerged victorious over the right-wing government.

1245. VanEeuwen, Daniel. NICARAGUA, L'AN II DE LA REVOLUTION: HEGEMONIE SANDINISTE ET MONTEE DES PERILS [Nicaragua, year two of the revolution: Sandinista hegemony and mounting dangers]. *Problèmes d'Amérique Latine [France] 1982 (63): 9-66.* Describes economic crises, advances in the campaign against illiteracy, polarization between the forces of the revolution and the bourgeoisie during 1979-80, and how, beginning in 1981, the forces of the Sandinista face destabilization of their regime and interference from outside.

1246. Vargas Escobar, Oscar René. NOTAS SOBRE EL NUEVO EJE DE ACUMULACIÓN CAPITALISTA EN CENTROAMÉRICA: EL CASO DE NICARAGUA [Notes on the new axis of capitalist accumulation in Central America: the case of Nicaragua]. *Estudios Sociales Centroamericanos [Costa Rice] 1979 8(22): 251-272.* The long depression cycle since the mid-1960's has led to a new axis of capitalist accumulation which is characterized by major participation of foreign capital in the productive process. This new strategy of capital accumulation in Nicaragua is not deliberate, but the product of tentative efforts to eliminate the contradiction of accumulation under the old system, which was in turn, a part of the worldwide capital accumulation system. Also, the inflationary process actually favors industrialization. Based on printed primary and secondary sources; 30 notes. T. D. Schoonover

1247. Velásquez, José Luis. LA INCIDENCIA DE LA FORMACIÓN DE LA ECONOMÍA AGROEXPORTADORA EN EL INTENTO DE FORMACIÓN DEL ESTADO NACIONAL EN NICARAGUA: (1860-1930) [The emergence of the agroexport economy in the effort to form the national state in Nicaragua: 1860-1930]. *Rev. del Pensamiento Centroamericano [Nicaragua] 1977 32(157): 11-31.* Explores the political structure that originated in Nicaragua when the agroexport economy began to develop between 1860 and 1911, and analyzes the political consequences that resulted from North American intervention after 1911. Relates Nicaraguan economic history to growth of the worldwide capitalist system and to the development of the conservative political oligarchy in Nicaragua. The result was an enclave economy dependent on the developed capitalist economies. R. L. Woodward, Jr.

1248. Walker, Thomas W. NICARAGUA CONSOLIDATES ITS REVOLUTION. *Current Hist. 1981 80(463): 79-82, 89-90.* Examines the social and economic impact of the Sandinista revolution on Nicaragua: the establishing of popular organizations, economic progress, social reforms, and a nonalignment foreign policy.

1249. Walker, Thomas W. THE SANDINISTA VICTORY IN NICARAGUA. *Current Hist. 1980 78(454): 57-61, 84.* Favorably compares the new Sandinista government of Nicaragua with the deposed government of Anastasio Somoza.

1250. Woodward, Ralph Lee, Jr. DR. PEDRO JOAQUIN CHAMORRO (1924-1978), THE CONSERVATIVE PARTY, AND THE STRUGGLE FOR DEMOCRATIC GOVERNMENT IN NICARAGUA. *Secolas Ann. 1979 10: 38-46.* Traces the anti-Somoza activities of Pedro Joaquín Chamorro, a leading member of the Partido Conservador Tradicional and editor of *La Prensa,* an anti-Somoza newspaper, in Nicaragua. Describes his consistent campaign to oust the dictatorship and secure religious, moral, economic, political, and social freedom through institution of a democracy, 1953-78.

1251. —. DOCUMENTO DE AUGUSTO CESAR SANDINO SOBRE CARLOS APONTE [A document of Augusto César Sandino on Carlos Aponte]. *Casa de las Américas [Cuba] 1982 22(130): 132-133.* The Venezuelan Carlos Aponte fought with Sandino in his guerrilla army in Nicaragua during the 1920's. He was executed in Cuba in 1935 during the Batista dictatorship with the leader of the revolutionary organization *Joven Cuba.* A letter of Sandino commending Aponte is reproduced here.
                                                                          J. V. Coutinho

1252. —. EL SANDINISMO Y LA LUCHA DE LIBERACIÓN NICARAGÜENSE, 1933-1939 [The Sandinista Movement and the Nicaraguan liberation struggle, 1933-39]. *Bol. del Archivo General de la Nación [Mexico] 1980 4(1): 50-62.* Reprints 10 documents concerning the Sandinista movement and internal politics in Nicaragua. Taken from the papers of Emilio Portes Gil, Abelardo L. Rodríguez, and Lázaro Cárdenas at the Archivo General de la Nación; photo.   J. A. Lewis

1253. —. THE KOCH-STATE DEPARTMENT CORRESPONDENCE ON U.S. RELATIONS WITH NICARAGUA. *Inter-Am. Econ. Affairs 1976 29(4): 85-93.* Reprints the correspondence between Congressman Edward Koch and the US State Department that appeared in the *Congressional Record* (18 February 1976) regarding US foreign aid to Nicaragua, characteristics of the Somoza regime, and military aid to Nicaragua. Table.   D. A. Franz

Panama

1254. Arosemena R., Jorge. LA UNITED FRUIT COMPANY ENCLAVE BANANERO EN PANAMÁ [The United Fruit Company banana enclave in Panama]. *Estudios Centro Americanos [El Salvador] 1974 29(313-314): 750-764.* Discusses the entrenchment of the United Fruit Company in Panama, giving a historical survey summarizing events from the end of the 19th century to the present and examining data since 1960 to show the company as an agent of US economic imperialism in Latin America.

1255. Bolivar Pedreschi, Carlos. EL NACIONALISMO PANAMEÑO Y LA CUESTIÓN CANALERA [Panamanian nationalism and the Canal Question]. *Anuario de Estudios Centroamericanos [Costa Rica] 1977 3: 295-310.* Panamanian nationalism demands immediate recovery of the Panama Canal, its demilitarization and neutralization. The neocolonial mentality of the United States government has opposed the nationalist position during the period 1960-77, but in treaty negotiations time is on the side of Panama. Panama must cultivate its relations with Communist states and developing nations to publicize its cause. Public opinion in the United States is becoming anticolonial and the time is ripe for Panama to dictate a treaty on its own terms. Based on newspapers; 5 notes.   H. J. Miller

1256. Burns, E. Bradford. PANAMA: A SEARCH FOR INDEPENDENCE. *Current Hist. 1977 72(424): 65-67, 82.* Examines the 73-year history of the Hay-Bunau-Varilla Treaty of 1903, Panama's repeated attempts at renegotiation of treaty terms, 1903-76, and the politics of treaty modification in the United States.

1257. Burns, E. Bradford. PANAMA'S STRUGGLE FOR INDEPENDENCE. *Current Hist. 1974 66(389): 19-22, 38.* Discusses Panama's position and goals in negotiating with the United States for total national sovereignty. One of seven articles on Latin America.   S

1258. Ciampi, Antonio. IL CANALE DI PANAMA IERI ED OGGI [The Panama Canal yesterday and today]. *Riv. Marittima [Italy] 1977 110(10): 49-62.* The history of the Panama Canal through two world wars until the eve of the Panama Canal treaty.

1259. Conte Porras, J. REFLEXIONES EN TORNO A LA GUERRA DE COTO Y DE LAS PRIMERAS DEMANDAS PANAMEÑAS PARA REFORMAR EL TRATADO DEL CANAL [Reflections on the Coto War and the first Panamanian demands for reform of the Canal Treaty]. *Lotería [Panama] 1971 (192): 19-34.* Traces from the mid-19th century the origins of the 1921 Panamanian-Costa Rican border war known as the Coto War, with emphasis on the role of Panamanian president Belisario Porras. These events reflect a general American strategy of guaranteeing US power over Panamanian territory.
                                                                          L. R. Atkins

1260. Davis, Enriqueta and Blanco, Freddy Enrique. EL PROBLEMA DEL INDIO EN PANAMÁ [The problem of the Indian in Panama]. *Am. Indígena [Mexico] 1978 38(1): 97-103.* Reviews Indian policies in Panama. Legislation has tended to guarantee cultural continuity to Indians, including their traditional habitat, divided for administrative purposes into four regions.   J

1261. Erice, Jesús. LA REVOLUCIÓN DE INDIOS KUNAS DE PANAMÁ (FEBRERO DE 1925) PARTE I [The revolution of the Cuna Indians of Panama (February 1925)]. *Estudios Centro Americanos [El Salvador] 1975 30(319-320): 283-304.* Discusses the 1925 rebellion by the Cuna Indians of Panama, utilizing maps and detailed descriptions of battles to show the process which led to the revolt. Article to be continued.

1262. Erice, Jesús. LA REVOLUCIÓN DE LOS INDIOS KUNAS DE PANAMÁ [The revolution of the Cuna Indians of Panama]. *Estudios Centro Americanos [El Salvador] 1975 30(321): 362-388.* Continued from a previous article (see preceding abstract). The diary of Father Jesús Erice narrating the revolution of the Cuna Indians in eastern Panama in 1925, including details of battles and the reaction of the Panamanian government.

1263. Gonzalez, Baldomero. NEW TRENDS IN RURAL PANAMA. *World Marxist R. [Canada] 1975 18(6): 124-129.* Identifies the political and agricultural reform of the collective *asentamientos* since 1962.   S

1264. Gorostiaga, Xavier. LA ZONA DEL CANAL Y EL SUB DESARROLLO PANAMEÑO [The Canal Zone and Panamanian underdevelopment]. *Estudios Centro Americanos [El Salvador] 1975 30(316-317): 129-143.* Discusses the economic-political-military presence of the United States in the Panama Canal Zone, seeing the US presence as a negative force acting against the economic development of the Canal Zone and therefore of the whole Latin American region; bases the analysis on 1970-71 economic data.

1265. Gutierrez, Roberto F. PODER LOCAL Y DESARROLLO RURAL EN PANAMÁ: EL EJEMPLO DEL DISTRITO DE GUARARÉ [Local power and rural development in Panama: the example of the district of Guararé]. *Cahiers du Monde Hispanique et Luso-Brésilien [France] 1981 (36): 41-61.* In spite of the administrative reforms of 1972, the system of decisionmaking in rural matters has remained poorly distributed, as exemplified by the Guararé district. The tradition of centralized control and the peasants' passivity are responsible. Administrative regulations of Guararé and neighboring districts; map, 5 tables, 5 notes.
                                                                          D. R. Stevenson

1266. Heinrichs, Waldo. THE PANAMA CANAL IN HISTORY, POLICY, AND CARICATURE. *Latin Am. Res. Rev. 1982 17(2): 247-261.* Reviews six books published since 1976 on the Panama Canal. Except for Walter LaFeber's *The Panama Canal: The Crisis in Historical Perspective,* the books fall into the traps of distortion and unreality. What is needed in the United States is sensitivity to the feelings and needs of Panamanians. The 1977 treaties showed signs of such sensitivity.
                                                                          J. K. Pfabe

1267. Iannettone, Giovanni.   SUL CANALE DI PANAMA [On the Panama Canal]. *Riv. di Studi Politici Int. [Italy] 1978 45(2): 209-228.* Traces the history of the Panama Canal, its building, acquisition by the United States, and revision of the US-Panamanian treaty regulating it, 1960's-77.

1268. Johnson, Harry G.   PANAMA AS A REGIONAL FINANCIAL CENTER: A PRELIMINARY ANALYSIS OF DEVELOPMENT CONTRIBUTION. *Econ. Development and Cultural Change 1976 24(2): 261-286.* Discusses the role of Panama as a regional financial center in banking and insurance for Latin America in the 1960's and 70's, including the valuation relationship between the Panamanian balboa and the American dollar.

1269. Kausch, Hans G.   THE 1977 PANAMA CANAL TREATIES: BEGINNING OF A NEW ERA? *World Today [Great Britain] 1978 34(11): 447-454.* Reviews conditions in Panama before the 1977 US-Panama treaty, and the treaty's provisions and political repercussions.

1270. Leeds, Roger S.   THE PANAMA CANAL TREATY: PAST AND PRESENT UNITED STATES INTERESTS. *Foreign Service J. 1976 53(3): 6-11, 27.* Offers a short history of Panama-United States relations over the Panama Canal; examines Gerald Ford's noncommittal attitude toward the Canal Zone and Congress's generally aggressive attitude toward American interests there. Concessions to the smaller country need not be interpreted as weaknesses.

1271. León, César A. de   LA GRAN REVOLUCIÓN DE OCTUBRE Y PANAMÁ [The Great October Revolution and Panama]. *Casa de las Américas [Cuba] 1977 18(105): 18-31.* The Russian Revolution plays a significant role in Latin America's struggle against capitalist imperialism. Panamanian independence coincided with the development of American imperialism, which exploited the masses with the support of the Panamanian bourgeoisie. Working-class parties in the 1920's organized to combat imperialism. The 1930's witnessed the founding of the Communist Party and the University of Panama. World War II brought more capital into the country and a greater number of American soldiers. Improved conditions did not resolve socioeconomic problems. The anti-imperialism struggle culminated in the 1964 insurrection to regain control of the Canal Zone, which was aided by a sympathetic national guard. Additional victories came with a labor code and a democratic constitution in 1972 and the abrogation of the Hay-Bunau-Varilla Treaty in 1977. The Communist Party deserves credit for these changes but the Panamanians must be aware of the continued threat of capitalist imperialism.
H. J. Miller

1272. Leonard, Thomas M.   THE UNITED STATES AND PANAMA: NEGOTIATING THE ABORTED 1926 TREATY. *Mid-America 1979 61(3): 189-203.* Disagreements between the United States and Panama over terms of the Hay-Bunau-Varilla Treaty of 1903 led to new negotiations in 1924, the major issues being commerce in the Canal Zone and land use by the United States. Talks were held in 1924 (March-August), 1925, and 1926. A treaty was signed in July 1926 covering the major issues. The Panama National Assembly refused to ratify because Article XI placed Panama on the American side during wars, and Panama was dissatisfied with the commercial clauses of the treaty. The US Senate Foreign Relations Committee then did not discuss the treaty. In the absence of a treaty Panama was forced to deal more explicitly with the United States and the United States to deal more sympathetically with Panama. These negotiations also led to another treaty in 1936. Based on State Department records, Panamanian newspaper accounts, and other primary sources; 56 notes.
J. M. Lee

1273. Major, John.   WASTING ASSET: THE U.S. RE-ASSESSMENT OF THE PANAMA CANAL, 1945-1949. *J. of Strategic Studies [Great Britain] 1980 3(2): 123-146.* The years 1945 to 1949 marked a decisive transitional phase in the history of the Panama Canal. Up to World War II, the canal had been the fulcrum of a US strategy whose chief areas of concern were Latin America and the Pacific, the spheres, respectively, of the Army and the Navy. The war years had witnessed a shift of US strategy to Europe. After the war the canal was no longer seen as crucial in government circles, and though old assumptions were to die hard among the American public, by the end of the 1940's it had been reduced to a subordinate place in official calculations. Based on State Department and other primary sources; 68 notes.
A. M. Osur

1274. Manduley, Julio.   PANAMA: DEPENDENT CAPITALISM AND BEYOND. *Latin Am. Perspectives 1980 7(2-3): 57-74.* Reviews the development of the Panamanian political economy since independence, its relation to the postwar international political and economic structure, and the influence of the Panama Canal and the canal negotiations with the United States that led to the 1977 treaty.
J. F. Vivian

1275. Osborne, Alfred E., Jr.   ON THE ECONOMIC COST TO PANAMA OF NEGOTIATING A PEACEFUL SOLUTION TO THE PANAMA CANAL QUESTION. *J. of Interam. Studies and World Affairs 1977 19(4): 509-521.* Recognizing that treaty negotiating is a difficult business, the economic costs to small countries, like Panama during current canal negotiations with United States, can be very high. Had the equal partner assumption been incorporated and accepted in the 1967 draft treaty, by 1974 Panama already would have accumulated an increased benefit of about one billion dollars. While the United States may lose politically and economically if an agreement is not signed, Panama is paying a high cost for economic opportunity. 6 tables, 10 notes, biblio.
T. D. Schoonover

1276. Rosenfeld, Stephen S.   THE PANAMA NEGOTIATIONS—A CLOSE-RUN THING. *Foreign Affairs 1975 54(1): 1-13.* Discusses the foreign and domestic controversy over the renegotiation of the Hay-Bunau-Varilla Treaty of 1903 concerning US sovereignty in the Panama Canal Zone. Since the "flag riots" of 1964, there have been 11 years of intermittent negotiation between the United States and Panama over whether to make only modest concessions leaving the 1903 treaty intact or to write a new treaty giving the Zone to Panama. General Omar Torrijos, Panama's president since 1968 has attempted to internationalize the issue through the United Nations. Secretary of State Henry Kissinger, attempting to conciliate the nationalism of Panama, signed the Eight Principles (7 February 1974) by which a new treaty would be negotiated yet congressional opposition has been powerful among those who dislike giving away vital strategic assets to the communists and among environmentalists who are opposed to mixing the sea life of the two oceans. The military establishment has been the strongest US proponent of the status quo. Note.
C. W. Olson

1277. Rubin, Barry.   PANAMA CANAL RETROSPECTIVE. *Contemporary Rev. [Great Britain] 1979 234(1357): 80-84.* Considers the controversy over the Panama Canal and outlines changes in US foreign policy concerning the canal since the 1903 treaty.

1278. Shay, Martha Jane.   THE PANAMA CANAL ZONE: IN SEARCH OF A JURIDICAL IDENTITY. *New York U. J. of Int. Law and Pol. 1976 9(1): 15-60.* The question of the legal definition of the Panama Canal Zone has never been satisfactorily resolved. Confusion began with the treaty of 1903 and has been complicated by subsequent treaties, court decisions, and laws. A permanent solution must address 70 years of dispute over the legal status of the zone, redefine it, and rearrange functions, powers, and responsibilities. Based on treaties and other legal documents and secondary sources.
K. E. Miller

1279. Souza, Ruben Dario.   EVENTS IN CHILE AND REVOLUTIONARY PROCESS IN PANAMA. *World Marxist R. [Canada] 1974 17(1): 95-101.* The General Secretary of Panama's Peoples' Party analyzes the Panamanian revolutionary movement in light of the right-wing coup d'etat in Chile.
S

1280. Souza, Ruben Dario.   PANAMA CHOOSES THE ROAD. *World Marxist R. [Canada] 1973 16(3): 50-56.* Explores the Communist Party's struggle against imperialism.
S

1281. Stiles, Martha Bennett.   A NEW TREATY FOR AN INDEPENDENT PEOPLE. *Mankind 1975 5(4): 44-52.* Provides the diplomatic background to the 1903 Hay-Bunau-Varilla Treaty in which, by somewhat devious methods, the US gained a highly favorable lease to the Panama Canal; and the 1967-74 renewal of treaty negotiations with Panama over the canal.

1282. Vaughn, Jack Hood.   A LATIN AMERICAN VIETNAM. *Foreign Service J. 1974 51(1): 15-17.* Still a United States colony in many important respects, Panama may be on the verge of becoming more independent.
S

1283. Vaughn, Jack Hood. A LATIN-AMERICAN VIETNAM. *Washington Monthly 1973 5(8): 30-34.* See preceding abstract.

1284. Westerman, George W. PANAMA TODAY. *Crisis 1974 81(9): 303-305.* Presents a short history of US-Panamanian foreign relations, 1903-74. S

1285. Zafesov, G. THE LAND OF TWO OCEANS. *Int. Affairs [USSR] 1977 (6): 127-132.* A review of American imperialism in the Panama Canal Zone and efforts by the heroic government of General Omar Torrijos to throw off colonial shackles and regain sovereignty in the Zone. Torrijos has made clear that nothing less than complete control will satisfy the Panamanian people. He has the support of the populace and is adjusting his foreign relationships to include the socialist countries. Impressive efforts are underway to cure the social and economic ills of the country, the inevitable accompaniments of imperialism.

V. L. Human

4. THE WEST INDIES AND THE GUIANAS

Regional Studies

1286. Abbott, George C. THE ASSOCIATED STATES AND INDEPENDENCE. *J. of Interamerican Studies and World Affairs 1981 23(1): 69-94.* Describes the dissolution of the West Indies Federation with the withdrawal of Jamaica and Trinidad and Tobago and the subsequent period of stability of the West Indies Associated States within the British Empire. The recent independence of the individual islands raises the question whether they can function as viable states. Perhaps soon the regional organizations and other synthesizing forces will make them aware that their common identity and mutual interests form a basis for reintegration. Based upon various printed national and international agency materials and secondary sources; 7 tables, 4 notes, ref.

T. D. Schoonover

1287. André, David J. GATHERING STORM IN THE EASTERN CARIBBEAN. *Military Rev. 1981 61(7): 2-14.* Traditionally, the United States has taken Latin America, and the Caribbean in particular, for granted as part of its sphere of influence. But due to past indifference, inattention and lack of imagination the islands of the Caribbean have been quickly, and often violently, drifting to the left. To correct this, a unilateral military approach is unacceptable. Instead, the United States should pursue a strong and steady course of economic and political cooperation to overcome longstanding local developmental problems. 2 maps, 21 notes.

D. H. Cline

1288. Axline, W. Andrew. INTEGRATION AND DEVELOPMENT IN THE COMMONWEALTH CARIBBEAN: THE POLITICS OF REGIONAL NEGOTIATIONS. *Int. Organization 1978 32(4): 953-973.* With the signing of the Treaty of Chaguaramas in 1973 and the subsequent adherence of all of the member countries of the Caribbean Free Trade Association (CARIFTA), the Caribbean Community and Common Market (CARICOM) was created; and the Caribbean integration movement became the first example of a free trade area moving to a customs union. This change provides an appropriate context for the study of the politics of regional integration in the Third World.

J

1289. Axline, W. Andrew and Landriault, France. SOUS-DÉVELOPPEMENT, INÉGALITÉ ET CRISE DE COOPÉRATION DANS LA COMMUNAUTÉ DES CARAÏBES [Underdevelopment, inequality, and crisis of cooperation in the Caribbean Community and Common Market]. *Can. J. of Development Studies [Canada] 1980 1(1): 47-74.* Provides a theory of integration based on the economics and politics of underdevelopment, focusing on the regional benefits of integration, their distribution, and the impact of dependency on the integration process, with a view to explaining the crisis of cooperation in the Caribbean and Community Common Market.

1290. Barrett, F. A. THE RISE AND DEMISE OF THE FEDERATION OF THE WEST INDIES. *Can. Rev. of Studies in Nationalism [Canada] 1974 1(2): 241-262.* A consideration of federalism and of island nationalism in the abortive ten-member Federation of the West Indies (1958-62). The federation disintegrated because the demands of several clashing island nationalisms could not be harmonized with the numerous compromises entailed in forging a political union. The terms of federation only barely concealed the awkwardness of accommodations. The choice of what the new nation's name should be and the selection of Trinidad as the federal capital occasioned sharp controversy. Member states also differed on whether the federal government ought to possess extensive or limited powers. Economic problems and difficulties in communications also intruded. In the face of these centrifugal pressures the federation succumbed. This union may have been the victim of the tide of nationalism that engulfed the world after World War II. The experience of federating merely sharpened the distinctive nationalisms and "island positions" of the ten participants. Based on secondary sources; 2 tables, 3 charts, 32 notes.

T. Spira

1291. Basdeo, Sahadeo. COLONIAL POLICY AND LABOUR ORGANISATION IN THE BRITISH CARIBBEAN 1937-1939: AN ISSUE IN POLITICAL SOVEREIGNTY. *Bol. de Estudios Latinoamericanos y del Caribe [Netherlands] 1981 (31): 119-129.* British policy in the Caribbean underwent major reassessment and change in the 1930's, and a labor policy was formulated for the first time to consider social and labor legislation for the colonies. The British Labour Party played a major role in these developments, which in turn contributed to trade union development in the West Indies. By 1940 it was clear that although the British had not given up *de jure* political sovereignty, it was prepared *de facto* to share that sovereignty. Primary sources; 73 notes.

R. L. Woodward, Jr.

1292. Bourne, Compton. CURRENT TRENDS AND PROBLEMS IN DOMESTIC DEBT FINANCING OF CARIBBEAN GOVERNMENTS. *Social and Econ. Studies [Jamaica] 1977 26(4): 412-431.* Traces public debt financing in Barbados, Guyana, Jamaica, and Trinidad from 1965 to 1976. Calls attention to the large proportion of the external debt, the need to increase the domestic financing of the public debt, and the problems involved. 11 tables, 8 notes, 5 ref. E. S. Johnson

1293. Cardenas, Osvaldo. LA VIABILIDAD DE LA INTEGRACION DEL CARIBE [Viability of the integration of the Caribbean]. *Estudios Sociales Centroamericanos [Costa Rica] 1981 10(30): 33-48.* Currently consisting of 13 independent and 14 other political entities, the Caribbean area has a long history of interest in integration. Dependency, underdevelopment, and colonial remnants have been obstacles to unification, but there are now various factors, such as the tendency to seek economic links outside the colonialists sphere, tendency to avoid alignment, and tendencies toward regional cooperation, which favor integration of the Caribbean political units. Based on printed sources; 5 tables, map, biblio.

T. D. Schoonover

1294. Castor, Suzy. THE AMERICAN OCCUPATION OF HAITI (1915-34) AND THE DOMINICAN REPUBLIC (1916-24). *Massachusetts R. 1974 15(1/2): 253-275.*

1295. Clarke, Colin G. THE QUEST FOR INDEPENDENCE IN THE CARIBBEAN. *J. of Latin Am. Studies [Great Britain] 1977 9(2): 337-345.* For nearly two centuries Caribbean nations have expressed their desire for independence. Recent literature on the struggle demonstrates that Haiti's slave rebellion may have provoked a harsher attitude toward the independence of other countries. It was not until the British began the postwar decolonization of their Caribbean territories that independence became the rule. Independence, federation with the mother country, and intermediate states have all existed in the area's emerging nations. The newest books on the subject show the preoccupation with constitutional solutions to domestic problems, and provide ample evidence for the rhetoric of Caribbean radicals. Secondary sources; 17 notes.

J. W. Leedom

1296. Collart, Yves. MENTALITÉ COLLECTIVE ET FONDEMENTS DE LA POLITIQUE ÉTRANGÈRE AUX ANTILLES: LE CAS DES TERRITOIRES ANGLOPHONES [Collective mentality and bases of foreign policy in the Antilles: the case of the English-speaking territories]. *Relations Int. [France] 1974 (2): 261-283.* Studies the collective mentality of the Commonwealth Caribbean, including Jamaica, the Bahamas, the British Virgin Islands, the Leeward and Windward Islands, and Guyana, and British Honduras. Suggests a better use of their common traits to stimulate cohesion and improve the education system and their concept of the tourist industry. 32 notes. G. P. Cleyet

1297. Cuthbert, Marlene. THE FIRST FIVE YEARS OF THE CARIBBEAN NEWS AGENCY. *Gazette [Netherlands] 1981 28(1): 3-15.* The Caribbean News Agency (CANA), formed in 1976 with the aid of UNESCO, is a regional news gathering cooperative independent of the major international news organizations and of government control, rare in Third World news agencies. However, the governments of the nations served by CANA have occasionally tried to undermine this independence for their own purposes. CANA's main problem now is the high cost of telecommunications facilities. Based on interviews and CANA documents; 2 fig., 6 notes, ref.   J. S. Coleman

1298. Duncan, W. Raymond. CARIBBEAN LEFTISM. *Problems of Communism 1978 27(3): 33-57.* Analyzes the social, economic, and political factors that contribute to the current turmoil in the Caribbean, and the four major variants of leftism: the Marxist-Leninists, socialists, ethnic nationalists, and moderate reformers. Identifies Guyana and Jamaica as the most important common sources of the region's volatility and increasing tilt toward the left. Stresses the differences in specific policy dilemmas and domestic political contexts that distinguish the prospects of leftist forces in each country. Map, 4 tables, 53 notes.
J. M. Lauber

1299. Green, J. E. A REVIEW OF POLITICAL SCIENCE RESEARCH IN THE ENGLISH-SPEAKING CARIBBEAN: TOWARD A METHODOLOGY. *Social and Econ. Studies [Jamaica] 1974 23(1): 1-47.* Reviews selected literature on Caribbean political science research and notes that most of the work has been data collecting. Argues for the use of scientific methodology in political science research in the Caribbean and cites areas that need further research. Fig., 36 notes.
E. S. Johnson

1300. Hall, Kenneth and Blake, Byron. THE CARIBBEAN COMMUNITY: ADMINISTRATIVE AND INSTITUTIONAL ASPECTS. *J. of Common Market Studies [Great Britain] 1978 16(3): 211-228.* Analyzes institutional and administrative aspects of the Caribbean Community (CARICOM) as they affect the economic integration of the 12 member nations, 1973-78.

1301. Hylton, Patrick. THE POLITICS OF CARIBBEAN MUSIC. *Black Scholar 1975 7(1): 23-29.* Discusses the Calypso and Reggae as political expression and protest against the exploitation and oppression of Africans in the New World.

1302. James, C. L. R. DE TOUSSAINT L'OUVERTURE A FIDEL CASTRO [From Toussaint L'Ouverture to Fidel Castro]. *Casa de las Américas [Cuba] 1975 16(91): 64-69.* Traces the history of black revolutionaries in the West Indies during the 19th century, the 20th-century interwar era, and since World War II. A reprint from the epilogue of the author's *The Black Jacobins: Toussaint L'Ouverture and Saint Domingo Revolution.*

1303. James, C. L. R. EXTRACTS FROM THE LIFE OF CAPTAIN CIPRIANI. *Jamaica J. [Jamaica] 1978 11(3-4): 78-84.* Extracts from the author's book, *The Life of Captain Cipriani,* on Cipriani's 1914-19 participation in forming Jamaican forces to fight in World War I, and his participation in and interpretation of the actions of the Legislative Council of Trinidad, 1919-31.

1304. Jensen, Peter Hoxcer. DEN DANSK VESTINDISKE ARBEJDERBEVAEGELSE OG STREJKEN I 1916 [The Danish West Indies' labor movement and the strike in 1916]. *Meddelelser om Forskning i Arbejderbevaegelsens Hist. [Denmark] 1981 (16): 5-19.* Looks at the growth of the Labour Union in the Danish West Indies (St. Thomas, St. Croix, and St. Jan) founded by David Hamilton Jackson in 1915 as a prelude to the wage strike against the sugar cane plantation owners in 1916, and contrasts this conflict with earlier ones in 1848 and 1878, which were basically concerned with workers' freedom and fundamental rights.

1305. Johnson, Caswell L. THE EMERGENCE OF POLITICAL UNIONISM IN ECONOMIES OF BRITISH COLONIAL ORIGIN: THE CASES OF JAMAICA AND TRINIDAD. *Am. J. of Econ. and Sociol. 1980 39(2): 151-164.* Examines the circumstances under which political unionism emerged in Jamaica and Trinidad and Tobago. The political activities of trade unions played a role in the process of economic development, helping to achieve political independence and then economic growth. But at that stage political unionism became incompatible with needed acceleration of growth rates. A significant deterioration in economic and social conditions produced a crisis and the unions traded support for the parties for some control over economic and social policy. This gave the political leaders the power they needed to negotiate for independence but, in Jamaica, it changed the focus and character of the labor movement. Secondary sources; 34 notes.   J

1306. Johnson, Caswell L. POLITICAL UNIONISM AND THE COLLECTIVE OBJECTIVE IN ECONOMIES OF BRITISH COLONIAL ORIGIN: THE CASES OF JAMAICA AND TRINIDAD. *Am. J. of Econ. and Sociol. 1975 34(4): 365-380.* Developing countries face an inconsistency between the need for more equitable distribution of income and wealth between classes and groups and the goals of an industrial relations system in which the trade unions have a systematic commitment to allied political parties to support them in exchange for some control over economic and social policy, or where unions compete with parties for popular support of certain social and political goals. This is designated as "political unionism" in contradistinction to "business unionism" where unions support any party whose overall strategy and objectives are most compatible. The analysis shows that "political unionism" led, in Jamaica and in Trinidad and Tobago, to lags in growth which make industrial relations reform a necessity of an effective program of social change.   J

1307. Johnson, Caswell L. POLITICAL UNIONISM AND AUTONOMY IN ECONOMIES OF BRITISH COLONIAL ORIGIN: THE CASES OF JAMAICA AND TRINIDAD. *Am. J. of Econ. and Sociol. 1980 39(3): 237-248.* Although the unions helped to achieve independence and thus economic growth in Jamaica, the country moved into independence with a legacy of bad labor-management relations. This became a permanent feature; the unions are encouraged to become militant political organizations, which in Trinidad were alienated from the formal political structure. The type of unions and industrial relations systems that emerged after independence proved unsuitable and undesirable for achieving sustained rapid rates of economic growth, making reform of the labor relations system and the electoral process mandatory.   J/S

1308. Jones, Edwin. SOME NOTES ON DECISION MAKING AND CHANGE IN CARIBBEAN ADMINISTRATIVE SYSTEMS. *Social and Econ. Studies [Jamaica] 1974 23(2): 292-310.* Discusses the nature of administrative decisionmaking in the Caribbean. The administrative decisionmaking process is derived from existing economic and political arrangements and tends to preserve the status quo. 3 notes, 14 refs.   E. S. Johnson

1309. Jones, Edwin. TENDENCIES AND CHANGE IN CARIBBEAN ADMINISTRATIVE SYSTEMS. *Social and Econ. Studies [Jamaica] 1975 24(2): 239-256.* Identifies the values and ideological tendencies that operated in the Caribbean colonial governments. These have carried over into the postindependence administrations and inhibit the development of governmental machinery that would bring social and economic transformation. 3 notes, 15 refs.   E. S. Johnson

1310. Joseph, Cedric L. THE STRATEGIC IMPORTANCE OF THE BRITISH WEST INDIES, 1882-1932. *J. of Caribbean Hist. [Barbados] 1973 7: 23-67.* The naval rivalry of the United States and the British Empire in the Caribbean was a potential cause of war until World War I. The withdrawal of the British from their Caribbean naval bases reached a logical conclusion with the destroyer-bases deal of 1940. Based on Cabinet Office papers, Foreign Office papers, General Board Records of the Navy Department (Foreign Relations); 112 notes.   M. Rippy

1311. Kaiser, Ernest. AN ANNOTATED BIBLIOGRAPHY OF THE CARIBBEAN. *Freedomways 1981 21(3): 210-225.* Reprints a session of an annotated bibliography listing books and pamphlets published from 1960 to 1981 that deal with the historical, political, social, economic, and educational conditions in the Caribbean.

1312. Karch, Cecilia. TOURISM AND PUBLIC POLICY IN THE COMMONWEALTH CARIBBEAN: "SWEETENING THE POT" IN THE FIRST DEVELOPMENT DECADE. *Rev. Interamericana [Puerto Rico] 1977-78 7(4): 647-665.* As a tool to promote development, tourism has disappointed its advocates. Since 1960 in the Caribbean, it has diverted precious resources from more productive areas. Its benefits have been limited to a small segment of the population and has destroyed the ecological balance on some islands. The future of tourism in the Commonwealth Caribbean depends on careful planning. 50 notes.
J. Lewis

1313. Lent, John A. OLDEST EXISTING COMMONWEALTH CARIBBEAN NEWSPAPERS. *Caribbean Q. [Jamaica] 1976 22(4): 90-106.* Only seven existing newspapers in the Caribbean Commonwealth region originated before the 20th century. The most important of these is the Jamaica *Daily Gleaner,* which originated in 1834. The author lists more than 500 newspapers in the region (Bahamas, Barbados, Bermuda, British Virgin Islands, Cayman Islands, Jamaica, Leeward Islands, Trinidad and Tobago, Turks Islands, and Windward Islands) by place and date, from the *Weekly Jamaica Courant* (1718-55) to the present. Biblio.
R. L. Woodward, Jr.

1314. Lewis, Vaughan A. THE US AND THE CARIBBEAN: ISSUES OF ECONOMICS AND SECURITY. *Caribbean Rev. 1982 11(2): 6-9, 50-51.* Discusses US interest in the Caribbean region, based on geographic proximity and such concerns as the mineral trade, immigration, and the drug trade. Focuses on national security issues and US fears of Communist intervention or Cuban presence in other Caribbean countries and on economic issues, because economic instability in the region could open the way for "nonhemispheric" intervention.

1315. Macmillan, Mona. THE MAKING OF *WARNING FROM THE WEST INDIES:* EXTRACT FROM A PROJECTED MEMOIR OF W. M. MACMILLAN. *J. of Commonwealth and Comparative Pol. [Great Britain] 1980 18(2): 207-219.* W. M. Macmillan's *Warning from the West Indies* (London, 1936) was written between March and October 1935 and was based on the small notebooks which Macmillan had compiled on a visit to the West Indies. This article provides information about the financing of Macmillan's visit to the West Indies, his personal impressions there, and the writing and publication of *Warning from the West Indies.* The years 1936-38 saw political disturbances in the West Indian islands, and in the West Indies report of 1939, Macmillan's suggestion of planned control through loans was adopted. Based on Macmillan's letters and notes; 37 notes.
F. P. Tudor

1316. Maingot, Anthony P. CUBA AND THE COMMONWEALTH CARIBBEAN: PLAYING THE CUBAN CARD. *Caribbean Rev. 1980 9(1): 7-10, 44-49.* Analyzes Cuba's relations with governments of the former British West Indies.

1317. Malmsten, Neal R. THE BRITISH LABOUR PARTY AND THE WEST INDIES, 1918-39. *J. of Imperial and Commonwealth Hist. [Great Britain] 1977 5(2): 172-205.* Growing concern within the Labour Party for a more comprehensive colonial policy, especially in the West Indies, brought about the Colonial Development Act, which though an employment stimulus, was the single bright spot in a period characterized by political rather than economic relief.

1318. Marshall, W. D. and Beckford, G. L. PEASANT MOVEMENTS AND AGRARIAN PROBLEMS IN THE WEST INDIES. *Cahiers Int. d'Hist. Écon. et Sociale [Italy] 1978 8: 187-219.* Part I. Analyzes West Indian peasant movements, 1838-1954. Demonstrates that the development of the peasantry has been constrained by the existence of the plantation system. The peasants were neglected by the governments until the 1940's. Part II. Discusses the conflict between the interests of the plantation and owners and those of the peasantry, primarily in Jamaica. The power of the plantations has retarded improvements in the peasants' standard of living. 109 notes, 2 tables, biblio.
F. X. Hartigan

1319. Martin, Tony. REPRESSION AND RESISTANCE IN WEST INDIAN HISTORY. *Pan-African J. [Kenya] 1975 8(2): 125-138.* Documents the repressive policies of successive governments in the West Indies, as well as the widespread resistance to them by the West Indian population. Before the abolition of slavery in the 1830's, the West Indian slaves were extremely rebellious. Between slavery and World War I, the black freedmen sought to escape continuing oppression, and many emigrated. From 1918 new radicalism swept through the islands and even after independence escalating resistance to repressive government continued. Based on newspapers and secondary sources; 15 notes.
M. Feingold

1320. Millett, Richard and Gaddy, G. Dale. ADMINISTERING THE PROTECTORATES: THE U.S. OCCUPATION OF HAITI AND THE DOMINICAN REPUBLIC. *Rev. Interamericana [Puerto Rico] 1976 6(3): 383-402.* Although the United States became a colonial power after 1898, it never developed a formal colonial office. Instead, administration of colonies and protectorates was turned over to the military, as in the case of Haiti (1915-34) and the Dominican Republic (1916-24). Military officials, however, lacked the training and understanding to be good colonial administrators. 97 notes.
J. A. Lewis

1321. Mills, G. E. PUBLIC POLICY AND PRIVATE ENTERPRISE IN THE COMMONWEALTH CARIBBEAN. *Social and Econ. Studies [Jamaica] 1974 23(2): 216-241.* Reviews the concept of government regulation of business and its specific manifestation in the Caribbean. The various forms of regulation in the Caribbean have largely been ineffective. 64 notes, 41 refs.
E. S. Johnson

1322. Milne, R. Stephen. IMPULSES AND OBSTACLES TO CARIBBEAN POLITICAL INTEGRATION: ACADEMIC THEORY AND GUYANA'S EXPERIENCE. *Internat. Studies Q. 1974 18(3): 291-316.*

1323. Mintz, Sidney W. THE RURAL PROLETARIAT AND THE PROBLEM OF RURAL PROLETARIAN CONSCIOUSNESS. *J. of Peasant Studies [Great Britain] 1974 1(3): 291-325.* The rural proletariat is a 25-year-old sociological category describing Caribbean populations, but confusion about such populations persists. The author discusses proletarianization, the definition of rural proletariats, and the Marxist conception of consciousness, as applicable to such groups. The Cuban case is described to exemplify the European bias of some analysts, and the difficulties created by an uncritical transfer of Western conceptions of class and class consciousness to a colonial agrarian situation. A special effort is made to conceptualize the rural proletariat in terms of its relationships to the peasantry, and the "concealment" of landless workers in peasant communities.
J

1324. Norton, Graham. THE CARIBBEAN, THE CARIBBEAN COMMON MARKET AND THE EEC. *World Survey [Great Britain] 1973 (57): 1-18.* Issue describing the region of the West Indies primarily since the 1950's, and discussing the Caribbean Free Trade Area and the region's trade with the European Economic Community.

1325. Odle, M. A. TAX STRUCTURE AND DEVELOPMENT: A NON-CAPITALIST INTERPRETATION. *Social and Econ. Studies [Jamaica] 1977 25(4): 395-411.* Reviews the history of taxation in the Caribbean, emphasizing that the burden of taxes has usually fallen on labor and not capital. Mixed capitalist-socialist economies have the same defect, and what is needed is the establishment of an ideal social system which taxation can then adapt to. 31 notes, 19 ref.
E. S. Johnson

1326. Ohiorhenuan, John F. E. DEPENDENCE AND NON-CAPITALIST DEVELOPMENT IN THE CARIBBEAN: HISTORICAL NECESSITY AND DEGREES OF FREEDOM. *Sci. and Soc. 1979-80 43(4): 386-408.* The concept of noncapitalist development is based on a recognition of the Marxist proposition that socialism requires highly developed productive forces. In the developing countries of the Caribbean, especially Jamaica, Guyana, and Trinidad and Tobago, the economic sector has depended on state capitalism, which can take two forms. The compensatory form involves the government's participation in national development either by supporting a transfer of surplus to capitalists or by undertaking activities in which private capital is not interested. The liquidatory form maintains allocative control over the surplus and attempts to prevent the development of local middle classes after the government has taken over or bought the economy from foreign capital. Caribbean development has differed from the experiences of the former colonies in Africa and the Asian republics of the USSR. 43 notes. S

1327. Paragg, Ralph. INTEGRATION AND REGIONAL DEVELOPMENT: THE CASE OF THE COMMONWEALTH CARIBBEAN. *J. of Interamerican Studies and World Affairs 1980 22(4): 495-500.* Review essay on S. Chermich, ed., *The Commonwealth Caribbean: The Integration Experience* (Baltimore: Johns Hopkins U. Pr., 1978) and W. A. Axline, *Underdevelopment, Dependence and the Politics of Integration: A Caribbean Application* (Ottawa: U. of Ottawa, 1977). Both authors work too much with the ideological conflict and must recognize that without a mass constituency and without raising the public consciousness Caribbean integration is not likely to rise above its present state.

T. D. Schoonover

1328. Payne, Anthony. THE RISE AND FALL OF CARIBBEAN REGIONALISATION. *J. of Common Market Studies [Great Britain] 1981 19(3): 255-280.* Discusses attempts among Caribbean nations to form an economic community along the lines of the European Economic Community, beginning in 1968 with the formation of the Caribbean Free Trade Association and ending with the creation in 1973 of the Caribbean Community and Common Market (CARICOM). Analyzes CARICOM's evolution from 1973 to 1981, the reasons for its limited success, and its prospects for survival.

1329. Payne, Richard J. U.S. POLICY TOWARD CARIBBEAN ECONOMIC PROBLEMS. *Round Table [Great Britain] 1981 (284): 360-372.* The United States is in danger of forgetting that national and global security rests on Third World support, and that demands for a New International Economic Order (NIEO) is part of the price of that support. Examination of the Commonwealth Caribbean interest in the establishment of NIEO and the US role shows the "basic obstacle to a successful U.S. policy appears to be stubborn economic difficulties in the Commonwealth Caribbean and a tendency in the United States to oversimplify these developments." 29 notes. D. H. Murdoch

1330. Pierre, Roland. CARIBBEAN RELIGION: THE VOODOO CASE. *Sociol. Analysis 1977 38(1): 25-36.* Interprets the voodoo religion in the West Indies as an expression of the racial and cultural resistance to colonial political, economic, social, psychological, and cultural oppression in the 18th-20th centuries.

1331. Ramsaran, Ramesh. COMMONWEALTH CARIBBEAN INTEGRATION: PROGRESS, PROBLEMS AND PROSPECTS. *Inter-Am. Econ. Affairs 1974 28(2): 39-50.* Discusses attempts at economic integration in the English speaking Caribbean through the Caribbean Free Trade Association (CARIFTA) and the Caribbean Community (CARACOM). Suggests that integration attempts will meet with limited success until preoccupation with national problems cease. Primary and secondary sources; 4 tables, 4 notes. D. A. Franz

1332. Rennie, Bukka. THE CONFLICTING TENDENCIES IN THE CARIBBEAN REVOLUTION. *Pan-African J. [Kenya] 1975 8(2): 153-176.* Examines the significance of the Russian Revolution of 1917 and the Black Power Movement of the 1960's for the Caribbean revolution. Their influence has produced three strains in the Caribbean revolution: black cultural nationalism, Caribbean Stalinism, and Caribbean Marxism. The author examines the conflicts among these tendencies as manifested in their attitude toward the New Beginning Movement (NBM) and the Communist Party of the Soviet Union.

M. Feingold

1333. Rodney, Walter. CONTEMPORARY POLITICAL TRENDS IN THE ENGLISH-SPEAKING CARIBBEAN. *Black Scholar 1975 7(1): 15-21.* Describes present Caribbean governments as petit bourgeois dictatorships, and argues that political independence has not substantially altered economic colonial relationships with the Western capitalist world.

1334. Rubin, Dale F. COMPETITION POLICY AND THE CARIBBEAN COMMUNITY. *J. of World Trade Law [Switzerland] 1975 9(4): 398-426.* Evolution of the market structure in many Caribbean countries has reached a point where merger activity is frequent and inefficiency resulting in exorbitant prices is evident in certain sectors. Industrial concentration has become a concern of government officials wishing to establish a competition policy within the appropriate regional framework. The author points out the differing political attitudes towards the creation and implementation of antitrust laws in the Caribbean, where the main concern is the proper economic performance of firms and not necessarily their fragmentation. J

1335. St. Pierre, Maurice. WEST INDIAN CRICKET—A SOCIO-HISTORICAL APPRAISAL. *Caribbean Q. [Jamaica] 1973 19(2): 7-27, (3): 20-35.* Part I. Despite a general trend toward shedding "the various vestiges of colonialism," cricket still figures prominently in the West Indian cultural and sporting scene. Whites dominated the game in the early part of the 20th century, but since the 1920's nonwhites have had an increasingly important share of the positions on the West Indian touring team. Through statistical analysis and historical narrative, the author examines the team until 1972, by which time it had become one of the world's best. The questions of white supremacy, violence, and divide-and-rule policies in colonial society contributed "to produce a type of cricket played by West Indians which is markedly different from that played in England." Based on secondary materials and personal observation; 5 tables, 13 notes. Part II. Before 1951 West Indian cricket teams visited England most often, but more recently Australia, New Zealand, India, and Pakistan. Many West Indian test cricketeers have by that means improved their economic status. Cricket has been an avenue for upward social mobility for nonwhite West Indian cricketeers. "The emergence of the West Indies, in the early 1960's, as world cricket champions has provided English-speaking West Indians all over the world with a sense of togetherness and regional identity." The author analyzes the situations that led to violent demonstrations in Guyana, Trinidad, and Jamaica. 15 notes. R. L. Woodward, Jr./E. P. Stickney

1336. Samaroo, Brinsley. THE POLITICS OF DISHARMONY: THE DEBATE ON THE POLITICAL UNION OF THE BRITISH WEST INDIES AND CANADA, 1884-1921. *Rev. Interamericana [Puerto Rico] 1977 7(1): 46-59.* Ever since 1884, a number of groups representing Canadian imperialists or hoping for certain economic benefits have proposed the political integration of Canada and the British West Indies. These proposals never had widespread popular appeal in Canada and the Caribbean and have always had to confront the problem of Canadian racism. 71 notes. J. A. Lewis

1337. Sánchez Robert, Gerardo. APUNTES SOBRE LA FEDERACIÓN DE LAS INDIAS OCCIDENTALES Y LAS CAUSAS DE SU FRACASO [Notes on the West Indies Federation and the causes of its failure]. *Santiago [Cuba] 1979 (34): 55-84.* The causes of the failure of the West Indies Federation can best be understood by analyzing the concept of federation and by a study of its chief component, Jamaica, and the reasons for its withdrawal from the association. Neither the general nor the particular objectives of economic union could be achieved by the Federation. Political and economic fragmentation, constitutional diversity, geographical dispersion, and the absence of a consciousness of unity were factors that worked against the Federation. 17 notes, biblio.

J. V. Coutinho

1338. Sanguin, Andre-Louis. "SMALL IS NOT BEAUTIFUL": LA FRAGMENTATION POLITIQUE DE LA CARAÏBE ["Small is not beautiful": political fragmentation in the Caribbean]. *Cahiers de Géog. du Québec [Canada] 1981 25(66): 343-359.* Describes how the political partitioning of the British West Indies by application of a 200-mile offshore economic zone limit and failure of the Caricom common market have contributed to ongoing regionalization of the Caribbean since the 1960's.

1339. Schreiber, Anna P. ECONOMIC COERCION AS AN INSTRUMENT OF FOREIGN POLICY: U.S. ECONOMIC MEASURES AGAINST CUBA AND THE DOMINICAN REPUBLIC. *World Pol. 1973 25(3): 387-413.* Traces the deterioration of US-Cuban relations following the accession to power of Fidel Castro and the subsequent US economic retaliation against Cuba and all countries that traded with it. Economic coercion was most disruptive 1961-64, creating shortages and slowing economic development, and Cuba's per capita production dropped 29%, 1961-68, despite massive aid from the USSR. The involvement of the USSR did not serve US interests in that it created another area of tension between the two superpowers. A similar policy of coercion was successfully applied against the Dominican Republic, 1960-62, in an attempt to bring down the dictatorship of Rafael Trujillo. Though often successful, economic coercion may depend on diplomatic and military pressure as well. Part of a research project conducted by the Royal Institute of International Affairs, London; 89 notes.

C. W. Olson

1340. Sherlock, Philip. THE WEST INDIAN EXPERIENCE. Proctor, Samuel, ed. Eighteenth-Century Florida and the Caribbean (Gainesville: U. of Florida Pr., 1976): 44-49. Describes the "West Indian experience," with which Florida is intimately linked. Colonialism, slavery, and the plantation system were the three major institutions that molded West Indian society. The author traces the history and impact of these institutions, the history of countermovements centered on New World blacks such as Marcus Garvey, and the growth of modern nationalism. Radical change has marked the last thirty years; today, the West Indian nations face formidable problems. West Indian history is now being treated from an indigenous viewpoint, rather than as a footnote to European or American history.   W. R. Hively

1341. Singham, A. W. THE CARIBBEAN, THE U.S. AND WORLD POLITICS. *Freedomways 1981 21(3): 151-160.* Traces the evolution of Caribbean nations from colonial entities to independent states since the end of World War II, focusing on the impact of Afro-Asian revolutionary movements on the region's political development, and discusses the region's relationship with the United States and its importance in the nonaligned movement of the 1970's.

1342. Singham, A. W. and Singham, N. L. CULTURAL DOMINATION AND POLITICAL SUBORDINATION: NOTES TOWARDS A THEORY OF THE CARIBBEAN POLITICAL SYSTEM. *Comparative Studies in Soc. and Hist. [Great Britain] 1973 15(3): 258-288.* There are a number of theoretical inadequacies in the analyses of the Caribbean political system. Literature on the economics of dependency is well advanced, but analyses of the mechanisms of dependency in the social and political spheres and the interdependency and complexity of these mechanisms are just beginning. "The peculiar needs of the plantation system resulted in the creation of a social order which was fundamentally different from both the feudal and the metropolitan capitalist models." The Caribbean can be postulated as a pure case of subordination. Based on primary and secondary sources; 63 notes.
                                                M. M. McCarthy

1343. Smart, Ian I. DISCOVERING THE CARIBBEAN: TWO IMPORTANT RESEARCH TOOLS. *Caribbean Rev. 1981 10(3): 32-34.* Review essay on Lambros Comitas's *The Complete Caribbeana 1900-1975* (1977) and *Caribbean Writers: a Bio-Bibliographical-Critical Encyclopedia* (1979), by Donald E. Herdeck et al., "the most important reference sources available to date for scholars and other persons interested in the multifaceted field of Caribbean studies."

1344. Thatcher, Terence L. NEW WAVES IN THE CARIBBEAN. *Worldview 1974 17(2): 37-39.* Discusses politics, economics, trade and population growth in the Caribbean region in the 1960's and 70's, including the influence of the Caribbean Free Trade Association.

1345. Tomasek, Robert D. CARIBBEAN EXILE INVASIONS: A SPECIAL REGIONAL TYPE OF CONFLICT. *Orbis 1974 17(4): 1354-1382.*

1346. Uchegbu, P. E. A. THE CARIBBEAN DEVELOPMENT BANK: IMPLICATIONS FOR INTEGRATION. *J. of World Trade Law [Switzerland] 1973 7(5): 568-586.* "The Caribbean Development Bank (1969) is legally distinct from CARIFTA, but it nevertheless constitutes CARIFTA's financial counterpart. This article discusses the principal features of the Bank and reviews its operational policies to date in the light of its objectives."   J

1347. Verner, Joel Gordon. THE RECRUITMENT OF CABINET MINISTERS IN THE FORMER BRITISH CARIBBEAN: A FIVE-COUNTRY STUDY. *J. of Developing Areas 1973 7(4): 635-652.* Examines 63 cabinet ministers who served in the Bahamas, Barbados, Guyana, Jamaica, and Trinidad-Tobago, 1966-71.   S

1348. Watson, Hilbourne A. THE POLITICAL ECONOMY OF U.S.-CARIBBEAN RELATIONS. *Black Scholar 1980 11(3): 30-41.* Examines US-Caribbean relations since the 1930's and traces recent development in US trade and investments in the West Indies, West Indian migration to the United States, and US attempts to stop the liberation movement in the Caribbean states.

1349. —. [THE POLITICAL USES OF COMMISSIONS OF ENQUIRY]. *Social and Econ. Studies [Jamaica] 1978 27(3): 256-312.*
Johnson, Howard. THE POLITICAL USES OF COMMISSIONS OF ENQUIRY (1): THE IMPERIAL COLONIAL WEST INDIES CONTEXT, THE FOSTER AND MOYNE COMMISSIONS, *pp. 256-283.* Describes the conditions that led to riots in Trinidad

in 1937, and the British Colonial Office's appointment of a commission (under Foster) to study the problems leading to the riots and to make recommendations. A second commission was appointed (under Walter Edward Guinness, 1st Baron Moyne) to examine overall conditions in the British West Indies. While as impartial as conditions would allow, in the end both commissions introduced changes desired by the Colonial Office without giving the appearance of Colonial Office intervention. 124 notes.
Jones, Edwin. THE POLITICAL USES OF COMMISSIONS OF ENQUIRY (2): THE POST COLONIAL JAMAICAN CONTEXT, *pp. 248-312.* Reviews the socioeconomic framework of Jamaica and summarizes the work of four post-independence commissions of enquiry. Argues that while neutral and objective such commissions have the purpose of maintaining the status quo for the benefit of the middle classes. 23 notes.   E. S. Johnson

Cuba

1350. Adams, Gordon. CUBA AND AFRICA: THE INTERNATIONAL POLITICS OF THE LIBERATION STRUGGLE. *Latin Am. Perspectives 1981 8(1): 108-125.* Cuba's "commitments in Africa, far from the personalistic, adventuristic actions of a Soviet puppet, have reflected a coherent world view and a historically consistent policy," according to the norms of nonaligned nations, and evoke "widespread support both in Africa and at home." 13 notes, biblio.
                                                J. F. Vivian

1351. Agudelo Díaz, María Mercedes. ANÁLISIS DEL CONTEXTO SOCIO-ECONÓMICO DE CUBA ANTERIOR A LA REFORMA AGRARIA [An analysis of the Cuban socioeconomic context prior to agrarian reform]. *U. Humanistica [Colombia] 1979 (10): 149-168.* While not a poor country, prerevolutionary Cuba had an agricultural economy dominated by sugar and large landholdings which produced instability.

1352. Aguilar, Luis E. FIDEL CASTRO: APUNTES SOBRE UN CAUDILLO SOCIALISTA [Fidel Castro: notes concerning a socialist caudillo]. *Revista/Review Interamericana [Puerto Rico] 1977 7(3): 372-399.* The autocratic nature of Castro's Cuba stems more from the personality of Fidel Castro than from the role of the Communist Party on the island, or the threat posed by the United States. 50 notes.
                                                J. A. Lewis

1353. Aguirre, Mirta; Garcia Ronda, Denia; and Monal, Isabel. EL LENINISMO EN *LA HISTORIA ME ABSOLVERÀ* [Leninism in "History Will Absolve Me"]. *Casa de las Américas [Cuba] 1975 16(93): 64-85.* Discusses the Leninist underpinnings of Fidel Castro's speech "History Will Absolve Me" at his 1953 trial for the assault on the Moncada barracks (26 July 1953), showing that while Castro did not copy Lenin or Martí, their influences are present in his thought.

1354. Aguirre, Mirta. KUBA I 60-LETIE VELIKOGO OKTIABRIA [Cuba and the 60th anniversary of the Great October Socialist Revolution]. *Novaia i Noveishaia Istoriia [USSR] 1977 (5): 84-93.* Reveals the specifics of the development of the revolutionary movement in Cuba under the impact of the Great October Revolution. The author underlines the principle of proletarian internationalism in the Soviet-Cuban relations, which found its manifestation in the USSR's rendering all possible assistance to Cuba in its struggle against imperialist aggression.   J

1355. Aguirre, Sergio. ALGUNAS LUCHAS SOCIALES EN CUBA REPUBLICANA [Some social struggles in republican Cuba]. *Rev. de la Biblioteca Nac. José Martí [Cuba] 1973 15(2): 5-40.* Continues an article published in *Cuba Socialista* in 1965, focusing on the years 1918-58, showing the building of the socialist revolution in Cuba.

1356. Ahmed, Samina. CUBAN FOREIGN POLICY UNDER CASTRO. *Pakistan Horizon [Pakistan] 1980 33(4): 50-83.* Summarizes Cuba's foreign policy since 1959, including the close ties with the USSR, relations with Latin America, intervention in Africa, and poor relations with the United States, which improved during the administration of Jimmy Carter.

1357. Alexander, Robert J. CASTRO'S GROWING DEPENDENCE ON THE USSR. *Freedom At Issue 1973 (22): 18-23, 24.*

1358. Alvarez, Oneida. REVOLUTIONARY CUBA'S ECONOMIC DEVELOPMENT. *World Marxist R. [Canada] 1974 17(11): 94-99.* Reports on the economic development of Cuba and the aid given by other Communist countries, 1958-73. S

1359. Anderle, Ádám. ALGUNOS PROBLEMAS DE LA EVOLUCIÓN DEL PENSAMIENTO ANTIMPERIALISTA EN CUBA ENTRE LAS DOS GUERRAS MUNDIALES: COMUNISTAS Y APRISTAS [Some problems in the evolution of anti-imperialist thought in Cuba between the two world wars: Communists and Apristas]. *Acta U. Szegediensis de Attila József Nominatae: Acta Hist. [Hungary] 1975 52: 3-81.* Discusses in great detail the formation of several anti-imperialist factions in Cuba during the 1920's and the consequences of their platforms in the development of Cuban revolutionary thought and action. Presents accounts of programs, speeches, and articles by members of the Communist Party, the Cuban Apra (PAC), Joven Cuba, and the PRC "Auténtico." Major figures discussed include Antonio Guiteras, Antonio Mella, Grau San Martin, and Rubén Martínez Villena. Although anti-imperialism provided a common ground, the opportunity to form a united effort was thwarted by continuous ideological and theoretical differences. Acceptance of the national bourgeoisie and the extent to which Marxian doctrines were implemented formed the basis of division. 94 notes, biblio. J. Perez

1360. Anderson, Paul A. JUSTIFICATIONS AND PRECEDENTS AS CONSTRAINTS IN FOREIGN POLICY DECISION-MAKING. *Am. J. of Pol. Sci. 1981 25(4): 738-761.* Foreign policy actions are accompanied, as a matter of course, by justifications in terms of precedent, consistency, and resolve. The proposition developed in this paper is that the necessity of justifying foreign policy decisions acts as a constraint on what counts as an acceptable alternative. Proposed courses of action which cannot by plausibly justified are considered, ceteris paribus, unacceptable. This constraint is supported by the nature of international politics and the politics of the policy setting. The uncertainty of international politics results in a premium on the appearance of consistency. The importance of justifications and precedents is reinforced within policy-making settings because of the shared belief in the importance of consistency. An examination of U.S. decisionmaking during the Cuban missile crisis provides support for the role of precedent and justification as constraints on acceptable alternatives. J

1361. Anillo, René. LA FEDERACIÓN ESTUDIANTIL UNIVERSITARIA EN EL PERÍODO DE 1951 A 1957: LA LUCHA DE LOS ESTUDIANTES CONTRA LA DICTADURA DE BATISTA [The Federation of University Students, 1951-57: student struggle against the Batista dictatorship]. *Rev. de la Biblioteca Nac. José Martí [Cuba] 1980 22(2): 113-142.* The Federation of University Students (FEU) was extremely active in opposing Fulgencio Batista during the 1950's. From its ranks came many of the revolution's martyrs as well as later leaders of Fidel Castro's Cuba. J. A. Lewis

1362. Annino, Antonio. CUBA E I PROBLEMI ISTITUZIONALI DELLA TRANSIZIONE AL SOCIALISMO [Cuba and the institutional problems of the transition to socialism]. *Pensiero Pol. [Italy] 1975 8(1): 87-93.* Much of the recent literature on Cuban history fails to consider sufficiently the relationship between political institutions and structural changes in Cuban society resulting from the 1959 revolution. The transition to socialism focused on institutional fluidity and on reconciling the divergent political views of Aníbal Escalante, Che Guevara, and Fidel Castro. The latter succeeded in effectively unifying the parties and the labor unions under the control of the Cuban Communist Party. The XIII Congress of Labor Unions and the First Party Congress of 1975 were the crucial and climactic point in the evolution of revolutionary political institutions. Based on secondary sources. S. Ruffo-Fiore

1363. Arias, Salvador. LITERATURA CUBANA (1959-1975) [Cuban literature, 1959-75]. *Casa de las Américas [Cuba] 1979 19(113): 14-26.* Focuses on revolutionary culture, defined as a concern with social and political problems. The revolutionary period is divided into the periods 1959-65 and 1966-75. During the first, authors stressed the need for the diffusion of knowledge that reflected revolutionary goals and national

interests. The second period witnessed increased literary productivity and greater maturity. Based mostly on secondary sources; 11 notes. H. J. Miller

1364. Auroi, Claude. L'AGRICULTURE CUBAINE [Cuban agriculture]. *Civilisations [Belgium] 1973/74 23-24(3/4): 213-232.* Land reform started in Cuba in 1957. From 1959 to 1963 measures were taken to centralize the holding of land in the state. The size of individual private holdings was greatly reduced. After 1968 the private sector was integrated into the national plan for production. Fidel Castro took steps in 1974 to suppress the status of the private landowner. 32 notes. H. L. Calkin

1365. Azicri, Max. CUBA AND THE US: ON THE POSSIBILITIES OF RAPPROCHEMENT. *Caribbean Rev. 1980 9(1): 26-29.* Traces the development of US-Cuban relations, noting that the possibility of detente during the early 1970's was destroyed by Cuban intervention in Africa.

1366. Azicri, Max. THE *INSTITUCIONALIZACIÓN* OF CUBA'S REVOLUTION. *Rev. Interamericana [Puerto Rico] 1978 8(2): 247-262.* Now that the Cuban revolution has become institutionalized, its goals are to stabilize the new socialist society. The government will continue to use a variety of moral and material incentives to keep popular support. Secondary sources; 37 notes. J. Lewis

1367. Azicri, Max. THE INSTITUTIONALIZATION OF THE CUBAN STATE: A POLITICAL PERSPECTIVE. *J. of Interamerican Studies and World Affairs 1980 22(3): 315-344.* The institutionalization of the Cuban revolution is not the outcome of a single historical happening, and specifically not of the regime's mistakes in the 1970 sugar harvest which produced a 15% shortfall. Fidel Castro's charismatic leadership was and remains a central legitimizing influence in the institutionalization of the revolution, but this process has been broadened to include the central government, state politico-administrative organs, and the central political institution, the Cuban Communist Party. Primary sources; 4 notes, ref. T. D. Schoonover

1368. Azicri, Max. POLITICAL PARTICIPATION AND SOCIAL EQUALITY IN CUBA: THE ROLE OF THE FEDERATION OF CUBAN WOMEN. *Secolas Ann. 1979 10: 66-80.* The Federation of Cuban Women has been responsible 1960-78 for the political participation and social equalization of women as well as their educational advancement and integration into the labor force.

1369. Azicri, Max. WOMEN'S DEVELOPMENT THROUGH REVOLUTIONARY MOBILIZATION: A STUDY OF THE FEDERATION OF CUBAN WOMEN. *Int. J. of Women's Studies [Canada] 1979 2(1): 27-50.* Discusses the achievements of the Federation of Cuban Women (FMC) which works within the political framework established under the revolution in the areas of education, labor, and politics to achieve social equality for women in Cuba.

1370. Bach, Robert L. THE NEW CUBAN EXODUS: POLITICAL AND ECONOMIC MOTIVATIONS. *Caribbean Rev. 1982 11(1): 22-25, 58-60.* Provides statistics showing that the Cuban refugees from Mariel who arrived by boat in 1980 in South Florida were not largely criminals or undesirables but were laborers and professionals, 74% of whom had held jobs for most of their adult lives. Discusses the debate over whether the refugees came to the United States for economic or political reasons, a debate that has continued since 1959.

1371. Baklanoff, Eric N. THE STRUCTURE OF CUBA'S DEPENDENCY PRECEDING THE REVOLUTION. *Secolas Ann. 1980 11: 23-39.* Cuba's economic dependency on the United States in the years immediately preceding the Revolution (1953-58) were characterized by a single crop economy (sugar), a dramatic rise in the national investment coefficient, accelerated capitalism, development of intermediate industries, and a growing tourist industry.

1372. Bambirra, Vania. LA POLÍTICA ECONÓMICA DE LA REVOLUCIÓN CUBANA, 1959-1960 [Economic policy of the Cuban Revolution, 1959-60]. *Investigación Econ. [Mexico] 1980 39(152): 99-118.* The 1959-60 economic program of the revolution in its democratic phase was prepared mostly by the UN Economic Commission for Latin America and was geared toward development and industrialization; foreign capital was to be used as little as possible, national capital to be encouraged. When Fidel Castro granted up to 200% wage increases and froze prices, rationing resulted, and government measures against counterrevolutionary behavior increased polarization. At the beginning of the transition to socialism, 40% of Cuban professionals and technicians had left. Smaller land holdings were combined into more easily managed agroindustrial complexes; American oil, banking, and communications interests were nationalized; but an enormous balance-of-payments deficit impeded the planned financing of the revolution by industrial growth.

1373. Bannikov, B. SLAVNYI IUBILEI (K 25-LETIIU REVOLIUTSIONNYKH VOORUZHENNYKH SIL RESPUBLIKI KUBA) [A glorious jubilee: the 25th anniversary of the Revolutionary Armed Forces of the Republic of Cuba]. *Voenno-Istoricheskii Zhurnal [USSR] 1981 23(11): 53-58*. Outlines the growth of the Cuban Revolutionary Armed Forces from 1956, when a detachment headed by Fidel Castro attempted an armed uprising against the Fulgencio Batista government. The revolution was not fully completed until Batista fled the country on 1 January 1959. In October 1959 a Ministry of the Revolutionary Armed Forces was formed to help counter growing American efforts to suppress the revolution, and by 1960 Cuba was receiving military aid from the USSR. The first external threat to peace in the shape of the Bay of Pigs landing was successfully countered by Cuban forces. Universal conscription was introduced in November 1963. 15 notes.   A. Brown

1374. Barkin, David. LA TRANSFORMACIÓN DEL ESPACIO EN CUBA POST-REVOLUCIONARIA [Spatial transformation in post-revolutionary Cuba]. *Bol. de Estudios Latinoamericanos y del Caribe [Netherlands] 1979 (27): 77-95*. Describes the spatial transformation of Cuba since the revolution and demonstrates that with changes in social and political relations, the organization of production, and the role of the state, Third World urban and housing problems can be overcome. With central planning and a real national development strategy, the regional disparities in a country can also be brought under control. Biblio.   M. Gormly

1375. Barkin, David. POPULAR PARTICIPATION AND THE DIALECTICS OF CUBAN DEVELOPMENT. *Latin Am. Perspectives 1975 2(4): 42-59*. Heavy investments made in the 1960's which are at last paying off and an increase in consumer goods which has sparked mass participation in economic development indicate that the development strategy of the Cuban government is experiencing success in the 1970's.

1376. Barquín, Ramón. CUBA: THE CYBERNETIC ERA. *Cuban Studies 1975 5(2): 1-24*. Cuba has begun to apply computer technology to problems of economic planning. So serious is the island's leadership about utilization of the latest technology that Cuba is manufacturing its own computers. Primary and secondary sources; 3 tables, 41 notes, biblio.   J. A. Lewis

1377. Barthélemy-Febrer, Françoise. CUBA DANS LA REALITE CENTRE-AMERICAINE ET CARAÏBE: QUELQUES REMARQUES SUR LES DIX DERNIERES ANNEES [Cuba in the Central American and Caribbean reality: some remarks of the last ten years]. *Problèmes d'Amérique Latine [France] 1982 (64): 143-167*. Demonstrates that Cuban political ideology focuses on the reclamation of Cuba by Cubans, through the instigation and development of revolutionary transformations.

1378. Béjar, Héctor and Castro, Nils. EL MONCADA EN AMERICA LATINA, 20 AÑOS DESPUES [Moncada in Latin America 20 years after]. *Santiago [Cuba] 1973 (11): 179-195*. Dictatorships supported by the United States typified post-1953 Latin America, as did a gradual awakening of the masses in Guatemala and Bolivia, particularly among the young. After the attack by Fidel Castro on the Moncada Barracks in Santiago de Cuba, public opinion turned away from parliamentary democracy and began demanding real social change and mass exercise of power. The attack on Moncada in 1953 had four results: it was a revolutionary triumph, it led to changes in the country, it identified the revolutionaries with the people, and it encouraged a rapid advance toward socialism. Thus 1953 marked the start of anti-imperialism in Latin America.   D. Wasserstein

1379. Belovolov, Iu. G. OKTIABR' I RABOCHEE DVIZHENIE NA KUBE [The October revolution and the working-class movement in Cuba]. *Voprosy Istorii [USSR] 1979 (4): 82-93*. Highlights the influence exercised by the ideas of the Great October Revolution on the working-class movement in Cuba. The author characterizes the level of consciousness and organization attained by the Cuban proletariat as well as the extent of the influence exerted by the anarcho-syndicalists and the reformists. Particular importance is attached in the article to Case No. 550 trumped up by the authorities. The government took advantage of the weaknesses of the working-class movement, resulting from its insufficient organization, ideological disunity, and the absence of a political party of the proletariat. The authorities succeeded in checking the spread of the strike movement and thwarting the development of the revolutionary situation in the country. Primary sources; 41 notes.   J

1380. Beltrán, Félix. ACERCA DEL DESEÑO GRÁFICO ANTES Y DESPUÉS DE LA REVOLUCIÓN [Graphic design before and after the revolution]. *Rev. de la Biblioteca Nac. José Martí [Cuba] 1979 21(2): 52-76*. Graphic design before the revolution served the interests of a small class of capitalists dominated by North American ties. After 1959, however, graphic design served the revolution and the people. 19 photos.   J. A. Lewis

1381. Bender, Lynn Darrell. *GUANTANAMO: ITS POLITICAL, MILITARY AND LEGAL STATUS*. *Caribbean Q. [Jamaica] 1973 19(1): 80-86*. The government of Fidel Castro has repeatedly insisted that the United States occupies the Guantánamo naval base illegally and has demanded its return, but has also recognized that it was powerless to evict the United States. The United States recognizes that Guantánamo no longer has much military or strategic value, but its political and psychological importance transcends its military utility. Castro's legal arguments are weak. (Gary Maris, in "International Law and Guantánamo" [*J. of Pol.* 1967 29(2): 261-286] offers more persuasive legal arguments than Cuba has.) Cuba could abrogate the treaty because of changed conditions (rule of *Rebus Sic Stantibus*). The assumptions on which the treaty was predicated, mutual friendship and common defense, no longer exist. Despite the legal argumentation, however, the issue is fundamentally political, and almost all US policymakers deem it inadvisable to make modification in the status of Guantánamo the first step toward settlement of US-Cuban differences. Based on published government documents, interviews, news media and secondary sources; 24 notes.   R. L. Woodward

1382. Bender, Lynn Darrell. U.S. CLAIMS AGAINST THE CUBAN GOVERNMENT: AN OBSTACLE TO RAPPROCHEMENT. *Inter-Am. Econ. Affairs 1973 27(1): 3-13*. An overall settlement with Cuba is "directly linked to the question of sugar trade and the type of relationship the United States is prepared to establish."   S

1383. Benjamin, Jules R. THE MACHADATO AND CUBAN NATIONALISM, 1928-1932. *Hispanic Am. Hist. Rev. 1975 55(1): 66-91*. Opposition developed toward President Gerardo Machado among all factions of Cuban society due to the severe economic depression, political repression, dictatorial methods, and nationalist anti-imperialist sentiment. Machado was overthrown in August 1933. US influence remained in spite of the nationalist sentiment. 48 notes.   B. D. Johnson

1384. Benjamin, Jules R. THE NEW DEAL, CUBA, AND THE RISE OF A GLOBAL FOREIGN ECONOMIC POLICY. *Business Hist. Rev. 1977 51(1): 57-78*. Revises the conventional thesis that isolationism characterized early New Deal foreign policy. US involvement in Cuba increased during this period, which helped to establish precedents for the global outlook of American policy in the 1940's and beyond. The new policy was especially visible in the use of the Reconstruction Finance Corporation and the Export-Import Bank to promote American interests. Based on State Department and other US governmental records; 39 notes.   C. J. Pusateri

1385. Blasier, Cole. THE CUBAN-U.S.-SOVIET TRIANGLE, CHANGING ANGLES. *Cuban Studies 1978 8(1): 1-9*. Through Cuba's own initiatives, its tense relations with both the United States and the USSR have eased greatly during the 1970's. Although complete rapprochement is in the interest of Cuba and the United States, it does not seem near.   J. A. Lewis

1386. Bondarchuk, Vladimir. FORMAS Y MÉTODAS DE INCORPORACIÓN DE LOS PEQUEÑOS AGRICULTORES A LA ECONOMÍA DE CUBA [Forms and methods of incorporating small landowners into the Cuban economy]. *Am. Latina [USSR] 1978 (4): 13-29.* Differences between Cuban agriculture and the agriculture of other socialist countries are more pronounced than among any other socialist countries. In Cuba, the development of small private agriculturists in a small market economy obey the general laws of Marxist-Leninist theory on socialist construction. The current agricultural policy in Cuba toward small agriculturalists enriches the theory and practice of building socialism. 21 notes.   J. D. Barnard

1387. Booth, David. CUBA, COLOR AND THE REVOLUTION. *Sci. and Soc. 1976 40(2): 129-172.* Racial classification in prerevolutionary Cuba was based on a color-class system in which physical appearance determined social status. In certain areas of public life talent, education, wealth, and ambition could override the single factor of color, but this did not mean that the white Cuban majority was free of racial prejudice, nor that it did not ascribe status on the basis of race. The revolutionary government has removed legal restrictions to the advancement of Negroes and has integrated the public areas of Cuban life. But private, especially social, vestiges of racial discrimination still remain. The elimination of these vestiges is not a high priority item on the government's action agenda. Based on observations in Cuba, 1968-1969.   N. Lederer

1388. Borisova, N. A. ISTORICHESKII PODVIG KUBINSKOGO NARODA [The historical feat of the Cuban people]. *Voprosy Istorii KPSS [USSR] 1979 (3): 143-147.* Summary of four papers delivered at a Moscow conference organized by the Institute of Marxism-Leninism, Academy of Social Sciences, and Academy of Sciences, 27-28 December 1978 to celebrate the 20th anniversary of the Cuban revolution. Three Soviet scholars (A. G. Egorov, B. S. Popov, and O. T. Bogomolov) and F. Grobart, Director of Cuba's Institute for the History of the Communist Movement and Socialist Revolution in Cuba, spoke on the history of the Cuban revolution and state. Based on published material; 4 notes.
                                                        L. E. Holmes

1389. Bosch, Aurora. DESARROLLO DE LA DANZA EN CUBA [Development of dance in Cuba]. *Rev. de la Biblioteca Nac. José Martí [Cuba] 1979 21(2): 89-102.* The revolution has given a significant boost to ballet in Cuba. The state has sponsored the creation of a National Ballet Company of Cuba (1959), the School of Modern Dance (1959), the School of National Folklore (1960), and the Ballet Company of Camagüey (1967).   J. A. Lewis

1390. Boughton, George J. SOVIET-CUBAN RELATIONS, 1956-1960. *J. of Inter-Am. Studies and World Affairs 1974 16(4): 436-453.* From 1956 to 1960 the USSR was actively interested in Cuban affairs as a result of both Cold War and world revolutionary leadership needs. The Soviets praised Castro for his military success but refrained from comment on his political ideas. In 1958 the Soviet Union openly supported some of Fidel Castro's political views while continuing to praise the Cuban Communist Party's program. Once Castro succeeded, the Soviet government quickly recognized his government and moved to establish economic ties. Based on Soviet newspapers, radio transcripts, and secondary works; 5 notes, biblio.   J. R. Thomas

1391. Bueno, Salvador. EL XV ANIVERSARIO DE LA ESCUELA DE TÉCNICOS DE BIBLIOTECA [The 15th anniversary of the School of Library Technicians]. *Rev. de la Biblioteca Nac. José Martí [Cuba] 1977 19(3): 170-177.* Discusses the ideological foundations of library service in Cuba after the revolution and considers the history of the Escuela de Técnicos de Biblioteca since its founding in 1962, its curriculum and certification requirements, and its work in fostering the growth of public libraries in Cuba. Based on a lecture, Havana, 7 June 1977.   R. D. Rodríguez

1392. Cabrera, Olga. LA REVOLUCIÓN DE OCTUBRE. SU REPERCUSIÓN EN EL MOVIMIENTO OBRERO DE CUBA [The October Revolution: its repercussion on the labor movement in Cuba]. *Santiago [Cuba] 1976 (21): 145-159.* Although reactionaries tried to hide the facts, the Cuban masses, whose optimism is reflected in contemporary verse, greeted the Russian Revolution with delight. Strikes in 1917, press reports in 1918, and other writings in 1919 show acceptance

of the principle of class struggle. Marxist texts were popular, although few were allowed to enter Cuba, and Lenin's writings clarified some ideological confusion, especially in 1921. The influence of the Russian Revolution led to the creation of a national workers' confederation and the formation of the first Communist Party of Cuba. 11 notes.
                                                    D. Wasserstein

1393. Cagan, Steve. DOCUMENTARY PHOTOGRAPHY IN CUBA. *Radical Am. 1980 14(5): 55-63.* During the 20 years since the revolution triumphed in Cuba, the practitioners of documentary photography have passed through three phases. Those active before the victory in 1959 focused on the contrasts of wealth and poverty. The photographers of the 1960's tended to concentrate on the concrete, the actuality of the moment, in a fashion less abstract than the Chinese photographs of industrial workers, for example. The third wave has taken this relaxed concern for the situation rather than the symbol even further. The work group is more often the subject rather than the mass or the rally. A fourth generation is emerging now.   C. M. Hough

1394. Cairo, Ana. EL PRESO POLÍTICO PABLO DE LA TORRIENTE-BRAU (BREVE COMENTARIO A LA PUBLICACIÓN DE UNAS CARTAS INÉDITAS) [The political prisoner Pablo de la Torriente: a brief commentary on some unpublished letters on their publication]. *Santiago [Cuba] 1976 (23): 65-97.* Twenty letters by the poet Pablo de la Torriente, written during his political imprisonment at the Isle of Pines in 1932. The introduction surveys Cuban affairs and Torriente's political involvements, and his success as chronicler of the imprisoned revolutionaries in the struggle against the dictatorship of Gerardo Machado, 1925-33.   D. Wasserstein

1395. Caldwell, Dan. A RESEARCH NOTE ON THE QUARANTINE OF CUBA—OCTOBER 1962. *Int. Studies Q. 1978 22(4): 625-633.* Both proponents and critics of the bureaucratic politics approach to the study of US foreign policymaking have acclaimed Graham Allison's *Essence of Decision* (Boston: Little, Brown, 1971). However, there are both intuitive and empirical reasons for challenging Allison's interpretation of the navy's implementation of the blockade during the Cuban missile crisis. Analysts employing a bureaucratic politics framework should check their interpretations against other data, particularly empirical evidence. It appears that the bureaucratic politics approach and its child, implementation analysis, may be more relevant to the analysis of budgetary decisions than to crisis decisions. Table, 13 notes.
                                                      E. S. Palais

1396. Carty, James W., Jr. CUBAN COMMUNICATORS. *Caribbean Q. [Jamaica] 1976 22(4): 59-67.* Summarizes literary and journalistic trends in Cuba since Castro came to power. Marxist-Leninist ideology has played a heavy role in the products of the Cuban press, ranging from technical publications through news reporting to the literary works of Nicolás Guillén and Alejo Carpentier. Cuban journalists have "seemed long on Marxist theory and short on communication techniques. But there has been improvement in their reporting and editing skills," and they are more honest than in the "bribe-prone" Batista era. Influence beyond Cuba is reflected in plans to start a Latin-American Centre for Journalism Studies "to counter US influence in . . . Latin American journalism schools." From a paper presented at the 3d International Media Conference, Pan-American University, November 1976.
                                                  R. L. Woodward, Jr.

1397. Casal, Lourdes. REVOLUTION AND *CONCIENCIA*: WOMEN IN CUBA. Berkin, Carol R. and Lovett, Clara M., ed. *Women, War & Revolution* (New York: Holmes & Meier, 1980): 183-206. The status of women in prerevolutionary Cuba was characterized paradoxically by advances in legal equality and by discrimination in the labor force in terms of concentration in low-paying and low-status jobs, limited varieties of jobs, and labor divisions in the family. Discusses the changes affecting women since the revolution in labor, education, community service, legislation, politics, and ideology. Also briefly mentions the Federation of Cuban Women (FMC), formed in 1960, and its role in mobilizing women into the political mainstream.

1398. Castro, Fidel. NUESTRA CAUSA HA TRIUNFADO [Our cause has triumphed]. *Casa de las Américas [Cuba] 1975 16(93): 5-10.* Reprints the text of a speech by Cuban Prime Minister Fidel Castro

Ruz, 22 August 1975, on the occasion of the 50th anniversary of the founding of the first Cuban Marxist-Leninist party.

1399. Chántez Oliva, Sara E. CONDICIONES DE VIDA DE LA CLASE OBRERA EN EL PERIODO PRE-REVOLUCIONARIO (1952-1958) [Conditions of life of the working class in the prerevolutionary period, 1952-58]. *Islas [Cuba] 1981 (69): 101-125.* Presents a social, political, economic and educational profile of the Cuban working class, with emphasis on demographics and the general standard of living.

1400. Chrisman, Robert and Allen, Robert L. THE CUBAN REVOLUTION: LESSONS FOR THE THIRD WORLD. *Black Scholar 1973 4(5): 2-15.* Discusses Cuba's colonial history, focusing on the revolution under Fidel Castro, 1961-73, as a model for other developing nations to follow.

1401. Chrisman, Robert. NATIONAL CULTURE IN REVOLUTIONARY CUBA. *Black Scholar 1977 8(8-10): 2-11, 81-96.* A delegation of eight black Americans visited Cuba in November 1976, the first such group to visit the revolution. They studied cultural developments in Cuba since the Castro takeover and found that the Cubans "are pursuing their revolution with an energy, an exuberance, a joy and a collective intelligence that borders upon genius."
B. D. Ledbetter

1402. Cole, Johnetta B. AFRO-AMERICAN SOLIDARITY WITH CUBA. *Black Scholar 1977 8(8-10): 73-80.* Discusses the unity between the black Americans and the Cuban people. Ties between the two communities began in the 19th century with the revolution which broke out in 1868 and have continued to the present. Currently the Afro-American people oppose US aggressions against Cuba and support the revolution which will bring equality to the Cuban people. 8 notes.
B. D. Ledbetter

1403. Cole, Johnetta B. RACE TOWARD EQUALITY: THE IMPACT OF THE CUBAN REVOLUTION ON RACISM. *Black Scholar 1980 11(8): 2-24.* Discusses the eradication of institutionalized racism in Cuba since the Cuban Revolution in 1959 and Fidel Castro's Proclamation against Racial Discrimination, although attitudes and behavior indicate that racism still exists there, and compares the Cuban experience with racism in America from the 1920's until 1978.

1404. Cole, Johnetta B. WOMEN IN CUBA: THE REVOLUTION WITHIN THE REVOLUTION. Lindsay, Beverly, ed. *Comparative Perspectives of Third World Women: The Impact of Race, Sex, and Class* (New York: Praeger, 1980): 162-178. Compares conditions for women in prerevolutionary Cuba with conditions after the 1959 revolution until 1979, focusing on the literacy campaign, the transformation of health care, the availability of work, housing, and women's participation in sports. While the revolution has changed the position of women, there are still prejudices and sexist attitudes that need changing.

1405. Connell-Smith, Gordon. CUBA AND THE AMERICAN HEMISPHERE. *Contemporary Rev. [Great Britain] 1975 226(1308): 1-5.* Discusses the effects of bad relations between Cuba and the United States on the Organization of American States, 1959-75.

1406. Crahan, Margaret E. RELIGIOUS PENETRATION AND NATIONALISM IN CUBA: U.S. METHODIST ACTIVITIES, 1898-1958. *Rev. Interamericana [Puerto Rico] 1978 8(2): 204-224.* Protestant missionary work began immediately after the Spanish-American War. American missionaries, viewing themselves as representatives of a superior culture and religion, were most effective among the island's middle class. In particular, Protestant schools attracted large numbers of students. Since 1958, however, these churches have been ambivalent in their attitude towards Castro's government. 49 notes.
J. Lewis

1407. Cruz-Luis, Adolfo. EL MOVIMIENTO TEATRAL CUBANO EN LA REVOLUCIÓN [The Cuban theatrical movement in the revolution]. *Casa de las Américas [Cuba] 1979 19(113): 40-50.* Cuban theater prior to 1959 reveals few noteworthy achievements. Government support fostered a theatrical revival in the 1960's. During the closing years of the decade the Escambray group was formed to bring drama to the masses. State cultural directives of the 1970's promoted

theater for the development of a socialist state. Schools, both in Cuba and socialist countries, trained dramatists.
H. J. Miller

1408. Darusenkov, O. CUBA ON THE ROAD TO SOCIALISM. *Int. Affairs [USSR] 1976 23(3): 49-53.* Report on Cuban socialist development on the conclusion of the First Congress of the Communist Party of Cuba 17-22 December 1975. Praises Cuba's social and economic progress, the strengthening of relations between Cuba and the Soviet bloc, the growing importance of Cuba as the leader of the anti-imperialist struggle in Latin America, and the CPC's strong adherence to a pro-Soviet line.
D. K. McQuilkin

1409. Darusenkov, O. CUBA STRIDES INTO SOCIALISM. *Int. Affairs [USSR] 1978 (8): 31-38.* From the time of the Moncada assault in July 1953, Cuba's revolutionary leadership has based its actions on Marxist principles, and especially since 1976 domestic and foreign policy progress has been great due to the activities of the Communist Party, active support from the socialist world, and coordination with Comecon economic guidelines.

1410. Darusenkov, O. CUBA-USSR: SOLID FRIENDSHIP. *Int. Affairs [USSR] 1974 (2): 16-21.* Surveys conditions in prerevolutionary Cuba, assesses the achievements of the Cuban revolution in the social sphere, and discusses the importance of Soviet-Cuban friendship to the economic development of Cuba.

1411. Darusenkov, O. T. BOEVOI AVANGARD KUBINSKOGO NARODA V BOR'BE ZA SOTSIALIZM [The militant vanguard of the Cuban people in the struggle for socialism]. *Voprosy Istorii KPSS [USSR] 1978 (12): 30-42.* Discusses some of the most important periods of the history of the Cuban Communist Party and stresses the leading role of the Party in the revolutionary movement of the masses.

1412. Darusenkov, O. T. "DVIZHENIE 26 IIULIA" V KUBINSKOI REVOLIUTSII [The July 26 Movement in the Cuban revolution]. *Novaia i Noveishaia Istoriia [USSR] 1979 (1): 13-30.* One of the main features of the Cuban revolution is the fact that Cuba's present-day Communist Party which leads the building of socialism in that country, was formed around the leadership of the July 26 Movement, the revolutionary and democratic organization that played the vanguard role in the revolution, 1953-60. The leadership of the July 26 Movement and its army headed by Fidel Castro ensured the unity of action by all the most consistent revolutionary forces in Cuba, which served as the basis for forming a single Marxist-Leninist party. The author traces the emergence and early activities of the July 26 Movement, between 1953 and 1957 when its leading role in the Cuban revolution was established.
J/S

1413. Darusenkov, O. T. KUBA STROIT SOTSIALIZM [Cuba constructs socialism]. *Novaia i Noveishaia Istoriia [USSR] 1977 (2); 137-152.* Surveys developments in Cuba from the beginning of the revolutionary movement until early 1977. Examines Fidel's life and revolutionary struggle to overthrow Fulgencio Batista and the American monopolies, with emphasis on socialist construction and the class struggle since 1959. Discusses the material and technical basis of socialism, the leading role of the Communist Party, and Cuba's foreign relations. Based on published documents and secondary works; 20 notes, biblio.
D. N. Collins

1414. De Los Angeles Ayón, Maria. DIE ARBEITERBEWEGUNG IM ELEKTRIZITÄTSMONOPOL IN HAVANA [The working-class movement in the electrical monopoly enterprise of Havana]. *Jahrbuch für Wirtschaftsgeschichte [East Germany] 1973 (2): 59-78.* Analyzes labor union activities in the electrical industry in the late 1920's and 1930's, within the context of Cuban political and labor history. Although moderate in its demands and generally apolitical, the electrical union was at first strongly opposed by the US owned monopoly company. But after the failure of the general strike of March 1935 the company adopted a public relations labor policy which the union hierarchy tacitly accepted. The workers' response took the form of negative attitudes to work. Based on company and union records and secondary works; 41 notes.
J. A. Perkins

1415. Dent, David and O'Brien, Carol. THE POLITICS OF THE U.S. TRADE EMBARGO OF CUBA, 1959-1977. *Towson State J. of*

Int. Affairs 1977 12(1): 43-60. Examines the rationale and effectiveness of the policy of economic coercion, through embargo, of Cuba's export production to the United States, 1959-77.

1416. Depestre, Rene. EL ASALTO AL MONCADA: REVÉS VICTORIOSO DE LA REVOLUCIÓN LATINOAMERICANO [The attack on Moncada: victorious turning point of the Latin American revolution]. *Casa de las Américas [Cuba] 1973 14(81): 6-40.* Discusses both battles of Moncada, emphasizing the second (1953) and showing the historical place of this battle in the continuum of the Cuban revolution.

1417. Díaz Roque, José. JOSÉ ANTONIO RAMOS: SU TEATRO Y SU IDEOLOGÍA CULTURAL CUBANA DE PRINCIPIOS [José Antonio Ramos: his theater and his principled Cuban cultural ideology]. *Islas [Cuba] 1979 (63): 91-150.* The work of José Antonio Ramos (1885-1946), characterized throughout by individualism, patriotism, and anti-imperialism, passed through nationalist reformist, revolutionary nationalist, and developing proletarian stages. He finally left behind the positivism and individualism of his class and his times to strengthen his anti-imperialism and socialist view of society.

1418. Díaz-Granados S., Consuelo. LA REFORMA AGRARIA EN CUBA E IMPLICACIONES [Cuban agrarian reform and its implications]. *U. Humanística [Colombia] 1979 (10): 169-187.* Land reform in Cuba ran up against North American subversive activities, the proletarian nature of the rural population, and the realities of sugar production.

1419. Dill, Hans-Otto. VALOR REVOLUCIONARIO Y VALOR ESTETICO-ARTISTICO DE LA POESIA DE NICOLAS GUILLEN [Revolutionary and aesthetic-artistic value of the poetry of Nicolás Guillén]. *Casa de las Américas [Cuba] 1982 22(132): 54-62.* The work of Cuban poet Guillén, described as artistic and revolutionary, is not the result of an artificial combination. The content of his work, whether political, social, or moral, is always aesthetic; the form always artistic. In his poetic consciousness and in the creation of some literary characters, Guillén has realized the new man of whom Che Guevara spoke. 12 notes.
J. V. Coutinho

1420. Dominguez, Jorge I. CUBA IN THE 1980's. *Problems of Communism 1981 30(2): 48-59.* The Cuban revolutionary government confronts a complex mixture of accomplishments and problems in the 1980's. While the former make it probable that the regime will stay in power, the latter make it likely that the leadership will have to exercise greater care in selecting objectives to pursue than it did in the last decade. In fact, it may have to sacrifice some goals it deems desirable in order to achieve others. Based on *Granma Weekly Review*; 37 notes.
J. M. Lauber

1421. Dominguez, Jorge I. CUBAN FOREIGN POLICY. *Foreign Affairs 1978 57(1): 83-108.* Because of heavy reliance on the Soviet connection, the Castro regime has traditionally conducted its foreign policy within externally defined boundaries. However, as long as Cuban policy has not been totally unharmonious with that of the Soviets, Castro has been able to operate quasi-autonomously. Cuba's achievements to date have been out of all proportion to its size and economic strength. Cuba has become a leading "nonaligned" force while simultaneously exporting revolution to the African continent.
M. R. Yerburgh

1422. Domínguez, Jorge I. INSTITUTIONALIZATION AND CIVIL-MILITARY RELATIONS. *Cuban Studies 1976 6(1): 39-66.* The armed forces in Cuba were among the first organizations on the island to become institutionalized, and the role of the military has included from the very beginning of the revolution work in areas besides that of defense and internal order. So successful have the armed forces been in their tasks that they have produced an administrative elite (the civic-soldier) that moves easily back and forth between civilian and military positions. 2 tables, 36 notes.
J. A. Lewis

1423. Dominguez, Jorge I. RACIAL AND ETHNIC RELATIONS IN THE CUBAN ARMED FORCES. A NON-TOPIC. *Armed Forces and Soc. 1976 2(2): 273-290.* Discusses race relations in the military of Cuba in the 1960's and 1970's, emphasizing the social disadvantages of Negroes.

1424. Dominguez, Jorge I. TAMING THE CUBAN SHREW. *Foreign Policy 1973 (10): 94-116.* Discusses the changes in Cuban foreign policy in the last four years.
S

1425. Dumoulin, John. EL MOVIMIENTO OBRERO EN CRUCES, 1902-1925: CORRIENTES IDEOLÓGICAS Y FORMAS DE ORGANIZACIÓN EN LA INDUSTRIA AZUCARERA [The labor movement in Cruces, 1902-25: ideological currents and forms of organization in the sugar industry]. *Islas [Cuba] 1979 (62): 83-121.* Discusses the general strike of 1902 and later strikes, the effects of economic and political conditions, ideological divisions between anarchists and socialists, the resolutions of the workers' congresses of 1912 and 1914, the formation and organization of unions and workers' associations, and their relations with political parties.

1426. Duncan, W. Raymond. CUBA: NATIONAL COMMUNISM IN THE GLOBAL SETTING. *Int. J. [Canada] 1976-77 32(1): 156-177.* Isolates essential features of Cuba's hybrid form of communism: the personal dominance of Fidel Castro, Cuban nationalism, and the institution of the revolution since 1970 along Soviet orthodox lines. Illuminates the foreign policy directions this brand of communism has generated. 49 notes.
R. V. Kubicek

1427. Dupuy, Alex and Yrchik, John. SOCIALIST PLANNING AND SOCIAL TRANSFORMATION IN CUBA: A CONTRIBUTION TO THE DEBATE. *Rev. of Radical Pol. Econ. 1978 10(4): 48-60.* An overview of the manner in which socialist planning has transformed Cuba since 1961.

1428. Durán Ros, Manuel M. EL TERRORISMO EN LA GUERRA MODERNA [Terrorism in modern war]. *Rev. General de Marina [Spain] 1975 188(6): 613-618.* Analyzes terrorism as a psychological weapon in guerrilla warfare. Terrorism comes in two basic forms (assassination and sabotage), two classes (selective and indiscriminate), and two operational levels (strategic and tactical). Examples of the theory of terrorism in the Algerian and Cuban revolutions are included. A people attacked by terrorism may lose its cohesion and surrender to the terrorists or rebel against the established government for not providing effective protection. But should there be an escalation of terrorism, the same people may become sufficiently indignant as to unite around the established government or form a force of its own to combat terrorism. The results of terrorism are so unpredictable that it is a dangerous weapon to utilize to further a specific political objective.
W. C. Frank

1429. Echevarría, Israel. CAMILO CIENFUEGOS: APORTE BIBLIOGRAFICO [Camilo Cienfuegos: bibliographical note]. *Rev. de la Biblioteca Nac. José Martí [Cuba] 1974 16(1): 135-170.* Gives a bibliography on the revolutionary commandant Camilo Cienfuegos, including his poetry and correspondence.

1430. Eckstein, Susan. CAPITALIST CONSTRAINTS ON CUBAN SOCIALIST DEVELOPMENT. *Comparative Pol. 1980 12(3): 253-274.* Utilizes Immanuel Wallerstein's view of a single, capitalist world economy in which production is geared to maximizing market profits, to discuss Cuba's socialist economic development. Prior to the revolution of 1959, sugar played a central role in the Cuban economy and Cuba was very dependent on US trade. In the postrevolutionary period, Cuba transferred its dependency to the Soviet bloc and made very little progress in expanding and diversifying its productive capacity. Cuba continues to be subject to world market forces, directly, to the extent that the Soviet bloc has not been able to absorb all of its exports and satisfy Cuba's consumer needs as well as capitalist countries could do, and, indirectly, to the extent that the Soviet bloc has not operated independently of the Western bloc and has been dependent on world market forces. Based on newspapers; 67 notes.
M. A. Kascus

1431. Eckstein, Susan. INCOME DISTRIBUTION AND CONSUMPTION IN POSTREVOLUTIONARY CUBA: AN ADDENDUM TO BRUNDENIUS. *Cuban Studies 1980 10(1): 91-98.* Replies to Claes Brundenius, "Measuring Income Distribution in Pre- and Post-Revolutionary Cuba," *[Cuban Studies, 1979 9(1): 19-44].* Although the revolution brought greater economic equality to Cuba, the principal beneficiaries of increased income on the island were the middle classes. 2 tables, 20 notes.
J. A. Lewis

1432. Eckstein, Susan. THE SOCIALIST TRANSFORMATION OF CUBAN AGRICULTURE: DOMESTIC AND INTERNATIONAL CONSTRAINTS. *Social Problems 1981 29(2): 178-196.* Discusses changes in the role of trade and the impact of the world economy on the structure of Cuba's domestic production and on the forces shaping the organization of Cuban agriculture since the revolution.

1433. Eckstein, Susan. STRUCTURAL AND IDEOLOGICAL BASES OF CUBA'S OVERSEAS PROGRAMS. *Pol. & Soc. 1982 11(1): 95-121.* Evaluation of the ideological, political, and economic factors involved in the expansion of Cuba's foreign aid programs in the 1970's. Military aid programs increased during this period, but civilian aid programs in the areas of construction, education, and medical projects also have exported a substantially larger amount of human capital that return significant percentages of Cuba's hard currency needs. Table, 101 notes.　　　　　　　　　　　　　　　　　　　D. G. Nielson

1434. Edwards, J. David. THE CONSOLIDATION OF THE CUBAN POLITICAL SYSTEM. *World Affairs 1976 139(1): 10-16.*

1435. Ellis, Keith. LITERARY AMERICANISM AND THE RECENT POETRY OF NICOLÁS GUILLÉN. *U. of Toronto Q. 1975 45(1): 1-18.* The work of black Cuban poet, Nicolás Guillén (b. 1904), was especially strong in attacking injustice in prerevolutionary Cuba, with political overtones for all of Latin America. Since the revolution, his poetry has assumed a profound creativity.

1436. Emel'ianov, Iu. V. KONGRESS S.SH.A. I REVOLIUTSION-NAIA KUBA [The US Congress and revolutionary Cuba]. *Voprosy Istorii [USSR] 1978 (3): 55-69.* Drawing on his close study of the US Congressional records, the author traces the progress of Congress debates on the Cuban question, which reflect the differences existing between the various groups within the US ruling circles and the evolution of US policy toward Cuba. The discussion of the different variants of American policy in the Senate and the House of Representatives revealed the existence in the US Congress of a group of realistic-minded politicians who clearly realized the futility of the US administration's anti-Cuban policy and from the very outset were fully aware of the need to recognize the fact of the revolutionary changes effected in Cuba. At the same time other Congressmen, complying with the will of the monopolies which had made big investments in the economy of prerevolutionary Cuba, the military-industrial circles and counter-revolutionary émigrés, took the initiative in organizing hostile acts against Cuba and openly demonstrated their vigorous opposition to any normalization of relations with it.　　　　　J

1437. Erisman, H. Michael. CUBA AND THE THIRD WORLD: THE SIXTH NONALIGNED NATIONS CONFERENCE. *Caribbean Rev. 1980 9(1): 21-25.* Examines Cuba's role in the controversies that confronted the Sixth Nonaligned Nations Conference, held in Havana during 1979, including the problems of Cambodian representation, membership of Egypt, and relations of members with the major East and West blocs.

1438. Erisman, H. Michael. CUBA'S LONG MARCH: THE STRUGGLE FOR THIRD WORLD LEADERSHIP. *Secolas Ann. 1980 11: 40-62.* Traces Cuba's rise in the nonaligned movement, 1959-79, examines the nature of conflict between Cuba and China, and speculates on the possibility of a future major leadership role for Cuba among the nonaligned nations.

1439. Erisman, H. Michael. CUBA'S STRUGGLE FOR THIRD WORLD LEADERSHIP. *Caribbean Rev. 1979 8(3): 8-12.* Cuba has gone through four distinct stages of development (consolidation of the revolution, 1959-61, hemispheric Fidelismo, 1962-68, incipient globalism, 1969-74, mature globalism, 1975-) and now wishes to become the leader of the Third World nonaligned movement, but China and others have opposed Cuba's membership in the nonaligned movement, claiming that it is but a surrogate for the USSR.

1440. Erisman, Michael. GLOBAL GUERRILLAS: TRAGEDIES AND TRIUMPHS OF CUBAN INTERNATIONALISM. *Revista/-Review Interamericana [Puerto Rico] 1979 9(3): 420-442.* Cuba's efforts to be a factor in world politics have been unique for such a small country. Its greatest successes have been in Africa rather than in Latin America. Based on sources in English; 40 notes.　　　　　　J. A. Lewis

1441. Farber, Samuel. GOING HOME TO CUBA. *Critique [Great Britain] 1981 (13): 138-150.* A native-born Cuban tells of his 1979 visit, after a 20-year absence, and compares pre- and postrevolutionary Cuba politically and economically.

1442. Farber, Samuel. POLITICS AND SOCIAL CLASSES IN PRE-REVOLUTIONARY CUBA. *Secolas Ann. 1980 11: 63-79.* A weak oligarchy characterized by ostentation rather than bigotry and by opportunism rather than ideology led to a lack of social and political consciousness within all Cuban social classes and allowed Batista's overthrow by Castro's coalition of working and middle classes and peasantry and the eventual establishment of a Communist state.

1443. Fernandez, Gaston A. THE FREEDOM FLOTILLA: A LEGITIMACY CRISIS OF CUBAN SOCIALISM? *J. of Interamerican Studies and World Affairs 1982 24(2): 183-209.* The present Cuban regime is experiencing a legitimacy problem among urban youth, unskilled laborers, and ex-prisoners. The regime's support remains strong among prerevolutionary landless peasants, rural poor, and the older generation. The regime's present problem is partly related to Cuba's prerevolutionary links to the world economy. Expectations and attitudes of urban workers are shaped by the urban past as a leisure and entertainment area for capitalists. This past created a certain standard of living in Havana and other large Cuban cities. Castro's revolutionary image is less effective than concrete economic gains in winning support in the urban areas. Based on interviews with 1980 "Freedom Flotilla" emigrants and printed primary materials; 2 notes, 4 tables, appendix, ref.
　　　　　　　　　　　　　　　　　　　　　T. D. Schoonover

1444. Fernández Barroso, Sergio. LA MÚSICA EN CUBA DURANTE LA ETAPA REVOLUCIONARIA [Music in Cuba during the revolutionary period]. *Rev. de la Biblioteca Nac. José Martí [Cuba] 1979 21(2): 119-132.* In spite of limited financial resources, classical music in Cuba has made great strides since the revolution. In addition to governmental support for all types of musical organizations, Cuban radio has set aside substantial time to play classical music for popular consumption.　　　　　　　　　　　　　　　　　　J. A. Lewis

1445. Fernández Retamar, Roberto. AL FINAL DEL COLOQUIO SOBRE LITERATURA CUBANA 1959-1981 [Concluding remarks at the colloquium on Cuban literature, 1959-81]. *Casa de las Américas [Cuba] 1982 22(131): 48-55.* The Cuban revolution has created a literature which is not only true literature and truly revolutionary but rich, multiform, and exacting. Whenever there was a previous tradition it has remained in continuity with it. Poetry, the short story, drama, essays, these have continued and deepened a tradition. Special mention must be made of the novel. The revolution has created a truly new literature for children and young people, and it has fostered two "ancillary" forms which are of great importance in a revolutionary period, namely oratory and the literature of testimony, beginning with the *Reminiscences of the Revolutionary War* of Che Guevara. Read at the closing session of the colloquium, November 1981.　　　　　　　　　J. V. Coutinho

1446. Figueroa, Isidro. EL COMPAÑERO RUBÉN [Comrade Rubén]. *Santiago [Cuba] 1974 (16): 95-149.* In a long interview in 1974, a colleague and fellow revolutionary describes his relations with Rubén Martínez Villena. An account of the discussions, the plottings, arrests, and meetings of members of the Communist Party; the activity of Martínez Villena as Party leader, his work among the masses, his arrest in 1928, his youth work and activity in various Party organizations, his role in the general strike of 1930, his departure from and return to Cuba, and his subsequent activities till his death in 1934.　　　D. Wasserstein

1447. Figueroa, María Antonia. UN CENTAVO DEL MAS HUMILDE DE LOS CUBANOS [A penny from the humblest of the Cubans]. *Santiago [Cuba] 1975 (18-19): 99-111.* An account of revolutionary activities and life in the 1950's in Santiago de Cuba and elsewhere. The author organized a mass movement in Oriente province during 1955-56 in close contact and cooperation with the leaders of the Cuban revolution. Revolutionary groups were successful in their infiltration tactics.　　　　　　　　　　　　　　　　　　D. Wasserstein

1448. Figueroa, O. Alvarez. A SZOCIALISTA EGYUTTM-ÜKÖDÉS SZEREPE KUBA GAZDASÁGI FEJLŐDÉSÉBEN

[Role of socialist cooperation in Cuba's economic development]. *Közgazdasági Szemle [Hungary] 1975 22(9): 1044-1053.* Surveys Cuba's economic development since the workers' seizure of power to the 1970's. In the wake of the agricultural reform, the measures leading to the nationalization of industry, the banks and foreign trade, and the imperialist blockade, the conditions for a deliberate conscious development have come about. In implementing its development policy, Cuba could rely on the efficient material, technological and financial assistance of the Comecon countries. Surveys the considerable economic results and the contributions of the individual socialist countries to developing various branches of the Cuban economy. J

1449. Fisher, Michael E. BLACK PEOPLE IN CUBA. *Southern Exposure 1975 3(1): 91-94.* Since Fidel Castro came to power in 1959, blacks in Cuba have entered the mainstream of society. This accomplishment was made possible by the total transformation of the economic and social arrangements imposed upon the Cubans by the United States after the Spanish-American War of 1898. Redistribution of political and economic power and educational reforms brought the blacks into equal standing. Secondary sources; 2 illus., 8 notes. G. A. Bolton

1450. Fitzgerald, Frank T. A CRITIQUE OF THE "SOVIETIZATION OF CUBA" THESIS. *Sci. and Soc. 1978 42(1): 1-32.* Carmelo Mesa-Lago among others has stated that the increased numbers of linkages between Cuba and the USSR have resulted in the Sovietization of domestic Cuban society. The Cuban replacement of moral by material incentives to production, an increase in social inequality, and the establishment of a decisionmaking matrix in which authoritarian dictates from the top have replaced mass participation in goal formulation and analysis of the economy highlights this supposed Sovietization process. A close examination of changes in the Cuban economy over the past decade indicates that Cuba's dependence on the Soviet Union is shallower than frequently believed and is not irreversible. The imposition of material incentives has not replaced moral incentives and has been accomplished in a setting which encourages collective consciousness. Greater social inequality has not resulted and Cuban workers fully participate in economic decisionmaking at all levels. The Cuban leaders are still emphatically interested in the creation of a "New Person" under Marxism. N. Lederer

1451. Forster, Nancy. CUBAN AGRICULTURAL PRODUCTIVITY: A COMPARISON OF STATE AND PRIVATE FARM SECTORS. *Cuban Studies 1981-82 11-12(2-1): 105-125.* Although data are somewhat limited, evidence suggests that private farms in Cuba are more productive than the large state farms. This does not mean, however, that there are inherent reasons preventing higher productivity on the state farms. 5 tables, 33 notes. J. A. Lewis

1452. Furtak, Robert K. KUBA: INSTITUTIONALISIERUNG EINES REVOLUTIONÄREN SYSTEMS [Cuba: institutionalization of a revolutionary system]. *Osteuropa [West Germany] 1978 28(6): 494-510.* Although the Cuban revolution from the outset tended toward socialism, Cuban political institutions and its economic system became socialist only in the 1970's.

1453. Galich, Manuel. PLAYA GIRÓN DESDE BUENOS AIRES, HACE DOS DÉCADAS [Playa Girón from Buenos Aires 20 years ago]. *Casa de las Américas [Cuba] 1981 21(125): 54-65.* Reprints six articles written for Argentine weeklies by the author during his exile in Buenos Aires in 1960 and 1961 on the preparation and outcome of the Bay of Pigs invasion sponsored by the Central Intelligence Agency. Articles reproduced from a periodical called successively *Propósitos, Conducta,* and *Principios.* J. V. Coutinho

1454. Gallo, Patrick J. CASTRO AND THE CUBAN REVOLUTION. *Riv. di Studi Politici Int. [Italy] 1974 41(1): 81-98.* Discusses the aims of the Cuban Revolution of 1959, the effect of US policy, how Fidel Castro became a Communist, and whether he promised one type of revolution but brought about another.

1455. García, Alejandro and Zanetti, Oscar. LOS MONOPOLIOS NORTEAMERICANOS Y LA LEY TARAFA [US monopolies and the Tarafa Law]. *Rev. de la Biblioteca Nac. José Martí [Cuba] 1980 22(2): 57-89.* The Ley Tarafa laid the groundwork for US monopolization of public railroads in Cuba. 64 notes. J. A. Lewis

1456. García del Pino, César. EN EL CINCUENTENARIO DE LA MUERTE DE CARLOS BALIÑO [On the 50th anniversary of the death of Carlos Baliño]. *Rev. de la Biblioteca Nac. José Martí [Cuba] 1976 18(1): 85-116.* Reviews the life of Carlos Baliño (1848-1926), the first Cuban Marxist and organizer of the first socialist and Communist organizations and newspapers in Cuba. Baliño's father, exiled to Fernando Póo in 1869 for participating in the Vuelta Abajo conspiracy, escaped to New Orleans where he died shortly after the younger Baliño joined him. Renouncing a career in architecture, Carlos Baliño organized immigrant Cuban tobacco and other workers in Key West and Tampa's Ibor City and established labor newspapers, which championed Cuban independence. He became an associate of José Martí in the 1896 revolution. Subsequently, Baliño remained in Cuba where he engaged in political and labor activities. In 1903, his Club de Propaganda Socialista was announced as Marxist. In 1920, he founded the Congreso Nacional Obrero, a labor union succeeded in 1923 by the Marxist-Leninist Agrupación Comunista de la Habana. 86 notes, 4 appendixes. R. D. Rodríguez

1457. García-Carranza, Araceli. BIO-BIBLIOGRAFÍA DE MARÍA VILLAR BUCETA [Biobibliography of María Villar Buceta]. *Rev. de la Biblioteca Nac. José Martí [Cuba] 1978 20(3): 149-180.* Biobibliography of Cuban poet, journalist, librarian, and revolutionary María Villar Buceta (1899-1976), including works by and about her and two indexes. She began publishing poetry in 1915, collaborating in magazine editing in 1920, and began a career in librarianship (with the National Library and subsequent lectureships) in 1924. She joined the Communist Party of Cuba in 1930. Biblio. R. D. Rodríguez

1458. Gebhardt, A. DIE FESTIGUNG DER REVOLUTIONÄREN EINHEIT DER KUBANISCHEN GEWERKSCHAFTSBEWEGUNG IM JAHRE 1960 AUF DER GRUNDLAGE DER BESCHLÜSSE DES X. CTC-KONGRESSES [The consolidation of the revolutionary unity of the Cuban trade union movement in 1960 on the foundation of the conclusions of the tenth congress of the Confederación de Trabajadores de Cuba]. *Lateinamerika [East Germany] 1979 (Spr): 25-40.* Trade union strength played an important part in the victory over domestic capitalism and US imperialism. The revolutionary consciousness of the workers was promoted by the party congresses, and it carried over to establish the new regime which enabled all Cubans to endure the immediate dislocations of the economy attendant upon the flight of upper-class bourgeoisie and pressure from the United States. Documents from the Cuban government and Party congresses; 43 notes. Summary in Spanish. D. R. Stevenson

1459. Gilbert, Jean Paul. LES ECHANGES ECONOMIQUES ENTRE CUBA ET L'UNION SOVIETIQUE [Economic exchanges between Cuba and the USSR]. *Problèmes d'Amérique Latine [France] 1982 (64): 91-121.* Examines economic relations between the two countries, demonstrating Cuba's economic dependency upon the Soviet Union.

1460. Goetze, Dieter. POLITISCHER ENTWICKLUNGSPROZESS UND MANIFESTATION DER GEWALT IN DER CUBANISCHEN REVOLUTION [Political development and manifestations of violence in the Cuban revolution]. *Jahrbuch für Geschichte von Staat, Wirtschaft und Gesellschaft Lateinamerikas [West Germany] 1978 15: 135-173.* The possibility of using force to drive the present Cuban regime out of power has been sharply reduced since the 1962 Playa Girón invasion attempt. The emigration of the elite and much of the middle class reduced structural conflicts and eliminated the prerevolutionary socioeconomic polarization by removing one of the poles. The socially accepted concentration of institutional and personal force during the early years of the revolution has helped stabilize revolutionary political rule in Cuba. Based on printed primary and secondary sources; 72 notes. T. D. Schoonover

1461. Gonzalez, Edward. CASTRO AND CUBA'S NEW ORTHODOXY. *Problems of Communism 1976 25(1): 1-19.* Analyzes the process of institutionalization of the Cuban Revolution since 1970. This period has seen an accompanying growth in Soviet influence, but Fidel Castro and his brother Raul remain very much in control. However, Fidel is likely to confront new pressures and demands on his leadership because of the broader elite coalition now ruling Cuba as well as the tighter links with Moscow. In view of this trend, Cuban policy in the future may well become more volatile. Based on primary and secondary English and Spanish sources; table, 75 notes.   J. M. Lauber

1462. Gonzalez, Edward. COMPLEXITIES OF CUBAN FOREIGN POLICY. *Problems of Communism 1977 26(6): 1-15.* The international behavior of Cuba in the 1970's has shown complex fluctuations between normalization of relations with the United States and an activist global policy supporting various national liberation movements in the Third World. Standard interpretations fail to explain these apparently divergent policy goals. A different approach concentrates instead on the views of three distinct elite groups discernible within Cuba's newly enlarged ruling coalition: the pragmatists, the revolutionists, and the military mission group. Chart, 60 notes.   J. M. Lauber

1463. Gonzalez, Edward. THE PARTY CONGRESS AND *PODER POPULAR. Cuban Studies 1976 6(2): 1-14.* Although the Communist Party of Cuba has emerged in the 1970's as a powerful force in Cuban politics, it still does not rival the power of the *fidelistas,* the *raulistas,* and the M-26-7 coalition—all groups of people tied to the revolutionary movement of the 1950's. Nevertheless, the strengthened Communist Party does illustrate the drive toward institutionalization within Cuba, a process which in time will naturally weaken the power of leaders such as Castro. 35 notes.   J. A. Lewis

1464. Gonzalez, Edward. POLITICAL SUCCESSION IN CUBA. *Studies in Comparative Communism 1976 9(1-2): 80-107.* Soviet control of Cuba has increased since 1970 and this will affect the succession. The candidates are Raul Castro, Osvaldo Dorticós, and Carlos Rodriguez. The army's role has grown since 1970 in part because its officers are superior to party cadres in education and training. The army has also developed a sense of corporate identity. The technocratic and bureaucratic groups may be expanded to include the military, which would make Raul's position strongest, but reduction of the perceived US threat might weaken it. 44 notes.   D. Balmuth

1465. González, Emilia T. THE DEVELOPMENT OF THE CUBAN ARMY. *Military Rev. 1981 61(4): 56-64.* Traces the development of the Cuban Revolutionary Armed Forces (FAR) from its formation in 1956 to the present day. Shortly after the rebel victory in 1959, Fidel Castro's brother Raúl was named head of the FAR and he has presided over the army's rise and evolution since. It has developed from a guerrilla force to an administrative force to an effective fighting force, primarily fighting overseas. 3 photos, 25 notes.   D. H. Cline

1466. González Acosta, Alejandro. A CINCUENTA Y CINCO AÑOS DE LA "AMERICA INDEFENSA" DE GAY CALBÓ [Fifty-five years after *América Indefensa* by Gay Calbó]. *Rev. de la Biblioteca Nac. José Martí [Cuba] 1981 23(1): 95-104.* Gay Calbó was one of the early student leaders in Cuba to understand the danger that the United States presented to the rest of the New World. In 1925 he published his most important work on this theme, *América Indefensa* [Defenseless America]. Based on printed sources.   J. A. Lewis

1467. González Bolaños, Aimée. LA LITERATURA FANTÁSTICA DE FÉLIX PITA RODRÍGUEZ EN LA REVOLUCIÓN: *LOS TEXTOS* [The literary fantasies of Félix Pita Rodríguez: *Los Textos*]. *Islas [Cuba] 1980 (65): 141-155.* Félix Pita Rodríguez's strength is the integration of idea and character, resulting in exemplary stories. *Los Textos* shows that one cannot separate principles of composition from their ideological base. Their source must be found in the experience of the socialist transformation of Cuban society.

1468. González-Echevarría, Roberto. CRITICISM AND LITERATURE IN REVOLUTIONARY CUBA. *Cuban Studies 1981 11(1): 1-17.* The Cuban Revolution, like the Mexican Revolution and the Spanish Civil War, marks a watershed in 20th-century Hispanic literature. Nevertheless, literary criticism, especially in Cuba, has not kept pace with the accomplishments of writers and poets inspired by the revolution. Biblio.   J. A. Lewis

1469. Gorbachev, B. DVA DESIATILETIIA REVOLUTSIONOI KUBY [Two decades of revolutionary Cuba]. *Mirovaia Ekonomika i Mezhdunarodnye Otnosheniia [USSR] 1979 (1): 25-32.* Deals with the economic, social, and political development of Cuba since 1959 and examines the course of Soviet-Cuban relations.

1470. Gorbachev, B. KUBA: REVOLIUTSIIA I EKONOMIKA [Cuba: revolution and the economy]. *Mirovaia Ekonomika i Mezhdunarodnye Otnosheniia [USSR] 1974 (3): 3-12.* Discusses the transformation and progress of the Cuban economy, 15 years after the revolution, with emphasis on management, planning, and labor incentives.

1471. Gordon, Gail and Bishop, Barbara. COMMUNITY CONTROL, CUBAN STYLE. *Freedomways 1981 21(3): 194-200.* Describes community participation in the National Health Service of Cuba from 1959 to 1981, comparing the status of health care in prerevolutionary Cuba to that after the nationalization of all medical institutions under Fidel Castro in 1965.

1472. Gottemoeller, Rose E. THE POTENTIAL FOR CONFLICT BETWEEN SOVIET AND CUBAN POLICIES IN THE THIRD WORLD. *Conflict 1982 3(4): 245-265.* Examines the evolution of the relationship between the USSR and Cuba since 1959, especially cooperation and conflict in their policies toward developing nations.

1473. Grabendorff, Wolf. CUBA'S INVOLVEMENT IN AFRICA: AN INTERPRETATION OF OBJECTIVES, REACTIONS, AND LIMITATIONS. *J. of Interamerican Studies and World Affairs 1980 22(1): 3-29.* Cuba's African policy is expected to help Cuba regain its vanguard position in the Third World, to aid socialism's victory in Africa, and to increase Cuba's bargaining power with both the USSR and the United Staes. Cuba risks undermining its credibility as a supporter of liberation movements, risks friction with friendly governments, and is restricted by collaboration with the USSR and the reaction of the West and nonaligned powers. 11 notes, ref.   T. D. Schoonover

1474. Graham, Margaret E. SALVATION THROUGH CHRIST OR MARX: RELIGION IN REVOLUTIONARY CUBA. *J. of Interamerican Studies and World Affairs 1979 21(1): 155-184.* In the 1960's Cuban churches, unlike those elsewhere in Latin America, did not enter a period of liberalization and innovation. At first a refuge from change, by the late 1960's the Cuban churches had entered a period of change due to the consolidation of the revolution and international developments. Still, even church members disposed to accept the revolution and Marxian economic analysis resisted the materialistic explanation of life. By retaining the transcendental explanation of life, they risked confrontation with the government. Table, 12 notes, ref.   T. D. Schoonover

1475. Granjon, Marie-Christine. LES RELATIONS ENTRE CUBA ET LES ETATS-UNIS DANS LES ANNEES SOIXANTE-DIX [Relations between Cuba and the United States in the 1970's]. *Problèmes d'Amérique Latine [France] 1982 (64): 123-141.* Explores the various phases of crisis and detente in relations between Cuba and the United States, noting that, since the election of Ronald Reagan, Central America and the Caribbean have become a potential area of confrontation.

1476. Grobart, Fabio. THE CUBAN WORKING CLASS MOVEMENT FROM 1925 TO 1933. *Sci. & Soc. 1975 39(1): 73-103.* The Cuban Communist Party played a major role in elevating the class consciousness of the working class during the events leading to the overthrow of dictator Gerardo Machado in 1933. Despite its illegal status, the party organized strikes and formed unions in the basic industries and gained adherents among university students. The party was not able, however, to gain sufficient power following the overthrow to enact the triumph of the agrarian and anti-imperialist revolutionary program.
                                                          N. Lederer

1477. Grobart, Fabio. EL CINCUENTENARIO DE LA FUNDACIÓN DEL PRIMER PARTIDO COMUNISTA DE CUBA [The 50th anniversary of the founding of the first Communist Party of Cuba]. *Casa de las Américas [Cuba] 1975 16(93): 48-63.* Traces the founding of the Communist Party in Cuba (1925) and details Cuban Communist development up to the present, including the revolution of 1959.

1478. Guevara, Ernesto Che. UNA REVOLUCIÓN QUE COMIENZA [A revolution which is starting]. *Santiago [Cuba] 1975 (18-19): 7-14.* Recounts his earliest memories of Fidel Castro in 1954 in Mexico, while undertaking military preparations for the invasion of Cuba. By then the failure of the Moncada attack had driven Castro to Mexico and caused division among his followers. Discusses the revolution's early success and failures, the disaster of the *Granma,* and the greatness of Castro as a leader. Reprinted from *O Cruzeiro* (1959).

D. Wasserstein

1479. Gugler, Josef. A MINIMUM URBANISM AND A MAXIMUM RURALISM: THE CUBAN EXPERIENCE. *Studies in Comparative Int. Development 1980 15(2): 27-44.* Examines Cuba's strategy for curtailing urban expansion, resultant social problems, and the rural-urban contradiction. The changing position of Havana as a mecca is outlined, as are the reasons for its decline in growth. Map, 4 tables, 22 notes, 47 ref.

S. A. Farmerie

1480. Gvozdaryov, B. USSR-CUBA: UNITY OF STAND AND VIEW. *Int. Affairs [USSR] 1974 (4): 3-8.* Reviews relations between Cuba and the Soviet Union, discusses Leonid Brezhnev's 1974 visit to Cuba, and analyzes Cuba's role as a socialist, anti-imperialist nation.

1481. Halperin, Maurice. FIDEL CASTRO IN RETROSPECT. *Queen's Q. 1974 81(4): 569-575.* Discusses the transformation of Fidel Castro's Cuba from an activist revolutionary state under charismatic leadership to a more traditional socialism in which the country falls in the mainstream of Russian objectives. The illusions of the early days of the revolution have practically disappeared and have been replaced by orthodox political regimentation.

J. A. Casada

1482. Halperin, Maurice. LOOKING BACK ON FIDEL. *Worldview 1976 19(10): 20-22.* The details of agronomist André Voisin's 1964 visit to Cuba reveal much about the character of Fidel Castro as a revolutionary leader.

1483. Halperin, Maurice. OSCAR LEWIS AND THE CUBAN REVOLUTION. *Queen's Q. [Canada] 1978-79 85(4): 677-685.* Review article of three works by Oscar Lewis, Ruth M. Lewis, and Susan M. Rigdon: *Four Men: Living the Revolution, An Oral History of Contemporary Cuba* (Urbana: U. of Illinois, 1977), *Four Women: Living the Revolution, An Oral History of Contemporary Cuba* (Urbana: U. of Illinois, 1977), *Neighbors: Living the Revolution, An Oral history of Contemporary Cuba* (Urbana: U. of Illinois, 1977). The trilogy was part of Project Cuba. In 1970 anthropologist Oscar Lewis gained permission from the Cuban government to freely interview Cubans. He was abruptly expelled, but not before he collected 20,000 pages of transcripts which form the basis of the books. The interviewees were poor prior to the Cuban Revolution and acknowledged that they were materially better off after 1959. Few, however, stressed the positive changes; most criticized the frustrations of daily life but were not concerned about the lack of political freedom. They admired Fidel Castro but only tolerated his government.

S

1484. Handelman, Howard. CUBAN FOOD POLICY AND POPULAR NUTRITIONAL LEVELS. *Cuban Studies 1981-82 11-12(2-1): 127-146* Fidel Castro's government has eliminated malnutrition in Cuba, but the diet of all sectors of the Cuban society (particularly the urban middle and working classes) has not necessarily improved. Secondary sources; 3 tables, 24 notes.

J. A. Lewis

1485. Harbron, John D. CUBA'S MARITIME OUTREACH. *US Naval Inst. Pro. 1978 104(9): 40-47.* Cuba is a fast-growing maritime power, having the third largest merchant fleet in the Western Hemisphere and a small but efficient navy of Soviet-built coastal craft and missile-firing torpedo boats. The Soviet Union and Eastern European countries have contributed much to Cuba's maritime development, but Cuba's own maritime efforts have been significant. Many Cuban merchant ships and tankers have been built for Cuba in non-Communist countries. Cuba's maritime development has taken on an increasingly indigenous style. 6 photos, table.

A. N. Garland

1486. Hernandez, Andres R. FILMMAKING AND POLITICS: THE CUBAN EXPERIENCE. *Am. Behavioral Scientist 1974 17(3): 360-392.*

1487. Heston, Thomas J. CUBA, THE UNITED STATES, AND THE SUGAR ACT OF 1948: THE FAILURE OF ECONOMIC COERCION. *Diplomatic Hist. 1982 6(1): 1-21.* In the years immediately following World War II, American diplomats, frustrated by their inabil-ity to gain Cuban cooperation on a number of economic issues, attempted to coerce Cuba via the Sugar Act (1948), which threatened to reduce the island's sugar sales to the United States by one-third. Cuba reacted vociferously, rallied Latin American support, and forced the United States to retreat from such an overt use of economic power. A direct result was the prohibition against economic coercion contained in the Charter of the Organization of American States. Based on US State Department records, congressional documents, and other primary sources; 75 notes.

A

1488. Horowitz, Irving Louis. AUTHENTICITY AND AUTONOMY IN THE CUBAN EXPERIENCE. *Cuban Studies 1976 6(1): 67-74.* Until now, most analyses of revolutions have found them to be either cyclical in nature (all revolutions pass through the same stages) or causal (all revolutions grow out of unique and noncomparable circumstances). Although both approaches are useful, there is a need to go beyond these explanations to determine what an authentic revolution is, especially in the Third World, and to understand what limits are placed on revolutions by economic dependence. The Cuban revolution offers an excellent place to start such studies.

J. A. Lewis

1489. Hostos y Ayala, Adolfo de. BREVE HISTORIA DE CUBA HASTA 1954 [Brief history of Cuba up to 1954]. *Bol. de la Acad. Puertorriqueña de la Hist. [Puerto Rico] 1974 3(12): 31-62.* Offers a historical synthesis of the island of Cuba from the pre-Columbian period to the present, analyzing the island's historical epochs from a cultural, political, and social point of view.

J. G. R. (IHE 96025)

1490. Iglesias, Fe. LA EXPLOTACIÓN DEL HIERRO EN EL SUR DE ORIENTE Y LA SPANISH AMERICAN IRON COMPANY [The working of iron in the south of Oriente and the Spanish American Company]. *Santiago [Cuba] 1975 (17): 59-106.* An account of the discovery and mining of iron in Cuba since 1883, and the dominant role of American interests in the iron industry. Describes the companies involved, their gradual conglomeration into the Spanish American Iron Company, this company's concessions, aspects of production and employment, and the benefits which the United States gained from the industry. 14 tables, 22 notes, biblio.

D. Wasserstein

1491. Irish, J. A. George. NICOLÁS GUILLÉN'S POSITION ON RACE: A REAPPRAISAL. *Rev. Interamericana [Puerto Rico] 1976 6(3): 335-347.* Nicolás Guillén (1902-) has long been Cuba's outstanding literacy advocate of *négritude.* Since 1959, however, Guillén has argued that the race problem in Cuba has been eliminated by the Castro Revolution. 33 notes.

J. A. Lewis

1492. Irish, J. A. George. THE REVOLUTIONARY FOCUS OF GUILLEN'S JOURNALISM. *Caribbean Q. [Jamaica] 1976 22(4): 68-78.* "Nicolás Guillén is a writer whose zest for his profession and zeal for human progress are combined with three basic streaks in his personality —genuine altruism, sharp-witted rationality and sustained militancy. The overriding interest and the burning passion of his selected prose is revolutionary struggle in the service of humanity and this expresses itself in his ardent fervour against Fascism and its related atrocities of racism, dictatorship and philistinism on the one hand, and on the other, capitalism and its inevitable corollary, imperialism. Guillén . . . has developed an approach to journalism that rises above the mere reporting of melodramatic and sensational scenes and incidents. He is a revolutionary thinker and a serious analyst, a committed 'pensador' within the Latin American tradition." The author demonstrates these qualities in Guillén through discussion of his career and references to his prose. Based on Guillén's writings; 24 notes.

R. L. Woodward, Jr.

1493. Jacquenay, Theodore. THE YELLOW UNIFORMS OF CUBA. *Worldview 1977 20(1-2): 4-10.* Reports on the treatment of political prisoners in Cuba 1959-76, especially the group of revolutionaries associated with Huberto Matos.

1494. James, Ariel. VANGUARDIA LITERARIA Y REVOLUCIÓN EN CUBA [Literary vanguard and revolution in Cuba]. *Santiago [Cuba] 1976 (21): 19-49.* Examines literary experiments in Cuba not as literature, but as a natural aspect of Cuba's history and national formation. In revolution a nation reaches its highest levels of expression. Literary movements in 19th-century Cuba, like that of Carlos Manuel de

Céspedes, played an important role in the creation of a specific Cuban national identity. The American occupation before World War I led to a slight decline in literary quality, but after 1915 the level rose again until the period of the republic in the 1930's.   D. Wasserstein

1495. Johnson, Leland L.   U.S. BUSINESS INTERESTS IN CUBA AND THE RISE OF CASTRO.   *World Pol. 1965 17(3): 440-459.* Discusses the role of US investment in Cuba in shaping relations between the United States and Cuba during Fidel Castro's early years (1959-64). "The presence and character of US investment in Cuba did play a role in Castro's ability to maintain a measure of popular support while simultaneously waging his propaganda campaign against the United States and moving toward the Soviet camp." Other sources of friction between the two countries, not obviously related to the presence and composition of US investment which Castro sought to exploit, are also outlined. 33 notes, 3 tables.   D. D. Cameron

1496. Kapcia, A. M.   CUBA'S AFRICAN INVOLVEMENT. *Survey [Great Britain] 1979 24(2): 142-159.* Rejecting conventional explanations, links Cuba's African intervention to the "mobilization" thesis. Mobilization has, all along, made an essential contribution to Cuba's survival as a revolutionary society, and the enthusiasm that the African involvement created and the mobilization it brought in its wake, were clear bonuses for the revolution. 86 notes.   V. Samaraweera

1497. Kapcia, Antoni M.   THE CUBAN ENIGMA.   *Problems of Communism 1980 29(1): 80-86.* A review article of six recent studies on Cuba. Over the two decades since its revolution, Cuba has evolved an "alternative" revolutionary model to that of the USSR. 33 notes.
J. M. Lauber

1498. Karl, Terry.   WORK INCENTIVES IN CUBA.   *Latin Am. Perspectives 1975 2(4): 21-41.* Moral incentives for workers in Cuba during 1963-73 did not achieve desired economic growth and production. But instituting added material gains coupled with a moral attitude instilled by earlier incentive programs have resulted in decentralization and mass participation in Cuba's progress.

1499. Khan, Anwar Naser.   THE CUBAN CRISIS OF 1962 AND INTERNATIONAL LAW.   *Pakistan Horizon [Pakistan] 1976 29(4): 73-84.* Discusses the Cuban missile crisis of 1962 with reference to international law and the UN Charter.

1500. Kline, Harvey F.   FIDEL CASTRO'S MARXIST REGIME: AN EVALUATION OF THE MAJOR POLICIES OF THE REVOLUTION.   *Rev. Interamericana [Puerto Rico] 1977 7(3): 400-416.* Reviews Fidel Castro's domestic policy, specifically agriculture, industrialization, diversification, education, health, housing, and minorities, and the constraints which it has faced during the 1960's and 1970's. Castro's drive to escape from the single-crop economy and his social and education programs have advanced Cuba's international position. Though accused of repression, Castro's regime seems an improvement over former regimes in the area of human rights.   G. A. Hewlett

1501. Kozol, Jonathan.   A NEW LOOK AT THE LITERACY CAMPAIGN IN CUBA.   *Harvard Educ. Rev. 1978 48(3): 341-377.* Traces the history of Cuba's literacy campaign initiated in 1960 by Fidel Castro, including teacher recruitment and training and the development of instructional methods, based on interviews and personal accounts.

1502. Kriukov, M. V.   KLANOVYE OBSHCHESTVA KITAIT-SEV-IMMIGRANTOV NA KUBE V PERVOI POLOVINE XX V. (K PROBLEME STRUKTURY I FUNKTSII TRADITSIONNYKH SOTSIAL'NYKH INSTITUTOV V INONATSIONAL'NOI SREDE) [Clan societies of Chinese immigrants in Cuba in the first half of the 20th century: the structure and functions of traditional social institutions in ethnically alien environments]. *Sovetskaia Etnografiia [USSR] 1977 (2): 55-67.* Characteristic of the structure of immigrant communities severed from their main ethnic area (and usually living under unfavorable conditions) is a resurrection of traditional social institutions: some in a peculiar, transformed shape. In the case of Chinese communities in America, imitative clan-type organizations are typical. The author discusses the structure and functions of such associations in the paper, particularly the Chinese community in Cuba of the late 19th and the first half of the 20th

century. It is demonstrated by materials from the Chinese press published in Cuba during this period that such "clan" organizations uniting compatriots bearing the same surname served not only as a consolidating but, at the same time, as a disintegrating factor. The predominance among Chinese immigrants of clan self-identification as against an all-national self-consciousness is evidence that the process of the formation of the Chinese nation was not yet completed in the early 20th century.   J

1503. Kukovecz, György.   DEMOCRÁCIA, ANTIIM-PERIALISMO Y ANTIFASCISMO EN LA POLÍTICA DE LOS COMUNISTAS CUBANOS (1935-1944) [Democracy, anti-imperialism and antifascism in the politics of the Cuban Communists, 1935-44]. *Acta U. Szegediensis de Attila József Nominatae: Acta Hist. [Hungary] 1980 68: 33-46.* Examines the popular front politics of the Communists during this period and its contradictions, in the context of the peculiar development of the first Cuban Communist Party, the general situation of the Cuban worker's movement and the political situation resulting from the failure of the bourgeois democratic revolution of 1933-35. 51 notes.   J. V. Coutinho

1504. Kula, Marcin.   LOS ASPECTOS INTERNACIONALES DE UN NACIONALISMO. LOS ESTUDIANTES DE LOS AÑOS VEINTE Y TREINTA EN LA LUCHA POR LA LIBERTAD DE CUBA Y DE AMÉRICA [International aspects of nationalism: students in the 1920's-30's in the struggle for the freedom of Cuba and America]. *Acta Poloniae Hist. [Poland] 1978 38: 199-208.* Traces the development of a revolutionary movement among Cuban students in the 1920's and 1930's. Shows that the Cuban nationalism manifested by these students was conceived by them as only a facet of a continent-wide movement for a free and united Republic of Latin America, and for the right of self-determination for colonial peoples on other continents. 18 notes.   J. C. Billigmeier

1505. Kunzle, David.   USES OF THE PORTRAIT: THE CHE POSTER.   *Art in Am. 1975 63(5): 66-73.* Discusses the use of portraits, especially that of Ernesto "Che" Guevara, as a mode of revolutionary idealism and political statement among Cuban artists, 1967-75.

1506. Labarre, Roland.   LA REVOLUCIÓN DEL 33 VISTA POR LA PRENSA FRANCESA DE LA ÉPOCA [The revolution of 1933 as seen by the French press of the time]. *Rev. de la Biblioteca Nac. José Martí [Cuba] 1980 22(2): 41-55.* The major Parisian newspapers gave considerable attention to the overthrow of the Cuban dictator Gerardo Machado and the subsequent revolution of 1933. French coverage of Cuban affairs reflected only a passing curiosity and there was almost no protest against American pressure to control events in Cuba. Based on eight Parisian newspapers.   J. A. Lewis

1507. Leal, Juan Felipe.   LAS CLASES SOCIALES EN CUBA EN VÍSPERAS DE LA REVOLUCIÓN [Social classes in Cuba prior to the revolution]. *Rev. Mexicana de Ciencia Pol. [Mexico] 1973 19(74): 99-109.* Studies the evolution of class structure in Cuba from 1513 to 1960 in order to categorize the events that led up to the Cuban Revolution.

1508. LeoGrande, William M.   THE COMMUNIST PARTY OF CUBA SINCE THE FIRST CONGRESS.   *J. of Latin Am. Studies [Great Britain] 1980 12(2): 397-419.* Since the First Congress in 1975, the Communist Party of Cuba (PCC) has been concerned to lead and supervise implementation of the resolutions adopted. The PCC has sought to consolidate its leading role by extending its influence among the masses and by establishing the Party's political hegemony over the political institutions, especially the administrative bureaucracy. There have been no major reorganizations of internal party operations since 1975. As the Cuban revolution enters its third decade, it has for the first time a Party organization capable of directing its future course.   Based in part on printed primary sources; 39 notes.   M. A. Burkholder

1509. LeoGrande, William M.   CONTINUITY AND CHANGE IN THE CUBAN POLITICAL ELITE.   *Cuban Studies 1978 8(2): 1-32.* The new political elite in Cuba has shown a remarkable continuity in membership since 1959. Nevertheless, during the 1960's there was a serious split in the Cuban Communist Party between the old guard leaders and new members recruited from the revolution itself. Since 1970, however, this split seems no longer important. 8 tables, 38 notes.
J. Lewis

1510. LeoGrande, William M.   CUBA: PARTY CONTROL AND POLITICAL SOCIALIZATION.   *Studies in Comparative Communism 1978 11(3): 278-291.* Immediately after the Cuban revolution the army, not the Party, was the controlling government institution. The old military had disappeared so there was no need to politically control the military. Also there was no clear differentiation between civil and military roles in Cuba. The Party's role increased in the 1970's when the army's role was reduced. 17 notes.   D. Balmuth

1511. LeoGrande, William M.   CUBAN DEPENDENCY: A COMPARISON OF PRE-REVOLUTIONARY AND POST-REVOLUTIONARY INTERNATIONAL ECONOMIC RELATIONS.   *Cuban Studies 1979 9(2): 1-29.* One of the principal goals of Castro's Revolution of 1959 was to lessen Cuba's economic dependency on the outside world. Most economic measurements show that some progress has been made in this area, but the level of dependence still remains very high. Primary sources; 14 tables, 18 notes.   J. A. Lewis

1512. LeoGrande, William M.   CUBAN POLICY RECYCLED.   *Foreign Policy 1982 (46): 105-119.* The United States must accept the reality of Cuba's alliance with the USSR and a hardline policy against Cuba by the Reagan administration will not succeed. In the face of US hostility, Cuba has no choice but to remain close to the Soviet Union. A strategy for dealing with US-Cuban conflict—gradual engagement of Cuba—offers the short-term advantages of removing Cuba as a flashpoint for superpower tension and moderating US-Cuban tensions. A long-term possibility is success in encouraging Cuban independence from the USSR.   M. K. Jones

1513. LeoGrande, William M.   PARTY DEVELOPMENT IN REVOLUTIONARY CUBA.   *J. of Interamerican Studies and World Affairs 1979 21(4): 457-480.* After unsuccessful attempts to organize the social and political revolution in the early and mid-1960's through the Integrated Revolutionary Organizations and the United Party of the Socialist Revolution, Fidel Castro restructured the latter organization, and changed its name to the Communist Party of Cuba. Given the tasks of fighting bureaucracy and supervising production and given considerable independence, the Party has served as the agency for institutionalizing the revolution with some success during the 1970's. It has served to reduce the future significance of Castro by facilitating the transition after his passing. Based on printed primary and secondary sources; table, ref.   T. D. Schoonover

1514. LeoGrande, William M.   THE POLITICS OF REVOLUTIONARY DEVELOPMENT: CIVIL-MILITARY RELATIONS IN CUBA, 1959-1976.   *J. of Strategic Studies [Great Britain] 1978 1(3): 260-294.* Examines the lengthy process by which revolutionary Cuba under Fidel Castro built a new political system, 1959-76. It was highly unusual for a Communist political system and reflects the character of the revolutionary struggle which preceded it. In Cuba the dynamism of institution-building was most clearly reflected in the sphere of civil-military relations because the revolution placed the military to the forefront as the leading institutional force. The process was completed 17 years after the insurrection. Based on Cuban and other primary sources; 3 tables, 81 notes.   A. M. Osur

1515. LeoGrande, William M.   THE THEORY AND PRACTICE OF SOCIALIST DEMOCRACY IN CUBA: MECHANISMS OF ELITE ACCOUNTABILITY.   *Studies in Comparative Communism 1979 12(1): 39-62.* The Cuban concept of democracy has expanded from an original definition of representation of the interests of proletarians and poor peasants and mass participation to include accountability. In 1966 local assemblies were established but these ended in 1970 with Cuba's economic failure. After 1970 the party established elections to party committees by secret ballot with more candidates than positions. A similar system was established for unions and in 1976 popular assemblies were created based on a secret ballot and requiring regular meetings of delegates with constituencies. A second election was held in 1979. These bodies are local authorities. Higher government bodies and national organs remain centrally controlled. 39 notes.   D. Balmuth

1516. Leogrande, William M.   TWO DECADES OF SOCIALISM IN CUBA.   *Latin Am. Res. Rev. 1981 16(1): 187-206.* Reviews eight works on Castro's Cuba. Many use comparative concepts and models that are cross-national in scope. Jorge Domínguez's *Cuba: Order and Revolution* and Carmelo Mesa-Lago's *The Economy of Socialist Cuba* are definitive works in their respective areas. 32 notes.   J. K. Pfabe

1517. Léresque, Jacques.   LA UNIÓN SOVIÉTICA Y CUBA: UNA RELACIÓN ESPECIAL   [The Soviet Union and Cuba: a special relationship].   *Foro Int. [Mexico] 1977 18(2): 219-242.* Discusses the strategic, political, and economic relations between Cuba and the USSR. 27 notes.   D. A. Franz

1518. Leuchter, W.   ZU PROBLEMEN DER HERAUSBILDUNG UND ENTWICKLUNG SOZIALISTISCHER WIRTSCHAFTSPLANUNG IN KUBA   [Concerning problems of the formation and development of socialist economic planning in Cuba].   *Lateinamerika [East Germany] 1979 (Spr): 41-67.* Cuba's problems in organizing a planned economy stemmed from its underdevelopment, ignorance, the poverty bequeathed by capitalism, inexperienced leadership, insufficient investment capital, and US hostility. Based on Cuban government documents and secondary literature from socialist bloc countries; 69 notes. Abstract in Spanish.   D. R. Stevenson

1519. Leuchter, W.   ZU WICHTIGEN ENTWICKLUNGSTENDENZEN BEI DER SCHAFFUNG DER MATERIELL-TECHNISCHEN BASIS DES SOZIALISMUS IN KUBA   [Developmental tendencies in the creation of the material and technological base for Cuban socialism].   *Lateinamerika [East Germany] 1980: 5-22.* Government planning and emphasis upon increasing industrial development were most important new directions in Cuban socialism. Based on official production statistics and secondary sources; chart, 33 notes. Spanish summary.   D. R. Stevenson

1520. Levesque, Jacques.   LA GUERRE D'ANGOLA ET LE ROLE DE CUBA EN AFRIQUE   [The Angola war and Cuba's role in Africa].   *Etudes Int. [Canada] 1978 9(3): 429-434.* Reviews the positions taken by Russia, China, and several South American and African states toward Cuba's military role in Angola in 1975. Notes Cuba's earlier involvement in Africa and suggests that this activity gives Havana greater latitude to develop its own foreign policy in Latin America. 19 notes.   J. F. Harrington, Jr.

1521. Lewis-Beck, Michael S.   SOME ECONOMIC EFFECTS OF REVOLUTION: MODELS, MEASUREMENT, AND THE CUBAN EXPERIENCE.   *Am. J. of Sociol. 1979 84(5): 1127-1149.* Using data from Cuba on the economic effects of revolution, rejects leading models (Conservative, Marxist, and Thermidorian), maintaining that economic effects are neither as disruptive nor as pervasive as is commonly thought.

1522. López Segrera, Francisco.   LA POLITICA DEL IMPERIALISMO YANQUI HACIA CUBA DE EISENHOWER A REAGAN   [Yankee imperialist policy toward Cuba from Eisenhower to Reagan].   *Casa de las Américas [Cuba] 1982 22(131): 22-33.* Traces the history of the US policy of nonrecognition and containment toward Cuba. Based on US opinion polls regarding attitudes to normalization of relations with Cuba, and a chronology of declarations and actions by Ronald Reagan from the time of the electoral campaign.   J. V. Coutinho

1523. Lucyga, C.   ZUR DARSTELLUNG VON GESCHICHTE UND GEGENWART IM NEUEN KUBANISCHEN ROMAN   [The representation of past and present in the new Cuban novel].   *Lateinamerika [East Germany] 1978 (Fall): 5-24.* The Cuban novel has reflected the social concerns and new nationalistic self-identity wrought by the revolutionary movements from the anti-Machado movement of 1933 to the successful Castro revolution of the late 1950's. Based on novels; 35 notes.   D. R. Stevenson

1524. Macaulay, Neill.   THE CUBAN REVOLUTION IN HISTORICAL PERSPECTIVE.   *Pro. of the South Carolina Hist. Assoc. 1978: 69-75.* Examines several interpretations of the Cuban Revolution and attempts to place it in historical perspective. After a discussion of the two major conspiracy theories of the Cuban Revolution, the author examines the recent history of Cuba and its leader Fidel Castro. He also discusses the 1956-58 guerrilla campaign against the Fulgencio Batista y Zaldivar government. Based on the author's personal knowledge of the Cuban Revolution gained by serving with Castro's forces, and published works; 9 notes.   J. W. Thacker, Jr.

1525. Macaulay, Neill. NOTES AND COMMENTS: THE CUBAN REBEL ARMY: A NUMERICAL SURVEY. *Hispanic Am. Hist. Rev. 1978 58(2): 284-295.* The number of guerrillas reported in the Cuban 26 of July Movement in 1958 has varied from 300 to 8,000. Fidel Castro reported 7,300 in 1958 but later claimed he had had only 3,000, apparently in an effort to emphasize the power of a small force. The author estimates there were 7,250 Fidelista guerrillas in December 1958. 4 tables, 58 notes.
B. D. Johnson

1526. MacEwan, Arthur. IDEOLOGY, SOCIALIST DEVELOPMENT, AND POWER IN CUBA. *Pol. and Soc. 1975 5(1): 67-82.* Contrasts what is termed the "sequential" (Russian) and the "simultaneous" (Cuban and Chinese) alternative transitions to socialism and the particular importance of ideology, especially concerning material versus social conditions, in opting for the latter route. Revolutionary Cuban experiences are presented as a case study of the "simultaneous route." Primary and secondary sources; 26 notes.
D. G. Nielson

1527. Marchant, Herbert. CASTRO'S CUBA AND THE SOVIET UNION. *World Survey [Great Britain] 1976 (91/92): 1-16.* Traces the development of Fidel Castro's "personal leadership" from 1959 and discusses Soviet predominance in shaping Cuban domestic and foreign policy, with emphasis on recent events in Angola.

1528. Marinello, Juan. RECUERDOS DE RUBÉN [Recollections of Rubén]. *Santiago [Cuba] 1974 (16): 43-49.* Memoirs describing his contemporary, Rubén Martínez Villena, their relations during the 1920's, Martínez Villena's conversion to communism, and his literary activities.
D. Wasserstein

1529. Márquez, Roberto. RACISM, CULTURE AND REVOLUTION: IDEOLOGY AND POLITICS IN THE PROSE OF NICOLAS GUILLEN. *Latin Am. Res. Rev. 1982 17(1): 43-68.* Nicolás Guillén's relatively unknown prose complements his poetry, often sharing identical themes. He was spokesman of the proletariat and gave himself totally to the struggle of the people. His prose persistently addressed three subjects: the condition of blacks, the Cuban cultural experience, and the overthrow of an unjust sociopolitical system. He fused a revolutionary spirit with art of enduring quality. Based on published and unpublished writings of Guillén; 27 notes.
J. K. Pfabe

1530. Marti, Jorge L. THE CUBAN SOCIETY AS REFLECTED IN ITS LITERATURE (1900-1930). *Secolas Ann. 1973 4: 80-93.* Shows the political events in Cuba—economic prosperity, financial bankruptcy, and political collapse—as reflected in the literature of the time. One of eight papers on Cuba and Chile read at the annual meeting of the Southeastern Conference on Latin American Studies.
S

1531. Mashkin, V. CUBA: A DISTANT COUNTRY CLOSE TO OUR HEARTS. *Int. Affairs [USSR] 1974 (1): 90-94.* Surveys Cuba's progress since 1961 and discusses the importance of Cuban-Soviet friendship to Cuba's achievements.

1532. Masud, Felix Roberto. CUBAN NATIONALISM. *Can. Rev. of Studies in Nationalism [Canada] 1980 7(biblio): 82-89.* Annotated bibliography of works published since 1971.
R. Aldrich

1533. Mateo, Maricela. EL EJÉRCITO OLIGÁRQUICO EN LA POLÍTICA NEOCOLONIAL CUBANA (1925-1952) [The oligarchic army in neocolonial Cuban politics, 1925-52]. *Santiago [Cuba] 1976 (22): 87-120.* Analyzes the important role of the army in Cuban politics. Its primary function was counterrevolutionary repression; this evolved parallel with national politics, 1899-1952. The military served not to defend the state, but rather as a means for rulers to impose decisions by force on matters of national importance. Whenever it failed, the United States stepped in to help. The army's composition reflected class distinctions and its actions always had a political tone. Fulgencio Batista made it a political party to support him, but in 1959 it was replaced by a genuine people's army. 20 notes.
D. Wasserstein

1534. McShane, John F. SMALL STATES IN THE INTERNATIONAL SYSTEM: A CUBAN CASE STUDY. *Secolas Ann. 1980 11: 80-102.* Using the McGowan and Gottwald model of foreign policy behavior (which is systemic and highly general) and Maurice East's foreign policy model (which is substantive with a policy-specific focus for small states), analyzes Cuba's foreign policy, 1959-79.

1535. Melon, Alfred. SOBRE TRES DISCURSOS DE JUAN MARINELLO [Three speeches of Juan Marinello]. *Casa de la Américas [Cuba] 1979 20(115): 46-59.* A major contribution of Juan Marinello to the Cuban Communist movement was his oratory. The analysis of three major addresses in the 1930's demonstrates that his oratorical skills carried emotional appeal, moralism that demanded action, and intellectual and didactic pronouncements. It was oratory equal to any other art form. His oratorical style made him an effective leader of the masses and therefore places him in the great oratorical tradition from José Marti to Fidel Castro. 12 notes.
H. J. Miller

1536. Méndez Díaz, Pedro. FEDERICO DE CÓRDOVA Y QUESADA: BREVE ESTUDIO (EN EL CENTENARIO DE SU NACIMIENTO) [Federico de Córdova y Quesada: brief study on the centenary of his birth]. *Rev. de la Biblioteca Nac. José Martí [Cuba] 1978 20(1): 101-121.* Homage to Federico de Córdova (1878-1960), Cuban lawyer, journalist, essayist, historian, and educator. Córdova served as legal consultant to the secretary of Public Education (1909-33) while working on several newspapers and journals and writing. After retiring from public life for political reasons, he lectured summers at the University of Havana (1943-53), where his interest in 19th-century Cuba and José Martí grew. Córdova was always a dissident, and a review of his best works (out of some 40 books) shows his progressive and anti-imperialist thought. Primary sources; 22 notes.
R. D. Rodríguez

1537. Mesa-Lago, Carmelo et al., comp. BIBLIOGRAPHY. *Cuban Studies 1973 4(1): 1-33.* A comprehensive bibliography of books, articles, and pamphlets on historical and contemporary Cuba published between 1971 and 1973.
J. A. Lewis

1538. Mesa-Lago, Carmelo. CASTRO'S DOMESTIC COURSE. *Problems of Communism 1973 22(5): 27-38.* In 1970 Cuba's leaders promised democratization of Cuban socialism. The contrasts between this promise and actual developments are explored with relation to the ruling Cuban Communist Party, the central administration, management of enterprises, trade unions, the private agricultural sector, and students and intellectuals. The concrete result has been more centralization and regimentation. Primary and secondary sources; 44 notes.
J. M. Lauber

1539. Mesa-Lago, Carmelo. FARM PAYMENT SYSTEMS IN SOCIALIST CUBA. *Studies in Comparative Communism 1976 9(3): 275-284.* Private farms created from private holdings of 400 hectares or more in 1959 have declined in significance in Cuba. Originally these holdings constituted 63% of arable land but since 1963 the share has fallen to 35%. After 1963 the government encouraged cooperatives, and since the late 1960's it has tried to curb the private sale of surpluses. The government purchases the surplus in return for a guaranteed income, a system known as *acopio.* Although the income of private farmers has been declining since 1967, it is still triple that of state farmers. Table, 10 notes.
D. Balmuth

1540. Mesa-Lago, Carmelo. THE SOVIETIZATION OF THE CUBAN REVOLUTION: ITS CONSEQUENCES FOR THE WESTERN HEMISPHERE. *World Affairs 1973 136(1): 3-35.*

1541. Miguez, Alberto. DOSSIER: CUBA ET LE MOUVEMENT DES NON-ALIGNES [Dossier: Cuba and the movement of nonaligned countries]. *Problèmes d'Amérique Latine [France] 1982 (64): 169-179.* Through summaries of positions taken at international conferences, shows the growth of Cuba to a commanding position among the nonaligned nations.

1542. Molina, Ernesto and Rodríguez, José Luis. ANÁLISIS DE LA ESTRUCTURA PRODUCTIVA DE LOS PAÍSES SOCIALISTAS A TRAVÉS DE LAS POLÍTICAS Y PLANES DE DESARROLLO: CUBA. [An analysis of the productive structure of socialist countries as seen through their development policies and plans: Cuba]. *Investigación Econ. [Mexico] 1980 39(154): 67-82.* In Cuba the problems of subjectivism and revolutionary voluntarism, so prominent in China, did not assume the character of an ideological rationalization, as in the thought of Mao. The struggle against sectarianism and dogmatism in the 1960's and the emphasis on the legitimacy and hegemony of the leadership prevented the mistakes and debates concerning development strategy from becoming a power struggle. Cuba's experience also underlines the importance of a politically and theoretically competent and self-critical leadership. The authors explain the Cuban way of socialization of agriculture and the role of the 1st Congress of the Cuban Communist Party in the definition of goals and methods of the current phase of socialist construction. Based on official documents. J. V. Coutinho

1543. Montaner, Carlos Alberto; Zayas-Bazán, Eduardo, transl. 20 YEARS AFTER THE CUBAN REVOLUTION. *Caribbean Rev. 1979 8(1): 4-9.* Examines the history of Cuban political, economic, social, and foreign policies since 1959 and concludes that neither the geography nor the history, not the economy nor Cuban social and political tradition indicates that the Communist dictatorship is an irreversible fact.

1544. Montiel, Pedro J. THE US AND CUBA, 1880-1934: THE POLITICAL ECONOMY OF HEGEMONY. *Caribbean Rev. 1979 8(1): 51-53.* Reviews Jules Robert Benjamin's *The United States and Cuba: Hegemony and Dependent Development, 1880-1934* (U. of Pittsburg, 1977) and finds the work an excellent study of Cuban economic and political problems—which led to the Revolution of 1933—related to the hegemonic presence of the United States and America's pursuit of its economic and security interests.

1545. Moran, Theodore H. THE INTERNATIONAL POLITICAL ECONOMY OF CUBAN NICKEL DEVELOPMENT. *Cuban Studies 1977 7(2): 145-166.* Cuba has the world's fourth largest nickel reserves but mines this metal on a very modest level. Expanded production of nickel would diversify the island's exports, but increased production will not come until Cuba and the United States resume normal diplomatic relations. Based on interviews and secondary sources; 3 tables, 40 notes. J. A. Lewis

1546. Moreno, Jose A. and Lardas, Nicholas O. INTEGRATING INTERNATIONAL REVOLUTION AND DETENTE: THE CUBAN CASE. *Latin Am. Perspectives 1979 6(2): 36-61.* Cuba's consistent support of international revolution has passed through four distinct phases since 1959. "Peaceful coexistence" ended in 1975 with Cuba's participation in the Angolan civil war. Since then Cuba seems to have moved toward detente with the United States. Several scenarios are possible in this context, all of them depending on mutually self-imposed restraints and limitations of policy. Table, 17 notes. J. F. Vivian

1547. Morowitz, Irving Louis. CUBA LIBRE? SOCIAL SCIENCE WRITINGS ON POSTREVOLUTIONARY CUBA 1959-1975. *Studies in Comparative Int. Development 1975 10(3): 101-123.* Views of the Cuban revolution have varied from C. Wright Mills's emphasis on the personal role of Fidel Castro to Jean Paul Sartre's belief in Cuba's moral radicalism and Maurice Zeitlin's argument that Castro became a Marxist because of US policy. Other interpretations have pointed to the failure of Castro's effort to replace material by moral incentives. The Cuban revolution has robbed Cuba of authentic scholars to interpret Cuba's experience. Emigré scholars like Carmelo Mesa Lago have put forth the accurate argument that the regime has inclined more and more to militarization. D. Balmuth

1548. Mraz, John G. *LUCIA:* HISTORY AND FILM IN REVOLUTIONARY CUBA. *Film & Hist. 1975 5(1): 8-14.* Focusing on Humberto Solás' film *Lucía,* considers historical films as powerful tools in the breakdown of colonial attitudes and the formation of a national identity in revolutionary Cuba. S

1549. Mühlemann, Christoph. AMERIKAS UNRUHIGER HINTERHOF [America's restless back yard]. *Schweizer Monatshefte [Switzerland] 1980 60(4): 301-308.* From 1959 Cuban foreign policy was one of export of revolutionary techniques to Latin America and Africa, although the economic weakness of Fidel Castro's regime allowed only individual doctors, teachers, and military advisers to be sent outside the country.

1550. Mühlemann, Christoph. CASTROS SPIELRAUM. GESCHICHTE EINER ABHÄNGIGKEIT [Castro's room for maneu-

ver: history of a dependency]. *Schweizer Monatshefte [Switzerland] 1977 57(3): 179-188.* From the outset the Cuban experiment was dependent on foreign assistance, leaving Fidel Castro's government no option, after the US embargo of 1960, but to accept Soviet economic, political, and military offers.

1551. Nicolau, Ramón. SOBRE RUBÉN MARTÍNEZ VILLENA [On Rubén Martínez Villena]. *Santiago [Cuba] 1974 (16): 85-94.* A fellow revolutionary describes some of his own activity, Rubén Martínez Villena's role in the revolution, and their close relations, 1920's-30's. D. Wasserstein

1552. Niess, Frank. NOTIZEN ZUM KUBANISCHEN SOZIALISMUS [Notes on Cuban socialism]. *Frankfurter Hefte [West Germany] 1977 32(7): 40-48, 32(8): 40-49.* Part I. Dominated by the martyred figure of José Martí (1853-95), the Cuban Revolution under Fidel Castro has been fairly realistic in confronting social and economic problems, as shown in its decision to develop agriculture rather than attempt rapid industrialization. Part II. Deals with developments in Cuba since 1970: the battle for sugar and its failure; the attempt at popular participation in decisionmaking known as Poder Popular; the First Congress of the Cuban Communist Party; and the trend toward the institutionalization of the Revolution.

1553. Nin de Cardona, José María. VISIÓN RETROSPECTIVA DE LA TRANSCENDENCIA INTERNACIONAL DE LA REVOLUCIÓN CUBANA DE 1959 [A retrospective vision of the international transcendency of the Cuba revolution of 1959]. *Rev. de Pol. Int. [Spain] 1977 (151): 209-221.* The author examines developments in Cuba, 1959-77, and sees the country as an enclave of political and economic interests and a latter-day utopia of considerable importance in international politics.

1554. Núñez, Ana. RUBÉN MARTÍNEZ VILLENA, EL PERIODISTA [Rubén Martínez Villena, the journalist]. *Santiago [Cuba] 1974 (16): 167-178.* Discusses Martínez Villena's work as a political journalist during the late 1920's and early 1930's, and his belief that the intellectual revolutionary ought to be a revolutionary first and an intellectual second. D. Wasserstein

1555. O'Ballance, Edgar. THE CUBAN FACTOR. *J. of the Royal United Services Inst. for Defence Studies [Great Britain] 1978 123(3): 46-51.* Discusses Cuban military power in contemporary Africa in the light of Cuban history since 1959.

1556. Pade, W. DIE KUBANISCHE ARBEITERKLASSE IN DER REVOLUTION UND BEIM AUFBAU DES SOZIALISMUS: EINIGE ÜBERLEGUNGEN [The Cuban working class in the revolution and in the building of socialism]. *Lateinamerika [East Germany] 1979 (Spr): 5-24.* The Communist Party has led the Cuban working class in accordance with Marxist-Leninist principles. Production has increased, and national independence is secure. Although economic inequalities still exist and vestiges of the old capitalist order remain, progress has been made toward economic equality and a workers' society. Based on documents from the Cuban government and secondary socialist bloc sources; 52 notes. Summary in Spanish. D. R. Stevenson

1557. Pade, Werner. ASPEKTE DER ZUSAMMENARBEIT ZWISCHEN DEN REVOLUTIONÄREN DEMOKRATEN UND DER ARBEITERKLASSE WÄHREND DER ANTIIMPERIALISTISCH-DEMOKRATISCHEN ETAPPE DER REVOLUTION IN KUBA (1959-1961) [Cooperation between the revolutionary Democrats and the working class during the anti-imperialistic democratic stages of the Cuban revolution, 1950-61]. *Lateinamerika [East Germany] 1978 (1): 127-137.* The international importance of the Cuban revolution lies in its demonstration of the need for a Leninist vanguard party to direct the revolution. This topples the reactionary leadership and paves the way for democratic participation and social reform. Based on papers presented at a Workers' Symposium in Sofia, Bulgaria, May 1977; 23 notes. D. R. Stevenson/S

1558. Padula, Alfred. FINANCING CASTRO'S REVOLUTION, 1956-1958. *Rev. Interamericana [Puerto Rico] 1978 8(2): 234-246.* Although ignored by the Castro government for political reasons and by the

Cuban middle class from embarrassment, it is clear that Fidel Castro financed his revolution with contributions from the island's bourgeoisie. Some of this cash was coerced, but most was given voluntarily. After the revolution, Castro used this money to destroy the very men who contributed it. Oral sources; 76 notes.   J. Lewis

1559.   Padula, Alfred.   THE RUIN OF THE CUBAN BOURGEOI-SIE, 1959-1961. *Secolas Ann. 1980 11: 5-22.* The destruction of the bourgeois class during Fidel Castro's revolution 1959-61, was due to its inability to build a modern nation despite adequate funds, its dependence on the United States, and its general lack of ethics, compounded by Castro's propaganda of fear, promise of employment, and ability to mold himself into a heroic savior figure.

1560.   Pascual, Sarah.   MIS RECUERDOS DE RUBÉN Y LA UNI-VERSIDAD POPULAR [My recollections of Rubén and the Popular University]. *Santiago [Cuba] 1974 (16): 51-84.* Rubén Martínez Villena was important to communism in Cuba in the 1920's, especially after 1923, when the Universidad Popular José Martí was founded. The university was very important for Martínez Villena's political and intellectual development, and in providing him with working-class contact. At that time the university functioned both as an educator and as a mobilizer of revolution, with teachers and students learning from each other. Martínez Villena's university experience led him to communist militancy, and in 1927 he joined the Communist Party. Describes also his role in the 1930 general strike.   D. Wasserstein

1561.   Perez, Louis A., Jr.   ARMY POLITICS, DIPLOMACY AND THE COLLAPSE OF THE CUBAN OFFICER CORPS: THE "SER-GEANTS' REVOLT" OF 1933. *J. of Latin Am. Studies [Great Britain] 1974 6(1): 59-76.* Commissioner Sergio Carbó of the unrecognized *Pentarguía* government promoted Sergeant Fulgencio Batista to colonel 8 September 1933 and appointed him Chief of Staff of the Army, "charging him to commission the officers required to preserve the integrity of the armed institution." Batista and other sergeants, corporals, and enlisted men organized a protest group at Camp Columbia on 3 September; they were joined on 4 September by civilians from the *Directorio Estudiantil Universitario.* They moved into the presidential palace later that day when a new government was declared and immediately sent directives throughout the island to noncommissioned officers and enlisted men to relieve their superiors of command. Ambassador Sumner Welles' support for the old (all-white) officer corps, together with the officers' reliance upon Welles, practically guaranteed the success of this accidental coup d'etat by "the sergeants," which was in full control by October. Primary and secondary works; 83 notes.   K. M. Bailor

1562.   Pérez, Louis A., Jr.   ARMY POLITICS IN SOCIALIST CUBA. *J. of Latin Am. Studies [Great Britain] 1976 8(2): 251-271.* The militarization of Cuban life in the 1970's began in 1956-58 in the Sierra Maestra. Military necessity demanded that the rebel army assume administrative control of civilian institutions in liberated areas such as schools, hospitals, and taxes. Between 1959 and 1961, political instability—domestic and international—forced Fidel Castro to use his veterans as the major political educators of the new Cuba. Between 1961 and 1970, production imperatives brought the veterans' experiences, rhetoric, discipline, and precision into every area and facet of Cuban life. Cuba in the 1970's is the rebel army experience, professionalized and modernized. Based on speeches, periodicals, literature, and secondary works; 67 notes.
                                                    K. M. Bailor

1563.   Perez, Louis A., Jr.   CAPITAL, BUREAUCRATS, AND POL-ICY: THE ECONOMIC CONTOURS OF UNITED STATES-CUBAN RELATIONS, 1916-1921. *Inter-Am. Econ. Affairs 1975 29(1): 65-80.* Discusses the interrelationship of US foreign policymakers and Americans associated with the rise of the Cuban sugar industry. Concludes that US foreign policy served the interests of Cuban and US financial and corporate interests. Primary and secondary sources; 3 notes.
                                                    D. A. Franz

1564.   Pérez, Louis A., Jr.   FULGENCIO BATISTA (1933-1939). *Rev. Interamericana [Puerto Rico] 1977 7(3): 361-371.* The bankruptcy of Cuba's social, economic, and political institutions as well as Fulgencio Batista's own organizational skills brought about his rise to political prominence, 1933-39. He used the army in promoting health, welfare, and

educational projects, which caused it to emerge as a modernizing elite. Military involvement in foreign relations (especially in economic relations with the United States) stabilized the government in a manner acceptable to world powers.   G. A. Hewlett

1565.   Pérez, Louis A., Jr.   IN THE SERVICE OF THE REVOLU-TION: TWO DECADES OF CUBAN HISTORIOGRAPHY, 1959-1979. *Hispanic Am. Hist. Rev. 1980 60(1): 79-89.* Cuban revisionist historians in the period 1900-59 emphasized the struggle against imperialism and exploitation. This concept of Cuban history has continued and has been used by Fidel Castro's government to unify all Cubans in support of the revolutionary government. Themes of struggle and continuity are salient features of historiography in today's Cuba where history is used by the state. Primary sources; 20 notes.   B. D. Johnson

1566.   Perez, Louis A., Jr.   "LA CHAMBELONA": POLITICAL PROTEST, SUGAR, AND SOCIAL BANDITRY IN CUBA, 1914-1917. *Inter-American Econ. Affairs 1978 31(4): 3-27.* Discusses the growth of the sugar industry in eastern Cuba and explores the relationship between the impact of sugar production and the Liberal uprising, *La Chambelona,* 1917. 80 notes.   D. A. Franz

1567.   Perez, Louis A., Jr.   THE PLATT AMENDMENT AND DYS-FUNCTIONAL POLITICS IN CUBA: THE ELECTORAL CRISES OF 1916-1917. *West Georgia Coll. Studies in the Social Sci. 1978 17: 49-60.* Announcement in 1915 of Mario G. Menocal's intention to seek reelection in 1916 set off a chain of political events reflecting fierce intraelite struggles for political hegemony in Cuba, in which each faction used the threat of American intervention under the Platt Amendment to gain political primacy.

1568.   Perez, Louis A., Jr.   SCHOLARSHIP AND THE STATE: NOTES ON *A HISTORY OF THE CUBAN REPUBLIC. Hispanic Am. Hist. R. 1974 54(4): 682-690.* Provides background notes to the writing of *A History of the Cuban Republic* (reprint, New York, 1969) by Charles E. Chapman, a project begun in the early 1920's with US government support. Chapman encountered difficulties with the State Department and Cuba over specific issues and interpretations, especially his criticism of the Cuban administration for corruption. The book "represents an early effort to employ scholarship in the pursuit of state policy." Based on the Enoch H. Crowder Papers at the University of Missouri, the Dwight Morrow Papers at Amherst College, and secondary sources; 35 notes.   N. J. Street

1569.   Perez, Louis A., Jr.   WOMEN IN THE REVOLUTIONARY WAR, 1953-1958: A BIBLIOGRAPHY. *Sci. & Soc. 1975 39(1): 104-108.* Compiles as completely as possible a collection of sources available in the United States dealing with the role of women in the Cuban revolutionary movement. It mainly covers materials printed during 1959-73 as available in the Center for Cuban Studies, the Library of Congress, the Hoover Institution and the University of Florida Library.
                                                    N. Lederer

1570.   Pérez, Luis A., Jr.   THE MILITARY AND POLITICAL AS-PECTS OF THE 1933 CUBAN REVOLUTION: THE FALL OF MA-CHADO. *Americas (Acad. of Am. Franciscan Hist.) 1974 31(2): 172-184.* Faced with economic crisis and growing political discontent, the regime of President Gerardo Machado (1871-1939) relied increasingly on the military forces to maintain control. This in turn fomented antimilitarism among both opponents of the government and "old line politicians." US pressure in 1933 upon Machado to resign was ostensibly justified by unsettled conditions in Cuba, but carried implicit a threat of open US intervention. Cuban armed forces forestalled this and other perceived dangers by moving to overthrow Machado themselves. Based on US archives and printed sources; 52 notes.   D. Bushnell

1571.   Pérez, Nancy.   ¿FUERON CELEBRADOS LOS CAR-NAVALES SANTIAGUEROS EN 1957? [Was the Santiago carnival celebrated in 1957?]. *Santiago [Cuba] 1981 (43): 69-105.* In 1957 the traditional carnival festivities in Santiago were to be renounced by the population due to the conditions created by the struggle against the government of Fulgencio Batista, but the authorities insisted that they take place. Examining all the relevant documentation of the times the author argues that although the carnival activities did take place, there cannot be said to have been a celebration. 30 notes.
                                                    J. V. Coutinho

1572.   Pérez-López, Jorge F. and Pérez-López, René.   A CALENDAR OF CUBAN BILATERAL AGREEMENTS 1959-1975: DESCRIPTION AND USES.   *Cuban Studies 1977 7(2): 167-182.* An introduction to a soon-to-be published list of all public, nonmilitary treaties made by Cuba under Fidel Castro. Cuban treaties since 1959 show that country to be the recipient in its agreements with developed nations and donor in its agreements with most Third World nations. Based on selected Cuban sources; 3 tables, 20 notes.   J. A. Lewis

1573.   Perez-Lopez, Jorge F.   NUCLEAR POWER IN CUBA: OPPORTUNITIES AND CHALLENGES.   *Orbis 1982 26(2): 495-516.* Examines Cuba's energy problems and its attempt to develop nuclear power with the help of the USSR and its Council for Mutual Economic Assistance (Comecon) since 1974. With no energy source of its own, Cuba has been forced to import large amounts of oil from the USSR to run its growing industrial plant, so in 1974 it decided to build a nuclear power plant, which is due to be completed in 1989 but is behind schedule. The Cubans' difficulties in building such a plant and the effects of the nuclear nonproliferation policy are examined. Based on published sources; 73 notes.   J. W. Thacker, Jr.

1574.   Pérez-Stable, Marifeli.   TOWARDS A MARXIST SCHOOL OF CUBAN STUDIES.   *Latin Am. Res. Rev. 1980 15(2): 248-256.* Reviews eight works which, with one exception, analyze facets of Cuba since the Castro revolution. A Marxist analysis of Cuba is urgently needed to offer an alternative to the dominant social science paradigm which has shaped Cuban studies. 6 notes.   J. K. Pfabe

1575.   Pérez-Stable, Marifeli.   WHITHER THE CUBAN WORKING CLASS.   *Latin Am. Perspectives 1975 2(4): 60-77.* Analyzes the labor movement in Cuba, 1959-73, especially the actions of the Confederación de Trabajadores de Cuba, 1959-70 and changes in bureaucracy, planning, and incentives 1970-73.

1576.   Pino-Santos, Oscar.   INTERVENCIONISMO YANQUI EN CUBA: DE MAGOON A BATISTA [Yankee interventionism in Cuba: From Magoon to Batista].   *Casa de las Américas [Cuba] 1973 14(80): 48-61.* Discusses US interventionism in Cuba in two separate periods: the semicolonial period (1902-33) and the neocolonial period (1934-58), emphasizing the response of the Cuban governments involved to US intervention in the different periods.

1577.   Piper, Don C.   THE CUBAN MISSILE CRISIS AND INTERNATIONAL LAW: PRECIPITOUS DECLINE OR UNILATERAL DEVELOPMENT.   *World Affairs 1975 138(1): 26-31.* Treats the incident with reference to the unilateral assertion of new rules by national decisionmakers.   S

1578.   Pollack, Benny.   MASS DEMOCRACY IN CUBA.   *Government and Opposition [Great Britain] 1977 12(4): 530-533.* Reviews Samuel Farber's *Revolution and Reaction in Cuba, 1933-1960, A Political Sociology from Machado to Castro* (1976).

1579.   Portuondo, José Antonio.   PABLO DE LA TORRIENTE, COMISARIO POLITICO [Pablo de la Torriente, political commissar].   *Santiago [Cuba] 1976 (23): 9-24.* Pablo de la Torriente was born in Puerto Rico, but moved around in various countries with his family, until settling finally in Cuba. In 1931-32 he was briefly detained for his revolutionary activities and wrote a book about his prison experiences. Deported from Cuba as an alien, he managed to return as a journalist. The suppression of the 1935 general strike led to his departure for New York, where he founded an anti-imperialist party. He has been compared with the Briton Christopher Caudwell, another author, killed in 1937 in the Spanish Civil War.   D. Wasserstein

1580.   Radosh, Ronald.   ON THE CUBAN REVOLUTION.   *Dissent 1976 23(3): 309-315.* Review article on Herbert L. Matthews' *Revolution in Cuba: An Essay in Understanding* (New York: Scribner's, 1975) and four other recent works on Cuba since the 1969 revolution. This recent group of books coincides with a softening of US policy toward Cuba.

1581.   Randall, Margaret.   LA MUJER CUBANA EN 1974 [The Cuban woman in 1974].   *Casa de las Américas [Cuba] 1975 15(88): 63-72.*

Studies the impact of the Cuban revolution on the status of women from 1971 to 1974. First the revolution had to resolve military and economic priorities and then address cultural problems, such as *machismo*. Progress in the liberation of women has been achieved both through public awareness and legal changes, such as elimination of job classifications based on sex and application of vagrancy laws equally to men and women. To assure greater opportunities for women in the labor force, women and men must share household duties equally, a spirit evident in the revision of the Family Code. Despite shortcomings, the revolution is effecting a true democratization for both men and women.
                                    H. J. Miller

1582.   Randall, Margaret.   VENCEREMOS: WOMEN IN THE NEW CUBA.   *Can. Dimension 1975 10(8): 49-55.*

1583.   Rincón, Carlos.   SOBRE ALEJO CARPENTIER Y LA POÉTICA DE LO REAL MARAVILLOSO AMERICANO   [On Alejo Carpentier and the poetry of America's marvelous reality].   *Casa de las Américas [Cuba] 1975 15(89): 40-65.* Discusses the life and works of Alejo Carpentier (b. 1904), Cuban novelist and essayist, stressing his ideological and artistic commitment to the Cuban revolution.

1584.   Ripoll, Carols.   THE CUBAN SCENE: CENSORS AND DISSENTERS.   *Partisan Rev. 1981 48(4): 574-587.* The Cuban Revolution is a tragically familiar story. Born with high revolutionary idealism, the Communists, with Castro's blessing, brought all aspects of Cuban life and culture under the state's control. Liberals suffered. The State became an end in itself; dissenters were jailed. The censors became the new cultural hero. Castro is a Latin American Stalin. All cultural activities became the handmaidens of state policy and objectives. It is a well known and sad history.   D. K. Pickens

1585.   Ritter, Archibald R. M.   THE CUBAN REVOLUTION: A NEW ORIENTATION.   *Current Hist. 1978 74(434): 53-56, 83-87.* Assesses the evolution of politics, economy, and government in Cuba during the 1970's, an evolution that points toward more popular voice in local politics and economic development decisions.

1586.   Ritter, Archibald R. M.   THE TRANSFERABILITY OF SOCIOECONOMIC DEVELOPMENT MODELS OF REVOLUTIONARY CUBA.   *Cuban Studies 1977 7(2): 183-204.* There has always been a messianic side to the Cuban Revolution which wished to expand the Cuban developmental model to other nations. Certain aspects of the revolution seem applicable to other societies, but there are many parts of the revolution that are so uniquely Cuban that their usefulness elsewhere is open to question. 24 notes.   J. A. Lewis

1587.   Roa, Raúl.   LAS PRIMAVERAS DE RUBÉN MARTÍNEZ VILLENA   [The spring of Rubén Martínez Villena].   *Santiago [Cuba] 1974 (16): 9-41.* The life of Rubén Martínez Villena, a communist and poet, in particular his education, political awakening, and discovery of communism. In 1922 he qualified as a lawyer and defended victims of government oppression. His political activity began in 1923 with the writing of articles and verse. He was arrested in the United States, but released and returned to Cuba, where he continued his writing and revolutionary activities. From 1926 he was frequently ill. He was a member of the Central Committee of the Cuban Communist Party and the main organizer of the 1930 general strike.   D. Wasserstein

1588.   Roca, Blas.   HISTORYCZNE DOŚWIADCZENIA REWOLUCJI KUBAŃSKIEJ [Historical experiences of the Cuban Revolution].   *Nowe Drogi [Poland] 1974 (6): 114-124.* Analyzes the Cuban Revolution, 1956-58, outlining the favorable domestic and international conditions, the effect of the attack on the Moncada Barracks, the participation of the masses, and the support of the USSR in bringing about the revolution's socialist phase.

1589.   Roca, Blas.   SPECIFIC FEATURES OF THE SOCIALIST DEMOCRACY OF CUBA.   *World Marxist Rev. [Canada] 1977 20(2): 14-20.* Discusses the evolution of popular rule in Cuba, 1960-76, through the institution of elections and revitalization and change within the administration of the socialist democracy.

1590. Roca, Sergio. CUBAN ECONOMIC POLICY IN THE 1970'S: THE TRODDEN PATHS. *Studies in Comparative Int. Development 1977 12(1): 86-114.* Explores the genesis, features, and high cost of the Guevara Moral Economic Model, which was characterized as a failure. Examines the process of change back to an older model and analyzes Cuban efforts to decentralize planning and management, utilize traditional methods of control, and renew the use of material incentives. In the course of rectifying the excesses of the moral economy Cuban communism has evolved from moral economics and pragmatic politics to moral politics and pragmatic economics with the latter subsidizing the former. This has forced dependence on Russia. The model is now the heroic guerrilla instead of the new man. It is too early to assess the results of the change. Primary sources; list of abbreviations, 2 tables, 7 notes, 52 refs.
S. A. Farmerie

1591. Roca, Sergio. REVOLUTIONARY CUBA. *Current Hist. 1981 80(463): 53-56, 84.* Assesses economic problems in Cuba during the late 1970's and their effect on domestic politics, and gives a brief overview of Cuba's internationalist and pro-Soviet foreign policy.

1592. Rodman, Peter W. THE MISSILES OF OCTOBER: TWENTY YEARS LATER. *Commentary 1982 74(4): 39-45.* An analysis of the Cuban missile crisis of October 1962, limited US objectives, and the reaction of the USSR. The crisis stimulated movement toward arms control and cooperation.

1593. Rodríguez, Carlos Rafael. EMILIO ROIG DE LEUCHSENRING [Emilio Roig de Leuchsenring]. *Islas [Cuba] 1980 (67): 169-178.* Emilio Roig de Leuchsenring was a forerunner of Cuba's socialist revolution, active since the 1920's with Alejo Carpentier, Juan Marinello, and Rubén Martínez Villena. Internationalist and revolutionary, he accepted V. I. Lenin's indictment of imperialism and was anticlerical because the Church was at the service of the oligarchy and thus of the Platt Amendment.

1594. Rodriguez, Ernesto E. PUBLIC OPINION AND THE PRESS IN CUBA. *Cuban Studies 1978 8(2): 51-65.* A statistical survey of the letters to the editor's column of *Granma,* 1974-76, official newspaper of the Cuban Communist Party, reveals that the values of the new socialist man have not yet been instilled in Cuba. Most Cubans are concerned with consumer problems, a characteristic of citizens in many capitalist countries. Primary sources; 2 tables, 33 notes, biblio.   J. Lewis

1595. Rodríguez Loeches, Enrique. UNA RADIO CLANDESTINA [A clandestine radio]. *Rev. de la Biblioteca Nac. José Martí [Cuba] 1980 22(2): 91-111.* Students opposed to the Fulgencio Batista coup of 1952 in Cuba operated an antigovernment radio station.   J. A. Lewis

1596. Rodríguez San Pedro, María del Carmen. LA ARTESANÍA EN CUBA SOCIALISTA [Arts and crafts in socialist Cuba]. *Rev. de la Biblioteca Nac. José Martí [Cuba] 1979 21(2): 103-118.* Because of governmental interest, popular arts and crafts have gone through a period of considerable growth since 1959. These arts and crafts reflect the spirit of the people and serve a useful purpose.   J. A. Lewis

1597. Rojas, Marta. 2 DE DICIEMBRE DE 1956. SE CUMPLÍA LA SEGUNDA PREMISA: LLEGAR [The second of December 1956. The fulfillment of the second premise: the arrival]. *Casa de las Américas [Cuba] 1976 16(99): 96-99.* Narrates Fidel Castro's activities in 1956 while he was in exile in Mexico. He faced the harassment of Batista spies and the vigilance of the Mexican police, which resulted in the arrest of several supporters. Their freedom was regained through the intervention of Lázaro Cárdenas. Castro had selected Mexico as the most convenient place to train a small expeditionary force to liberate Cuba. Members of the force included Raúl Castro, Antonio López, and Ernesto Che Guevara. In November 1956, a group of 82 men left for Cuba—the fulfillment of Castro's promise to return and liberate Cuba from the Batista dictatorship.   H. J. Miller

1598. Ronfeldt, David F. SUPERCLIENTS AND SUPERPOWERS: CUBA: SOVIET UNION/IRAN: UNITED STATES. *Conflict 1979 1(4): 273-302.* Discusses the military, geopolitical, and strategic significance of Cuba and Iran to the USSR and the United States during the 1970's.

1599. Rouquié, Alain. CUBA DANS LES RELATIONS INTERNATIONALES: PREMIERS ROLES ET VULNERABILITE [Cuba's foreign relations: initial roles and vulnerability]. *Problèmes d'Amérique Latine [France] 1982 (64): 81-90.* Explores Cuba's multiple roles on the international scene and the apparent contradiction between revolutionary language and the interests of the state, and the socialist state as it related to the USSR.

1600. Safford, Jeffrey J. THE NIXON-CASTRO MEETING OF 19 APRIL 1959. *Diplomatic Hist. 1980 4(4): 425-431.* Reprints the text of a memorandum written by US Vice-President Richard Nixon on his conversation with Cuban revolutionary Fidel Castro during the latter's visit to the United States in 1959. Nixon judged Castro as non-Communist, but "incredibly naive with regard to the Communist threat"; praised his "indefinable qualities which make him a leader of men"; and criticized his "almost slavish subservience to prevailing majority opinion," his shallow understanding of how to run a government or an economy, and his reluctance to welcome American investment in Cuba. In addition, the document reveals Nixon's concept of leadership. 5 notes.
T. L. Powers

1601. Salas, Argeo. DISTINGUIDOS CORRELIGIONARIOS... [Distinguished coreligionists...]. *Santiago [Cuba] 1973 (10): 137-150.* Analyzes the electoral situation, especially municipal level returns and electoral malpractices, in the province of Oriente, Cuba, 1902-25. Discusses the varying political attitudes of three cities, Santiago de Cuba, Holguín, and Guantánamo, which dominated the administrative and economic life of Oriente through the republican period. Based on documents in the Archivo Histórico Provincial of Santiago de Cuba; table, 6 notes.
D. Wasserstein

1602. Sánchez, Germán. EL MONCADA: CRISIS DEL SISTEMA NEOCOLONIAL, INICIO DE LA REVOLUCIÓN LATINOAMERICANA [Moncada: the crisis of the neocolonial system, the beginning of the Latin American revolution]. *Casa de las Américas [Cuba] 1973 14(79): 44-90.* Gives an economic and political history of Cuba, 1934-53, showing how the assault on Moncada barracks was the culmination of the failures of imperialism in Cuba and stressing the importance of Moncada in light of subsequent revolutionary events.

1603. Sánchez Bermúdez, Juan Alberto. POLITICA ECONOMICA Y SOCIAL DEL GOBIERNO DE MACHADO [Social and economic policies of Machado's government]. *Islas [Cuba] 1981 (68): 151-161.* Through the Platt Amendment and the treaty of Reciprocity, the United States dominated the Cuban economy and Gerardo Machado and the ruling oligarchy were obliged to maneuver to survive without offending US interests.

1604. Sarracino, Rodolfo. LOS ASESORES YANQUIS Y LA REFORMA TRIBUTARIA EN LA DÉCADA DEL 30 [US advisers and tax reform in the 1930's]. *Rev. de la Biblioteca Nac. José Martí [Cuba] 1978 20(3): 131-148.* The Cuban government contracted US economists in 1932 and 1939 to advise on improvement of the fiscal and tax system of Cuba. The recommendations of Edwin Seligman in 1932 and Roswell Magill and Carl Shoup in 1939 differ in reflecting the influence of the New Deal, but both studies concluded that administrative corruption was extensive and that either the state must reform or increased taxation would continue. Based on primary sources; 3 tables, 38 notes.   R. D. Rodríguez

1605. Sass, U. and Holtz, C. DIE KUBANISCHE REVOLUTION IN DEN WERKEN VON JOSÉ SOLER PUIG [The Cuban revolution in the works of José Soler Puig]. *Lateinamerika [East Germany] 1978 (Fall): 25-34.* José Soler Puig in his works signals a new direction and depth in Cuban national literature: a commitment to illuminate and discuss the material needs of the common people and the socialist vision to cope with them.

1606. Savin, V. M. and Torshin, M. P. A. GARSIA, P. MIRONCHUK: OKTIABR'SKAIA REVOLIUTSIIA I EE VLIIANIE NA KUBU. GABANA 1977 [A. Garcia and P. Mironchik's *The October Revolution and its Influence on Cuba* (Havana, 1977)]. *Istoriia SSSR [USSR] 1979 (1): 236-238.* Reviews *La Revolución de Octubre y su influencia en Cuba.* From the moment of its creation Soviet Russia has

exerted a great influence on the development of the working class movement in Latin America. In Cuba the ideas of the Russian Revolution accompanied the working class in all the phases of its struggle for national independence which culminated in the Revolution of 1959. 5 notes.
J. M. Chambers

1607. Segal, Aaron. DANCE AND DIPLOMACY: THE CUBAN NATIONAL BALLET. *Caribbean Rev. 1980 9(1): 30-32.* Led by Alicia Alonso, the Cuban National Ballet is the only Caribbean cultural group to win international acclaim; it has been concerned with expressing Cuban culture rather than ideology, and owes its success to government support and broad recruitment of dancers from all sections of society.

1608. Seraev, S. A. KOOPERIROVANIE MELKIKH SEMLEDEL'TSEV V RESPUBLIKE KUBA [Cooperation of small farmers in Cuba]. *Voprosy Istorii [USSR] 1979 (7): 76-85.* As distinct from the USSR and some other socialist countries, the restructuring of the system of farming along socialist lines in Cuba began with the creation of a powerful state sector in agriculture. Parallel with this sector there exists a considerable number of small and middle farmers in Cuban agriculture. At its First Congress in 1975 the Communist Party of Cuba adopted a decision steadfastly to pursue a policy of uniting small peasant farms in agricultural cooperatives side by side with integrating their land into state farms. The appropriate material, technical, social and political prerequisites have been created in Cuba for the voluntary and gradual production cooperation of the mass of small farmers. J

1609. Sergeev, F. OPERATSIIA V ZALIVE KOCHINOS [Operation in the Bay of Pigs]. *Novaia i Noveishaia Istoriia [USSR] 1981 (4): 129-142, (5): 116-135.* Part 1. Surveys the history of Cuba since the takeover by Fulgencio Batista in March 1952 and analyzes the efforts by the US government and the sugar monopolies to undermine the regime of Fidel Castro. The USSR provided economic assistance to Cuba to counter the blackmail of the United States. When it became clear that economic blockade could not destabilize Castro's regime, the United States resorted to organizing an invasion by Cuban emigres. President-elect John F. Kennedy was informed of the preparations and sanctioned them. There was disagreement about the precise date of the invasion and the president hesitated, preferring to continue with preparations. Part 2. In early April 1961 the CIA decided that the invasion was adequately prepared. The military planners concluded that the invasion should take place at night in the area of the Bay of Pigs. Further progress would be made with the help of tanks. The invasion was to be supported by air attacks. The invaders miscalculated, thinking they would be supported by the Cuban population, and they underestimated the preparedness of the revolutionary government. The invasion took place on 16-17 April and on the 19th it was clear that the counterrevolution would fail. The Cuban revolution won an important military and moral victory. Based on US, Cuban, Soviet, and other press and secondary sources; 87 notes.
V. Sobell

1610. Shcheglov, A. BOR'BA ZA ARMIIU V KHODE KUBINSKOI REVOLIUTSII [The struggle for the army during the Cuban revolution]. *Voenno-Istoricheskii Zhurnal [USSR] 1980 22(12): 40-45.* An analysis of the role played by the Cuban army during the revolution. Western writers who claim that one of the first tasks of the Cuban insurgents was to exterminate Batista's army are wrong. They were changed from an antipopular force led by American advisers by a sustained propaganda campaign and reeducation of deserters and prisoners. Based on published sources in Spanish and Russian; 19 notes.
D. N. Collins

1611. Shcheglov, A. OB IDEINOI ZAKALKE KUBINSKIKH VOINOV [The ideological training of Cuban soldiers]. *Voenno-Istoricheskii Zhurnal [USSR] 1979 21(1): 64-68.* Political education of the Cuban army has been vital since the start of the anti-Batista struggle. Organs of agitation and propaganda included *El Cubano Libre,* first published in 1956, and Radio Rebelde, which went on the air in 1958. Until Batista's defeat ideological education was subordinated to the main objective, the earliest possible overthrow of the regime. After the Castro movement took power, political education was combined with the drive against illiteracy. By the end of 1966, all military and naval units had Communist Party organizations within them, and by 1976 86% of the armed forces officers were members of the Party or of the Union of Young Communists. 16 notes.
P. R. Taylor

1612. Shelnin, E. SOZDANIE MATERIAL'NO-TEKHNICHESKOI BAZY SOTSIALIZMA NA KUBE [The creation of a material and technical basis of socialism in Cuba]. *Voprosy Ekonomiki [USSR] 1976 (6): 80-89.* Post-revolutionary figures, 1962-75, indicate economic growth in Cuba which has proved to be a major condition for the creation of socialism.

1613. Silverman, Bertram. A NEW DIRECTION IN CUBAN SOCIALISM. *Current Hist. 1975 68(401): 24-28, 38, 42.* Notes the economic strategy of Cuba since 1963 and Castro's 1970 Work Organization and Work Norms plan. S

1614. Sokolova, Z. I. SOVETSKAIA ISTORIOGRAFIIA KUBINSKOI REVOLIUTSII [Soviet historiography of the Cuban revolution]. *Voprosy Istorii [USSR] 1980 (11): 33-44.* Deals with the works by Soviet historians on the problems of the Cuban revolution and gives an assessment of the contribution made by each of them to the study of various aspects of the development of the revolutionary process in Cuba. The author pays particular attention to the study by Soviet historiographers of such cardinal problems as the revolutionary situation of the 1950's and the character and the driving forces of the Cuban revolution. J

1615. Sommerfeld, Piotr. PARTIA KOMUNISTYCZNA W SYSTEMIE PARTYJNO-POLITYCZNYM KUBY W LATACH 1939-1947 [The Communist Party in Cuba party political systems, 1939-47]. *Z Pola Walki [Poland] 1980 23(2): 45-68.* Describes the activities of the Communist Party in Cuba as it took on the characteristics of a mass party after the passage of the bourgeois-democratic constitution of 1940 enabled it to be legally active and participate as a member of the ruling alliance.

1616. Sommerfeld, Piotr. STRATEGIA I TAKTYKA SOCJALISTYCZNEJ PARTII LUDOWEJ KUBY W LATACH 1952-1959 [Strategic and tactical lines of the Socialist People's Party of Cuba, 1952-59]. *Z Pola Walki [Poland] 1977 (2): 29-56.* The 1952 coup d'etat of Fulgencio Batista was founded on internal Cuban tensions together with the US tendency to rely on dictatorial governments in satellite countries. Acting illegally after 1953 the Socialist People's Party (SPL) opposed the coup and led the working class in the struggle for democracy, Cuban sovereignty, and socialism. It established grass roots organizations with the working class as the base and organized political action and protest strikes in support of the 26th July insurgents. Its tactic was to develop a broad political struggle. The SPL leadership and guerrilla headquarters established close contacts. Success crowned the unity of action between the SPL and the July 26th Movement with the fall of the Batista regime in early 1959. Strengthening the unity of revolutionary forces became the main task of the SPL.
J/S

1617. Sorhegui, Arturo, and Quiñones, Mirna. EL TRATADO HAY-QUESADA; CONSIDERACIONES HISTÓRICAS [The Hay-Quesada Treaty: historical considerations]. *Rev. de la Biblioteca Nac. José Martí [Cuba] 1980 22(1): 151-171.* One objective of American expansion in the Caribbean was the Isle of Pines, an island close to Cuba. At several points before the ratification of the Hay-Quesada Treaty in 1925, the United States considered annexing the island. This interest in Cuban territory helped radicalize public opinion in Cuba against the United States. 3 tables, 2 charts, 15 notes.
J. A. Lewis

1618. Statsenco, Igor. SOBRE ALGUNOS ASPECTOS POLÍTICO-MILITARES DE LA CRISIS DEL CARIBE [Political-military aspects of the Caribbean crisis]. *Am. Latina [USSR] 1978 (3): 140-150.* After US-trained Cuban exiles failed at the Bay of Pigs in 1961 and in response to Soviet military aid sent to Cuba, especially missiles, US reinforcements were sent to Guantanamo naval base, reserves were called up, and a blockade ("quarantine") was put around Cuba. The actions of the US government frightened many of its own citizens. But the USSR stood firm and the UN called on the countries involved to settle the crisis peacefully. The Soviet Union saved the Cuban revolution. Contrary to US propaganda, Soviet missiles in Cuba did not cause the crisis, but were the response to US threats against the Cuban revolution. Note.
J. D. Barnard

1619. Steinberg, Blema S. GOALS IN CONFLICT: ESCALATION, CUBA, 1961. *Can. J. of Pol. Sci. [Canada] 1981 14(1): 83-105.* Studies of dyadic interstate conflict assume that a state's coercive behavior is a function either of its opponent's behavior (an open or stimulus-response model) or its own prior behavior (a closed or organizational process model). Both approaches largely ignore the role of purpose—the goals articulated by decisionmakers. Quantitative and qualitative analysis of the Cuban missile crisis in the light of Soviet and American goals suggests that increases in their coercive behavior were a product of a mixture of prior incompatible objectives and conflict behavior and that both parties contributed mutually to escalating the conflict. Behavior models alone are inadequate to explain either country's conflict actions; objectives add an important dimension. Fig., 3 tables, 55 notes.　　　　K. E. Miller

1620. Stepan, Alfred. MAKERS OF THE 20TH CENTURY: CASTRO. *Hist. Today [Great Britain] 1981 31(May): 26-30.* Reexamines Fidel Castro's activity and role in the Cuban revolution, and argues that the official Cuban version of the revolution, Régis Débray's *Revolution in the Revolution?* (1967), which stresses the military aspects of the struggle against Batista, neglects the political tactics used by Castro in his march to power and seriously distorts our view of his achievements.

1621. Surí Quesada, Emilio. EL MEJOR HOMBRE DE LA GUERRILLA [The best man in the guerrilla movement]. *Casa de las Américas [Cuba] 1981 21(124): 142-145.* Pays tribute to the memory of a fighter variously called Cachungo, Capitán San Luis, and Rolando during the revolutionary guerrilla war in Cuba.　　　　J. V. Coutinho

1622. Swan, Harry. THE NINETEEN TWENTIES: A DECADE OF INTELLECTUAL CHANGE IN CUBA. *Rev. Interamericana [Puerto Rico] 1978 8(2): 275-288.* The so-called Generation of 1923 was united only in that it opposed foreign intrusion and administrative corruption, and never on the means to achieve their ends. This generation did, however, succeed in spreading political activity beyond the island's elite to the lower classes. 42 notes.　　　　J. Lewis

1623. Sweezy, Paul M. FIFTEENTH AND TWENTIETH ANNIVERSARIES FOR CUBA. *Monthly R. 1973 25(4): 23-27.* Briefly discusses the Cuban socialist revolution and the country's foreign relations and politics, 1953-73.　　　　S

1624. Tamayo, Irma. LA REFORMA AGRARIA EN CUBA [Agricultural reform in Cuba]. *Santiago [Cuba] 1976 (21): 175-194.* Agrarian reform has been an important element of social change in Cuba. In the last 20 years before the revolution, agriculture was in the hands of a small oligarchy, and many latifundia existed even though the 1940 constitution had outlawed them. Half a million workers became landless laborers after 1952, when monopolies began to operate. The 1959 and 1963 laws of agrarian reform replaced the latifundia system with a two-tier system of large and small estates, partly state and partly privately owned. 4 tables, biblio.　　　　D. Wasserstein

1625. Thomas, Hugh. CASTRO PLUS 20: CUBA'S MARTIAL APOTHEOSIS. *Encounter [Great Britain] 1978 51(4): 112-120.* Discusses the regime of Cuba's Fidel Castro, with regard to the country's economy and political structure since his ascent to power in 1959.

1626. Thomas, Hugh. THE U.S. AND CASTRO, 1959-1962. *Am. Heritage 1978 29(6): 26-35.* Castro, a caudillo, needed and used the support of Cuban communists from the beginning of his revolution. Until the revolution the United States played a negligible role in Cuba. Castro's background and personality combined with strong anti-Americanism to lead to his public declaration in 1961 of his Marxist position. 7 illus.　　　　J. F. Paul

1627. Toro, Carlos del. CARLOS BALIÑO, PERSEVERANTE PUBLICISTA DE LAS IDEAS REVOLUCIONARIAS [Carlos Baliño, constant advocate of revolutionary ideas]. *Santiago [Cuba] 1975 (20): 261-268.* Carlos Benigno Baliño López left Cuba in 1869 for political exile. He established contact with other exiles involved in revolutionary activities, was active in the formation of political parties and clubs, and supported the Russian Revolution of 1917. Baliño played an important part in the Communist congress of 1925 in Cuba. Analyzes his short story, *El Militarista.*　　　　D. Wasserstein

1628. Toro, Carlos del. LOS PROBLEMAS FUNDAMENTALES DEL PUEBLO CUBANO EN "LA HISTORIA ME ABSOLVERÁ" [The fundamental problems of the Cuban people in "History will absolve me"]. *Acta U. Szegediensis de Attila József Nominatae: Acta Hist. [Hungary] 1980 68: 47-52.* In his historic speech delivered at his trial for assault on the Moncada garrison Fidel Castro touched on the fundamental problems of the Cuban people, unemployment, industrialization, housing, education, and public health. The constitutional and institutional decadence of the colonial republic demanded drastic changes, which began on 26 July 1953 and culminated with the triumph of the revolution on 1 January 1959.　　　　J. V. Coutinho

1629. Torres, Armando. LA RUTA DEL 26 [The route of the 26th]. *Santiago [Cuba] 1973 (11): 55-65.* A transcript of an April 1973 interview with Armando Torres, minister of justice in the Cuban revolutionary government. Discusses his revolutionary activities from 1952, student action before that date and reactions to the coup of 1952, his detention and interrogation in 1953, his contacts with other revolutionaries after 1956, the significance of unity both among revolutionaries and in the populace at large, underground activities, and his work for people detained during the Batista regime.　　　　D. Wasserstein

1630. Torriente Brau, Pablo de la. PABLO DE LA TORRIENTE BRAU, CONTRIBUCIÓN A SU BIBLIOGRAFÍA [Pablo de la Torriente Brau: a contribution to his bibliography]. *Rev. de la Biblioteca Nac. José Martí [Cuba] 1980 22(2): 17-39.* Publication of five previously unknown letters and two magazine articles by Pablo de la Torriente Brau (1901-36), a prominent Cuban revolutionary of the 1930's. Based on manuscripts in the Cuban National Library; note.　　　　J. A. Lewis

1631. Torriente-Brau, Zoe de la. MIS RECUERDOS DE PABLO EN SANTIAGO DE CUBA [My recollections of Pablo in Santiago de Cuba]. *Santiago [Cuba] 1976 (23): 25-46.* The life of the author, Pablo de la Torriente, by his sister. Describes his family influences on his intellectual development; the sports he played; his education, particularly under his father and other teachers; and his death in the defense of Madrid, 1936, against the Nationalists during the Spanish Civil War. He went to Spain originally as a reporter for various Communist Party papers, but soon became a soldier.　　　　D. Wasserstein

1632. Torshin, M. P. STANOVLENIE SOVETSKO-KUBINSKIKH EKONOMICHESKIKH I KUL'TURNYKH OTNOSHENII (1959-1965) [The formation of Soviet-Cuban economic and cultural relations, 1959-65]. *Istoriia SSSR [USSR] 1975 (5): 118-133.* Official diplomatic relations between the Soviet Union and Cuba were established in May 1960; the first trade contacts were established in October 1959. In February 1960, a five-year trade treaty was signed between the two countries, and Cuba obtained 100 million dollars worth of credit from the Soviet Union for the purchase of Soviet machinery and equipment. The Soviet Union bought Cuban sugar during 1960-67 at higher prices than prevalent on the world market, freeing Cuba from dependence on the US market. The Soviet Union also supplied Cuba with oil, making the oil boycott of Cuba by imperialist monopolies worthless. Many other treaties between the two countries followed, showing a wide range of contacts in all fields. Primary and secondary sources; 89 notes.

L. Kalinowski

1633. Travieso, Julio. EL VIAJE DE UN COMBATIENTE [The journey of a combatant]. *Santiago [Cuba] 1973 (11): 67-81.* Describes the revolutionary development of Oscar Quintela, a worker and trade unionist from a small village near Havana, Cuba. Repeatedly detained by the police for unionist work, he lost 15 pounds in a 50 day hunger strike in 1947, but won a 10% pay rise. At this time he got to know Fidel Castro and came to support him. On Fulgencio Batista's coup in 1953, he immediately called a strike at his factory; shortly thereafter a group of 10 Castro supporters began their revolutionary activities there, also taking part in the legendary attack on the Moncada barracks in 1953. Based on an interview with Oscar Quintela.　　　　D. Wasserstein

1634. Useem, Bert. PEASANT INVOLVEMENT IN THE CUBAN REVOLUTION. *J. of Peasant Studies [Great Britain] 1977 5(1): 99-111.* Existing explanations of peasant involvement in the Cuban revolution emphasize such sociopsychological factors as the peasants' purported "land hunger." An alternative explanation focuses on the meshing of a localized landlord-squatter conflict with a state-guerrilla conflict. The case study lends further evidence to the contention that explanations relying on social organisational factors, rather than state of mind factors, are better able to account for why people become involved in social movements. J

1635. Valdés, Nelson P. CUBA Y ANGOLA: UNA POLÍTICA DE SOLIDARIDAD INTERNACIONAL [Cuba and Angola: a policy of international solidarity]. *Estudios de Asia y África [Mexico] 1979 14(4): 601-668.* Shows the continuity of the foreign policy of revolutionary Cuba, especially in its relation to African liberation movements and briefly describes Cuba's relationships with the liberation movements in former Portuguese colonies, especially Angola. The real reason for Cuban assistance to Angola is revolutionary solidarity. 145 notes.
J. V. Coutinho

1636. Valdés, Nelson P. CUBA Y LA GUERRA ENTRE SO-MALIA Y ETIOPÍA [Cuba and the Somalia-Ethiopia war]. *Estudios de Asia y África [Mexico] 1979 14(2): 244-267.* Explores Cuba's relations with Somalia and Ethiopia and the reasons for its alliance with Ethiopia. Based on statements of Cuban officials published in the official press.
J. V. Coutinho

1637. Valdés, Nelson P. THE CUBAN REVOLUTION: ECO-NOMIC ORGANIZATION AND BUREAUCRACY. *Latin Am. Perspectives 1979 6(1): 13-37.* Overview of the Guevarist, Fidelista, and institutional policy models applied to the political and economic organization of Cuba. By 1978 the Cuban system had achieved a working communist ideal by trial and error. However, the risk of suffocation by bureaucracy which now comprises 25% of the total labor force, is real. 8 notes, biblio.
J. F. Vivian

1638. Valdés, Nelson P. REVOLUTION AND INSTITUTIONALI-ZATION IN CUBA. *Cuban Studies 1976 6(1): 1-38.* Cuban leaders have made a serious effort since 1970 to replace charismatic government by institutionalizing the revolution. Yet institutionalizing the revolution contains some serious dangers, chief of which is the possibility that the Cuban bureaucracy will become self-serving and isolated from the people. 78 notes.
J. A. Lewis

1639. Valdés Paz, Juan. NOTAS SOBRE LA SOCIALIZACIÓN DE LA PROPIEDAD EN CUBA [Notes about the socialization of property in Cuba]. *Estudios Sociales Centroamericanos [Costa Rica] 1980 9(27): 251-275.* The triumphant revolution permitted the initial development of economic and social transformation while the socialization of private property created the condition for economic transformation. Suppression of the private economic base of the propertied classes reenforced by migration simplified the Cuban social structure. The socialization of production and consumption has generated a theoretical material base of socialism guaranteeing the defense of the revolution and establishing social priorities. Based on Cuban publications; 8 tables, annex, 13 notes.
T. D. Schoonover

1640. Valenta, Jiri. THE SOVIET-CUBAN INTERVENTION, 1975. *Studies in Comparative Communism 1978 (1-2): 3-33.* Soviet military intervention in Angola was opportunistic, a response to American unwillingness to risk another Vietnam-like war in Angola and Chinese influence in Africa. Cuba acted not as a Soviet pawn but as an ally and gained much as a result. Soviet action demonstrated its ability to undertake large-scale airborne aid, sending $300 million. The Angolan situation is still muddled as a guerrilla war continues. The West's willingness to reduce the opportunities available to the USSR and Cuba may restrict future Soviet efforts in Africa. 72 notes.
D. Balmuth

1641. Varela, Teodosio. MONCADA—SYMBOL OF THE PEO-PLE'S HEROISM. *World Marxist R. [Canada] 1973 16(8): 122-125.*

1642. Vázquez, Antonio. CUARTEL MONCADA: REPRESIÓN VS. REVOLUCIÓN [Moncada barracks: repression versus revolution]. *Santiago [Cuba] 1973 (11): 9-32.* The history of the Moncada barracks in Santiago, 1859-1960. The barracks, also a military hospital and prison, served as an assembly point for troops during all major insurrections after 1870. They also played an important role in the city's defense during the War of Independence, and later housed various regiments. In 1953 Fidel

Castro led an unsuccessful but legendary attack on it. Table, 49 notes.
D. Wasserstein

1643. Vellinga, M. L. THE MILITARY AND THE DYNAMICS OF THE CUBAN REVOLUTIONARY PROCESS. *Comparative Pol. 1976 8(2): 245-271.* Examines the Cuban military sector and its relation to society at large. Analyzes the development of a new type of military organization, military professionalism, and the development of a new formula to explain the relationship of the armed forces and the state. The Cubans emphasized the militia over the regular army because it was supposedly a better defensive weapon and had a greater social and political goal. Castro introduced compulsory military service as a leveling device as well as for defensive purposes, and attached the military career to the continuation of the Cuban revolution. Therefore, the military sector provides an area for the maintenance and spread of ideology. 83 notes.
R. I. Vexler

1644. Vladimirov, V. "KAMPANII VTORZHENIIA" I IKH ZNACHENIE V NATSIONAL'NOI-OSVOBODITEL'NOI BOR'BE NA KUBE ["The campaigns of diversion" and their significance in the national liberation struggle in Cuba]. *Novaia i Noveishaia Istoriia [USSR] 1974 (4): 43-55.* Nineteenth-century Cubans, hampered by strong concentrations of Spanish troops in the wealthier western regions of the country, successfully took up diversionary tactics in the eastern regions. When the Spanish left in 1898, Cuba was not independent because US influence grew. In 1951 Cubans, led by Fidel Castro, started actions against the Batista dictatorship and in 1958 began diversionary military campaigns. These revolutionary forces drove out the corrupt government and opened up the road to socialism. Based on the speeches of Fidel Castro and Leonid Brezhnev, and Cuban documents and periodicals; 21 notes.
A. J. Evans

1645. Volsky, George. CUBA FIFTEEN YEARS LATER. *Current Hist. 1974 66(389): 10-14, 35.* Discusses the leadership of Fidel Castro since 1959 and Cuba's foreign policy. One of seven articles on Latin America.
S

1646. Volsky, George. CUBA: PROPAGANDA AS AN INSTRU-MENT OF POWER AND SOCIO-ECONOMIC DEVELOPMENT. *Secolas Ann. 1973 4: 5-10.* One of eight papers on Cuba and Chile read at the annual meeting of the Southeastern conference on Latin American Studies.
S

1647. Volsky, George. CUBA TWENTY YEARS LATER. *Current Hist. 1979 76(444): 54-57, 83-84.* Discusses the ideological move to the left in socialist Cuba on the occasion of the 20th anniversary of the revolution, the relaxing of US attitudes, and the economic realities Fidel Castro has had to face.

1648. Volsky, George. CUBA'S FOREIGN POLICY. *Current Hist. 1976 70(413): 69-72, 81.* Despite Fidel Castro's indication in 1975 that Cuba wanted diplomatic rapprochement with the US, the prospects are unlikely, judging from the US censure of Cuba's international position and from the foreign trade needs of the Cuban government.

1649. Volsky, George. THE SOVIET-CUBAN CONNECTION. *Current Hist. 1981 80(468): 325-328, 335, 346.* Discusses USSR-Cuban relations from the Cuban revolution in 1959 to the recent use of Cuban troops in conjunction with Soviet foreign policy objectives in Africa.

1650. Wirth, Dieter. DIE BEDEUTUNG DER GEWALT IM ENT-WICKLUNGSPROZESS CUBAS [The meaning of violence in the Cuban development process]. *Jahrbuch für Geschichte von Staat, Wirtschaft und Gesellschaft Lateinamerikas [West Germany] 1978 15: 175-189.* Violence can be assumed to be a part of the Latin American political culture, even though it does not appear everywhere, continuously, or always in the same form. Despite use of force in Cuba, the overwhelming majority of the Cuban people recognize that regime as legitimate. Unlike the Eastern European regimes, the Cuban example of permitting the emigration of middle classes is not only relatively humane, but has reduced the potential opposition and contributed greatly to the regime's stability. Based on printed primary and secondary sources; 32 notes.
T. D. Schoonover

1651. Wolpin, Miles D. CUBAN POLITICAL SCIENCE IN THE SEVENTIES: SOME OBSERVATIONS. *Caribbean Q. [Jamaica] 1975 21(1-2): 20-34*. The development of political science as an academic discipline in Cuba has labored under many handicaps, including serious budgetary limitation for the social sciences and humanities. The primary function of the School of Political Science of the University of Havana is "to enhance the efficacy of mobilization and administrative elites by training them in political analysis and exposing them to a broad and appropriate range of empirical data." Analyzes the types of course offerings and the changes in the direction toward "practical" orientations to fill the above mobilization and administrative needs. There has been considerable restructuring of curriculum reflecting party philosophy and needs. 28 notes.　　　　　　　　　　　　　　　R. V. Ritter

1652. Woodyard, George W. PERSPECTIVES ON CUBAN THEATER. *Revista/Review Interamericana [Puerto Rico] 1979 9(1): 42-49*. Castro's revolution has had a profound effect on Cuban theater. Like most art forms, Cuban theater is now a branch of the state, with all the advantages and disadvantages such sponsorship entails. It is one of the most active art forms in Cuba today. 21 notes.　　　J. A. Lewis

1653. Yebra, Rita. PROCESO DE URBANIZACIÓN EN CUBA EN DOS DÉCADAS DE REVOLUCIÓN [The process of urbanization in Cuba in the two decades since the revolution]. *Rev. de la Biblioteca Nac. José Martí [Cuba] 1979 21(2): 77-88*. Urbanization in Cuba has undergone three stages since 1959. From 1959 to 1962, the revolutionary government made efforts to lessen the influence of Havana upon the island. From 1962 to 1970, public leaders concentrated on consolidating this decentralization. Since 1970, technocrats focused on strengthening the agrarian and industrial sectors outside Havana. Based on a thesis submitted to the École Pratique des Hautes Études, Paris, 1979.
　　　　　　　　　　　　　　　　　　　　　　J. A. Lewis

1654. Zeuske, Max. ZUR ENTWICKLUNG DER REVOLUTIONÄREN STREITKRÄFTE KUBAS BIS 1963 [The development of the revolutionary armed forces of Cuba to 1963]. *Militärgeschichte [East Germany] 1979 18(1): 17-30*. Proceeding from Cuba's specific conditions and from Fidel Castro's concept of revolution, interprets the place and role of armed struggle in the Cuban revolution. In the development of revolutionary armed forces, the author distinguishes the two stages: from the guerrilla to rebel army, 1956-58; and from the latter to the socialist peoples army, 1959-63. Proposes a detailed division of these stages into five and three phases respectively. With the deepening of the socialist traits of the revolution in 1960 Cuba began intensive military cooperation with socialist countries, and the delivery of Soviet weapons took on special importance. 3 illus., 56 notes.
　　　　　　　　　　　　　　　　　　J/T (H. D. Andrews)

1655. Zubatsky, David S. UNITED STATES DOCTORAL DISSERTATIONS ON CUBAN STUDIES. *Cuban Studies 1974 4(2): 33-55*. A comprehensive, classified guide to dissertations in the humanities and social sciences on Cuba.　　　　　　　　J. A. Lewis

1656. —. [ANGOLA, CUBA, AND THE UNITED STATES]. *Foreign Policy 1978 (31): 3-33*.
Bender, Gerald J. ANGOLA, THE CUBANS, AND AMERICAN ANXIETIES, *pp. 3-30*. The presence of Cuban troops in Angola has unsettled both the Carter administration and many Americans. The author seeks to clarify the background and events leading to the Cuban presence and help allay fears of a Soviet victory over American foreign policy interests in Africa.
Crocker, Chester A. COMMENT: MAKING AFRICA SAFE FOR THE CUBANS, *pp. 31-33*. Bender largely masked the USSR's sinister role in Angola and overly romanticized its entanglement with Cuba.　　　　　　　　　　　　H. R. Mahood

1657. —. CRONOLOGÍA DE LA REVOLUCIÓN CUBANA [Chronology of the Cuban revolution]. *Rev. de la Biblioteca Nac. José Martí [Cuba] 1979 21(2): 21-26*. A yearly list of the accomplishments of the Cuban revolution, 1959-78.　　　　　　　J. A. Lewis.

1658. —. [CUBA IN AFRICA]. *Cuban Studies 1980 10(1): 1-48*.

LeoGrande, William M. CUBAN-SOVIET RELATIONS AND CUBAN POLICY IN AFRICA, *pp. 1-36*. The presence of Cuban troops in Africa is consistent with earlier objectives of Cuban foreign policy to provide aid to national liberation movements and to support progressive governments. This policy does not necessarily stem from the dictates of the USSR's foreign policy in Africa. Revised from a paper given to the International Studies Association, Toronto, 1979; 3 tables, 110 notes.
Blasier, Cole. COMMENT: THE CONSEQUENCES OF MILITARY INITIATIVES, *pp. 37-42*. Cuba's activity in Africa has had a cost at home that Cubans may not be willing to pay forever.
Gonzalez, Edward. COMMENT: OPERATIONAL GOALS OF CUBAN POLICY IN AFRICA, *pp. 43-48*. Castro's success in Africa has allowed the island to exert leverage on the USSR for increased economic and military aid.　　　　J. A. Lewis

1659. —. [CUBA IN AFRICA: PART II]. *Cuban Studies 1980 10(2): 1-90*.
Domínguez, Jorge I. POLITICAL AND MILITARY LIMITATIONS AND CONSEQUENCES OF CUBAN POLICIES IN AFRICA, *pp. 1-35*. Continued from a previous article (see preceding entry). Although Cuba has suffered some reverses in Africa, it has generally maintained its goals and influence better than more powerful nations. 7 tables, 49 notes.
Valenta, Jiri. COMMENT: THE SOVIET-CUBAN ALLIANCE IN AFRICA AND FUTURE PROSPECTS IN THE THIRD WORLD, *pp. 36-43*. Relates the possible significance of new factors, especially the Soviet invasion of Afghanistan, the election of Ronald Reagan, and the growing importance of the Caribbean. 13 notes.
Bender, Gerald J. COMMENT: PAST, PRESENT, AND FUTURE PERSPECTIVES OF CUBA IN AFRICA, *pp. 44-54*. Cuba's involvement in Africa was and is much more modest than commonly thought. Table, 10 notes.
Roca, Sergio. ECONOMIC ASPECTS OF CUBAN INVOLVEMENT IN AFRICA, *pp. 55-80*. The economic cost-benefit to Cuba of its activities in Africa has generally been unfavorable to the island. 4 tables, 101 notes.
Pérez-López, Jorge F. COMMENT: ECONOMIC COSTS AND BENEFITS OF AFRICAN INVOLVEMENT, *pp. 80-85*. It is very difficult to assess the cost-benefit to Cuba of its involvement in Africa. 20 notes.
Eckstein, Susan. COMMENT: THE GLOBAL POLITICAL ECONOMY AND CUBA'S AFRICAN INVOLVEMENT, *pp. 85-90*. Cuba's place in the world capitalist economy encourages involvement in African affairs. 9 notes.　　　　　　　　J. A. Lewis

1660. —. [CUBA'S POSTREVOLUTIONARY ECONOMY]. *Am. J. of Sociol. 1981 86(5): 1124-1133*.
Pilarski, Adam M. and Snyder, Donald. ECONOMIC EFFECTS OF REVOLUTION: A REEVALUATION OF CUBAN EVIDENCE, *pp. 1124-1129*. Michael S. Lewis-Beck's study of short-run shifts in the level of output and long-run shifts in the rate of growth of output after the 1958 Cuban Revolution fails to consider that the energy consumption figures which Lewis-Beck used to measure output may have been distorted for political purposes so as to exaggerate short-run output and that the US embargo in 1960 was not the only factor in Cuba's drop in long-run economic output.
Lewis-Beck, Michael S. CAN WE ASSESS THE EFFECTS OF REVOLUTION? A THIRD LOOK AT THE CUBAN EVIDENCE, *pp. 1130-1133*. Pilarski and Snyder's theory that Castro manipulated the figures on energy consumption for 1957 and 1958 (based on a discrepancy between Castro's figures and Batista's) fails to consider the more likely possibility that Batista altered the data or, more likely still, that Batista's figures were based on measurement errors whereas Castro, with more data available to him, could measure energy consumption more accurately. Further, the confounding of internal and external variables, such as the US embargo, in an attempt to explain the drop in long-run output is not overcome by the procedure Pilarski and Snyder propose.

1661. —. FORUM ON INSTITUTIONALIZATION: A POSTSCRIPT. *Cuban Studies 1981 11(1): 87-92*.

Fitzgerald, Frank T. REVIEWING THE LITERATURE ON THE INSTITUTIONALIZATION OF THE CUBAN REVOLUTION: A RESPONSE TO MAX AZICRI, *pp. 87-89*. Fitzgerald objects to an earlier article by Max Azicri, reviewing the literature on the institutionalization of the Cuban Revolution. Azicri's article was neither comprehensive nor accurate in the literature that it surveyed. In particular, Azicri misinterpreted the significance of Carmelo Mesa-Lago's *Cuba in the 1970's*, a work that most literature on the Cuban Revolution must consider. 12 notes.

Mesa-Lago, Carmelo. REVOLUTIONARY EMPATHY VS. CALCULATED DETACHMENT IN THE STUDY OF THE CUBAN REVOLUTION: A REPLY TO FITZGERALD, *pp. 90-92*. Fitzgerald's criticism of the Azicri article is unfair. Moreover, Fitzgerald's suggestion that Mesa-Lago's *Cuba in the 1970's* lacks objectivity because it does not express empathy with the Cuban Revolution has to be rejected. 7 notes.   J. A. Lewis

1662. —. THE MILITARIZATION OF CUBA. *Armed Forces and Soc. 1977 3(4): 609-632*.

Leogrande, William M. THE DEMILITARIZATION OF THE CUBAN REVOLUTION: A REJOINDER TO IRVING LOUIS HOROWITZ, *pp. 609-616*. Contrary to Horowitz's assertion of a militaristic trend in Cuba since 1970, [see *Armed Forces and Soc.* 1975 1(4): 402-418], there has been a decline in the military presence among the Cuban revolutionaries. 23 notes.

Horowitz, Irving Louis. CASTROLOGY REVISITED: FURTHER OBSERVATIONS ON THE MILITARIZATION OF CUBA, *pp. 617-632*. Vigorously restates his thesis. Militarism in Cuba is a consequence of the inner history of the revolution. 32 notes.   J. P. Harahan

Dominican Republic

1663. Alemán, José Luis. CIENCIA, TECNOLOGÍA Y POLÍTICA DE INVERSIONES EN R.D., 1966-1974 [Science, technology and the politics of investments in the Dominican Republic, 1966-74]. *Estudios Sociales [Dominican Republic] 1975 8(1): 3-68*. Discusses the political economy of the Dominican Republic, 1966-74, focusing primarily on the impact of foreign investments on the economy as a whole, including the impact of technology on investments; utilizes numerous tables of economic data.

1664. Alemán, José Luis. POLÍTICAS DE DESARROLLO ECONÓMICO Y POBLACIÓN [Policies of economic development and population]. *Estudios Sociales [Dominican Republic] 1974 7(1/2): 83-115*. Discusses the importance of demographic characteristics of the population of the Dominican Republic—birth, fertility, and voluntary infant mortality—in relation to contemporary politics of economic development.

1665. Augelli, John P. NATIONALIZATION OF DOMINICAN BORDERLANDS. *Geographical Rev. 1980 70(1): 19-35*. In the mid-1930's, the Dominican dictator, Rafael Trujillo, embarked on a systematic program of erasing Haitian influence and otherwise nationalizing the frontier zone adjacent to Haiti. The policy proposed to stabilize what had been the most contested and unstable border in the Americas, to block further penetration of Dominican territory by Haitians, and to foster a strong sense of national identity among the people of the Dominican border provinces. By using his absolute political and economic power and by playing on the traditional fear and hatred that Dominicans harbored for Haitians, Trujillo was able to achieve some of his nationalization goals. On the basis of occurrences since 1960, the long-range success of his policies is questionable. The Dominican experience with nationalization of borderlands suggests generalizations applicable to frontier problems elsewhere in Latin America. 14 notes.   J

1666. Calder, Bruce J. CAUDILLOS AND GAVILLEROS VERSUS THE UNITED STATES MARINES: GUERRILLA INSURGENCY DURING THE DOMINICAN INTERVENTION, 1916-1924. *Hispanic Am. Hist. Rev. 1978 58(4): 649-675*. A series of revolutionary incidents in the Dominican Republic led to occupation by the US Marines in 1916. Guerrilla warfare increased in the eastern sec-

tion, due to unemployment, landlessness, and attempts by the Marines to destroy the local caudillo [leader] system. The Marines considered themselves racially superior to the Dominicans, and their abuse of peasants created more insurgents. Describes cases of torture and other abuses. The guerrillas surrendered in the spring of 1922 in return for almost total amnesty, shortly after the United States and the Dominican Republic agreed to terminate the occupation. 2 maps, 87 notes.
                    B. D. Johnson

1667. Calder, Bruce J. THE DOMINICAN TURN TOWARD SUGAR. *Caribbean Rev. 1981 10(3): 18-21, 44-45*. Traces the rise of the sugar industry in the Dominican Republic during the late 19th and early 20th centuries that transformed independent small farmers into workers at the mercy of the sugar companies for food, shelter, and employment and made the country dependent on the world commodity market while the United States controlled the industry almost entirely by the 1920's.

1668. Calder, Bruce J. VARIETIES OF RESISTANCE TO THE UNITED STATES OCCUPATION OF THE DOMINICAN REPUBLIC, 1916-1924. *Secolas Ann. 1980 11: 103-119*. Initial complacency in the Dominican Republic following the American occupation in 1916 was replaced by a determined guerrilla resistance among the peasantry and sugar workers in the eastern sector and a campaign of noncooperation and propaganda among the intellectual and upper classes in the towns and cities, which combined with military and administrative blunders within the occupying government to necessitate withdrawal of American interventionists in 1924.

1669. Dilla Alfonso, Haroldo. PENETRACION IMPERIALISTA, CORRELACION DE CLASES Y POLITICA EN REPUBLICA DOMINICANA (1900-1924) [Imperialist penetration, class relations, and politics in the Dominican Republic, 1900-24]. *Santiago [Cuba] 1981 (42): 9-42*. The first capitalist relations of production in the Dominican Republic appeared in the 1870's with the sugar industry and to some extent the export-oriented cocoa plantations. The protagonist of this change was the new middle class, which came from Cuba, Puerto Rico, Europe, and the United States. After 1888 the need to have recourse to foreign capital gradually led to the Dominico-American convention of 1907, which was a great leap forward in neocolonial dependence. After the 1916 military occupation by the United States, the native middle classes became totally subordinated to imperialist interests. American investments reshaped the social structure of the late 19th century as well as the legal, political, and ideological superstructure in the direction of an ever greater dependence. 28 notes.   J. V. Coutinho

1670. Doré y Cabral, Carlos. REFORMA AGRARIA Y LUCHAS SOCIALES EN LA REPÚBLICA DOMINICANA: 1966-1978 (PARTE II) [Land reform and social conflict in the Dominican Republic: 1966-78 (Part II)]. *Estudios Sociales Centroamericanos [Costa Rica] 1980 9(26): 9-36*. Continued from an earlier article (see following entry). The Dominican Republic's domestic oligarchy has been displaced by the international bourgeoisie. Hence, the United States has financed its hegemony over the combined nationality of the Dominicans. Possibly in the future those political parties which do not form part of the informal domination agreement may recognize that through the agrarian laws the peasants are excluded from the political process. Those who have joined ranks with the peasants may not have succeeded in achieving a national dimension with their reformist activity, but their work is evident in the political class and rank organization of the Dominican peasants. Based on newspapers and printed government documents; 2 tables, 36 notes, biblio.   T. D. Schoonover

1671. Doré y Cabral, Carlos. REFORMA AGRARIA Y LUCHAS SOCIALES EN LA REPUBLICA DOMINICANA: 1966-1978. (PARTE I) [Land reform and social struggles in the Dominican Republic: 1966-78. Part I]. *Estudios Sociales Centroamericanos [Costa Rica] 1980 9(25): 91-123*. Since the civil war of 1965, the pact forced upon the dominant classes by the United States has been under strain. Under the leadership of Joaquín Balaguer the Agrarian Reform Law of 1972 aided the bourgeoisie as it modernized the economy. 7 tables, 17 notes. Article to be continued.   T. D. Schoonover

1672. Ferguson, Yale H. THE DOMINICAN INTERVENTION OF 1965: RECENT INTERPRETATIONS. *Internat. Organization 1973 27(4): 517-548.* Reviews current articles and books on the Dominican Republic crisis of 1965. Concludes that the Constitutionalists would have won if the United States had not intervened. From the beginning the US was deeply suspicious of the rebels and saw the coup as possibly Communist or Castro oriented. Discusses the US intervention and post-intervention objectives, negotiations, provisional government, and elections. Analyzes the role of the Organization of American States and the UN. Discusses "the problem of determining the validity of studies that draw heavily upon interviews and classified materials provided on a not-for-direct-attribution basis." 7 notes.   E. P. Stickney

1673. Kryzanek, Michael J. POLITICAL PARTY DECLINE AND THE FAILURE OF LIBERAL DEMOCRACY: THE PRD IN DOMINICAN POLITICS. *J. of Latin Am. Studies [Great Britain] 1977 9(1): 115-143.* Factionalism over whether and how to cooperate with the Balaguer regime beset the Partido Revolucionario Dominicana (PRD), 1965-74. It was unable to resolve conflicts between politics and ideology, the generation gap between the older politicos and the younger ideologues, and the tactical problem of personalism versus democratic decisionmaking in crises. The consequences were losses in membership, decline in financial support, lack of visibility, and proliferation of other opposition political parties. Forced stability, the beginnings of reform, a stronger economy, and overt US support made the PRD irrelevant to a population which wanted simple and uncomplicated government and politics. Based on periodicals, interviews, and secondary works; 48 notes.   K. M. Bailor

1674. Malck, R. Michael. RAFAEL LEONIDAS TRUJILLO: A REVISIONIST CRITIQUE OF HIS RISE TO POWER. *Rev. Interamericana [Puerto Rico] 1977 7(3): 436-445.* Reviews interpretations on the political rise of Rafael Trujillo, 1911-61. Study of the Trujillo regime is difficult because of limited academic freedom in the Dominican Republic. Moreover, national statistics have been manufactured for political reasons and official correspondence has been confiscated or destroyed. Foreign and domestic propaganda from both pro- and anti-Trujillo groups has also impaired study of the regime. Contrary to many interpretations, Trujillo was a typical product of the lower classes and his political rise, aided by local elites and the US military, resulted from the divisive and revolutionary forces within the country.   G. A. Hewlett

1675. Malek, R. Michael. DOMINICAN REPUBLIC'S GENERAL RAFAEL L. TRUJILLO M. AND THE HAITIAN MASSACRE OF 1937: A CASE OF SUBVERSION IN INTERCARIBBEAN RELATIONS. *Secolas Ann. 1980 11: 137-155.* Racism, economic depression, and Dominican nationalism, along with express permission from General Rafael Trujillo, were responsible for the massacre (and subsequent concealment of the act) of several thousand Haitians living within the Dominican Republic's borders in 1937.

1676. Mann, Arthur J. AGRICULTURAL PRICE STABILIZATION POLICY IN A DEVELOPING ECONOMY: THE CASE OF THE DOMINICAN REPUBLIC. *Social and Econ. Studies [Jamaica] 1977 26(2): 190-201.* Describes the functioning of the agricultural price stabilization policy in the Dominican Republic. Notes problems, including political interference and a lack of data with which to evaluate the success or failures of the policy. 2 tables, 11 notes, 6 references.   E. S. Johnson

1677. Mann, Arthur J. PUBLIC EXPENDITURE PATTERNS IN THE DOMINICAN REPUBLIC AND PUERTO RICO 1930-1970. *Social and Econ. Studies [Jamaica] 1975 24(1): 47-82.* Provides data on the growth of public expenditures in the Dominican Republic and Puerto Rico and attempts to identify the reasons for the growth of the public sector. The surplus earned during World War II and increased public acceptance are important reasons for the growth. Finds many similarities in the public spending of the two countries. 6 tables, 24 notes, biblio., 3 appendixes.   E. S. Johnson

1678. Persia, Pedro Juan. THE DOMINICAN REPUBLIC: PROBLEMS AND PROSPECTS. *World Marxist Rev. [Canada] 1977 20(5): 124-129.* A review of the deteriorating structural crisis occurring in the

Dominican Republic, caused by the drop in sugar prices, the rise in fuel prices, a steadily increasing foreign debt, costlier international loans, and an unfavorable ratio between foreign investment and profit export by the multinationals. Examines the role of the Communist Party in the amelioration of this situation.

1679. Sharpe, Kenneth E. LA LUCHA CAMPESINA EN LA REPÚBLICA DOMINCANA: PODER, COMUNIDAD, IGLESIA [The peasant battle in the Dominican Republic: power, community, church]. *Estudios Sociales [Dominican Republic] 1975 8(4): 191-238.* Discusses the political impact of social reform programs in the contemporary Dominican Republic, focusing on the rural community, Catholic Church, and political structure.

1680. Thomas, J. THE DOMINICAN MODEL. *Monthly Rev. 1982 33(10): 34-43.* Analyzes the history of the Dominican Republic since 1965 in order to better understand the transfer of power from Joaquín Balaguer to Antonio Guzmán following the 1978 elections, with special attention to the influence of US policy.

1681. Vilas, Carlos M. NOTAS SOBRE LA FORMACIÓN DEL ESTADO EN EL CARIBE: LA REPÚBLICA DOMINICANA [Notes on the formation of the state in the Caribbean: the Dominican Republic]. *Estudios Sociales Centroamericanos [Costa Rica] 1979 8(24): 117-177.* The development since the last third of the 19th century of monopoly capitalism on an international scale has transformed Caribbean society. The importation of new industries into the Dominican Republic transformed its economic structure and initiated the differentiation of its social classes. The international bourgeoisie helped shape a domestic bourgeoisie to administer its peripheral interests. A centralized and militarized state best satisfied the local bourgeoisie's need for control, culminating in the Trujillo dictatorship. The diverse factions of the domestic bourgeoisie and the multinational businesses have appropriated the state to serve their ends. The suppressed economic interests move toward opposition and conflict, followed by US intervention in various forms. 92 notes.   T. D. Schoonover

1682. Vilas, Carlos María. DESARROLLO CAPITALISTA PERIFÉRICO Y LAS TRANSFORMACIONES POLÍTICAS EN LA REPÚBLICA DOMINICANA [Peripheral capitalist development and political transformations in the Dominican Republic]. *Rev. de Ciencias Sociales [Puerto Rico] 1978 20(3-4): 347-377.* Suggests that recently held elections in the Dominican Republic mark not only the end of Joaquín Balaguer's lengthy presidency, but also the transition to another period of economic growth. The author analyzes economic and sociopolitical aspects of the history of the Dominican Republic, 1965-78.   J/S

1683. Wiarda, Howard J. and Kryzanek, Michael J. DOMINICAN DICTATORSHIP REVISITED: THE CAUDILLO TRADITION AND THE REGIMES OF TRUJILLO AND BALAGUER. *Rev. Interamericana [Puerto Rico] 1977 7(3): 417-435.* A general model for the political, psychological, and military elements in caudillo rule is applied for comparative purposes to the regimes of two Dominican Republic leaders, Rafael Trujillo, 1930-61, and Joaquín Balaguer, 1965-77. The two regimes are remarkably similar, despite differences in individual personalities, demeanor, style, and background, in fitting the model of 16th-century imperialist Spain. It is thus difficult to conceive of a change in the politics of the Dominican Republic.   G. A. Hewlett

1684. Wiarda, Howard J. THE UNITED STATES AND THE DOMINICAN REPUBLIC: INTERVENTION, DEPENDENCY, AND TYRANNICIDE. *J. of Interamerican Studies and World Affairs 1980 22(2): 247-260.* Reviews Piero Gleijeses's *The Dominican Crisis: The 1965 Constitutionalist Revolt and the American Intervention* (Baltimore: Johns Hopkins U. Pr., 1978), and Bernard Diederich, *Trujillo: The Death of the Goat* (Boston: Little, Brown, 1978). Given the hundred-year presence of the United States in Dominican affairs, the Dominican Republic's chances of becoming a viable nation and breaking out of the vicious circles of underdevelopment and dependency remains a question mark. 3 notes, ref.   T. D. Schoonover

The Guianas

1685. Andic, Suphan. GOVERNMENT FINANCES IN SURI-NAM. *Social and Econ. Studies [Jamaica] 1977 26(4): 531-554.* De-scribes Surinam and its economy, examining proposed government development plans through 1990, and concludes that most of the invest-ment will have to be financed by foreign sources. Additional investment will promote inflation. 15 tables, 12 notes, 7 ref.   E. S. Johnson

1686. Ankum-Houwink, J. C. GUYANA, 1953-1966. *Spiegel Hist. [Netherlands] 1973 8(12): 651-660.* A brief survey of the political history of Guyana from 1953 until independence and the role played by such controversial figures as Cheddi Jagan (1918-). Biblio.
    G. D. Homan

1687. Babtiste, Fitzroy A. THE ANTI-VICHYITE MOVEMENT IN FRENCH GUIANA, JUNE TO DECEMBER 1940. *Social and Econ. Studies [Jamaica] 1977 26(3): 294-307.* Describes the events and personalities involved in the anti-Vichyite movement in French Guiana in 1940. The movement failed, in part because it lacked American sup-port. 68 notes, 9 ref.   E. S. Johnson

1688. Bourne, Compton. THE POLITICAL ECONOMY OF IN-DIGENOUS COMMERCIAL BANKING IN GUYANA. *Social and Econ. Studies [Jamaica] 1974 23(1): 97-126.* Demonstrates that the open-ing of indigenous commercial banks in the Caribbean is a political re-sponse to the perceived weaknesses in expatriate banks. Discusses the problems of indigenous banking including the lack of banking skills, the increased fragmentation of banking, and the conflict of financial and political goals. 8 tables, 21 notes.   E. S. Johnson

1689. Brana-Shute, Gary. POLITICS IN UNIFORM: SURINA-ME'S BEDEVILED REVOLUTION. *Caribbean Rev. 1981 10(2): 24-27, 49-50.* Discusses the 25 February 1980 coup d'etat against the constitutionally established government in Surinam carried out by 16 noncommissioned army officers, with special attention to its causes and implications.

1690. Campbell, Trevor A. THE MAKING OF AN ORGANIC IN-TELLECTUAL: WALTER RODNEY (1942-1980). *Latin Am. Per-spectives 1981 8(1): 49-63.* Traces the career of Walter Rodney, historian and leader of the Marxist opposition party, the Working People's Alliance in Guyana, who was killed in a bomb blast in 1980. 13 notes, biblio.
    J. F. Vivian

1691. Crist, Raymond E. JUNGLE GEOPOLITICS IN GUYANA: HOW A COMMUNIST UTOPIA THAT ENDED IN MASSACRE CAME TO BE SITED. *Am. J. of Econ. and Sociol. 1981 40(2): 107-114.* Examines why the Jonestown utopia was sited in the Guyana jungle. Given the human and geographical circumstances, its siting in the Guyana rainforest was highly probable, affording evidence that, to some extent, at least, people and their geography determine human events.
    J/S

1692. Dew, Edward. ANTI-CONSOCIATIONALISM AND INDE-PENDENCE IN SURINAM. *Bol. de Estudios Latinoamericanos y del Caribe [Netherlands] 1976 (21): 3-15.* From 1948 to 1973, the politics of Surinam, a self-governing Dutch dominion, generally supported the "con-sociational" theory of Arend Lijphart, according to which leaders of a plural society's principal ethnic groups exercise veto power over govern-ment decisions. In 1973 Surinamese politics became a confrontation be-tween Negro and Hindustani parties over the issue of independence, promoted by the Negro government and opposed by the principal Hin-dustani party. Just when civil war seemed likely to erupt, the contending politicians agreed to sink their differences and cooperate in making inde-pendence a success. This about-face, leading to restoration of minimal consociationalism, is attributed to the government's successful bluff, as well as to fear of ethnic strife and loss of Dutch financial aid. Based on Surinamese newspapers and secondary sources; 55 notes.
    D. M. Cregier

1693. Dew, Edward. TESTING ELITE PERCEPTIONS OF DE-PRIVATION AND SATISFACTION IN A CULTURALLY PLU-RAL SOCIETY. *Comparative Pol. 1974 6(2): 271-286.* Examines the 1971 Surinam parliament, with its Creole, Hindustani, and Indonesian representation, in order to identify conflict potential.   S

1694. Grant, C. H. POLITICAL SEQUENCE TO ALCAN NA-TIONALIZATION IN GUYANA—THE INTERNATIONAL AS-PECTS. *Social and Econ. Studies [Jamaica] 1973 22(2): 249-271.* Discusses the dependency of the developing nations on multinational corporations, and suggests a model that describes the situation leading to nationalization. Relates the international political effects of the nationali-zation of Alcan properties in Guyana. 31 notes.   E. S. Johnson

1695. Greene, J. E. THE POLITICS OF ECONOMIC PLANNING IN GUYANA. *Social and Econ. Studies [Jamaica] 1974 23(2): 186-203.* Examines the philosophy of cooperative socialism and its use as a devel-opmental goal in Guyana. Assesses the ability of this philosophy to bring change, and suggests some changes which might reduce the political impediments to planning. 3 tables, 5 notes, 23 refs.
    E. S. Johnson

1696. Hansen, William W. WALTER RODNEY: AN EXEM-PLARY LIFE. *Monthly Rev. 1981 32(11): 24-31.* Describes the writ-ings of Walter Rodney, principally his *How Europe Underdeveloped Africa* (1972), which assesses the impact of European colonialism on Africa, using 1960 as its focal point, with a view to formulating the strategy and tactics of African development.

1697. Hendrickson, Embert J. THE QUEST FOR IDENTITY IN DEVELOPING NATIONS: THE EXPERIENCE OF GUYANA. *Indian Pol. Sci. Rev. [India] 1976 10(1): 37-46.* The population of Guyana is composed of seven ethnic groups, of which the East Indians and the Africans are the largest. Prime Minister Forbes Burnham's gov-ernment has sought to unify and inspire these groups by establishing a cooperative republic and by encouraging the local culture. Nevertheless, tension between the two major groups continues.   J. C. English

1698. Hope, Kempe R. NATIONAL COOPERATIVE COMMER-CIAL BANKING AND DEVELOPMENT STRATEGY IN GUYANA. *Am. J. of Econ. and Sociol. 1975 34(3): 309-322.* The evolution of the cooperative movement in Guyana resulted in the adop-tion of a new development strategy. In it a leadership role is given to a new type of government bank, the Guyana National Cooperative Bank. Its mission is to protect and nurture the developing country's cooperative societies, organized mostly on Rochdale principles or on those of the Scandinavian marketing cooperatives. Basically a development savings bank, the GNCB is also an organ through which the Government mini-mizes the role of foreign banks in the export sector of the national econ-omy.   J

1699. Hope, Kempe R. and David, Wilfred L. PLANNING FOR DEVELOPMENT IN GUYANA: THE EXPERIENCE FROM 1945 TO 1973. *Inter-Am. Econ. Affairs 1974 27(4): 27-46.*

1700. Hoppe, R. HET POLITIEK SYSTEM VAN SURINAME: ELITE-KARTEL DEMOKRATIE [The political system of Surinam: elite-cartel democracy]. *Acta Pol. [Netherlands] 1976 11(2): 145-177.* States that the functioning of the Surinamese political system may fruit-fully be studied by conceptualizing it as an elite-cartel democracy. A brief analysis of Surinam's economic history combined with a class analysis provides the basis of identifying the privileged and the underprivileged elements in the political-economic system. Racial and class position are closely interwoven, and the ways in which class and race have affected the development of political parties after World War II are traced. The elites govern by means of compromises, made possible by keeping their respective constituencies isolated from each other and fostering strong client-patron relationships between politicians and their constituencies. In the concluding section, it is hypothesized that this unfavorable system will continue to operate and that Surinam, now on the verge of indepen-dence, probably awaits a long period of political instability.   J/S

1701. Jagan, Cheddi. GUYANA: A REPLY TO THE CRITICS. *Monthly Rev. 1977 29(4): 36-49.* Distinguishes the ideologies and roles of Guyana's two major political parties, his own People's Progressive Party and the governing People's National Congress, in recent history.

1702. Jagan, Cheddi. GUYANA AT THE CROSSROADS. *Black Scholar 1974 5(10): 43-47.* Outlines the decline in the standard of living and economic "collapse" brought on by the economic policies of the People's National Congress regime in Guyana, 1965-74.

1703. Jameson, Kenneth. AN INTERMEDIATE REGIME IN HISTORICAL CONTEXT: THE CASE OF GUYANA. *Development and Change [Netherlands] 1980 11(1): 77-95.* Examines economic changes in Guyana and the problems of the intermediate regime, dominated by the lower middle class, which has antagonized the wealthy and done little to benefit the poor.

1704. Litvak, Isaiah and Maule, Christopher J. NATIONALISATION IN THE CARIBBEAN BAUXITE INDUSTRY. *Internat. Affairs [Great Britain] 1975 51(1): 43-59.* Examines the role of the Canadian government in the light of the Guyana government's nationalization of a bauxite subsidiary of Alcan Aluminium, Ltd. Suggests implications for Canadian foreign policy and Canadian-based multinational corporations. Primary and secondary sources; 30 notes. P. J. Beck

1705. Litvak, Isaiah A. and Maule, Christopher J. FORCED DIVESTMENT IN THE CARIBBEAN. *Int. J. [Canada] 1977 32(3): 501-532.* Analyze, with the aid of models delineating government-business relations in the development and management of natural resources, the events leading up to Guyana's nationalization of the Demerara Bauxite Company, a subsidiary of Alcan Aluminium, Canada's largest multinational, in 1971. 3 tables, 23 notes. R. V. Kubicek

1706. Litvak, Isaiah A. and Maule, Christopher J. FOREIGN CORPORATE SOCIAL RESPONSIBILITY IN LESS DEVELOPED ECONOMIES. *J. of World Trade Law [Switzerland] 1975 9(2): 121-135.* Direct investment by the multinational corporation has been the primary instrument by which the resources of the less developed countries have been developed. But in spite of the benefits accompanying this capital inflow, their presence is often felt as a form of economic neo-colonialism. The effort of host governments to find a more evenly-balanced relationship with the MNC and to encourage a greater sense of corporate social responsibility can range from persuasive dialogue to the ultimate policy tool of nationalization, as the authors point out in this case study of Guyana. J

1707. Litvak, Isaiah A. and Maule, Christopher J. FOREIGN FIRMS: SOCIAL COSTS AND BENEFITS IN DEVELOPING COUNTRIES. *Public Policy 1975 23(2): 167-187.* Developing nations, which are beginning to exercise permanent sovereignty over their natural resources, are pressuring foreign firms in an attempt to increase economic and social contributions to the host country. The Guyanese government's perception of the costs and benefits derived from two foreign corporations, Booker McConnell Ltd. (a sugar producer) and Demerara Bauxite Company, provides a case study of the differing community relations strategies employed by these two firms. The Booker approach, which opted for local control and ownership, led to goodwill at the same time that the Demerara operation was nationalized. While bargaining room exists, foreign firms will need to adjust their behavior to meet new political realities. Table, 39 notes. S. Bruntjen

1708. Long, Frank. IS SIZE A DISADVANTAGE IN DEALING WITH TRANSNATIONAL CORPORATIONS? *Inter-American Econ. Affairs 1980 33(4): 61-75.* Guyana's nationalization of bauxite and sugar industries and introduction of the Cooperative Bank in competition with foreign-owned banking in the period 1970-78 and its constrained and selective approach to foreign investment since then demonstrate that small states need not be at a disadvantage in dealing with multinational corporations.

1709. Mandle, Jay R. CONTINUITY AND CHANGE IN GUYANESE UNDERDEVELOPMENT. *Rev. Interamericana [Puerto Rico] 1977 7(2): 216-226.* One major hurdle to economic development in Guyana has been the country's failure to diversify its agricultural production. Guyana's monocultural dependence upon sugar, however, has been lessened recently with the nationalization of that segment of the rural economy. 3 tables, 8 notes. J. A. Lewis

1710. Mandle, Jay R. CONTINUITY AND CHANGE IN GUYANESE UNDERDEVELOPMENT. *Monthly Rev. 1976 28(4): 37-50.* Guyana remained a British colony until 1966. Since that time, economic development has been extremely unimpressive. Until the recent nationalization of the enormous sugar industry, Guyana never really met its goal of becoming a cooperative socialist republic. Accomplished under difficult political circumstances, this bold takeover virtually ended foreign financial intrusion, erased the last vestiges of colonialism, and stimulated badly needed diversification within the agricultural sector. 9 notes. M. R. Yerburgh

1711. Petras, James. A DEATH IN GUYANA HAS MEANING FOR THIRD WORLD. *Latin Am. Perspectives 1981 8(1): 47-48.* Personal statement about Guyana political leader Walter Rodney (assassinated, 1980), who "symbolized a new generation of political leaders emerging in the Caribbean and Central America." J. F. Vivian

1713. Premdas, Ralph R. GUYANA: COMMUNAL CONFLICT, SOCIALISM AND POLITICAL RECONCILIATION. *Inter-Am. Econ. Affairs 1977 30(4): 63-83.* Discusses the conflict between African and East Indian communities in Guyana, attempts at political reconciliation of the two groups, and the development of socialism there. Provides theoretical considerations on the political development of multiethnic states. Table, 38 notes. D. A. Franz

1714. Premdas, Ralph R. GUYANA: SOCIALIST RECONSTRUCTION OR POLITICAL OPPORTUNISM? *J. of Interamerican Studies and World Affairs 1978 20(2): 133-164.* The joint Anglo-American intervention in Guyana politics in 1965, which ousted Prime Minister Cheddi Jagan from and elevated Forbes Burnham to office, appeared to have safely established a US client capitalist state. But economic necessity has led to the nationalization of industry under Burnham, who now leads the Maoist while Jagan heads the Moscow faction. Both factions and leaders pledge cooperation in the new program, especially against external efforts to destabilize the government. Ref. T. D. Schoonover

1715. Premdas, Ralph R. THE RISE OF THE FIRST MASS-BASED MULTI-RACIAL PARTY IN GUYANA. *Caribbean Q. [Jamaica] 1974 20(3-4): 5-20.* Traces the rise of the original People's Progressive Party (PPP), before its leadership split over tactics and strategy. It represented an independence movement which sought to eliminate colonialism from Guyana and institute a socialist society on a multiracial basis. Concentrates on the political aspects of the PPP's formation. There were various voluntary cultural and economic organizations that existed before the Political Affairs Committee (PAC), the PPP's immediate predecessor. The PAC was useful in mobilizing popular opinion against the British colonial presence. PAC developed from a predominantly Georgetown-based pressure group to a countrywide mass party. A single mass party with an integrated ideology that transcends sectional interests is vital for welding the disparate ethnic parts of the Guyanese population into a viable united working force. 49 notes. R. V. Ritter

1716. Prince, Ethlyn. THE DEVELOPMENT OF PUBLIC ENTERPRISE IN GUYANA. *Social and Econ. Studies [Jamaica] 1974 23(2): 204-215.* Describes the nature of public ownership in Guyana and government attempts to gain reasonable and responsible control over government corporations. 15 notes, 7 refs. E. S. Johnson

1717. Rodney, Walter. PEOPLE'S POWER, NO DICTATOR. *Latin Am. Perspectives 1981 8(1): 64-78.* Reprint of pamphlet published in 1979, the last political statement written by Walter Rodney (assassinated, 1980) for Guyana's Working People's Alliance (WPA). J. F. Vivian

1718. Sackey, James A. DEPENDENCE, UNDERDEVELOPMENT AND SOCIALIST-ORIENTED TRANSFORMATION IN GUYANA. *Inter-American Econ. Affairs 1979 33(1): 29-50.* Analyzes the possibilities of social transformation and freedom from economic imperialism in Guyana by focusing on the degree of dependency of Guyana on other nations, entrenched social classes, and political ideologies; internal and external economic inequalities are interrelated.

1719. St. Pierre, Maurice. RACE, THE POLITICAL FACTOR AND THE NATIONALIZATION OF DEMERARA BAUXITE

COMPANY, GUYANA. *Social and Econ. Studies [Jamaica] 1975 24(4): 481-503.* Describes how policies of the Demerara Bauxite Company eventually led to the politicization of the work force and the creation of an atmosphere which led to the nationalization of the company. 9 tables, 18 notes, biblio., appendix.   E. S. Johnson

1720. Spackman, Ann. OFFICIAL ATTITUDES AND OFFICIAL VIOLENCE: THE RUIMVELDT MASSACRE, GUYANA 1924. *Social and Econ. Studies [Jamaica] 1973 22(3): 315-334.* Describes the official attitudes surrounding a military shooting into a civilian crowd. Attempts to place the shooting in the colonial context and to deflate the image of liberal British colonial rule. Based on newspaper and colonial office reports; 49 notes.   E. S. Johnson

1721. Speckman, Ann. THE ROLE OF PRIVATE COMPANIES IN THE POLITICS OF EMPIRE: A CASE STUDY OF BAUXITE AND DIAMOND COMPANIES IN GUYANA IN THE EARLY 1920'S. *Social and Econ. Studies [Jamaica] 1975 24(3): 341-378.* Uses case studies of the role of the Aluminum Company of America and De Beers Company in attempting to monopolize mineral resources in Guyana to illustrate the role of private interest in political decisions. Also notes the power of large international corporations to influence governments in their favor. 93 notes, biblio.   E. S. Johnson

1722. Spinner, Thomas J., Jr. THE EMPEROR BURNHAM HAS LOST HIS CLOTHES: GUYANA'S POLITICAL LIFE IN DISARRAY. *Caribbean Rev. 1980 9(4): 4-8.* Traces Forbes Burnham's rise to power 1950's-70's and his current unpopularity due to corruption, economic troubles, unemployment, food shortages, and hostility between East Indians and blacks.

1723. Spinner, Thomas J., Jr. NATIONALISM, SOCIALISM, AND CULTURAL PLURALISM IN GUYANA. *Queen's Q. [Canada] 1977 84(4): 582-592.* The president of Guyana, his prime minister, and the leader of the largest opposition party were descendants of three non-Western civilizations—China, Africa, and India. Large numbers of each came at different periods. Those of East Indian descent made up half the population by 1970. In the early 1940's the independence movement gained momentum with the return of Cheddi Jagan to British Guiana. Although the new generation of leaders has begun to emerge, ethnic hostility has overcome its accomplishments. The country has accepted socialism in order to modernize rapidly and to achieve greater equality and a better standard of living. 15 notes.   E. P. Stickney

1724. Vernooij, J. SURINAME: NIEUW VOLK EN NIEUWE KERK [Surinam: a new people and a new church]. *Wereld en Zending [Netherlands] 1977 6(1): 47-52.* Together with the people of Surinam the Dutch Christian churches there, mostly Roman Catholic, are preparing for their own independence from the strong ties that have bound them spiritually and materially to the metropolis, keeping them isolated from Surinam's political and social life. The image of the Surinam Christian Church is one of charitable action lacking a theology, but it is now beginning to formulate a theological clarification of its place in Surinam's religious syncretism.   G. Herritt

1725. Vining, James W. THE RICE ECONOMY OF GOVERNMENT SCHEMES IN GUYANA. *Inter-Am. Econ. Affairs 1975 29(1): 3-20.* Compares the operation of government-sponsored rice-producing settlements with private rice production in Guyana and discusses reasons for the economic failure of government settlements. Primary and secondary sources; map, 2 tables, 29 notes.   D. A. Franz

1726. Waters, Donald J. JUNGLE POLITICS: GUYANA, THE PEOPLES TEMPLE, AND THE AFFAIRS OF STATE. *Caribbean Rev. 1980 9(2): 8-13.* Jonestown and its aftermath must be viewed in the context of Guyana and local and international politics of the 1970's.

Haiti

1727. Bellegarde-Smith, Patrick. DANTÈS BELLEGARDE: HAITIAN STATESMAN. *Américas (Organization of Am. States) 1978 30(8): 18-21.* Provides a biography of Haitian statesman and diplomat Dantès Bellgarde (1877-1966).

1728. Bellegarde-Smith, Patrick. HAITI: PERSPECTIVES OF FOREIGN POLICY: AN ESSAY ON THE INTERNATIONAL RELATIONS OF A SMALL STATE. *Caribbean Q. [Jamaica] 1974 20(3-4): 21-38.* Attempts to isolate and define the salient factors of Haitian foreign policy as typical of small states' international relations. Its foreign policy, recognizing internal limitations, has had limited goals. Its resource base has been meager, with the majority of its population outside the national economy. Haiti understood the US goal of Caribbean stability as a *sine qua non* to American security. Although it could not guarantee domestic tranquility it endeavored to meet all external debt obligations. "Through its foreign policy, Haiti sought to insure a wide latitude of domestic freedom of action or control which in effect, would guarantee national survival." 37 notes.   R. V. Ritter

1729. Bellegarde-Smith, Patrick D. DANTES BELLEGARDE AND PAN-AFRICANISM. *Phylon 1981 42(3): 233-244.* Louis Dantes Bellegarde (1877-1966) led the struggle for the political liberation of Haiti and made a significant contribution to worldwide black awareness. At various times he was a presidential adviser, cabinet member, diplomat, and public speaker. He worked against United States occupation of Haiti and for black consciousness.   A. G. Belles

1730. Fauriol, Georges A. CANADIAN RELATIONS WITH HAITI: AN OVERVIEW. *Rev. Interamericana [Puerto Rico] 1977 7(1): 109-117.* Canada's diplomatic and economic ties with Haiti have traditionally been minimal. In recent years, however, contact between the two nations has increased because of their common French background. 28 notes.   J. A. Lewis

1731. Fleurant, Gerdes. THE PRESENT SITUATION IN HAITI AND ANTI-DUVALIER STRUGGLE. *Pan-African J. [Kenya] 1975 8(4): 355-370.* The period 1957-74 was marked by sinister political repression, violence, and corruption in Haiti under the dictatorship of the Duvalier family. This situation conforms to the existence of a feudal socioeconomic structure dating from the colonial period, and to the growing US influence in the economic and political life of Haiti. Thousands of people have been imprisoned, and large numbers of Haitians have fled the country. An anti-Duvalier political opposition has developed among the one million Haitian emigrés. The aim of the struggle is not only the overthrow of Duvalierism but the complete liberation of the Haitian people.   R. G. Neville

1732. Goninski, S. A. GAITANSKAIA TRAGEDIIA [The tragedy of Haiti]. *Voprosy Istorii [USSR] 1973 (7): 112-127.* The history of Haiti since its independence in 1804 is largely a chronicle of misfortunes. The United States continually harassed the country, especially during 1847-1915, and actually occupied it during 1915-34. Modern Haiti's history has been shaped by the dictatorship of François Duvalier, who became president on 22 October 1957. He systematically eliminated all opposition, established a reign of terror, stirred up racial hatred, and repressed religion. The assassination of John F. Kennedy was greeted with jubilation by his regime, which remains unchanged under Jean-Claude Duvalier, who became ruler after his father died. 78 notes.

1733. Laraque, Paul. BREVE EXPOSICION SOBRE RELACIONES DIALECTICAS DE POLITICA Y CULTURA EN HAITI [Brief exposition on dialectical relations between politics and culture in Haiti]. *Casa de las Américas [Cuba] 1981 22(129): 140-146.* Until the US occupation of Haiti in 1915, Haitian literature was mostly a servile imitation of the French. After that date the reaction of the intellectuals expressed itself in two parallel currents: one had its source in the work of Jean Price Mars, the author of *Ainsi Parla l'Oncle* (1928), and the other in the indigenist movement centered around the *Revue Indigène* (1927-28). Price Mars denounced the "collective bovarism" of his countrymen. The group of the *Revue Indigène* formed by young men recently returned from France sought to identify itself with the people, especially the African heritage of the peasant masses. The article describes some aspects of this struggle for identity in the political context of the time.

J. V. Coutinho

1734. Lutskov, N. D. OKKUPATSIIA GAITI SOEDINENNYMI SHTATAMI AMERIKI (1915-1934 GG.) [The US occupation of Haiti, 1915-34]. *Novaia i Noveishaia Istoriia [USSR] 1976 (6): 66-79.* Examines the causes and course of the US armed intervention in Haiti and the Haitian people's heroic struggle for independence. The author proves that the occupation of Haiti has resulted in its complete economic and political enslavement by US imperialism.   J

1735. Martin, Edwin M. HAITI: A CASE STUDY IN FUTILITY. *SAIS Rev. 1981 (2): 61-70.* Reviews US foreign aid efforts in Haiti since the 1960's, when the Alliance for Progress and diplomatic offensive against Cuba introduced the massive aid programs, still largely ineffective.

1736. Nicholls, David. IDEOLOGIE ET MOUVEMENTS POLITIQUES EN HAITI, 1915-1946 [Ideology and political movements in Haiti 1915-46]. *Ann.: Econ., Soc., Civilisations [France] 1975 30(4): 654-679.* An analysis of protest movements in Haiti in the 20th century with particular attention to the role ideology played in them. Three main currents are discussed: nationalism, which is seen as broadly class based; negritude, which is seen as the ideology of black middle class intellectuals; and socialism, which is to be identified with the mulatto elite. The political events of 1946 in Haiti are only explicable in terms of those ideological conflicts of the preceding period and of their relation to the evolving class structure of the country. 119 notes.   R. Howell

1737. Nicholls, David. IDEOLOGY AND POLITICAL PROTEST IN HAITI, 1930-46. *J. of Contemporary Hist. [Great Britain] 1974 9(4): 3-26.* Three movements between 1930 and 1946 and their accompanying ideologies may be distinguished as culminating in the revolution of 1946: *noirisme* (the Black question), really an ethnological nationalism; Marxism; and technocratic socialism. Primary sources; 77 notes.

M. P. Trauth

1738. Obichere, Boniface I. BLACK POWER AND MAGIC IN HAITIAN POLITICS: DR. FRANCOIS DUVALIER, 1957-1971. *Pan-African J. [Kenya] 1973 6(2): 109-125.* Discusses the life and career of François Duvalier, president of Haiti, 1957-71, and a controversial figure due to the unorthodox nature of his dictatorship.

1739. Remy, Anselme. EL FENÓMENO DUVALIER [The Duvalier phenomenon]. *Revista/Review Interamericana [Puerto Rico] 1977 7(3): 446-467.* In the eyes of many people in the West, Dr. François Duvalier was nothing more than a bizarre dictator of Haiti, 1957-71, who was supported by voodoo. To believe this is to misunderstand Haitian history. Duvalier represented an important element in his country's society, the nationalistic black middle class struggling against a Francophile mulatto elite. Photo, 30 notes.   J. A. Lewis

1740. Stepick, Alex. THE NEW HAITIAN EXODUS. THE FLIGHT FROM TERROR AND POVERTY. *Caribbean Rev. 1982 11(1): 14-17, 55-57.* Traces emigration from Haiti over the last century, focusing on emigration to the United States since François (Papa Doc) Duvalier's regime began in 1958 and effects on Haiti's economy.

1741. Vernon, John A. RACIAL GAMESMANSHIP AND THE U.S. OCCUPATION OF HAITI: AN ILLUSTRATIVE EPISODE. *Alabama Hist. Q. 1978 40(3-4): 144-161.* Examines the racial implication of President Hoover's appointment of the president of the Tuskegee Institute, Robert R. Moton, to head a committee to investigate educational conditions in Haiti. Attention is paid to Moton's demands that the group be transported on a battleship. Based on a dissertation by Hans Schmidt, Rutgers University, 1968; 44 notes.

Jamaica

1742. Bell, Wendell and Robinson, Robert V. EUROPEAN MELODY, AFRICAN RHYTHM, OR WEST INDIAN HARMONY? CHANGING CULTURAL IDENTITY AMONG LEADERS IN A NEW STATE. *Social Forces 1979 58(1): 249-279.* Compares the cultural identities of 83 leaders in 1974, twelve years after Jamaica's political independence, with a study completed just before independence in 1962. With a largely slave-descendant, black population, Jamaica has a mixed creole culture with Anglo-European and African features combined with local modifications and innovations. Historically, cultural domination followed political domination, and the Anglo cultural features were most influential and positively correlated with social class. Over the last several years, however, the African elements have been asserted by a number of groups, including Black Power advocates. From 1962 to 1974, Jamaican leaders became dramatically less Anglo-European and more West Indian in their cultural identities. By 1974, there was a noticeable tendency for the two major political parties to polarize on the question of the African heritage. 4 tables, fig., 14 notes, appendix, biblio.   J/S

1743. Bell, Wendell. INDEPENDENT JAMAICA ENTERS WORLD POLITICS: FOREIGN POLICY IN A NEW STATE. *Pol. Sci. Q. 1977-78 92(4): 683-703.* Traces the behavior of the new state of Jamaica from the time it entered world politics as a politically independent actor through its first 14 years of nationhood. Divides Jamaica's foreign policy into three stages: increasing consciousness of black Africa, anticolonialism, and antiracism. Additionally, he shows that for a small state with a "penetrated economy," foreign and domestic policies often merge.   J

1744. Bell, Wendell and Gibson, J. William, Jr. INDEPENDENT JAMAICA FACES THE OUTSIDE WORLD: ATTITUDES OF ELITES AFTER TWELVE YEARS OF NATIONHOOD. *Int. Studies Q. 1978 22(1): 5-48.* A comparison of the foreign policy attitudes of Jamaican leaders in 1962, just prior to independence, and in 1974 shows a dramatic change. Favorable attitudes toward Jamaica's alignment with Western nations declined from 71% of the leaders in 1962 to 36% in 1974. The shift was toward association with any country as long as Jamaica's self-interest was served. The social characteristics, roles, and values of leaders affected their foreign policy attitudes. Based on interviews and secondary sources; 6 tables, fig., 38 notes.

E. S. Palais

1745. Bell, Wendell. INEQUALITY IN INDEPENDENT JAMAICA: A PRELIMINARY APPRAISAL OF ELITE PERFORMANCE. *Rev. Interamericana [Puerto Rico] 1977 7(2): 294-308.* Most Jamaican leaders who favored independence a decade ago hoped that it would bring social and economic equality. Although strides have been made in achieving the former, the latter still shows little change from colonial times. Table, 44 notes.   J. A. Lewis

1746. Bilby, Kenneth. JAMAICA'S MAROONS AT THE CROSSROADS: LOSING TOUCH WITH TRADITION. *Caribbean Rev. 1980 9(4): 18-21, 49.* History of the Jamaican Maroons, descendants of African slaves who escaped and settled in the interior mountains in the late 17th and early 18th centuries, focusing on British attempts to control them, sacking their settlement in the early 1730's, and the Maroons' current identity crisis due to a changing social and political climate.

1747. Boulton, Adam. JAMAICA'S BAUXITE STRATEGY: THE CARIBBEAN FLIRTS WITH THE INTERNATIONAL SYSTEM. *SAIS Review 1981 (2): 81-91.* The political interpretation of Jamaica's poor performance in bauxite production in the 1970's, which places the blame on Michael Manley's leftist stridency, is misguided; the history of the bauxite industry shows real gains—a fairer revenue and a Jamaican repossession of territory—but it is also demonstrating the dominance of vertically integrated multinational corporations.

1748. Brown, Adlith. PLANNING AS A POLITICAL ACTIVITY: SOME ASPECTS OF THE JAMAICAN EXPERIENCE. *Social and Econ. Studies [Jamaica] 1975 24(1): 1-14.* Social and economic planning by technical experts is ineffective because it is conducted without consideration of the political process. For planning to be effective there must

be defined and agreed political goals toward which the planning can be oriented. 4 notes, 19 refs.
E. S. Johnson

1749. Burt, Arthur E. THREE RESISTANCE MOVEMENTS IN JAMAICA: THE MAROONS, GARVEYISM, AND THE RASTAFARIANS. *J. of the Afro-American Hist. and Geneal. Soc. 1982 3(1): 33-39.* Maroons (escaped African slaves in the Jamaican interior) fought a guerrilla war against the British in the early 1660's, Marcus Garvey's Back-to-Africa movement sought to make blacks aware of themselves as a race to resist British colonial racism, 1927-35, and the Rastafarians, who believed in the divinity of Ras Tafari (Haile Selassie), also believed that Africa was "the legitimate and righteous home of all Negroes," 1930-62.

1750. Campbell, Horace. JAMAICA: THE MYTH OF ECONOMIC DEVELOPMENT AND RACIAL TRANQUILITY. *Black Scholar 1973 4(5): 16-23.* Examines the history of Jamaica, 19th-20th centuries, focusing on the last 40 years, current political trends among the black population, and the institution of Rastafarianism, 1938-73, noting as well the incursion of non-Jamaican industries and US economic interests.

1751. Carnegie, James Alexander. EL INSTITUTO DE JAMAICA: UN SIGLO DE CULTURA [The Jamaica Institute: a century of culture]. *Américas (Organization of Am. States) 1979 31(11-12): 36-43.* The Jamaica Institute was founded in 1879 by the British colonial governor Sir Anthony Musgrave for the purpose of fostering letters, science, and the arts and supplementing military and political power with intellectual control of the islands, but it has sponsored many useful activities in many fields.

1752. Eaton, George. OSMOND DYCE—LABOUR LEADER—A LIFE AND ITS TIMES, 1918-1970. *Caribbean Q. [Jamaica] 1974 20(3-4): 59-73.* A study of the life of Osmond Dyce as a Jamaican labor leader and organizer. Surveys the development of trade unionism during his early years and his indoctrination in Marxist-Socialist ideology through the Left Book Club. In 1942 Osmond Dyce became a full-time organizer of the People's National Party (PNP) and increasingly involved in violent labor disputes between rival organizations. After a left-wing purge of PNP he became more directly involved in politics, which ultimately led to new horizons and a new career as an administrator in Caribbean and international labor organizations, devoting himself also to educational activities.
R. V. Ritter

1753. Girling, R. K. THE MIGRATION OF HUMAN CAPITAL FROM THE THIRD WORLD: THE IMPLICATIONS AND SOME DATA ON THE JAMAICAN CASE. *Social and Econ. Studies [Jamaica] 1974 23(1): 84-96.* Discusses the costs to the developing nations of the "brain drain", using the example of Jamaica. The emigration of trained individuals represents a gift to the receiving country and a loss to the originating country. This loss includes the costs of education and the loss of income to the originating country. 2 figs., table, 3 notes.
E. S. Johnson

1754. Girvan, Norman and Bernal, Richard. THE IMF AND THE FORECLOSURE OF DEVELOPMENT OPTIONS: THE CASE OF JAMAICA. *Monthly Rev. 1982 33(9): 34-48.* Summarizes Jamaica's experience with the International Monetary Fund (IMF) in the period 1975-80 and suggests lessons for other Third World countries.

1755. Gorden, Derek. WORKING CLASS RADICALISM IN JAMAICA: AN EXPLORATION OF THE PRIVILEGED WORKER THESIS. *Social and Econ. Studies [Jamaica] 1978 27(3): 313-341.* Tests the hypothesis that workers in a developing nation feel sufficiently privileged not to be receptive to revolutionary political ideology. Statistically analyzing data on the social and economic status of workers, as well as the type of industry, the author indicates that, contrary to the privileged worker thesis, industrial workers in Jamaica appear to be more receptive to radical and socialist ideas. Based on data collected from 346 industrial workers in metropolitan Kingston. 5 tables, 2 fig., 56 notes, appendix.
E. S. Johnson

1756. Holzberg, Carol S. SOCIAL STRATIFICATION, CULTURAL NATIONALISM, AND POLITICAL ECONOMY IN JAMAICA: THE MYTHS OF DEVELOPMENT AND THE ANTI-

WHITE BIAS. *Can. Rev. of Sociol. and Anthrop. [Canada] 1977 14(4): 368-380.* It is only by mapping the organization and composition of the island's economic elite and by documenting the role of these national entrepreneurs in Jamaican big business that it becomes possible to determine the extent to which white strategic command of political, economic, and cultural resources has changed since the advent to power of the People's National Party in 1972.
J/S

1757. Jones, E. S. SOCIAL CHANGE AND ORGANISATIONAL TRANSFER. *African Social Res. [Zambia] 1973 (15): 387-392.* Reviews Jeffrey Harrod's *Trade Union Foreign Policy: a Study of British and American Trade Union Activities in Jamaica* (London, 1972). This is the first study of foreign penetration in union structures. Notes the major reasons for union involvement and outlines earlier essays on this topic.
H. G. Soff

1758. Jones, Edwin. ADMINISTRATIVE INSTITUTION BUILDING IN JAMAICA—AN INTERPRETATION. *Social and Econ. Studies [Jamaica] 1974 23(2): 264-291.* Describes the nature of the pre- and post-independence administrative institutions in Jamaica. Many of the motivating values for the administrative personnel were not changed by independence. The ideal time for a broad-based institutional reconstruction would have been at independence. Fig., 4 notes, 23 refs.
E. S. Johnson

1759. Keith, Sherry. AN HISTORICAL OVERVIEW OF THE STATE AND EDUCATIONAL POLICY IN JAMAICA. *Latin Am. Perspectives 1978 5(2): 37-52.* The Jamaican government committed itself to democratic socialism in 1974. The subsequent conflict between the masses and the middle classes has affected the educational system.

1760. Kopkind, Andrew. JAMAICA: "SOCIALISM SOON COME." *Working Papers for a New Society 1977 5(1): 44-52.* Examines the economic policies of the socialist administration of Michael Manley in Jamaica, 1972-77.

1761. Lewin, Arthur. THE FALL OF MICHAEL MANLEY: A CASE STUDY OF THE FAILURE OF REFORM SOCIALISM. *Monthly Rev. 1982 33(9): 49-60.* The crux of the recently deposed prime minister of Jamaica, Michael Manley's, and by extension the nation's, problem is the two-party political system of Jamaica which created him and by which he was bound. In fact, Manley's Development Program, while appearing to be revolutionary, was merely a natural outgrowth of the Jamaican political system.

1762. Lewis, Vaughan A. PRINCIPIOS Y TENDENCIAS DE LA POLÍTICA EXTERIOR JAMAIQUINA [Principles and tendencies of Jamaican foreign policy]. *Foro Int. [Mexico] 1981 22(1): 22-69.* Discusses post-1972 use of foreign policy to stimulate internal economic development in Jamaica. 85 notes.
D. A. Franz

1763. Mason, Clifford. JAMAICA NOW. *Crisis 1981 88(4): 192-197.* In 1980, Edward Seaga became prime minister of Jamaica. The peaceful transfer of power that took place was considered an important lesson in democracy for Central and South America. The nation still has tremendous problems in its economy and educational structure, but Seaga will be a practical and effective leader who may find some solutions.
A. G. Belles

1764. Miller, Errol. SELF AND IDENTITY PROBLEMS IN JAMAICA. *Caribbean Q. [Jamaica] 1973 19(2): 108-142.* PART II: AN ANALYSIS OF ATTEMPTED SOLUTIONS. Continued from a previous article. Analyzes the four 20th-century attempts of the Jamaican people to solve the problems of self-worth evaluation: Garveyism (1910-40), which challenged the assumed superiority of white and British culture and developed an Afro-Jamaican national identity; the National Movement (1935-55), which rejected African identification; Black Power (1965-), which emphasized African identification; and the Development Movement (1955-), successor to the National Movement once political independence became a fait accompli, which emphasized economic and technological growth. The acceptance of these movements depended on both internal and external factors, and none of the movements was truly comprehensive, all being concerned only with the oppressed classes. Improvements in self-identity among Jamaicans have occurred, but there is still a need for the development of a national identity which includes every member of the society; the development of black multiracial pluralism; and the phasing out of a class identity which implies differences in worth between classes.   R. L. Woodward, Jr.

1765. Mills, G. E. and Robertson, Paul D. THE ATTITUDES AND BEHAVIOR OF SENIOR CIVIL SERVICE IN JAMAICA. *Social and Econ. Studies [Jamaica] 1974 23(2): 311-343.* Reviews the ideal role of the bureaucrat in a developing country. The current civil service staff is still functioning in a colonial fashion and radical change is needed to bring about effective development. Based on interviews; 14 figs., 12 notes, 29 refs.   E. S. Johnson

1766. Nowicka, Ewa. THE JAMAICAN ROOTS OF THE GARVEY IDEOLOGY. *Acta Poloniae Hist. [Poland] 1978 37: 129-161.* A biography of Marcus Garvey (1887-1940), creator of an international Negro movement, who was born and raised in Jamaica and who insisted that the races should be separated, not integrated, and that the blacks, who once ruled the world, would eventually return to their own glory. The author shows the Jamaican social background of Garvey's ideas, their application to America, the British influence on his thinking, and his founding of the United Negro Improvement Association and its Pan-Africanism. 48 notes.   H. Heitzman Wojcicka

1767. Nunes, F. E. THE DECLINING STATUS OF THE JAMAICAN CIVIL SERVICE. *Social and Econ. Studies [Jamaica] 1974 23(2): 344-357.* Questionnaire responses establish that the civil service has declined in status as an occupation since independence. Though the decline may be more relative than real, it is detrimental to effective government leadership. 4 tables, 4 notes, 10 refs.   E. S. Johnson

1768. O'Flaherty, J. Daniel. FINDING JAMAICA'S WAY. *Foreign Policy 1978 (31): 137-158.* During the 1970's relations between the United States and Jamaica were severely strained. Reasons for this stress are analyzed in light of the fact that the Carter administration has a stake both in the survival of the Jamaican political system and the Michael Manley regime.   H. R. Mahood

1769. Reid, Hazel. BOB MARLEY: UP FROM BABYLON. *Freedomways 1981 21(3): 171-179.* Discusses the life and musical career of Jamaican Robert Nesta Marley (1945-81), commenting on the religious basis of his music and its political implications for the Third World.

1770. Robinson, Robert V. and Bell, Wendell. ATTITUDES TOWARDS POLITICAL INDEPENDENCE IN JAMAICA AFTER TWELVE YEARS OF NATIONHOOD. *British J. of Sociol. [Great Britain] 1978 29(2): 208-233.* Reviews changed attitudes among 83 Jamaican leaders, 1962-74, to political independence.

1771. St. Pierre, Maurice. THE 1938 JAMAICAN DISTURBANCES. A PORTRAIT OF MASS REACTION AGAINST COLONIALISM. *Social and Econ. Studies [Jamaica] 1978 27(2): 171-196.* The economic strains of the underprivileged masses of Jamaica in 1938 are documented and identified as the cause of the riots and strikes of that year. The fact that such disturbances did lead to some amelioration encouraged further disturbances and established the need for acceptable leaders. 6 tables, 2 fig., 8 notes, 35 ref.   E. S. Johnson

1772. Sewell, Lileth. MUSIC IN THE JAMAICAN LABOUR MOVEMENT. *Jamaica J. [Jamaica] 1979 (43): 42-47.* Analyzes the content and style of political music, 1930's-70's.

1773. Stephenson, Olivier. "WHO THE CAP FIT . . .": WHITHER GOEST JAMAICA? *Freedomways 1976 16(4): 245-250.* Examines political conditions, black marketing, poverty, growing violence, and the political parties opposing and supporting the term of Prime Minister Michael Manley, who has come under attack for his role in Jamaica's plight, 1972-76.

1774. Stone, Carl. CLASS AND STATUS VOTING IN JAMAICA. *Social and Econ. Studies [Jamaica] 1977 26(3): 279-293.* Analyzes voting and voting behavior in metropolitan Kingston for elections in 1970, 1972, and 1976. There was an increase in lower-class votes for the center-left People's National Party (PNP), though public opinion surveys reveal a

much more conservative attitude among the voters. 3 tables, fig., 9 notes, 8 ref.   E. S. Johnson

1775. Stone, Carl. DEMOCRACY AND SOCIALISM IN JAMAICA, 1962-1979. *J. of Commonwealth and Comparative Pol. [Great Britain] 1981 19(2): 115-133.* Analyzes attempts to promote democratization in the Jamaican political system between 1962 and 1979, principally efforts by the People's National Party to implement populist demands for greater control over the public and private domains of power in Jamaica. Based on the author's quarterly polls, conducted for the *Daily Gleaner;* 7 tables, 11 notes.   M. K. Hogg

1776. Stone, Carl. JAMAICA'S 1980 ELECTIONS: WHAT MANLEY DID DO; WHAT SEAGA NEED DO. *Caribbean Rev. 1981 10(2): 5-7, 40-43.* Discusses the accomplishments and defeat of Jamaica's People's National Party led by former Prime Minister Michael Manley in the 1980 parliamentary election by Prime Minister Edward Seaga, especially the role of public opinion in the election.

1777. Stone, Carl. POLITICAL ASPECTS OF POSTWAR AGRICULTURAL POLICIES IN JAMAICA (1945-1970). *Social and Econ. Studies [Jamaica] 1974 23(2): 145-175.* Governmental agricultural policy in Jamaica has been determined by the politically influential planter class. While reforms have occurred, they have been slow and of little impact. In the future more radical land reform programs will be more likely, due to an increasingly liberal government. 9 tables, 34 notes, 26 refs.

                                                        E. S. Johnson

1778. Stone, Carl. REGIONAL PARTY VOTING IN JAMAICA (1959-1976). *J. of Interamerican Studies and World Affairs 1978 20(4): 393-420.* Produces a picture of voting patterns over the past 20 years between the Jamaica Labor Party (JLP) and the People's National Party (PNP). The PNP has broad geographical strength, hence popular national voting superiority, but the JLP's highly competitive activity in some rural areas works to balance electoral outcomes. Based on aggregate statistics by regions and districts and supplemental sample surveys; 4 notes, ref.   T. D. Schoonover

1779. Stone, Carl. URBANISATION AS A SOURCE OF POLITICAL DISAFFECTION: THE JAMAICAN EXPERIENCE. *British J. of Sociol. [Great Britain] 1975 26(4): 448-464.* Reexamines the theory of the distruptive effects of rapid urbanization on political authority in the context of recent Jamaican experience. The author relates the lower socio-political integration of the urban Jamaican, as compared to the Latin American, to Jamaica's social history as a slave plantation colony.

1780. Stone, Carl. THE 1976 PARLIAMENTARY ELECTION IN JAMAICA. *J. of Commonwealth and Comparative Pol. [Great Britain] 1977 15(3): 250-265.* The People's National Party (PNP) won the 1976 Jamaican elections, continuing the cyclical pattern of governments since 1962. The election, against the background of economic problems, was characterized by the opposition Jamaican Labour Party's (JLP) campaign which emphasized efficient political and financial management under the leadership of Edward Seaga. The PNP emphasized its socialism, establishing the credibility of past policies under its leader Michael Manley. Violence reached new peaks and issues became intense, leading to class polarization and realignment: the PNP lost its middle-class support to the JLP. Continuing economic problems have forced the PNP government to abandon its initial radical policy and to lose credibility. 7 tables, 39 notes.

                                                        S. G. Jackson

1781. Swaby, R. A. SOME PROBLEMS OF PUBLIC UTILITY REGULATION BY A STATUTORY BOARD IN JAMAICA: THE JAMAICAN OMNIBUS SERVICES CASE. *Social and Econ. Studies [Jamaica] 1974 23(2): 242-263.* Describes the operation of the Public Passenger Transport Board and the inability of the lay board to adequately supervise the activity of a multinationally owned public utility. A well trained regulatory body is needed to supervise large corporations. 54 notes, 17 refs, appendix.   E. S. Johnson

1782. Tramm, Madeleine Lorch. MULTINATIONALS IN THIRD WORLD DEVELOPMENT: THE CASE OF JAMAICA'S BAUXITE INDUSTRY. *Caribbean Q. [Jamaica] 1977 23(4): 1-16.* Weighs the effects of multinational corporations on economic growth and social mobility in Jamaica using the aluminum industry as a case study. Their influence is more negative than positive. Based on extensive research in Jamaica during 1972-73, especially in Mandeville; 36 notes, biblio.

R. L. Woodward, Jr.

1783. Watson, G. Llewellyn. PATTERNS OF BLACK PROTEST IN JAMAICA: THE CASE OF THE RAS-TAFARIANS. *J. of Black Studies 1974 4(3): 329-343.* The Rastafarians—poor, black, lower-class Jamaicans who advocate the overthrow of the current Jamaican government—combine violence with Marxism and religion. 4 notes, biblio.

K. Butcher

1784. —. JAMAICA: A CROSS-ROADS IN THE NEW WORLD. *Australian Foreign Affairs Record [Australia] 1975 46(3): 121-124.* Describes Jamaica's development and its present role in international relations, on the eve of the 1975 British Commonwealth heads of government meeting there.

Other West Indies

Including the Bahamas, Bermuda, and the islands of the Eastern Caribbean

1785. Anderson, William A. and Dynes, Russell R. CIVIL DISTURBANCES AND SOCIAL CHANGE: A COMPARATIVE ANALYSIS OF THE UNITED STATES AND CURAÇAO. *Urban Affairs Q. 1976 12(1): 37-56.* Civil disturbances in Curaçao, May 1969, and the United States, mid-1960's, were general attacks by the disadvantaged on traditional social arrangements and were also part of broader political and social movements. They developed specific political demands and ushered in periods of nonwhite innovation which engendered reform and counter-protest activity. The Curaçaoan disturbance had the greater immediate impact because of its rapid politicization, undeveloped indigenous social control mechanisms, and the larger percentage of the total population involved. Networks of organization are crucial to the crystallization of new movements. Based on semistructured interviews and on published primary and secondary sources; 4 notes, biblio.

L. N. Beecher

1786. Anderson, William A. and Dynes, Russell R. ORGANIZATIONAL AND POLITICAL TRANSFORMATION OF A SOCIAL MOVEMENT: A STUDY OF THE 30TH OF MAY MOVEMENT IN CURACAO. *Social Forces 1973 51(3): 330-341.* Examines the transformation of the May Movement in Curacao, Netherland Antilles, in the context of social movement theory. Initiated by an economic strike, the movement became increasingly politicized. Its initial protopolitic phase was characterized by a violent outburst, then a political strike. The resulting labor solidarity led to the resignation of the government. The movement eventuated in the formation of a new labor party which was successful in a subsequently called election. Internal conflict within the labor movement promoted rather than hindered political mobilization. The structural setting, however, maintained the movement, in Smelser's terms, at a norm-oriented rather than in a value-oriented direction.

J

1787. Baptise, Patrick. PUBLIC FINANCE IN TRINIDAD AND TOBAGO. *Social and Econ. Studies [Jamaica] 1977 26(4): 477-500.* Summarizes the Keynesian, Monetarist, and New Cambridge school approaches to fiscal policy. Analyzes the financial operations of the government of Trinidad and Tobago in respect to the three theories. Finds that more economic planning is needed to increase the effect of government fiscal policy and reduce the negative impacts. 9 tables, 4 fig., 8 notes.

E. S. Johnson

1788. Baptiste, F. A. LE RÉGIME DE VICHY À LA MARTINIQUE (JUIN 1940 A JUIN 1943) [The Vichy regime in Martinique, June 1940 to June 1943]. *Rev. d'Hist. de la Deuxième Guerre Mondiale [France] 1978 28(111): 1-24.* In 1940 Admiral Georges Robert became high commissioner of Martinique, Guadeloupe, and French Guiana and commander of French naval forces in the Caribbean under the Vichy government. Robert chose to support Pétain and took strong measures against supporters of de Gaulle's Free French movement. The policies were anti-British and anti-American. The British attempted to undermine Robert but the United States recognized Vichy and Robert's government in the French West Indies. The Vichy government purged the West Indian civil service and reduced the liberal democratic general council and municipal council to impotence. It also established censorship and other information controls, concentration camps for Communists and Freemasons, and coordinated police systems. In addition to Robert, lower ranking "Quisling-Laval" types carried out pro-German policies. The Catholic bishop and creole leaders regarded Vichy as a bulwark against communism and gave it strong support. 100 notes.

G. H. Davis

1789. Beckford, George L. SOCIOLOGICAL CHANGE AND POLITICAL CONTINUITY IN THE ANGLOPHONE CARIBBEAN. *Studies in Comparative Int. Development 1980 15(1): 3-14.* Tests the hypothesis that contemporary Caribbean economy and society in the former British West Indies maintain basic features rooted in slavery and the plantation system. Outlines economic, demographic, political, and social change. The present dependence of West Indian economies on the international capitalist system tends to support the hypothesis. 4 tables, fig., 2 notes, 15 ref.

S. A. Farmerie

1790. Berleant-Schiller, Riva. THE FAILURE OF AGRICULTURAL DEVELOPMENT IN POST-EMANCIPATION BARBUDA: A STUDY OF SOCIAL AND ECONOMIC CONTINUITY IN A WEST INDIAN COMMUNITY. *Bol. de Estudios Latinoamericanos y del Caribe [Netherlands] 1978 (25): 21-36.* Environmental disadvantages, outsiders' misconceptions, and a sturdy culture evolved during slavery enabled post-emancipation Barbudans to resist damage to their community by colonizers and developers. The latter, biased in favor of intensive cultivation, private land ownership, and profitability, misunderstood and despised the communal land tenure system favored by the islanders. The Barbudans' belief that the island was theirs strengthened resistance to encroachment, 1860-1923. Based mainly on British Colonial Office records; 79 notes.

D. M. Cregier

1791. Brewster, Havelock. ECONOMIC DEPENDENCE: A QUANTITATIVE INTERPRETATION. *Social and Econ. Studies [Jamaica] 1973 22(1): 90-95.* Defines economic dependence and suggests means to measure it and its politico-cultural impact with reference to Trinidad and Tobago. Based on personal observation.

E. S. Johnson

1792. Carson, Edward. THE ESTABLISHMENT OF THE PUBLIC RECORD OFFICE OF THE BAHAMAS. *J. of the Soc. of Archivists [Great Britain] 1974 5(1): 31-37.* A Public Record Office of the Bahamas was established in 1970 under the auspices of the United Nations by Edward Carson of H. M. Customs and Excise Office in 1970. Describes the writer's visits to record offices in the United States and Canada, the selection of a site in the Bahamas, preparation of enabling legislation, the construction of the building, the physical movement of the records, assembling an archive system, and drafting of a guide. Appendix.

L. A. Knafla

1793. Castañeda Fuertes, Digna. ANÁLISIS HISTÓRICO DE LAS CLASES EXPLOTADAS EN MARTINICA [A historical analysis of the exploited classes in Martinique]. *Santiago [Cuba] 1976 (24): 67-127.* The historical, ideological, and strategic aspects of class struggle in a typical Caribbean island colony. Discusses the geography, economy, and society of Martinique and their effect on the country's insular development. The workers' struggle against exploitation has been continuous and falls into four periods: pre-1848, 1848-1900, 1900-36, and 1936-76. Rebellions were conditioned by the cultural level of the population and the ideological level of the world labor movement, but ultimately by the colonial context and French cultural and economic policy on the island. 57 notes, biblio., appendix.

D. Wasserstein

1794. Crusol, Jean. LES DÉSÉQUILIBRES DE LA CROISSANCE EXCENTRÉE EN ÉCONOMIE DE PLANTATION INSULAIRE. LE CAS DES ANTILLES FRANÇAISES [The imbalances of eccentric growth in an island plantation economy: the example of the French Antilles]. *Rev. d'Écon. Pol. [France] 1977 87(1): 1-32.* Views the principal problems facing the politicians and administrators of the French West Indies since World War II: the weak rate of economic growth, the low standard of living for workers in agriculture, and the low level of development.

1795. Deosaran, Ramesh. SOME ISSUES IN MULTICUL-TURALISM: THE CASE OF TRINIDAD AND TOBAGO IN THE POST-COLONIAL ERA. *Ethnic Groups 1981 3(3): 199-225.* Discusses cultural pluralism in Trinidad and Tobago and the social and economic basis for the tensions that persist between East Indians and Africans. Examines psychological factors, the Black power ideology, political institutions, the distribution of socioeconomic resources, and the philosophical basis for multicultural harmony.   J/S

1796. Deosaran, Ramesh. SOME ISSUES IN MULTICUL-TURALISM: THE CASE OF TRINIDAD AND TOBAGO IN THE POST-COLONIAL ERA. *Plural Soc. [Netherlands] 1981 12(1-2): 15-35.* Discusses the social, political, and psychological implications of cultural pluralism in Trinidad and Tobago during the 20th century, focusing on multiculturalism's impact on the growth of democratic institutions and on socioeconomic reforms.

1797. Duller, H. J. LA ECONOMÍA Y LA ACTIVIDAD EM-PRESARIAL DE LAS ANTILLAS [Economy and entrepreneurial activity of the Antilles]. *Bol. de Estudios Latinoamericanos y del Caribe [Netherlands] 1976 (20): 54-81.* With its history of diversified entrepreneurship and prosperous middle class, the Netherlands Antilles has many of the standard features of a successfully developing country. But the economy of the Antilles is not flourishing and recently has experienced a per capita decline of growth. The author attributes the regression of the Antillean economy chiefly to the exhaustion of its mainstay, oil refining, and the failure of tourism to take up the slack. Recommends linkage of the Antilles with the Andean Group's capital market, redirection of Dutch economic aid into support for job-creating small industries, and steps to reduce the highly unfavorable balance of trade. Based on interviews and published sources in Dutch and English; 72 notes.
D. M. Cregier

1798. Elkins, W. F. TRINIDAD'S LONGSHOREMEN'S STRIKE. *Jamaica J. [Jamaica] 1978 11(3-4): 76-77.* Growing racial consciousness, nationalism, and a desire to oust the British government resulted in the outbreak of violence during a longshore strike in Port of Spain, Trinidad, 1919.

1799. Emmanuel, Patrick. ELECTIONS AND PARTIES IN THE EASTERN CARIBBEAN: A HISTORICAL SURVEY. *Caribbean Rev. 1981 10(2): 14-17.* Surveys elections and political parties in the eastern Caribbean from 1930 to 1981, especially the dominance of labor movements and the emergence of alternative parties and radical political organization.

1800. Fraser, H. A. THE LAND AND CANNABIS IN THE WEST INDIES. *Social and Econ. Studies [Jamaica] 1974 23(3): 361-385.* Summarizes and relates the origins of cannabis legislation in the British West Indies. Because of cultural differences, there is difficulty in enforcing laws concerning cannabis. 6 notes.
E. S. Johnson

1801. Gontier, Fernande. AIMÉ CÉSAIRE, POET AND POLITICIAN. *Negro Hist. Bull. 1975 38(3): 377-379.* Aimé Césaire (b. 1913), black writer and social philosopher from Martinique, compares himself to an old volcano with few but violent eruptions. In the play, *The Tragedy of King Christophe* (New York: Grove Press, 1969), he portrays the dilemma of ends and means. The end is human dignity and liberty; the means are violence and brutality. 26 notes.   M. J. Wentworth

1802. Green, Timothy. IN TRINIDAD, CONSERVATIONISTS BATTLE NATIONALIZED GAS PLANT TO PRESERVE THE SCARLET IBIS AND OTHER BIRDS. *Smithsonian 1975 6(2): 34-41.* Traces a long controversy over the future of a 79,000-acre swamp around the tributaries of Trinidad's largest river, the Caroni. The Ministry of Agriculture's Wildlife Conservation Committee has pressed for extension of the existing sanctuary. An LPG barge operated by the government oil company in the swamp threatens roosting areas. In 1974 the government agreed to accept arbitration but reneged on the arbitrator's recommendation that barge operations be terminated and the Caroni swamp be designated a national park. A subsequent cabinet, however, decided in principle on the Caroni National Park and retaining barge operations.
K. A. Harvey

1803. Hendricks, Robert E. and Redlhammer, Paul R. EDUCATIONAL CHANGE IN THE ISLANDS: AN ASSESSMENT OF BAHAMIAN TRENDS. *J. of Negro Educ. 1980 49(1): 85-90.* Since independence in 1973, the government of the Bahamas has sought to reorient Bahamian education away from the elitist notions fostered by colonialism and toward an educational system stressing socially useful skills. To date, however, little has been accomplished on the classroom level. Based on secondary sources and interviews; 14 notes.
R. E. Butchart

1804. Hughes, Alister and Redman, John. REVOLUTION IN GRENADA: AN INTERVIEW WITH MAURICE BISHOP. *Black Scholar 1980 11(3): 50-58.* Discusses the career of radical political activist Maurice Bishop of Grenada. Beginning his activism while he was a law student in London in the 1960's, he became prime minister in the revolutionary government of Grenada after the 13 March 1979 overthrow of the government of Eric Gairy.

1805. Ince, Basil A. THE MEDIA AND FOREIGN-POLICY FORMATION IN SMALL STATES: TRINIDAD AND TOBAGO. *Int. J. [Canada] 1976 31(2): 270-292.* Analyzes the role of mass media in small developing nations like Trinidad as disseminators of information including that on foreign policy for the specific purpose of fostering development. 57 notes.   R. V. Kubicek

1806. Jackman, Oliver Hamlet. SOVEREIGNTY AND INTERDEPENDENCE: A BIOGRAPHY OF BARBADOS. *Américas (Organization of Am. States) 1979 31(3): 22-29.* Traces the history of Barbados, independent in 1966, including the beginnings of British colonization in 1625.

1807. Johnson, Howard. OIL, IMPERIAL POLICY AND THE TRINIDAD DISTURBANCES, 1937. *J. of Imperial and Commonwealth Hist. [Great Britain] 1975 4(1): 29-54.* Labor disturbances among sugar and oil workers in Trinidad in the 1930's brought fairly quick and positive response from the British Colonial Office. It genuinely attempted to improve social, economic, and working conditions for the laborers, because of the economic importance of the oil which the colony was producing.

1808. Khan, Jamal. DEVELOPMENT ADMINISTRATION AND DEVELOPMENT PROJECT: A STUDY OF THE INTERNATIONAL SEA FOODS LIMITED. *Caribbean Q. [Jamaica] 1977 23(4): 71-89.* Studies the International Sea Foods Limited in Barbados as an example of a development project and administration. The administration of development "is in more ways than one the administration of development programmes and projects in the developing world." Improvement in project administration not only reinforces development but also makes a significant contribution to the process of national development. Based on primary published sources and interviews in Barbados; 2 tables, 3 fig., 10 ref.   R. L. Woodward, Jr.

1809. Laing, Edward A. INDEPENDENCE AND ISLANDS: THE DECOLONIZATION OF THE BRITISH CARIBBEAN. *New York U. J. of Int. Law and Pol. 1979 12(2): 281-312.* Examines Great Britain's procedure for granting independence to the British West Indies, the tactics employed by the islanders to gain independence, the role of the UN, and the international implications of decolonization.

1810. Layne, Anthony. RACE, CLASS AND DEVELOPMENT IN BARBADOS. *Revista/Review Interamericana [Puerto Rico] 1979 9(3): 358-367.* Although independence has brought some economic development to Barbados, it is not clear yet whether the economic gains in recent years are enough to head off radicalization of the island's politics. 4 tables, 38 notes.   J. A. Lewis

1811. Layne, Anthony. RACE, CLASS AND DEVELOPMENT IN BARBADOS. *Caribbean Q. [Jamaica] 1979 25(1-2): 40-51.* Political independence in Barbados (1966) was accompanied by the assumption that this would lead to national development, including economic growth, social justice, and satisfaction of the expectations of historically underprivileged blacks and Indians. Analysis of occupational structure of the three major racial groups in Barbados (Negroes, whites and coloureds) reveals considerable upward mobility on the part of Negroes and substantial improvement in educational levels during the 1960's, but there has not been a "fundamental change" in the government's philosophy of development. Based on published government reports and other published materials; 38 notes, 4 tables.   R. L. Woodward, Jr.

1812. Lowe, Arbon Jack. BARBADOS. *Américas (Organization of Am. States) 1975 27(10): s1-s24.* An overview of Barbados since prehistoric times, covering population, political and economic development, and culture.

1813. Lowenthal, David and Clarke, Colin G. ISLAND ORPHANS: BARBUDA AND THE REST. *J. of Commonwealth and Comparative Pol. [Great Britain] 1980 18(3): 293-307.* Rivalries among West Indian islands have inhibited cooperation and thwarted wider national or supranational aims since 1960, and the same differences and particularism have stimulated demands for autonomy even in the poorest and smallest of them. The inhabitants of Barbuda fear that domination by Antigua will disrupt long-established patterns of social cohesion, communal access to resources, and ecological restraint. Based on newspapers and secondary works; 44 notes.   D. J. Nicholls

1814. Lynch, Charles. EDUCATION AND THE NEW GRENADA. *Black Scholar 1981 12(4): 13-24.* Briefly traces the history of the island of Grenada in the Caribbean since its discovery by Christopher Columbus in 1498. It was colonized by France in 1650 and became a British possession in 1763. Focusing on Grenada's educational system since the 1979 revolution when the People's Revolutionary Government of Prime Minister Maurice Bishop took over.

1815. Manning, Frank E. THE BIG BROTHER: CANADIAN CULTURAL SYMBOLISM AND BERMUDIAN POLITICAL THOUGHT. *Rev. Interamericana [Puerto Rico] 1977 7(1): 60-72.* Canadian presence in Bermuda has been particularly strong in the fields of religion and education. This presence is soon likely to expand to other areas. As ties with Great Britain are slowly loosened, many Bermuda citizens favor an official political tie with Canada. 3 notes, biblio.   J. A. Lewis

1816. Manning, Frank E. RELIGION AND POLITICS IN BERMUDA: REVIVALIST POLITICS AND THE LANGUAGE OF POWER. *Caribbean Rev. 1979 8(4): 18-21, 42-43.* Interjection of religious morality into the rhetoric of the left-wing opposition Progressive Labour Party, has made it a threat to the ruling United Bermuda Party, 1960's-70's.

1817. Martin, Tony. REVOLUTIONARY UPHEAVAL IN TRINIDAD, 1919: VIEWS FROM BRITISH AND AMERICAN SOURCES. *J. of Negro Hist. 1973 58(3): 313-326.* A longshoremen's strike in Trinidad in 1919 was the reflection of a growing resentment of nonwhite subjects toward British colonialism in the Caribbean. The official stance of both the British and U.S. governments was unfavorably disposed toward this and other manifestations of hostility against whites. Based on primary sources in the Public Record Office and the U.S. National Archives and secondary sources; 48 notes.   N. G. Sapper

1818. Murch, Arvin W. MARTINIQUE IN TRANSITION: SOME IMPLICATIONS OF SECONDARY MODERNIZATION IN A DEPENDENT SOCIETY. *Rev. Interamericana [Puerto Rico] 1977 7(2): 207-215.* By standards elsewhere in the Third World, Martinique should be a society interested in independence, but it is not. The island's rapid and recent modernization has effectively undermined what sentiment there was to break the colonial ties with France. 11 notes.   J. A. Lewis

1819. Nancoo, Stephen. MASS MEDIA ROLES IN ELECTORAL CAMPAIGN: THE TRINIDAD AND TOBAGO 1976 GENERAL ELECTION. *Indian J. of Pol. Studies [India] 1978 2(2): 118-129.* Discusses the role of the mass media in the 1976 elections in Trinidad and Tobago, particularly the possible partisanship of newspaper coverage.

1820. Nunes, F. E. A MINISTRY AND ITS COMMUNITY: TOBAGO—A CASE STUDY IN PARTICIPATION. *Social and Econ. Studies [Jamaica] 1974 23(2): 176-185.* Discusses the problem of creating a participatory government for Tobago. Institutionalized public

involvement is necessary before a satisfactory administrative system can be developed. 16 notes, 6 refs.   E. S. Johnson

1821. Romalis, Rochelle. ECONOMIC CHANGE AND PEASANT POLITICAL CONSCIOUSNESS IN THE COMMONWEALTH CARIBBEAN. *J. of Commonwealth and Comparative Pol. [Great Britain] 1975 13(3): 219-241.* Examines the impact of colonialism on St. Lucia's rural political experience. The transition from sugar to bananas as the main plantation product in the 1950's transformed the impoverished subsistence and wage-bound rural dwellers into a population of small farmers involved in the international export market. This in turn has created enormous political changes. During the 1960's the newly developed peasant political consciousness resulted in a political polarization which culminated in a power struggle among various island factions. Describes how the government, when threatened locally by loss of control, enlisted metropolitan assistance to curtail small grower involvement in the banana industry. Discusses the implications of these events for the island's political development as a whole. Based on Reports of the Agriculture Department, St. Lucia, and various secondary works; 34 notes.   C. Anstey

1822. Singh, Kelvin. ADRIAN COLA RIENZI AND THE LABOUR MOVEMENT IN TRINIDAD (1925-44). *J. of Caribbean Hist. [Barbados] 1982 16: 10-35.* Traces the importance of Adrian Cola Rienzi in the development of the labor movement in Trinidad, especially in the period 1937-40. Rienzi was an attorney and political organizer and gave critical leadership to the organization of labor unions and to their recognition by employers. Primary sources; 163 notes.
                                      R. L. Woodward, Jr.

1823. Šlessers, Mārtiņš. DEURBANIZĀCIJA TRINIDĀDE UN TOBAGO [Resettlement to rural areas in Trinidad and Tobago]. *Akad. Dzīve 1982 24: 28-31.* Discusses the resettlement plan in Trinidad and Tobago, which allocated parcels of land and government loans to the poor, enabling them to become self-sufficient and even contribute to the economic welfare of the country.

1824. Thorndike, Tony. GRENADA: MAXI-CRISIS FOR MINI-STATE. *World Today [Great Britain] 1974 30(10): 436-444.* "Examines the colonial heritage and the teething troubles of the new Caribbean state which has just taken its seat in the United Nations."   J

1825. Verton, Peter. EMANCIPATION AND DECOLONIZATION: THE MAY REVOLT AND ITS AFTERMATH IN CURAÇAO. *Rev. Interamericana [Puerto Rico] 1976 6(1): 88-100.* The 1969 riot of workers in Curaçao had serious repercussions in the Dutch Antilles. It brought the Afro-Curaçaoans into the political scene for the first time, it convinced the Dutch public to speed up independence, and it increased the political division between Curaçao and Aruba. Primary and secondary sources; 28 notes.   J. A. Lewis

1826. Verton, Peter. MODERNIZATION IN TWENTIETH CENTURY CURAÇAO: NEW ELITES AND THEIR FOLLOWERS. *Rev. Interamericana [Puerto Rico] 1977 7(2): 248-259.* Independence has meant in Curaçao the emergence of a new political elite. This ruling group has not, however, improved the island's economic situation. Nor has it completed the emancipation of the Afro-Curaçaoans. 5 tables, 8 notes.   J. A. Lewis

1827. Will, W. Marvin. MASS POLITICAL PARTY INSTITUTIONALISATION IN BARBADOS: AN ANALYSIS OF THE ISSUES AND DYNAMICS OF THE POST-INDEPENDENCE PERIOD. *J. of Commonwealth and Comparative Pol. [Great Britain] 1981 19(2): 134-156.* Analyzes the electoral and adaptive party functions in the Barbadian political system following independence in 1966. Briefly reviews preindependence political development, and describes the agricultural diversification, manufacturing, and tourism that formed the socio-economic setting for the critical 1971 election. The process of party institutionalization, clearly seen in the 1971 election, continued into the 1980's. Based on government records, newspaper articles, and political party manifestoes; 2 tables, 66 notes.   M. K. Hogg

1828. Williams, Marion. ASPECTS OF PUBLIC POLICY IN BARBADOS 1964-1976. *Social and Econ. Studies [Jamaica] 1977 26(4):*

432-445. Examines the factors, both public and private, that have influenced public financial policy. Economic necessity has regularly been the prime factor influencing public policy. 5 tables, fig., 17 notes, 2 ref.

E. S. Johnson

1829. Zéndegui, Guillermo de. IMAGE OF TRINIDAD AND TOBAGO. *Américas (Organization of Am. States) 1974 26(2): S1-16.* An overview of the Republic of Trinidad and Tobago since prehistoric times, covering its history, political, social and economic development, culture, population and agriculture.

1830. —. DOCUMENTS FROM THE NATIONAL UNITED FREEDOM FIGHTERS OF TRINIDAD. *Pan-African J. [Kenya] 1975 8(2): 203-225.* Publishes three documents prepared by the National United Freedom Fighters (NUFF) of Trinidad. The first is an ideological statement intended to provide a historical and ethical justification for the organization's anti-imperialist struggle in the Caribbean. The second consists of an interview conducted by the NUFF with some of its members, both men and women, who were asked to explain their revolutionary attitudes. The third is an appeal issued by the NUFF which calls on the population of Trinidad and Tobago to petition their government against its repression of revolutionaries.

S

1831. —. [NATIONALISM IN THE FRENCH CARIBBEAN]. *Rev. Interamericana [Puerto Rico] 1976 6(1): 102-119.*
Austin, Roy L. NATIONALISM IN THE FRENCH ANTILLES: EVALUATION OF MURCH'S THESIS, *pp. 102-114.* Questions the explanation in Arvin Murch's *Black Frenchmen* (Cambridge, 1971) that nationalism did not appear in the French Caribbean because political, social, and economic satisfaction was quite high in the French islands during the 20th century. Primary and secondary sources; 3 tables, 2 notes, biblio.
Murch, Arvin. BLACK FRENCHMEN REVISITED: A REPLY TO ROY AUSTIN, *pp. 115-119.* Defends his earlier conclusions and argues that no one can understand the French Caribbean in recent decades without taking into account progress made by the metropolitan French administration. Note.

J. A. Lewis

5. THE ANDEAN NATIONS

Regional Studies

1832. Alvarez Garcia, Marcos. LE PACTE ANDIN, UN PROCESSUS POSITIF D'INTÉGRATION EN AMÉRIQUE LATINE [The Andean Pact: a positive process of integration in Latin America]. *Rev. de l'Inst. de Sociologie [Belgium] 1975 (3-4): 415-436.* The 1969 Andean Pact united Bolivia, Chile, Ecuador, Peru, and Venezuela economically. The author discusses the pact's objectives, achievements, and prospects.

1833. Avery, William P. and Cochrane, James D. INNOVATION IN LATIN AMERICAN REGIONALISM: THE ANDEAN COMMON MARKET. *Internat. Organization 1974 27(2): 181-223.* "The Andean Common Market, the most recent attempt at regional integration in Latin America, differs from the other Latin American efforts both in the factors that prompted its formation and in the support it had when it was established. More importantly, it differs in its terms and provisions, providing for a higher level of integration than any other Latin American effort. Several of its features—a common policy on foreign investment, regional planning and coordination in such fields as industry and agriculture, a quasi-supranational secretariat—make it an innovative approach to integration in Latin America. Numerous factors enhance the integrative potential of Andean integraiton. Among these are relatively favorable ratings on several of the neo-functional variables of regional integration. These indicators suggest that the effort may attain its objectives and perhaps even set an example to be followed by other economic groupings among Latin American countries. Still, projections about the future of the Andean Common Market must remain mixed. Some negative factors exist within the movement that could, if they triumph over the positive factors, lead to the same stagnation that now characterizes LAFTA and the CACM." J

1834. Ciccarelli, Orazio. THE LETICIA DISPUTE, 1932-1934: A RECONSIDERATION OF PERUVIAN MOTIVATIONS. *Southern Q. 1973 11(4): 277-296.* An analysis of a dispute between Peru and Colombia concerning the territory of Leticia. The property in question was given to Colombia in 1922 as the result of the Salmon-Lozano treaty of that year. Peruvian troops occupied the area on the heels of Japan's invasion of Manchuria in 1932 and the Leticia incident attracted more international attention than it might have. Political and military events are studied along with eventual peace provisions. 78 notes.
R. W. Dubay

1835. Ferris, Elizabeth G. THE ANDEAN PACT: A SELECTED BIBLIOGRAPHY. *Latin Am. Res. Rev. 1978 13(3): 108-124.* Provides a bibliography on the Andean Pact with emphasis on Spanish sources generally not catalogued in North American libraries. Most materials are available in the United States. It is organized in four sections: 1) background studies; 2) general studies; 3) specific programs; and 4) single national experience in the pact. Biblio.
J. K. Pfabe

1836. Ferris, Elizabeth G. FOREIGN INVESTMENT AS AN INFLUENCE ON FOREIGN POLICY BEHAVIOR: THE ANDEAN PACT. *Inter-American Econ. Affairs 1979 33(2): 45-69.* Examines the role of the six governments that make up the Andean Pact: Bolivia, Colombia, Chile, Ecuador, Peru, and Venezuela in supporting the Andean Pact and the decision to treat foreign capital in common.

1837. Ferris, Elizabeth G. NATIONAL POLITICAL SUPPORT FOR REGIONAL INTEGRATION: THE ANDEAN PACT. *Int. Organization 1979 33(1): 83-104.* National political support for integration is essential for the success of a regional integration scheme, yet the dynamics of such support have not been adequately researched. National support is conceptualized here as a multidimensional phenomenon, encompassing national activity in the Andean Pact, supportive attitudes toward the pact, and national implementation of group decisions. These three dimensions of support are empirically as well as conceptually distinct; nations support the Andean Pact to different degrees and manifest their support in different ways. Nations which are more supportive of trade liberalization measures tend to be less supportive of joint policies in the areas of industrial programming and foreign investment. The ultimate success of the Andean Pact depends on the ability of its members to formulate mutually satisfactory ways of maintaining political support from all pact members. J

1838. Gros Espiell, Héctor. UN EPISODIO EN LA HISTORIA DIPLOMÁTICA: GIL FORTOUL Y EL LAUDO SUIZO DE 24 DE MARZO DE 1922 [An incident in diplomatic history: Gil Fortoul and the Swiss arbitration award of 24 March 1922]. *Bol. de la Acad. Nac. de la Hist. [Venezuela] 1979 62(247): 696-700.* Analyzes a section of Tomás Polanco's *Gil Fortoul: A Light in the Dark,* which deals with the arbitration by the Swiss government in 1922 whereby Venezuela lost to Colombia a significant part of its territory. Gil Fortoul, as a Venezuelan negotiator, was unfairly blamed for the loss. The Venezuelan Foreign Office was to blame because of its submission of unrequired information to the Swiss government, and its refusal to participate in the direct negotiations with Colombia, proposed by the Swiss arbiter. L. Makin

1839. Grosse, Robert. FOREIGN INVESTMENT REGULATION IN THE ANDEAN PACT: THE FIRST TEN YEARS. *Inter-American Econ. Affairs 1980 33(4): 77-92.*

1840. Hoelscher, David H. S. STRUCTURAL CHANGE IN CHILEAN TRADE PATTERNS. *Inter-Am. Econ. Affairs 1977 31(1): 65-75.* Examines the direction and composition of Chilean trade flows to determine the structure of trade patterns from 1969 to 1975 when the dominant factors influencing trade were Andean Pact commitments and domestic inflation and recession. Based on secondary sources and statistical interpretation; 8 tables, 4 notes, biblio. D. A. Franz

1841. Hojman, David E. THE ANDEAN PACT: FAILURE OF A MODEL OF ECONOMIC INTEGRATION? *J. of Common Market Studies [Great Britain] 1981 20(2): 139-160.* Discusses the elimination of intraregional trade barriers, the common external tariff, the treatment of foreign investment, and the sectoral program for industrial development of the Andean Pact, which seems to be destined to fail in its objective of balanced development of its members, its survival dependent on the richer members; if they behave rationally, the poorer members should choose to stay in the group.

1842. Lemos, María Luisa Ortega de. LA CONFERENCIA DEL MAR Y LA CONTROVERSIA COLOMBO-VENEZOLANA [The sea rights conference and the Colombian-Venezuelan controversy]. *U. Humanistica [Colombia] 1974-75 (8-9): 241-280.* Examines the history of the Colombian-Venezuelan controversy over sea rights, 1815-1974, with special reference to the international sea rights conferences of 1958, 1960, and 1974.

1843. Levine, Daniel H. CHURCH ELITES IN VENEZUELA AND COLOMBIA: CONTEXT, BACKGROUND AND BELIEFS. *Latin Am. Res. Rev. 1979 14(1): 51-79.* Compares Venezuelan and Colombian bishops' views regarding the relation of the Catholic Church to social problems. In both nations a majority views structural problems as more important than moral. Over 80% of the bishops believe the Church should either continue its traditional role or activate the laity; a small minority supported Church activism. Venezuelan bishops were more accepting of dialogue with Marxists, owing perhaps to differences in education, experience, and the less secure and influential role of the Church there. Based on interviews with bishops and secondary sources; 8 tables, 17 notes, biblio. J. K. Pfabe

1844. Mace, Gordon. THE ANDEAN GROUP AT THE TEN YEAR MARK. *Int. Perspectives [Canada] 1979 (Sept-Dec): 30-34.* The Cartagena Agreement of 1969 initiated the process of economic integration for the Andean countries of Bolivia, Chile, Colombia, Ecuador, Peru and Venezuela. The encouraging progress of the first four years, particularly an increase in regional trade, came to a standstill 1974-76, primarily because of changes in the economic development models of some members and the loss of Chile. The experiment includes some novel approaches, such as joint planning for industrial development and the introduction of common textbooks, but it has been unable to avoid the difficulties that have affected similar efforts elsewhere in the Third World.

E. S. Palais

1845. Middlebrook, Kevin J. REGIONAL ORGANIZATIONS AND ANDEAN ECONOMIC INTEGRATION, 1969-75. *J. of Common Market Studies [Great Britain] 1978 17(1): 62-82.* Functioning as principal instruments of the Andean Group's Commission and Junta, overseeing economic affairs for Bolivia, Chile, Colombia, Ecuador, Peru, and Venezuela, regional organizations assist in local industrialization and infrastructure, regional development programs, harmonizing socioeconomic policy, directing growth and distribution, and promoting automatic tariff reduction programs, 1969-75.

1846. Milenky, Edward S. DEVELOPMENTAL NATIONALISM IN PRACTICE: THE PROBLEMS AND PROGRESS OF THE ANDEAN GROUP. *Inter-Am. Econ. Affairs 1973 26(4): 49-68.*

1847. Petras, James F. and Morley, Morris H. THE RISE AND FALL OF REGIONAL ECONOMIC NATIONALISM IN THE ANDEAN COUNTRIES 1969-1977. *Social and Econ. Studies [Jamaica] 1978 27(2): 153-170.* In May of 1969 five western South American countries entered into an agreement that would form the Andean Common Market and restrict foreign investment. Changes in government among the five and pressure from international financial institutions led, in 1977 to the effective removal of foreign investment restrictions.

E. S. Johnson

1848. Salomon, Frank. THE ANDEAN CONTRAST. *J. of Int. Affairs 1982 36(1): 55-71.* Examines socioeconomic factors that have prevented the Quechua- and Aymara-speaking Indians, who constitute a majority in the Andean regions of Peru, Ecuador, and Bolivia, from forming the strong, effective political movements that might ameliorate their status in those three countries, and offers comparisons between policies toward Indians in those Andean countries and the government policies of countries in the Amazonian region.

1849. Slaght, Dale V. THE NEW REALITIES OF ECUADORIAN-PERUVIAN RELATIONS: A SEARCH FOR CAUSES. *Inter-American Econ. Affairs 1973 27(2): 3-14.* Discusses the causes of improved relations between Ecuador and Peru.   S

1850. Sudarev, V. ANDSKAIA GRUPPA NA POROGE 80-YKH GODOV [The Andean group on the eve of the 1980's]. *Mirovaia Ekonomika i Mezhdunarodnye Otnosheniia [USSR] 1980 (12): 136-142.* Examines the policy and relations within the Andean group and its relations with other countries of Latin America.

1851. Switzer, Kenneth A. THE ANDEAN GROUP; A REAPPRAISAL. *Inter-Am. Econ. Affairs 1973 26(4): 69-81.* "The major question for the Andean Group then remains to be whether or not the group can continue its course while maintaining satisfaction within each member nation (Bolivia, Chile, Colombia, Ecuador, and Peru)."   S

1852. Tironi, Ernesto. LAS ESTRATEGÍAS REGIONALES DE DESARROLLO Y LA INTEGRACIÓN DE LOS PAÍSES ANDINOS [Regional development strategies and the integration of the Andean Group]. *Estudios Int. [Chile] 1976 9(34): 58-102.* Discusses the development and economic integration of the Andean Group and the framework of the Cartagena Agreement, the members' political and ideological views on integration, and their particular interests.

1853. Vargas-Hidalgo, Rafael. THE CRISIS OF THE ANDEAN PACT: LESSONS FOR INTEGRATION AMONG DEVELOPING COUNTRIES. *J. of Common Market Studies [Great Britain] 1979 17(3): 213-226.* Analyzes the problems inherent in the South American economic integration, the Andean Pact, and in economic agreements between developing nations in general which include divergent political views, differing rates of development, and rivalry between member nations.

1854. Vargas-Hidalgo, Rafael. LA CRISIS DEL PACTO ANDINO [The crisis of the Andean Pact]. *Rev. de Pol. Int. [Spain] 1977 (151): 101-111.* Analyzes the causes of the crisis of the Andean Pact which culminated in the withdrawal of Chile in 1976.

1855. Vickers, William T. ETHNOLOGICAL METHODS, RESULTS, AND THE QUESTION OF ADVOCACY IN ANDEAN RESEARCH. *Latin Am. Res. Rev. 1980 15(3): 229-239.* Reviews Gabriel Escobar's *Sicaya: Cambios culturales en una comunidad mestiza andina* (Lima: Inst. de Estudios Peruanos, 1973), Billie Jean Isbell's *To Defend Ourselves: Ecology and Ritual in an Andean Village* (Austin: Inst. of Latin American Studies, U. of Texas, 1978), Stephen B. Brush's *Mountain, Field and Family: The Economy and Human Ecology of an Andean Valley* (Philadelphia: U. of Pennsylvania Pr., 1977), Ted Lewellen's *Peasants in Transition. The Changing Economy of the Peruvian Aymara: A General Systems Approach* (Boulder, Colo.: Westview Pr., 1978), and Norman E. Whitten, Jr.'s *Sacha Runa: Ethnicity and Adaptation of Ecuadorian Jungle Quichua* (Urbana: U. of Illinois Pr., 1976). These books show that the ethnological community study is a viable method of investigating the impact of industrialism and the process of sociocultural change.

J. K. Pfabe

1856. Villacres Moscoso, Jorge. LAS NORMAS REGULADORAS DEL DOMINIO LACUSTRE EN EL NUEVO DERECHO ECONÓMICO INTERNACIONAL [The regulatory norms of ownership of lakes in the new international economic law]. *Estudios de Derecho [Colombia] 1974 33(86): 243-257.* Discusses international law governing the control and possession of lakes in Latin America since the 19th century, paying particular attention to Lake Titicaca, the Sea of the Andes.

1857. Villegas, Maria Adriana de. MIGRATIONS AND ECONOMIC INTEGRATION IN LATIN AMERICA: THE ANDEAN GROUP. *Int. Migration Rev. 1977 11(1): 59-76.* Migration in the Andean Group of Latin America is often caused by unfair income distribution and the prevailing division of labor, 1970-77.

Bolivia

1858. Alba, Carlos. NATIONALISM IS CONTRARY TO NATIONAL INTERESTS. *World Marxist R. [Canada] 1973 16(7): 75-83.* Analyzes the present Bolivian Nationalist Popular Front government terrorist tactics. Continuing series on "Political Portrait of Latin America."   S

1859. Arauco, Fernando. LA LUCHA DEL PUEBLO BOLIVIANO [The struggle of the Bolivian people]. *Rev. Mexicana de Ciencias Pol. y Soc. [Mexico] 1975 21(82): 57-70.* Discusses the Bolivian opposition to the US-imposed dictatorship in the 1970's, mobilized by the Federation of Bolivian Mine Workers and the Bolivian Workers' Central (COB).

1860. Barrios de Chungara, Domitila and Viezzer, Moema. LET ME SPEAK! *Monthly Rev. 1979 30(9): 42-54.* Presents excerpts from *Let Me Speak!* by Domitila Barrios de Chungara, wife of a Bolivian tin miner and leader of the Housewive's Committee of the Siglo XX Mines, a participant in the struggles of the mining community with mine administrators and their CIA and United States Embassy "advisors."

1861. Burke, Melvin and Malloy, James M. FROM NATIONAL POPULISM TO NATIONAL CORPORATISM; THE CASE OF BOLIVIA (1952-70). *Studies in Comparative Internat. Development 1974 9(1): 49-73.* Analyzes the Bolivian attempt at a populist resolution of its socioeconomic problems. The Movimiento Nacionalista Revolucionario failed to achieve its populist goals and was replaced by the military. This new government sacrificed economic growth for stability, wasted much of its wealth on nationalistic projects, fostered the development of a healthy private sector of the economy at the expense of the masses, and did not produce long-term solutions to Bolivia's economic problems. Primary and secondary sources; 9 tables, 19 notes, biblio.

S. A. Farmerie

1862. Campbell, Leon G. and Cortés, Carlos E. FILM AS A REVOLUTIONARY WEAPON: A JORGE SANJINÉS RETROSPECTIVE.

Hist. Teacher 1979 12(3): 383-402. Discusses five full length revolutionary films of Jorge Sanjinés, Bolivian filmmaker and radical, *Ukamu, Blood of the Condor, Night of San Juan, The Principal Enemy,* and *Small Town.* His first films not only documented the peasants' oppressive living-conditions but also were an active call to revolutionary activity. Later films were not as revolutionary but were still reflective of a new people's cinema. His films have "given promise of developing mass consciousness, and furthering the understanding of Bolivia's authentic popular culture." 21 notes.   L. C. Smith

1863. DeSantis, Sergio. IL "SOCIALISMO MILITARE" IN BOLIVIA (1936-1946) [Military Socialism in Bolivia, 1936-46]. *Storia Contemporanea [Italy] 1973 4(4): 821-877.* Bolivian politics reached a turning point in the Chaco War, fought with Paraguay over the region between the two countries. This war was a disaster for Bolivia and occasioned the formation of the Legion of Ex-Combatants (LEC). The LEC became a true political party headed by German Busch, whose military coup initiated military socialism in 1936 and displaced the traditional oligarchy. After Busch's suicide in 1939 and the 1946 lynching of his successor Gualberto Villaroel, military socialism in Bolivia ended. Based on secondary sources; 85 notes.   G. Pizzimenti

1864. Echevarría, Evelio. PANORAMA Y BIBLIOGRAFÍA DE LA NOVELA SOCIAL BOLIVIANA [Overview and bibliography of the Bolivian social protest novel]. *Inter-Am. Rev. of Biblio. 1977 27(2): 143-152.* Novels of social protest in Bolivia follow certain themes: the Indians, the mines and miners, the Chaco War, the jungle, the mixed-bloods, and the politics. Discusses characteristics and examples of these types published between 1904 and the National Revolution of 1952, comparing them with those published 1952-70. 5 notes, biblio.   B. D. Johnson

1865. Fletcher, G. Richard. SANTA CRUZ: A STUDY OF ECONOMIC GROWTH IN EASTERN BOLIVIA. *Inter-Am. Econ. Affairs 1975 29(2): 23-41.* Surveys the economic growth of Bolivia's Santa Cruz department since 1825, indicating the effect of central government policy on economic development in the area. Based on personal observation and secondary sources; 11 notes.   D. A. Franz

1866. Gomez, Walter. BOLIVIA: PROBLEMS OF A PRE- AND POST-REVOLUTIONARY EXPORT ECONOMY. *J. of Developing Areas 1976 10(4): 461-484.* Bolivia's significant dependence on one major export is typical of underdeveloped economies. Bolivia's economy is based on traditional agriculture and modern and export-oriented mining. During the first third of the century mining profits were very high (48 percent of the value of exports) and taxes very low (2-12 percent of value). The railway system completed in 1920 with heavy government indebtedness benefited only the mineowners at the peak of their profit-taking and exacerbated the nation's economic dualism. After the 1952 nationalization, the government mining corporation, Comibol, took over operation of the mines, and by 1958 production had declined to half the 1952 level —and still there was no money for needed investment in mine modernization. Private mining failed to stimulate economic development, 1900-30, and excessive postrevolutionary taxes hurt the mining sector. 4 tables, 5 figs., 48 notes.   O. W. Eads, Jr.

1867. Greño Velasco, José Enrique. BOLIVIA Y SU RETORNO AL MAR [Bolivia and her return to the sea]. *Rev.de Política Int. [Spain] 1977 (150): 199-230.* Discusses Bolivia's failure since the late 19th century to regain a corridor to the sea from Chile or from Peru.

1868. Guillet, David. INTEGRACIÓN SOCIOPOLÍTICA DE LAS POBLACIONES NUEVAS EN BOLIVIA: DESCRIPCIÓN DE UN CASO Y DISCUSION [Socio-political integration of new peoples in Bolivia: a description and discussion]. *Estudios Andinos 1973 3(7): 111-128.* Describes the social, economic, and political reforms in the canton of Omereque in the Valley of Cochabamba, Bolivia. The region was very successful in integrating a large new population of Indians (Cholas) while simultaneously proceeding with reforms. Omereque was able to develop and absorb the new population because it possessed a favorable agricultural and marketing base. The Bolivian mining unions played a major role in developing the needed reforms. 16 notes.   R. Scott

1869. Gutiérrez, Héctor and Héran, François. BOLIVIE: DE GRAVES PROBLÈMES SOCIO-DÉMOGRAPHIQUES; PRÉSENTATION DE QUELQUES DONNÉES RÉCENTES [Bolivia: serious sociodemographic problems, recent data]. *Problèmes d'Amérique Latine [France] 1981 (62): 11-30.* Early returns of the 1976 Bolivian national census illustrate the grave demographic, social, and agrarian situation in Bolivia.

1870. Heath, Dwight B. JUSTICIA DE CONTRABANDO: LOS JUZGADOS REVOLUCIONARIOS DE LOS CAMPESINOS BOLIVIANOS [Contraband justice: the revolutionary courts of the Bolivian peasants]. *Estudios Andinos 1974-76 4(2): 53-58.* Prior to the 1952 Bolivian revolution peasants had been largely integrated into national life. Ironically, however, they became increasingly isolated from mestizo- and white-dominated institutions. One example is the system for management of conflict. Peasants, mostly Indians, had little recourse to the civil courts. Peasants' unions established during the revolution formed the nucleus for a separate tribunal system under the Ministry of Peasant Affairs. The new court system implies greater barriers to social integration of peasants. Secondary sources; 3 notes.   J. L. White

1871. Heyduk, Daniel. BOLIVIA'S LAND REFORM HACENDADOS. *Inter-Am. Econ. Affairs 1973 27(1): 87-96.*

1872. Huizer, Gerrit. PEASANT MOVEMENTS FROM THE END OF THE XIXTH CENTURY UP TO OUR TIME. *Cahiers Int. d'Hist. Écon. et Sociale [Italy] 1978 8: 117-126.* Analyzes Bolivian peasant movements, 1866-1955. During the colonial period the communal property of the Indian villages was respected to a certain degree, but after independence a small ruling minority tried to gain control over the vast Indian lands. This provoked strong peasant reaction, and though the peasants were defeated in the Chaco War, 1932-35, they had exposed weakness in the traditional social system and this increased unrest. Various new peasant political parties were formed about 1940, and the Indian Congress in 1945 demanded an end to compulsory services. Violence grew after 1946, culminating in the Land Reform Decree of 1953 which ended feudalism in Bolivia. Secondary sources; 16 notes, biblio.   F. X. Hartigan

1873. Keehn, Norman H. BUILDING AUTHORITY: A RETURN TO FUNDAMENTALS. *World Pol. 1974 26(3): 331-352.* In newly established regimes, building and maintaining authority is the fundamental task. It is on the basis of their authority that leaders secure compliance and support to achieve public purposes. The conferring of benefits constitutes the incentive designed to attract support and to motivate compliance. In postrevolutionary Bolivia, inflationary fiscal and monetary policies underpinned the government's support-building policies. Inflationary outputs helped to create the consent that facilitated governing. By 1956 inflation had become so acute that the Bolivian government was impelled to administer a stabilization program. Stabilization reduced the government's capacity to confer benefits; this led to a shift in support and loyalties. Failure to consider the political aspects of inflation threatened the viability of the government.   J

1874. Klein, Herbert S. BOLIVIA AND ITS AGRARIAN REFORM: A REVIEW OF RECENT LITERATURE. *Peasant Studies Newsletter 1976 5(4): 20-24.* Discusses recent historiography of the impact of the Movimiento Nacionalista Revolucionario's 1952 coup d'etat and land reform for peasants in Bolivia, 1952-60's.

1875. Knudson, Jerry W. LICENSING NEWSMEN: THE BOLIVIAN EXPERIENCE. *Gazette [Netherlands] 1979 25(3): 163-175.* Bolivian President General Hugo Banzer issued a decree in 1972 stipulating that all journalists must be eligible for inclusion in the National Register of Professional Journalists in order to practice their craft. The two most prominent professional organizations for journalists, the Association of La Paz Journalists and the Federation of Workers of the Bolivian Press, supported the licensing of newsmen and have some share in the licensing process, along with the Ministry of Education and the Bolivian Catholic University. In Bolivia, the licensing of newsmen reflects a desire by journalists to upgrade their professional and economic status rather than an attempt by the government to control the press. Based on interviews and secondary sources; 32 notes.   J. S. Coleman

1876. Kohl, James V. PEASANT AND REVOLUTION IN BOLIVIA, APRIL 1, 1952-AUGUST 2, 1953. *Hispanic Am. Hist. Rev. 1978 58(2): 238-259.* The Bolivian revolution of 9 April 1952, which placed the National Revolutionary Movement (MNR) in power, was largely an urban revolution. During the next 16 months, however, the Indian peasants revolted, refusing to work and violently seizing land. On 2 August 1953, the Agrarian Reform Decree was passed to bring order to the expropriations. 84 notes.   B. D. Johnson

1877. Lavaud, Jean-Pierre. BOLIVIE, LA DÉMOCRATIE ENTRE-VUE [Bolivia, democracy glimpsed]. *Problèmes d'Amérique Latine [France] 1979 (54): 9-61.* Analyzes the political situation created in Bolivia by military governments beginning with General Hugo Banzer Suarez's regime, 1971-76, and ending with the election of Lidia Gueiler Tejada as the president of a civilian government in 1979.

1878. Lavaud, Jean-Pierre. BOLIVIE: LE RETOUR DES MILI-TAIRES [Bolivia: the return of the military]. *Problèmes d'Amérique Latine [France] 1981 (62): 79-109.* Describes Bolivia's successive coups d'état since November 1979, centering on the struggle between the military and its opposition, in particular the leftist and union sectors.

1879. LeBot, Yves. LE MOUVEMENT SYNDICAL BOLIVIEN À LA CROISÉE DES CHEMINS (1978-1980) [The Bolivian labor movement at the crossroads, 1978-80]. *Problèmes d'Amérique Latine [France] 1981 (62): 111-158.* Analysis of the Bolivian trade union movement since 1952, centering on the role of the Bolivian Workers' Central (COB), as an important political force, particularly since 1978.

1880. Maffucci, Mario. UNA QUESTIONE SUDAMERICANA: LO SBOCCO AL MARE DELLA BOLIVIA [A South American question: Bolivia's outlet to the sea]. *Civitas [Italy] 1977 28(2): 53-68.* Traces the history of Bolivia's quest for an outlet to the sea in the foreign relations among Bolivia, Chile, and Peru; defining borders has been a continual problem in those countries since the end of Spanish colonialism in the 19th century.

1881. Mansilla, H. C. F. LA REVOLUCIÓN DE 1952 EN BOLI-VIA: UN INTENTO REFORMISTA DE MODERNIZACIÓN [The Bolivian revolution of 1952: a reformist attempt at modernization]. *Folia Humanistica [Spain] 1980 18(215): 751-761.* Regional fragmentation prevents the appearance of homogeneous social class structures valid for all of Bolivia. The reformist movement started with the Nationalist Revolutionary Movement (MNR) in 1941, which achieved power in 1952, implementing the nationalization of the mining industry (unsuccessful for increasing national income) in 1952 and land reform (much more successful) in 1953. The first regime to introduce economic planning in Latin America, it became repressive and totalitarian.

1882. Mansilla, H. C. F. LA REVOLUCIÓN DE 1952 EN BOLI-VIA: UN INTENTO REFORMISTA DE MODERNIZACIÓN [The 1952 revolution in Bolivia: a reformist attempt at modernization]. *Rev. de Estudios Pol. [Spain] 1980 (17): 117-128.* The social and economic changes that occurred in Bolivia after the 1952 revolution represented attempts to avoid both the socialist State-led attempt at rapid accumulation of capital of the Cuban type, and the dependent capitalism of the Brazilian model. These changes implied an important break in the history of the country, separating a traditional phase from a modernizing one. Economic change was hampered by the inherited structures and the landlocked position of the country. In the political field, demagogic and manipulative elements predominated. 20 notes.   J. V. Coutinho

1883. Mayorga, Rene Antonio. NATIONAL-POPULAR STATE, STATE CAPITALISM AND MILITARY DICTATORSHIP IN BOLIVIA: 1952-1975. *Latin Am. Perspectives 1978 5(2): 89-119.*

1884. McEwen, William. LOS CAMBIOS POLÍTICOS DESPUÉS DE LA REVOLUCIÓN BOLIVIANA: EL PODER EN UNA COMUNIDAD PROVINCIAL [Political change after the Bolivian revolution: power in a provincial community]. *Estudios Andinos 1973 3(7): 91-110.* A study of the economic, political, and social changes that have occurred in the rural Bolivian town of Sorata. The changes, traced to the Bolivian Revolution of 1952, introduced the local Indian population as a new political force in the region. The Indians, in unison with the

mining unions, became a new and powerful force in local and national politics. The sometimes violent struggle between the new and old political groups in the region continued from the election of the new Movimiento Nacionalista Revolucionario (MNR) in 1952 until 1964. Following the MNR's fall in 1964 various groups of *sindicatos,* inactive since 1952, again took up the struggle against the central government.
                                                            R. Scott

1885. Mitchell, Christopher. THE NEW AUTHORITARIANISM IN BOLIVIA. *Current Hist. 1981 80(463): 75-78, 89.* Examines the chaotic economic situation and the lack of substantial social support that hampers the rule of the present Bolivian junta, headed by General Luís Garcá Meza.

1886. Morales, Waltraud Queiser. BOLIVIA MOVES TOWARD DEMOCRACY. *Current Hist. 1980 78(454): 76-79, 86-88.* Reviews electoral politics and the succession of unstable military governments in Bolivia during the 1970's, discusses economic problems, and analyzes conditions for a successful democratic government.

1887. Moreno, Nahuel. THE ANTI-IMPERIALIST FRONT IN BOLIVIA. *Internat. Socialist R. 1973 34(2): 30-43.*

1888. Nash, June. CONFLICTO INDUSTRIAL EN LOS ANDES: LOS MINEROS BOLIVIANOS DEL ESTAÑO [Industrial conflict in the Andes: the Bolivian tin miners]. *Estudios Andinos 1974-76 4(2): 219-257.* Industrial conflict in Bolivian mining is best analyzed by the Marxist model. Since national independence mine workers have pursued a revolutionary strategy. High unemployment has increased class conflict. Analysis of major incidents reveals that violence has historically been precipitated by owners' rejection of labor demands. The labor movement took a pragmatic attitude in the 1920's, and was strengthened by the violence of the 1940's. Civil war erupted in the mines in 1949, and continued through the 1960's, destroying labor organization. Labor has rejected participation in national governments. Bolivian miners are the most proletarian and exploited workers in Latin America. Primary and secondary sources; 14 notes.   J. L. White

1889. Parrenin, Georges. GENÈSE DES MOUVEMENTS INDI-ENS-PAYSANS EN BOLIVIE (1900-1952) [Genesis of the Indian-peasant movements in Bolivia, 1900-52]. *Problèmes d'Amérique Latine [France] 1981 (62): 31-53.* Analyzes the evolution of Indian peasant movements in Bolivia since 1900 and their political involvement during the national revolution of 1952-53.

1890. Rivera Cusicanqui, Silvia. LA ANTROPOLOGÍA Y AR-QUEOLOGÍA EN BOLIVIA: LÍMITES Y PERSPECTIVAS [Anthropology and archaeology in Bolivia: limits and prospects]. *Am. Indígena [Mexico] 1980 40(2): 217-224.* The absence of academic anthropology in Bolivia is due to the racist attitudes of the Bolivian elite and their attempts to control and manipulate the oppressed ethnic groups. Following the Mexican model, Bolivia instituted several cultural anthropology institutes in an attempt to provide a viable bridge to the past and to gloss over the cultural heterogeneity with an ideology of national unity. But governmental restrictions limited these activities to a kind of tourist-oriented window-dressing anthropology with little space for critical and independent work. This situation is, however, being challenged by the rise of self-conscious Indian groups opposed to the official view.
                                                            J/S

1891. Rivière d'Arc, Hélène and Lavaud, Jean-Pierre. LES FONC-TIONS CIVILES DE L'ARMÉE BOLIVIENNE: DE L'AMÉNAGE-MENT À L'INDUSTRIE [Civilian functions of the Bolivian army: from planning to industrialization]. *Cahiers des Amériques Latines [France] 1979 20: 159-180.* Analyzes the Bolivian army's takeover of civilian matters even beyond its political powers, mainly in economic planning and the management of the nation's business and industrial development. Examines the stages in the army's involvement in planning since 1961, and the creation in 1972 of the Confederation of the Armed Forces for National Development (COFADENA), with foreign help. The economic involvement generated political conflict among military groups, ending in 1974 in victory for followers of Colonel Hugo Banzer. 2 tables, appendix, 37 notes.   G. P. Cleyet

1892. Roca, Omar. EL SESQUICENTENARIO DE LA INDEPEN-
DENCIA DE BOLIVIA [The sixtieth anniversary of Bolivian indepen-
dence]. *Casa de las Américas [Cuba] 1976 16(94): 92-103.* A survey of
Bolivian revolutions from the independence era to the present, focusing
on the struggle of indigenous and mestizo classes against aristocratic,
bourgeois, and 20th-century foreign monopolisitic domination. The Indian struggle starting in the latter half of the 18th century subsequently
joined forces with the mestizos. The benefits of independence went to the
Creoles who allied themselves with old Spanish landowners to safeguard
common economic interests. The eventual liberal victory in the revolutions of the 19th century was a bourgeois triumph. The 20th-century
revolutions showed the growing power of the working masses in achieving
their rights. The masses suffered a setback with the arrival of the Hugo
Banzer government. Secondary works.   H. J. Miller

1893. Rojas, Antonio. LAND AND LABOR IN THE ARTICULA-
TION OF THE PEASANT ECONOMY WITH THE HACIENDA.
Latin Am. Perspectives 1980 7(4): 67-82. The short-term consequences
of land reform in Omasuyos province, Bolivia, following the revolution
of 1952 were favorable to small landowners and peasants. Long-term,
however, the results have been a harsh capitalism exploiting a large
migrant labor force and production units incapable of competing equally.
3 tables, 8 notes, biblio.   J. F. Vivian

1894. Rybalkin, I. E. POD ZNAMENEM BOR'BY ZA INTERESY
NARODA [Under the banner of the struggle for the people's interests].
Voprosy Istorii KPSS [USSR] 1980 (1): 115-119. Surveys the history of
the Bolivian Communist Party from its formation in 1950 to its cooper-
ation with other parties in successfully opposing a military coup in 1980.
Published documents; 15 notes.   L. E. Holmes

1895. Sanders, G. Earl. THE QUIET EXPERIMENT IN AMERI-
CAN DIPLOMACY: AN INTERPRETATIVE ESSAY ON UNITED
STATES AID TO THE BOLIVIAN REVOLUTION. *Americas
(Acad. of Am. Francisan Hist.) 1976 33(1): 25-49.* Though the United
States had long distrusted Bolivia's Movimiento Nacionalista Revolucionario (MNR), after the latter seized power in 1952 it obtained both
American recognition and other assistance. Fundamentally, the State
Department decided that MNR offered the best chance of stability and
that United States aid could consolidate the party's "pragmatic center"
against its labor-left wing. A new spurt of aid followed the Cuban Revolution. United States policy did have a moderating effect on the MNR and
the Bolivian government and strengthened the military, which took over
in 1964 and provided relative stability. Stability was still fragile under
MNR rule and basic problems remained unsolved, while the seeming
success of policy toward Bolivia may have misled United States diplomacy elsewhere. Secondary sources and published official documents; 88
notes.   D. Bushnell

1896. Sanz, Fernando Ortiz. 150 YEARS OF BOLIVIAN INDE-
PENDENCE. *Américas (Organization of Am. States) 1975 27(8): 2-4.*
Short chronicle of the events which followed Bolivia's independence,
1825-1975.

1897. Stafford, Joseph D., III. THE BOLIVIAN MILITARY IN
POLITICS. *Secolas Ann. 1979 10: 81-94.* Application of three models
of political systems, clientelism, corporatism, and praetorianism, to Bolivia's government since the 1964 military coup concludes that the lack of
mediating power contenders, the broad range of power contenders and
power capabilities, and the instability of governing coalitions indicates the
application of praetorianism as the best-fitting model.

1898. Urquidi, Arturo. ANTEPROYECTO DE LEY GENERAL
DE COMUNIDADES INDÍGENAS [Bill for general legislation concerning Indian communities]. *Anuario Indigenista [Mexico] 1977 37:
131-159.* In order to encourage socioeconomic development among
Bolivian Indians, the government must recognize and guarantee to Indian
communities the right to freely determine their systems of land tenure and
their political, social, cultural, and economic structures; extend the benefits of agrarian reform to these communities; provide economic assistance;
and include Indian communities in the scope of national plannng. A
National Institute of Indian Communities should be created to implement
the provisions of the Indian communities' law by identifying Indian communities, helping settle boundary disputes, and providing administrative
and technical assistance.   G.-A. Patzwald

1899. Useem, Bert. THE WORKERS' MOVEMENT AND THE
BOLIVIAN REVOLUTION. *Pol. & Soc. 1980 9(4): 447-469.* The
influence of the international political economy on Third World labor
movements can be illustrated by an examination of the decline of labor's
power in postrevolutionary Bolivia. Even though the success of the 1952
Movimiento Nacionalista Revolucionario (Nationalist Revolutionary
Movement, MNR) rested in large part on the power of labor, especially
the power of the mine workers, the country's changing position in the
international political economy, brought about by the declining importance of tin, resulted in the elimination of worker participation in the
coalition MNR government within a four-year period. 113 notes.
                                                              D. G. Nielsen

1900. Volk, Steven S. CLASS, UNION, PARTY: THE DEVELOP-
MENT OF A REVOLUTIONARY UNION MOVEMENT IN
BOLIVIA (1905-1952). *Sci. & Soc. 1975 39(1): 26-43, (2): 180-198.* Part
I. HISTORICAL BACKGROUND. Unlike the labor situation in much
of the rest of Latin America, labor unions in Bolivia provided a revolutionary thrust to its nation's political developments. Generally speaking,
Bolivian unions since the early years of the 20th century have fought for
economic and political rights while opposing capitalism, imperialism and
the forces within their own ranks calling for class collaboration. Part II.
FROM THE CHACO WAR TO 1952. The political organization of the
labor movement in Bolivia became important only following the end of
the Chaco War in 1935. Labor was influenced by bourgeois-reformist and
revolutionary-socialist ideologies. A revolutionary movement based on
miner support and participation developed, dominated by spontaneity
and isolated from socialist parties. Although the miners were the decisive
force in the revolution of 1952, they lacked the leadership and the political
party necessary to control the bourgeois-democratic revolution. Secondary sources.   N. Lederer

1901. Waghelstein, John D. CHE'S BOLIVIAN ADVENTURE.
Military Rev. 1979 59(8): 39-48. Ernesto "Che" Guevara's attempt to
introduce Cuban-style revolution in Bolivia failed for tactical and political
reasons. Tactical errors included weakness in supply systems, inadequate
river-crossing security, lack of intelligence security, and insufficient communication networks with urban centers. Che's insistence on dominating
revolution leadership, excluding Bolivian Communist Party members,
and the lack of anti-U.S. propaganda are seen as political errors. 52 notes.
                                                                J. Moore

1902. Whitehead, Laurence. BANZER'S BOLIVIA. *Current Hist.
1976 70(413): 61-64, 80.* General Hugo Banzer, in power in Bolivia since
1971, has recently tried to win favor through economic and territorial
negotiations with Chile, mainly to gain a seaport, but his military regime
has little to bargain with.

1903. Whitehead, Laurence. EL ESTADO Y LOS INTERESES SEC-
CIONALES: EL CASO BOLIVIANO [The state and sectional interests: the case of Bolivia]. *Estudios Andinos 1974-75 4(1): 85-118.* None
of the theories of state power propounded by Max Weber, Karl Marx, and
others fits the case of Bolivia. Bolivia is susceptible to manipulation by
foreign interests and intimidation by armed domestic factions. In this
context all interest groups tend to become pressure groups. The major
interest groups in Bolivia are the military corporations, workers, students,
and peasants. The government maintains a weak posture toward these
groups, yielding alternately to the demands of each. Bolivia, however, is
a geographically vulnerable, socially fragmented, exceptionally poor, and
traditionally ungovernable country. Observations regarding interest
groupings in Bolivia cannot, therefore, be extended to other Latin American or developing countries. 16 notes.   J. L. White

1904. Whitehead, Laurence. MINERS AS VOTERS: THE ELEC-
TORAL PROCESS IN BOLIVIA'S MINING CAMPS. *J. of Latin
Am. Studies [Great Britain] 1981 13(2): 313-346.* Electoral politics in
Bolivia in the 1940's paved the way for the revolution of 1952. Minework-
ers, as a result of the system of representation, enjoyed a disproportionate
influence once they were organized to vote as a bloc. Elections in 1923
and 1931 did not benefit the miners, but the 1940 elections provided the
first significant opportunity for political organization in mining zones
since 1923. For the first time, the system of electorate management
seemed breached. Not until 1944, however, did the Nationalist Revolutionary Movement (MNR) under Victor Paz Estenssoro achieve major

gains. In the 1951 election, Paz Estenssoro, strongly supported by miners, won a plurality, if not a majority, of votes for the presidency. Only a coup prevented him from assuming office. The election was important in preparing the way for the 1952 revolution and demonstrated the miners' willingness to vote as well as to take subversive action. Based largely on printed primary sources; 42 notes, 4 tables.　　　M. A. Burkholder

1905. Widerkehr, Doris E. AUTONOMY OVERSHADOWED: A BOLIVIAN COOPERATIVE WITHIN THE NATIONALIZED MINING INDUSTRY. *Human Organization 1980 39(2): 153-160.* Studies Highpoint, a Bolivian mining community owned by the state corporation, COMIBOL, and organized as a workers' cooperative, during the 1970's, and concludes that COMIBOL's power has tended to dominate local autonomy.

1906. Zavaleta Mercado, René. LA FUERZA DE LA MASA: DE BANZER A GUEVARA ARZE [The power of the mass: from Banzer to Guevara Arze]. *Estudios Sociales Centroamericanos [Costa Rica] 1980 9(26): 131-152.* Following political thought from President Hugo Banzer, 1971-78, to President Walter Guevara Arze, 1979, one ends up with Guevara expressing Bonapartist or Caesarian ideology, which if not taken into account by the Marxist working-class movement may succeed in putting an end to that movement—which seems to be the objective of revolutionary nationalism as judged by its political activity in Bolivia.
　　　T. D. Schoonover

1907. Zéndegui, Guillermo de. IMAGE OF BOLIVIA. *Américas (Organization of American States) 1973 25(10): S1-S24.* Overview of Bolivia covering geography, history, political development, culture, population, and social development, 1550-1973.

Colombia

1908. Agosin, Manuel R. DEVELOPMENT PATTERNS AND LABOUR ABSORPTION IN COLOMBIAN MANUFACTURING. *J. of Development Studies [Great Britain] 1976 12(4): 351-363.* Explains low growth rates in employment in Colombia's manufacturing sector, offering evidence that industrial growth fostered by trade policies may be to blame, 1970's.

1909. Asociación Nacional de Usuarios Campesinos. EL CAFÉ Y EL MOVIMIENTO CAMPESINO [Coffee and the peasant movement]. *Latin Am. Perspectives 1975 2(3): 53-83.* Analyzes rural social classes, sharecropping, and the effects of US economic imperialism on the coffee industry in Colombia. Discusses the economic policies of the middle classes involved in the coffee industry and various peasant movements, 1955-70. Reprinted from *Uno en Dos,* June 1972.

1910. Bailey, John J. BUREAUCRATIC POLITICS AND SOCIAL SECURITY POLICY IN COLOMBIA. *Inter-Am. Econ. Affairs 1976 29(4): 3-20.* Uses social security policy in Colombia as a case study of administrative policymaking within a political system comprised of competing elitist groups. Adapted from a paper presented to the American Political Science Association, San Francisco, 2-5 September 1975. Primary and secondary sources; 5 tables, 23 notes, appendix.
　　　D. A. Franz

1911. Bailey, John J. LA IMPLEMENTACIÓN POLÍTICA EN UN RÉGIMEN NEOCORPORATIVO: ALGUNOS EJEMPLOS DE LA EDUCACIÓN COLOMBIANA [Political implementation in a neocorporative regime: some examples from Colombian education]. *Estudios Andinos 1974/75 4(1): 203-239.* Analyzes the political significance of two educational agencies in Colombia: the Colombian Institute for the Promotion of Higher Education (ICFES) and the National Apprenticeship Service (SENA). Their functions reveal decentralization of power in a neocorporatist regime. Both founded in the 1950's, ICFES and SENA are quasi-public agencies. Both formulate educational policy and allocate resources with minimal governmental control. Corporatism, then, does not mean centralized direction. The two Colombian examples are not typical merely of Latin America, but of the corporatist model elsewhere. Neocorporatism is seen as an effective means of formulating public policy. Primary and secondary sources; 25 notes.　　　J. L. White

1912. Berry, Albert. RURAL POVERTY IN TWENTIETH-CENTURY COLOMBIA. *J. of Interamerican Studies and World Affairs 1978 20(4): 355-376.* Colombia's urban-based economic policy has slighted the enduring rural poverty. In the last half-century little progress has been made in rural housing and health. The record in education has been better although still far from strong. 12 notes, ref.
　　　T. D. Schoonover

1913. Booth, John A. RURAL VIOLENCE IN COLOMBIA, 1948-1963. *Western Political Q. 1974 27(4): 657-679.* An application of factor analysis to certain social, economic, and political variables and the intensity and persistence of violence in rural Colombia, 1948-63.　　　S

1914. Catanese, Anthony James. PLANNING IN A STATE OF SIEGE: THE COLOMBIA EXPERIENCE. *Land Econ. 1973 49(1): 35-43.*

1915. Christie, Keith H. ANTIOQUEÑO COLONIZATION IN WESTERN COLOMBIA: A REAPPRAISAL. *Hispanic Am. Hist. Rev. 1978 58(2): 260-283.* Social historians have written of the egalitarian nature of the development of the Antioquia area of Colombia. However, while some poor families did succeed here, inequalities of initial opportunity, of wealth, and of political influence limited social mobility. Well-connected families did better than the others. 4 tables, 38 notes.
　　　B. D. Johnson

1916. Dailey, Suzanne. RELIGIOUS ASPECTS OF COLOMBIA'S LA VIOLENCIA: EXPLANATIONS AND IMPLICATIONS. *J. of Church and State 1973 15(3): 381-406.* Discusses the religious persecution of Protestants in Colombia in the 1950's.　　　S

1917. Dalgaard, Bruce R. MONETARY REFORM, 1923-30: A PRELUDE TO COLOMBIA'S ECONOMIC DEVELOPMENT. *J. of Econ. Hist. 1980 40(1): 98-104.* Examines two financial missions to Colombia headed by Edwin Walter Kemmerer to determine their impact on Colombia's financial system and on the flow of American investment to Colombia. The 1923 and 1930 missions established a central bank and completely reorganized the Colombian financial and fiscal system. These reforms served to provide enough stability to encourage American investment, which helped to develop a financial and economic infrastructure in Colombia.　　　J

1918. Delgado, Alvaro. AGAINST THE DANGER OF MILITARISM. *World Marxist R. [Canada] 1974 17(2): 103-108.* Analyzes the impact of the military coup d'etat in Chile (1973) on the Communist-led revolutionary movement in Colombia.　　　S

1919. Dix, Robert H. CONSOCIATIONAL DEMOCRACY: THE CASE OF COLOMBIA. *Comparative Pol. 1980 12(3): 303-321.* Discusses Arend Lijphart's theory of consociational democracy as applied to Colombia. Colombia is unique among consociational democracies to the extent that its elites failed to prevent conflict during the National Union Period (1945-49) and yet succeeded during the National Front Period (1958-74). Most of the conditions Lijphart believes promote consociational democracy were ineffective in Colombia. Changes in elite behavior are a factor contributing to the success or failure of consociational democracy, a factor that Lijphart does not indicate. 46 notes.
　　　M. A. Kascus

1920. Dix, Robert H. THE VARIETIES OF POPULISM: THE CASE OF COLOMBIA. *Western Pol. Q. 1978 31(3): 334-351.* Delineates two major varieties of Latin American populism, represented in Colombia by Jorge Eliécer Gaitán in the late 1940's and Gustavo Rojas Pinilla in the 1960's and early 1970's. Comparisons are made of the sources of their support, the composition of their leadership, their ideologies and programs, and their organization and leadership style.　　　J/S

1921. Dudley, Leonard and Sandilands, Roger J. THE SIDE EFFECTS OF FOREIGN AID: THE CASE OF PUBLIC LAW 480 WHEAT IN COLOMBIA. *Econ. Development and Cultural Change 1975 23(2): 325-336.* By constructing a theoretical model, the authors analyze the relative effects of US foreign aid wheat on Colombia between 1955 and 1971. Domestic production suffered because Colombian producers averaged 20% lower prices than the estimated socially optimal level. "In effect, the marketing agency sold imported wheat at a price low enough to eliminate the greater part of domestic production, but still high enough to yield substantial revenues on the imports which replaced it." Based on published sources; 3 tables, 23 notes.

J. W. Thacker, Jr.

1922. Ebel, Roland H. FOUR TOWNS IN COLOMBIA: A COMPARATIVE STUDY OF COMMUNITY POLITICAL CULTURE. *Secolas Ann. 1974 5: 82-101.* Assesses the attitudes and values according to 1) community view, 2) view of the political role of decisionmaker, 3) community resources, 4) community priorities, and 5) the political process in four Colombian cities, El Cerrito, La Cumbre, Roldanillo, and Puerto Tejada.   S

1923. Ebel, Roland H. and Henderson, James. PATTERNS OF CONTINUITY IN LATIN AMERICAN SOCIETY: POLITICAL AND HISTORICAL PERSPECTIVES. *Secolas Ann. 1976 7: 89-122.* Latin American politics in general and Colombian politics in particular demonstrate political continuity of values and behavior since the colonial period. Secondary materials; 2 figs., 90 notes.   J. A. Lewis

1924. Egginton, Everett and Ruhl, J. Mark. THE INFLUENCE OF AGRARIAN REFORM PARTICIPATION ON PEASANT ATTITUDES: THE CASE OF COLOMBIA. *Inter-Am. Econ. Affairs 1974 28(3): 27-43.* Evaluates the impact of an agrarian reform program by comparing the attitudes of rural "participants and non-participants with regard to economic satisfaction, confidence in the political system, and future expectations." Concludes that agrarian reform participation in Colombia contributes to the disparity between peasant expectations and benefits. Primary and secondary sources; 10 tables, 13 notes, appendixes.

D. A. Franz

1925. Fenoy, Gérard. L'ARMÉE EN COLOMBIE [The army in Colombia]. *Cahiers du Monde Hispanique et Luso-Brésilien [France] 1976 26: 83-104.* Studies the history and development of the armed forces in Colombia and the influence of the military on government and politics. Describes how successive regimes worked to transform rival bands into a regular army after the Thousand Day War (1899-1902), how mandatory military service began, and how the military academies were established. After 1925, the mainly upper-class army shifted to a middle-class, rural, uneducated membership. The army remained inactive throughout the period of agrarian reform, unionism, and fiscal reform (1934-38). After the return of the Conservative Party, the army under General Gustavo Rojas Pinilla became actively involved in the government of Mariano Ospina Perez, and entered full force into the period of civil war called *La Violencia.* Describes the strong US influence on the development of the Colombian army, through its involvement in the Interamerican Defense League (1942), in providing planes and matériel, and in the Rio Pact (1947) and other treaties. Also views the aggressions of Generals Ruiz Novoa and Valencia Tovar against the governments in power, 1962-72. Secondary sources; biblio.   S. Sevilla

1926. Fernández, Raúl A. IMPERIALIST CAPITALISM IN THE THIRD WORLD: THEORY AND EVIDENCE FROM COLOMBIA. *Latin Am. Perspectives 1979 6(1): 38-64.* Analysis of finance, manufacturing, and agriculture indicates that a neocolonial character pervades the Colombian economy. A feeble domestic capitalism is dependent upon or serves an efficient foreign capitalism, mainly North American. The quasi feudalism of the 19th century has been continued into the 20th century under exploitative conditions. 6 tables, 13 notes, biblio.

J. F. Vivian

1927. Fleet, Michael. HOST COUNTRY MULTINATIONAL RELATIONS IN THE COLOMBIAN AUTOMOBILE INDUSTRY. *Inter-American Econ. Affairs 1978 32(1): 3-32.* Discusses relations between foreign multinational automobile companies and the Colombian government showing that although initial contracts favorable to Colombian interests are awarded, compliance with their provisions has been ineffectively pursued. Concludes that "in some cases 'controlling' one's multinationals can be more expensive than it is worth." Paper originally presented at an ASA-LASA meeting in Houston, Texas. 64 notes.

D. A. Franz

1928. Fleet, Michael. THE POLITICS OF AUTOMOBILE INDUSTRY DEVELOPMENT IN COLOMBIA. *J. of Interamerican Studies and World Affairs 1982 24(2): 211-239.* Colombia's government has maintained a balanced policy toward the automobile industry, and its placement between caution and commitment has sought to achieve some tangibles while holding options open. Thus, it seems neither to be caving in to the transnationals nor imposing itself upon the domestic elite, and it has not faced significant opposition from either group. Based upon printed primary materials; 23 notes, 5 tables, ref.

T. D. Schoonover

1929. Galli, Rosemary. RURAL DEVELOPMENT AS SOCIAL CONTROL: INTERNATIONAL AGENCIES AND CLASS STRUGGLE IN THE COLOMBIAN COUNTRYSIDE. *Latin Am. Perspectives 1978 5(4): 71-89.* A review of recent efforts at agricultural reform in Colombia. The early pattern of large farms and impoverished peasants and part-time rural workers aroused protests, and gradual and ineffective reforms were instituted. The 1960's witnessed the advent of the Green Revolution, which greatly increased production, but which also starved out peasants who did not have the capital to finance it. This was followed in the 1970's by foreign-financed and controlled efforts to keep the peasants in the countryside. Not economic nor humanistic at all, this latest agrarian "reform" was designed solely to prevent rural uprisings and revolutions. Chart, 3 notes, ref.   V. L. Human

1930. Galli, Rosemary. THE UNITED NATIONS DEVELOPMENT SYSTEM AND COLOMBIA. *Latin Am. Perspectives 1975 2(3): 36-52.* Preinvestment assistance to Colombia through the UN development system (the UNDP and the specialized agencies), 1971, demonstrated the function of the UN system to open the host country to the international capitalist world.

1931. García, Antonio. LA CRISIS DEL MODELO LIBERAL DE CRECIMIENTO ECONOMICO: ANALISIS DE LA EXPERIENCIA COLOMBIANA [The crisis of the liberal model of economic growth: analysis from the Colombian experience]. *Estudios Sociales Centroamericanos [Costa Rica] 1980 9(26): 103-130.* Certain limits of perception in the liberal ideology permit present economic and social plans to be introduced as if they treat only technical operations and are not political instruments which relate on structural levels to a strategic and global conception of development. In the present situation in Latin America, the crisis in the liberal model of economic growth not only signifies the exhaustion of the possibilities to continue operating as before but the opening of a new historical way, of the emergence of the people as the creative force and as the conductors of historical plans and projects of life and of the imagination of a new society determining what makes up development. Based on newspapers and institutional documents; 18 notes.   T. D. Schoonover

1932. Geithman, David T. and Landers, Clifford E. POLITICAL AND ECONOMIC FORCES IN COLOMBIAN SOCIETY AS REFLECTED IN THE LITERATURE OF *LA VIOLENCIA.* *Secolas Ann. 1975 (6): 75-93.* The period of *La Violencia* (1946-58) has yet to spawn a great novel, but many good novels have emerged from the events. The best of these works, especially those of Alvaro Valencia Tovar, Gabriel Garciá Márquez, and Eduardo Caballero Calderón, are nonpartisan and show the bewildering forces turned loose during this social upheaval. Primary and secondary sources; 32 notes.   J. Lewis

1933. Gilhodès, Pierre. LA VIOLENCE EN COLOMBIE, BANDITISME ET GUERRE SOCIALE [La Violencia in Colombia, banditry and social war]. *Cahiers du Monde Hispanique et Luso-Brésilien [France] 1976 26: 70-81.* A critical study of *La Violencia* in Colombia as a peasant uprising and harsh interparty competition, comparing it to the Zapatista revolution in Mexico or the Vietnamese civil war. Defines *La Violencia* as a confused accumulation of thefts, rapes, assassinations, tortures, forced migrations, arrests, and military occupations within the indefinite dates of about 1946-64. The assassination of liberal leftist leader Jorge Eliécer Gaitán (1948) marked one of the first stages. Conservative pressure and police activity to control popular mobilization ensued, but the new government of General Gustavo Rojas Pinilla had difficulty handling the growing Communist activity, 1953-58. Outlines the final degeneration of the guerrilla warfare into banditry in the early 1960's. Concludes that the *Violencia* brought important social effects, such as accelerated urbanization, liberalization of the labor force, and a rise in peasant consciousness and effectiveness in national political affairs. 2 charts, 8 notes.   S. Sevilla

1934. González G., Fernán E.   ELECCIONES Y PARTICIPACIÓN POPULAR EN COLOMBIA [Elections and popular participation in Colombia]. *Estudios Centro Americanos [El Salvador] 1974 29(305-306): 211-221.* The lack of equal opportunity in all of the territories impedes real democracy, since there cannot be true political equality when the majority of the population has no access to national goods and services.
                                                                        L. Russell

1935. Goulet, Denis.   A SUBVERSIVE AGENT FROM CO-LOMBIA. *Worldview 1974 17(6): 29-34.* Colombian sociologist Orlando Fals-Borda (1925-) was a "moral agent in revolutionary times, whose ethical dilemmas and ideological options are those faced by countless others." The author stresses his major contribution to the study of social change and his analysis of subversion "as a moral category." Primary and secondary sources; 4 notes.   M. L. Frey

1936. Gros, Christian.   COLONISATION DE LA FORÊT ET RÔLE DE L'ÉTAT: QUELQUES REMARQUES SUR LE CAS DE L'"ORIENTE COLOMBIEN" [Settlement of the forest and the state's role: the situation in eastern Colombia]. *Travaux & Mémoires de l'Inst. des Hautes Études de l'Amérique Latine [France] 1979 (32): 133-139.* History of the settlement of the forested regions of eastern Colombia, centering on the government's participation.

1937. Groves, Roderich T.   THE COLOMBIAN NATIONAL FRONT AND ADMINISTRATIVE REFORM. *Administration and Society 1974 6(3): 316-336.* The 1958 National Front agreement, based on a coalition of the Conservative Party and the Liberal Party, has not had the sort of beneficial impact on national life that the Colombian leadership had hoped.   S

1938. Haney, Emil B., Jr. and Haney, Wava G.   SOCIAL AND ECO-LOGICAL CONTRADICTIONS OF COMMUNITY DEVELOP-MENT AND RURAL MODERNIZATION IN A COLOMBIAN PEASANT COMMUNITY. *Human Organization 1978 37(3): 225-234.* Describes problems of community development resulting from power centralization and unequal reward allocation, especially in education and agricultural management in the peasant community of Fómeque since the 1930's.

1939. Henderson, James D.   ANOTHER ASPECT OF THE *VI-OLENCIA*. *Secolas Ann. 1980 11: 120-136.* Examines the strong anti-Communist nature of Colombia's *Violencia*, 1940's-65.

1940. Hobsbawm, Eric.   PEASANT MOVEMENTS IN CO-LOMBIA. *Cahiers Int. d'Hist. Écon. et Sociale [Italy] 1978 8: 166-186.* Colombia has few records of powerful economic and social peasant movements before the mid-19th century. However, there is evidence of considerable peasant violence, 1925-48, which changed colonial Colombia, a society of exploitation and lordship into a modern state governed by an effective two-party system which reached down to the village and the peasantry. Major conflicts erupted over land ownership and the cultivation of cash crops, especially coffee. 5 tables, 6 notes.
                                                                  F. X. Hartigan

1941. Hoskin, Gary and Swanson, Gerald.   POLITICAL PARTY LEADERSHIP IN COLOMBIA: A SPATIAL ANALYSIS. *Comparative Pol. 1974 6(3): 395-424.* Political parties impede political change in Colombia.   S

1942. Kirby, J. M.   COLOMBIAN LAND-USE CHANGE AND THE SETTLEMENT OF THE ORIENTE. *Pacific Viewpoint [New Zealand] 1978 19(1): 1-25.* Discusses land use and government encouragement of colonization in Colombia in order to incorporate unused lands into the national economy.

1943. Kline, Harvey F.   THE COAL OF "EL CERREJÓN": AN HISTORICAL ANALYSIS OF MAJOR COLOMBIAN POLICY DE-CISIONS AND MNC ACTIVITIES. *Inter-American Econ. Affairs 1981 35(3): 69-90.* Studies the development of the El Cerrejón coalfields

by the Colombian government and a consortium of multinational corporations in response to the oil crisis of the 1970's, and the questions that this huge economic development scheme pose for the financial and managerial future of Colombia.

1944. Kline, Harvey F.   INTEREST GROUPS IN THE COLOM-BIAN CONGRESS: GROUP BEHAVIOR IN A CENTRALIZED, PATRIMONIAL POLITICAL SYSTEM. *J. of Inter-Am. Studies and World Affairs 1974 16(3): 274-300.* A study of interest groups in the Colombian Congress reveals that congressmen form an elite group. As new groups appear they are coopted by the elites to strengthen its position still more. Interest groups are also found in the highest social stratum which pressure the congress elite. Based on Colombian government records and secondary sources; 4 tables, 4 notes, biblio.
                                                                   J. Thomas

1945. König, Hans-Joachim.   THEORETISCHE UND METHODIS-CHE ÜBERLEGUNGEN ZUR ERFORSCHUNG VON NATION-ALISMUS IN LATEINAMERIKA [Theoretical and methodological reflections on studies of Latin American nationalism]. *Can. Rev. of Studies in Nationalism [Canada] 1979 6(1): 13-32.* The central question in studying nationalism is its connection with the socioeconomic and political development of the area concerned. Nationalism may have arisen as a result of partial social change or it may have been used by the elite as an instrument of development. Thus, it is closely tied to modernization, whether favoring solidarity and liberty or oppression. This functional approach is used with particular reference to Colombia, from the independence movements of the early 1800's to the Frente Nacional (1958-74).
                                                                   R. Aldrich

1946. Leal, Magdalena Leon de and Deere, Carmen Diana.   ESTU-DIO DE LA MUJER RURAL Y EL DESARROLLO DEL CAPI-TALISMO EN EL AGRO COLOMBIANO [Rural women and the development of capitalism in agrarian Colombia]. *Am. Indígena [Mexico] 1978 38(2): 341-381.* Elaborates on the general characteristics of capitalism's development process, its significance in four different regions of Colombia, and the division of labor by sex. The analysis of capitalist development in these regions illustrates three forms of regional integration within the national economy: production for the international market, capitalistic production in response to internal market development, and the function of providing manual labor. Each form of integration has had its special agrarian structure and an internal process of change in production relationships, with important repercussions for the rural economy.   J/S

1947. Legrand, Catherine C.   PERSPECTIVES FOR THE HISTORI-CAL STUDY OF RURAL POLITICS AND THE COLOMBIAN CASE: AN OVERVIEW. *Latin Am. Res. Rev. 1977 12(1): 7-36.* A "national" bias in the writing of Colombian history has ignored the study of localities and of rural history. Further research into specific rural problems and regions is essential. Such research should incorporate four perspectives: structural motivations of peasant unrest, national-local interaction, patron-client relationships, and regionalism. Based on secondary sources; 15 notes, biblio.   J. K. Pfabe

1948. Loy, Jane M.   REBELLION IN THE COLOMBIAN LLA-NOS: THE ARAUCA AFFAIR OF 1917. *Americas (Acad. of Am. Franciscan Hist.) 1978 34(4): 502-531.* At the end of 1916 a band of malcontents and adventurers led by Humberto Gómez seized the town of Arauca on the Venezuelan border, repudiated the government of President José Vicente Concha (1867-1929), and proceeded to carry out depredations in the surrounding country. Though soon suppressed, the movement briefly called attention to the situation of a neglected frontier community and provided various pretexts for political recrimination among politicians of the interior. Based on printed sources, especially press and official documents; 124 notes.   D. Bushnell

1949. Mármora, Lelio.   LABOR MIGRATION POLICY IN CO-LOMBIA. *Int. Migration Rev. 1979 13(3): 440-454.* Discusses the context and application of Colombian government programs, begun in 1975, to develop a systematic labor migration policy.

1950. McGreevey, William Paul.   REINTERPRETING COLOM-BIAN ECONOMIC HISTORY. *J. of Interamerican Studies and World*

Affairs 1981 23(3): 352-363. Review essay of M. Arango, *Café e Industria, 1850-1930* (1977), C. W. Bergquist, *Coffee and Conflict in Colombia, 1886-1910* (1978), R. Brew, *El Desarrollo Económico de Antioquia desde la Independencia hasta 1920* (1977), and M. Palacios, *Coffee in Colombia, 1850-1970* (1980), and *El Café en Colombia, 1850-1970: Una Historia Económica, Social y Política* (1979). Bergquist, Palacios, and Arango offer good analysis and interpretation, although Palacios neglects theory. These works will serve well as the basis for an ongoing debate. Brew's monograph is essentially a useful collection of data, which awaits an analyst to place it in a coherent framework. 6 notes, ref.   T. D. Schoonover

1951. Misas Arango, Gabriel. LA POLITIQUE INDUSTRIELLE DU GOVERNEMENT LÓPEZ (1974-1978) [President López's industrial policy, 1974-78]. *Problèmes d'Amérique Latine [France] 1979 (52): 89-104.* The neoliberal industrial policy of Alfonso López Michelsen, president of Colombia 1974-78, neither reduced inflation nor increased industry's efficiency.

1952. Mosquera, A. APUNTES CRÍTICOS SOBRE ALGUNAS TENDENCIAS IDEOLÓGICAS EN COLOMBIA [Critical notes on some ideological tendencies in Colombia]. *Lateinamerika [East Germany] 1977 (Aut): 37-49.* Criticizes the ultrarevolutionary movements in Colombia for being anarchistic and adventuristic suggesting that they have failed to organize the masses properly and have opposed the mainstream Soviet-oriented movement. Based on these organizations' writings and Lenin's works; 28 notes.   D. R. Stevenson

1953. Ocampo, José F. THE PRESENT STAGE OF THE COLOMBIAN REVOLUTION. *Latin Am. Perspectives 1975 2(3): 5-18.* Analyzes the political climate in Colombia, 1968-74, including social classes, the strategy and tactics of the upper classes, the economic and political activism of the lower classes, and the rise of nonrevisionist political parties within the proletariat.

1954. Pabón Núñez, Lucio. EL RÉGIMEN CONCORDATARIO EN LA HISTORIA DE COLOMBIA [The system of concordats in the history of Colombia]. *Boletíen de Hist. y Antigüedades [Colombia] 1975 62(709): 205-223.* The earliest concordat in force in what is now Colombia was that of 1753 between the Spanish crown and the Vatican. Following independence, Colombia rulers earnestly sought the conclusion of a national concordat, but the initial disinclination of the papacy to deal with the new republic and later the development of church-state conflict delayed realization of a concordat until 1887. That agreement underwent certain changes but remained essentially intact until the new concordat of 1973. 35 notes.   D. Bushnell

1955. Pécaut, Daniel. LA COLOMBIE DE 1974 À 1979: DU MANDAT CLAIR À LA CRISE MORALE [Colombia from 1974 to 1979: from a clear mandate to a moral crisis]. *Problèmes d'Amérique Latine [France] 1979 (52): 7-61.* Analyzes the evolution of the policies initiated by Colombian President Alfonso López Michelsen in 1974, centering on the rise of coffee prices, illegal export of drugs, social unrest, and the consequences of these issues on Colombian economic and political institutions.

1956. Pécaut, Daniel. LA CONSTITUTION DES *GREMIOS* EN INSTANCE QUASI-GOUVERNEMENTALE: L'EXEMPLE COLOMBIEN DANS LES ANNÉES 1945-1950 [The creation of a quasi-governmental role for the Gremios; the Colombian example in the years 1945-50]. *Rev. Française d'Hist. d'Outre-mer [France] 1979 66(3-4): 331-341.* In the troubled political climate of Colombia in the late 1940's the political lobbies of such groups as the Coffee Growers' National Federation developed a role that reinforced and underpinned the state. 9 notes.   D. G. Law

1957. Pécaut, Daniel. LA PHÉNOMÈNE DE "LA VIOLENCE" EN 1945-53 [The phenomenon of *La Violencia* in 1945-53]. *Cahiers du Monde Hispanique et Luso-Brésilien [France] 1976 26: 55-67.* Studies the social and political consequences of the first part of *La Violencia,* the civil war in Colombia. Attempts to align the violence with the process of national modernization, offering an explanation behind the development resulting from the movement. Points out that the cities were mainly involved in the battle, and that the systematic offensive of the dominant

class in blocking popular mobilization was strongest in cities such as Rio Magdalena, Bogota, and Cali, (ca. 1945-47). Examples of cohesion to block *La Violencia* were efforts by industrialists to maintain the agrarian structure, the counter-reform law of 1944, and the dislocation of the government resulting from the adoption of a new economic policy. Based largely on G. Guzman's *La Violencia en Colombia* (1962); note.   S. Sevilla

1958. Pécaut, Daniel. POLITIQUE DU CAFÉ ET DÉMOCRATIE CIVILE RESTREINTE: LE CAS DE LA COLOMBIE [Coffee policy and restricted civil democracy: the Colombian case]. *Cultures et Développement [Belgium] 1980 12(3-4): 477-506.* Examines the evolution of the policy on the production and export of coffee followed by Colombia since the 1930's and its relation to the country's political regime.

1959. Peeler, John A. COLOMBIAN PARTIES AND POLITICAL DEVELOPMENT: A REASSESSMENT. *J. of InterAm. Studies and World Affairs 1976 18(2): 203-224.* A narrow, exploitative elite has dominated Colombian political parties and as such they are responsible for Colombia's social problems today. Yet, the political system remains healthy and the 1974 elections gave no indication of an impending breakdown. In the case of Colombia it is not true that a corrupt system is automatically a decaying system, doomed to quick extinction. On the contrary, the Colombian party system, while corrupt, appears viable and stable for the foreseeable future. Based on Colombian government and political party documents and secondary sources; table, biblio.   J. R. Thomas

1960. Plazas S., Francisco de Paula. GENEALOGIAS [Genealogies]. *Bol. de Hist. y Antigüedades [Colombia] 1976 63(715): 537-546.* Traces the genealogy of the Echandía family, descended from Francisco de Echandía Landa (1713-88), which became established in the Colombian department of Tolima and whose best-known member is the Liberal leader and former presidential candidate Darío Echandía Olaya (b. 1897). Based on local archives and published works; biblio.   D. Bushnell

1961. Pollock, John C. VIOLENCE, POLITICS, AND ELITE PERFORMANCE: THE POLITICAL SOCIOLOGY OF *LA VIOLENCIA* IN COLOMBIA. *Studies in Comparative Int. Development 1975 10(2): 22-50.* Investigates the wave of widespread violence in Colombia, 1948-60, exploring the relationship between social mobilization, violence, and coffee. Analyzes several hypotheses purporting to explain the violence. The savage, widespread violence was unusual, even for Colombia; the violence arose in the context of relatively rapid social and economic mobilization; and it was associated with demands for change. Primary sources; 4 tables, 9 notes, biblio.   S. A. Farmerie

1962. Ramsey, Russell W. CRITICAL BIBLIOGRAPHY ON LA VIOLENCIA IN COLOMBIA. *Latin Am. Res. Rev. 1973 8(1): 3-44.* Bibliography of *La Violencia* in Colombia, 1946-65; examines the growth of civil strife in 1946, the first guerrilla war, 1953, the *entrega* of 1954, and the alternation plan of 1958.

1963. Randall, Stephen J. THE BARCO CONCESSION IN COLOMBIAN-AMERICAN RELATIONS, 1926-1932. *Americas (Acad. of Am. Franciscan Hist.) 1976 33(1): 96-108.* Though committed to the necessity of foreign investment, Colombian leaders were concerned about US predominance, particularly in the petroleum industry. The resulting confrontation involved several concrete disagreements but focused on the cancellation, in 1926, of the Barco concession, located near the Venezuelan border and largely controlled by Gulf Oil. The State Department added its protest against Colombia's action and over the next years indicated that the Barco cancellation threatened Colombia's credit rating and ultimately its economic stability. The pro-US Enrique Olaya Herrera, who became president in 1930, restored the concession despite nationalist protests. Primary sources; 45 notes.   D. Bushnell

1964. Randall, Stephen J. THE INTERNATIONAL CORPORATION AND AMERICAN FOREIGN POLICY: THE UNITED STATES AND COLOMBIAN PETROLEUM, 1920-1940. *Can. J. of Hist. [Canada] 1974 9(2): 179-196.*

1965. Real, John P. COLOMBIA—1970: A CASE STUDY. *Military Rev. 1974 54(10): 58-60.* Discusses riot suppression tactics successfully employed in disorders in Bogotá, Colombia, surrounding the 1970 presidential elections.

1966. Rounds, Christopher. LA REFORMA AGRARIA EN CO-LOMBIA Y OTROS TÓPICOS RELACIONADOS: INVESTIGA-CIÓN BIBLIOGRÁFICA [Agrarian reform in Colombia and related topics: a bibliographic investigation]. *U. Humanística [Colombia] 1979 (10): 129-147.* Bibliography of land reform in Colombia.

1967. Rubbo, Anna and Taussig, Michael. EL SERVICIO DOMÉS-TICO EN EL SUROESTE DE COLOMBIA [Domestic servants in southwestern Colombia]. *Am. Indígena [Mexico] 1981 41(1): 85-112.* Examines the inner character and external consequences of female ser-vanthood in a region of marked capitalist development centered around Cali, Colombia. Female servanthood embodies and molds the basis of all power relations and plays an important part in the reproduction of social relations because servants are the essential link between the macrostruc-ture of political life and the microstructure of domestic personal existence.
J/S

1968. Ruhl, J. Mark. AN ALTERNATIVE TO THE BUREAU-CRATIC-AUTHORITARIAN REGIME: THE CASE OF COLOM-BIAN MODERNIZATION. *Inter-American Econ. Affairs 1981 35(2): 43-69.* Examines the bureaucratic and authoritarian model of Latin American military regimes, and demonstrates the manner in which Co-lombia seems to have escaped this pattern of development.

1969. Ruhl, J. Mark. CIVIL-MILITARY RELATIONS IN COLOMBIA: A SOCIETAL EXPLANATION. *J. of Interamerican Studies and World Affairs 1981 23(2): 123-146.* Colombia maintains a tradition of civil control of the military unlike most other Latin American countries. Colombia has not yet faced the modernization pressures that have disturbed political and civilian institutions elsewhere. 6 notes, ref.
T. D. Schoonover

1970. Schmidt, Steffen W. BUREAUCRATS AS MODERNIZING BROKERS? CLIENTELISM IN COLOMBIA. *Comparative Pol. 1974 6(3): 425-450.* The relationship of the bureaucracy to political par-ties in Colombia.
S

1971. Schmidt, Steffen W. *LA VIOLENCIA* REVISITED: THE CLIENTELIST BASES OF POLITICAL VIOLENCE IN CO-LOMBIA. *J. of Latin Am. Studies [Great Britain] 1974 6(1): 97-111.* Between 1930 and 1964, 300,000 Colombians were killed in the struggle for power between Liberals and Conservatives. If the town of Salado is a representative experience, then the effects of this struggle, characterized by great self-righteousness and continuing patron-client relations which tie people together, still linger. Prospective violence is still perceived by Saladeños as the most important problem today. Thus, "party-based patron-client networks were strengthened, preserved and brought into play during the worst of *La Violencia*," so much so that "in Salado, people still perceive violence in terms of political parties, still conserve a large amount of partisan consciousness, continue to hate the opposition for what they believe it did and to a great degree still trust and rely upon their own party as a source of security." Based on interviews and second-ary works; 28 notes.
K. M. Bailor

1972. Schmidt, Steffen W. WOMEN'S CHANGING ROLES IN CO-LOMBIA. Iglitzin, Lynne B. and Ross, Ruth, eds. *Women in the World* (Santa Barbara, Calif.: Clio Books, 1976): 243-255. Conventional indica-tors—voting rights, party membership, education, careers, and percent of work force—all place women on the outskirts of Colombian society and politics. Their significant role has been in parapolitical activity, such as prison work and campaign activity. Few women have a secondary educa-tion; most work "marginally" in domestic and agricultural labor. Repre-sentation in party leadership and government is minor; and despite variance in ideology, political parties remain sexist. Although they have had the right to vote since 1957, turnout is lower among women. But competitive politics has only been reinstituted since 1974 and Colombia can expect change in the near future. Primary and secondary sources; 11 notes.
N. Barron

1973. Serrano Camargo, Rafael. ¿QUE PASO EN LAS BANAN-ERAS? [What happened in the banana zone?]. *Bol. de Hist. y An-*

tigüedades [Colombia] 1981 68(732): 203-215. The repression of the 1928 banana strike continues to evoke heated discussion. The scope of the events was clearly exaggerated for political reasons.
D. Bushnell

1974. Sing, Horst. CAMILO TORRES RESTREPO—APOSTAT ODER PROPHET? [Camilo Torres Restrepo: apostate or prophet?]. *Civitas [Switzerland] 1977 33(4): 223-240.* The Colombian Camilo Tor-res's (1929-66) revolutionary ideas were based not on Marxist views, but on traditional and conservative ideals of Christianity and the priesthood, influenced by Christian anthropology.

1975. Sloan, John W. REGIONALISM, POLITICAL PARTIES AND PUBLIC POLICY IN COLOMBIA. *Inter-American Econ. Af-fairs 1979 33(3): 25-46.* Explains the survival of Colombia's civilian politi-cal system by outlining the relationship between regionalism, the Conservative and Liberal parties and public policy.

1976. Thirsk, W. R. THE DISTRIBUTION OF LAND REFORM BENEFITS IN COLOMBIA. *Land Econ. 1976 52(1): 77-87.* Examines the changing need for and impact on rural labor as the result of land reform. Though the small farmer and the landless rural laborer should benefit from land reform, it might mean higher food cost for the urban poor. 15 notes, biblio.
E. S. Johnson

1977. Uribe T., Carlos A. LA ANTROPOLOGÍA EN COLOMBIA [Anthropology in Colombia]. *Am. Indígena [Mexico] 1980 40(2): 281-308.* The anthropological community has always reacted to, and been affected by, political and economic trends that have influenced the society as a whole. In short, scientific activity is determined and influenced by the phenomenon of power in society and the interplay of diverse social forces in Colombian society that take place outside of the narrower limits in which the scientific community is contained.
J/S

1978. Williams, Miles W. URBANIZATION AND THE BREAK-DOWN OF THE TWO PARTY SYSTEM IN BOGOTA. *Secolas Ann. 1976 7: 79-89.* Urbanization in Colombia has brought profound change to recent politics. It has destroyed the power of the Conservative party, thus upsetting the traditional balance between Conservative and Liberal voters, and has created a group of young people who give alle-giance to neither of the two traditional political parties. Based on primary and secondary sources; 6 tables, 10 notes.
J. A. Lewis

1979. Wright, Philip. THE ROLE OF THE STATE AND THE POLITICS OF CAPITAL ACCUMULATION IN COLOMBIA. *Development and Change [Netherlands] 1980 11(2): 229-255.* Identifies specific historical factors in class formation and political conflict that have circumscribed the economic role of government in Colombia.

1980. Zelinsky, Ulrich. STRATEGIEN INSTITUTIONELLER GE-WALT ZUR HERRSCHAFTSSICHERUNG IN KOLUMBIEN, 1970-1973 [Strategies of institutional violence for the securing of au-thority of Colombia, 1970-73]. *Jahrbuch für Geschichte von Staat, Wirt-schaft und Gesellschaft Lateinamerikas [West Germany] 1978 15: 259-293.* Institutional violence produces its own dynamic in Colombia, by perpetuating limited conflicts between the Liberals and Conservatives who identify with the state and the political opposition groups. On one hand, to grant more freedom to the opposition lends aid to their demands to alter the governing relationships. On the other hand, to undermine the opposition via agricultural reforms implies modifying the given scheme for distributing privileges. Based on printed and secondary sources; 2 tables, 45 notes.
T. D. Schoonover

1981. —. [COLOMBIA AND THE ANDEAN GROUP: ECO-NOMIC AND POLITICAL DETERMINANTS OF REGIONAL IN-TEGRATION POLICY]. *Q. Rev. of Econ. and Business 1981 21(2): 182-203.*
Urrutia M., Miguel. COLOMBIA AND THE ANDEAN GROUP: ECONOMIC AND POLITICAL DETERMINANTS OF RE-GIONAL INTEGRATION POLICY, *pp. 182-199.* An attempt is made to identify the economic, political, and bureaucratic forces that determine Colombian policy toward the Andean Group. The analysis of this area of policymaking is used as a case study in decisionmaking in Colombia, and of the limits that exist to the influence special interest groups can exert on policymaking. The

analysis also helps to explain the diminishing level of support by Colombia for an ambitious economic integration effort in the Andean Group.

Williamson, John. COMMENT ON "COLOMBIA AND THE ANDEAN GROUP," *pp. 199-203.*   J

Ecuador

1982. Brownrigg, Leslie Ann. INTEREST GROUPS IN REGIME CHANGES IN ECUADOR. *Inter-Am. Econ. Affairs 1974 28(1): 3-17.* Analyzes Ecuadorian politics in terms of interest group activity. Holds that the political instability of the years 1960-72 reflected interest group counterbalancing and interplay while subsequent stability reflected "the paralysis of the political impact of key interest groups." Notes the impact of petroleum production on the nation. Primary and secondary sources; 13 notes.   D. A. Franz

1983. Collin-Delavaud, Anne. L'ENCADREMENT DES PAYSANS DANS UN SECTEUR D'AMÉNAGEMENT HYDRAULIQUE DE LA CÔTE ÉQUATORIENNE: LE PROJET BABAHOYO [The process of settlement of the peasantry in an area of water development in the Ecuadorian coast: the Babahoyo project]. *Travaux & Mémoires de l'Inst. des Hautes Études de l'Amérique Latine [France] 1979 (32): 37-42.* An analysis of the project of settlement of the peasantry for the development of the region near Babahoyo through modern technical methods and land reform based on expropriation and the creation of cooperatives.

1984. Drekonja, Gerhard. ECUADOR: HOW TO HANDLE THE BANANA REPUBLIC TURNED OIL STATE. *Bol. de Estudios Latinoamericanos y del Caribe [Netherlands] 1980 (28): 77-94.* Traditional histories of Ecuador are now irrelevant; an economic history that takes cognizance of the new role of petroleum must be pursued more aggressively. Some Ecuadorean historians are now doing this, but there are side differences in approach and analysis between national and foreign historians of Ecuador. 2 tables, 59 notes, biblio.
                                                                 R. L. Woodward, Jr.

1985. Goncharov, V. M. PEDRO SAAD [Pedro Saad]. *Voprosy Istorii KPSS [USSR] 1979 (5): 129-131.* A biographical sketch of Pedro Saad (b. 1909), member of the Communist Party of Ecuador since 1934 and of its Executive Committee since 1938. He has served as the Party's General Secretary since 1952.   L. E. Holmes

1986. Goncharov, V. M. ZACHAROVANNYE OSTROVA (ISTORIIA BOR'BY ZA GALAPAGOSY) [The enchanted islands: istoriia history of the struggle for the Galápagos Islands]. *Voprosy Istorii [USSR] 1975 (8): 139-147.* Discusses repeated efforts by the United States and Europe to dominate politically the beautiful and strategically important Galápagos Islands. Discovered in 1535, the islands became the property of Ecuador at its independence in 1830, and since then have become the object of overt and covert negotiations between the United States, major European powers and the government of Ecuador, in which the latter has often been unfairly pressurized to sell or lease at least part of the islands. America gained a foothold during World War II but US naval forces were eventually forced to depart in June 1946 after public protest against their continued presence. 46 notes.   V. Sobeslavsky

1987. Grayson, George W. POPULISM, PETROLEUM AND POLITICS IN ECUADOR. *Current Hist. 1975 68(401): 15-19, 39-40.*

1988. Handelman, Howard. DEVELOPMENT AND MISDEVELOPMENT IN ECUADOR. *J. of Interamerican Studies and World Affairs 1982 24(1): 115-122.* Reviews Gerhard Drekonja's, ed. *Ecuador Hoy* (1978); Osvaldo Hurtado's *Political Power in Ecuador* (1980); Miguel Murmis, Jose Bengoa, and Osvaldo Barksy's *Terratenientes y Desarrollo Capitalistis en el Argo* (1978); and Moritz Thomsen's *The Farm on the River of Emeralds* (1978) and concludes Ecuador is entering an important new stage of political development deserving more careful attention.   T. D. Schoonover

1989. Iturralde G., Diego. NACIONALIDADES ETNICAS Y POLÍTICA CULTURAL EN ECUADOR [Ethnic nationalities and cultural policy in Ecuador]. *Am. Indígena [Mexico] 1981 41(3): 387-397.* While the state pays lip service to policies designed to respect Indian cultural values, at the same time it implements *indigenista* policies whose objective is precisely the opposite. The problem arises out of the nature of the issue: Indians as a class and Indians as cultural groups. State policies have mostly concerned themselves with Indians as a class, and since independence, its efforts have been directed toward removing the obstacles that the Indians present for capitalist development by transforming them into wage laborers and consumers. The implementation of these policies necessarily implies the destruction of ethnic and cultural identities. It is only when these efforts begin to bear fruit that the state begins to institute policies aimed at respecting different cultural forms at a time when these forms have almost lost their real meaning.   J

1990. Kasza, Gregory J. REGIONAL CONFLICT IN ECUADOR: QUITO AND GUAYAQUIL. *Inter-American Econ. Affairs 1981 35(2): 3-41.* Describes and explains the character of regional competition between Quito and Guayaquil over the past two decades and the sentiments that have made this a matter of national importance in Ecuador.

1991. Luzuriaga, Gerardo. LA GENERACIÓN DEL 60 Y EL TEATRO [The 1960's generation and the theater]. *Cahiers du Monde Hispanique et Luso-Brésilien [France] 1980 (34): 157-170.* The so-called 1960's generation theatrical movement in Ecuador consists of three definable phases. The period of experimentalism, 1955-63, is typified by the University Experimental Theater founded in Quito in 1955 under the direction of Sixto Salguero and the Independent Theater founded by Francisco Tobar García in 1954. In the popularization period of 1964-70, as a reflection of political events, the theatrical form involved the popular sectors of Ecuadorean society: Fabio Pacchioni made a substantial contribution in the 1960's by creating several theater groups. The years 1971-79 reflect the mood of Latinamericanization, as the national theater became associated with the Latin American movement of political awareness and cultural pride, and achieved international prestige. Based on studies of Ecuadorean theater; biblio.   P. J. Durell

1992. Maldonado Lince, Guillermo. LA REFORMA AGRARIA EN EL ECUADOR [Agrarian reform in Ecuador]. *Cahiers du Monde Hispanique et Luso-Brésilien [France] 1980 (34): 33-56.* Outlines the state of agriculture, living conditions, and land ownership of the rural population and general economic picture of Ecuador in the 1970's. Increasing population and rural poverty dictated the need for land reform, resulting in the agricultural reform bill of October 1973 which had been preceded by the first agricultural reform bill in 1964. Such legislation was and continues to be opposed by conservative forces, as the prosperity of large estates has been based on the exploitation of manpower. Under the present government their view dominates. The author studies the background and content of the bill, powers of implementation, and results as part of an overall national agricultural policy for coordination and production. Based mainly on government statistical data; table.
                                                                      P. J. Durell

1993. Martz, John D. MARXISM IN ECUADOR. *Inter-American Econ. Affairs 1979 33(1): 3-28.* Provides a historical sketch of Marxism in Ecuador from 1926 to the present, focusing on factional weakening of the movement.

1994. Martz, John D. THE QUEST FOR POPULAR DEMOCRACY IN ECUADOR. *Current Hist. 1980 78(454): 66-70, 84.* Discusses political developments in Ecuador during the 1970's leading to the inauguration of President Jaime Roldós Aguilera in 1979.

1995. Martz, John D. REGIONALIST EXPRESSION OF POPULISM: GUAYAQUIL AND THE CFP, 1948-1960. *J. of Interamerican Studies and World Affairs 1980 22(3): 289-314.* Many scholars have sought to dismiss populism from Latin American history. The Concentración de Fuerzas Populares (CFP) offered welfare programs for the poor, redistribution of goods and services, and rapid improvement of human conditions. The CFP's leadership style, which was personalistic, messianic, and authoritarian, suggested populism. Mid-century Ecuadorian demography indicated Guayaquil as the natural core for populism, and this city provided the legions of followers of the CFP. Primary sources; table, 9 notes.   T. D. Schoonover

1996. Pyne, Peter. LEGISLATURES AND DEVELOPMENT: THE CASE OF ECUADOR, 1960-1961. *Comparative Pol. Studies 1976 9(1): 69-92.* Discusses the function of politics and legislative bodies in Ecuador in the context of developing nations in 1960-61.

1997. Pyne, Peter. THE POLITICS OF INSTABILITY IN ECUADOR: THE OVERTHROW OF THE PRESIDENT, 1961. *J. of Latin Am. Studies [Great Britain] 1975 7(1): 109-133.* Since coups d'etat are the long-term norm in Ecuadorian politics, the 1961 overthrow of José Velasco Ibarra was a return to "that convention which had been dormant since 1947." Specifically, increasing economic stagnation since 1956, the Bay of Pigs' impact on Velasco Ibarra's promised recovery from Peru of Ecuador's lost lands, hostility to his programs by the elites' representatives in Congress, his caudillistic distrust of all potential institutional and personal rivals, and the continued absence of organized mass political parties all contributed to this return to instability. Based on newspaper accounts and secondary sources; 3 tables, 112 notes.

K. M. Bailor

1998. Pyne, Peter. PRESIDENTIAL CAESARISM IN LATIN AMERICA: MYTH OR REALITY? A CASE STUDY OF THE ECUADORIAN EXECUTIVE DURING THE PRESIDENCY OF JOSÉ MARÍA VELASCO IBARRA, 1960-1961. *Comparative Pol. 1977 9(3): 281-304.* Examines the presidency of José María Velasco Ibarra, showing that the alleged system of caesarism—the existence of caudillos—in Latin American politics is not a viable one; there is a need for constant reassessment and questioning of broadly held ideas and theories in political science.

1999. Redclift, M. R. AGRARIAN CLASS STRUCTURE AND THE STATE: THE CASE OF COASTAL ECUADOR. *Bol. de Estudios Latinoamericanos y del Caribe [Netherlands] 1976 (21): 16-31.* The abolition by the Ecuadorian government in 1970 of sharecropping in the coastal rice zone has helped to form a new social class of peasant laborers belonging to marketing and production cooperatives. These agricultural cooperatives are advised or managed by government-employed technologists. The peasants, identifying with the state apparatus and perceiving a community of interest with owners of large estates also using modern technology, do not develop class values in opposition to capitalism. Based on the author's research in the rice zone of Ecuador, Ecuadorian primary sources, and secondary sources; 66 notes.

D. M. Cregier

2000. Redclift, M. R. AGRARIAN REFORM AND PEASANT ORGANIZATION IN THE GUAYAS BASIN, ECUADOR. *Inter-Am. Econ. Affairs 1976 30(1): 3-27.* Examines the termination of rice sharecropping in the Guayas Basin by government decree and the development of ex-sharecropper agricultural cooperatives aided by government patronage. Indicates that state patronage has replaced money lenders and landlords. Primary and secondary sources; 44 notes, biblio.

D. A. Franz

2001. Redclift, M. R. THE INFLUENCE OF THE AGENCY FOR INTERNATIONAL DEVELOPMENT (AID) ON ECUADOR'S AGRARIAN DEVELOPMENT POLICY. *J. of Latin Am. Studies [Great Britain] 1979 11(1): 185-201.* Extant studies of Agency for International Development (AID) impact are inadequate. Analysis of the Ecuadorian case (until 1972) indicates that AID succeeded in establishing "a pattern for state intervention in the agrarian sector." AID fomented a developmental ideology that Ecuador itself pursued independently. 51 notes.

J. F. Vivian

2002. Saint-Geours, Yves. L'ÉQUATEUR: RETOUR À LA DÉMOCRATIE, DÉCOLLAGE ÉCONOMIQUE? (1976-1980) [Ecuador: return to democracy, economic take-off? 1976-80]. *Problèmes d'Amérique Latine [France] 1981 (59): 6-41.* Studies the economic growth, political transitions, and employment objectives of Ecuador, which has in the last five years benefited from large petroleum revenues, but which also faces problems of agricultural stagnation, industrialization, and returning to a constitutional regime.

2003. Whitten, Norman E., Jr. ECUADORIAN ETHNOCIDE AND INDIGENOUS ETHNOGENESIS: AMAZONIAN RESURGENCE AMIDST ANDEAN COLONIALISM. *J. of Ethnic Studies 1976 4(2): 1-22.* Analyzes the plight of the central Ecuadorian "Canelos

Quichua" forest Indians, threatened by modernization programs and a government "national culture" ideology aimed at racial mixture, to produce a homogeneous population. Indian commune leaders have refused to participate in the nationalist development of the Oriente until the government prevents encroachment by outside colonists on their lands. Close links between the trespassers and the political regime in Quinto have meant frustration of the Indians' claims in the courts, and attempts to reduce the free Indians to agricultural laborers for the white colonists. Official ethnocide, or extermination of the total lifeway of a people, is Quito's stated policy and is well underway; yet the Quichua have heightened their determination to preserve their ethnicity while at the same time adapting new technology to their known environment. They may yet survive while maintaining cultural integrity, but the balance is most tenuous. Based on field research and the author's forthcoming book on the *Sacha Runa*; 13 notes.

G. J. Bobango

2004. Zuvekas, Clarence, Jr. AGRARIAN REFORM IN ECUADOR'S GUAYAS RIVER BASIN. *Land. Econ. 1976 52(3): 314-329.* Describes the need for land reform in Ecuador, and cites the possibilities for reform in the Guayas basin. Describes one land reform program initiated in 1970 and its transformation from an innovative program to a rather traditional one. 4 tables, 39 notes, biblio.

E. S. Johnson

Peru

2005. Albertocchi, Giovanni. MANUEL SCORZA, IL QUINTO CANTARE PERUVIANO: VERSO LA "SOLUZIONE" DEL MITO [Manuel Scorza's fifth Peruvian chant: toward the "solution" of the myth]. *Ponte [Italy] 1981 37(5): 446-453.* Reviews *La tumba del relámpago* [The tomb of the lightning], concluding volume of a series of novels that Peruvian writer Manuel Scorza has devoted to the struggle of the native Indian *comuneros* of the Central Andes in the 1960's.

2006. Alisky, Marvin. GOVERNMENT-PRESS RELATIONS IN PERU. *Journalism Q. 1976 53(4): 661-665.* Reviews government control of the media in Peru, 1968-76 and describes varying degrees of suppression as responses to political and economic situations, concluding that the Peruvian model of governmental guidance of the media may well be adapted by other reform governments in the Western hemisphere.

2007. Anderle, Ádám. COMUNISTAS Y APRISTAS EN LOS AÑOS TREINTA EN EL PERÚ (1930-1935) [Communists and apristas in Peru, 1930-35]. *Acta. U. Szegediensis de Attila József Nominatae: Acta Hist. [Hungary] 1978 63: 43-99.* Analyzes the effects of the 1929 world depression in Peru, and explains how the Communist Party played an important role in organizing the workers in labor unions, and how the Aprista Party channelled the masses into political action. Nevertheless, the Aprista Party lost the elections and the oligarchy organized a strong anticommunist campaign. In spite of the repression enforced against them, both parties showed solid political structure, by 1935.

L. Makin

2008. Anderle, Ádám. J. C. MARIÁTEGUI ÉS A PERUI MUNKÁSMOZGALOM AZ 1920-AS ÉVEKBEN [J. C. Mariátegui and the Peruvian workers' movement in the 1920's]. *Acta U. Szegediensis de Attila József Nominatae: Acta Hist. [Hungary] 1976 59: 57-83.* Peruvian workers' movements, 1906-16, were basically anarchistic. In 1919, a labor union center was set up and between 1919 and 1923 students engaged in a reform movement. In 1921 the People's University was founded. Anarchist groups left the labor movement and José Carlos Mariátegui played a crucial role in organizing the workers, 1923-26. He gave 18 lectures at the People's University, introducing Marxist-Leninist ideas. Based on Peruvian archival material; 83 notes.

R. Hetzron

2009. Anderle, Ádám. A PERUI KOMMUNISTA PÁRT MÚKÖDÉSÉNEK KEZDETE (1930-1936) [The beginnings of the activities of the Peruvian Communist Party, 1930-36]. *Párttörténeti Közlemények [Hungary] 1977 23(1): 69-108.* The American Popular Revolutionary Alliance (APRA), broke with the international workers' movement in 1927 and started a new party in Peru in 1928. This move to the Right speeded up the organizing of Communist and socialist groups

into a party. A Socialist Party was founded in 1928 and in 1930 it adopted the name Communist Party (PCP). The PCP assumed leadership of the syndicalist movement (CGTP) but in 1931, the prevailing sectarian orientation drove the workers' masses to APRA. The workers later corrected their errors and in 1932-35, led the antiwar movement. Yet in spite of disappointment with the politics of APRA a popular front was not created and this resulted in a strengthening of the Right. 133 notes.
R. Hetzron/S

2010. Atwood, Rita and Mattos, Sergio Augusto Soares. MASS MEDIA REFORM AND SOCIAL CHANGE: THE PERUVIAN EXPERIENCE. *J. of Communication 1982 32(2): 33-45.* Radical media reforms instituted by the government of Juan Velasco Alvarado, during 1968-75 in order to transform Peruvian society by encouraging the participation of the lower classes in Peru's redevelopment efforts ultimately failed. Discusses the successes and failures of media reform in structural reorganization in general and traces the development of Peru's mass media from the founding of the newspaper *El Comercio* in 1839.

2011. Barker, Mary L. NATIONAL PARKS, CONSERVATION, AND AGRARIAN REFORM IN PERU. *Geographical Rev. 1980 70(1): 1-18.* Park planning and conservation policies in Peru have evolved from an inadequate legal base. The first reserves were established in the 1960's, and a major policy revision in 1975 laid the foundation for a national system of conservation units to include areas of three major biophysical zones: the coastal desert, the Andes, and tropical forest of the Amazon basin. The success of the Peruvian system depends on policy integration with an agricultural reform program designed to bring landless and low-income peasants into the economic mainstream of Peru. Huascarán National Park serves to illustrate the objectives and the managerial constraints embodied in the Peruvian system. 39 notes. J

2012. Basadre, Jorge. LEYES ELECTORALES PERUANAS (1890-1917) THEORÍA Y REALIDAD [Peruvian electoral laws: theory and reality, 1890-1917]. *Historica [Peru] 1977 1(1): 1-36.* Examines changes in electoral law and the system of parliamentary politics in Peru. Electoral law reforms during this period restricted rather than expanded political participation. Politics was depicted as the exclusive domain of the upper classes who formed numerous factions. These engaged in bitter and often comic intramural battles. Long quotations from period novels demonstrate the recreational aspects of politics. Based on parliamentary debates; 35 notes. Article to be continued in *Rev. de Derecho y Ciencias Políticas.*
G. M. Yeager

2013. Benites, Alfredo. LES RAPPORTS ECONOMIQUES ENTRE LES SECTEURS AGRICOLE ET INDUSTRIEL DANS LE DEVELOPPEMENT CAPITALISTE AU PEROU (1968-1980) [Economic ties between the agricultural and industrial sectors in the capitalist development of Peru, 1968-80]. *Problèmes d'Amérique Latine [France] 1982 (63): 147-174.* Discusses agrarian and industrial reforms in 1969 and 1970, and their implementation within two distinct politico-economic contexts: the presidency of General Juan Velasco Alvarado (1968-75) and that of General Francisco Morales Bermúdez (1975-80).

2014. Blanchard, Peter. A POPULIST PRECURSOR: GUILLERMO BILLINGHURST. *J. of Latin Am. Studies [Great Britain] 1977 9(2): 251-273.* Guillermo Billinghurst, president of Peru, 1912-14, is a good example of a Latin American populist, for throughout his career he consciously strove to forge alliances with the masses. Billinghurst early in his career sided with Peru's emerging labor movement, and these groups, in turn supported his candidacy for president. In October 1912, Billinghurst's small reforms in a textile strike averted a potentially disastrous general strike. Billinghurst's prolabor actions, even after he broke a strike of brewery workers, led to his rejection by his party and, in 1914, to a coup. Although he died in exile in 1915, Billinghurst's career showed future politicians the importance of the workers. Based on archival materials in Peruvian national and provincial archives, the British Public Record Office, and printed sources; 91 notes. J. W. Leedom

2015. Bollinger, William. THE BOURGEOIS REVOLUTION IN PERU: A CONCEPTION OF PERUVIAN HISTORY. *Latin Am. Perspectives 1977 4(3): 18-56.* Interprets Peruvian history since the end of the colonial period, examining changes in the mode of production, tracing the rise of the Peruvian bourgeoisie to state power, and explaining

why other writers have ignored or denied this process. Initial capitalist development in the agricultural sector did not result from a sudden break with precapitalist relations of production. Resulting hybrid forms of exploitation created serious problems for historical research. Tables.
J. Dietz

2016. Bonilla, Heraclio. THE NEW PROFILE OF PERUVIAN HISTORY. *Latin Am. Res. Rev. 1981 16(3): 210-224.* Explains the achievements of recent Peruvian historiography, which traces Peru from its entry into the international economy in the 16th century until the 1929 economic crisis. Research in the last decade has deepened the level of analysis and expanded the areas of knowledge. Factors influencing historiographical change include greater mass political consciousness, a Marxism stripped of dogmatism, and the influence of the social sciences.
J. K. Pfabe

2017. Bridges, Thomas. HAYA DE LA TORRE: REFLECTIONS OF A REVOLUTIONARY. *Américas (Organization of Am. States) 1980 32(4): 4-8.* Interview with Víctor Raúl Haya de Torre, founder of the Aprista Party in Peru.

2018. Caballero, José María. SOBRE EL CARÁCTER DE LA REFORMA AGRARIA PERUANA [On the character of the Peruvian agrarian reform]. *Latin Am. Perspectives 1977 4(3): 146-159.* The post-1968 land reform created a variety of state property institutions aimed at consolidation of land holdings and "modernization" of production. The result has been the spread of capitalist relations under state administration, though the persistence of precapitalist forms may block its progress. J. Dietz

2019. Campbell, Leon G. THE HISTORIOGRAPHY OF THE PERUVIAN GUERRILLA MOVEMENT, 1960-1965. *Latin Am. Res. Rev. 1973 8(1): 45-70.* Critical bibliography of writings on Peruvian guerrilla warfare, 1960-65.

2020. Caravedo Molinari, Baltazar. THE STATE AND THE BOURGEOISIE IN THE PERUVIAN FISHMEAL INDUSTRY. *Latin Am. Perspectives 1977 4(3): 103-121.* Explores the role of the state in aiding the development of capitalist relations of production within the fishing industry. With the collapse of the availability of anchovies, the state was forced to nationalize to protect the interests of the large capitalists, not to benefit all Peruvians. Once profitability had been restored, and concentration of production assured, much of the industry was returned to private owners after August 1976. Table. J. Dietz

2021. Clayton, Lawrence A. A SHARED PROSPERITY: W. R. GRACE AND COMPANY AND MODERN PERU. *West Georgia Coll. Studies in the Social Sci. 1978 17: 1-12.* Chronicles the development of the relationship between W. R. Grace & Co. and the successive governments of Peru, 1852-1960's, which remained a sound one for over a century and contributed to social change and economic development in Peru.

2022. Clinton, Richard L. MILITARY-LED REVOLUTION IN PERU: A POSTMORTEM. *Latin Am. Res. Rev. 1980 15(1): 198-205.* A review article of seven books which deal primarily with Peru since 1968. J. K. Pfabe

2023. Collin-Delavaud, Claude. LE PÉROU ET SES FRONTIÈRES NON CONSOLIDÉES: LES DIFFICULTÉS DE L'INTÉGRATION ÉCONOMIQUE [Peru and its nonconsolidated borders: the difficulties of economic integration]. *Cahiers des Amériques Latines [France] 1978 18: 77-85.* Peru's borders with Chile and Ecuador are still as unstable as they were a century ago. The difficulty of achieving economic integration is as important as political irredentism in making these borders issues of conflict. D. R. Stevenson

2024. Collin-Delavaud, Claude. L'ENCADREMENT DE LA PAYSANNERIE DANS LES ZONES D'IRRIGATION DE LA CÔTE PÉRUVIENNE [Infrastructure of the peasantry in the zones of irrigation on the Peruvian coast]. *Travaux & Mémoires de l'Inst. des Hautes Études de l'Amérique Latine [France] 1979 (32): 123-128.* An analysis of agricultural reform since 1950, centering on irrigation projects on the Peruvian coast and the government's structural investment.

2025. Collin-Delavaud, Claude. PÉROU: VERS UN RÉGIME CIVIL [Peru: toward a civilian regime]. *Problèmes d'Amérique Latine [France] 1979 (54): 62-88.* Analyzes the political, social, and economic situation in Peru, centering on the measures for economic recovery attempted since 1968 by the successive military governments, which since 1977 have allowed civilian leaders growing authority.

2026. Collings, Richard J. DEPENDENCY AND MILITARY RULE: A PERUVIAN CASE STUDY. *Secolas Ann. 1979 10: 15-37.* Though Peru relied heavily on American foreign aid, 1963-73, there was a gradual reduction in that dependency due to punitive measures taken by the United States and to Peru's desire to reduce US control in favor of aid from other sources.

2027. Cometta Manzoni, Aída. VIGENCIA DE JOSÉ CARLOS MARIÁTEGUI [The continued relevance of José Carlos Mariátegui]. *Rev. Nac. de Cultura [Venezuela] 1981 41(246): 79-89.* José Carlos Mariátegui (1895-1930), the outstanding Peruvian essayist, was a self-taught intellectual of extensive culture. In 1926, he founded the journal *Amauta,* which became popular in all of Latin America as the free voice of the new anticolonial thought sweeping the continent. Similarly successful was the journal *Labor,* which Mariátegui published 1928-30, effective in forming a proletarian class awareness among the Peruvian working masses. His two most important works were *La escena contemporánea* (1925), which describes the Europe of the years 1920-25, and *Siete ensayos de una realidad peruana* (1928), which presents a historical study of Peru's national problems from an economic perspective. Primary sources; 12 notes.　　　　　　　　　　　　　G. Pizzimenti

2028. Covarrubias, A. and Vanek, J. SELF-MANAGEMENT IN THE PERUVIAN LAW OF SOCIAL PROPERTY. *Administration and Society 1975 7(1): 55-64.* Explains the basic features of Peru's unique Law of the Sector of Social Property (1974), intended to direct the country towards a social democracy based on full worker participation.　S

2029. Deere, Carmen Diana and Janvry, Alain de. DEMOGRAPHIC AND SOCIAL DIFFERENTIATION AMONG NORTHERN PERUVIAN PEASANTS. *J. of Peasant Studies [Great Britain] 1981 8(3): 335-366.* Analyzes social inequality among the peasantry of the northern Peruvian department of Cajamarca in the 1970's, using and assessing the Marxist class framework of V. I. Lenin's *Development of Capitalism in Russia* and the demographic approach of A. V. Chayanov's *Theory of Peasant Economy.* These opposed analyses need not be mutually exclusive. The Cajamarca case shows that social differentiation determined by access to the means of production is more significant in explaining inequality, but demographic differentiation as discussed by Chayanov is an important variable when applied to the division of labor by sex and age and to sources of income over the life cycle. Based on fieldwork and secondary sources; 15 tables, 7 notes, biblio.
　　　　　　　　　　　　　D. J. Nicholls

2030. DeWind, Adrian. DE CAMPESINOS A MINEROS: EL ORIGEN DE LAS HUELGAS EN LAS MINAS PERUANAS [From peasant to miner: the origin of the strikes in the Peruvian mines]. *Estudios Andinos 1974-76 4(2): 1-31.* Increased mechanization and concentration on industrial metals after 1950 forced the Peruvian mining industry to seek a more dependable labor force. Previously the mines recruited casual labor from agriculture. The change to full-time, contracted labor resulted in greater commercialization of agriculture and alienation of workers from the land. Labor unions, vigorous after World War II, encouraged proletarianization of mine workers. The major mining company attempted to institute various social service programs for workers, but with little success. From 1969 to 1971 a wave of strikes hit the Peruvian mining industry. Target of these strikes was the Cerro y Pasco Corporation, then Peru's largest employer. Primary and secondary sources; 5 notes.
　　　　　　　　　　　　　J. L. White

2031. Dewind, Adrian. FROM PEASANTS TO MINERS: THE BACKGROUND TO STRIKES IN THE MINES OF PERU. *Sci. & Soc. 1975 39(1): 44-72.* The gradual growth of militancy of miners working in the former Cerro de Pasco Corporation mines has been intensified by the increase in the number of permanent, proletarianized laborers demanding better living and working conditions. The transformation of the labor system from a largely temporary, semi-agriculturalized work

force to one divorced from the land and compelled to rely on wages for survival resulted in the creation of a class conscious group not placated by government nationalization of their place of employment. Based largely on research in Peru, 1970-71.　　　　　　N. Lederer

2032. Dickerson, Mark O. PERU INSTITUTES SOCIAL PROPERTY AS PART OF ITS "REVOLUTIONARY TRANSFORMATION." *Inter-Am. Econ. Affairs 1975 29(3): 23-33.* Discusses the concept of social property, outlines its structural organization, and examines its place in the context of change in Peru. Primary and secondary sources; chart, 32 notes.　　　　　　　　D. A. Franz

2033. Dore, Elizabeth and Weeks, John. CLASS ALLIANCES AND CLASS STRUGGLE IN PERU. *Latin Am. Perspectives 1977 4(3): 4-17.* Argues the need to analyze and determine the dominant mode of production in understanding the present historical juncture in Peru. Identifies the divergent classes (local bourgeoisie, landowners, petite bourgeoisie, comprador elements, proletariat) and their differences. The 1968 "revolution" was the culmination of the bourgeois revolution and not a socialist revolution, as some have argued, nor a "Bonapartist" military takeover. The author also considers the role of the state and the possibility of revolutionary alliances and develops a critique of dependency theory.
　　　　　　　　　　　　　J. Dietz

2034. Dore, Elizabeth. CRISIS AND ACCUMULATION IN THE PERUVIAN MINING INDUSTRY, 1968-1974. *Latin Am. Perspectives 1977 4(3): 77-102.* Discusses the crisis within the mining industry in the 1960's. The necessary reorganization of production was beyond the financial capabilities of individual capitalists and was unprofitable. Nationalization—reorganization of production by the state—was thus necessary to maintain the interests of capital as a whole, including the mining interests. Nationalizations were not anticapitalist. Tables, charts.
　　　　　　　　　　　　　J. Dietz

2035. Dore, Elizabeth and Weeks, John. THE INTENSIFICATION OF THE ASSAULT AGAINST THE WORKING CLASS IN "REVOLUTIONARY" PERU. *Latin Am. Perspectives 1976 3(2): 55-83.* Sees the Peruvian military government not as nationalistic but as an attempt by the Peruvian bourgeoisie to ally itself with international capital to gain power over the landlord class. Examines changes under the military government, and compares credit and production statistics for manufacturing and agriculture. Uses Marxist class analysis for analyzing the society of Peru and for understanding its economy. Tables.
　　　　　　　　　　　　　J. L. Dietz

2036. Eeuwen, Daniel van. LE PROJET THÉORIQUE DE LA RÉVOLUTION PÉRUVIENNE [The theoretical project of the Peruvian revolution]. *Cultures et Développement. Rev. Int. des Sci. du Développement [Belgium] 1979 11(4): 527-550.* Analyzes the political theory of the anti-imperialist, anticapitalist and anticommunist revolutionary regime of General Juan Velasco Alvarado.

2037. Einaudi, Luigi R. REVOLUTION FROM WITHIN? MILITARY RULE IN PERU SINCE 1968. *Studies in Comparative Internat. Development 1973 8(1): 71-87.*

2038. Emmerson, John K. JAPANESE AND AMERICANS IN PERU, 1942-43. *Foreign Service J. 1977 54(5): 40-47, 56.* Recalls his duties in the US embassy in Peru, 1942-43, helping to gather leaders of the Japanese community there for internment in the United States. Chapter from the forthcoming *The Japanese Thread.*

2039. Epstein, Erwin H. PEASANT CONSCIOUSNESS UNDER PERUVIAN MILITARY RULE. *Harvard Educ. Rev. 1982 52(3): 280-300.* Examines how the military government in Peru from 1968 to 1980 initially won the support of Peru's oppressed highland Indians through educational programs and describes subsequent program failures.

2040. Ferner, Anthony. THE DOMINANT CLASS AND INDUSTRIAL DEVELOPMENT IN PERU. *J. of Development Studies [Great Britain] 1979 15(4): 268-288.* Examines the acceptance by the dominant class of the industrial development of Peru following the coup of 1968 and the installation of the military regime; such industrialization had always been favored by the elite.

2041. Fishel, John T. ATTITUDES OF PERUVIAN HIGHLAND VILLAGE LEADERS TOWARD MILITARY INTERVENTION. *J. of InterAm. Studies and World Affairs 1976 18(2): 155-178.* If the military revolution of 1968 is to be totally successful in Peru the highland villages must be satisfied with the basic alterations or the revolution will be only partially realized. Village leaders expect large governmental participation in the economy, especially in the area of planning. This political leadership is generally nationalistic and expresses a desire for Peruvian autonomy. A majority of the leaders also accept the idea of oligarchical rule and support constitutional government. Based on a questionnaire sent to village leaders and secondary sources; 14 notes, biblio.
J. R. Thomas

2042. Fitzgerald, E. V. K. PERU: THE POLITICAL ECONOMY OF AN INTERMEDIATE REGIME. *J. of Latin Am. Studies [Great Britain] 1976 8(1): 53-71.* Examines Peru's state capitalism as a case study in dependency theory, discussing continued reliance on foreign enterprise and finance and agrarian stagnation. The weakening of the bourgeoisie's hegemony, the late emergence of the petite bourgeoisie, and the strengthening of labor, 1950-62, created more foreign penetration and labor unrest from 1962 to 1968. Utilizing radical land reform, and nationalization of mining, oil, heavy industry, fishing, and banking concerns, the regime broke the bourgeoisie's control and reduced foreign investment. The author discusses the resultant state capitalism, 1969-75, especially in export production, finance, support industries, and commerce. Secondary sources; 32 notes.
K. M. Bailor

2043. Fitzgerald, E. V. K. THE POLITICAL ECONOMY OF PERU 1968-75. *Development and Change [Netherlands] 1976 7(1): 7-33.* Explores the political economy of Peru since the 1968 military takeover, discussing the political and economic options for a dependent, dual export economy.

2044. Fitzgerald, E. V. K. STATE CAPITALISM IN PERU. *Bol. de Estudios Latinoamericanos y del Caribe [Netherlands] 1976 (20): 17-33.* The Peruvian military government in power since 1968 has been state capitalist in the sense of becoming the dominant owners of the export and industrial sectors of the economy and controlling planning and investment. The state has largely replaced the Peruvian bourgeoisie as the source of domestic capital, the latter continuing its pre-1968 conversion from an entrepreneurial to a rentier class. Peruvian state capitalism has had little impact on the household sectors of peasants, artisans, and service personnel constituting over 60% of the work force. Although the regime has reduced foreign ownership and established new relationships with multinational corporations and international banks, most of the traditional constraints on Peruvian economic development remain operative. Based on secondary sources in English and Spanish; 8 tables, 29 notes.
D. M. Cregier

2045. Frankman, Myron J. SECTORAL POLICY PREFERENCES OF THE PERUVIAN GOVERNMENT, 1946-1968. *J. of Latin Am. Studies [Great Britain] 1974 6(2): 289-300.* From 1950 to 1959, only export producers enjoyed dominance in the Peruvian economy, being supported by the Central Bank's exchange policies, the Central Reserve Bank's extensive credit, and special tax preferences. From 1959 to the 1968 coup, the government tried to elevate industry to dominance as well as through tariff protection and tax credits. As a result, nonexport agriculture was neglected, and taxes increased for nondominant sectors such as agriculture and commerce. Representation on public bodies from national interest groups was "a key to obtaining preferential treatment for a sector." Peru's experience during these years disproves two widely-believed generalizations, i.e., that prospects are dim for the exports of primary producing countries in the modern world, and that "the granting of extensive privileges to the export sector by developing countries is a thing of the distant past." Based on government publications and secondary works; 2 tables, 40 notes.
K. M. Bailor

2046. Gallavresi, Lucilla. LA RIVOLUZIONE PERUVIANA ALLA PROVA [The Peruvian revolution examined]. *Affari Esteri [Italy] 1975 7(28): 654-675.* Examines the reforms carried out in Peru by the revolutionary military government since 1968; though the direction of the revolution is still an enigma, it cannot be excluded as a possible model for other nations in Latin America.

2047. Gavrikov, Iu. P. KHOSE KARLOS MARIATEGI: BORETS ZA IDEI MARKIZMA-LENINIZMA V LATINSKOI AMERIKE (1894-1930) [José Carlos Mariátegui, fighter for Marxism-Leninism in Latin America, 1894-1930]. *Novaia i Noveishaia Istoriia [USSR] 1978 (5): 103-111.* Mariátegui developed the ideas of Marxism-Leninism in his book *Seven interpretative essays on Peruvian life* (1928). He stated that the Incas had reached a highly developed and harmonious Communist system. His treatment of the social structure in Peru, his discussion of Peru's independence from Britain and North America, and of the history of Peruvian literature, follow Marxist-Leninist class-analysis principles.
M. R. Colenso

2048. Gilbert, Dennis. THE END OF THE PERUVIAN REVOLUTION: A CLASS ANALYSIS. *Studies in Comparative Int. Development 1980 15(1): 15-38.* Explores factors related to the end of the Peruvian Revolution: economic crisis, short range economic problems, the class orientation of the development model, the role of oligarchs and industrialists, and relations with foreign capital. The Peruvian Revolution was a neat replication of precursor revolutions in Argentina, Brazil, and Chile. 3 tables, 11 notes, 67 ref.
S. A. Farmerie

2049. Gilbert, Dennis. SOCIETY, POLITICS, AND THE PRESS: AN INTERPRETATION OF THE PERUVIAN PRESS REFORM OF 1974. *J. of Interamerican Studies and World Affairs 1979 21(3): 369-393.* On 27 July 1974, Peruvian President Juan Velasco Alvarado's government seized control of the country's press in order to reorganize it along progressive nationalist lines. While the old press represented the socioeconomic class structure—right-wing government repression, wealthy family ownership, and oligopolistic advertisers—the new press has no clear social base. It is rooted only in the shifting politics of the regime itself. 11 notes, ref.
T. D. Schoonover

2050. Golte, Juergen. DETERMINATEN DES ENTSTEHENS UND DES VERLAUFS BAEUERLICHER REBELLION IN DEN ANDEN VOM 18. ZUM 20. JAHRHUNDERT [Determinants of the origins and course of peasant rebellion in the Andes, 18th-20th centuries]. *Jahrbuch für Geschichte von Staat, Wirtschaft und Gesellschaft Lateinamerikas [West Germany] 1978 15: 41-74.* Examination of peasant rebellions in Peru permits the formation of hypotheses regarding the factors determining the origins and course of violent peasant movements. All the movements originate in alternations which limit peasant forms of production. Normally the peasants cannot coordinate action beyond their area of production, but broad transformations in production bring peasants from various regions together in bigger movements. These movements, however, are only effective on the economic, not on the political level. Based on manuscript, published primary, and secondary sources; 6 maps, table, 70 notes.
T. D. Schoonover

2051. Goodsell, Charles T. THE MULTINATIONAL CORPORATION AS POLITICAL ACTOR IN A CHANGING ENVIRONMENT: PERU. *Inter-Am. Econ. Affairs 1975 29(3): 3-21.* Compares the activity of multinational corporations in Peru to the environmental model proposed by F. E. Emery and E. L. Trist ["The Causal Texture of Organizational Environments," *Human Relations* February 1965 18: 21-32]. Secondary sources; 14 notes.
D. A. Franz

2052. Goodsell, Charles T. THAT CONFOUNDING REVOLUTION IN PERU. *Current Hist. 1975 68(401): 20-23.* Discusses the military government of Juan Velasco Alvarado, who seized power in 1968.
S

2053. Gorman, Stephen M. CORPORATISM WITH A HUMAN FACE? THE REVOLUTIONARY IDEOLOGY OF JUAN VELASCO ALVARADO. *Inter-American Econ. Affairs 1978 32(2): 25-38.* Examines key points of the political ideology of Juan Velasco Alvarado's presidency in Peru, 1968-75, including his views on social justice, revolutionary ideology and participation, nationalism and dependency, development, history, and destiny.

2054. Gorman, Stephen M. PERU BEFORE THE ELECTION FOR THE CONSTITUENT ASSEMBLY: TEN YEARS OF MILITARY RULE AND THE QUEST FOR SOCIAL JUSTICE. *Government and Opposition [Great Britain] 1978 13(3): 288-306.* Reviews events in Peru from the coup in 1968 to the preparations for elections for a constitutional assembly in 1978. The military has been willing to relinquish power after initiating reforms, but socioeconomic expectations have increased, and the population has become organized and politically active while the military has been unable to control the organizations it has engendered.

2055. Grayson, George W. PERU'S REVOLUTIONARY GOVERNMENT. *Survival [Great Britain] 1973 15(3): 130-136.* Traces the domestic and foreign policies of the Juan Velasco Alvarado government in Peru, 1968-72, and the resultant problems from implementing them.

2056. Gulyás, András. AZ INDIÁNKÉRDÉS AZ 1920-AS ÉVEK IRODALMÁBAN ÉS MARIÁTEGUI MARXISTA KONCEPCIÓJA [The Indian question in the literature of the 1920's and Mariátegui's Marxist conception]. *Acta. U. Szegediensis de Attila József Nominatae: Acta Hist. [Hungary] 1976 59: 25-41.* National consciousness arose in Peru after 100 years of independence, and in the 1920's nationalists attempted to solve the Indian question. *Indigenismo* was a political and ideological-cultural movement set up to promote understanding of the life of Indians and mestizos who formed the majority of the population. The *indigenistas* tried to assure a place for Indian heritage in Peruvian national development. José Carlos Mariátegui introduced a Marxist point of view which saw the problem as a socioeconomic rather than a national question. 36 notes.   R. Hetzron

2057. Hazen, Dan C. THE POLITICS OF SCHOOLING IN THE NONLITERATE THIRD WORLD: THE CASE OF HIGHLAND PERU. *Hist. of Educ. Q. 1978 18(4): 419-444.* Examines the impact of education on socioeconomic and political conditions of the Department of Puno in southern Peru. Rather than judging the impact by the expectations of the promoters, the author examines the complex interaction between the subjects and promoters. Education may be sought as a means to conserve the traditional but now threatened social order, but the whole picture changes as education progresses and its rationale and the interrelationships of the groups change in response to its effects. 36 notes.
                                                                        R. V. Ritter

2058. Heigert, Hans. "PLAN INCA," OR THE PERUVIAN REVOLUTION: LETTER FROM LIMA. *Encounter [Great Britain] 1975 44(4): 53-56.* Discusses socialism and capitalism in the revolutionary government of Peru from 1968-70's, emphasizing issues involving unemployment and freedom of the press.

2059. Hobsbawm, E. J. PEASANT LAND OCCUPATIONS. *Past And Present [Great Britain] 1974 (62): 120-152.* Analyzes the mass invasion and occupation of land by peasants mainly in the light of 20th-century evidence from Peru but with several additional references to other countries. Attempts to assess the social and political assumptions and the strategic thinking which underlies this form of peasant militancy by examining a number of peasant land invasions. The author also investigates the connections between land occupation and peasant revolutionism. Primary and secondary sources; 95 notes.   R. G. Neville

2060. Horna, Hernan. SOUTH AMERICA'S MARGINAL HIGHWAY. *J. of Developing Areas 1976 10(4): 409-424.* Peru's President Fernando Belaúnde Terry, 1963-68, encouraged a far-reaching infrastructural development in the form of a 3,720-mile road to connect Venezuela, Colombia, Ecuador, Peru, and Bolivia. The project is opening millions of acres of land for colonization while promoting geographic, political, and economic integration of South America. Beginning in 1963, 30 percent of Peru's 1,536-mile segment was under way by 1967. Belaúnde was overthrown in 1968 but subsequent governments continued the road so that by 1976 most of the Peru section was finished except for bridges that would require foreign equipment and materials. Consequences of the roadway include feeder and penetration roads and establishment of numerous technical and agricultural institutes. Furthermore oil was discovered in Peru. The other nations are working more slowly on the highway and it will probably not be finished by the projected completion date of 1995. 2 tables, fig., 46 notes.   O. W. Eads, Jr.

2061. Huerta, John E. PERUVIAN NATIONALIZATIONS AND THE PERUVIAN-AMERICAN COMPENSATION AGREEMENTS. *New York U. J. of Int. Law and Pol. 1977 10(1): 1-66.* Offers an overview of nationalization of American interests in Peru, 1974-76, discussing individual cases and the American reaction, and examines the political,

legal, and diplomatic ramifications of negotiations for lump-sum payment of compensatory fees by Peru.

2062. Jameson, Kenneth P. DESIGNED TO FAIL: TWENTY-FIVE YEARS OF INDUSTRIAL DECENTRALIZATION POLICY IN PERU. *J. of Developing Areas 1979 14(1): 55-70.* Nations faced with the problem of balancing regional desires with perceived national requirements often seek a solution in some greater equity in the sharing out of political power and economic activity. Peru, with industrial concentration centered in the Lima-Callao area, faced similar problems and attempted some infrastructure in the rural villages. Most programs were designed to consolidate regional support for the central government without any substantial decentralization of industry, a policy of dependent capitalist development. Based on official Peruvian statistics; 2 tables, 29 notes, 2 appendixes.   O. W. Eads, Jr.

2063. Jaquette, Jane S. REVOLUCIÓN POR DECRETO: EL CONTEXTO DE LA FORMULACIÓN POLÍTICA EN EL PERU [Revolution by decree: the context of political formulation in Peru]. *Estudios Andinos 1974/75 4(1): 279-308.* The military government in Peru which assumed power in October of 1968 under President Juan Velasco Alvarado has achieved a social revolution. The military has replaced the former landed oligarchy in a paternalistic national economy. Economic participation by the state and encouragement of industry has produced a regulated economy in contrast to a previous policy of laissez-faire. Agrarian reform has improved agricultural production. Banking and investment reform have taken place. The goal of this economic reform has been to chart a course between capitalism and Marxism and to create controlled pluralism, a new model of political participation. Primary and secondary sources; 32 notes.   J. L. White

2064. Jonkind, Fred. A REAPPRAISAL OF THE ROLE OF REGIONAL ASSOCIATIONS IN LIMA, PERU: AN EPISTEMOLOGICAL PERSPECTIVE. *Comparative Studies in Soc. and Hist. [Great Britain] 1974 16(4): 471-482.*

2065. Kay, Cristóbal. ACHIEVEMENTS AND CONTRADICTIONS OF THE PERUVIAN AGRARIAN REFORM. *J. of Development Studies [Great Britain] 1982 18(2): 141-170.* Analyzes the Peruvian agrarian reform in the context of alternative transitions to capitalist agriculture and alternative agrarian reforms and evaluates its contribution to rural development. Reformers must understand the rationality of the preexisting agrarian system to achieve a successful restructuring of economy and society. Discusses the contradictions that arose between the state model and the competing peasants' models of agrarian reform.

2066. Kerekes, György. JOSÉ CARLOS MARIÁTEGUI, LATIN-AMERIKA KIEMELKEDŐ GONDOLKODÓJA [José Carlos Mariátegui, an outstanding Latin American thinker]. *Acta U. Szegediensis de Attila József Nominatae: Acta Hist. [Hungary] 1976 59: 9-23.* The Marxist thinker José Carlos Mariátegui was born in 1895, in Lima, Peru. He was an autodidact. He became a reporter, which brought him into contact with the political opposition, and in 1918 he founded his own magazine *Nuestra Época*, followed by *La Razón* which became a theoretical and political forum. In 1919 he was exiled from Peru, and he spent 1920-23 in Europe, mainly in Italy, returning to Peru in 1923 as a mature revolutionary. He died of tuberculosis in 1930. He was a universal thinker and an important theoretician. He did display some racial bias, but reinterpreted ethnic questions as class problems. Note, biblio.
                                                                        R. Hetzron

2067. Klaiber, Jeffrey L. THE POPULAR UNIVERSITIES AND THE ORIGINS OF APRISMO, 1921-1924. *Hispanic Am. Hist. Rev. 1975 55(4): 693-715.* The Peruvian popular universities (1921-24) were established by the Federación de Estudiantes Peruanos, led by Victor Raul Haya de la Torre. The government deported Haya de la Torre and other politically active students in 1923 and closed the popular universities in 1924. Haya de la Torre founded the Aprista Party (the Alianza Popular Revolucionaria Americana—APRA) in Mexico in 1924. The Aprista program was closely allied with the concept of the popular university. 72 notes.   B. D. Johnson

2068. Klaiber, Jeffrey L. RELIGION AND REVOLUTION IN PERU: 1920-1945. *Americas (Acad. of Am. Franciscan Hist.) 1975*

31(3): 289-312. The leftist generation that emerged after 1920, including Peruvian Marxist José Carlos Mariátegui (1891-1930), Aprista party founder Víctor Raúl Haya de la Torre (b. 1895), and Indianist writers, moved away from doctrinaire liberal anticlericalism and sought to convert "popular Catholicism . . . into a source of energy for the coming revolution." Their attitude toward the generally conservative established Church was in the main hostile. However, they preferred not to antagonize the religious sentiments of the lower classes and incorporated certain spiritual and moral overtones and religious symbolism into their thought and doctrine and (in the case of Apra) their party organization. 79 notes.

D. Bushnell

2069. Korovina, E. F. and Korovin, A. F. THE FIRST MARXIST IN PERU. *Soviet Studies in Hist. 1973-74 12(3): 88-97.* José Carlos Mariátegui (1895-1930), founder of the Peruvian Communist Party, was first a proponent of various eclectic notions of an anarcho-syndicalist type, who became a firm adherent to Marxism-Leninism in 1923. An author of political works, a theorist and practical worker in the cause of socialism, he died prematurely of tuberculosis, having given his life and knowledge to the proletariat.

2070. Kuczynski, Pedro-Pablo. THE PERUVIAN EXTERNAL DEBT: PROBLEM AND PROSPECT. *J. of Interamerican Studies and World Affairs 1981 23(1): 3-27.* Since the last civilian government left power in 1968, Peru's economy has undergone major changes, including the state assumption of foreign trade and land redistribution, and has experienced unemployment, stagnation, and a greatly increased debt. The debt has sharply limited Peruvian development and its ability to manage its financial affairs. Based upon published and unpublished documents of international agencies; 4 tables, 6 notes, ref.

T. D. Schoonover

2071. Kuczynski, Pedro-Pablo. RECENT STUDIES OF PERU. *Latin Am. Res. Rev. 1981 16(1): 225-228.* Reviews six books on Peruvian economy and society. To some extent, all reflect the point of view of the "first phase" of the Peruvian revolution.

J. K. Pfabe

2072. Laidlaw, Karen A. CIVILIAN VERSUS MILITARY RULE AS AN AID TO DEVELOPMENT: PERU, 1963-1974. *Int. J. of Contemporary Sociol. 1980 17(1-2): 59-81.* Compares the effects of civilian and military government on the economic development of Peru, analyzing two periods, the 1963-68 civilian reformist regime of Fernando Belaúnde Terry; and the 1968-74 military government of General Juan Velasco Alvarado. Strong dictatorial governments may be necessary to promote economic growth in the unstable countries of the Third World.

2073. Laite, Julian. MINERS AND NATIONAL POLITICS IN PERU, 1900-1974. *J. of Latin Am. Studies [Great Britain] 1980 12(2): 317-340.* From the founding of the Cerro de Pasco Mining Company in 1902 until the nationalization of its mines in 1974, working-class politics developed cyclically, moving from compromise to confrontation and back again. Locally this cyclical development resulted from the organization of the labor force, the strength of trade unions, and the support given by the rural sector. Nationally, Peru has faced repeated dilemmas over matching the aspirations of the labor movement and the interests of foreign investment. Based partly on printed primary sources; 49 notes.

M. A. Burkholder

2074. Landry, David M. A CASE STUDY OF THE EVOLUTION OF A MONETARY ECONOMY IN THE SIERRA REGION OF PERU. *Southern Q. 1975 13(4): 313-322.* Examines economic changes affecting a portion of Peru's Indian population, with emphasis on the transition from a barter to a monetary economy. Such changes were expected to improve the social and political aspects of Indian culture. The author focuses on the historical background and barriers that restricted economic innovation and the organization of contemporary credit unions. The credit union movement came to be dominated by government bureaucracy and failed to substantially alter social and political conditions. 19 notes.

R. W. Dubay

2075. Laurinchukas, A. THE TROUBLED LAND OF PERU. *Int. Affairs [USSR] 1973 (6): 76-80.* Discusses President Juan Velasco Alvarado's attempts to institute agricultural reform, the resistance of the elites, and the social, political, and economic conditions of Peru, 1969-73.

2076. Long, Norman and Winder, David. FROM PEASANT COMMUNITY TO PRODUCTION CO-OPERATIVE: AN ANALYSIS OF RECENT GOVERNMENT POLICY IN PERU. *J. of Development Studies [Great Britain] 1975 12(1): 75-94.* Discussions concerning rural development in Peru since the military coup of 1968 have focused mainly on the large-scale land reform program under which the coastal estates and many of the livestock and agricultural haciendas in the highlands have been expropriated. This has tended to deflect interest from other important aspects of rural development policy. It would be wrong to assume that, prior to the latest reforms, the Peruvian scene consisted almost entirely of latifundia agriculture, for a substantial proportion of the productive agricultural land in both the highlands and coastal valleys was, and remains, in the control of smallholder farmers, or is held under communal ownership by peasant communities. In an attempt to incorporate these nonhacienda zones into the plan for national development *[Plan del Peru: 1971-1975],* the government is encouraging the expansion of smallholder commercial production, the establishment of new, or the improvement of existing, marketing and servicing cooperatives, and is promoting a reorganization of peasant communities with the long-term objective of transforming them into modern production or multipurpose cooperatives. This paper outlines recent legislation aimed at reforming these peasant communities and examines the social consequences of the new policy, particularly as it affects smallholder regions. The authors assess the effectiveness of the policy in transferring the benefits of community resources to the poorer strata of the rural population, a central aim of the reforms, and isolate the factors which inhibit the emergence of viable modes of cooperative organization and which limit the role that community institutions can play in promoting local development. The situation in the Matahuasi district of the Mantaro Valley in Central Peru is analyzed.

J

2077. López, Jaime Alejo. TRANSFORMACIONES ECONÓMICAS Y SOCIALES DEL GOBIERNO MILITAR DE PERÚ [Economic and social transformations by the military government of Peru]. *Investigación Econ. [Mexico] 1973 32(128): 775-787.* Describes the political situation in Peru prior to 1968 when the military takeover occurred and outlines subsequent legislation concerning agriculture, industry, government control over currency exchange, precious metals and mining, working conditions, and education.

2078. López Soria, José Ignacio. CULTURA E IDEOLOGÍA EN EL PERÚ [Culture and ideology in Peru]. *Casa de las Américas [Cuba] 1980 20(119): 78-87.* Discusses the economic bases of Peru's modern capitalist system originating in the latter half of the 19th century and the development of the present social class structure, the cultural values and ideology of the dominant bourgeoisie, the proletariat, intellectuals, and clerics, and the movement of romantic anticapitalism and the utopianism of contemporary literature.

P. J. Durell

2079. Lowenthal, Abraham F. DATELINE PERU: A SAGGING REVOLUTION. *Foreign Policy 1980 (38): 182-190.* Peru's heralded 1968 revolution has not lived up to its promise, but it has caused significant alterations in the structure and distribution of power within that country. The old landed oligarchy is out of touch, the press is controlled, the Catholic Church is nearly invisible, US influence is sharply reduced, and the military is discredited. Power now rests with a new entrepreneurial elite, the expanded state technocracy and bureaucracy, the "private and official international finance community," and, most significantly, the increasingly mobilized population. This shift may make possible more substantial changes in the future.

T. L. Powers

2080. Lowenthal, Abraham F. PERU'S AMBIGUOUS REVOLUTION. *Foreign Affairs 1974 52(4): 799-817.* An experiment is underway in Peru which tests whether soldiers as rulers can use their power to implement major structural change sufficient to open the way to equitable and integrated national development without turning to repression. How this experiment fares may influence the tendencies in other Third World countries. Note. Also published in Spanish in *Foreign Affairs* 1974 52(4).

R. Riles

2081. Luna Vegas, Ricardo. GENARO CARNERO CHECA: GRAN PERIODISTA, DISCIPULO DE MARIATEGUI [Genaro Carnero Checa, great journalist, disciple of Mariátegui]. *Casa de las Américas [Cuba] 1981 22(128): 104-107.* The Peruvian journalist Carnero Checa (1910-80) was a creative and revolutionary fighter in the struggles of his people and his time.   J. V. Coutinho

2082. Malloy, James M. AUTHORITARIANISM, CORPORA-TISM AND MOBILIZATION IN PERU. *R. of Pol. 1974 36(1): 52-84.* Focuses on Juan Velasco Alvarado's attempt to mobilize mass support through the state organization Sistema Nacional de Apoyo a la Movilización Social (National System in Support of Social Mobilization).   S

2083. Martinez, Arthur D. THE POLITICS OF TERRITORIAL WATERS: 12 MILES OR 200? *Studies in Comparative Internat. Development 1973 8(2): 213-223.* Peru guards its fishing rights in the interest of the national economy.   S

2084. Martínez, Héctor. REFORMA AGRARIA PERUANA: EM-PRESAS ASOCIATIVAS [Peruvian agrarian reform: cooperative enterprises]. *Bol. de Estudios Latinoamericanos y del Caribe [Netherlands] 1981 (30): 103-123.* Describes the variety of programs under the Peruvian Agrarian Reform Law of 1969 and analyzes the experience of the agricultural cooperatives established under that law. These cooperatives represent 66% of the 7,405,508 hectares and 77% of the families in the reform program. Based on observation and publications of the Dirección General de Reforma Agraria; 2 tables, 15 notes.
                    R. L. Woodward, Jr.

2085. Mazet, Claude. CROISSANCE DEMOGRAPHIQUE ET CONCENTRATION URBAINE AU PÉROU: L'ACCENTUATION DES DÉSÉQUILIBRES À LA FIN DU XXᵉ SIÈCLE [Demographic growth and urban concentration in Peru: emphasis on the imbalance at the end of the 20th century]. *Jahrbuch für Geschichte von Staat, Wirtschaft und Gesellschaft Lateinamerikas [West Germany] 1979 16: 379-406.* The urban network is distorted in favor of the agglomeration Lima-Callao. Consequently, the largest part of Peruvian national space lacks adequate material investment and infrastructure. The absence of the state or its insufficient and indirect role is flagrant. Thus, in the Comas district of Lima, 80% of the commercial establishments function without a license and avoid taxes. Map, 10 tables, 57 notes.
                    T. D. Schoonover

2086. Moncloa, Francisco. SEBASTIÁN SALAZAR BONDY EN LO COTIDIANO EN LA HISTORIA DEL PERÚ [Sebastián Salazar Bondy in the day-to-day history of Peru]. *Casa de las Américas [Cuba] 1980 21(121): 74-81.* More than in the case of any other Peruvian writer the life and work of Sebastián Salazar Bondy (1924-65) serves as a reflection of the changing pattern of history in Peru from the 1920's to the 1960's. With quotations from his writings the author discusses the Peruvian's life as a poet, dramatist, storyteller, critic of art, literature, and the theater, uncompromising critic of defects in the political and social system, and opponent of the abuse of power by the rich and influential, and sets it against the background of Peruvian political, economic, and social developments.   P. J. Durell

2087. Montoya, Rodrigo. CHANGES IN RURAL CLASS STRUC-TURE UNDER THE PERUVIAN AGRARIAN REFORM. *Latin Am. Perspectives 1978 5(4): 113-126.* Analyzes the sociopolitical consequences of the recent land reform program in Peru. Obvious, perhaps permanent, changes have been made in the Peruvian countryside and its inhabitants. The author discusses the conditions which led to the reform, the elimination of feudal classes and feudal holdings, the impact on the peasantry and rural laborers, and the rise of a technical rural labor force. 10 notes.   V. L. Human

2088. Neersø, Peter. PERU, ANDES-PAGTEN OD GE TRANS-NATIONALE SELSKABER [Peru, the Andean Pact and the transnationals]. *Nationaløkonomisk Tidsskrift [Denmark] 1981 119(1): 64-77.* Reviews Peru's policies toward foreign investments since 1968. The restrictive policies introduced by the military government were inconsistent and therefore were doomed to failure. The introduction of common Andean investment restrictions could not prevent the failure. However, the present liberal Peruvian investment policies may prove to be just as unsuccessful due to growing social unrest.   J

2089. Neersø, Peter. PERUS POLITIK OVERFOR UDEN-LANDSKE INVESTERINGER [Peru's policy vis à vis foreign invest-

ments]. *Internasjonal Politikk [Norway] 1975 (2): 241-257.* Surveys reforms and regulations introduced by Peru's military regime in changing the industrialization strategy and policy vis-à-vis foreign investments; assesses the impact and effects of the various measures.   J

2090. Neff, Richard E. PERU: AN END TO THE RULING CLASS. *Contemporary Rev. [Great Britain] 1978 233(1350): 14-20.* Discusses the declining political power of the traditional landed oligarchy in Peru, 1968-78.

2091. Neira, Hugo. AU PÉROU, LE RETOUR DE L'OLIGAR-CHIE [The return of the oligarchy in Peru]. *Études [France] 1980 353(4): 293-309.* The divisions among the leftist parties do not fully explain the return to power of Fernando Belaúnde Terry, elected first in 1963, in the elections of 1980 which ended the rule of a progressive military regime.

2092. North, Llisa. REVIEW ESSAY: THE PERUVIAN APRISTA PARTY AND HAYA DE LA TORRE: MYTHS AND REALITIES. *J. of Inter-Am. Studies and World Affairs 1975 17(2): 245-253.* Reviews five books dealing with the Peruvian Aprista Party and the movement's founder, Victor Raul Haya de la Torre.   J. R. Thomas

2093. Nunn, Frederick M. NOTES ON THE "JUNTA PHENOME-NON" AND THE "MILITARY REGIME" IN LATIN AMERICA WITH SPECIAL REFERENCE TO PERU, 1968-1972. *Americas: A Q. Rev. of Inter-Am. Cultural Hist. 1975 31(3): 237-251.* Military regimes, which often feature a junta of some sort, have long been a familiar phenomenon in Latin America. The terms are used, however, in widely differing ways. The term military regime applies currently in Peru in the strict sense that "national defense, as defined and practiced by military leaders, became the chief determinant in the shaping of national policy." 37 notes.   D. Bushnell

2094. Nunn, Frederick M. PROFESSIONAL MILITARISM IN TWENTIETH-CENTURY PERU: HISTORICAL AND THEORETI-CAL BACKGROUND TO THE *GOLPE DE ESTADO* OF 1968. *Hispanic Am. Hist. Rev. 1979 59(3): 319-417.* Literature by Peruvian military authors of the 20th century illustrates a common belief among graduates of the Centro de Altos Estudios Militares that the military was a civilizing influence, an agent of culture and democracy, and an integrator of Peruvians. The 1968 military overthrow of Fernando Belaúnde Terry's government was a natural culmination of this philosophy that the military elite could best run the country. 66 notes.
                    B. D. Johnson

2095. Olson, Richard Stuart. ECONOMIC COERCION IN INTER-NATIONAL DISPUTES: THE UNITED STATES AND PERU IN THE IPC EXPROPRIATION DISPUTE OF 1968-1971. *J. of Developing Areas 1975 9(3): 395-413.* When President Belaúnde of Peru in 1968 agreed to compensate the American-owned International Petroleum Company (subsidiary of the Standard Oil Company of New Jersey), the military exiled him to Argentina, expropriated all IPC holdings, and declared that no compensation would be paid for seized oil fields. Controlling 80% of Peru's domestic petroleum market at the time of the seizure, IPC had previously been accused of tax evasion and intervention in internal politics. Under Belaúnde's compromise, IPC would have ceded its subsoil claims to the state in return for absolution of all past debts, taxes, and claims against the company. The 1962 Hickenlooper Amendment (under which the US President could cut off aid to a country that expropriated American-owned property without reaching a compensation agreement within six months) was applied to a limited extent, limited because US interests own most of Peru's copper and there was fear that they would also be expropriated. Indirect sanctions were more effective since the perpetrator could not so easily be identified. Other expropriations were made by the military government of General Juan Velasco Alvarado but fair compensation was usually paid. Developing nations are vulnerable to several direct and indirect economic sanctions which encourage them to work within the Western capitalist system. 3 tables, 3 figs., 44 notes.   O. W. Eads, Jr.

2096. Pásara, Luis. DIAGNOSING PERU. *Latin Am. Res. Rev. 1982 17(1): 235-243.* Reviews literature on the Peruvian military regime from 1968 to 1975. Useful are general studies by E. V. K. Fitzgerald and

Julio Cotner. The rise and fall of the military reform government are well studied, although consensus still is lacking. Still requiring study is how the military changed Peruvian society. Biblio.   J. K. Pfabe

2097. Petras, James and Havens, A. Eugene. PERU: ECONOMIC CRISES AND CLASS CONFRONTATION. *Monthly Rev. 1979 30(9): 25-41.* Analyzes the historical basis of the rise of the revolutionary left taking place in Peru in 1978 and discusses possible responses by Peru's national bourgeoisie and imperialist forces.

2098. Philip, G. D. E. THE POLITICAL ECONOMY OF EXPRO-PRIATION: THREE PERUVIAN CASES. *Millennium: J. of Int. Studies [Great Britain] 1977-78 6(3): 221-235.* Examines three cases of radical nationalization in Peru, 1968-76, the takeovers of IPC (1968-69), Cerro de Pasco (1973), and Marcona (1975-76). There was no Peruvian program for expropriation, but there was a predisposition to expropriation that took advantage of opportunities as they occurred. Political gains, except during the dispute with the United States after the IPC takeover, have been small, and Peru has also failed to realize the full economic potential of its measures, partly because the use of foreign loans to finance expropriation has often led to an increased dependence on international finance. Secondary sources; 31 notes.   P. J. Beck

2099. Philip, George. THE PERUVIAN TIGHTROPE. *World Today [Great Britain] 1977 33(12): 464-471.* Examines politics in Peru, 1956-77.

2100. Piel, Jean. LES MOUVEMENTS PAYSANS AU PÉROU DE LA FIN DU XVIIIe SIÈCLE À NOS JOURS [The peasant movements of Peru from the end of the 18th century to the present]. *Cahiers Int. d'Hist Écon. et Sociale [Italy] 1978 8: 282-310.* Analyzes peasant movements in Peru, 1780-1970's. Four distinct periods emerge: 1) the colonial period characterized by serfdom and slavery, 1780-1823; 2) the period from independence to the consolidation of the Peruvian nation, 1823-66; 3) the rebellion of the Indian peasantry, 1866-1919; and 4) from 1920 to 1978 when the constitution recognized the existence of native communities and the inalienability of their lands. Violence arose again, 1956-64, but efforts by supporters of Fidel Castro ultimately failed to win over the peasants, who gave their backing to government programs. Biblio.   F. X. Hartigan

2101. Pike, Frederick B. PERU'S HAYA DE LA TORRE AND ARCHETYPAL REGENERATION MYTHOLOGY. *Inter-American Econ. Affairs 1980 34(2): 25-65.* Discusses the role that mythopoetic studies can play in historical interpretations, and examines the importance of the mythopoetic imagination in the attempt by Víctor Raúl Haya de la Torre and his Alianza Popular Revolucionaria Americana (Aprista Party) during the 1920's to create a new national synthesis by incorporating values of the Peruvian Indians into the settlers' worldview.

2102. Pike, Frederick B. RELIGION, COLLECTIVISM AND IN-TRAHISTORY: THE PERUVIAN IDEAL OF DEPENDENCE. *J. of Latin Am. Studies [Great Britain] 1978 10(2): 239-262.* Surveys the Peruvian elite's quest for a status quo 1600-1960's, mainly by means of religion and collectivism, in which the working class is controlled by and dependent on individualistic upper classes.

2103. Prado, Jorge del. THE REVOLUTION CONTINUES. *World Marxist R. [Canada] 1973 16(1): 64-72.* Peru is moving inexorably toward communism.   S

2104. Quijano, Aníbal. RECENT DEVELOPMENTS IN PERU: AN INTERVIEW WITH ANÍBAL QUIJANO. *Monthly R. 1973 24(11): 53-61.* Discusses social and economic reforms of the current military government and the leftist response.   S

2105. Reuter, W. DIE IDEOLOGISCHE ENTWICKLUNG DER PERUANTISCHEN MILITARS UND DER PROZESS DER ANTI-IMPERIALISTISCHEN UND ANTIOLIGARCHISCHEN UMGES-TALTUNGEN IN PERU [The ideological development of the Peruvian armed forces and the process of anti-imperialist and anti-oligarchistic changes in Peru]. *Lateinamerika [East Germany] 1977 (Spr): 57-66.*

2106. St. John, Ronald Bruce. THE END OF INNOCENCE: PERUVIAN FOREIGN POLICY AND THE UNITED STATES, 1919-1942. *J. of Latin Am. Studies [Great Britain] 1976 8(2): 325-344.* Peru's increasingly belligerent nationalism and increased involvement in international organizations, awareness of the complexity of foreign relations, and distrust of the US government can be traced directly to Augusto B. Leguía's (1863-1932) "ill-advised dependency on the US government, coupled with his tendency to promise territorial resolutions totally beyond the capacity" of Peru to achieve in its disputes with Chile, Colombia, and Ecuador during his second presidential term, 1919-30. The attempts of his three successors, Luis M. Sánchez Cerro (1930-33), Oscar R. Benavides (1933-39), and Manuel Prado Ugarteche (1939-45), either to fulfill or reduce Leguía's promises reinforced these four trends. Based on US and Peruvian diplomatic documents, periodicals, and secondary works; 50 notes.   K. M. Bailor

2107. Sanchez, Juan Chong. EL PROCESO DE PLANIFICACIÓN SOCIAL EN EL PERÚ [The process of national planning in Peru]. *Estudios Andinos 1973 3(7): 29-56.* Planning in Peru consists of four main aspects: agrarian reform, national unification ("Andina" concept) both within Peru and among its neighbors, the nationalization of the petroleum industry, and complete economic independence. The author outlines planning in Peru, 1962-71, and traces political factors influencing planning. 2 tables, 3 graphs, 24 notes.   R. Scott

2108. Saulniers, Alfred H. ENCI: PERU'S BANDIED MONOPO-LIST. *J. of Interamerican Studies and World Affairs 1980 22(4): 441-462.* After very little use of government enterprise before 1968, Peru expanded such activity after 1968 and in 1974 created the Empresa Nacional de Comercialización de Insumos (ENCI) to oversee domestic and foreign marketing of basic products from industry, mining, agriculture, and any other product classified as fundamental to the Peruvian economy. Yet no clear government policy for marketing has appeared as ENCI undergoes regular transformation. Case studies of other such enterprises would be useful for understanding the Peruvian economy and to aid in generating well-based theory. Based on ENCI and other Peruvian official publications; 3 tables, 8 notes, ref.   T. D. Schoonover

2109. Scheina, Robert L. THE NEW PERUVIAN NAVY, 1885-1976. *Warship Int. 1978 15(3): 204-211.*

2110. Scott, Chris. THE LABOUR PROCESS, CLASS CONFLICT AND POLITICS IN THE PERUVIAN SUGAR INDUSTRY. *Development and Change [Netherlands] 1979 10(1): 57-89.* Examines economic and political impact of the 1969 land reform program in the Peruvian sugar industry from the standpoint of the labor process, social relationships, and political struggle.

2111. Skinner, Geraldine. JOSÉ CARLOS MARIÁTEGUI AND THE EMERGENCE OF THE PERUVIAN SOCIALIST MOVE-MENT. *Sci. & Soc. 1979-80 43(4): 447-471.* José Carlos Mariátegui (1895-1930) is considered a political forebear by both the latest Peruvian government and many factions on the Left, including the Communist Party of Peru and the Aprista party. He did not, however, have a fully developed and mature Marxist ideology, although he was a socialist and was instrumental in the development of both the political and industrial wings of the Peruvian labor movement. His subjective approach led him to an erroneous belief in the spontaneous socialist consciousness of the Peruvian Indians and he rejected the Leninist model of organization. 29 notes.   S

2112. Slater, David. THE STATE AND TERRITORIAL CEN-TRALIZATION: PERU, 1968-1978. *Bol. de Estudios Latinoamericanos y del Caribe [Netherlands] 1979 (27): 43-67.* Analysis of certain spatial effects of state intervention in Peru after the military takeover in 1968, particularly the primary effect of the reinforcement of territorial centralization as well as spatial concentration. The political implications of these effects are briefly considered. 2 tables, 98 notes.

M. Gormly

2113. Smith, Richard Chase. LIBERAL IDEOLOGY AND IN-DIGENOUS COMMUNITIES IN POST-INDEPENDENCE PERU. *J. of Int. Affairs 1982 36(1): 73-82.* Examines the impact of the history of colonialism and the early liberal ideologies of South American nations on the relationship between the Peruvian government and Peru's Indians from the first Belaúnde Terry government, 1963-68, of Belaúnde to the 1980's, commenting on the formulation of Indian policies in Peru and elsewhere during the independence movements of the 19th century.

2114. Sylvers, Malcolm. JOSE CARLOS MARIATEGUI E L'ITA-LIA: LA FORMAZIONE DI UN RIVOLUZIONARIO PERUVIANO [José Carlos Mariátegui and Italy: The formation of a Peruvian revolutionary]. *Movimento Operaio e Socialista [Italy] 1975 21(1/2): 57-120.* José Carlos Mariátegui (1894-1930) a Peruvian intellectual was transformed into a Marxist revolutionary by his five-year exile in Europe. Mariátegui lived mostly in Italy, experiencing both the Red Years and the Fascist reaction. His articles, especially on intellectual subjects, reflect the influence of Croce and Gobetti, two major Italian students of Marx. After his return to Peru in 1924, Mariátegui constantly used his European experiences for his analysis of Peruvian affairs. Based on Mariátegui's published writings, press, and secondary materials; 205 notes.
J. E. Miller

2115. Thévenin, Chantal. LE RÔLE DU FONDS MONÉTAIRE INTERNATIONAL DANS LA POLITIQUE ÉCONOMIQUE PÉRU-VIENNE (1975-1978) [The role of the International Monetary Fund (IMF) in the economic policy of Peru, 1975-78]. *Rev. Française d'Hist. d'Outre-mer [France] 1979 66(3-4): 301-319.* When the troubled Peruvian economy sought IMF help in 1975, stringent conditions intended to stabilize the economy were laid down before money was lent. The economy did not improve under IMF direction, and it may be that the IMF's strict financial analysis misunderstood a number of factors. The Peruvian government certainly seems unlikely to heed IMF advice in future. Based on official publications; biblio.
D. G. Law

2116. Tufano, Vincent J. CIVIL-MILITARY RELATIONS AND THE PERUVIAN COUP D'ETAT OF 1914. *Centerpoint 1978 2(4): 54-59.* Discusses the civilian support of the 1914 military coup d'etat in Peru, which overthrew the unpopular administration of President Guillermo Billinghurst.

2117. Uzzell, Douglas. "CHOLOS" Y AGENCIAS GUBER-NAMENTALES EN LIMA: ANTECEDENTES Y ANÁLISIS ["Cholos" and governmental agencies in Lima: antecedents and analysis]. *Estudios Andinos 1974-76 4(2): 33-42.* Recent migration into Lima, Peru, has brought newer cholo (predominantly Indian) residents into confrontation with institutions dominated by creoles (predominantly white). The terms used here do not indicate ethnic groups so much as voluntary social identification. Cholo residents have more direct contacts with civic government agencies than do creoles, and a greater opportunity for conflict arises. Cholos have thus devised imaginative means, called "the game," to contravene creole bureaucracy. The fight over the licensing of privately owned buses in Lima, 1968-71, provides an example of how the game operates. Secondary sources; 5 notes.
J. L. White

2118. Valcárcel, Luis E. EL INDIGENISMO PERUANO [Peruvian Indianism]. *Am. Indígena [Mexico] 1975 35(2): 247-249.* Describes the development of Indianism in Peru since colonial days, reporting the deeds and names of distinguished Indianists. This Indianist process has reached its pinnacle due to the political, economic, and social changes that are taking place in Peru.

2119. VanCleve, John V. THE LATIN AMERICAN POLICY OF PRESIDENT KENNEDY: A REEXAMINATION: CASE: PERU. *Inter-Am. Econ. Affairs 1977 30(4): 29-44.* The Latin American policy of the Kennedy Administration was pragmatic rather than idealistic, hardly a break from previous foreign policy, and geared to obtain favorable publicity. United States-Peruvian relations in 1962 are used as a case study. 52 notes.
D. A. Franz

2120. Vanden, Harry E. MARIÁTEGUI: MARXISMO, COMU-NISMO, AND OTHER BIBLIOGRAPHIC NOTES. *Latin Am. Res. Rev. 1979 14(3): 61-86.* José Carlos Mariátegui sought to apply Marxism-Leninism within the specific context of Latin American realities. In Peru he worked for a broadly based socialist party which would incorporate elements of Incan communalism. Such ideas were rejected by Soviet and some Latin American Communists during the Stalinist era. Recent Soviet, Peruvian, and other writers on Mariátegui have defended him as

a genuine Marxist-Leninist who attempted to integrate this ideology into specific national realities. Based on Mariátegui family archives and writings of Mariátegui; 12 notes, biblio.
J. K. Pfabe

2121. Vanden, Harry E. THE PEASANTS AS A REVOLUTION-ARY CLASS: AN EARLY LATIN AMERICAN VIEW. *J. of Interamerican Studies and World Affairs 1978 20(2): 191-209.* The peasant is the least understood and most abused actor on the modern political stage, particularly the Latin American peasant, stereotyped as a lazy, sleepy, frightened figure. In addition to Lenin, Mao, and Guevara, Peruvian intellectual José Carlos Mariátegui (1894-1930) said much of value about peasants and revolution. His works are not well-known outside Peru, but as his newly republished works become better-known, he will take a high place among Latin American peasant-revolution theorists. 15 notes, ref.
T. D. Schoonover

2122. Varese, Stefano. ETNOLOGÍA DE URGENCIA, CON-CIENCIA ÉTNICA Y PARTICIPACIÓN SOCIAL EN EL PERÚ [Emergency ethnology, ethnic consciousness, and social participation in Peru]. *Am. Indígena [Mexico] 1975 35(2): 251-262.* Points out that the Peruvian revolution that started in 1968 has resulted in a series of important modifications in the economic, political, and social structure of the country, and within this context considers and proposes an emergency ethnology policy, an active participation of the Peruvian towns in the construction of a multicultural and multiethnic national consciousness.
J/S

2123. Vazquez Ayllón, Carlos. POLÍTICA EXTERIOR DEL PERÚ [Peruvian foreign policy]. *Rev. de Política Int. [Spain] 1978 (158): 23-39.* Summarizes Peruvian foreign policy since the creation of the Foreign Office in 1821 to the present day.

2124. Villanueva, Victor. THE PETTY BOURGEOIS IDEOLOGY OF THE PERUVIAN APRISTA PARTY. *Latin Am. Perspectives 1977 4(3): 57-76.* Historical analysis of the Alianza Popular Revolucionaria Americana (APRA) in Peru. Analyzes the class base of the party and the actions of its leader, Victor Raul Haya de la Torre. Demonstrates the futility of a petit bourgeois party like APRA's leading an anti-imperialist struggle without proletarian leadership.
J. Dietz

2125. Vorozheikina, Tatiana. LOS MILITARES EN PODER: EX-PERIENCIA PERUANA [The military in power: the Peruvian experience]. *Am. Latina [USSR] 1978 (4): 53-70.* The progressive transformation of Peruvian society which began 10 years ago was a peculiar phenomenon and a failure. The regime did nationalize foreign holdings and tried to help the masses by forming cooperatives and other methods. The Peruvian experiment failed because it failed to eliminate the old aristocracy and their capitalist cohorts and because it treated the masses paternalistically and thus failed to mobilize sufficient mass support. Secondary sources; 24 notes.
J. D. Barnard

2126. Weeks, Jack. CRISIS AND ACCUMULATION IN THE PERUVIAN ECONOMY, 1967-1975. *Rev. of Radical Pol. Econ. 1976 8(4): 56-72.* Presents a Marxian analysis of economic crisis in Peru, 1967-75, asserting that the barrier to accumulation arises not from deficiencies in demand in either the foreign or domestic markets, but rather from basic contradictions within the realm of production.

2127. Weeks, John. BACKWARDNESS, FOREIGN CAPITAL, AND ACCUMULATION IN THE MANUFACTURING SECTOR OF PERU, 1954-1975. *Latin Am. Perspectives 1977 4(3): 124-145.* Criticizes the view of dependency theory that foreign capital inhibits industrialization. In Peru, foreign capital has contributed to overall development of production. The influx of foreign capital has continued, resulting in a fierce competitive struggle by capital from different countries for an advantage. This view helps to explain the crises of 1967-69 and 1974 and reveals nationalization to be a means of aiding capitalists, not driving them out. Tables.
J. Dietz

2128. Werlich, David P. ENCORE FOR BELAÚNDE IN PERU. *Current Hist. 1981 80(463): 66-69, 85-86.* Summarizes political and economic developments in Peru during the 1970's up to the election in July 1980, which restored constitutional government and reinstated Fernando Belaúnde Terry as president, and examines party alignments and platforms contributing to the landslide victory.

2129. Werlich, David P. PERU: THE LAME DUCK "REVOLU-TION." *Current Hist. 1979 76(444): 62-65, 85-87.* Because of problems incurred when it overextended itself economically since 1972, the military government of Peru, led by General Francisco Morales Bermudez convened a constituent assembly, calling the first election in 12 years.

2130. Whyte, William Foote and Alberti, Giorgio. THE INDUS-TRIAL COMMUNITY IN PERU. *Ann. of the Am. Acad. of Pol. and Social Sci. 1977 (431): 103-112.* The Industrial Community is a government-imposed economic reform program for private industry in Peru. Created in 1970, the Industrial Community was designed to improve relations between labor and management, to increase productivity, to redistribute income and enhance social justice, and to accelerate economic progress. The record shows that the Industrial Community has fallen far short of the expectations of government leaders on all of these points. Reasons for the generally negative outcomes are examined. J

2131. Wise, David O. MARIÁTEGUI'S *AMAUTA* (1926-1930), A SOURCE FOR PERUVIAN CULTURAL HISTORY. *Inter-American Rev. of Biblio. 1979 29(3-4): 285-304.* The Peruvian journal *Amauta*, founded by José Mariátegui, was founded in 1926. It was known for its high literary quality, Marxist interpretations, anti-imperialism, and Indianist leanings. After Mariátegui's death in April 1930, Ricardo Martínez de la Torre became editor, and it became a virtual organ of the Peruvian Communist Party. The magazine ceased publication in September 1930. 49 notes. B. D. Johnson

2132. Womack, John, Jr. MARIÁTEGUI, MARXISM, & NA-TIONALISM. *Marxist Perspectives 1980 3(2): 170-174.* Reviews *José Carlos Mariátegui and the Rise of Modern Peru, 1890-1930* by Jesús Chavarría which traces Mariátegui's attempt to reconcile nationalism and socialism for Peru.

2133. Zavaleta, C. E. EL ENSAYO EN EL PERÚ, 1950-1975 [The essay in Peru, 1950-75]. *Cuadernos Hispanoamericanos [Spain] 1979 116(347): 428-435.* Relates the essay to the history of ideas and by way of background charts the course of intellectual development in Peru since 1950, including the effects of prevailing political conditions, philosophical trends, the study of history, sociology, and philosophy of education in Peruvian universities and educational institutions, and the limitations through lack of resources in research facilities and publishing. Three essay types are listed, together with the main writers and their publications: 1) interpretation of the historical-social development of Peru in order to present the true essence of the country; 2) discourse on individual themes, characterized by formal harmony and reasoned presentation; and 3) periodical articles, combining elements of the essay and commentary. P. J. Durell

2134. Ziółkowska, Lidia. PROBLEM INDIAŃSKI W PISARST-WIE JOSÉ CARLOSA MARIÁTEGUI [The Indian problem in the writings of José Carlos Mariátegui]. *Przegląd Socjologiczny [Poland] 1977 29: 101-119.* Discusses the history of the social movement known as Peruvian Indianism and interprets the views of Peruvian intellectual José Carlos Mariátegui on the Indian problem.

2135. —. FORUM. *Hispanic Am. Hist. Rev. 1980 60(2): 303-312.* García, José Z. CRITIQUE OF FREDERICK M. NUNN'S "PRO-FESSIONAL MILITARISM IN TWENTIETH-CENTURY PERU: HISTORICAL AND THEORETICAL BACKGROUND TO THE *GOLPE DE ESTADO* OF 1968," *pp. 303-307.* Frederick M. Nunn's thesis (see abstract 2094) that Peru's post-1968 military government had its roots in doctrines introduced by French training officers between 1896 and 1940 is credible. Nunn's thesis that the post-1968 regime was not leftist but was essentially conservative is unproven. The author briefly discusses works on the regime by Luigi Einaudi and Víctor Villanueva. 2 notes. Nunn, Frederick M. FREDERICK M. NUNN'S REPLY, *pp. 308-312.* Despite some structural reforms during the 1968-75 regime, the officer corps was not predominantly leftist, although there were some leftist factions. 8 notes. B. D. Johnson

Venezuela

2136. Alexander, Robert J. DEMOCRACY IN VENEZUELA. *Latin Am. Res. Rev. 1980 15(2): 241-247.* Reviews the following works on Venezuela since World War II: Harrison Sabin Howard, *Rómulo Gallegos y la Revolución Burguesa en Venezuela* (Caracas: Monte Avila Editores, C.A., n.d.), John D. Martz and David J. Myers, ed., *Venezuela: The Democratic Experience* (New York: Praeger, 1977), Robert Bond, ed., *Contemporary Venezuela and Its Role in International Affairs* (New York: New York U. Pr., 1977), James F. Petras, Morris Morley, and Steven Smith, *The Nationalization of Venezuelan Oil* (New York: Praeger, 1977), and Aníbal Fernández, Alejo Planchart, and Gene E. Bigler, *Modelo Demo-Económico de Venezuela* (Caracas: Instituto de Estudios Superiores de Administración, 1975). J. K. Pfabe

2137. Ameringer, Charles. LEONARDO RUIZ PINEDA: LEADER OF VENEZUELAN RESISTANCE, 1949-1952. *J. of Interamerican Studies and World Affairs 1979 21(2): 209-232.* Leonardo Ruiz Pineda, a middle-class intellectual who was essentially nonviolent and moderate has been made into a hero by the leadership of the Acción Democrática (AD). Police killed Ruiz Pineda during the dictatorship of Marcos Perez Jimenez. In the last several decades, the AD leadership has manipulated Ruiz Pineda as a symbol to undermine those factions or groups within its ranks which seek to resort to urban guerrilla activity or violence. Ruiz Pineda's hero-image militates against violence and revolutionary action. 4 notes, ref. T. D. Schoonover

2138. Arráiz, Antônio. GÓMEZ: EVOLUCIÓN DEL PAÍS [Gómez: the country's evolution]. *Fuerzas Armadas de Venezuela [Venezuela] 1980 (276): 45-48.* General Juan Vicente Gómez (1857?-1935) Venezuelan dictator, 1908-35 was undeniably evil, but he played an important role in the modernization of Venezuela.

2139. Arvelo-Jimenez, Nelly. THE POLITICAL STRUGGLE OF THE GUAYANA REGION'S INDIGENOUS PEOPLES. *J. of Int. Affairs 1982 36(1): 43-54.* Examines factors affecting prospects for the indigenous peoples of the Guayana region of Venezuela during the 1970's and 1980's, including the industrial expansion into the region, differences between the national interest and that of the Indians, and the impact of the economic and political development on official Amerindian policy in Venezuela.

2140. Avery, William P. OIL, POLITICS, AND ECONOMIC POL-ICY MAKING: VENEZUELA AND THE ANDEAN COMMON MARKET. *Int. Organization 1976 30(4): 541-571.* Venezuela's entry into the Andean Common Market (ACM) represents a case of systems transformation. Venezuelan membership has led both to major changes in economic provisions of the Common Market, and to significant alterations in foreign relations among members. Analysis of these changes depends on an understanding of the political debate in Venezuela, which was prolonged, and which led to membership under favorable terms earned through hard negotiations. J

2141. Baloyra, Enrique A. OIL POLICIES AND BUDGETS IN VENEZUELA, 1938-1968. *Latin Am. Research Rev. 1974 9(2): 28-72.*

2142. Barthélemy-Febrer, Françoise. LE RETOUR DES SOCIAUX-CHRÉTIENS AU VÉNÉZUÉLA: PREMIER BILAN (MARS 1979-MARS 1981) [The return of the Social Christian Party (COPEI) in Venezuela: a first evaluation, March 1979-March 1981]. *Problèmes d'Amérique Latine [France] 1981 (60): 7-48.* Analyzes economic conditions since 1979 and discusses Venezuelan leaders' struggle for a New International Economic Order to remedy the present international crisis.

2143. Blake, R. Norris. NOGALES MÉNDEZ: ACTION WAS HIS BYWORD. *Rev. Interamericana [Puerto Rico] 1977 7(3): 547-557.* The biography of Venezuelan Rafael Nogales Méndez, including his involvement in the Russo-Japanese War, the Turkish army, and the French Foreign Legion. His nonmilitary life included cattle rustling, Amazon exploration, and itinerant labor throughout the Near East, Asia, Europe, the United States, and Latin America. His final military escapade was involvement in the abortive overthrow of Venezuelan dictator Juan Vicente Gómez in 1937. G. A. Hewlett

2144. Blank, David Eugene. OIL AND DEMOCRACY IN VENE-ZUELA. *Current Hist. 1980 78(454): 71-75, 84-85.* Discusses the politics of oil and its role in the social and economic development of a democratic Venezuela, 1970's.

2145. Burggraaff, Winfield J. ANDEANISM AND ANTI-ANDEANISM IN TWENTIETH CENTURY VENEZUELA. *Americas: A Q. Rev. of Inter-Am. Cultural Hist. (Acad. of Am. Franciscan Hist.) 1975 32(1): 1-12.* Discusses the political dominance of one province, Táchira, in Venezuela, 1899-1958.

2146. Butler, Robert. REVIEW ESSAY: CONTEMPORARY VEN-EZUELA. *J. of Inter-Am. Studies and World Affairs 1975 17(2): 237-244.* Reviews six books on the problems of contemporary Venezuela, focusing on economic questions.　　　　　　　J. R. Thomas

2147. Bye, Vegard. NATIONALIZATION OF OIL IN VENEZU-ELA: RE-DEFINED DEPENDENCE AND LEGITIMIZATION OF IMPERIALISM. *J. of Peace Research [Norway] 1979 16(1): 57-78.* Studies the effects of the 1976 oil nationalization in Venezuela to establish whether the previous structure of foreign dominance has been fundamentally altered. Dominance structures persisted, but with some differences between indicators. The expected long-term effect of increased oil prices, oil nationalization, and the new development strategy is that the degree of monoproduction will be reduced, whereas economic and technological penetration as well as dependence on foreign trade will actually increase. This points to the need for more fundamental changes in power relationships inside the country. Nationalization alone does not guarantee a development in the interests of the majority.　　　　　　　J

2148. Carbonell, José Antonio. JUAN VICENTE GOMEZ VISTO POR J. FRED RIPPY [Juan Vicente Gomez as seen by J. Fred Rippy]. *Bol. Hist. [Venezuela] 1975 (38): 251-261.* Briefly introduces a Spanish translation of J. Fred Rippy's analysis of Gomez contained in the chapter "Dictators of Venezuela," in *South American Dictators* (New York, 1937), the last volume of the series *Studies in Hispano-American Affairs.* J. V. Gomez (1857-1935) ruled Venezuela with an iron hand from 1908 to his death. Rippy emphasized the more positive aspects of his rule and refered in some detail to the group of contemporary Venezuelan writers who tried to justify the rule of a strongman in a wild country of political passions and constant upheavals.　　　　　　　F. Pollaczek

2149. Carrera, Jeronimo. INVESTIGATING THE ECONOMY. *World Marxist Rev. [Canada] 1977 20(5): 102-109.* An analysis of the political and economic realities surrounding the Venezuelan Communist Party that have impeded scientific research by party members.

2150. Carrera, Jeronimo. VENEZUELA: PROBLEMS UNSOLVED BY NATIONALIZATION. *World Marxist Rev. [Canada] 1976 19(7): 94-100.* Describes the progress made toward the nationalization of the oil industry in Venezuela from 1900 to 1976 and the Venezuelan Communist Party's position in 1976 on nationalization of oil and other industries.

2151. Carrillo Moreno, José. GUILLERMO MORÓN: UNA CON-CEPCIÓN DINÁMICA DE LA HISTORIA [Guillermo Morón: a dynamic concept of history]. *Bol. de la Acad. Nac. de la Hist. [Venezuela] 1973 56(221): 100-112.* Reviews Guillermo Morón's *Historia de Venezuela,* new edition, 5 vols. (Caracas: Italgráfica, 1971); English edition, ed. John Street, *History of Venezuela* (New York: Roy, 1963).
　　　　　　　M. C. F. (IHE 87680)

2152. Conaway, Mary Ellen. CIRCULAR MIGRATION IN VENE-ZUELAN FRONTIER AREAS. *Int. Migration [Netherlands] 1977 15(1): 35-42.* Discusses migratory patterns among selected indigenous groups in the marginal frontier area bordering the Orinoco River in Venezuela. Governmental efforts, promoting national integration through economic and other means, have disrupted traditional native economic and political systems. The author describes and compares the extent of adaptation among the Guahibos and other tribes who participate in the traditional and introduced economic systems through different kinds of circular migratory patterns. "Circular movement patterns are a measure of the degree of both national integration and frontierness." 5 notes, biblio.　　　　　　　R. C. Alltmont

2153. Cross, Benedict. MARXISM IN VENEZUELA. *Problems of Communism 1973 22(6): 51-70.* The Soviet invasion of Czechoslovakia in 1968 caused a split in the Venezuelan Communist Party and the birth of a new party, the *Movimiento al Socialismo* (MAS). Under the leadership of theoretician Teodoro Petkoff, the MAS denounces all revolutionary models, strikes a strong anti-Stalinist stance, and has shifted its attention from the politics of international Communism toward purely national issues. Primary and secondary sources; 37 notes.
　　　　　　　J. M. Lauber

2154. Dabaguian, Emil. VENEZUELA, EVOLUCIÓN IDEOLÓGICA Y POLÍTICA DEL PARTIDO ACCIÓN DEMO-CRÁTICA [Venezuela: the political and ideological evolution of the Democratic Action Party]. *Am. Latina [USSR] 1978 (3): 94-113.* The roots of Acción Democrática (AD) are to be found in Aprismo. Aprismo appeared as a petit bourgeois reaction to the ideas of Marxism-Leninism. National reform ideologues such as Víctor Raúl Haya de la Torre and Rómulo Betancourt borrowed ideas from scientific socialism and then proclaimed them as an original ideology for Latin America. National reform leaders in Latin America kept shifting their positions in response to the radical changes in the world, hoping in this way to conserve their influence with the masses. The major events in Acción Democrática's development in Venezuela illustrate this. 23 notes.
　　　　　　　J. D. Barnard

2155. Deas, Malcolm. VENEZUELA. *World Survey [Great Britain] 1976 (88): 1-16.* Reviews the political and economic history of Venezuela from its discovery in 1498, tracing its exploitation by the Spaniards, the 19th-century wars of independence, and its 20th-century experience with the oil industry.

2156. Dodge, Stephen C. VENEZUELA'S BRIGHT FUTURE. *Current Hist. 1976 70(413): 65-68, 85-86.* Oil-rich Venezuela, with enough money to industrialize before its wells run dry, stands a good chance of becoming South America's major industrial nation, to judge from the situation in 1976.

2157. Eguizabal, Cristina. LE VENEZUELA ET L'AMÉRIQUE LATINE, 1974-1976 [Venezuela and Latin America, 1974-76]. *Cahiers des Amériques Latines [France] 1979 19: 267-275.* Venezuela pursues a foreign policy dedicated to the program of regional and national development. Seeking to be internally strong and internationally respected, Venezuela relies heavily on its oil resources and its ties with OPEC.
　　　　　　　D. R. Stevenson

2158. Ellner, Steve. DIVERSE INFLUENCES ON THE VENEZU-ELAN LEFT: FIVE BOOKS BY VENEZUELAN LEFTISTS. *J. of Interamerican Studies and World Affairs 1981 23(4): 483-493.* Reviews A. Blanco Muñoz's *La Lucha Armada: Hablan 5 Jefes* (1980), R. Iarrazábal's *Estrategía de Poder* (1979), Proceso Político's *CAP: 5 Años: Un Juicio Crítico* (1978), J. V. Rangel's *Seguridad, Defensa y Democracia: Un Tema para Civiles y Militares* (1980), and J. A. Silva Michelana and H. R. Sonntag's *El Proceso Electoral de 1978: Su Perspectiva Histórica Estructural* (1979), which reveal how the guerrilla defeat and competition among leftists in the 1960's and 1970's have made the various factions define their positions more clearly. A recent consensus, however, recognized the need to combine for the 1983 political presidential elections. Venezuela may see a host of small leftist parties merge to form a serious contender for power. 5 notes, ref.　　　　　　　T. Schoonover

2159. Ellner, Steve. FACTIONALISM IN THE VENEZUELAN COMMUNIST MOVEMENT, 1937-1948. *Sci. & Soc. 1981 45(1): 52-70.* Follows the complicated 1940's popular front debate in Communist ranks that anticipated the present situation in Venezuela, where brothers Gustavo and Eduardo Machado head rival Communist organizations. In South America, the official Communist party has seen the national bourgeoisie as a positive and important force in the struggle for national liberation. But left dissidents view it as a false ally in the more important anti-imperialistic struggles. Primary sources, particularly interviews.
　　　　　　　L. V. Eid

2160. Ellner, Steve. LOOKING BOTH WAYS IN VENEZUELA. *Contemporary Rev. [Great Britain] 1979 235(1365): 196-199.* Discusses the Venezuelan presidential elections of 1978 in the context of the country's history since 1973.

2161. Ellner, Steve. POLITICAL PARTY DYNAMICS IN VENE- ZUELA AND THE OUTBREAK OF GUERRILLA WARFARE. *Inter-American Econ. Affairs 1980 34(2): 3-24.* Examines the relations between the leftists (Venezuelan Communist Party and Movimiento de Izquierdo Revolucionaria) and the moderates in Venezuela from General Marcos Pérez Jiménez's forced departure in 1958 to President Rafael Caldera's fulfillment of an election promise in 1969 to legalize the two leftist parties and to grant amnesty to leftists not involved in terrorist activities; explains why the attempts to unite leftist and moderate political parties of the opposition failed.

2162. Ellner, Steven. THE VENEZUELAN LEFT IN THE ERA OF THE POPULAR FRONT, 1936-45. *J. of Latin Am. Studies [Great Britain] 1979 11(1): 169-184.* The Venezuelan left failed to unite during the era of the popular front. International events and World War II explained part of the division. More important, however, were domestic issues that kept the Communist Party and Accíon Democrática (AD) mutually suspicious and strained within their ranks. These internal tensions persist in both political parties today. Primary and secondary sources, including oral interviews; 44 notes. J. F. Vivian

2163. Ewell, Judith. THE EXTRADITION OF MARCOS PEREZ JIMENEZ, 1959-1963: PRACTICAL PRECEDENT FOR ENFORCE- MENT OF ADMINISTRATIVE HONESTY? *J. of Latin Am. Studies [Great Britain] 1977 9(2): 291-313.* Marcos Perez Jimenez, president of Venezuela from 1952 to 1958, fled to the United States after his overthrow in 1958. In 1959 the new government of Venezuela sought his extradition on charges of murder, embezzlement, and criminal malversation. The extradition hearings lasted until 1963, when it was finally decided that the United States would hand him over for trial only on grounds of malversation and petty peculation. The hearings themselves illustrate the difficulties in trying a former head of state: the United States government could not afford to appear ungrateful to former allies, nor could it offend the new government; and as a point of law, it showed how difficult it was to separate political crimes (for which extradition cannot be sought) from impeachable felonies. His extradition cannot, therefore, be seen as a precedent either for or against extradition. Based on US and Venezuelan archival sources and printed records; 85 notes. J. W. Leedom

2164. Ewell, Judith. MARCOS PÉREZ JIMÉNEZ: VENEZUELA'S CRUCIAL DECADE, 1948-1958. *Rev. Interamericana [Puerto Rico] 1977 7(3): 509-523.* Although Marcos Pérez Jiménez was in some respects a ruthless dictator, he was less so than other Latin American caudillos. He was not actually tyrannical or fanatical, but he did bring about corruption in Venezuela's economy, especially in the oil industry. Oil profits if properly spent could have brought Venezuela modernization and influence in world trade. His regime, earmarked by conspicuous consumption, deprivation among the lower classes, and massive imports, set a standard for current Venezuela. G. A. Hewlett

2165. Faría, Jesús. STANOVLENIE KOMMUNISTA [The making of a Communist]. *Novaia i Noveishaia Istoriia [USSR] 1981 (1): 91-104, (2): 73-84.* Part I. Autobiographical sketch of Jesús Faría (b. 1910), general secretary of the Communist Party of Venezuela, covering the period 1910-36. He was born into a large and poor peasant family and got his first job at 13, working 16 hours a day in a tavern. He then worked in the petroleum industry and got his first taste of revolution when he took part in the disturbances that followed the death in 1935 of the Venezuelan dictator Juan Vicente Gómez. He became a member of the Communist Party and the trade-union movement shortly afterwards, helping to organize a general strike in December 1936. Part II. Describes Faría's career from the Venezuelan general strike of 1936-37 until 1944. In 1937 Faría took part in the clandestine first national conference of the Communist Party of Venezuela, which then grew in strength, especially among petroleum workers. In 1941 he took part in the Conference of Latin American Workers in Mexico. In 1944 a new wave of antitrade union and anti-Communist repression was unleashed by the government, forcing the Communist Party even deeper underground. 2 photos, 6 notes. A. Brown

2166. Febrer, Françoise. LE QUINQUENNAT DE CARLOS AN- DRÉS PÉREZ AU VENEZUELA (1974-1979) [The five-year term of Carlos Andrés Pérez in Venezuela, 1974-79]. *Problèmes d'Amérique Latine [France] 1979 (51): 6-54.* Analyzes the five-year term of Venezuelan President Carlos Andrés Pérez, the candidate from the strongest Social Democratic party in Latin America, the Acción Democrática (AD), and examines his influence on the country's accelerated economic, social and demographic development, its foreign policy, and the political forces confronting his administration.

2167. Fejes, Fred. PUBLIC POLICY IN THE VENEZUELAN BROADCASTING INDUSTRY. *Inter-American Econ. Affairs 1979 32(4): 3-32.* Provides a brief history of Venezuelan broadcasting from 1930 to the present and discusses how it is an expression of the country's political and economic dependence rather than a creative force in its development.

2168. Fleet, Michael H. VENEZUELAN COMMUNISM: ALEX- ANDER'S CONSTRUCTION OF A STRAWMAN. *Studies in Comparative Communism 1973 6(4): 445-451.* Reviews R. J. Alexander's *The Communist Party of Venezuela* (Stanford, 1969). Alexander is mistaken in believing that the Communists turned to guerrilla warfare because of the success of the Acción Democrática. Support for democracy in Venezuela is weak. The book ignores the internal debate in the party, which flourishes despite the contention that the success of the Acción Democrática has undercut any possibility of the party's success. 9 notes. D. Balmuth

2169. Gall, Norman. THE CHALLENGE OF VENEZUELAN OIL. *Foreign Policy 1975 (18): 44-67.* Traces the recent background of Venezuelan oil policies in the context of world oil supplies as they affect the United States. With Arab oil embargos threatening US access to oil, Venezuelan oil becomes increasingly necessary. Venezuela has supplied and continues to supply more oil to the US than any other single producing nation. But Venezuela is committed to nationalizing the oil industry, and since the US can no longer oppose nationalization effectively it should negotiate long-range price and supply arrangements with Venezuela. Primary and secondary sources; 12 notes, biblio. R. F. Kugler

2170. Gilhodès, Pierre. VENEZUELA, GENÈSE DE SON SYS- TÈME DE PARTIS [Venezuela: the origin of its party system]. *Cahiers du Monde Hispanique et Luso-Brésilien [France] 1979 (32): 71-105.* Outlines the social and economic factors and circumstances that shaped the political system in Venezuela throughout the 19th century. Traces successive governments and their leaders to the 1970's and discusses reasons for the lack of a strong conservative party in the 20th century, the development of Christian Democracy and Acción Democrático, the role of the Catholic Church, the influence of the United States, Venezuela's international relations, the petroleum industry, multinational interests, the rise of communism, and the stability of the 1961 constitution. Secondary sources; 43 notes. P. J. Durell

2171. Gill, Henry S. UNDERSTANDING VENEZUELA'S FOR- EIGN POLICY. *Social and Econ. Studies [Jamaica] 1978 27(3): 350-363.* Reviews Robert Bond, ed., *Contemporary Venezuela and its Role in International Affairs* (1977) noting that this is the first comprehensive work on Venezuelan foreign policy. Reviews previous studies of various aspects of Venezuelan foreign relations, ca. 1899-1977, with particular reference to Venezuela's Latin American and Caribbean policies. 41 notes. E. S. Johnson

2172. Grayson, George W. VENEZUELA'S PRESIDENTIAL POL- ITICS. *Current Hist. 1974 66(389): 23-27, 39-40.* Describes the political parties and their candidates for the presidential election of 9 December 1973 and the administration of the outgoing President Rafael Caldera. One of seven articles on Latin America. S

2173. Guistet, Louis. LE VENEZUELA [Venezuela]. *Défense Natl. [France] 1976 32(4): 79-89.* Examines the background to the establishment of a liberal democracy in Venezuela, stressing the characteristics of underdevelopment in the social and economic structure of this wealthy country, which is aspiring to international influence.

2174. Hudon, Gérald. STORMY VENEZUELAN OIL POLITICS PAVED WAY FOR CREATION OF OPEC. *Int. Perspectives [Canada] 1975 (3): 36-40.* Venezuela's history of oil development, governmental oil policy, and role as an oil power are discussed.

2175. Huizer, Gerrit. PEASANT ORGANIZATIONS AND AGRARIAN REFORM SINCE 1900. *Cahiers Int. d'Hist. Écon. et Sociale [Italy] 1978 8: 326-333.* Analyzes peasant movements in Venezuela, 1900-78. Romulo Betancourt, following the presidency of Juan Vicente Gómez, started to organize the peasants politically, allowing the peasant union movement to gain strength, 1945-48. Following the overthrow of the Betancourt government by Carlos Delgado Chalbaud and Marcos Pérez Jiménez in 1948, however, the peasant and labor movements were severely repressed. The peasant movement grew again in 1958 when Jiménez was overthrown and Betancourt returned to power. Based mainly on secondary sources; 36 notes. F. X. Hartigan

2176. Kaplan, Marcos. PETRÓLEO Y DESARROLLO: EL IMPACTO INTERNO [Petroleum and development: the internal impact]. *Foro Int. [Mexico] 1980 21(1): 83-106.* Discusses the internal political and economic development of oil exporting countries (primarily Venezuela, Iran, and Saudi Arabia) and argues that oil income should be used to foster economic diversification and lessen dependence on oil income. Reworking of paper prepared for a conference at the National Autonomous University of Mexico, 15-18 October 1979. Secondary sources; 23 notes. D. A. Franz

2177. Kirby, John. VENEZUELA'S LAND REFORM: PROGRESS AND CHANGE. *J. of Interam. Studies and World Affairs 1973 15(2): 205-220.* Venezuelan agrarian reform began with the overthrow of the Pérez Jiménez government in 1958. Various government programs since that time have failed to produce much improvement in crop yields or the rural standard of living in rural agricultural regions. The large landholders still have their power, and total production has not increased significantly. However, social benefits have accrued. Based on state and business reports and secondary books and articles; 4 notes, biblio. J. R. Thomas

2178. Kozlov, Iu. K. GUSTAVO MACHADO [Gustavo Machado]. *Voprosy Istorii KPSS [USSR] 1978 (7): 121-124.* A biographical sketch of Gustavo Machado (b. 1898), Latin American revolutionary and one of the founders and leaders of the Communist Party of Venezuela. Machado helped organize radical groups and Communist parties throughout Latin America. Despite frequent arrests and exile, Machado served the Venezuelan Communist Party as a member of the Secretariat, parliamentary delegate, and from 1971 as chairman. Based on published documents and secondary sources; 3 notes. L. E. Holmes

2179. Levine, Daniel H. DEMOCRACY AND THE CHURCH IN VENEZUELA. *J. of Interam. Studies and World Affairs 1976 18(1): 3-23.* The Roman Catholic Church in Venezuela supported military regimes and dictatorships until 1958. At that time, when democratic government took over, there was some fear that Church leaders would oppose the new political system. But the Church has supported democracy and has prospered. However, those within the Church who advocate more than an accommodation of democracy champion social change. However, there is no prospect for such Church action. Based on Venezuelan church publications; 14 notes, biblio. J. R. Thomas

2180. Levine, Daniel H. PORTRAITS OF VENEZUELA. *J. of Interamerican Studies and World Affairs 1981 23(2): 203-223.* Reviews Victor E. Childers's *Human Resources Development: Venezuela* (1974), *The Venezuela Peasant in Country and City* (1979), edited by Luise Margolies, John D. Martz and Enrique A. Baloyra's *Electoral Mobilization and Public Opinion: The Venezuela Campaign of 1973* (1976), John D. Martz and Enrique A. Baloyra's *Political Attitudes in Venezuela: Societal Cleavages and Public Opinion* (1979), Stan Steiner's *In Search of the Jaguar: Growth and Paradox in Venezuela* (1979), and Angela Zago's *Aquí No Ha Pasado Nada* (1972), which reveal the difficulty and elusiveness of concepts and categories needed to explain recent Venezuelan life. 4 notes, ref. T. D. Schoonover

2181. Levine, Daniel H. REVIEW ESSAY: URBANIZATION, MIGRANTS AND POLITICS IN VENEZUELA. *J. of Inter-Am. Studies and World Affairs 1975 17(3): 358-372.* Venezuela is one of the few nations in Latin America today that enjoys democratic government. A predominantly urban country, the growth of cities has outpaced industrial expansion, and unemployment is high, creating social problems for the cities. Based on the six books reviewed and secondary books and articles; 12 notes, biblio. J. R. Thomas

2182. Mamalakis, Markos. THE NEW INTERNATIONAL ECONOMIC ORDER: CENTERPIECE VENEZUELA. *J. of Interamerican Studies and World Affairs 1978 20(3): 265-295.* President Carlos Andrés Pérez's emphasis on the moral and ideological aspects of the New International Economic Order (NIEO) have focused attention on Venezuela's role with regard to the NIEO. The author examines operations of economic order in Venezuela, 1973-77, revealing a complicated, diverse, and at times unclear system. Relates NIEO projects and the course of Venezuelan oil-related prosperity. 11 notes. T. D. Schoonover

2183. Martz, John D. POLICY-MAKING AND THE QUEST FOR CONSENSUS. *J. of Interam. Studies and World Affairs 1977 19(4): 483-508.* The nationalization of Venezuelan oil permits the study of the dynamics of that country's decisionmaking. While there was broad national consensus on national values and on policy objectives to be obtained through nationalization, the policy instrument created to institute the nationalization revealed deep divisions among groups in Venezuela, particularly after President Carlos Andrés Pérez decided to alter the policy instrument proposed by the *Comisión Presidencial de Reversión Petrolera* which he had created. Specifically, Pérez revised Article 5 to facilitate agreements with private foreign entities, rather than merely permit those agreements with private foreign entities which were deemed necessary. Political factions in Venezuela have taken strong exception to this instrument of nationalization. Fig., 4 notes, biblio. T. D. Schoonover

2184. Martz, John D. and Harkins, Peter B. URBAN ELECTORAL BEHAVIOR IN LATIN AMERICA: THE CASE OF METROPOLITAN CARACAS, 1958-1968. *Comparative Politics 1973 5(4): 523-549.* A consideration of local politics in Caracas, Venezuela, preceded by a review of recent politics in the nation as a whole. Several districts, reflecting class interests, were selected for the study, and reflect a polarization of ideas along a Left-Right axis. The poverty-stricken barrios tend to vote increasingly for leftist candidates; a drift toward authoritarianism is evident. Based on an analysis of Venezuelan elections returns, 1958-68; 9 tables, chart, fig., 38 notes. V. L. Human

2185. Mayobre, José Antonio. DESDE 1936 HASTA NUESTROS DÍAS [From 1936 to our times]. *Pol. y econ. en Venezuela, 1810-1976* (Caracas: Fundación John Boulton, 1976): 275-292. At the death of dictator Juan Vicente Gómez in 1935, the Venezuelan economy was in a state of crisis, with low standards of living and education. Oil, controlled by foreign interests, bore the economic promise. From 1936 to 1945, there was a gradual movement toward democracy, with slow improvement in the economy. The years 1945-48 saw feverish attempts at reform, while 1948-58 was a decade of dictatorship and repression. Since 1958, Venezuela has experienced democracy, along with rapid economic and industrial growth due to the now nationalized petroleum industry. Table. S

2186. Moron, Guillermo. HISTORIA POLÍTICA CONTEMPORANEA DE VENEZUELA (1936-1976) [The contemporary political history of Venezuela, 1936-76]. *Jahrbuch für Geschichte von Staat, Wirtschaft und Gesellschaft Lateinamerikas [West Germany] 1977 14: 350-368.* In search for national unity, Venezuela has wavered between democracy and dictatorship. Caudillismo has been modified but remains important in modern Venezuelan political history. Since 1936, the politician who has most markedly stamped Venezuelan caudillismo is Rómulo Betancourt. Despite his preeminence, the historical, political, and media treatment of Betancourt has been neither accurate nor revealing. 24 notes. T. D. Schoonover

2187. Myers, David J. URBAN VOTING, STRUCTURAL CLEAVAGE, AND PARTY SYSTEM EVOLUTION: THE CASE OF VENEZUELA. *Comparative Pol. 1975 8(1): 119-151.* On the whole the social cleavages of periphery-center, traditionalism-modernism, and poverty-nonpoverty can explain the voting patterns in the 1958, 1963, and 1968 Venezuelan elections. In the 1973 election the COPEI and Acción Democrática, both traditionalist parties, increased their votes in "modern areas," contrary to expectations. This is a short-lived phenomenon, and modernism will continue to work against the traditionalist parties. Primary and secondary sources; 53 notes, appendix. B. J. LaBue

2188. Myers, David J. VENEZUELA'S MAS. *Problems of Communism 1980 29(5): 16-27.* Since its birth in 1971, Venezuela's Movement

Toward Socialism (MAS) has become the most significant electoral force on the Venezuelan Left. Its Eurocommunist-style appeal to Venezuelan nationalism and to Iberian instincts of unity and harmony among leftists contrasts favorably in voters' eyes with the rigid sectarianism and loyalty to Moscow demonstrated by the traditional Venezuelan Communist Party. Despite its multifaceted electoral strategy, MAS is unlikely to pass up any good chance to seize power by force. Based on numerous Venezuelan and US scholarly publications; 2 tables, 37 notes.

J. M. Lauber

2189. Ortega Diaz, Pedro. FOR THE OVERTHROW OF MONOPOLY POWER. *World Marxist R. [Canada] 1973 16(10): 65-73.* An overview of political parties in Venezuela as they prepare for the national elections, particularly of the Communists, who as part of the New Force seek to overthrow monopoly power. Continuing the series "Political Portrait of Latin America."

S

2190. Ortega Pérez, Carlos. FUERZA AÉREA VENEZOLANA: ALCANCE Y SIGNIFICADO DEL 10 DE DICIEMBRE [Venezuelan Air Force: the significance of 10 December]. *Fuerzas Armadas de Venezuela [Venezuela] 1980 (276): 86-91.* On 10 December 1920 a group of French and Venezuelan officers founded the School of Military Aviation in the little airfield of Maracay, which was the beginning of the history of aviation in the country.

2191. Pérez Sáinz, Juan Pablo and Zarembka, Paul. ACCUMULATION AND THE STATE IN VENEZUELAN INDUSTRIALIZATION. *Latin Am. Perspectives 1979 6(3): 5-29.* The oil industry inhibited a viable import substitution policy in Venezuela until the 1960's. Since then industrialization and the nationalization of foreign-owned oil and iron interests have given the state the major role in accumulating capital and fomenting investment. A policy of export promotion, particularly through the Andean Pact, confirms the dominant role of the state in economic development. 4 tables, 12 notes, biblio.

J. F. Vivian

2192. Petras, James and Morley, Morris. THE VENEZUELAN DEVELOPMENT "MODEL" AND US POLICY. *Development and Change [Netherlands] 1976 7(4): 391-412.* The case of nationalization of certain industries in Venezuela, 1973-76, following the election of a leftist regime which maintains that nationalization actually strengthens ties with imperialism and capitalist development; examines the effects of nationalization on Venezuela's social class structure and imperialism and the view of US official agencies of the Venezuelan example.

2193. Revel-Mouroz, Jean. ADMINISTRATION DE L'ESPACE ET DÉVELOPPEMENT RÉGIONAL AU VENEZUELA [Administration of space and regional development in Venezuela]. *Cahiers du Monde Hispanique et Luso-Brésilien [France] 1979 (32): 129-147.* After years of planning the Venezuelan government initiated regional development policies in the period 1960-70. Regional programs were directed toward the utilization of natural resources, particularly energy, in marginal zones. The most important regional institution was the Venezuelan Corporation of Guayana (GVG). Venezuela has undergone a thorough administrative regional reorganization under the direction of the Central Office of Coordination and Planning of the Presidency of the Republic (CORDIPLAN). Based on government information sources; table, 3 fig., 19 notes.

P. J. Durell

2194. Serbin, Andres; Schneiderman, Stephanie and Droste, James F., transl. THE VENEZUELAN RECEPTION: HUMAN RESOURCES AND DEVELOPMENT. *Caribbean Rev. 1982 11(1): 42-45.* Discusses Venezuela's open immigration policy and the social problems that have resulted since massive immigration began in the 1940's, and particularly during the last 20 years, when the petroleum industry and political stability have provided a more attractive lure.

2195. Suárez Figueroa, Naudy. LA PRENSA DE OPOSICIÓN ANTIGOMECISTA EN EL EXILIO [The anti-Gómez opposition press in exile]. *Bol. Hist. [Venezuela] 1976 (41): 209-219.* Venezuela hoped for political freedoms from Juan Vicente Gómez, interim president in 1913. However, as elections approached, a newspaper's sponsorship of a second candidate precipitated Gómez's subsequent dictatorial suppression of all civil liberty. He imprisoned his opponent, and forced the journalist to flee.

Successively, newspapers opposed to Gómez were closed and opposition journalists imprisoned, including those associated with student publications. Political exiles continued their anti-Gómez campaign in the press of other Latin American countries and in the United States, in some cases founding newspapers themselves. Biblio.

G. Pizzimenti

2196. Sullivan, William M. THE HARASSED EXILE: GENERAL CIPRIANO CASTRO, 1908-1924. *Americas (Acad. of Am. Franciscan Hist.) 1976 33(2): 282-297.* Cipriano Castro (b. 1858?) took leave of the Venezuelan presidency in November 1908 to seek medical treatment in Europe. Acting president Juan Vicente Gómez (1857?-1935) staged a coup soon afterward to prevent his return. Castro did scheme to return, working with Gómez's other opponents to do so. However, his movements were watched and repeatedly restricted by the US and other foreign governments, which had experienced difficulties with Castro when in power. Afflicted by ill health, he wandered from one place of exile to another until his death in Puerto Rico in 1924. Primary sources; 65 notes.

D. Bushnell

2197. Sullivan, William M. SITUACIÓN ECONÓMICA Y POLÍTICA DURANTE EL PERÍODO DE JUAN VICENTE GÓMEZ, 1908-1935 [Economic and political situation during the period of Juan Vicente Gómez, 1908-35]. *Pol. y econ. en Venezuela, 1810-1976 (Caracas: Fundación John Boulton, 1976): 249-271.* After the 1908 coup d'état, Juan Vicente Gómez (1854-1935) consolidated his position with moves promoting peace and confidence. He also, however, modernized the military, assuming dictatorial powers in 1914. Venezuela was still a one-crop economy until foreign, primarily US, investors developed petroleum, which by 1925 was the leading export. Gómez and his intimates had grown rich with a highly repressive government, but in 1925 he relaxed his grip somewhat, his position secure. At his death, the oil industry had caused the appearance of a proletariat, a middle class, and educated young people.

S

2198. Tornes, Kristin. VENEZUELA—EN UNDERUTVIKLET OLJEGIGANT [Venezuela—An underdeveloped oil giant]. *Internasjonal Politikk [Norway] 1974 3: 665-677.* Traces the main lines of Venezuela's development during the last 50 years. Describes the economic, social and political conditions today, and shows how the profit from the oil sector has contributed to the maintaining of a mono-economy.

J

2199. Tugwell, Franklin. PETROLEUM POLICY IN VENEZUELA: LESSONS IN THE POLITICS OF DEPENDENCE MANAGEMENT. *Studies in Comparative Internat. Development 1974 9(1): 84-120.* Considers the bargaining position of nations having a single major export commodity that has been developed by foreign investors. Focuses on related strategies and conflicts, describing the general model of negotiating for an increased share of the profits. Relates as an example the Venezuelan oil experience. Traces the several strategies adopted since 1958; "an aggressive and openly experimental strategy is likely to be the best in dealing with foreign companies." Table, 16 notes, biblio.

S. A. Farmerie

2200. Valdez, Alberto. LA DOTACIÓN DE TIERRAS A COMUNIDADES INDÍGENAS EN VENEZUELA [The granting of land to Indian communities in Venezuela]. *Am. Indígena [Mexico] 1974 34(1): 215-223.* By approaching from a historical viewpoint the subject of land distribution among Indian communities in Venezuela from colonial times to the present, the author shows that the story is one of monopolization of Indian lands. The present agrarian reform law amply supports the right of Indian communities to land, implementing land distribution with two basic principles: community and inalienability.

J/S

2201. Wright, Winthrop R. RACE, NATIONALITY, AND IMMIGRATION IN VENEZUELAN THOUGHT, 1890 TO 1937. *Can. Rev. of Studies in Nationalism [Canada] 1979 6(1): 1-12.* Although 75% of the population of Venezuela is racially mixed, the white elite has consistently pursued a policy of Europeanization. They have believed that only an influx of white immigrants could assure the economic and political development of the nation and solve its social problems. This translated into immigration laws in 1891, renewed in 1936, which barred nonwhites from settling in the country. The policy has eroded only since 1958. Based on the writing of Venezuelan nationalists and materials in Venezuelan national archives; 43 notes.

R. Aldrich

2202. Zschock, Dieter; Fernandez, Anibal; Schuyler, George W.; and Duncan, W. Raymond. THE EDUCATION-WORK TRANSITION OF VENEZUELAN UNIVERSITY STUDENTS. *J. of Inter-Am. Studies and World Affairs 1974 16(1): 96-118.* Venezuela's economic and social development is in the hands of young university-trained professionals. Since a growing number of these professional people emerged from lower-middle-class backgrounds it has been assumed that they are in the forefront of social and political reform movements. However, a survey taken by the authors reveals the opposite to be true. Students from lower-middle-class backgrounds want to achieve elite status for personal security rather than to influence national development. This attitude could make them even more conservative than present Venezuelan leaders. Based on the author's survey and secondary sources; 6 notes, biblio.

J. R. Thomas

6. BRAZIL

General

2203. Aguiar, Neuma. REVIEW ESSAY: INDUSTRIALIZATION, ORGANIZATION AND UNIONIZATION IN SÃO PAULO. *Studies in Comparative Int. Development 1975 10(1): 100-106.* Three complimentary and valuable contributions on the sociology of work are *Sindicato e Estado, Suas Relações na Formacão do Proletariado de São Paulo* by Azis Simão, *Sindicato e Desenvolvimento no Brasil* by Jose A. Rodrigues, and *Industrializacão e Atitudes Operarias: Estudo de um Grupo de Trabalhadores* by Leoncio Rodrigues. Writing on the history of unionism, Simão focuses on the São Paulo region and Jose Rodrigues on a broader geographical area. Both works utilize the same approach, methods, and attack the same general hypothesis. Both fail to conduct a wider theoretical discussion involving comparisons with other countries. Leoncio Rodrigues, delving into workers' attitudes toward their firms, the union, and politics, fails to explore topics systematically.
S. A. Farmerie

2204. Alexander, Robert J. THE BRAZILIAN TENENTES AFTER THE REVOLUTION OF 1930. *J. of Interam. Studies and World Affairs 1973 15(2): 221-248.* The Tenente Revolt in Brazil in 1922 and again in 1924 was a military uprising of young, lower ranking officers. After the 1924 uprising, some went into exile but others joined together and moved through the Brazilian hinterland trying to enlist support for their social and political reform programs from the Brazilian peasantry. When this attempt was crushed, the officers were punished, but subsequently many were reassigned to military posts in Rio de Janeiro, where the movement continued to operate underground. The Tenentes have since been influential in several governments, and reemerged to support the military government that was launched in 1964. They are not a prime motivating force in the current military regime, because their ideology remains as vague today as it was in 1922. Based on memoirs, personal interviews, secondary books and articles; biblio.
J. R. Thomas

2205. Antonov, Iu. A. CHEST' I SOVEST' BRAZIL'SKOGO NARODA (K 80-LETIIU SO DNIA ROZHDENIIA LUISA KARLOSA PRESTESA) [The honor and conscience of the Brazilian people: the 80th birthday of Luis Carlos Prestes]. *Voprosy Istorii KPSS [USSR] 1978 (1): 95-99.* Traces the career of L. C. Prestes (b. 1898), general secretary of the Brazilian Communist Party. From a military background, Prestes spent much of his life in exile, leading a party that was mostly illegal but still able to exert force in Brazilian politics.

2206. Apesteguy, Christine; Martiniere, Guy; and Thery, Hervé. FRONTIÈRES EN AMAZONIE: LA POLITIQUE DU BRÉSIL ET L'INTÉGRATION DE L'AMÉRIQUE DU SUD [Boundaries in the Amazon Basin: Brazilian policy and the integration of South America]. *Problèmes d'Amérique Latine [France] 1979 (53): 76-98.* Examines changes in the borders of Amazon basin countries and the various agreements made since 1500 to limit Brazilian expansion to the west, concluding with the 1978 Amazonian Pact to develop harmony among South American nations and perhaps lead to the economic integration of the whole continent.

2207. Apesteguy, Christine and Thery, Hervé. LES FRONTIÈRES DU NORD-BRÉSIL: DE L'INDÉPENDANCE AU PACTE AMAZONIEN [The borders of north Brazil: from independence to the Amazon Pact]. *Cahiers des Amériques Latines [France] 1978 18: 69-75.* The Amazon Pact (1978), the latest attempt to arbitrate the boundaries of northern and western Brazil, has imperfectly contained the imperialistic expansionism of Brazil. In general, since independence in 1822, all pacts and treaties have been favorable to Brazil and have enabled her to establish de facto sovereignty over the vast territory. Note.
D. R. Stevenson

2208. Armando Frazao, Sergio. LA BÚSQUEDA DEL ORDEN INTERNACIONAL: LAS RELACIONES DEL PODER Y LOS CAMBIOS QUE SE VISLUMBRAN EN EL MUNDO DE HOY [The search for international political order: power relations and glimpsed changes in today's world]. *Foro Internacional [Mexico] 1973 13(52): 442-454.* Discusses role of political and economic stability, power relations, and intermediate states in establishing a stable international order. Brazil is used as an example of an intermediate state.
D. A. Franz

2209. Arruda, Marcos. A STUDY OF CAPITALISM IN BRAZIL. *Latin Am. Perspectives 1979 6(4): 32-44.* Peter Evans's *Dependent Development: The Alliance of Multinational, State and Local Capital in Brazil* (1979) is one of the most thorough and comprehensive approaches thus far to understanding the Brazilian economy. His assertion that the state bourgeoisie forms a competitive part of the world capitalist alliance should be modified, for the state bourgeoisie may be in competition with international factions "for control over the Brazilian productive process." 4 notes, biblio.
J. F. Vivian

2210. Azevedo, Thales de. LA "RELIGION CIVILE." INTRODUCTION AU CAS BRÉSILIEN [Civil religion: introduction to the Brazilian case]. *Arch. de Sci. Sociales des Religions [France] 1979 47(1): 7-22.* In order to study the formation of a civil religion in Brazil, two fundamental facts should be taken into account: that Brazil has always been considered a Catholic country, and that close ties have linked church and state since the 16th century. The author considers three moments of Brazilian history as decisive in the formation of an official religious value system: the long submission of church to state before and after the country's independence, the proclamation of the republic in 1891, and the revolutions of 1930 and 1964.
J

2211. Bailey, Norman A. and Schneider, Ronald M. BRAZIL'S FOREIGN POLICY: A CASE STUDY OF UPWARD MOBILITY. *Inter-Am. Econ. Affairs 1974 27(4): 3-25.* Examines Brazil's foreign policy in the last 20 years, the influence of the military, diplomats, economic technocrats, and industrial and commercial sectors, and the rise of Brazil as a "minor power."
S

2212. Barrett, Chris. UNITED STATES FOREIGN AID AND SUDENE: THE DESTRUCTION OF THE BRAZILIAN NORTHEAST. *New Scholar 1974 4(2): 263-273.* Reviews *The Politics of Foreign Aid in the Brazilian Northeast* by Reardan Roett (Vanderbilt U. Press, 1972).
S

2213. Bento, Cláudio Moreira. O ESPADIM DE CAXIAS DOS CADETES DO EXERCITO: HISTORICO, TRADICÕES, SIMBOLISMO [The Caxias saber ceremony of the army cadets: history, traditions, symbolism]. *Rev. do Inst. Hist. e Geog. Brasileiro [Brazil] 1980 (326): 93-105.* Since 1932, the first-year cadets of the military school have received a miniature copy of the saber used by the Duke of Caxias, the father of the Brazilian army, in his campaigns in central and southern Brazil in 1842-70. Describes the historical background, symbolism, and traditions associated with the ceremony. Based on bulletins of the Military Academy and secondary sources; 11 notes.
J. V. Coutinho

2214. Bonavides, Paulo. O ESTADO SOCIAL E A TRADIÇÃO POLITICAL LIBERAL DO BRASIL [The social state and the liberal political tradition of Brazil]. *Rev. Brasileira de Estudos Pol. [Brazil] 1981 (53): 63-90.* The "law state" emerged from bourgeois and constitutionalist ideas of the late 18th century, and the proper role of the state was extended to the "social state" in the 19th century by Marx, Saint-Simon, and Bismarck in different ways to give the state responsibility for social justice and public welfare. The theoretical and practical evolution of such a state is described, as is the attempt to combine the two without falling into the trap of socialist totalitarianism. The constitution and judicial interpretations of West Germany are used to illustrate the points made. The transition of Brazil from liberal to social state is illustrated through reference to the constitutions of 1824 (the monarchy), 1891 (the liberal republic), and 1934 (the social republic). The constitution of 1946 is seen as a retreat to liberalism. 11 notes.
R. Garfield

2215. Brummel, Jürgen. GEWALT IN DEN AUSSENPOLITISCHEN BEZIEHUNGEN LATEINAMERIKAS AM BEISPIEL DER BRASILIANISCHEN SICHERHEITS- UND EXPANSION-SPOLITIK [Force in Latin America's political relations as exemplified by Brazil's security and expansionist policies]. *Jahrbuch für Geschichte von Staat, Wirtschaft und Gesellschaft Lateinamerikas [West Germany] 1978 15: 425-435.* In the 20th century force has played a very minor role in the relations between Latin American states. However latent, indirect force is common, for which Brazil's foreign policy in South America offers an especially good example. Based on printed primary and secondary sources; 12 notes. T. D. Schoonover

2216. Byrd, Pratt. A LOOK AT FOUR FOREIGN SERVICES: BRAZIL, WEST GERMANY, ISRAEL, JAPAN. *Foreign Service J. 1973 50(10): 10-13, 36-37, (11): 16, 21-22, 28.*

2217. Cachapuz de Medeiros, Antônio Paulo. PROJEÇÕES DO CASTILHISMO NA POLITICA AUTORITARIA BRASILEIRA [Influence of Julio de Castilhos's ideas on Brazilian authoritarian politics]. *Veritas [Brazil] 1981 26(104): 469-492.* Julio de Castilhos (1860-1903) was a journalist and politician and an early member of the republican movement in Rio Grande do Sul. His authoritarian character and wide personal power made him a very influential figure. His positivism influenced the development of authoritarian ideas among politicians and the military. This influence spread to the whole country, especially through Getulio Vargas, the revolution of 1930, and the Estado Novo of 1937-1945, and affecting the governments that came to power after the 1964 revolution. 33 notes. J. V. Coutinho

2218. Caldeira, José Ribamar. ESTABILIDADE SOCIAL E CRISE POLÍTICA: O CASO DO MARANHÃO [Social stability and political crisis: the case of Maranhão]. *Rev. Brasileira de Estudos Pol. [Brazil] 1978 (46): 55-101.* The changes experienced by the state of Maranhão, Brazil between 1956 and 1976 were incapable of reorienting the direction of the society. The major rupture in the process of regulation of political power, 1965-66, did not alter this circumstance. Even then, the stability of the society was preserved by the continuation of historically established patterns of conflict resolution. 6 charts, 24 notes. B. J. Chandler

2219. Cardoso, Fernando Henrique. EXPANSION ÉTATIQUE ET DÉMOCRATIE [State-controlled expansion and democracy]. *Rev. de l'Inst. de Sociologie [Belgium] 1981 (1-2): 231-238.* Studies the expansion of public investments in seven Latin American countries with an emphasis on Brazil, the role of the public sector in their economies, and the democratization of the state in the interest of the people.

2220. Cardoso, Fernando Henrique. POLITICAL REGIME AND SOCIAL CHANGE: SOME REFLECTIONS CONCERNING THE BRAZILIAN CASE. *Bol. de Estudios Latinoamericanos y del Caribe [Netherlands] 1981 (30): 3-20.* Acknowledging the failure of great theoretical systems to explain the dynamics of historical change, reviews the theoretical approaches to the understanding of political power and applies them to Brazil, which is in transition from the "liberal-democratic" paradigm to a political "grassrootism." 19 notes. R. L. Woodward, Jr.

2221. Cavalcanti, Themistocles Brandão. A CIÊNCIA POLÍTICA, O DIREITO, A ECONOMIA [Political science, jurisprudence, economics]. *Rev. de Ciência Política [Brazil] 1977 (Oct, special issue): 79-92.* Examines the extent to which legal education, the traditional discipline which dealt with the social sciences, has been and should be replaced by the independent disciplines of sociology, politics, economics, and anthropology. Pays particular attention to Brazil in the 20th century and to the relationship between judicial institutions and the role and working of governments.

2222. Cavalcanti, Themistocles Brandão. A FORMAÇÃO JURÍDICA DO BRASIL [The development of Brazil's judicial system]. *Rev. de Ciência Política [Brazil] 1977 20(3): 3-16.* Examines the sources of Brazilian law, judicial developments under the Republic 1822-1977, the Recife school, the Faculty of Law at São Paulo University, and contemporary judicial culture.

2223. Cavalcanti, Themistocles Brandão. INSTITUTO DE DIREITO PÚBLICO E CIENCIA POLÍTICA. REFORMA DO PODER JUDICIÁRIO [Institute of public law and political science: reform of the judiciary]. *Rev. de Ciência Pol. [Brazil] 1978 21(2): 23-46.* Discusses the reform of the judiciary proposed by the government of Brazil to the National Congress, to rationalize the judicial process and break its traditional patterns.

2224. Cavalcanti, Themistocles Brandão. A MODERNIZAÇÃO DO PODER JUDICIÁRIO [Modernization of the judiciary]. *Rev. de Ciência Pol. [Brazil] 1978 21(2): 3-15.* Explains the need for modernizing the judiciary, to adapt it to changes in Brazilian society.

2225. Cervo, Amado Luis. FONTES PARLAMENTARES BRASILEIRAS E OS ESTUDOS HISTÓRICOS [Brazilian Parliamentary sources and historical studies]. *Latin Am. Res. Rev. 1981 16(2): 172-181.* Provides a guide to the voluminous but little known riches of historical resources pertaining to the Brazilian parliament. Study of parliamentary documents can be particularly useful in comprehending the foreign relations of Brazil. 10 notes. J. K. Pfabe

2226. Chacon, Vamireh. FEDERALISMO APARENTE E UNITARISMO PERMANENTE NO BRASIL [Apparent federalism and permanent centralism in Brazil]. *Rev. Brasileira de Estudos Pol. [Brazil] 1976 (42): 107-126.* Surveys the opposing tendencies toward federalism and centralism in Brazilian history. Brazil was born as a centralized colony but since independence there have been attempts to force the country toward federalism. Nonetheless, past experiences forecast the replacement of this nominal federalism by a centralism whose vitality is undoubted. 21 notes. B. J. Chandler

2227. Chacon, Vamireh. A SOCIAL DEMOCRACIA BRASILEIRA [Brazilian Social Democracy]. *Rev. Brasileira de Estudos Pol. [Brazil] 1980 (51): 123-154.* Social democracy in Brazil can be traced from the antislavery campaign of the late 19th century and 19th-century Brazilian Krausist socialism centered in São Paulo, a Church-related social reform movement inspired by Pope Leo XIII. Reviews Brazilian attempts to define socialism, especially in the Brazilian context, and to describe its doctrines, methods, and goals, which ranged from mere social melioration to communism. Brazilian socialism has been, for the most part, Social Democracy—nondogmatic, nearly non-Marxist, emphasizing personal liberty as much as social and economic reform, and willing to work peacefully within the capitalist order for gradual change. 46 notes. R. Garfield

2228. Chawla, R. L. MULTINATIONALS AS AGENTS OF EXPORT PROMOTION: THE CASE OF BRAZILIAN MANUFACTURING EXPORTS. *Int. Studies [India] 1977 16(2): 275-286.* Recognizing the possible damage to the development of indigenous manufactures for export, studies multinational corporations (MNC) in Brazil. The export targets the Brazilian government set for itself were not capable of realization without MNC assistance. Being alert to possible detrimental effects, Brazil has carefully defined sectors of operation with sufficient care and wisdom as to obviate the dangers, and has thereby demonstrated the values which can accrue to the country when the policy has been both cautious and imaginative. 4 tables, 23 notes. R. V. Ritter

2229. Chilcote, Ronald H. and Harding, Timothy F. INTRODUCTION. *Latin Am. Perspectives 1979 6(4): 2-15.* Introduction to issue devoted to contemporary Brazil. Discussion divided between theoretical interpretations and workers' challenge in a controlled capitalist system. Biblio. J. F. Vivian

2230. Cintra, Miguel Conçalves de Ulhôa. OS PARTIDOS POLÍTICOS E REPRESENTAÇÃO POPULAR [Political parties and representation of the people]. *Rev. de Ciência Política [Brazil] 1977 20(4): 55-71.* Examines political representation in Brazil in the 20th century. In the period ca. 1970-76, only 0.1% of the population participated in party associations and the majority of electors were disinterested, voting out of obligation and regional interest. The author stresses the importance of candidate selection procedures under such conditions.

2231. Dias, Gentil Martins. NEW PATTERNS OF DOMINATION IN RURAL BRAZIL: A CASE STUDY OF AGRICULTURE IN THE

BRAZILIAN NORTHEAST. *Econ. Development and Cultural Change 1978 27(1): 169-182.* Examines the patterns of rural settlement and tenure in Northeastern Brazil and the effect of the emergence of the state and its bureaucracy as the local patron. Until recently, farmers either lived on *fazendas* (large scale plantations) or on *rocas* (small holdings loosely connected to each other and to the towns). As the *fazendas* declined, the government became a sort of super-patron with the *rocas* system continuing to operate, causing an unstable system. Based on published sources; table, 25 notes.   J. W. Thacker, Jr.

2232. Díaz de Arce, Omar; Castañeda, Digna; and Galich, Manuel. NACIONALISMO BURGUÉS EN BRASIL [Bourgeois nationalism in Brazil]. *Santiago [Cuba] 1977 (28): 9-30.* The government of João Goulart was a temporary reemergence of the bourgeois nationalism of Getulio Vargas following the transitory governments of João Café Filho, Jânio Quadros, and Juscelino Kubitschek. The author traces the rise of Getulio Vargas to power, and the motivations behind his policies, 1934-45, and 1951-54. The 1960's witnessed the increase in foreign investments to the detriment of Brazilian industry, a situation only slightly alleviated by Quadros's tax policies. After reinvesting the executive with some of its lost power, Goulart was used by the middle classes because of his influence over the labor movement as a disciple of Getulio Vargas. His government was replaced by a military one. Based on discussion of Omar Díaz de Arce's article in *Santiago* [Cuba] 1973 (12) at the University of Havana; 2 notes.   R. O. Khan

2233. Donnelly, John T. EXTERNAL FINANCING AND SHORT-TERM CONSEQUENCES OF EXTERNAL DEBT SERVICING FOR BRAZILIAN ECONOMIC DEVELOPMENT, 1947-1968. *J. of Developing Areas 1973 7(3): 411-430.*

2234. Drury, Bruce. CIVIL-MILITARY RELATIONS AND MILITARY RULE: BRAZIL SINCE 1964. *J. of Pol. and Military Sociol. 1974 2(2): 191-203.* "Social scientists contend that prolonged, effective government by the armed forces in a developing nation is improbable because of the inability of the officers to act as proficient political brokers vis-a-vis the major civilian groups within the society. The experience of Brazil, 1964-1970, indicates that the success of military rule may be enhanced by the following factors. First, if interest associations are weak and subservient to the State, there may be no effective opposition to military rule. Second, if the boundaries of the military institutions are fragmented, the officers may acquire extensive political and administrative experience while remaining somewhat insulated against societal cleavages. Third, if the armed forces can acquire institutional pride and a generally accepted political doctrine, the officers may gain the confidence needed to assume an expanded political role and the armed forces may be able to sublimate or avoid profound internal conflicts."   J

2235. Dzidzienyo, Anani and Turner, L. Michael. RELACIONES ENTRE AFRICA Y BRASIL: UNA RECONSIDERACION [Africa-Brazil relations: another look]. *Estudios de Asia y Africa [Mexico] 1981 16(4): 651-674.* In the last seven years Brazil has adopted a policy of expansion of its interests in West Africa, and this policy has been characterized by Brazilians themselves as "conquest." The authors analyze the extent of Brazil's commercial ties with Nigeria, Angola, and Gabon and its historical and cultural ties with those countries. Given Africa's colonial experience and the importance of the racial question in both national and international politics, Africans would be well advised to look closely into any attempts at foreign penetration of their markets. 61 notes.   J. V. Coutinho

2236. Evans, Peter. MULTINATIONALS, STATE-OWNED CORPORATIONS, AND THE TRANSFORMATION OF IMPERIALISM: A BRAZILIAN CASE STUDY. *Econ. Development and Cultural Change 1977 26(1): 43-64.* Analyzes the development of the petrochemical industry in Brazil, 1954-75, showing the transformation of imperialism from foreign exploitation to a partnership between the multinational corporations and government. Discusses the growth of the petrochemical industry through a combination of private initiative and state participation in the 1950's-60's, and the emergence of state capitalism in partnership with multinational corporations in the 1970's. Describes the advantages and disadvantages of the system. Based on published sources; illus., 2 tables, 17 notes.   J. W. Thacker, Jr.

2237. Evans, Peter B. CONTINUITIES AND CONTRADICTIONS IN THE EVOLUTION OF BRAZILIAN DEPENDENCE. *Latin Am. Perspectives 1976 3(2): 30-54.* Dependency, like capitalism in general, requires change. The author shows how the relations of classic dependence generated forces which brought about a transformation in the relation of foreign capitalism to the periphery. Dependency was transformed, but not ended. In some ways, Brazilian dependence became more thorough. The transformed dependence is more severe and is still in motion. Includes an analysis of the economy. Tables.

J. L. Dietz

2238. Ferreira Filho, Manoel Gonçalves. O PLANEJAMENTO ECONÔMICO NA CONSTITUIÇÃO BRASILEIRA [Economic planning in the Brazilian constitution]. *Rev. Brasileira de Estudos Pol. [Brazil] 1980 (51): 101-121.* Surveys the constitutional role of government economic planning in the constitutions of several social democratic and Communist countries. Summarizes the economic articles of the Brazilian constitutions of 1937, 1946, and 1967 (as amended). Economic planning for development today is nondoctrinal and nonideological, simply an accepted technique of government.   R. Garfield

2239. Fishlow, Albert. BRAZILIAN DEVELOPMENT IN LONG-TERM PERSPECTIVE. *Am. Econ. Rev. 1980 70(2): 102-108.* Committed to a pragmatic program rather than an ideological one, Brazilian policy, subject to occasional modification, has been based on transferring resources from agriculture to industry, monetary expansion, and a reliance on foreign capital. A discussion by Morris D. Morris and Samuel A. Morley, who question Fishlow's optimism about Brazil's economic future, follows on pages 109-112. 7 ref.   D. K. Pickens

2240. Fleischer, David V. A BANCADA FEDERAL MINEIRA: TRINTA ANOS DE RECRUTAMENTO POLÍTICO, 1945/1975 [The federal delegation from Minas Gerais: 30 years of political recruitment, 1945-75]. *Rev. Brasileira de Estudos Pol. [Brazil] 1977 (45): 7-58.* Studies the sociopolitical, regional, party, and career backgrounds of 154 federal deputies elected in Minas Gerais state, Brazil, 1945-75, and analyzes their significance. Since 1945, there have been significant changes in the patterns of political recruitment, among them, tendencies toward drawing from a broader occupational and social base, declining influence of the political bosses in selection, and a more rapid emergence of newer figures. There has also been a seeming reluctance of local prefects to seek election to congress because of the low prestige of federal service in recent years. 12 charts, 3 fig., 69 notes.   B. J. Chandler

2241. Fleischer, David V. EL COMPONENTE POLITICO ELECTORAL DE LA ESTRATEGIA DE "APERTURA" DEL GOBIERNO MILITAR BRASILEÑO [The electoral policy component of the Brazilian military government's *apertura* strategy]. *Rev. de Estudios Pol. [Spain] 1981 (24): 55-91.* The present Brazilian authoritarian government is in basic continuity with the experience of the Estado Novo after 1930, though it preserves certain minimal attributes of formal democracy. When the legitimacy of the authoritarian regime was called into question, the strategists of the system followed the precept of the 1930 conspirators: to make the revolution before the people make it. This idea of "anticipation" has guided the majority of politicians and administrators since 1945, including those who came after the 1964 coup. 45 notes.   J. V. Coutinho

2242. Flynn, Peter. BRAZIL: AUTHORITARIANISM AND CLASS CONTROL (A REVIEW ARTICLE). *J. of Latin Am. Studies [Great Britain] 1974 6(2): 315-333.* Reviews ten recent books on the political and social history of modern Brazil that concentrate on the topics of democracy, authoritarianism, nationalism, social classes, elites, and bureaucracy; evalutes the areas in need of further research.

K. M. Bailor/S

2243. Fox, Jonathan. HAS BRAZIL MOVED TOWARD STATE CAPITALISM? *Latin Am. Perspectives 1980 7(1): 64-84.* Analyzes interpretive literature on the direction of Brazil's economic policy. From the second of two issues devoted to Brazil. 18 notes, biblio.

J. F. Vivian

2244. Franco, Afonso Arinos de Melo. CONTINUIDADE E ATUALIDADE POLÍTICA DE MINAS [Continuity and present political state of affairs in Minas Gerais]. *Veritas [Brazil] 1977 22(86): 126-144.* An account of the origins of the Minas Gerais region, the subsequent course of its history, and high points in its development as a state.

2245. Franco, Celina do Amaral Peixoto Moreira and Bomeny, Regina Helena Diniz. ARQUIVOS PRIVADOS NA HISTÓRIA CONTEMPORÂNEA BRASILEIRA [Private archives in contemporary Brazilian history]. *Rev. de Ciência Política [Brazil] 1977 20(1): 15-24.* Describes the development of private archives in Brazil 19th-20th centuries, their current state, the establishment and functioning of the Center for Research and Documentation of Contemporary Brazilian History, its procedure for organizing and classifying donated private collections, and its connections with similar institutions.

2246. Gall, Norman. THE RISE OF BRAZIL. *Commentary 1977 63(1): 45-55.* Brazil has recently become a new political force in the Western Hemisphere, developing into the world's 10th largest economy. It is uncertain whether it can continue to grow in a slowing world economy. Dramatic increases in population and energy consumption, particularly the expanded use of the internal combustion engine, have since 1945 opened the country up and supported rapid economic development. Brazil has become a competitor for world energy resources, a consumer forced to exploit marginal production areas. The triumph of authoritarian government in Brazil has duplicated itself in several Latin American states. Brazil's relation to the United States is also a question mark as it is beginning to conduct a pragmatic "ecumenical" foreign policy, shifting away from traditional friendships.   S. R. Herstein

2247. Garg, Ramesh C. BRAZILIAN EXTERNAL DEBT: A STUDY OF CAPITAL FLOWS AND TRANSFER OF RESOURCES. *J. of Interamerican Studies and World Affairs 1978 20(3): 341-351.* Non-oil-exporting countries confronting the increased costs of oil have had to choose between a domestically unpopular slowdown of economic development or external borrowing. Choosing borrowing, they have rapidly built large external debts and now confront debt servicing problems. Despite greatly increased coffee prices, already by 1975 Brazil required 15% of its foreign trade exchange for debt service. 11 notes.
T. D. Schoonover

2248. Goertzel, Ted. AMERICAN IMPERIALISM AND THE BRAZILIAN STUDENT MOVEMENT. *Youth and Soc. 1974 6(2): 123-150.* Reports on issues the author observed in a study of Brazilian student politics in the mid-1960's.   S

2249. Goldfrank, Walter. ESSENCE AND VARIATION: APPROACHES TO THE STUDY OF CONTEMPORARY BRAZIL. Rubinson, Richard, ed. *Dynamics of World Development* (Beverly Hills, Calif.: Sage, 1981): 89-99. Contrasts the analyses of Brazil in Noam Chomsky and E. S. Herman's *The Political Economy of Human Rights* (1979), and in Peter Evans's *Dependent Development* (1979). Chomsky and Herman focus on one aspect of the essence of Brazilian development—brutal repression undertaken with the support of the United States. Evans's work, by contrast, focuses on both essence and variation in his study of the triple alliance of multinational firms, local capital, and state actors as the institutional crux of semiperipheral Brazil. The essence is the workings of dependent development, while the variation is the awareness of Brazil's shift from the periphery to the semiperiphery and critical problem in the success of its development strategy. The two works are analyzed to demonstrate how a proper conceptualization of world development is necessary for understanding any particular case and to point out strategies for analysis. 2 notes.   J. Powell

2250. Haddad, Paulo Roberto. BRAZIL: ECONOMISTS IN A BUREAUCRATIC-AUTHORITARIAN SYSTEM. *Hist. of Pol. Econ. 1981 13(3): 656-680.* Examines problems in the academic training of Brazilian economists, the increase in the penetration of economists in various institutions, and the economist's role in the formulation and implementation of public policies. In the 1980's, economists in Brazil will have to play a crucial role in laying the basis of a new pattern of economic growth and development; this action may reinforce the process of political redemocratization. Secondary sources; 3 tables, 22 notes, biblio.
T. P. Richardson

2251. Hahner, June E. FEMINISM, WOMEN'S RIGHTS, AND THE SUFFRAGE MOVEMENT IN BRAZIL. *Latin Am. Res. Rev. 1980 15(1): 65-111.* Brazilian feminism originated in the mid-19th century with a small group of pioneer feminists who expressed dissatisfaction with female roles. Some women participated in the abolition movement, but not in policymaking roles. Journals and newspapers disseminated feminist ideas, urging an improved position in the family and access to better education and careers. After the late 1880's, suffrage became the focal point, and the women's movement, led by professional women and relatives of the elite, became more conservative and thus more acceptable. Suffrage was achieved in 1932. Based on feminist journals and newspapers and Brazilian government documents; 134 notes.
J. K. Pfabe

2252. Hanson, Carl A. DISSERTATIONS ON LUSO-BRAZILIAN TOPICS: A BIBLIOGRAPHY OF DISSERTATIONS COMPLETED IN THE UNITED STATES, GREAT BRITAIN AND CANADA, 1892-1970. *Americas [Acad. of Am. Franciscan Hist.] 1974 30(3): 373-403.* Continued from a previous article. Lists dissertations on Brazilian history since 1808, by chronological and topical subdivisions. An addendum lists 1971 dissertations and others that came to light too late for inclusion in their proper place.   D. Bushnell

2253. Herescu, Mariana. O PRINCÍPIO DA NÃO-EXTRADIÇÃO POR CRIME POLÍTICO [The principle of nonextradition for political crimes]. *Rev. de Ciência Política [Brazil] 1975 (Special no.): 79-95.* Outlines the legal basis for extradition, the definition of political crime, the history of the principle of nonextradition for political crimes, and the relevant legislation in 20th-century Brazil.

2254. Jaguaribe, Helio. EL BRAZIL Y LA AMÉRICA LATINA [Brazil and Latin America]. *Foro Int. [Mexico] 1975 15(60): 607-637.* Discusses Brazil's Latin American policies (1945-74), and examines Brazil's alternatives of economic integration or independent action to stimulate development and achieve autonomy. Originally presented at a Round Table on the Latin American Subsystem and its Participation in the International System held in Buenos Aires, 3-5 July 1974. Table, 3 notes.
D. A. Franz

2255. Johnson, Phil Brian. UP-TIGHT ABOUT RUY: AN ESSAY ON BRAZILIAN CULTURAL NATIONALISM AND MYTHOLOGY. *J. of Interam. Studies and World Affairs 1973 15(2): 191-204.* Ruy Barbosa was a famous Brazilian statesman in the late 19th and early 20th century. He held a number of government positions and he wrote widely in journals and reviews expounding his views on any number of subjects. Following his death in 1923 he was widely praised and soon emerged as a great hero. This assessment of Barbosa continued until a critical biography appeared in 1964. However, Brazilian intellectuals defended the earlier interpretation and condemned the 1964 work as mere debunking. By 1973 Barbosa's larger-than-life image was still intact and no objective history had been produced. Based on works by and about Ruy Barbosa; note, biblio.   J. R. Thomas

2256. Kalwa, Erich. DER BRASILIANISCHE TENENTISMO. EINE STUDIE ZUR POLITISCHEN FUNKTION DER AKTUELLEN POLEMIK [Brazilian tenentismo: the political function of current polemics]. *Zeitschrift für Geschichtswissenschaft [East Germany] 1980 28(7): 640-650.* Examines the traditional function of the armed forces in the states of South America as a keeper and guard of ruling systems, a role that is in decline. The growing economic and social crisis in Latin America has made the armed forces a carrier of progressive ideas and a vehicle of change. Explores the modern development of Brazil and the contribution of the *tenentes* movement of the 1920's. 44 notes.
G. E. Pergl

2257. Kaplan, Stephen S. and Bonsor, Norman C. DID UNITED STATES AID REALLY HELP BRAZILIAN DEVELOPMENT? THE PERSPECTIVE OF A QUARTER-CENTURY. *Inter-Am. Econ. Affairs 1973 27(3): 25-46.*

2258. Kiemen, Mathias C. THE POLITICAL TRANSFORMATION OF THE BRAZILIAN CATHOLIC CHURCH. *Americas: A Q. Rev. of Inter-Am. Cultural Hist. (Acad. of Am. Franciscan Hist.) 1975 32(1): 134-144.*

2259. Kiracofe, Clifford A., Jr. BRAZIL: AN EMERGING STRATEGIC FACTOR IN THE SOUTHERN ATLANTIC. *J. of Social and Pol. Studies 1980 5(3): 199-230.* Analyzes the increasing economic, military, and global importance of Brazil from 1822 to 1980 and discusses the possible formation of a South Atlantic defense organization similar to the North Atlantic Treaty Organization.

2260. Krasner, Stephen D. MANIPULATING INTERNATIONAL COMMODITY MARKETS: BRAZILIAN COFFEE POLICY 1906 TO 1962. *Public Policy 1973 21(4): 493-523.*

2261. Kuznesof, Elizabeth Anne. BRAZILIAN URBAN HISTORY: AN EVALUATION. *Latin Am. Res. Rev. 1982 17(1): 263-275.* Reviews Eulalia María Lahmeyer Lobo's *Historia do Rio de Janeiro,* 2 vol. (1978), Katia M. de Queiros Mattoso's *Bahía: A Cidade do Salvador e seu Mercado no Seculo XIX* (1978), Victor Nunes Leal's *Coronelismo: The Municipality and Representative Government in Brazil,* translated by June Henfrey (1977), and Eul Soo Pang's *Bahía in the First Brazilian Republic: Coronelismo and Oligarchs, 1889-1934* (1979). Though each volume is useful, none is completely satisfactory because of failure to integrate political and economic development and urban-rural relationships. 16 notes. J. K. Pfabe

2262. Lafer, Celso. EVOLUÇÃO DA POLÍTICA EXTERNA BRASILEIRA [Evolution of Brazilian foreign policy]. *Rev. Brasileira de Pol. Int. [Brazil] 1975 18(69-72): 59-65.* Outlines general points for the study of international relations, with particular reference to the 1960's and 1970's and to Brazil. Foreign policy is shaped and directed less by the Ministry of Foreign Affairs than by institutions and organizations controlling imports and exports and the international transfer of resources and technology. P. J. Taylorson

2263. Lafer, Celso. LA POLÍTICA EXTERIOR BRASILEÑA: BALANCE Y PERSPECTIVAS [Brazil's foreign policy: balance and perspectives]. *Estudios Int. [Chile] 1980 13(51): 309-327.* Analyzes Brazil's external policy in terms of its international economic connections.

2264. Lamare, Judith L. CAUSAL VS. CONTEXTUAL ANALYSIS: A CASE STUDY OF BRAZILIAN LOCAL POLITICAL PARTICIPATION. *Western Pol. Q. 1974 27(1): 117-142.*

2265. Landry, David M. BRAZIL'S NEW REGIONAL AND GLOBAL ROLES. *World Affairs 1974 127(1): 23-37.* Projects Brazil's diplomatic role as a bargainer between industrialized countries and developing nations. S

2266. Lauerhass, Ludwig, Jr. WHO WAS GETÚLIO? THEME AND VARIATIONS IN BRAZILIAN POLITICAL LORE. *J. of Latin Am. Lore 1979 5(2): 273-290.* Compares and contrasts the image of Getúlio Vargas, president of Brazil from 1930 to 1954, in folklore and in the stories of the elites.

2267. Lebreton, Jean-Pierre. LE BRÉSIL ET SA STRATÉGIE DE DÉVELOPPEMENT [Brazil and Brazilian development strategy]. *Défense Natl. [France] 1978 34(6): 99-113.* Surveys ways in which increasing economic power since 1960 has aided Brazilian expansionist ambitions in developing nations and the Amazon Basin, 1960-78.

2268. Leite, Cleantho de Paiva. BRASIL-JAPÃO: UM "RELAÇÃO ESPECIAL" [Brazil-Japan: a special relationship]. *Rev. Brasileira de Pol. Int. [Brazil] 1974 17(65-68): 27-42.* Presents the background of Portuguese-Japanese foreign relations and the commercial links established in the 16th century in the wake of the first Christian missions. Focuses on Japanese emigration in the late 19th century, the encouragement of immigration to Brazil in order to satisfy manpower requirements in the coffee boom, the imposition of restrictions in the 1930's, the breaking of Brazilian-Japanese relations during World War II and the resumption of commercial links in 1949, statistical data on the increasing trade between the two countries in the 1960's, recent Japanese investment in Brazilian industries, and the formation of a binational committee of industrialists. Secondary sources; 2 tables, 13 notes, biblio. P. J. Taylorson

2269. Leite, Miriam Lifchitz Moreira. COLEÇÃO PARTICULAR DE AGENOR MACHADO [The private collection of Agenor Machado]. *Rev. de Hist. [Brazil] 1977 55(111): 225-227.* An inventory of maps, photographs, books, papers, and objects donated to the Historical Documentation Section of the History Department of the University of São Paulo, presented as characterizing the interests and activities of Agenor Machado, 1920-53, especially in the contemporary history of São Paulo and Minas Gerais. R. O. Khan

2270. Levine, Robert M. THE BURDEN OF SUCCESS: *FUTEBOL* AND BRAZILIAN SOCIETY THROUGH THE 1970S. *J. of Popular Culture 1980 14(3): 453-464.* Traces the evolution of soccer in Brazil from its beginnings as an upper-class import in the 1890's, through its changing styles of play and its development as a national sport, to its politicization in the 1970's and the decline in popular support for professional teams. 3 plates, 23 notes. D. G. Nielson

2271. Lewin, Linda. SOME HISTORICAL IMPLICATIONS OF KINSHIP ORGANIZATION FOR FAMILY-BASED POLITICS IN THE BRAZILIAN NORTHEAST. *Comparative Studies in Soc. and Hist. [Great Britain] 1979 21(2): 262-292.* Examines the relationship between the descent system and preferred marital patterns as they illustrate the integral relationship between kinship and the political role of power families (or *parentalas)* in northeastern Brazil, 1889-1930.

2272. Lima Sobrinho, Barbosa. EVOLUÇÃO DOS SISTEMAS ELEITORAIS [The evolution of electoral systems]. *Rev. de Ciência Política [Brazil] 1977 (Oct, special issue): 101-110.* Traces the development of universal suffrage and electoral procedures in Brazil, 1791-1977, comparing their development with that of others countries, especially France.

2273. Macedo, Roberto. EFEMÉRIDES CARIOCAS, 1565-1965 [Ephemera of Rio de Janeiro, 1565-1965]. *Rev. do Inst. Hist. e Geográfico Brasileiro [Brazil] 1974 (302): 3-146.* A collection of notes concerning events occurring on the dates 1 and 31 May in the years 1565-1965 in Rio de Janeiro. Considers religious, political, educational, artistic, sporting, commercial, medical, and social events. K. A. Ross

2274. Macedo, Roberto. EFEMÉRIDES CARIOCAS [A chronological register of past events in Rio de Janeiro]. *Rev. do Inst. Hist. e Geográfico Brasileiro [Brazil] 1974 (304): 5-157.* Lists in chronological order, events relevant to the history of Rio de Janeiro that occurred in the month of June, 1557-1965. Events listed include many aspects of local, cultural, religious, social, and political history. Based mainly on local archive sources. P. J. Taylorson

2275. Macedo, Roberto. EFEMÉRIDES CARIOCAS [Cariocan calendar]. *Rev. do Inst. Hist. e Geográfico Brasileiro [Brazil] 1978 (319): 121-256, (320): 162-345, (321): 53-221.* Reproduces extracts from a daily calendar of events in Rio de Janeiro covering August, September, and October, 1530's-1965. The extracts record births, marriages, executions, shipwrecks, foundations, academic appointments, and many other activities. J. P. H. Myers

2276. Madeira, Felicia R. and Singer, Paul. STRUCTURE OF FEMALE EMPLOYMENT AND WORK IN BRAZIL, 1920-1970. *J. of Inter-Am. Studies and World Affairs 1975 17(4): 490-496.* Technological changes have altered the social division of work in Brazil and have enabled women to aspire to careers beyond homemaking. But the jobs available for women are linked to the development level of the nation and educational opportunities for women. Up to 1940, 70% of the Brazilian work force was in agriculture, where women had many opportunities to perform productive activities without leaving the home. During that period, women who did work in urban centers were employed as housemaids and seamstresses, which did not conflict with their traditional training. City and country women participated in work only as aids to men. Since 1940, however, there have been deep changes due to increased industrialization. There are more opportunities for women in banking, textile factories, and social services. There are still too few jobs open to women, but the future appears to hold promise. J. R. Thomas

2277. Malloy, James M. SOCIAL INSURANCE POLICY IN BRAZIL: A STUDY IN THE POLITICS OF INEQUALITY. *Inter-Am.*

Econ. Affairs 1976 30(3): 41-67. Examines the impact of the Brazilian social insurance system on income redistribution and suggests that the system works to the disadvantage of the poor. 6 notes.

                                                    D. A. Franz

2278. Maranhão, Jarbas. ORIGEM, IMPORTÂNCIA E COMPE-TÊNCIA DO TRIBUNAL DE CONTAS [Origin, importance, and competence of the Fiscal Court]. *Rev. de Ciência Pol. [Brazil] 1980 23(1): 43-48.* Describes the origins, establishment, and concept of the Fiscal Court in Brazil. Recounts the popular struggle to distinguish public finances from the ruler's private property and for the control of those finances. Provides a brief history of the court, with a definition of its functions and its relations to the executive power.

                                                    J. V. Coutinho

2279. Marinho, Armando de Oliveira; Maduro, Lídice Aparecida Pontes; Porto, Adonia Prado Marques; and Medeiros, Jarbas. O CON-GRESSO NACIONAL E A POLÍTICA EXTERNA BRASILEIRA [The national congress and Brazilian foreign policy]. *Rev. de Ciência Política [Brazil] 1975 (special no.): 56-78.* Discusses the concepts of revival, modernization, and representativeness of Brazilian legislative powers and the present national political situation.

2280. McCann, Frank D., Jr. ORIGINS OF THE "NEW PROFES-SIONALISM" OF THE BRAZILIAN MILITARY. *J. of Interameri-can Studies and World Affairs 1979 21(4): 505-522.* Alfred Stephan's assertion that the "new professionalism" of the Brazilian military contributed to the expanding role of the military in contemporary politics does not take into consideration the ideologies developing since the late 19th century which seek to explain the relationship of the soldier to the state. Contemporary Brazilian military intervention into politics can be traced to 19th- and early 20th-century concepts about the citizen soldier, the professional soldier, and the corporative soldier. Thus the "new professionalism" in Brazil is deeply rooted in the past. Table, 7 notes, ref.

                                                    T. D. Schoonover

2281. Meade, Teresa. THE TRANSITION TO CAPITALISM IN BRAZIL: NOTES ON A THIRD ROAD. *Latin Am. Perspectives 1978 5(3): 7-26.* A history and analysis of the social, political, and economic development of Brazil and its conversion to capitalism. Colonial and early postcolonial production consisted primarily of sugarcane for export. Later came coffee in the south, also for export, and the commercial development of the port cities, devoted primarily to facilitating the coffee trade. Brazil followed neither the socialist nor the capitalist roads to economic development. The middle-man and small merchant never appeared in important numbers, nor the factories to develop a working class. Not until the 20th century was the alliance between rural landlords and urban merchants broken. 10 notes, ref.   V. L. Human

2282. Meira, Silvio. OS PARTIDOS POLITICOS [Political parties]. *Rev. de Ciência Política [Brazil] 1975 18(2): 9-27.* Refers to the origins of political parties in general and their history in Brazil from 1822, and discusses the constitutions of 1967 and 1969.

2283. Mendes de Almeida, Angela and Lowy, Michael. UNION STRUCTURE AND LABOR ORGANIZATION IN THE RECENT HISTORY OF BRAZIL. *Latin Am. Perspectives 1976 3(1): 98-119.* Analyzes the role and limits imposed on Brazilian labor by the labor movement since 1946. Considers the historic roots of the lack of labor resistance to the 1964 coup, the coup's impact on unions, and the new forms of labor resistance which are emerging in Brazil.

                                                    J. L. Dietz

2284. Mendonça, Otávio. PARTIDOS POLITICOS BRASILEIROS [Brazilian political parties]. *Rev. de Ciência Pol. [Brazil] 1981 24(1): 18-29.* Briefly sketches the evolution, present situation, and future prospects of Brazilian political parties. Studies the place of the parties in the Brazilian constitution, the two-party and multiparty system as experienced in Brazil, and the majority and proportional vote system.

                                                    J. V. Coutinho

2285. Moises, Jose Alvaro. CURRENT ISSUES IN THE LABOR MOVEMENT IN BRAZIL. *Latin Am. Perspectives 1979 6(4): 51-70.* The Brazilian labor movement since 1945 has experienced bureaucratiza-

tion, failure to define its relationship to the social order, a leadership overly concerned with controlling the rank and file rather than leading it, and vulnerability to co-optation by the government. Table, 8 notes, biblio.

                                                    J. F. Vivian

2286. Morris, Michael. TRENDS IN U.S.-BRAZILIAN MARI-TIME RELATIONS. *Inter-Am. Econ. Affairs 1973 27(3): 3-24.*

2287. Munck, Ronaldo. STATE INTERVENTION IN BRAZIL: IS-SUES AND DEBATES. *Latin Am. Perspectives 1979 6(4): 16-31.* Examines state political and economic intervention 1930-74. Scarcity and incapacity of private capital generates intervention as do times of recession, but state intervention need not be antithetical to capitalism. 4 tables, 9 notes, biblio.

                                                    J. F. Vivian

2288. Niani (Dee Brown). BLACK CONSCIOUSNESS VS. RAC-ISM IN BRAZIL. *Black Scholar 1980 11(3): 59-70.* Discusses the United Black Movement Against Racial Discrimination (MNU) in Brazil, a movement less than two years old, and the MNU's activities against racial and class oppression of Afro-Brazilians. Traces the history of black oppression in Brazil since emancipation in 1888.

2289. Nicholls, William H. PROFESSOR FORMAN ON THE BRAZILIAN PEASANTRY. *Econ. Development and Cultural Change 1978 26(2): 359-383.* Reviews Shepard Forman, *The Brazilian Peasantry* (Columbia U. Pr., 1975) which discusses "the manner by which the Brazilian peasantry has been related to other population segments and to particular social, economic, political and cultural phenomena over time." 12 notes.   J. W. Thacker, Jr.

2290. Oliveira, Ismarth Araujo de. POLÍTICA INDIGENISTA BRASILEÑA [Brazilian Indian policy]. *Am. Indígena [Mexico] 1977 37(1): 41-63.* A general review of Indianism in Brazil from the establishment of the SPI until its transformation as FUNAI, and of the achievements and difficulties the latter has had to face. The policies followed by the organism agree with the general principles established in the Estatuto do Indio. The Federal government's aim is to prepare indigenous populations for the future assimilation into national society. This task poses multiple challenges, among them the wide dispersion of the Indian population on the land and the different degrees of acculturation of some of the groups.   J/S

2291. Olson, Richard Stuart. EXPROPRIATION AND ECO-NOMIC COERCION IN WORLD POLITICS: A RETROSPECTIVE LOOK AT BRAZIL IN THE 1960'S. *J. of Developing Areas 1979 13(3): 247-262.* The state government of Rio Grande do Sul in 1959 and 1962 expropriated US-owned public utilities. The author analyzes Brazil's economic growth and the effect of the US response under the Hicken-looper Amendment which mandates suspension of US foreign aid in cases of uncompensated expropriation. The US companies received compensation, as Brazil critically needed large-scale foreign aid and investment in the early 1960's. "Value deprivation" was the sanction applied against Brazilian President João Goulart, but not against previous presidents or the military governments that succeeded him. Based upon US-AID sources; 4 tables, 28 notes.   O. W. Eads, Jr.

2292. Pang, Eul-Soo. THE CHANGING ROLES OF PRIESTS IN THE POLITICS OF NORTHEAST BRAZIL, 1889-1964. *Americas [Acad. of Am. Franciscan Hist.] 1974 30(3): 341-372.* The "village priests," representing both the traditions of folk Catholicism and the official church," have functioned as "active politicians," "partisan bureaucrats," "reform-mongers," and "pressure group lobbyists." During the Old Republic (1889-1930), the first role was predominant, and back-country priests were significantly more successful than those of the coastal region, thanks to a popular mentality that readily turned to the priest as a source of help and leadership combined with a highly personalistic and loosely structured political system. Under the "state paternalism" of Getúlio Vargas (1930-45), the priest as "pressure group lobbyist" came increasingly to the fore, while the "bourgeois-democratic republic" of 1945-64 saw priests predominantly acting as "lobbyist and then reform-monger." These shifts of emphasis were related to changes in both state and church and to the emergence in the Northeast of agrarian unrest. Primary and secondary sources; 83 notes.   D. Bushnell

2293. Pang, Eul-Soo. FROM REGIONALISM TO GAUCHO CHAUVINISM IN BRAZILIAN POLITICS: OLD AND NEW VIEWS. *Luso-Brazilian Rev. 1979 16(1): 104-114.* Review article on Joseph Love's *Rio Grande do Sul and Brazilian Regionalism, 1882-1930* (Stanford: Stanford U. Pr., 1971) and Carlos E. Cortés's *Gaúcho Politics in Brazil: The Politics of Rio Grande do Sul, 1930-1964* (Albuquerque: U. of New Mexico Pr., 1974). Love's analysis of federal elections concludes that Rio Grande was the pivotal power in the First Republic. Cortés describes the development of Rio Grande into a national power, 1930-64, but his dependence on the role of personalities does not adequately explain the period. 18 notes. J. M. Walsh

2294. Paoli, Arturo. UN CHOIX POLITIQUE ET RELIGIEUX (AU BRÉSIL) [A political and religious choice (in Brazil)]. *Esprit [France] 1973 (7/8): 149-154.* Eighteen religious figures from northeastern Brazil published a declaration in which they analyzed the economic and social situation of the region. They doubt that the government's policies can aid the situation. They point out that the church cannot live separated from the world as a spiritual ghetto, but must act in support of its members during a time of hardship. Citing scriptural precedents, they maintain that the church must come out against the prevalent oppression. G. F. Jewsbury

2295. Pederosa, Bernadette. PERSPECTIVAS DO FEDERALISMO BRASILEIRO [Perspectives on Brazilian federalism]. *Rev. Brasileira de Estudos Pol. [Brazil] 1981 (52): 105-128.* Discusses the nature of federalism and a federal state, and the forms that such states can assume. Notes that modern federal states tend to concentrate power in the central government, rather than the member states. In Brazil, federal ideas existed in colonial and imperial times, but Brazil only became a federal state after the republican revolution of 1889. Describes the evolution of Brazilian federalism since then, noting the tendency for greater central power and concentration of that power in executive, rather than legislative, hands. This is a common tendency in Latin America; in federal systems, economic questions tend to promote central-regional partnerships at the expense of the states. 23 notes. R. Garfield

2296. Pereira, Luiz Carlos Bresser. EL NUEVO MODELO BRASILEÑO DE DESARROLLO [The new Brazilian model of development]. *Investigación Econ. [Mexico] 1974 33(132): 727-747.* Outlines the economic development of Brazil from the 19th century and focuses on the problems of the distribution of income in Brazil, the fostering of dynamic industries since 1970, and the new model of development that took shape after 1964.

2297. Pérez Llana, Carlos E. BRASIL Y EUROPA: EL PROBLEMA DE LAS PERCEPCIONES [Brazil and Europe: a problem of perceptions]. *Estudios Int. [Chile] 1981 14(56): 553-567.* Both Europe and Brazil have seen each other from distorted perspectives, affecting their economic and political relations and the balance of world power.

2298. Pessar, Patricia R. UNMASKING THE POLITICS OF RELIGION: THE CASE OF BRAZILIAN MILLENARIANISM. *J. of Latin Am. Lore 1981 7(2): 255-277.* Examines four Brazilian millenarian movements based on Folk Catholicism in which poor rural Brazilians accept misfortune and suffering as a result of transgressions or "failure to fulfill the norms of reciprocity and cooperation" vis-à-vis the saints or God. They are the Canudos in Bahia led by Antonio Conselheiro, 1893-99; the Contestado in Santa Catarina led by several "monks," 1910-16; the Joaseiro in Ceará founded by Padre Cícero, 1872-1980; and Santa Brígida in Bahia led by Pedro Batista, 1939-80.

2299. Pimentel, Waldemiro. CONTRIBUIÇÃO AO ESTUDO DOS PRISIONEIROS DE GUERRA DO BRASIL [Contribution to the study of Brazilian prisoners of war]. *Rev. do Inst. Hist. e Geográfico Brasileiro [Brazil] 1975 (306): 174-201.* Discusses the Luso-Brazilian military tradition regarding prisoners of war, and the country's adherence to international conventions since 1863, and outlines the specifications applied in the war against the Dutch in the Northeast, the occupation of French Guiana, the Paraguay war, and World War II. Based on military and legal sources. P. J. Taylorson

2300. Prestes, Luis Carlos. THREAT TO DEMOCRACY IN LATIN AMERICA. *World Marxist R. [Canada] 1973 16(11): 46-54.*

Brazil's conservative, military-dominated government has followed an expansionist policy while neglecting social needs. Part of the continuing series, "Political Portrait of Latin America." S

2301. Queiroz, Maria Isaura Pereira de. COLLECTIVITÉS NOIRES ET MONTÉE SOCIO-ÉCONOMIQUE DES NOIRS AU BRÉSIL [Black groups and the social mobility of blacks in Brazil]. *Cahiers du Monde Hispanique et Luso-Brésilien [France] 1974 (22): 105-131.* Studies the social mobility of blacks in Brazil, particularly in São Paulo, since the abolition of slavery. Racial conflicts within Brazilian society have only erupted when blacks felt their ascent blocked by white opposition. Thus far, it has happened in the 1930's and 1940's, with the blacks reacting through the formation of politically aggressive associations. Based on sociological studies; 40 notes, biblio. L. Garon

2302. Queiroz, Suely Robles Reis de. SÃO PAULO (1875-1975) [São Paulo, 1875-1975]. *Rev. de Hist. [Brazil] 1976 54(108): 419-502.* Provides a comprehensive survey of São Paulo, 1875-1975, from an economic and political perspective, dealing with the subject in two phases: 1) 1875-1930, when agricultural expansion based on coffee was the most significant event in Brazil's economic history, and the undeveloped hinterland grew into the dynamic center of the nation's economy; 2) the postdepression years, when coffee ceased to be the prime mover in the factors of production and profit. First published in *O Estado de São Paulo*, January 1975. 202 notes. P. J. Taylorson

2303. Rachum, Ilan. FROM YOUNG REBELS TO BROKERS OF NATIONAL POLITICS: THE *TENENTES* OF BRAZIL (1922-1967). *Bol. de Estudios Latinoamericanos y del Caribe [Netherlands] 1977 (23): 41-60.* Young officers who led several armed rebellions between 1922 and 1930, the tenentes, remained politically active between 1930 and 1964 and (in some cases) held influential positions in the post-1964 military regimes. Promoting an ideology of "controlled democracy" and technocracy, these politically tenacious officers gave Brazil a measure of institutional stability during an era of great economic and social change. Yet the role of the tenentes was somewhat counterproductive, as their combativeness and intransigence thwarted the careers of three generations of civilian politicians. Only in Castro's Cuba has there been such close identification in a modern Latin American state between the military and authentic political leadership. Based on memoirs and secondary sources in Portuguese and English; 51 notes. D. M. Cregier

2304. Resende, Antônio de Lara. SETENTA E CINCO ANOS DE ELEIÇÕES EM MINAS GERAIS [Seventy-five years of elections in Minas Gerais]. *Rev. Brasileira de Estudos Políticos [Brazil] 1977 (44): 165-187.* A memoir on various elections, 1900-76, in the state of Minas Gerais, Brazil. B. J. Chandler

2305. Resende, Expedito. A EVOLUÇÃO DA POLÍTICA EXTERIOR DO BRASIL [The evolution of the foreign policy of Brazil]. *Rev. Brasileira de Pol. Int. [Brazil] 1975 18(69-72): 117-126.* Continuing objectives of Brazilian government policy have been the maintaining of independence, sovereignty, and territorial integrity and the establishing of foreign relations to insure these aims. The author traces the development of Brazilian foreign relations in six stages: diplomacy of independence to 1825, national unity to 1875, progress toward the proclamation of the republic, boundary diplomacy to 1912, diplomacy of legal construction to the late 1950's, and the diplomacy of development to the present. P. J. Taylorson

2306. Robock, Stefan H. ARE THERE DEVELOPMENT LESSONS FROM BRAZIL? *Int. Development Rev. 1976 18(1): 16-22.* Examines the social and political conditions which have permitted Brazil's economic development "miracle."

2307. Roett, Riordan. BRAZIL ASCENDANT: INTERNATIONAL RELATIONS AND GEOPOLITICS IN THE LATE 20TH CENTURY. *J. of Int. Affairs 1975 29(2): 139-154.* Analyzes Brazilian foreign policy; Brazil's history and current political and economic development facilitate the attainment of the international position of power and prestige it seeks.

2308. Roett, Riordan. BRAZIL'S INTERNATIONAL RELATIONS IN PERSPECTIVE. *Orbis 1982 26(1): 257-267.* Reviews Robert Wesson's *The United States and Brazil: Limits of Influence* (1982) and Wayne A. Selcher's, ed., *Brazil in the International System: The Rise of a Middle Power* (1981). While Wesson emphasizes the relations between the United States and Brazil, the volume edited by Selcher tries to put Brazil in a global context. 6 notes.   J. W. Thacker, Jr.

2309. Rondon, Frederico. O PROBLEMA INDÍGENA BRASILEIRO: ASPECTOS POLÍTICOS [The Brazilian native Indian problem: political aspects]. *Rev. Brasileira de Pol. Int. [Brazil] 1973 16(63-64): 41-62.* Considers the influence of Old World prejudices in the treatment of the indigenous population since 1500, and Indian policy from the colonial to the republican period, including governmental organization of reservations and the involvement of the military. Biblio.
P. J. Taylorson

2310. Sampaio, Nelson de Sousa. PERFIL HISTÓRICO DO BRASIL, 1822-1972 [Historical profile of Brazil, 1822-1972]. *Rev. Brasileira de Estudos Pol. [Brazil] 1976 (42): 5-67.* An inquiry into the major facets of Brazil's historical development during its first 150 years of independence. Discusses and interprets such matters as the slow pace of change, absence of a national hero, relatively low level of violence, spirit of tolerance, generally nonauthoritarian leadership, governance by elites, ever-increasing centralization, absence of ideological commitment, and racial composition and race relations.   B. J. Chandler

2311. Schliemann, Peter-Uwe. LES INVESTISSEMENTS ÉTRANGERS DIRECTS AU BRÉSIL [Direct foreign investments in Brazil]. *Problèmes d'Amérique Latine [France] 1980 (55): 30-61.* A statistical analysis of the role of direct foreign investments in Brazil from 1950 to 1978, focusing on both its technical and political aspects. Stresses the evolution, particularly since 1970, to a "Brazilian pattern of development."

2312. Schmink, Marianne. WOMEN IN BRAZILIAN *ABERTURA* POLITICS. *Signs 1981 7(1): 115-134.* During the 1930's a moderate women's movement successfully achieved women's suffrage in Brazil. This upper- and middle-class reformist movement was not interested in revolutionary models in other countries. When a new movement began in 1975, conservative working women were recruited for the general struggle for political democracy. In neighborhood and working-class organizations, conflicts within the women's movement emerged and the meetings literally dissolved into fistfights. Coalitions were achieved, but elasticity was crucial and the historical context of the movement cannot be ignored. Secondary and primary sources; 44 notes.
S. P. Conner

2313. Selcher, Wayne A. BRAZILIAN RELATIONS WITH PORTUGUESE AFRICA IN THE CONTEXT OF THE ELUSIVE "LUSO-BRAZILIAN COMMUNITY." *J. of Interam. Studies and World Affairs 1976 18(1): 25-58.* The Brazilian government has shown a willingness to work with and assist newly independent African states that formerly belonged to Portugal, but it has refused to deal with extreme left-wing governments. Brazil has sent ambassadors to the new nations and some technical aid and relief assistance has been furnished. In return, Brazil expects to enhance its foreign trade through commercial agreements with Portuguese-speaking Africa. Based on Brazilian public documents, newspapers, and magazines; 5 notes, biblio.   J. R. Thomas

2314. Silva, Carlos Medeiros. EVOLUÇÃO DO REGIME FEDERATIVO [The evolution of Federalism]. *Rev. de Ciência Política [Brazil] 1977 (Oct, special issue): 111-126.* Examines the development of the federal concept in Brazil and elsewhere, ca. 1824-1977. Asserts that the federalism of the 1891 Brazilian constitution is anachronistic and an inadequate check on the disordered tendency toward centralization.

2315. Skidmore, Thomas E. THE HISTORIOGRAPHY OF BRAZIL, 1889-1964. *Hispanic Am. Hist. Rev. 1975 55(4): 716-748.* Reviews recent ideological trends in the study of Brazilian history, economics, and politics for the period 1889-1964. Article to be continued (see next abstract). 72 notes.   B. D. Johnson

2316. Skidmore, Thomas E. THE HISTORIOGRAPHY OF BRAZIL, 1889-1964. *Hispanic Am. Hist. Rev. 1976 56(1): 81-109.* Continued from a previous article (see preceding abstract). A review of the

literature of the economic history and foreign relations of Brazil during the years 1889-1964, with a briefer treatment of state and local politics. Covers articles on the single-product economy, the policy of grand designs, and the increasing obsession with petroleum. Foreign affairs, with authors too numerous to mention, generally has a Leftist tinge, whether from Brazil or the United States. The literature is extensive and is increasing rapidly, rendering many traditional standard works obsolete. 62 notes.
V. L. Human

2317. Smith, Peter Seaborn. BRAZILIAN OIL: FROM MYTH TO REALITY. *Inter-Am. Econ. Affairs 1977 30(4): 45-61.* Discusses the two myths surrounding Brazilian oil—i.e., that Brazil has vast reserves of oil and that international oil companies are anxious to exploit those reserves. These myths affected Brazilian oil policy since the late 1920's and the discovery of large offshore reserves in the 1970's, which gave some support to the myths. Based on newspaper and journal articles; 59 notes.   D. A. Franz

2318. Soares, Glaucio Ary Dillon. DESIGUALDADES ELEITORAIS NO BRASIL [Electoral inequalities in Brazil]. *Rev. de Ciência Política [Brazil] 1973 7(1): 25-48.* Points out the imperfections of the Brazilian electoral system which gives inadequate representation to all social groups and states in the Chamber of Deputies and Senate.

2319. Sobrinho, Raphael Valentino. POLITICA E COMÉRCIO INTERNACIONAL [Politics and international trade]. *Rev. de Ciência Política [Brazil] 1973 7(4): 53-74.* Discusses the imperialism of liberalism, Brazil's economic policy, and the problem of the responsibility of rich and powerful nations, particularly the United States, to give foreign aid to developing nations.

2320. Soiffer, Stephen M. and Howe, Gary N. PATRONS, CLIENTS AND THE ARTICULATION OF MODES OF PRODUCTION: AN EXAMINATION OF THE PENETRATION OF CAPITALISM INTO PERIPHERAL AGRICULTURE IN NORTHEASTERN BRAZIL. *J. of Peasant Studies [Great Britain] 1982 9(2): 176-206.* Describes the evolution of the relationship between elite and mass in Barro, a small town in rural northeastern Brazil, 1897-1975, in terms of its relationship to the penetration of capitalism in agriculture. Eight stages are proposed: the patron as mechanism of ecological adaptation, 1897-1905; as the most powerful among conflicting elites, 1905-15; as a point of reconciliation, 1915-22; as point of resistance to capitalism, 1922; as intermediary between state and local elites, 1922-35; as direct representative of the state, 1935-55; as means of access to the state, 1955-75; as alternative to the state, 1975. Throughout, the style of relationship between elite and mass has been crucial in regulating the penetration of capitalism as a mode of production. Based on secondary works; 15 notes.
D. J. Nicholls

2321. Théry, Hervé. L'AMÉNAGEMENT DE LA VALLÉE DU SÃO FRANCISCO [The São Francisco valley development]. *Travaux & Mémoires de l'Inst. des Hautes Études de l'Amérique Latine [France] 1979 (32): 9-15.* Reviews government attempts to develop the São Francisco valley, noting the inadequacy of the results, which are marked more by commercial exploitation of resources than an improvement in the peasants' welfare.

2322. Trindade, Antônio Augusto Cançado. POSIÇÕES INTERNACIONAIS DO BRASIL NO PLANO MULTILATERAL [Brazil and multilateral international relations]. *Rev. Brasileira de Estudos Pol. [Brazil] 1981 (52): 147-218.* Discusses the Brazilian position and activities in major international conferences and organizations, including the UN founding conference (1945), the UN General Assembly and Security Council, UNCTAD, the Law of the Sea Conference, and UN forums on population and environment and the reasons (including questions of internal politics) for Brazil's participation and position in each. Notes that multilateral and international solutions to world problems have been generally unsuccessful in the face of a world of sovereign states, but that Brazil has come more and more to support a multilateral approach to world problems, and the author expects that this approach will become more common as world interdependence, especially in the economic sphere, grows. 253 notes, appendix.   R. Garfield

2323. Valdes, Luis. VOTING PATTERNS IN RURAL AND UR-
BAN BRAZIL. *Secolas Ann. 1974 5: 66-81.*

2324. Vianna, Helio. O PENSAMENTO MILITAR DE CAS-
TELLO BRANCO [The military ideas of Castello-Branco]. *Rev. do
Inst. Hist. e Geográfico Brasileiro [Brazil] 1978 (321): 242-249.* Reviews
an anthology of the writings of Marshal Humberto Castello-Branco
(1900-67), whose papers were collected by Colonel Francisco Ruas Santos, and cover most of his career. Castello-Branco's historical research is
included in the anthology, as well as papers relating to his period as Chief
of Operations with the Brazilian Expeditionary Force in Italy, 1944-45.
Although a strong opponent of military intervention in politics, Castello-
Branco was forced to become president in 1964.

                                                    J. P. H. Myers.

2325. Villas-Boas, Pedro L. ÍNDICE DA REVISTA DO IN-
STITUTO HISTÓRICO E GEOGRÁFICO DO RIO GRANDE DO
SUL [Index of the *Revista do Instituto Histórico e Geográfico do Rio
Grande do Sul*]. *Rev. do Inst. Hist. e Geográfico Brasileiro [Brazil] 1975
(306): 217-355.* A comprehensive author, title, and subject index covering
the period 1921 (the first issue) to 1971. Authors appear in capital letters,
titles in italics, and subjects in lower case. The material is presented as
an aid to historical research.   P. J. Taylorson

2326. Wagner, F. E. and Ward, John O. URBANIZATION AND
MIGRATION IN BRAZIL. *Am. J. of Econ. and Sociol. 1980 39(3):
249-259.* Brazil's rural to urban migration has been dramatic, as urban
population moved from 15% of the total to more than half between 1940
and 1970. Studies of population shifts in Brazil based on choice models
of decisionmaking are inconclusive. The current trend in urban migration
reflects the impact of structural changes in Brazil's economy including
industrialization, agricultural automation, and accompanying public policy changes. Governmental policies designed to stem the flow of population to the cities will require structural changes in the economy
comparable to those which precipitated the migration.   J/S

2327. Walker, Thomas W. O SURGIMENTO DO POPULISMO NO
BRASIL: UM ESTUDO DO MUNICÍPIO DE RIBEIRÃO PRETO
[The emergence of populism in Brazil: a study of the municipality of
Ribeirão Preto]. *Rev. de Ciência Pol. [Brazil] 1978 21(4): 73-93.* Analyzes
the birth and evolution of populism in Brazil, 1900-64, as shown by the
example of Ribeirão Preto, where social, political, and economic conditions were particularly favorable to the growth of populism.

2328. Westphalen, C. M.; Balhana, A. P.; and Machado, B. P.
MOUVEMENTS AGRAIRES AU PARANÁ MODERNE [Agrarian
movements in modern Paraná]. *Cahiers Int. d'Hist. Écon. et Sociale
[Italy] 1978 8: 127-155.* Analyzes agrarian movements and social change
in the Brazilian state of Paraná from the 17th to the 20th centuries.
Primary sources; 3 maps, 5 notes.   F. X. Hartigan

2329. —. [BRAZILIAN COOPERATIVE MOVEMENT]. *Com-
munautés [France] 1979 (50): 42-57.*
Pinho, D. Benevides. ANATOMIE DU MOUVEMENT COOPÉR-
    ATIF BRÉSILIEN [Anatomy of the Brazilian cooperative move-
    ment], *pp. 42-56.* Describes the rise of cooperatives in Brazil,
    1960-80.
N. D. L. R. UN GROUPE COPASP [The COPASP group], *p. 57.*
    Describes emergence of Co-operativa de Pesquisas-Ação de São
    Paolo (COPASP), a cooperative organization.

2330. —. [BRAZILIAN FOREIGN POLICY IN SOUTHERN
AFRICA]. *Munger Africana Lib. Notes 1974 23: 4-37.*
Glasgow, Roy. PRAGMATISM AND IDEALISM IN BRAZILIAN
    FOREIGN POLICY IN SOUTHERN AFRICA, *pp. 4-20.* From
    a paper given at the 1973 African Studies Association meeting,
    Syracuse, New York.
Spitzer, Manon L. COMMENT, *pp. 21-23.*
Glasgow, Roy. REPLY, *p. 24.*
Sanders, Thomas. COMMENT, *pp. 25-26.*
Glasgow, Roy. REPLY, *pp. 27-28.*
—. INTERVIEW, *pp. 29-37.*

2331. —. [BRAZIL'S AGRICULTURAL SECTOR]. *Luso-Brazilian Rev. 1978 15(2): 195-227.*
DeMello, Fernando Homen. ECONOMIC POLICY AND THE AG-
    RICULTURAL SECTOR IN BRAZIL, *pp. 195-223.* The eco-
    nomic development model of the 1950's was designed to achieve
    industrial growth and the agricultural sector was to ensure that
    food was available in urban areas. The subsidization of some agri-
    cultural commodities encouraged the growth of latifundia. In the
    1960's there was a move away from strict import subsidies to in-
    clude industrial products. This was reflected in a more favorable
    agricultural exchange policy, a growth of urban credit, and more
    interest in agricultural research. After 1974 there was a balance of
    payments problem, however, and policies designed to provide
    cheaper agricultural products for consumers and higher incomes
    for farmers had to be modified. Based on Brazilian government
    documents and journals; 5 tables, 63 notes.
Schuh, G. Edward. COMMENT, *pp. 223-227.* Examines de Mello's
    analysis and asserts that greater attention should be paid to a fiscal
    interpretation of the policies pursued as well as to the effect of
    subsidies, cheap credit, trade, income distribution, and internal
    migration.   J. M. Walsh/S

2332. —. A DEMOCRACIA NA HISTÓRIA POLÍTICA DO BRA-
SIL [Democracy in Brazil's political history]. *Rev. de Ciência Pol.
[Brazil] 1980 23(1): 99-120.* Discusses periods of Brazilian history that
could be called democratic, the notion of "crowned democracy" proposed
by the monarchists, the democratic processes of the first republic, obstacles resulting from the inheritance of the Portuguese political and administrative style, whether there has been in Brazil a system of education
conducive to democratic aims, and recent political processes. A transcript of a round-table discussion at the Institute of Public Law and
Political Science of the Getulio Vargas Foundation, 16 October 1979.
                                                    J. V. Coutinho

2333. —. [INDUSTRIALIZATION IN BRAZIL]. *Luso-Brazilian
Rev. 1978 15(2): 178-194.*
Baer, Werner. EVALUATING THE IMPACT OF BRAZIL'S IN-
    DUSTRIALIZATION, *pp. 178-190.* Reviews the development
    and current position of Brazil's industrial sector in terms of 10
    major factors: growth, employment, technology, income distribu-
    tion, regional balances, balance of payments, dependence on foreign
    nations, the role of the public sector, environment, and energy.
    Indicates that: industry did not become the leading sector of the
    economy until the 1930's; the type of growth that has occurred has
    led to a further concentration of income; recent policies to diversify
    exports have conflicted with measures designed to increase employ-
    ment; and import substitution in industry has encouraged a new
    and complex dependence on foreign countries. Based on Brazilian
    government publications; 6 notes.
Haddad, Paulo Roberto. COMMENT, *pp. 191-194.* Suggests that
    Brazil's policy makers have failed to implement rational compre-
    hensive plans and to establish satisfactory economic priorities.
    Moreover, there has been a centralization of decisions without con-
    sidering their impact on efficiency.   J. M. Walsh/S

Interwar Years, 1914-1945

2334. Abreu, Dióres Santos. COMUNICAÇÕES ENTRE O SUL DE
MATO GROSSO E O SUDOESTE DE SÃO PAULO. O COMÉRCIO
DE GADO [Communications between the south of Mato Grosso and
the southwest of São Paulo: the cattle trade]. *Rev. de Hist. [Brazil] 1976
53(105): 191-214.* Examines the political and economic objectives in the
government initiatives for the exploration and opening up of the central-
south territory in the late 19th and early 20th century. Establishing road
and river communications between the Mato Grosso and São Paulo were
important in order to satisfy the increasing demand for cattle in the São
Paulo market. Private undertakings, such as those of Major Cecílio,
improved means of transporting stock. Map, 41 notes.
                                                    P. J. Taylorson

2335. Andrada, Antonio Carlos Ribeiro de and Campos, Francisco
Luiz da Silva. LEI NO. 995 DE 20.9.27 INSTITUI O VOTO SE-

CRETO E CUMULATIVO [Law No. 995, 20 September 1927 instituting the secret ballot and cumulative vote]. *Rev. de Ciência Política [Brazil] 1977 20(1): 33-37.* Transcribes the text of the first law to institute the secret ballot and cumulative vote in Minas Gerais, Brazil, in accordance with the 1891 constitution permitting states to legislate on electoral matters.

2336. Barbosa, Eni. ENFOQUE ECONOMICO DO RIO GRANDE DO SUL—1891 A 1930 [Economic look at Rio Grande do Sul: 1892-1930]. *Veritas [Brazil] 1982 27(105): 140-146.* Part of a study of the factors that enabled other states to economically surpass the state of Rio Grande do Sul. Examines revenue, expenditure, and other aspects of federal fiscal policy, as well as administrative and economic policies at the state and municipal levels and the influence of the means of communication on the economy and financial situation. J. V. Coutinho

2337. Benzaquen De Araujo, Ricardo. AS CLASSIFICAÇÕES DE PLÍNIO: UMA ANÁLISE DO PENSAMENTO DE PLÍNIO SALGADO ENTRE, 1932-38 [Plínio's classifications: analysis of Plínio Salgado's thought, 1932-38]. *Rev. de Ciência Pol. [Brazil] 1978 21(3): 161-179.* Analyzes the ideas of Plínio Salgado, founder and head of Acao Integralista Brasileira (Integralist Brazilian Movement), the right-wing political movement of the 1930's which was against individualism and materialism and wanted a return to medieval values.

2338. Buescu, Mircea. LE COMMERCE EXTÉRIEUR DU BRÉSIL PENDANT LA SECONDE GUERRE MONDIALE [Foreign trade of Brazil during the Second World War]. *Rev. d'Hist. de la Deuxième Guerre Mondiale [France] 1974 24(94): 65-84.* During World War II the Brazilian economy expanded its industrial exports despite the closure of European markets, primarily because of war production. A drastic reduction in imports was accompanied by a great increase in consumer prices. Export expansion promoted industrial development and agricultural expansion, but import restrictions limited industrial expansion and reduced tariff revenues. 9 notes. G. H. Davis

2339. Cardoso, Eliana A. THE GREAT DEPRESSION AND COMMODITY-EXPORTING LDCS: THE CASE OF BRAZIL. *J. of Pol. Econ. 1981 89(6): 1239-1250.* Discusses government support of the Brazilian coffee industry in the 1930's, in order to emphasize the importance of fiscal and monetary policies in a developing nation with a major commodity export.

2340. Castro Gomes, Angela Maria. A REPRESENTAÇÃO DE CLASSES NA CONSTITUINTE DE 1934 [Class representation in the 1934 Constitutional Assembly]. *Rev. de Ciência Pol. [Brazil] 1978 21(3): 53-115.* Analyzes social classes represented at the Brazilian Constitutional Assembly of 1934, suggesting that the presence of both employers and employees meant that the assembly dealt mainly with matters of economic and social policy which gave a pragmatical approach to the problems of state organization.

2341. Cavalcanti, Themistocles Brandão. TOPICS DE UMA HISTÓRIA POLÍTICA [Subjects of a political history]. *Rev. de Ciência Pol. [Brazil] 1978 21(3): 5-26.* Analyzes the revolutionary justice of 1930 in Brazil, the professional representation of the 1934 Constitution, the repercussions of unconstitutionalities and the struggle between federal and state powers.

2342. Coelho, Inocênco Mártires. ASPECTOS POSITIVOS DA CONSTITUÇÃO DE 1937 [Positive aspects of the Constitution of 1937]. *Rev. de Ciência Pol. [Brazil] 1978 21(2): 103-108.* Analyzes the 1937 Brazilian Constitution giving more power to the executive.

2343. Conniff, Michael L. THE TENENTES IN POWER: A NEW PERSPECTIVE ON THE BRAZILIAN REVOLUTION OF 1930. *J. of Latin Am. Studies [Great Britain] 1978 10(1): 61-82.* Most influential in 1931-32, the Club 3 de Octubro played a central role in the "lieutenants" movement, which began in the early 1920's as a revolt among army cadets and officers. Two-thirds of the club's membership was military officers, a surgeon led it, and it was organized to counteract traditional regionalisms. Ideologically, the club's *Outline of the Revolutionary Program for Political and Social Reconstruction of Brazil* was a hodge-podge intended to rationalize the economy and provide numerous social and

progressive reforms. Getulio Dornelles Vargas's relationship with the club was initially intimate and dependent but declined rapidly after mid-1932. Socially, the club's appeal was greatest among lower-class skilled and clerical workers. Based on *Centro de Pesquisas e Documentação em História Contemporânea,* periodicals, and secondary works; table, 58 notes. K. M. Bailor

2344. Cruz de Ravagni, Leda Almada. LES INVESTISSEMENTS FRANÇAIS AU BRESIL (1890-1930) [French investments in Brazil, 1890-1930]. *Cahiers des Amériques Latines [France] 1977 16: 107-124.* French investments in Brazil are analyzed despite scarce statistical data and scattered sources. French investment never reached the scale of British investment and was hampered in southern Brazil during World War I by the area's large German population. The analysis focuses on French loans to the Brazilian government. Based on archives of French ministries and secondary sources; 27 notes, biblio. D. R. Stevenson

2345. Doles, Dalísia E. Martins. GOIÁS E A PRIMEIRA REPÚBLICA [Goiás and the first republic]. *Rev. de Hist. [Brazil] 1976 54(107): 147-152.* Sketches political and economic conditions in Goiás state, 1889-1930. At the end of the 19th century Goiás underwent a phase of stagnation due to the exhaustion of the mining industry, the unstable economy, isolation, inadequate transportation and communications facilities, and small-scale cattle raising and farming. Electoral corruption and *coronelismo,* resulting from the semifeudal agricultural economy and the politics of the governors installed by Manuel Ferraz de Campos Salles (president, 1898-1902) created the political oligarchies of Bulhões, Eugênio Jardim, and Antonio Ramos Caiado that continued until 1930. P. J. Taylorson

2346. Dutra, Eliana Regina de Freitas. A IGREJA E AS CLASSES POPULARES EM MINAS NA DÉCADA DE VINTE [The Church and the common classes in Minas in the decade of the 1920's]. *Rev. Brasileira de Estudos Pol. [Brazil] 1979 (49): 71-98.* Discusses the ways in which the Catholic Church, which had prospered under the Brazilian monarchy, dealt with its new position under the Republic after 1889. The Church had to deal with a regime that was anticlerical and Positivist in its philosophy. The Church took as its guide the instructions of the encyclical *Rerum Novarum* of Pope Leo XIII (1891). Gradually, it won the right to have catechism in schools, organize Catholic trade unions, and operate politically, especially by claiming the need to represent and defend the rights of Brazilian workers. This was seen especially in the creation of a Catholic Labor Confederation and the publication of its official newspaper. By the time of the Revolution of 1930, the Church with its "popular" arms was an important force. 72 notes. R. Garfield

2347. Fleischer, David V. A CÚPULA POLÍTICA MINEIRA NA REPÚBLICA VELHA: AS ORIGENS SOCIOECONOMICA E RECRUTAMENTO DE GOVERNADORES VICE-GOVERNADORES E DEPUTADOS FEDERAIS [Higher administration in Minas Gerais under the República Velha: the socioeconomic backgrounds and recruitment of governors, vice-governors, and federal deputies]. *Rev. de Ciência Política [Brazil] 1977 20(4): 9-54.* Examines the appointments in key categories of officials in Minas Gerais, 1890-1937, with special regard to their contrasting backgrounds. Based on computer analyzed data from the Arquivo Público Mineiro.

2348. Garcia-Zamor, Jean-Claude. REGIONALISM AND POLITICAL STABILITY IN BRAZIL. *R. Interamericana [Puerto Rico] 1973 3(2): 143-158.* Political scientists have often blamed regionalism for much of Latin America's political instability. However, Brazil has experienced its most stable governments during periods when the provinces had the most power and the central authorities the least (1889-1930). Primary and secondary sources; 4 tables, 32 notes. J. A. Lewis

2349. Gordon-Ashworth, Fiona. AGRICULTURAL COMMODITY CONTROL UNDER VARGAS IN BRAZIL, 1930-1945. *J. of Latin Am. Studies [Great Britain] 1980 12(1): 87-105.* President Getúlio Vargas employed commodity control not only for coffee, Brazil's major source of foreign exchange earnings, but also for sugar, cassava, cotton, hides, meat, maté, and cacao. The important domestic commodities of maize, rice, and beans were still free of control in 1945. Coffee and cotton received particular attention because of their export value. Between 1930 and 1945 Vargas introduced changes that tightened and centralized control of commodities through the use of *autarquias,* semi-autonomous administrative units, which today serve as instruments for the administration of centralized agricultural planning. 56 notes, 4 appendixes.   M. A. Burkholder

2350. Hall, Michael M. and Pinheiro, Paulo Sérgio. THE CLARTÉ GROUP IN BRAZIL. *Mouvement Social [France] 1980 (111): 217-234.* The Clarté group in Brazil was founded at the end of 1921, when there was still enthusiasm for the Russian Revolution, but also when an already weak labor movement was in serious disarray. The lessons of the First World War were thus difficult to draw. The members of the group were mostly politicians and journalists who advocated moderate reformism. They were at some distance from the local Communist party. Many Clarté figures had contacts with nationalist movements run by young officers. Thus the group, originally marked by Barbusse's idealistic and pacifist themes, was finally much more a precursor of the Vargas government of the 1930's.   J

2351. Hendricks, Craig and Levine, Robert M. PERNAMBUCO'S POLITICAL ELITE AND THE RECIFE LAW SCHOOL. *Americas (Acad. of Am. Franciscan Hist.) 1981 37(3): 291-313.* From the establishment of the Brazilian republic in 1889 to the beginning of the Estado Novo in 1937, the state of Pernambuco was controlled by a political elite whose members were mostly of upper-class origin, based in the state capital or coastal plain, and linked to each other by close kinship and other ties. Changes that occurred in composition of the elite did not alter its essential features. Throughout the period, though tending gradually to diminish in importance, the Recife Law School served as a mechanism of acculturation and training for sons of elite families. Based on statistical analysis of biographical data in printed sources and some interviews; 3 tables, 26 notes.   D. Bushnell

2352. Hilton, Stanley E. BRAZIL AND THE POST-VERSAILLES WORLD: ELITE IMAGES AND FOREIGN POLICY STRATEGY, 1919-1929. *J. of Latin Am. Studies [Great Britain] 1980 12(2): 341-364.* The Brazilian foreign policy elite after Versailles considered that Machiavellian principles governed the international behavior of states. It thought Argentina aggressive and expansionist while Brazil was militarily vulnerable and diplomatically isolated. The defensive strategy it followed relied on diplomacy. Until 1926 Brazil sought prestige in the League of Nations, but failure to secure a permanent seat led to withdrawal. Regarding Argentina, Brazilian officials opposed disarmament proposals that would freeze the country in a militarily inferior position. Finally, the government sought a special relationship with the United States. Based on materials in the Arquivo Histórico do Itamaraty, other Brazilian archives, and limited printed primary sources; 92 notes.
M. A. Burkholder

2353. Hilton, Stanley E. BRAZILIAN DIPLOMACY AND THE WASHINGTON-RIO DE JANEIRO "AXIS" DURING THE WORLD WAR II ERA. *Hispanic Am. Hist. Rev. 1979 59(2): 201-231.* The major work on wartime Brazilian-American relations, Frank D. McCann's *The Brazilian-American Alliance, 1937-1945* (Princeton U. Pr., 1973) indicates that the United States was deceitful in dealing with Brazil and aimed its policy toward "economic and political hegemony." The author shows that, on the contrary, Brazil juggled the Axis and the United States to gain the most benefits for Brazil. The United States government cultivated Brazil while respecting its sovereignty. Based on documents and letters of Americans and Brazilians of the period, including those of Getúlio Vargas; 114 notes.   B. D. Johnson

2354. Hilton, Stanley E. MILITARY INFLUENCE ON BRAZILIAN ECONOMIC POLICY, 1930-1945: A DIFFERENT VIEW. *Hispanic Am. Hist. R. 1973 53(1): 71-94.* Analyzes the impact of military demands on policymaking on trade and steel issues facing the Getúlio Vargas (1883-1954) government of Brazil, 1930-45. "Under the impact of international turbulence, with a relatively strong and potentially aggressive neighbor on its southern flank, the high command gave top priority during the period to purchases abroad. Army planners also sought expanded production of munitions and small arms, and to the extent that they provided technical assistance and granted contracts to certain existing civilian factories, they encouraged manufacturing. The establishment

of basic industry on a large scale, such as the Volta Redonda steel complex was, however, part of the high command's general and much less urgent vision of Brazil as an industrial power." 81 notes.
D. D. Cameron

2355. Hilton, Stanley E. VARGAS AND BRAZILIAN ECONOMIC DEVELOPMENT, 1930-1945: A REAPPRAISAL OF HIS ATTITUDE TOWARD INDUSTRIALIZATION AND PLANNING. *J. of Econ. Hist. 1975 35(4): 754-778.* Demonstrates that the prevailing interpretation of federal economic thought and policies in Brazil during the Depression is untenable. The Getúlio Vargas government (1930-45) was, in fact, profoundly interested in planning from 1930 on, and committed itself at the outset, for politico-strategic as well as economic reasons, to a structural transformation of the economy via industrialization. The late 1930's do not, therefore, represent the watershed in federal policies that previous historians have argued. Based on archival material.

2356. Holloway, Thomas H. CREATING THE RESERVE ARMY? THE IMMIGRATION PROGRAM OF SÃO PAULO, 1886-1930. *Int. Migration Rev. 1978 12(2): 187-209.* Analyzes the immigration policy of the state government of São Paulo, Brazil, 1886-1930, and its relationship to the labor needs of coffee culture.

2357. Johnson, Phil Brian. RUI BARBOSA E A REFORMA DE ENSINO DE 1882: RECORDAÇÕES E REPERCOSSÕES PARTE 1, 1882-1930 [Ruy Barbosa and the 1882 educational reform: recollections and repercussions, 1882-1930]. *Rev. do Inst. Hist. e Geográfico Brasileiro [Brazil] 1976 (312): 241-262.* Ruy Barbosa's reform was rejected largely because it had depended on the support of the Imperial government, which changed in 1882, and because of the decentralized administration and lack of money due to inefficient taxation. However, the reform's influence continued as its various parts were gradually incorporated into subsequent reforms. Its conception of a national educational organization appealed to nationalist deputies who opposed the political and economic limitations of decentralized government and state favoritism toward the south central region. The reform's influence also reflected the rising status of Ruy Barbosa, who came to be regarded as one of the greatest republican statesmen. Based principally on Brazilian parliamentary records and the works of Ruy Barbosa; 53 notes. Article to be continued.
R. O. Khan

2358. Khenkin, S. M. NEPOBEDIMAIA KOLONNA [The invincible column]. *Voprosy Istorii [USSR] 1976 (2): 86-98.* Recreates the campaign launched by the column of Luis Carlos Prestes, 1924-27, a major revolutionary action undertaken by a group of patriotic minded officers in Brazil with the aim of overthrowing the reactionary oligarchic regime and democratizing the country's social and political life. Analyzes the political aims and social connections of the revolutionaries. The chief cause for the failure of the patriotic officers was their inability to form an alliance with the working masses of Brazil. A careful study of the experience furnished by the Tenentists' heroic raid enables one to gain a better understanding of the role played by democratic minded officers in the liberation movement of a number of countries. Based on documentary materials and the memoirs of insurgents.   J

2359. Levine, Robert M. PERSPECTIVES ON THE MID-VARGAS YEARS: 1934-1937. *J. of Interamerican Studies and World Affairs 1980 22(1): 57-80.* American and British diplomatic dispatches reported that Getulio Vargas's government in its first years was inept and unstable. They did not report the significant progress achieved in Brazil during the 1930's. Based on manuscripts and printed primary and secondary sources; 14 notes, ref.   T. D. Schoonover/S

2360. Lins, Maria de Lourdes Ferreira. LA FORCE EXPÉDITIONNAIRE BRÉSILIENNE: ESSAI D'INTERPRETATION [The Brazilian Expeditionary Force: an interpretive essay]. *Rev. d'Hist. de la Deuxième Guerre Mondiale [France] 1978 28(111): 87-94.* The Brazilian Expeditionary Force within American General Mark Clark's Fifth Army in Italy in World War II comprised 25,000 soldiers. As they suffered a high rate of physical and psychological disability, their strength was very slight. Furthermore, they had to be retrained for American equipment and so were completely supplied by the United States. Ideologically the government of Getulio Vargas stood closer to the Axis powers, but it was more practical to fight on the side of the United States. Participation in the war had a significant effect on the subsequent history of Brazil. 19 notes.　　　　　　　　　　　　　　　　　　　G. H. Davis

2361. Lustosa, Oscar de Figueiredo. A IGREJA E O INTE-GRALISMO NO BRASIL—1932-1939 [The Church and fascism in Brazil, 1932-39]. *Rev. de Hist. [Brazil] 1976 54(108): 503-532.* Describes the political climate in Brazil during the beginning and growth of the fascist movement, analyzing the ideology of Ação Integralista Brasileira, which attempted to identify with Brazilian traditions despite its foreign origins. Attention is directed to the role and functions that its leaders ascribed to the religious element in the corporate state and the reaction of the Catholic Church at various levels (episcopal hierarchy, clergy, laity, Liga Eleitoral Católica, and Ação Católica). Many Catholics were seen to be easy prey to the messianic fervor that was artificially stimulated and carefully fomented by a massive propaganda campaign. 72 notes.
　　　　　　　　　　　　　　　　　　　P. J. Taylorson

2362. Machado, Maria Cristina Russi da Matta. ASPECTOS DO FENÓMENO DO CANGAÇO NO NORDESTE BRASILEIRO [Aspects of the *cangaço* (bandit) phenomenon in northeast Brazil]. *Rev. de Hist. [Brazil] 1973 46(93): 139-175, 47(95): 177-212, (96): 473-489; 1974 47(97): 161-200, 49(99): 145-174.* Part I. Outlines the background circumstances and conditions that gave rise to the outbreak of banditry in northeast Brazil in the early 20th century, focusing on the inequitable social structure and poverty of the *sertão.* Local government was controlled by colonels, representing the oligarchy, who directed social and economic policies. Part II. The abuse of power by the colonels led to banditry on the part of the *sertejanos.* From 1900 to 1930 revenge was the chief motive, during 1930-38 persecution and torture by government soldiers. The bandit movement began to disintegrate during the 1930's because of internal disunity and the promise of government amnesty. Part III. Examines urban public opinion and the press concerning the bandits. Part IV. Examines the values of the *cangaçeiro,* including honesty, masculinity, and mysticism. Robbery was justified by the severity of their lives. Part V. Changes in Brazilian society after the 1930 revolution contributed to the decline of the *cangaço* phenomenon: feminism, decline in bandit motivation, and the death of the leader, Lampião.
　　　　　　　　　　　　　　　　P. J. Taylorson/C. A. Preece/S

2363. Manor, Paul. THE LIGA NACIONALISTA DE SÃO PAULO. A POLITICAL REFORMIST GROUP IN PAULISTA ACADEMIC OF YORE: 1917-1924. *Jahrbuch für Geschichte von Staat, Wirtschaft und Gesellschaft Lateinamerikas [West Germany] 1980 17: 317-353.* The Liga Nacionalista de São Paulo lacked the decisiveness to fulfill its own political credo and disappeared after 1924 when confronted by the military. Its legacy was the idea of the creation of a popular base of reform and the so-called Partido da Mocidade (the party of youth). Likewise, its leadership did not disappear with the party's demise, but continued to act or communicate in Brazil particularly in the Partido Democratico de São Paulo, formed in 1926. Based on published primary sources; 89 notes.　　　　　　　　　　　　　T. D. Schoonover

2364. Maram, Sheldon L. LABOR AND THE LEFT IN BRAZIL, 1890-1921: A MOVEMENT ABORTED. *Hispanic Am. Hist. Rev. 1977 57(2): 254-272.* Trade unionism in Brazil was retarded by the large number of immigrants in the work force, ethnic conflicts, the workers' belief in upward mobility, and the immigrants' vulnerability to deportation. Domination of the union movement by the forces of anarcho-syndicalism between 1906 and 1921 led to further government repression of unions. 44 notes.　　　　　　　　　　　　　B. D. Johnson

2365. Maram, Sheldon L. URBAN LABOR AND SOCIAL CHANGE IN THE 1920'S. *Luso-Brazilian Rev. 1979 16(2): 215-223.* Scholars have paid little attention to the continued sharp decline of Brazilian labor organization in the 1920's. Fear of labor encouraged repression beginning in 1917 and continuing despite the weakness of the movement. Destruction of leadership and grassroots support resulted. Immigrant worker attitudes and an unfavorable economic situation further diminished union opportunities. The Communist Party of Brazil was the first sustained political action by a portion of the working class but could not save the labor movement. Based mainly on Brazilian newspapers and government reports; 32 notes.　　　　　　　J. M. Walsh

2366. Medeiros, Jarbas. INTRODUÇÃO AO ESTUDO DO PENSAMENTO POLÍTICO AUTORITÁRIO BRASILEIRO 1914-1945 [An introduction to the study of Brazilian authoritarian political thought, 1914-45]. *Rev. de Ciência Política [Brazil] 1974 17(1): 59-102, 17(2): 31-87, 17(3): 3-106, 17(4): 67-124; 1975 18(1): 17-100, 18(2): 68-180, 18(3): 49-138.* Part I. FRANCISCO CAMPOS [Francisco Campos]. Part II. OLIVEIRA VIANNA [Oliveira Vianna]. Part III. AZEVEDO AMARAL [Azevedo Amaral]. Part IV. ALCEU AMOROSO LIMA [Alceu Amoroso Lima]. Part IV. ALCEO AMOROSO LIMA CONTINUAÇÃO [Alceu Amoroso Lima—continuation]. Part V. PLINIO SALGADO. PRIMEIRA PARTE [Plinio Salgado, part one]. Part V. PLINIO SALGADO CONTINUAÇÃO [Plinio Salgado, continuation]. Discusses the careers, views, and activities of five Brazilian political authoritarians, 1914-45.

2367. Monteiro, Norma de Góes. FRANCISCO CAMPOS: TRAJETORIA POLITICA [Francisco Campos: political trajectory]. *Rev. Brasileira de Estudos Pol. [Brazil] 1981 (53): 183-210.* Describes the life, career and thought of Francisco Campos, one of the major theorists and actors of the Brazilian revolution of 1930. His activities in the Provisional Government, 1930-1934, are described in detail, especially his work as Minister of Education and Public Health, and, after 1934, his work as Minister of Justice. Many of the ideas of the new 1934 constitution were his, as were many laws and interpretations following upon it. He resigned in 1942, and his effective power ended with the overthrow of President Vargas in 1945. He remained active and continued to teach until his death in 1968. 75 notes.　　　　　　　　　　　　　R. Garfield

2368. Mota, Carlos Guilherme. REPÚBLICA VELHA, TESE NOVA [Old republic, new thesis]. *Rev. de Hist. [Brazil] 1973 47(96): 579-583.* Refers to the completion in 1971 of three theses on the first Brazilian republic, focusing on Paulo Sérgio de Moraes Sarmento Pinheiro "La fin de la Première République au Brésil: crise politique et révolution (1920-1930)," (University of Paris), which covers the social structure, the political setting, and the 1930 Revolution. Thesis sources; 5 notes.　　　　　　　　　　　　　　P. J. Taylorson

2369. Oliveira, Antônio Camilo de. A AÇÃO DIPLOMÁTICA DE MELO FRANCO [Diplomatic activities of Melo Franco]. *Rev. do Inst. Hist. e Geográfico Brasileiro [Brazil] 1973 (298): 81-104.* Text of a speech praising Afrânio de Melo Franco, prominent Brazilian politician and diplomat. Melo Franco, beginning his public career in 1906, served his nation in many capacities, including as its representative to the League of Nations and foreign minister. His last notable service came in 1938 when he headed the Brazilian delegation to the Pan-American Conference in Lima.　　　　　　　　　　　　　　　B. J. Chandler

2370. Pang, Eul-Soo. ABERTURA IN BRAZIL: A ROAD TO CHAOS? *Current Hist. 1981 80(463): 57-61, 88.* Outlines the economic and political situation in Brazil in the second half of the 1970's with a discussion on the possibilities for survival of *abertura,* conceived in the final years of the Ernesto Geisel administration and designed to promote greater social, economic, and cultural freedom.

2371. Pimenta Velloso, Mônica. A ORDEM: UMA REVISTA DE DOUTRINÁ, POLÍTICA E CULTURA CATÓLICA [The Order: a magazine of the catechism, politics, and culture of the Catholic Church]. *Rev. de Ciência Pol. [Brazil] 1978 21(3): 117-159.* Analyzes the topics dealt with by A Ordem (The Order) the magazine of Brazil's Catholic Church and emphasizes its conservative and elitist outlook, 1921-37.

2372. Pimentel, Waldemiro. A REVOLUÇÃO NO ESTADO DE SÃO PAULO EM 1924 [The uprising in São Paulo State in 1924]. *Rev. do Inst. Hist. e Geográfico Brasileiro [Brazil] 1974 (304): 285-337.* Reproduces documents on federal military operations in the São Paulo State during the uprising of 1924 and shows the scope of the revolutionary movement, the composition and organization of the army, naval and air force personnel involved in the actions, names of commanders and leaders, the disposition of combat units, statistics on the dead and wounded, and the political and military measures that were put into effect. Based on military archive sources.　　　　　　　　　　　P. J. Taylorson

2373. Prestes, Luis Carlos. HOW I BECAME A COMMUNIST. *World Marxist R. [Canada] 1973 16(1): 114-122.* Reminiscences of the general secretary of the now banned (since 1947) Communist Party of Brazil.   S

2374. Rachum, Ilan. THE BRAZILIAN REVOLUTION OF 1930: A REVISION. *Inter-Am. Econ. Affairs 1975 29(3): 59-84.* Discusses Brazil's revolution of 1930 and concludes that 1) the oligarchy supported the revolution because of demoralization caused by the unsettled political situation, 2) the military coup during the revolution was a face-saving action, and 3) the Depression did not cause the revolution although it was a contributing factor. Based on secondary sources and newspaper articles; 59 notes.   D. A. Franz

2375. Rachum Ilan. FEMINISM, WOMEN SUFFRAGE, AND NATIONAL POLITICS IN BRAZIL: 1922-1937. *Luso-Brazilian Rev. 1977 14(1): 118-134.* Discusses feminism in Brazil during the 1880's, after World War I, and in the 1960's. Growth of protest movements and radical political parties aided the rise of feminist interest, and liberal governments assisted by approval or acquiescence, but these governments were replaced by authoritarian and conservative ones hostile to feminist movements. In the post-World War I period, Bertha Lutz was the most prominent and active feminist. She organized the Brazilian Federation for the Advancement of Women (FBPF) and was instrumental in achieving the franchise for women in 1932. Secondary sources; 49 notes.
J. M. Walsh

2376. Rosenberg, Emily S. ANGLO-AMERICAN ECONOMIC RIVALRY IN BRAZIL DURING WORLD WAR I. *Diplomatic Hist. 1978 2(2): 131-152.* Great Britain's long-standing economic hegemony in Brazil was fatally weakened during World War I. The mobilization of capital and resources for war needs necessitated withdrawal from overseas investment, and allowed their replacement by increasingly aggressive US influences. In Brazil, as in other developing countries around the world, this "wartime shift in the locus of economic power heralded a new international economic order, one centered in the United States rather than Great Britain." 3 tables, 69 notes.   T. L. Powers

2377. Ruas Santos, Francisco. LES FORCES ARMÉES BRÉSILIENNES DANS LA SECONDE GUERRE MONDIALE [The Brazilian armed forces in World War II]. *Rev. Hist. des Armées [France] 1975 2(4): 105-130.* Brazil declared war on Germany and Italy on 22 August 1942 as a consequence of German submarine attacks on Brazilian merchant shipping following a breach in diplomatic relations between the two countries. Prior to its actual entry into the war, Brazil had signed an agreement with the United States (on 23 May) providing for coordinated military and economic policy. This study describes that policy generally, with particular attention to the role of the 25,000-man Brazilian Expeditionary Force, commanded by Divisional Commander João Batista Masca Renhas de Morais, which fought in Italy from August 1944 until May 1945. The author, today Professor of Military History at the Agulhas Negras Military Academy, was a member of that expeditionary force and much of his account is a primary source. 5 illus., 4 maps, 4 notes.   A. Blumberg

2378. Singlemann, Peter. POLITICAL STRUCTURE AND SOCIAL BANDITRY IN NORTHEAST BRAZIL. *J. of Latin Am. Studies [Great Britain] 1975 7(1): 59-83.* Offering an ideal-typical interpretation of outlawry and politics, the author uses the 1926 commissioning of Lampião ("The King of the Northeast" in the years 1918-38) as the captain of the federal government's *batalhão patriotico* for southern Ceará as his major example of the interchangeability of outlawry and respectability in rural Brazil, thus agreeing with much of E. J. Hobsbawm's argument. The structure of Brazilian politics—a vertical set of alliances reaching from its base in the great landowners up to the central government—was a highly personalized system; the landowner's primary local allies (horizontal alliances) were his private police and the state police, and his political enemies were often designated outlaws. If his political fortunes shifted, his private police became outlaws, and his opponent's local allies became the law. Secondary sources; 106 notes.
K. M. Bailor

2379. Smith, Joseph. AMERICAN DIPLOMACY AND THE NAVAL MISSION TO BRAZIL, 1917-30. *Inter-American Econ. Affairs 1981 35(1): 73-91.* Traces US trade and political relations with Brazil from 1889 to 1930, focusing on US domestic and foreign maneuverings

designed to win a contract from Brazil for a naval mission, which Brazil had requested in order to upgrade its navy.

2380. Soares, Álvaro Teixeira. ARAÚJO JORGE: O DIPLOMATA E O HISTORIADOR [Araújo Jorge: the diplomat and historian]. *Rev. do Inst. Hist. e Geográfico Brasileiro [Brazil] 1978 (318): 74-78.* Reminiscences of the diplomatic career and historical writings of Araújo Jorge (b. 1884) by a former subordinate, which include details of his publications, his period as ambassador to Portugal, and his membership of the Brazil-Bolivia boundary commission.

2381. Soares d'Araújo, Maria Celina and Moura, Gerson. O TRATADO COMERCIAL BRASIL-EUA DE 1935 OS INTERESSES INDUSTRIALS BRASILEIROS [Brazilian-US Commercial Treaty of 1935 and Brazilian industrial interests]. *Rev. de Ciência Pol. [Brazil] 1978 21(1): 55-73.* Analyzes the international context in which the Brazilian-US Commercial Treaty of 1935 was signed, the treaty itself, the process of its approval, the debate in Parliament and its supporters and opposers.

2382. Taylor, Quintard. FRENTE NEGRA BRASILEIRA: THE AFRO-AMERICAN CIVIL RIGHTS MOVEMENT, 1924-1937. *UMOJA: A Scholarly J. of Black Studies 1978 2(1): 25-40.* Seeking to protect the political and economic rights of Afro-Brazilians, the Frente Negra Brasileira, met with defeat since most blacks, indoctrinated for decades with the national myth of "racial democracy," believed that no problem of racism existed.

2383. Topik, Steven. THE EVOLUTION OF THE ECONOMIC ROLE IN THE BRAZILIAN STATE, 1889-1930. *J. of Latin Am. Studies [Great Britain] 1979 11(2): 325-342.* The Brazilian state actively intervened in the economy during the First Republic, 1889-1930, despite the fact that it was a country relying on an agricultural base. The politicians were forced, by Brazil's close involvement in the world economy and its reliance on foreign capital, to enact measures it would have preferred to leave to private business. Although the state increased its control over the economy, it did not increase national autonomy, for its measures made Brazil more dependent on foreign capital and markets. Based on printed sources; 2 tables, 48 notes.   E. J. Adams

2384. Topik, Steven. MIDDLE-CLASS BRAZILIAN NATIONALISM, 1889-1930: FROM RADICALISM TO REACTION. *Social Science Q. 1978 59(1): 93-104.* Examines the uses of nationalism as a political tool by two Brazilian movements—the politically reactionary Ação Social Nacionalista (ASN) of the 1920's and the radical Jacobins of the 1890's. Although the two movements shared similar constituencies, they differed in ideology because of changes in social and economic conditions between 1889 and 1930.   J

2385. Topik, Steven. STATE ENTERPRISE IN A LIBERAL REGIME: THE BANCO DO BRASIL, 1905-1930. *J. of Interamerican Studies and World Affairs 1980 22(4): 401-422.* The Banco do Brasil, as representative of government enterprises, made no substantial contribution to industrial and agricultural development during the First Republic. Its goals were the modest ones of stabilizing exchange, discounting and rediscounting, and lending to the government, which it did well, earning sizeable profits. Its powers to participate in the economy were gradually increased, however, until it was called upon to fill new roles after the Depression and World War II had put the liberal economic model to rest. Based on Banco do Brasil publications and other Brazilian private and public primary publications; 3 notes, table, ref.
T. D. Schoonover

2386. Topik, Steven. STATE INTERVENTIONISM IN A LIBERAL REGIME: BRAZIL, 1889-1930. *Hispanic Am. Hist. Rev. 1980 60(4): 593-616.* Brazil's First Republic (1889-1930) was formed on liberal principles as a loosely bound federation of near-autonomous states. The author's thesis is that power was more centralized in the federal government than others have noted. The government played an active role in the economy through regulation, incentives for private enterprise, and direct ownership (for example, of some railroads). Such variations from classic liberalism were necessary for an underdeveloped country, but the ruling class maintained the essence of liberalism. The 1930 revolution led by Getúlio Vargas was a logical culmination of the First Republic, not a sharp departure. Based on the *Anuário Estatístico, 1939/1940* (Brasil,

Diretoria Geral de Estatística) and other Brazilian government publications; 3 fig., 63 notes.
                                                              B. D. Johnson

2387. Trindade, Hélgio Henrique. PLÍNIO SALGADO E A REVO-LUÇÃO DE 30: ANTECEDENTES [Plínio Salgado and the revolution of 1930: antecedents]. *R. Brasileira de Estudos Pol. 1974 (38): 9-56.* Discusses the people, ideas and publications which contributed to the rise of the fascist Integralist movement of the 1930's in Brazil. It was generated by the rise of European fascism and native factors. Many young Brazilian intellectuals, discontented with the oligarchical liberalism of the Old Republic (1889-1930), were attracted to the antiliberal, authoritarian, corporatist ideas of Mussolini's Italy and the New State in Portugal. Among them was Plínio Salgado, who after a trip to Europe in 1930 became the leader of the Integralist movement. Based on the writings of Salgado and other Integralist writers; 156 notes.
                                                              B. J. Chandler

2388. Vassilieff, Irina. UM DOCUMENTO INTERESSANTE DE 1930 [An interesting document from 1930]. *Rev. de Hist. [Brazil] 1977 55(111): 219-223.* Publishes an Electoral Act from Varpa illustrating electoral procedures, with an introduction outlining contemporary conditions.

2389. Vianna Moog, Clodomir. LINDOLFO COLLOR E A QUESTÃO SOCIAL DO BRASIL [Lindolfo Collor and the Brazilian social question]. *Rev. do Inst. Hist. e Geográfico Brasileiro [Brazil] 1978 (318): 188-206.* Reminiscences of a friendship with Lindolfo Collor (1891-1942), first minister of labor in Brazil, 1930-32, including details of Collor's early career in *riograndense* politics, his views on labor legislation, and his resignation from the Vargas government.

2390. Vieira Macabu, Adilson. A EXTRADIÇÃO: SUA EVO-LUÇÃO NA DOUTRINA E NA PRÁTICA INTERNACIONAL (PRIMEIRA PARTE) [Extradition: its evolution in international theory and practice, Part I]. *Rev. de Ciência Pol. [Brazil] 1980 23(2): 143-190.* Studies the evolution of the practice of extradition, the concept of the state's punitive rights extending beyond its frontiers, and the foundations and juridical sources of extradition. Ends with a list of applications for extradition decided on by the Brazilian Supreme Court between 1912 and 1938. Article to be continued. 48 notes, biblio.
                                                              J. V. Coutinho

2391. Williams, Margaret Todaro. INTEGRALISM AND THE BRAZILIAN CATHOLIC CHURCH. *Hispanic Am. Hist. R. 1974 54(3): 431-452.* Discusses the symbiotic relationship between the Brazilian Catholic Church and the Integralist movement in the 1930's. In a drive to regain some of the church's political power, Dom Sebastião Cardinal Leme organized lay defense groups, political pressure groups, and a Catholic elite and encouraged support of Plinio Salgado's *Ação Integralista Brasiliera* (AIB) without maintaining a formal alliance with Integralism. The two were ideologically compatible, sharing a belief in order, hierarchy, obedience to authority, anti-communism, conservatism, and a desire for a strong corporative state. Based on a medieval Catholic framework, Integralism propagandized the Catholic mystique. In 1937 the establishment of the *Estado Novo* eliminated political parties, suppressing integralism. Though the Church adjusted, it had to resume a dependent political role. Based on documents of the Brazilian Catholic Church, personal interviews, and secondary sources; 53 notes.
                                                              N. J. Street

2392. Williams, Margaret Todaro. JACKSON DE FIGUEIREDO, CATHOLIC THINKER: A PSYCHOBIOGRAPHICAL STUDY. *Americas [Acad. of Am. Franciscan Hist.] 1974 31(2): 139-163.* Fanatically devoted to the Church and influenced by 19th-century traditionalist and contemporary rightist European thinkers, Jackson de Figueiredo (1891-1928) saw in Catholicism "the most fundamental element of the Brazilian heritage" and a bulwark against threatening forces of disorder. As a publicist in the 1920's, he "sparked a powerful Catholic political movement based on the concept of national moral regeneration." His political passion and intolerance contrasted, however, with a private gentleness and Bohemianism. Following his sudden conversion in 1918, Catholic activism had given him a "solution to his problems of aggression and identity." Based on Figueiredo writings; 63 notes.
                                                              D. Bushnell

2393. Williams, Margaret Todaro. THE POLITICIZATION OF THE BRAZILIAN CATHOLIC CHURCH: THE CATHOLIC ELEC-TORAL LEAGUE. *J. of Inter-Am. Studies and World Affairs 1974 16(3): 301-325.* The Brazilian Catholic Electoral League functioned from 1932 to 1937, during which time the Church regained some of the privileges and influence it had lost with the fall of the monarchy in the 19th century. The league demanded religious instruction in public schools and the maintenance of existing restrictions such as those banning divorce. The league, hoping to create a nonpartisan Catholic voting block to influence all parties, was so successful as a pressure group that the government finally took action against it, forcing its demise. Its leaders, however, continued to cooperate with the government, thereby limiting their potential for assisting the masses. Based on government and church records and secondary sources; 8 notes, biblio.
                                                              J. Thomas

2394. —. [BRAZILIAN-AMERICAN RELATIONS DURING WORLD WAR II]. *Hispanic Am. Hist. Rev. 1979 59(4): 691-701.*
McCann, Frank D. CRITIQUE OF STANLEY E. HILTON'S "BRA-ZILIAN DIPLOMACY AND THE WASHINGTON-RIO DE JANEIRO 'AXIS' DURING THE WORLD WAR II ERA," *pp. 691-700.* Hilton's article (see abstract 2353) indicated that Frank D. McCann in *The Brazilian-American Alliance, 1937-1945* (Princeton, 1973) concluded that the United States was deceitful in dealing with Brazil during World War II and sought to rule it. This interpretation of the book is incorrect.
Hilton, Stanley E. STANLEY E. HILTON'S REPLY, *p. 701.* Defends his article and interpretation, referring to the "conceptual fuzziness" of McCann's work. 37 notes.
                                                              B. D. Johnson

The Democratic Governments, 1945-1964

2395. Cardoso, Eliana A. CELSO FURTADO REVISITED: THE POSTWAR YEARS. *Econ. Development and Cultural Change 1981 30(1): 117-128.* Examines the relationship between industrialization and postwar agricultural exports in Brazil, recalculating on the basis of new data the estimates of Brazilian economist Celso Furtado (1959). "The accelerated industrialization of the 1940's and 1950's had a marked antiagricultural bias and therefore implied a weak long-range growth strategy. The trade policies of the Brazilian government in the immediate postwar period certainly were not optimal in this sense, even though they undoubtedly fostered the industrialization process of the country during the period." 2 illus., 16 notes.
                                                              J. W. Thacker, Jr.

2396. Daly, Herman E. THREE VIEWS OF CURRENT BRAZIL-IAN ECONOMIC DEVELOPMENT. *Rev. Interamericana [Puerto Rico] 1975 5(2): 250-257.* Of the three principal approaches to economic development today (neo-Marxist, neoclassicist, and neo-Malthusian), the Brazilians generally accept neoclassical economic theory. This approach has helped bring on the Brazilian economic miracle of the postwar years, yet it also ignores the fact that Brazil's prosperity has bypassed most of its population. Secondary sources; 13 notes.
                                                              J. A. Lewis

2397. Fleischer, David V. O PLURIPARTIDARISMO NO BRA-SIL: DIMENSÕES SOCIO-ECONOMICAS E REGIONAIS DO RE-CRUTAMENTO LEGISLATIVO, 1946-1967 [The multiparty system in Brazil: socioeconomic and regional aspects of legislator recruitment, 1946-67]. *Rev. de Ciência Pol. [Brazil] 1981 24(1): 49-75.* Describes and analyzes party recruitment during the multiparty phase of Brazilian political development. Studies the socioeconomic and political background of 1,047 deputies and compares three major political parties in terms of occupation, geographical origin, education level, and previous political career. Notes regional differences and differences in recruitment styles of the three parties. 8 tables, 43 notes.
                                                              J. V. Coutinho

2398. Hilton, Stanley E. THE UNITED STATES, BRAZIL, AND THE COLD WAR, 1945-1960: END OF THE SPECIAL RELATION-SHIP. *J. of Am. Hist. 1981 68(3): 599-624.* Analyzes US policy decisions during the Truman and Eisenhower years that drove Brazil away from its traditional special relationship with the United States and toward a position of solidarity with Spanish America. US neglect of Brazil plus

Brazil's demands for preferential treatment combined to alienate Brazil and cost the United States influence in Latin America. Based on State Department records and private correspondence; 89 notes.

T. P. Linkfield

2399. Huddle, Donald L. MEASUREMENTS OF STATIC WELFARE LOSSES, DISTRIBUTION INEQUITIES, AND REVENUES IN THE BRAZILIAN MULTIPLE AUCTION EXCHANGE RATE SYSTEM. *Q. J. of Econ. 1975 89(3): 490-503.* Measures the costs to Brazil (1953-58) from the imposition of a multiple exchange rate system on foreign trade.   S

2400. Leacock, Ruth. JFK, BUSINESS, AND BRAZIL. *Hispanic Am. Hist. Rev. 1979 59(4): 636-673.* President John F. Kennedy's Alliance for Progress was launched without business support on the assumption that the communist threat would come from the poor in Latin America. When leftist João Goulart became president of Brazil, this policy began to change. The expropriation of an ITT subsidiary by the Brazilian state of Rio Grande do Sul, the suggested nationalization of AMFORP, which wished to sell to Brazil, and Brazil's attempts to control iron properties of Hanna Mining Corporation were regarded as communistic, anti-United States moves. The Kennedy administration became more business-oriented in its dealings with Brazil. US businessmen and the CIA played a financial part in the 1962 elections in Brazil in an attempt to overthrow Goulart. The roles of US Ambassador Lincoln Gordon and ITT president Harold S. Geneen are discussed. 128 notes.

B. D. Johnson

2401. Mallon, Florencia E. PEASANTS AND RURAL LABORERS IN PERNAMBUCO, 1955-1964. *Latin Am. Perspectives 1978 5(4): 49-70.* An analysis of events leading to a strike of sugarcane workers in Pernambuco, an area of northeastern Brazil. The prime problem in rural radicalization is the differing degrees of radicalism exhibited by peasants and rural workers, the former thought to be more conservative, though that is not always so. These difficulties were overcome in Pernambuco, and the alliance between the two resulted in a successful strike. These revolutionary beginnings were cut short by a Stalinist leadership that had not learned its lessons well. 8 notes, ref.   V. L. Human

2402. Manor, Paul. FACTIONS ET IDÉOLOGIE DANS L'ARMÉE BRÉSILIENNE: "NATIONALISTES" ET "LIBÉRAUX," 1946-1951 [Factions and ideology in the Brazilian army: Nationalists and Liberals, 1946-51]. *Rev. d'Hist. Moderne et Contemporaine [France] 1978 25(Oct.-Dec.): 556-586.* Traces the ideological confrontation between Nationalists and Liberals in the Brazilian army in the light of post-World War II issues, and describes the events and ideologies which characterized this rivalry during the presidency of Marshal Eurico Dutra, 1946-51. Corrects popular misconceptions about this era while asserting that this rivalry led to changes in the political-military structure of the Brazilian state. Based on archival and secondary sources.

W. D. Wrigley

2403. Manor, Paul. LA *CRUZADA DEMOCRÁTICA* UN GROUPE MILITAIRE DE PRESSION DE LA DROITE LIBÉRALE DANS L'ARMÉE BRÉSILIENNE, 1952-1962 [The Cruzada Democrática: a military pressure group of the liberal right in the Brazilian army, 1952-62]. *Rev. Française d'Hist. d'Outre-mer [France] 1979 66(3-4): 435-460.* Discusses a Christian, liberal, pro-Western group that gradually allied itself with political parties of the right and center with the aim of moving the country away from its neutral posture. It developed an increasing influence, which culminated in its providing all the presidents of Brazil since 1964. Primary sources; 35 notes.   D. G. Law

2404. McCann, Frank D., Jr. THE BRAZILIAN ARMY AND THE PROBLEM OF MISSION, 1939-1964. *J. of Latin Am. Studies [Great Britain] 1980 12(1): 107-126.* From its inception, Brazil's army had no clear vision of its mission. Prior to World War II the army's focus was almost exclusively internal. Active participation in the war held out the promise of increased prominence in the postwar world, yet it revealed to the army Brazil's underdevelopment and its reliance upon foreign supplies. From this realization came the army's belief that Brazil could have internal security and rational economic development only with alterations in the economic and political structure. Direct military involvement in politics and governance followed. With economic growth, however, the

military is again turning more attention to its own institution. 45 notes.

M. A. Burkholder

2405. Mota, Carlos Guilherme. OS ANOS 50: LINHAS DE PRODUÇÃO CULTURAL [The 1950's: trends in cultural output]. *Rev. de Hist. [Brazil] 1977 55(111): 155-175.* Characterizes intellectual developments in Brazil in the 1950's as a transformation from the academic to the political, from attitudes concerned with overcoming underdevelopment to nationalist ideological tendencies. The author considers intellectual trends by examining the works of Roland Corbisier, Antônio Cândido, and Raymundo Faoro. 16 notes.   R. O. Khan/S

2406. Mota, Carlos Guilherme. PARA A HISTÓRIA DAS IDÉIAS NO BRASIL: A PLATAFORMA DA NOVA GERACÃO (1945) (TRAÇOS DO PENSAMENTO RADICAL) [Toward the history of ideas in Brazil: the tenets of the "new generation" (1945) (Aspects of radical thought)]. *Rev. de Hist. [Brazil] 1975 52(103, part 2): 519-546.* Studies the 1945 publication of *Plataforma da Nova Geração,* edited by Mário Neme, the results of a survey of 29 young Brazilian intellectuals on the cultural heritage and ideology of their country. The author discusses the views of Edgar da Mata-Machado, Paulo Emílio, Antônio Cândido, and Mário Schenberg, citing their opinions on the political generation, the disappearance of the "formal" Brazil, the fight against reactionary thought, and new theoretical elements to establish parameters different from those already present in the history of ideologies. Secondary sources; 15 notes.   P. J. Taylorson

2407. Nichols, Glenn A. CLASS AND MASS IN PRE-1964 BRAZIL: THE CASE OF RIO DE JANEIRO. *J. of Interam. Studies and World Affairs 1976 18(3): 323-356.* Some scholars explain the 1964 Brazilian coup as due to class polarization and middle-class fear of developing lower class electoral strength. Others trace the coup, and the durability of the military government that succeeded it, precisely to the weakness of Brazilian class lines and institutional organization. The author presents and analyzes data developed from Rio de Janeiro precinct records, 1947-62, to test the relative validity of the mass and class hypotheses. Rio's voting patterns suggest increasing polarization between the classes after 1955. 13 tables, 14 notes, biblio., appendix.   S

2408. Nichols, Glenn A. PARTY FAILURE IN PRE-1964 BRAZIL: A RESEARCH NOTE. *Luso-Brazilian Rev. 1977 14(2): 185-194.* There has been a tendency in the study of pre-1964 Brazilian politics to downplay the role of environment and overemphasize the personal influence of leaders such as Getúlio Vargas, Jânio Quadros, João Goulart, and Carlos Lacerda. While the National Democratic Union (UDN) suffered from the excesses of such leaders, its failure to solve problems can be linked to attempts to adjust to its role as the party of the middle class. Greater lower-class participation in politics after World War II forced the UDN to alter its campaign strategies in order to win elections. This conduct encouraged personal success and decreased party unity substantially. Secondary sources; tables, 23 notes.   J. M. Walsh

2409. Nichols, Glenn A. VOTING IN PRE-1964 BRAZIL: THE NEED FOR REASSESSMENT. *Luso-Brazilian Rev. 1980 17(1): 63-78.* Reassessment of the role of the Brazilian voter is necessary because: 1) there is now evidence that certain voters were becoming issue-oriented, responsive, and consistent within a particular election; 2) criteria for defining a rational voter must be applied within the environment of the developing nation; 3) the voting data from *urna* (precincts) now available are more refined than aggregate figures from the Tribunal Superior Eleitoral (Superior Electoral Tribunal) but not as limited as survey analyses. These precinct data are deteriorating and should be saved to help in assessing the present Brazilian situation. Table, 33 notes.

J. M. Walsh

2410. Peregrino, Umberto. JUSCELINO KUBITSCHEK PERANTE A HISTÓRIA [Juscelino Kubitschek before history]. *Rev. do Inst. Hist. e Geog. Brasileiro [Brazil] 1979 (325): 61-89.* Juscelino Kubitschek's place among the Brazilian presidents of exceptional merit is assured by his creation of the new capital, Brasília, which from the architectural and urbanistic point of view exemplifies the city of the future.   J. V. Coutinho

2411. Williams, Margaret Todaro. CHURCH AND STATE IN VARGAS' BRAZIL: THE POLITICS OF COOPERATION. *J. of Church and State 1976 18(3): 443-462.* During the rule of Brazil by Getulio Vargas (d. 1954), the Roman Catholic Church gained government favor through the activities of Cardinal Sebastião Leme. Leme controlled the Church through an elite coterie of high clergy and lay persons. The author describes the methods he used to gain his end, a church-state alliance. The conclusion assesses the cost and benefits to the Church. 36 notes.   E. E. Eminhizer

2412. —. [THE COLLAPSE OF DEMOCRACY IN BRAZIL]. *Latin Am. Res. Rev. 1980 15(3): 3-43.*
Wallerstein, Michael. THE COLLAPSE OF DEMOCRACY IN BRAZIL: ITS ECONOMIC DETERMINANTS, *pp. 3-40.* Rejects theories that the breakdown of democracy in Brazil occurred because of 1) a movement to a late stage of import substitution industrialization and 2) a distributional conflict between classes. Instead, it was the result of political consequences of economic stabilization. The need to fight inflation and to restore economic growth, along with a balance of payments crisis, destroyed the existing political coalition. 8 tables, 18 notes, biblio.
Baer, Werner. COMMENT, *pp. 41-43.* Identifies topics that need further investigation. 3 notes.   J. K. Pfabe

The Military Regime since 1964

2413. Alencastro, Luiz-Felipe de. L'IMPÉRATIF ÉLECTORAL AU BRÉSIL (1964-1981) [Electoral imperative in Brazil, 1964-81]. *Problèmes d'Amérique Latine [France] 1981 (61): 41-76.* An analysis of the Brazilian regime after the 1964 coup, centering on the formation of political parties and the parliamentary elections of 1966-78.

2414. Alves, Marcio Moreira. NEW POLITICAL PARTIES. *Latin Am. Perspectives 1979 6(4): 108-120.* Proposes creation of a popular front in Brazil composed of all groups and factions in opposition to the established regime, in association with labor unions. Such a front would produce Brazil's first truly popular party with a national scope. Secondary sources; 15 notes.   J. F. Vivian

2415. Anglarill, Nilda B. LA POLÍTICA EXTERIOR DE BRASIL PARA AFRICA NEGRA [Brazil's foreign policy toward black Africa]. *Rev. de Estudios Int. [Spain] 1980 1(1): 93-106.* There have been two stages in recent Brazilian foreign policy toward black Africa. The first stage, 1970-74, emphasized friendship with Portugal and defense of the West. The second stage, 1974-79, during General Ernesto Geisel's presidency, hoped to establish an Afro-Luso-Brazilian community and intensify horizontal cooperation among developing countries in Brazil's favored geopolitical areas of activity, Latin America, and Africa. Some examples of cooperative policies between Brazil and some Arab countries of Africa and the Middle East are given. 34 notes.   D. Ardia

2416. Apesteguy, Christine. LA COLONISATION DIRIGÉE EN AMAZONIE ET LA MISE AU PAS DE L'INCRA [Planned settlement in the Amazon region of Brazil and INCRA's withdrawal]. *Travaux & Mémoires de l'Inst. des Hautes Études de l'Amérique Latine [France] 1979 (32): 119-122.* Discusses the planning policy for the settlement of the Amazon region in Brazil by the Instituto Nacional de Colonização e de Reforma Agraria (INCRA). Criticizes its methods and comments on its partial failure.

2417. Apesteguy, Christine. L'INTERVENTION FÉDÉRALE EN AMAZONIE: ÉLÉMENTS POUR UNE DEFINITION DE L'ÉTAT MILITAIRE AU BRÉSIL [Federal intervention in the Amazon region: elements for a definition of the military state in Brazil]. *Cahiers des Amériques Latines [France] 1979 19: 89-100.* The Brazilian military state is analyzed by looking at its intervention in the Amazon region. The state, legitimated ideologically, monopolized the administration of the region and opened it up to capitalist development. Biblio., glossary.   D. R. Stevenson

2418. Araújo, Aloizio G. de Andrade. AS ELEIÇÕES LEGISLATIVAS DE 1978: II. AS ELEIÇÕES EM MINAS GERAIS

[The legislative elections of 1978: II. The elections in Minas Gerais]. *Rev. Brasileira de Estudos Pol. [Brazil] 1980 (51): 37-70.* Traces the changing fortunes of the Aliança Renovadora Nacional (ARENA) and Movimiento Democrático Brasileira (MDB), in the state of Minas Gerais, particularly their relative success in legislative elections, 1966-78. Analyzes ARENA's initial success, the MDB's advantage by 1974, and both parties' growth and improved hold on the electorate since then. Describes the intense factionalism in both parties in Minas Gerais, due to the parties' origin in government fiat. Part 2 of a series of three articles in this series on the 1978 legislative elections in Brazil; 7 tables.
R. Garfield

2419. Atroshenko, A. BRAZIL: PROBLEMS OF DEVELOPMENT. *Int. Affairs [USSR] 1977 (3): 62-68.* The military regime which came to power in Brazil in 1964 inaugurated a neocapitalist program for economic development, featuring the creation of favorable conditions for foreign capital. The program's success, for example a 150% growth in real per capita income since the takeover, has been noted in the bourgeois press. Nonetheless, the profits of foreign-owned companies are often not reinvested in Brazil, and foreign loans must be serviced even after the inflow of new capital has slackened. Thus a capital drain is created which has been aggravated by an adverse shift in the terms of trade with the Common Market. Also, wage restraints plus controlled inflation have resulted in a drop in real wages since 1964. The poor have no part in Brazil's economic miracle.   L. W. Van Wyk

2420. Atroshenko, A. SOVREMENNYE TENDENTSII RAZVITIIA BRAZILII [Current trends in Brazil's development]. *Mirovaia Ekonomika i Mezhdunarodnye Otnosheniia [USSR] 1981 (8): 83-96.* Focuses on contemporary changes in the political, economic, and social life of Brazil, discussing the severe military rule of the regime established in the mid-1960's, which created extremely favorable conditions for foreign capital activities, yet aggravated the social situation and balance of payments problems and the "denaturalization" of Brazil's economy by multinational corporations. Current economic difficulties, following a short-lived prosperity, have caused the emergence of opposition in all strata of Brazilian society and the rise of the workers' movement.

2421. Baer, Werner and Villela, Annibal V. THE CHANGING NATURE OF DEVELOPMENT BANKING IN BRAZIL. *J. of Interamerican Studies and World Affairs 1980 22(4): 423-440.* In the late 1960's Brazil's policymakers were concerned with the weakness in the domestic private sector of the Brazilian economy compared to the state and multinational sectors. They chose the National Bank for Economic Development (BNDE) as the agency to strengthen the private sector. It is not clear, however, what role the BNDE has had in private sector growth, since much of its resources are automatically channeled. Based on BNDE published sources; 3 tables, 8 notes, ref.
T. D. Schoonover

2422. Bertrand, Jean-Pierre. LES TROIS GRANDS AXES DE LA POLITIQUE AGRICOLE BRÉSILIENNE: MODERNISATION DE L'AGRICULTURE, DÉVELOPPEMENT DU COMMERCE EXTÉRIEUR ET DE L'AGRO-INDUSTRIE [The three important lines of Brazilian agricultural policy: modernization of agriculture, development of foreign trade, and industrial farming]. *Problèmes d'Amérique Latine [France] 1980 (56): 62-101.* Analyzes the agricultural policy of Brazil since the 1960's, centering on the modernization of farming and the development of agricultural exports. The agricultural sector improved greatly, but the program failed to ameliorate inflation.

2423. Black, Jan Knippers. THE MILITARY AND POLITICAL DECOMPRESSION IN BRAZIL. *Armed Forces and Soc. 1980 6(4): 625-638.* Decompression, a growing freedom of both political and cultural expression, has taken place in Brazil during the late 1970's. Censorship has been lifted, wildcat strikes have occurred, the official opposition party has become more than a formality, and civilians no longer seem to be intimidated. Although the military government under General João Baptista de Figueiredo claims to be relinquishing power to civilians voluntarily, it is actually succumbing to pressure from the business community, both national and international. The restiveness of labor is giving the business community second thoughts about the value of further decompression. Primary sources; 3 notes.   E. L. Keyser

2424. Blay, Eva Alterman. THE POLITICAL PARTICIPATION OF WOMEN IN BRAZIL: FEMALE MAYORS. *Signs 1979 5(1): 42-59.* Between 1972 and 1976, 60 women mayors were elected in Brazil. Although statistics are difficult to gather, the phenomenon warrants explanation because politics in Brazil have always been a male domain. Since 1964, however, municipalities have exercised less power, particularly in areas where women are now assuming leadership roles. These women are typically less educated, of a lower socioeconomic status, younger, and with less political experience than their male counterparts. Based on statistical evidence, interviews, and secondary sources; 6 tables, 21 notes.   S. P. Conner

2425. Bohne, Regina. DIE ENTDECKUNG DER GERECHTIG-KEIT [The discovery of justice]. *Frankfurter Hefte [West Germany] 1974 29(9): 647-655.* Since the Rightist revolution of 1964 in Brazil, the leaders of the Roman Catholic Church have shown an increasing willingness to oppose political repression.

2426. Brasileiro, Ana Maria. O COMPORTAMENTO ELEITORAL NOS MUNICÍPIOS FLUMINENSES [Electoral behavior in the Greater Rio de Janeiro area municipalities]. *Rev. de Ciência Política [Brazil] 1977 20(3): 109-118.* Examines developments in the party political system before and during the elections in Rio de Janeiro State in 1966, 1970, and 1972 and the combined Guanabara-Rio de Janeiro elections of 1975, as well as developments in voting patterns and the recruitment of candidates.

2427. Britto, Luiz Navarro de. AS ELEIÇÕES LEGISLATIVAS DE 1978: I. AS ELEIÇÕES NACIONAIS [The legislative elections of 1978: I. The national elections]. *Rev. Brasileira de Estudos Pol. [Brazil] 1980 (51): 7-35.* Examines the Brazilian national elections of 1978, which exemplify a party realignment, especially within and between the two major parties, the government's Aliança Renovadora Nacional (ARENA) and the opposition Movimiento Democrático Brasileira (MDB). Surveys the parties' results in recent elections and their response to apportionment changes in the Brazilian constitution. In a continuing bipartisan realignment, each party is becoming stronger in particular areas of the country, ARENA in the poorer states and the MDB in the more developed. However, the situation is still fluid and subject to the actions of the government. First of three articles in this issue on the 1978 legislative elections; 7 tables, 3 graphs.   R. Garfield

2428. Brooks, Edwin. THE BRAZILIAN ROAD TO ETHNICIDE. *Contemporary Rev. [Great Britain] 1974 224(1300): 232-238.* Discusses the results of government policy toward the aborigines of Brazil, 1967-74.

2429. Bruneau, Thomas C. POWER AND INFLUENCE: ANALYSIS OF THE CHURCH IN LATIN AMERICA AND THE CASE OF BRAZIL. *Latin Am. Res. Rev. 1973 8(2): 25-52.* Examines the power and influence of the Catholic Church in Latin America, from the 16th to the 20th century, with emphasis on studies done since 1960 on its political power in Brazil.

2430. Cardoso, Fernando Henrique. LES IMPASSES DU RÉGIME AUTORITAIRE: LE CAS BRÉSILIEN [The impasses of a dictatorial regime: the Brazilian case]. *Problèmes d'Amérique Latine [France] 1979 (54): 89-108.* Analyzes the problems faced by dictatorships in Latin America, focusing on Brazil since 1964 and the attempts since 1974 to liberalize the government.

2431. Carvalho, Carlos Alberto Penna Rodrigues de. AS ELEIÇÕES LEGISLATIVAS DE 1978: III. AS ELEIÇÕES MUNICIPIO DE BARBACENA [The legislative elections of 1978: III. The elections in the municipality of Barbacena]. *Rev. Brasileira de Estudos Pol. [Brazil] 1980 (51): 71-99.* Studies the elections of 1974 and 1978 in the city of Barbacena, Minas Gerais state, the effect of economic changes on political behavior, and the role of local political leadership in political change. Analyzes the relative power and campaign techniques of the two main parties, Aliança Renovadora Nacional (ARENA) and the Movimiento Democrático Brasileiro (MDB). While economic considerations played a part in deciding the outcome, politics was still really dominated by personalist factions with origins antedating the "bipartisan" era which began in 1965. One of three articles in this issue on the 1978 legislative elections; 9 tables, 2 charts.   R. Garfield

2432. Castro, Sofia de. FASCISM AND THE "REPRESENTATIVE DEMOCRACY" TACTIC. *World Marxist Rev. [Canada] 1976 19(11): 101-107.* Examines the reactionary military coup in Brazil in 1964 and the Communist Party's resistance to it.

2433. Courson, J. de. LE "MODÈLE BRÉSILIEN" OU L'ULTRA CAPITALISME POUR PAYS PAUVRES [The "Brazilian model," or ultracapitalism for poor countries]. *Esprit [France] 1974 (5): 815-849.* A detailed economic analysis of the "Brazilian model." Criticizes the massive inequity of Brazilian economic development, the military regime that runs the country, and the international economy that supports it. Examines the economic "miracle," its impact on the people, the productivity increases, capital accumulation, and theoretical underpinnings of the system, and the country's relations with the international capitalist world at large. 48 notes.   G. F. Jewsbury

2434. Coutinho, Luciano Galvão. INVERSIÓN ESTATAL Y POLÍTICA ECONÓMICA EN BRASIL 1974-80 [Government investment and economic policy in Brazil, 1974-80]. *Investigación Econ. [Mexico] 1980 39(152): 175-217.* After 1974 public sector investment was adjusted to balance overall investment and soften business cycles. Public corporations became independent, practically controlled sector development, and obtained their financing outside Brazil. Inflation rose from 26% in 1974 to 42% in 1977, and the balance of payments deteriorated, limiting the maneuverability of the public sector, with investments primarily in electric energy, oil, steel, mining and some nonproductive sectors. The 1979-80 oil price increases worsened the balance-of-payments situation and inflation.

2435. Dassin, Joan R. A REPORT ON HUMAN RIGHTS IN BRAZIL: A REPORT AS OF MARCH, 1979. *Universal Human Rights 1979 1(3): 35-49.* Analyzes present conditions in Brazil and the problems and prospects for the continuation of President João Baptista Figueiredo's "redemocratization" policies.

2436. de Meira Penna, J. O. BRASILIA, FIFTEEN YEARS LATER. *Diogenes [Italy] 1975 (91): 57-69.* Discusses political, economic, and social change in Brasilia, Brazil in the 1960's and 70's, emphasizing the role of industrialization and the federal government.

2437. Dillman, Daniel C. LAND AND LABOR PATTERNS IN BRAZIL DURING THE 1960'S. *Am. J. of Econ. and Sociol. 1976 35(1): 49-70.* Much of the agricultural regions of Brazil in the 1960's were under the autocratic domination of *latifundismo,* which regulated interpersonal relationships and those between man and land. Polyvalency of employment acted in concert with farm management to strengthen *latifundismo* and to impede the socioeconomic aspirations of most rural dwellers. High frequency of multiple farm ownership by the landed elite suggested that the extension of *latifundismo* encountered little resistance. The Estatuto da Terra (1964) was unsuccessful as a means of land reform. Beneficiaries of land were almost nonexistent under the military regime.   P. Travis

2438. Dumont, Cícero. SUBLEGENDA [Subtickets]. *Rev. Brasileira de Estudos Pol. [Brazil] 1977 (45): 113-123.* Analyzes the practice in Brazil, authorized since 1965, of permitting multiple candidates to contest the same post in general elections, all running as candidates of the same party, with the candidate receiving the most votes credited with all votes cast for candidates of his party. Over the 10 years that the system has been in effect, it has been much debated, but further study needs to be done before definitive conclusions may be drawn.   B. J. Chandler

2439. Dye, David R. and Silva, Carlos Eduardo de Souza e. A PERSPECTIVE ON THE BRAZILIAN STATE. *Latin Am. Res. Rev. 1979 14(1): 81-98.* Philippe C. Schmitter's 1973 interpretation of the post-1964 regime as a reflection of "Bonapartism" and "restoration/Portugalization" takes Brazilian reality out of historical context and obscures genuinely new facets of Brazil's political economy. The Brazilian state does not have the autonomy of the French state in the mid-19th century. The regime's authoritarianism is designed to promote modernization, not to preserve privileges of the traditional social structure. 13 notes, biblio.   J. K. Pfabe

2440. Evans, Peter B. THE MILITARY, THE MULTINATION-ALS AND THE "MIRACLE": THE POLITICAL ECONOMY OF THE "BRAZILIAN MODEL" OF DEVELOPMENT. *Studies in Comparative Int. Development 1974 9(3): 26-45.* The current military regime in Brazil has exercised greater control over the economy than previous governments. Its policy, which includes intervention in banking and industry and establishing wage controls, has generated much support from the business community. The primary beneficiaries of this development policy are the multinational corporations and the national bourgeoisie. Meanwhile, the masses, plagued by such ills as a subsistence economy, high infant mortality, and widespread illiteracy, remain unaffected by the military regime's economic miracle. The continuance of this revolution from above is precarious because it depends on foreign capital and is vulnerable to international economic crises. Table, 3 notes, biblio.
                                                                S. A. Farmerie

2441. Faucher, Philippe. CROISSANCE ET RÉPRESSION, LA DOUBLE LOGIQUE DE L'ÉTAT DÉPENDANT: LE CAS DU BRÉSIL [Growth and repression, the ambiguous logic of the dependent state: the case of Brazil]. *Can. J. of Pol. Sci. [Canada] 1979 12(4): 747-774.* Examines the Brazilian economy, which was stabilized after 1964 and grew rapidly from 1968 to 1974. Analyzes the political structure of Brazil and the social changes resulting from the development of a dependent association among the repressive military, the civilian technocracy, and foreign investors. That association rests on the distribution of power within the state and brings conflicts and a bargaining situation, well illustrated by the government of Ernesto Geisel since 1974. 25 notes.
                                                                G. P. Cleyet

2442. Fleischer, David V. CONDIÇÕES DE SOBREVIVENCIA DA BANCADA FEDERAL MINEIRA EM ELEIÇÕES DISTRITAIS [Conditions for survival of the federal Minas bloc in district elections]. *Rev. Brasileira de Estudos Pol. [Brazil] 1981 (53): 153-181.* Analyzes vote distribution in districts of Minas Gerais in the 1978 elections, testing the effects that alternative systems of apportionment and election would have on the outcome. Concludes that a mixed system of district and proportional representation would produce victories for candidates and parties most in accord with the perceived wishes of the Minas Gerais electorate. Shows graphically the differing political orientations of the geographic and economic subregions of the state. 8 tables, 12 maps, 9 notes.
                                                                R. Garfield

2443. Fleischer, David V. A EVOLUÇÃO DO BIPARTIDARISM BRASILEIRO, 1966-1979 [The evolution of Brazilian bipartisanism, 1966-79]. *Rev. Brasileira de Estudos Pol. [Brazil] 1980 (51): 155-185.* Surveys the rise of a two-party system in Brazil since 1966 in place of the old multiparty situation, and analyzes the structure of the two parties, Aliança Renovadora Nacional (ARENA) and the Movimiento Democrático Brasileiro (MDB) in terms of their elected members in state and national legislatures. Shows how the older were fused into the new ones, and traces the realignments through the Sixth to Ninth Legislatures (1967-83) analyzing the profession, region, and previous political experience of the elected deputies. The two parties retain deep cleavages, both doctrinal and regional, and a proportional system of election could lead to the rise of other parties. 9 charts, 22 notes.   R. Garfield

2444. Fleisher, David V. RENOVAÇÃO POLÍTICA—BRASIL 1978: ELEIÇÕES PARLAMENTARES SOB A ÉGIDE DO "PACOTE DE ABRIL" [Political renewal, Brazil 1978: parliamentary elections under the aegis of the April Package]. *Rev. de Ciência Pol. [Brazil] 1980 23(2): 57-82.* Studies the 1978 Brazilian elections from the point of view of parliamentary stability and renewal, both quantitatively and qualitatively. Quantitative data is analyzed by states and regions. Qualitatively, in terms of occupation, university education, recruitment, political experience of the elected members, and their affinities with the former political parties. The new 1977 electoral law—known as the April Package—which based state representation in the Federal Chamber on the state's actual population instead of on the electoral rolls and introduced the notion of "indirect senator," had no effect on the elections to the Chamber but some influence on the Senate elections. 11 tables, 25 notes.
                                                                J. V. Coutinho

2445. Freire, Antonio. A NATIONAL AUTHORITARIAN BRAZIL SEEKS STATUS OF A GREAT POWER. *Int. Perspectives [Can-*

ada] 1973 (9-10): 41-45. Examines political events in Brazil, 1970-73, including the opening of diplomatic relations with Communist and underdeveloped countries, the lessening of economic dependency, the occasional belligerency toward the United States, and the changes in internal political structure, which indicate that Brazil has begun a move toward world status as a new superpower.

2446. Garruccio, Ludovico. L'EGEMONIA MILITARE IN BRASILE. LE ALTERNATIVE E IL NUOVO MODELLO POLITICO [Military hegemony in Brazil: the alternatives and the new political model]. *Storia Contemporanea [Italy] 1973 4(4): 879-937.* Brazilian President João Goulart was deposed in 1964 and the armed forces assumed power. Assuming the role of protectors of national unity, the military replaced the faltering civil government. The military's political ideology includes the use of their professional and technological expertise to maintain unity and national security. This new model combines economic development, reformism, and supremacy of the elite, with minimal political participation by the masses. 112 notes.   G. Pizzimenti

2447. Germain, Louis. LA MONTÉE EN PUISSANCE DU BRÉSIL [Brazil's rise in power]. *Défense Natl. [France] 1974 30(4): 57-75.* Considers Brazil's increasing economic, diplomatic, and military power, 1964-74, under the military government, while the problem of normalizing internal politics has been kept in the background.

2448. Greenfield, Sydney M. PATRONAGE, POLITICS, AND THE ARTICULATION OF LOCAL COMMUNITY AND NATIONAL SOCIETY IN THE PRE-1968 BRAZIL. *J. of Interam. Studies and World Politics 1977 19(2): 139-172.* Examination of the activities of a local doctor and lawyer from two municipios in Minas Gerais during the 1965 election reveals the interrelationship between patronage-clientage and politics and how local communities articulated their desires to the state and national institutions. However, when the military candidate was bested in 1965 by a three-week campaign from an opposition candidate who promised more to local leaders, and then, when subsequent demonstrations and elections further challenged the military government, they resorted to arguments other than popular consent to justify their continued rule. While patronage appears to remain a central institution in the articulation of community ideas, the precise process is unclear and must be researched. Based on secondary sources; 4 notes, biblio.
                                                                T. D. Schoonover

2449. Gross, Daniel R. THE INDIANS AND THE BRAZILIAN FRONTIER. *J. of Int. Affairs 1982 36(1): 1-14.* Discusses the role of the Fundação Nacional do Indio in the exploitation and mistreatment of Brazil's Indians during the 1970's and 1980's by landowners, investors, and industrial groups involved in Brazil's program for the modernization of the interior.

2450. Hewlett, Sylvia. THE DYNAMICS OF ECONOMIC IMPERIALISM: THE ROLE OF DIRECT FOREIGN INVESTMENT IN BRAZIL. *Latin Am. Perspectives 1975 2(1): 136-148.* Direct foreign investment in Brazil, 1960's-74, brought about industrial growth but failed to promote social development because of its exploitation of cheap labor and the concentration of wealth in the upper classes.

2451. Horvath, Giorgio. BRASILE: IL COSTO SOCIALE DI UNA CORSA SFRENATA ALLO SVILUPPO [Brazil: the social cost of an unbridled rush to development]. *Civitas [Italy] 1973 24(9): 37-60.* "The present political and economic system of Brazil is very similar to 'colonial-fascism,' that is, to a system characterized by an extreme authoritarianism, by the leading role of foreign capital, and by economic development without any change in the social order of the country. It is probable that Brazil will thus grow so much economically that it will reach the level of the most developed nations. But the social cost of such an unbridled rush to development is already high, and the risk is that it will become higher and higher. In a wider prospect Brazil will be able to realize its size limit only if the population sharing in the productive process increases, thus enriching itself with new persons having a national and social consciousness and being interested in enterprise. In short, it is necessary that a new middle class arise, a class to the national feelings of which the dependence on foreign capital must be repugnant, a class which is not worried only about its own power, but is interested in the problems of misery and social justice."   J

2452. Jarnaes, Johan. SITUASJONEN I BRASIL [The situation in Brazil]. *Samtiden [Norway] 1978 87(2): 65-75.* Examines political tensions in Brazil in the years since the installation of the military government, with particular attention on the influence of the US government and multinational corporations.

2453. Karaváev, Alexandr. CONCENTRACIÓN Y FUSIÓN DEL CAPITAL EN BRASIL [Concentration and fusion of capital in Brazil]. *Am. Latina [USSR] 1978 (4): 30-52.* One of the notable results of the 1964 military takeover in Brazil has been the strengthening and consolidation of big capitalistic interests, both Brazilian and international. Although there are more than 40,000 incorporated businesses in Brazil they are actually dependent on the great capitalist enterprises. Monopolistic capital is determining the socioeconomic development of Brazil and making it into a dependency of foreign capitalism. 28 notes.
J. D. Barnard

2454. Kellman, Shelly. THE YANOMAMIS: THEIR BATTLE FOR SURVIVAL. *J. of Int. Affairs 1982 36(1): 15-42.* Traces the history of the Fundação Nacional do Indio from its creation in 1969 to 1982, focusing on its collaboration with the forces of modernization in the exploitation and mistreatment of the Yanomami Indians in northwestern Brazil during the period 1960's-80's, when highway projects into the interior brought epidemics and cultural disruption to the region's indigenous peoples.

2455. Kluck, Patricia. SMALL FARMERS AND AGRICULTURAL DEVELOPMENT POLICY: A LOOK AT BRAZIL'S LAND REFORM STATUTE. *Human Organization 1979 38(1): 44-51.* Though created to reduce conflicting demands of increased production and improvement of the lot of small farmers, Brazil's Land Reform Statute (1964) stands to jeopardize the economic output of small farmers and make it increasingly difficult for young persons to enter farming, as indicated by data collected in Rio Grande do Sul, 1964-78.

2456. Laurand, Didier. EST-CE LA FIN DU "MIRACLE BRÉSILIEN"? [Is it the end of the Brazilian miracle?]. *Défense Natl. [France] 1976 32(4): 91-98.* Reviews the nature and causes of the economic crisis which hit Brazil in 1975, contrasting it with the sustained growth of 1967-74.

2457. Leacock, Ruth. "PROMOTING DEMOCRACY": THE UNITED STATES AND BRAZIL, 1964-68. *Prologue 1981 13(2): 77-99.* Discusses the American effort to promote democracy in Brazil during the Johnson administration. In 1964 conditions seemed ideal for the encouragement of democratic institutions in Brazil, but during the period 1964-68 Brazil moved steadily toward a more authoritarian state. The American failure to promote democracy in Brazil is attributed in part to a lack of a clear definition or plan of action, a lack of understanding of the Brazilian military, and a general unwillingness to use economic aid as a leverage in bringing about political change when it could have been effectively used. Based on Public Papers of the Presidents, U.S. Congress, House and Senate Committee on Foreign Affairs Hearings, Oral History Interview, CIA Information Cables; 13 photos, 81 notes.
M. A. Kascus.

2458. Levien, Robert M. BRAZIL: THE AFTERMATH OF "DECOMPRESSION". *Current Hist. 1976 70(413): 53-56, 81.* Despite economic gains, the people of Brazil have advanced little and military regime head Ernesto Geisel seems unable in 1976 to control the regime's machinery of repression.

2459. Levine, Robert M. BRAZIL: DEMOCRACY WITHOUT ADJECTIVES. *Current Hist. 1980 78(454): 49-52, 82-83.* Political and economic review, including the liberalization, of General João Baptista Figueiredo's regime in Brazil since the coup of 1964.

2460. Levine, Robert M. BRAZIL: THE DIMENSIONS OF DEMOCRATIZATION. *Current Hist. 1982 81(472): 60-63, 86-87.* Brazil's "abertura" process, the opening up of the democratization process, begun in 1977, has been spontaneously extended to the arena of public expectations, taking the debate far beyond the initial arena of elite-level conflict to discussions of the relationship between the 1964 revolution and the very fabric of Brazilian society.

2461. Levine, Robert M. BRAZIL'S DEFINITION OF DEMOCRACY. *Current Hist. 1979 76(444): 70-73, 83.* Expectations in 1975 of a civilian government in Brazil by 1978 were unfulfilled, although President Ernesto Geisel had eased up on some of the military's repressive policies.

2462. Lopes, J. Leites. ATOMS IN DEVELOPING COUNTRIES. *Bull. of the Atomic Scientists 1978 34(4): 31-34.* Examines the relative evils of military dictatorships and American imperialism as they affect the development of nuclear physics in Brazil, and the political and economic strings attached to the sale of nuclear materials and technology by imperialist countries, 1937-78.

2463. Löwy, Michael. STUDENTS AND CLASS STRUGGLE IN BRAZIL. *Latin Am. Perspectives 1979 6(4): 101-107.* Brazilian students remain the most active and organized social sector in opposition to the current military regime, yet also an isolated force only imperfectly linked to rural and urban workers. It is not clear that the workers' strikes of 1978-79 witnessed the emergence of a united urban proletariat. 2 notes, biblio.
J. F. Vivian

2464. Macedo, Murillo. REFLECTIONS ON THE PROBLEM OF EMPLOYMENT IN BRAZIL. *Luso-Brazilian Rev. 1981 18(1): 5-28.* Describes plans for a national employment policy. For some time, Brazilian planners believed that employment problems would be solved with economic growth. But Brazil's rising unemployment and chronic underemployment, related, in part, to development and strong demographic growth, require a policy to achieve an employment level consistent with population increases and rises in productivity. In the short term, jobs must be generated particularly for certain sectors in the population. From an address to a 1980 symposium in Madison, Wisconsin. 11 tables.
J. M. Walsh

2465. Malloy, James M. AUTHORITARIANISM AND THE EXTENSION OF SOCIAL SECURITY PROTECTION TO THE RURAL SECTOR IN BRAZIL. *Luso-Brazilian Rev. 1977 14(2): 195-210.* Brazil pioneered in Latin America in establishing a social security system for agricultural labor (FUNRURAL) in 1971. This program was based on the concept of national integration, important to the modernizing goals of the military dictatorship, and represents a victory for Brazilian technocrats. Nonetheless, the rural program was founded forty years following the urban (INPS), benefits are still substantially less, and losses in personal independence have been high. While the politicization of the social security system began under Getúlio Vargas, the recent military regimes have been most successful in using it as a tool for controlling social unrest and for increasing economic development through forced savings. Based on personal interviews, primary and secondary sources; 31 notes.
J. M. Walsh

2466. Malloy, James M. SOCIAL SECURITY POLICY AND THE WORKING CLASS IN TWENTIETH-CENTURY BRAZIL. *J. of Interam. Studies and World Politics 1977 19(1): 35-60.* One aspect of the growing role of the Brazilian state as regulator of social, economic, and political life has been its expansion into social protection via the social insurance system. Developments since 1964 reveal a return to the early Vargas era policies, indicated by efforts to exclude labor from the state-dominated coalition. The creation of an administrative-technocratic model in the social insurance system has eliminated any meaningful influence from labor leaders. The victory of the centralizing technical-administrative model over the decentralized, political participation model has converged with and reinforced the centralizing goals of the military regime. 7 notes, biblio.
T. D. Schoonover

2467. Martinez-Alier, Verena and Boito Júnior, Armando. THE HOE AND THE VOTE: RURAL LABOURERS AND THE NATIONAL ELECTION IN BRAZIL IN 1974. *J. of Peasant Studies [Great Britain] 1977 4(3): 147-170.* Questions notions about the political attitudes of rural laborers in present-day Brazil that hold that laborers have no opinion and vote for whom they are told. Among a group of laborers in the interior of the state of São Paulo there is a well-developed sense of class identity and of the need for solidarity, although actual solidarity is very limited. Their lack of involvement in national politics is in contrast with their activity in local politics. The author demonstrates how the experience of the group and the resulting world view help explain the laborer's ideas of political struggle and their approach to the electoral process. Shows how the structurally different roles of men and women are reflected in their respective political attitudes.   J/S

2468. Martins, Luciano.   LA RÉORGANISATION DES PARTIS POLITIQUES ET LA CRISE ÉCONOMIQUE AU BRÉSIL [The reorganization of political parties and the economic depression in Brazil]. *Problèmes d'Amérique Latine [France] 1980 (55): 21-29.* Analyzes the 1979 reorganization of Brazilian political parties. Stresses the influence of the economic depression on the political crisis in the contradictory aspects of the government's policies of liberalization and austerity.

2469. Mauro, Frédéric.   CHRONIQUE BIBLIOGRAPHIQUE: LE BRÉSIL [A bibliographical chronicle: Brazil]. *Ann.: Écon., Soc., Civilisations [France] 1980 35(6): 1194-1203.* Gives a record of recent books and journals on general, economic, and political history of Brazil since the 15th century. 56 notes, biblio.   G. P. Cleyet

2470. McDonough, Peter.   DEVELOPMENT PRIORITIES AMONG BRAZILIAN ELITES. *Econ. Development and Cultural Change 1981 29(3): 535-559.* Analyzes the variation in development priorities among Brazilian leaders in 1972-73. Discusses the developmental agendas of elite subgroups as well as the political considerations that favor aggregate growth over "premature" distribution. The same groups divide over the issue of authoritarian government versus democracy. Based on interviews with 250 Brazilian leaders in 1972-73; 2 tables, 2 graphs, 32 notes, appendix.   J. W. Thacker, Jr.

2471. McDonough, Peter.   MAPPING AN AUTHORITARIAN POWER STRUCTURE: BRAZILIAN ELITES DURING THE MEDICI REGIME. *Latin Am. Res. Rev. 1981 16(1): 79-106.* Several conditions mark the Brazilian power structure during the presidency of Emílio Garrastazú Médici, 1969-74. First, it is composed of three polarities: 1) class cleavage; 2) cleavage between governmental officials and economic leaders; and 3) the isolated position of Church leaders. Second, the Brazilian power structure renews itself; it is not a closed group. However, the capitalist class is more closely knit through endogamy and kinship ties than bureaucratic elites. Third, ideological issues divide the elite. Least divisive are moral questions, such as legalization of divorce. More polarizing are social issues, such as agrarian reform, and particularly political matters, such as freedom of opposition parties. Based on statistical sampling of Brazilian elites; 3 tables, 5 figs., 41 notes.   J. K. Pfabe

2472. Mendonça, Lycia de.   A POLÍTICA HABITACIONAL A PARTIR DE 1964 [Housing policy since 1964]. *Rev. de Ciência Pol. [Brazil] 1980 23(3): 141-161.* The housing crisis in Brazil has its origin in the process of industrialization that began in the 1940's. Between 1940 and 1970 a marked redistribution of the population took place, with concentration in the urban areas. Inflation slowed construction of housing. In 1964 a National Housing Plan was set up by the military government. The article describes the objectives and programming of the plan and achievements to 1974. Adaptation of a doctoral dissertation at the Sorbonne; 65 notes.   J. V. Coutinho

2473. Mendonça de Barros, José Roberto and Graham, Douglas H. THE BRAZILIAN ECONOMIC MIRACLE REVISITED: PRIVATE AND PUBLIC SECTOR INITIATIVE IN A MARKET ECONOMY. *Latin Am. Res. Rev. 1978 13(2): 5-38.* Despite professed governmental goals of strengthening the private sector, state interference and activity in production, finance, marketing, and pricing have led to continued growth and dominance of the public sector, with a corresponding decline in influence of the private. Three factors contributed to this development: the need for rapid economic growth as a legitimating factor for the government; the traditional weakness of the private sector; and the absence of effective means of obtaining low-cost, long-term capitalization for private firms. Based on secondary sources; 7 tables, 45 notes.
                    J. K. Pfabe

2474. Moises, Jose Alvaro and Stolcke, Verena.   URBAN TRANSPORT AND POPULAR VIOLENCE: THE CASE OF BRAZIL. *Past & Present [Great Britain] 1980 (86): 174-192.* Between 1974 and 1976 Brazil's largest industrial cities, Rio de Janeiro and São Paulo, were swept by a series of riots directed at suburban railroads. Real wages were

at their lowest since 1964 and the railroads—the condition of which threatened workers with loss of wages, unemployment, and even death— became the targets for riots, which were the only form of political expression available, as legitimate means were repressed. As the government and rail company tried to explain away accidents as the result of irresponsibility and "subversive elements" the crowd took to wholesale destruction as a way of trying to force the authorities to take action. Based on newspaper reports; 68 notes.   D. J. Nicholls

2475. Molotnik, J. R.   POLITICS AND POPULAR CULTURE IN BRAZIL. *Massachusetts Rev. 1976 17(3): 507-524.* On 3 December 1968 the repression initiated by the 1964 Brazilian Revolution was legally confirmed by the declaration of Institutional Act No. 5 which dissolved Congress, suspended *habeas corpus* and the freedom of the press, and gave repressive powers to the military. Since 1964 art has become a vehicle for registering political protest. As soon as the censors tried to inhibit expression, the artists' resistance increased. But further restrictions have produced a cultural vacuum inhabited only by inoffensive plays or works with erotic themes. Thus the fine arts have to some extent replaced political action in Brazil. There is a continued need for artistic contributions to the freedom struggle so that this conflict might be successful. Based on letters, interviews, and secondary works; 7 notes.
                    E. R. Campbell

2476. Monteiro, Lois A.   POPULATION POLICY AND THE PRESS: THE EXAMPLE OF BRAZIL. *Contemporary Rev. [Great Britain] 1975 226(1309): 76-81.* Discusses the role of the press in the controversy over birth control in Brazil, 1967-75.

2477. Moreira Alves, Marcio.   LA POLÍTICA DE LOS TECNÓCRATAS EN EL BRASIL [The policy of the technocrats in Brazil]. *Casa de las Américas [Cuba] 1973 14(81): 44-53.* Discusses the power of Brazilian technocrats which lies behind the military government in Brazil since 1964, showing how the economic power of technocrats has pushed industrialization in the country without concomitant social benefits for the Brazilian people.

2478. Murphy, Thomas.   TWILIGHT FOR THE BRAZILIAN MILITARY. *Contemporary Rev. [Great Britain] 1979 234(1356): 16-22.* Considers the policy of Brazil's military government to return to full democratic norms following 14 years of repressed political tension, in particular the liberalizing administrations of generals Ernesto Geisel and João Baptista Figueiredo.

2479. Narayanan, R. and Chawla, R. L.   LIMITS TO EXPORT-LED GROWTH: THE BRAZILIAN EXPERIENCE DURING 1964-1974. *Int. Studies [India] 1978 17(2): 331-345.* Analyzes Brazil's deliberate economic policy of export-led growth, 1964-74, and assesses this policy's impact on the economy. Although exports, especially manufactured goods and nontraditional agricultural products like soybeans, increased during this period, Brazil's export sector eventually suffered a serious setback. Brazil's policy was successful, but at the expense of the agricultural sector and with increased domination by multinational corporations. 19 notes.   T. P. Linkfield

2480. Nepomuceno, Eric.   BRASIL: LA GENERACION QUE SALIO DEL SILENCIO [Brazil: the generation that broke its silence]. *Casa de las Américas [Cuba] 1981 22(129): 93-96.* It took almost 10 years for the Brazilian authors who began to write after the 1964 coup to find their voice and an audience. Each writer of this generation became a chronicler of his time, recording what the collective memory had experienced and the official memory was trying to conceal. Those who believe that literature is more than a play on words and that writers are not more than common mortals would find that a journey through the productions of the writers of this time is rewarding. Biblio.   J. V. Coutinho

2481. Oliveira, Roberto Cardoso de.   MOVIMIENTOS INDÍGENAS E INDIGENISMO EN BRASIL [Indian movements and *indigenismo* in Brazil]. *Am. Indígena [Mexico] 1981 41(3): 399-405.* In Brazil today there is a growing crisis in the ideology behind Indian policy. Indian representatives are excluded from the apparatus of the Brazilian state, and Indians live in a constant state of deprivation. Although the Indian population is estimated to be about 0.2% of the total, it would be a mistake to assume that they play an insignificant role in Brazil. Brazilian public opinion is profoundly concerned with the Indian question, and there are now 16 organizations in 11 states working for Indian causes. They were formed in response to government pressure on the National Indian Foundation (FUNAI) to emancipate the Indians, but they could no longer appeal to previous legislation enacted to protect Indians. Indian leaders, with the assistance of the Missionary Indianist Council (CIMI), put pressure on FUNAI and the federal government to meet specific demands. CIMI has been instrumental in organizing meetings of Indian chiefs, first on a regional and later on a national basis. Since 1974 there have been 15 such assemblies. The Union of Indian Nations (UNIND) was launched in June 1980 in a series of meetings and has managed to unite leaders of those Indian groups that have been most outspoken in the defense of their rights.   J/S

2482. Pang, Eul-Soo. BRAZIL'S PRAGMATIC NATIONALISM. *Current Hist.* 1975 68(401): 5-10, 38. The nationalist policy of the new Ernesto Geisel administration.   S

2483. Pedreira, Fernando.   DECOMPRESSION IN BRAZIL? *Foreign Affairs* 1975 53(3): 498-512. The editor-in-chief of *O Estado de São Paulo* traces the political and economic history of the Brazilian military government as its fourth president, Ernesto Geisel, completed his first year in office. Brazil is in the initial stage of the industrial revolution which brings on political and social instability, requiring repression much as in 19th-century France under Adolphe Thiers and Napoleon III. Outsiders must understand that the military establishment has always had a full-fledged participation in decision-making in Brazil, for which there is no counterpart in Anglo-Saxon countries.   C. W. Olson

2484. Peixoto, Antonio Carlos. LA POLITIQUE DE DÉTENTE AU BRÉSIL ET LES ÉLECTIONS DE 1974 ET 1978 [The policy of detente in Brazil and the 1974 and 1978 elections]. *Problèmes d'Amérique Latine [France]* 1980 (55): 7-20. Analyzes the policy of detente in Brazil since its inception by the Geisel government in March 1974, centering on the progress made in the 1974 and 1978 congressional elections toward a greater liberalization.

2485. Peixoto, Antonio Carlos.   LES NOUVEAUX CENTRES DE POUVOIR DANS LE SYSTÈME INTERNATIONAL: LA MONTÉE EN PUISSANCE DU BRÉSIL: CONCEPTS ET RÉALITIÉS [The new centers of power in the international system: Brazil's rise to power, concepts and realities]. *Rev. Française de Sci. Pol. [France]* 1980 30(2): 328-355. Analyzes Brazil's emergence as a new world power, due to its natural resources, the extent of its territory, population, economic growth, and growing participation in the international market, discussing its hegemonic role and influence in other countries, its economic strength due to industrialization, political strategy based on economic development, its relationship to the other world powers, and its development of nuclear energy and nuclear policy.

2486. Pereira, Potyara A. P. BUROCRACIA E PLANEJAMENTO REGIONAL NA AMAZÔNIA [Bureaucracy and regional planning in Amazonia]. *Rev. Brasileira de Estudos Pol. [Brazil]* 1978 (46): 127-157. Since 1966 the Brazilian government has planned to integrate the Amazon region into national economic development. But the bureaucratic procedures of SUDAM (Superintendency of the Development of the Amazon region), the agency concerned, have been paradoxical. The agency has not given priority to rapid economic development for the reason that the interests of the national power structure are centered in the south. Thus, the economic development of the Amazon is likely to be pursued at a slow pace and subordinated to the national developmental model.   B. J. Chandler

2487. Perry, William. THE BRAZILIAN ARMED FORCES: MILITARY POLICY AND CONVENTIONAL CAPABILITIES OF AN EMERGING POWER. *Military Rev.* 1978 58(9): 10-24. Chronicles the growth in Brazil's military power, 1965-76, including naval, air, and land strength, as a result of economic growth and development.

2488. Poppino, Rollie E.   BRAZIL AFTER A DECADE OF REVOLUTION. *Current Hist.* 1974 66(389): 1-5, 35-38. Studies the political, economic, and social changes in Brazil since 1964. One of seven articles on Latin America.   S

2489. Portes, Alejandro. HOUSING POLICY, URBAN POVERTY, AND THE STATE: THE *FAVELAS* OF RIO DE JANEIRO, 1972-1976. *Latin Am. Res. Rev.* 1979 14(2): 3-24. Attempts by the Brazilian military government to eradicate *favelas* and to move *favelados* to housing on the periphery of the city failed because of the capitalist orientation of the government and the need for the National Housing Bank (BNH) to earn a profit. The inability of the *favelados* to pay for new housing led to middle-class occupation of these housing projects. The government finally abandoned the program of *favela* eradication. Based on government publications and secondary sources; 6 notes, biblio.
                                                   J. K. Pfabe

2490. Prestes, L. C. THE COMMUNISTS' HISTORICAL OPTIMISM. *World Marxist Rev. [Canada]* 1976 19(10): 17-26. Briefly outlines historical events in Brazil, 1964-75, which supply a political background for Communist Party operations today; extensive discussion of the 25th CPSU Congress.

2491. Ribeiro, Luis.   BEHIND THE FACADE OF THE BRAZILIAN "MIRACLE." *World Marxist R. [Canada]* 1973 16(11): 55.

2492. Rivière D'Arc, Hélène and Apestéguy, Christine.   LES NOUVELLES FRANGES PIONNIÈRES EN AMAZONIE BRÉSILIENNE: LA VALLÉE DE L'ARAGUAIA [New frontiers in the Amazon region of Brazil: the Araguaia valley]. *Études Rurales [France]* 1978 (69): 81-100. The construction of the Trans-Amazon and Belém-Brasília highways symbolizes the policy of integrating the Amazon region with the rest of Brazil. Since 1974, more realistic ventures followed the ideological action which the political situation of 1968-70 required. At present, however, the objective of Amazonian policy is to reinforce the expansion of capitalist agriculture. The problems encountered in the colonization of the Araguaia Valley have resulted from the conflict between the new methods of organizing agriculture brought in by São Paulo businessmen and the rural economy which several generations of poor settlers from northeastern Brazil had developed in various parts of the area. Secondary sources; map, 13 notes, biblio.   J. S. Gassner

2493. Rosenbaum, H. Jon and Tyler, William G.   ZEHN JAHRE MILITÄRHERRSCHAFT IN BRASILIEN [Ten years' military rule in Brazil]. *Europa Archiv [West Germany]* 1973 28(24): 863-876. Politics in Brazil after 1964 was characterized by a continuous centralization and depoliticization and the total suppression of organized opposition. There was increasing growth of production and exports and a slow decline in inflation rates.

2494. Savonnet-Guyot, Claudette.   RACES ET CLASSES AU BRÉSIL: LA DÉMOCRATIE RACIALE EN QUESTION [Races and classes in Brazil: racial democracy in question]. *Rev. Française de Sci. Pol. [France]* 1979 29(4-5): 877-894. Analyzes the problem of interaction of races and social classes in Brazil on the basis of recent studies that have questioned the existence of racial democracy.

2495. Schwartzman, Simon. THE MIRACLE AND ITS COSTS. *Latin Am. Res. Rev.* 1980 15(2): 269-272. Reviews the following books which analyze economic development in Brazil, primarily since 1964: Jan Knippers Black, *United States Penetration of Brazil* (U. of Pennsylvania Pr., 1977), Shelton H. Davis, *Victims of the Miracle: Development and the Indians of Brazil* (Cambridge U. Pr., 1977), Martin T. Katzman, *Cities and Frontiers in Brazil: Regional Dimensions of Economic Development* (Harvard U. Pr., 1977), Wayne A. Selcher, *Brazil's Multilateral Relations: Between First and Third Worlds* (Boulder, Colo.: Westview Pr., 1978), and Flavio Rabelo Versiani and José Roberto Mendonça de Barros, ed., *Formação Econômica do Brasil: A Experiência da Industrialização* (São Paulo: Editora Saraiva, 1977).   J. K. Pfabe

2496. Skidmore, Thomas E.   THE YEARS BETWEEN THE HARVESTS: THE ECONOMICS OF THE CASTELO BRANCO PRESIDENCY, 1964-1967. *Luso-Brazilian Rev.* 1978 15(2): 153-177. An adequate understanding of the Brazilian growth model cannot be achieved without careful consideration of the policies of the Castelo Branco government, 1964-67. While precedents were established in political and other spheres, economic policies were of top priority. Roberto Campos and Octavio Gouvéia de Bulhões led a team of technocrats in a gradualist strategy which aimed at minimizing rather than eliminating inflation. Domestic stabilization policies included indexing in the public sector and control of private credit and wages. Foreign financing was actively sought, particularly from the United States. While some achievements were made, policies chosen encouraged foreign ownership while curtailing domestic entrepreneurship, created high social costs for certain sectors via real wage reductions of 25% and failed to revitalize economic growth. Based on interviews and government documents; 32 notes.

J. M. Walsh

2497. Soares, Gláucio Ary Dillon. MILITARY AUTHORITARIANISM AND EXECUTIVE ABSOLUTISM IN BRAZIL. *Studies in Comparative Int. Development 1979 14(3-4): 104-126.* Discusses the sources of political legitimacy vis-à-vis the old pre-1964 regime. Considered are economic stagnation and inflation; the corruptible nature of politicians; chaos and inefficiency; inefficiency of the legislature; and communism. Since 1964 a military government has existed. Its goals and means involved a move toward executive supremacy and a decrease in the congress's legislative and oversight function. Basic contradictions of the system are examined. Support for improvement of the system is apparent but, "In the long run, the Brazilian military will either have to step down altogether or end all pretense of an electoral democracy." Secondary sources; 10 tables, 11 notes, 15 ref.   S. A. Farmerie

2498. Tyson, Brady. BRAZIL: NINE YEARS OF MILITARY TUTELAGE. *Worldview 1973 16(7): 29-34.* Brazil's military government, though allegedly aiming at development, 1964-73, produced torture and political brutality, media censorship, income and educational disparities among social classes, legal and political repression, and economic exploitation.

2499. Verner, Joel G. THE STRUCTURE OF THE PUBLIC CAREERS OF BRAZILIAN LEGISLATORS, 1963-1970: A RESEARCH NOTE. *Int. J. of Comparative Sociol. [Canada] 1975 16(1-2): 64-80.* Describes and analyzes the role of public officers in the recruitment of legislators for the Brazilian Chamber of Deputies by examining the careers of 477 Brazilian legislators who served in the Chamber, 1963-71. The typical legislator had experience in at least two public offices, most

probably at state level; initial and end offices were important in his experience, transitional offices were not. No single pattern of advancement emerged but the most significant path of promotion was from private life to state level to Chamber. Secondary sources; 4 tables, 9 notes.

R. G. Neville

2500. Wonder, Edward. NUCLEAR COMMERCE AND NUCLEAR PROLIFERATION: GERMANY AND BRAZIL, 1975. *Orbis 1977 21(2): 277-306.* Although nuclear proliferation is considered a major problem on the international scene, politics at the national level have caused deep divisions among the various exporter nations as how best to control the problem. Commercial self-interest also plays a significant role, as do other domestic factors. It was these latter factors that played an important role in West Germany's decision to transfer nuclear fuel technology to Brazil in 1975. West Germany ignored US opposition considering it to arise more from commercial self-interest than the proliferation issue. 50 notes.   A. N. Garland

2501. —. [THE STATE AND SOCIOECONOMIC CHANGE IN BRAZIL]. *Luso-Brazilian Rev. 1978 15(2): 278-307.*
Soares, Gláucio Ary Dillon. AFTER THE MIRACLE, *pp. 278-301.* All commentators agree that since 1964 the Brazilian government has become very powerful. Government policies have had a profound impact on public enterprises, labor, income concentration, land tenure, and regional economic disparities. However, the goverment's inability to control inflation indicates the limitation of economic growth as an ideology. Based on unpublished papers and Brazilian government publications. 5 notes.
Portes, Alejandro. LEGITIMACY, CO-OPTATION, AND THE AUTHORITARIAN STATE: COMMENTS ON "AFTER THE MIRACLE," *pp. 302-307.* Soares's paper provides a broad and well-documented view of Brazil in the 1970's. The author asserts that the problem of legitimacy needs further discussion and that middle-class cooptation may sustain the military regime even if it fails in its policy of providing more jobs and higher wages.

J. M. Walsh/S

7. THE SOUTHERN CONE

Regional Studies

2502. Epstein, Edward C. ANTIINFLATION POLICIES IN ARGENTINA AND CHILE: OR, WHO PAYS THE COST. *Comparative Pol. Studies 1978 11(2): 211-230.* Studies various methods adopted for price control in Argentina and Chile from the early 1950's through the 1970's.

2503. F. V. THE BEAGLE CHANNEL AFFAIR. *Am. J. of Int. Law 1977 71(4):733-740.* The Beagle Channel is located in Tierra del Fuego at the southern tip of the South American continent. The diplomatic history of the conflict between Argentina and Chile is traced. The boundaries were fixed by the treaty of 23 July 1881 and reaffirmed by British arbiters, 18 April 1977. Map. R. J. Jirran

2504. González Novoa, Rafael. LUIS GALDAMES GALDAMES [Luis Galdames Galdames]. *Rev. Chilena de Hist. y Geog. [Chile] 1980 (148): 297-313.* A short biography of the activities of Luis Galdames, a prominent Chilean educator, intellectual, and political figure. W. F. Sater

2505. Grenier, Philippe. LE DIFFÉREND FRONTALIER CHILENO-ARGENTIN [The border dispute between Chile and Argentina]. *Cahiers des Amériques Latines [France] 1978 18: 87-92.* The ongoing border dispute between Chile and Argentina over the Patagonian area prevents the territorial integration of the latter into either country. Chile's attitude is one of nationalistic pride reinforced by her interpretation of the treaty between Chile and Argentina in 1881. Argentina's interests are strategic and economic, based on her concern to control the resources of the area. Note. D. R. Stevenson

2506. Greño Velasco, José Enrique. ARGENTINA, URUGUAY; PUNTO FINAL A UNA LARGA CONTROVERSIA [Argentina and Uruguay, the end of a long controversy]. *Rev. de Política Int. [Spain] 1974 (132): 43-72.* Discusses the background to the Treaty of Rio de la Plata of November 1973, which provides a basis for viable regional integration.

2507. Greño Velasco, José Enrique. CANAL DE BEAGLE: EL LAUDO ARBITRAL DE LA CORONA BRITÁNICA [Beagle Channel: arbitration by the British Crown]. *Rev. de Política Int. [Spain] 1978 (155): 65-102.* Outlines the dispute over Beagle Channel between Chile and Argentina from 1902 until the arbitration by the British in 1977 over Beagle Channel.

2508. Greño Velasco, José Enrique. URUGUAY: DEL TRATADO DEL RIO DE LA PLATA A LOS ACUERDOS DE RIVERA [Uruguay: from the treaty of the Rio de la Plata to the Rivera accords]. *Rev. de Política Int. [Spain] 1976 (143): 205-222.* Studies, in detail, foreign relations between Uruguay and Argentina following the signing of border agreements and treaties of friendship in 1973.

2509. Jhabvala, Farrokh. STORM OVER CAPE HORN. *Caribbean Rev. 1979 8(4): 12-17.* Describes Chilean and Argentine claims to several small islands at Cape Horn, 1876-1978.

2510. Marín Madrid, Alberto. EL CASO DEL CANAL BEAGLE [The case of the Beagle Channel]. *Rev. Chilena de Hist. y Geografía [Chile] 1977 (145): 185-199.* Jurisdiction over the islands in the Beagle Channel, Tierra del Fuego, has consistently been disputed between Chile and Argentina. To avoid confrontation Chile accepted British mediation culminating in the Pactos de Mayo in 1902. Argentina continued, however, to claim certain areas, refusing to allow Chile to exercise its legal jurisdiction. W. F. Sater/S

2511. Primack, Joel. HUMAN RIGHTS IN THE SOUTHERN CONE. *Bull. of the Atomic Scientists 1981 37(2): 24-29.* Discusses the work of the American Association for the Advancement of Science (AAAS) Clearinghouse on Science and Human Rights in Argentina, Bolivia, Brazil, Chile, Paraguay, and Uruguay, countries under the rule of repressive military regimes who control the universities and have dismissed or imprisoned many professors and scientists since the late 1960's.

2512. Whiteford, Scott. MARGINALIDAD ASOCIACIONAL: LOS TRABAJADORES TEMPORALES Y UN SINDICATO [Associational marginality: seasonal workers and union]. *Estudios Andinos 1974-76 4(2): 33-42.* Seasonal workers, predominantly Bolivian, constitute the bulk of the labor force on the sugar cane plantations of northeast Argentina. Despite this they have traditionally received inadequate labor union representation. Unionization of sugar workers dates to 1944; the largest strike occurred in 1945. Discrimination against migrant labor is based on fear of foreign influence and the vulnerability of seasonals to outside pressures. In addition, labor unions in Latin America derive their power from government recognition, not majority support. Labor leadership is enabled to follow its own goals. In the Argentine sugar industry the interests of seasonal workers are sacrificed. Primary and secondary sources; 5 notes. J. L. White

Argentina

General

2513. Abalo, Carlos. POLÍTICA ECONÓMICA Y MOVIMIENTO POPULAR EN ARGENTINA [Economic policy and popular movements in Argentina]. *Investigación Econ. [Mexico] 1980 39(152): 149-158.* In Latin America, populism has been just a capitalist reordering of society, usually in times of state crisis. An agreement between the classes is struck, as in 1946 Argentina with Juan Peron, when workers and armed forces agreed to restructure society. Industrialization was to be facilitated by government control of economy and finances; capital was mostly national, delaying the access to modern technology and thus competitiveness. The military governments of 1955, 1962, and 1966 were unable to resolve the continued crisis, and in 1973 Peron was brought back with a new social pact that also failed. The military intervention of 1976 changed the entire economic direction, in an attempt by the upper class to modernize and increase capital accumulation.

2514. Béarn, Guy. LE POUVOIR MILITAIRE EN ARGENTINE [Argentina's military leadership]. *Histoire [France] 1978 (2): 84-87.* Discusses the role of the military in Argentina in reversing the results of democratic elections in the 20th century.

2515. Bologna, Alfredo Bruno. OCUPACION DE LAS ISLAS GEORGIAS DEL SUR (SAN PEDRO) Y SANDWICH DEL SUR [Occupation of South Georgia (San Pedro) and South Sandwich Islands]. *Rev. de Ciência Pol. [Brazil] 1982 25(1): 44-53.* Argentina was the first country to occupy the South Georgia Islands, and from November 1904 to March 1906 it was, through the Compañia Argentina de Pesca, the only occupant. Whaling attracted other nations, and in 1908 Great Britain signed a contract with the Compañia Argentina and gradually consolidated its position on the islands. Great Britain and Argentina maintained joint occupation until 1961 when Argentine activity ceased, although the Argentine claim to sovereignty was retained. The South Sandwich Islands were occupied by Argentina several times beginning in 1908, and Argentina maintains a permanent scientific base there. 40 notes. J. V. Coutinho

2516. Bono, Agostino. THE TROUBLED JEWS OF ARGENTINA. *Worldview 1977 20(11): 10-13.* Discusses anti-Semitism in Argentina from the arrival of masses of Jewish immigrants from Spain and Italy in the late 1800's to the present.

2517. Bourdé, Guy. LE MONDE DES AFFAIRES ET L'INDUSTRIE DE SUBSTITUTION EN ARGENTINE (1929-1949) [The business world and import substitution industry in Argentina, 1929-49].

Travaux & Mémoires de l'Inst. des Hautes Études de l'Amérique Latine [France] 1980 33: 47-79. Traces the complex relationships which linked businessmen, landed proprietors, entrepreneurs, and politicians during the first age of import substitution industrialization.

2518. Ciria, Alberto. ARGENTINA AT THE CROSSROADS. *J. of Interamerican Studies and World Affairs 1978 20(2): 211-220.* Reviews five books related to key issues of modern Argentina which reveal the state of current research on that country. Sources of Argentina's political instability are to be found in structural processes rather than random activities, power hungry groups, or personalities. The interrelation between economic and political developments can be employed as a pivotal axis for analysis of Argentina's alternating civil-military administrations.   T. D. Schoonover

2519. Couselo, Jorge Miguel. THE CONNECTION: THREE ESSAYS ON THE TREATMENT OF HISTORY IN THE EARLY ARGENTINE CINEMA. *J. of Latin Am. Lore 1975 1(2): 211-230.* Discusses three early Argentine films, their treatment of Argentina's history, and the nationalism inherent in their making: Enrique García Velloso's *Mariano Moreno y la Revolución de Mayo* (1915), Acedes Greca's *El Ultimo Malón* (1917), and Clemente Onelle's *El Misionero de Atacoma* (1922).

2520. Deiner, John T. RADICALISM IN THE ARGENTINE CATHOLIC CHURCH. *Government and Opposition [Great Britain] 1975 10(1): 70-89.* Discusses the political doctrines of the Argentine Catholic Church and the Movement of Priests for the Third World, particularly focusing on the violence which has occurred in Argentina since 1969.

2521. DiTella, Torcuato S. WORKING-CLASS ORGANIZATION AND POLITICS IN ARGENTINA. *Latin Am. Res. Rev. 1981 16(2): 33-56.* Several factors explain why the Peronist government was able to control labor while previous and subsequent governments failed. This government made concessions to labor and was more clearly pro-labor. Of greater significance is that the system of working-class representation was unable to defend itself against government efforts. Partly this was due to mass internal migration. In addition, masses of previously passive workers were aroused and insisted on results. As a result, a system of representation was changed to one of caudillista mobilization. Based on interviews from the Oral History Program, Instituto Di Tella, and publications of working-class organizations; 52 notes.   J. K. Pfabe

2522. Dolgopol, Hugo. ARGENTINA: UNA LITERATURA URBANA [Argentina: an urban literature]. *Bol. Cultural y Bibliográfico [Colombia] 1979 16(4): 217-227.* Argentine cities, especially Buenos Aires, as centers of economic, political, and social power, also became centers of cultural power, a trend reinforced by the arrival of capitalism and massive growth of cities, with their depersonalization and other attendant problems, magnificently captured by writers as diverse as Florencio Sánchez, Raúl Scalabrini Ortiz, Jorge Luis Borges, Lucio V. López, Julián Martel, Ernesto Sábato, Manuel Gálvez, Eduardo Mallea, Julio Cortázar, Roberto Arlt, Vicente Bioy Casares, Manuel Mujica Lainez and others.

2523. Etchepareborda, Roberto. ARGENTINA Y LA POLÍTICA DEL BUEN VECINO [Argentina and the good neighbor policy]. *Inter-American Rev. of Biblio. 1979 29(3-4): 345-350.* Reviews Randall Bennett Woods's *The Roosevelt Foreign-Policy Establishment and the Good Neighbor Policy: the United States and Argentina, 1941-1945* (Regents Pr. of Kansas, 1979) in which Woods tells how rivalry among Cordell Hull, Sumner Welles, Henry Wallace, and Henry Morgenthau led to a very uneven US policy toward Argentina. US concern about Argentine neutrality led to interference in Argentine internal politics. The book is a valuable contribution, but has a number of errors attributable to Woods's lack of knowledge about Argentina. Use of more Argentine documents would have been helpful.   B. D. Johnson

2524. Etchepareborda, Roberto; Butt, John W., transl. THE NATIONAL ARTS FUND OF ARGENTINA. *Cultures [France] 1980 7(3): 31-48.* Examines the development of an institution created by the Argentinian state with the aim of promoting cultural activities, the National Arts Fund, founded by the Provisional Government under Lt. General Pedro Eugenio Aramburu on 3 February 1958.

2525. Fennell, Lee C. REASON FOR ROLL CALLS: AN EXPLORATORY ANALYSIS WITH ARGENTINE DATA. *Am. J. of Pol. Sci. 1974 18(2): 395-403.* "Despite numerous studies dealing with patterns of roll call voting, little attention has been given to the reasons for this form of voting in legislative bodies. Using both historical and interview data from the Argentine Chamber of Deputies, the article examines the propositions that use of roll calls is related to 1) representational role concepts of the members, 2) level of conflict within the chamber, and 3) nature of the legislative bloc system."   J

2526. Ferrari, Gustavo. LA POLÍTICA EXTERIOR ARGENTINA A TRAVÉS DE LA BIBLIOGRAFÍA GENERAL [Argentine foreign policy through general bibliography]. *Inter-American Rev. of Biblio. 1980 30(2): 133-147.* An examination of Argentine writings in diplomatic history shows that the Argentine people have little interest in foreign affairs. They are isolationist and pacifistic, partly due to their geographic position. The works of J. B. Alberdi and Vicente G. Quesada (both of the 19th century) and 20th-century Ramón J. Cárcano, Norberti Piñero, Víctor Lascano, Carlos A. Silva, Lucio M. Moreno Quintana, and 19 others are examined to illustrate this thesis. Revision of an article published in 1973; 33 notes.   B. D. Johnson

2527. Flichman, Guillermo. AGRICULTURE ET INDUSTRIALISATION: ARTICULATION ET CONFLIT: LE CAS ARGENTIN [Agriculture and industrialization, articulation and conflict: the Argentine case]. *Problèmes d'Amérique Latine [France] 1981 (59): 64-83.* Discusses Argentina's agricultural and industrial development, the crisis of 1930, the reforms of Juan Perón, the new stage of industrialization from 1958 to 1964, the effects of agricultural expansion from 1964 to 1973, the Peronist interregnum 1973-76, and the influence of the military government's economic policy in agriculture and industry.

2528. Ghioldi, Orestes. WHITHER ARGENTINA? *World Marxist R. [Canada] 1973 16(12): 73-80.* Discusses Argentina's political situation, its historical background, and future. Continues the series "Political Portrait of Latin America."   S

2529. Goncharov, V. M. VERNYI SYN TRUDOVOGO NARODA ARGENTINY (K 80-LETIIU SO DNIA ROZHDENIIA KHERONIMO ARNEDO AL'BARESA) [A true son of the workers of Argentina: on the 80th birthday of Gerónimo Arnedo Alvarez]. *Voprosy Istorii KPSS [USSR] 1977 (10): 142-144.* A sketch of the career of Gerónimo Arnedo Alvarez (b. 1897), General Secretary of the Argentine Communist Party, who first visited Moscow in 1933.

                                                    J. P. H. Myers

2530. Greño Velasco, José Enrique. LA APERTURA ARGENTINA HACIA EL PACÍFICO [The Argentine opening toward the Pacific]. *Rev. de Pol. Int. [Spain] 1975 (141): 211-233.* Gives a brief geographical history of Argentina since 1494, then discusses Argentina's attempts to integrate its economic use of the Atlantic and Pacific Oceans, focusing on Argentina's attempts to promote Andean political unity.

2531. Grondona, Mariano. RECONCILING INTERNAL SECURITY AND HUMAN RIGHTS. *Int. Security 1978 3(1): 3-16.* Discusses the theory of undersecurity, wherein a nation's security forces cannot maintain order without infringing on democratic principles or calling upon the military, and applies this theory to the political history of Argentina after the eruption of terrorism and guerrilla warfare against the military government between 1969 and 1977.

2532. Jordan, David C. AUTHORITARIANISM AND ANARCHY IN ARGENTINA. *Current Hist. 1975 68(401): 1-4, 40-41.*

2533. Kaplan, Marcos. LA POLÍTICA DEL PETRÓLEO (1907-1955) [The politics of petroleum, 1907-55]. *Foro Internacional [Mexico] 1973 14(53): 85-105.* Surveys the government oil policy of Argentina, 1907-55. Primary and secondary sources; 12 notes, appendixes.

                                                    D. A. Franz

2534. Kohen, Alberto. ARGENTINA: LIGHT AND SHADE IN THE SOUTH ATLANTIC. *World Marxist Rev. [Canada] 1976 19(12): 68-79.* Examines the relation of US imperialism and control of fascist regimes in order to exploit natural resources and maintain political control over various Latin American countries; focuses on the American involvement in Argentina, 1930-76.

2535. Liebman, Seymour B. ARGENTINE JEWS AND THEIR INSTITUTIONS. *Jewish Social Studies 1981 43(3-4): 311-328.* A survey of the historical and contemporary situation of Argentine Jews, stressing communal divisions and problems. The author devotes considerable attention to the Jacob Kovadloff and Jacobo Timerman affairs which have generated recent discussion of Argentine anti-Semitism. An appendix describes six major Argentine Jewish institutions. Secondary sources; 60 notes.   J. D. Sarna

2536. MacDonald, C. A. THE POLITICS OF INTERVENTION: THE UNITED STATES AND ARGENTINA, 1941-1946. *J. of Latin Am. Studies [Great Britain] 1980 12(2): 365-396.* Between 1941 and 1945 the United States treated Argentina differently from the rest of Latin America. Misinformation about the extent of German influence led the State Department to distinguish between the Argentine people (good, pro-democracy, pro-Allies) and their government (evil, repressive, pro-Axis). This provided an ideological framework for intervention that culminated in an unsuccessful effort to discredit Juan Domingo Perón and to prevent his election as president. To the end the United States did not understand that the choice was among degrees of nationalism, not between "nationalists" and "pro-Americans." The article concludes with a postscript reviewing *The Roosevelt Foreign Policy Establishment and the "Good Neighbour"* by Randall Bennett Woods. Based on the US National Archives, the Public Record Office, papers in the Franklin D. Roosevelt Library and printed sources; 149 notes.
                                                          M. A. Burkholder

2537. Maechling, Charles, Jr. THE ARGENTINE PARIAH. *Foreign Policy 1981-82 (45): 69-83.* Traces 30 years of political chaos and four years of terrorism and repression in Argentina and examines its serious economic problems, political strife, and repressive military government, which give the Argentine military regime of the early 1980's little future and provide little common ground for US-Argentine friendship. The attempts of President Ronald Reagan's administration to bridge the gap bring no benefit to the United States, and the United States should instead keep relations on a "cool, correct, and impersonal plane."
                                                          M. K. Jones

2538. Martin, Markos. V AVANGARDE BOR'BY RABOCHEGO KLASSA (K 60-LETIIU SO DNIA OSNOVANIIA KOMMUNISTI-CHESKOI PARTII ARGENTINY) [In the vanguard of the working class struggle: the 60th anniversary of the founding of the Argentine Communist Party]. *Voprosy Istorii KPSS [USSR] 1978 (1): 99-101.* A tribute to the Communist Party of Argentina, founded in 1918, claiming substantial and increasing popular support, but nonetheless an underground, or at best semilegal party for most of its existence.

2539. Merkx, Gilbert W. RECESSIONS AND REBELLIONS IN ARGENTINA, 1870-1970. *Hispanic Am. Hist. R. 1973 53(2): 285-295.* Examines the economic circumstances surrounding armed rebellions against the control authority in Argentina, 1870-1970. Rebellions are likely 60% of the time in downturn years (the first year the economic indicators show a decline) and 31% of the time in poor years (continued decline), while only 7% of the time in upturn and prosperous years. Seventy-three percent of rebellions occur in the first part of a downturn, or within two years of its beginning. During 1870-80, rebellions were regional in character, from 1890 to the 1930's they were party rebellions, and since 1930 military rebellions. Rebellions were led by new groups seeking power or older groups trying to maintain it. 5 tables, 21 notes.
                                                          C. W. Olsen

2540. Milenky, Edward S. ARMS PRODUCTION AND NATIONAL SECURITY IN ARGENTINA. *J. of Interamerican Studies and World Affairs 1980 22(3): 267-288.* Although the developing countries' production of world arms is small, it can be significant in some local and regional contexts. Argentina's case illustrates the difficulty of entering the armaments industry above the rifle-and-ammunition stage. Factors such as prestige, a strong military bureaucracy, national economic and strategic independence, resentment of feelings of dependence and inequities in wealth and power, declining faith in Great Power security

guarantees, and a sense of independence may lead some middle powers to choose to develop a sophisticated arms production capacity. Ref.
                                                          T. D. Schoonover

2541. Most, Benjamin A. AUTHORITARIANISM AND THE GROWTH OF THE STATE IN LATIN AMERICA: AN ASSESSMENT OF THEIR IMPACTS ON ARGENTINE PUBLIC POLICY, 1930-1970. *Comparative Pol. Studies 1980 13(2): 173-203.* Examines conflicting theories on the nature of recent authoritarian regimes in Latin America and their economic policies, emphasizing the experience of Argentina.

2542. Neilson, James. ARGENTINA: THE PROCESS & THE PUZZLE. *Encounter [Great Britain] 1981 56(1): 88-92.* Discusses political apathy and nationalist trends in Argentina in the 1970's, as reflected in political and cultural affairs.

2543. Pasquino, Gianfranco. MUTAMENTI SOCIO-ECONOMICI, ELITES E DECADENZA POLITICA: IL CASO ARGENTINO [Socioeconomic changes, elites, and political decay: the Argentine case]. *Riv. Italiana di Sci. Pol. [Italy] 1973 3(2): 355-387.* In the light of some influential hypotheses on political development and institutionalization, the author analyzes the Argentine experience from the Saenz Peña law [providing for compulsory vote and secret ballot, 1912] to the Peronist era and its legacy. The first major break in the process of democratization took place mainly because of a split within the Radical Party and because the old ruling classes had never accepted the rules of the democratic game. The system that was slowly assimilating vast immigration and urbanization waves had not yet been able to offer avenues of political integration. This integration, albeit subordinate and of populistic nature, was the main accomplishment of the Peronist movement. Its subsequent discrimination, until March 1973, has been the major source of instability, but there is no evidence that the rules of the game are acceptable to the military nor that interference from external powers can be stopped.
                                                          J

2544. Perez Lindo, Augusto. ÉTAT OLIGARCHIQUE, DÉSINTÉGRATION SOCIALE ET VIOLENCE POLITIQUE EN ARGENTINE [Oligarchic state, social disintegration, and political violence in Argentina]. *Rev. de l'Inst. de Sociologie [Belgium] 1981 (1-2): 319-356.* Discusses state militarism, social classes and ideologies, the historical constitution and power of Argentina's oligarchy and how it causes the social, economic, and political disintegration of its dependent society, and the conflict between oligarchy and democracy.

2545. Rock, David. REVOLT AND REPRESSION IN ARGENTINA. *World Today [Great Britain] 1977 33(6): 215-222.* Examines events in Argentina, including guerrilla and terrorist activities, the Peronist revival, and the decline of the populist government, 1973-77.

2546. Rock, David. REVOLT AND REPRESSION IN ARGENTINA. *Current Hist. 1978 74(434): 57-60, 83.* Reviews the rise of disparate guerrilla groups, 1969-73, the chaos of populist governments, and the guerrilla resurgence and political repression under the military government, 1976-78, in a country where class and political relationships remain permanently distorted by the Peronist heritage.

2547. Rodríguez Bustamante, Norberto. SOCIOLOGY AND REALITY IN LATIN AMERICA: THE CASE OF ARGENTINA. *Int. Social Sci. J. [France] 1979 31(1): 86-97.* Debate over whether sociology or other social sciences would have a theoretical or a research orientation came to an end in 1966 when the military government determined that political objectives rather than intellectual ones would determine subject content in colleges and universities.

2548. Rouquié, Alain. ARGENTINE: LES FAUSSES SORTIES DE L'ARMÉE ET L'INSTITUTIONNALISATION DU POUVOIR MILITAIRE [Argentina: the sham exits of the army and the institutionalization of military power]. *Problèmes d'Amérique Latine [France] 1979 (54): 109-129.* Examines the pattern of succession of Argentinian governments since 1930, which is characterized by military hegemony despite periods of civilian rule. Attempts to return to constitutionalism have been ineffectual.

2549. Rouquié, Alain. GROUPES DE PRESSION ET FORCES AR-MÉES EN ARGENTINE: LA LOGIQUE DE L'ETAT PRÉTORIEN [Pressure groups and the armed forces in Argentina: the logic of the praetorian state]. *Rev. Française d'Hist. d'Outre-mer [France] 1979 66(3-4): 377-383.* Since 1930 the army has been the central point of power in Argentina, which has led to a reversal of roles in which political struggles take place within the armed forces, while the political parties become pressure groups and lobbies. The character and structure of this "praetorian" society is examined. D. G. Law

2550. Russel, Charles A.; Schenkel, James F.; and Miller, James A. URBAN GUERRILLAS IN ARGENTINA: A SELECT BIBLIOG-RAPHY. *Latin Am. Res. Rev. 1974 9(3): 53-92.* Lists the various groups of urban guerrillas operating in Argentina during the 1960's and 1970's and chronicles their activities.

2551. Russell, Dora Isella. THE LAST ROMANTIC IN NEW WORLD POLITICS. *Américas (Organization of Am. States) 1979 31(9): 26-30.* Examines the life of Argentinian Alfredo L. Palacios, the flamboyant first socialist deputy in the Americas.

2552. Smith, Peter H. ARGENTINA: THE UNCERTAIN WARRI-ORS. *Current Hist. 1980 78(454): 62-65, 85-86.* Discusses the political and economic disintegration of Argentina during the 1970's.

2553. Sosa, Juan. ARGENTINA AT THE CROSSROADS. *Critique [Great Britain] 1978 (9): 143-151.* Surveys the present political situation in Argentina vis-à-vis the working classes based on a review of the Peronist period, 1945-55, the new capitalist strategy after Peron, the return to power of Peronism, and the 1976 military coup and its repressive aftermath.

2554. Tulchin, Joseph S. UNA PERSPECTIVA HISTÓRICA DE LA POLÍTICA ARGENTINA FRENTE AL BRASIL [An historical view of Argentinian policy toward Brazil]. *Estudios Int. [Chile] 1980 13(52): 460-480.* Discusses the historical roots of Argentina's foreign policy and some characteristic attitudes of its governments to explain Argentinian perceptions of Brazil.

2555. Turner, Frederick C. THE STUDY OF ARGENTINE POLI-TICS THROUGH SURVEY RESEARCH. *Latin Am. Res. Rev. 1975 10(2): 73-116.* Public opinion surveys, with in-depth questionnaires, can be used as a method of understanding what has gone on in recent political history of Argentina since 1930.

2556. Tutino, Saverio. LA VIOLENZA DI STATO IN AMERICA LATINA: L'ESEMPIO ARGENTINO [State violence in Latin Amer-ica: the Argentine example]. *Problemi di Ulisse [Italy] 1978 14(86): 43-49.* Chronicles the violent repression to combat terrorism in Argentina under both the Perón regime (1973-76) and the military junta that followed it.

2557. Vent, Herbert J. ARGENTINA: ITS PHYSICAL-CUL-TURAL BACKGROUNDS AND IMPLICATIONS FOR UNITED STATES FOREIGN POLICY. *Social Studies 1974 65(5): 208-211.* Analyzes Argentina's physical-cultural background in relation to US-Argentina foreign relations. Note. L. R. Raife

2558. Waldmann, Peter. URSACHEN DER GUERRILLA IN AR-GENTINIEN [Origins of the guerrillas in Argentina]. *Jahrbuch für Geschichte von Staat, Wirtschaft und Gesellschaft Lateinamerikas [West Germany] 1978 15: 295-348.* In an attempt to repair the lack of back-ground analysis of the urban guerrilla warfare in Argentina, 1960's-70's, the author develops an intensive examination of its roots. Based upon printed primary and secondary sources; 108 notes, 4 tables. T. D. Schoonover

2559. Weisbrot, Robert. ANTI-SEMITISM IN ARGENTINA. *Midstream 1978 24(5): 12-23.* Examines the experiences of Jewish settlers in Argentina from the late 19th century to the present. Jews were identi-fied with Russian revolutionaries and greedy capitalists, and they have suffered systematic discrimination, violence, and destruction of property in regimes that either tolerated or actively encouraged such behavior, although some individual Jews have risen to places of prominence.

2560. Wellhofer, E. Spencer. BACKGROUND CHARACTERIS-TICS AND DISSIDENT BEHAVIOR: TESTS WITH ARGENTINE PARTY ELITES. *J. of Developing Areas 1975 9(2): 237-252.* Analyzes the Argentine Socialist Party under the assumption that profiles of elite social and occupational characteristics will help predict the political goals such leaders are likely to seek. Dissidents were more likely to have joined the party at a later age than loyalists, had less political experience and a higher proportion of native-born fathers, become active in politics at a later age, and originated from the interior of the country where the proportion of European immigrants was lower. Dissidents were more likely to be those members who would suffer the least and gain the most from dissent, were less tied to the party by family, and less successful in holding party offices. Loyalists also invested the most in the party, re-ceived the most rewards, and were tied by blood or marriage. Career characteristics were a common dimension to the six party schisms of 1915, 1917, 1921, 1927, 1938, and 1957. Based on Socialist Party and newspaper data and interviews; 5 tables, 17 notes. O. W. Eads, Jr.

2561. Wellhofer, E. Spencer. THE POLITICAL INCORPORA-TION OF THE NEWLY ENFRANCHISED VOTER: ORGANIZA-TIONAL ENCAPSULATION AND SOCIALIST LABOR PARTY DEVELOPMENT. *Western Pol. Q. 1981 34(3): 399-414.* The effective-ness of party organization is modeled by a modified Cobb-Douglas pro-duction function where inputs are the characteristics of party organization and output is the popular vote of the party. The mathemati-cal properties of the function suggest the dynamics of party organizational efforts to voter mobilization. The findings of the model have implications for understanding the transformation of limited franchise regimes to mass suffrage polities. The model is tested with time-series data for the Argen-tine, British, Norwegian, and Swedish socialist and labor parties. J

2562. Wellhofer, E. Spencer. POLITICAL PARTIES AS "COMMU-NITIES OF FATE": TESTS WITH ARGENTINE PARTY ELITES. *Am. J. of Pol. Sci. 1974 18(2): 347-363.* "Stratification systems are impor-tant to the degree they define a 'community of fate' influencing behavior. Social background and organizational career data are indicators of differ-ent stratification systems. These two indicators are compared for their predictive utility in determining loyalist and dissident behavior of politi-cal party elites." J

2563. Wellhofer, E. Spencer. POLITICAL PARTY DEVELOP-MENT IN ARGENTINA: THE EMERGENCE OF SOCIALIST PARTY PARLIAMENTARIANISM. *J. of Inter-Am. Studies and World Affairs 1975 17(2): 153-174.* In the United States office-seeking has always been a major thrust of political parties, but the Socialist Party of Argentina has not until recently shown any inclination to dwell upon the acquisition of offices. Instead, the Argentine socialists, in their early years, devoted their energies to building a working-class subculture. More recently, however, the socialists have moved to create a predominantly electoral organization. Based on archival material and secondary sources; 6 tables, biblio. J. R. Thomas

2564. Winn, Peter. FROM MARTÍN FIERRO TO PERONISM: A CENTURY OF ARGENTINE SOCIAL PROTEST. *Americas (Acad. of Am. Franciscan Hist.) 1978 35(1): 89-94.* The themes of protest against social and political oppression and defense of native cultural traditions found in the poem *Martín Fierro* by José Hernández, whose first edition appeared in 1872, can be seen again in the movement led by Juan Domingo Perón in Argentina in the present century. 14 notes. D. Bushnell

2565. Woods, Randall B. CONFLICT OR COMMUNITY? THE UNITED STATES AND ARGENTINA'S ADMISSION TO THE UNITED NATIONS. *Pacific Hist. Rev. 1977 46(3): 361-386.* Despite appearances, American sponsorship of Argentina's membership in the UN in 1945 does not support the revisionist interpretation of American foreign policy. Although Argentina had maintained diplomatic ties with the Axis powers, served as a base for German espionage in the Western Hemisphere, and submitted to the rule of two autocratic militaristic governments, American policymakers supported its admission because they were committed to the principles of nonintervention, international-ism, and respect for the sovereignty of all nations. Based on documents in manuscript collections and National Archives, on published primary sources, and on secondary sources; 77 notes. W. K. Hobson

Interwar Years, 1914-1943

2566. Ambri, Mariano. I MILITARI NELLA POLITICA ARGEN-TINA: LA "RIVOLUZIONE" DEL 1930 [The military in Argentine politics: the "revolution" of 1930]. *Civitas [Italy] 1975 26(7/8): 95-106.* The "revolution" of 1930 had, in perspective, a continental importance. Up to that time Argentina had been a steady point in the political and constitutional development of South American events. The coup d'état that removed Hipólito Yrigoyen destroyed the traditional datum of stability and it therefore was a fundamental moment in the history of South America.   J/S

2567. Cheresky, Isidoro. SINDICATOS Y FUERZAS POLITICAS EN LA ARGENTINA PREPERONISTA (1930-1943) [Labor unions and political forces in pre-Peronist Argentina, 1930-43]. *Bol. de Estudios Latinoamericanos y del Caribe [Netherlands] 1981 (31): 5-42.* Reviews in considerable detail the Argentine labor movement, 1930-43, explaining its relationship especially to the Socialist Party and to the General Confederation of Workers (CGT). 78 notes, 8 tables.
                                                R. L. Woodward, Jr.

2568. Floria, Carlos. LE CRISI ARGENTINE [The Argentine crises]. *Affari Esteri [Italy] 1975 7(28): 629-653.* Argentina, a land rich in resources, culturally well-developed, is prevented from achieving the status to which it is entitled because of its social conditions and political instability.

2569. Gravil, Roger. THE ANGLO-ARGENTINE CONNECTION AND THE WAR OF 1914-1918. *J. of Latin Am. Studies [Great Britain] 1977 9(1): 59-89.* The World War I experience does not substantiate Andre Gunder Frank's hypothesis that substantial economic growth in Latin America has occurred in wartime. Although Argentina's economic ties with Great Britain and the United States were tightened during 1914-18, Argentinian industry regressed, and Britain in particular thoroughly manipulated Argentinian trade and investments. Based on British Foreign Office documents and secondary works; 13 tables, 106 notes.
                                                K. M. Bailor

2570. Mirelman, Victor A. THE *SEMANA TRAGICA* OF 1919 AND THE JEWS IN ARGENTINA. *Jewish Social Studies 1975 37(1): 61-73.* The violent attacks on Argentinian Jews occurring in Buenos Aires and elsewhere 10-12 January 1919 were generated by native fears of Jewish revolutionary involvement, Catholic anti-Semitism, and anti-foreign feelings among the Christian populace. Jews responded by appealing to the government for aid and in extending prompt succor to the victims. Briefly united by the tragedy in the *Comité de la Colectividad,* the Jewish community could not sustain a permanent collective front once the emergency passed. The impact of the assault on the Jewish quarters was only temporary. Based on Spanish-language primary and secondary sources.   N. Lederer

2571. Nálevka, Vladimír. ODRAZ SVĚTOVÉ HOSPODÁŘSKÉ KRIZE V ARGENTINĚ [The effect of the world economic crisis on Argentina]. *Acta Universitatis Carolinae Philosophica et Hist. [Czechoslovakia] 1974 (3): 45-82.* The world Depression of the 1930's revealed the weakness of Argentina's political and economic nature. The author describes the changes in Argentina after the 1930 coup d'état of landlords and generals. The economic crisis in Argentina lasted until 1945 and gradually created the basis for the changes of the 1950's. Based on documents; 144 notes.   G. E. Pergl

2572. Pade, Werner. DIE HANDELSBEZIEHUNGEN DES DEUTSCHEN IMPERIALISMUS ZU ARGENTINIEN (1918 BIS 1933) [German imperialist trade relations with Argentina, 1918-33]. *Jahrbuch für Wirtschaftsgeschichte [East Germany] 1977 (3): 47-66.* Discusses the reestablishment of German trade relations with Argentina after their decline in World War I. Despite the German postwar position and competition from America and Britain, German companies reestablished themselves, 1918-23, trading German industrial exports for Argentine raw materials and foodstuffs. Relations reached their peak in 1928-29, when Germany made important investments in Argentina in the fields of communications, electrochemicals, and transport. Economic involvement led to political influence especially between 1929 and 1933, and German

influence spread through Argentina to other areas of Latin America. 88 notes.
                                                S. G. Jackson/S

2573. Potter, Anne L. THE FAILURE OF DEMOCRACY IN ARGENTINA, 1916-1930: AN INSTITUTIONAL PERSPECTIVE. *J. of Latin Am. Studies [Great Britain] 1981 13(1): 83-109.* From 1912 to 1930 Argentina was a functioning liberal democracy. In the latter year, however, the military overthrew the civilian government. Earlier hypotheses to explain the failure of Argentine democracy tend to miss the point that in 1930 the political opposition to Radical President Hipólito Yrigoyen and his Personalist party saw his policies as quickly leading to their complete extinction. This perception, more than military discontents or economic difficulties, led to the coup. The structural and institutional nature of politics needs to be included as a variable for studying conditions of democratic success and failure. Based in part on printed primary sources; 53 notes.   M. A. Burkholder

2574. Randall, Laura. RESPUESTAS ARGENTINAS A LAS CRISIS ECONÓMICAS, DESDE 1914 A PERÓN (PRIMERA GUERRA MUNDIAL Y GRAN DEPRESIÓN) [Argentina's response to economic crises from 1914 to Perón: World War I and the Great Depression]. *Rev. de Hist. [Costa Rica] 1977 3(5): 47-64.* Argentinian response to the economic challenges produced by World War I and the Depression was slow and conservative; the economy diversified somewhat, banking remained inadequate, and British interests largely prevailed. 64 notes.
                                                J. P. H. Myers

2575. Rodriguez, Celso. CANTONISMO: A REGIONAL HARBINGER OF PERONISM IN ARGENTINA. *Americas (Acad. of Am. Franciscan Hist.) 1977 34(2): 170-201.* The political movement led by Federico Cantoni in the Argentine province of San Juan in the 1920's bitterly opposed both traditional conservative forces in San Juan and the nationally predominant branch of the Radical Party led by Hipólito Yrigoyen. In and out of office at provincial level, it foreshadowed the later nationwide movement of Juan Domingo Perón in its dedication to "social redemption of the underdogs," better distribution of economic benefits within the existing system, and personalist and populist political style. Based on newspapers and other published sources; 87 notes.
                                                D. Bushnell

2576. Scroggins, Daniel C. LEOPOLDO LUGONES' DEFENSE OF THE MONROE DOCTRINE IN THE *REVUE SUD-AMÉRICAINE.* *Inter-American Rev. of Biblio. 1978 28(2): 169-175.* In his *Revue Sud-Américaine* published in Paris, January-July 1914, the Argentine poet Leopoldo Lugones supported President Woodrow Wilson and the Monroe Doctrine, as modified by Luis María Drago (1859-1921), as a basis for hemispheric solidarity. His change from a socialist to an arch-conservative is briefly discussed. 11 notes.   B. D. Johnson

2577. Solberg, Carl. FARM WORKERS AND THE MYTH OF EXPORT-LED DEVELOPMENT IN ARGENTINA. *Americas [Acad. of Am. Franciscan Hist.] 1974 31(2): 121-138.* Argentina's outwardly impressive material development, based on export growth, from late 19th century to the Great Depression was flawed by major inequalities. Especially acute was the plight of native-born landless farm workers. Discriminated against in favor of immigrants in colonization schemes, sometimes even expelled from their homes, they were further victimized by vagrancy laws, neglect of rural education, precarious working conditions, and official repression. Primary and secondary sources; table, 62 notes.   D. Bushnell

2578. Solberg, Carl. THE ORIGINS OF YACIMIENTOS PETROLÍFEROS FISCALES: PROTOTYPE OF STATE MONOPOLY PETROLEUM COMPANIES. *New Scholar 1978 7(1-2): 121-128.* Studies the origins of the oil industry in Argentina and the political struggle surrounding the attempt by the Yacimientos Petrolíferos Fiscales (YPF) to turn itself into a viable state-owned oil industry, 1907-27.
                                                G. L. Neville

2579. Solberg, Carl. THE TARIFF AND POLITICS IN ARGENTINA 1916-1930. *Hispanic Am. Hist. R. 1973 53(2): 260-284.* Analyzes the Argentine political struggle over the tariff issue. After World War I had ended Argentina's prosperity, President Hipólito Irigoyen (1916-22 and 1928-30) initially supported a mild protectionism. He was supported by the powerful landed interest group, the *Sociedad Rural,* which believed that industries which bought cattle by-products ought to receive tariff support. The tariffs raised the cost of living, and this burden fell most heavily on the urban masses. President Marcelo T. de Alvear (1922-28) slashed tariffs and broke with the Sociedad, which reversed itself under heavy pressure from Great Britain, the market for 25-30% of Argentina's total exports. Viscount D'Abernon's 1929 visit to Buenos Aires amounted to a total Argentine capitulation, though the D'Abernon Pact never went into effect. Irigoyen was overthrown by a coup in September 1930. 4 tables, 79 notes.   C. W. Olson

2580. Solberg, Carl E. PEOPLING THE PRAIRIES AND THE PAMPAS: THE IMPACT OF IMMIGRATION ON ARGENTINE AND CANADIAN AGRARIAN DEVELOPMENT, 1870-1930. *J. of Interamerican Studies and World Affairs 1982 24(2): 131-161.* Immigration did not change the prevailing social or political systems in Argentina or Canada. The millions of European and American immigrants quickly adjusted to the prevailing land tenure system and patterns of social and community life. Immigrants joined agrarian protest but could not end the control of dominant political groups in Argentina and Canada over agrarian economic policy. Both pampas and prairie farmers remained peripheral groups within the larger national frameworks, which experienced rapid industrialization and urbanization. Based on official printed primary materials; note, 7 tables, ref.   T. D. Schoonover

2581. Sosnowski, Saúl. "LOS DUEÑOS DE LA TIERRA", DE DAVID VIÑAS: CUESTIONAMIENTO E IMPUGNACION DEL LIBERALISMO [*The Masters of the Earth,* by David Viñas: inquiry and argument for liberalism]. *Cahiers du Monde Hispanique et Luso-Brésilien [France] 1975 25: 57-75.* Through the fiction of David Viñas, *The Masters of the Earth,* published in 1958, studies labor battles in Argentina, 1900-20, especially the strikes in Patagonia, and their "solution," and the role of the Argentinian Army in the conflict. The novel describes the relationship of Vincente Vera and his wife, Yuda Singer, but focuses on the progression of violence and mediation in the strike. Presents a portrait of national politics, including the bourgeois culture and the Radical Party's blind loyalty to its ideology. The initial triumph of the strikes led to voting rights for the working class, but ultimately this success was limited. Describes the second stage of intervention by the army which put an end to revolutionary progress. Viñas concludes his book with the implication that only total transformation of the social and economic structure of Argentina could resolve the conflict. Based on the Viñas book and secondary sources; 33 notes.   S. Sevilla

2582. Walter, Richard J. ELECTIONS IN THE CITY OF BUENOS AIRES DURING THE FIRST YRIGOYEN ADMINISTRATION: SOCIAL CLASS AND POLITICAL PREFERENCES. *Hispanic Am. Hist. Rev. 1978 58(4): 595-624.* This study of six elections in Buenos Aires 1916-20 during the administration of President Hipólito Yrigoyen shows a correlation between social class and the party the voters favored. Most support of the Socialist Party came from blue-collar workers while the Radicals received the support of the public employee sector. The minor Democratic Progressive Party garnered support from professionals and students. 6 tables, 64 notes.   B. D. Johnson

2583. Walter, Richard J. MUNICIPAL POLITICS AND GOVERNMENT IN BUENOS AIRES, 1918-1930. *J. of Inter-American Studies and World Affairs 1974 16(2): 173-197.* Buenos Aires city politics in 1918-30 were marked by electoral reform that opened up municipal politics to a large segment of the electorate. This in turn led to the formation of new political groups. Men who served on the city council in this era used that experience to move into national politics. The political developments of this period also provide some insight into the urbanization process that took place throughout the nation. Based on Buenos Aires city government documents and secondary books and articles; 4 tables, note, biblio.   J. R. Thomas

2584. —. EL PLAN DE REACTIVACIÓN ECONÓMICA ANTE EL HONORABLE SENADO [Plan for economic reactivation submitted to the Senate]. *Desarrollo Econ. [Argentina] 1979 19(75): 403-426.* Transcribes the 1940 Pinedo Plan for economic recovery, drawn up after almost a decade of conservative rule by Raul Pinedo, in collaboration with Raul Prebisch, Ernesto Malaccorto, and Guillermo Walter Klein. The plan was aimed at overcoming the difficulties Argentina's economy

was encountering as a result of the crisis of the 1930's and World War II. The plan influenced economic and political debate for over three decades. The plan outlines the economic difficulties perceived by the conservative administration between 1935 and 1940, emphasizing problems resulting from the war. An industrializing strategy is outlined.
G. A. Makin

Perón, Reconstruction, and Revival, 1943-1976

2585. Allen, Julia Coan and Weaver, Frederick Stirton. THE FISCAL CRISIS OF THE ARGENTINE STATE. *Latin Am. Perspectives 1979 6(3): 30-45.* An application of James O'Connor's *The Fiscal Crisis of the State* (1973) to the Argentine economy under Juan Perón, 1946-55. The model, slightly modified, explains Perón's political success and economic failure because it avoids the weakness of both dependency and class-analysis models. 6 tables, 8 notes, biblio.   J. F. Vivian

2586. Alschuler, Lawrence R. ASYMÉTRIE ET ASYNCHRONIE DANS LE DÉVELOPPEMENT ARGENTIN [Asymmetry and asynchrony in Argentinian development]. *Études Int. [Canada] 1976 7(4): 499-515.* Studies Argentina's attempts to encourage socioeconomic growth and at the same time equalize income distribution, 1950-70, with special emphasis on the Peron years and the Argentinian revolution, 1966-69. Identifies the strategies aimed at reconciling growth and equality, and proposes a theory based on the relationship between asymmetry and international exchange and the asynchrony of development. Secondary sources; 2 tables, 4 graphs, 33 notes.
J. F. Harrington, Jr.

2587. Alschuler, Lawrence R. THE STRUGGLE OF ARGENTINA WITHIN THE NEW INTERNATIONAL DIVISION OF LABOR. *Can. J. of Development Studies [Canada] 1980 1(2): 219-241.* Examines the major political regimes in Argentina between 1950 and 1970 in the light of the attempts to move Argentina to a more favorable position within the changing international division of labor.

2588. Ambri, Mariano. IL PRIMO AVVENTO DI PERON [Peron's first ascent to power]. *Civitas [Italy] 1973 24(9): 17-36.* "Because of Peron's return to leadership in Argentina, the historical period of his first ascent to power is now gaining a renewed interest. The author, while examining the events which led Peron to power on February 24th, 1946, points out the demagogic character of the Peronist movement, and underlines the errors made by the democratic parties, which had formed an alliance named Democratic Union. The originality of that movement which was later named 'justicialist' is not to be underestimated, but the opposition's errors—which still are frequent—were mainly responsible for Peron's electoral success in 1946."   J

2589. Best, John. THE NEW FOREIGN POLICY THRUST IN PERON'S TROUBLED ARGENTINA. *Internat. Perspectives [Canada] 1974 (3): 35-38.* Discusses the problems and policies of President Juan Peron, 1973-74.   S

2590. Bourdé, Guy. LA CGT ARGENTINE ET LES OCCUPATIONS D'USINES DE MAI-JUIN 1964 [The CGT and the sit-down strikes of May-June 1964 in Argentina]. *Mouvement Social [France] 1978 103: 53-86.* Repressed during 1955-58, the Argentine labor movement regained its former strength and secured new freedom during 1958-66. But this was accompanied by galloping inflation and heavy unemployment. The Peronists initiated the wave of sit-down strikes, implemented by the General Confederation of Labor (CGT) in May-June 1964, to secure not only economic reform but also Juan Peron's return to Argentina. Reactionary business sectors and the army disapproved of the government's capitulation in granting a minimum wage and a sliding scale. The CGT's strike effort failed in December 1964, and in June 1966 the ruling class brought the army back to power.   J/S

2591. Bowen, Nicholas. THE END OF BRITISH ECONOMIC HEGEMONY IN ARGENTINA: MESSERSMITH AND THE EADY-MIRANDA AGREEMENT. *Inter-Am. Econ. Affairs 1975 28(4): 3-24.* Surveys the role of US Ambassador George S. Messersmith in breaking the impasse in the Eady-Miranda negotiations of 1946 on

Argentine-British economic relations. Primary and secondary sources; 51 notes.
D. A. Franz

2592. Cantón, Darío and Jorrat, Jorge Raúl. EL VOTO PERONISTA EN 1973: DISTRIBUCION, CRECIMIENTO MARZO-SEPTIEM-BRE Y BASES OCUPACIONALES [The Peronist vote in 1973: distribution, growth between March and September and occupational basis]. *Desarrollo Econ. [Argentina] 1980 20(77): 71-92.* Explores the hypothesis that Peronism had an electorate of workers and that nonworkers rejected Peronism. Argentina is broken up into four large regions, according to the moment political participation began and according to degrees of development. The increase in the Peronist vote between March and September 1973 is described. The occupational basis of the Peronist vote is analyzed at provincial, departmental, and voting center levels. Concludes that the FREJULI electoral victory was unrestricted and that worker support and nonworker rejection were even stronger in 1973. 29 notes, 12 tables, appendix with Spearman correlation values.
G. Makin

2593. Canton, Darío and Jorrat, Jorge R. OCCUPATION AND VOTE IN URBAN ARGENTINA: THE MARCH 1973 PRESIDENTIAL ELECTION. *Latin Am. Res. Rev. 1978 13(1): 146-157.* A study of five urban areas reveals that workers strongly supported Peronism. Patterns of occupational support for major political parties have changed little since 1946. Yet because workers do not produce the total Peronist vote, Peronism may not be a working-class party in every electoral unit. Based on 1973 election returns and secondary sources; 4 tables, 16 notes.
J. K. Pfabe

2594. Ciria, Alberto. PERONISM YESTERDAY AND TODAY. *Latin Am. Perspectives 1974 1(3): 21-41.* A history of Peronism in Argentina.
S

2595. Corradi, Juan E. ARGENTINA: DEPENDENCY AND POLITICAL CRISIS. *Monthly R. 1973 25(7): 28-42.* Reviews political developments in Argentina from 1955 to 1973 emphasizing Peronism and popular resistance to control of the economy by multinational corporations.
S

2596. Corradi, Juan Eugenio. ARGENTINA AND PERONISM: FRAGMENTS OF THE PUZZLE. *Latin. Am. Perspectives 1974 1(3): 3-20.* Peronism and the role of agrarian and industrial classes in Argentina.
S

2597. Craig, Alexander. PERÓN AND PERONISM: PERSONALISM PERSONIFIED. *Int. J. [Canada] 1976 31(4): 703-717.* A critical assessment of Juan Peron's application of military techniques and the personalization of power to government. 27 notes.
R. V. Kubicek

2598. D'Amico, David F. RELIGIOUS LIBERTY IN ARGENTINA DURING THE FIRST PERON REGIME, 1943-1955. *Church Hist. 1977 46(4): 490-503.* Describes religious liberty in Argentina, 1943-55, concentrating on the restrictions of Protestant liberties. Evaluates the role of the Catholic Church in the developments which led to the coercion of Protestants, examining the role of Juan Peron, to show how the regime affected Roman Catholic and Protestant Christianity. Peron limited Protestants' freedom to propagate their views by radio broadcasts, move and act without the government checking their personnel, finances, and property, and freedom to buy property and erect church buildings. 58 notes.
D. Dibert

2599. Deiner, John T. EVA PERON AND THE ROOTS OF POLITICAL INSTABILITY IN ARGENTINA. *Civilisations [Belgium] 1973/74 23/24(3/4): 195-212.* Eva Peron from 1945 to 1952 helpd transform Argentine politics by her activities with the workers, women, and the poor. She made them feel they were a part of the Argentine political system and they made demands on the system and received benefits from it. Eva Peron was a charismatic political figure who managed to generate strong empathy for others. 27 notes.
H. L. Calkin

2600. Deiner, John T. THE ILO AND PERON'S ARGENTINA. *Social Sci. 1973 48(4): 222-231.* "During Juan Peron's presidency, Argentina made a major effort to gain world influence and prestige. In a series of confrontations at the International Labor Organization, the United States and its allies in the international labor movement successfully contested various Argentine attempts to win world labor support. This article provides a detailed account of the frustrations Argentine labor leaders encountered at the International Labor Organization, and discusses the political repercussions within Argentina of those unsuccessful encounters."
J

2601. Epstein, Edward C. CONTROL AND CO-OPTATION OF THE ARGENTINE LABOR MOVEMENT. *Econ. Development and Cultural Change 1979 27(3): 445-465.* Analyzes the growth of the industrial labor force and the increase in urban labor agitation in Argentina, 1955-73. The control Juan Peron exercised over the labor unions, 1943-55, was not continued by his successors. Their attempts for successful union cooptation were successful for short periods only because they failed to integrate the working class into the general population. In order to minimize labor hostility the government focused its attention on the labor union leadership rather than the membership. Based on published sources; 79 notes.
J. W. Thacker, Jr.

2602. Epstein, Edward C. POLITICIZATION AND INCOME REDISTRIBUTION IN ARGENTINA: THE CASE OF THE PERONIST WORKER. *Econ. Development and Cultural Change 1975 23(4): 615-631.* Analyzes the reasons for the popularity of Juan Peron and Peronism among Argentine workers between 1955 and 1973 by an examination of the economic and social policies adopted by Peron while in office (1943-55) and his successors after 1955. The Peronist workers continued their loyalty to Peron because of memories of favorable treatment received during Peron's rule, the unsatisfactory treatment received under his successors, and the presence of the Peronist General Confederation of Labor (CGT) as a means for reminding them of what they had lost. Based on published sources; 10 tables, 56 notes.
J. W. Thacker, Jr.

2603. Escudé, Carlos. LAS RESTRICCIONES INTERNACIONALES EN LA ECONOMIA ARGENTINA, 1945-49 [International restrictions on the Argentine economy, 1945-49]. *Desarrollo Econ. [Argentina] 1980 20(77): 3-40.* Concentrates on aspects of the relations among the United States, Great Britain, and Argentina, which led to a deterioration of the Argentine economy. The US boycott of Argentina resulted in restrictions that are held to be one of the main reasons for the stagnation of Argentine economic growth after World War II. Based on British Foreign Office papers and State Department files; 146 notes.
G. Makin

2604. Fernandez, Julio A. THE CRISIS OF AUTHORITY IN ARGENTINA. *Current Hist. 1974 66(389): 15-18, 38.* Traces the political career of Juan Peron and the political atmosphere in Argentina which favored his return to power in 1973. One of seven articles on Latin America.
S

2605. Fernández, Julio A. POLITICAL IMMOBILITY IN ARGENTINA. *Current Hist. 1976 70(413): 73-76, 86-87.* The military of Argentina has been watching Isabel Martínez de Perón since her rise to power in 1975, waiting for her regime to collapse under its own weight and so end the myths of Peronism.

2606. Goetz, Arturo. ARGENTINA. *World Survey [Great Britain] 1973 (55): 1-17.* Outlines the historical development of Argentina, the nature and role of Peronism, the 1973 presidential election, and the state of the economy.
P. J. Beck

2607. Gomáriz Moraga, Enrique. SOBRE LAS CAUSAS DEL FENÓMENO PERONISTA [On the causes of the Peronist phenomenon]. *Rev. de Política Int. [Spain] 1979 (163): 127-138.* Peronism developed from the economic conditions created by the depression and World War II, which broke Latin America's traditional relationship with the centers of the world economy, provoked internal tensions, fomented nationalism, and gave greater autonomy to the ruling classes.

2608. Goncharov, V. M. VIKTORIO KODOVIL'IA—REVOLIUTSIONER, INTERNATSIONALIST, PATRIOT [Victorio Codovilla, revolutionary, internationalist, patriot]. *Novaia i Noveishaia Istoriia [USSR] 1979 (1): 68-82, (2): 100-115.* Part I. The life and work of Victorio

Codovilla (1894-1970), a leader of the Communist Party. Germany attacked the USSR in 1941, Codovilla returned illegally from exile in Chile to Argentina and organized a solidarity movement in support of the Soviet Union. In 1954 he was the main proponent of the view that the Communist Party should play a leading role in a broad democratic opposition against Argentinian dictatorship. In the immediate postwar years Codovilla called for support for some of Juan Peron's reformist measures. Codovilla was imprisoned and constantly persecuted by the reactionary authorities. Part II. The establishment of Latin America's first socialist state in Cuba raised new hopes for all the progressive forces in the area. The Argentine Party expressed its sympathies with Cuba and Codovilla went there in 1964. Argentina lived through yet another of its structural crises and the government ruthlessly followed International Monetary Fund strictures. Codovilla advocated cooperation with left-wing Peronists and fought for internal party unity. He organized against US imperialism and the Vietnam War and sided with the USSR against China. He died in Moscow in April 1970 after a long illness. 62 notes.

V. Sobeslavsky

2609. Goodwin, Paul B., Jr. THE POLITICS OF RATE-MAKING: THE BRITISH-OWNED RAILWAYS AND THE UNIÓN CÍVICA RADICAL, 1921-1928. *J. of Latin Am. Studies [Great Britain] 1974 6(2): 257-287.* In contrast to some of today's multinational corporations, the British-owned Argentine railways respected Argentina's sovereignty, as shown in the 1922 and 1928 elections. In the 1920-22 post-war recession, the railways' requests for higher rates were used by President Hipólito Yrigoyen as the major reason for Argentina's economic malaise; but once his Radical Party's successor was safely elected, the requested rate increases were granted. Subsequently, the new President Marcelo T. de Alvear and Yrigoyen fought over party policy and control, split the party into two wings, and confronted each other in the 1928 elections. Alvear forced a reduction in rates prior to the election in order to embarrass Yrigoyen into raising them to provide wage increases for the railway unions. In spite of his public baiting of the railways, Yrigoyen considered them as integral parts of his "vast plan of public works." The companies "never sought the intervention of the British government," but were "unwilling pawns" and "handy scapegoats" in the arena of Argentine politics. Based on company and government records, newspaper accounts, and secondary works; 2 tables, 107 notes.   K. M. Bailor

2610. Hirzy, Jacques. RÉFLEXIONS SUR LA POLITIQUE D'INDUSTRIALISATION DU GOUVERNEMENT PÉRONISTE (ACCOMPAGNÉES DE RÉFÉRENCES BIBLIOGRAPHIQUES) [Reflections on the industrialization of the Peronist government with bibliographical references]. *Travaux & Mémoires de l'Inst. des Hautes Études de l'Amérique Latine [France] 1980 33: 81-101.* In the postwar era, when industrialization was considered a key element in the search for economic emancipation, Juan Peron established what was in fact a fascist regime that, in spite of its advanced social legislation, was essentially based on the army.

2611. Hollander, Nancy Caro. SI EVITA VIVIERA. *Latin Am. Perspectives 1974 1(3): 42-57.* The role of women in the Peronism of Argentina.   S

2612. Hollander, Nancy Caro. WOMEN WORKERS AND THE CLASS STRUGGLE: THE CASE OF ARGENTINA. *Latin Am. Perspectives 1977 4(1-2): 180-193.* Analyzes the political organization of working women that occurred in the Peronist movement in the 1940's. While early capitalist development brought women into the labor force, futher expansion led to the substitution of immigrant European workers for women. The case raises important political questions about the role of women in populist coalitions; Peronism actually served to reinforce the oppression of women under capitalist development.   J. L. Dietz

2613. Hornos, Axel. PERON'S LEGACY. *Mankind 1975 4(11): 54-65.* Examines Juan Perón's legacy of social reform for the working class in Argentina.

2614. James, Daniel. THE PERONIST LEFT, 1955-1975. *J. of Latin Am. Studies [Great Britain] 1976 8(2): 273-296.* From June 1973 to November 1974, the combative unions, Revolutionary Peronism, and the Peronist Youth suffered a series of blows which exposed the severe differences underlying these three groups' loyalties to Juan Peron himself.

The Argentine unions were forced to choose between continued change and job security; by opting for the latter out of loyalty to Peron they have become the right wing of the *Peronistas.* Revolutionary Peronism and the Peronist Youth were driven to choose between loyalty to the old anti-imperialist front, loyalty to Perón, and genuine socialist, but non-Marxist, goals. Both chose the latter, and thus became the left wing. Based on periodicals, correspondence, and secondary sources; 48 notes.

K. M. Bailor

2615. James, Daniel. POWER AND POLITICS IN PERONIST TRADE UNIONS. *J. of Interamerican Studies and World Affairs 1978 20(1): 3-36.* An examination of the internal power base of the Peronist union leadership and of the ramifications of this power in society. Union power was extensive, though ambiguous, oligarchic, and undemocratic. The development and transformation of Peronist union power and leadership can only be understood within the historical context of Argentina's working class in the post-1955 period. It was not the result of a bureaucratic process nor of the personal wishes of union leaders. Based on primary and secondary sources as well as interviews; 16 notes, ref.

T. D. Schoonover

2616. James, Daniel. RATIONALISATION AND WORKING CLASS RESPONSE: THE CONTEXT AND LIMITS OF FACTORY FLOOR ACTIVITY IN ARGENTINA. *J. of Latin Am. Studies [Great Britain] 1981 13(2): 375-402.* Examines state efforts to increase worker productivity in Argentina in the 1950's and 1960's and worker responses. Employers and government spokesmen considered worker productivity too low by the early 1950's and sought ways to redefine legitimate work effort. Rewriting clauses in contracts regulating working conditions could be rendered meaningless by an opposed work force and their internal commissions of shop floor delegates. The military government of General Pedro Aramburu, 1955-58, provided decrees allowing employers to "rationalize" productivity, but some ambiguity remained. The Arturo Frondizi government, 1958-62, made the most systematic and successful effort to solve the problem. During these years employers won the right to transfer personnel, and shop floor delegates were limited in number and activity. Union acceptance of rationalization, however, brought gains in fringe benefits for workers and greater ability to control their membership. Based in part on printed primary sources; 60 notes.

M. A. Burkholder

2617. Janke, Peter. TERRORISM IN ARGENTINA. *J. of the Royal United Services Inst. for Defence Studies [Great Britain] 1974 119(3): 43-48.* Describes and analyzes the activities of the Trotskyist People's Revolutionary Army (ERP) and its guerrilla warfare in Argentina since 1968. ERP's tactics have included kidnapping for ransom or propaganda effect and minor military actions. The aim of the ERP's terrorist policies is "to provoke the government into over-reacting so as to drive the country's left wing generally into a common policy of violence."

D. H. Murdoch

2618. Jelin, Elizabeth. LABOUR CONFLICTS UNDER THE SECOND PERONIST REGIME, ARGENTINA 1973-76. *Development and Change [Netherlands] 1979 10(2): 233-257.* Briefly examines industrialization in Argentina since the 1940's; describes the labor strikes which occurred between 1973 and 1976 under the second Peronist regime, specifically the causes of the strikes and the attitudes of the government.

2619. Kenworthy, Eldon. THE FUNCTION OF THE LITTLE-KNOWN CASE IN THEORY FORMATION OR WHAT PERONISM WASN'T. *Comparative Pol. 1973 6(1): 17-46.* Examines the application of the Peronist case as a species of fascism in the writings of Seymour Martin Lipset and Kenneth Organski.   S

2620. Knowles, Christopher. REVOLUTIONARY TRADE UNIONISM IN ARGENTINA: INTERVIEW WITH AUGUSTIN TOSCO. *Radical Am. 1975 9(3): 17-37.* Interviews the Marxist leader of the Light and Power Union in the industrial city of Córdoba, who discusses the governments of Juan Perón and Isabel Perón, the ideological conflict between Peronism and Marxism, and the Cordobazo, the spontaneous mass economic protest of 1969.

2621. Kohen, A. CLAVES PARA LA COMPRENSIÓN DE UNA ÉPOCA: 1945-1955 [Keys toward understanding an epoch: 1945-55].

Lateinamerika [East Germany] 1977 (Aut): 5-35. The role of the Communists in combating Juan Perón and "peronismo" in Argentina is fitted into the larger context of the cold war between the United States and the USSR. "Peronismo" failed to take into account the economic realities and needs of the Argentinian people, and as a result it failed to mobilize the working class. In the 1973 return of Perón, the left-wing peronistas responded to the economic consciousness of the workers. Secondary sources; 26 notes.

D. R. Stevenson

2622. Leonard, Virginia W. EDUCATION AND THE CHURCH-STATE CLASH IN ARGENTINA, 1954-1955. *Catholic Hist. Rev. 1980 66(1): 34-52.* An analysis of the role of the Church in the downfall of Juan Peron of Argentina in 1955. Covers early friendly relations between Peron and the Church, the beginnings and development of the crisis caused by Peron's totalitarian ambitions, his efforts to wrest control of education from the grasp of the clergy, and growing Church opposition to him. Peron lost an ally that would later bring about his downfall, but absolute control of the nation was not possible without control of education.

V. L. Human

2623. Lewis, Paul H. WAS PERÓN A FASCIST? AN INQUIRY INTO THE NATURE OF FASCISM. *J. of Pol. 1980 42(1): 242-256.* The Argentine dictatorship of Juan Peró, 1946-55, was fascist in its use of a single party and corporativist economic structures, its stated ideals of government-imposed class collaboration, obedience, and national power, and its extension of coercive powers in a totalitarian fashion. In its main features, it closely resembled Mussolini's Italy. While Peronist party and corporatist organizations were not as highly developed as in Italy, Perón was in power for only nine years in Argentina while Mussolini dominated Italy for over two decades. In mass support and indoctrination of the military, Argentine fascism was more radical than the Italian version. 25 notes.

A. W. Novitsky

2624. Little, Walter; Seibert, Sibila, transl. LA ORGANIZACIÓN OBRERA Y EL ESTADO PERONISTA, 1943-1955 [Labor organizations and the Peronist state, 1943-55]. *Desarrollo Econ. [Argentina] 1979 19(75): 331-376.* Since the vast literature on the subject has concentrated on populist features and the apparently irrational attributes of working-class support for Peronism, the author seeks to analyze in detail institutional and rational aspects of the relationship. The emerging alliance of 1943-46 was precarious. Reviews Peron's perception of the needs of the working class and his understanding of the role of the state in fulfilling them and offers a periodization and a typology. New unions were Peron's staunchest supporters, old unions more critical; but positions ultimately depended on the position of the union leadership. Union membership was homogeneous, and the explanatory capability of the dualist thesis prevalent in the initial literature is not supported by empirical evidence. Based on Peron's speeches and papers from trade union archives; 3 tables, 116 notes.

G. A. Makin

2625. Little, Walter. PARTY AND STATE IN PERONIST ARGENTINA, 1945-1955. *Hispanic Am. Hist. Rev. 1973 53(4): 644-662.* Juan Peron of Argentina failed to build an effective political party. He perceived that the masses were leaderless and set out to make himself their leader. He reasoned that personalism was more important than traditional political parties, which the people distrusted. The scheme worked wonderfully; Peron beat back his enemies and reigned supreme. He always feared the organized masses, even under his leadership, and this reluctance to trust the people produced ingrown leadership, erratic rule, and the eventual downfall of the regime. 27 notes.

V. L. Human

2626. Lumsden, Ian. PERON'S LAST STAND. *Can. Dimension 1974 10(2): 36-41, 55.* Discusses political unrest in Argentina and Juan Domingo Peron's (1895-1974) relationship to the radical and right wing of the Peronista movement.

S

2627. Merkx, Gilbert W. ARGENTINA: PERONISM AND POWER. *Monthly Rev. 1976 27(8): 38-51.* Assesses the current political crisis in Argentina. Juan Peron broadened his political base before the September 1973 elections, but during his short tenure in office he displayed a steady shift to the right. His widow's administration has been marked by the tactless maneuvers of Jose Lopez Rega, the resurgence of anti-Communist death squads, and complete inability to meet the demands of workers for uniform wage adjustments.

M. R. Yerburgh

2628. Moneta, Carlos Juan. LA POLÍTICA EXTERIOR DEL PERONISMO: 1973-1976 [Peronist foreign policy, 1973-76]. *Foro Int. [Mexico] 1979 20(2): 220-276.* Provides a critical analysis of the formulation and application of Argentina's foreign policy from 1973 to 1976. 77 notes.

D. A. Franz

2629. Morón, Guillermo. NOTICIA SOBRE ERNESTO SÁBATO [Note on Ernesto Sábato]. *Bol. de la Acad. Nac. de la Hist. [Venezuela] 1977 60(238): 225-235.* Reviews the work of Ernesto Sábato (b. 1911), an Argentine anti-Peronist essayist and novelist. Examines his work in terms of its meaning and symbolism. A bibliography of Sábato's major works precedes the analysis. Based on Sábato's works; 24 notes.

J. R. Grusin

2630. Navarro, Marysa. THE CASE OF EVA PERÓN. *Signs: J. of Women in Culture and Soc. 1977 3(1): 229-240.* Traces the rise of Eva Perón (1919-52) and explains how she used her position as Juan Perón's wife to establish her own unique power position. She operated especially through control of the ministry of labor, which had been the original basis of her husband's influence, and through the Fundación Eva Perón. Nevertheless, her power and leadership remained dependent on him and showed no sign of rivalry. 22 notes.

L. M. Maloney/S

2631. Navarro, Marysa. EVITA AND THE CRISIS OF 17 OCTOBER 1945: A CASE STUDY OF PERONIST AND ANTI-PERONIST MYTHOLOGY. *J. of Latin Am. Studies [Great Britain] 1980 12(1): 127-138.* At her death in 1952, Eva Perón (Evita) had become the source of opposing myths that she was a saint or an ambitious *parvenue*. The author analyzes Argentina's crisis of 17 October 1945 and subsequent references to Evita's participation in it to discover the development of the myths. Evita, in fact, was not important in the crisis that paved the way for Juan Perón's election as president, but both Peronists and opponents found it useful to credit her with a significant role. For Peronists this demonstrated that she was a traditional wife supporting her husband; for anti-Peronists, involvement proved she was a domineering, masculine figure whose own strength undermined respect for her husband. Based on oral interviews and other sources; 42 notes.

M. A. Burkholder

2632. O'Donnell, Guillermo. STATE AND ALLIANCES IN ARGENTINA, 1956-1976. *J. of Development Studies [Great Britain] 1978 15(1): 3-33.* Examines the relationship between patterns of economic development and the interests of the different social classes, and the impact of both on politics in Argentina.

2633. Pasquini, Giancarlo. IL GRANDE MAGMA PERONISTA [The great Peronist magma]. *Ponte [Italy] 1973 29(5): 593-598.* During his nine years in power (1946-55), Juan Peron stood for a more equitable distribution of Argentina's riches in favor of the common people, which explains his strong hold over the working class.

2634. Peralta Ramos, Monica. THE ECONOMY: LIBERATION OR DEPENDENCY? *Latin Am. Perspectives 1974 1(3): 82-92.* A contribution to the economic dependency debate which focuses on basic questions: What is the concrete expression of dependency in Argentina today? How does imperialism maintain its domination? What are its local allies? Which forces are capable of participating in liberation? Shows that the most powerful sectors of the propertied classes have long tied their interest to American imperialism, while other sectors of the middle class have been displaced and discriminated against by foreign monopoly capital. These sectors are now directing economic policy, as Peronism attempts to modify the forces within the bourgeois camp in favor of state and national capital. Present objective conditions make it necessary that revolutionary change precede national liberation; thus Peronism is not viable.

J. L. Dietz

2635. Portantiero, Juan C. DOMINANT CLASSES AND POLITICAL CRISIS IN ARGENTINA TODAY. *Latin Am. Perspectives 1974 1(3): 93-120.* Analyzes the deep-running processes of social and political change in Argentina that began in 1966, when foreign capital launched an offensive on Argentina's productive structure and tried to consolidate an authoritarian regime similar to Brazil's. Contributes to an understanding of contradictions within Argentine society, the role of foreign investments, the stalemate in class conflict, the limits of the "Brazilian" model for Argentina, and the features of Peronism as a compromise "solution" to stalemated conflict. Points out that the predominant dependent monopolist middle class has not been able to consolidate itself against the older economic groups. 　　　　　　　　　　J. L. Dietz

2636. Queiroz, Maria José de. PERÓN E O PERONISMO: UMA VISÃO LITERÁRIA [Peron and Peronism: a literary vision]. *Rev. Brasileira de Estudos Pol.* *[Brazil] 1979 (48): 85-100.* Describes the nature and impact of the Peronist era in Argentina and discusses the possibility of the rise of "neo-Peronism." Peronism assumed the dimensions of a cultural as well as political movement, and its ideology penetrated all aspects of Argentine life. Surveys many of the most notable literary expressions of Peronism, noting its anti-intellectual, hypernationalistic qualities, especially outside of Buenos Aires. Describes press and literary opposition to the regime and comments on leading authors. Peronism and its opposition were both caught up in generational conflict and xenophobic ideology, and the end of Peronism has not yet been seen in Argentina. 25 notes. 　　　　　　　　　　　　　R. Garfield

2637. Ranis, Peter. EARLY PERONISM AND THE POST-LIBERAL ARGENTINE STATE. *J. of Interamerican Studies and World Affairs 1979 21(3): 313-338.* Juan Perón remained the pivotal figure in all coalition politics since 1943 and demonstrated an ability to marshal a varied intellectual and political clientele. His unique ability to mobilize society was reflected in his reorganization of Argentina's economic development, his relationship to organized labor, and his ability to persuade labor and the bourgeoisie to accept each other's national role. 6 notes, ref. 　　　　　　　　　　　　　　　T. D. Schoonover

2638. Ranis, Peter. PERONISTAS WITHOUT PERON. *Society 1973 10(3): 53-59.* Compares Juan Domingo Perón's (1895-1974) policies of 1943-55 to those of the contemporary Peronista movement in Argentina. 　　　　　　　　　　　　　　　　　　　　　S

2639. Rock, David. ARGENTINA'S QUEST FOR STABILITY. *World Today [Great Britain] 1974 30(7): 306-314.* "The restoration of Peronism can be seen as an attempt to ward off the forces of the Left, but the success of this venture is not assured." 　　　　　　　　　　J

2640. Rommel, Waldemar. PERONISM AND ARGENTINA'S FOREIGN POLICY. *Studies on the Developing Countries [Poland] 1974 (6): 47-69.* Analyzes the four periods in the rise of Peronism, 1943-74, and the effect of Peronism on Argentina's foreign policy in each of these periods.

2641. Rouquie, Alain. LE VOTE PÉRONISTE EN 1973 [The Peronist vote in 1973]. *R. Française de Sci. Pol. [France] 1974 24(3): 469-499.* Traditional interpretations of the Peronist phenomenon stress the emotional nature of the faithfulness of the rank and file of Argentinians to the mythical General Peron. Can an approach such as this account for the victory of the Justicialist movement in the March 1973 election? Why did the Argentinian electorate bring the Peronists to power after 18 years in exile and 17 years of military dictatorship? Examination of the results of the March 1973 presidential election suggests that the Peronist vote which has been astonishingly stable since 1946 was based on relatively rational political grounds. By virtue of its own intrinsic nature and its place in the Argentinian political system, Peronism was able to channel the contradictory grievances of the poorer strata of the social and economic classes neglected or unfairly treated by previous regimes. Personal affection for General Peron, nostalgia for past prosperity, and the authoritarian ideology of the movement played only a secondary role. Paradoxically, the Peronist vote in 1973 was a vote for democracy and political pluralism. 　　　　　　　　　　　　　　　　　　　　J

2642. Santos Martínez, Pedro. POLÍTICA Y RIQUEZA AGROPECUARIA DURANTE EL PERONISMO (1946-1955) [Politics and agricultural wealth during the Peron era, 1946-55]. *Jahrbuch für Geschichte von Staat, Wirtschaft und Gesellschaft Lateinamerikas [West Germany] 1977 14: 332-349.* The worldwide depression of the 1930's sharply reduced Argentina's exports. The Peronist government attempted technical agricultural reform in order to improve productivity. It also attempted to establish a national monopoly over agricultural marketing to promote industrialization. The plan met major setbacks. 8 tables, 35 notes. 　　　　　　　　　　　　　　　　T. D. Schoonover

2643. Schoultz, Lars. THE SOCIOECONOMIC DETERMINANTS OF POPULAR-AUTHORITARIAN ELECTORAL BEHAVIOR: THE CASE OF PERONISM. *Am. Pol. Sci. Rev. 1977 71(4): 1423-1446.* In several highly mobilized developing nations rising levels of working-class political activism seem to have encouraged the development of political movements which are both popular and authoritarian. This popular authoritarianism melds intensive political mobilization of previously excluded social sectors with political structures which severely limit these groups' ability to affect public policy. Much of the research on popular authoritarianism has attempted to explain the phenomenon by identifying the socioeconomic determinants of popular-authoritarian electoral behavior. In an effort to clarify the relative merit of contending explanations, this study uses data from the prototypic case of Argentine Peronism to test six common hypotheses and then to construct a model which optimizes the explanatory ability of five major socioeconomic variables. The results indicate that an area's rate of industrial growth and the size of its working-class population account for more than four-fifths of the variation in Peronist electoral behavior that can be attributed to socioeconomic variables. 　　　　　　　　　　　　　　　　　　J

2644. Serbín, Andrés. LAS ORGANIZACIONES INDÍGENAS EN LA ARGENTINA [Indian organizations in Argentina]. *Am. Indígena [Mexico] 1981 41(3): 407-434.* Describes the Indian populations of Argentina and the ways in which these groups have been incorporated into the national economy and society. Examines official domestic policy and its effects on the organization and political participation of the Indians. In the 1960's Indian organizations articulated with political events as a function of the potential links of these movements with the federal and provincial governments and popular political organizations with differing ideological and organizational points of view. The general national political process has resulted in the evolution and subsequent repression of the Indian movement. 　　　　　　　　　　　　　　　　　　J/S

2645. Sidicaro, Ricardo. CONSIDERACIONES SOCIOLOGICAS SOBRE LAS RELACIONES ENTRE EL PERONISMO Y LA CLASE OBRERA EN LA ARGENTINA, 1943-1955 [Sociological consideration of the relations between Peronism and the working class in Argentina, 1943-1955]. *Bol. de Estudios Latinoamericanos y del Caribe [Netherlands] 1981 (31): 43-60.* Examines the reasons for working class support of Peronism in the period 1943-46, the more general ties between workers and the state from 1946 to 1955, and the manner in which relations between the state and the labor unions developed in this period. Statistical data shows the rise of labor power and participation until about 1950 and its decline thereafter. Primary sources; 40 notes, 3 tables. 　　　　　　　　　　　　　　　　　R. L. Woodward, Jr.

2646. Sofer, Eugene F. TERROR IN ARGENTINA: JEWS FACE NEW DANGERS. *Present Tense 1977 5(1): 19-25.* Discusses the birth, development, and renascence of Peronism, focusing on Jewish contributions and repercussions for the Jewish community. Describes the current atmosphere of intimidation, violence, and terrorism; the suspension of constitutional law; the extension of martial law; and the official tolerance of overt anti-Semitism. Details the David Graiver case, the American Jewish Committee's difficulties, the efforts of the *Delegación de Asociaciones Israelitas de la Argentina* to combat anti-Semitism, the legacy of Isabel Peron, the impact of the Montoneros (left Peronistas) and the para-militarists (right-wing Nationalists), and the policies of Lopez Rega. Incorporates a reprint of Kathleen Teltsch's "Jewish Group Closes Argentine Office, Cites Threats" *(New York Times,* 8 July 1977). 4 photos. 　　　　　　　　　　　　　　　　　　　　R. B. Mendel

2647. Suarez, Carlos Oscar. ARGENTINA: LA CRISIS DEL PROYECTO PERONISTA [Argentina: the crisis of the Peronist project]. *Rev. Mexicana de Ciencia Pol. [Mexico] 1975 21(80): 121-130.* Maintains that the political, cultural, and economic crisis in Argentina, 1943-73, developed primarily as a result of the political activities of General Juan Peron, whose liberation schemes have failed because of adherence to capitalistic goals.

2648. Teichman, Judith. INTEREST CONFLICT AND ENTREPRENEURIAL SUPPORT FOR PERÓN. *Latin Am. Res. Rev. 1981 16(1): 144-155.* The Confederation of Light Metallurgical Industries supported the Perón regime. It consisted of newer firms which developed during the import substitution era of World War II. Made up primarily of light industries producing for consumers, it benefited from Peronist policies such as distribution of foreign exchange. Older, neoliberal trade associations, especially manufacturers of machinery, equipment, and machine tools, felt alienated by Peronist actions. Based on publications of trade associations, newspaper accounts, and recollections of trade association leaders; table, 15 notes, biblio., appendix. J. K. Pfabe

2649. Torre, Juan Carlos. WORKERS STRUGGLE AND CONSCIOUSNESS. *Latin Am. Perspectives 1974 1(3): 73-81.* A study of current working class struggles in Argentina. Class struggles between the base and the union bureaucracies are at the center of the Peronist coalition. Income redistribution in favor of the working class is more difficult for Peronism today than 20 years ago; it cannot be sufficient relative to the present state of proletarian consciousness. The inability to control the labor movement through populist devices is likely to speed the historic closure of Peronism and lead to a more advanced revolutionary movement. J. L. Dietz

2650. Turner, Frederick C. DAS ERBE DES PERONISMUS [The heritage of Peronism]. *Europa-Archiv [West Germany] 1977 32(14): 467-474.* Juan Peron became a hero to the common people in Argentina, but much of his domestic policy was intended only to delude the masses and win their support.

2651. Ul'ianova, S. I. "KORDOBASO" [The Cordobazo]. *Voprosy Istorii [USSR] 1979 (10): 184-188.* The strike and demonstrations against the military regime in Argentina in May 1969 showed the correctness of the Leninist view that the only force capable of bringing about change is the revolutionary energy of the masses. An analysis of the forces involved shows them to have been a broad spectrum of opponents of the dictatorship. Based on printed primary sources; 35 notes. C. J. Read

2652. —. ARGENTINA SINCE THE RETURN OF CIVILIAN GOVERNMENT. *Australian Foreign Affairs Record 1974 45(8): 508-515.* Traces the events leading to the return of a Peronist civilian government in Argentina in May 1973 after seven years of military rule. The death of President Juan Domingo Perón on 1 July 1974, drew international attention not only to Argentina but to Perón himself and has left Argentina with a political void that will be difficult to fill. J

2653. Virasoro, I. FÉ, PUEBLO, PODER EN LA ARGENTINA [Faith, people, and power in Argentina]. *Estudios Centro Americanos [El Salvador] 1974 29(312): 687-704.* Discusses popular participation in political movements in Argentina since 1946, focusing particularly on the appeal and analysis of Peronism and populism.

2654. Wellhofer, E. Spencer. THE MOBILIZATION OF THE PERIPHERY: PERON'S 1946 TRIUMPH. *Comparative Pol. Studies 1974 7(2): 239-251.*

2655. Wellhofer, E. Spencer. PERONISM IN ARGENTINA: THE SOCIAL BASE OF THE FIRST REGIME, 1946-1955. *J. of Developing Areas 1977 11(3): 335-356.* While Juan Perón attracted support from all social classes outside metropolitan Buenos Aires, some class polarization existed. He received more support from the rural lower strata than from the rural middle classes. The regime's economic policy was responsible for loss of commercial-agricultural support, and it was unable to increase urban lower-class support. It is not true that Perón drew disproportionately from the less politically experienced. He appealed to a broad spectrum of voters. Based on election statistics, national census data, and secondary sources; 7 tables, 44 notes. O. W. Eads, Jr.

2656. Zylberberg, Jacques. DE PERON À PERON: 30 ANS D'HISTOIRE ARGENTINE [From Peron to Peron: 30 years of Argentine history]. *Civilisations [Belgium] 1973-1974 23-24(1-2): 117-131.* Analyzes Juan Peron's place in Argentine history, 1943-73, his years in power, the reasons for his falls, difficulties during the interregnum period, and the return of Peronism to Argentina. H. L. Calkin

2657. —. SUBVERSION IN THE ARGENTINE. *Patterns of Prejudice [Great Britain] 1975 9(4): 13-17.* Discusses political subversion, terrorism, and anti-Semitism in Argentina in 1975, including the role of the Roman Catholic Church.

2658. —. VICE-PRESIDENCIA DE LA NACION ARGENTINA. CONSEJO NACIONAL DE POSGUERRA. ORDENAMIENTO ECONOMICO Y SOCIAL [Vice-presidency of the Argentine nation. National Postwar Council. Economic and social planning]. *Desarrollo Econ. [Argentina] 1980 20(77): 93-120.* The Argentine government created the National Post-War Council on 25 August, 1944 so as to begin studies which would allow economic planning. The director of the council was the Vice-President, Juan Perón. Dr. José Figuerola was the Secretary and author of the document transcribed here. Reproduces chapters 1, 2, and 4 of the document; 34 tables. G. Makin

Military Hegemony since 1976

2659. Bender, Lynn Darrell. ARGENTINE FOREIGN POLICY: HISTORY OF A CHAMELEONIC NATIONALISM. *Rev. Interamericana [Puerto Rico] 1976 6(3): 317-320.* Traditionally, Argentina has pursued an independent position in world diplomacy, separate from the struggles of the world powers. Under the present military junta (1976-), however, Argentina has become a client state of the West in an effort to attract foreign capital. J. A. Lewis

2660. Canitrot, Adolfo. LA DISCIPLINA COMO OBJETIVO DE LA POLITICA ECONOMICA: UN ENSAYO SOBRE EL PROGRAMA ECONOMICO DEL GOBIERNO ARGENTINO DESDE 1976 [Discipline as an aim of economic policy: an essay on the economic program of the Argentine government since 1976]. *Desarrollo Econ. [Argentina] 1980 19(76): 453-475.* Nondemocratic liberalism is shown to have secured military consent for a lowering of tariffs and a halt to industrial expansion. The liberals stated that plans for political transformations must be preceded by economic reform to remove alleged distortions in relative prices, the outcome, to the liberals, of industrialization and an overgrown state sector. 35 notes. G. Makin

2661. Falcoff, Mark. THE TIMERMAN CASE. *Commentary 1981 72(1): 15-23.* Examines the case of the 1977 kidnapping and imprisonment of Argentine newspaper publisher Jacobo Timerman and his subsequent release following international pressure to assess both the extent of human rights violations among leftist and right-wing forces in Argentina, and of Argentine anti-Semitism during and after the overthrow of the government of Juan Peron.

2662. Ferrer, Aldo. THE ARGENTINE ECONOMY, 1976-1979. *J. of Interamerican Studies and World Affairs 1980 22(2): 131-162.* Describes and evaluates the performance of the Argentine economy under policies inaugurated in April 1976. Inadequate economic growth, poor development strategies, and targeted underemployment are aspects of the current economic policies which also reveal a recurrent theme in Argentine history over the past 50 years: the failure to implement economic programs compatible with a democratic political system. A developed, open society should be possible in a country with Argentina's vast economic potential. Based on printed government documents; 3 tables, 4 notes, ref. T. D. Schoonover

2663. Floria, Carlos. LA SITUAZIONE POLITICA ARGENTINA [The political situation in Argentina]. *Affari Esteri [Italy] 1978 10(37): 135-151.* The military government of post-Peronist Argentina has been unified by its fight against guerilla forces within the country, but claims to transform the government into a representative democracy seem no more than vague promises.

2664. Frenkel, Roberto. EL DESARROLLO RECIENTE DEL MERCADO DE CAPITALES EN LA ARGENTINA [The recent development of the capital market in Argentina]. *Desarrollo Econ. [Argentina] 1980 20(78): 215-248.* Analyzes the financial reforms applied in Argentina from 1 June 1977, contending that such measures constituted the most fundamental institutional reform of the "liberal" program. Describes the anti-inflationary policies of 1976-79 and the policies applied on the external sector, and examines the workings of the financial markets, paying attention to interest rates and external capital flows and the demand for goods and services as well as the evolution of the industrial product. 10 graphs, 12 tables, 27 notes, based on Central Bank data and Forex Club data. G. Makin

2665. Grabendorff, Wolf. ¿DE PAÍS AISLADO A ALIADO PREFERIDO? LAS RELACIONES ENTRE ARGENTINA Y LOS ESTADOS UNIDOS: 1976-1981 [From isolated country to preferred ally? Relations between Argentina and the United States: 1976-81]. *Estudios Int. [Chile] 1982 15(58): 232-239.* Discusses the asymmetrical economic and political relationships between Argentina and the United States, 1976-81, and the need and possibility for change in those relationships.

2666. Green, Raul H. LES ENTREPRISES PUBLIQUES EN ARGENTINE FACE À LA NOUVELLE STRATÉGIE ÉCONOMIQUE [Public enterprises in Argentina facing the new economic strategy]. *Problèmes d'Amérique Latine [France] 1981 (61): 19-39.* Analyzes the situation of Argentine public enterprises after the 1976 military coup, when a liberal economic policy was adopted, tending to reduce the role of the state and allow the private sector to take the lead.

2667. Janke, Peter. GUERRILLA POLITICS IN ARGENTINA. *Military Rev. 1977 57(1): 62-70.* The modern history of guerrilla movements in Latin America dates from Castro's Cuban victory in 1959—because that victory made guerrilla warfare appear successful. Argentina is ripe for such activity owing to the confusion of post-Peronist political alignments. The next 12 months will show which of the several groups in the field will ultimately find the broad support necessary for a successful movement.   G. E. Snow

2668. Jordan, David C. ARGENTINA'S MILITARY COMMONWEALTH. *Current Hist. 1979 76(444): 66-69, 89-90.* Describes the military government of retired General Jorge Videla, that has peacefully governed Argentina since the overthrow of Maria Estela Martinez de Peron's regime on 24 March 1976.

2669. Patria Grande Economic and Political Research Center. ARGENTINA 1976-1980: EL MODELO NEOLIBERAL DE LA OLIGARQUIA [Argentina, 1976-80: the neoliberal model of the oligarchy]. *Investigación Econ. [Mexico] 1981 40(156): 339-369.* Since March 1976 the dominant sectors in Argentina have been implementing an organic social and economic project that aims not merely at their own enrichment but at a redefinition of the socioeconomic structure of the country. It incorporates new productive sectors like the automotive and petrochemical industries and requires and assumes the support of imperialism.
                                                    J. V. Coutinho

2670. Riquet, Michel. L'ARGENTINE ENTRE LA DICTATURE MILITAIRE ET L'ÉGLISE [Argentina between military dictatorship and the Church]. *Nouvelle Rev. des Deux Mondes [France] 1978 (9): 526-537.* Analyzes Argentina's economic problems, condemns the dictatorial methods of the Argentinian government, its persecution of the Church, and the American trusts helped by the CIA, of which the Church does not wish to be either accomplice or dupe.

2671. Rock, David. REPRESSION AND REVOLT IN ARGENTINA. *New Scholar 1978 7(1-2): 105-120.* Examines the background to the social crisis in Argentina, 1976-78, and considers the impact of political disturbances, guerrilla warfare, the resurgence of the Left, the actions of the security forces, the rise of the Montonero movement and its followers, 1969-72, and Peronism.   G. L. Neville

2672. Rouquié, Alain. L'ARGENTINE À L'HEURE MILITAIRE: LA FIN DES ILLUSIONS [Argentina in the military hour: the end of illusions]. *Défense Natl. [France] 1976 32(7): 87-101.* Assesses the significance of the March 1976 coup d'etat in light of the three years of Peronism and the ideological currents prevalent in the armed forces.

2673. Wynia, Gary W. THE ARGENTINE REVOLUTION FALTERS. *Current Hist. 1982 81(472): 74-77, 87-88.* The military regime was created during conflict and crisis, but as the crisis faded, familiar political forces reasserted themselves and challenged the government's single-minded pursuit of its own political vision. The Jacobo Timerman case is a good example of the military government's repressive measures, which grossly violate human rights.

2674. Wynia, Gary W. ILLUSION AND REALITY IN ARGENTINA. *Current Hist. 1981 80(463): 62-65, 84-85.* Evaluates alleged and

actual changes in Argentina under the current government led by Jorge Videla, emphasizng developments within the economic sector, the human rights issue, the political sphere, and labor organizations.

Chile

General

2675. Aguilera, Manuel Villa. CHILE: LA CONTRARREVOLUCIÓN EN LA REVOLUCIÓN [Chile: the counterrevolution in the revolution]. *Rev. Mexicana de Ciencia Pol. [Mexico] 1973 19(74): 69-80.* Examines the ideological contradictions to be found in the Chilean bourgeoisie from 1970 to 1976 in an effort to explain the causes behind the abrupt change from a democratic system supported by the bourgeoisie to a politically repressive one.

2676. Álvarez García, Marcos. LE RÔLE DE L'ÉTAT ET LA NOUVELLE LÉGISLATION D'EXCEPTION AU CHILI [The role of the state and new emergency legislation in Chile]. *Rev. de l'Inst. de Sociologie [Belgium] 1981 (1-2): 239-283.* Examines Chile's legal system, the political and legal supremacy of the National Congress, the constitutional rights of individuals, "exception legislation" or restraint of an individual's constitutional guarantees by the State in the event of a state of emergency, revolutionary changes in the legal framework, the military junta, states of siege and legislative exceptions affecting them, and the amnesty and antiterrorist "decree-laws."

2677. Bengoa, José. LA EVOLUCIÓN DE LA TENENCIA DE LA TIERRA Y LAS CLASES SOCIALES AGRARIAS EN CHILE [The evolution of land tenure and rural social classes in Chile]. *Investigación Econ. [Mexico] 1979 38(147): 127-158.* During Chile's industrialization, 1940-60, agricultural labor wage rates were kept low and production oriented to the internal market. The subdivision of properties began at the end of that period, and the number of units doubled 1955-65. The 1965 reform encouraged cooperatives and small agribusinesses and started expropriations. The process accelerated under the Allende government, but with undercapitalization production fell in 1972 and 1973, creating serious distortions. After 1973, 60% of expropriated land was returned to private hands, and 30% of public lands were distributed, but the rural economic structure had changed fundamentally. It is more complex, more dynamic, reflecting the emergence of a rural middle class.

2678. Bock, Peter G. THE TRANSNATIONAL CORPORATION AND PRIVATE FOREIGN POLICY. *Society 1974 11(2): 44-49.* Examines the foreign policy of the International Telephone and Telegraph Company in Chile.   S

2679. Boron, Atilio A. NOTAS SOBRE LAS RAÍCES HISTÓRICO-ESTRUCTURALES DE LA MOVILIZACIÓN POLÍTICA EN CHILE [Notes on the historical-structural roots of political mobilization in Chile]. *Foro Int. [Mexico] 1975 16(61): 64-121.* Discusses political mobilization of peasants and proletariat in Chile, 1909-73, emphasizing the growth of labor unions and agrarian reform activities. Secondary sources; 5 tables, 65 notes.   D. A. Franz

2680. Bossert, Thomas John. THE AGRARIAN REFORM AND PEASANT POLITICAL CONSCIOUSNESS IN CHILE. *Latin Am. Perspectives 1980 7(4): 6-28.* An attitudinal survey conducted among peasants in Chile's central valley, 1971-72, found that *asentados* [collectivized farm workers] were more politically conscious than *inquilinos* [private estate workers] or *afuerinos* [day laborers]. Paradoxically, peasants involved in land reform were politically more active than those uninvolved. 5 tables, 16 notes, biblio.   J. F. Vivian

2681. Carrière, Jean. CONFLICT AND COOPERATION AMONG CHILEAN SECTORAL ELITES. *Bol. de Estudios Latinoamericanos y del Caribe [Netherlands] 1975 (19): 16-27.* Examines the actions and policies of the National Society of Agriculture (SNA), the dominant organization of and lobby for the landowning elite, to determine the degree of elite cohesion in Chile, 1932-64. The author clarifies the realities of elite behavior in Chile, and points out the deficiencies of the liberal and

Marxist approaches. Analyzes and classifies the conflict situations which mobilized SNA political activity. 6 tables, 13 notes.   J. B. Reed

2682. Chinchilla, Norma Stoltz and Sternberg, Marvin. THE AGRARIAN REFORM AND CAMPESINO CONSCIOUSNESS. *Latin Am. Perspectives 1974 1(2): 106-126.* Describes the pre-reform latifundia-minifundia agrarian structure of Chile with its rapidly growing dependence on an agricultural work force of wage laborers rather than permanent tenants (inquilinos). Compares this structure to that resulting from the agrarian reform of the Christian Democrats (1964-70) and accelerated by the Socialist-Communist government of the Popular Unity (1970-73). Land reform created a new, relatively privileged group by providing land to many former tenants but not to wage laborers. The political consciousness of the peasantry increased but support for the Christian Democrats, Communists, and Socialists varied by sector of the estate workforce. The most serious problems were not technical but political.   J. L. Dietz

2683. Chinchilla, Norma Stoltz and Bollinger, William. THEORETICAL ISSUES OF THE CHILEAN EXPERIENCE. *Latin Am. Perspectives 1974 1(2): 3-8.* Attempt to "synthesize the political significance of events in Chile since 1970."   S

2684. Chonchol, Jacques. EL SISTEMA BUROCRÁTICO: INSTRUMENTO Y OBSTÁCULO EN EL PROCESO DE REFORMA AGRARIA CHILENO [The bureaucratic system: instrument and obstacle in the process of Chilean agricultural reform]. *Cahiers des Amériques Latines [France] 1977 (15): 87-100.* Chile's bureaucratic system was born of a traditional bureaucracy and took no responsibility to promote agricultural production. The Salvador Allende government could not reorganize such a system in order to promote agricultural reform. Secondary sources; 4 notes.   D. R. Stevenson

2685. Collins, Joseph. AGRARIAN REFORM AND COUNTER-REFORM IN CHILE. *Monthly Rev. 1979 31(6): 28-40.* Shows how the land reform and free trade policies of the postrevolutionary Chilean government, 1973-78, compare unfavorably with those of the Allende administration, 1970-73.

2686. Constantin, Elio E. INTERVIEW WITH LUIS CORVALAN, GENERAL SECRETARY, C.P. OF CHILE. *Communist Viewpoint 1973 5(1): 36-43.*

2687. Couyoumojian, Ricardo. EL MERCADO DEL SALITRE DURANTE LA PRIMERA GUERRA MUNDIAL Y LA POST-GUERRA, 1914-1921: NOTAS PARA SU ESTUDIO [The nitrate market during World War I and the postwar period, 1914-21: notes for its study]. *Historia [Chile] 1974-75 (12): 13-55.* The nitrate industry was in a crisis before World War I as a result of competition from other nitrogenous fertilizers, but after wartime dislocation, Allied demand for nitrate as a component of explosives revived it. Then, surpluses again depressed the market for Chilean producers. As a direct result, the Association of Nitrate Producers of Chile was formed, both as a response to world conditions and demands by the Chilean government that the industry be organized. The Chileanization of the industry also resulted from the refusal of the US Guggenhiem firm to adequately modernize nitrate mining in Chile as it had done for copper. These developments reflected the growing economic nationalism during the postwar period in Latin America.   L. G. Campbell

2688. Fagen, Richard R. THE UNITED STATES AND CHILE: ROOTS AND BRANCHES. *Foreign Affairs 1975 53(2): 297-313.* Criticizes US intervention in Chilean affairs before and after the election of Salvador Allende to the presidency. US Chilean policy must be reviewed in the light of Cold War thinking as well as the American attitude toward Third World countries. Marxist Allende was regarded as a serious threat to American interests; aside from the made-to-order copper issue, both covert and overt means were undertaken to undermine his regime. 10 notes.   C. W. Olson

2689. Falcoff, Mark. EDUARDO FREI MONTALVA (1911-1982). *Rev. of Pol. 1982 44(3): 323-327.* Highlights the political career of Eduardo Frei, leader of Chile's Christian Democratic Party and president from 1964 to 1970. During his presidency, Frei promulgated reforms in

agriculture, social services, education, and tax collection. A split within the Christian Democrats paved the way for the Allende victory in 1970. Frei's years after his term in office were largely spent in leading the Christian Democrats, now officially proscribed, against Communist and Socialist forces.   G. A. Glovins

2690. Fazio, Hugo. ANALYZING LESSONS OF THE PAST IN THE INTEREST OF THE FUTURE. *World Marxist Rev. [Canada] 1976 19(4): 91-100.* Analyzes the economic policies of the Popular Unity government and the military government in Chile in the 1970's.

2691. Gall, Norman. CHILE: THE STRUGGLE IN THE COPPER MINES. *Dissent 1973 20(1): 99-109.*

2692. Gil, Federico G. SOCIALIST CHILE AND THE UNITED STATES. *Inter-American Econ. Affairs 1973 27(2): 29-48.*

2693. Grigulevich, I. AMERIKANSKII IMPERIALIZM PROTIV CHILIISKOGO NARODA [US imperialism against the Chilean people]. *Voprosy Istorii [USSR] 1978 (11): 51-67.* Illustrates the interference of US ruling circles in the internal affairs of Chile, including the organization of subversive activities against the Popular Unity government, and direct participation in overthrowing it. The author convincingly shows that the ruling element of the United States of America bears direct responsibility for the establishment of a fascist dictatorship in Chile and for the heinous crimes perpetrated by the fascist junta against the Chilean people. Based on official American sources, Congress documents and other materials.   J

2694. Hackethal, Eberhard. ZUR GESCHICHTE DER SOZIALISTISCHEN PARTEI CHILES [On the history of the Socialist Party of Chile]. *Zeitschrift für Geschichtswissenschaft [East Germany] 1973 21(8): 893-911.* The Chilean Socialist Party, founded in 1912, organically developed into a Marxist-Leninist party. In 1933 various Chilean left-wing movements formed a single Socialist Party. After World War II differences over tactics produced party splits. In 1955-56 this stage was overcome. With the cooperation of the Communist Party a Popular Front was organized. Secondary sources; 50 notes.   R. Wagnleitner

2695. Hansen, Roy A. PUBLIC ORIENTATIONS TO THE MILITARY IN CHILE. *Pacific Sociol. R. 1973 16(2): 192-208.* Analyzes public opinion toward the military role in defense and maintenance of internal order.   S

2696. Hellinger, Daniel. ELECTORAL CHANGE IN THE CHILEAN COUNTRYSIDE: THE PRESIDENTIAL ELECTIONS OF 1958 AND 1970. *Western Pol. Q. 1978 31(2): 253-273.* Contradicts the notion that there was no significant partisan realignment of the masses during the last 20 years in Chile, finding more polarization in 1970 than in 1958. Generally, the vote for the Left became more highly identified with the proportion of wage earners in the agricultural sector, with some types of poverty, and with the poorest form of land tenure. The centrist vote became more associated with the landed peasantry and permanently employed wage earners. Finally, the vote for the Right became more strongly associated with the importance of moderate land holdings, perhaps reflecting a more general shift of the middle class to the Right. These results cast doubt on the theory that the electoral system itself placed insurmountable constraints upon those who sought to travel a democratic road to socialism. Based on aggregate data for 155 rural communes.   J

2697. Huerta de Pacheco, María Antonieta. REFORMA AGRARIA CHILENA: 1938-1978 [Chilean agrarian reform: 1938-78]. *U. Humanistica [Colombia] 1979 (11): 159-188.* Little reform occurred until the Frei administration launched its goals of 100,000 new owners, increased productivity, and improvements in the living standard of rural workers; under the Allende administration, 21% (in addition to Frei's 13%) of productive land was expropriated, benefiting 70,000 families, but from 1973 to 1976 about 26.5% of these lands were returned, and agricultural reform changed direction, shifting to market economy adjustments.

2698. Hurley, Neil. CHILEAN TELEVISION: A CASE STUDY OF POLITICAL COMMUNICATION. *Journalism Q. 1974 51(4): 683-689, 725.* Television, originally an instrument of education and develop-

ment in Chile, has become the tool of political and commercial interests.
S

2699. Kay, Cristóbal. AGRARIAN REFORM AND THE CLASS STRUGGLE IN CHILE. *Latin Am. Perspectives 1978 5(3): 117-141.* Discusses agricultural reform in Chile under both democratic and socialist regimes. The Christian Democratic Party began the land reform process, which consisted of redistributing land from large farms to landless peasants, unionization of farm labor, and the incorporation of the peasantry into the mainstream of the nation. The landlords sought to increase production and thereby bypass expropriation, or at worst to reserve the best land for themselves. The socialist regime of Salvador Allende challenged this policy, wishing to go much further. But Allende had to have the peasants on his side, and though they were eager enough for expropriation, they were less than eager for collectivization. The strategy was inadequate; at best Allende pushed the Christian Democrat program to its limits. 4 tables, 14 notes, ref.   V. L. Human

2700. Kay, Cristóbal. CHILE: AGRARIAN REFORM 1965-1973. *Am. Latina [Brazil] 1976 17: 18-31.* Description of the uses made by the Christian Democrats (1964-70) and the Popular Unity government (1970-73) of the same agrarian reform legislation. The former tried to modernize agriculture within the capitalist framework, while the latter created a new landowning group through expropriation and peasant unionization. The rest of Chile did not accept socialism to the extent the peasants did, and the fall of the Popular Unity was inevitable. 19 notes.
C. B. Fitzgerald

2701. Kay, Cristobal. THE CHILEAN ROAD TO SOCIALISM: POST MORTEM. *Sci. and Soc. 1976 40(2): 220-231.* A review of recent books and articles on the Allende government in Chile indicates serious disagreements among radical observers in explaining the regime's failure and overthrow. Paul Sweezy's statement of the need for a revolutionary insurrection in 1971 fails to take into account the imperative need for timing in revolutionary evolution. Criticism of Salvador Allende's lack of decisive action in certain situations ignores the patent reality of his limited freedom of maneuver. The triumph of the military junta and the bloody repression which followed has failed to eradicate revolutionary consciousness among the Chilean workers and peasants. Because of this consciousness the present government is wholly dependent for its existence on US support and a policy of permanent repression.   N. Lederer

2702. Kay, Cristóbal. POLITICAL ECONOMY, CLASS ALLIANCES AND AGRARIAN CHANGE IN CHILE. *J. of Peasant Studies [Great Britain] 1981 8(4): 485-513.* Analyzes the changing internal balance of social and political forces in Chilean agriculture, 1850 to the present, and the effects of Chile's dependent-peripheral position in the international capitalist economy. Between 1850 and 1930, agriculture provided substantial marketable surpluses and significant export earnings while releasing abundant cheap labor to the growing towns. Its technical and social relations of production remained largely precapitalist, and the political dominance of the large landowners prevented a full transition to agrarian capitalism and hindered the growth of modern industry. The stagnation of agricultural production after 1930 sharpened agrarian discontent and retarded industrialization. The benefits of the radical land reforms of 1964-73 in increasing production and peasant living standards have largely been lost since the coup of 1973. Based on Chilean official publications and Chilean, American, and British secondary sources; ref.
M. J. Clark

2703. Kerbo, Harold R. FOREIGN INVOLVEMENT IN THE PRECONDITIONS FOR POLITICAL VIOLENCE: THE WORLD SYSTEM AND THE CASE OF CHILE. *J. of Conflict Resolution 1978 22(3): 363-391.* Studies US influence in Chile, 1966-73. While there was relatively little political unrest in Chile up to 1970, American interests—with the aid of the CIA—began to foment unrest among Chile's middle class and this interference, in addition to other indigenous factors, led to the coup which ousted President Salvador Allende in 1973.

2704. Korovin, A. F. PROOBRAZ NARODNOGO FRONTA V CHILI (1925 G) [Prototype of the Popular Front in Chile, 1925]. *Voprosy Istorii [USSR] 1979 (7): 185-188.* A Fascist plot in Chile in 1973 overthrew the Chilean Government of Popular Unity. The experience of the formation of that front is especially important for the international

revolutionary movement. In 1925 the Chilean Communist Party began the unification of all progressive forces in the country and formed the Assembly. This first attempt was not successful, but in the 1930's a Popular Front was created and remains an important reality in Chilean life today. 25 notes.   J. L. Evans

2705. Kunzle, David. CHILE'S *LA FIRME* VERSUS ITT. *Latin Am. Perspectives 1978 5(1): 119-133.* Traces the background of the International Telephone and Telegraph Corporation's activities in Chile since the early 1900's, and the Chilean satirical magazine, *La Firme*'s attacks on ITT since the early 1970's.

2706. Kusnetzoff, Fernando. HOUSING POLICIES OR HOUSING POLITICS: AN EVALUATION OF THE CHILEAN EXPERIENCE. *J. of Inter-Am. Studies and World Affairs 1975 17(3): 281-310.* The housing problems of Chile from 1958 to 1973 can be instructive to other nations of the third world. Three different Chilean presidents attacked the problem of too little housing in urban centers, as well as the substandard quality of housing that did exist. All three failed to resolve the difficulty. The matter of housing has become a national issue and has tended to politicize those living in the new ghetto areas. This has led to growing state participation in the formulation and financing of housing policies. Based on government statistics and secondary books and articles; 12 notes, biblio.   J. R. Thomas

2707. Lalive d'Epinay, Christian and Zylberberg, Jacques. UNE VARIABLE OUBLIÉE DE LA PROBLÉMATIQUE AGRAIRE: LE PROLÉTARIAT URBAIN (LE CAS DU CHILE) [Urban proletariat, a variable neglected in agrarian problems: the case of Chile]. *Civilisations [Belgium] 1973-1974 23-24(1-2): 51-64.* Analyzes surveys of 441 workers in Santiago and 200 in Concepción, Chile, to determine their attitude toward agricultural reform. The attitudes of the proletariat show that they approve agrarian reform but object to the way the Christian Democratic government implemented it. As a result of geographical isolation and social structure in Chile, rural groups are not integrated with other groups. 11 notes.   H. L. Calkin

2708. Leahy, Edward P. CHILENOS AND AGRARIAN REFORM. *Secolas Ann. 1973 4: 56-70.* Describes the agricultural reform program in Chile, which includes expropriation and redistribution of land, and its impact on the people. One of eight papers on Cuba and Chile read at the annual meeting of the Southeastern Conference on Latin American Studies.   S

2709. LeGates, Richard T. A DECADE OF STRUGGLE FOR HOUSING IN CHILE. *Inter-Am. Econ. Affairs 1974 28(2): 51-75.* Describes "the strategies attempted by Frei and Allende in the housing area and [attempts] to explain the strengths and weaknesses of both approaches." Primary and secondary sources; 24 notes, biblio.
D. A. Franz

2710. Letelier, Crescente Donoso. NOTAS SOBRE EL ORIGEN, ACATAMIENTO Y DESGATE DEL REGIMEN PRESIDENCIAL, 1925-1973 [Notes on the origin, respect, and waste of the presidential regime, 1925-73]. *Historia [Chile] 1976 13: 271-352.* Study of the constitution of 1925, largely through the actions, speeches, and correspondence of Carlos Ibáñez, twice president of Chile, 1927-31 and 1952-58. Military discontent, 1924-25, accurately reflected public opinion. The constitution effectively established presidential authority based on popular will and removed the evils of parliamentarianism, yet succumbed to interparty strife after 1960. Ibáñez remained the leading interpreter of the constitution throughout his career. 99 notes.   J. F. Vivian

2711. Lippard, Lucy R. THE DEATH OF A MURAL MOVEMENT. *Art in Am. 1974 62(1): 35-37.* Leftist political art has been suppressed by the new Chilean regime.   S

2712. Llanos, M. A. Huesbe and Shaver, Barbara M. ALLENDE: THE COMMUNIST STRATEGY IN CHILE. *North Dakota Q. 1977 45(2): 6-23.* Chronicles the political career of Salvador Allende Gossens, 1932-71, in Chile focusing on his involvement with the Communist Party.

2713. Lovemen, Brian. RURAL RADICALISM AND AGRARIAN REFORM IN CHILE. *New Scholar 1974 4(2): 245-250.* Review article on James Petras and Hugo Z. Merino, *Peasants In Revolt: A Chilean Case Study, 1965-1971,* (U. of Texas Press, 1972). Petras and Merino analyze the Culiprán, one of a number of large farms with a full history of peasant rebellions. With "land seizure" in 1965, the "bourgeoisification" of the peasants began. Based on peasant interviews, *Peasants in Revolt* fails at its primary task—to place the uprisings in a historical context. The peasant enterprise failed because of the "failure of Christian Democratic and Marxist party officials and governmental personnel to rely upon extended campesino participation in the agrarian program instead of centrally imposed policies."   D. K. Pickens

2714. Mamalakis, Markos. HISTORICAL STATISTICS OF CHILE: AN INTRODUCTION. *Latin Am. Res. Rev. 1978 13(2): 127-137.* Describes and evaluates economic historical statistics of Chile since 1830 in the following categories: national accounts, demography, agriculture, industry, prices, mining, the public sector, money and banking, and trade and balance of payments. Based on government documents and secondary sources; 3 notes, biblio.   J. K. Pfabe

2715. Michaels, Albert L. THE ALLIANCE FOR PROGRESS AND CHILE'S "REVOLUTION IN LIBERTY," 1964-1970. *J. of Interam. Studies and World Affairs 1976 18(1): 74-99.* The Alliance for Progress achieved some of its goals in Chile, such as the continuation of parliamentary democracy, a redistribution of some wealth, and the streamlining of educational programs. But ultimately the Alliance failed because its purpose—economic development in Latin America—conflicted with US policy of protecting markets and investments. Based on newspapers, journals and secondary books and articles; 8 notes, biblio.   J. R. Thomas

2716. Monteón, Michael. THE *ENGANCHE* IN THE CHILEAN NITRATE SECTOR, 1880-1930. *Latin Am. Perspectives 1979 6(3): 66-79. Enganche,* the practice of contracting day laborers from afar, including neighboring countries, was introduced early in the nitrate industry of northern Chile and continued virtually unchanged through World War I, despite growing labor violence and radicalism. State regulation followed the depressed conditions of the 1920's, which with the end of open immigration in 1919, effectively undercut the Left while paternalistically responding to public and capitalist concern for social and economic order. 2 notes, biblio.   J. F. Vivian

2717. Montupil Inaipil, Fernando. EL PROBLEMA INDIGENA EN CHILE: UNA DESMISTIFICACION NECESARIA [The Indian problem in Chile: a necessary demystification]. *Casa de las Américas [Cuba] 1982 22(131): 34-47.* Chile has claimed to be a racially democratic country, but, with the exception of the Allende government (1970-73), traditional policies and the sentiments of the oligarchy and the creole bourgeoisie have treated the indigenous populations with contempt and have tried forcibly to assimilate them. The Mapuche has been treated as if he were identified with the rest of the national society, as if his problems were the same as those of the marginalized peasantry, aggravated only by his cultural backwardness. The traditional policy of integration as well as the colonial nature of interethnic relations have denied and ignored the specificity of the problems of the indigenous people. This tendency has become intensified with the new law promulgated in 1979. Chapter of the book *Inche Tati: el Pueblo Mapuche, Tradición Indómita en Chile.* 18 notes.   J. V. Coutinho

2718. Nef, Jorge. CHILE: A POST-MORTEM. *New Scholar 1978 7(1-2): 271-281.* Surveys the situation in Chile since the military coup and death of Salvador Allende, 11 September 1973, and analyzes two studies which constitute "critiques from the Left": Stefan de Vylder's *Allende's Chile: The Political Economy of the Rise and Fall of the Unidad Popular,* Cambridge Latin American Studies, No. 25. (1976), and Carlos Altamirano's *Dialéctica de una Derrota,* (1977). The reviewer maintains that Vylder's study presents a systematic interpretation of the formulation and extension of policies by the Allende administration from a conceptual framework of political economy through a study of the structural and operational constraints of the economic program of the Unidad Popular. Altamirano's work is a partisan and polemic essay and lacks documentation and references. Its aims are to probe the factors leading to the failure of Chile's socialist experiment to formulate a new political strategy for the popular movement. Secondary sources; 6 notes.   G. L. Neville

2719. Nef, Jorge. CHILEAN POLITICS: DREAMS AND NIGHTMARES. *Revista/Review Interamericana [Puerto Rico] 1979 9(1): 144-148.* A review article on Arturo Valenzuela's *Political Brokers in Chile: Local Government in a Centralized Polity* (Durham: Duke U. Pr., 1977), which fills an important gap in Chilean studies by examining local government.   J. A. Lewis

2720. Nunn, Frederick M. LATIN AMERICAN MILITARYLORE: AN INTRODUCTION AND A CASE STUDY. *Americas (Acad. of Am. Franciscan Hist.) 1979 35(4): 429-474.* The military profession in modern Latin America is characterized by a body of thought and self-perceptions which are transmitted from one generation of officers to another and to a large extent cut across national boundaries. Such lore can be studied through oral and written sources, military service journals being among the most valuable. The Chilean army, as an example, adhered from the early 20th century to a set of beliefs strongly influenced by European military thought that posited the superiority of military discipline over civilian political disorder. Faced with the multiple crises of the Salvador Allende administration (1970-73), the military easily found justification in this traditional thought for their intervention to oust Allende. Based on military publications, interviews; 128 notes.   D. Bushnell

2721. Pollack, Benny. THE CHILEAN SOCIALIST PARTY: PROLEGOMENA TO ITS IDEOLOGY AND ORGANIZATION. *J. of Latin Am. Studies [Great Britain] 1978 10(1): 117-152.* The Chilean Socialist Party emerged in the 1920's, consolidated during 1933-39, experienced internal division during 1939-53, and emerged as a clear ideological power during 1953-73. It has developed independently from the Communist Party, though often competing or working with it. It has practiced Marxist tactics and ideology rather than dogmatically imposing them, has been the only Marxist party to achieve power by the electoral process, has always relied on voluntary rank-and-file workers rather than professional organizers, and has provided a continuous forum for many working- and middle-class sectors. Based on party records and documents; 77 notes, 4 "organigrams."   K. M. Bailor

2722. Pugh Gillmore, Kenneth. ACADEMIA DE GUERRA NAVAL: SETENTA AÑOS [The Naval War Academy: seventy years]. *Rev. de Marina [Chile] 1981 98(5): 547-552.* The Naval Warfare Academy was founded in 1911, at a time when only the United States, the United Kingdom, and France had similar institutions. To organize and direct it, Chile engaged Commander Charles Burns of the Royal Navy, who remained in Chile until 1914. The first Chilean director was Captain Agustín Fontaine Calvo; because of political problems, no conferences were held from 1924 to 1928. In 1938 the conference system was replaced by regular classes, to last two years, now mandatory for promotion to General Staff. Current programs include military, political, economic and administrative sciences; the academy also exchanges students with other nations.

2723. Ramaswamy, C. R. THE END OF THE EXPERIMENT. *Indian Rev. [India] 1973 69(7): 73-75.* Discusses the poetry and political attitudes of Pablo Neruda in Chile from the 1930's to 1973.

2724. Remmer, Karen L. THE TIMING, PACE AND SEQUENCE OF POLITICAL CHANGE IN CHILE, 1891-1925. *Hispanic Am. Hist. Rev. 1977 57(2): 205-230.* Following the Chilean 1891 civil war, a competitive political system developed during the parliamentary government period of 1891-1925. The Radicals, Democrats, Liberal Democrats, Liberals, Nationals, and Independents were important political forces. This period created in Chile a strong tradition of constitutional government and procedural democracy. 100 notes.   B. D. Johnson

2725. Rosenkranz, Hernan and Pollack, Benny. ESTRATEGIAS POLÍTICAS DIVERGENTES, MOVILIZACIÓN CONVERGENTE Y SECTORES MEDIOS: LA IZQUIERDA Y LA DEMOCRACIA CRISTIANA EN CHILE, 1963-1973 [Divergent political strategies, convergent mobilization and middle sectors: the Left and the Christian Democrats in Chile, 1963-73]. *Foro Int. [Mexico] 1976 17(2): 215-243.* Discusses political strategies of Chile's leftist parties and the Christian Democrats from 1963 to the fall of the Popular Unity regime. The overthrow of Salvador Allende was not only a reaction against leftist government but against increased political participation by new sectors of the population stimulated by rising expectations under Christian Democrat and Popular Unity governments. Secondary sources; 27 notes.

D. A. Franz

2726. Salvadori, Roberto Giuliano. IL CILE NELLA PUBBLICISTICA E NEGLI STUDI ITALIANI [Chile in Italian publications and studies]. *Ann. della Fondazione Luigi Einaudi [Italy] 1975 9: 217-282.* Italian publications on Chile published between the end of the 19th century and World War II are few and of little value; they are based on second-hand information and are mere travel books. Between 1946 and September 1974, in addition to general works with geographic, historical, economic, and statistical information, the author found theoretical books on underdevelopment, banks, and colonial market. Eduardo Frei's and Salvador Allende's presidencies have stimulated many works on political parties, trade unions, the Catholic Church, the armed forces, the policy of Unidad Popular's government, the coup d'état, and the military government. Biblio.

M. de Leonardis

2727. Santana, Roberto. LES ENSEIGNEMENTS DE LA POLITIQUE AGRAIRE CHILIENNE [Lessons of Chilean agricultural policy]. *Cahiers des Amériques Latines [France] 1977 (15): 101-112.* Programs to increase agricultural productivity in Chile, 1965-73, have benefited the dominant groups of agrarian society and have hurt the poor and marginal groups. Technology has strengthened those who can help themselves and has increased the proletarianization of the peasants. Based on government documents and secondary sources; table, 8 notes.

D. R. Stevenson

2728. Sater, William F. A SURVEY OF RECENT CHILEAN HISTORIOGRAPHY, 1965-1976. *Latin Am. Res. Rev. 1979 14(2): 55-88.* Reviews and evaluates studies of Chilean history completed between 1965 and 1976, excluding the Allende period. Considerable work has been done on colonial politics and the Balmaceda era (1886-91). Numerous investigations of the Chilean economy both support and offer challenges to the dependency model. Areas which need further study are the 1833-91 period, the parliamentary years (1891-1924), the post-Alessandri era, and the nature of the Chilean elite. Secondary sources; 141 notes.

J. K. Pfabe

2729. Schnelle, Kurt. PABLO NERUDA Y LOS ELEMENTOS DE LA POESIA POPULAR EN LOS *VERSOS DEL CAPITAN* [Pablo Neruda and the elements of popular poetry in the *Versos del Capitán*]. *Islas [Cuba] 1981 (68): 105-115.* Chilean poet Pablo Neruda (1904-73) united political struggle with literature. He wrote for simple and modest folk and believed that poetry is like bread, which must be shared by all.

2730. Seron, Jorge Barria. THE CHILEAN PEASANT MOVEMENT. *Cahiers Int. d'Hist. Écon. et Sociale [Italy] 1978 8: 156-165.* Analyzes peasant movements in Chile, 1810-1973. These were affected by the gradual process of territorial occupation, semifeudal labor organization, and a slow process of urbanization. A massive popular movement began in the 1920's as a corollary to local and world conditions. The first political program containing peasant claims was issued in 1923 by the newly-founded Communist Party. The First National Peasant Congress was held in 1939 and this resulted in the formation of the National Peasant Federation. In 1940 the organization of peasant labor unions was permitted, and in 1967 union strength was split between Christian Democrats and Marxists. 5 notes, biblio.

F. X. Hartigan

2731. Sigmund, Paul E. THE CIA IN CHILE. *Worldview 1976 19(4): 11-17.* Analyzes CIA involvement in Chile, 1960-76. This involvement "show[s] the astonishing degree to which an open society can be penetrated by political and economic means and demonstrates the danger of uncontrolled covert activity. When that covert activity results in the establishment of a repressive military regime that denies basic civil liberties—which is what Chile now has—it raises all the more graphically the questions of responsibility and culpability." Based on the investigations of the Senate Select Committee on Intelligence Activities. Primary and secondary sources; 3 notes.

M. Frey

2732. Suarez, Felipe. CHILE: TEAR OUT THE ROOTS OF FASCISM. *World Marxist R. [Canada] 1973 16(12): 48-52.*

2733. Tapia-Videla, Jorge. THE CHILEAN PRESIDENCY IN A DEVELOPMENTAL PERSPECTIVE. *J. of Interam. Studies and World Affairs 1977 19(4): 451-481.* In the course of Chilean political development, the role of the presidency and the presidency's relationship to congress have been fundamental. The anarchy of the independence era produced a consensus for a strong executive, but the enormous wealth and state revenue produced by the nitrate industry induced the weak presidency of the Parliamentary Republic. The nitrate crisis of the 1920's led to conciliation politics, which survived until the confrontation politics of the recent years. In this light, the collapse of Chilean democracy was unavoidable. Secondary sources; 3 notes, biblio.

T. D. Schoonover

2734. Thijssen, Gerardus G. DE POLITIEKE DISSIDENTEN VAN CHILI [The political dissidents of Chile]. *Annalen van het Thijmgenootschap [Netherlands] 1974 62(2): 60-75.* The author, a priest in Chile in 1953-73, reports on the growing consciousness of the common people of their oppressed state. Describes his own role and those of Juan Costa and Isaias Montes in its advancement. In spite of Allende's defeat and the present physical and spiritual suppression by the Junta, socialism in Chile and the Third World will ultimately dominate. Based on personal experience.

G. Herritt

2735. Valdés S., Ximena. LA PETITE EXPLOITATION AGRICOLE AU CHILI. FRONT POPULAIRE, GOUVERNEMENT MILITAIRE (1938-1979) [The small Chilean agricultural enterprise: Popular Front, military government (1938-79)]. *Études Rurales [France] 1981 (81-82): 73-88.* The small agricultural household has undergone during the past 40 years all the consequences of the social and economic transformations of the country. The small farmers who had been until 1962 subordinated to the hacienda system, became suddenly dependent on the cooperative and agro-food industries created by the various reforms promoting the modernization of agriculture, 1962-73. Rare were the *minifundios* that managed to survive though they were the main supply of basic food items consumed by the poor rural and urban population. The rural depopulation increased in spite of the fact that the urban labor market has been saturated since 1950. Migrants have settled on small plots on the outskirts of the towns and formed a rural proletariat surviving only due to the multiplicity of its occupations, while concentration has brought land into the hands of a few wealthy people.

J/S

2736. Valenzuela, Arturo. POLITICAL PARTICIPATION, AGRICULTURE, AND LITERACY: COMMUNAL VERSUS PROVINCIAL VOTING PATTERNS IN CHILE. *Latin Am. Res. Rev. 1977 12(1): 105-114.* Examines voting and voting behavior by using aggregate analysis based on communes and challenges previous conclusions based on the provincial level. Data from communes invalidate the hypothesis that political participation is higher among rural Chileans. In rural areas urbanization is more strongly related to participation; in predominantly urban areas the rural citizen participates more. Based on provincial and communal election returns and secondary sources; 5 tables, 16 notes.

J. K. Pfabe

2737. Vega, Hector. L'ÉFFRITEMENT DE L'ÉTAT AU CHILI: ITINÉRAIRE D'UNE CRISE (1970-1973) [The disintegration of the state in Chile: itinerary of a crisis, 1970-73]. *Rev. de l'Inst. de Sociologie [Belgium] 1981 (1-2): 357-376.* Discusses the late 1960's conflict between social sectors in Chile, involving the reformist, modernizing sectors of the bourgeois economy and workers, the primitive sectors of the economy and traditional industries, the urban and rural poor, and the political parties, or "political class." Divides the Popular Unity era into the periods 1970-72 and 1972-73, characterized by the interaction between these sectors in search of reconciliation.

2738. Vicuña, Francisco Orrego. SOME INTERNATIONAL LAW PROBLEMS POSED BY THE NATIONALIZATION OF THE COPPER INDUSTRY BY CHILE. *Am. J. of Internat. Law 1974 67(4): 711-727.*

2739. Voigt, Arnold. ZUM VERHÄLTNIS VON FEUDALISMUS UND KAPITALISMUS IN LATEINAMERIKA—DAS BEISPIEL DER GROSSGRUNDBESITZVERHÄLTNISSE IN DER LANDWIRTSCHAFT CHILES [Feudalism and capitalism in Latin America: the role of the large landed estates in the agriculture of Chile]. *Jahrbuch für Wirtschaftsgeschichte [East Germany] 1980 (4): 27-47.* Marxist analysis of the economic and social structure of Latin America shows it to be partially feudal and partially capitalist. The ultra-leftists incorrectly argue that colonialism was capitalist and that the region is ready for socialist revolution. Latin America was conquered and restructured with feudal latifundia, which continue today. The latifundist is both feudal landowner and capitalist producer. But the social classes tend to be precapitalist. Following the Chilean revolution the military junta restored power to the latifundists. Based on Chilean government statistics and monographs; 33 notes. — E. L. Turk

2740. Waterman, Harvey. POLITICAL MOBILIZATION AND THE CASE OF CHILE. *Studies in Comparative Int. Development 1978 13(1): 60-70.* Criticizes research for its poorly delimited area of inquiry and its lack of clarity on the factors resulting in political mobilization. Illustrates the problem through a critique of an article, "Hypermobilization in Chile, 1970-73" (see abstract 2823). Of the two generalized approaches to the study of political mobilization—the causal mode and the purposive mode—the author prefers the latter. Secondary sources; 21 ref. — S. A. Farmerie

2741. Wilhelmy, Manfred. ANALYZING CHILEAN FOREIGN RELATIONS. *Latin Am. Res. Rev. 1982 17(1): 244-254.* Reviews Walter Sánchez and Teresa Pereira's *Ciento Cincuenta Años de Política Exterior Chilena* (1979), the Instituto de Estudios Sociales, Económicos y Culturales' *Chile y El Fin de La Guerra Fría* (1974), Francisco Orrego Vicuña's *La Participación de Chile en el Sistema Internacional* (1974), and Genaro Arriagada's and Manuel Antonio Garretón's "América Latina a la Hora de las Doctrinas de la Seguridad Nacional," in *Las fuerzas armadas en la sociedad civil* (1978). Though of varied scope and value, these works reflect common concerns with the deep crisis of the Chilean political system and with the issue of the decline in Chile's international standing. — J. K. Pfabe

2742. Wilhelmy, Manfred. HACIA UN ANÁLISIS DE LA POLÍTICA EXTERIOR CHILENA CONTEMPORÁNEA [Toward an analysis of contemporary Chilean foreign policy]. *Estudios Int. [Chile] 1979 12(48): 440-471.* Chile's postwar foreign policy is explained in terms of an evolution from consensual forms in internal affairs and compatibility in external relations toward internal conflict and external incompatibility.

2743. Wolpin, Miles D. SYSTEMIC CONSTRAINTS ON CHILEAN SOCIALISM IN COMPARATIVE PERSPECTIVE. *Politics and Society 1973 3(3): 347-378.* Examines 1) the "relationships between egalitarian and nationalistic measures in Cuba" and their impact on the Left in Chile, and 2) the "possibility of modernizing mass political roles" in Chile. Discusses the "normative commitments of counterelites," mass attitudes, and behavioral patterns which allow "for the maintenance of corporate-owning-upper-class-dominated parliamentary systems in Chile and the North Atlantic Community." — S

2744. Zylberberg, Jacques. LES LIMITATIONS DU DÉVELOPPEMENT CHILIEN [The limits of Chilean development]. *Civilisations [Belgium] 1972 22(3): 405-430.* Continued from an earlier article. Chile's democracy has been one of the chief obstacles to its economic development, as intermediate social classes have emerged to exert political blackmail on the traditional establishment. Movements of students, workers, and the military against the Frei government gave rise to the Popular Unity coalition in 1969-70 and the election of Salvador Allende, a part of the blackmail. Economic boom in 1971 was followed by growing economic anarchy in 1972. — H. L. Calkin

2745. —. AN OFFICIAL HISTORY OF THE CHILEAN AIR FORCE. *Aerospace Hist. 1978 25(1): 25-30.* The aviation history of Chile goes back to 1785 when a hot air balloon was tested in the city of Concepción. Ballooning continued to draw interest until 1910 when the first airplane flew from Batuco, Chile's first airport. In 1913 the Aviation School was established. This article details several noteworthy flights by Chilean pilots, including the first crossing of the Andes into Argentina, 1918, the double crossing of the Andes, 1919, and the Santiago-Rio de Janeiro connection in 1922. The first airline in Chile was established in 1930. The Chilean Air Force became autonomous in 1930. Besides its professional mission the air force contributes to the social and economic development of the country. 4 photos. — C. W. Ohrvall

2746. —. SUPPLEMENT: CHILE: THE LAND AND THE PEOPLE. *Américas (Organization of Am. States) 1976 28(6/7): s1-s16.* A general article on the culture, history, art, and development of Chile, 1750-1976, including information on colonization and independence, geographical contrasts, land, resources, politics, government, and educational system.

Parliamentary Republic and Presidential Power, 1914-1970

2747. Antonov, Iu. A. LUIS EMILIO REKABARREN SERRANO [Luis Emilio Recabarren Serrano]. *Voprosy Istorii KPSS [USSR] 1976 (7): 109-113.* Marks the centenary of the birth of Recabarren describing his revolutionary party activities in Chile until his death in 1924, when a military junta took power in Chile.

2748. Barnard, Andrew. CHILEAN COMMUNISTS, RADICAL PRESIDENTS AND CHILEAN RELATIONS WITH THE UNITED STATES, 1940-1947. *J. of Latin Am. Studies [Great Britain] 1981 13(2): 347-374.* Economic and financial ties formed the bases for US interest in Chile and the framework within which these foreign relations were conducted during the 1940's. In 1940, 1946, and 1947, Radical presidents in Chile broke ties with the Communist Party of Chile (PCCh). The PCCh suspected US influence behind these breaks. However, changes in domestic and international circumstances, not US suggestion, prompted the action in 1940. The break in 1946 can be explained in exclusively Chilean terms. In 1947, the US State Department, as part of its Cold War policy, did indeed place pressure on President Gabriel González Videla to break with the PCCh. For his own political reasons, however, González Videla found the action acceptable. Based largely on British Foreign Office Records, US Department of State Archives, and contemporary newspapers; 134 notes. — M. A. Burkholder

2749. Carrière, Jean. LANDOWNERS AND THE RURAL UNIONIZATION QUESTION IN CHILE: 1920-1948. *Bol. de Estudios Latinoamericanos y del Caribe [Netherlands] 1977 (22): 34-52.* Argues that the low level of unionization of Chilean rural workers before the mid-1960's was due not to their apathy and fatalism, as has been widely believed, but to the crushing blows they received whenever they tried to organize. The force behind the movement to prevent rural unionization was the Sociedad Nacional de Agricultura (SNA), a powerful landowners' pressure group. Supported by the Communist Party, agricultural workers were militant and often effective but were repeatedly suppressed. Adoption in 1947 of a law severely regulating agricultural unions ended a decade of pressure by the SNA and ensured that the state's coercive apparatus would be used to keep the peasants powerless and unorganized. Based on Chilean archival material and periodicals; 79 notes, appendix. — D. M. Cregier

2750. Corkill, David R. THE CHILEAN SOCIALIST PARTY AND THE POPULAR FRONT 1933-41. *J. of Contemporary Hist. [Great Britain] 1976 11(2-3): 261-273.* The Chilean Socialist Party organized in 1922 as the result of dissonance over the affiliation of the Communists with Moscow. For the next decade there were a congeries of small socialist parties until their merger in 1933. Within five years the new party became a major force in Chilean politics. It linked with the Popular Front again in the 1938 presidential election, but the union was shortlived. Socialist views were broader than the Communists' and in 1941 the split occurred again. Published primary sources; 35 notes. — M. P. Trauth

2751. Drake, Paul W. THE CHILEAN SOCIALIST PARTY AND COALITION POLITICS, 1932-1946. *Hispanic Am. Hist. Rev. 1973 53(4): 619-643.* The Chilean Socialist Party was born as a consequence of the Great Depression. The party found itself in an advantageous position in the Chilean system of coalition politics, wielding power out of all proportion to its actual strength. The war in Europe and returning prosperity tended to institutionalize the party and blunt the impetus for reform. By 1946, the party had declined alarmingly, a victim of unfulfilled reform promises and internal squabbles. 62 notes. — V. L. Human

2752. Hackethal, Eberhard. LUIS EMILIO RECABARREN UND DIE ANFÄNGE DER ARBEITERBEWEGUNG IN CHILE [Luis Emilio Recabarren and the beginnings of the workers' movement in Chile]. *Beiträge zur Geschichte der Arbeiterbewegung [East Germany] 1974 16(5): 861-875.* Recabarren (1876-1924) was one of the influential early leaders of the Chilean workers' movement. His native Valparaiso had mutual help societies of dock and railraod workers in the 1890's. In October 1903, he published the first number of *El Trabajo,* the first of 11 workers' journals he founded in the last two decades of his life. An ardent follower of Lenin and observer of the Bolshevik revolution, Recabarren founded the Communist Party of Chile in 1922. Based on Recabarren's works and on secondary materials; 89 notes.   G. H. Libbey

2753. Hackethal, Eberhard. ZUM KAMPF DER KOMMUNISTISCHEN PARTEI CHILES UM DIE EINHEIT DER ARBEITERKLASSE UND DIE ANTIIMPERIALISTISCHE VOLKSEINHEIT (1956-69) [The struggle of the Communist Party of Chile for unity of the working class and anti-imperialist unity of the people, 1956-69]. *Beiträge zur Geschichte der Arbeiterbewegung [East Germany] 1973 15(5): 739-756.* The Communist Party of Chile opposed simplified theories of the sudden introduction of the dictatorship of the proletariat and the dogmatic application of the armed guerrilla warfare. It aimed instead at winning a majority of the supporters of the Christian Democrats, increasingly disillusioned by the policies of the government. To realize the united front policy of a broad people's front, the Party first had to develop and improve its agrarian theories. Cooperation with the Socialist Party of Chile and involvement in the trade unions prepared the ground for a united front. In the sixties this resulted in the development of a Communist mass movement and the foundation of the Popular Unity in 1969. Primary and secondary sources; 91 notes.   R. Wagnleitner

2754. Isuani, Ernesto Aldo and Cervini, Rubén Alberto. ANÁLISIS DEL VOTO DE IZQUIERDA EN SANTIAGO DE CHILE: UN MODELO CAUSAL [An analysis of the leftist vote in Santiago de Chile: a causal model]. *Latin Am. Res. Rev. 1975 10(3): 103-120.* Develops a causal model of the radical vote in the 1964 presidential election in Santiago de Chile. Provides socioeconomic explanations for leftist voting among the economically deprived and shows how interaction between the working class and those who had economic advantages produced some leftist voting among the latter.   E. Rodenburg

2755. Kawai, Tsuneo. AMERIKA TEIKOKUSHUGI NO BŌCHŌ TO IBAÑEZ TAISEI NO JURITSU [Expansion of American imperialism and the establishment of the Ibáñez regime]. *Rekishigaku Kenkyū [Japan] 1974 (414): 30-38.* Attempts to clarify the relationship between US imperialism in Chile and Chilean domestic politics, stressing the regime of Carlos Ibáñez (1927-31). The Ibáñez regime pushed forward modernization policies with the backing of American capital. The Ibáñez government controlled the Chilean society fascistically by suppressing the Communist and labor movements and organizing legal trade unions from above. The Ibáñez government fostered simultaneously processes of modernization and subordination to imperialism; it could not solve the Chilean economic and political crises which came to the surface in the early 1920's, but rather accumulated and exacerbated domestic contradictions. These contradictions burst out again with the Depression and led to the advance of the revolutionary struggles of the Chilean people in the thirties and the establishment of the government of the Popular Front.   S. Itō

2756. Korolev, Iu. N. BOR'BA ZA EDINSTVO RABOCHEGO KLASSA V CHILI (1956-1970 GG.) [The struggle for the unity of the working class in Chile, 1956-70]. *Voprosy Istorii [USSR] 1973 (1): 62-77.* Highlights the acute political and ideological struggle attending the emergence and consolidation of the United Trade Union Centre of Chile—a powerful organization of the country's working population uniting about one million workers, office employees and peasants. Analyzes the peculiarities in the structure of the Chilean working class and its organizations, and emphasizes the outstanding role played by the Chilean Communist Party in the struggle to achieve labour unity. The unity of the Chilean working class provided the groundwork for the establishment of a broad alliance of democratic and anti-imperialist forces, on the basis of which there emerged a coalition of the Left political parties—the Popular Unity Bloc, which gained victory in the presidential elections of September 1970. The country's working class is the chief motive force which directs the process of revolutionary transformations taking place in Chile.   J

2757. Lehmann, A. D. COSCIENZA CONTADINA E RIFORMA AGRARIA IN CILE [Peasant consciousness and agrarian reform in Chile]. *Quaderni di Sociologia [Italy] 1973 22(3): 201-242.* Proposes a model of peasant consciousness development in Chile during the 1965-1970 period. The conceptual framework used refers to the problems that the peasant culture faces in the process of social transformation. Applying this framework to the Chilean situation, the author builds a model of behavior inclusive of both the subjective world of the representations and the objective world in which political and social action develops. After explaining the essential concepts used by the country-workers to define their social condition (the *cumplir,* the relations with the parties, with the *patron;* the individual or collective working, etc.), the author analyzes the peasant consciousness in three different structures: the traditional *fundo,* the reunited *fundo* and the *asentamiento.* This consciousness shows three patterns (i.e. dependent, integrated and antagonistic consciousness), while the union membership is taken as an independent variable. In the conclusion the author emphasizes the insuperable political subordination of the Chilean peasant's world. Based on field research in the Colchagua area (Central Chile).   J

2758. Millar Carvacho, René. INTERVENCIONES Y FRAUDES ELECTORALES EN EL PERIODO PARLAMENTARIO: LA ELECCIÓN PRESIDENCIAL DE 1920 [Electoral fraud and intervention in the parliamentary regime: the presidential elections of 1920]. *Rev. Chilena de Hist. del Derecho [Chile] 1978 (7): 179-193.* Most of the widespread fraud of the 1920 election was the work of political parties, not the central government. In the countryside, the hacienda owners manipulated the elections by denying free suffrage. Thus, rural workers generally voted as their employer required. Urban labor, while freer, nonetheless had their votes manipulated by electoral agents although, sometimes, party discipline did exert some influence.   W. F. Sater

2759. Ramírez Rivera, Hugo Rodolfo. EL PRESIDENTE IBAÑEZ Y LA MASONERIA [President Carlos Ibañez and Freemasonry]. *Historia [Chile] 1981 16: 343-366.* Reproduces, with an introduction, two documents of the Chilean Grand Lodge relating to the second presidential term, 1952-58, of General Carlos Ibáñez del Campo. One is the annual message read before the members of the lodge in 1957. In it the Grand Master reveals his apprehensions regarding the weaknesses of the political constitution of Chile, the concentration of power in the hands of the president, and the citizens' indifference to public affairs. The other document contains the texts of two interviews with President Ibáñez in which members of the lodge seem to wish to warn him against possible dictatorial tendencies. Texts of documents preserved in private archives; 43 notes.   J. V. Coutinho

2760. Roddick, Jackie. THE FAILURE OF POPULISM IN CHILE: LABOUR MOVEMENT AND POLITICS BEFORE WORLD WAR II. *Bol. de Estudios Latinoamericanos y del Caribe [Netherlands] 1981 (31): 61-90.* Traces the history of the Chilean labor movement from about 1880 to 1940, noting its strong commitment to revolutionary ideology and involvement in the nation's politics. In the early years, 1880-1920, it utilized the general strike as a political weapon (a table indicates 32 general strikes between 1890 and 1927). Strong organization characterized its development throughout the period, and indicated the importance of the Chilean working class. Based largely on secondary sources; 7 tables, 40 notes, biblio.   R. L. Woodward, Jr.

2761. Sater, William F. THE ABORTIVE KRONSTADT: THE CHILEAN NAVAL MUTINY OF 1931. *Hispanic Am. Hist. Rev. 1980 60(2): 239-268.* General Carlos Ibáñez was unseated as dictator of Chile in July 1931, partly due to economic difficulties. Free elections were planned for 18 September, but late on 31 August enlisted men in the navy rebelled at planned pay cuts and seized ships in Coquimbo. The mutiny spread, and demands for social and economic changes in Chile were added to demands relating to the navy. The administration tried to compromise but failed. Air attacks on the ships, though doing no damage, led to the surrender of the mutineers. There is evidence of Communist agitation. The mutiny apparently led to the election of the conservative presidential candidate, Juan Esteban Montero. Based on Chilean newspapers

of the period and reports and correspondence in the Public Records Office, London, Records of the Foreign Office and Records of the US Department of State and Military Intelligence Division in the National Archives, Washington, D. C.; 89 notes.
B. D. Johnson

2762. Stemplowski, Ryszard. CHILE I OBCE KONCERNY NAFT-OWE W OKRESIE WIELKIEGO KRYZYSU [Chile and foreign oil companies during the great depression]. *Przegląd Hist. [Poland] 1978 69(3): 445-457.* During the great depression, Chile's socialist government sought to cope with an unfavorable balance of payments by exchanging Chilean saltpeter for Soviet oil, and by rationing gasoline. It asked the West India Oil Company and Shell-Mex (Chile) Ltd., to store this oil, but both rejected the suggestion. The refusal gave rise to a project to establish a state oil monopoly, which prompted the diplomatic intervention of the American and British ambassadors on orders from Washington and London. Despite Chilean efforts to reduce the oil companies' control they managed to preserve their dominant position. 56 notes.
J. T. Hapak

2763. Sweeney, Ernest S. ALLENDE'S ELECTION AND THE CATHOLIC CHURCH IN CHILE: THE OVERLAPPING OF PAS-TORAL CONCERNS AND POLITICAL REALITIES. *Thought 1981 56(223): 371-386.* Discusses the response of the Catholic Church to the 1970 presidential campaign in Chile and evaluates that response in terms of the Church's commitment to social justice. The problem for the Church in a highly politicized society was to find a means to express in a nonpolitical way its position on the need for radical social change to achieve social justice. The Church was successful in repeatedly and publicly urging economic and institutional reforms without tying its position to any political party or program. The Church insisted that personal and social liberation must be promoted in whatever political option the people of Chile should choose. When the Marxist Salvador Allende became president, the Church supported his program for socioeconomic change. Despite the differences in ideology, the concrete measures promoted by Allende were in harmony with the Church's social doctrine. Based on official Catholic Church publications and secondary sources; 42 notes.
R. D. Rahmes

2764. Szymanski, Albert. THE RISE AND DECLINE OF THE CHRISTIAN DEMOCRATIC PARTY IN CHILE: AN ANALYSIS OF THE 1961 AND 1965 CONGRESSIONAL ELECTIONS. *Social and Econ. Studies [Jamaica] 1975 24(4): 458-482.* Analyzes the voter support for the Christian Democratic Party in Chile to explain the rise and fall of the party. Suggests and examines several hypotheses concerning party support and concludes that, among other factors, new voter support was significant in the growth, and later shift in those voters in the decline. Makes some comparisons with European Christian Democratic parties. 9 tables, 28 notes, 16 refs., statistical appendix.
E. S. Johnson

2765. Turner, Barbara. LA REFORMA EDUCACIONAL CHILENA: 1964-1970 [Chilean educational reform: 1964-70]. *Estudios Andinos 1973 3(3): 105-118.* Analyzes the objectives and results of the Chilean government program *Reforma Educacional Chilena* initiated in 1964. Its objectives included the expansion of educational opportunities on all levels, an increased quality of education, changes in the educational structure and the establishment of procedures for continuous evaluation and reform. By 1970 the program had met or exceeded all of its goals, except for the attempt to establish a government department for educational planning and evaluation. Based on governmental reports and secondary sources; 5 tables, biblio.
J. L. White

2766. Vargas Gariola, Juan Eduardo. LA SOCIEDAD DE FOMENTO FABRIL, 1883-1928 [The Society for Promotion of Manufacturing, 1883-1928]. *Historia [Chile] 1976 13: 5-53.* Founded in 1883 at the instigation of the government of President Domingo Santa Maria, the society reflected a faith in science, social progress, and the civilizing impact of education and foreign immigration. It stood for the economic protection of agriculture and mining according to traditional liberal tenets. The society resisted economic nationalism at the turn of the century and opposed the tax and social reforms of 1924. 95 notes, membership lists, occupational charts.
J. F. Vivian

2767. Voigt, Arnold. DIE AGRARREFORM DER CHILENISC-HEN CHRISTDEMOKRATIE UND IHR EINFLUSS AUF DIE ENTWICKLUNG DER REVOLUTIONÄREN SITUATION IN CHILE BIS ZUM JAHRE 1970 [Agrarian reform by Chilean Christian Democrats and its influence on the development of the revolutionary situation in Chile, to 1970]. *Jahrbuch für Wirtschaftsgeschichte [East Germany] 1978 (4): 19-38.* Salvador Allende's election as head of state, and the formation of the people's government in Chile in 1970, can be interpreted as a climax of revolutionary action. Examines the agrarian question as well as other basic elements of liberation movements. The rural reform launched by the Christian Democrats did not succeed and the victorious Unidad Popular adopted a different solution to Chile's agrarian question. 37 notes.
G. E. Pergl

2768. Wolpin, Miles D. THE TRANS-NATIONAL APPEAL OF THE CUBAN REVOLUTION: CHILE, 1958-1970. *Caribbean Q. [Jamaica] 1973 19(1): 7-48.* Inspired by Cuban success in expropriating US corporations, Chilean leftists radicalized their immediate goals by 1961. The leftist constituency among the lower class did not expand significantly during the 1960's partly due to dogmatic Marxist tactics despite the rapid extension of bourgeois political culture. The defeat of the bourgeois parties in 1970 resulted from: 1) the close identification of Eduardo Frei's officials with domestic and foreign capital; 2) defection of populistic Christian Democrats, many inspired by the Cuban Revolution after visiting Cuba; 3) seizure of the Radical Party by similar individuals; and 4) tactical inflexibility, ambition and overconfidence by bourgeois political elites. Forecasts a military coup (1971-73) due to 1) the corporate expansionist goal of US foreign policies; and 2) systematic negative indoctrination on communism applied to most Chilean military and police officers by the United States. Primary and secondary sources; 81 notes .
R. L. Woodward

2769. Wright, Thomas C. AGRICULTURE AND PROTECTION-ISM IN CHILE, 1880-1930. *J. of Latin Am. Studies [Great Britain] 1975 7(1): 45-58.* Free trade advocacy by the large landowners was not a major hindrance to Chilean development; the Sociedad Nacional de Agricultura (central provinces landowners' association) obtained specific duties on livestock imports in 1897, and subsequently broadened its protectionist interests until 1930. The resultant coalition of mining, agriculture, and commerce retarded Chilean development, because prosperity after 1900 allowed for moderate protectionist tariffs whereas what was needed was more extreme protectionism. Based on *Bol. de la Soc. Nac. de Agricultura* articles, newspaper and legislative records, and secondary works; 2 tables, 43 notes.
K. M. Bailor

2770. Yeager, Gertrude M. THE CLUB DE LA UNION AND KIN-SHIP: SOCIAL ASPECTS OF POLITICAL OBSTRUCTIONISM IN THE CHILEAN SENATE, 1920-1924. *Americas (Acad. of Am. Franciscan Hist.) 1979 35(4): 539-572.* In 1920 Arturo Alessandri was elected president of Chile at the head of a broad social and political alliance and with a reformist program, against the opposition of a rival coalition that represented more traditional political forces. Santiago's Club de la Unión, whose membership included the principal families of the Chilean aristocracy, became one focus of continued opposition to Alessandri after his inauguration. Elite politicians in the Chilean Senate gave expression to the same attitude by systematic obstruction of administration initiatives. Press and published sources; 3 tables, 99 notes.
D. Bushnell

2771. Zeitlin, Maurice; Neuman, Lawrence W.; Ratcliff, Richard Earl. CLASS SEGMENTS: AGRARIAN PROPERTY AND POLITICAL LEADERSHIP IN THE CAPITALIST CLASS OF CHILE. *Am. Sociol. Rev. 1976 41(6): 1006-1029.* Analyzes the relationship between large landownership and "representative political activity" as one expression of political hegemony in the capitalist class of Chile in the mid-1960's. Landed corporate executives and principal owners of capital and their nonlanded counterparts in the largest corporations are distinct "class segments." The authors analyze their comparative officeholding in parliament and cabinet ministries and in the leadership of the political parties of the Right, as well as the officeholding of their fathers and others in their immediate families. The landed segment played a distinctive role in the political leadership of the capitalist class. The problem of the "coalescence" of agrarian property and corporate capital as a self-contradictory class situation and its relevance for state policy is posed for further analysis.
J

2772. —. [CHILE: MILITARY TAKEOVER AND LEFTIST RE-ACTION]. *World Marxist R. [Canada] 1973 16(11): 3-16.*
—. THE PEOPLE CANNOT BE VANQUISHED!, pp. 3-5.
Teitelboim, Volodia. FOR A VICTORIOUS REVOLUTION, WITH ACCOUNT OF THE TRAGIC EXPERIENCE, pp. 5-16.

Popular Unity in Power, 1970-1973

2773. Alatalu, T. POLITICHESKIE PROBLEMY RAZVITIIA REVOLIUTSII V CHILI [Problems of revolutionary developments in Chile]. *Eesti NSV Teaduste Akad. Toimetised. Ühiskonnateadused [USSR] 1982 31(3): 249-261.* Although President Salvador Allende resorted to radical reforms the opinion that Chile's problems could be solved by constitutional means prevailed. This was the main reason for his later defeat. Attempts by the opposition to overthrow the government in 1971 and 1972 failed because the government was supported by the masses and the army. During the June 1973 coup d'etat the army defended the revolution until its commanders were replaced in August 1973. The Popular Unity Party demanded the army's neutrality and undermined the authority of its commanders. Then the army joined the reactionaries in the 11 September 1973 fascist coup. Secondary sources; 74 notes.   S. P. Forgus

2774. Álvarez Quiñones, Roberto. GÉNESIS IMPERIALISTA DEL GOLPE FASCISTA EN CHILE [Imperialist genesis of the fascist coup in Chile]. *Casa de las Américas [Cuba] 1974 14(83): 61-68.* Discusses the role of the International Telephone & Telegraph Corporation in opposing the Salvador Allende regime from 1970, and its work to help the fascist coup d'etat which overthrew the regime in 1973.

2775. Andreas, Carol. THE CHILEAN WOMEN: REFORM, RE-ACTION, AND RESISTANCE. *Latin Am. Perspectives 1977 4(4): 121-125.* Though not specifically feminist in nature, Popular Unity reforms enacted in Chile in 1970-73 benefited women by providing socialized medical care and day care centers, broadening employment prospects, and encouraging local political participation.

2776. Angell, Alan. COUNTERREVOLUTION IN CHILE. *Current Hist. 1974 66(389): 6-9.* Discusses the 1973 coup d'etat. One of seven articles on Latin America.   S

2777. Ayres, Robert L. ELECTORAL CONSTRAINTS AND THE CHILEAN WAY TO SOCIALISM. *Studies in Comparative Internat. Development 1973 8(2): 128-161.* Examines the possibility of a socialist revolution headed by Allende within the existing political structure.
                                                                       S

2778. Ayres, Robert L. POLITICAL HISTORY, INSTITUTIONAL STRUCTURE, AND PROSPECTS FOR SOCIALISM IN CHILE. *Comparative Politics 1973 5(4): 497-522.* Analyzes the prospects for success of the Marxist Allende government in Chile as suggested by the historical tradition and institutional structure of the nation. The social conditions which determine the occurrence of revolution are, and have been, primarily absent. Political violence has been rare, free elections traditional, and hatred for the wealthy uncommon. The press has been free, the government relatively successful. The best Allende can hope for is reform rather than total revolution. 46 notes.   V. L. Human

2779. Bosch, Juan. SALVADOR ALLENDE EN LAS *MEMORIAS* DE KISSINGER [Salvador Allende in Kissinger's memoirs]. *Casa de las Américas [Cuba] 1981 22(128): 100-103.* The chapter in Kissinger's *White House Years* devoted to Chile and the overthrow of the Allende government makes it clear that the assassins of Allende would not have dared to do away with the president without the overwhelming power and support of the United States.   J. V. Coutinho

2780. Bourdé, Guy. L'ECHEC D'ALLENDE (1970-1973) [The defeat of Allende, 1970-73]. *Histoire [France] 1982 (48): 10-23.* Debates on the cause of the fall of the Allende government in Chile center on Chilean perspectives on socialism, internal and external economic strains, North American conspiracies, and deterioration of the government.

2781. Bourricaud, François. CHILE: WHY ALLENDE FELL. *Dissent 1974 21(3): 402-415.* Discusses the political crisis surrounding the administration of Salvadore Allende, 1970-73.   S

2782. Briones, Álvaro and Witker, Jorge. EL GOBIERNO DE LA UNIDAD POPULAR EN CHILE Y LA INTEGRACIÓN LATINOAMERICANA [The government of the Popular Unity in Chile and Latin American integration]. *Rev. Mexicana de Ciencia Pol. [Mexico] 1974 20(76): 81-88.* Treats the effects of Salvador Allende's anti-imperialist political program in Chile upon the previously established Latin American strategy of economic integration, 1960-73.

2783. Caceres, Ernesto. NOTAS SOBRE LOS PROBLEMAS DE ORGANIZACIÓN POLÍTICA DE LA UNIDAD POPULAR CHILENA Y LA LUCHA DE CLASES [Problems of political organization in the Popular Unity of Chile and class struggle]. *Rev. Mexicana de Ciencia Pol. [Mexico] 1973 19(74): 61-67.* Examines the organizational problems of the Popular Unity, a coalition of left-wing political parties formed in 1970 in Chile and disbanded with the coup of 11 September 1973, as representative of larger socioeconomic problems in Chile.

2784. Campa, Riccardo. LA VIA CILENA [The Chilean way]. *Comunità [Italy] 1974 28(171): 65-110.* A detailed analysis of the situation in Chile before and during Salvador Allende's popular coalition government of left-wing parties, 1970-73, when it was overthrown by a military coup.

2785. Castelain-Meunier, Christine. ESPACE, IDÉOLOGIE, LUTTES URBAINES (CHILI 1971-1973) [Space, ideology, and urban conflicts: Chile, 1971-73]. *Recherche Sociale [France] 1977 (63): 61-79.* Describes how urban space was affected by government policies under the Presidency of Salvador Allende, 1970-73, in Chile, including urban renewal and birth control.

2786. Castillo, Rene. LESSONS AND PROSPECTS OF THE REVOLUTION. *World Marxist R. [Canada] 1974 17(7): 83-95.* A letter by the author, a member of Chile's Communist Party, analyzes reasons for the defeat of the leftist Popular Unity alliance in the 1973 military coup d'etat.   S

2787. Collier, Simon. ALLENDE'S CHILE: CONTEMPORARY HISTORY AND THE COUNTERFACTUAL. *J. of Latin Am. Studies [Great Britain] 1980 12(2): 445-452.* Reviews 12 books published from 1974 to 1977 as they view Salvador Allende's Chile from the perspective of what might (or ought to) have happened instead of what did happen. Paul E. Sigmund's *The Overthrow of Allende* is unique among the books in that he convincingly vindicates contemporary history as an exercise. Not even Sigmund, however, can totally avoid the attraction of the counterfactual. 23 notes.   M. A. Burkholder

2788. Condamines, Charles. LES CHRÉTIENS CHILIENS ENTRE LE FASCISME, LA DEMOCRATIE ET LE SOCIALISME [The Chilean Christians between fascism, democracy, and socialism]. *Esprit [France] 1974 (2): 249-273.* An overview of the events in Chile under Allende and the challenges presented to the Roman Catholic Church. The Church's position in Latin America is so great that its implicit political power is decisive. In Chile during the Allende years certain parts of the Church went beyond the reformist tradition and became revolutionary. The "Social-Christian" movement became extremely powerful in the first years of the 1970's. After the coup the Church found itself in a contradictory position from which it is still trying to withdraw. The upper levels of the hierarchy may well have recognized the Junta which removed Allende, but there still remain the lower segments of the Church who were involved with a major social change.   G. F. Jewsbury

2789. Cortés, Fernando and Yocelevsky, Ricardo. LA DISTRIBUCIÓN DEL INGRESO EN EL GOBIERNO DE LA UNIDAD POPULAR (1970-1972) [Income distribution under the Popular Unity government: 1970-72]. *Demografía y Econ. [Mexico] 1980 14(3): 349-388.* Part of a research project on political and economic factors in the change in income distribution in Chile during 1970-72.

2790. Craig, Alexander. CHILE: THE DOWNFALL OF THE ALLENDE GOVERNMENT. *Behind the Headlines [Canada] 1974 33(2):*

1-24. Salvador Allende's attempts to radically redistribute the national wealth and legally control the economy in Chile raised grave social and political questions and provoked more conflict than the constitutional system could withstand. Extremists of both left and right, the rapidly deteriorating economy, the governmental weaknesses and mistakes, and to a much lesser extent, the US economic warfare, threatened to collapse the system. The military, acting as representatives of the nation and defenders of the constitution, intervened by staging a very thorough counterrevolution that lacks popular support and bodes ill for Chile.

R. D. Frederick

2791. Crummett, Maria de los Angeles. EL PODER FEMENINO: THE MOBILIZATION OF WOMEN AGAINST SOCIALISM IN CHILE. *Latin Am. Perspectives 1977 4(4): 103-113.* Composed of upper-class women, El Poder Femenino sought to overthrow the government of Salvador Allende which threatened to deprive them of their elite status.

2792. Cuadra, Claudio. REGIME WITHOUT A FUTURE. *World Marxist R. [Canada] 1974 17(12): 99-107.* Outlines the events leading to the military junta's coup d'etat in Chile in 1973, and compares junta political tactics to those used by the Nazis.   S

2793. Fagen, Patricia. THE MEDIA IN ALLENDE'S CHILE. *J. of Communication 1974 24(1): 59-70.* Uncertainty of power within the Popular Unity government and the dichotomy between social progress and individual freedom are reasons for the failure of Chile's mass media to support leftist social change during the rule of Salvador Allende.
                                                                        S

2794. Falcoff, Mark. WHY ALLENDE FELL. *Commentary 1976 62(1): 38-45.* Chile has come to represent a set of issues concerning the problems of social change in underdeveloped countries and the relationship between primary producing countries and the capitalist world. Salvador Allende ignored danger signals in Chile and failed to realize that military bolstering of the social order in 1973 could only come with a military assumption of total power. American involvement in Allende's fall is in question. The hostility of the United States to the regime is clear, but evidence suggests that US involvement amounted to an attempt to discredit Allende before the forthcoming Chilean elections of 1976, not support for violent overthrow. Chilean responsibility for events in the country is greater than has been admitted. Allende's base was not broad or deep enough to maintain the regime. The fact that the world economy could do without Chilean copper led, once foreign aid became a trickle, to a complete collapse of the regime.   S. R. Herstein

2795. Faúndez, Julio. THE DEFEAT OF POLITICS: CHILE UNDER ALLENDE. *Bol. de Estudios Latinoamericanos y del Caribe [Netherlands] 1980 (28): 59-75.* Reviews and analyzes the considerable volume of writings by contemporaries of Salvador Allende's Popular Unity government of Chile (1970-73). These works, both from the Right and the Left, reveal the need for reassessment of Leftist strategy in Chile during the past fifty years.   R. L. Woodward, Jr.

2796. Faúndez B., Julio. THE CHILEAN ROAD TO SOCIALISM. *Social Policy 1974 5(4): 11-20.* Discusses various interpretations of the Allende government's policies and its opposition by the Chilean right.
                                                                        S

2797. Feinberg, Richard E. DEPENDENCY AND THE DEFEAT OF ALLENDE. *Latin Am. Perspectives 1974 1(2): 30-43.* Chile's dependency on outside forces and on internal centralization was a factor in the coup d'etat which overthrew Salvador Allende.   S

2798. Fredborg, Arvid. MYTEN ALLENDE [The Allende myth]. *Svensk Tidskrift [Sweden] 1974 61(2): 68-76.* Discusses the political situation of Chile, 1973-74, and claims that there was a lack of support from voters and no majority in parliament for the Marxist policies of President Salvador Allende.

2799. Galich, Manuel. ALGUNOS PRECEDENTES OLIGÁRQUICO-CASTRENSES AL 11 DE SEPTIEMBRE DE 1973 [Some oligarchical and military precedents for 11 September 1973]. *Casa de las Américas [Cuba] 1974 14(83): 25-49.* Discusses military and oligarchic precedents in Chilean history from the 19th century until 11 September 1973, when the military and oligarchy combined to overthrow Marxist president Salvador Allende.

2800. Galjart, B. F. ALLENDE EN DE BOEREN: EEN ANALOGISCHE ANALYSE VAN DE PRESIDENTS-VERKIEZINGEN VAN 1970 IN CHILI [Allende and the peasants]. *Acta Politica [Netherlands] 1974 9(1): 3-23.* Various more or less explicit Marxian theories are current about the diretion of political behavior to be expected of poor peasants in the Third World. In Chile in 1970, peasants did get a chance to vote a government into power that had promised to take the country along the road to socialism. How did they vote? Using as units the more agrarian municipalities of Chile, an ecological analysis of the presidential elections was carried out. The possibility of a categorical error being admitted, the results seem to indicate that the peasants did not vote as a bloc, but according to their position in the productive process as independent owners, tenants, fixed or temporal wage earners. Each of the three presidential candidates appears to have found a particular structural niche in the Chilean countryside. For Allende, this niche is characterized by irrigated plantation type agriculture, that makes use of temporal wage labor provided by minifundia. The results also indicate that the syndical policies of the Frei government may have benefited the candidate of the governing party, but not its land reform policy.   J

2801. Garrett-Schesch, Pat. THE MOBILIZATION OF WOMEN DURING THE POPULAR UNITY GOVERNMENT. *Latin Am. Perspectives 1975 2(1): 100-104.* Refutes claims made by David Belnap in a 1974 Los Angeles *Times* article which held that women in Chile were overwhelmingly pro-Allende.

2802. Gedicks, Al. THE NATIONALIZATION OF COPPER IN CHILE: ANTECEDENTS AND CONSEQUENCES. *R. of Radical Pol. Econ. 1973 5(3): 1-25.* Reviews the role of copper in the Chilean economy to 1973, focusing on control by US and European multinational corporations.   S

2803. Genest, Jean. SALVADOR ALLENDE (1908-1973). *Action Natl. [Canada] 1973 63(3): 206-227.* Salvador Allende's attempt to establish a Marxist system compatible with democratic liberties in Chile was defeated by Chile's economic conditions and his own lack of administrative capabilities and economic inexperience.

2804. Goldberg, Peter A. THE POLITICS OF THE ALLENDE OVERTHROW IN CHILE. *Pol. Sci. Q. 1975 90(1): 93-116.* Discusses the violent overthrow of Chilean President Salvador Allende. Examines the paradox of the occurrence of such a coup d'etat in a country noted for its history of stable and democratic institutions.

2805. Gonzalez, Ernesto. UNIDAD POPULAR: A MARCH TO DISASTER ON THE "PEACEFUL ROAD." *Internat. Socialist R. 1973 34(9): 6-11, 25-42.* Examines the situation in Chile prior to the military coup d'etat and criticizes the Popular Unity.   S

2806. Goodsell, James. ALLENDE AND CHILE IN POST-ELECTION PERIOD. *Int. Perspectives [Canada] 1973 (July-Aug): 38-41.* Examines Chile's economic conditions during the political crisis which Salvador Allende faced, 1970-73, including discussion of his removal of several military officials.

2807. Gutiérrez, Joaquín. GÉNESIS Y PERSPECTIVAS DEL FACISMO EN CHILE [Genesis and perspectives of fascism in Chile]. *Casa de las Américas [Cuba] 1975 15(90): 77-82.* Discusses the development of the Chilean dictatorship 1970-75, showing how the situation in Chile is interconnected with the worldwide imperialist crisis.

2808. Handelman, Howard. THE POLITICAL MOBILIZATION OF URBAN SQUATTER SETTLEMENTS. *Latin Am. Res. Rev. 1975 10(2): 35-72.* Before and during the administration of Chilean Marxist President Salvador Allende, the Popular Unity coalition supporting him had great success in organizing the urban poor of Santiago and other Chilean cities.

2809. Hanson, Simon G. KISSINGER ON THE CHILEAN COUP. *Inter-Am. Econ. Affairs 1973 27(3): 61-85.* Reviews the interest, or lack of it, in Latin American policy during the hearings on the nomination of Henry A. Kissinger as secretary of state, 1973.   S

2810. Holden, David. ALLENDE AND THE MYTHMAKERS. *Encounter [Great Britain] 1974 42(1): 12-24.* The exaggerated reaction of Western liberals and socialists to the military coup in Chile, which destroyed the regime of Salvador Allende, amounts to a romantic vision which obscures reality. Analysis shows that Allende was not overthrown by covert American intervention nor by a revolt of the privileged classes; serious doubts must also be raised about his commitment to constitutionalism—or indeed to a genuine revolutionary position. Allende was basically "a political romantic, dealing in sensation rather than sense."
D. H. Murdoch

2811. Horne, Alistair. "CUNNING IN MINE OVERTHROW." *Int. Rev. [Great Britain] 1974 (1): 81-83.* Reviews Robert Moss' *Chile's Marxist Experiment* (Newton-Abbot, England: David & Charles; New York: Halsted Pr., 1974), examining the Marxist regime of Salvador Allende, 1970-73, and discussing the implications of the regime for the international Left.

2812. Hudson, Rexford A. THE ROLE OF THE CONSTITUTIONAL CONFLICT OVER NATIONALIZATION IN THE DOWNFALL OF SALVADOR ALLENDE. *Inter-American Econ. Affairs 1978 31(4): 63-79.* Argues that Salvador Allende's violations of the law and constitution created the milieu in which the Chilean military was able to overthrow the regime. 31 notes.   D. A. Franz

2813. Hurley, Neil P. THE RISE AND FALL OF SALVADOR ALLENDE. *Thought 1975 50(197): 188-198.* During the three years of Salvador Allende's government a polarization of the Chilean public and a reciprocal spiral of misunderstanding and passionate hatred took place. Erroneous perceptions of reality, due in large part to differences in social conditioning, were often maintained in spite of contradictory evidence.
J. C. English

2814. Ietswaart, Heleen F. P. LABOR RELATIONS LITIGATION: CHILE, 1970-1972. *Law & Soc. Rev. 1981-82 16(4): 625-668.* On the basis of data dealing with the processing of labor grievances by state institutions in Chile in the period of 1970-72, the author argues that litigiousness—the propensity to pursue grievances—was growing during that time. The Labor Inspectorate responded positively to increased demand for justice, but the labor courts were insensitive to the process of change. Developments in litigiousness and litigation rates are analyzed in the light of the macrosocial process of change that took place at the time.
J/S

2815. Kaufman, Edy. LA POLÍTICA EXTERIOR DE LA UNIDAD POPULAR CHILENA [The foreign policy of Chile's Popular Unity government]. *Foro Int. [Mexico] 1976 17(2): 244-274.* Discusses the foreign policy of the Allende regime in Chile, characterizing it as generally successful although internal policy considerations reduced resources and talent allocated to foreign affairs. Primary and secondary sources; 101 notes.   D. A. Franz

2816. Kay, Cristobal. AGRARIAN REFORM AND THE TRANSITION TO SOCIALISM IN CHILE, 1970-1973. *J. of Peasant Studies [Great Britain] 1975 2(4): 418-445.* Examines Popular Unity's agrarian policy in the light of the failure of the revolutionary forces to capture power and initiate a transition to socialism in Chile. Although Allende's agrarian reform was extensive, drastic and rapidly executed, it nevertheless limited the peasantry's contribution to the revolutionary struggle for power. The author briefly examines the agrarian legacy left by the Christian Democratic government of Frei to the Popular Unity. The analysis includes the effect of the Allende government's agrarian program on peasant mobilization and organization, focusing on land seizures and peasant councils. Although Popular Unity's agrarian policy produced an accumulation of revolutionary forces in the rural sector, its contradictions demonstrate why socialist relations of production failed to develop.
J

2817. Kay, Cristóbal. CHILE: THE MAKING OF A COUP D'ETAT. *Sci. & Soc. 1975 39(1): 3-25.* The Chilean experience vindicates the theories that it is impossible to begin a transition to socialism while

working within a bourgeois institutional framework and that when capitalism is undergoing an acute economic crisis and is being challenged by proletarian power, the petty bourgeoisie and the middle classes will turn to the extreme political right. The case of Chile also indicates that the seizure of power must precede and not follow the revolutionary transformation of society. Based partly on personal observations.
N. Lederer

2818. Kay, Cristóbal. RÉFORME AGRAIRE ET RÉVOLUTION DANS LE CHILI D'ALLENDE [Agrarian reform and revolution in Allende's Chile]. *Études Rurales [France] 1975 (59): 51-71.* The agrarian policy of the Popular Unity movement reflects the limitations and contradictions of its political strategy. Although President Salvador Allende's agrarian reform was extensive, drastic, and rapidly executed, it nevertheless limited the peasants' contribution to the revolutionary struggle for power. After a brief examination of the rural legacy of the Christian Democrat government to the Popular Unity government, the article presents Allende's agrarian program. Analyzes peasant mobilization and organization, focusing on land seizures and peasant councils. Studies the organization and functioning of the expropriated latifundia and analyzes why socialist relations of production failed to develop. Assesses the Popular Unity agrarian policy in the light of the failure of the revolutionary forces to capture power and initiate a transition to socialism. Secondary sources; 54 notes.   J. S. Gassner

2819. Kudachkin, M. F. LUIS KORVALAN: VIDNYI DEIATEL' KOMMUNISTICHESKOGO DVIZHENIIA [Luis Corvalán: a prominent figure in the Communist movement]. *Voprosy Istorii KPSS [USSR] 1976 (9): 101-106.* Describes the revolutionary work of the Secretary General of the Chilean Communist Party under Salvador Allende.

2820. Kudachkin, M. F. OPYT BOR'BY KOMPARTII CHILI ZA EDINSTVO LEVYKH SIL I REVOLIUTSIONNYE PREOBRAZOVANIIA [The struggle of the Chilean Communist Party for unity of leftist forces and revolutionary transformation]. *Voprosy Istorii KPSS [USSR] 1974 (5): 48-60.* From its election in 1970, the Chilean government of Popular Unity headed by Salvador Allende attempted by legal and peaceful means to transform Chilean society and economy. But such a complete transformation was precluded by opposition forces in the congress, reliance on the old state apparatus by the new government, the opposition's use of illegal means including an armed coup, and failure to create armed units capable of defending the revolution. Based on published Chilean and Soviet sources; 20 notes.   L. E. Holmes

2821. Kunzle, David. ART IN CHILE'S REVOLUTIONARY PROCESS: GUERILLA MURALIST BRIGADES. *New World R. 1973 41(3): 42-53.* Describes the activities of the Ramona Parra Brigades, Communist mural painters who expressed Allende's revolutionary programs.   S

2822. Kyle, Patricia A. and Francis, Michael J. WOMEN AT THE POLLS: THE CASE OF CHILE, 1970-1971. *Comparative Pol. Studies 1978 11(3): 291-310.* Analyzes women's voting patterns from data collected in Chile's 1970 election.

2823. Landsberger, Henry A. and McDaniel, Tim. HYPERMOBILIZATION IN CHILE, 1970-1973. *World Pol. 1976 28(4): 502-541.* The accelerating mobilization of Chile's working class from 1965 onward, instead of resulting in more massive support for Salvador Allende's minority-based Popular Unity government, resulted in 1) heightened but unattainable economic demands; 2) increased support for the extreme Left (a severe threat to the regime's policies and even existence, as Allende recognized); 3) increased support for the opposition Christian Democrats; and 4) a general deauthorization of all institutions, including those tailored specifically to working-class needs. In some situations, mobilization may sweep away the remnants of an old regime. But where that is not possible or not the real issue, it may overwhelm rather than aid an already weak government, even if it is change-oriented.   J

2824. Langton, Kenneth P. and Rapoport, Ronald. SOCIAL STRUCTURE, SOCIAL CONTEXT, AND PARTISAN MOBILIZATION: URBAN WORKERS IN CHILE. *Comparative Pol. Studies 1975 8(3): 318-344.* A study of Chile under Salvador Allende shows that when workers identify subjectively with their class and hold a conflict image of politics, they tend to support the Left.

2825. Lavretski, I. R.   TOVARISHCH PREZIDENT: ZHIZN' I GE-
BEL' SAL'VADORA AL'ENDE   [The life and death of Comrade President Salvador Allende]. *Novaia i Noveishaia Istoriia [USSR] 1974 (2):
98-115, (3): 118-140, (4): 137-161.* Part I. Outlines Allende's early life and
career before 1942: his student days, conversion to socialism, political
activities, involvement with the Socialist Party of Chile, and arrest and
exile. 17 notes. Part II. Discusses Allende's political activities, 1946-70,
the influence of the Cuban revolution on him, his electoral victory in
1970, and the opposition he faced from right-wing Chilean groups which
collaborated with foreign capitalist forces. 29 notes. Part III. Examines
the right-wing political opposition to Allende's government, which led to
the coup d'etat, and Allende's death on 11 September 1973. Describes the
subsequent reign of terror directed by Allende's successor Augusto Pinochet. 37 notes.   L. Smith/A. J. Evans

2826. Lawrence, R. T.   WHY THE ARMED FORCES INTER-
VENED IN CHILE.   *Marine Corps Gazette 1978 62(2): 18-26.* Examines the background of Chile's political struggles and military
governments, 1970-74, including the junta in 1973, for which the author
voices support based on Latin American pride in its military tradition.

2827. Lehmann, David.   ALLENDE'S CHILE: THE JUDGEMENT
OF HISTORY AND THE VERDICT OF FRINGE MARXISM.
J. of Development Studies [Great Britain] 1978 14(2): 249-253. Reviews
Allende's Chile (New York: Praeger, 1976), edited by Philip O'Brien, and
Ian Roxborough's, Philip O'Brien's, and Jackie Roddick's *Chile: State
and Revolution* (London: Macmillan, 1977).

2828. Liebman, Arthur and Petras, James F.   CLASS AND STU-
DENT POLITICS IN CHILE.   *Politics and Society 1973 3(3): 329-345.*
A case study of university student radicalism in Latin America through
an examination of the working-class base of the Allende government and
the shift in the political outlook of University of Chile students, 1971-72.
Given the usual Latin American university student's social origins, "long-
term commitments to upward mobility and higher status appear as formidable obstacles to furthering student ties with radical
working-class-backed administrations." Based on primary and secondary
sources; 4 tables, 29 notes.   D. G. Nielson

2829. Loveman, Brian.   ALLENDE'S CHILE: THE PEACEFUL
ROAD TO DISASTER.   *New Scholar 1978 5(2): 309-323.* Salvador
Allende was a revolutionary in rhetoric only. He lacked the Leninist will
to move beyond the politics of reform and establish a workers' dictatorship. In his desire for a constitutional means to socialism, he failed to
disarm Chile's army, and when the time was right it destroyed both the
revolution and Allende. Small property owners and entrepreneurs distrusted Allende and joined with Allende's domestic and foreign enemies
to quiet the language of liberation by force. 35 notes.
                                                             D. K. Pickens

2830. Loveman, Brian.   UNIDAD POPULAR IN THE COUN-
TRYSIDE: NI RAZON, NI FUERZA.   *Latin Am. Perspectives 1974
1(2): 147-155.* There are many reasons for the failure of the Popular Unity
government in Chile. Among these were US intervention in Chilean
politics, lack of a unified program, lack of a revolutionary armed forces,
corruption and dissension within the coalition, and a strong multi-class
opposition. In great part, however, the failure of the Unidad Popular,
especially in the rural areas, can be attributed to a mistrust of the rural
working class and a disdain for the "peasant mentality" that led the
government to adopt an essentially conservative, statist approach to national political economy. Thus the repression of the workers and peasants
that followed the coup of 11 September 1973 is in great part the responsibility of those who adopted an elitist, statist program for 1970-73.   J

2831. Lovemen, Brian, ed., and Sasturian, Gloria, trans.   POLITICAL
POLARIZATION IN CHILE, TWO VIEWS OF THE CRISIS.
New Scholar 1974 4(2): 251-262. Presents two letters from Chile about
events of 11 September 1973, the destruction of the Allende government.
A Rightist argues that Marxist propaganda distorts events in Chile. A
moderate Leftist notes the contribution of North American business firms
to the coming of the bloody military rebellion.   D. K. Pickens

2832. Maira, Luis.   ALGUNOS ANTECEDENTES DE LA VICTO-
RIA DE LA UNIDAD POPULAR EN CHILE Y SU POSTERIOR
CONFLICTO CON ESTADOS UNIDOS   [Some antecedents of the
Popular Unity in Chile and its subsequent conflict with the United
States]. *Foro Internacional [Mexico] 1974 15(2): 252-278.* Analyzes the
political conditions contributing to the 1970 electoral victory of the Popular Unity coalition and discusses US political and economic intervention
in Chile up to the overthrow of the Allende government. Primary sources;
table, 9 notes.   D. A. Franz

2833. Marin, Gladys.   LESSONS OF CHILE.   *World Marxist Rev.
[Canada] 1977 20(7): 63-74.* An evaluation of the Popular Unity's alliances with the other Chilean political parties and its relationship to the
working class as a whole leads the author to conclude that the main
problem of the Chilean revolutionary process was that no solid and
homogeneous revolutionary leadership was brought into being.

2834. Mattelart, Armand.   NOTAS SOBRE EL "GREMIALISMO"
Y LA LÍNEA DE MASAS DE LA BURGUESÍA CHILENA
[Note on "corporatism" and the mass line of the Chilean bourgeoisie].
Casa de las Américas [Cuba] 1974 14(83): 69-84. Describes the development in the 19th and 20th centuries of bourgeois mass organizations
(*gremios,* or guilds) and their use in mass actions (truckdrivers' strikes,
etc.) to undermine the Allende government (1971-72)—a practice reflecting an ideology strikingly similar to Lenin's "mass line."

2835. Mattelart, Michele.   CHILE: EL GOLPE DE ESTADO EN
FEMENINO O CUANDO LAS MUJERES DE LA BURGUESÍA
SALEN A LA CALLE   [Chile: the women's coup d'etat or when the
women of the bourgeoisie hit the street]. *Casa de las Américas [Cuba]
1975 15(88): 75-90.* Studies the role women played in the overthrow of
the Allende government (1970-73). Shows how the reactionaries successfully utilized women in the coup d'etat and suggests the need for leftists
to learn from this experience. Depicts the role of women in the anti-
Allende movement as organizers and participants in street demonstrations, as supporters of strikes by miners and truck drivers, and as
organizers of women from all socioeconomic classes to combat the socialist government. Women in *barrio* agencies and cultural centers proved
effective organizers of women in poorer classes. Reactionaries spread
propaganda by the mass media about the evils of communism. Past
conservative governments had a poor record in granting women political
and civil rights but they realized that women were an important tool for
the coup d'etat, without giving up their reactionary views of a woman's
place. Based on newspaper sources.   H. J. Miller

2836. Millas, Orlando.   STAGES IN THE STRUGGLE.   *World
Marxist Rev. [Canada] 1977 20(2): 50-61.* Reassesses events in Chile from
1970 to 1973, when failure to defend the gains of the democratic stage in
the revolutionary process led to the temporary victory of fascist, imperialist interests.

2837. Modell, Hilary and Waitzkin, Howard.   HEALTH CARE AND
SOCIALISM IN CHILE.   *Monthly Rev. 1975 27(1): 29-41.* Analyzes
the changes in public health during the Unidad Popular government, its
dismantling by the present regime, and the relationship of health care and
social change.

2838. Morley, Morris and Smith, Steven.   IMPERIAL "REACH":
U.S. POLICY AND THE CIA IN CHILE.   *J. of Pol. and Military
Sociol. 1977 5(2): 203-216.* This study of the role of US covert activities
in Chile between 1970 and 1973 has two basic purposes: to locate the CIA
and its activities within the overall US executive branch response to the
Allende government, showing how the CIA only executes and applies
already thought out policies, and to show how peripheral nations with a
history of investment, commercial, and financial dependence on core
capitalist countries are particularly susceptible to covert politics and subversion. Briefly examines the historical roots of Chilean economic dependence on US capital, and the conditioning impact of this phenomenon on
the internal class structure, which allows us to locate the sources of
instability that plagued the Allende government throughout its tenure in
office. Concludes that the Popular Unity government in Chile was vulnerable to political and economic and financial manipulation from the outside because of the ease with which the CIA was able to locate economic
pressure points and set up liaisons inside the Chilean class structure, state,
and private institutions.   J/S

2839. Moss, Robert. THE CLOAK-AND-DAGGER CONTROVERSY. *Int. Rev. [Great Britain] 1974 (3): 19-24, 61.* Discusses the controversy surrounding the involvement of Cubans and the US Central Intelligence Agency in covert operations in the 1973 coup d'etat in Chile.

2840. Mottet, George. THE CHILEAN DRAMA. *Lock Haven R. 1974 (15): 57-64.* Traces the political and economic events leading to the fall of Salvador Allende's revolutionary government in 1973.   S

2841. Mujal-León, Eusebio M. THE COMMUNIST PARTY OF CHILE, 1969-1973: THE LIMITS OF PLURALISM. *World Affairs 1973 136(2): 132-151.*

2842. Nogee, Joseph L. and Sloan, John W. ALLENDE'S CHILE AND THE SOVIET UNION: A POLICY LESSON FOR LATIN AMERICAN NATIONS SEEKING AUTONOMY. *J. of Interamerican Studies and World Affairs 1979 21(3): 339-368.* While much has been written about Allende's fall and the US role in his downfall, the issue of the USSR's willingness to aid the Popular Unity has been unexplored. Allende's road to socialism required large financial support which the United States would not appreciably provide. The Soviet Union supplied only limited foreign aid, nothing like its support to the Cuban revolution. Table, 10 notes, ref.   T. D. Schoonover

2843. North, Liisa. THE MILITARY IN CHILEAN POLITICS. *Studies in Comparative Int. Development 1976 11(2): 73-106.* Focuses on the attempts of the Popular Unity of Chilean President Salvador Allende to neutralize the military establishment as a potential perpetrator of a coup. The military system and army officer corps are intensively analyzed and reveal the military's basically apolitical nature. The government's strategy, in both theory and practice, vis-à-vis the military is discussed, as is the strategy of the political opposition to incite a coup. Evidence indicates that military involvement in the process set in motion with the election of Allende was unavoidable, but the success of the reactionary coup which unseated him was by no means inevitable. Based on primary and secondary sources; 39 notes.   S. A. Farmerie

2844. O'Brien, Phil. SOVIETS IN EMBRYO: CHILE 1973. *Critique [Great Britain] 1973 1(2): 79-82.* Discusses the regime of Salvador Allende in Chile (1970-73), giving an analysis of Chile's beginning steps toward socialism which ended in the 1973 coup.

2845. Obyden, K. M. CHILIISKAIA REVOLIUTSIIA: USPEKHI PROBLEMY [The Chilean revolution: successes and problems]. *Novaia i Noveishaia Istoriia [USSR] 1973 (2): 20-38.* The victory of the National Front in Chile, led by Salvador Allende, was the greatest victory for the progressive forces in Latin America since the Cuban revolution. The Chilean Communists played a vital role in the victory. Salvador Allende came to power peacefully, and began to reform the country to benefit the poor, but no attempt was made to dispossess the wealthy. Local and foreign reaction began to foment internal trouble, which was, however, countered by the people in Leninist fashion. Based on Soviet and Chilean sources; 39 notes.   A. J. Evans

2846. Ogles, Richard H. EDWARD BOORSTEIN AND THE LESSONS TO BE LEARNED FROM THE CHILEAN EXPERIENCE DURING THE ALLENDE YEARS: A REVIEW ESSAY. *Rev. of Radical Pol. Econ. 1979 11(1): 62-67.* An analytical and critical review of Edward Boorstein's *Allende's Chile: an Inside View* (New York: Int. Pub., 1977), which attempts to explain the failure and eventual downfall of the Marxist Allende government in Chile. Boorstein's main error lies in arguing after the fact, in deciding what should have been done rather than what could have been done. Allende's failure to infiltrate the army, his strict reliance on Moscow, and ultimate dependence on the electoral apparatus culminated in his downfall. 19 notes.   V. L. Human

2847. Pannoni, Gregory A. OVERTHROW OF ALLENDE: AN ANALYSIS OF U.S. INVOLVEMENT. *Towson State J. of Int. Affairs 1979 13(2): 97-116.* Through economic pressure and covert weapons action (notably by the CIA) the United States sought to prevent Salvador Allende from coming to power in Chile, destabilize his government once it had attained power, and secure US-owned multinational corporations, 1970-73.

2848. Paz, Octavio and Fong, Monique, trans. THE CENTURIONS OF SANTIAGO. *Dissent 1974 21(2): 354-356.* Comments on the Chilean coup d'état and its implications for the Left in Latin America. From the Mexican journal *Plural.*   S

2849. Petras, James. NACIONALIZACIÓN, CAMBIO SOCIO-ECONÓMICO Y PARTICIPACIÓN POPULAR BAJO EL GOBIERNO DE LA UNIDAD POPULAR EN CHILE [Nationalization, socioeconomic change, and popular participation under the Popular Unity government in Chile]. *Estudios Andinos 1973 3(3): 5-24.* Examines the process of radicalization and popular political participation in four sectors of the Chilean working class during the presidency of Salvador Allende, 1970-73. The author visited a copper mine, a textile factory, the countryside, and an urban encampment of unemployed workers. Interest and participation in the political process was found to be inversely proportional to social and economic status. Employees in the nationalized copper and textile industries were more concerned with wages and working conditions. Parties of the Left found strong support in the countryside and succeeded in mobilizing the urban poor to a high degree. Based on interviews, primary documents, and secondary sources; 7 notes.   J. L. White

2850. Petras, James; Deaton, Richard; Panitch, Leo; Swartz, Don; and Whitaker, Reg. REPORT: CHILE. *Can. Dimension [Canada] 1973 9(7/8): 16 pp.* The Socialist struggle in Chile did not end with Salvador Allende's victory, rather a new and difficult phase began. The real situation in Chile had little relationship to media accounts. Allende's support had increased and the left parties were approaching an absolute majority: "Allende's Government was not overthrown because of 'economic chaos' but because it was attacking the wealth, power and prestige of Chilean propertied groups." The epitaph for Chile is "there is no parliamentary road to socialism." Illus.   E. P. Stickney

2851. Petras, James F. CHILE AFTER THE ELECTIONS. *Monthly R. 1973 25(1): 15-23.* Political opposition to the reform policies of the Allende government accounts for the economic dislocation experienced.   S

2852. Petras, James F. CHILE: NATIONALIZATION, SOCIO-ECONOMIC CHANGE AND POPULAR PARTICIPATION. *Studies in Comparative Internat. Development 1973 8(1): 24-51.* Examines inverse relationship between income level and active participation in labor organization.   S

2853. Rai, Lajpat. ALLENDISM AND ITS PROSPECTS IN LATIN AMERICA. *India Q. [India] 1974 30(1): 12-24.* Examines the rule of Salvador Allende from the viewpoint of the contradictions within the Popular Unity, the roles of the US government, ITT, the CIA, and the Chilean military, 1970-73.

2854. Ratcliffe, Richard E. CAPITALISTS IN CRISIS: THE CHILEAN UPPER CLASS AND THE SEPTEMBER 11 COUP. *Latin Am. Perspectives 1974 1(2): 78-91.* The role of the upper classes in Chile during the coup d'état which overthrew Salvador Allende.   S

2855. Rodríguez Monegal, Emir. PABLO NERUDA: LA ULTIMA PALABRA [Pablo Neruda: The last word]. *Rev. Nac. de Cultura [Venezuela] 1975/76 34(222/223): 20-34.* After his autobiographic *Memorial de Isla Negra* (1964), Pablo Neruda completed 19 books of poetry, two dramas, a volume of prose, and one of memoirs. From then until his death, he engaged in public activity, both literary and civic, working for socialism in Chile and the presidential campaigns of Salvador Allende and traveling abroad to meetings in Western Europe and Russia. In 1971, Neruda was named the Chilean Ambassador to France and received the Nobel Prize for literature. Forced to resign by illness, he returned to Chile, where he died twelve days after the military coup of 1973, which took the life of his friend Allende. Based on primary and secondary sources.   G. Pizzimenti

2856. Rossum, R. G. van NABESCHOUWING OP CHILI'S ZWARTE SEPTEMBER [Reflections in Chile's Black September]. *Wereld en Zending [Netherlands] 1973 2(6): 414-424.* Considers the role of the Church in Salvador Allende's downfall in 1973, examining the Church both in Chile and in Latin America and the influence of the European Churches.

2857. Ruiz-Tagle, Jaime. L'EXPÉRIENCE CHILIENNE FACE AUX ÉLECTIONS [The elections in Chile]. *Études [France] 1973 338(2): 225-242.* Previews situation in Chile prior to the March 1973 elections. Reviews Allende's election in 1970, agrarian reform, copper, national unity, the nationalization of private banks, partial industrial expropriation, the suppression of news media, and the reactions of the Right and Left, in the transition to socialism. Considers the peculiarities of the class struggle in a country where political parties do not coincide with the social classes.   R. K. Adams

2858. Rybáček-Mlýnková, Jiřina. CHILE UNDER ALLENDE: A BIBLIOGRAPHICAL SURVEY. *Am. Latina [Brazil] 1976 17: 32-69.* Survey of the interpretations of political events in Chile, 1970-73. The author describes the works of Marxist and non-Marxist writers. Based on books, newspapers, journal articles, academic studies, speeches, and official position papers; 108 notes, biblio.   C. B. Fitzgerald

2859. Sandri, Renato. CHILE: ANALYSIS OF AN EXPERIMENT AND A DEFEAT. *Sci. and Soc. 1976 40(2): 194-219.* The economic factor was the primary cause of the defeat of the Popular Unity, given the failure of the Allende government to effectively cope with inflation generated by the increased buying power of the masses and the lack of supplies available for purchase. Agrarian reform led to stiffened opposition on the part of rural capitalists, while expropriated lands were used for small-scale, family production rather than for the urban market. Overriding these items was the dependent nature of the Chilean economy. The Popular Unity lost the political struggle because it failed to highlight the national and democratic nature of its program. It made many mistakes in a situation in which making a single error was fatal. Translated from *Critica marxista* (1973).   N. Lederer

2860. Sergeev, F. ROL' TSRU V VOENNO-FASHISTSKOM PEREVOROTE V CHILI [The role of the CIA in the military-fascist coup in Chile]. *Novaia i Noveishaia Istoriia [USSR] 1977 (3): 91-102, (4): 101-116.* An examination of the role of the Central Intelligence Agency in the 1973 military coup which displaced the Communist government of Salvador Allende. The CIA began plotting the coup as early as 1970, when Allende was elected. The investigative journalism and disclosures of the American press about their government's involvement in Chilean politics were stage-managed by the CIA. US interference in Chile must be seen as a part of a larger pattern of interference in Latin American politics and military organization. Based on US newspapers and secondary sources; 55 notes.   D. N. Collins/S

2861. Sigmund, Paul E. ALLENDE AND THE MYTHMAKERS IN THE WAKE OF CHILE'S COUP. *Internat. Perspectives [Canada] 1974 (2): 49-53.*

2862. Sigmund, Paul E. ALLENDE IN RETROSPECT. *Problems of Communism 1974 23(3): 45-62.* Investigates the major questions left unanswered since the overthrow of President Salvador Allende in September, 1973. Allende's policies resulted in the polarization of Chilean politics, which involved the previously aloof military. His downfall resulted from specific aspects of the Chilean political system, the policies of the Allende regime, and inherent contradictions in the Marxist theory to which he appealed. Primary and secondary sources; 2 tables, 33 notes.   J. M. Lauber

2863. Sigmund, Paul E. THE DRAMA OF CHILEAN POLITICS. *Worldview 1973 16(7): 41-45.* Reviews eight works on Chilean political culture, concentrating on land reform, socialism, labor, and Salvador Allende, 1964-73.

2864. Sigmund, Paul E. THE "INVISIBLE BLOCKADE" AND THE OVERTHROW OF ALLENDE. *Foreign Affairs 1974 52(2): 322-340.* If persuasive evidence exists that the US government or US interests contributed to the overthrow of the Allende government it should be acknowledged. However, ample data show that international lending agencies and governments continued to make loans and issue credit to Chile. In fact in August 1973 Allende had more short-term credits available to him ($574 million) than when he had come to the presidency ($310 million). His regime was overthrown because of his domestic policies, not the international policies of the United States. Based on U.S. Congressional hearings, governmental publications, other

primary and secondary sources; 14 notes. (For comment, see abstract 2897).   R. Riles

2865. Sigmund, Paul E. SEEING ALLENDE THROUGH THE MYTHS. *Worldview 1974 17(4): 16-21.* Explodes leftist, rightist, and Christian Democratic myths about Salvador Allende's 1970-73 government in Chile and the military coup d'etat that overthrew him.

2866. Spence, Jack. CLASS MOBILIZATION AND CONFLICT IN ALLENDE'S CHILE: A REVIEW ESSAY. *Pol. and Soc. 1978 8(2): 131-164.* Discussion of the Allende period and eight recent works (1976-78) concerning it from a Marxist class-conflict perspective. Barbara Stallings's *Economic Development and Class Conflict in Chile, 1958-1973* (1978) provides a historical backdrop for Allende's election in 1970. Stefan De Vylder's *Allende's Chile: The Political Economy of the Rise and Fall of the Unidad Popular* (1976) draws the social implications of Allende's three-point economic program. Kyle Steenland's *Agrarian Reform under Allende* (1978) clarifies the political conditions which hindered rural reform, while Juan Espinosa and Andrew Zimbalist's *Economic Democracy: Workers' Participation in the Management of Industrial Enterprise in Chile, 1970-1973* (1978) examines these dynamics of the newly socialized industrial sector. Edward Boorstein's *Allende's Chile, An Inside View* (1977) provides insights based on the author's association with the Chile Trading Company. Ian Roxborough, Phil O'-Brien, and Jackie Roddick's *Chile: The State and Revolution* (1977) is sympathetic to the left's criticism of the Popular Unity's confidence in a parliamentary revolution. Paul Sigmund's *The Overthrow of Allende and the Politics of Chile, 1964-76* (1977) focuses on the political maneuvering preceding the coup and is critical of Allende and the Popular Unity, while Robinson Rojas Sanford's *The Murder of Allende and the End of the Chilean Way to Socialism* (1976) examines the role of the military bureaucracy in the seizure of power. Secondary sources; 33 notes.
D. G. Nielson

2867. Spence, Jack. INSTITUTIONALIZING NEIGHBORHOOD COURTS: TWO CHILEAN EXPERIENCES. *Law and Soc. Rev. 1978 13(1): 139-182.* The convergence of national competition among political parties with the development of a squatter settlement movement in the Allende period brought the issue of neighborhood courts to national attention. Two local experiments emerged, one employing professional judges holding regular informal hearings beyond their normal judicial duties for poor urban residents, the other involving left-organized squatter settlements' establishment of their own "extra-official" court systems using locally elected lay judges. The professional court tended to routinize disputes, arbitrate, and rely on state police power; the lay court tended to mediate, focus on sociological and political causes of disputes, and use formal and informal enforcement power. Both were constrained by the lack of organizational resources and clear-cut goals and reflected the class-based conflict of Chilean politics during the period.   J

2868. Stallings, Barbara and Zimbalist, Andy. THE POLITICAL ECONOMY OF THE UNIDAD POPULAR. *Latin Am. Perspectives 1975 2(1): 69-88.* Examines the economic policy of Chile's Popular Unity, 1970-73, and considers the possibility of applying the Brazilian economic model to Chile to encourage economic recovery.

2869. Steenland, Kyle. THE COUP IN CHILE. *Latin Am. Perspectives 1974 1(2): 9-29.* There were two main currents in the Popular Unity government. One believed in the "Chilean road to socialism," in the possibility of a peaceful transition. The other current believed in the necessity of preparing for an armed confrontation between the working class and government on one side, and the Armed Forces and the bourgeoisie on the other. The predominance of the group which believed in the peaceful transition meant that the Popular Unity was unprepared for the military coup. The coup took place once 1) the top Army officers who supported constitutionality were removed; 2) the armed threat of the working class *cordones* (factory districts) had become apparent; and 3) the evidence of leftist infiltration among the troops surfaced. These three factors consolidated the officers of the armed forces, enabling them to achieve a unity which was impossible before.   J

2870. Steenland, Kyle. RURAL STRATEGY UNDER ALLENDE. *Latin Am. Perspectives 1974 1(2): 129-146.* The rural policies under Allende were quantitatively but not qualitatively different from those of the previous Frei government, and the reformed sector never constituted the bulk of agricultural production or of the labor force. The rural bourgeoisie was weakened but not destroyed. The strategy of the Popular Unity in the countryside therefore suffered from the same weaknesses as it did in the cities, i.e., overreliance on bourgeois legality, insufficient control of production, and nonexistent control of distribution. The rural sector took on exceptional importance due to the increased consumption and massive imports of food with scarce dollars and the tense and nearly balanced political struggle.   J

2871. Sweezy, Paul M. THE ROAD TO SOCIALISM: CHILE. *Monthly Rev. 1975 27(6): 33-35.* Reply to Julio Faúndez on the Chilean situation during the years 1970-73, reprinted from *Social Policy,* June 1975.

2872. Tannahill, R. Neal. ALLENDE AND THE CHILEAN ARMED FORCES. *Armed Forces and Soc. 1979 5(3): 487-494.* A review essay on Robinson Rojas Sandford's, *The Murder of Allende* (New York: Harper & Row, 1975); Ian Roxborough, Phil O'Brien, and Jackie Roddick's, *Chile: The State and Revolution* (New York: Holmes & Meier, 1976); Stefan de Vylder's, *Allende's Chile: The Political Economy of the Rise and Fall of the Unidad Popular* (London: Cambridge U. Pr., Latin American Studies, no. 25, 1976); Frederick M. Nunn's, *The Military in Chilean History: Essays in Civil-Military Relations, 1810-1973* (Albuquerque: U. of New Mexico Pr., 1976). All attempt to explain why the Unidad Popular government of Salvador Allende Gossens was a "blind alley, leading the Chilean people not to socialism by peaceful means but to fascism by violent means." The answers must be found not by consideration of the military alone, but in the total political, social, and economic context.   R. V. Ritter

2873. Teitelboim, Volodia. PRELUDE TO FUTURE VICTORIES. *World Marxist R. [Canada] 1974 17(3): 83-90.* Analyzes the revolutionary strategy of Chile's Communist Party and the lessons of the 1973 coup d'etat.   S

2874. Teitelboim, Volodia. REFLECTIONS ON THE 1,000 DAYS OF POPULAR UNITY RULE. *World Marxist Rev. [Canada] 1977 20(1): 50-62.* Assesses the rule of Popular Unity in Chile and studies the methods and devices of the counterrevolutionary forces in order to eventually return Chile to popular rule.

2875. Torres-Peñuela, Julio E. LA PRENSA AL SERVICIO DEL "ORDEN": EL CASO DE CHILE [The press in the service of "order": the case of Chile]. *Estudios Centro Americanos [El Salvador] 1973 28(300): 685-704.* Discusses the concept of freedom of the press and shows how it can be distorted, and then analyzes the case of Chile (1973) during the fall of Salvador Allende to illustrate the theoretical findings.

2876. —. ASSESSING THE LITERATURE SINCE THE COUP. *Latin Am. Perspectives 1974 1(2): 156-160.* An assessment of the literature dealing with the coup d'etat which overthrew Salvador Allende and Popular Unity in Chile.   S

2877. —. CHILEAN DEFEAT CARRIES VITAL LESSONS ON BUILDING WORKERS' REVOLUTION. *Progressive Labor 1973 9(3): 11-14.* "Fascism does not fall from the sky, but is openly prepared for by the bourgeoisie. The Allende government invited the military heads to take over key ministries at the very time these men were plotting their coup. But this period of fascism's preparation can also be used for the preparation of worker's revolution—if revolutionaries draw a clear line between themselves and the fake socialists like Allende and the 'Communist' Party."   J

2878. Valdés, Pablo. CHILE IN SEARCH OF A NEW DESTINY. *Secolas Ann. 1973 4: 71-79.* Gives an overview of Chilean politics, society, and economy from 1830 to the present and describes the achievements and problems of Salvador Allende's regime. One of eight papers on Cuba and Chile read at the annual meeting of the Southeastern Conference on Latin American Studies.   S

2879. Valenzuela, Arturo. IL CROLLO DELLA DEMOCRAZIA IN CILE [The breakdown of democracy in Chile]. *Riv. Italiana di Scienza Pol. [Italy] 1975 5(1): 83-129.* The Chilean election of 1970 brought into office a minority coalition dominated by Marxist parties dedicated to a fundamental transformation of that country's social and political structures within the framework of democratic institutions. From the outset the experiment of President Salvador Allende encountered a multiplicity of constraints inherent in Chile's highly polarized political system. The Popular Unity government was simply not able to deviate substantially from the incrementalist style of Chilean politics with its overriding concern for wage readjustments and particularistic transactions, nor was it able to overcome the sharp rivalries among the parties of its own coalition, some of which continually pressured the government to move faster in changing society. At the same time, elements, both foreign and domestic, wedded to the status quo reacted with vigor at any encroachment on their privileges.   J

2880. Valenzuela, Arturo and Valenzuela, J. Samuel. VISIONS OF CHILE. *Latin Am. Res. Rev. 1975 10(3): 155-176.* Bibliographical and historiographical review of 31 books pertaining to the junta, 1970-73.

2881. Vanderwood, Paul. LATIN AMERICA IN FERMENT: THE VISION OF SAUL LANDAU. *Film & Hist. 1975 5(1): 1-7, 23.* One of three articles in a special issue on Latin American history in film. Concentrates on Saul Landau's film *Que Hacer?* [What is to be done?], about the 1970 accession of Salvador Allende to the presidency of Chile. Landau attempts to raise the political awareness of his viewers, specifically American audiences.   S

2882. Vincenot, Jacques. LA NATIONALISATION DES BANQUES AU CHILI [The nationalization of banks in Chile]. *Nouvelle Rev. des Deux Mondes [France] 1981 (7): 68-73.* Discusses the procedure of nationalization of banks in Chile under Chilean President Salvador Allende, 1970-73.

2883. Vuskovic, Pedro Bravo. SIGNIFICACIÓN LATINOAMERICANA DE LA EXPERIENCIA CHILENA RECIENTE [The Latin American significance of the recent Chilean experience]. *Foro Int. [Mexico] 1974 15(2): 145-163.* Discusses dependent capitalism in Chile, the attempt to break from it through an indigenous socialist response led by the Popular Unity government, and the return to dependence and neofascism under a military government.   D. A. Franz

2884. Wallis, Victor. IMPERIALISM AND THE "VIA CHILENA." *Latin Am. Perspectives 1974 1(2): 44-57.* Attempts to lay the groundwork for comparisons between the Chilean experience under Allende and any possible future attempts at using legal accession to office for revolutionary ends. The uniqueness of the Chilean case, apart from its being the first, is seen to lie in the degree of foreign domination which prevailed at the outset. Examines in detail how the issue of foreign domination contributed to Allende's victory. Discusses both the direct and the indirect role of imperialism in bringing about his downfall, and concludes with some reflections on how a "legal approach" might work in advanced countries.   J

2885. Whitehead, Laurence. SALVADOR ALLENDES UNTERGANG [Salvador Allende's end]. *Europa Archiv [West Germany] 1973 28(22): 767-780.* Salvador Allende, facing the hostility not only of the Chilean Right but also of US business and government, could have avoided the coup d'etat only by voluntarily giving up his power.

2886. Whitehead, Laurence. WHY ALLENDE FELL. *World Today [Great Britain] 1973 29(11): 461-473.* "The extreme polarization of political forces before the coup aggravated the regime's economic difficulties and thereby made confrontation unavoidable. In the final analysis, the *Unidad Popular* was the almost inevitable victim."   J

2887. Winn, Peter and Kay, Cristobal. AGRARIAN REFORM AND RURAL REVOLUTION IN ALLENDE'S CHILE. *J. of Latin Am. Studies [Great Britain] 1974 6(1): 135-159.* "The most profound land reform in history without violent revolution" was accomplished in Chile between 1967 and mid-1972. The conservative Alessandri government initiated it in its 1962 land reform laws, Frei's coalition government implemented and expanded it in its 1967 law, and Allende's *Unidad Popular* coalition completed the reform between 1970 and 1972, chiefly by interpreting and applying the 1967 law in the most radical ways possible. The results were the end of the *latifundio,* the redistribution of

those lands to transitional peasant cooperatives and some state farms, and a massive redistribution of income. Income redistribution led to a sharp increase in the demand for food and clothing, which, in spite of maintaining productivity, has in turn led to increased imports in an economy already suffering from an unfavorable trade balance. Thus, by 1973, agrarian reform was subordinated to the government's broader economic policies. Based on government documents and secondary works; 23 notes.
K. M. Bailor

2888. Winn, Peter. LOOSING THE CHAINS: LABOR AND THE CHILEAN REVOLUTIONARY PROCESS, 1970-1973. *Latin Am. Perspectives 1976 3(1): 70-84.* Salvador Allende was elected largely on the support of the working class, united by a history of social solidarity and struggle, but divided by differences in social origin, income, age, and consciousness. Chilean workers were rewarded with redistributive policies and increased political access. The Allende victory transformed the Chilean working class into an active protagonist of change, which ultimately came into conflict with the more legalistic reforms of Popular Unity. The result was a paralyzing polarization of consciousness and politics within the working class, which took a counterrevolution to erase.
J. L. Dietz

2889. Woll, Allen L. THE COMIC BOOK IN A SOCIALIST SOCIETY: ALLENDE'S CHILE, 1970-1973. *J. of Popular Culture 1976 9(4): 1039-1045.* Salvador Allende's government politicized all facets of life in Chile, and attempted to force artists to take a political stand. The government attempted to limit American influence in all areas of life. Walt Disney comic books were seen as capitalist propaganda, and their view of underdeveloped nations as inhabited by savages smacked of imperialism. In 1971 the government began printing *La Firme*, a comic book in which the characters desired only peace and security without the accumulation of capital. Rich women were shown as ornate caricatures, and businessmen were portrayed as bourgeois fools; only workers were seen with some nobility. Americans, especially CIA agents, became the villains. *La Firme* was discontinued after the 1973 coup, and replaced again by Disney comics. 12 notes.
J. W. Leedom

2890. Yanez, Alexandro and Banchero, Gabriel. CHILE: CONTINUING CONFRONTATION. *World Marxist R. [Canada] 1973 16(9): 95-101.* In Chile there is a continuing confrontation between the reactionaries supported by U.S. commercial interests and Allende's Popular Unity government.
S

2891. Zapata S., Francisco. THE CHILEAN LABOR MOVEMENT UNDER SALVADOR ALLENDE: 1970-1973. *Latin Am. Perspectives 1976 3(1): 85-97.* Analyzes the relation of the Central Unica de Trabajadores (CUT) to the Salvador Allende government and the role of labor and labor management under Popular Unity. Considers some of the problems encountered by a labor movement in the transition to socialism and specifically along the "Chilean road to socialism."
J. L. Dietz

2892. Zimbalist, Andrew. THE DYNAMIC OF WORKER PARTICIPATION: AN INTERPRETIVE ESSAY ON THE CHILEAN AND OTHER EXPERIENCES. *Administration and Society 1975 7(1): 43-54.* Discusses "some of the analytical implications of our survey on worker participation in management in Chilean socialized industry during the Allende period."
S

2893. Zimbalist, Andrew. WORKERS' CONTROL: ITS STRUCTURE UNDER ALLENDE. *Monthly R. 1974 25(10): 39-43.* Examines the successes and failures of socialized labor under the Allende regime in Chile.
S

2894. Zimbalist, Andy and Stallings, Barbara. SHOWDOWN IN CHILE. *Monthly R. 1973 25(5): 1-24.* Recounts the political and economic conditions in Chile during the last year of Salvador Allende's socialist regime.
S

2895. —. CHILE: AN UNPRECEDENTED SITUATION. *Monthly Rev. 1973 24(9): 30-34.* Two anonymous communications from Chile describing the political situation at the end of 1972.

2896. —. CHILE AND THE WORLD BANK. *Inter-Am. Econ. Affairs 1976 30(2): 81-91.* Reprint of a World Bank background paper dated September 1974 reviewing its actions in Chile during the Allende regime.
D. A. Franz

2897. —. CHILE: WHAT WAS THE U.S. ROLE? *Foreign Policy 1974 (16): 126-156.*
Farnsworth, Elizabeth. MORE THAN ADMITTED, pp. 127-141. Challenges Paul E. Sigmund's *Foreign Affairs* article (see abstract 2864). Cites various authorities, including US officials and bankers, to prove that the US used economic weapons and pressures to weaken Salvador Allende. By denying loans and credit to Chile, the US Export-Import Bank initiated an "invisible blockade." Based partially on primary sources. 11 notes.
Sigmund, Paul E. LESS THAN CHARGED, pp. 142-156. Farnsworth commits factual errors and errs from lack of documentation, jumps to illogical conclusions, and fails to see Allende's contribution to his own downfall. Denies that there was an "invisible blockade," conceding that the US did delay help. Allende hurt himself politically by counterproductive economic policies, such as the redistribution of income and the expropriation of farms. Primary and secondary sources; 11 notes.
R. F. Kugler

2898. —. EL APARATO CONTRARREVOLUCIONARIO DE LOS ESTADOS UNIDOS: LA OFENSIVA CHILENA [The counterrevolutionary apparatus of the United States: the Chilean offensive]. *Casa de las Américas [Cuba] 1975 16(92): 3-28.* Discusses the Chilean response to US imperialism since 1970, including military, paramilitary, corporate, and CIA intervention in Chile, detailing the covert but continuing fight against imperialism.

2899. —. [UNDERSTANDING CHILE: A PEACE RESEARCHER'S DILEMMA]. *J. of Peace Res. [Norway] 1974 11(2): 95-113.*
Krippendorff, Ekkehart. CHILE, VIOLENCE AND PEACE RESEARCH, pp. 95-103. The defeat of Chile's Popular Unity, 1970-73, demonstrates the futility of nonviolence in achieving social reform and requires a reassessment of the assumptions of peace researchers.
Rivera, Deodato. LET US FACE CHILE, YES: BUT WHICH CHILE? pp. 105-113. Krippendorff's article is nonfactual, which the author demonstrates through analysis of Chilean social classes and the supposed irreversibility of Chilean affairs as well as the importance of foreign influence on the 1973 coup.

The Pinochet Regime since 1973

2900. Agor, Weston H. PUBLIC SUPPORT FOR THE MILITARY GOVERNMENT OF CHILE. *Freedom at Issue 1976 (37): 12-14.* Discusses Chilean public opinion of the military government in power there since 1973, comparing that government's record of violence and negation of civil liberties to that of the government of Salvador Allende, 1970-73.

2901. Alarcón, Haydée. A CHILEAN WOMAN SPEAKS. *Monthly Rev. 1977 29(1): 58-62.* A Chilean dentist who participated in public health reform during the Popular Unity period, 1970-73, recalls the political imprisonment and torture of women following the coup d'etat of 1973.

2902. Alexander, Robert J. CHILE A YEAR AFTER THE MILITARY COUP. *Freedom at Issue 1974 (28): 4-6, 15-20.*

2903. Angell, Alan. CHILE AFTER FIVE YEARS OF MILITARY RULE. *Current Hist. 1979 76(444): 58-61, 88-89.* General Augusto Pinochet Ugarte has controlled Chile since 1973, despite the uproar over the 1976 Orlando Letelier assassination and popular opposition.

2904. Angell, Alan. CHILE ONE YEAR AFTER THE COUP. *Current Hist. 1975 68(401): 11-14, 42.* Describes the repressive nature of the military junta, economic conditions in Chile, and US involvement in Chilean politics during the Allende government.
S

2905. Angell, Alan. THE CHILEAN ROAD TO MILITARISM. *Internat. J. [Canada] 1974 29(3): 393-411.* Explains the unexpected brutality of the counterrevolution following the long-expected fall of the Allende government. 15 notes.   R. V. Kubicek

2906. Arroyo, Gonzalo. NOTA SOBRE LA IGLESIA Y LOS CRISTIANOS DE IZQUIERDA A LA HORA DEL PUTSCH EN CHILE [A note about the Church and the Christians of the Left at the time of the coup in Chile]. *Latin Am. Perspectives 1975 2(1): 89-99.* Examines the role played by the Catholic Church following the coup d'etat in Chile and analyzes the options left to revolutionary Christians by the victorious putschists and the Church's accommodation with them.

2907. Bianchi, Soledad. EL MOVIMIENTO ARTISTICO CHILENO EN EL CONFLICTO POLITICO ACTUAL [The Chilean artistic movement in the current political conflict]. *Casa de las Américas [Cuba] 1982 22(130): 146-154.* The institutionalization of the Chilean military government has affected the system of education, daily life, and the arts. Describes the cultural policy of the regime, its stages, and its effects on artistic life. The artists have been living in a strategy of survival which has affected their means of expression. Social relations have lost their transparency, which could lead to hypocrisy, atomization, and withdrawal of the individual into private life. However, many think that the hermetic passivity and immobilism could be just the conditions for the preservation of tradition and of memory, which would again come to the surface at the moment of an eventual institutional break. 21 notes.
J. V. Coutinho

2908. Bizzarro, Salvatore. CHILE UNDER THE JACKBOOT. *Current Hist. 1976 70(413): 57-60, 81-83.* Since its takeover in 1973, the military regime of Augusto Pinochet Ugarte in Chile has faced economic failure and mounting opposition to its violations of human rights.

2909. Calderón, José. APUNTES SOBRE LA REFORMA AGRARIA CHILENA [Points on Chile's agrarian reform]. *Foro Internacional [Mexico] 1974 15(2): 292-302.* Discusses Chilean agrarian reform, 1965-73, and action taken by the military government since 1973 to nullify it. Secondary sources; note.   D. A. Franz

2910. Castillo, Rene. LESSONS AND PROSPECTS OF THE REVOLUTION. *World Marxist R. [Canada] 1974 17(8): 107-116.* Analyzes the actions which the Communist Party and other democratic elements in Chile must take in order to depose the country's military junta.   S

2911. Catalán, Oscar and Arrate, Jorge. CHILE: LA POLÍTICA DEL RÉGIMEN MILITAR Y LAS NEUVAS FORMAS DE DESARROLLO EN AMÉRICA LATINA [Chile: the politics of the military regime and new modes of development in Latin America]. *Bol. de Estudios Latinoamericanos y del Caribe [Netherlands] 1978 (25): 51-71.* Chile's military government has implemented monetarist development policies, 1973-78, similar to those in vogue elsewhere in Latin America. It has emphasized capital accumulation for investment in domestic industries potentially profitable in international markets. This program, beneficial chiefly to multinational corporations has been promoted at the expense of the rest of Chilean society, including the middle sectors and industrialists unaffiliated to international capitalism. As the regime's inept political and ideological tactics have failed to win support for its unpopular economic policies, only repression and coercion have ensured public compliance. Based on data in Chilean and European publications, and secondary sources; 10 tables, 11 notes.
D. M. Cregier

2912. Chossudovsky, Michel. CHICAGO ECONOMICS, CHILEAN STYLE. *Monthly Rev. 1975 26(11): 14-17.* Discusses the repercussions of the economic policy of Chile's military junta.

2913. Collins, Joseph D. ESTUDIO DE UN CASO: LA GUERRA ECONÓMICA CONTRA CHILE [Case study: the economic war against Chile]. *Rev. Mexicana de Ciencias Pol. y Soc. [Mexico] 1975 21(81): 131-151.* Examines US intervention in the economic development in Chile after the 1973 coup d'etat and exposes the US disclaimer of involvement in Chilean political affairs.

2914. DeVylder, Stefan. CHILE 1973-81: ETT EKONOMISKT LABORATORIUM [Chile, 1973-81: an economic laboratory]. *Int. Pol. [Norway] 1982 (2): 311-335.* Since 1973, Chile has been converted into a test case of neoliberal economic theories. The coherence with which these theories have been put into practice gives Chile under Augusto Pinochet an importance which goes far beyond the Chilean borders. This article is an assessment of the ends, means, and major economic results of this experiment. Divides economic development since 1973 into three phases, hyperstagflation, 1973-75, recovery, 1976-80, and, finally, the present crisis, which began in the latter half of 1981 and which has been aggravated during 1982. Assesses the policies pursued with the help of 10 preliminary conclusions, which all point in the same direction: the "Chilean model" does not seem to represent a road to social and economic progress.   J/S

2915. Drake, Paul W. CORPORATISM AND FUNCTIONALISM IN MODERN CHILEAN POLITICS. *J. of Latin Am. Studies [Great Britain] 1978 10(1): 83-116.* Since 1973, the Chilean junta has made "the most concerted attempt at corporate government in Chilean history," primarily inspired by two indigenous sources: one, the private economic organizations *(gremios)* which have traditionally mediated between individuals and the state; and two, the persistent undercurrents of politico-ideological corporatism which emerged in the early 20th century, which included minor political parties, theorists, and movements and which also was often influenced by and paralleled contemporary European trends since World War I. Secondary studies; 85 notes.   K. M. Bailor

2916. Falabella, Gonzalo. LES SYNDICATS SOUS UN RÉGIME AUTORITAIRE: LE CAS DU CHILI [Labor unions under an authoritarian regime: the Chile case]. *Problèmes d'Amérique Latine [France] 1980 (58): 143-173.* A study of the evolution in the situation of labor unions in Chile since 1974 and their resistance to the restrictive measures of the Pinochet government.

2917. Fazio, Hugio. RESULTS OF JUNTA RULE. *World Marxist Rev. [Canada] 1976 19(12): 94-97.* Examines the economic situation of Chile following the 1973 coup, comparing it to Chilean economy, 1960.

2918. Fazio, Hugo. THE DARK NIGHT WILL END. *World Marxist R. [Canada] 1975 18(5): 128-133.* Discusses economic conditions and the Communist Party in Chile, 1974-75.   S

2919. Figueroa, Humberto. INTERNATIONAL SOLIDARITY IN ACTION. *World Marxist Rev. [Canada] 1976 19(11): 89-91.* A 60th birthday tribute to Luis Corvalán, leader in the Chilean Communist Party and symbol of liberation against the fascist regime which overthrew Salvador Allende in 1973.

2920. Garcés, Joan E. WORLD EQUILIBRIUM, CRISIS AND MILITARIZATION OF CHILE. *J. of Peace Res. [Norway] 1974 11(2): 81-93.*

2921. Garreaud, Jacqueline and Kauffmann, Lane. THE COUP IN CHILE AND THE DEATH OF NERUDA, INTERVIEWS AND COMMENTARY FROM RADIO-TELEVISION BELGIUM. *New Scholar 1975 5(1): 143-159.* Presents extracts from a videotape program made by Radio-Television Belgium in Santiago, Chile, covering the events of the 1974 coup d'état and its aftermath.

2922. Gonzalez, Heliodoro. ARMS-SALES POLICY: THE CHILEAN CASE. *Inter-American Econ. Affairs 1980 34(3): 3-24.* Reviews Great Britain's 1980 decision to lift its arms embargo against Chile, and the US decision in the same year to cease all deliveries of military equipment to Chile.

2923. Grenier, Philippe. LE CHILI DU GÉNÉRAL PINOCHET [Chile under General Pinochet]. *Problèmes d'Amérique Latine [France] 1980 (58): 9-68.* An overall study of the economic and social situation in Chile since General Augusto Pinochet took over the government (1973), including the regime's political evolution, economic reorganization and its social consequences, and repression and resistance.

2924. Grishaev, P. I. FARS S "LIBERALIZATSIEI" FASHISTSKOGO REZHIMA V CHILI [The farce of "liberalizing" the fascist regime in Chile]. *Sovetskoe Gosudarstvo i Pravo [USSR] 1980 (5): 110-116.* The fascist military junta that seized power in Chile in a coup d'etat on 11 September 1973 has attempted to create an atmosphere of liberalization, particularly through disclosure in October 1978 of a draft of a new constitution. Analysis of this draft reveals that it provides the opportunity for the military to concentrate power in its own hands and to prevent representatives of the people from participating in the administration of the country. Articles in the Fundamental Law of 1925 guaranteeing citizens' rights to take part in the political, social, and economic life of the country have been excluded from the draft, political parties have been dissolved, and trade unions have been placed under strict junta supervision.   J/S

2925. Guy, Jim. THE CASE OF THE MAPUCHE AND CHILE'S "BAD" LAW 2568. *Int. Perspectives [Canada] 1981 (Sept-Oct): 14-16.* The Mapuche, a tribe of about a half million Indians, mostly concentrated in Chile's province of Cautín, appear to be the chief victims of a law passed by the Pinochet government in March 1979. The new law, which threatens to terminate the practice of communal title to Indian lands, is already having disastrous consequences for the Mapuche, and may ultimately result in the destruction of their institutions, customs, language, and religion. Their only hope is that international pressure can be brought upon Chile by means of international groups such as the Toronto-based World Council of Indigenous People.   E. Palais

2926. Hurtado-Beca, Cristina. CHILE 1973-1981: DESARTICULACION Y REESTRUCTURACION AUTORITARIA DEL MOVIMIENTO SINDICAL [Chile 1973-81: arbitrary disarticulation and restructuring of the labor movement]. *Bol. de Estudios Latinoamericanos y del Caribe [Netherlands] 1981 (31): 91-117.* Since 1973 the Chilean labor movement has been deprived of its traditionally strong voice in Chilean politics and has been restructured by the authoritarian Chilean government. The Labor Code has been modified to diminish labor's power and other "reforms" have further limited the effectiveness of labor organization and political action. Nevertheless, the labor movement in Chile continues to maintain its organization and support of the Left. The real value of wages slipped substantially between 1971 and 1981. Primary sources; 82 notes, 8 tables.   R. L. Woodward, Jr.

2927. Hurtado-Beca, Cristina. LE PROCESSUS D'INSTITUTIONNALISATION AU CHILI [The making of new institutions in Chile]. *Problèmes d'Amérique Latine [France] 1980 (58): 78-101.* Chilean President Augusto Pinochet's constitutional actions since 1973.

2928. Jencks, Christopher. EQUALITY: LAISSEZ-FAIRE ECONOMICS AND REPRESSIVE POLITICS. *Working Papers for a New Soc. 1977 4(4): 8-10.* The free market and laissez-faire economic policy of the military junta of Chile has made the rich richer and other classes of society poorer and has led to political repression, 1973-76.

2929. Jofré, Manuel A. LITERATURA CHILENA DE TESTIMONIO [Witness literature from Chile]. *Casa de las Américas [Cuba] 1981 22(129): 150-156.* Examines works written by Chileans in Chile and abroad after the 1973 coup that overthrew the government of Salvador Allende. The themes these works treat are not literary themes but nuclear units of lived experience, where human life is portrayed in its fullness. They are introspective works that delve into the subjective life of individuals deprived of the possibility of choice and forced to define themselves in other terms.   J. V. Coutinho

2930. Kehoe, Mary. CHILE: DEATH OF A DEMOCRACY. *Can. Labour 1974 19(1): 28-35.* The Chilean military coup which toppled Salvador Allende has damaged workers' economic security and their human rights.   S

2931. Knudson, Jerry W. THE CHILEAN PRESS SINCE ALLENDE. *Gazette: Int. J. for Mass Communication Studies [Netherlands] 1981 27(1): 5-20.* Although Salvador Allende's regime engaged in some efforts to stifle freedom of the press, the Chilean mass media have suffered much more under the Pinochet government. Not only has the number of newspapers declined, but those still being published generally follow a policy of self-censorship in order to avoid problems with the authorities. More critical of the government are the nation's magazines, although in this sector also there exists self-censorship and restraint.

Radio and television are effectively muted by government control. The Chilean media are not now in as bad a position as they were during the early days of Pinochet's rule, but this improvement seems threatened by a proposed new constitution. Based on interviews and secondary sources; 41 notes.   J. S. Coleman

2932. Labbé, Dominique and Montès, Arturo. L'HYPER-INFLATION: STRATÉGIE ÉCONOMIQUE DE LA JUNTE CHILIENNE [Hyperinflation: the Chilean junta's economic strategy]. *Esprit [France] 1976 461(10): 377-391.* The junta's political strategy since 1973 has been to leave galloping inflation in Chile unrestrained in order to hide its economic policy of reducing the standard of living of the masses while increasing the income of the privileged classes. The result has been a 50% drop in labor income and the collapse of domestic markets.

2933. Laffitte, Bernard. L'ARMÉE ET LE POUVOIR AU CHILI [The army and power in Chile]. *Défense Natl. [France] 1974 30(11): 51-66.* Examines the history of Chile to explain the most violent of Latin American military coups d'etat in September 1973, and also considers the problems which subsequently confronted the Chilean junta.

2934. Lagos, Ricardo and Rufatt, Oscar A. MILITARY GOVERNMENT AND REAL WAGES IN CHILE: A NOTE. *Latin Am. Res. Rev. 1975 10(2): 139-146.* Real wages for Chile's lower classes plummeted in the first year the military junta was in power; the economic situation could be summed up in the words of a Brazilian general: "the economy is doing fine, it is the people who are doing badly."

2935. Letelier, Orlando. ECONOMIC 'FREEDOM'S' AWFUL TOLL: THE 'CHICAGO BOYS' IN CHILE. *Rev. of Radical Pol. Econ. 1976 8(3): 44-52.* Discusses the effects of Chicago school economic theorists (notably Milton Friedman) on the economic policies of Chile and especially the irresponsibility of their aid to the Pinochet government.

2936. Mauro Marini, Ruy. ECONOMÍA POLÍTICA DE UN GOLPE MILITAR [Political economy of a military coup]. *Foro Internacional [Mexico] 1974 15(2): 279-291.* Discusses the economic policies of the Popular Unity government and the succeeding military regime in Chile. Secondary sources; 6 notes.   D. A. Franz

2937. Millas, Orlando. ECONOMIC CHAOS IN CHILE; ONE YEAR OF JUNTA MISRULE. *World Marxist R. [Canada] 1974 17(9): 113-122.* Military junta policies after the coup of 1973 have depressed Chile's economy.   S

2938. Mistral, Carlos. CHILE: THE MILITARY JUNTA AND ITS PERSPECTIVES. *Monthly R. 1974 25(10): 28-38.* Discusses the social, economic, and political ramifications of the Chilean military takeover of 1973.   S

2939. Moreno, Francisco José. THE BREAKDOWN OF CHILEAN DEMOCRACY. *World Affairs 1975 138(1): 19-25.* Examines the role of the military and of the Christian Democrats in recent Chilean politics.   S

2940. Nef, Jorge. THE POLITICS OF REPRESSION: THE SOCIAL PATHOLOGY OF THE CHILEAN MILITARY. *Latin Am. Perspectives 1974 1(2): 58-77.*

2941. Nunn, Frederick M. MILITARY-CIVILIAN RELATIONS IN CHILE: THE LEGACY OF THE GOLPE OF 1973. *Inter-Am. Econ. Affairs 1975 29(2): 43-58.* Explores the effect of the Chilean coup of 1973 on civil-military relations, speculates on the character of continuing military or reconstituted civilian government, and concludes that "the armed forces are now a vital component of Chilean political life." Primary and secondary sources; 20 notes.   D. A. Franz

2942. Petras, James F. CHILE AND LATIN AMERICA. *Monthly Rev. 1977 28(9): 13-24.* Discusses the consolidation of the dictatorship in Chile and social conditions there, 1973-77, especially economic planning and the role of the University of Chicago economists.

2943. Petras, James F. and Morley, Morris. CHILEAN DESTABILISATION AND ITS AFTERMATH: AN ANALYSIS AND A CRI-

TIQUE. *Politics [Australia] 1976 11(2): 140-148.* The conservative interpretation of the overthrow of Allende has been weakened by new evidence. US influence in the Christian Democratic Party and rightist political forces helped to weaken the democratically elected Allende regime. CIA-directed funding and penetration of Chilean military forces during the Allende regime caused further economic disruption which led to the coup and allowed much US influence in the financing and designing of postcoup military regime policies. Contrary to media reports, the economy experienced a sharp increase in productivity particularly in the socialized sector. The short-range result of the September 1973 coup has been to redistribute political and economic power from the working class to the upper classes, confirming the thesis that the coup was not the product of impersonal forces reacting to a crisis, but an attempt to restore the former power of the Chilean upper classes and foreign US power. 31 notes.   K. A. McLean

2944. Pike, Fredrick B. CHILEAN LOCAL GOVERNMENT AND SOME REFLECTIONS ON DEPENDENCE. *Inter-American Econ. Affairs 1977 31(2): 63-70.* A review of Arturo Valenzuela's book *Political Brokers in Chile: Local Government in a Centralized Polity* (Durham: U. of North Carolina Pr., 1977) is the basis for a discussion of political dependence in Chile and other areas. Contends that in the Chilean case, international political dependence may well be a logical extension of internal local political dependence and that political dependence is not necessarily a negative condition. Based on quotations from reviewed text; 2 notes.   D. A. Franz

2945. Pollock, John and Dickinson, Torry. APOLOGISTS FOR TERROR: THE CHILEAN JUNTA AND THE U.S. PRESS. *Worldview 1974 17(3): 27-32.* Following the 1973 military coup which overthrew the regime of the Marxist Salvador Allende in Chile, the junta leaders and leading US newspapers agreed that economic and social dislocation justified the coup; threats to political stability were exclusively leftist in origin and justified repression; and the military was trustworthy because it was nonpolitical.

2946. Prieto, Roberto. FIVE WEEKS IN JUNTA TORTURE CHAMBERS; LETTER TO THE EDITOR. *World Marxist R. [Canada] 1974 17(2): 109-112.* A Communist Party member describes his imprisonment after the 1973 military coup in Chile.   S

2947. Remmer, Karen L. POLITICAL DEMOBILIZATION IN CHILE, 1973-1978. *Comparative Pol. 1980 12(3): 275-301.* Discusses the process of demobilization resulting from the military coup of 11 September 1973 and examines its relationship to the central policy goals of the Chilean junta. High levels of coercion and political repression characterized the process of demobilization as a special effort was made to control the chief vehicles for spreading political awareness, the trade unions and the political parties. Demobilization created problems to replace those it solved. The coercive measures applied to group political activity deprived the junta of the resources that it needed to reach its long-term goals. Based on survey data and newspapers; 2 tables, 100 notes.   M. A. Kascus

2948. Remmer, Karen L. PUBLIC POLICY AND REGIME CONSOLIDATION: THE FIRST FIVE YEARS OF THE CHILEAN JUNTA. *J. of Developing Areas 1979 13(4): 441-461.* Analyzes the process whereby authoritarian regimes consolidate their power and attempt to restructure the political order focusing on the coup of 1973 in Chile, a nation with a long tradition of formal democracy. Findings included a high level of political repression; junta efforts to restucture the economy along free enterprise principles by stimulating private investments, removing free market restrictions, and reallocating productive resources, and drastic cutbacks in the number of government employees. In 1978, however, GNP levels were below those of 1970-72. But inflation fell from 505% in 1974 to 30% in 1978 and the national balance of payments improved, while unemployment reached its highest level in 40 years. Support for the military government gradually eroded and high levels of repression remained necessary for the junta to continue in control. 107 notes.   O. W. Eads, Jr.

2949. Rivas Espejo, Mario. LIBÉRALISME ÉCONOMIQUE ET ESPACE RURAL AU CHILI DEPUIS 1973 [Economic imperialism and rural space in Chile since 1973]. *Études Rurales [France] 1980 (77):*

21-37. Discusses the agricultural counterreform which has been taking place in Chile since 1973 and which aims to develop a capitalist agriculture oriented toward export. The introduction of liberal economic ideas into the domain of agriculture has substantially transformed its characteristics, as it has put an end to the method of development induced by the two previous agricultural reforms. Measures taken include the selling of public land to private owners and the concentration of capital in the hands of a new rural bourgeoisie able to integrate agricultural and industrial concerns. Beside this new bourgeoisie, a peasant population still exists but is being pauperized or turned into a proletariat. Shows the rationality of economic liberalism and concludes that solving the agricultural problem in Chile does not depend on the transformation of the agricultural structure, but on a total questioning of society.   J

2950. Rosenkranz-Schikler, Hernán. ACTITUDES NORTEAMERICANAS HACIA LA JUNTA MILITAR CHILENA: CONTINUIDAD Y CAMBIO, 1973-1978 [North American attitudes toward the Chilean military junta: continuity and change, 1973-78]. *Foro Int. [Mexico] 1981 22(1): 70-89.* Examines official US attitudes toward Chile and US private investment in the country. Based on primary and secondary sources; 5 tables, 29 notes.   D. A. Franz

2951. Rosett, Claudia. CHILE'S ECONOMIC REVOLUTION. *Reason 1982 13(12): 32-39.* Discusses the free-market economic policy recommendations of Roberto Kelly and his colleagues at Chile's Catholic University, 1972-73. The reforms were enacted in part in 1973 and almost in their entirety in 1975.

2952. Touraine, A. and Frachon, G. LA VOIE CHILIENNE: LE PAYS DE LA PEUR [The Chilean way: the country of fear]. *Esprit [France] 1973 (11): 582-610.* An outline of the long- and short-range causes of the revolution that overthrew Salvador Allende in Chile and a description of the state of mind of the people of Santiago after the overthrow.   G. F. Jewsbury

2953. Valenzuela, Arturo. EIGHT YEARS OF MILITARY RULE IN CHILE. *Current Hist. 1982 81(472): 64-68, 88.* After seven years in office, the military government of General Augusto Pinochet in Chile is very weak, and any significant economic or political crisis—say, a split within the armed forces or increased repression against the middle classes —could easily undermine the present regime.

2954. VanRossum, R. G. CHILI, EEN ARZELENDE KERK [Chile, a wavering Church]. *Wereld en Zending [Netherlands] 1976 5(3): 162-171.* Despite an impressive program of charitable work, 1973-76, the Catholic Church in Chile by its failure to condemn the military government formed in 1973 has done a disservice to the cause of evangelization.

2955. Whitehead, Laurence. THE CHILEAN DICTATORSHIP. *World Today [Great Britain] 1976 32(10): 366-375.* Examines the Chilean dictatorship of Augusto Pinochet, citing three motives for his takeover: to rescue the economy, prove a monetarist doctrine, and restore class rule; touches on economic conditions and opposition forces within the country, 1973-76.

2956. Winn, Peter. THE ECONOMIC CONSEQUENCES OF THE CHILEAN COUNTER REVOLUTION: AN INTERIM ASSESSMENT. *Latin Am. Perspectives 1974 1(2): 92-105.*

2957. Zapata, Francisco. LAS RELACIONES ENTRE LA JUNTA MILITAR Y LOS TRABAJADORES CHILENOS: 1973-1978 [Relations between the military junta and Chilean workers 1973-78]. *Foro Int. [Mexico] 1979 20(2): 191-219.* Examines government-labor relations from 1973 to 1978 in an attempt to characterize current (1978) state-labor relations. 4 tables, 12 notes, biblio.   D. A. Franz

Falklands/Malvinas

2958. Barsegov, Iu. and Imnadze, L. FOLKLENDSKIE (MAL'-VINSKIE) OSTROVA: STARYI SPOR V NOVYKH USLOVIIAKH [Falkland (Malvinas) Islands: old argument under new conditions]. *Mirovaia Ekonomika i Mezhdunarodnye Otnosheniia [USSR] 1982 (6): 129-134.* Examines the history and present relations of the Falkland Islands with Great Britain, Argentina and the United States.

2959. Beck, Peter J. COOPERATIVE CONFRONTATION IN THE FALKLAND ISLANDS DISPUTE: THE ANGLO-ARGENTINE SEARCH FOR A WAY FORWARD, 1968-1981. *J. of Interamerican Studies and World Affairs 1982 24(1): 37-58.* Geopolitical aspects—off-shore resources and communications—have heightened interest in the Falkland Islands. Whether developments in the late 1970's and early 1980's are moving toward confrontation or collaboration will probably become clearer after the Falkland Island Council election of November 1981. It is easier for a European than for a Latin American nation to make territorial concessions in Latin America. Based on British Foreign Office manuscripts, British newspapers, and Parliamentary debates; 7 notes, ref. T. D. Schoonover

2960. Bologna, Alfredo Bruno. CONFLICTO REINO UNIDO DE GRAN BRETAÑA Y REPUBLICA ARGENTINA POR LAS ISLAS MALVINAS [British-Argentine conflict over the Falkland Islands]. *Rev. de Ciência Pol. [Brazil] 1981 24(2): 9-17.* Gives a brief history of the conflict in the context of the United Nations resolutions on nonautonomous territories. Distinguishes periods of cooperation, conflict, and negotiation. 34 notes. J. V. Coutinho

2961. Hickey, John. KEEP THE FALKLANDS BRITISH? THE PRINCIPLE OF SELF-DETERMINATION OF DEPENDENT TERRITORIES. *Inter-Am. Econ. Affairs 1977 31(1): 77-88.* Examines the political and economic position of the Falkland Islands and relations between Great Britain and Argentina concerning them. Based on secondary sources; 6 notes. D. A. Franz

2962. Jackman, S. W. RUDOLPH VERNER AND THE BATTLE OF THE FALKLAND ISLANDS. *Am. Neptune 1973 33(1): 34-40.* Publication of a report on the battle of the Falkland Islands by Rudolph Verner, gunnery commander on one of the British ships involved. The German squadron appeared while the British ships were refueling. Had they entered the harbor and attacked, the battle might have gone differently. Instead the German squadron sailed to open sea, where the light cruisers scattered to reach neutral ports and the heavy ships remained to fight. The short battle was the first British victory in World War I naval action. V. L. Human

2963. Jhabvala, Farrokh. TWO HUNDRED ISLANDS OF SOLEDAD: INTERNATIONAL LAW OF THE SOUTH ATLANTIC. *Caribbean Rev. 1982 11(3): 8-11, 42-43.* The Falkland Islands were discovered either in 1520, as Argentina claims, or in 1592 by an Englishman, John Davis. Great Britain and Argentina ultimately went to war over ownership of the Malvinas, as they are called in Argentina.

2964. Johnson, Richard. THE FUTURE OF THE FALKLAND ISLANDS. *World Today [Great Britain] 1977 33(6): 223-231.* Following a survey conducted by the government of Great Britain on the economic future of the Falkland Islands, the author discusses Argentinian claims, agricultural reform, social organization, and the gas, oil, and fishing industries, 1973-75.

2965. Kelsey, Robert J. MANEUVERING IN THE FALKLANDS. *US Naval Inst. Pro. 1982 108(9): 36-38.* British strategy and operations during the Falkland Islands campaign provide an excellent example of a maneuver-oriented naval strategy. They illustrate the use of containment, control, and destruction. K. J. Bauer

Paraguay

2966. Alexander, Robert J. THE TYRANNY OF GENERAL STROESSNER. *Freedom at Issue 1977 (41): 16-18.* Friendly relations with the military and police elements in Paraguay, popular support through association with a traditional political party, suppression of opposition, and inattention from the outside world have preserved the dictatorship of General Alfredo Stroessner for 22 years.

2967. Baer, Werner. THE PARAGUAYAN ECONOMIC CONDITION: PAST AND CURRENT OBSTACLES TO ECONOMIC MODERNIZATION. *Inter-Am. Econ. Affairs 1975 29(1): 49-63.* Analyzes Paraguay's economic conditions and discusses the obstacles to socioeconomic modernization as represented in three books: Joseph Pincus, *The Economy of Paraguay* (Praeger, 1968); Henry D. Ceuppens, *Paraguay Año 2000* (Asuncion, 1971); and Adlai F. Arnold, *Foundations of an Agricultural Policy in Paraguay* (Praeger, 1971). Primary and secondary sources; 3 tables, 7 notes. D. A. Franz

2968. Báez, Julia. PANORAMA DE LA SITUACIÓN INDÍGENA EN PARAGUAY [Panorama of the Indians' situation in Paraguay]. *Casa de las Américas [Cuba] 1976 14(95): 66-74.* In October 1974 a congress of Indian representatives convened in Paraguay. The 23 delegates represented indigenous groups from Paraguay, Argentina, Brazil, Bolivia and Venezuela. The convention dealt with major problems confronting present-day Indian groups such as economic exploitation, loss of lands and destruction of cultures. The Paraguayan government, religious missionaries, and business firms carry the major responsibility for these injustices. These have been denounced by scholars, political and religious leaders throughout the world. The manifesto drafted at the conference called for return of Indian lands, preservation of indigenous cultures, better health services and an end to low discriminatory wages. Secondary sources; 6 notes. H. J. Miller

2969. Maidana, Antonio. KOMMUNISTY PARAGVAIA VO GLAVE PROGRESSIVNYKH SIL V BOR'BE PROTIV VOENNOI DIKTATURY [Paraguay's Communists at the head of progressive forces in the struggle against the military dictatorship]. *Voprosy Istorii KPSS [USSR] 1978 (3): 81-92.* Survey of the history of the Communist Party of Paraguay from its founding in 1928, with primary attention devoted to its most recent past. Paraguay has been victimized by the combined forces of foreign capital, foreign- and native-owned latifundia, and the military dictatorship of Alfredo Stroessner. Paraguay's Communist Party proposes a popular program of sweeping political, economic, cultural, and social changes for the democratization of the nation's life. 16 notes. L. E. Holmes

2970. Rivarola, Domingo. FREINS ET OBSTACLES À LA RÉFORME AGRAIRE AU PARAGUAY [Agrarian reform restrained and obstructed in Paraguay]. *Civilisations [Belgium] 1975 25(3-4): 286-293.* Land reform in Paraguay had a political origin in the middle of the 19th century when the government put estates up for sale. Effective attempts to assist the rural class were initiated in 1926 and in 1940, hindered by lack of financial means and political disorder. Farmers have no definite status but are compelled to cultivate their own land or rented property or act as seasonal workers. Failure at agrarian reform has led to extensive migration to Argentina. H. L. Calkin

2971. Varon, Benno Weiser. BIG FROG IN A SMALL POND. *Midstream 1980 26(2): 35-39.* A memoir of Israel's first ambassador to Paraguay, 1968-1973, dealing with diplomatic relations as illustrated by a children's story.

2972. Vasquez, Pedro. AN ANTI-DICTATORIAL FRONT IN THE MAKING. *World Marxist R. [Canada] 1974 17(4): 82-87.* Paraguay's Communist Party is leading a growing anti-dictatorial front against the country's ruler, Alfredo Stroessner. S

2973. Vasquez, Pedro. UNITY AGAINST THE DICTATORSHIP. *World Marxist R. [Canada] 1975 18(6): 32-37.* Discusses the Communist Party in Paraguay since 1971. S

2974. Westhues, Kenneth. CURSES VERSUS BLOWS: TACTICS IN CHURCH-STATE CONFLICT. *Sociol. Analysis 1975 36(1): 1-16.* Parameters for the analysis of church-state conflict are set forth and illustrated by a case-study of relations between the Catholic Church and the Stroessner government in Paraguay since the late 1960s. Four models by which to study this phenomenon are described: factional, institutional, and inter-organizational conflict models, as well as an open-systems model. The last is suggested as the most adequate. The conflict in Paraguay is shown to have erupted with the breakdown of common referees between the two parties. Analysis of the dynamics of the conflict reveals incongruity between the tactics used by the church and those used by the government. Some effects of such incongruity are reviewed, and alternative outcomes of church-state conflict are suggested.　　J

2975. Westhues, Kenneth. THE ESTABLISHED CHURCH AS AN AGENT OF CHANGE. *Sociol. Analysis 1973 34(2): 106-123.* "The revolutionary potential of sectarian religion and a common anti-organizational bias result in the common assumption that by definition an established church does not serve as a change agent in its society. This assumption is challenged and a model is set forth which states conditions under which a national established church which is a sub-unit of an international religion can assume the role of agent of change. The results of a case-study of Roman Catholicism in Paraguay lend support to the model. It is shown that Catholicism in Paraguay is in a position of power, and that its present radical stance is due largely to its acceptance of new theology from its Roman parent. The critical and innovative role of Paraguayan Catholicism is regarded as a rational response of the organization of Catholicism to the Paraguayan environment. The limits of its change-agent role are discussed. The research, based on a variety of field methods, was done in May-July, 1972."　　J

2976. Zéndegui, Guillermo de. IMAGE OF PARAGUAY. *Américas (Organization of Am. States) 1975 27(2): S1-24.* An overview of Paraguay since prehistoric times, covering its political and social development, economic base, culture, history, and population.

Uruguay

2977. Burns, E. Bradford. A *STATE OF SIEGE* THAT NEVER WAS. *J. of Latin Am. Lore 1976 2(2): 257-264.* Assesses Constantin Costa-Gavras's film *State of Siege* (1973) on Uruguay in light of Latin American documentary films, 1917-70. Use of historical imagination and social perception to interpret the oppressive interplay of dependency and imperialism are of greater theoretical and philosophical importance than strict historical documentation of fact.

2978. Delgado Rodríguez, Francisco. URUGUAY: EVOLUCION INDUSTRIAL Y SOCIEDAD [Uruguay: industrial development and society]. *Santiago [Cuba] 1982 (45): 9-31.* The economic development of Uruguay during the last century and a half is a case of the evolution and subsequent involution of a sector of the national industrial bourgeoisie. Its characteristic traits are the emergence of the capitalist mode of production, which no doubt led to the struggle for independence and an economic system based on bonds with an outside free-exchange and later imperialist environment under the hegemony of the cattle-exporting bourgeoisie. The article describes the vicissitudes of this system from independence to the 1973 coup. The old national bourgeoisie could not measure up to the new monopolies and to the impact of international imperialism. 4 tables, 40 notes.　　J. V. Coutinho

2979. Falcoff, Mark. THE URUGUAY THAT NEVER WAS: A HISTORIAN LOOKS AT COSTA-GAVRAS'S *STATE OF SIEGE.* *J. of Latin Am. Lore 1976 2(2): 239-256.* Discusses Constantin Costa-Gavras's film *State of Siege* (1973) as a historical document, offering a comparison of the film's analysis of Uruguayan politics, 1968-72, and the actual data on the country's foreign and domestic policies.

2980. Geffner, Daniel I. and Wilkie, James W. CINEMALORE: *STATE OF SIEGE* AS A CASE STUDY. *J. of Latin Am. Lore 1976 2(2): 221-238.* Examines Constantin Costa-Gavras's film *State of Siege* (1973). It documents the guerrilla warfare carried on during 1963-72 by the Tupamaro guerrillas against the government of Uruguay. It portrays the warfare as moral history and in terms of its impact as cinema lore or historical documentation.

2981. Gonzalez, Julio. AGAINST THE DICTATORSHIP. *World Marxist R. [Canada] 1975 18(4): 97-104.* Portrays the role of the Communist Party toward the liberation of Uruguay, 1973-75.　　S

2982. Handelman, Howard. LABOR-INDUSTRIAL CONFLICT AND THE COLLAPSE OF URUGUAYAN DEMOCRACY. *J. of Interamerican Studies and World Affairs 1981 23(4): 371-394.* The last two decades have revealed the difficult and tortuous path toward political and economic development in Latin America. The Latin American countries with the more advanced indicators of socioeconomic development—Argentina, Chile, Uruguay, and Brazil—have instituted the most repressive bureaucratic and authoritarian regimes. Uruguay, despite some anomalies, fits into Guillermo O'Donnell's bureaucratic authoritarian scheme because it is a regime of the economic and military elite seeking to resolve political crises related to economic bottlenecks. Interviews, memoirs, Ecuadorian government documents, and secondary sources; 15 notes, ref.　　T. Schoonover

2983. Israel, Guillermo and Kiessling, Wolfgang. DEUTSCHE ANTIFASCHISTEN IN URUGUAY (1933-1943) [German antifascists in Uruguay, 1933-43]. *Beiträge zur Geschichte der Arbeiterbewegung [East Germany] 1976 18(4): 666-682.* German emigrants after 1933 organized antifascist propaganda and activities in Uruguay. Although the antidemocratic military dictatorship established in Uruguay in March 1933 opposed the antifascists, various organizations continued with their resistance work. In July 1941 a German Antifascist Committee for Aid to the Soviet Union was founded. Based on printed documents, newspapers, and secondary literature; 27 notes.　　R. Wagnleitner

2984. Kirby, John. ON THE VIABILITY OF SMALL COUNTRIES: URUGUAY AND NEW ZEALAND COMPARED. *J. of Inter-Am. Studies and World Affairs 1975 17(3): 259-280.* Uruguayans believe that they can perform miracles. Although smaller than several of Brazil's states, the nation has sought to consume products like any viable nation. However, Uruguayans have not produced enough to pay for this consumption. Progress is possible if Uruguay uses New Zealand as a model. Uruguay must diversify its export trade and use manufactured articles to reduce its dependence on limited markets and products. More importantly, however, Uruguayans must understand that their industrial buildup can be successful only if it is aided by a strong agricultural base. Based on government publications and secondary works; 5 tables, 5 notes, biblio.　　J. R. Thomas

2985. Lefever, Ernest W. MURDER IN MONTEVIDEO: THE AID/MITRIONE STORY. *Freedom At Issue 1973 (21): 14-16.* Defense of the U.S. Agency for International Development's "public safety program" against criticisms from Uruguayan leftists.　　S

2986. Lines, Chris. A URUGUAYAN APPRAISAL. *Contemporary Rev. [Great Britain] 1976 229(1329): 189-193.* Surveys the political and economic development of Uruguay under President Juan Marie Bordaberry Arocena, 1971-76.

2987. Little, Cynthia Jeffress. MORAL REFORM AND FEMINISM: A CASE STUDY. *J. of Inter-Am. Studies and World Affairs 1975 17(4): 386-396.* A Uruguayan physician, Paulina Luisi (1875-1950) was dedicated to both moral reform and feminism. She fought for women's rights and for the establishment of one sexual moral standard. She worked to destroy white slavery and alcoholism while at the same time urging the acceptance of women in institutions of higher education. Her own career served as a model for other women because she was Uruguay's first woman bachelor's degree holder, its first woman physician and surgeon, and a member of the Uruguayan diplomatic corps. She believed that women possessed a moral superiority and that feminine values, if adopted by society, could alleviate the major social ills of the time. Based on Uruguayan newspapers, organization documents, and secondary sources.　　J. R. Thomas

2988. Mallin, Jay. THE MILITARY VS. URBAN GUERRILLAS. *Marine Corps Gazette 1973 57(1): 18-25.* Outlines the socioeconomic conditions in Uruguay that fomented the Tupamaro movement in the early 1960's and refers to urban guerrilla activities and their suppression by the government authorities in the early 1970's.

2989. McDonald, Ronald H.   THE RISE OF MILITARY POLITICS IN URUGUAY.   *Inter-Am. Econ. Affairs 1975 28(4): 25-43.* Traces the military's rise and route to political power in Uruguay, emphasizing the role of Tupamaro violence and the political deinstitutionalization of Uruguay by its military. Primary and secondary sources; table, 31 notes.
D. A. Franz

2990. McDonald, Ronald H.   THE STRUGGLE FOR NORMALCY IN URUGUAY.   *Current Hist. 1982 81(472): 69-73, 85-86.* The consistent theme of the military regime in Uruguay and its policies has been "transition," and even the new presidency of General Alvarez has been characterized as transitional by the military leaders and their puppet institutions. However, "transition" and "normalcy" need to be defined in Uruguayan terms, considering the enormous power of the military in the government.

2991. Mottet, George J.   EL URUGUAY Y LAS GUERRILLAS URBANAS   [Uruguay and urban guerrillas]. *Lock Haven R. 1973 (14): 21-35.* Presents a brief history of the Tupamaros, their motives and ideology.
S

2992. Oliveira, Sergio L. d'.   URUGUAY AND THE TUPAMARO MYTH.   *Military R. 1973 53(4): 25-36.* Describes the development of Uruguay's subversive Tupamaro movement. The Tupamaros reached their peak strength in 1971 and then declined as a result of their own vulnerabilities and effective government antisubversive measures. These measures included assignment of the principal antisubversive mission to the armed forces, adequate legislation, and creation of functional organizations to cope with subversive activity. 4 illus., table.
J. K. Ohl

2993. Otero, Mario.   OPPRESSION IN URUGUAY.   *Bull. of the Atomic Scientists 1981 37(2): 29-31.* Discusses the combination of economic crisis and the fascist government in Uruguay which has resulted in the stagnation of scientific work and cultural activity as well as the persecution of countless trade union and political activists, scientists, and professors.

2994. Pastorino, Enrique.   STOP THE TERROR!   *World Marxist R. [Canada] 1974 17(7): 108-110.* In 1974 Uruguay's rulers used terror to defeat the Communist Party and the revolutionary movement.   S

2995. Porzecanski, Arturo C.   AUTHORITARIAN URUGUAY.   *Current Hist. 1977 72(424): 73-75, 85-86.* Despite economic growth and the establishment of law and order, Uruguay's four-year authoritarian regime has eroded individual liberty, 1972-76.

2996. Porzecanski, Arturo C.   URUGUAY'S CONTINUING DILEMMA.   *Current Hist. 1974 66(389): 28-30, 38-39.* Describes the lively politics and stagnant economic conditions of Uruguay since the 1960's. One of seven articles on Latin America.   S

2997. Rama, C. M.   MOUVEMENTS PAYSANS ET PROBLÈMES AGRAIRES EN URUGUAY DE LA FIN DU XVIIIᵉ SIÈCLE À NOS JOURS   [Peasant movements and agrarian problems in Uruguay from the end of the 18th century to the present]. *Cahiers Int. d'Hist. Écon. et Sociale [Italy] 1978 8: 311-325.* Analyzes the agrarian problems of Uruguay which are essentially those of a small livestock-producing country. Also examines peasant movements which existed during the period of colonization, during the struggle for independence, 1811-30, and during the consolidation of national independence. In the 20th century, agrarian associations and cooperatives were formed. 25 notes.
F. X. Hartigan

2998. Rodriguez, Enrique.   URUGUAY AFTER THE COUP.   *World Marxist R. [Canada] 1974 17(5): 135-142.* Describes the 1973 military coup in Uruguay and the resulting changes in political strategy adopted by the Uruguayan Communist Party.   S

2999. Rouquie, A.   L'URUGUAY, DE L'ÉTAT PROVIDENCE À L'ÉTAT GARNISON   [Uruguay, from welfare state to garrison state]. *Études [France] 1979 350 (6): 741-758.* Studies the political conditions which contributed to the reign of the state terror in Montevideo, Uruguay in 1973.

3000. Saxlund, Ricardo.   THE QUIET HEROISM OF THE REVOLUTIONARY.   *World Marxist Rev. [Canada] 1977 20(2): 70-78.* Discusses the continuing struggle of the Communist Party in Uruguay, through examination of letters and statements of relatives of political prisoners, or those active in the cause, 1970-1977.

3001. Sierra, Sergio.   INTERNATIONAL ASPECTS OF THE URUGUAYAN DRAMA.   *World Marxist Rev. [Canada] 1976 19(12): 86-94.* Examines the growth of the Communist Party in Uruguay as both a weapon against a fascist regime and a method of presenting anti-imperialism sentiments, 1972-76.

3002. Suarez, Alberto.   THE OLIGARCHY OF THE PEOPLE.   *World Marxist R. [Canada] 1973 16(2): 77-85.* The revolution of socialism is being assisted by Uruguay's Communist Party. Part of the continuing series "Political Portrait of Latin America."   S

3003. Torres, Cristina.   URUGUAY: L'ECHEC DE LA TENTATIVE D'INSTITUTIONNALISATION DU REGIME   [Uruguay: the failure of the attempt at institutionalization of the regime]. *Problèmes d'Amérique Latine [France] 1982 (64): 7-34.* Details the attempted creation of a civilian-military government, and the various stages of development of that concept; explains the people's defeat of the initiative and of the military constitution.

3004. Van Aken, Mark J.   THE RADICALIZATION OF THE URUGUAYAN STUDENT MOVEMENT.   *Americas (Acad. of Am. Franciscan Hist.) 1976 33(1): 109-129.* Student political protest in Uruguay was rekindled in 1917 by a preparatory students' strike which, though unsuccessful, resulted in establishment of the Centro de Estudiantes "Ariel." Concerned at first with educational and cultural questions, the Center turned gradually to espouse social change under the influence of foreign contacts and intellectual ferment. The Ariel Center expired in the 1930's, but its radical posture was taken up by the *Federación de Estudiantes Universitarios del Uruguay* founded in 1929. The latter ultimately gave expression to widespread disillusion among Uruguayan students with both representative democracy and capitalism. This further radicalization drew much of its inspiration from the creed of anti-imperialism. Based on the student press, interviews, secondary works; 73 notes.
D. Bushnell

3005. Viejra, E.   BOR'BA URUGVAISKIKH KOMMUNISTOV V USLOVIIAKH PODPOL'IA I REPRESSII DIKTATURY   [The struggle of Uruguayan Communists as an underground movement during dictatorial repression]. *Voprosy Istorii KPSS [USSR] 1976 (12): 95-99.* Despite arrests of many Communists and a general repression of the Communist Party since October 1975 the Party retains its ideological and organizational strength as well as unity. Its struggle to uphold its principles, especially the creation of an antifascist front, has been inspired by the Party's previous success in the face of repression following the military coup of June 1973. 2 notes.
L. E. Holmes

3006. Zéndegui, Guillermo de.   JOSÉ ANTONIO MORA: A LIFE DEVOTED TO THE HEMISPHERE.   *Américas (Organization of American States) 1975 27(3): 25-27.* Discusses the diplomatic career of José Antonio Mora, a Uruguayan who filled several OAS posts, including Secretary-General, 1956-58.

SUBJECT INDEX

Subject Profile Index (SPIndex) carries both generic and specific index terms. Begin a search at the general term but also look under more specific or related terms. Cross-references also appear in this index.

Each string of index descriptors is intended to present a profile of a given article; however, no particular relationship between any two terms in the profile is implied. Terms within the profile are listed alphabetically after the leading term. The variety of punctuation and capitalization reflects production methods and has no intrinsic meaning; e.g., there is no difference in meaning between 'History, study of' and 'History (study of).'

Cities, towns, and other small geographical subdivisions are normally listed in parentheses following their respective countries e.g., 'Brazil (Minas Gerais).' However, certain regions of divided, disputed, changed or indeterminate sovereignty do appear as leading terms listed alphabetically in the index, e.g., 'Falkland Islands.'

Terms beginning with an arabic numeral are listed after the letter Z. Chronology of a particular article appears at the end of the string of index descriptors. In the chronological descriptor, 'c' stands for century, e.g., '19c' means '19th century.'

The last number in the index string, in italics, refers to the bibliographic entry number.

—. Colombia. 1930-80. *1977*

Anti-Americanism. Communism. Costa-Gavras, Constantin. Films. Foreign Relations. 1964-82. *71*

Anticlericalism. Church and State. Constitutional Congress. Mexico. 1916-17. *795*

Anticolonialism. Voodoo. West Indies. 18c-20c. *1330*

Anti-Communism. Diplomacy. Mexico. Nationalism. USA. 1924-27. *758*

Anti-Communist Movements. Colombia. *Violencia*. 1940's-65. *1939*

Anti-dictatorial front. Communist Party. Paraguay. Stroessner, Alfredo. 1973-74. *2972*

Anti-Fascist Movements. Germans. Uruguay. 1933-41. *2983*

Antigua *See also* West Indies Associated States.

—. Antigua (Barbuda). Autonomy. 1960-80. *1813*

Antigua (Barbuda). Agriculture. Colonization. Land Tenure. 1860-1923. *1790*

—. Antigua. Autonomy. 1960-80. *1813*

Anti-Imperialism *See also* Imperialism; Nationalism.

—. Alvarado Quirós, Alejandro. Costa Rica. Diplomacy. USA. 1920-45. *1080*

—. Belize. Great Britain. Strikes. 1930's-60's. *1055*

—. Chile. Economic integration. Popular Unity. 1960-73. *2782*

—. Communist Party. Panama. 1903-77. *1271*

—. Documents. National United Freedom Fighters (NUFF). Revolutionary Movements. Trinidad and Tobago. 1970's. *1830*

—. Foreign Policy. USA. 1970's. *320*

—. Foreign Relations. USA. 1891-1929. *19*

—. Literature. 1930's. *144*

—. Multinational corporations. Socialists. 1945-76. *382*

Anti-imperialist front. Argentina. Bolivia. Communism (Trotskyism). Lora, Guillermo. 1971-74. *1887*

Anti-imperialist groups. Costa Rica. Nicaragua. Puerto Rico. USA (domination). 1958-73. *1048*

Anti-imperialist struggle. Communists. 1969-73. *193*

Anti-Semitism *See also* Jews.

—. Argentina. 19c-20c. *2516*

—. Argentina. 20c. *2559*

—. Argentina. Catholic Church. Subversion. Terrorism. 1975. *2657*

—. Argentina. Riots. 1919. *2570*

Antisubversive measures. Tupamaros. Uruguay. 1962-72. *2992*

Antitrust laws. Caribbean Region. Competition policy. Regionalism. 20c. *1334*

Aponte, Carlos. Cuba. Nicaragua. Revolution. Venezuela. 1900-40. *184*

—. Letters. Nicaragua. Sandino, Augusto César. 1929. *1251*

APRA. Catholicism, popular. Leftists. Peru. 1920-45. *2068*

—. Communist Party. Peru. 1924-36. *2009*

—. Communist Party. Peru. Political Change. 1930-35. *2007*

—. Haya de la Torre, Víctor Raúl. Ideology. Peru. 1924-32. *450*

—. Haya de la Torre, Víctor Raúl. Indians. Peru. 1920-29. *2101*

—. Haya de la Torre, Víctor Raúl. Peru. Students. Universities, popular. 1921-31. *2067*

—. Haya de la Torre, Víctor Raúl (interview). Peru. 1913-79. *2017*

—. Ideology. Middle Classes. Peru. 1920's-70's. *2124*

APRA (review article). Haya de la Torre, Víctor Raúl. Peru. 1870-1974. *2092*

Aprismo. Acción Democrática. Ideology. Venezuela. 1900-79. *2154*

Aprista Party. *See* APRA.

Apristas. Communist Party. Cuba. Revolutionary theory. 1920's-30's. *1359*

Aquirre Beltrán, Gonzalo. Acculturation (review article). Mexico (Cuajinicuilapa). Negroes. 20c. *623*

Arab-Israeli conflict. Foreign Policy. 1947-75. *296*

—. UN. 1947-76. *303*

Arabs. Jews. 1948-70's. *258*

Árbenz, Gustavo. Arévalo, Juan José. Guatemala. 1944-54. *1145*

Arbenz, Jacobo. Guatemala. Land reform. 1954-78. *1135*

Arbitration, International *See also* Boundaries; Disarmament.

—. Boundaries. Colombia. Diplomacy. Fortoul, Gil. Switzerland. Venezuela. 1922. *1838*

—. Organization of American States. Rio Treaty. 1970-76. *526*

Archaeology *See also* Anthropology; Indians.

—. Anthropology. Bolivia. 1899-1980. *1890*

—. Anthropology. Nicaragua. 1980. *1184*

Archival Catalogs and Inventories. Brazil. Machado, Agenor (papers). São Paulo University (History Department). 1920-53. *2269*

Archives *See also* names of individual archives; Documents.

—. Bahamas. Public Record Office. 1970's. *1792*

—. Church and State. Mexico. 20c. *667*

—. Mexico (Baja California). 1744-1950. *644*

Archives, private. Brazil. Center for Research and Documentation of Contemporary Brazilian History. 19c-20c. *2245*

Arellano, Edward. General Confederation of Labor (CGT). Labor Unions and Organizations. Mendoza, Ciro. Mexico. Textile industry. 1920-78. *563*

Arévalo, Juan José. Árbenz, Gustavo. Guatemala. 1944-54. *1145*

—. Guatemala. Military. Revolution. Ubico Castañeda, Jorge. 1944. *1146*

Argentina. Agricultural Labor (native-born). Discrimination. Economic Development. ca 1860-1930. *2577*

—. Agricultural Policy. Industrialization. ca 1935-55. *2642*

—. Agriculture. Canada. Immigration. Social Organization. 1870-1930. *2580*

—. Agriculture. Industrialization. 1930's-70's. *2527*

—. Allende, Salvador. Chile. Communism. Perón, Juan. 1970's. *90*

—. Alliances. Atlantic, South. Brazil. South Africa. USSR. 1960's-70's. *77*

—. Alvear, Marcelo T. de. Great Britain. Irigoyen, Hipólito. Politics. Tariff. 1916-30. *2579*

—. Anarchy. Authoritarianism. 1974. *2532*

—. Anti-imperialist front. Bolivia. Communism (Trotskyism). Lora, Guillermo. 1971-74. *1887*

—. Anti-Semitism. 19c-20c. *2516*

—. Anti-Semitism. 20c. *2559*

—. Anti-Semitism. Catholic Church. Subversion. Terrorism. 1975. *2657*

—. Anti-Semitism. Riots. 1919. *2570*

—. Armaments industry. Developing Nations. National security. ca 1930-79. *2540*

—. Arnedo Alvarez, Gerónimo. Communist Party. 20c. *2524*

—. Art and State. National Arts Fund. 1958-80. *2524*

—. Authoritarianism. Brazil. Bureaucracies. Political Change. ca 1964-76. *132*

—. Authoritarianism. Economic Policy. 1930-70. *2541*

—. Authoritarianism, popular. Peronism. Voting and Voting Behavior. 1940's-70's. *2643*

—. Authors. Bibliographies. Peronism. Political Protest. Sábato, Ernesto. 1940's-70's. *2629*

—. Bay of Pigs invasion. Cuba. Puerto Rico. 1960-61. *1453*

—. Beagle Channel. Chile. Foreign Relations. 1810-1977. *2503*

—. Beagle Channel. Chile. Great Britain. 1902-77. *2507*

—. Beagle Channel. Chile. Territorial claims. Tierra del Fuego. 1881-1977. *2510*

—. Bibliographies. Foreign policy. 1879-1978. *2526*

—. Bibliographies. Guerrilla warfare, urban. 1960-75. *2550*

—. Bibliographies. Industrialization. Perón, Juan. 1944-60. *2610*

—. Bolivia. Brazil. Ecuador. Military Government. Peru. Political Change. 1960-80. *436*

—. Boundaries (disputes). Chile. 1843-1978. *2505*

—. Boundaries (disputes). Chile. Horn, Cape. 1876-1978. *2509*

—. Boycotts. Economic relations. Great Britain. USA. 1945-49. *2603*

—. Brazil. Censorship. Military Government. Press (academic). 1964-75. *88*

—. Brazil. Chile. Labor movement. Working class. 1960-74. *45*

—. Brazil. Cuba. Peru. Revolution. 1920-33. *146*

—. Brazil. Economic Policy. Inflation. Perón, Juan. Vargas, Getúlio. 1946-55. *391*

—. Brazil. Exports. Mexico. Unemployment. 1953-70. *333*

—. Brazil. Foreign policy. 19c-20c. *2554*

—. Brazil. Foreign policy. Mexico. 18c-1975. *286*

—. Brazil. Military Service (enlistees). Poles. World War II. 1940-44. *442*

—. Brazil. Paraguay (Alto Paraná). Yacireta, Treaty of. ca 1970-73. *519*

—. Business. Import substitution. 1929-49. *2517*

—. Capital Market. Economic Policy. 1975-79. *2664*

—. Catholic Church. Clergy. Movement of Priests for the Third World. Radicals and Radicalism. Violence. 1969-70's. *2520*

—. Catholic Church. Dictatorship. 1970's. *2670*

—. Censorship. Colleges and universities. Military government. Sociology. 1966-79. *2547*

—. Chile. Economic dependency. Elites. Modernization. Political conflict. 1900-25. *154*

—. Chile. Economic Policy. Inflation. 1950's-70's. *2502*

—. Church and State. Education. Perón, Juan. 1954-55. *2622*

—. Civil Rights. Domestic policy. Indians. 1960's. *2644*

—. Civil-Military Relations. Political Systems. Pressure groups. 1930-76. *2549*

—. Class consciousness. Labor Unions and Organizations. Peronism. 1960-73. *2649*

—. Class Struggle. Democratization. Political Parties. 1946-73. *2528*

—. Coalition politics. Perón, Juan. ca 1940-73. *2637*

—. Codovilla, Victorio. Communist Party. Political Leadership. 1958-70. *2608*

—. Communist Parties and Movements. Revolutionary movements. ca 1910-75. *125*

—. Communist Party. 1918-78. *2538*

—. Communists. Perón, Juan. Political Leadership. 1945-73. *2621*

—. "Communities of fate." Elites (behavior). Political parties. -1974. *2562*

—. Cordobazo. Labor Unions and Organizations. Marxism. Peronism. Tosco, Augustín (interview). 1960's-70's. *2620*

—. Coups d'Etat. Democracy. Political Systems. 1912-30. *2573*

—. Coups d'etat. Depressions. 1930-45. *2571*

—. Coups d'Etat. Military. Yrigoyen, Hipólito. 1930. *2566*

—. Coups d'Etat. Peronism. Politics and the Military. Working class. 1945-78. *2553*

—. Decisionmaking. Diplomacy. Inter-American Conference (Rio de Janeiro). USA. World War II. 1942. *553*

—. Democratic Union. Elections. Peronist movement. Politics. 1946. *2588*

—. Depressions. Economic Policy. World War I. 1910-40. *2574*

—. Development, historical. Economic Conditions. Peronism. 19c-20c. *2606*

—. Diplomacy. Eady-Miranda Agreement. Economic relations. Great Britain. Messersmith, George S. USA. 1930-48. *2591*

—. Dissident behavior. Elites. Political Surveys. Socialist Party. 1915-57. *2560*

—. Documents. Economic Policy. Pinedo Plan. 1935-40. *2584*

—. Domestic policy. Perón, Juan. 1940's-70's. *2650*

—. Drago Doctrine. Foreign relations. Perón, Juan. USA. 1823-1974. *2557*

—. Economic Conditions. Government. Political Change. 1978-80. *2674*

—. Economic Conditions. Multinational corporations. Peronism. Political crisis. 1955-73. *2595*

—. Economic conditions. Political Indicators. 1970's. *2552*

—. Economic dependency debate. Imperialism. Landowning class. Middle classes. Peronism. 1940-73. *2634*

—. Economic development. Politics. Social classes. 1956-76. *2632*

—. Economic growth. Exploitation. Frank, Andre Gunder. Great Britain. 1900-24. *2569*

—. Economic growth. Income distribution. 1950-70. *2586*

—. Economic Integration. Pacific Ocean. 16c-1970's. *2530*

—. Economic planning. National Postwar Council. Perón, Juan. 1943-44. *2658*

—. Economic Policy. 1976-79. *2662*

—. Economic Policy. Government Enterprise. 1976-80. *2666*

—. Economic Policy. Liberalism. 1976-80. *2669*

—. Economic policy. Liberalism. Military. 1946-79. *2660*

—. Economic policy. Military government. Populism. 1946-76. *2513*

—. Economic Policy. Models. Perón, Juan. 1946-55. *2585*

—. Economic policy. Perón, Juan. Public Opinion. Quantitative Methods. Social classes. 1946-55. *2655*

—. Elections. Military Leadership. 20c. *2514*

—. Elections, presidential. Justicialist movement. Peronist vote. 1973. *2641*

—. Elections (presidential). Peronism. Working Class. 1973. *2593*

—. Electoral organization. Socialist Party. Working class subculture. 1900-46. *2563*

—. Elites. Peronist movement. Political development. 1912-70's. *2543*

—. Falkland Islands. Foreign Relations. Great Britain. 1960-81. *2959*

—. Falkland Islands. Foreign Relations. Great Britain. 1976-77. *2961*

—. Falkland Islands. Foreign Relations. Great Britain. UN (resolutions). 1965-77. *2960*

—. Falkland Islands. Great Britain. International law. War. 1520-1982. *2963*

—. Falkland Islands. Great Britain. Naval strategy. 1982. *2965*

—. Falkland Islands. Great Britain. USA. 1975-81. *2958*

—. Fascism. Perón, Juan. 1920-55. *2623*

—. Fascism, species of. Lipset, Seymour Martin. Organski, Kenneth. Peronism. 1938-69. *2619*

—. Films. García Velloso, Enrique. Greca, Acedes. History. Onelle, Clemente. 1915-22. *2519*

—. Foreign Investments. Foreign policy. Nationalism. 1816-1976. *2659*

—. Foreign Investments. Germany. Trade. 1918-33. *2572*

—. Foreign Investments. Great Britain. Railroads and State. Unión Cívica Radical. Yrigoyen, Hipolito. 1891-1928. *2609*

—. Foreign investments. Peronism. Political change. Social Classes. 1960-73. *2635*

—. Foreign Policy. Intervention. Nationalism. USA. 1941-46. *2536*

—. Foreign policy. Perón, Juan. 1973-74. *2589*

—. Foreign policy. Peronism. 1943-74. *2640*

—. Foreign policy. Peronism. 1973-76. *2628*

—. Foreign policy. UN (membership). USA. 1942-45. *2565*

—. Foreign Relations. Military Government. USA. 1940-81. *2537*

—. Foreign relations. Treaties. Uruguay. 1973-76. *2508*

—. Foreign Relations. USA. 1976-81. *2665*

—. Foreign Relations (review article). Good neighbor policy. USA. Woods, Randall Bennett. 1941-45. *2523*

—. General Confederation of Labor (CGT). Labor movement. Political Parties. Socialist Party. 1930-43. *2567*

—. General Confederation of Labor (CGT). Labor movement. Strikes. 1964. *2590*

—. General Confederation of Labor (CGT). Peronism. Working Class. 1943-73. *2602*

—. Government. Industry. Productivity. Working Conditions. 1953-62. *2616*

—. Government. International division of labor. 1950-70. *2587*

—. Government. Labor. 1900-70. *2521*

—. Government. Perón, Juan. 1930's-55. *2607*

—. Government. Perón, Juan. Personalism. 1946-74. *2597*

—. Government, civilian. Perón, Juan. Politics and the Military. 1973-75. *2652*

—. Government Enterprise. Oil Industry and Trade. Politics. Yacimientos Petrolíferos Fiscales. 1907-27. *2578*

—. Great Britain. South Georgia Islands. South Sandwich Islands. Sovereignty. 1904-82. *2515*

—. Guerrilla movements. 1959-70's. *2667*

—. Guerrilla Warfare. Political repression. 1969-78. *2546*

—. Guerrilla Warfare. Political repression. 1973-77. *2545*

—. Guerrilla warfare, urban. 1960-77. *2558*

—. Hernández, José (*Martín Fierro*). Perón, Juan. Political Protest. 1872-1974. *2564*

—. Human rights. Military government. National Security. 1969-77. *2531*

—. Human rights. Timerman, Jacobo. 1973-81. *2661*

—. Imperialism. USA. 1930-76. *2534*

—. International Labor Organization. Perón, Juan. USA. 1946-55. *2600*

—. Jews. 1620-1981. *2535*

—. Jews. Peronism. 1940-77. *2646*

—. Labor. Peronism. Voting and Voting Behavior. 1973. *2592*

—. Labor movement. 1943-78. *2601*

—. Labor Unions and Organizations. Peronism. 1943-55. *2624*

—. Labor Unions and Organizations. Peronism. Politics. 1955-73. *2615*

—. Labor Unions and Organizations. Peronism. Working class. 1943-55. *2645*

—. Labor unions, representation. Migrant labor. Sugar industry. 1944-76. *2512*

—. Legislative bodies. Voting, roll call. -1974. *2525*

—. Literature. Peronism. 1945-79. *2636*

—. Military. Perón, Isabel. 1975. *2605*

—. Military. Peronism. Political Attitudes. 1973-76. *2672*

—. Military Government. 1930-79. *2548*

—. Military government. 1963-78. *2663*

—. Military Government. 1981-82. *2673*

—. Military government. Videla, Jorge. 1976-79. *2668*

—. Nationalism. Political Attitudes. 1970-81. *2542*

—. Novels. Social Conditions. Strikes. Viñas, David (*Masters of the Earth*). Working class. 1900-20. *2581*

—. Oil policies. 1907-55. *2533*

—. Oligarchy. Social Conditions. Violence, political. 1880-1980. *2544*

—. Palacios, Alfredo L. 1900-55. *2551*

—. People's Revolutionary Army (ERP). Terrorism. 1968-74. *2617*

—. Perón, Eva. Political Crises. 1945. *2631*

—. Perón, Eva. Political instability, roots of. 1945-52. *2599*

—. Perón, Eva. Political Leadership. 1944-52. *2630*

—. Perón, Juan. Peronist movement (radical, right-wing split). Political unrest. 1955-74. *2626*

—. Perón, Juan. Political parties. 1945-55. *2625*

—. Perón, Juan. Politics. 1943-73. *2656*

—. Perón, Juan. Protestants. Religious Liberty. 1943-55. *2598*

—. Perón, Juan. Social reform. Working class. 1946-55. *2613*

—. Perón, Juan. Voting and Voting Behavior. 1940-46. *2654*

—. Perón, Juan. Working class. 1946-73. *2633*

—. Perón, Juan (political biography). Politics. 1943-73. *2604*

—. Peronism. 1943-73. *2647*

—. Peronism. 1943-74. *2594*

—. Peronism. Political crisis. 1972-75. *2627*

—. Peronism. Political Factions. 1955-75. *2614*

—. Peronism. Political Participation. 1946-74. *2653*

—. Peronism. Social Classes (agrarian, industrial). 1974. *2596*

—. Peronism. Women. 1974. *2611*

—. Peronism. Women. Working Class. 1940's. *2612*

—. Peronism, restoration of. 1973-74. *2639*

—. Peronistas. Political Parties (programs). 1943-55. 1973. *2638*

—. Political instability. Social conditions. 20c. *2568*

—. Political repression. Revolution. 1930-78. *2671*

—. Political repression. Violence. 1970's. *2556*

—. Political stability. 1890-1976. *2518*

—. Politics. Public opinion surveys. 1930-75. *2555*

—. Rebellions. Recessions. 1870-1970. *2539*

—. Rio de la Plata, Treaty of. Uruguay. ca 1970-73. *2506*

—. Strikes. 1973-76. *2618*

Argentina (Buenos Aires). Authors. Cities. 19c-20c. *2522*

—. City Government. Politics (municipal, national). 1918-30. *2583*

—. Political Parties. Social Classes. Voting and Voting Behavior. Yrigoyen, Hipólito. 1916-20. *2582*

Argentina (Córdoba). Demonstrations. Political Change. Social Classes. Strikes. 1966-69. *2651*

Argentina (San Juan). Cantoni, Federico. Peronism. Political movements. 1920's. *2575*

Arias Sanchez, Oscar. Cerdas Cruz, Rodolfo. Costa Rica. Politics (review article). Stone Zemurray, Samuel. ca 1940's-75. *1066*

Armaments industry. Argentina. Developing Nations. National security. ca 1930-79. *2540*

Armed Forces *See also* Military.

—. Brazil. Economic growth. 1965-76. *2487*

Armies *See also* National Guard.

—. Batista, Fulgencio. Cuba. Politics and the Military. Social Classes. 1899-1959. *1533*

—. Bolivia. Civil-Military Relations. Economic Development. Political Factions. 1961-79. *1891*

—. Brazil. Cruzada Democrática. Politics and the Military. Pressure Groups. 1952-62. *2403*

—. Brazil. Liberals. Nationalists. Political Factions. 1946-51. *2402*

—. Castro, Fidel. Cuba. Guerrilla warfare. 1958. *1525*

—. Chile. Coups d'Etat. Political Factions. Popular Unity. 1970-74. *2869*

—. Colombia. Politics and the Military. 1900-72. *1925*

—. Communist Party. Cuba. Political education. 1956-79. *1611*

—. Cuba. 1956-80. *1373*

—. Cuba. 1956-81. *1465*

—. Cuba. Guerrilla Warfare. Revolution. 1956-63. *1654*

—. Cuba. Militarization. Social Change. 1950-70. *1562*

—. Cuba. Revolution. 1952-58. *1610*

—. Drugs. Mexico. Pershing, John J. Prostitution. USA. Venereal disease. 1916-17. *802*

—. Logistics. Mexico. USA. 1916. *777*

—. Mexico. Revolution. 1910-30. *775*

—. Military Government. Revolutionary process. USA. 1810-1973. *469*

Armies (professionalization). Carías Andino, Tiburcio. Honduras. Politics and the Military. 1918-74. *1180*

Arms control. Cuban missile crisis. 1962-82. *1592*

Arms race. International law. Nuclear nonproliferation (denuclearized zones). USSR. 1962-73. *137*

Arms Trade *See also* Armaments Industry.

—. 1966-75. *420*

—. Brazil. Dominican Republic. USA. 1945-74. *429*

—. Chile. Embargo. Great Britain. USA. 1980. *2922*

—. USA. 1961-71. *414*

—. USA. 1976-78. *427*

Arms transfers. Air Forces. Military budgets. Public Finance. 1960-70. *446*

Arnedo Alvarez, Gerónimo. Argentina. Communist Party. 20c. *2529*

Art *See also* Artists; Arts and Crafts; Painting.

—. Mexico. Political Protest. 1950-69. *860*

Art and State. Argentina. National Arts Fund. 1958-80. *2524*

Art (murals). Censorship. Chile. Ramona Parra Brigades. 1969-73. *2711*

Artists. Chile. Mural painters. Ramona Parra Brigades. Revolutionary process. 1969-73. *2821*

—. Mexico. Murals. USA. 1920's-82. *611*

—. Revolution. Siqueiros, David Alfaro. 1939-61. *914*

Arts. Chile. Cultural policy. Military government. 1973-82. *2907*

Arts and crafts. Cuba. 1959-79. *1596*

Arts policy. Cuesta, George (theater review). Intellectuals. Mexico. Revolution. Theater. 1929-30. *776*

Asama (vessel). Japan. Mexico (Baja California; Turtle Bay). Navies. 1911-16. *818*

Asentamientos. Agricultural reform. Panama. 1962-75. *1263*

Assassination. Chile. Letelier, Orlando. Military Government. Pinochet, Augusto. 1973-78. *2903*

—. El Salvador. Revolution. Romero, Oscar. 1970's-80. *1107*

—. Foreign Policy. Human rights. Nicaragua. Somoza, Anastasio. USA. 1974-80. *1208*

—. Guatemala. Politics. 1954-81. *1160*

Assimilation *See also* Integration.

—. Brazil. Indian policy. 16c-20c. *2290*

Association of Nitrate Producers. Chileanization. Nitrate industry. World War I. 1914-30. *2687*

Association of Regional History. Local History. Mexico. National Institute of Anthropology and History. 20c. *654*

Asturias, Miguel Angel (*Señor Presidente*). Authors. Dictatorship. 20c. *8*

Athletes. Cricket. Negroes. Social mobility. West Indies. 1900-73. *1335*

Athletics. *See* Physical Education and Training; Sports.

Atlantic, South. Alliances. Argentina. Brazil. South Africa. USSR. 1960's-70's. *77*

—. Amazon Basin. Boundaries. Economic integration. Foreign Relations. 16c-1978. *2206*

—. Amazon Basin. Treaties. Venezuela. 1960-78. *500*

—. Amazon Pact. Boundaries. Treaties. 1822-1978. *2207*

—. Anarcho-syndicalism. Immigrants. Labor Unions and Organizations. 1890-1921. *2364*

—. Archival Catalogs and Inventories. Machado, Agenor (papers). São Paulo University (History Department). 1920-53. *2269*

—. Archives, private. Center for Research and Documentation of Contemporary Brazilian History. 19c-20c. *2245*

—. Argentina. Authoritarianism. Bureaucracies. Political Change. ca 1964-76. *132*

—. Argentina. Bolivia. Ecuador. Military Government. Peru. Political Change. 1960-80. *436*

—. Argentina. Censorship. Military Government. Press (academic). 1964-75. *88*

—. Argentina. Chile. Labor movement. Working class. 1960-74. *45*

—. Argentina. Cuba. Peru. Revolution. 1920-33. *146*

—. Argentina. Economic Policy. Inflation. Perón, Juan. Vargas, Getúlio. 1946-55. *391*

—. Argentina. Exports. Mexico. Unemployment. 1953-70. *333*

—. Argentina. Foreign policy. 19c-20c. *2554*

—. Argentina. Foreign policy. Mexico. 18c-1975. *286*

—. Argentina. Military Service (enlistees). Poles. World War II. 1940-44. *442*

—. Argentina. Paraguay (Alto Paraná). Yacireta, Treaty of. ca 1970-73. *519*

—. Armed forces. Economic growth. 1965-76. *2487*

—. Armies. Cruzada Democrática. Politics and the Military. Pressure Groups. 1952-62. *2403*

—. Armies. Liberals. Nationalists. Political Factions. 1946-51. *2402*

—. Arms trade. Dominican Republic. USA. 1945-74. *429*

—. Assimilation. Indian policy. 16c-20c. *2290*

—. Atlantic, South. International Security. 1822-1980. *2259*

—. Authoritarianism. Castilhos, Julio de. Politics. Vargas, Getúlio. 19c-20c. *2217*

—. Authoritarianism. Economic Conditions. Government. Social Change. 1964-78. *2501*

—. Authoritarianism. Political Theory. 1914-45. *2366*

—. Authors. Coups d'Etat. Literature. 1964-80. *2480*

—. Balance of Payments. Debt, external. Economic development. 1947-68. *2233*

—. Banco do Brasil. Economic Development. Government enterprise. Liberalism. 1905-30. *2385*

—. Banking. Development. National Bank for Economic Development. 1950-79. *2421*

—. Barbosa, Ruy. Biography, critical. Mythology. Nationalism, cultural. ca 1890-1973. *2255*

—. Barbosa, Ruy. Educational reform. 1882-1930. *2357*

—. Bibliographies. 15c-1980. *2469*

—. Bibliographies. Dissertations. Portugal. 1892-1971. *2252*

—. Bibliographies. Politics (review article). Social Conditions. 1882-1972. *2242*

—. Birth control. Press. 1967-75. *2476*

—. Bonapartism. Political Systems. Schmitter, Philippe C. 1964-78. *2439*

—. Boundaries. Colombia. García Ortiz, Laureano. Peru. Treaties. 1920-30. *56*

—. Campos, Francisco. Constitutions. Government. Revolution. 1930-68. *2367*

—. Capital. Economic Structure. Monopolies. 1964-77. *2453*

—. Capitalism. 17c-20c. *2281*

—. Capitalism. Chile. Cuba. Economic development. Human rights (panel discussion). Socialism. 1960's. *214*

—. Capitalism, foreign. Dependency. Economic change. 20c. *2237*

—. Capitalism (review article). Evans, Peter. 1970's. *2209*

—. Castello-Branco, Humberto (anthology; review article). Military. 1900-67. *2324*

—. Catholic Church. Church and state. Leme, Sebastião, Cardinal. Vargas, Getúlio. 1930-54. *2411*

—. Catholic Church. Fascism. Integralist movement. 1930's. *2361*

—. Catholic Church. Figueiredo, Jackson de. Political movements. Publicists. 1918-28. *2392*

—. Catholic Church. *Ordem* (periodical). 1921-37. *2371*

—. Catholic Church. Political power. 16c-20c. *2429*

—. Catholic Church. Political repression. 1964-74. *2425*

—. Catholic Church. Political transformation. 1950-64. *2258*

—. Catholic Electoral League. Church and State. Pressure groups. 1932-37. *2393*

—. Catholicism, Folk. Millenarianism. Politics. Religion. 1893-1980. *2298*

—. Centralism. Federalism. Government. 19c-20c. *2226*

—. Chamber of Deputies. Legislators, recruitment of. 1963-71. *2499*

—. Chile. Civil War. Diplomacy (review article). Spain. Valladão, Alfredo *(Brazil and Chile in the Imperial Era)*. 1817-1930's. *547*

—. Chile. Foreign policy. Repression. USA. Working class. 20c. *44*

—. Church and state. Civil religion. 1891-1964. *2210*

—. Cities (review article). Historiography. 1500-1945. *2261*

—. Civil Rights. Indians. Indigenismo. National Indian Foundation. 1970's. *2481*

—. Civil Rights Organizations. Frente Negra Brasileira. 1924-37. *2382*

—. Civil-military relations. Military government. 1964-70. *2234*

—. Clarté group. Communism. Nationalism. 1921-32. *2350*

—. Class struggle. Students. 1964-77. *2463*

—. Club 3 de Octubro. Revolution. Tenentes. Vargas, Getúlio. 1922-35. *2343*

—. Coffee. Economic Policy. 1930-39. *2339*

—. Coffee policy. Commodity markets, international. 1906-62. *2260*

—. Collor, Lindolfo. Labor. Vianna Moog, Clodomir (memoirs). 1891-1942. *2389*

—. Commerce. Foreign Relations. Industry. Treaties. USA. 1935. *2381*

—. Communist Party. 1964-76. *2432*

—. Communist Party. Labor Unions and Organizations. 1917-30. *2365*

—. Communist Party. Prestes, Luis Carlos. 1922-78. *2205*

—. Communist Party. Prestes, Luis Carlos (reminiscences). 1922-34. *2373*

—. Communist Party (25th Congress, 1976). USSR. 1964-76. *2490*

—. Constitution of 1937. 1937. *2342*

—. Constitutional Assembly. Social classes. 1934. *2340*

—. Constitutions. Economic planning. 1946-69. *2238*

—. Constitutions. Liberalism. Politics. 1821-1969. *2214*

—. Constitutions. Political parties. 1822-1969. *2282*

—. Co-operativa de Pesquisas-Ação de São Paolo. Cooperatives. 1960-80. *2329*

—. Courts. Fiscal Court. Public finance. 1890-1980. *2278*

—. Cultural development. Intellectuals. Nationalism. 1950-59. *2405*

—. Debt, external. 1967-77. *2247*

—. Debt, external. Economic Policy. Mexico. Uruguay. 1973-78. *412*

—. Democracy. Electoral policy. Military government. Political Change. 1964-81. *2241*

—. Democracy. Foreign Policy. USA. 1964-68. *2457*

—. Democracy. Government Enterprise. 1950-71. *2219*

—. Democracy. Military government. 1960-80. *2497*

—. Democracy. Political Culture. 19c-20c. *2332*

—. Democracy, breakdown of. Economic Conditions. 1950-64. *2412*

—. Democratization. 1977-82. *2460*

—. Democratization. Military government. 1964-79. *2478*

—. Dependency. Economic Development. Economic Policy. Mexico. Multinational corporations. 1955-80. *347*

—. Detente. Elections. Political Parties. 1974-80. *2484*

—. Developing Nations. Economic Growth. Expansionism. 1960-78. *2267*

—. Development. Elites. 1972-73. *2470*

—. Dictatorship. 1964-79. *2430*

—. Diplomacy. Jorge, Araújo. Soares, Álvaro T. (memoirs). 1906-44. *2380*

—. Diplomacy. McCann, Frank D. USA. 1937-45. *2394*

—. Diplomacy. Melo Franco, Afrânio de. 1906-37. *2369*

—. Diplomacy. Mexico. USA. 1913-15. *319*

—. Diplomacy. Navies. 1917-36. *2379*

—. Diplomacy. USA. World War II. 1935-45. *2353*

—. Diplomatic dispatches. Great Britain. Political Leadership. USA. Vargas, Getúlio. 1934-37. *2359*

—. Documents. Foreign relations. Parliaments. 1823-1975. *2225*

—. Domestic Policy. Housing. 1964-74. *2472*

—. Domestic Policy. Military government. Power. 1964-74. *2447*

—. Economic Conditions. 1967-76. *2456*

—. Economic Conditions. Foreign Policy. 1960-79. *2263*

—. Economic Conditions. Political parties. 1979-80. *2468*

—. Economic development. 1945-70's. *2246*

—. Economic development. 1964-74. *2296*

—. Economic development. 1964-74. *2433*

—. Economic development. 1964-76. *2419*

—. Economic development. 1968-74. *2306*

—. Economic Development. Economic Policy. 1830-1980. *2239*

—. Economic development. Economic Theory. 1945-75. *2396*

—. Economic Development. Foreign Aid. USA. 1946-70. *2257*

—. Economic Development. Foreign investments. 1950-78. *2311*

—. Economic Development. Military Government. Social Classes. 1964-73. *2440*

—. Economic Development. Social Conditions. 1960's-80. *2420*

—. Economic development. Social cost. 1973. *2451*

—. Economic Development (review article). 1964-77. *2495*

—. Economic Development (review article). Political Systems. 20c. *2249*

—. Economic Growth. Imperialism. 1971-73. *2491*

—. Economic Growth. Political Change. Social change. 1964-74. *2488*

—. Economic Growth. Political Repression. 1964-79. *2441*

—. Economic Growth. Trade. World War II. 1939-45. *2338*

—. Economic Growth (social costs). Foreign Policy. Military-dominated government. 1930-72. *2300*

—. Economic history. Foreign relations. Historiography. 1889-1964. *2316*

—. Economic Planning. Employment. 1964-70's. *2464*

—. Economic Planning. Industrialization. 1890-1977. *2333*

—. Economic Planning. Industrialization. Vargas, Getúlio. 1930-45. *2355*

—. Economic policy. 1930-79. *2243*

—. Economic Policy. 1964-67. *2496*

—. Economic Policy. Exports. 1964-74. *2479*

—. Economic Policy. Federal government. Liberalism. 1889-1930. *2386*

—. Economic Policy. Foreign Policy. 1945-74. *2254*

—. Economic Policy. Government Enterprise. 1889-1930. *2383*

—. Economic Policy. Government Enterprise. 1964-75. *2473*

—. Economic policy. Investments. 1974-80. *2434*

—. Economic policy. Military influence. Vargas, Getúlio. 1930-45. *2354*

—. Economic power. Foreign Investments. Great Britain. USA. World War I. 1914-19. *2376*

—. Economic relations. Mexico. USA. 1950-74. *358*

—. Economic Structure. Foreign policy. 1960's-70's. *2262*

—. Economics. Government. Law. Political Science. 20c. *2221*

—. Economists. Government. 1801-1980. *2250*

—. Education. Elites (political). Guatemala. Legislators. Uruguay. 1964-72. *191*

—. Elections. 1978. *2444*

—. Elections. Political parties. 1964-81. *2413*

—. Elections (procedures; *sublegenda*). 1967-77. *2438*

—. Electoral system. 20c. *2318*

—. Electoral system. Suffrage, universal. 1791-1977. *2272*

—. Electoral system (document). 1930. *2388*

—. Elites. 1969-74. *2471*

—. Elites. Folklore. Vargas, Getúlio (image). 1930-54. *2266*
—. Elites. Foreign policy. 1919-29. *2352*
—. Employment (structure). Industrialization. Women. 1920-70. *2276*
—. Europe. Foreign Relations. 1945-81. *2297*
—. Exchange rates, multiple. Trade. 1953-58. *2399*
—. Expeditionary Force. Morais, João Batista Masca Renhas de. World War II. 1942-45. *2377*
—. Export promotion. Manufactures. Multinational corporations. ca 1964-77. *2228*
—. Exports. Germany, West. Nuclear Science and Technology. Technology transfer. 1975. *2500*
—. Expropriation. Foreign Relations. Hickenlooper Amendment. Public utilities. USA. 1959-67. *2291*
—. Extradition. 1912-38. *2390*
—. Extradition. Legislation. Political crimes. 20c. *2253*
—. Fascism. Integralist movement. Salgado, Plínio. ca 1920's-30's. *2387*
—. Federalism. 1824-1977. *2314*
—. Federalism. 1834-1964. *2295*
—. Feminism. Lutz, Bertha. Politics. Suffrage. 1864-1964. *2375*
—. Force. Foreign policy. 1950's-70's. *2215*
—. Foreign Aid. Politics. Trade. USA. 20c. *2319*
—. Foreign Investments. France. 1890-1930. *2344*
—. Foreign investments. Industrial growth. Social development. 1960's-74. *2450*
—. Foreign policy. 1820's-1975. *2305*
—. Foreign policy. 1822-1975. *2307*
—. Foreign Policy. 1948-74. *2265*
—. Foreign policy. 1950's-73. *2211*
—. Foreign Policy. Foreign Relations. UN. 1945-80. *2322*
—. Foreign policy. Political Change. 20c. *2279*
—. Foreign Policy. USA. 1960-74. *284*
—. Foreign relations. Immigration. Japan. Trade. 19c-1960's. *2268*
—. Foreign Relations. Maritime relations. USA. 1967-73. *2286*
—. Foreign Relations. Political structure. USA. 1973. *2445*
—. Foreign Relations. USA. 1945-60. *2398*
—. Foreign Relations (review article). USA. 1950's-81. *2308*
—. Foreign services. Germany, West. Israel. Japan. -1973. *2216*
—. Forman, Shepard. Peasants (review article). 1975. *2289*
—. Geisel, Ernesto. Industrialization. Military government. Social instability. 1964-75. *2483*
—. Geisel, Ernesto. Military Government. 1975-78. *2461*
—. Geisel, Ernesto. Military government. Repression. 1976. *2458*
—. Geisel, Ernesto. Nationalist policy. 1974-. *2482*
—. Goulart, João. Nationalism. Political Leadership. Vargas, Getúlio. 1930-64. *2232*
—. Government. Imperialism, transformation of. Multinational corporations. Petrochemical industry. 1954-75. *2236*
—. Government. Labor movement. 1940's-70's. *2283*
—. Government. Political Change. 1975-79. *2370*
—. Government Enterprise. 1920-74. *2287*
—. Historiography. 1889-1964. *2315*
—. Human rights. 1964-79. *2435*
—. Idealism. Krausism. Positivism. Yrigoyen, Hipólito. 1800-1970. *176*
—. Ideology. Intellectuals. *Plataforma da Nova Geração.* 1940's. *2406*
—. Ideology. Military Government. 1960-71. *2446*
—. Imperialism. Student movements. USA. 1954-68. *2248*
—. Income redistribution. Social insurance. 1889-1976. *2277*
—. Indian policy. 19c-20c. *2309*
—. Indians. Modernization. Public Policy. 1970's-80's. *2449*
—. Indians. Modernization. Yanomami. 1960's-80's. *2454*
—. Industrialization. Military government. Technocrats. 1964-70's. *2477*
—. Integralist movement. Leme, Sebastião, Cardinal. 1920-40. *2391*
—. Intermediate states. International order. Power relations. 1945-73. *2208*
—. International system. Political Power. 1964-80. *2485*

—. Judicial process. Law Reform. 1933-76. *2223*
—. Judicial Process. Modernization. 20c. *2224*
—. Judicial system. 1822-1977. *2222*
—. Labor. Land Tenure *(latifundismo)*. 1960's. *2437*
—. Labor movement. 1930's-78. *2285*
—. Legislators. Political Recruitment. 1946-67. *2397*
—. Liga Nacionalista de São Paulo. Political Parties. Political reform. 1917-24. *2363*
—. Local Politics. Political participation. 1960-1975. *2264*
—. Mayors. Political participation. Women. 1972-76. *2424*
—. Migration. Urbanization. 1940-80. *2326*
—. Military Government. 1964-73. *2493*
—. Military government. 1964-78. *2452*
—. Military government. 1964-79. *2459*
—. Military government. Peru. Political Culture. 1964-74. *416*
—. Military government. Political Change. 1964-80. *2423*
—. Military Government. Political Repression. 1964-73. *2498*
—. Military officers. Prestes, Luis Carlos. Rebellions. Tenentes. 1924-27. *2358*
—. Moraes Sarmento Pinheiro, Paulo Sérgio de (review article). 1920-30. *2368*
—. National Democratic Union. Political Leadership. Political Parties. 1930-65. *2408*
—. Negroes. Political Participation. Social mobility. 1850's-1974. *2301*
—. Negroes. Racism. 1888-1979. *2288*
—. Nuclear physics. Technology transfer. 1937-78. *2462*
—. Oil. 1929-76. *2317*
—. Political Economy. 1964-79. *2229*
—. Political parties. 1889-1978. *2414*
—. Political Parties. 1966-79. *2443*
—. Political parties. 19c-20c. *2284*
—. Political Parties. Voting and Voting Behavior. 19c-20c. *2230*
—. Political protest. Popular culture. ca 1964-75. *2475*
—. Political stability. Regionalism. 1889-1974. *2348*
—. Politics. 1930-55. *2341*
—. Politics. Social change. 19c-20c. *2220*
—. Politics. Social Classes. Women. 1930-81. *2312*
—. Politics and the Military. 1824-1973. *2280*
—. Politics and the Military. 1939-64. *2404*
—. Politics and the Military. Reform programs. Tenentes. 1922-73. *2204*
—. Politics and the Military. Tenentes. 1922-67. *2303*
—. Prisoners of war. 1800-1969. *2299*
—. Race Relations. Social classes. 1972-78. *2494*
—. Revolution. 1922-30. *2374*
—. Soccer. 1890-1979. *2270*
—. Social security policy. Working class. 1964-77. *2466*
—. Socialism. 1879-1969. *2227*
—. Tenentes. 1920's-70's. *2256*
—. Voting and Voting Behavior. 1930-64. *2409*
—. Voting patterns. 1952-63. *2323*
—. Woman Suffrage. 1850-1932. *2251*
Brazil (Amazon region). Economic Development. Ideology. Military Government. 1965-74. *2417*
—. Instituto Nacional de Colonização e de Reforma Agraria. Settlement. 1970-78. *2416*
Brazil (Amazon region; Araguaia Valley). Agriculture. Development. 1960's-70's. *2492*
Brazil (Amazonia). Bureaucracies. Economic development. Regional planning. 1966-78. *2486*
Brazil (Brasilia). Economic Conditions. Industrialization. 1960-75. *2436*
Brazil (Goiás). Economic conditions. Politics. 1889-1930. *2345*
Brazil (Maranhão). Political crisis. Social Conditions. 1956-76. *2218*
Brazil (Mato Grosso, São Paulo). Cattle industry. Trade. Transportation, Commercial. 1876-1920's. *2334*
Brazil (Minas Gerais). Catholic Church. Church and State. Working Class. 1891-1930. *2346*
—. Chamber of Deputies. Congress. Political recruitment. 1945-75. *2240*
—. Election Laws (secret ballot). Voting and Voting Behavior (cumulative). 1927. *2335*
—. Elections. 1978. *2442*
—. Elections. Local Government. Military government. Patronage. 1965-68. *2448*

—. Elections. Resende, Antônio de Lara (memoirs). 1900-76. *2304*
—. Elections, legislative. Political Parties. 1964-78. *2418*
—. Political Change. 16c-1970's. *2244*
—. Public Administration (appointments). 1890-1937. *2347*
Brazil (Minas Gerais; Barbacena). Elections, legislative. 1974-78. *2431*
Brazil (Northeast). Agrarian unrest. Catholic Church. Church and State. Clergy (political role). 1889-1964. *2292*
—. Agriculture. Government. Social Organization. 1960's-70's. *2231*
—. Bandits. 1900-30's. *2362*
—. Catholic Church. Church and State. 1973. *2294*
—. Families. Kinship organization. Politics. 1889-1930. *2271*
Brazil (Northeast; Barro). Agriculture. Capitalism. Patron-client Relations. Production, modes of. 1897-1975. *2320*
Brazil (Northeast; Ceará). Banditry, social. Hobsbawm, E. J. Lampião. Political structure. ca 1900-30. *2378*
Brazil (Northeast, destruction of). Foreign aid. Roett, Reardan. SUDENE. USA. 1960-72. *2212*
Brazil (Parana). Agriculture. Business. Investments. Multinational corporations. Paraguay. 1965-78. *335*
—. Peasant movements. Social Change. 17c-1960. *2328*
Brazil (Pernambuco). Agricultural Labor. Peasants. Radicalization. Strikes. 1955-64. *2401*
—. Elites (political). Recife Law School. 1889-1938. *2351*
Brazil (Riberião Preto). Populism. 1900-64. *2327*
Brazil (Rio de Janeiro). 1565-1965. *2273*
—. Calendars. 1534-1965. *2275*
—. Coups d'Etat. Social Classes. Voting patterns. 1947-64. *2407*
—. Favelas. Housing policy. 1972-76. *2489*
—. Favelas. Marginality theory. Poor. 1968-73. *383*
—. Political Parties. Voting and Voting Behavior. 1964-76. *2426*
—. Urban History. 1557-1965. *2274*
Brazil (Rio de Janeiro, São Paulo). Railroads, suburban. Riots. 1974-76. *2474*
Brazil (Rio Grande do Sul). Cortés, Carlos E. Love, Joseph. Regionalism (review article). 1880's-1960's. *2293*
—. Economic Conditions. Economic Policy. Intergovernmental Relations. 1891-1930. *2336*
—. Farmers, small. Land reform. 1964-78. *2455*
—. Index. *Revista do Instituto Histórico e Geográfico do Rio Grande do Sul.* 1921-71. *2325*
Brazil (São Francisco valley). Economic Development. Government. 1958-78. *2321*
Brazil (São Paulo). Coffee. Economic Development. 1875-1975. *2302*
—. Coffee. Immigration policy. Labor Force. 1886-1930. *2356*
—. Elections (national). Labor. Local politics. Peasants. Political attitudes. 1974. *2467*
—. Labor Unions and Organizations. Work, sociology of (review article). 20c. *2203*
—. Military Campaigns (documents). Rebellions. 1924. *2372*
Brazilian Expeditionary Force. Military Ground Forces. World War II. 1941-45. *2360*
Brezhnev, Leonid (visit). Cuba. USSR. 1961-74. *1480*
British Commonwealth *See also* Great Britain.
—. Cuba. Foreign Relations. West Indies. 1960's-70's. *1316*
—. International relations. Jamaica. 1494-1975. *1784*
British Honduras *See also* Belize; Central America.
—. Boundaries (disputes). Great Britain. Guatemala. Ubico Castañeda, Jorge. USA. 1933-42. *1147*
British West Indies *See also* West Indies.
—. Canada. Political integration. 1884-1974. *1336*
—. Colonialism. Commissions of Enquiry. Great Britain. Jamaica. Trinidad and Tobago. 1934-77. *1349*
—. Decolonization. 1960's-70's. *1809*
—. Drugs. Legislation. Marijuana. 1912-73. *1800*
Budgets (deficits). Capital accumulation. Mexico. 1940's-70's. *894*
Bureaucracies. Agricultural reform. Allende, Salvador. Chile. 1971-73. *2684*

—. Caribbean Free Trade Association. Economic integration. West Indies. 1963-73. *1331*
—. Chaguaramas, Treaty of. Economic Integration. Negotiations. 1973. *1288*
—. Economic Integration. 1980. *1289*
—. Economic integration. Political institutions. West Indies. 1973-78. *1300*
—. Economic Integration. West Indies. 1968-81. *1328*
Caribbean Development Bank. Economic integration. West Indies. 1969-73. *1346*
Caribbean Free Trade Association. Andean Pact. Central American Common Market. Economic integration. Latin American Free Trade Association. Mexico. 1960's-70's. *523*
—. Caribbean Community. Economic integration. West Indies. 1963-73. *1331*
—. Economics. Politics. West Indies. 1967-70's. *1344*
—. European Economic Community. Trade. West Indies. 1950's-73. *1324*
Caribbean News Agency. News agencies. West Indies. 1976-81. *1297*
Caribbean Region. Africa. Bibliographies. Negroes. 1973-74. *102*
—. Antitrust laws. Competition policy. Regionalism. 20c. *1334*
Caricatures. *See* Cartoons and Caricatures.
Carnero Checa, Genaro. Journalists. Peru. 1935-80. *2081*
Carnival. Cuba (Santiago). Revolutionary Movements. 1957. *1571*
Carpentier, Alejo. Cuba. Ideology. Literature. Revolution. 20c. *1583*
—. Dictatorship (review article). García Márquez, Gabriel. Novels. Roa Bastos, Augusto. 1840-1975. *64*
Carranza, Venustiano. *America* (weekly). Catholic Church. Mexico. Revolution. Tierney, Richard Henry. 1914-17. *733*
—. Cabrera, Luis. Diplomacy. Mexico. USA. Wilson, Woodrow. 1914-17. *731*
—. Casa del Obrero Mundial. Documents. Government. Mexico. 1915-16. *823*
—. Diplomacy. Mexico. Pershing, John J. USA. Villa, Pancho. Wilson, Woodrow. 1915-17. *801*
—. Economic Policy. Mexico. Nationalism. Obregón, Álvaro. Political Development. 1917-24. *809*
—. Emigration. Labor. Mexico. USA. 1916-20. *725*
—. Foreign Relations. Mexico. Plan of San Diego. USA. 1915-16. *750*
—. Mexicans. Mexico. Rebellions. USA (Texas). 1848-1920. *792*
—. Mexico. Nationalism. Reform. 1915-20. *790*
Carrillo Puerto, Felipe. Alvarado, Salvador. Mexico (Yucatán). Women's liberation movement. 1920-24. *772*
—. Caciquism. Mexico (Yucatán). Socialism. 1922-24. *763*
Carrington, 6th Baron. Belize. Documents. Great Britain. Guatemala. Treaties. 1981. *1064*
Carrizosa, Rubén C. Land Reform. Mexico (Tlaxcala; Huamantla). Patron-client Relations. 1930-39. *575*
Cartagena Agreement. Andean Group. Economic integration. Regional development. 1969-76. *1852*
Cartoons and Caricatures (review article). Johnson, John J. Tyler, Ron. USA. ca 1880-1975. *170*
Casa del Obrero Mundial. Cárdenas, Lázaro. Documents. Mexico. 1938. *849*
—. Carranza, Venustiano. Documents. Government. Mexico. 1915-16. *823*
—. Documents. Labor, Department of. Labor Unions and Organizations. Mexico. 1914-15. *825*
—. Documents. Labor, Department of. Labor Unions and Organizations. Mexico. Political Factions. 1915. *828*
—. Documents. Labor Unions and Organizations. Mexico. Political Factions. 1915. *826*
—. Labor Unions and Organizations. Mexico. Revolution. Strikes. Working class. 1909-16. *753*
—. Labor Unions and Organizations. Mexico (Mexico City). Peasants. Working Class. 1910-16. *727*
—. Letters. Mexico. Mexico. Zapata, Emiliano. 1914-15. *827*
Castello-Branco, Humberto (anthology; review article). Brazil. Military. 1900-67. *2324*
Castilhos, Julio de. Authoritarianism. Brazil. Politics. Vargas, Getúlio. 19c-20c. *2217*

Castillo, Rene (letter). Chile. Communist Party. Coups d'etat. Popular Unity. 1970-73. *2786*
Castro, Cipriano. Exile. Gómez, Juan Vicente. Venezuela. 1908-24. *2196*
Castro, Fidel. Armies. Cuba. Guerrilla warfare. 1958. *1525*
—. Batista, Fulgencio. Bay of Pigs invasion. Cuba. Kennedy, John F. USA. USSR. 1952-62. *1609*
—. Communist Parties and Movements. Cuba. Guatemala. Labor Party. Revolution. 1959-68. *457*
—. Communist Party. Cuba. Dictatorship. USA. 1940-77. *1352*
—. Communist Party. Cuba. Institutionalization. Revolution. 1959-70. *1367*
—. Cuba. Domestic policy. 1960's-70's. *1500*
—. Cuba. Domestic Policy. Foreign policy. USSR. 1959-76. *1527*
—. Cuba. Economic Conditions. Ideology. 1959-79. *1647*
—. Cuba. Economic Structure. Political Systems. 1958-78. *1625*
—. Cuba. Exile. Mexico. Revolutionary Movements. 1956. *1597*
—. Cuba. Financial support. Middle Classes. Revolution. 1956-58. *1558*
—. Cuba. Foreign Aid. USSR. 1959-77. *1550*
—. Cuba. Foreign policy. 1959-74. *1645*
—. Cuba. Foreign policy. 1968-73. *1424*
—. Cuba. Foreign Policy. Revolution. USA. 1959-62. *1626*
—. Cuba. Foreign Relations. Nixon, Richard M. (memorandum). USA. 1959. *1600*
—. Cuba. Foreign Relations. USSR. 1956-60. *1390*
—. Cuba. Historiography. Revolution. 1957-80. *1620*
—. Cuba. Independence Movements. Military campaigns. Socialism. 1860-1959. *1644*
—. Cuba. Labor Disputes. Quintela, Oscar. Revolutionary activities. 1946-53. *1633*
—. Cuba. Land reform. 1957-74. *1364*
—. Cuba. Political Leadership. Voisin, André. 1964. *1482*
—. Cuba. Politics and the Military. 1959-76. *1514*
—. Cuba. Revolution. Social Sciences (review article). 1959-75. *1547*
—. Cuba. Revolution. USA. 1959-74. *1454*
—. Cuba. Socialism, traditional. 1959-74. *1481*
—. Cuba (dependence). USSR. 1968-73. *1357*
—. Cuba, invasion of. Guevara, Ernesto "Che" (memoirs). Military preparations. Revolution. 1954-56. *1478*
—. Cuba (Santiago). Military Camps and Forts. Moncada barracks. 1859-1960. *1642*
Castro, Fidel ("History Will Absolve Me" speech). Cuba. Social Problems. 1953-59. *1628*
—. Cuba (Moncada). Leninism. Political Speeches. 1953. *1353*
Castro, Fidel (speech). Communist Party (50th anniversary). Cuba. 1959-75. *1398*
Catholic Church *See also* religious orders by name, e.g. Jesuits, etc.; Vatican.
—. 1965-79. *105*
—. Agrarian unrest. Brazil (Northeast). Church and State. Clergy (political role). 1889-1964. *2292*
—. Agricultural cooperatives. El Salvador. Peasants. 1960's-70's. *1124*
—. Allende, Salvador. Chile. Coups d'Etat. 1973. *2856*
—. Allende, Salvador. Chile. Elections. Social change. 1968-70. *2763*
—. *America* (weekly). Carranza, Venustiano. Mexico. Revolution. Tierney, Richard Henry. 1914-17. *733*
—. Anti-Semitism. Argentina. Subversion. Terrorism. 1975. *2657*
—. Argentina. Clergy. Movement of Priests for the Third World. Radicals and Radicalism. Violence. 1969-70's. *2520*
—. Argentina. Dictatorship. 1970's. *2670*
—. Authority. Social Organization. 1940's-70's. *106*
—. Bishops. Colombia. Social problems. Venezuela. 1968-78. *1843*
—. Brazil. Church and state. Leme, Sebastião, Cardinal. Vargas, Getúlio. 1930-54. *2411*
—. Brazil. Fascism. Integralist movement. 1930's. *2361*
—. Brazil. Figueiredo, Jackson de. Political movements. Publicists. 1918-28. *2392*
—. Brazil. *Ordem* (periodical). 1921-37. *2371*
—. Brazil. Political power. 16c-20c. *2429*
—. Brazil. Political repression. 1964-74. *2425*

—. Brazil. Political transformation. 1950-64. *2258*
—. Brazil (Minas Gerais). Church and State. Working Class. 1891-1930. *2346*
—. Brazil (Northeast). Church and State. 1973. *2294*
—. Capitalism. Church and State. Cristero Movement. Mexico. 1926-29. *800*
—. Central America. Independence Movements. 1820-1980. *1000*
—. Chile. Coups d'Etat. 1970-73. *2906*
—. Chile. Military government. 1973-76. *2954*
—. Chile. Revolutionary change. 1970's. *2788*
—. Church and State. 1970's. *203*
—. Church and State. Guatemala (Quiché). 1950-59. *1154*
—. Church and state. Mexico. 1810-1970. *662*
—. Church and state. Mexico. 1910-40. *821*
—. Clergy (conferences). Social justice. 1968-73. *221*
—. Democracy. Venezuela. 1958-75. *2179*
—. Development theory. Leftism. ca 1960-77. *463*
—. Dominican Republic. Peasants. Social reform. 1970's. *1679*
—. El Salvador. Jesuits. Political Factions. 1977-81. *1114*
—. Folk saint movements. Mexico. Religious cults. 1880-1958. *641*
—. Liberation movements. 1960's-70's. *476*
—. Medellín conference. Social Reform. Theology. 1968-78. *140*
—. Military government. National security. 1960's-70's. *21*
—. Paraguay. Social Change. 1972. *2975*
—. Politics. 1960's-70's. *108*
—. Puebla conference. Revolutionary movements. Theology. 1970's. *3*
—. Puebla Conference. Social Problems. ca 1968-79. *202*
—. Socialism. 1970's. *158*
Catholic Church (review article). Câmara, Helder. Social change. 1960-74. *120*
—. Politics. 1960-80. *165*
Catholic clergy. Communist Parties and Movements. 1968-72. *461*
—. Guatemala. Political participation. -1975. *1167*
Catholic clergy, limits on. Church and state. Mexico. Tejeda, Adalberto. 1930's. *847*
Catholic Electoral League. Brazil. Church and State. Pressure groups. 1932-37. *2393*
Catholicism. Human rights. Social change. 1961-79. *117*
—. Left, opening to the. 1973. *171*
—. Nationalism. ca 1960-67. *188*
Catholicism, Folk. Brazil. Millenarianism. Politics. Religion. 1893-1980. *2298*
Catholicism, popular. APRA. Leftists. Peru. 1920-45. *2068*
Catholics. Marxism. Politics. Religion (review article). 20c. *107*
Cattle industry. Brazil (Mato Grosso, São Paulo). Trade. Transportation, Commercial. 1876-1920's. *2334*
—. Mexico. Revolution. USA. 1910-23. *771*
Caudillo tradition. Balaguer, Joaquín. Dominican Republic. Trujillo, Rafael. 1931-77. *1683*
Caxias, Duke of. Military Decorations, Flags, and Symbols. Military Education. 1932-82. *2213*
Cedillo, Saturnino. Local Government. Mexico (San Luis Potosí). Modernization. Peasants. Revolution. 1920-38. *769*
Censorship *See also* Freedom of the Press.
—. Argentina. Brazil. Military Government. Press (academic). 1964-75. *88*
—. Argentina. Colleges and universities. Military government. Sociology. 1966-79. *2547*
—. Art (murals). Chile. Ramona Parra Brigades. 1969-73. *2711*
—. Chile. Press. 1973-79. *2931*
—. Peru. Politics. Press. Social Conditions. ca 1919-79. *2049*
—. Peru. Press. 1968-76. *2006*
Censorship Commission of Publications and Illustrated Magazines. Mexico. 1970's. *622*
Census *See also* Statistics.
—. Bolivia. Demography. 1976. *1869*
Center for Research and Documentation of Contemporary Brazilian History. Archives, private. Brazil. 19c-20c. *2245*
Central America. Acosta, Julio. Costa Rica. Federalism. 1920-23. *1081*
—. Acosta, Julio. Costa Rica. Foreign policy (isthmian recognition). Jiménez, Ricardo. Politics. ca 1900-1930's. *1082*

—. Autonomy. Colleges and Universities. 1676-1944. *1006*

—. Bananas. Exports. Multinational corporations. 1947-75. *1012*

—. Bibliographies. Military. 1915-80. *1040*

—. Bibliographies. Nationalism. 1970-80. *1026*

—. Bibliographies. Political Culture. 1930-79. *1023*

—. Capital accumulation. Foreign Investments. Nicaragua. ca 1913-77. *1246*

—. Capital accumulation. Government. 1950's-70's. *1030*

—. Capitalism. Regionalism. 16c-1970. *1033*

—. Catholic Church. Independence Movements. 1820-1980. *1000*

—. Christianity. Reform. Social Policy. 20c. *1031*

—. Civil-Military Relations (review article). Military aid. USA. 20c. *1238*

—. Class struggle. 1960-80. *1007*

—. Colombia. Urbanization. Venezuela. West Indies. 1930-76. *17*

—. Conflict and Conflict Resolution. Mexico. Persian Gulf. 1978-80. *118*

—. Costa Rica. Foreign Relations. 1923-34. *1083*

—. Cuba. Revolution. USSR. 1973-81. *1044*

—. Defense. Military Strategy. 1970's. *1019*

—. Democracy. Elections. Mexico. West Indies. 1960's-82. *453*

—. Demography. Economic Conditions. Political history. ca 1912-75. *1042*

—. Dependency. 19c-20c. *1025*

—. Dictatorship. Foreign Relations. 1934-45. *1020*

—. Documents. Foreign policy. Mexico. 1923-37. *556*

—. Economic Conditions. Foreign Relations. Social Conditions. USA. 1979-81. *998*

—. Economic integration. Foreign Policy. USA. 1960-73. *1024*

—. Economic integration. Nicaragua. Political Systems. Somoza family. 1960-76. *1218*

—. Economic Integration. USA. 19c-20c. *1015*

—. Economic Policy. Integration. 1950-78. *1039*

—. Economic Structure. Political Systems. 1929-76. *1032*

—. Foreign Policy. Government. Honduras. USA. 1871-1981. *1174*

—. Foreign Policy. USA. 1960-78. *1045*

—. Foreign policy. USA. 1960-80. *1013*

—. Foreign Policy. USA. 1978-80. *1002*

—. Foreign Policy. USA. 1980's. *1001*

—. Foreign Relations. Quantitative Methods (small group theory). West Indies. 1948-64. *549*

—. Foreign Relations. USA. 1960's-81. *1018*

—. Foreign relations. Venezuela. West Indies. 1936-78. *499*

—. Imperialism. United Fruit Company. USA. West Indies. 1870's-1950's. *84*

—. Political Change. 1970's-80's. *1011*

—. Political profiles. Regional integration. 1969. *1021*

—. Terrorism. 1970's. *997*

—. USA. West Indies. 1979-81. *291*

Central American Bank of Economic Integration. Economic Integration. 1960-71. *1004*

Central American Common Market. Agricultural development. Institutional dualism. Social Conditions. 1950-70. *1010*

—. Agriculture. Economic Structure. Guatemala. 1953-78. *1159*

—. Andean Pact. Caribbean Free Trade Association. Economic integration. Latin American Free Trade Association. Mexico. 1960's-70's. *523*

—. Economic Development. 1955-79. *1043*

—. Economic Development. Government. Monopolies. USA. 1900-77. *1049*

—. Economic Development. USA. 1954-70. *1047*

—. Economic integration. El Salvador. Honduras. War. 1969-77. *995*

—. Economic integration. Latin American Free Trade Association. 1960's. *507*

—. Economic Integration. Latin American Free Trade Association. 1960-77. *524*

—. Foreign Policy. Mexico. 1960's-70's. *527*

—. Mexico. Trade. 1951-72. *493*

—. Trade intensification. 1961-68. *1008*

—. Trade, intra-area. Urbanization. 1960-71. *1046*

Central American Peace Conferences (Washington, 1907, 1923). Diplomatic recognition. International Law. Tobar Doctrine. USA. 1900-30. *548*

Central Campesina Independiente. Agricultural Organizations. Central Independiente de Obreros Agrícolas y Campesinos. Mexico. Political Factions. 1962-70's. *955*

Central Independiente de Obreros Agrícolas y Campesinos. Agricultural Organizations. Central Campesina Independiente. Mexico. Political Factions. 1962-70's. *955*

Central Intelligence Agency. Chile. Coups d'Etat. Foreign Policy. USA. 1970-73. *2838*

—. Chile. Coups d'etat. USA. 1972-73. *2839*

—. Chile. Coups d'Etat. USA. ca 1970-77. *2860*

—. Chile. USA. 1960-76. *2731*

Central Intelligence Agency (review article). USA. 1970-79. *283*

Central Unica de Trabajadores. Allende, Salvador. Chile. Labor movement. Popular Unity. 1970-73. *2891*

—. Chile. Communist Party. Labor Unions and Organizations. Popular Unity. Working class. 1956-70. *2756*

Centralism. Brazil. Federalism. Government. 19c-20c. *2226*

—. Díaz, Porfirio. Government. Mexico. Political authority. 1876-1928. *961*

—. Véliz, Claudio (review article). 19c-20c. *189*

Centralist tradition. 16c-1970's. *190*

Centralization. Agricultural Commodities. Brazil. Economic Policy. Vargas, Getúlio. 1930-45. *2349*

—. Communist Party. Cuba. Domestic Policy. 1970-73. *1538*

Centralization, territorial. Government Enterprise. Peru. 1968-78. *2112*

Cerdas Cruz, Rodolfo. Arias Sanchez, Oscar. Costa Rica. Politics (review article). Stone Zemurray, Samuel. ca 1940's-75. *1066*

Cerro de Pasco Corporation. Foreign Investments. Labor movement. Mines. Peru. 1900-74. *2073*

—. Miners. Peru. Working class (class consciousness). 1970's. *2031*

Césaire, Aimé (Tragedy of King Christophe). Drama. Martinique. 1960's-73. *1801*

Chaco War. Bolivia. Foreign Policy. Historiography. Paraguay. USA. 1932-35. *98*

—. Bolivia. Paraguay. 1911-38. *42*

Chaguaramas, Treaty of. Caribbean Community. Economic Integration. Negotiations. 1973. *1288*

Chambelona. Cuba, eastern. Political protest. Sugar. 1900-19. *1566*

Chamber of Deputies. Brazil. Legislators, recruitment of. 1963-71. *2499*

—. Brazil (Minas Gerais). Congress. Political recruitment. 1945-75. *2240*

Chamorro, Pedro Joaquín. Democracy. Nicaragua. 1953-78. *1250*

Chapman, Charles E. (History of the Cuban Republic). Cuba. Government patronage. State Department. USA. 1920-27. *1568*

Chavarría, Jesús. Mariátegui, José Carlos (review article). Marxism. Peru. 1890-1930. *2132*

Chayanov, A. V. Lenin, V. I. Peasants. Peru (Cajamarca). Social Classes. 1970's. *2029*

Chile. 1750-1976. *2746*

—. Academia de Guerra Naval. Military Education. Navies. 1911-81. *2722*

—. Agricultural policy. 1965-73. *2727*

—. Agricultural policy. Land Reform. Peasant mobilization. Popular Unity. 1970-73. *2816*

—. Agricultural Reform. Allende, Salvador. 1964-70. *2767*

—. Agricultural reform. Allende, Salvador. Bureaucracies. 1971-73. *2684*

—. Agricultural reform. Allende, Salvador. Land reform. 1964-73. *2708*

—. Agricultural reform. Capitalism. Rural Development. Social Change. 1973-79. *2949*

—. Agricultural reform (review article). Merino, Hugo Z. Peasants. Petras, James. Radicals and Radicalism, rural. 1965-71. *2713*

—. Agriculture. Capitalism. Estates. Feudalism. 16c-20c. *2739*

—. Agriculture. Economic Conditions. Land reform. Social Organization. 1850-1977. *2702*

—. Agriculture. Literacy. Political participation. Voting and voting behavior. 1920-60. *2736*

—. Agriculture. Protectionism. 1880-1930. *2769*

—. Air Forces. 1785-1978. *2745*

—. Alessandri, Arturo. Club de la Unión. Elites. Senate. 1920-24. *2770*

—. Allende, Salvador. 1830-1973. *2878*

—. Allende, Salvador. Argentina. Communism. Perón, Juan. 1970's. *90*

—. Allende, Salvador. Birth control. City Planning. 1971-73. *2785*

—. Allende, Salvador. Blockade, invisible. Economic weapons. Export-Import Bank. Foreign Policy. USA. 1970-74. *2897*

—. Allende, Salvador. Catholic Church. Coups d'Etat. 1973. *2856*

—. Allende, Salvador. Catholic Church. Elections. Social change. 1968-70. *2763*

—. Allende, Salvador. Central Unica de Trabajadores. Labor movement. Popular Unity. 1970-73. *2891*

—. Allende, Salvador. Christian Democratic Party. Land reform. 1964-73. *2699*

—. Allende, Salvador. Communist Party. 1932-71. *2712*

—. Allende, Salvador. Constitutional conflict. Coups d'Etat. 1970-73. *2812*

—. Allende, Salvador. Coups d'Etat. 1960-73. *2780*

—. Allende, Salvador. Coups d'Etat. 1970-73. *2794*

—. Allende, Salvador. Coups d'Etat. 1970-73. *2829*

—. Allende, Salvador. Coups d'Etat. 1973. *2790*

—. Allende, Salvador. Coups d'etat. Dependency. 1970-74. *2797*

—. Allende, Salvador. Coups d'Etat. Fascism. Revolution (planning). 1973. *2877*

—. Allende, Salvador. Coups d'etat. Government. Myths. 1970-73. *2865*

—. Allende, Salvador. Coups d'etat. International Telephone & Telegraph Corporation. USA. 1970-73. *2774*

—. Allende, Salvador. Coups d'Etat. Liberals, Western. 1971-74. *2810*

—. Allende, Salvador. Coups d'Etat. Pinochet, Augusto. Political opposition. 1916-73. *2825*

—. Allende, Salvador. Coups d'Etat. Political writings. 1973-81. *2929*

—. Allende, Salvador. Coups d'Etat. Subversive Activities. USA. 1970-73. *2847*

—. Allende, Salvador. Coups d'Etat (antecedents). Multinational Corporations. USA. 1955-73. *2840*

—. Allende, Salvador. Coups d'Etat (justification of). Political Leadership (junta). Press. USA. 1973. *2945*

—. Allende, Salvador. Economic conditions. 1970-73. *2806*

—. Allende, Salvador. Economic conditions. Marxist system. 1908-73. *2803*

—. Allende, Salvador. Economic conditions. Politics. 1972-73. *2894*

—. Allende, Salvador. Economic dislocation. Political opposition. Reform policies. 1970-73. *2851*

—. Allende, Salvador. Elections. Politics. 1970-73. *2857*

—. Allende, Salvador. Elections, presidential. Peasants. 1970. *2800*

—. Allende, Salvador. Elitism. Peasants. Political economy. Popular Unity. 1970-73. *2830*

—. Allende, Salvador. Films. Landau, Saul (Que Hacer). Political consciousness. USA. 1975. *2881*

—. Allende, Salvador. Foreign Investments. Socialism. USA. 1912-73. *2850*

—. Allende, Salvador. Frei, Eduardo. Housing. 1964-73. *2709*

—. Allende, Salvador. Historiography. Popular Unity (review article). 1970-75. *2701*

—. Allende, Salvador. Imperialism. Legal accession. Revolutionary Movements. 1970's. *2884*

—. Allende, Salvador. Intervention. Kissinger, Henry A. (White House Years). 1973. *2779*

—. Allende, Salvador. Marxism. Political opposition. 1973-74. *2798*

—. Allende, Salvador. Marxism. Politics (polarization). 1970-73. *2862*

—. Allende, Salvador. Mass media. Social change. 1970-74. *2793*

—. Allende, Salvador. Methodology (counterfactuals). Sigmund, Paul E. (review article). 1970-73. *2787*

—. Allende, Salvador. Myths. 1970-73. *2861*

—. Allende, Salvador. Political crisis. 1970-73. *2781*

—. Allende, Salvador. Political polarization. 1970-73. *2813*

—. Allende, Salvador. Politics. 1960-73. *2784*

—. Allende, Salvador. Politics and the Military. 1970-73. *2773*

—. Allende, Salvador. Popular Unity. 1970-73. *2853*

—. Allende, Salvador. Popular Unity. Working class. 1970-73. *2888*

—. Allende, Salvador. Popular Unity (review article). Social Conditions. 1970-73. *2866*
—. Allende, Salvador. Revolution. 1970-73. *2845*
—. Allende, Salvador. Social conditions. Socialism, prospects for. ca 1950-73. *2778*
—. Allende, Salvador. Socialism. 1971-73. *2796*
—. Allende, Salvador (review article). Altamirano, Carlos. Popular Unity. Vylder, Stefan de. 1964-77. *2718*
—. Allende, Salvador (review article). Boorstein, Edward. 1970-72. *2846*
—. Alliance for Progress. Economic development. USA. 1964-70. *2715*
—. Andean Pact. 1973-76. *1854*
—. Andean Pact. Trade patterns. 1953-75. *1840*
—. Anti-Imperialism. Economic integration. Popular Unity. 1960-73. *2782*
—. Argentina. Beagle Channel. Foreign Relations. 1810-1977. *2503*
—. Argentina. Beagle Channel. Great Britain. 1902-77. *2507*
—. Argentina. Beagle Channel. Territorial claims. Tierra del Fuego. 1881-1977. *2510*
—. Argentina. Boundaries (disputes). 1843-1978. *2505*
—. Argentina. Boundaries (disputes). Horn, Cape. 1876-1978. *2509*
—. Argentina. Brazil. Labor movement. Working class. 1960-74. *45*
—. Argentina. Economic dependency. Elites. Modernization. Political conflict. 1900-25. *154*
—. Argentina. Economic Policy. Inflation. 1950's-70's. *2502*
—. Armies. Coups d'Etat. Political Factions. Popular Unity. 1970-74. *2869*
—. Arms Trade. Embargo. Great Britain. USA. 1980. *2922*
—. Art (murals). Censorship. Ramona Parra Brigades. 1969-73. *2711*
—. Artists. Mural painters. Ramona Parra Brigades. Revolutionary process. 1969-73. *2821*
—. Arts. Cultural policy. Military government. 1973-82. *2907*
—. Assassination. Letelier, Orlando. Military Government. Pinochet, Augusto. 1973-78. *2903*
—. Authoritarianism. Labor Unions and Organizations. 1974-79. *2916*
—. Banks. Nationalization. 1970-73. *2882*
—. Banzer, Hugo. Bolivia. Diplomacy. Trade. 1971-76. *1902*
—. Bibliographies. Coups d'etat. Popular Unity. 1973-74. *2876*
—. Bibliographies. Historiography. Military Government. 1970-73. *2880*
—. Bibliographies. Politics. 1970-73. *2858*
—. Bolivia. Boundaries. Foreign relations. Peru. 19c-20c. *1880*
—. Bolivia. Boundaries (disputes). Peru. 1879-1976. *68*
—. Bolivia. Coups d'etat, counter-revolutionary. Guyana. 1961-73. *212*
—. Boundaries (disputes). Economic integration. Ecuador. Peru. 1866-1976. *2023*
—. Brazil. Capitalism. Cuba. Economic development. Human rights (panel discussion). Socialism. 1960's. *214*
—. Brazil. Civil War. Diplomacy (review article). Spain. Valladão, Alfredo (*Brazil and Chile in the Imperial Era*). 1817-1930's. *547*
—. Brazil. Foreign policy. Repression. USA. Working class. 20c. *44*
—. Capitalism. Dependency. Military government. Popular Unity. 1936-74. *2883*
—. Capitalism. Dictatorship. Military. 1960-80. *46*
—. Castillo, Rene (letter). Communist Party. Coups d'etat. Popular Unity. 1970-73. *2786*
—. Catholic Church. Coups d'Etat. 1970-73. *2906*
—. Catholic Church. Military government. 1973-76. *2954*
—. Catholic Church. Revolutionary change. 1970's. *2788*
—. Censorship. Press. 1973-79. *2931*
—. Central Intelligence Agency. Coups d'Etat. Foreign Policy. USA. 1970-73. *2838*
—. Central Intelligence Agency. Coups d'etat. USA. 1972-73. *2839*
—. Central Intelligence Agency. Coups d'Etat. USA. ca 1970-77. *2860*
—. Central Intelligence Agency. USA. 1960-76. *2731*

—. Central Unica de Trabajadores. Communist Party. Labor Unions and Organizations. Popular Unity. Working class. 1956-70. *2756*
—. Christian Democratic Party. Elections (congressional). 1938-73. *2764*
—. Christian Democratic Party. Frei, Eduardo. Presidency. 1964-82. *2689*
—. Christian Democrats. Democracy, breakdown of. Military. 1970-75. *2939*
—. Christian Democrats. Land Reform. Popular Unity. 1964-73. *2700*
—. Christian Democrats. Political participation. Popular Unity. 1963-73. *2725*
—. Cities. Political mobilization. Poor. 1960's-73. *2808*
—. Civil liberties. Military government. Public opinion. Violence. 1970-75. *2900*
—. Civil-military relations. 1973-75. *2941*
—. Class Struggle. Poder Femenino. Upper Classes. Women. 1970-73. *2791*
—. Class struggle. Political organization. Popular Unity. 1970-73. *2783*
—. Coalition politics. Socialist Party. 1932-46. *2751*
—. Colombia. Coups d'etat. Revolutionary movements. 1973-74. *1918*
—. Comic books. *La Firme*. Propaganda. 1970-73. *2889*
—. Communism. Labor Unions and Organizations. Peasant movements. 1810-1973. *2730*
—. Communist Parties and Movements (decentralization). Cuba. Democracy. Political Science (value analysis). 1962-73. *452*
—. Communist Party. Corvalán, Luis. 1970-76. *2919*
—. Communist Party. Corvalán, Luis. Economic Conditions. Popular Unity. 1972. *2686*
—. Communist Party. Corvalán, Luis. Revolutionary activities. 1916-76. *2819*
—. Communist Party. Coups d'etat. Revolutionary strategy. 1973-74. *2873*
—. Communist Party. Economic conditions. 1974-75. *2918*
—. Communist Party. Foreign relations. González Videla, Gabriel. Radical Party. USA. 1940-47. *2748*
—. Communist Party. Labor Unions and Organizations. Recabarren, Luis Emilio. 1890's-1924. *2752*
—. Communist Party. Military junta. Revolution. 1973-74. *2910*
—. Communist party. Pluralism. Political Parties (coalition). 1969-73. *2841*
—. Communist Party. Popular Unity. 1970-73. *2874*
—. Communist Party. Popular Unity. Revolutionary transformation. 1970-73. *2820*
—. Communist Party. Popular Unity. Socialist Party. United front policy. 1956-69. *2753*
—. Communist Party. Prieto, Roberto (letter). Prisons. 1973. *2946*
—. Constitutions. Pinochet, Augusto. Political Systems. 1973-80. *2927*
—. Constitutions. Politics and the Military. 1973-78. *2924*
—. Constitutions. Presidency. 1920-70. *2710*
—. Copper. Multinational corporations. Nationalization. 1970. *2802*
—. Copper Mines and Mining. International law. Nationalization. 1970. *2738*
—. Copper mines and Mining. Nationalization. 1964-73. *2691*
—. Corporatism. Functionalism. Politics. 16c-20c. *2915*
—. Costa, Juan. Dissent. Montes, Isaias. Political consciousness. 1953-73. *2734*
—. Coups d'Etat. 1973-74. *2902*
—. Coups d'Etat. 1973. *2776*
—. Coups d'etat. 1973. *2804*
—. Coups d'etat. Economic Conditions. Human rights. Labor. 1973-74. *2930*
—. Coups d'Etat. Economic consequences. 1973-74. *2956*
—. Coups d'Etat. Economic policy. Popular Unity. 1960-74. *2936*
—. Coups d'Etat. Foreign Policy. USA. 1971-73. 1970's. *2693*
—. Coups d'Etat. Freedom of the press. 1973. *2875*
—. Coups d'Etat. Ideas, History of. Military. 20c. *2720*
—. Coups d'Etat. Intervention. USA. 1966-73. *2703*
—. Coups d'Etat. Intervention (economic). USA. 1970-73. *2943*
—. Coups d'Etat. Kissinger, Henry A. (confirmation hearings). USA. 1971-73. *2809*

—. Coups d'Etat. Left. Politics and the Military. 1974. *2848*
—. Coups d'etat. Middle Classes. Women. 1973. *2835*
—. Coups d'Etat. Military. Repression, politics of. Social pathology. 1973. *2940*
—. Coups d'etat. Military junta. 19c-1973. *2933*
—. Coups d'etat. Military junta. Political tactics. 1912-74. *2792*
—. Coups d'Etat. Military tradition. 1970-74. *2826*
—. Coups d'etat. Panama. Peoples' Party. Revolutionary movements. 1973-74. *1279*
—. Coups d'Etat. Peace research. Popular Unity. Social classes. Violence. 1970-73. *2899*
—. Coups d'Etat. Political polarization. 1973. *2831*
—. Coups d'Etat. Political Systems (bourgeois). Socialism, transition to. 1970-73. *2817*
—. Coups d'Etat. Politics and the Military. Socialism. 1973. *2772*
—. Coups d'etat. Politics (polarization). Popular Unity. 1973. *2886*
—. Coups d'etat. Popular Unity. -1973. *2805*
—. Coups d'etat. Upper classes. 1973. *2854*
—. Coups d'Etat (motives). Economic conditions. Pinochet, Augusto. 1973-76. *2955*
—. Coups d'Etat (precedents). 19c-1973. *2799*
—. Courts, neighborhood. Political Parties. Social Classes. 1971-73. *2867*
—. Cuba. Dominican Republic. Foreign Policy (review article). USA. 1930-72. *225*
—. Cuba. Revolution. 1960's-70's. *454*
—. Cuban revolution. Frei, Eduardo. Leftists. USA. 1958-73. *2768*
—. Democracy. Economic development. Popular Unity. 1969-72. *2744*
—. Democracy, breakdown of. Political Parties. Popular Unity. ca 1970's. *2879*
—. Dependency, political. Local Government (review article). Valenzuela, Arturo. 1880-1977. *2944*
—. Depressions. Monopolies. Oil Industry and Trade. 1930-39. *2762*
—. Dictatorship. Imperialism. 1970's. *2807*
—. Diplomatic negotiations. Peru. Tacna-Arica dispute. USA. 1922-29. *6*
—. Documents. Freemasonry. Ibáñez, Carlos. Politics. 1952-58. *2759*
—. Domestic policy. Echeverría, Luis. Foreign policy. Mexico. 1970-76. *926*
—. Economic Conditions. 1960-76. *2917*
—. Economic Conditions. Human rights. Military government. Pinochet, Augusto. 1973-76. *2908*
—. Economic Conditions. Ibáñez, Carlos. Imperialism. Modernization. USA. 1925-31. *2755*
—. Economic Conditions. Military junta. 1971-74. *2937*
—. Economic conditions. Military junta. USA. 1975. *2904*
—. Economic Conditions. Nationalization. Political participation. Popular Unity. Working class. 1970-73. *2849*
—. Economic Conditions. Pinochet, Augusto. Social Conditions. 1973-80. *2923*
—. Economic Conditions. Statistics. 1830-1976. *2714*
—. Economic Conditions. Wages. 1968-74. *2934*
—. Economic Conditions. World Bank. 1970-73. *2896*
—. Economic development. Foreign Aid. USA. 1973-75. *2913*
—. Economic Growth. Labor Unions and Organizations. Nationalization. 1945-71. *2852*
—. Economic planning. Social conditions. USA. 1973-77. *2942*
—. Economic Policy. 1973-81. *2914*
—. Economic policy. Friedman, Milton. Technical assistance. USA. 1973-75. *2935*
—. Economic policy. Inflation. 1973-75. *2932*
—. Economic policy. Kelly, Roberto. 1973-81. *2951*
—. Economic Policy. Military Government. Monetary policy. 1973-78. *2911*
—. Economic policy. Military government. Popular Unity. 1970's. *2690*
—. Economic policy. Military junta. 1967-74. *2912*
—. Economic policy. Political repression. 1973-76. *2928*
—. Economic policy. Popular Unity. 1970-73. *2868*
—. Educational Reform. 1964-70. *2765*
—. Elections. Military aid. USA. Venezuela. 1963-64. *430*

—. Elections, presidential. Political Change. Social Classes. Voting and Voting Behavior. 1958-70. *2696*

—. Elections, presidential. Political Corruption. 1920. *2758*

—. Electoral constraints. Socialism. 1952-71. *2777*

—. Elites. Land Tenure. Political leadership. Social Classes. 1960's. *2771*

—. Elites. Landowners. National Society of Agriculture. Political Participation. 1932-64. *2681*

—. Farmers, small. Military government. Popular Front. Social Change. 1938-79. *2735*

—. Fascism. Political Reform. 1973. *2732*

—. *Firme* (periodical). International Telephone & Telegraph Corporation. 1900's-70's. *2705*

—. Foreign aid. USSR. 1971-73. *2842*

—. Foreign Investments. Foreign Policy. USA. 1960-78. *2950*

—. Foreign policy. 1945-79. *2742*

—. Foreign Policy. International lending agencies. USA. 1970-73. *2864*

—. Foreign policy. International Telephone & Telegraph Corporation. Multinational Corporations. USA. 1971-74. *2678*

—. Foreign Policy. Intervention. USA. 1970-74. *2688*

—. Foreign policy. Popular Unity. 1970-73. *2815*

—. Foreign Relations. USA. 1970-73. *2692*

—. Foreign Relations (rapprochement). Mexico. 1972-73. *495*

—. Foreign Relations (review article). Political Systems. 19c-20c. *2741*

—. Galdames, Luis. Intellectuals. Politics. 1910-41. *2504*

—. Government. Popular Unity. Social Classes. 1967-73. *2737*

—. Government, Resistance to. Gremialismo. Ideology. Middle Classes. 19c-1973. *2834*

—. Historiography. 1965-76. *2728*

—. Historiography (review article). Marxism. 1972-73. *2827*

—. Housing policy. 1958-73. *2706*

—. Human rights. Military junta. 1975. *70*

—. Ideology. Middle Classes. Political Change. 1970-76. *2675*

—. Imperialism, fight against. USA. 1970-74. *2898*

—. Income distribution. Popular Unity. 1970-72. *2789*

—. Indians. Land Tenure. Legislation. Mapuche. 1979-81. *2925*

—. Indians. Mapuche. Social Policy. 20c. *2717*

—. Interest Groups. Labor Unions and Organizations (suppression). Landowners. National Society of Agriculture. Peasants. 1920-48. *2749*

—. Interest Groups. Society for Promotion of Manufacturing. 1883-1928. *2766*

—. Intervention. USA. ca 1930's-77. *275*

—. Intervention, economic. Popular Unity. USA. 1960-74. *2832*

—. Labor Code. Labor movement. Political Participation. 1973-81. *2926*

—. Labor grievances. Public Administration. Social Change. 1970-72. *2814*

—. Labor movement. Military Government. 1973-78. *2957*

—. Labor movement. Politics. Populism. 1880-1940. *2760*

—. Labor, socialized. 1971-74. *2893*

—. Labor Unions and Organizations. Peasants. Political mobilization. Working Class. 1909-73. *2679*

—. Land Reform. 1938-78. *2697*

—. Land reform. 1960-73. *2887*

—. Land Reform. Military government. 1965-74. *2909*

—. Land Reform. Peasant consciousness. 1965-70. *2757*

—. Land reform. Peasants. Political Attitudes. 1965-72. *2680*

—. Land reform. Peasants (political consciousness). Tenants. Wage laborers. 1950-73. *2682*

—. Land reform. Trade policies. 1970-78. *2685*

—. Land tenure. Social classes. 1965-79. *2677*

—. Law. Legislation. State of emergency. 1925-79. *2676*

—. Left. Politics (review article). Popular Unity. 1970-73. *2795*

—. Literature. Neruda, Pablo. Politics. Socialism. 1964-73. *2855*

—. Local Government (review article). 1960-77. *2719*

—. Management. Worker participation. 1971-74. *2892*

—. Mass attitudes. Political Participation. Social Classes. Socialism. ca 1950's-73. *2743*

—. Migrant Labor (contract). Nitrate industry. 1880-1930. *2716*

—. Militarism. USA. USSR. 1962-74. *2920*

—. Militarism. Violence, political. 1970-74. *2905*

—. Military. Popular Unity. 1970's. *2843*

—. Military Government. 1973. *2938*

—. Military government. Pinochet, Augusto. 1973-82. *2953*

—. Military Government. Political Participation. 1973-78. *2947*

—. Military government. Public policy. 1973-78. *2948*

—. Military role. Public opinion. 1964-65. *2695*

—. Mutinies. Navies. 1931. *2761*

—. Neruda, Pablo. Poetry. 1920's-73. *2729*

—. Neruda, Pablo. Poetry. Political attitudes. 1930's-73. *2723*

—. Nitrate industry. Political development. Presidency. 1920's-76. *2733*

—. Parliamentary government. Political systems. 1891-1925. *2724*

—. Political Attitudes. Popular Unity. Women. 1970-73. *2801*

—. Political communication. Television. 1964-74. *2698*

—. Political Conditions. 1972. *2895*

—. Political culture (review article). 1964-73. *2863*

—. Political Factions. Popular Front. Socialist Party. 20c. *2694*

—. Political imprisonment. Women. 1973-77. *2901*

—. Political Leadership. Popular Unity. Revolution. 1958-72. *2833*

—. Political mobilization. 1976. *2740*

—. Political Participation (leftist). Working Class (class consciousness). 1970-73. *2824*

—. Political significance. Radicals and Radicalism. 1970-74. *2683*

—. Politics. Rural policies. 1970-73. *2870*

—. Politics and the Military (review article). Popular Unity. 1970-73. *2872*

—. Popular Front. 1925-79. *2704*

—. Popular Front. Socialist Party. 1922-38. *2750*

—. Popular Unity. Reactionaries. 1970-73. *2890*

—. Popular Unity. Reform. Women. 1970-73. *2775*

—. Popular Unity, defeat of. 1970-73. *2859*

—. Public health. Socialism. 1950's-75. *2837*

—. Recabarren, Luis Emilio. Revolutionary activities. 1876-1924. *2747*

—. Revolutionary process. 1970-73. *2836*

—. Socialism. 1970-73. *2844*

—. Socialism. 1970-73. *2871*

—. Socialist Party. 1970-73. *2721*

—. Voting and Voting Behavior. Women. 1970. *2822*

—. Working Class (mobilization). 1970-73. *2823*

Chile (Concepción, Santiago). Agricultural reform. Political Attitudes. Working Class. 1968-73. *2707*

Chile (Santiago). Allende, Salvador. Coups d'Etat. Political Attitudes. 1973. *2952*

—. Coups d'etat. 1974. *2921*

—. Leftism. Models. Voting and Voting Behavior. 1964. *2754*

Chile, University of. Radicals and Radicalism. Social Classes. Students. 1971-72. *2828*

Chilean studies. Italy. 20c. *2726*

Chileanization. Association of Nitrate Producers. Nitrate industry. World War I. 1914-30. *2687*

China. Cuba. Foreign Relations. Leadership. Nonaligned nations. 1959-79. *1438*

—. Foreign Policy. 1970's. *266*

Chinese. Cuba. Social Organization. 19c-20c. *1502*

—. Discrimination. Mexico (Sonora). Social Classes. 1910-33. *736*

—. Immigration. Mexico, Northern. 1875-1932. *760*

—. Immigration. Mexico (Sonora). Persecution. 1890's-1931. *761*

Cholos. Bureaucracies. Creoles. Peru (Lima). Race Relations. 1968-71. *2117*

Chorti. Capitalism. Guatemala, eastern. Indians. Rites and Ceremonies. 1971-73. *1141*

Christian churches, Dutch. Surinam. 17c-1975. *1724*

Christian Democratic Party. Allende, Salvador. Chile. Land reform. 1964-73. *2699*

—. Chile. Elections (congressional). 1938-73. *2764*

—. Chile. Frei, Eduardo. Presidency. 1964-82. *2689*

Christian Democrats. Chile. Democracy, breakdown of. Military. 1970-75. *2939*

—. Chile. Land Reform. Popular Unity. 1964-73. *2700*

—. Chile. Political participation. Popular Unity. 1963-73. *2725*

Christianity *See also* Catholic Church; Missions and Missionaries; Protestantism; Theology.

—. Central America. Reform. Social Policy. 20c. *1031*

—. Leftism. 1960's. *473*

—. Political theory. Revolution. Torres, Camilo. 1929-66. *1974*

—. Radicals and Radicalism. Theology, liberation. 1945-77. *464*

Chronology. Cuba. Revolution. 1959-78. *1657*

—. Nicaragua. Revolutionary Movements. 1850-1979. *1225*

Church and State. Agrarian unrest. Brazil (Northeast). Catholic Church. Clergy (political role). 1889-1964. *2292*

—. Anticlericalism. Constitutional Congress. Mexico. 1916-17. *795*

—. Archives. Mexico. 20c. *667*

—. Argentina. Education. Perón, Juan. 1954-55. *2622*

—. Brazil. Catholic Church. Leme, Sebastião, Cardinal. Vargas, Getúlio. 1930-54. *2411*

—. Brazil. Catholic Electoral League. Pressure groups. 1932-37. *2393*

—. Brazil. Civil religion. 1891-1964. *2210*

—. Brazil (Minas Gerais). Catholic Church. Working Class. 1891-1930. *2346*

—. Brazil (Northeast). Catholic Church. 1973. *2294*

—. Capitalism. Catholic Church. Cristero Movement. Mexico. 1926-29. *800*

—. Catholic Church. 1970's. *203*

—. Catholic Church. Guatemala (Quiché). 1950-59. *1154*

—. Catholic Church. Mexico. 1810-1970. *662*

—. Catholic Church. Mexico. 1910-40. *821*

—. Catholic clergy, limits on. Mexico. Tejeda, Adalberto. 1930's. *847*

—. Models. Paraguay. 1972. *2974*

—. Protestantism. 20c. *121*

Church and State (review article). Historiography. Mexico. 1917-29. *770*

Cienfuegos, Camilo. Bibliographies. Cuba. 1950's-60's. *1429*

Cinema Novo. Films. Radicals and Radicalism. 1950's-70's. *18*

Cipriani, Arthur Andrew. Jamaica. Politics. Trinidad and Tobago. World War I. 1914-31. *1303*

Cities *See also* headings beginning with the word city and the word urban; names of cities and towns; Housing; Sociology; Urbanization.

—. Argentina (Buenos Aires). Authors. 19c-20c. *2522*

—. Attitudes. Colombia. Community Participation in Politics. Political culture. 1970. *1922*

—. Bibliographies. Guerrilla Warfare. 1962-72. *163*

—. Chile. Political mobilization. Poor. 1960's-73. *2808*

—. Country Life. Ideology. 16c-20c. *157*

—. Government. Squatter settlements. 1950's-70. *151*

—. Political opposition. Political Theory. 1945-77. *34*

Cities (review article). Brazil. Historiography. 1500-1945. *2261*

City Government *See also* Cities; Public Administration.

—. Argentina (Buenos Aires). Politics (municipal, national). 1918-30. *2583*

City Planning *See also* Housing; Regional Planning.

—. Allende, Salvador. Birth control. Chile. 1971-73. *2785*

—. Cuba (Havana). Social Conditions. 1959-79. *1479*

—. Mexico (Lázaro Cárdenas City). New towns. 1970-78. *869*

Civil Disturbances *See also* Revolution; Riots.

—. Colombia. Novels. *Violencia*. 1946-58. *1932*

—. Colonial rule. Guyana. Ruimveldt massacre. 1924. *1720*

—. Curaçao. Political Protest. Social change. USA. 1960's-70's. *1785*

Civil liberties. Chile. Military government. Public opinion. Violence. 1970-75. *2900*

Civil Liberty. See Civil Rights.

Civil religion. Brazil. Church and state. 1891-1964. *2210*

Civil Rights *See also* Freedom of the Press; Human Rights.

—. Argentina. Domestic policy. Indians. 1960's. *2644*

—. Brazil. Indians. Indigenismo. National Indian Foundation. 1970's. *2481*

—. Constitutions. El Salvador. 1883-1976. *1119*

Civil Rights Organizations. Brazil. Frente Negra Brasileira. 1924-37. *2322*

Civil Service *See also* Federal Government; Public Administration; Public Employees.

—. Jamaica. Social Status. 1930-70. *1767*

—. Local Government. Trinidad and Tobago (Tobago). 1925-70. *1820*

Civil Service, senior (attitudes). Jamaica. 1972. *1765*

Civil War. Brazil. Chile. Diplomacy (review article). Spain. Valladão, Alfredo *(Brazil and Chile in the Imperial Era).* 1817-1930's. *547*

—. Costa Rica. Honduras. 1923-25. *1037*

—. Costa Rica. Physicians. Political Factions. Social reform. Strikes. 1946-48. *1076*

—. Cuba (Santiago). Spain (Madrid). Torriente-Brau, Pablo de la. Torriente-Brau, Zoe de la (memoirs). 1901-36. *1631*

—. El Salvador. Farabundo Martí National Liberation Front. Revolutionary Democratic Front. USA. 1981. *1108*

—. El Salvador. Leadership. 1972-81. *1122*

—. El Salvador. Military Government. 1961-79. *1087*

Civilian regimes. Economic Policy. Military government. 1961-70. *33*

Civil-Military Relations *See also* Politics and the Military.

—. Argentina. Political Systems. Pressure groups. 1930-76. *2549*

—. Armies. Bolivia. Economic Development. Political Factions. 1961-79. *1891*

—. Billinghurst, Guillermo. Coups d'Etat. Peru. 1914. *2116*

—. Bolivia. Coups d'Etat. 1979-81. *1878*

—. Brazil. Military government. 1964-70. *2234*

—. Chile. 1973-75. *2941*

—. Colombia. ca 1950-80. *1969*

—. Corporatism. Politics and the Military. 19c-1975. *441*

—. Cuba. Institutionalization. 1959-76. *1422*

—. Economic Development. Peru. 1968-80. *2025*

—. Guatemala. Military Aid. USA. 1953-78. *1150*

—. Military aid. USA. 1946-78. *426*

—. Military Education. Military officers. Professionalism. 1960's-70's. *417*

Civil-Military Relations (review article). 1960-74. *439*

—. Central America. Military aid. USA. 20c. *1238*

Claims. Cuba. Foreign Relations. Sugar. Trade. USA. 1957-73. *1382*

Clarté group. Brazil. Communism. Nationalism. 1921-32. *2350*

Class conflict. Campesino movements. Modernization. 1918-74. *389*

Class consciousness. Argentina. Labor Unions and Organizations. Peronism. 1960-73. *2649*

—. Methodology. Peasantry. Rural proletariat. West Indies. 1950's-. *1323*

Class Struggle. Argentina. Democratization. Political Parties. 1946-73. *2528*

—. Brazil. Students. 1964-77. *2463*

—. Central America. 1960-80. *1007*

—. Chile. Poder Femenino. Upper Classes. Women. 1970-73. *2791*

—. Chile. Political organization. Popular Unity. 1970-73. *2783*

—. Communism. Dictatorship. Guatemala. Osorio, Araña. 1954-73. *1166*

—. Dependency theory. Imperialism. 1960-80. *359*

—. Dictatorship. Duvalier, François. Haiti. ca 1957-71. *1739*

—. Economic Conditions. Leftism. Peru. 1968-78. *2097*

—. Economic Conditions. Middle Classes. Military government. Peru. 1970's. *2035*

—. Education, Elementary. Educational policy. Mexico. Revolution. 1890-1930. *691*

—. Guatemala. Violence. 1812-1978. *1127*

—. Guatemala. Violence. 1960-75. *1169*

—. Martinique. Rebellions. 1635-1976. *1793*

Clergy *See also* specific denominations by name.

—. Argentina. Catholic Church. Movement of Priests for the Third World. Radicals and Radicalism. Violence. 1969-70's. *2520*

Clergy (conferences). Catholic Church. Social justice. 1968-73. *221*

Clergy (political role). Agrarian unrest. Brazil (Northeast). Catholic Church. Church and State. 1889-1964. *2292*

Clientelism. Bureaucracies. Colombia. Political Systems. 19c-1974. *1970*

Club de la Unión. Alessandri, Arturo. Chile. Elites. Senate. 1920-24. *2770*

Club 3 de Octubro. Brazil. Revolution. Tenentes. Vargas, Getúlio. 1922-35. *2343*

Coal Mines and Mining. Colombia (Guajira peninsula; Cerrejón). Economic development. Multinational corporations. 1970's. *1943*

Coalition politics. Argentina. Perón, Juan. ca 1940-73. *2637*

—. Chile. Socialist Party. 1932-46. *2751*

Codovilla, Victorio. Argentina. Communist Party. Political Leadership. 1958-70. *2608*

Coffee. Agricultural policy. Costa Rica. Economic Development. ca 1650-1970's. *1084*

—. Balance of power. Guatemala. 1950's-70's. *1171*

—. Brazil. Economic Policy. 1930-39. *2339*

—. Brazil (São Paulo). Economic Development. 1875-1975. *2302*

—. Brazil (São Paulo). Immigration policy. Labor Force. 1886-1930. *2356*

—. Colombia. Economic Policy. Peasant movements. Social classes. 1955-70. *1909*

—. Colombia. Economic Policy. Political Systems. 1930-80. *1958*

—. Colombia. Economic Structure. 19c-20c. *1950*

Coffee policy. Brazil. Commodity markets, international. 1906-62. *2260*

Cold War *See also* Detente.

—. Detente. Foreign Relations. Medina Echavarría, José. USA. 1948-68. *288*

—. Foreign relations. Historiography (US). USA. 1945-50. 1950-75. *265*

—. Foreign Relations. Organization of American States. USA. 1944-49. *312*

Colleges and Universities *See also* names of individual institutions; Dissertations; Students.

—. Argentina. Censorship. Military government. Sociology. 1966-79. *2547*

—. Authoritarianism. Autonomy. Mexico. Mexico, National Autonomous University of. 1929-75. *635*

—. Autonomy. Central America. 1676-1944. *1006*

—. Communism. Cuba. Martínez Villena, Rubén. Pascual, Sarah (memoirs). Universidad Popular José Martí. 1920-30. *1560*

—. Cultural development. 1500-1978. *187*

—. Educational Policy. Mexico. 1812-1979. *589*

—. Educational reform. Student movements. 1917-30. *2*

—. Graduates. Mexico, National Autonomous University of (National School of Economics). Public Employees. 1929-52. *181*

—. Mexico. Mexico, National Autonomous University of. Radicals and Radicalism. 1966-72. *946*

—. Mexico. Political Leadership. Political Socialization. 1920-70. *584*

—. Political Systems. Politics. Students. 1970's. *109*

Colleges and Universities (political role). Educational Policy. ca 1950-73. *67*

Colleges and Universities (politicization). Elites. Modernization. 20c. *76*

Collor, Lindolfo. Brazil. Labor. Vianna Moog, Clodomir (memoirs). 1891-1942. *2389*

Colombia. Agricultural Labor. Land reform. 1960. *1976*

—. Agricultural reform. ca 1870-1978. *1929*

—. Agricultural reform participation. Peasant attitudes. 1970-74. *1924*

—. Agriculture. Capitalism. Economic Development. Women. 20c. *1946*

—. Andean Group. Decisionmaking. Economic integration. Foreign Policy. 1974-80. *1981*

—. Anthropology. 1930-80. *1977*

—. Anti-Communist Movements. *Violencia.* 1940's-65. *1939*

—. Arbitration, International. Boundaries. Diplomacy. Fortoul, Gil. Switzerland. Venezuela. 1922. *1838*

—. Armies. Politics and the Military. 1900-72. *1925*

—. Attitudes. Cities. Community Participation in Politics. Political culture. 1970. *1922*

—. Authoritarianism. Bureaucracies. Military. 1964-73. *1968*

—. Automobile Industry and Trade. Economic Policy. Politics. 1965-80. *1928*

—. Automobile industry and Trade. Government regulation. Multinational Corporations. 1969-76. *1927*

—. Bananas. Strikes. 1928-29. *1973*

—. Barco concession. Economic Policy. Oil industry and trade. USA. 1926-32. *1963*

—. Bibliographies. Land reform. 1979. *1966*

—. Bibliographies. *Violencia.* 1946-65. *1962*

—. Bishops. Catholic Church. Social problems. Venezuela. 1968-78. *1843*

—. Boundaries. Brazil. García Ortiz, Laureano. Peru. Treaties. 1920-30. *56*

—. Boundaries. Leticia incident. Peru. Salmon-Lozano treaty. 1922. 1932-34. *1834*

—. Bureaucracies. Clientelism. Political Systems. 19c-1974. *1970*

—. Bureaucracies. Public Administration (policymaking). Social security policy. 1920-75. *1910*

—. Central America. Urbanization. Venezuela. West Indies. 1930-76. *17*

—. Chile. Coups d'etat. Revolutionary movements. 1973-74. *1918*

—. Civil Disturbances. Novels. *Violencia.* 1946-58. *1932*

—. Civil-Military Relations. ca 1950-80. *1969*

—. Coffee. Economic Policy. Peasant movements. Social classes. 1955-70. *1909*

—. Coffee. Economic Policy. Political Systems. 1930-80. *1958*

—. Coffee. Economic Structure. 19c-20c. *1950*

—. Colombian Institute for the Promotion of Higher Education. Corporatism. Decentralization. Educational policy. National Apprenticeship Service. 1950's-74. *1911*

—. Communist Parties and Movements. Ideology. 20c. *1952*

—. Concordats. Vatican. 1753-1973. *1954*

—. Congress. Elites, political. Interest groups. 1974. *1944*

—. Democracy, consociational. Elites. Elites (behavior). Lijphart, Arend. 1945-74. *1919*

—. Drug traffic. Mexico. USA. 1920's-80's. *376*

—. Economic aid (preinvestment assistance). UN. 1970-73. *1930*

—. Economic Conditions. Elections. Political Participation. 1960's-74. *1934*

—. Economic Conditions. López Michelsen, Alfonso. Social Conditions. 1974-79. *1955*

—. Economic development. Foreign Investments. Kemmerer, Edwin Walter. Monetary reform. USA. 1923-30. *1917*

—. Economic Development. Imperialism. USA. 1920-74. *1926*

—. Economic growth. Liberalism. ca 1950-79. *1931*

—. Economic Planning. Political instability. 1973. *1914*

—. Economic Policy. Politics. 1880-1978. *1979*

—. Economic policy. Poverty. Rural Development. ca 1900-76. *1912*

—. Elite performance. Violence. 1948-60. *1961*

—. Employment. Industrialization. 1960's-70's. *1908*

—. Factor analysis. Violence, rural. 1948-63. *1913*

—. Fals-Borda, Orlando. Social change. 1925-74. *1935*

—. Foreign aid. Public Law 480. USA. Wheat. 1955-71. *1921*

—. Foreign policy. Multinational Corporations. Oil Industry and Trade. USA. 1920-40. *1964*

—. Forests and Forestry. Government. Settlement. 1926-78. *1936*

—. Gaitán, Jorge Eliécer. Populism. Rojas Pinilla, Gustavo. 1940's-70's. *1920*

—. Government. Pressure Groups. 1945-50. *1956*

—. Historiography. Politics, rural. Regionalism. 1900-40. *1947*

—. Industrial policy. López Michelsen, Alfonso. 1974-78. *1951*

—. Labor. Migration policy. 1975-79. *1949*

—. Land ownership. Peasant movements. 1537-1969. *1940*

—. Land use. Settlement. 1950's-70's. *1942*

—. Modernization. Nationalism. 1819-1974. *1945*

—. Modernization. *Violencia.* 1945-53. *1957*

—. National Front. Political Reform. Public Administration. 1958-74. *1937*

—. Panama. Treaties. Uribe, Antonio José. USA. 1901-22. *234*

—. Persecution, religious. Protestants. 1950's. *1916*

—. Political continuity. Values. -20c. *1923*
—. Political opposition. Violence, institutional. 1970's. *1980*
—. Political parties. 1957-75. *1959*
—. Political parties. Social classes. 1968-74. *1953*
—. Political parties. Urbanization. 1970's. *1978*
—. Political party leadership. 1969-70. *1941*
—. Political systems. Regionalism. 1863-1979. *1975*
—. Territorial Waters (conference). Venezuela. 1815-1974. *1842*
—. *Violencia*. 1946-64. *1933*
—. Women. 1948-70's. *1972*
Colombia (Antioquia). Colonization. Social mobility. 1835-1974. *1915*
Colombia (Arauca). Gómez, Humberto. Rebellions. 1916-18. *1948*
Colombia (Bogotá). Elections, presidential. Riot suppression tactics. 1970. *1965*
Colombia (Cali). Political Systems. Servants. Social Organization. Women. 1938-79. *1967*
Colombia (Fómeque). Community development. Modernization, rural. 1936-70's. *1938*
Colombia (Guajira peninsula; Cerrejón). Coal Mines and Mining. Economic development. Multinational corporations. 1970's-81. *1943*
Colombia (Salado). Patron-client networks. *Violencia*. 1930-73. *1971*
Colombia (Tolima). Echandía family. Genealogy. 18c-20c. *1960*
Colombian Institute for the Promotion of Higher Education. Colombia. Corporatism. Decentralization. Educational policy. National Apprenticeship Service. 1950's-74. *1911*
Colonial Development Act. Great Britain. Labour Party. West Indies. 1918-39. *1317*
Colonial Government *See also* Imperialism; Neocolonialism.
—. Dominican Republic. Haiti. Military Occupation. 1898-1940. *1320*
—. Great Britain. Labor policy. West Indies. 1931-40. *1291*
—. Great Britain. Macmillan, W. M. *(Warning from the West Indies)*. West Indies. 1934-39. *1315*
—. Public Administration. West Indies. 1900-73. *1309*
Colonial Office. Great Britain. Labor Disputes. Oil. Trinidad and Tobago. 1937-38. *1807*
Colonial practices, Spanish. Bureaucracies. Modernization. Organizational model. Venezuela. -1970's. *75*
Colonial rule. Civil Disturbances. Guyana. Ruimveldt massacre. 1924. *1720*
Colonialism *See also* Imperialism; Neocolonialism.
—. ca 1821-1973. *115*
—. Africa. Rodney, Walter. 1960-72. *1696*
—. Belize. Ideology. Social Classes. 17c-20c. *1050*
—. British West Indies. Commissions of Enquiry. Great Britain. Jamaica. Trinidad and Tobago. 1934-77. *1349*
—. Communications. 1940's-70's. *168*
—. Culture. Great Britain. Jamaica Institute. Musgrave, Anthony. 1879-1979. *1751*
—. Exploitation. Spain. 17c-20c. *180*
—. Jamaica. Political Protest. 1938. *1771*
—. Peasants. Political Participation. St. Lucia. 1950's-70's. *1821*
—. Racism. Strikes, longshoremen's. Trinidad and Tobago. 1919. *1817*
Colonization *See also* Settlement.
—. Agriculture. Antigua (Barbuda). Land Tenure. 1860-1923. *1790*
—. Colombia (Antioquia). Social mobility. 1835-1974. *1915*
—. Costa Rica. Land Reform. Peasants. 1942-78. *1085*
—. Cultural imperialism. Nationalism. Pan-Americanism. Revolution. 16c-20c. *208*
—. Guatemala (Petén). Land reform. 1954-79. *1158*
Colorado River. Mexico. Salinity problem. Treaties (water; 1944). USA. 1944-74. *574*
Comecon. Cuba. Nuclear power. USSR. 1974-81. *1573*
Comibol. Bolivia. Economic Development. Export economy. Mines. 1900-70's. *1866*
Comic books. Chile. *La Firme*. Propaganda. 1970-73. *2889*
Comitas, Lambros. Herdeck, Donald E. Reference Books (review article). West Indies. 1900-75. *1343*
Comité Nacional de Unidad Sindical. Guatemala. Labor Unions and Organizations. 1953-78. *1130*

Commerce *See also* Banking; Business; International Trade; Monopolies; Prices; Statistics; Tariff; Trade; Transportation.
—. Brazil. Foreign Relations. Industry. Treaties. USA. 1935. *2381*
Commissions of Enquiry. British West Indies. Colonialism. Great Britain. Jamaica. Trinidad and Tobago. 1934-77. *1349*
Commodity markets, international. Brazil. Coffee policy. 1906-62. *2260*
Common Market. *See* European Economic Community.
Communications *See also* Mass Media; Newspapers.
—. Colonialism. 1940's-70's. *168*
Communism *See also* Anarchism and Anarchists; Anti-Communist Movements; Leftism; Leninism; Marxism; Socialism.
—. Allende, Salvador. Argentina. Chile. Perón, Juan. 1970's. *90*
—. Anti-Americanism. Costa-Gavras, Constantin. Films. Foreign Relations. 1964-82. *71*
—. Brazil. Clarté group. Nationalism. 1921-32. *2350*
—. Chile. Labor Unions and Organizations. Peasant movements. 1810-1973. *2730*
—. Class struggle. Dictatorship. Guatemala. Osorio, Araña. 1954-73. *1166*
—. Colleges and Universities. Cuba. Martínez Villena, Rubén. Pascual, Sarah (memoirs). Universidad Popular José Martí. 1920-30. *1560*
—. Cuba. Foreign policy. 1953-76. *1426*
—. Cuba. Foreign relations. Political Change. Revolution. 1953-73. *1623*
—. Exiles. Mariátegui, José Carlos. 1910-23. *468*
—. Nationalization. Peru. Social Reform. 1969-73. *2103*
Communism (Trotskyism). Anti-imperialist front. Argentina. Bolivia. Lora, Guillermo. 1971-74. *1887*
Communist Countries *See also* Western Nations.
—. Cuba. Economic development. Foreign Aid. 1958-73. *1358*
—. Economic dependency. Socialism. ca 1945-70's. *60*
Communist Parties and Movements *See also* specific parties by country.
—. Argentina. Revolutionary movements. ca 1910-75. *125*
—. Castro, Fidel. Cuba. Guatemala. Labor Party. Revolution. 1959-68. *457*
—. Catholic clergy. 1968-72. *461*
—. Colombia. Ideology. 20c. *1952*
—. Petkoff, Teodoro. Venezuela. 1968-73. *2153*
—. Political Factions. Venezuela. 1937-81. *2159*
—. Russian Revolution. 1917-34. *479*
—. Russian Revolution. 20c. *474*
Communist Parties and Movements (decentralization). Chile. Cuba. Democracy. Political Science (value analysis). 1962-73. *452*
Communist Parties and Movements (general secretaries; discussion). Honduras. Paraguay. Socialism. 1972-73. *147*
Communist Parties and Movements (seminar). Revolutionary movements. 1974. *490*
Communist Party. Allende, Salvador. Chile. 1932-71. *2712*
—. Anti-dictatorial front. Paraguay. Stroessner, Alfredo. 1973-74. *2972*
—. Anti-imperialism. Panama. 1903-77. *1271*
—. APRA. Peru. 1924-36. *2009*
—. APRA. Peru. Political Change. 1930-35. *2007*
—. Apristas. Cuba. Revolutionary theory. 1920's-30's. *1359*
—. Argentina. 1918-78. *2538*
—. Argentina. Arnedo Alvarez, Gerónimo. 20c. *2529*
—. Argentina. Codovilla, Victorio. Political Leadership. 1958-70. *2608*
—. Armies. Cuba. Political education. 1956-79. *1611*
—. Bolivia. 1950-79. *1894*
—. Brazil. 1964-76. *2432*
—. Brazil. Labor Unions and Organizations. 1917-30. *2365*
—. Brazil. Prestes, Luis Carlos. 1922-78. *2205*
—. Brazil. Prestes, Luis Carlos (reminiscences). 1922-34. *2373*
—. Castillo, Rene (letter). Chile. Coups d'etat. Popular Unity. 1970-73. *2786*
—. Castro, Fidel. Cuba. Dictatorship. USA. 1940-77. *1352*

—. Castro, Fidel. Cuba. Institutionalization. Revolution. 1959-70. *1367*
—. Central Unica de Trabajadores. Chile. Labor Unions and Organizations. Popular Unity. Working class. 1956-70. *2756*
—. Centralization. Cuba. Domestic Policy. 1970-73. *1538*
—. Chile. Corvalán, Luis. 1970-76. *2919*
—. Chile. Corvalán, Luis. Economic Conditions. Popular Unity. 1972. *2686*
—. Chile. Corvalán, Luis. Revolutionary activities. 1916-76. *2819*
—. Chile. Coups d'etat. Revolutionary strategy. 1973-74. *2873*
—. Chile. Economic conditions. 1974-75. *2918*
—. Chile. Foreign relations. González Videla, Gabriel. Radical Party. USA. 1940-47. *2748*
—. Chile. Labor Unions and Organizations. Recabarren, Luis Emilio. 1890's-1924. *2752*
—. Chile. Military junta. Revolution. 1973-74. *2910*
—. Chile. Pluralism. Political Parties (coalition). 1969-73. *2841*
—. Chile. Popular Unity. 1970-73. *2874*
—. Chile. Popular Unity. Revolutionary transformation. 1970-73. *2820*
—. Chile. Popular Unity. Socialist Party. United front policy. 1956-69. *2753*
—. Chile. Prieto, Roberto (letter). Prisons. 1973. *2946*
—. Costa Rica. Foreign Relations. USA. 1920's-48. *1075*
—. Coups d'etat. Political strategy. Uruguay. 1968-74. *2998*
—. Cuba. 1939-47. *1615*
—. Cuba. Elites (political). 1959-76. *1509*
—. Cuba. Figueroa, Isidro (memoirs). Martínez Villena, Rubén. 1920-34. *1446*
—. Cuba. Institutionalization. Political Leadership. 1959-76. *1463*
—. Cuba. Machado, Gerardo. 1925-33. *1476*
—. Cuba. Marinello, Juan. Political Speeches. 1930's. *1535*
—. Cuba. Political Development. Revolution. 1961-78. *1513*
—. Cuba. Political institutions. Socialism, transition to. 1962-75. *1362*
—. Cuba. Political Leadership. 1952-78. *1411*
—. Cuba. Political socialization. Politics and the Military. 1959-70's. *1510*
—. Cuba. Political Systems. 1975-79. *1508*
—. Cuba. Politics. Popular front. 1935-44. *1503*
—. Dictatorship. Paraguay. 1928-77. *2969*
—. Economic Conditions. Research. Social Conditions. Venezuela. 1931-77. *2149*
—. Economic development. Honduras. Military government. Social reform. 1971-73. *1172*
—. Ecuador. Saad, Pedro. 1934-78. *1985*
—. El Salvador. Elections. Political parties. 1968-73. *1094*
—. El Salvador. National Opposition Union. 1930-75. *1110*
—. El Salvador. Nicaragua. Politics. Right. USA. 1960-81. *1027*
—. El Salvador. Revolution. 1970's-81. *1097*
—. Faría, Jesús. Memoirs. Venezuela. 1936-44. *2165*
—. Honduras. 1954-75. *1176*
—. Honduras. Padilla, Rigoberto (interview). 1929-77. *1182*
—. Imperialism. Panama. Settlement program (asentamiento). USA (Canal Zone). 1968-73. *1280*
—. Labor movement. Mexico. Popular Front. 1935-38. *837*
—. Labor Unions and Organizations. Mexico. 1935-39. *840*
—. Machado, Gustavo. Venezuela. 1919-78. *2178*
—. Mexico. Political Leadership. Siqueiros, David Alfaro. 1962-74. *618*
—. Nationalization. Oil industry and trade. Venezuela. 1900-76. *2150*
—. Paraguay. 1971-75. *2973*
—. Political repression. Uruguay. 1955-76. *3005*
—. Revolutionary movements. Terrorism (governmental). Uruguay. 1974. *2994*
—. Tupamaros. Uruguay. 1952-73. *3002*
—. Uruguay. 1970-1977. *3000*
—. Uruguay. 1972-76. *3001*
—. Uruguay. 1973-76. *2981*
Communist Party (founding). Cuba. 1925-75. *1477*
Communist Party (Party of Labor). Guatemala. Revolution. 1944-74. *1163*

Communist Party (review article). Acción Democrática. Alexander, Robert J. Venezuela. 20c. *2168*

Communist Party (1st Congress). Baliño y López, Carlos B. *(Militarista)*. Cuba. Exiles. Revolutionary activities. 1869-1926. *1627*

—. Costa Rica. 1900-73. *1072*

Communist Party (1st Congress, 1975). Cuba. USSR. 1970's. *1408*

Communist Party (3d Congress). Honduras. Political Factions. Reformism. 1972-77. *1175*

Communist Party (25th Congress, 1976). Brazil. USSR. 1964-76. *2490*

Communist Party (50th anniversary). Castro, Fidel (speech). Cuba. 1959-75. *1398*

Communists. Anti-imperialist struggle. 1969-73. *193*

—. Argentina. Perón, Juan. Political Leadership. 1945-73. *2621*

—. Cuba. Mariátegui, José Carlos. 1920's. *481*

—. Detente. Politics. 1970's. *127*

—. Elections. Political parties. Venezuela. 1973. *2189*

"Communities of fate." Argentina. Elites (behavior). Political parties. -1974. *2562*

Community development. Colombia (Fómeque). Modernization, rural. 1936-70's. *1938*

Community Participation in Politics. Attitudes. Cities. Colombia. Political culture. 1970. *1922*

Community relations. Booker McConnell Ltd. Demerara Bauxite Company. Developing nations. Firms, foreign. Guyana. 1920-73. *1707*

Compañía Nacional de Subsistencias Populares. Entrepreneurship. Government Enterprise. 1937-76. *610*

—. Government Enterprise. Marketing. Mexico. 1960-79. *923*

—. Mexico. Public Welfare. 1968-73. *851*

Competition. Ecuador (Guayaquil, Quito). 1960-80. *1990*

Competition policy. Antitrust laws. Caribbean Region. Regionalism. 20c. *1334*

Computer technology. Cuba. Economic planning. 1970's. *1376*

CONASUPO. Bureaucracies. Career networks. Mexico. Patron-client model. 1964-75. *915*

Concentración de Fuerzas Populares. Ecuador (Guayaquil). Populism. ca 1940-60. *1995*

Concordats. Colombia. Vatican. 1753-1973. *1954*

Confederación de Trabajadores de Cuba. Cuba. Economic Policy. Labor movement. 1959-73. *1575*

Confederation of Labor (CTC). Cuba. Labor Unions and Organizations. Revolution. 1959-61. *1458*

Confederation of Light Metallurgical Industries. Business. Interest Groups. Perón, Juan. 1944-55. *2648*

Confederation of Mexican Workers (CTM). Cárdenas, Lázaro. Labor movement. Regional Confederation of Mexican Labor (CROM). 1936-40. *848*

Conflict and Conflict Resolution. Central America. Mexico. Persian Gulf. 1978-80. *118*

—. Ethnic Groups. Guyana. Socialism. 1953-76. *1713*

Conflict, management of. Bolivia. Court system. Peasants. 1952-76. *1870*

Conflict potential. Elites (political). Parliaments. Political Attitudes. Surinam. 1955-76. *1693*

Congo crisis. Intervention. Suez crisis. UN. Voting patterns. 1956-60. *227*

Congress *See also* Legislation.

—. Brazil (Minas Gerais). Chamber of Deputies. Political recruitment. 1945-75. *2240*

—. Colombia. Elites, political. Interest groups. 1974. *1944*

—. Cuba. Foreign Policy. Revolution. USA. 1960's-70's. *1436*

Conservation of Natural Resources *See also* types of resource conservation, e.g. Soil Conservation, Water Conservation, Wildlife Conservation, etc.; Ecology; Forests and Forestry.

—. Agricultural reform. National Parks and Reserves. Peru. 1960's-70's. *2011*

Conservatism. Ação Social Nacionalista. Brazil. Middle Classes. Nationalism. Radicals and Radicalism. 1889-1930. *2384*

—. Military. Radicals and Radicalism. USA. ca 1960-80. *447*

Consociationalism. Ethnic groups. Independence. Politics. Surinam. 1948-75. *1692*

Constitution of 1917. Flores Magón, Ricardo. Liberal Party (program). Mexico. 1906-17. *779*

Constitution of 1937. Brazil. 1937. *2342*

Constitutional Assembly. Brazil. Social classes. 1934. *2340*

Constitutional conflict. Allende, Salvador. Chile. Coups d'Etat. 1970-73. *2812*

Constitutional Congress. Anticlericalism. Church and State. Mexico. 1916-17. *795*

—. Democracy. Mexico. 1916-17. *796*

Constitutional convention. Mexico. Political Factions. Regionalism. 1916-17. *805*

Constitutional Law *See also* Civil Rights; Democracy; Federal Government; Legislation; Legislative Bodies; Political Science; Suffrage.

—. Mexico. 20c. *588*

Constitutions. Brazil. Campos, Francisco. Government. Revolution. 1930-68. *2367*

—. Brazil. Economic planning. 1946-69. *2238*

—. Brazil. Liberalism. Politics. 1821-1969. *2214*

—. Brazil. Political parties. 1822-1969. *2282*

—. Chile. Pinochet, Augusto. Political Systems. 1973-80. *2927*

—. Chile. Politics and the Military. 1973-78. *2924*

—. Chile. Presidency. 1920-70. *2710*

—. Civil Rights. El Salvador. 1883-1976. *1119*

—. Government. 1811-1980. *15*

—. Legislative Bodies. Mexico. 1824-1977. *690*

Conventions, International. *See* Treaties.

Co-operativa de Pesquisas-Ação de São Paolo. Brazil. Cooperatives. 1960-80. *2329*

Cooperative movement. Banking, commercial. Economic Development (strategy). Guyana National Cooperative Bank. 1945-75. *1698*

Cooperative socialism. Economic planning. Guyana. 1960-76. *1695*

Cooperatives *See also* Agricultural Cooperatives.

—. Bolivia. Government Ownership. Local Government. Mines. 1951-79. *1905*

—. Brazil. Co-operativa de Pesquisas-Ação de São Paolo. 1960-80. *2329*

Copper. Chile. Multinational corporations. Nationalization. 1973. *2802*

Copper Mines and Mining. Chile. International law. Nationalization. 1970. *2738*

—. Chile. Nationalization. 1964-73. *2691*

Cordemex. Fibers Industry. Mexico (Yucatán). Nationalization. 1961-77. *870*

Cordobazo. Argentina. Labor Unions and Organizations. Marxism. Peronism. Tosco, Augustín (interview). 1960's-70's. *2620*

Córdova, Federico de. Authors. Cuba. Politics. 1878-1960. *1536*

Corporatism. Authoritarianism. National System in Support of Social Mobilization (SINAMOS). Peru. Social Mobilization. Velasco Alvarado, Juan. 1968-74. *2082*

—. Bolivia. Economic Conditions. Movimiento Nacionalista Revolucionario. Politics and the Military. Populism. 1952-70. *1861*

—. Chile. Functionalism. Politics. 16c-20c. *2915*

—. Civil-military relations. Politics and the Military. 19c-1975. *441*

—. Colombia. Colombian Institute for the Promotion of Higher Education. Decentralization. Educational policy. National Apprenticeship Service. 1950's-74. *1911*

—. Dependency. Honduras. 20c. *1173*

—. Echeverría, Luis. Government. Mexico. Social security. 1970-76. *985*

—. Foreign Relations. USA. 1900's-74. *287*

—. Politics. Social Change. 20c. *201*

—. Populism. State development. 1800-1975. *210*

—. Populism, passing of. 16c-1974. *128*

Corporatism (review article). Military Government. 1964-79. *438*

Cortés, Carlos E. Brazil (Rio Grande do Sul). Love, Joseph. Regionalism (review article). 1880's-1960's. *2293*

Corvalán, Luis. Chile. Communist Party. 1970-76. *2919*

—. Chile. Communist Party. Economic Conditions. Popular Unity. 1972. *2686*

—. Chile. Communist Party. Revolutionary activities. 1916-76. *2819*

Cosío Villegas, Daniel. Intellectuals. Mexico. Political Commentary. 1968-76. *979*

—. Mexico. Political Systems (review article). 1946-76. *950*

Cosmopolitism. Ideas, history of. Internationalism. 16c-20c. *164*

Costa, Juan. Chile. Dissent. Montes, Isaias. Political consciousness. 1953-73. *2734*

Costa Rica. Acosta, Julio. Central America. Federalism. 1920-23. *1081*

—. Acosta, Julio. Central America. Foreign policy (isthmian recognition). Jiménez, Ricardo. Politics. ca 1900-1930's. *1082*

—. Agricultural Organizations. Peasants. ca 1970-7. *1065*

—. Agricultural policy. Coffee. Economic Development. ca 1650-1970's. *1084*

—. Agricultural Policy. Indians. Land use. 1500-1973. *1068*

—. Alvarado Quirós, Alejandro. Anti-Imperialism. Diplomacy. USA. 1920-45. *1080*

—. Anti-imperialist groups. Nicaragua. Puerto Rico. USA (domination). 1958-73. *1048*

—. Arias Sanchez, Oscar. Cerdas Cruz, Rodolfo. Politics (review article). Stone Zemurray, Samuel. ca 1940's-75. *1066*

—. Boundaries. Panama. USA. 1846-1921. *1259*

—. Calderón Guardia, Rafael Ángel. Social security. 1940-44. *1077*

—. Central America. Foreign Relations. 1923-34. *1083*

—. Civil war. Honduras. 1923-25. *1037*

—. Civil war. Physicians. Political Factions. Social reform. Strikes. 1946-48. *1076*

—. Colonization. Land Reform. Peasants. 1942-78. *1085*

—. Communist Party. Foreign Relations. USA. 1920's-48. *1075*

—. Communist Party (1st Congress). 1900-73. *1072*

—. Demilitarization. Public policy. 1948-80. *1074*

—. Democracy. Political Leadership. Puerto Rico. Venezuela. 1940's-70's. *449*

—. Diplomacy (secret). Intervention. Jiménez, Ricardo. Nicaragua. USA. 1912-27. *1038*

—. Figueres, José. Foreign Relations. Nicaragua. Somoza family. 1940's-70's. *996*

—. Government. National Development. 1821-1978. *1071*

—. Intervention, foreign. Nicaragua. USA. 1925-26. *1036*

—. National Development. 1821-1978. *1073*

—. Partido Liberación Nacional. Presidency. 1940-78. *1079*

—. Peasants. Political participation. 1972-76. *1067*

—. Policymaking. Social security. 1920-78. *1078*

—. Politics. 1943-80. *1086*

—. Social Democratic Party. 1930-49. *1070*

Costa Rica (Puerto Limón). Bananas. 1880-1940. *1069*

Costa-Gavras, Constantin. Anti-Americanism. Communism. Films. Foreign Relations. 1964-82. *71*

—. Films. Guerrilla warfare. *State of Siege* (film; review article). Uruguay. 1963-73. *2980*

—. Films. Politics. *State of Siege* (film; review article). Uruguay. 20c. *2979*

—. Films, documentary. Methodology. *State of Siege* (film; review article). 1917-70. *2977*

Counterinsurgency *See also* Guerrilla Warfare.

—. Economic Conditions. Social Conditions. Tupamaros. Uruguay. ca 1960-72. *2988*

—. Guatemala. Political parties. 1944-78. *1170*

—. Guatemala. Violence. 1960-78. *1129*

—. Military aid. USA. 1963-73. *444*

Country Life *See also* Agricultural Organizations; Rural Settlements.

—. Cities. Ideology. 16c-20c. *157*

Coups d'Etat. Allende, Salvador. Catholic Church. Chile. 1973. *2856*

—. Allende, Salvador. Chile. 1960-73. *2780*

—. Allende, Salvador. Chile. 1970-73. *2794*

—. Allende, Salvador. Chile. 1970-73. *2829*

—. Allende, Salvador. Chile. 1973. *2790*

—. Allende, Salvador. Chile. Constitutional conflict. 1970-73. *2812*

—. Allende, Salvador. Chile. Dependency. 1970-74. *2797*

—. Allende, Salvador. Chile. Fascism. Revolution (planning). 1973. *2877*

—. Allende, Salvador. Chile. Government. Myths. 1970-73. *2865*

—. Allende, Salvador. Chile. International Telephone & Telegraph Corporation. USA. 1970-73. *2774*

—. Allende, Salvador. Chile. Liberals, Western. 1971-74. *2810*

—. Allende, Salvador. Chile. Pinochet, Augusto. Political opposition. 1916-73. *2825*

—. Allende, Salvador. Chile. Political writings. 1973-81. *2929*

—. Allende, Salvador. Chile. Subversive Activities. USA. 1970-73. *2847*

—. Allende, Salvador. Chile (Santiago). Political Attitudes. 1973. *2952*
—. Allende, Salvador. Politics. 1972-73. *2885*
—. Argentina. Democracy. Political Systems. 1912-30. *2573*
—. Argentina. Depressions. 1930-45. *2571*
—. Argentina. Military. Yrigoyen, Hipólito. 1930. *2566*
—. Argentina. Peronism. Politics and the Military. Working class. 1945-78. *2553*
—. Armies. Chile. Political Factions. Popular Unity. 1970-74. *2869*
—. Authors. Brazil. Literature. 1964-80. *2480*
—. Batista, Fulgencio. Cuba. Sergeants' revolt. Welles, Sumner. 1933-34. *1561*
—. Bibliographies. Chile. Popular Unity. 1973-74. *2876*
—. Billinghurst, Guillermo. Civil-military relations. Peru. 1914. *2116*
—. Bolivia. Civil-Military Relations. 1979-81. *1878*
—. Bolivia. Historiography. Land reform. Movimiento Nacionalista Revolucionario. Peasants. 1952-60's. *1874*
—. Brazil (Rio de Janeiro). Social Classes. Voting patterns. 1947-64. *2407*
—. Castillo, Rene (letter). Chile. Communist Party. Popular Unity. 1970-73. *2786*
—. Catholic Church. Chile. 1970-73. *2906*
—. Central Intelligence Agency. Chile. Foreign Policy. 1970-73. *2838*
—. Central Intelligence Agency. Chile. USA. 1972-73. *2839*
—. Central Intelligence Agency. Chile. USA. ca 1970-77. *2860*
—. Chile. 1973-74. *2902*
—. Chile. 1973. *2776*
—. Chile. 1973. *2804*
—. Chile. Colombia. Revolutionary movements. 1973-74. *1918*
—. Chile. Communist Party. Revolutionary strategy. 1973-74. *2873*
—. Chile. Economic Conditions. Human rights. Labor. 1973-74. *2930*
—. Chile. Economic consequences. 1973-74. *2956*
—. Chile. Economic policy. Popular Unity. 1960-74. *2936*
—. Chile. Foreign Policy. USA. 1971-73. 1970's. *2693*
—. Chile. Freedom of the press. 1973. *2875*
—. Chile. Ideas, History of. Military. 20c. *2720*
—. Chile. Intervention. USA. 1966-73. *2703*
—. Chile. Intervention (economic). USA. 1970-73. *2943*
—. Chile. Kissinger, Henry A. (confirmation hearings). USA. 1971-73. *2809*
—. Chile. Left. Politics and the Military. 1974. *2848*
—. Chile. Middle Classes. Women. 1973. *2835*
—. Chile. Military. Repression, politics of. Social pathology. 1973. *2940*
—. Chile. Military junta. 19c-1973. *2933*
—. Chile. Military junta. Political tactics. 1912-74. *2792*
—. Chile. Military tradition. 1970-74. *2826*
—. Chile. Panama. Peoples' Party. Revolutionary movements. 1973-74. *1279*
—. Chile. Peace research. Popular Unity. Social classes. Violence. 1970-73. *2899*
—. Chile. Political polarization. 1973. *2831*
—. Chile. Political Systems (bourgeois). Socialism, transition to. 1970-73. *2817*
—. Chile. Politics and the Military. Socialism. 1973. *2772*
—. Chile. Politics (polarization). Popular Unity. 1973. *2886*
—. Chile. Popular Unity. -1973. *2805*
—. Chile. Upper classes. 1973. *2854*
—. Chile (Santiago). 1974. *2921*
—. Communist Party. Political strategy. Uruguay. 1968-74. *2998*
—. Ecuador. Velasco Ibarra, José. 1960-61. *1997*
—. Ideology. Literature. Militarism. Peru. 1900-68. *2094*
—. Military Government. Surinam. 1980. *1689*
—. Nicaragua. Sacasa, Juan Bautista (*Como y por que caí del poder*). Somoza, Anastasio. 1933-36. *1237*
Coups d'Etat (antecedents). Allende, Salvador. Chile. Multinational Corporations. USA. 1955-73. *2840*
Coups d'etat, counter-revolutionary. Bolivia. Chile. Guyana. 1961-73. *212*
Coups d'Etat (data). Politics and the Military. 1946-70. *445*

Coups d'Etat (justification of). Allende, Salvador. Chile. Political Leadership (junta). Press. USA. 1973. *2945*
Coups d'Etat (motives). Chile. Economic conditions. Pinochet, Augusto. 1973-76. *2955*
Coups d'Etat (precedents). Chile. 19c-1973. *2799*
Court system. Bolivia. Conflict, management of. Peasants. 1952-76. *1870*
Courts *See also* Judicial Process.
—. Brazil. Fiscal Court. Public finance. 1890-1980. *2278*
Courts, neighborhood. Chile. Political Parties. Social Classes. 1971-73. *2867*
Crafts. *See* Arts and Crafts.
Creole culture. Black Power. Cultural Imperialism. Jamaica. 1962-74. *1742*
Creoles. Bureaucracies. Cholos. Peru (Lima). Race Relations. 1968-71. *2117*
Cricket. Athletes. Negroes. Social mobility. West Indies. 1900-73. *1335*
Cristero Movement. Capitalism. Catholic Church. Church and State. Mexico. 1926-29. *800*
Cruzada Democrática. Armies. Brazil. Politics and the Military. Pressure Groups. 1952-62. *2403*
Cuba. 15c-1954. *1489*
—. Accountability. Democracy. Local Government. 1958-79. *1515*
—. Africa. Angola. Foreign policy. Intervention. 1966-77. *1520*
—. Africa. Foreign Policy. 1959-79. *1440*
—. Africa. Foreign Policy. 1978-81. *1350*
—. Africa. Foreign Policy. ca 1960-79. *1473*
—. Africa. Foreign policy. USSR. 1959-78. *1658*
—. Africa. Foreign Relations. Military. USSR. 1959-81. *1649*
—. Africa. Foreign Relations. Political economy. 1959-80. *1659*
—. Africa. Intervention. Mobilization thesis. 1959-79. *1496*
—. Africa. Military. 1959-78. *1555*
—. Agricultural cooperatives. 1975-79. *1608*
—. Agricultural policy. Landowners, small. Socialist construction. 1959-77. *1386*
—. Agricultural Policy (payment systems). Land Tenure. 1959-76. *1539*
—. Agricultural productivity. Farms, private. State farms. 1959-81. *1451*
—. Agricultural reform. 1940-63. *1624*
—. Agriculture. Economic Structure. Sugar. 1886-1958. *1351*
—. Agriculture. Socialism. 1959-81. *1432*
—. Americas (North and South). Revolution (Sovietization). 1960's-73. *1540*
—. Angola. Foreign Policy. Intervention. USA. USSR. 1975-77. *1656*
—. Angola. Foreign Policy. Revolution. 1959-78. *1546*
—. Angola. Foreign policy. Revolutionary Movements. 1975-78. *1635*
—. Angola. Intervention, military. USSR. 1975-76. *1640*
—. Aponte, Carlos. Nicaragua. Revolution. Venezuela. 1900-40. *184*
—. Apristas. Communist Party. Revolutionary theory. 1920's-30's. *1359*
—. Argentina. Bay of Pigs invasion. Puerto Rico. 1960-61. *1453*
—. Argentina. Brazil. Peru. Revolution. 1920-33. *146*
—. Armies. 1956-80. *1373*
—. Armies. 1956-81. *1465*
—. Armies. Batista, Fulgencio. Politics and the Military. Social Classes. 1899-1959. *1533*
—. Armies. Castro, Fidel. Guerrilla warfare. 1958. *1525*
—. Armies. Communist Party. Political education. 1956-79. *1611*
—. Armies. Guerrilla Warfare. Revolution. 1956-63. *1654*
—. Armies. Militarization. Social Change. 1950-70. *1562*
—. Armies. Revolution. 1952-58. *1610*
—. Arts and crafts. 1959-79. *1596*
—. Authors. Córdova, Federico de. Politics. 1878-1960. *1536*
—. Balance of Power. Iran. Military Strategy. USA. USSR. 1970's. *1598*
—. Baliño y López, Carlos B. Labor Unions and Organizations. Revolutionary Movements. ca 1860-1930. *1456*
—. Baliño y López, Carlos B. (*Militarista*). Communist Party (1st Congress). Exiles. Revolutionary activities. 1869-1926. *1627*
—. Ballet. Diplomacy. 1960's-70's. *1607*

—. Batista, Fulgencio. Bay of Pigs invasion. Castro, Fidel. Kennedy, John F. USA. USSR. 1952-62. *1609*
—. Batista, Fulgencio. Coups d'etat. Sergeants' revolt. Welles, Sumner. 1933-34. *1561*
—. Batista, Fulgencio. Federation of University Students. Revolutionary Movements. Students. 1951-57. *1361*
—. Batista, Fulgencio. Political Leadership. Politics and the Military. 1933-39. *1564*
—. Bibliographies. -1970's. 1971-73. *1537*
—. Bibliographies. Cienfuegos, Camilo. 1950's-60's. *1429*
—. Bibliographies. Nationalism. 1971-80. *1532*
—. Bibliographies. Revolutionary movements. USA. Women. 1953-58. *1569*
—. Bolivia. Political parties. Revolution. 1952-76. *465*
—. Brazil. Capitalism. Chile. Economic development. Human rights (panel discussion). Socialism. 1960's. *214*
—. Brezhnev, Leonid (visit). USSR. 1961-74. *1480*
—. British Commonwealth. Foreign Relations. West Indies. 1960's-70's. *1316*
—. Bureaucracies. Economic Development. 1959-78. *1637*
—. Calbó, Gay (*América Indefensa*). USA. 1925-86. *1466*
—. Capitalism. Economic development. Economy, world. 1959-77. *1430*
—. Carpentier, Alejo. Ideology. Literature. Revolution. 20c. *1583*
—. Castro, Fidel. Communist Parties and Movements. Guatemala. Labor Party. Revolution. 1959-68. *457*
—. Castro, Fidel. Communist Party. Dictatorship. USA. 1940-77. *1352*
—. Castro, Fidel. Communist Party. Institutionalization. Revolution. 1959-70. *1367*
—. Castro, Fidel. Domestic policy. 1960's-70's. *1500*
—. Castro, Fidel. Domestic Policy. Foreign policy. USSR. 1959-76. *1527*
—. Castro, Fidel. Economic Conditions. Ideology. 1959-79. *1647*
—. Castro, Fidel. Economic Structure. Political Systems. 1958-78. *1625*
—. Castro, Fidel. Exile. Mexico. Revolutionary Movements. 1956. *1597*
—. Castro, Fidel. Financial support. Middle Classes. Revolution. 1956-58. *1558*
—. Castro, Fidel. Foreign Aid. USSR. 1959-77. *1550*
—. Castro, Fidel. Foreign policy. 1959-74. *1645*
—. Castro, Fidel. Foreign policy. 1968-73. *1424*
—. Castro, Fidel. Foreign Policy. Revolution. USA. 1959-62. *1626*
—. Castro, Fidel. Foreign Relations. Nixon, Richard M. (memorandum). USA. 1959. *1600*
—. Castro, Fidel. Foreign Relations. USSR. 1956-60. *1390*
—. Castro, Fidel. Historiography. Revolution. 1957-80. *1620*
—. Castro, Fidel. Independence Movements. Military campaigns. Socialism. 1860-1959. *1644*
—. Castro, Fidel. Labor Disputes. Quintela, Oscar. Revolutionary activities. 1946-53. *1633*
—. Castro, Fidel. Land reform. 1957-74. *1364*
—. Castro, Fidel. Political Leadership. Voisin, André. 1964. *1482*
—. Castro, Fidel. Politics and the Military. 1959-76. *1514*
—. Castro, Fidel. Revolution. Social Sciences (review article). 1959-75. *1547*
—. Castro, Fidel. Revolution. USA. 1959-74. *1454*
—. Castro, Fidel. Socialism, traditional. 1959-74. *1481*
—. Castro, Fidel ("History Will Absolve Me" speech). Social Problems. 1953-59. *1628*
—. Castro, Fidel (speech). Communist Party (50th anniversary). 1959-75. *1398*
—. Central America. Revolution. USSR. 1973-81. *1044*
—. Centralization. Communist Party. Domestic Policy. 1970-73. *1538*
—. Chapman, Charles E. (*History of the Cuban Republic*). Government patronage. State Department. USA. 1920-27. *1568*
—. Chile. Communist Parties and Movements (decentralization). Democracy. Political Science (value analysis). 1962-73. *452*

—. Chile. Dominican Republic. Foreign Policy (review article). USA. 1930-72. *225*

—. Chile. Revolution. 1960's-70's. *454*

—. China. Foreign Relations. Leadership. Nonaligned nations. 1959-79. *1438*

—. Chinese. Social Organization. 19c-20c. *1502*

—. Chronology. Revolution. 1959-78. *1657*

—. Civil-military relations. Institutionalization. 1959-76. *1422*

—. Claims. Foreign Relations. Sugar. Trade. USA. 1957-73. *1382*

—. Colleges and Universities. Communism. Martínez Villena, Rubén. Pascual, Sarah (memoirs). Universidad Popular José Martí. 1920-30. *1560*

—. Comecon. Nuclear power. USSR. 1974-81. *1573*

—. Communism. Foreign policy. 1953-76. *1426*

—. Communism. Foreign relations. Political Change. Revolution. 1953-73. *1623*

—. Communist countries. Economic development. Foreign Aid. 1958-73. *1358*

—. Communist Party. 1939-47. *1615*

—. Communist Party. Elites (political). 1959-76. *1509*

—. Communist Party. Figueroa, Isidro (memoirs). Martínez Villena, Rubén. 1920-34. *1446*

—. Communist Party. Institutionalization. Political Leadership. 1959-76. *1463*

—. Communist Party. Machado, Gerardo. 1925-33. *1476*

—. Communist Party. Marinello, Juan. Political Speeches. 1930's. *1535*

—. Communist Party. Political Development. Revolution. 1961-78. *1513*

—. Communist Party. Political institutions. Socialism, transition to. 1962-75. *1362*

—. Communist Party. Political Leadership. 1952-78. *1411*

—. Communist Party. Political socialization. Politics and the Military. 1959-70's. *1510*

—. Communist Party. Political Systems. 1975-79. *1508*

—. Communist Party. Politics. Popular front. 1935-44. *1503*

—. Communist Party (founding). 1925-75. *1477*

—. Communist Party (1st Congress, 1975). USSR. 1970's. *1408*

—. Communists. Mariátegui, José Carlos. 1920's. *481*

—. Computer technology. Economic planning. 1970's. *1376*

—. Confederación de Trabajadores de Cuba. Economic Policy. Labor movement. 1959-73. *1575*

—. Confederation of Labor (CTC). Labor Unions and Organizations. Revolution. 1959-61. *1458*

—. Congress. Foreign Policy. Revolution. USA. 1960's-70's. *1436*

—. Cultural development. 1959-76. *1401*

—. Cultural relations. Trade. Treaties. USSR. 1959-65. *1632*

—. Dance. 1959-79. *1389*

—. Decentralization. Urbanization. 1959-79. *1653*

—. Democracy. 1960-76. *1589*

—. Democracy. Leninism. Revolution. Working Class. 1959-61. *1557*

—. Democracy. Revolution (review article). 1933-60. *1578*

—. Dependency. 1959-78. *1511*

—. Dependency. Economic Structure. Economic Structure. 1953-58. *1371*

—. Dependency (review article). Foreign Relations. USA. 1880's-1930's. *1544*

—. Developing nations. Foreign Relations. USSR. 1959-79. *1472*

—. Developing Nations. Revolution. 1868-1973. *1400*

—. Dissertations. 1905-73. *1655*

—. Documents. Letters. Revolution. Torriente-Brau, Pablo de la. 1935. *1630*

—. Domestic Policy. 1970-81. *1420*

—. Domestic Policy. Economic Conditions. Foreign policy. 1975-80. *1591*

—. Domestic Policy. Economic development. Ideology. Mexico. 20c. *387*

—. Domestic Policy. Nutrition. Social Classes. 1959-81. *1484*

—. Domínguez, Jorge. Mesa-Lago, Carmelo. Socialism (review article). 1960-80. *1516*

—. Dominican Republic. Economic coercion. Foreign policy. USA. 1960-72. *1339*

—. Economic Conditions. Political development. Social Conditions. 1959-79. *1469*

—. Economic Conditions. Political Systems. 1959-79. *1441*

—. Economic Conditions. Politics. 1970's. *1585*

—. Economic Conditions. Production. Statistics. 1957-76. *1660*

—. Economic Conditions. Revolution. 1960's-70's. *1521*

—. Economic dependency. Political Theory. Revolution. 1959-76. *1488*

—. Economic Development. 1959-74. *1470*

—. Economic development. Foreign Relations. USSR. 1960-73. *1410*

—. Economic Development. Power, instrument of. Propaganda. Social Change. 1962-72. *1646*

—. Economic development. Socialist cooperation. 1960-75. *1448*

—. Economic development model. 1960-76. *1586*

—. Economic growth. Socialism. 1962-75. *1612*

—. Economic planning. 1959-65. *1518*

—. Economic Planning. Industrialization. Socialism. 1959-80. *1519*

—. Economic Planning. Social Change. Socialism. 1961-78. *1427*

—. Economic policy. 1959-61. *1372*

—. Economic Policy. 1960's-70's. *1375*

—. Economic policy. Foreign policy. USA. 1933-34. *1384*

—. Economic policy. Incentives, material. 1959-77. *1590*

—. Economic Policy. Labor Reform. Work Organization and Work Norms plan. 1963-75. *1613*

—. Economic Policy. Machado, Gerardo. Social Policy. USA. 1929-32. *1603*

—. Economic relations. USSR. 1960-82. *1459*

—. Economic Structure. Political Leadership. 1959-80. *1542*

—. Economics. Foreign aid. Ideology. 1970-81. *1433*

—. Economists, US. Magill, Roswell. Seligman, Edwin. Shoup, Carl. Tax reform. 1932-39. *1604*

—. Emigration. Force, use of. Government, Resistance to. Middle classes. Political culture. 1960's-70's. *1650*

—. Escambray group. Government. Theater. 1959-76. *1407*

—. Ethiopia. Foreign Relations. Somalia. 1978-79. *1636*

—. Federation of Cuban Women. Political participation. Social Status. Women. 1960-78. *1368*

—. Federation of Cuban Women. Women. 1960's-70's. *1369*

—. Films. Politics. 1897-1971. *1486*

—. Films (historical) (review article). National self-image. Solás, Humberto. 1895-1970's. *1548*

—. Foreign Investments. USA. 1959-64. *1495*

—. Foreign policy. 1959-80. *1356*

—. Foreign policy. 1959-80. *1549*

—. Foreign policy. 1960's-78. *1421*

—. Foreign Policy. Guantánamo Bay (status of). Military Bases. USA. 1960-72. *1381*

—. Foreign policy. International Trade. USA. 1975. *1648*

—. Foreign policy. Mexico. USA. 1960-74. *561*

—. Foreign Policy. Nonaligned Nations. 1959-79. *1439*

—. Foreign Policy. Nonaligned nations. 1961-79. *1541*

—. Foreign policy. Political Factions. 1970-77. *1462*

—. Foreign policy. States, small. 1959-79. *1534*

—. Foreign policy. Sugar industry. USA. 1914-21. *1563*

—. Foreign Policy. USA. 1959-82. *1512*

—. Foreign Policy. USA. 1961-81. *1522*

—. Foreign relations. 1960-82. *1599*

—. Foreign Relations. Mexico. 1959-73. *531*

—. Foreign Relations. Negroes. USA. 1868-1977. *1402*

—. Foreign Relations. Nicaragua. 1960's-70's. *103*

—. Foreign Relations. Nickel. USA. 1975-76. *1545*

—. Foreign Relations. Organization of American States. USA. 1959-75. *1405*

—. Foreign Relations. Panama. 1960's-70's. *543*

—. Foreign Relations. Reagan, Ronald (administration). 1970-82. *1475*

—. Foreign Relations. Revolutionary Movements. USSR. 20c. *1354*

—. Foreign Relations. Sugar Act (1948). Tariff. USA. 1945-48. *1487*

—. Foreign Relations. USA. 1960's-70's. *1365*

—. Foreign Relations. USA. ca 19c-1974. *498*

—. Foreign Relations. USA. USSR. 1959-76. *1385*

—. Foreign Relations. USSR. 1959-77. *1517*

—. Foreign Relations. USSR. 1961-74. *1531*

—. France (Paris). Machado, Gerardo. Newspapers. Revolution. USA. 1933. *1506*

—. Generation of 1923. Intellectuals. 1920-29. *1622*

—. Government, Resistance to. Radio. Students. 1945-52. *1595*

—. *Granma* (newspaper). Public opinion. 1974-76. *1594*

—. Graphic design. Revolution. 1959-79. *1380*

—. Guerrilla Warfare. Revolution. Rolando (guerrilla). 1950's. *1621*

—. Guevara, Ernesto "Che" (portraits). Posters. 1967-75. *1505*

—. Guillén, Nicolás. Ideology. Literature. 1920-65. *1529*

—. Guillén, Nicolás. Literature. Race Relations. 1920-76. *1491*

—. Guillén, Nicolás. Poetry. ca 1930's-75. *1435*

—. Guillén, Nicolás. Poetry. Revolution. 1920's-82. *1419*

—. Havana Conference. Nonaligned Nations. 1979. *1437*

—. Havana, University of. Political science. ca 1960-75. *1651*

—. Historiography. Revolution. 1956-78. *1524*

—. Historiography. Revolution. 1959-79. *1565*

—. Historiography (review article). Marxism. 1933-77. *1574*

—. Historiography, Soviet. Revolution. 1952-59. *1614*

—. Ideology. 1970-82. *1377*

—. Ideology. Military. Revolution. 1959-76. *1643*

—. Ideology. Socialism, transition to. 1960-. *1526*

—. Incentives. Labor. 1963-73. *1498*

—. Income distribution. 1959-78. *1431*

—. Institutionalization. Revolution. 1959-76. *1638*

—. Institutionalization. Revolution. 1959-78. *1366*

—. Institutionalization. Socialism. 1950-78. *1452*

—. International law. Missile crisis. USA. 1962-75. *1577*

—. International politics. Revolution. 1959-77. *1553*

—. Intervention. Platt Amendment. Political Factions. 1916-17. *1567*

—. Interventionism. USA. 1902-58. *1576*

—. Journalism. 1959-76. *1396*

—. Journalism. Martínez Villena, Rubén. Political Attitudes. 1920's-30's. *1554*

—. Labor movement. Russian Revolution. 1917-25. *1392*

—. Land reform. Subversive activities. Sugar. 1958-69. *1418*

—. Legitimacy. Social Classes. 1970-81. *1443*

—. Lewis, Oscar. Oral History (review article). Revolution. 1950's-70. *1483*

—. Libraries. School of Library Technicians. 1962-77. *1391*

—. Literacy campaign. 1960-77. *1501*

—. Literary criticism. Revolution. 1900-79. *1468*

—. Literary movements. National Characteristics. Revolution. 1800-1940. *1494*

—. Literature. 1959-75. *1363*

—. Literature. 1959-81. *1445*

—. Literature. Politics. 1900-30. *1530*

—. Machado, Gerardo. Nationalism. 1928-33. *1383*

—. Machado, Gerardo. Politics and the Military. Revolution. USA. 1933. *1570*

—. Marinello, Juan (memoirs). Martínez Villena, Rubén. 1920's. *1528*

—. Martínez Villena, Rubén. Nicolau, Ramón (memoirs). Revolution. 1920's-30's. *1551*

—. Martínez Villena, Rubén. Revolutionary activities. 1899-1934. *1587*

—. Matos, Huberto. Political Imprisonment. 1959-76. *1493*

—. Medicine. National Health Service. Nationalization. 1959-81. *1471*

—. Merchant Marine. Navies. 1960's-70's. *1485*

—. Mesa-Lago, Carmelo. Social Conditions. Sovietization. 1960's-70's. *1450*

—. Methodist Church. Missions and Missionaries. Nationalism. USA. 1898-1958. *1406*

—. Mexico. Political tensions. Revolution. 1910-75. *131*

—. Middle Classes (destruction). Revolution. 1959-61. *1559*

—. Militarism. 1970-78. *1662*

Elites (political). Brazil. Education. Guatemala. Legislators. Uruguay. 1964-72. *191*

—. Brazil (Pernambuco). Recife Law School. 1889-1938. *2351*

—. Colombia. Congress. Interest groups. 1974. *1944*

—. Communist Party. Cuba. 1959-76. *1509*

—. Conflict potential. Parliaments. Political Attitudes. Surinam. 1955-76. *1693*

—. Mexico. 1935-73. *639*

—. Mexico. 1935-78. *582*

—. Mexico. 1946-70. *580*

—. Mexico. Women. 1910-74. *668*

—. Mexico. Women. 1920-79. *585*

Elites (review article). Mexico. Social Control. 1917-70's. *621*

Elites (white). Jamaica. Political Change. Social Classes. 1972-77. *1756*

Elitism. Allende, Salvador. Chile. Peasants. Political economy. Popular Unity. 1970-73. *2830*

Embargo. Arms Trade. Chile. Great Britain. USA. 1980. *2922*

Emigration *See also* Demography; Immigration; Population; Race Relations; Refugees.

—. Brain drain. Developing nations. Jamaica. 1967-75. *1753*

—. Carranza, Venustiano. Labor. Mexico. USA. 1916-20. *725*

—. Cuba. Force, use of. Government, Resistance to. Middle classes. Political culture. 1960's-70's. *1650*

—. Haiti. 1804-1982. *1740*

—. Mexico. Policymaking. Politics. USA. 1920-78. *653*

Emmerson, John K. (memoir). Diplomacy. Japanese. Peru. USA. World War II. 1942-43. *2038*

Employment *See also* Unemployment.

—. Agricultural production. Income distribution. Land reform. Mexico. 1960's. *951*

—. Brazil. Economic Planning. 1964-70's. *2464*

—. Colombia. Industrialization. 1960's-70's. *1908*

—. Education. Social Conditions. Youth. 1970-74. *47*

Employment (structure). Brazil. Industrialization. Women. 1920-70. *2276*

Employment trends. Mexico. 1950-70. *856*

Empresa Nacional de Comercialización de Insumos. Government enterprise. Marketing. Peru. 1968-78. *2108*

Energy. Canada. Economic Integration. Mexico. Political systems. USA. 1930-80. *616*

—. Foreign policy. Mexico. Tomatoes. Trade Regulations. USA. 1969-80. *937*

—. Natural resources. Regional Planning. Venezuela. 1960-78. *2193*

Energy policy. Foreign Relations. Mexico. 1910-79. *560*

Entrepreneurs. Economic analyses. Politics. 1910-76. *339*

Entrepreneurship. Compañía Nacional de Subsistencias Populares. Government Enterprise. 1937-76. *610*

Equality. Jamaica. Social Classes. 1960-77. *1745*

Erice, Jesús (diary). Cuna. Indians. Panama. Rebellions. 1925. *1262*

Escalation. Cuban missile crisis. National Goals. 1962. *1619*

Escambray group. Cuba. Government. Theater. 1959-76. *1407*

Escobarista Rebellion. Calles, Plutarco Elías. Documents. Mexico. 1929. *830*

Essays. Ideas, history of. Peru. 1950-75. *2133*

Estates. Agriculture. Capitalism. Chile. Feudalism. 16c-20c. *2739*

Ethiopia. Cuba. Foreign Relations. Somalia. 1978-79. *1636*

Ethnic Groups *See also* Minorities.

—. Azuela, Mariano. Mexico. Novels. Politics. Revolution. Social Classes. 1910's-20's. *710*

—. Conflict and Conflict Resolution. Guyana. Socialism. 1953-76. *1713*

—. Consociationalism. Independence. Politics. Surinam. 1948-75. *1692*

—. East Indians. Negroes. Trinidad and Tobago. 1950-80. *1795*

—. Government. Miskito. Nicaragua. 1770-1980. *1191*

—. Guatemala. Panama. Social Status. 20c. *1003*

—. Guyana. Jagan, Cheddi. Nationalism. Pluralism, cultural. Socialism. 1940-70's. *1723*

—. Guyana. National Self-image. 1966-76. *1697*

—. Miskito. Nicaragua. Revolution. 1979-82. *1213*

—. Political development. Social Conditions. Trinidad and Tobago. 20c. *1796*

Ethnic policy. Guatemala. Indigenismo. 1822-20c. *1142*

Ethnicity. Guyana. Malaysia. Political parties. Social Classes. 1953-76. *122*

Ethnology (review article). Andes. Indians. Methodology. Social Change. 16c-20c. *1855*

Europe. Brazil. Foreign Relations. 1945-81. *2297*

—. Capitalism. Fascism. 1920's-70's. *466*

—. Economic development. Imperialism. North America. 16c-20c. *404*

—. Ecuador. Foreign Relations. Galápagos Islands. USA. 1830-1946. *1986*

—. Fascism. Italy. League of Nations. Mexico. Peace. 1919-25. *784*

—. Foreign Policy. Italy. 1970-81. *231*

—. Foreign Relations. 1945-81. *282*

—. Foreign Relations. Trade. 1970-82. *268*

—. Militarism, professional. 1890-1940. *437*

—. Trade. 1960's-75. *355*

European Economic Community. Caribbean Free Trade Association. Trade. West Indies. 1950's-73. *1324*

—. Economic negotiations. USA. 1960-75. *492*

—. Trade. 1970-80. *12*

Evans, Peter. Brazil. Capitalism (review article). 1970's. *2209*

Exchange Rates. Economic Policy. Inflation. 1957-72. *289*

—. Mexico. Political economy. 1955-77. *945*

—. Mexico. Politics. 1960-78. *939*

Exchange rates, multiple. Brazil. Trade. 1953-58. *2399*

—. Industrial efficiency. International competition. Schydlowsky, Daniel M. Trade policies. 1967-70's. *408*

Executive Power. Economic Policy (budgetary). Ideology. Mexico. Wilkie, James W. (thesis). 1935-64. *594*

—. Mexico. Presidency. 20c. *587*

Exile. Castro, Cipriano. Gómez, Juan Vicente. Venezuela. 1908-24. *2196*

—. Castro, Fidel. Cuba. Mexico. Revolutionary Movements. 1956. *1597*

Exile invasions. USA. War. West Indies. 1945-74. *1345*

Exiles. Baliño y López, Carlos B. *(Militarista)*. Communist Party (1st Congress). Cuba. Revolutionary activities. 1869-1926. *1627*

—. Communism. Mariátegui, José Carlos. 1910-23. *468*

—. Diaries. Mexico. Rühle-Gerstel, Alice. Trotsky, Leon. 1937. *846*

—. Gómez, Juan Vicente. Newspapers. Venezuela. 1913-35. *2195*

—. Italy. Mariátegui, José Carlos. Marxism. Peru. 1919-29. *2114*

Expansionism *See also* Imperialism.

—. Brazil. Developing Nations. Economic Growth. 1960-78. *2267*

Expeditionary Force. Brazil. Morais, João Batista Masca Renhas de. World War II. 1942-45. *2377*

Exploitation. Argentina. Economic growth. Frank, Andre Gunder. Great Britain. 1900-24. *2569*

—. Colonialism. Spain. 17c-20c. *180*

—. Indians. Paraguay. 1974. *2968*

—. Western nations. 16c-1973. *52*

Export economy. Bolivia. Comibol. Economic Development. Mines. 1900-70's. *1866*

Export promotion. Automobile Industry and Trade. Mexico. Multinational Corporations. 1960's-70's. *865*

—. Brazil. Manufactures. Multinational corporations. ca 1964-77. *2228*

Export-Import Bank. Allende, Salvador. Blockade, invisible. Chile. Economic weapons. Foreign Policy. USA. 1970-74. *2897*

Exports. Argentina. Brazil. Mexico. Unemployment. 1953-70. *333*

—. Bananas. Central America. Multinational corporations. 1947-75. *1012*

—. Brazil. Economic Policy. 1964-74. *2479*

—. Brazil. Germany, West. Nuclear Science and Technology. Technology transfer. 1975. *2500*

—. Economic growth. Foreign investments. 1960's-75. *407*

—. Foreign policy. Mexico. Oil. 1960-79. *959*

—. Foreign Relations. Israel. Mexico. Oil. Politics. 1975-79. *953*

Expressionism. Mexico. Painting. Politics. 20c. *652*

Expropriation. Brazil. Foreign Relations. Hickenlooper Amendment. Public utilities. USA. 1959-67. *2291*

—. Foreign Investments. Mexico. Oil Industry and Trade. 1850-1938. *718*

Extradition. Brazil. 1912-38. *2390*

—. Brazil. Legislation. Political crimes. 20c. *2253*

—. Pérez Jiménez, Marcos. USA. Venezuela. 1959-63. *2163*

F

Factor analysis. Colombia. Violence, rural. 1948-63. *1913*

Faletto, Enzo. Cardoso, Fernando Henrique. Democracy. Dependency. Developmentalism. Political Systems. 19c-20c. *338*

Falkland Islands. Argentina. Foreign Relations. Great Britain. 1960-81. *2959*

—. Argentina. Foreign Relations. Great Britain. 1976-77. *2961*

—. Argentina. Foreign Relations. Great Britain. UN (resolutions). 1965-77. *2960*

—. Argentina. Great Britain. International law. War. 1520-1982. *2963*

—. Argentina. Great Britain. Naval strategy. 1982. *2965*

—. Argentina. Great Britain. USA. 1975-81. *2958*

—. Economic Conditions. 1973-75. *2964*

Falkland Islands (battle). Germany. Great Britain. Naval Battles. Verner, Rudolph (report). World War I. 1914. *2962*

Fals-Borda, Orlando. Colombia. Social change. 1925-74. *1935*

Families. Brazil (Northeast). Kinship organization. Politics. 1889-1930. *2271*

Family Histories. *See* Genealogy.

Family planning. Birth control policies. El Salvador. Politics. 1970's. *1109*

—. Politics. World Population Conference (1974). 1950's-70's. *198*

Farabundo Martí National Liberation Front. Civil war. El Salvador. Revolutionary Democratic Front. USA. 1981. *1108*

Faría, Jesús. Communist Party. Memoirs. Venezuela. 1936-44. *2165*

Farmers, small. Brazil (Rio Grande do Sul). Land reform. 1964-78. *2455*

—. Chile. Military government. Popular Front. Social Change. 1938-79. *2735*

—. Economic growth. El Salvador. Foreign aid. 1955-74. *1091*

Farms, private. Agricultural productivity. Cuba. State farms. 1959-81. *1451*

Fascism *See also* Anti-Fascist Movements.

—. Allende, Salvador. Chile. Coups d'Etat. Revolution (planning). 1973. *2877*

—. Americas (North and South). 1860-1981. *489*

—. Argentina. Perón, Juan. 1920-55. *2623*

—. Brazil. Catholic Church. Integralist movement. 1930's. *2361*

—. Brazil. Integralist movement. Salgado, Plínio. ca 1920's-30's. *2387*

—. Capitalism. Europe. 1920's-70's. *466*

—. Chile. Political Reform. 1973. *2732*

—. Europe. Italy. League of Nations. Mexico. Peace. 1919-25. *784*

—. Political development. 1945-76. *484*

—. Political theory. 20c. *472*

—. USA. 1960's-70's. *451*

Fascism, species of. Argentina. Lipset, Seymour Martin. Organski, Kenneth. Peronism. 1938-69. *2619*

Favelas. Brazil (Rio de Janeiro). Housing policy. 1972-76. *2489*

—. Brazil (Rio de Janeiro). Marginality theory. Poor. 1968-73. *383*

Federal Government *See also* Civil Service; Congress; Constitutions; Government; Legislation.

—. Brazil. Economic Policy. Liberalism. 1889-1930. *2386*

—. Decentralization. Mexico. ca 1970's. *877*

Federal revenues, allocation of. Mexico. Political leadership. 1934-73. *583*

Federalism *See also* Federal Government.

—. Acosta, Julio. Central America. Costa Rica. 1920-23. *1081*

—. Brazil. 1824-1977. *2314*

—. Brazil. 1834-1964. *2295*

—. Brazil. Centralism. Government. 19c-20c. *2226*

—. Nationalism. West Indies Federation. 1945-68. *1290*

—. West Indies Federation. 1958-61. *1337*

Federation *See also* Confederation.

Federation of Bolivian Mine Workers. Bolivia. Nationalism. USA. Workers' Central (COB). 1970's. *1859*

Federation of Cuban Women. Cuba. Political participation. Social Status. Women. 1960-78. *1368*

—. Cuba. Women. 1960's-70's. *1369*

Federation of University Students. Batista, Fulgencio. Cuba. Revolutionary Movements. Students. 1951-57. *1361*

Feminism *See also* Women's Liberation Movement.

—. Brazil. Lutz, Bertha. Politics. Suffrage. 1864-1964. *2375*

—. Luisi, Paulina. Moral reform. Uruguay. 1875-1950. *2987*

Feudalism. Agriculture. Capitalism. Chile. Estates. 16c-20c. *2739*

Fibers Industry. Cordemex. Mexico (Yucatán). Nationalization. 1961-77. *870*

Figueiredo, Jackson de. Brazil. Catholic Church. Political movements. Publicists. 1918-28. *2392*

Figueres, José. Costa Rica. Foreign Relations. Nicaragua. Somoza family. 1940's-70's. *996*

Figueroa, Isidro (memoirs). Communist Party. Cuba. Martínez Villena, Rubén. 1920-34. *1446*

Figueroa, María A. (memoirs). Cuba (Oriente; Santiago de Cuba). Revolutionary Movements. 1953-56. *1447*

Films. Allende, Salvador. Chile. Landau, Saul *(Que Hacer)*. Political consciousness. USA. 1975. *2881*

—. Anti-Americanism. Communism. Costa-Gavras, Constantin. Foreign Relations. 1964-82. *71*

—. Argentina. García Velloso, Enrique. Greca, Acedes. History. Onelle, Clemente. 1915-22. *2519*

—. Bolivia. Revolutionary Movements. Sanjinés, Jorge. 1960-75. *1862*

—. Cinema Novo. Radicals and Radicalism. 1950's-70's. *18*

—. Costa-Gavras, Constantin. Guerrilla warfare. *State of Siege* (film; review article). Uruguay. 1963-73. *2980*

—. Costa-Gavras, Constantin. Politics. *State of Siege* (film; review article). Uruguay. 20c. *2979*

—. Cuba. Politics. 1897-1971. *1486*

—. Ideology. Marxism. 19c-20c. *101*

Films, documentary. Costa-Gavras, Constantin. Methodology. *State of Siege* (film; review article). 1917-70. *2977*

Films, historical. Social conditions. 1930's-70's. *138*

Films (historical) (review article). Cuba. National self-image. Solás, Humberto. 1895-1970's. *1548*

Financial center, regional. Banking. Insurance. Panama. 1960's-70's. *1268*

Financial support. Castro, Fidel. Cuba. Middle Classes. Revolution. 1956-58. *1558*

Firme (periodical). Chile. International Telephone & Telegraph Corporation. 1900's-70's. *2705*

Firms, foreign. Booker McConnell Ltd. Community relations. Demerara Bauxite Company. Developing nations. Guyana. 1920-73. *1707*

Fiscal Court. Brazil. Courts. Public finance. 1890-1980. *2278*

Fiscal policy. Economic planning. Public finance. Trinidad and Tobago. 1964-75. *1787*

Fishing Rights *See also* Maritime Law.

—. Ecology. Tariff. Territorial Waters. 1952-73. *40*

—. Foreign Relations. Guatemala. Mexico. 1958-59. *206*

—. Marine resources. 1930's-73. *7*

—. Peru. Politics. Territorial waters. 1945-72. *2083*

Fishmeal industry. Nationalization. Peru. 1968-76. *2020*

Fletcher, Henry P. Diplomacy. Mexico. Revolution. USA. 1917-20. *743*

Flores Magón, Ricardo. Constitution of 1917. Liberal Party (program). Mexico. 1906-17. *779*

Flores Magón, Ricardo (prison letters). Anarchism and Anarchists. Mexico. Sarnoff, Lilly. USA. 1920-22. *713*

Folk saint movements. Catholic Church. Mexico. Religious cults. 1880-1958. *641*

Folklore. Brazil. Elites. Vargas, Getúlio (image). 1930-54. *2266*

—. Guatemala. Indians. Nationhood. Symbols. 1524-1974. *1161*

Food Industry *See also* Nutrition.

—. Agriculture. Government Regulation. Mexico. Multinational corporations. 1960-75. *968*

Force. Brazil. Foreign policy. 1950's-70's. *2215*

—. Foreign relations. 1945-76. *246*

Force, use of. Cuba. Emigration. Government, Resistance to. Middle classes. Political culture. 1960's-70's. *1650*

Foreign Aid *See also* Economic Aid; Industrialization; Military Aid; Modernization.

—. Agricultural Policy. Ecuador. 1964-75. *2001*

—. Brazil. Economic Development. USA. 1946-70. *2257*

—. Brazil. Politics. Trade. USA. 20c. *2319*

—. Brazil (Northeast, destruction of). Roett, Reardan. SUDENE. USA. 1960-72. *2212*

—. Castro, Fidel. Cuba. USSR. 1959-77. *1550*

—. Chile. Economic development. USA. 1973-75. *2913*

—. Chile. USSR. 1971-73. *2842*

—. Colombia. Public Law 480. USA. Wheat. 1955-71. *1921*

—. Communist countries. Cuba. Economic development. 1958-73. *1358*

—. Cuba. Economics. Ideology. 1970-81. *1433*

—. Dependency. Military Government. Peru. USA. 1963-73. *2026*

—. Economic growth. El Salvador. Farmers, small. 1955-74. *1091*

—. Haiti. Social Change. 1960's-80. *1735*

—. Human rights. USA. 1970-79. *299*

—. Israel. Technical assistance. 1960-75. *302*

—. Koch, Edward (correspondence). Nicaragua. USA. 1970's. *1253*

—. Police. Public safety program. USA. 1960's-73. *325*

—. USA. 1960-71. *160*

Foreign Aid (distribution). USA. 1946-73. *93*

Foreign influence. Political institutions. USA. 1776-1976. *280*

Foreign Investments. 1811-1970. *400*

—. 1958-78. *112*

—. Allende, Salvador. Chile. Socialism. USA. 1912-73. *2850*

—. Andean Common Market. 1969-77. *1847*

—. Andean group. Caribbean Community. Economic Integration. Regionalism. 1966-74. *497*

—. Andean Pact. Economic Policy. Peru. 1968-80. *2088*

—. Andean Pact. Foreign policy. 1968-79. *1836*

—. Andean Pact. Government regulation. 1969-79. *1839*

—. Argentina. Foreign policy. Nationalism. 1816-1976. *2659*

—. Argentina. Germany. Trade. 1918-33. *2572*

—. Argentina. Great Britain. Railroads and State. Unión Cívica Radical. Yrigoyen, Hipólito. 1891-1928. *2609*

—. Argentina. Peronism. Political change. Social Classes. 1960-73. *2635*

—. Brazil. Economic Development. 1950-78. *2311*

—. Brazil. Economic power. Great Britain. USA. World War I. 1914-19. *2376*

—. Brazil. France. 1890-1930. *2344*

—. Brazil. Industrial growth. Social development. 1960's-74. *2450*

—. Capital accumulation. Central America. Nicaragua. ca 1913-77. *1246*

—. Capital accumulation. Economic policy. Mexico. 1920-55. *612*

—. Capitalism. Mexico. 20c. *677*

—. Capitalist countries. Economic Development. 1961-72. *363*

—. Cerro de Pasco Corporation. Labor movement. Mines. Peru. 1900-74. *2073*

—. Chile. Foreign Policy. USA. 1960-78. *2950*

—. Colombia. Economic development. Kemmerer, Edwin Walter. Monetary reform. USA. 1923-30. *1917*

—. Cuba. USA. 1959-64. *1495*

—. Dependency theory. Industrialization. Peru. 1967-77. *2127*

—. Diplomacy. Mexico. Nationalization. Oil Industry and Trade. USA. 1938-45. *630*

—. Dominican Republic. Technology. 1966-74. *1663*

—. Economic growth. Exports. 1960's-75. *407*

—. Economic Policy. Military Government. Peru. 1968-75. *2089*

—. Economic Regulations. Oil Industry and Trade. Venezuela. 1958-74. *2199*

—. Expropriation. Mexico. Oil Industry and Trade. 1850-1938. *718*

—. Foreign Relations. Mexico. USA. 1910-80. *700*

—. International law. USA. 1896-1977. *293*

—. Japan. 1960's-74. *239*

—. Japan. 1970's. *94*

—. Mining industry. Multinational corporations. Politics. 1950-77. *377*

—. Oil Industry and Trade. 1920-30. *406*

—. Social Classes. 1964-81. *384*

—. USA. 1890-1929. *271*

Foreign Investments (private; review article). Developing nations. 1965-75. *370*

Foreign Policy *See also* Detente; International Relations (discipline).

—. 1945-81. *236*

—. 1960's-70's. *261*

—. Africa. Angola. Cuba. Intervention. 1966-77. *1520*

—. Africa. Brazil. Geisel, Ernesto. 1970-79. *2415*

—. Africa. Cuba. 1959-79. *1440*

—. Africa. Cuba. 1978-81. *1350*

—. Africa. Cuba. ca 1960-79. *1473*

—. Africa. Cuba. USSR. 1959-78. *1658*

—. Africa, southern. Brazil. Portugal. 1970's. *2330*

—. Allende, Salvador. Blockade, invisible. Chile. Economic weapons. Export-Import Bank. USA. 1970-74. *2897*

—. Allison, Graham. Blockade. Cuban missile crisis. Methodology (implementation analysis; review article). USA. 1962. *1395*

—. Andean Group. Colombia. Decisionmaking. Economic integration. 1974-80. *1981*

—. Andean Pact. Foreign investments. 1968-79. *1836*

—. Angola. Cuba. Intervention. USA. USSR. 1975-77. *1656*

—. Angola. Cuba. Revolution. 1959-78. *1546*

—. Angola. Cuba. Revolutionary Movements. 1975-78. *1635*

—. Anti-Imperialism. USA. 1970's. *320*

—. Arab-Israeli conflict. 1947-75. *296*

—. Argentina. Bibliographies. 1879-1978. *2526*

—. Argentina. Brazil. 19c-20c. *2554*

—. Argentina. Brazil. Mexico. 18c-1975. *286*

—. Argentina. Foreign Investments. Nationalism. 1816-1976. *2659*

—. Argentina. Intervention. Nationalism. USA. 1941-46. *2536*

—. Argentina. Perón, Juan. 1973-74. *2589*

—. Argentina. Peronism. 1943-74. *2640*

—. Argentina. Peronism. 1973-76. *2628*

—. Argentina. UN (membership). USA. 1942-45. *2565*

—. Assassination. Human rights. Nicaragua. Somoza, Anastasio. USA. 1974-80. *1208*

—. Attitudes (mentalité). West Indies (English-speaking). 1974. *1296*

—. Bolivia. Chaco War. Historiography. Paraguay. USA. 1932-35. *98*

—. Boundaries. Leguía, Augusto B. Peru. USA. 1908-42. *2106*

—. Brazil. 1820's-1975. *2305*

—. Brazil. 1822-1975. *2307*

—. Brazil. 1948-74. *2265*

—. Brazil. 1950's-73. *2211*

—. Brazil. Chile. Repression. USA. Working class. 20c. *44*

—. Brazil. Democracy. USA. 1964-68. *2457*

—. Brazil. Economic Conditions. 1960-79. *2263*

—. Brazil. Economic Growth (social costs). Military-dominated government. 1930-72. *2300*

—. Brazil. Economic Policy. 1945-74. *2254*

—. Brazil. Economic Structure. 1960's-70's. *2262*

—. Brazil. Elites. 1919-29. *2352*

—. Brazil. Force. 1950's-70's. *2215*

—. Brazil. Foreign Relations. UN. 1945-80. *2322*

—. Brazil. Political Change. 20c. *2279*

—. Brazil. USA. 1960-74. *284*

—. Castro, Fidel. Cuba. 1959-74. *1645*

—. Castro, Fidel. Cuba. 1968-73. *1424*

—. Castro, Fidel. Cuba. Domestic Policy. USSR. 1959-76. *1527*

—. Castro, Fidel. Cuba. Revolution. USA. 1959-62. *1626*

—. Central America. Documents. Mexico. 1923-37. *556*

—. Central America. Economic integration. USA. 1960-73. *1024*

—. Central America. Government. Honduras. USA. 1871-1981. *1174*

—. Central America. USA. 1960-78. *1045*

—. Central America. USA. 1960-80. *1013*

—. Central America. USA. 1978-80. *1002*

—. Central America. USA. 1980's. *1001*

—. Central American Common Market. Mexico. 1960's-70's. *527*

—. Central Intelligence Agency. Chile. Coups d'Etat. USA. 1970-73. *2838*
—. Chile. 1945-79. *2742*
—. Chile. Coups d'Etat. USA. 1971-73. 1970's. *2693*
—. Chile. Domestic policy. Echeverría, Luis. Mexico. 1970-76. *926*
—. Chile. Foreign Investments. USA. 1960-78. *2950*
—. Chile. International lending agencies. USA. 1970-73. *2864*
—. Chile. International Telephone & Telegraph Corporation. Multinational Corporations. USA. 1971-74. *2678*
—. Chile. Intervention. USA. 1970-74. *2688*
—. Chile. Popular Unity. 1970-73. *2815*
—. China. 1970's. *266*
—. Colombia. Multinational Corporations. Oil Industry and Trade. USA. 1920-40. *1964*
—. Communism. Cuba. 1953-76. *1426*
—. Congress. Cuba. Revolution. USA. 1960's-70's. *1436*
—. Cuba. 1959-80. *1356*
—. Cuba. 1959-80. *1549*
—. Cuba. 1960's-78. *1421*
—. Cuba. Domestic Policy. Economic Conditions. 1975-80. *1591*
—. Cuba. Dominican Republic. Economic coercion. USA. 1960-72. *1339*
—. Cuba. Economic policy. USA. 1933-34. *1384*
—. Cuba. Guantánamo Bay (status of). Military Bases. USA. 1960-72. *1381*
—. Cuba. International Trade. USA. 1975. *1648*
—. Cuba. Mexico. USA. 1960-74. *561*
—. Cuba. Nonaligned Nations. 1959-79. *1439*
—. Cuba. Nonaligned nations. 1961-79. *1541*
—. Cuba. Political Factions. 1970-77. *1462*
—. Cuba. States, small. 1959-79. *1534*
—. Cuba. Sugar industry. USA. 1914-21. *1563*
—. Cuba. USA. 1959-82. *1512*
—. Cuba. USA. 1961-81. *1522*
—. Cuban missile crisis. Decisionmaking. USA. 1962. *1360*
—. Debt, External. Mexico. 1965-77. *913*
—. Decisionmaking. GATT. Mexico. USA. 1980. *986*
—. Democracy. Venezuela. ca 1830-1976. *2173*
—. Dependency. Trade. UN General Assembly. USA. Voting and Voting Behavior. 1950-73. *155*
—. Developing Nations. Great powers. Mexico. 1910-30's. *742*
—. Developing nations. Mass media. Trinidad and Tobago. 1962-76. *1805*
—. Diplomacy. 1967-77. *317*
—. Domestic Policy. Economic integration. 1958-70. *367*
—. Domestic Policy. Mexico. Revolution. Social change. ca 1910-30's. *764*
—. Domestic Policy. Peru. Velasco Alvarado, Juan. 1968-72. *2055*
—. Dominican Republic. Intervention (review article). Organization of American States. UN. USA. 1965-72. *1672*
—. Echeverría, Luis. Mexico. 1970-76. *983*
—. Echeverría, Luis. Mexico. Mexico. 1968-76. *981*
—. Echeverría, Luis. Mexico. Regional organization. 1974. *496*
—. Economic Conditions. New International Economic Order. USA. West Indies. 1970's-81. *1329*
—. Economic Conditions. Nicaragua. Social Policy. 1979-80. *1248*
—. Economic development. USA. 1970's. *522*
—. Economic interests. Germany. 1933-41. *300*
—. El Salvador. Nicaragua. Venezuela. 1970-81. *501*
—. El Salvador. USA. USSR. 1981. *1099*
—. Energy. Mexico. Tomatoes. Trade Regulations. USA. 1969-80. *937*
—. Europe. Italy. 1970-81. *231*
—. Exports. Mexico. Oil. 1960-79. *959*
—. Good Neighbor Policy. 1933-70's. *324*
—. Great Britain. Harrod, Jeffrey. Jamaica. Labor Unions and Organizations (review article). USA. 20c. *1757*
—. Guatemala. Politics. Ubico Castañeda, Jorge. USA. 1931-44. *1148*
—. Haiti. States, small. ca 1804-1974. *1728*
—. Human rights. Mexico. 1945-77. *906*
—. Human rights. USA. 1946-79. *263*
—. Independence. Jamaica. 1962-76. *1743*
—. Jamaica. 1972-77. *1762*

—. Jamaica. Political Leadership. Public Opinion. 1962-74. *1744*
—. Kennedy, John F. (administration). Peru. USA. 1960-62. *2119*
—. Kissinger, Henry A. USA. 1968-76. *260*
—. Leftism. Military. USA. 1970-77. *41*
—. Lobbying. USA. 1960-79. *310*
—. López Mateos, Adolfo. Mexico. 1958-74. *929*
—. Mexico. 1960's-70's. *532*
—. Mexico. 1970-75. *917*
—. Mexico. 1972-74. *962*
—. Mexico. Oil Industry and Trade. USA. 1921-28. *927*
—. Mexico. Revolution. Scott, Hugh Lenox. USA. Wilson, Woodrow. 1914-17. *749*
—. Mexico. Tlatelolco Conference. 1973-74. *534*
—. Nationalization. Social classes. USA. Venezuela. 1973-76. *2192*
—. Panama Canal. USA. 1903-79. *1277*
—. Panama Canal. USA. 1945-49. *1273*
—. Peru. 1821-1978. *2123*
—. Rockefeller, Nelson. Roosevelt, Franklin D. 1933-42. *252*
—. Treaties. USA. 1939-45. *267*
—. USA. 1900-76. *274*
—. USA. 1950's-76. *240*
—. USA. 1953-70. *321*
—. USA. 1977-80. *264*
—. USA. 20c. *249*
—. USA. West Indies. 1959-81. *1287*
—. Venezuela. 1974-76. *2157*
Foreign Policy (coordination of). Regional subsystem. 1970-74. *551*
Foreign policy distance, comparative. USA. 1953-70. *322*
Foreign policy (isthmian recognition). Acosta, Julio. Central America. Costa Rica. Jiménez, Ricardo. Politics. ca 1900-1930's. *1082*
Foreign Policy (review article). Bond, Robert. Venezuela. 1899-1977. *2171*
—. Chile. Cuba. Dominican Republic. USA. 1930-72. *225*
—. Mexico. ca 1950-75. *615*
Foreign Relations *See also* Boundaries; Detente; Diplomacy; Disarmament; International Relations (discipline); Tariff; Treaties.
—. 1970's. *244*
—. Africa. 1974-78. *314*
—. Africa. Cuba. Military. USSR. 1959-81. *1649*
—. Africa. Cuba. Political economy. 1959-80. *1659*
—. Africa. Pakistan. 1970's. *83*
—. Africa (Portuguese). Brazil. 1970-75. *2313*
—. Africa, West. Brazil. Trade. 1970's. *2235*
—. Amazon Basin. Boundaries. Brazil. Economic integration. 16c-1978. *2206*
—. Americas (North and South). Historiography. 1970's. *511*
—. Andean Common Market. Economic policy. Venezuela. 1959-74. *2140*
—. Andean group. 1979-80. *1850*
—. Andean Pact. Mexico. 1968-72. *515*
—. Anderson, Chandler. Business. Mexico. USA. 1913-20. *752*
—. Antarctic. 1959-79. *530*
—. Anti-Americanism. Communism. Costa-Gavras, Constantin. Films. 1964-82. *71*
—. Anti-Imperialism. USA. 1891-1929. *19*
—. Argentina. Beagle Channel. Chile. 1810-1977. *2503*
—. Argentina. Drago Doctrine. Perón, Juan. USA. 1823-1974. *2557*
—. Argentina. Falkland Islands. Great Britain. 1960-81. *2959*
—. Argentina. Falkland Islands. Great Britain. 1976-77. *2961*
—. Argentina. Falkland Islands. Great Britain. UN (resolutions). 1965-77. *2960*
—. Argentina. Military Government. USA. 1940-81. *2537*
—. Argentina. Treaties. Uruguay. 1973-76. *2508*
—. Argentina. USA. 1976-81. *2665*
—. Australia. Trade. 1945-73. *326*
—. Balaguer, Joaquín. Dominican Republic. Elections. Guzmán, Antonio. USA. 1965-80. *1680*
—. Belize. Boundaries (disputes). Great Britain. Guatemala. 1859-1979. *1028*
—. Bibliographies. USA. 1973-75. *276*
—. Bolivia. Boundaries. Chile. Peru. 19c-20c. *1880*

—. Bonner, Raymond. Bushnell, John A. Democracy. El Salvador. Military. Ramos, Arnold. USA. Williams, Murat. 1982. *1125*
—. Brazil. Commerce. Industry. Treaties. USA. 1935. *2381*
—. Brazil. Documents. Parliaments. 1823-1975. *2225*
—. Brazil. Economic history. Historiography. 1889-1964. *2316*
—. Brazil. Europe. 1945-81. *2297*
—. Brazil. Expropriation. Hickenlooper Amendment. Public utilities. USA. 1959-67. *2291*
—. Brazil. Foreign Policy. UN. 1945-80. *2322*
—. Brazil. Immigration. Japan. Trade. 19c-1960's. *2268*
—. Brazil. Maritime relations. USA. 1967-73. *2286*
—. Brazil. Political structure. USA. 1973. *2445*
—. Brazil. USA. 1945-60. *2398*
—. British Commonwealth. Cuba. West Indies. 1960's-70's. *1316*
—. Canada. 1970's. *254*
—. Canada. Haiti. 20c. *1730*
—. Canada. Mexico. 1944-73. *872*
—. Canada. USA. 1970-76. *262*
—. Cárdenas, Lázaro. Mexico. Nationalization. Oil Industry and Trade. USA. 1945-50. *928*
—. Carranza, Venustiano. Mexico. Plan of San Diego. USA. 1915-16. *750*
—. Castro, Fidel. Cuba. Nixon, Richard M. (memorandum). USA. 1959. *1600*
—. Castro, Fidel. Cuba. USSR. 1956-60. *1390*
—. Central America. Costa Rica. 1923-34. *1083*
—. Central America. Dictatorship. 1934-45. *1020*
—. Central America. Economic Conditions. Social Conditions. USA. 1979-81. *998*
—. Central America. Quantitative Methods (small group theory). West Indies. 1948-64. *549*
—. Central America. USA. 1960's-81. *1018*
—. Central America. Venezuela. West Indies. 1936-78. *499*
—. Chile. Communist Party. González Videla, Gabriel. Radical Party. USA. 1940-47. *2748*
—. Chile. USA. 1970-73. *2692*
—. China. Cuba. Leadership. Nonaligned nations. 1959-79. *1438*
—. Claims. Cuba. Sugar. Trade. USA. 1957-73. *1382*
—. Cold War. Detente. Medina Echavarría, José. USA. 1948-68. *288*
—. Cold War. Historiography (US). USA. 1945-50. 1950-75. *265*
—. Cold War. Organization of American States. USA. 1944-49. *312*
—. Communism. Cuba. Political Change. Revolution. 1953-73. *1623*
—. Communist Party. Costa Rica. USA. 1920's-48. *1075*
—. Corporatism. USA. 1900's-74. *287*
—. Costa Rica. Figueres, José. Nicaragua. Somoza family. 1940's-70's. *996*
—. Cuba. 1960-82. *1599*
—. Cuba. Dependency (review article). USA. 1880's-1930's. *1544*
—. Cuba. Developing nations. USSR. 1959-79. *1472*
—. Cuba. Economic development. USSR. 1960-73. *1410*
—. Cuba. Ethiopia. Somalia. 1978-79. *1636*
—. Cuba. Mexico. 1959-73. *531*
—. Cuba. Negroes. USA. 1868-1977. *1402*
—. Cuba. Nicaragua. 1960's-70's. *103*
—. Cuba. Nickel. USA. 1975-76. *1545*
—. Cuba. Organization of American States. USA. 1959-75. *1405*
—. Cuba. Panama. 1960's-70's. *543*
—. Cuba. Reagan, Ronald (administration). 1970-82. *1475*
—. Cuba. Revolutionary Movements. USSR. 20c. *1354*
—. Cuba. Sugar Act (1948). Tariff. USA. 1945-48. *1487*
—. Cuba. USA. 1960's-70's. *1365*
—. Cuba. USA. ca 19c-1974. *498*
—. Cuba. USA. USSR. 1959-76. *1385*
—. Cuba. USSR. 1959-77. *1517*
—. Cuba. USSR. 1961-74. *1531*
—. Dependency model. USA. 1910-73. *295*
—. Disarmament. Mexico. 1957-77. *938*
—. Documents. Great Britain. Mexico. Nicaragua. 1926-34. *705*
—. Documents. Intervention. Mexico. Nicaragua. USA. 1922-29. *327*
—. Echeverría, Luis. Economic relations. Mexico. 1973. *992*

—. Economic Conditions. Economic policy. Mexico. 1976-78. *976*
—. Economic Conditions. Mexico. USA. 1970-77. *954*
—. Economic Conditions. National security. USA. West Indies. 1962-82. *1314*
—. Economic Conditions. USA. 1950-80. *226*
—. Economic development. Mexico. Natural gas. Oil Industry and Trade. USA. 1977-79. *965*
—. Ecuador. Europe. Galápagos Islands. USA. 1830-1946. *1986*
—. Ecuador. Peru. 1941-73. *1849*
—. El Paso-Juárez Conference. Mexico. USA (New Mexico). USA (New Mexico; Columbus, raid). Villa, Pancho. 1916. *748*
—. El Salvador. Honduras. 1969-79. *1017*
—. El Salvador. Honduras. War. 1969-76. *999*
—. Energy policy. Mexico. 1910-79. *560*
—. Europe. 1945-81. *282*
—. Europe. Trade. 1970-82. *268*
—. Exports. Israel. Mexico. Oil. Politics. 1975-79. *953*
—. Fishing Rights. Guatemala. Mexico. 1958-59. *206*
—. Force. 1945-76. *246*
—. Foreign investments. Mexico. USA. 1910-80. *700*
—. Historiography. USA. 1970's. *222*
—. Historiography. USA. 20c. *297*
—. Historiography (Latin American). USSR. 1917-79. *304*
—. Independence. USA. 1969-77. *229*
—. International division of labor. Mexico. Tomatoes. Trade. USA (Florida). 1970-80. *977*
—. International Relations (discipline). 1945-79. *248*
—. International system. USA. 1960-74. *245*
—. Intervention. Mexico. Pershing, John J. USA. Wilson, Woodrow. 1916. *810*
—. Jamaica. Political systems. USA. 1972-77. *1768*
—. Japan. Mexico. Revolution. 1916-17. *767*
—. Japan. Trade. 1960-79. *281*
—. Korea, South. Trade. 1950-80. *123*
—. Mexico. Meyer, Lorenzo. Nationalism. Oil Industry and Trade (review article). USA. 1917-42. *680*
—. Mexico. Naturalization. Oil. USA. 1915-42. *671*
—. Mexico. Obregón, Álvaro. USA. 1913-23. *756*
—. Mexico. Oil Industry and Trade. USA. 1910-72. *564*
—. Mexico. Political change. Reform. USA. 1923-77. *944*
—. Mexico. Revolution. Steffens, Lincoln. USA. 1913-27. *807*
—. Mexico. USA. 1940-80. *958*
—. Mexico. USA. 1973-80. *875*
—. Mexico. USA (New Mexico; Columbus, raid). Villa, Pancho. 1913-16. *816*
—. Mexico. USSR. 1917-24. *678*
—. Monroe Doctrine. Rio Treaty. USA. 19c-20c. *228*
—. National development. Río de la Plata Basin. 1941-80. *538*
—. Nationalism. Panama Canal. USA. 1960-77. *1255*
—. Nationalism. USSR. 1973. *323*
—. Nicaragua. Revolution. USA. 1978-79. *1212*
—. Nicaragua. Sandinista National Liberation Front. 1970's. *1235*
—. Nuclear Nonproliferation. 1970's-80's. *145*
—. Organization of American States. USA. 1948-78. *503*
—. Panama. Sovereignty. USA. 1964-74. *1257*
—. Panama. Torrijos, Omar. USA. 1969-73. *1283*
—. Panama. 1903-74. *1284*
—. Panama Canal. USA. 1898-1975. *1270*
—. Panama Canal Zone. Torrijos, Omar. USA. 1903-77. *1285*
—. Poland. 1918-74. *294*
—. Regional development. USA. ca 1880-1973. *5*
—. Romania. 1880-1980. *224*
—. Spain. 1492-1978. *270*
—. USA. -1975. *242*
—. USA. 1823-1980. *269*
—. USA. 1944-60. *285*
—. USA. 1945-70's. *243*
—. USA. 1960's-70's. *247*
—. USA. 1961-75. *309*
—. USA. 20c. *272*
—. USA. West Indies. 1945-81. *1341*
—. USA. West Indies. 1970-76. *1348*

—. USSR. 1930's. *305*
Foreign Relations (Commission, 2d report). Linowitz, Sol M. USA. 1976. *256*
Foreign Relations (rapprochement). Chile. Mexico. 1972-73. *495*
Foreign Relations (review article). Alliance for Progress. USA. 1946-74. *313*
—. Argentina. Good neighbor policy. USA. Woods, Randall Bennett. 1941-45. *2523*
—. Brazil. USA. 1950's-81. *2308*
—. Chile. Political Systems. 19c-20c. *2741*
—. Dependency theory. 16c-1979. *55*
—. Germany. ca 1889-1945. *298*
—. Linowitz Commission Report. USA. 1976. *279*
—. Rangel, Carlos. USA. 16c-1979. *292*
—. UN. 1946-74. *232*
—. USA. 1970-74. *233*
—. USA. 1974. *306*
Foreign services. Brazil. Germany, West. Israel. Japan. -1973. *2216*
Foreign Trade. *See* International Trade.
Forests and Forestry *See also* Lumber and Lumbering.
—. Colombia. Government. Settlement. 1926-78. *1936*
Forman, Shepard. Brazil. Peasants (review article). 1975. *2289*
Fortoul, Gil. Arbitration, International. Boundaries. Colombia. Diplomacy. Switzerland. Venezuela. 1922. *1838*
France. Bibliographies. Dissertations. 1976-78. *217*
—. Bibliographies. Dissertations. Research. 1979. *220*
—. Brazil. Foreign Investments. 1890-1930. *2344*
—. Independence Movements (lack of). Martinique. Modernization. 1960's-70's. *1818*
France (Paris). Cuba. Machado, Gerardo. Newspapers. Revolution. USA. 1933. *1506*
Franchise. *See* Suffrage.
Frank, Andre Gunder. Argentina. Economic growth. Exploitation. Great Britain. 1900-24. *2569*
Free World. *See* Western Nations.
Freedom of the Press *See also* Censorship.
—. 1945-75. *78*
—. Chile. Coups d'Etat. 1973. *2875*
—. El Salvador. 1970's. *1118*
—. Peru. Revolutionary government. Unemployment. 1968-70's. *2058*
Freemasonry. Chile. Documents. Ibáñez, Carlos. Politics. 1952-58. *2759*
Frei, Eduardo. Allende, Salvador. Chile. Housing. 1964-73. *2709*
—. Chile. Christian Democratic Party. Presidency. 1964-82. *2689*
—. Chile. Cuban revolution. Leftists. USA. 1958-73. *2768*
French Guiana. Government, Resistance to. Vichy Regime. World War II. 1940. *1687*
French West Indies. Agriculture. Economic growth. Politics. 1945-76. *1794*
—. Nationalism. 1945-76. *1831*
Frente Negra Brasileira. Brazil. Civil Rights Organizations. 1924-37. *2382*
Friedman, Milton. Chile. Economic policy. Technical assistance. USA. 1973-75. *2935*
Functionalism. Chile. Corporatism. Politics. 16c-20c. *2915*
Furtado, Celso. Agricultural Production. Brazil. Economic Policy. Industrialization. 1946-52. *2395*

G

Gaitán, Jorge Eliécer. Colombia. Populism. Rojas Pinilla, Gustavo. 1940's-70's. *1920*
Galápagos Islands. Ecuador. Europe. Foreign Relations. USA. 1830-1946. *1986*
Galdames, Luis. Chile. Intellectuals. Politics. 1910-41. *2504*
Galeano, Eduardo. Imperialism (review article). USA. 1970's. *51*
Garcia, Antonio. Mexico. Peasants. Poetry. Revolutionary Movements. 1968-73. *903*
García Márquez, Gabriel. Carpentier, Alejo. Dictatorship (review article). Novels. Roa Bastos, Augusto. 1840-1975. *64*
García Ortiz, Laureano. Boundaries. Brazil. Colombia. Peru. Treaties. 1920-30. *56*
García Velloso, Enrique. Argentina. Films. Greca, Acedes. History. Onelle, Clemente. 1915-22. *2519*

Garvey, Marcus. Belize. Black Cross Nurses Association. 1920-70. *1059*
—. Belize. Negroes. Peoples United Party. Political Parties. Universal Negro Improvement Association. 1914-49. *1052*
—. Government, Resistance to. Jamaica. Maroons. Rastafarianism. 1517-1962. *1749*
—. Ideology. Jamaica. Negroes. Pan-Africanism. USA. 1887-1927. *1766*
GATT. Decisionmaking. Foreign policy. Mexico. USA. 1980. *986*
Geisel, Ernesto. Africa. Brazil. Foreign policy. 1970-79. *2415*
—. Brazil. Industrialization. Military government. Social instability. 1964-75. *2483*
—. Brazil. Military Government. 1975-78. *2461*
—. Brazil. Military government. Repression. 1976. *2458*
—. Brazil. Nationalist policy. 1974-. *2482*
Genealogy. Colombia (Tolima). Echandía family. 18c-20c. *1960*
General Confederation of Labor (CGT). Arellano, Edward. Labor Unions and Organizations. Mendoza, Ciro. Mexico. Textile industry. 1920-78. *563*
—. Argentina. Labor movement. Political Parties. Socialist Party. 1930-43. *2567*
—. Argentina. Labor movement. Strikes. 1964. *2590*
—. Argentina. Peronism. Working Class. 1943-73. *2602*
—. Labor movement. Mexico. Regional Confederation of Mexican Labor (CROM). 1920's. *730*
—. Labor Unions and Organizations. Mexico. 1921-31. *714*
Generation of 1923. Cuba. Intellectuals. 1920-29. *1622*
Generations. Intellectuals. Mexico. 1907-64. *685*
Geography *See also* Boundaries; Ethnology.
—. Guyana (Jonestown; siting). Utopias. 1978. *1691*
Geopolitics *See also* Boundaries; Demography; International Waters.
—. 1953. *54*
Germans. Anti-Fascist Movements. Uruguay. 1933-41. *2983*
Germany. Argentina. Foreign Investments. Trade. 1918-33. *2572*
—. *Dresden* (cruiser). Intervention. Mexico (Tampico, Veracruz). Revolution. 1913-14. *755*
—. Economic interests. Foreign Policy. 1933-41. *300*
—. Falkland Islands (battle). Great Britain. Naval Battles. Verner, Rudolph (report). World War I. 1914. *2962*
—. Foreign Relations (review article). ca 1889-1945. *298*
—. Great Britain. Imperialism. Trade. USA. 1918-39. *31*
—. Intelligence. Mexico. USA. Witzke affair. World War I. 1914-23. *751*
Germany, East. Latin American studies. 1950's-70's. *30*
Germany, West. Brazil. Exports. Nuclear Science and Technology. Technology transfer. 1975. *2500*
—. Brazil. Foreign services. Israel. Japan. -1973. *2216*
Gómez, Humberto. Colombia (Arauca). Rebellions. 1916-18. *1948*
Gómez, Juan Vicente. Castro, Cipriano. Exile. Venezuela. 1908-24. *2196*
—. Dictatorship. Rippy, J. Fred. Venezuela. ca 1908-35. *2148*
—. Economic Conditions. Oil industry and trade. Venezuela. 1908-35. *2197*
—. Exiles. Newspapers. Venezuela. 1913-35. *2195*
—. Modernization. Venezuela. 1908-35. *2138*
Gompers, Samuel. Labor Unions and Organizations. Pan-American Federation of Labor. World War I. 1918-27. *552*
González Casanova, Pablo. Cardoso, Fernando Henrique. Sociology. 1930's-70's. *92*
—. Labor movement. Mexico. Working Class (review article). 19c-20c. *660*
González Videla, Gabriel. Chile. Communist Party. Foreign relations. Radical Party. USA. 1940-47. *2748*
Good neighbor policy. Argentina. Foreign Relations (review article). USA. Woods, Randall Bennett. 1941-45. *2523*
—. Foreign Policy. 1933-70's. *324*
Goulart, João. Brazil. Nationalism. Political Leadership. Vargas, Getúlio. 1930-64. *2232*

I

—. Argentina. Government. Productivity. Working Conditions. 1953-62. *2616*

—. Banking. Guyana. Multinational corporations. Nationalization. 1970-79. *1708*

—. Brazil. Commerce. Foreign Relations. Treaties. USA. 1935. *2381*

—. Capital accumulation. Economic Conditions. Mexico. 1960-79. *924*

—. Economic Policy (preferences). Government. Peru. 1946-68. *2045*

Inflation. Argentina. Brazil. Economic Policy. Perón, Juan. Vargas, Getúlio. 1946-55. *391*

—. Argentina. Chile. Economic Policy. 1950's-70's. *2502*

—. Bolivia. Political stability. 1950's. *1873*

—. Chile. Economic policy. 1973-75. *2932*

—. Devaluation. Mexico. Peso. 1976-79. *882*

—. Economic Policy. Exchange Rates. 1957-72. *289*

—. Economic Policy. Mexico. Social Organization. 1935-81. *565*

—. Monetary factors. 1950-69. *403*

Institutional dualism. Agricultural development. Central American Common Market. Social Conditions. 1950-70. *1010*

Institutional Revolutionary Party (PRI). Agricultural Organizations. Mexico. Peasants. 1938-79. *949*

—. Elections. Mexico. National Action Party (PAN). Political reform. 1967-73. *980*

—. Elections (presidential). Mexico. National Action Party (PAN). Political Campaigns. 1969-70. *947*

—. Mexico. Obregón, Álvaro. Political Factions. 1914-28. *744*

—. Mexico. Political Reform. 1979-81. *930*

Institutionalization. Castro, Fidel. Communist Party. Cuba. Revolution. 1959-76. *1367*

—. Civil-military relations. Cuba. 1959-76. *1422*

—. Communist Party. Cuba. Political Leadership. 1959-76. *1463*

—. Cuba. Revolution. 1959-76. *1638*

—. Cuba. Revolution. 1959-76. *1366*

—. Cuba. Socialism. 1950-78. *1452*

—. Ideology. Mexico. Political Systems. Revolution. 20c. *651*

Instituto Indigenista Interamericano. Indians. Racism. ca 1940-74. *216*

Instituto Nacional de Colonização e de Reforma Agraria. Brazil (Amazon region). Settlement. 1970-78. *2416*

Insurance. Banking. Financial center, regional. Panama. 1960's-70's. *1268*

Insurrections. *See* Rebellions.

Integralist movement. Brazil. Catholic Church. Fascism. 1930's. *2361*

—. Brazil. Fascism. Salgado, Plínio. ca 1920's-30's. *2387*

—. Brazil. Leme, Sebastião, Cardinal. 1920-40. *2391*

Integration *See also* Assimilation.

—. Central America. Economic Policy. 1950-78. *1039*

—. Indians. Migration, Internal (circular). Venezuela (Orinoco). 1920-74. *2152*

Integration, national. Developmentalism. Natural Resources (use of). Political thought (continuity). Secularization. 1800-1970. *204*

Intellectuals. Arts policy. Cuesta, George (theater review). Mexico. Revolution. Theater. 1929-30. *776*

—. Brazil. Cultural development. Nationalism. 1950-59. *2405*

—. Brazil. Ideology. *Plataforma da Nova Geração.* 1940's. *2406*

—. Chile. Galdames, Luis. Politics. 1910-41. *2504*

—. Cosío Villegas, Daniel. Mexico. Political Commentary. 1968-76. *979*

—. Cuba. Generation of 1923. 1920-29. *1622*

—. Generations. Mexico. 1907-64. *685*

—. Government. Mexico. 20c. *646*

—. Guyana. Political Leadership. Rodney, Walter. 1960's-80. *1690*

—. Mexico. Political Protest. 1900-71. *672*

Intelligence. Germany. Mexico. USA. Witzke affair. World War I. 1914-23. *751*

Inter-American Conference (Rio de Janeiro). Argentina. Decisionmaking. Diplomacy. USA. World War II. 1942. *553*

Inter-American Development Bank. Industrialization. 1960-75. *409*

Inter-American Institute of Agricultural Sciences. Agriculture. -1973. *529*

Interest Groups *See also* Political Factions; Pressure Groups.

—. Bolivia. Social Organization. State power. ca 1950-74. *1903*

—. Business. Confederation of Light Metallurgical Industries. Perón, Juan. 1944-55. *2648*

—. Business. Economic Policy. Government. Mexico. 20c. *684*

—. Chile. Labor Unions and Organizations (suppression). Landowners. National Society of Agriculture. Peasants. 1920-48. *2749*

—. Chile. Society for Promotion of Manufacturing. 1883-1928. *2766*

—. Colombia. Congress. Elites, political. 1974. *1944*

—. Ecuador. Oil Industry and Trade. Politics (regime changes). 1960-72. *1982*

Intergovernmental Relations. Brazil (Rio Grande do Sul). Economic Conditions. Economic Policy. 1891-1930. *2336*

—. Irrigation. Mexico. Rural development. 1930-78. *936*

Intermediate states. Brazil. International order. Power relations. 1945-73. *2208*

Internal Migration. *See* Migration, Internal.

International Boundary and Water Commission. Bilateral commissions. International Organizations (judicial). Mexico. USA. 19c-1974. *624*

—. Irrigation. Mexico (Tamaulipas). Rio Grande Basin. USA (Texas). 1900-20. *676*

International Committee of Bankers on Mexico. Banking. Dollar diplomacy. Lamont-de la Huerta Agreement (1922). Mexico. USA. 1919-38. *626*

International competition. Exchange rates, multiple. Industrial efficiency. Schydlowsky, Daniel M. Trade policies. 1967-70's. *408*

International division of labor. Argentina. Government. 1950-70. *2587*

—. Foreign Relations. Mexico. Tomatoes. Trade. USA (Florida). 1970-80. *977*

International Institute of Social History. Bibliographies. Mexico. Netherlands (Amsterdam). 1880-1940. *576*

International Labor Organization. Argentina. Perón, Juan. USA. 1946-55. *2600*

International Law *See also* Arbitration, International; Boundaries; International Relations (discipline); Maritime Law; Refugees; Treaties; War.

—. 1883-1945. *539*

—. 1930-80. *521*

—. Argentina. Falkland Islands. Great Britain. War. 1520-1982. *2963*

—. Arms race. Nuclear nonproliferation (denuclearized zones). USSR. 1962-73. *137*

—. Canal Zone. Panama. 1903-76. *1278*

—. Central American Peace Conferences (Washington, 1907, 1923). Diplomatic recognition. Tobar Doctrine. USA. 1900-30. *548*

—. Chile. Copper Mines and Mining. Nationalization. 1970. *2738*

—. Cuba. Missile crisis. USA. 1962-75. *1577*

—. Cuban Missile Crisis. UN. 1962. *1499*

—. Economic zone. Territorial Waters. 1952-70's. *401*

—. Foreign Investments. USA. 1896-1977. *293*

—. International Waters. 1945-73. *554*

—. Lake Titicaca. Territorial Waters (lakes). 19c-20c. *1856*

International law (doctrines). Mexico. USA. 1907-69. *692*

International Law (problems). Labor Unions and Organizations (international). Multinational corporations. North America. 1937-73. *411*

International lending agencies. Chile. Foreign Policy. USA. 1970-73. *2864*

International Military Education and Training Program. Human rights. Military Education. USA. 1978. *424*

International Monetary Fund. Developing Nations. Jamaica. 1975-80. *1754*

—. Economic policy. Peru. 1975-78. *2115*

International order. Brazil. Intermediate states. Power relations. 1945-73. *2208*

International Organizations (high-level, proposed). Economic Integration. 1973-. *520*

International Organizations (judicial). Bilateral commissions. International Boundary and Water Commission. Mexico. USA. 19c-1974. *624*

International Petroleum Company. Economic coercion. Nationalization. Peru. USA. 1968-71. *2095*

International politics. Cuba. Revolution. 1959-77. *1553*

International Red Aid. USSR. Working class. 1917-77. *311*

International regulation. Multinational corporations. 1970's. *205*

International relations. British Commonwealth. Jamaica. 1494-1975. *1784*

International Relations (discipline) *See also* Foreign Relations.

—. 1967-79. *183*

—. Foreign Relations. 1945-79. *248*

International Sea Foods Limited. Barbados. Development. Public Administration. 1966-74. *1808*

International Security *See also* Arbitration, International; Disarmament; Peace.

—. Atlantic, South. Brazil. 1822-1980. *2259*

—. Atomic energy. Tlatelolco, Treaty of. 1963-77. *235*

—. Economic Integration. Regional system. 1960's-70's. *550*

—. Nuclear nonproliferation (denuclearized zones). Tlatelolco, Treaty of. USA. USSR. 1950's-80. *509*

—. Organization of American States (meeting). Rio Treaty. USA. 1947-75. *525*

—. Regionalism. 1970-81. *544*

International system. Brazil. Political Power. 1964-80. *2485*

—. Foreign Relations. USA. 1960-74. *245*

—. Latin American Economic System. 1940's-70's. *32*

International Telephone & Telegraph Corporation. Allende, Salvador. Chile. Coups d'etat. USA. 1970-73. *2774*

—. Chile. *Firme* (periodical). 1970's-70's. *2705*

—. Chile. Foreign policy. Multinational Corporations. USA. 1971-74. *2678*

International Trade *See also* Foreign Investments.

—. Cuba. Foreign policy. USA. 1975. *1648*

International trade negotiations. 1980. *369*

International Waters *See also* Maritime Law.

—. International Law. 1945-73. *554*

Internationalism. Cosmopolitism. Ideas, history of. 16c-20c. *164*

Intervention. Africa. Angola. Cuba. Foreign policy. 1966-77. *1520*

—. Africa. Cuba. Mobilization thesis. 1959-79. *1496*

—. Allende, Salvador. Chile. Kissinger, Henry A. (*White House Years*). 1973. *2779*

—. Alliances. Documents. Mexico. Nicaragua. Sandino, Augusto César. USA. 1926-30. *219*

—. Angola. Cuba. Foreign Policy. USA. USSR. 1975-77. *1656*

—. Argentina. Foreign Policy. Nationalism. USA. 1941-46. *2536*

—. Attitudes. Government. Peru. Political leadership. Villages. 1964-75. *2041*

—. Canada. El Salvador. Navies. Political Attitudes. Revolution. 1932. *1100*

—. Chile. Coups d'Etat. USA. 1966-73. *2703*

—. Chile. Foreign Policy. USA. 1970-74. *2688*

—. Chile. USA. ca 1930's-77. *275*

—. Congo crisis. Suez crisis. UN. Voting patterns. 1956-60. *227*

—. Costa Rica. Diplomacy (secret). Jiménez, Ricardo. Nicaragua. USA. 1912-27. *1038*

—. Cuba. Platt Amendment. Political Factions. 1916-17. *1567*

—. Documents. Foreign Relations. Mexico. Nicaragua. USA. 1922-29. *327*

—. Documents. Mexico. Nicaragua. Press. USA. 1926-27. *218*

—. Dominican Republic. Economic Development. Social classes. ca 1870-1976. *1681*

—. Dominican Republic. Economic Growth. Haiti. Imperialism. USA. 1915-34. *1294*

—. Dominican Republic. Guerrilla warfare. Marines. USA. 1916-22. *1666*

—. *Dresden* (cruiser). Germany. Mexico (Tampico, Veracruz). Revolution. 1913-14. *755*

—. Foreign relations. Mexico. Pershing, John J. USA. Wilson, Woodrow. 1916. *810*

—. Guatemala. Historiography. USA. 1954-78. *1152*

—. Guatemala. USA. 1945-54. *1149*

—. Mexico (Veracruz). Military occupation. USA. 1914. *739*

—. Multinational Corporations. USA. 1953. *53*

—. Nicaragua. Political change. USA. 19c-20c. *1234*

—. Nicaragua. Sandino, Augusto César. USA. 1909-34. *1196*

Intervention (economic). Chile. Coups d'Etat. USA. 1970-73. *2943*

—. Chile. Popular Unity. USA. 1960-74. *2832*

Intervention, foreign. Costa Rica. Nicaragua. USA. 1925-26. *1036*

—. Cuba. 1959-75. *1363*
—. Cuba. 1959-81. *1445*
—. Cuba. Guillén, Nicolás. Ideology. 1920-65. *1529*
—. Cuba. Guillén, Nicolás. Race Relations. 1920-76. *1491*
—. Cuba. Politics. 1900-30. *1530*
—. Culture. Haiti. Politics. Price Mars, Jean. 1915-20's. *1733*
—. Dictatorship (theme). 1846-1976. *22*
—. Guillén, Nicolás. Journalism. Revolutionary Movements. 1936-75. *1492*
—. Hungary. Immigration. 1919-45. *230*
—. Marxism. Mexico. Politics. Revueltas, José. 1910-76. *597*
—. Nicaragua. Pérez, Fernando. Revolution. 1970's. *1198*
Lobbying *See also* Interest Groups; Political Factions.
—. Foreign policy. USA. 1960-79. *310*
Local Government *See also* Local Politics; Public Administration.
—. Accountability. Cuba. Democracy. 1958-79. *1515*
—. Bolivia. Cooperatives. Government Ownership. Mines. 1951-79. *1905*
—. Brazil (Minas Gerais). Elections. Military government. Patronage. 1965-68. *2448*
—. Caciquism. Ejidos. Land Tenure. 1917-77. *673*
—. Cargo system. Mexico, central. 1520-1975. *606*
—. Cedillo, Saturnino. Mexico (San Luis Potosí). Modernization. Peasants. Revolution. 1920-38. *769*
—. Civil Service. Trinidad and Tobago (Tobago). 1925-70. *1820*
—. Echeverría, Luis. Juntas de Vecinos. López Portillo, José. Mexico (Mexico City). Political Participation. 1971-81. *991*
—. Panama (Guararé). Reform. Rural development. 1972-81. *1265*
Local Government (Maya liaison officer). Belize (Crique Sarco). Indians. Kekchi. Modernization. 1951-62. *1060*
Local Government (review article). Chile. 1960-77. *2719*
—. Chile. Dependency, political. Valenzuela, Arturo. 1880-1977. *2944*
Local History. Association of Regional History. Mexico. National Institute of Anthropology and History. 20c. *654*
Local Politics *See also* Local Government.
—. Brazil. Political participation. 1960-1975. *2264*
—. Brazil (São Paulo). Elections (national). Labor. Peasants. Political attitudes. 1974. *2467*
—. Elites. Mexico (Tlaxcala). 1932-40. *834*
—. Social Classes. Venezuela (Caracas). Voting and Voting Behavior. 1958-68. *2184*
Logistics *See also* Military Strategy; Naval Strategy.
—. Armies. Mexico. USA. 1916. *777*
Longshoremen. Strikes. Trinidad and Tobago (Port of Spain). Violence. 1919. *1798*
López Mateos, Adolfo. Authoritarianism. Decisionmaking. Mexico. Profit-sharing. 1917-73. *967*
—. Foreign policy. Mexico. 1958-74. *929*
López Michelsen, Alfonso. Colombia. Economic Conditions. Social Conditions. 1974-79. *1955*
—. Colombia. Industrial policy. 1974-78. *1951*
López Portillo, José. Echeverría, Luis. Juntas de Vecinos. Local Government. Mexico (Mexico City). Political Participation. 1971-81. *991*
—. Echeverría, Luis. Mexico. 1970's. *889*
—. Echeverría, Luis. Mexico. Presidency. 1976. *908*
—. Economic policy. Mexico. 1977-80. *970*
—. Elections. Mexico. Political reform. 1977. *896*
—. Mass media. Mexico. Reform. 1970's. *893*
—. Mexico. Political Reform. 1976-81. *935*
—. Mexico. Reform. Social Conditions. 1977-79. *863*
Lora, Guillermo. Anti-imperialist front. Argentina. Bolivia. Communism (Trotskyism). 1971-74. *1887*
Love, Joseph. Brazil (Rio Grande do Sul). Cortés, Carlos E. Regionalism (review article). 1880's-1960's. *2293*
Lugones, Leopoldo. Drago, Luis María. Monroe Doctrine. *Revue Sud-Américaine*. Wilson, Woodrow. 1914. *2576*
Luisi, Paulina. Feminism. Moral reform. Uruguay. 1875-1950. *2987*
Lumber and Lumbering. Mexico (Chiapas, Tabasco). Traven, B. Working Conditions. 1870-1946. *569*

Lutz, Bertha. Brazil. Feminism. Politics. Suffrage. 1864-1964. *2375*

M

Machado, Agenor (papers). Archival Catalogs and Inventories. Brazil. São Paulo University (History Department). 1920-53. *2269*
Machado, Gerardo. Communist Party. Cuba. 1925-33. *1476*
—. Cuba. Economic Policy. Social Policy. USA. 1929-32. *1603*
—. Cuba. France (Paris). Newspapers. Revolution. USA. 1933. *1506*
—. Cuba. Nationalism. 1928-33. *1383*
—. Cuba. Politics and the Military. Revolution. USA. 1933. *1570*
Machado, Gustavo. Communist Party. Venezuela. 1919-78. *2178*
Macmillan, W. M. (*Warning from the West Indies*). Colonial Government. Great Britain. West Indies. 1934-39. *1315*
Madero, Francisco. Independence Movements. Mexico. Revolution. USA. 1910-17. *720*
Magazines. *See* Periodicals.
Magic. Dictatorship. Duvalier, François. Haiti. Negroes. 1957-71. *1738*
Magill, Roswell. Cuba. Economists, US. Seligman, Edwin. Shoup, Carl. Tax reform. 1932-39. *1604*
Maiakovski, Vladimir. Mexico. Poets. Travel. USA. 1925. *789*
Malaysia. Ethnicity. Guyana. Political parties. Social Classes. 1953-76. *122*
Malvinas. *See* Falkland Islands.
Management *See also* Industrial Relations.
—. Chile. Worker participation. 1971-74. *2892*
—. Law of the Sector of Social Property. Peru. Poland. Worker participation. 1974-75. *2028*
Manley, Michael. Economic Conditions. Jamaica. Socialism. 1972-77. *1760*
—. Elections. Jamaica. Seaga, Edward. 1976-80. *1776*
—. Jamaica. Political conditions. 1972-76. *1773*
—. Jamaica. Political Systems. Socialism. 1970's-82. *1761*
Manufactures *See also* names of articles manufactured; names of industries; Prices.
—. Brazil. Export promotion. Multinational corporations. ca 1964-77. *2228*
Mapuche. Chile. Indians. Land Tenure. Legislation. 1979-81. *2925*
—. Chile. Indians. Social Policy. 20c. *2717*
Marginality theory. Brazil (Rio de Janeiro). Favelas. Poor. 1968-73. *383*
Mariátegui, José Carlos. *Amauta* (periodical). Marxism. Periodicals. Peru. 1926-30. *2131*
—. Communism. Exiles. 1910-23. *468*
—. Communists. Cuba. 1920's. *481*
—. Exiles. Italy. Marxism. Peru. 1919-29. *2114*
—. Indians. Marxism. Nationalism. Peru. 1925-75. *2056*
—. Indigenismo. Peru. 19c-1929. *2134*
—. Labor movement. Marxism. Peru. ca 1920-26. *2008*
—. Labor movement. Peru. Socialism. 1916-29. *2111*
—. Lenin, V. I. Political thought. Russian Revolution. Zapata, Emiliano. 1917-70's. *485*
—. Marxism. Peru. 1920-78. *2120*
—. Marxism. Peru. Political Theory. 1895-1930. *2066*
—. Marxism-Leninism. Peru. 1910's-30's. *2069*
—. Peasants. Peru. Political Theory. Revolution. ca 1920-70's. *2121*
—. Peru. Political theory. 1914-30. *2027*
Mariátegui, José Carlos (review article). Chavarría, Jesús. Marxism. Peru. 1890-1930. *2132*
Mariátegui, José Carlos (*Seven interpretative essays on Peruvian life*). Marxism-Leninism. Peru. 1894-1930. *2047*
Marijuana. British West Indies. Drugs. Legislation. 1912-73. *1800*
Marine resources. Fishing rights. 1930's-73. *7*
Marinello, Juan. Communist Party. Cuba. Political Speeches. 1930's. *1535*
Marinello, Juan (memoirs). Cuba. Martínez Villena, Rubén. 1920's. *1528*
Marines *See also* Military Ground Forces; Navies.
—. Dominican Republic. Guerrilla warfare. Intervention. USA. 1916-22. *1666*
Maritime Law *See also* Fishing Rights; International Waters.
—. Territorial Waters. 1945-74. *57*

Maritime relations. Brazil. Foreign Relations. USA. 1967-73. *2286*
Marketing. Compañía Nacional de Subsistencias Populares. Government Enterprise. Mexico. 1960-79. *923*
—. Empresa Nacional de Comercialización de Insumos. Government enterprise. Peru. 1968-78. *2108*
Marley, Bob. Jamaica. Music. 1970's. *1769*
Maroons. Garvey, Marcus. Government, Resistance to. Jamaica. Rastafarianism. 1517-1962. *1749*
—. Jamaica. 17c-1980. *1746*
Martínez Villena, Rubén. Colleges and Universities. Communism. Cuba. Pascual, Sarah (memoirs). Universidad Popular José Martí. 1920-30. *1560*
—. Communist Party. Cuba. Figueroa, Isidro (memoirs). 1920-34. *1446*
—. Cuba. Journalism. Political Attitudes. 1920's-30's. *1554*
—. Cuba. Marinello, Juan (memoirs). 1920's. *1528*
—. Cuba. Nicolau, Ramón (memoirs). Revolution. 1920's-30's. *1551*
—. Cuba. Revolutionary activities. 1899-1934. *1587*
Martinique. Césaire, Aimé (*Tragedy of King Christophe*). Drama. 1960's-73. *1801*
—. Class struggle. Rebellions. 1635-1976. *1793*
—. France. Independence Movements (lack of). Modernization. 1960's-70's. *1818*
—. Robert, Georges. Vichy regime. World War II. 1940-43. *1788*
Marxism *See also* Anarchism and Anarchists; Class Struggle; Communism; Leninism; Socialism.
—. Agriculture. Land reform. Peasants (review article). Social conditions. 1900-75. *372*
—. Allende, Salvador. Chile. Political opposition. 1973-74. *2798*
—. Allende, Salvador. Chile. Politics (polarization). 1970-73. *2862*
—. *Amauta* (periodical). Mariátegui, José Carlos. Periodicals. Peru. 1926-30. *2131*
—. Argentina. Cordobazo. Labor Unions and Organizations. Peronism. Tosco, Augustín (interview). 1960's-70's. *2620*
—. Catholics. Politics. Religion (review article). 20c. *107*
—. Chavarría, Jesús. Mariátegui, José Carlos (review article). Peru. 1890-1930. *2132*
—. Chile. Historiography (review article). 1972-73. *2827*
—. Cuba. Historiography (review article). 1933-77. *1574*
—. Economic dependency (theory). Imperialism, theory of. Revolution. 1974. *467*
—. Ecuador. Political Factions. 1926-79. *1993*
—. Exiles. Italy. Mariátegui, José Carlos. Peru. 1919-29. *2114*
—. Films. Ideology. 19c-20c. *101*
—. Indians. Mariátegui, José Carlos. Nationalism. Peru. 1925-75. *2056*
—. Labor movement. Mariátegui, José Carlos. Peru. ca 1920-26. *2008*
—. Literature. Mexico. Politics. Revueltas, José. 1910-76. *597*
—. Mariátegui, José Carlos. Peru. 1920-78. *2120*
—. Mariátegui, José Carlos. Peru. Political Theory. 1895-1930. *2066*
Marxism (international). Allende, Salvador. Moss, Robert (review article). 1970-73. *2811*
Marxism-Leninism. Mariátegui, José Carlos. Peru. 1910's-30. *2069*
—. Mariátegui, José Carlos (*Seven interpretative essays on Peruvian life*). Peru. 1894-1930. *2047*
Marxist system. Allende, Salvador. Chile. Economic conditions. 1908-73. *2803*
Masons. *See* Freemasonry.
Mass attitudes. Chile. Political Participation. Social Classes. Socialism. ca 1950's-73. *2743*
Mass Media *See also* Films; Newspapers; Radio; Television.
—. Allende, Salvador. Chile. Social change. 1970-74. *2793*
—. Developing nations. Foreign policy. Trinidad and Tobago. 1962-76. *1805*
—. López Portillo, José. Mexico. Reform. 1970's. *893*
—. Peru. Reform. Velasco Alvarado, Juan. 1839-1975. *2010*
Massacres. Capitalism. Guatemala (Panzós). Peasants. 1978. *1126*
—. Depressions. Dominican Republic. Haitians. Nationalism. Racism. Trujillo, Rafael. 1937. *1675*

—. Ejidos. Land Tenure. ca 1920-70's. *708*
—. El Paso-Juárez Conference. Foreign Relations. USA (New Mexico). USA (New Mexico; Columbus, raid). Villa, Pancho. 1916. *748*
—. El Salvador. Guatemala. Land Reform. 1910-74. *1014*
—. Elections. Institutional Revolutionary Party (PRI). National Action Party (PAN). Political reform. 1967-73. *980*
—. Elections. López Portillo, José. Political reform. 1977. *896*
—. Elections. National Action Party (PAN). 1976. *855*
—. Elections, presidential. Henríquez Guzman, Miguel. Political opposition. 1950-54. *957*
—. Elections (presidential). Institutional Revolutionary Party (PRI). National Action Party (PAN). Political Campaigns. 1969-70. *947*
—. Electrical workers. Labor Unions and Organizations (independence). Politics. Railroad workers. 1955-72. *918*
—. Elite identification. Presidency. Quantitative methods. 1822-1970. *595*
—. Elites. House of Deputies. Political Recruitment. 1940-73. *901*
—. Elites. Political mobility. 1946-71. *984*
—. Elites. Political power. Social History (review article). 1428-1973. *694*
—. Elites. Political Systems. 1910-80. *665*
—. Elites. Revolution. ca 1910-20. *806*
—. Elites, political. 1935-73. *639*
—. Elites, political. 1935-78. *582*
—. Elites, political. 1946-70. *580*
—. Elites, political. Women. 1910-74. *668*
—. Elites, political. Women. 1920-79. *585*
—. Elites (review article). Social Control. 1917-70's. *621*
—. Emigration. Policymaking. Politics. USA. 1920-78. *653*
—. Employment trends. 1950-70. *856*
—. Energy. Foreign policy. Tomatoes. Trade Regulations. USA. 1969-80. *937*
—. Energy policy. Foreign Relations. 1910-79. *560*
—. Europe. Fascism. Italy. League of Nations. Peace. 1919-25. *784*
—. Exchange rates. Political economy. 1955-77. *945*
—. Exchange Rates. Politics. 1960-78. *939*
—. Executive power. Presidency. 20c. *587*
—. Exports. Foreign policy. Oil. 1960-79. *959*
—. Exports. Foreign Relations. Israel. Oil. Politics. 1975-79. *953*
—. Expressionism. Painting. Politics. 20c. *652*
—. Expropriation. Foreign Investments. Oil Industry and Trade. 1850-1938. *718*
—. Federal revenues, allocation of. Political leadership. 1934-73. *583*
—. Fishing Rights. Foreign Relations. Guatemala. 1958-59. *206*
—. Foreign investments. Foreign Relations. USA. 1910-80. *700*
—. Foreign Policy. 1960's-70's. *532*
—. Foreign policy. 1970-75. *917*
—. Foreign policy. 1972-74. *962*
—. Foreign policy. Human rights. 1945-77. *906*
—. Foreign policy. López Mateos, Adolfo. 1958-74. *929*
—. Foreign policy. Oil Industry and Trade. USA. 1921-28. *927*
—. Foreign policy. Revolution. Scott, Hugh Lenox. USA. Wilson, Woodrow. 1914-17. *749*
—. Foreign Policy. Tlatelolco Conference. 1973-74. *534*
—. Foreign Policy (review article). ca 1950-75. *615*
—. Foreign Relations. International division of labor. Tomatoes. Trade. USA (Florida). 1970-80. *977*
—. Foreign relations. Intervention. Pershing, John J. USA. Wilson, Woodrow. 1916. *810*
—. Foreign Relations. Japan. Revolution. 1916-17. *767*
—. Foreign Relations. Meyer, Lorenzo. Nationalism. Oil Industry and Trade (review article). USA. 1917-42. *680*
—. Foreign Relations. Naturalization. Oil. USA. 1915-42. *671*
—. Foreign Relations. Obregón, Álvaro. USA. 1913-23. *756*
—. Foreign Relations. Oil Industry and Trade. USA. 1910-72. *564*
—. Foreign Relations. Political change. Reform. USA. 1923-77. *944*

—. Foreign Relations. Revolution. Steffens, Lincoln. USA. 1913-27. *807*
—. Foreign Relations. USA. 1940-80. *958*
—. Foreign Relations. USA. 1973-80. *875*
—. Foreign Relations. USA (New Mexico; Columbus, raid). Villa, Pancho. 1913-16. *816*
—. Foreign Relations. USSR. 1917-24. *678*
—. Garcia, Antonio. Peasants. Poetry. Revolutionary Movements. 1968-73. *903*
—. General Confederation of Labor (CGT). Labor movement. Regional Confederation of Mexican Labor (CROM). 1920's. *730*
—. General Confederation of Labor (CGT). Labor Unions and Organizations. 1921-31. *714*
—. Generations. Intellectuals. 1907-64. *685*
—. Germany. Intelligence. USA. Witzke affair. World War I. 1914-23. *751*
—. González Casanova, Pablo. Labor movement. Working Class (review article). 19c-20c. *660*
—. Government. Intellectuals. 20c. *646*
—. Government. Labor movement. 1958-59. *933*
—. Government. Revolution (review article). 1910-79. *637*
—. Government Enterprise. Labor Unions and Organizations. Radicals and Radicalism. 1972-78. *881*
—. Historiography. Labor movement. Social classes. ca 1940-69. 1970-78. *703*
—. Historiography. Peasants. Revolution. Tradition. 20c. *811*
—. Historiography. Politics. 1970's. *934*
—. Historiography. Revisionism. Revolution. 1930-77. *715*
—. Historiography. Revolution. 1910-75. *778*
—. Historiography (review article). 1000 BC-1977. *666*
—. Historiography (review article). West Indies. 17c-1979. *82*
—. Hormonal steroid industry. Industrial development. Multinational corporations. 1940-76. *608*
—. Ideology. Institutionalization. Political Systems. Revolution. 20c. *651*
—. Ideology. Nationalism. Politics. 1940-70. *941*
—. Ideology. Revolution. Social Customs. 19c-20c. *663*
—. Ideology. USA. 16c-20c. *888*
—. Import control. Protectionism. Trade. 1930-70. *627*
—. Income tax. Taxation. 1920-64. *603*
—. Independence Movements. Madero, Francisco. Revolution. USA. 1910-17. *720*
—. Indians. 1910-81. *655*
—. Indigenization. Multinational corporations. 1971-80. *864*
—. Industrial development. Protectionism. Tariff policy. 1930-65. *628*
—. Industrialization. 1917-76. *701*
—. Institutional Revolutionary Party (PRI). Obregón, Álvaro. Political Factions. 1914-28. *744*
—. Institutional Revolutionary Party (PRI). Political Reform. 1978-81. *930*
—. Intellectuals. Political Protest. 1900-71. *672*
—. Intergovernmental Relations. Irrigation. Rural development. 1930-78. *936*
—. International law (doctrines). USA. 1907-69. *692*
—. Journalism. Revolution. USA. 1916-29. *717*
—. Juárez, Benito. National myth. 19c-20c. *698*
—. Juárez, Benito (myth of). Politics. 19c-20c. *699*
—. Labor movement. 1917-75. *601*
—. Labor Unions and Organizations. Railroads. USA. 1880-1933. *650*
—. Labor Unions and Organizations. Teachers. 1931-45. *572*
—. Land reform. Obregón, Álvaro. 1920-24. *745*
—. Law (private, public). 1798-1974. *695*
—. Legislative Bodies. Party deputy system. Political parties. 1963-73. *640*
—. Literature. Marxism. Politics. Revueltas, José. 1910-76. *597*
—. López Portillo, José. Mass media. Reform. 1970's. *893*
—. López Portillo, José. Political Reform. 1976-81. *935*
—. López Portillo, José. Reform. Social Conditions. 1977-79. *863*
—. Maiakovski, Vladimir. Poets. Travel. USA. 1925. *789*

—. Mexico, National Autonomous University of. Revolution. Students. 1910-40. *719*
—. Middle Classes. Politics. 20c. *567*
—. Middle Classes. Reformism. 1930's. *839*
—. Migrant Labor. Repatriation. USA. 1920-23. *724*
—. Migration, internal. Population Policy. 1978-82. *871*
—. Military reform. Obregón, Álvaro. Professionalization. 1920-24. *747*
—. Mining industry. 1877-1970. *707*
—. Missions and Missionaries. Protestant Churches. USA (Southwestern). 1867-1930. *726*
—. Modernization. 1917-70's. *658*
—. Modernization. Standard of living. 1940-70. *952*
—. Naco (battle). Revolution. USA. 1914-15. *781*
—. Naco (battle). Revolution. USA (Arizona; Naco). 1914-15. *746*
—. National Action Party (PAN). Political reform. 1970's. *925*
—. Natural gas. Oil Industry and Trade. USA. 1901-78. *617*
—. Natural gas. USA. 1977-80. *911*
—. Novels. Revolution. 1900-70. *780*
—. Novels. Revolution. Values. Violence. 1910-60's. *598*
—. Nuevo León, University of. 1947-48. *942*
—. Oil Industry and Trade. Political Corruption. 1970's. *909*
—. Oil Industry and Trade. Politics. 1981. *910*
—. Oil Industry and Trade. Social Problems. 1980's. *987*
—. Oil policies. Petróleos Mexicanos. 1915-79. *990*
—. Paz, Octavio *(El Ogro Filantrópico)*. Philosophy (review article). 1979. *940*
—. Peasant movements. 1770-1978. *604*
—. Peasants. Populism, agrarian. Rural development. 1950-79. *788*
—. Peasants. Social Conditions. 20c. *993*
—. Peasants. Sugar. 1920-75. *607*
—. Political analysis. Saltillo Industrial Group. Strikes. 1974. *879*
—. Political Campaigns. Political leadership. Vasconcelos, José. 1929-77. *723*
—. Political change. Political recruitment. 1976-79. *874*
—. Political Change. Revolution. Social Conditions. 1910-74. *634*
—. Political development. 20c. *689*
—. Political Leadership. Presidentialism. 20c. *636*
—. Political life. 1900-75. *648*
—. Political Protest. Strikes. Students. 1972. *994*
—. Political Protest. Students. 1968. *956*
—. Political recruitment. Universities. 1935-74. *873*
—. Political stability. 1913-82. *931*
—. Political systems. 1940-77. *579*
—. Political systems. Regime support, diffuse. Symbols, political. 1975. *599*
—. Political Systems. Revolution. 1917-70. *803*
—. Politics. Welfare bureaucracy. 1960's-70's. *661*
—. Politics (rumors). Presidency. Succession. 1968-76. *932*
—. Population explosion. Social Conditions. Social policy. 1950's-1974. *558*
—. Presidency. 1876-1976. *619*
—. Press. 1917-74. *593*
—. Press. Rebellions. Romania. 1910-17. *813*
—. Public Administration. Reform. Secretariat of Programming and Budget. 1958-79. *858*
—. Regional development. 1940-73. *578*
—. Regional studies. Research. Revolution. ca 1910-25. *729*
—. Revolution. 1910-20. *762*
—. Revolution. 1910-38. *766*
—. Revolution. Salazar, José Inés. ca 1910-18. *814*
—. Revolution. Social Classes. Violence. 1910-30's. *812*
—. Revolution. Vasconcelos, José. 1925-59. *782*
—. Revolution. Villa, Pancho. 1910-20. *768*
—. Revolution. Women. 1910-20. *773*
—. San Pedro de la Cueva (massacre). Sonora campaign. Villa, Pancho. 1915-16. *783*
—. Sinarquismo. 1937-44. *638*
—. Social Classes (review article). 1970's. *919*
—. Social policy. 1900-74. *687*
—. Supreme Court. 1917-70's. *590*
—. USA (New Mexico). USA (New Mexico; Columbus, raid). Villa, Pancho. 1916. *765*

—. Women. 19c-20c. *704*
Mexico (Baja California). Archives. 1744-1950. *644*
Mexico (Baja California; Turtle Bay). *Asama* (vessel). Japan. Navies. 1911-16. *818*
Mexico (border region). Industrialization. Tariff. Unemployment. USA. 1974. *857*
Mexico (Cancún). Economic Development. USA. 1950's-82. *343*
Mexico, central. Cargo system. Local Government. 1520-1975. *606*
Mexico (Chiapas). Agriculture. Development. Indians. 1528-1975. *697*
—. Landowners. Rebellions. 1914-20. *754*
Mexico (Chiapas; Selva Lacandona). Government. Settlement. 1962-78. *963*
Mexico (Chiapas, Tabasco). Lumber and Lumbering. Traven, B. Working Conditions. 1870-1946. *569*
Mexico (Ciudad Juárez). Transportation. USA (Texas; El Paso). 1950's-70's. *964*
Mexico (Coahuila). Political Factions. 1910-20. *791*
Mexico (Coatzacoalcos, Minatitlán). Oil Workers Union. Petróleos Mexicanos. Political Systems. 1960's-70's. *786*
Mexico (Cuajinicuilapa). Acculturation (review article). Aquirre Beltrán, Gonzalo. Negroes. 20c. *623*
Mexico (Guerrero). Peasant movements. Vázquez, Jenaro. 1960-66. *904*
Mexico (Guerrero; Sierra Madre). Capitalism. Development. Government. 1964-76. *887*
Mexico (Hidalgo; San Antonio Tochatlaco). Agricultural production. Haciendas. Land Reform. 1880-1920. *716*
Mexico (Laguna). Agricultural Reform. Capitalism. Cárdenas, Lázaro. Economic Development. 1936-73. *842*
Mexico (Lázaro Cárdenas City). City Planning. New towns. 1970-78. *869*
Mexico (Mexico City). Casa del Obrero Mundial. Labor Unions and Organizations. Peasants. Working Class. 1910-16. *727*
—. Echeverría, Luis. Juntas de Vecinos. Local Government. López Portillo, José. Political Participation. 1971-81. *991*
—. Government. Labor movement. Streetcar workers. 1922-28. *794*
Mexico (Michoacán). Bibliographies. Cárdenas, Lázaro. Military. Politics. 1910-40. *573*
—. Educational Reform. Political Change. Schools, rural. Social Change. 1915-29. *787*
Mexico (Monterrey). Economic conditions. Politics. 1810-1974. *674*
Mexico (Morelos). Peasants. Social Organization. Urban growth. ca 1545-1970. *609*
Mexico, National Autonomous University of. Authoritarianism. Autonomy. Colleges and Universities. Mexico. 1929-75. *635*
—. Colleges and universities. Mexico. Radicals and Radicalism. 1966-72. *946*
—. Mexico. Revolution. Students. 1910-40. *719*
Mexico, National Autonomous University of (National School of Economics). Colleges and Universities. Graduates. Public Employees. 1929-52. *581*
Mexico (Nayarit). Elections. 1959-75. *907*
Mexico, Northern. Agricultural production. Land expropriation. Political Factions. 1976. *854*
—. Chinese. Immigration. 1875-1932. *760*
—. Political Leadership. Revolutionary Movements. 1880-1937. *728*
Mexico (Nuevo León). Benítez family. Governors. 19c-20c. *632*
Mexico (Papaloapan basin). Development. Settlement. 1975-78. *559*
Mexico (Puebla). Modernization. Politics. Programa de Inversiones Públicas para el Desarrollo Rural. Rural Development. 1940-78. *890*
Mexico (Quintana Roo). Government. Investments. Rural settlements. 1977. *897*
Mexico (San Bartolomé, Chiapas). Indians (Tzotzil). Mayan community. Political participation. Political systems. 1975. *675*
Mexico (San Cosme). Patronage. Social Classes. 1940-74. *975*
Mexico (San Luis Potosí). Cedillo, Saturnino. Local Government. Modernization. Peasants. Revolution. 1920-38. *769*
—. Economic development. Mines. Prehistory-1978. *577*
Mexico (Sonora). Aguilar Camín, Héctor. Revolution (review article). 1910-20. *793*
—. Chinese. Discrimination. Social Classes. 1910-33. *736*

—. Chinese. Immigration. Persecution. 1890's-1931. *761*
—. Diaries. Kibbey, William Beckford. Rebellions. 1929. *737*
—. Maytorena, José María. Reform. Revolution. 1913-15. *735*
Mexico, southern. Peasants. Revolution. Zapata, Emiliano. 1910-20. *799*
Mexico (Tamaulipas). International Boundary and Water Commission. Irrigation. Rio Grande Basin. USA (Texas). 1900-20. *676*
Mexico (Tampico). Labor Unions and Organizations. Oil Industry and Trade. Strikes. 1923-24. *709*
Mexico (Tampico, Veracruz). *Dresden* (cruiser). Germany. Intervention. Revolution. 1913-14. *755*
Mexico (Tlaxcala). Elites. Local Politics. 1932-40. *834*
—. Land Reform. Peasant movements. Social conditions. 1910-17. *722*
Mexico (Tlaxcala; Huamantla). Carrizosa, Rubén C. Land Reform. Patron-client Relations. 1930-39. *575*
Mexico (Tlaxcala; Natívitas valley). Land Reform. Land Tenure. Peasants. 1917-23. *721*
Mexico (Veracruz). Intervention. Military occupation. USA. 1914. *739*
Mexico (Yucatán). Alvarado, Salvador. Carrillo Puerto, Felipe. Women's liberation movement. 1920-24. *772*
—. Caciquismo. Carrillo Puerto, Felipe. Socialism. 1922-24. *763*
—. Cordemex. Fibers Industry. Nationalization. 1961-77. *870*
—. Economic development. Political corruption. 1910-74. *614*
—. Political Change. 1910-40. *625*
Mexico (Zongolica). Economic Development. Population growth. 1900-72. *605*
Meyer, Lorenzo. Foreign Relations. Mexico. Nationalism. Oil Industry and Trade (review article). USA. 1917-42. *680*
Microforms. Bibliographies. Books, Early. 1500-1940. *182*
Middle Classes. Ação Social Nacionalista. Brazil. Conservatism. Nationalism. Radicals and Radicalism. 1889-1930. *2384*
—. APRA. Ideology. Peru. 1920's-70's. *2124*
—. Argentina. Economic dependency debate. Imperialism. Landowning class. Peronism. 1940-73. *2634*
—. Bolívar, Simón. Democracy. Monism. 1813-1974. *460*
—. Capitalism. Dominican Republic. Imperialism. USA. 1900-24. *1669*
—. Capitalism. Government. 1970's. *27*
—. Castro, Fidel. Cuba. Financial support. Revolution. 1956-58. *1558*
—. Chile. Coups d'etat. Women. 1973. *2835*
—. Chile. Government, Resistance to. Gremialismo. Ideology. 19c-1973. *2834*
—. Chile. Ideology. Political Change. 1970-76. *2675*
—. Class Struggle. Economic Conditions. Military government. Peru. 1970's. *2035*
—. Cuba. Emigration. Force, use of. Government, Resistance to. Political culture. 1960's-70's. *1650*
—. Democratic Union of Liberation. Nicaragua. 1974-78. *1243*
—. Dependency. Economic Development. Nicaragua. 1950-80. *1224*
—. Industrialization. USA. 1914-79. *142*
—. Mexico. Politics. 20c. *567*
—. Mexico. Reformism. 1930's. *839*
—. Military. Politics. 1960's-70's. *418*
Middle Classes (destruction). Cuba. Revolution. 1959-61. *1559*
Migrant labor. Argentina. Labor unions, representation. Sugar industry. 1944-76. *2512*
—. Mexico. Repatriation. USA. 1920-23. *724*
Migrant Labor (contract). Chile. Nitrate industry. 1880-1930. *2716*
Migrants. Politics. Urbanization (review article). Venezuela. 20c. *2181*
Migration *See also* Emigration; Immigration; Refugees.
—. Andean Group. Income distribution. Labor. 1970-77. *1857*
—. Brazil. Urbanization. 1940-80. *2326*
Migration, internal. Methodology. Radicals and Radicalism. Social Surveys. 1950's-75. *175*
—. Mexico. Population Policy. 1978-82. *871*
Migration, Internal (circular). Indians. Integration. Venezuela (Orinoco). 1920-74. *2152*

Migration policy. Colombia. Labor. 1975-79. *1949*
Militarism *See also* Civil-Military Relations; Disarmament; Imperialism; Military Government; Politics and the Military.
—. Chile. USA. USSR. 1962-74. *2920*
—. Chile. Violence, political. 1970-74. *2905*
—. Coups d'Etat. Ideology. Literature. Peru. 1900-68. *2094*
—. Cuba. 1970-78. *1662*
Militarism, professional. Europe. 1890-1940. *437*
Militarization. Armies. Cuba. Social Change. 1950-70. *1562*
Military *See also* Air Warfare; Armies; Civil-Military Relations; Disarmament; Guerrilla Warfare; Logistics; Navies; Politics and the Military; Tactics; War.
—. Africa. Cuba. 1959-78. *1555*
—. Africa. Cuba. Foreign Relations. USSR. 1959-81. *1649*
—. Arévalo, Juan José. Guatemala. Revolution. Ubico Castañeda, Jorge. 1944. *1146*
—. Argentina. Coups d'Etat. Yrigoyen, Hipólito. 1930. *2566*
—. Argentina. Economic policy. Liberalism. 1946-79. *2660*
—. Argentina. Perón, Isabel. 1975. *2605*
—. Argentina. Peronism. Political Attitudes. 1973-76. *2672*
—. Authoritarianism. Bureaucracies. Colombia. 1964-73. *1968*
—. Bibliographies. Cárdenas, Lázaro. Mexico (Michoacán). Politics. 1910-40. *573*
—. Bibliographies. Central America. 1915-80. *1040*
—. Bonner, Raymond. Bushnell, John A. Democracy. El Salvador. Foreign Relations. Ramos, Arnold. USA. Williams, Murat. 1982. *1125*
—. Brazil. Castello-Branco, Humberto (anthology; review article). 1900-67. *2324*
—. Capitalism. Chile. Dictatorship. 1960-80. *46*
—. Chile. Christian Democrats. Democracy, breakdown of. 1970-75. *2939*
—. Chile. Coups d'Etat. Ideas, History of. 20c. *2720*
—. Chile. Coups d'Etat. Repression, politics of. Social pathology. 1973. *2940*
—. Chile. Popular Unity. 1970's. *2843*
—. Conservatism. Radicals and Radicalism. USA. ca 1960-80. *447*
—. Cuba. Ideology. Revolution. 1959-76. *1643*
—. Cuba. Race relations. 1960's-70's. *1423*
—. Economic development. Statism. 20c. *428*
—. Foreign Policy. Leftism. USA. 1970-77. *41*
—. Middle classes. Politics. 1960's-70's. *418*
Military aid. Central America. Civil-Military Relations (review article). USA. 20c. *1238*
—. Chile. Elections. USA. Venezuela. 1963-64. *430*
—. Civil-Military Relations. Guatemala. USA. 1953-78. *1150*
—. Civil-Military Relations. USA. 1946-78. *426*
—. Counterinsurgency. USA. 1963-73. *444*
—. Politics and the Military. 1950's-70's. *425*
Military Bases *See also* names of military bases.
—. Cuba. Foreign Policy. Guantánamo Bay (status of). USA. 1960-72. *1381*
Military budgets. Air Forces. Arms transfers. Public Finance. 1960-70. *446*
Military campaigns. Castro, Fidel. Cuba. Independence Movements. Socialism. 1860-1959. *1644*
Military Campaigns (documents). Brazil (São Paulo). Rebellions. 1924. *2372*
—. Castro, Fidel. Cuba (Santiago). Moncada barracks. 1859-1960. *1642*
Military Capability. Treaties. 1940-75. *448*
Military Decorations, Flags, and Symbols. Caxias, Duke of. Military Education. 1932-82. *2213*
Military Education. Academia de Guerra Naval. Chile. Navies. 1911-81. *2722*
—. Air Forces. Aviation. School of Military Aviation. Venezuela. 1920-80. *2190*
—. Caxias, Duke of. Military Decorations, Flags, and Symbols. 1932-82. *2213*
—. Civil-military relations. Military officers. Professionalism. 1960's-70's. *417*
—. Human rights. International Military Education and Training Program. USA. 1978. *424*
Military expenditure. 1961-70. *421*
Military Government *See also* Military Occupation.
—. 1960's-70's. *434*

—. 19c-20c. *440*
—. Agriculture. Economic Structure. Industry. Peru. 1968-80. *2013*
—. Argentina. 1930-79. *2548*
—. Argentina. 1963-78. *2663*
—. Argentina. 1981-82. *2673*
—. Argentina. Bolivia. Brazil. Ecuador. Peru. Political Change. 1960-80. *436*
—. Argentina. Brazil. Censorship. Press (academic). 1964-75. *88*
—. Argentina. Censorship. Colleges and universities. Sociology. 1966-79. *2547*
—. Argentina. Economic policy. Populism. 1946-76. *2513*
—. Argentina. Foreign Relations. USA. 1940-81. *2537*
—. Argentina. Human rights. National Security. 1969-77. *2531*
—. Argentina. Videla, Jorge. 1976-79. *2668*
—. Armies. Revolutionary process. USA. 1810-1973. *469*
—. Arts. Chile. Cultural policy. 1973-82. *2907*
—. Assassination. Chile. Letelier, Orlando. Pinochet, Augusto. 1973-78. *2903*
—. Authoritarianism. Industrialization. 1964-78. *422*
—. Belaúnde Terry, Fernando. Peru. 1960-80. *2091*
—. Bibliographies. Chile. Historiography. 1970-73. *2880*
—. Bolivia. 1971-79. *1877*
—. Bolivia. 1980. *1885*
—. Bolivia. Democracy. Political Systems. 1970's. *1886*
—. Brazil. 1964-73. *2493*
—. Brazil. 1964-78. *2452*
—. Brazil. 1964-79. *2459*
—. Brazil. Civil-military relations. 1964-70. *2234*
—. Brazil. Democracy. 1960-80. *2497*
—. Brazil. Democracy. Electoral policy. Political Change. 1964-81. *2241*
—. Brazil. Democratization. 1964-79. *2478*
—. Brazil. Domestic Policy. Power. 1964-74. *2447*
—. Brazil. Economic Development. Social Classes. 1964-73. *2440*
—. Brazil. Geisel, Ernesto. 1975-78. *2461*
—. Brazil. Geisel, Ernesto. Industrialization. Social instability. 1964-75. *2483*
—. Brazil. Geisel, Ernesto. Repression. 1976. *2458*
—. Brazil. Ideology. 1960-71. *2446*
—. Brazil. Industrialization. Technocrats. 1964-70's. *2477*
—. Brazil. Peru. Political Culture. 1964-74. *416*
—. Brazil. Political Change. 1964-80. *2423*
—. Brazil. Political Repression. 1964-73. *2498*
—. Brazil (Amazon region). Economic Development. Ideology. 1965-74. *2417*
—. Brazil (Minas Gerais). Elections. Local Government. Patronage. 1965-68. *2448*
—. Capitalism. Chile. Dependency. Popular Unity. 1936-74. *2883*
—. Catholic Church. Chile. 1973-76. *2954*
—. Catholic Church. National security. 1960's-70's. *21*
—. Chile. 1973. *2938*
—. Chile. Civil liberties. Public opinion. Violence. 1970-75. *2900*
—. Chile. Economic Conditions. Human rights. Pinochet, Augusto. 1973-76. *2908*
—. Chile. Economic Policy. Monetary policy. 1973-78. *2911*
—. Chile. Economic policy. Popular Unity. 1970's. *2690*
—. Chile. Farmers, small. Popular Front. Social Change. 1938-79. *2735*
—. Chile. Labor movement. 1973-78. *2957*
—. Chile. Land Reform. 1965-74. *2909*
—. Chile. Pinochet, Augusto. 1973-82. *2953*
—. Chile. Political Participation. 1973-78. *2947*
—. Chile. Public policy. 1973-78. *2948*
—. Civil war. El Salvador. 1961-79. *1087*
—. Civilian regimes. Economic Policy. 1961-70. *33*
—. Class Struggle. Economic Conditions. Middle Classes. Peru. 1970's. *2035*
—. Communist Party. Economic development. Honduras. Social reform. 1971-73. *1172*
—. Corporatism (review article). 1964-79. *438*
—. Coups d'Etat. Surinam. 1980. *1689*
—. Democratization. 1940's-70's. *413*
—. Dependency. Foreign aid. Peru. USA. 1963-73. *2026*
—. Economic Conditions. 1970's. *223*

—. Economic development. Government (civilian). Peru. 1963-74. *2072*
—. Economic Policy. Foreign investments. Peru. 1968-75. *2089*
—. Economic Reform. Legislation. Peru. Social Reform. 20c. *2077*
—. Economic reform. Peru. 1968-74. *2063*
—. Economic reform. Peru. Quijano, Aníbal (interview). Social Reform. 1968-73. *2104*
—. El Salvador. Elites. Reform. 1979-80. *1098*
—. El Salvador. Revolutionary Democratic Front. 1970-80. *1102*
—. Elections. Peru. 1968-78. *2054*
—. Historiography. Peru. 1968-75. *2096*
—. Human rights. Religion. 1970's. *174*
—. Ideology. Nunn, Frederick M. Peru. 1968-75. *2135*
—. Military junta phenomenon. Peru. 1968-72. *2093*
—. Peasants. Peru. 1968-80. *2039*
—. Peru. 1968-77. *2125*
—. Peru. Reform. 1968-75. *2046*
—. Peru. Revolution. 1968-71. 1930's-71. *2037*
—. Peru. Velasco Alvarado, Juan. 1968-75. *2052*
—. Political Development. Uruguay. 1976-82. *3003*
—. Political repression. 1970's. *431*
—. Political Systems. Uruguay. 1970-80's. *2990*
Military Government (review article). Peru. 1968-70's. *2022*
Military Ground Forces. Brazilian Expeditionary Force. World War II. 1941-45. *2360*
Military influence. Brazil. Economic policy. Vargas, Getúlio. 1930-45. *2354*
Military junta. Chile. Communist Party. Revolution. 1973-74. *2910*
—. Chile. Coups d'etat. 19c-1973. *2933*
—. Chile. Coups d'Etat. Political tactics. 1912-74. *2792*
—. Chile. Economic Conditions. 1971-74. *2937*
—. Chile. Economic conditions. USA. 1975. *2904*
—. Chile. Economic policy. 1967-74. *2912*
—. Chile. Human rights. 1975. *70*
Military junta phenomenon. Military government. Peru. 1968-72. *2093*
Military Leadership. Argentina. Elections. 20c. *2514*
Military Occupation *See also* Military Government.
—. Colonial Government. Dominican Republic. Haiti. 1898-1940. *1320*
—. Dominican Republic. Government, Resistance to. USA. 1916-24. *1668*
—. Elections. McCoy, Frank R. Nicaragua. Sandino, Augusto César. USA. 1927-28. *1187*
—. Haiti. USA. 1910's-30's. *1734*
—. Intervention. Mexico (Veracruz). USA. 1914. *739*
—. Nicaragua (Puerto Cabezas). Ridgway, Matthew B. (report). USA. 1927-33. *1209*
Military officers. Brazil. Prestes, Luis Carlos. Rebellions. Tenentes. 1924-27. *2358*
—. Civil-military relations. Military Education. Professionalism. 1960's-70's. *417*
Military officers (motives). Power, seizure of. 1954-68. *435*
Military preparations. Castro, Fidel. Cuba, invasion of. Guevara, Ernesto "Che" (memoirs). Revolution. 1954-56. *1478*
Military Reform. Ideology. Peru. 1970-77. *2105*
—. Mexico. Obregón, Alvaro. Professionalization. 1920-24. *747*
Military role. Chile. Public opinion. 1964-65. *2695*
Military Service (enlistees). Argentina. Brazil. Poles. World War II. 1940-44. *442*
Military Service, Professional. Politics and the Military. 1950-73. *423*
—. Politics and the Military. 1960's-. *432*
Military Socialism. Bolivia. Busch, German. Legion of Ex-Combatants. Villaroel, Gualberto. 1936-46. *1863*
Military spending. National security problem. 1970's. *186*
Military Strategy *See also* Logistics; Naval Strategy.
—. Balance of Power. Cuba. Iran. USA. USSR. 1970's. *1598*
—. Central America. Defense. 1970's. *1019*
—. USA. 1850-1979. *419*
—. USA. 20c. *58*
Military Strategy (indirect strategy). Guerrilla environment. 1974. *99*
Military tradition. Chile. Coups d'Etat. 1970-74. *2826*

Military-dominated government. Brazil. Economic Growth (social costs). Foreign Policy. 1930-72. *2300*
Millenarianism. Brazil. Catholicism, Folk. Politics. Religion. 1893-1980. *2298*
Mineral resources. Aluminum Company of America. De Beers Company. Guyana. 1920's. *1721*
Mineral resources, exploitation of. Oceans. Regional policy. UN. USA. 1969-76. *13*
Miners. Barrios de Chungara, Domitila. Bolivia. Memoirs. Political Protest. USA. 1961-70's. *1860*
—. Bolivia. Elections. Paz Estenssoro, Victor. Politics. Revolution. 1923-52. *1904*
—. Bolivia. Labor movement. Tin. 1918-76. *1888*
—. Cerro de Pasco Corporation. Peru. Working class (class consciousness). 1970's. *2031*
Mines. Bolivia. Comibol. Economic Development. Export economy. 1900-70's. *1866*
—. Bolivia. Cooperatives. Government Ownership. Local Government. 1951-79. *1905*
—. Cerro de Pasco Corporation. Foreign Investments. Labor movement. Peru. 1900-74. *2073*
—. Economic development. Mexico (San Luis Potosí). Prehistory-1978. *577*
Mining industry. Foreign investments. Multinational corporations. Politics. 1950-77. *377*
—. Mexico. 1877-1970. *707*
—. Nationalization. Peru. 1960's. *2034*
—. Peru. Strikes. 1950-76. *2030*
Ministers. *See* Clergy.
Minorities *See also* Discrimination; Ethnic Groups; Nationalism; Population; Racism.
—. Discrimination. Nationalism. 19c-20c. *104*
—. Indians. Nicaragua. 1980's. *1194*
Miskito. Ethnic Groups. Government. Nicaragua. 1770-1980. *1191*
—. Ethnic Groups. Nicaragua. Revolution. 1979-82. *1213*
—. Indians. Nicaragua. Revolution. 1970's. *1207*
—. Indians. Nicaragua. Sumo. 1979-81. *1240*
Missile crisis. Cuba. International law. USA. 1962-75. *1577*
Missions and Missionaries. Cuba. Methodist Church. Nationalism. USA. 1898-1958. *1406*
—. Ideology. Summer Institute of Linguistics. Wycliffe Bible Translators. 1917-79. *177*
—. Mexico. Protestant Churches. USA (Southwestern). 1867-1930. *726*
Mitrione, Dan A. Agency for International Development. Tupamaros. Uruguay. USA. 1969-73. *2985*
Mobility. *See* Social Mobility.
Mobilization thesis. Africa. Cuba. Intervention. 1959-79. *1496*
Models *See also* Methodology.
—. Argentina. Economic Policy. Perón, Juan. 1946-55. *2585*
—. Chile (Santiago). Leftism. Voting and Voting Behavior. 1964. *2754*
—. Church and State. Paraguay. 1972. *2974*
Moderates. Left. Political parties. Venezuela. 1958-69. *2161*
Modernization *See also* Developing Nations; Economic Theory; Foreign Aid; Industrialization; Social Change.
—. Agriculture. Domestic Policy. Irrigation. Mexico. Political power. 1970-76. *899*
—. Argentina. Chile. Economic dependency. Elites. Political conflict. 1900-25. *154*
—. Belize (Crique Sarco). Indians. Kekchi. Local Government (Maya liaison officer). 1951-62. *1060*
—. Bolivia. Nationalist Revolutionary Movement (MNR). Nationalization. Reform. Revolution. Social Classes. 1952-56. *1881*
—. Brazil. Indians. Public Policy. 1970's-80's. *2449*
—. Brazil. Indians. Yanomami. 1960's-80's. *2454*
—. Brazil. Judicial Process. 20c. *2224*
—. Bureaucracies. Colonial practices, Spanish. Organizational model. Venezuela. -1970's. *75*
—. Burns, E. Bradford. Elites. Labor. Skidmore, Thomas E. 19c-20c. *69*
—. Campesino movements. Class conflict. 1918-74. *389*
—. Cedillo, Saturnino. Local Government. Mexico (San Luis Potosí). Peasants. Revolution. 1920-38. *769*

—. Cuba. Films (historical) (review article). Solás, Humberto. 1895-1970's. *1548*
—. Cuba. Novels. Revolutionary Movements. 1958-75. *1523*
—. Ethnic groups. Guyana. 1966-76. *1697*
—. Jamaica. Social Classes. 1910-73. *1764*
National Society of Agriculture. Chile. Elites. Landowners. Political Participation. 1932-64. *2681*
—. Chile. Interest Groups. Labor Unions and Organizations (suppression). Landowners. Peasants. 1920-48. *2749*
National System in Support of Social Mobilization (SINAMOS). Authoritarianism. Corporatism. Peru. Social Mobilization. Velasco Alvarado, Juan. 1968-74. *2082*
National United Freedom Fighters (NUFF). Anti-Imperialism. Documents. Revolutionary Movements. Trinidad and Tobago. 1970's. *1830*
Nationalism *See also* Anti-Imperialism; Independence Movements; Minorities.
—. Ação Social Nacionalista. Brazil. Conservatism. Middle Classes. Radicals and Radicalism. 1889-1930. *2384*
—. Anti-Communism. Diplomacy. Mexico. USA. 1924-27. *758*
—. Argentina. Foreign Investments. Foreign policy. 1816-1976. *2659*
—. Argentina. Foreign Policy. Intervention. USA. 1941-46. *2536*
—. Argentina. Political Attitudes. 1970-81. *2542*
—. Bibliographies. Central America. 1970-80. *1026*
—. Bibliographies. Cuba. 1971-80. *1532*
—. Bolivia. Federation of Bolivian Mine Workers. USA. Workers' Central (COB). 1970's. *1859*
—. Boundaries. Dominican Republic. Haiti. Trujillo, Rafael. 1930's-70's. *1665*
—. Brazil. Clarté group. Communism. 1921-32. *2350*
—. Brazil. Cultural development. Intellectuals. 1950-59. *2405*
—. Brazil. Goulart, João. Political Leadership. Vargas, Getúlio. 1930-64. *2232*
—. Carranza, Venustiano. Economic Policy. Mexico. Obregón, Álvaro. Political Development. 1917-24. *809*
—. Carranza, Venustiano. Mexico. Reform. 1915-20. *790*
—. Catholicism. ca 1960-67. *188*
—. Colombia. Modernization. 1819-1974. *1945*
—. Colonization. Cultural imperialism. Pan-Americanism. Revolution. 16c-20c. *208*
—. Cuba. Machado, Gerardo. 1928-33. *1383*
—. Cuba. Methodist Church. Missions and Missionaries. USA. 1898-1958. *1406*
—. Cuba. Ramos, José Antonio. Theater. 1906-46. *1417*
—. Cuba. Revolutionary Movements. Students. 1920's-30's. *1504*
—. Dependency. Economic development. Imperialism. 1960's-70's. *357*
—. Depressions. Dominican Republic. Haitians. Massacres. Racism. Trujillo, Rafael. 1937. *1675*
—. Discrimination. Minorities. 19c-20c. *104*
—. Eight Principles. Hay-Bunau-Varilla Treaty. Kissinger, Henry A. Panama Canal. Torrijos, Omar. USA. 1964-75. *1276*
—. Ethnic Groups. Guyana. Jagan, Cheddi. Pluralism, cultural. Socialism. 1940-70's. *1723*
—. Federalism. West Indies Federation. 1945-68. *1290*
—. Foreign Relations. Mexico. Meyer, Lorenzo. Oil Industry and Trade (review article). USA. 1917-42. *680*
—. Foreign Relations. Panama Canal. USA. 1960-77. *1255*
—. Foreign Relations. USSR. 1973. *323*
—. French West Indies. 1945-76. *1831*
—. Ideology. Mexico. Politics. 1940-70. *941*
—. Indians. Mariátegui, José Carlos. Marxism. Peru. 1925-75. *2056*
—. Negroes. Social Conditions. West Indies. 16c-20c. *1340*
—. Revolutionary Movements. 1946-79. *486*
Nationalism, cultural. Barbosa, Ruy. Biography, critical. Brazil. Mythology. ca 1890-1973. *2255*
Nationalism, developmental. Andean Group. 1969-72. *1846*
Nationalist policy. Brazil. Geisel, Ernesto. 1974-. *2482*
Nationalist Popular Front. Bolivia. Terrorism (governmental). 1971-73. *1858*

Nationalist Revolutionary Movement (MNR). Bolivia. Economic Structure (international). Labor movement. Revolution. 1952-57. *1899*
—. Bolivia. Modernization. Nationalization. Reform. Revolution. Social Classes. 1952-56. *1881*
—. Bolivia (Sorata). Indians. Political change. Revolution. 1952-65. *1884*
Nationalists. Armies. Brazil. Liberals. Political Factions. 1946-51. *2402*
Nationalization. Agricultural production. Economic development. Sugar. 1960's-70's. *1709*
—. Alcan Aluminium Ltd. Bauxite industry. Canada. Guyana. Multinational corporations. 1960-. *1704*
—. Alcan Aluminium Ltd. Booker McConnell Ltd. Developing Nations. Guyana. Multinational corporations. Neocolonialism. 1970's. *1706*
—. Alcan Aluminium Ltd. Demerara Bauxite Company. Guyana. 1970-75. *1705*
—. Alcan Aluminium Ltd. Developing nations. Guyana. Multinational corporations. 1953-71. *1694*
—. Alliance for Progress. Brazil. Business. USA. 1961-63. *2400*
—. Banking. Guyana. Industry. Multinational corporations. 1970-79. *1708*
—. Banks. Chile. 1970-73. *2882*
—. Bolivia. Modernization. Nationalist Revolutionary Movement (MNR). Reform. Revolution. Social Classes. 1952-56. *1881*
—. Cárdenas, Lázaro. Foreign Relations. Mexico. Oil Industry and Trade. USA. 1945-50. *928*
—. Cárdenas, Lázaro. Labor. Mexico. Railroads. Worker Management. 1937-38. *844*
—. Chile. Copper. Multinational corporations. 1973. *2802*
—. Chile. Copper mines and Mining. 1964-73. *2691*
—. Chile. Copper Mines and Mining. International law. 1970. *2738*
—. Chile. Economic Conditions. Political participation. Popular Unity. Working class. 1970-73. *2849*
—. Chile. Economic Growth. Labor Unions and Organizations. 1945-71. *2852*
—. Communism. Peru. Social Reform. 1969-73. *2103*
—. Communist Party. Oil industry and trade. Venezuela. 1900-76. *2150*
—. Cordemex. Fibers Industry. Mexico (Yucatán). 1961-77. *870*
—. Cuba. Medicine. National Health Service. 1959-81. *1471*
—. Decisionmaking. Oil Industry and Trade. Pérez, Carlos Andrés. Political factions. Venezuela. 1974-77. *2183*
—. Demerara Bauxite Company. Guyana. Racism. 1946-71. *1719*
—. Dependency. Oil. Venezuela. 1976. *2147*
—. Diplomacy. Foreign Investments. Mexico. Oil Industry and Trade. USA. 1938-45. *630*
—. Economic coercion. International Petroleum Company. Peru. USA. 1968-71. *2095*
—. Economic development. Industrialization. Oil industry and trade. Venezuela. 1960's-70's. *2191*
—. Fishmeal industry. Peru. 1968-76. *2020*
—. Foreign Policy. Social classes. USA. Venezuela. 1973-76. *2192*
—. Mining industry. Peru. 1960's. *2034*
—. Peru. Political economy. 1968-76. *2098*
—. Peru. Treaties (compensation). USA. 1974-76. *2061*
Nationhood. Folklore. Guatemala. Indians. Symbols. 1524-1974. *1161*
Natural gas. Economic development. Foreign Relations. Mexico. Oil Industry and Trade. USA. 1977-79. *965*
—. Mexico. Oil Industry and Trade. USA. 1901-78. *617*
—. Mexico. USA. 1977-80. *911*
Natural Resources *See also* Conservation of Natural Resources; Forests and Forestry; Marine Resources; Mineral Resources.
—. Energy. Regional Planning. Venezuela. 1960-78. *2193*
Natural Resources (use of). Developmentalism. Integration, national. Political thought (continuity). Secularization. 1800-1970. *204*
Naturalization. Cuba. Property. Socialism. 1929-68. *1639*
—. Foreign Relations. Mexico. Oil. USA. 1915-42. *671*
Naval Battles. Falkland Islands (battle). Germany. Great Britain. Verner, Rudolph (report). World War I. 1914. *2962*
Naval Construction. *See* Shipbuilding.

Naval Engineering. *See* Marine Engineering.
Naval Recruiting and Enlistment. *See* Military Conscription; Military Recruiting.
Naval rivalry. Great Britain. USA. West Indies. 1882-1940. *1310*
Naval strategy. Argentina. Falkland Islands. Great Britain. 1982. *2965*
Navies *See also* headings beginning with the word naval; Military.
—. Academia de Guerra Naval. Chile. Military Education. 1911-81. *2722*
—. *Asama* (vessel). Japan. Mexico (Baja California; Turtle Bay). 1911-16. *818*
—. Brazil. Diplomacy. 1917-30. *2379*
—. Canada. El Salvador. Intervention. Political Attitudes. Revolution. 1932. *1100*
—. Caperton, William B. Diplomacy. USA. World War I. 1915-26. *255*
—. Chile. Mutinies. 1931. *2761*
—. Cuba. Merchant Marine. 1960's-70's. *1485*
—. Peru. 1885-1976. *2109*
Negotiations. Caribbean Community. Chaguaramas, Treaty of. Economic Integration. 1973. *1288*
Negroes *See also* Black Power; Discrimination; Race Relations; Racism.
—. Acculturation (review article). Aquirre Beltrán, Gonzalo. Mexico (Cuajinicuilapa). 20c. *623*
—. Africa. Bibliographies. Caribbean Region. 1973-74. *102*
—. Athletes. Cricket. Social mobility. West Indies. 1900-73. *1335*
—. Belize. Garvey, Marcus. Peoples United Party. Political Parties. Universal Negro Improvement Association. 1914-49. *1052*
—. Brazil. Political Participation. Social mobility. 1850's-1974. *2301*
—. Brazil. Racism. 1888-1979. *2288*
—. Cuba. Foreign Relations. USA. 1868-1977. *1402*
—. Cuba. Race. Social status. 16c-20c. *1387*
—. Cuba. Social Change. 1950-75. *1449*
—. Dictatorship. Duvalier, François. Haiti. Magic. 1957-71. *1738*
—. East Indians. Ethnic Groups. Trinidad and Tobago. 1950-80. *1795*
—. Garvey, Marcus. Ideology. Jamaica. Pan-Africanism. USA. 1887-1927. *1766*
—. Ideology. Revolution. West Indies. 1917-73. *1332*
—. Music (Calypso, Reggae). Political Protest. West Indies. 1975. *1301*
—. Nationalism. Social Conditions. West Indies. 16c-20c. *1340*
—. Politics. Racism. 20c. *37*
—. Revolutionaries. West Indies. 19c-20c. *1302*
Neocolonialism *See also* Colonialism.
—. Alcan Aluminium Ltd. Booker McConnell Ltd. Developing Nations. Guyana. Multinational corporations. Nationalization. 1970's. *1706*
—. Cuba. Moncada barracks, attack on. Revolution. 1934-53. *1602*
—. Political trends. West Indies (English-speaking). 1975. *1333*
Neruda, Pablo. Chile. Literature. Politics. Socialism. 1964-73. *2855*
—. Chile. Poetry. 1920's-73. *2729*
—. Chile. Poetry. Political attitudes. 1930's-73. *2723*
Netherlands (Amsterdam). Bibliographies. International Institute of Social History. Mexico. 1880-1940. *576*
Netherlands Antilles. Curaçao. Independence. May revolt. Riots. 1969-76. *1825*
—. Economic Conditions. 20c. *1797*
Netherlands Antilles (Curacao). Labor movement. May Movement. Political mobilization. 1955-69. *1786*
New International Economic Order. Economic Conditions. Foreign Policy. USA. West Indies. 1970's-81. *1329*
—. Pérez, Carlos Andrés. Venezuela. ca 1920-77. *2182*
New towns. City Planning. Mexico (Lázaro Cárdenas City). 1970-78. *869*
New Zealand. Economic Policy. Small countries (viability). Uruguay. 20c. *2984*
News agencies. Caribbean News Agency. West Indies. 1976-81. *1297*
Newspapers *See also* Freedom of the Press; Journalism; Periodicals; Press; Reporters and Reporting.
—. Canada (Quebec). Editorials. 1959-73. *241*
—. Cuba. France (Paris). Machado, Gerardo. Revolution. USA. 1933. *1506*
—. Elections. Trinidad and Tobago. 1976. *1819*
—. Exiles. Gómez, Juan Vicente. Venezuela. 1913-35. *2195*

Revolutionary process. Armies. Military Government. USA. 1810-1973. *469*
—. Artists. Chile. Mural painters. Ramona Parra Brigades. 1969-73. *2821*
—. Chile. 1970-73. *2836*
Revolutionary strategy. Chile. Communist Party. Coups d'etat. 1973-74. *2873*
Revolutionary theory. Apristas. Communist Party. Cuba. 1920's-30's. *1359*
—. Cuba. Roig de Leuchsenring, Emilio. 1916-65. *1593*
Revolutionary transformation. Chile. Communist Party. Popular Unity. 1970-73. *2820*
Revue Sud-Américaine. Drago, Luis María. Lugones, Leopoldo. Monroe Doctrine. Wilson, Woodrow. 1914. *2576*
Revueltas, José. Literature. Marxism. Mexico. Politics. 1910-76. *597*
Rice. Agricultural cooperatives. Ecuador. Government Enterprise. Peasants. Social Classes. 1964-75. *1999*
—. Government Enterprise. Guyana. 1974. *1725*
Ridgway, Matthew B. (report). Military occupation. Nicaragua (Puerto Cabezas). USA. 1927-33. *1209*
Rienzi, Adrian Cola. Labor movement. Trinidad and Tobago. 1925-44. *1822*
Right. Communist Party. El Salvador. Nicaragua. Politics. USA. 1960-81. *1027*
—. Government. 1964-79. *482*
Rio Conference (1942). USA. World War II. 1941-42. *238*
Río de la Plata Basin. Foreign Relations. National development. 1941-80. *538*
Rio de la Plata, Treaty of. Argentina. Uruguay. ca 1970-73. *2506*
Rio Grande Basin. International Boundary and Water Commission. Irrigation. Mexico (Tamaulipas). USA (Texas). 1900-20. *676*
Rio Treaty. Arbitration, International. Organization of American States. 1970-76. *526*
—. Foreign Relations. Monroe Doctrine. USA. 19c-20c. *228*
—. International Security. Organization of American States (meeting). USA. 1947-75. *525*
Riot suppression tactics. Colombia (Bogotá). Elections, presidential. 1970. *1965*
Riots *See also* Civil Disturbances; Demonstrations; Strikes.
—. Anti-Semitism. Argentina. 1919. *2570*
—. Brazil (Rio de Janeiro, São Paulo). Railroads, suburban. 1974-76. *2474*
—. Curaçao. Independence. May revolt. Netherlands Antilles. 1969-76. *1825*
Rippy, J. Fred. Dictatorship. Gómez, Juan Vicente. Venezuela. ca 1908-35. *2148*
Rites and Ceremonies. Capitalism. Chorti. Guatemala, eastern. Indians. 1971-73. *1141*
Roa Bastos, Augusto. Carpentier, Alejo. Dictatorship (review article). García Márquez, Gabriel. Novels. 1840-1975. *64*
Robert, Georges. Martinique. Vichy regime. World War II. 1940-43. *1788*
Rockefeller, Nelson. Foreign Policy. Roosevelt, Franklin D. 1933-42. *252*
Rodney, Walter. Africa. Colonialism. 1960-72. *1696*
—. Guyana. Intellectuals. Political Leadership. 1960's-80. *1690*
—. Guyana. Political Leadership. 1960's-80. *1711*
—. Guyana. Working People's Alliance. 1953-79. *1717*
Roett, Reardan. Brazil (Northeast, destruction of). Foreign aid. SUDENE. USA. 1960-72. *2212*
Roig de Leuchsenring, Emilio. Cuba. Revolutionary theory. 1916-65. *1593*
Rojas Pinilla, Gustavo. Gaitán, Jorge Eliécer. Populism. 1940's-70's. *1920*
Rolando (guerrilla). Cuba. Guerrilla Warfare. Revolution. 1950's. *1621*
Roman Catholic Church. *See* Catholic Church.
Romania. Foreign Relations. 1880-1980. *224*
—. Mexico. Press. Rebellions. 1910-17. *813*
Romero, Oscar. Assassination. El Salvador. Revolution. 1970's-80. *1107*
Roosevelt, Franklin D. Foreign Policy. Rockefeller, Nelson. 1933-42. *252*
Rose, Vernon J. Business. Calles, Plutarco Elías. Mexico. Oil policies. Rath, Arthur C. USA. 1923-24. *712*
Rühle-Gerstel, Alice. Diaries. Exiles. Mexico. Trotsky, Leon. 1937. *846*
Ruimveldt massacre. Civil Disturbances. Colonial rule. Guyana. 1924. *1720*

Ruiz Pineda, Leonardo. Acción Democrática. Hero-image. 1949-52. *2137*
Rural Development. Agricultural reform. Capitalism. Chile. Social Change. 1973-79. *2949*
—. Colombia. Economic policy. Poverty. ca 1900-76. *1912*
—. Intergovernmental Relations. Irrigation. Mexico. 1930-78. *936*
—. Land Reform. Peru. 1969-80. *2065*
—. Local Government. Panama (Guararé). Reform. 1972-81. *1265*
—. Mexico. Peasants. Populism, agrarian. 1950-79. *788*
—. Mexico (Puebla). Modernization. Politics. Programa de Inversiones Públicas para el Desarrollo Rural. 1940-78. *890*
—. Resettlement. Trinidad and Tobago. 1960's. *1823*
Rural development policy. Agricultural Cooperatives. Peasant communities. Peru (Matahuasi). 1968-. *2076*
Rural Life. *See* Country Life.
Rural policies. Chile. Politics. 1970-73. *2870*
Rural proletariat. Class consciousness. Methodology. Peasantry. West Indies. 1950's-. *1323*
Rural Settlements. Government. Investments. Mexico (Quintana Roo). 1977. *897*
Russian Revolution. 1917-77. *487*
—. Communist Parties and Movements. 1917-34. *479*
—. Communist Parties and Movements. 20c. *474*
—. Cuba. Labor movement. 1917-25. *1392*
—. Cuba. Revolutionary Movements (review article). 1917-59. *1606*
—. Cuba. Working Class. 1917-20. *1379*
—. Lenin, V. I. Mariátegui, José Carlos. Political thought. Zapata, Emiliano. 1917-70's. *485*

S

Saad, Pedro. Communist Party. Ecuador. 1934-78. *1985*
Sábato, Ernesto. Argentina. Authors. Bibliographies. Peronism. Political Protest. 1940's-70's. *2629*
Sacasa, Juan Bautista *(Como y por que caí del poder).* Coups d'Etat. Nicaragua. Somoza, Anastasio. 1933-36. *1237*
Saint Lucia *See also* West Indies Associated States.
—. Colonialism. Peasants. Political Participation. 1950's-70's. *1821*
Salaries. *See* Wages.
Salazar Bondy, Sebastián. Authors. Peru. 1924-65. *2086*
Salazar, José Inés. Mexico. Revolution. ca 1910-18. *814*
Salazar Viniegra, Leopold. Drug policy. Law enforcement. Mexico. USA. 1936-40. *696*
Salgado, Plínio. Acao Integralista Brasileira. Brazil. Political Theory. 1932-38. *2337*
—. Brazil. Fascism. Integralist movement. ca 1920's-30's. *2387*
Salinity problem. Colorado River. Mexico. Treaties (water; 1944). USA. 1944-74. *574*
Salmon-Lozano treaty. Boundaries. Colombia. Leticia incident. Peru. 1922. 1932-34. *1834*
Saltillo Industrial Group. Mexico. Political analysis. Strikes. 1974. *879*
San Pedro de la Cueva (massacre). Mexico. Sonora campaign. Villa, Pancho. 1915-16. *783*
Sandinista National Directorate. Nicaragua. Politics. 1978-80. *1221*
Sandinista National Liberation Front. Cuba. Nicaragua. 1925-78. *1203*
—. Documents. Nicaragua. 1933-39. *1252*
—. Economic Policy. Nicaragua. Revolution. 1976-80. *1192*
—. Foreign Relations. Nicaragua. 1970's. *1235*
—. Government. Nicaragua. Political Systems. Somoza, Anastasio. 1970's. *1249*
—. Guerrilla warfare. Nicaragua. Somoza, Anastasio. 1967-78. *1236*
—. Ideology. Nicaragua. Revolution. 1961-82. *1244*
—. Nicaragua. Poets. 1926-78. *1185*
—. Nicaragua. Political power. 1979-80. *1220*
—. Nicaragua. *Prensa* (newspaper). Press. 1920-80. *1227*
—. Nicaragua. Revolution. 1950's-79. *1233*
—. Nicaragua. Revolution. 1979-80. *1211*
—. Nicaragua. Revolutionary Movements. 1920's-70's. *1206*
—. Nicaragua. Somoza, Anastasio. 1936-78. *1231*

—. Nicaragua. Somoza (family). 1909-80. *1230*
Sandino, Augusto César. Alliances. Documents. Intervention. Mexico. Nicaragua. USA. 1926-30. *219*
—. Aponte, Carlos. Letters. Nicaragua. 1929. *1251*
—. Elections. McCoy, Frank R. Military occupation. Nicaragua. USA. 1927-28. *1187*
—. Independence Movements. Nicaragua. USA. 1904-36. *1195*
—. Intervention. Nicaragua. USA. 1909-34. *1196*
—. Nicaragua. Political thought. 1909-33. *1204*
Sandino, Augusto César (last writings). Nicaragua. Revolution. 1933-34. *1214*
Sanjinés, Jorge. Bolivia. Films. Revolutionary Movements. 1960-75. *1862*
São Paulo University (History Department). Archival Catalogs and Inventories. Brazil. Machado, Agenor (papers). 1920-53. *2269*
Sarnoff, Lilly. Anarchism and Anarchists. Flores Magón, Ricardo (prison letters). Mexico. USA. 1920-22. *713*
Saudi Arabia. Economic Policy. Iran. Oil. Venezuela. 1920-80. *2176*
Scarlet ibis. Oil. Trinidad and Tobago (Caroni River). Wildlife Conservation. 1960-74. *1802*
Schmitter, Philippe C. Bonapartism. Brazil. Political Systems. 1964-78. *2439*
School of Library Technicians. Cuba. Libraries. 1962-77. *1391*
School of Military Aviation. Air Forces. Aviation. Military Education. Venezuela. 1920-80. *2190*
Schools, rural. Educational Reform. Mexico (Michoacán). Political Change. Social Change. 1915-29. *787*
Schydlowsky, Daniel M. Exchange rates, multiple. Industrial efficiency. International competition. Trade policies. 1967-70's. *408*
Scientific Experiments and Research. Government. Higher Education. 1940-81. *179*
Scorza, Manuel. Indians (review article). Novels. Peru. 20c. *2005*
Scott, Hugh Lenox. Foreign policy. Mexico. Revolution. USA. Wilson, Woodrow. 1914-17. *749*
Sea (corridor to). Bolivia. 19c-20c. *1867*
Seaga, Edward. Democracy. Jamaica. 1941-81. *1763*
—. Elections. Jamaica. Manley, Michael. 1976-80. *1776*
Secretariat of Programming and Budget. Mexico. Public Administration. Reform. 1958-79. *858*
Secularization. Developmentalism. Integration, national. Natural Resources (use of). Political thought (continuity). 1800-1970. *204*
Seligman, Edwin. Cuba. Economists, US. Magill, Roswell. Shoup, Carl. Tax reform. 1932-39. *1604*
Senate *See also* Legislation.
—. Alessandri, Arturo. Chile. Club de la Unión. Elites. 1920-24. *2770*
Sergeants' revolt. Batista, Fulgencio. Coups d'etat. Cuba. Welles, Sumner. 1933-34. *1561*
Serials. *See* Periodicals.
Servants. Colombia (Cali). Political Systems. Social Organization. Women. 1938-79. *1967*
Settlement *See also* Colonization; Resettlement; Rural Settlements.
—. Brazil (Amazon region). Instituto Nacional de Colonização e de Reforma Agrária. 1970-78. *2416*
—. Colombia. Forests and Forestry. Government. 1926-78. *1936*
—. Colombia. Land use. 1950's-70's. *1942*
—. Development. Mexico (Papaloapan basin). 1975-78. *559*
—. Ecuador (Babahoyo). Land reform. 1976-78. *1983*
—. Government. Guatemala, northern. Peasants. 1954-78. *1140*
—. Government. Mexico (Chiapas; Selva Lacandona). 1962-78. *963*
Settlement program (asentamiento). Communist Party. Imperialism. Panama. USA (Canal Zone). 1968-73. *1280*
Short stories. Authors. Honduras. 1920's-70's. *1181*
Shoup, Carl. Cuba. Economists, US. Magill, Roswell. Seligman, Edwin. Tax reform. 1932-39. *1604*
Sigmund, Paul E. (review article). Allende, Salvador. Chile. Methodology (counterfactuals). 1970-73. *2787*
Sinarquismo. Mexico. 1937-44. *638*

—. Mexico. Population explosion. Social policy. 1950's-1974. *558*

—. Nationalism. Negroes. West Indies. 16c-20c. *1340*

Social Conditions (review article). 19c-20c. *87*

Social Control. Elites (review article). Mexico. 1917-70's. *621*

Social cost. Brazil. Economic development. 1973. *2451*

Social Customs. Ideology. Mexico. Revolution. 19c-20c. *663*

Social Democratic parties. 1970-80. *136*

Social Democratic Party *See also* Marxism; Socialism.

—. Costa Rica. 1930-49. *1070*

Social development. Brazil. Foreign investments. Industrial growth. 1960's-74. *2450*

—. Economic structure. El Salvador. 1965-80. *1089*

Social History (review article). Elites. Mexico. Political power. 1428-1973. *694*

Social Indicators. Methodology. Political development. Urbanization. ca 1950-70. *161*

Social instability. Brazil. Geisel, Ernesto. Industrialization. Military government. 1964-75. *2483*

Social insurance. Brazil. Income redistribution. 1889-1976. *2277*

Social justice. Catholic Church. Clergy (conferences). 1968-73. *221*

Social mobility. Athletes. Cricket. Negroes. West Indies. 1900-73. *1335*

—. Brazil. Negroes. Political Participation. 1850's-1974. *2301*

—. Colombia (Antioquia). Colonization. 1835-1974. *1915*

—. Students. Venezuela. 1960-74. *2202*

Social Mobilization. Authoritarianism. Corporatism. National System in Support of Social Mobilization (SINAMOS). Peru. Velasco Alvarado, Juan. 1968-74. *2082*

Social Organization. Agricultural production. Industrialization. Land Reform. 1967-73. *385*

—. Agriculture. 18c-20c. *365*

—. Agriculture. Argentina. Canada. Immigration. 1870-1930. *2580*

—. Agriculture. Brazil (Northeast). Government. 1960's-70's. *2231*

—. Agriculture. Chile. Economic Conditions. Land reform. 1850-1977. *2702*

—. Authority. Catholic Church. 1940's-70's. *106*

—. Barbados. Economic development. Race Relations. 1960-79. *1810*

—. Bolivia. Interest groups. State power. ca 1950-74. *1903*

—. Chinese. Cuba. 19c-20c. *1502*

—. Colombia (Cali). Political Systems. Servants. Women. 1938-79. *1967*

—. Cuba. Peasants. Political Participation. Revolution. 1959. *1634*

—. Culture. Economic Structure. Ideology. Peru. 20c. *2078*

—. Dominican Republic. Economic Structure. Sugar. 19c-1920's. *1667*

—. Economic Policy. Inflation. Mexico. 1935-81. *565*

—. Economic Structure (review article). Peru. 1890-1975. *2071*

—. El Salvador. Political Systems. 1969-79. *1103*

—. Government. Land reform. 1960-80. *395*

—. Government. Nicaragua. Somoza family. 1912-79. *1242*

—. Land reform. Peru. 1969-76. *2087*

—. Mexico (Morelos). Peasants. Urban growth. ca 1545-1970. *609*

Social Organization (index of fragmentation). Politics. 1945-79. *130*

Social pathology. Chile. Coups d'Etat. Military. Repression, politics of. 1973. *2940*

Social Policy. Central America. Christianity. Reform. 20c. *1031*

—. Chile. Indians. Mapuche. 20c. *2717*

—. Cuba. 1959-78. *1374*

—. Cuba. Economic Policy. Machado, Gerardo. USA. 1929-32. *1603*

—. Economic Conditions. Foreign policy. Nicaragua. 1979-80. *1248*

—. Economic Structure. El Salvador. 1960-80. *1088*

—. Mexico. 1900-74. *687*

—. Mexico. Population explosion. Social Conditions. 1950's-1974. *558*

—. Political determinants. 1940-60. *178*

Social Problems *See also* Emigration; Housing; Immigration; Migrant Labor; Prostitution; Public Welfare; Race Relations; Unemployment.

—. Bishops. Catholic Church. Colombia. Venezuela. 1968-78. *1843*

—. Castro, Fidel ("History Will Absolve Me" speech). Cuba. 1953-59. *1628*

—. Catholic Church. Puebla Conference. ca 1968-79. *202*

—. Economic Conditions. 20c. *172*

—. Economic Development. Immigration policy. Venezuela. 1930-82. *2194*

—. Mexico. Oil Industry and Trade. 1980's. *987*

—. Political crisis. 1970-74. *110*

Social property, concept of. Modernization. Peru. 1974-75. *2032*

Social Reform *See also* names of reform movements; Social Problems.

—. Argentina. Perón, Juan. Working class. 1946-55. *2613*

—. Catholic Church. Dominican Republic. Peasants. 1970's. *1679*

—. Catholic Church. Medellín conference. Theology. 1968-78. *140*

—. Civil war. Costa Rica. Physicians. Political Factions. Strikes. 1946-48. *1076*

—. Communism. Nationalization. Peru. 1969-73. *2103*

—. Communist Party. Economic development. Honduras. Military government. 1971-73. *1172*

—. Economic Reform. Legislation. Military Government. Peru. 20c. *2077*

—. Economic reform. Military government. Peru. Quijano, Aníbal (interview). 1968-73. *2104*

—. Jamaica. Labor Unions and Organizations. Political unionism. Trinidad and Tobago. 1945-75. *1306*

Social Revolutions. Bolivia. Economic growth. Mexico. 1952-64. *39*

Social Sciences (review article). Castro, Fidel. Cuba. Revolution. 1959-75. *1547*

Social Security *See also* Social Insurance.

—. Agricultural labor. Authoritarianism. Brazil. Economic development. Vargas, Getúlio. 1930's-70's. *2465*

—. Calderón Guardia, Rafael Ángel. Costa Rica. 1940-44. *1077*

—. Corporatism. Echeverría, Luis. Government. Mexico. 1970-76. *985*

—. Costa Rica. Policymaking. 1920-78. *1078*

Social security policy. Brazil. Working class. 1964-77. *2466*

—. Bureaucracies. Colombia. Public Administration (policymaking). 1920-75. *1910*

Social Status. Civil service. Jamaica. 1930-70. *1767*

—. Cuba. Federation of Cuban Women. Political participation. Women. 1960-78. *1368*

—. Cuba. Negroes. Race. 16c-20c. *1387*

—. Decisionmaking. Elites. Political parties. 20c. *24*

—. Ethnic groups. Guatemala. Panama. 20c. *1003*

Social Structure. *See* Social Organization; Social Status.

Social Surveys *See also* Sociology.

—. Methodology. Migration, internal. Radicals and Radicalism. 1950's-75. *175*

Social Welfare. *See* Public Welfare.

Socialism *See also* Capitalism; Communism; Government Ownership; Labor; Labor Unions and Organizations; Leftism; Leninism; Marxism; Utopias.

—. Agriculture. Cuba. 1959-81. *1432*

—. Allende, Salvador. Chile. 1971-73. *2796*

—. Allende, Salvador. Chile. Foreign Investments. USA. 1912-73. *2850*

—. Brazil. 1879-1969. *2227*

—. Brazil. Capitalism. Chile. Cuba. Economic development. Human rights (panel discussion). 1960's. *214*

—. Caciquism. Carrillo Puerto, Felipe. Mexico (Yucatán). 1922-24. *763*

—. Capitalism. Economic development. 1964-76. *352*

—. Castro, Fidel. Cuba. Independence Movements. Military campaigns. 1860-1959. *1644*

—. Catholic Church. 1970's. *158*

—. Chile. 1970-73. *2844*

—. Chile. 1970-73. *2871*

—. Chile. Coups d'Etat. Politics and the Military. 1973. *2772*

—. Chile. Electoral constraints. 1952-71. *2777*

—. Chile. Literature. Neruda, Pablo. Politics. 1964-73. *2855*

—. Chile. Mass attitudes. Political Participation. Social Classes. ca 1950's-73. *2743*

—. Chile. Public health. 1950's-75. *2837*

—. Communist Countries. Economic dependency. ca 1945-70's. *60*

—. Communist Parties and Movements (general secretaries; discussion). Honduras. Paraguay. 1972-73. *147*

—. Conflict and Conflict Resolution. Ethnic Groups. Guyana. 1953-76. *1713*

—. Cuba. 1918-58. *1355*

—. Cuba. 1970-77. *1552*

—. Cuba. 1976-78. *1409*

—. Cuba. Economic growth. 1962-75. *1612*

—. Cuba. Economic Planning. Industrialization. 1959-80. *1519*

—. Cuba. Economic Planning. Social Change. 1961-78. *1427*

—. Cuba. Institutionalization. 1950-78. *1452*

—. Cuba. Naturalization. Property. 1929-68. *1639*

—. Cuba. Pita Rodríguez, Félix (*Los Textos*). Revolution. 1971-77. *1467*

—. Democracy. Jamaica. People's National Party. 1962-79. *1775*

—. Economic Conditions. Jamaica. Manley, Michael. 1972-77. *1760*

—. Economic development. Economic policy. Guyana. Jamaica. 1950's-70's. *378*

—. Ethnic Groups. Guyana. Jagan, Cheddi. Nationalism. Pluralism, cultural. 1940-70's. *1723*

—. Jamaica. Manley, Michael. Political Systems. 1970's-82. *1761*

—. Labor movement. Mariátegui, José Carlos. Peru. 1916-29. *2111*

—. Political Parties. Suffrage. 1860-1980. *2561*

Socialism, building of. Cuba. Revolution. Working class. 1970-79. *1556*

Socialism, Democratic. 1889-1980. *477*

Socialism, prospects for. Allende, Salvador. Chile. Social conditions. ca 1950-73. *2778*

Socialism (review article). Cuba. Domínguez, Jorge. Mesa-Lago, Carmelo. 1960-80. *1516*

Socialism, traditional. Castro, Fidel. Cuba. 1959-74. *1481*

Socialism, transition to. Chile. Coups d'etat. Political Systems (bourgeois). 1970-73. *2817*

—. Communist Party. Cuba. Political institutions. 1962-75. *1362*

—. Cuba. Ideology. 1960-. *1526*

Socialist construction. Agricultural policy. Cuba. Landowners, small. 1959-77. *1386*

—. Cuba. Revolutionary movements. 1950-77. *1413*

Socialist cooperation. Cuba. Economic development. 1960-75. *1448*

Socialist International. Political Factions. 1976-82. *471*

Socialist Party. Argentina. Dissident behavior. Elites. Political Surveys. 1915-57. *2560*

—. Argentina. Electoral organization. Working class subculture. 1900-46. *2563*

—. Argentina. General Confederation of Labor (CGT). Labor movement. Political Parties. 1930-43. *2567*

—. Chile. 1920-73. *2721*

—. Chile. Coalition politics. 1932-46. *2751*

—. Chile. Communist Party. Popular Unity. United front policy. 1956-69. *2753*

—. Chile. Political Factions. Popular Front. 20c. *2694*

—. Chile. Popular Front. 1922-38. *2750*

Socialist People's Party. Cuba. Revolution. 26th of July Movement. 1952-59. *1616*

Socialists. Anti-imperialism. Multinational corporations. 1945-76. *382*

Society for Promotion of Manufacturing. Chile. Interest Groups. 1883-1928. *2766*

Society of Jesus. *See* Jesuits.

Sociology *See also* Cities; Emigration; Immigration; Labor; Population; Race Relations; Social Classes; Social Conditions; Social Organization; Social Problems.

—. Argentina. Censorship. Colleges and universities. Military government. 1966-79. *2547*

—. Cardoso, Fernando Henrique. González Casanova, Pablo. 1930's-70's. *92*

Solás, Humberto. Cuba. Films (historical) (review article). National self-image. 1895-1970's. *1548*

Soler Puig, José. Cuba. Novels. Revolution. 1960-75. *1605*

Somalia. Cuba. Ethiopia. Foreign Relations. 1978-79. *1636*

T

Tacna-Arica dispute. Chile. Diplomatic
negotiations. Peru. USA. 1922-29. *6*
Tactics *See also* Air Warfare; Guerrilla Warfare.
—. Bolivia. Guevara, Ernesto "Che". Revolution.
1956-67. *1901*
Tarafa Law. Cuba. Monopolies. Railroads. USA.
1920-25. *1455*
Tariff *See also* Economic Integration; Protectionism.
—. Alvear, Marcelo T. de. Argentina. Great
Britain. Irigoyen, Hipólito. Politics. 1916-30.
2579
—. Border Industrialization Program.
Industrialization. Mexico. USA. 1970-80.
972
—. Cuba. Foreign Relations. Sugar Act (1948).
USA. 1945-48. *1487*
—. Ecology. Fishing rights. Territorial Waters.
1952-73. *40*
—. Industrialization. Mexico (border region).
Unemployment. USA. 1974. *857*
Tariff policy. Industrial development. Mexico.
Protectionism. 1930-65. *628*
Tax reform. Cuba. Economists, US. Magill,
Roswell. Seligman, Edwin. Shoup, Carl.
1932-39. *1604*
Taxation *See also* Income Tax; Tariff.
—. Income tax. Mexico. 1920-64. *603*
—. West Indies. 1800-1976. *1325*
Teacher Training. Education. Nicaragua.
Revolution. 1960's-81. *1200*
Teachers. Labor Unions and Organizations.
Mexico. 1931-45. *572*
Teapot Dome Scandal. Diplomacy. Mexico.
Oil. USA. 1926-27. *757*
Technical assistance. Chile. Economic policy.
Friedman, Milton. USA. 1970-80. *2935*
—. Foreign Aid. Israel. 1960-75. *302*
Technical Education. Economic Commission for
Latin America. Economic planning. UN.
1953-74. *334*
Technocrats. Brazil. Industrialization. Military
government. 1964-70's. *2477*
Technology *See also* Manufactures; Technical
Education.
—. Dominican Republic. Foreign investments.
1966-74. *1663*
Technology transfer. Brazil. Exports. Germany,
West. Nuclear Science and Technology. 1975.
2500
—. Brazil. Nuclear physics. 1937-78. *2462*
Tejeda, Adalberto. Catholic clergy, limits on.
Church and state. Mexico. 1930's. *847*
Television. Chile. Political communication.
1964-74. *2698*
—. Public policy. Radio. Venezuela. 1930-79.
2167
Tenants. Chile. Land reform. Peasants (political
consciousness). Wage laborers. 1950-73.
2682
Tenentes. Brazil. 1920's-70's. *2256*
—. Brazil. Club 3 de Octubro. Revolution.
Vargas, Getúlio. 1922-35. *2343*
—. Brazil. Military officers. Prestes, Luis Carlos.
Rebellions. 1924-27. *2358*
—. Brazil. Politics and the Military. 1922-67.
2303
—. Brazil. Politics and the Military. Reform
programs. 1922-73. *2204*
Territorial claims. Argentina. Beagle Channel.
Chile. Tierra del Fuego. 1881-1977. *2510*
—. Belize. Guatemala. 1839-1975. *1005*
Territorial Waters *See also* International Waters;
Maritime Law.
—. Ecology. Fishing rights. Tariff. 1952-73.
40
—. Economic zone. International Law. 1952-70's.
401
—. Fishing rights. Peru. Politics. 1945-72. *2083*
—. Maritime Law. 1945-74. *57*
Territorial Waters (conference). Colombia.
Venezuela. 1815-1974. *1842*
Territorial Waters (lakes). International law.
Lake Titicaca. 19c-20c. *1856*
Terrorism *See also* Assassination; Guerrilla Warfare.
—. 1970-78. *162*
—. Anti-Semitism. Argentina. Catholic Church.
Subversion. 1975. *2657*
—. Argentina. People's Revolutionary Army
(ERP). 1968-74. *2617*
—. Central America. 1970's. *997*
—. Political repression. Politics and the Military.
20c. *20*
—. War. 1950's-70's. *1428*
Terrorism (governmental). Bolivia. Nationalist
Popular Front. 1971-73. *1858*

—. Communist Party. Revolutionary movements.
Uruguay. 1974. *2994*
Textile industry. Arellano, Edward. General
Confederation of Labor (CGT). Labor Unions
and Organizations. Mendoza, Ciro. Mexico.
1920-78. *563*
Theater *See also* Ballet; Drama; Films.
—. Arts policy. Cuesta, George (theater review).
Intellectuals. Mexico. Revolution. 1929-30.
776
—. Cuba. 1959-79. *1652*
—. Cuba. Escambray group. Government.
1959-76. *1407*
—. Cuba. Nationalism. Ramos, José Antonio.
1906-46. *1417*
—. Ecuador. 1955-79. *1991*
Theater (revues). Popular Culture. 1910-43. *808*
Theology *See also* Christianity; Religion.
—. 1950-78. *173*
—. Catholic Church. Medellín conference. Social
Reform. 1968-78. *140*
—. Catholic Church. Puebla conference.
Revolutionary movements. 1970's. *3*
Theology, liberation. Christianity. Radicals and
Radicalism. 1945-77. *464*
Theology, liberation (review article). 1973. *65*
Theses, Doctoral. *See* Dissertations.
Third World. *See* Developing Nations, Non-aligned
Nations.
Tierney, Richard Henry. *America* (weekly).
Carranza, Venustiano. Catholic Church.
Mexico. Revolution. 1914-17. *733*
Tierra del Fuego. Argentina. Beagle Channel.
Chile. Territorial claims. 1881-1977. *2510*
Timerman, Jacobo. Argentina. Human rights.
1973-81. *2661*
Tin. Bolivia. Labor movement. Miners. 1918-76.
1888
Tlatelolco Conference. Foreign Policy. Mexico.
1973-74. *534*
—. USA. 1974. *213*
Tlatelolco, Treaty of. Atomic energy. International
Security. 1963-77. *235*
—. International security. Nuclear nonproliferation
(denuclearized zones). USA. USSR. 1950's-80.
509
—. Nuclear arms. Nuclear policy. USA.
1960's-70's. *541*
—. Nuclear arms control. 1967-75. *540*
—. Nuclear Nonproliferation. 1969-80. *542*
Tobar Doctrine. Central American Peace
Conferences (Washington, 1907, 1923).
Diplomatic recognition. International Law.
USA. 1900-30. *548*
Tomatoes. Energy. Foreign policy. Mexico.
Trade Regulations. USA. 1969-80. *937*
—. Foreign Relations. International division of
labor. Mexico. Trade. USA (Florida).
1970-80. *977*
Torres, Armando (interviews). Cuba. Revolutionary
activities. Students. 1945-68. *1629*
Torres, Camilo. Christianity. Political theory.
Revolution. 1929-66. *1974*
Torriente-Brau, Pablo de la. Civil War. Cuba
(Santiago). Spain (Madrid). Torriente-Brau,
Zoe de la (memoirs). 1901-36. *1631*
—. Cuba. Documents. Letters. Revolution.
1935. *1630*
—. Cuba. Political Imprisonment. Revolutionary
activities. 1901-36. *1579*
Torriente-Brau, Pablo de la (letters). Cuba (Isle of
Pines). Political imprisonment. Revolutionaries.
1932-35. *1394*
Torriente-Brau, Zoe de la (memoirs). Civil War.
Cuba (Santiago). Spain (Madrid).
Torriente-Brau, Pablo de la. 1901-36. *1631*
Torrijos, Omar. Eight Principles.
Hay-Bunau-Varilla Treaty. Kissinger, Henry A.
Nationalism. Panama Canal. USA. 1964-75.
1276
—. Foreign Relations. Panama. USA. 1969-73.
1283
—. Foreign Relations. Panama Canal Zone.
USA. 1903-77. *1285*
Tosco, Augustín (interview). Argentina.
Cordobazo. Labor Unions and Organizations.
Marxism. Peronism. 1960's-70's. *2620*
Tourism. Economic Development. West Indies.
1960-77. *1312*
Trade *See also* Exports; International Trade; Tariff.
—. Africa, West. Brazil. Foreign Relations.
1970's. *2235*
—. Argentina. Foreign Investments. Germany.
1918-33. *2572*
—. Australia. Foreign Relations. 1945-73. *326*
—. Banzer, Hugo. Bolivia. Chile. Diplomacy.
1971-76. *1902*

—. Brazil. Economic Growth. World War II.
1939-45. *2338*
—. Brazil. Exchange rates, multiple. 1953-58.
2399
—. Brazil. Foreign Aid. Politics. USA. 20c.
2319
—. Brazil. Foreign relations. Immigration. Japan.
19c-1960's. *2268*
—. Brazil (Mato Grosso, São Paulo). Cattle
industry. Transportation, Commercial.
1876-1920's. *2334*
—. Caribbean Free Trade Association. European
Economic Community. West Indies. 1950's-73.
1324
—. Central American Common Market. Mexico.
1951-72. *493*
—. Claims. Cuba. Foreign Relations. Sugar.
USA. 1957-73. *1382*
—. Cuba. Cultural relations. Treaties. USSR.
1959-65. *1632*
—. Debt, external. 1973-80. *375*
—. Dependency. Foreign policy. UN General
Assembly. USA. Voting and Voting Behavior.
1950-73. *155*
—. Europe. 1960's-75. *355*
—. Europe. Foreign Relations. 1970-82. *268*
—. European Economic Community. 1970-80.
12
—. Foreign Relations. International division of
labor. Mexico. Tomatoes. USA (Florida).
1970-80. *977*
—. Foreign Relations. Japan. 1960-79. *281*
—. Foreign Relations. Korea, South. 1950-80.
123
—. Germany. Great Britain. Imperialism. USA.
1918-39. *31*
—. Import control. Mexico. Protectionism.
1930-70. *627*
—. Reciprocal Trade Agreement Act (1934).
USA. 1933-39. *315*
Trade Embargo. Cuba. USA. 1959-77.
1415
Trade intensification. Central American Common
Market. 1961-68. *1008*
Trade, intra-area. Central American Common
Market. Urbanization. 1960-71. *1046*
Trade patterns. Andean Pact. Chile. 1953-75.
1840
Trade policies. Chile. Land reform. 1970-78.
2685
—. Exchange rates, multiple. Industrial efficiency.
International competition. Schydlowsky, Daniel
M. 1967-70's. *408*
Trade Regulations *See also* Protectionism; Tariff.
—. Energy. Foreign policy. Mexico. Tomatoes.
USA. 1969-80. *937*
Trade Union Movements. *See* Labor Movements.
Trade Unions. *See* Labor Unions and
Organizations.
Tradition. Historiography. Mexico. Peasants.
Revolution. 20c. *811*
—. National Development. West Indies.
1960's-70's. *114*
Traditionalism. Political Theory. 1825-1950.
458
Transport Board. Jamaica. Public utility regulation.
1947-70. *1781*
Transportation *See also* names of transportation
vehicles, e.g. Railroads, etc.; Commerce.
—. Mexico (Ciudad Juárez). USA (Texas; El
Paso). 1950's-70's. *964*
Transportation, Commercial. Brazil (Mato Grosso,
São Paulo). Cattle industry. Trade.
1876-1920's. *2334*
Travel. Maiakovski, Vladimir. Mexico. Poets.
USA. 1925. *789*
Traven, B. Lumber and Lumbering. Mexico
(Chiapas, Tabasco). Working Conditions.
1870-1946. *569*
Treaties *See also* names of treaties, e.g. Tlatelolco,
Treaty of; Arbitration, International.
—. Amazon Basin. Brazil. Venezuela. 1960-78.
500
—. Amazon Pact. Boundaries. Brazil. 1822-1978.
2207
—. Annexation. Cuba (Isle of Pines). Hay, John.
Public opinion. Quesada, Gonzalo de. USA.
1898-1980. *1617*
—. Argentina. Foreign relations. Uruguay.
1973-76. *2508*
—. Belize. Carrington, 6th Baron. Documents.
Great Britain. Guatemala. 1981. *1064*
—. Boundaries. Brazil. Colombia. García Ortiz,
Laureano. Peru. 1920-30. *56*
—. Brazil. Commerce. Foreign Relations.
Industry. USA. 1935. *2381*
—. Colombia. Panama. Uribe, Antonio José.
USA. 1901-22. *234*

—. Cuba. Cultural relations. Trade. USSR.
1959-65. *1632*
—. Diplomacy. Panama. USA. 1924-26. *1272*
—. Economic costs. Panama Canal. USA.
1964-75. *1275*
—. El Salvador. Honduras. War. 1969-77. *1016*
—. Foreign policy. USA. 1939-45. *267*
—. Military Capability. 1940-75. *448*
—. Nuclear arms. USA. 1973-77. *237*
—. Panama Canal. USA. 1903-77. *1269*
—. Panama Canal. USA. 19c-20c. *1267*
Treaties (bilateral agreement). Cuba. 1959-75.
1572
Treaties (compensation). Nationalization. Peru.
USA. 1974-76. *2061*
Treaties (water; 1944). Colorado River. Mexico.
Salinity problem. 1944-74. *574*
Trials. Nicaragua. Somocistas. 1979-81. *1239*
Trinidad and Tobago. Prehistory-1974. *1829*
—. Anti-Imperialism. Documents. National
United Freedom Fighters (NUFF).
Revolutionary Movements. 1970's. *1830*
—. British West Indies. Colonialism. Commissions
of Enquiry. Great Britain. Jamaica. 1934-77.
1349
—. Cipriani, Arthur Andrew. Jamaica. Politics.
World War I. 1914-31. *1303*
—. Colonial Office. Great Britain. Labor Disputes.
Oil. 1937-38. *1807*
—. Colonialism. Racism. Strikes, longshoremen's.
1919. *1817*
—. Developing Nations. Economic dependency.
1960's. *1791*
—. Developing nations. Foreign policy. Mass
media. 1962-76. *1805*
—. East Indians. Ethnic Groups. Negroes.
1950-80. *1795*
—. Economic growth. Independence. Jamaica.
Labor Unions and Organizations. Politics.
1930's-50's. *1305*
—. Economic planning. Fiscal policy. Public
finance. 1964-75. *1787*
—. Elections. Newspapers. 1976. *1819*
—. Ethnic Groups. Political development. Social
Conditions. 20c. *1796*
—. Jamaica. Labor Unions and Organizations.
Political unionism. Social Reform. 1945-75.
1306
—. Jamaica. Labor Unions and Organizations.
Politics. 1948-77. *1307*
—. Labor movement. Rienzi, Adrian Cola.
1925-44. *1822*
—. Resettlement. Rural Development. 1960's.
1823
Trinidad and Tobago (Caroni River). Oil. Scarlet
ibis. Wildlife Conservation. 1960-74. *1802*
Trinidad and Tobago (Port of Spain).
Longshoremen. Strikes. Violence. 1919.
1798
Trinidad and Tobago (Tobago). Civil Service.
Local Government. 1925-70. *1820*
Trotsky, Leon. Diaries. Exiles. Mexico.
Rühle-Gerstel, Alice. 1937. *846*
Trujillo, Rafael. Balaguer, Joaquín. Caudillo
tradition. Dominican Republic. 1931-77.
1683
—. Boundaries. Dominican Republic. Haiti.
Nationalism. 1930's-70's. *1665*
—. Depressions. Dominican Republic. Haitians.
Massacres. Nationalism. Racism. 1937.
1675
—. Dictatorship. Dominican Republic.
Historiography. 1911-61. *1674*
Tupamaros. Agency for International Development.
Mitrione, Dan A. Uruguay. USA. 1969-73.
2985
—. Antisubversive measures. Uruguay. 1962-72.
2992
—. Communist Party. Uruguay. 1952-73. *3002*
—. Counterinsurgency. Economic Conditions.
Social Conditions. Uruguay. ca 1960-72.
2988
—. Guerrilla Warfare (urban). Uruguay. 1962-73.
2991
—. Politics and the Military. Uruguay. 1964-74.
2989
Tyler, Ron. Cartoons and Caricatures (review
article). Johnson, John J. USA. ca 1880-1975.
170

U

Ubico Castañeda, Jorge. Arévalo, Juan José.
Guatemala. Military. Revolution. 1944.
1146

—. Boundaries (disputes). British Honduras.
Great Britain. Guatemala. USA. 1933-42.
1147
—. Foreign Policy. Guatemala. Politics. USA.
1931-44. *1148*
UN. Arab-Israeli conflict. 1947-76. *303*
—. Brazil. Foreign Policy. Foreign Relations.
1945-80. *2322*
—. Colombia. Economic aid (preinvestment
assistance). 1970-73. *1930*
—. Congo crisis. Intervention. Suez crisis. Voting
patterns. 1956-60. *227*
—. Cuban Missile Crisis. International Law.
1962. *1499*
—. Dominican Republic. Foreign Policy.
Intervention (review article). Organization of
American States. 1945-72. *1672*
—. Economic Commission for Latin America.
Economic planning. Technical Education.
1953-74. *334*
—. Foreign Relations (review article). 1946-74.
232
—. Israeli issues. Voting and Voting Behavior.
1947-68. *316*
—. Mineral resources, exploitation of. Oceans.
Regional policy. USA. 1969-76. *13*
UN General Assembly. Dependency. Foreign
policy. Trade. USA. Voting and Voting
Behavior. 1950-73. *155*
UN (membership). Argentina. Foreign policy.
USA. 1942-45. *2565*
UN (resolutions). Argentina. Falkland Islands.
Foreign Relations. Great Britain. 1965-77.
2960
Underdeveloped Nations. *See* Developing Nations.
Unemployment *See also* Employment.
—. Argentina. Brazil. Exports. Mexico. 1953-70.
333
—. Freedom of the press. Peru. Revolutionary
government. 1968-70's. *2058*
—. Industrialization. Mexico (border region).
Tariff. USA. 1974. *857*
Unión Cívica Radical. Argentina. Foreign
Investments. Great Britain. Railroads and
State. Yrigoyen, Hipólito. 1891-1928. *2609*
Unions. *See* Labor Unions and Organizations.
United front policy. Chile. Communist Party.
Popular Unity. Socialist Party. 1956-69.
2753
United Fruit Company. Central America.
Imperialism. USA. West Indies. 1870's-1950's.
84
—. Panama. 1960-74. *1254*
United States. *See* USA; US; and entries beginning
with the word American.
Universal Negro Improvement Association. Belize.
Garvey, Marcus. Negroes. Peoples United
Party. Political Parties. 1914-49. *1052*
Universidad Popular José Martí. Colleges and
Universities. Communism. Cuba. Martínez
Villena, Rubén. Pascual, Sarah (memoirs).
1920-30. *1560*
Universities. Mexico. Political recruitment.
1935-74. *873*
Universities, popular. APRA. Haya de la Torre,
Víctor Raúl. Peru. Students. 1921-31. *2067*
Upper Classes. Chile. Class Struggle. Poder
Femenino. Women. 1970-73. *2791*
—. Chile. Coups d'etat. 1973. *2854*
—. Industrialization. Peru. 1969-79. *2040*
Urban concentration. Peru. 1940-78. *2085*
Urban growth. Mexico (Morelos). Peasants.
Social Organization. ca 1545-1970. *609*
Urban History. Brazil (Rio de Janeiro). 1557-1965.
2274
Urbanization *See also* City Planning; Modernization.
—. Brazil. Migration. 1940-80. *2326*
—. Central America. Colombia. Venezuela.
West Indies. 1930-76. *17*
—. Central American Common Market. Trade,
intra-area. 1960-71. *1046*
—. Colombia. Political parties. 1970's. *1978*
—. Cuba. Decentralization. 1959-79. *1653*
—. Jamaica. Political Protest. 1945-70. *1779*
—. Methodology. Political development. Social
Indicators. ca 1950-70. *161*
Urbanization (review article). Migrants. Politics.
Venezuela. 20c. *2181*
Uribe, Antonio José. Colombia. Panama. Treaties.
USA. 1901-22. *234*
Uruguay. Agency for International Development.
Mitrione, Dan A. Tupamaros. USA. 1969-73.
2985
—. Anti-Fascist Movements. Germans. 1933-41.
2983
—. Antisubversive measures. Tupamaros. 1962-72.
2992

—. Argentina. Foreign relations. Treaties.
1973-76. *2508*
—. Argentina. Rio de la Plata, Treaty of. ca
1970-73. *2506*
—. Authoritarianism. 1972-76. *2995*
—. Bordaberry Arocena, Juan Marie. Economic
Development. Political Change. 1971-76.
2986
—. Brazil. Debt, external. Economic Policy.
Mexico. 1973-78. *412*
—. Brazil. Education. Elites (political).
Guatemala. Legislators. 1964-72. *191*
—. Communist Party. 1970-1977. *3000*
—. Communist Party. 1972-76. *3001*
—. Communist Party. 1973-75. *2981*
—. Communist Party. Coups d'etat. Political
strategy. 1968-74. *2998*
—. Communist Party. Political repression.
1955-76. *3005*
—. Communist Party. Revolutionary movements.
Terrorism (governmental). 1974. *2994*
—. Communist Party. Tupamaros. 1952-73.
3002
—. Costa-Gavras, Constantin. Films. Guerrilla
warfare. *State of Siege* (film; review article).
1963-73. *2980*
—. Costa-Gavras, Constantin. Films. Politics.
State of Siege (film; review article). 20c. *2979*
—. Counterinsurgency. Economic Conditions.
Social Conditions. Tupamaros. ca 1960-72.
2988
—. Democracy. Economic development. Politics.
ca 1955-78. *2982*
—. Diplomatic career. Mora, José Antonio.
1945-75. *3006*
—. Economic conditions. Politics. 1960's-74.
2996
—. Economic development. Social Change.
1872-1973. *2978*
—. Economic Policy. New Zealand. Small
countries (viability). 20c. *2984*
—. Feminism. Luisi, Paulina. Moral reform.
1875-1950. *2987*
—. Guerrilla Warfare (urban). Tupamaros.
1962-73. *2991*
—. Military Government. Political Development.
1976-82. *3003*
—. Military Government. Political Systems.
1970-80's. *2990*
—. Peasant movements. 1726-1978. *2997*
—. Political protest. Radicalization. Student
movements. 1917-60's. *3004*
—. Political repression. 1972-79. *2999*
—. Political repression. 1973-81. *2993*
—. Politics and the Military. Tupamaros. 1964-74.
2989
USA. Agency for International Development.
Mitrione, Dan A. Tupamaros. Uruguay.
1969-73. *2985*
—. Air Warfare. Mexico. 1916. *774*
—. Allende, Salvador. Blockade, invisible. Chile.
Economic weapons. Export-Import Bank.
Foreign Policy. 1970-74. *2897*
—. Allende, Salvador. Chile. Coups d'etat.
International Telephone & Telegraph
Corporation. 1970-73. *2774*
—. Allende, Salvador. Chile. Coups d'Etat.
Subversive Activities. 1970-73. *2847*
—. Allende, Salvador. Chile. Coups d'Etat
(antecedents). Multinational Corporations.
1955-73. *2840*
—. Allende, Salvador. Chile. Coups d'Etat
(justification of). Political Leadership (junta).
Press. 1973. *2945*
—. Allende, Salvador. Chile. Films. Landau, Saul
(Que Hacer). Political consciousness. 1975.
2881
—. Allende, Salvador. Chile. Foreign Investments.
Socialism. 1912-73. *2850*
—. Alliance for Progress. Brazil. Business.
Nationalization. 1961-63. *2400*
—. Alliance for Progress. Chile. Economic
development. 1964-70. *2715*
—. Alliance for Progress. Foreign Relations
(review article). 1946-74. *313*
—. Alliances. Documents. Intervention. Mexico.
Nicaragua. Sandino, Augusto César. 1926-30.
219
—. Allison, Graham. Blockade. Cuban missile
crisis. Foreign policy. Methodology
(implementation analysis; review article). 1962.
1395
—. Alvarado Quirós, Alejandro. Anti-Imperialism.
Costa Rica. Diplomacy. 1920-45. *1080*
—. Ambassadors. Diplomacy. Mexico. 1935-79.
592
—. American Federation of Labor. Imperialism.
Labor movement. 1945-70. *277*

—. American Institute for Free Labor Development. Imperialism. Labor movement. 20c. *307*

—. Anarchism and Anarchists. Flores Magón, Ricardo (prison letters). Mexico. Sarnoff, Lilly. 1920-22. *713*

—. Anderson, Chandler. Business. Foreign Relations. Mexico. 1913-20. *752*

—. Angola. Cuba. Foreign Policy. Intervention. USSR. 1975-77. *1656*

—. Annexation. Cuba (Isle of Pines). Hay, John. Public opinion. Quesada, Gonzalo de. Treaties. 1898-1980. *1617*

—. Anti-Communism. Diplomacy. Mexico. Nationalism. 1924-27. *758*

—. Anti-Imperialism. Foreign Policy. 1970's. *320*

—. Anti-Imperialism. Foreign Relations. 1891-1929. *19*

—. Argentina. Boycotts. Economic relations. Great Britain. 1945-49. *2603*

—. Argentina. Decisionmaking. Diplomacy. Inter-American Conference (Rio de Janeiro). World War II. 1942. *553*

—. Argentina. Diplomacy. Eady-Miranda Agreement. Economic relations. Great Britain. Messersmith, George S. 1930-48. *2591*

—. Argentina. Drago Doctrine. Foreign relations. Perón, Juan. 1823-1974. *2557*

—. Argentina. Falkland Islands. Great Britain. 1975-81. *2958*

—. Argentina. Foreign Policy. Intervention. Nationalism. 1941-46. *2536*

—. Argentina. Foreign policy. UN (membership). 1942-45. *2565*

—. Argentina. Foreign Relations. 1976-81. *2665*

—. Argentina. Foreign Relations. Military Government. 1940-81. *2537*

—. Argentina. Foreign Relations (review article). Good neighbor policy. Woods, Randall Bennett. 1941-45. *2523*

—. Argentina. Imperialism. 1930-76. *2534*

—. Argentina. International Labor Organization. Perón, Juan. 1946-55. *2600*

—. Armies. Drugs. Mexico. Pershing, John J. Prostitution. Venereal disease. 1916-17. *802*

—. Armies. Logistics. Mexico. 1916. *777*

—. Armies. Military Government. Revolutionary process. 1810-1973. *469*

—. Arms Trade. 1961-71. *414*

—. Arms trade. 1976-78. *427*

—. Arms trade. Brazil. Dominican Republic. 1945-74. *429*

—. Arms Trade. Chile. Embargo. Great Britain. 1980. *2922*

—. Artists. Mexico. Murals. 1920's-82. *611*

—. Assassination. Foreign Policy. Human rights. Nicaragua. Somoza, Anastasio. 1974-80. *1208*

—. Balaguer, Joaquín. Dominican Republic. Elections. Foreign Relations. Guzmán, Antonio. 1965-80. *1680*

—. Balance of payments components. Dependency, economic. Mexico. 1970-75. *960*

—. Balance of Power. Cuba. Iran. Military Strategy. USSR. 1970's. *1598*

—. Banking. Dollar diplomacy. International Committee of Bankers on Mexico. Lamont-de la Huerta Agreement (1922). Mexico. 1919-38. *626*

—. Banks. Debt, external. Dependency. Mexico. 1824-1979. *912*

—. Barco concession. Colombia. Economic Policy. Oil industry and trade. 1926-32. *1963*

—. Barrios de Chungara, Domitila. Bolivia. Memoirs. Miners. Political Protest. 1961-70's. *1860*

—. Batista, Fulgencio. Bay of Pigs invasion. Castro, Fidel. Cuba. Kennedy, John F. USSR. 1952-62. *1609*

—. Bibliographies. Cuba. Revolutionary movements. Women. 1953-58. *1569*

—. Bibliographies. Foreign Relations. 1973-75. *276*

—. Bibliographies. Historiography. Mexico. -1974. *159*

—. Bilateral commissions. International Boundary and Water Commission. International Organizations (judicial). Mexico. 19c-1974. *624*

—. Birth control. Ideology. Women. 1950's-70's. *148*

—. Bolivia. Chaco War. Foreign Policy. Historiography. Paraguay. 1932-35. *98*

—. Bolivia. Development project, international. Lake Titicaca. Peru. 1935-78. *368*

—. Bolivia. Diplomacy. Movimiento Nacionalista Revolucionario. Revolution. 1952-64. *1895*

—. Bolivia. Federation of Bolivian Mine Workers. Nationalism. Workers' Central (COB). 1970's. *1859*

—. Bonner, Raymond. Bushnell, John A. Democracy. El Salvador. Foreign Relations. Military. Ramos, Arnold. Williams, Murat. 1982. *1125*

—. Border Industrialization Program. Economic Conditions. Mexico. Multinational corporations. 1940-70. *602*

—. Border Industrialization Program. Industrialization. Mexico. Tariff. 1970-80. *972*

—. Boundaries. Costa Rica. Panama. 1846-1921. *1259*

—. Boundaries. Diplomacy. Groundwater. Mexico. 1940's-70's. *948*

—. Boundaries. Foreign policy. Leguía, Augusto B. Peru. 1908-42. *2106*

—. Boundaries (disputes). British Honduras. Great Britain. Guatemala. Ubico Castañeda, Jorge. 1933-42. *1147*

—. Bracero program. Immigration. Mexico. 1942-46. *922*

—. Brazil. Chile. Foreign policy. Repression. Working class. 20c. *44*

—. Brazil. Commerce. Foreign Relations. Industry. Treaties. 1935. *2381*

—. Brazil. Democracy. Foreign Policy. 1964-68. *2457*

—. Brazil. Diplomacy. McCann, Frank D. 1937-45. *2394*

—. Brazil. Diplomacy. Mexico. 1913-15. *319*

—. Brazil. Diplomacy. World War II. 1935-45. *2353*

—. Brazil. Diplomatic dispatches. Great Britain. Political Leadership. Vargas, Getúlio. 1934-37. *2359*

—. Brazil. Economic Development. Foreign Aid. 1946-70. *2257*

—. Brazil. Economic power. Foreign Investments. Great Britain. World War I. 1914-19. *2376*

—. Brazil. Economic relations. Mexico. 1950-74. *358*

—. Brazil. Expropriation. Foreign Relations. Hickenlooper Amendment. Public utilities. 1959-67. *2291*

—. Brazil. Foreign Aid. Politics. Trade. 20c. *2319*

—. Brazil. Foreign Policy. 1960-74. *284*

—. Brazil. Foreign Relations. 1945-60. *2398*

—. Brazil. Foreign Relations. Maritime relations. 1967-73. *2286*

—. Brazil. Foreign Relations. Political structure. 1973. *2445*

—. Brazil. Foreign Relations (review article). 1950's-81. *2308*

—. Brazil. Imperialism. Student movements. 1954-68. *2248*

—. Brazil (Northeast, destruction of). Foreign aid. Roett, Reardan. SUDENE. 1960-72. *2212*

—. Business. Calles, Plutarco Elías. Mexico. Oil policies. Rath, Arthur C. Rose, Vernon J. 1923-24. *712*

—. Cabrera, Luis. Carranza, Venustiano. Diplomacy. Mexico. Wilson, Woodrow. 1914-17. *731*

—. Calbó, Gay (*América Indefensa*). Cuba. 1925-80. *1466*

—. Canada. Economic Integration. Energy. Mexico. Political systems. 1930-80. *616*

—. Canada. Foreign Relations. 1970-76. *262*

—. Caperton, William B. Diplomacy. Navies. World War I. 1915-26. *255*

—. Capitalism. Dominican Republic. Imperialism. Middle classes. 1900-24. *1669*

—. Capitalism. Economic structure. Mexico. Social Conditions. 1950-70. *859*

—. Cárdenas, Lázaro. Foreign Relations. Mexico. Nationalization. Oil Industry and Trade. 1945-50. *928*

—. Carranza, Venustiano. Diplomacy. Mexico. Pershing, John J. Villa, Pancho. Wilson, Woodrow. 1915-17. *801*

—. Carranza, Venustiano. Emigration. Labor. Mexico. 1916-20. *725*

—. Carranza, Venustiano. Foreign Relations. Mexico. Plan of San Diego. 1915-16. *750*

—. Cartoons and Caricatures (review article). Johnson, John J. Tyler, Ron. ca 1880-1975. *170*

—. Castro, Fidel. Communist Party. Cuba. Dictatorship. 1940-77. *1352*

—. Castro, Fidel. Cuba. Foreign Policy. Revolution. 1959-62. *1626*

—. Castro, Fidel. Cuba. Foreign Relations. Nixon, Richard M. (memorandum). 1959. *1600*

—. Castro, Fidel. Cuba. Revolution. 1959-74. *1454*

—. Cattle industry. Mexico. Revolution. 1910-23. *771*

—. Central America. Civil-Military Relations (review article). Military aid. 20c. *1238*

—. Central America. Economic Conditions. Foreign Relations. Social Conditions. 1979-81. *998*

—. Central America. Economic Integration. 19c-20c. *1015*

—. Central America. Economic integration. Foreign Policy. 1960-73. *1024*

—. Central America. Foreign Policy. 1960-78. *1045*

—. Central America. Foreign policy. 1960-80. *1013*

—. Central America. Foreign Policy. 1978-80. *1002*

—. Central America. Foreign Policy. 1980's. *1001*

—. Central America. Foreign Policy. Government. Honduras. 1871-1981. *1174*

—. Central America. Foreign Relations. 1960's-81. *1018*

—. Central America. Imperialism. United Fruit Company. West Indies. 1870's-1950's. *84*

—. Central America. West Indies. 1979-81. *291*

—. Central American Common Market. Economic Development. 1954-70. *1047*

—. Central American Common Market. Economic Development. Government. Monopolies. 1900-77. *1049*

—. Central American Peace Conferences (Washington, 1907, 1923). Diplomatic recognition. International Law. Tobar Doctrine. 1900-30. *548*

—. Central Intelligence Agency. Chile. 1960-76. *2731*

—. Central Intelligence Agency. Chile. Coups d'etat. 1972-73. *2839*

—. Central Intelligence Agency. Chile. Coups d'Etat. ca 1970-77. *2860*

—. Central Intelligence Agency. Chile. Coups d'Etat. Foreign Policy. 1970-73. *2838*

—. Central Intelligence Agency (review article). 1970-79. *283*

—. Chapman, Charles E. (*History of the Cuban Republic*). Cuba. Government patronage. State Department. 1920-27. *1568*

—. Chile. Communist Party. Foreign relations. González Videla, Gabriel. Radical Party. 1940-47. *2748*

—. Chile. Coups d'Etat. Foreign Policy. 1971-73. 1970's. *2693*

—. Chile. Coups d'Etat. Intervention. 1966-73. *2703*

—. Chile. Coups d'Etat. Intervention (economic). 1970-73. *2943*

—. Chile. Coups d'Etat. Kissinger, Henry A. (confirmation hearings). 1971-73. *2809*

—. Chile. Cuba. Dominican Republic. Foreign Policy (review article). 1930-72. *225*

—. Chile. Cuban revolution. Frei, Eduardo. Leftists. 1958-73. *2768*

—. Chile. Diplomatic negotiations. Peru. Tacna-Arica dispute. 1922-29. *6*

—. Chile. Economic Conditions. Ibáñez, Carlos. Imperialism. Modernization. 1925-31. *2755*

—. Chile. Economic conditions. Military junta. 1975. *2904*

—. Chile. Economic development. Foreign Aid. 1973-75. *2913*

—. Chile. Economic planning. Social conditions. 1973-77. *2942*

—. Chile. Economic policy. Friedman, Milton. Technical assistance. 1973-75. *2935*

—. Chile. Elections. Military aid. Venezuela. 1963-64. *430*

—. Chile. Foreign Investments. Foreign Policy. 1960-78. *2950*

—. Chile. Foreign Policy. International lending agencies. 1970-73. *2864*

—. Chile. Foreign policy. International Telephone & Telegraph Corporation. Multinational Corporations. 1971-74. *2678*

—. Chile. Foreign Policy. Intervention. 1970-74. *2688*

—. Chile. Foreign Relations. 1970-73. *2692*

—. Chile. Imperialism, fight against. 1970-74. *2898*

—. Chile. Intervention. ca 1930's-77. *275*

—. Chile. Intervention, economic. Popular Unity. 1960-74. *2832*

—. Chile. Militarism. USSR. 1962-74. *2920*

—. Civil disturbances. Curaçao. Political Protest. Social change. 1960's-70's. *1785*

—. Civil war. El Salvador. Farabundo Martí National Liberation Front. Revolutionary Democratic Front. 1981. *1108*

—. Civil-Military Relations. Guatemala. Military Aid. 1953-78. *1150*

—. Civil-Military Relations. Military aid. 1946-78. *426*

—. Claims. Cuba. Foreign Relations. Sugar. Trade. 1957-73. *1382*

—. Cold War. Detente. Foreign Relations. Medina Echavarría, José. 1948-68. *288*

—. Cold War. Foreign relations. Historiography (US). 1945-50. 1950-75. *265*

—. Cold War. Foreign Relations. Organization of American States. 1944-49. *312*

—. Colombia. Drug traffic. Mexico. 1920's-80's. *376*

—. Colombia. Economic development. Foreign Investments. Kemmerer, Edwin Walter. Monetary reform. 1923-30. *1917*

—. Colombia. Economic Development. Imperialism. 1920-74. *1926*

—. Colombia. Foreign aid. Public Law 480. Wheat. 1955-71. *1921*

—. Colombia. Foreign policy. Multinational Corporations. Oil Industry and Trade. 1920-40. *1964*

—. Colombia. Panama. Treaties. Uribe, Antonio José. 1901-22. *234*

—. Colorado River. Mexico. Salinity problem. Treaties (water; 1944). 1944-74. *574*

—. Communist Party. Costa Rica. Foreign Relations. 1920's-48. *1075*

—. Communist Party. El Salvador. Nicaragua. Politics. Right. 1960-81. *1027*

—. Congress. Cuba. Foreign Policy. Revolution. 1960's-70's. *1436*

—. Conservatism. Military. Radicals and Radicalism. ca 1960-80. *447*

—. Corporatism. Foreign Relations. 1900's-74. *287*

—. Costa Rica. Diplomacy (secret). Intervention. Jiménez, Ricardo. Nicaragua. 1912-27. *1038*

—. Costa Rica. Intervention, foreign. Nicaragua. 1925-26. *1036*

—. Counterinsurgency. Military aid. 1963-73. *444*

—. Cuba. Dependency (review article). Foreign Relations. 1880's-1930's. *1544*

—. Cuba. Dominican Republic. Economic coercion. Foreign policy. 1960-72. *1339*

—. Cuba. Economic policy. Foreign policy. 1933-34. *1384*

—. Cuba. Economic Policy. Machado, Gerardo. Social Policy. 1929-32. *1603*

—. Cuba. Foreign Investments. 1959-64. *1495*

—. Cuba. Foreign Policy. 1959-82. *1512*

—. Cuba. Foreign Policy. 1961-81. *1522*

—. Cuba. Foreign Policy. Guantánamo Bay (status of). Military Bases. 1960-72. *1381*

—. Cuba. Foreign policy. International Trade. 1975. *1648*

—. Cuba. Foreign policy. Mexico. 1960-74. *561*

—. Cuba. Foreign policy. Sugar industry. 1914-21. *1563*

—. Cuba. Foreign Relations. 1960's-70's. *1365*

—. Cuba. Foreign Relations. ca 19c-1974. *498*

—. Cuba. Foreign Relations. Negroes. 1868-1977. *1402*

—. Cuba. Foreign Relations. Nickel. 1975-76. *1545*

—. Cuba. Foreign Relations. Organization of American States. 1959-75. *1405*

—. Cuba. Foreign Relations. Sugar Act (1948). Tariff. 1945-48. *1487*

—. Cuba. Foreign Relations. USSR. 1959-76. *1385*

—. Cuba. France (Paris). Machado, Gerardo. Newspapers. Revolution. 1933. *1506*

—. Cuba. International law. Missile crisis. 1962-75. *1577*

—. Cuba. Interventionism. 1902-58. *1576*

—. Cuba. Machado, Gerardo. Politics and the Military. Revolution. 1933. *1570*

—. Cuba. Methodist Church. Missions and Missionaries. Nationalism. 1898-1958. *1406*

—. Cuba. Monopolies. Railroads. Tarafa Law. 1920-25. *1455*

—. Cuba. Racism. Revolution. 1920-78. *1403*

—. Cuba. Trade Embargo. 1959-77. *1415*

—. Cuba (Oriente). Iron industry. Spanish American Company. 1883-1959. *1490*

—. Cuban missile crisis. Decisionmaking. Foreign policy. 1962. *1360*

—. Cuban Missile Crisis. USSR. 1959-1962. *1618*

—. Decisionmaking. Foreign policy. GATT. Mexico. 1980. *986*

—. Democracy. Human rights. -1970's. *200*

—. Dependency. Dominican Republic. Intervention (review article). ca 1964-79. *1684*

—. Dependency. Foreign aid. Military Government. Peru. 1963-73. *2026*

—. Dependency. Foreign policy. Trade. UN General Assembly. Voting and Voting Behavior. 1950-73. *155*

—. Dependency model. Foreign relations. 1910-73. *295*

—. Dependency theory. 1960-76. *337*

—. Development. Economic relations. 1942-54. *290*

—. Diplomacy. 1950-74. *318*

—. Diplomacy. Economic policy. Mexico. Punitive expeditions. ca 1914-17. *711*

—. Diplomacy. Emmerson, John K. (memoir). Japanese. Peru. World War II. 1942-43. *2038*

—. Diplomacy. Fletcher, Henry P. Mexico. Revolution. 1917-20. *743*

—. Diplomacy. Foreign Investments. Mexico. Nationalization. Oil Industry and Trade. 1938-45. *630*

—. Diplomacy. Hay-Bunau-Varilla Treaty. Panama Canal. 1903. 1967-74. *1281*

—. Diplomacy. Mexico. Oil. Teapot Dome Scandal. 1926-27. *757*

—. Diplomacy. Mexico. Politics. Social Conditions. 1969-80. *966*

—. Diplomacy. Mexico. Revolution. *Vida Nueva* (newspaper). Villa, Pancho. 1914-15. *741*

—. Diplomacy. Mexico. Water. 1848-1979. *568*

—. Diplomacy. Panama. Treaties. 1924-26. *1272*

—. Diplomacy (review article). 19c-20c. *308*

—. Documents. Foreign Relations. Intervention. Mexico. Nicaragua. 1922-29. *327*

—. Documents. Intervention. Mexico. Nicaragua. Press. 1926-27. *218*

—. Dominican Republic. Economic Growth. Haiti. Imperialism. Intervention. 1915-34. *1294*

—. Dominican Republic. Foreign Policy. Intervention (review article). Organization of American States. UN. 1965-72. *1672*

—. Dominican Republic. Government, Resistance to. Military Occupation. 1916-24. *1668*

—. Dominican Republic. Guerrilla warfare. Intervention. Marines. 1916-22. *1666*

—. Dominican Republic. Intervention, military. Mexico. 1914-65. *253*

—. Drug policy. Law enforcement. Mexico. Salazar Viniegra, Leopold. 1936-40. *696*

—. Drug traffic. Mexico. 1948-77. *885*

—. Drugs. Mexico. Operation Intercept. Smuggling. 1968-69. *886*

—. Duvalier family. Government, resistance to. Haiti. Political repression. 1957-74. *1731*

—. Economic coercion. International Petroleum Company. Nationalization. Peru. 1968-71. *2095*

—. Economic conditions. Elites. Nicaragua. Somoza family. 1870-1976. *1188*

—. Economic Conditions. Foreign Policy. New International Economic Order. West Indies. 1970's-81. *1329*

—. Economic Conditions. Foreign Relations. 1950-80. *226*

—. Economic Conditions. Foreign Relations. Mexico. 1970-77. *954*

—. Economic Conditions. Foreign Relations. National security. West Indies. 1962-82. *1314*

—. Economic Conditions. Mexico. Political Commentary. 1973-74. *891*

—. Economic costs. Panama Canal. Treaties. 1964-75. *1275*

—. Economic development. Foreign Policy. 1970's. *522*

—. Economic development. Foreign Relations. Mexico. Natural gas. Oil Industry and Trade. 1977-79. *965*

—. Economic Development. Mexico (Cancún). 1950's-82. *343*

—. Economic development. Panama Canal. 1970-71. *1264*

—. Economic negotiations. European Economic Community. 1960-75. *492*

—. Economic relations. 1914-15. *66*

—. Economic Relations. 1959-80. *129*

—. Ecuador. Europe. Foreign Relations. Galápagos Islands. 1830-1946. *1986*

—. Education. Haiti. Hoover, Herbert C. Moton, Robert R. 1930. *1741*

—. Eight Principles. Hay-Bunau-Varilla Treaty. Kissinger, Henry A. Nationalism. Panama Canal. Torrijos, Omar. 1964-75. *1276*

—. El Salvador. Foreign policy. USSR. 1981. *1099*

—. El Salvador. Political crisis. 1972-81. *1112*

—. El Salvador. Political Repression. 1970-81. *1111*

—. Elections. McCoy, Frank R. Military occupation. Nicaragua. Sandino, Augusto César. 1927-28. *1187*

—. Elections, supervision of. Nicaragua. 1927-32. *1210*

—. Emigration. Mexico. Policymaking. Politics. 1920-78. *653*

—. Energy. Foreign policy. Mexico. Tomatoes. Trade Regulations. 1969-80. *937*

—. Exile invasions. War. West Indies. 1945-74. *1345*

—. Extradition. Pérez Jiménez, Marcos. Venezuela. 1959-63. *2163*

—. Fascism. 1960's-70's. *451*

—. Foreign Aid. 1960-71. *160*

—. Foreign aid. Human rights. 1970-79. *299*

—. Foreign aid. Koch, Edward (correspondence). Nicaragua. 1970's. *1253*

—. Foreign Aid. Police. Public safety program. 1960's-73. *325*

—. Foreign Aid (distribution). 1946-73. *93*

—. Foreign influence. Political institutions. 1776-1976. *280*

—. Foreign investments. 1890-1929. *271*

—. Foreign investments. Foreign Relations. Mexico. 1910-80. *700*

—. Foreign Investments. International law. 1896-1977. *293*

—. Foreign Policy. 1900-76. *274*

—. Foreign Policy. 1950's-76. *240*

—. Foreign policy. 1953-70. *321*

—. Foreign Policy. 1977-80. *264*

—. Foreign policy. 20c. *249*

—. Foreign Policy. Great Britain. Harrod, Jeffrey. Jamaica. Labor Unions and Organizations (review article). 20c. *1757*

—. Foreign Policy. Guatemala. Politics. Ubico Castañeda, Jorge. 1931-44. *1148*

—. Foreign Policy. Human rights. 1946-79. *263*

—. Foreign Policy. Kennedy, John F. (administration). Peru. 1960-62. *2119*

—. Foreign Policy. Kissinger, Henry A. 1968-76. *260*

—. Foreign Policy. Leftism. Military. 1970-77. *41*

—. Foreign policy. Lobbying. 1960-79. *310*

—. Foreign policy. Mexico. Oil Industry and Trade. 1921-28. *927*

—. Foreign policy. Mexico. Revolution. Scott, Hugh Lenox. Wilson, Woodrow. 1914-17. *749*

—. Foreign Policy. Nationalization. Social classes. Venezuela. 1973-76. *2192*

—. Foreign policy. Panama Canal. 1903-79. *1277*

—. Foreign Policy. Panama Canal. 1945-49. *1273*

—. Foreign policy. Treaties. 1939-45. *267*

—. Foreign Policy. West Indies. 1959-81. *1287*

—. Foreign policy distance, comparative. 1953-70. *322*

—. Foreign Relations. -1975. *242*

—. Foreign Relations. 1823-1980. *269*

—. Foreign Relations. 1944-60. *285*

—. Foreign relations. 1945-70's. *243*

—. Foreign relations. 1960's-70's. *247*

—. Foreign relations. 1961-75. *309*

—. Foreign Relations. 20c. *272*

—. Foreign Relations. Historiography. 1970's. *222*

—. Foreign Relations. Historiography. 20c. *297*

—. Foreign Relations. Independence. 1969-77. *229*

—. Foreign Relations. International system. 1960-74. *245*

—. Foreign relations. Intervention. Mexico. Pershing, John J. Wilson, Woodrow. 1916. *810*

—. Foreign Relations. Jamaica. Political systems. 1972-77. *1768*

—. Foreign Relations. Mexico. 1940-80. *958*

—. Foreign Relations. Mexico. 1973-80. *875*

—. Foreign Relations. Mexico. Meyer, Lorenzo. Nationalism. Oil Industry and Trade (review article). 1917-42. *680*

—. Foreign Relations. Mexico. Naturalization. Oil. 1915-42. *671*
—. Foreign Relations. Mexico. Obregón, Álvaro. 1913-23. *756*
—. Foreign Relations. Mexico. Oil Industry and Trade. 1910-72. *564*
—. Foreign Relations. Mexico. Political change. Reform. 1923-77. *944*
—. Foreign Relations. Mexico. Revolution. Steffens, Lincoln. 1913-27. *807*
—. Foreign Relations. Monroe Doctrine. Rio Treaty. 19c-20c. *228*
—. Foreign Relations. Nationalism. Panama Canal. 1960-77. *1255*
—. Foreign Relations. Nicaragua. Revolution. 1978-79. *1212*
—. Foreign Relations. Organization of American States. 1948-78. *503*
—. Foreign relations. Panama. 1903-74. *1284*
—. Foreign Relations. Panama. Sovereignty. 1964-74. *1257*
—. Foreign Relations. Panama. Torrijos, Omar. 1969-73. *1283*
—. Foreign Relations. Panama Canal. 1898-1975. *1270*
—. Foreign Relations. Panama Canal Zone. Torrijos, Omar. 1903-77. *1285*
—. Foreign Relations. Regional development. ca 1880-1973. *5*
—. Foreign Relations. West Indies. 1945-81. *1341*
—. Foreign Relations. West Indies. 1970-76. *1348*
—. Foreign Relations (Commission, 2d report). Linowitz, Sol M. 1976. *256*
—. Foreign Relations (review article). 1970-74. *233*
—. Foreign Relations (review article). 1974. *306*
—. Foreign Relations (review article). Linowitz Commission Report. 1976. *279*
—. Foreign Relations (review article). Rangel, Carlos. 16c-1979. *292*
—. Galeano, Eduardo. Imperialism (review article). 1970's. *51*
—. Garvey, Marcus. Ideology. Jamaica. Negroes. Pan-Africanism. 1887-1927. *1766*
—. Germany. Great Britain. Imperialism. Trade. 1918-39. *31*
—. Germany. Intelligence. Mexico. Witzke affair. World War I. 1914-23. *751*
—. Great Britain. Naval rivalry. West Indies. 1882-1940. *1310*
—. Guatemala. Historiography. Intervention. 1954-78. *1152*
—. Guatemala. Intervention. 1945-54. *1149*
—. Guatemala. National Democratic Front. 1954. *1165*
—. Haiti. Military Occupation. 1910's-30's. *1734*
—. Hay-Bunau-Varilla Treaty. Panama. Politics. 1903-76. *1256*
—. Human rights. International Military Education and Training Program. Military Education. 1978. *424*
—. Ideology. Mexico. 16c-20c. *888*
—. Imperialism. 19c-20c. *301*
—. Imperialism. Revolutionary Movements. Working class. 1950-74. *143*
—. Independence Movements. Madero, Francisco. Mexico. Revolution. 1910-17. *720*
—. Independence Movements. Nicaragua. Sandino, Augusto César. 1904-36. *1195*
—. Industrialization. Mexico (border region). Tariff. Unemployment. 1974. *857*
—. Industrialization. Middle classes. 1914-79. *142*
—. International law (doctrines). Mexico. 1907-69. *692*
—. International security. Nuclear nonproliferation (denuclearized zones). Tlatelolco, Treaty of. USSR. 1950's-80. *509*
—. International Security. Organization of American States (meeting). Rio Treaty. 1947-75. *525*
—. Intervention. Mexico (Veracruz). Military occupation. 1914. *739*
—. Intervention. Multinational Corporations. 1953. *53*
—. Intervention. Nicaragua. Political change. 19c-20c. *1234*
—. Intervention. Nicaragua. Sandino, Augusto César. 1909-34. *1196*
—. Intervention (military; review article). ca 1900-79. *250*
—. Journalism. Mexico. Revolution. 1916-29. *717*

—. Labor Unions and Organizations. Mexico. Railroads. 1880-1933. *650*
—. Maiakovski, Vladimir. Mexico. Poets. Travel. 1925. *789*
—. Mexico. Migrant Labor. Repatriation. 1920-23. *724*
—. Mexico. Naco (battle). Revolution. 1914-15. *781*
—. Mexico. Natural gas. 1977-80. *911*
—. Mexico. Natural gas. Oil Industry and Trade. 1901-78. *617*
—. Military occupation. Nicaragua (Puerto Cabezas). Ridgway, Matthew B. (report). 1927-33. *1209*
—. Military Strategy. 1850-1979. *419*
—. Military Strategy. 20c. *58*
—. Mineral resources, exploitation of. Oceans. Regional policy. UN. 1969-76. *13*
—. Nationalization. Peru. Treaties (compensation). 1974-76. *2061*
—. Nuclear arms. Nuclear policy. Tlatelolco, Treaty of. 1960's-70's. *541*
—. Nuclear arms. Treaties. 1973-77. *237*
—. Oil Industry and Trade. Venezuela. 1920-75. *2169*
—. Organization of American States. 1948-74. *528*
—. Panama Canal. Treaties. 1903-77. *1269*
—. Panama Canal. Treaties. 19c-20c. *1267*
—. Panama Canal (review article). ca 1890-1977. *1266*
—. Pan-Americanism. Wilson, Woodrow. 1914-17. *517*
—. Political change. Reporters and reporting. ca 1960-75. *141*
—. Press. Revolution. 1910-73. *96*
—. Reciprocal Trade Agreement Act (1934). Trade. 1933-39. *315*
—. Rio Conference (1942). World War II. 1941-42. *238*
—. Tlatelolco Conference. 1974. *213*
—. Western Hemisphere idea. 1808-1976. *405*
USA (Arizona; Naco). Mexico. Naco (battle). Revolution. 1914-15. *746*
USA (Canal Zone). Communist Party. Imperialism. Panama. Settlement program (asentamiento). 1968-73. *1280*
USA (domination). Anti-imperialist groups. Costa Rica. Nicaragua. Puerto Rico. 1958-73. *1048*
USA (Florida). Foreign Relations. International division of labor. Mexico. Tomatoes. Trade. 1970-80. *977*
USA (New Mexico). El Paso-Juárez Conference. Foreign Relations. Mexico. USA (New Mexico; Columbus, raid). Villa, Pancho. 1916. *748*
—. Mexico. USA (New Mexico; Columbus, raid). Villa, Pancho. 1916. *765*
USA (New Mexico; Columbus, raid). El Paso-Juárez Conference. Foreign Relations. Mexico. USA (New Mexico). Villa, Pancho. 1916. *748*
—. Foreign Relations. Mexico. Villa, Pancho. 1913-16. *816*
—. Mexico. USA (New Mexico). Villa, Pancho. 1916. *765*
USA (Oklahoma). Boundaries. Mexico. National Guard. 1916. *759*
USA (Southwestern). Mexico. Missions and Missionaries. Protestant Churches. 1867-1930. *726*
USA (Texas). Carranza, Venustiano. Mexicans. Mexico. Rebellions. 1848-1920. *792*
—. International Boundary and Water Commission. Irrigation. Mexico (Tamaulipas). Rio Grande Basin. 1900-20. *676*
USA (Texas; El Paso). Mexico (Ciudad Juárez). Transportation. 1950's-70's. *964*
USSR. Africa. Cuba. Foreign policy. 1959-78. *1658*
—. Africa. Cuba. Foreign Relations. Military. 1959-81. *1649*
—. Alliances. Argentina. Atlantic, South. Brazil. South Africa. 1960's-70's. *77*
—. Angola. Cuba. Foreign Policy. Intervention. USA. 1975-77. *1656*
—. Angola. Cuba. Intervention, military. 1975-76. *1640*
—. Arms race. International law. Nuclear nonproliferation (denuclearized zones). 1962-73. *137*
—. Balance of Power. Cuba. Iran. Military Strategy. USA. 1970's. *1598*
—. Batista, Fulgencio. Bay of Pigs invasion. Castro, Fidel. Cuba. Kennedy, John F. USA. 1952-62. *1609*
—. Brazil. Communist Party (25th Congress, 1976). 1964-76. *2490*

—. Brezhnev, Leonid (visit). Cuba. 1961-74. *1480*
—. Castro, Fidel. Cuba. Domestic Policy. Foreign policy. 1959-76. *1527*
—. Castro, Fidel. Cuba. Foreign Aid. 1959-77. *1550*
—. Castro, Fidel. Cuba. Foreign Relations. 1956-60. *1390*
—. Castro, Fidel. Cuba (dependence). 1968-73. *1357*
—. Central America. Cuba. Revolution. 1973-81. *1044*
—. Chile. Foreign aid. 1971-73. *2842*
—. Chile. Militarism. USA. 1962-74. *2920*
—. Comecon. Cuba. Nuclear power. 1974-81. *1573*
—. Communist Party (1st Congress, 1975). Cuba. 1970's. *1408*
—. Cuba. Cultural relations. Trade. Treaties. 1959-65. *1632*
—. Cuba. Developing nations. Foreign Relations. 1959-79. *1472*
—. Cuba. Economic development. Foreign Relations. 1960-73. *1410*
—. Cuba. Economic relations. 1960-82. *1459*
—. Cuba. Foreign Relations. 1959-77. *1517*
—. Cuba. Foreign Relations. 1961-74. *1531*
—. Cuba. Foreign Relations. Revolutionary Movements. 20c. *1354*
—. Cuba. Foreign Relations. USA. 1959-76. *1385*
—. Cuba. Revolution (institutionalization). 1959-76. *1461*
—. Cuban Missile Crisis. USA. 1959-1962. *1618*
—. El Salvador. Foreign policy. USA. 1981. *1099*
—. Foreign Relations. 1930's. *305*
—. Foreign Relations. Historiography (Latin American). 1917-79. *304*
—. Foreign Relations. Mexico. 1917-24. *678*
—. Foreign Relations. Nationalism. 1973. *323*
—. Historiography. 1947-80. *79*
—. International Red Aid. Working class. 1917-77. *311*
—. International security. Nuclear nonproliferation (denuclearized zones). Tlatelolco, Treaty of. USA. 1950's-80. *509*
Utilities. *See* Public Utilities.
Utopias. Geography. Guyana (Jonestown; siting). 1978. *1691*

V

Valenzuela, Arturo. Chile. Dependency, political. Local Government (review article). 1880-1977. *2944*
Valladão, Alfredo *(Brazil and Chile in the Imperial Era)*. Brazil. Chile. Civil War. Diplomacy (review article). Spain. 1817-1930's. *547*
Values *See also* Attitudes; Public Opinion.
—. Colombia. Political continuity. -20c. *1923*
—. Mexico. Novels. Revolution. Violence. 1910-60's. *598*
Vargas, Getúlio. Agricultural Commodities. Brazil. Centralization. Economic Policy. 1930-45. *2349*
—. Agricultural labor. Authoritarianism. Brazil. Economic development. Social security. 1930's-70's. *2465*
—. Argentina. Brazil. Economic Policy. Inflation. Perón, Juan. 1946-55. *391*
—. Authoritarianism. Brazil. Castilhos, Julio de. Politics. 19c-20c. *2217*
—. Brazil. Catholic Church. Church and state. Leme, Sebastião, Cardinal. 1930-54. *2411*
—. Brazil. Club 3 de Octubro. Revolution. Tenentes. 1922-35. *2343*
—. Brazil. Diplomatic dispatches. Great Britain. Political Leadership. USA. 1934-37. *2359*
—. Brazil. Economic Planning. Industrialization. 1930-45. *2355*
—. Brazil. Economic policy. Military influence. 1930-45. *2354*
—. Brazil. Goulart, João. Nationalism. Political Leadership. 1930-64. *2232*
Vargas, Getúlio (image). Brazil. Elites. Folklore. 1930-54. *2266*
Varon, Benno. Diplomacy. Israel. Memoirs. Paraguay. 1968-73. *2971*
Vasconcelos, José. Mexico. Political Campaigns. Political leadership. 1929-77. *723*
—. Mexico. Revolution. 1925-59. *782*
Vatican. Colombia. Concordats. 1753-1973. *1954*
Vázquez, Jenaro. Mexico (Guerrero). Peasant movements. 1960-66. *904*

Velasco Alvarado, Juan. Agricultural reform. Economic conditions. Elites. Peru. 1969-73. *2075*

—. Authoritarianism. Corporatism. National System in Support of Social Mobilization (SINAMOS). Peru. Social Mobilization. 1968-74. *2082*

—. Domestic Policy. Foreign Policy. Peru. 1968-72. *2055*

—. Ideology. Peru. 1968-75. *2053*

—. Mass media. Peru. Reform. 1839-1975. *2010*

—. Military government. Peru. 1968-75. *2052*

—. Peru. Political theory. 1968-75. *2036*

Velasco Ibarra, José. Coups d'etat. Ecuador. 1960-61. *1997*

—. Ecuador. Presidency. 1960-61. *1998*

Véliz, Claudio (review article). Centralism. 19c-20c. *189*

Venereal disease. Armies. Drugs. Mexico. Pershing, John J. Prostitution. USA. 1916-17. *802*

Venezuela. Acción Democrática. Alexander, Robert J. Communist Party (review article). 20c. *2168*

—. Acción Democrática. Aprismo. Ideology. 1900-79. *2154*

—. Agricultural production. Land reform. Social benefits. Standard of living, rural. 1958-73. *2177*

—. Agricultural Reform. Peasant movements. 1900-78. *2175*

—. Air Forces. Aviation. Military Education. School of Military Aviation. 1920-80. *2190*

—. Amazon Basin. Brazil. Treaties. 1960-78. *500*

—. Andean Common Market. Economic policy. Foreign relations. 1959-74. *2140*

—. Aponte, Carlos. Cuba. Nicaragua. Revolution. 1900-40. *184*

—. Arbitration, International. Boundaries. Colombia. Diplomacy. Fortoul, Gil. Switzerland. 1922. *1838*

—. Betancourt, Rómulo. Political Leadership. 1936-76. *2186*

—. Bishops. Catholic Church. Colombia. Social problems. 1968-78. *1843*

—. Bond, Robert. Foreign Policy (review article). 1899-1977. *2171*

—. Bureaucracies. Colonial practices, Spanish. Modernization. Organizational model. -1970's. *75*

—. Caldera, Rafael. Elections, presidential. Political parties. 1968-73. *2172*

—. Castro, Cipriano. Exile. Gómez, Juan Vicente. 1908-24. *2196*

—. Catholic Church. Democracy. 1958-75. *2179*

—. Central America. Colombia. Urbanization. West Indies. 1930-76. *17*

—. Central America. Foreign relations. West Indies. 1936-78. *499*

—. Chile. Elections. Military aid. USA. 1963-64. *430*

—. Colombia. Territorial Waters (conference). 1815-1974. *1842*

—. Communist Parties and Movements. Petkoff, Teodoro. 1968-73. *2153*

—. Communist Parties and Movements. Political Factions. 1937-81. *2159*

—. Communist Party. Economic Conditions. Research. Social Conditions. 1931-77. *2149*

—. Communist Party. Faría, Jesús. Memoirs. 1936-44. *2165*

—. Communist Party. Machado, Gustavo. 1919-78. *2178*

—. Communist Party. Nationalization. Oil industry and trade. 1900-76. *2150*

—. Communists. Elections. Political parties. 1973. *2189*

—. Costa Rica. Democracy. Political Leadership. Puerto Rico. 1940's-70's. *449*

—. Decisionmaking. Nationalization. Oil Industry and Trade. Pérez, Carlos Andrés. Political factions. 1974-77. *2183*

—. Democracy. Economic Development. Oil. 1936-76. *2185*

—. Democracy. Foreign Policy. ca 1830-1976. *2173*

—. Democracy (review article). 1945-77. *2136*

—. Dependency. Nationalization. Oil. 1976. *2147*

—. Dictatorship. Gómez, Juan Vicente. Rippy, J. Fred. ca 1908-35. *2148*

—. Economic Conditions. Gómez, Juan Vicente. Oil industry and trade. 1908-35. *2197*

—. Economic Conditions. Oil industry and trade. Political Change. 1498-1976. *2155*

—. Economic conditions. Social Christian Party (COPEI). 1979-81. *2142*

—. Economic Development. Immigration policy. Social problems. 1930-82. *2194*

—. Economic development. Industrialization. Nationalization. Oil industry and trade. 1960's-70's. *2191*

—. Economic development. Oil. Political Change. 1970's. *2144*

—. Economic Development. Oil. Politics. Social Conditions. 1920's-70's. *2198*

—. Economic Policy. Iran. Oil. Saudi Arabia. 1920-80. *2176*

—. Economic Policy. Oil. Pérez Jiménez, Marcos. 1948-58. *2164*

—. Economic Regulations. Foreign Investments. Oil Industry and Trade. 1958-74. *2199*

—. El Salvador. Foreign policy. Nicaragua. 1970-81. *501*

—. Elections. National Development. 1973-79. *2160*

—. Energy. Natural resources. Regional Planning. 1960-78. *2193*

—. Exiles. Gómez, Juan Vicente. Newspapers. 1913-35. *2195*

—. Extradition. Pérez Jiménez, Marcos. USA. 1959-63. *2163*

—. Foreign policy. 1974-76. *2157*

—. Foreign Policy. Nationalization. Social classes. USA. 1973-76. *2192*

—. Gómez, Juan Vicente. Modernization. 1908-35. *2138*

—. Immigration. Political Theory. Race. 1890-1937. *2201*

—. Indians. Land distribution. 18c-20c. *2200*

—. Industrialization. Oil. 1976. *2156*

—. Left. Moderates. Political parties. 1958-69. *2161*

—. Left. Movement Toward Socialism. 1968-80. *2188*

—. Left. Political parties. Popular Front. 1931-78. *2162*

—. Left. Politics (review article). 1970's. *2158*

—. Migrants. Politics. Urbanization (review article). 20c. *2181*

—. Modernization. Political Parties. Voting patterns. 1950-73. *2187*

—. Morón, Guillermo (review article). -1973. *2151*

—. New International Economic Order. Pérez, Carlos Andrés. ca 1920-77. *2182*

—. Nogales Méndez, Rafael. 1900's-37. *2143*

—. Oil. Politics. 1914-75. *2174*

—. Oil Industry and Trade. USA. 1920-75. *2169*

—. Oil policies. Public Finance. 1938-68. *2141*

—. Pérez, Carlos Andrés. Presidency. 1973-79. *2166*

—. Political Parties. 1820-20c. *2170*

—. Political Systems. Social Change (review article). 1960's-70's. *2180*

—. Public policy. Radio. Television. 1930-79. *2167*

—. Social Mobility. Students. 1960-74. *2202*

Venezuela (Caracas). Local politics. Social Classes. Voting and Voting Behavior. 1958-68. *2184*

Venezuela (Guayana). Economic Development. Indians. Political development. 1970's-80's. *2139*

Venezuela (Orinoco). Indians. Integration. Migration, Internal (circular). 1920-74. *2152*

Venezuela (review article). Economic Conditions. 1959-74. *2146*

Venezuela (Táchira). Andeanism. Political dominance. 1899-1958. *2145*

Verner, Rudolph (report). Falkland Islands (battle). Germany. Great Britain. Naval Battles. World War I. 1914. *2962*

Vianna Moog, Clodomir (memoirs). Brazil. Collor, Lindolfo. Labor. 1891-1942. *2389*

Vichy Regime. French Guiana. Government, Resistance to. World War II. 1940. *1687*

—. Martinique. Robert, Georges. World War II. 1940-43. *1788*

Vida Nueva (newspaper). Diplomacy. Mexico. Revolution. USA. Villa, Pancho. 1914-15. *741*

Videla, Jorge. Argentina. Military government. 1976-79. *2668*

Villa, Pancho. Carranza, Venustiano. Diplomacy. Mexico. Pershing, John J. USA. Wilson, Woodrow. 1915-17. *801*

—. Diplomacy. Mexico. Revolution. USA. *Vida Nueva* (newspaper). 1914-15. *741*

—. El Paso-Juárez Conference. Foreign Relations. Mexico. USA (New Mexico). USA (New Mexico; Columbus, raid). 1916. *748*

—. Foreign Relations. Mexico. USA (New Mexico; Columbus, raid). 1913-16. *816*

—. Mexico. Revolution. 1910-20. *768*

—. Mexico. San Pedro de la Cueva (massacre). Sonora campaign. 1915-16. *783*

—. Mexico. USA (New Mexico). USA (New Mexico; Columbus, raid). 1916. *765*

Villages See also Rural Settlements.

—. Attitudes. Government. Intervention. Peru. Political leadership. 1964-75. *2041*

Villar Buceta, María. Bibliographies. Poets. 1915-78. *1457*

Villaroel, Gualberto. Bolivia. Busch, German. Legion of Ex-Combatants. Military Socialism. 1936-46. *1863*

Viñas, David (*Masters of the Earth*). Argentina. Novels. Social Conditions. Strikes. Working class. 1900-20. *2581*

Violence. Argentina. Catholic Church. Clergy. Movement of Priests for the Third World. Radicals and Radicalism. 1969-70's. *2520*

—. Argentina. Political repression. 1970's. *2556*

—. Chile. Civil liberties. Military government. Public opinion. 1970-75. *2900*

—. Chile. Coups d'Etat. Peace research. Popular Unity. Social classes. 1970-73. *2899*

—. Class struggle. Guatemala. 1812-1978. *1127*

—. Class struggle. Guatemala. 1960-75. *1169*

—. Colombia. Elite performance. 1948-60. *1961*

—. Counterinsurgency. Guatemala. 1960-78. *1129*

—. Cuba. Political development. 1960's-70's. *1460*

—. El Salvador. Social Conditions. 1980. *1092*

—. Longshoremen. Strikes. Trinidad and Tobago (Port of Spain). 1919. *1798*

—. Mexico. Novels. Revolution. Values. 1910-60's. *598*

—. Mexico. Revolution. Social Classes. 1910-30's. *812*

Violence, institutional. Colombia. Political opposition. 1970's. *1980*

—. Government. 1900-76. *1104*

Violence, political. Argentina. Oligarchy. Social Conditions. 1880-1980. *2544*

—. Chile. Militarism. 1970-74. *2905*

—. El Salvador. Guatemala. 1970-79. *1029*

—. Government. Guatemala. 1966-80. *1128*

—. Guatemala. 1966-72. *1134*

Violence, rural. Colombia. Factor analysis. 1948-63. *1913*

Violencia. Anti-Communist Movements. Colombia. 1940's-65. *1939*

—. Bibliographies. Colombia. 1946-65. *1962*

—. Civil Disturbances. Colombia. Novels. 1946-58. *1932*

—. Colombia. 1946-64. *1933*

—. Colombia. Modernization. 1945-53. *1957*

—. Colombia (Salado). Patron-client networks. 1930-73. *1971*

Voisin, André. Castro, Fidel. Cuba. Political Leadership. 1964. *1482*

Voodoo. Anticolonialism. West Indies. 18c-20c. *1330*

Voting and Voting Behavior See also Elections; Suffrage.

—. Agriculture. Chile. Literacy. Political participation. 1920-60. *2736*

—. Argentina. Authoritarianism, popular. Peronism. 1940's-70's. *2643*

—. Argentina. Labor. Peronism. 1973. *2592*

—. Argentina. Perón, Juan. 1940-46. *2654*

—. Argentina (Buenos Aires). Political Parties. Social Classes. Yrigoyen, Hipólito. 1916-20. *2582*

—. Brazil. 1930-64. *2409*

—. Brazil. Political Parties. 19c-20c. *2230*

—. Brazil (Rio de Janeiro). Political Parties. 1964-76. *2426*

—. Chile. Elections, presidential. Political Change. Social Classes. 1958-70. *2696*

—. Chile. Women. 1970. *2822*

—. Chile (Santiago). Leftism. Models. 1964. *2754*

—. Dependency. Foreign policy. Trade. UN General Assembly. USA. 1950-73. *155*

—. Elections. Jamaica. Labour Party. People's National Party. 1976. *1780*

—. Israeli issues. UN. 1947-68. *316*

—. Jamaica. Labor Party. People's National Party. 1959-76. *1778*

—. Jamaica (Kingston). Public opinion. Social Classes. 1967-76. *1774*

—. Local politics. Social Classes. Venezuela (Caracas). 1958-68. *2184*

—. Political participation. Women. 1949-. *85*

—. Argentina. Brazil. Chile. Labor movement. 1960-74. *45*

—. Argentina. Coups d'Etat. Peronism. Politics and the Military. 1945-78. *2553*

—. Argentina. Elections (presidential). Peronism. 1973. *2593*

—. Argentina. General Confederation of Labor (CGT). Peronism. 1943-73. *2602*

—. Argentina. Labor Unions and Organizations. Peronism. 1943-55. *2645*

—. Argentina. Novels. Social Conditions. Strikes. Viñas, David *(Masters of the Earth)*. 1900-20. *2581*

—. Argentina. Perón, Juan. 1946-73. *2633*

—. Argentina. Perón, Juan. Social reform. 1946-55. *2613*

—. Argentina. Peronism. Women. 1940's. *2612*

—. Brazil. Chile. Foreign policy. Repression. USA. 20c. *44*

—. Brazil. Social security policy. 1964-77. *2466*

—. Brazil (Minas Gerais). Catholic Church. Church and State. 1891-1930. *2346*

—. Cárdenas, Lázaro. Mexico. Political Factions. 1935-36. *838*

—. Casa del Obrero Mundial. Labor Unions and Organizations. Mexico. Revolution. Strikes. 1909-16. *753*

—. Casa del Obrero Mundial. Labor Unions and Organizations. Mexico (Mexico City). Peasants. 1910-16. *727*

—. Central Unica de Trabajadores. Chile. Communist Party. Labor Unions and Organizations. Popular Unity. 1956-70. *2756*

—. Chile. Economic Conditions. Nationalization. Political participation. Popular Unity. 1970-73. *2849*

—. Chile. Labor Unions and Organizations. Peasants. Political mobilization. 1909-73. *2679*

—. Cuba. Democracy. Leninism. Revolution. 1959-61. *1557*

—. Cuba. Revolution. Socialism, building of. 1970-79. *1556*

—. Cuba. Russian Revolution. 1917-20. *1379*

—. Cuba. Standard of living. 1952-58. *1399*

—. Dependency. Elites. Individualism. Peru. 1600-1970. *2102*

—. Economic structure. Mexico. Political Systems. 1938-81. *600*

—. Imperialism. Revolutionary Movements. USA. 1950-74. *143*

—. International Red Aid. USSR. 1917-77. *311*

—. Jamaica. Radicals and Radicalism. 1972. *1755*

Working class (class consciousness). Cerro de Pasco Corporation. Miners. Peru. 1970's. *2031*

—. Chile. Political Participation (leftist). 1970-73. *2824*

Working Class (mobilization). Chile. 1970-73. *2823*

Working Class (review article). González Casanova, Pablo. Labor movement. Mexico. 19c-20c. *660*

Working class subculture. Argentina. Electoral organization. Socialist Party. 1900-46. *2563*

Working Conditions. Argentina. Government. Industry. Productivity. 1953-62. *2616*

—. Lumber and Lumbering. Mexico (Chiapas, Tabasco). Traven, B. 1870-1946. *569*

Working People's Alliance. Guyana. Rodney, Walter. 1953-79. *1717*

World Bank. Chile. Economic Conditions. 1970-73. *2896*

World Population Conference (1974). Family planning. Politics. 1950's-70's. *198*

World War I *See also* battles and campaigns by name.

—. Argentina. Depressions. Economic Policy. 1910-40. *2574*

—. Association of Nitrate Producers. Chileanization. Nitrate industry. 1914-30. *2687*

—. Brazil. Economic power. Foreign Investments. Great Britain. USA. 1914-19. *2376*

—. Caperton, William B. Diplomacy. Navies. USA. 1915-26. *255*

—. Cipriani, Arthur Andrew. Jamaica. Politics. Trinidad and Tobago. 1914-31. *1303*

—. Falkland Islands (battle). Germany. Great Britain. Naval Battles. Verner, Rudolph (report). 1914. *2962*

—. Germany. Intelligence. Mexico. USA. Witzke affair. 1914-23. *751*

—. Gompers, Samuel. Labor Unions and Organizations. Pan-American Federation of Labor. 1918-27. *552*

World War II *See also* battles and campaigns by name.

—. Argentina. Brazil. Military Service (enlistees). Poles. 1940-44. *442*

—. Argentina. Decisionmaking. Diplomacy. Inter-American Conference (Rio de Janeiro). USA. 1942. *553*

—. Brazil. Diplomacy. USA. 1935-45. *2353*

—. Brazil. Economic Growth. Trade. 1939-45. *2338*

—. Brazil. Expeditionary Force. Morais, João Batista Masca Renhas de. 1942-45. *2377*

—. Brazilian Expeditionary Force. Military

Ground Forces. 1941-45. *2360*

—. Diplomacy. Emmerson, John K. (memoir). Japanese. Peru. USA. 1942-43. *2038*

—. French Guiana. Government, Resistance to. Vichy Regime. 1940. *1687*

—. Martinique. Robert, Georges. Vichy regime. 1940-43. *1788*

—. Rio Conference (1942). USA. 1941-42. *238*

Wycliffe Bible Translators. Ideology. Missions and Missionaries. Summer Institute of Linguistics. 1917-79. *177*

Y

Yacimientos Petrolíferos Fiscales. Argentina. Government Enterprise. Oil Industry and Trade. Politics. 1907-27. *2578*

Yacireta, Treaty of. Argentina. Brazil. Paraguay (Alto Paraná). ca 1970-73. *519*

Yanomami. Brazil. Indians. Modernization. 1960's-80's. *2454*

Youth. Developing Nations. Ideology. Revolutionary Movements. 1970-77. *62*

—. Education. Employment. Social Conditions. 1970-74. *47*

Yrigoyen, Hipólito. Argentina. Coups d'Etat. Military. 1930. *2566*

—. Argentina. Foreign Investments. Great Britain. Railroads and State. Unión Cívica Radical. 1891-1928. *2609*

—. Argentina (Buenos Aires). Political Parties. Social Classes. Voting and Voting Behavior. 1916-20. *2582*

—. Brazil. Idealism. Krausism. Positivism. 1800-1970. *176*

Z

Zapata, Emiliano. Casa del Obrero Mundial. Letters. Mexico. Mexico. 1914-15. *827*

—. Lenin, V. I. Mariátegui, José Carlos. Political thought. Russian Revolution. 1917-70's. *485*

—. Mexico, southern. Peasants. Revolution. 1910-20. *799*

26th of July Movement. Cuba. Revolution. 1953-60. *1412*

—. Cuba. Revolution. Socialist People's Party. 1952-59. *1616*

AUTHOR INDEX

A

Aas, Solveig 1074
Abad, Diana 184
Abalo, Carlos 2513
Abbott, George C. 1286
Abreu, Dióres Santos 2334
Acevedo de Silva, María
  Guadalupe 850
Adams, Gordon 1350
Adams, Richard N. 1183
Adie, Robert F. 708
Adleson, S. Lief 709
Aftalión, Marcelo E. 492
Agor, Weston H. 2900
Agosin, Manuel R. 1908
Agudelo Díaz, María
  Mercedes 1351
Aguiar, Neuma 2203
Aguilar, Luis E. 1352
Aguilera, Manuel Villa 2675
Aguilera Peralta, Gabriel 1050
  1126 1127 1128 1129
Aguirre, Mirta 1353 1354
Aguirre, Sergio 1355
Ahmed, Samina 1356
Alarcón, Haydée 2901
Alatalu, T. 2773
Alba, Carlos 1858
Alberti, Giorgio 2130
Albertocchi, Giovanni 2005
Albizurez, Miguel Angel 1130
Alcalá Quintero, Francisco
  493
Aleixo, José Carlos Brandi
  995
Alemán, José Luis 1663 1664
Alencastro, Luiz-Felipe de
  2413
Alexander, Robert J. 1357
  2136 2204 2902 2966
Alisky, Marvin 558 851 2006
Allemann, Fritz René 413
Allen, Elisabeth A. 559
Allen, Julia Coan 2585
Allen, Robert L. 1400
Almeida, Rómulo 494
Alschuler, Lawrence R. 1
  2586 2587
Alvarez, Alejandro 852
Alvarez, Oneida 1358
Alvarez, Orieta 2
Álvarez García, Marcos 1832
  2676
Álvarez Quiñones, Roberto
  2774
Alvarez Uriarte, Miguel 853
Alves, Marcio Moreira 2414
Ambri, Mariano 2566 2588
Ameringer, Charles 449 996
  2137
Ames, Barry 328 329
Anderle, Ádám 450 1359
  2007 2008 2009
Anderson, Paul A. 1360
Anderson, Thomas P. 997
Anderson, William A. 1785
  1786
Andic, Suphan 1685
Andino, Alberto 710
Andrada, Antonio Carlos
  Ribeiro de Campos 2335
André, David J. 1287
Andreas, Carol 2775
Ángeles Sánchez N., Maria de
  los 854
Angelier, Jean-Pierre 560
Angell, Alan 2776 2903 2904
  2905
Anglarill, Nilda B. 2415
Anillo, René 1361
Ankum-Houwink, J. C. 1686
Annino, Antonio 1362
Antoine, Charles 3
Antonov, Iu. A. 2205 2747
Aoki, Yoshio 711 832
Apesteguy, Christine 2206
  2207 2416 2417 2492
Arauco, Fernando 1859
Araújo, Aloizio G. de
  Andrade 2418
Arellano, Jorge Eduardo 1184
Arenal, Electa 1185

Arias, Salvador 1363
Arismendi, Rodmy 451
Arismendi, Rodnei 1186
Armando Frazao, Sergio 2208
Arosemena R., Jorge 1254
Arráiz, António 2138
Arrate, Jorge 2911
Arriola, Carlos 495 496 855
Arriola, Enrique 712
Arroyo, Gonzalo 330 2906
Arroyo, Luis Leobardo 856
Arruda, Marcos 2209
Arvelo-Jimenez, Nelly 2139
Ashdown, Peter 1051 1052
  1063
Asociación Nacional de
  Usuarios Campesinos
  1909
Astiz, Carlos A. 561
Atroshenko, A. 2419 2420
Atwood, Rita 2010
Aubey, Robert T. 610
Augelli, John P. 1665
Auroi, Claude 1364
Austin, Roy L. 1831
Avery, William P. 414 1833
  2140
Aviel, JoAnn Fagot 4
Avrich, Paul 713
Axline, W. Andrew 497 1288
  1289
Ayala, José 562
Ayres, Robert L. 331 2777
  2778
Azevedo, Thales de 2210
Azicri, Max 1365 1366 1367
  1368 1369
Aznar Sánchez, Juan 1053

B

Babtiste, Fitzroy A. 1687
Bacevich, Andrew J., Jr. 1187
Bach, Robert L. 1370
Baena Paz, Guillermina 563
  714
Baer, Werner 2333 2412 2421
  2967
Baerresen, Donald W. 857
Báez, Julia 2968
Bailey, David C. 715
Bailey, John J. 858 1910 1911
Bailey, Norman A. 2211
Baklanoff, Eric N. 870 1371
Balassa, Bela 408 412
Balhana, A. P. 2328
Baloyra, Enrique A. 2141
Baltodano, Emilio 1131
Băluţă-Kiss, Lucreţia 224
Bambirra, Vania 1372
Banchero, Gabriel 2890
Bannikov, B. 1373
Baptise, Patrick 1787
Baptiste, F. A. 1788
Barahona Portocarrero,
  Amaru 1188
Barahona Riera, Francisco
  1065
Barber, Willard F. 225
Barbosa, Eni 2336
Barcia Trelles, Camilo 5 498
  564
Barker, Mary L. 2011
Barkin, David 565 859 1374
  1375
Barnard, Andrew 2748
Barnett, Alan W. 860
Barnhart, Harley E. 415
Barquín, Ramón 1376
Barrett, Chris 2212
Barrett, F. A. 1290
Barrios de Chungara,
  Domitila 1860
Barsegov, Iu 2958
Barthélémy-Febrer, Françoise
  1377 2142
Bartra, Armando 861
Bartra, Roger 566 862
Basadre, Jorge 6 2012
Basdeo, Sahadeo 1291
Basurto, Jorge 567
Bataillon, Claude 863
Bath, C. Richard 568

Bath, Richard 7
Batz, Manuel Ajquij 1132
Bauer Paiz, Alfonso 1133
Béarn, Guy 2514
Beck, Peter J. 2959
Beckford, G. L. 1318 1789
Béjar, Héctor 1378
Bejarano, Dionisio Ramos
  1172
Belfrage, Cedric 1126
Bell, John Patrick 1066
Bell, Wendell 1742 1743 1744
  1745 1770
Bellegarde-Smith, Patrick
  1727 1728 1729
Belli, Humberto 1189
Bellingeri, Marco 1134
Bellini, Giusseppe 8
Belovolov, Iu. G. 1379
Beltrán, Félix 1380
Bender, Gerald J. 1656 1659
Bender, Lynn Darrell 1381
  1382 2659
Bender, Lynn-Darrell 9
Benedetti, Annibale 10
Benedetti, Mario 11
Bengoa, José 2677
Benites, Alfredo 2013
Benjamin, Jules R. 1383 1384
Benjamin, Thomas 569
Benneth, Douglas 864
Bennett, Douglas 570 571 865
  866
Bento, Cláudio Moreira 2213
Benzaquen De Araujo,
  Ricardo 2337
Berberoglu, Berch 332
Berkin, Carol R. 1397
Berleant-Schiller, Riva 1790
Bernal, Richard 1754
Bernhard, Virginia 69 392
Berrocal, Luciano 12
Berry, Albert 1912
Berryman, Phillip 998
Bertrand, Jean-Pierre 2422
Best, John 2589
Bianchi, Soledad 2907
Biggs, Gonzalo 13
Bilby, Kenneth 1746
Binder, Wolfgang 489
Bishop, Barbara 1471
Bitar, Sergio 226
Bizarro, Salvatore 867 2908
Black, Jan Knippers 2423
Blake, Byron 1300
Blake, R. Norris 2143
Blanchard, Peter 2014
Blanco, Freddy Enrique 1260
Blanco, José 2144
Blank, David Eugene 869
Blanksten, George I. 452
Blasier, Cole 1385 1658
Blay, Eva Alterman 2424
Boardman, Thomas 227
Boatler, Robert W. 333
Bock, Peter G. 2678
Boersner, Demetrio 499
Bohne, Regina 228 2425
Bohning, Don 453
Boito Júnior, Armando 2467
Bolivar Pedreschi, Carlos
  1255
Bollinger, William 2015 2683
Bologna, Alfredo Bruno 229
  999 2515 2960
Bomeny, Regina Helena Diniz
  2245
Bonavides, Paulo 2214
Bond, Robert D. 500 501
Bondarchuk, Vladimir 1386
Bonfil Batalla, Guillermo 14
Bonilla, Heraclio 2016
Bono, Agostino 2516
Bonpane, Blase 1000
Bonsor, Norman C. 2257
Booth, David 1387
Booth, John A. 1067 1134
  1190 1913
Borisova, N. A. 1388
Boron, Atilio A. 2679
Bosch, Aurora 1389
Bosch, Juan 2779
Bossert, Thomas John 2680

Boughton, George J. 1390
Boulton, Adam 1747
Bourdé, Guy 2517 2590 2780
Bourdillat, Nicole 1087
Bourgois, Philippe 1191
Bourne, Compton 1292 1688
Bourricaud, François 2781
Bowen, Nicholas 2591
Bozbag, Ali F. 416
Bozzoli de Wille, María E.
  1068
Bradley, Leo H. 1054
Brana-Shute, Gary 1689
Brandt, Niels 502
Brannon, Jeffery 870
Brasileiro, Ana Maria 2426
Bravo Lira, Bernardino 15
Brewster, Havelock 1791
Bridges, Thomas 2017
Briones, Álvaro 2782
Britto, Luiz Navarro de 2427
Britton, John A. 16 572 717
  833
Brock, Lothar 503
Brodersohn, Victor 1088 1089
Brogan, Christopher 417
Brooks, Edwin 2428
Brown, Adlith 1748
Brown, Jerry B. 718
Brown, Lyle C. 573
Brown, Shirley Vining 489
Brownell, Herbert 574
Brownrigg, Leslie Ann 1982
Bruce, David C. 334
Brummel, Jürgen 2215
Bruneau, Thomas C. 2429
Brunet, Yves 17
Bueno, Salvador 230 1391
Buescu, Mircea 2338
Bulmer-Thomas, Victor 1135
Bulychev, I. 1192
Burbach, Roger 1001 1193
Burggraaff, Winfield J. 2145
Burke, Melvin 1861
Burke, Michael E. 719
Burns, E. Bradford 1256 1257
  2977
Burstein, John N. 1194
Burt, Arthur E. 1749
Burton, Julianne 18
Buşe, Constantin 19 720 1195
  1196
Bushuyev, V. 454
Butler, Robert 2146
Butt, John W. 2524
Buve, Raymond 575 576 721
  722 834
Bye, Vegard 1002 2147
Byrd, Pratt 2216

C

Caballero, José María 2018
Cabarrús, Carlos Rafael 1003
Cabrera, Herman Hooker
  1004
Cabrera, Olga 1392
Cabrera A., Gustavo 871
Cabrera Ipina, Octaviano 577
Caceres, Ernesto 2783
Cáceres Prendes, Jorge Rafael
  1090
Cachapuz de Medeiros,
  Antônio Paulo 2217
Cádenas, Arturo 578
Cagan, Steve 1393
Cail-Coms, Michèle 335
Cairo, Ana 1394
Calamai, Marco 20
Caldeira, José Ribamar 2218
Calder, Bruce J. 1666 1667
  1668
Calderón, José 2909
Caldwell, Dan 1395
Calkin, G. A. 872
Calvert, Peter 1005
Calvo, Roberto 21
Camacho, Manuel 579
Cambranes, Julio C. 1136
Camp, Roderic Ai 557 580
  581 582 583 584 585 639
  723 873 874
Campa, Riccardo 2784

Campbell, Horace 1750
Campbell, Leon G. 1862 2019
Campbell, Trevor A. 1690
Campos, Francisco Luiz da
  Silva 2335
Campos Icardo, Salvador 875
Cañedo, Patricia Salcido 586
Canitrot, Adolfo 2660
Cantón, Darío 2592 2593
Caporaso, James A. 336
Caraveo Molinari, Baltazar
  2020
Carbonell, José Antonio 2148
Cardenal, Fernando 1197
Cardenas, Osvaldo 1293
Cardona, Rokael 1137
Cardoso, Eliana A. 2339 2395
Cardoso, Fernando Henrique
  337 2219 2220 2430
Cardoso, Lawrence A. 724
  725 726
Caregorodcev, V. A. 455
Carmagnani, Marcello 231
Carnegie, James Alexander
  1751
Carpizo, Jorge 587
Carr, Barry 727 728 729
Carrera, Jeronimo 2149 2150
Carrière, Jean 418 2681 2749
Carrillo Flores, Antonio 588
  589 590
Carrillo Moreno, José 2151
Carson, Edward 1792
Carty, James W., Jr. 1396
Carvalho, Carlos Alberto
  Penna Rodrigues de 2431
Casal, Lourdes 1397
Casanova, Manuel 504
Casaus, Víctor 1198
Casey Gaspar, Jeffrey 1069
Castañeda, Digna 1793 2232
Castasñeda, Jorge G. 1199
Castelain-Meunier, Christine
  2785
Castell Cancino, Jorge 876
Castellanos, Jorge 22
Castilla Urbina, Miguel de
  1200
Castillo, Oscar Mauricio 1201
Castillo, Rene 2786 2910
Castor, Suzy 1294
Castro, Alejandro Carrillo 877
Castro, Fidel 1398
Castro, Héctor David 505
Castro, José Rivera 730
Castro, Nils 1378
Castro, Sofia de 2432
Castro Gomes, Angela Maria
  2340
Castro Torres, Carlos Felipe
  1138
Catalán, Oscar 2911
Catanese, Anthony James
  1914
Cavaioli, Frank J. 489
Cavalcanti, Themistocles
  Brandão 2221 2222 2223
  2224 2341
Cavarozzi, Marcelo 338
Cazali Avila, Augusto 1006
Cazanga Moncada, Osvaldo
  1070
Cerdas Cruz, Rodolfo 1071
Cerutti-Gulberg, Horacio V.
  23
Cervini, Rubén Alberto 2754
Cervo, Amado Luis 2225
Chacon, Vamireh 2226 2227
Chafee, Wilbur A., Jr. 339
Chalmers, Douglas A. 24
Chántez Oliva, Sara E. 1399
Chapin, Jorge 1139
Chawla, R. L. 2228 2479
Cheresky, Isidoro 2567
Chilcote, Ronald H. 2229
Child, John 419 506
Chinchilla, Norma Stoltz 25
  1007 2682 2683
Chonchol, Jacques 2684
Chossudovsky, Michel 2912
Chrisman, Robert 1400 1401
Christie, Keith H. 1915
Christou, G. 1008 1046
Ciampi, Antonio 1258

LIST OF PERIODICALS

A

Acta Politica [Netherlands]
Acta Poloniae Historica [Poland]
Acta Universitatis Carolinae Philosophica et
 Historica [Czechoslovakia]
Acta Universitatis Szegediensis de Attila József
 Nominatae: Acta Historica [Hungary]
Action Nationale [Canada]
Actualidad Bibliográfica de Filosofía y Teología;
 Selecciones de Libros (IHE) [Spain]
Administration & Society
Administrative Science Quarterly
Aerospace Historian
Affari Esteri [Italy]
African Social Research [Zambia]
Agricultural History
Air Force Magazine
Air University Review
Ajia Afurika Kenkyū [Japan]
Akademiskă Dzīve
Alabama Historical Quarterly
América Indígena [Mexico]
América Latina [Brazil]
America Latina [Union of Soviet Socialist Republic]
American Behavioral Scientist
American Economic Review
American Heritage
American Historical Review
American Journal of Economics and Sociology
American Journal of International Law
American Journal of Political Science
American Journal of Sociology
American Neptune
American Political Science Review
American Society of International Law. Proceedings
 (issues for 1970-73 appeared under the title
 American Journal of International Law)
American Sociological Review
Americas: A Quarterly Review of Inter-American
 Cultural History (Academy of American
 Franciscan History)
Américas (Organization of American States)
Amerikanskii Ezhegodnik [Union of Soviet Socialist
 Republic]
Analele Universității București: Istorie [Romania]
Annalen van het Thijmgenootschap [Netherlands]
Annales Canadiennes d'Histoire (see Canadian
 Journal of History = Annales Canadiennes
 d'Histoire) [Canada]
Annales d'Etudes Internationales (see Annals of
 International Studies = Annales d'Etudes
 Internationales) [Switzerland]
Annales: Economies, Sociétés, Civilisations [France]
Annali della Fondazione Luigi Einaudi [Italy]
Annals of International Studies = Annales d'Études
 Internationales [Switzerland]
Annals of the American Academy of Political and
 Social Science
Anuario de Estudios Americanos [Spain]
Anuario de Estudios Centroamericanos (IHE)
 [Costa Rica]
Anuario Indigenista [Mexico]
Arbejder Historie [Denmark]
Archives de Sciences Sociales des Religions [France]
Arizona and the West
Armed Forces and Society
Army Quarterly and Defence Journal [Great
 Britain]
Art in America
Asian Affairs: An American Review
Australian Foreign Affairs Record [Australia]
Australian Journal of Politics and History
 [Australia]
Aviation Quarterly
Aztlán

B

Behind the Headlines [Canada]
Beiträge zur Geschichte der Deutschen
 Arbeiterbewegung (see Beiträge zur Geschichte
 der Arbeiterbewegung) [German Democratic
 Republic]
Belfagor: Rassegna di Varia Umanità [Italy]
Belizean Studies [Belize]
Black Scholar
Boletín Cultural y Bibliográfico (IHE) [Colombia]
Boletín de Estudios Latinoamericanos y del Caribe
 [Netherlands]
Boletín de Historia y Antigüedades [Colombia]
Boletín de la Academia Nacional de la Historia
 [Venezuela]

Boletín de la Academia Puertorriqueña de la
 Historia (IHE) [Puerto Rico]
Boletín del Archivo General de la Nación [Mexico]
Boletín Histórico [Venezuela]
British Journal of Sociology [Great Britain]
Bulletin of the Atomic Scientists (briefly known as
 Science and Public Affairs)
Business History Review

C

Cahiers de Géographie de Québec [Canada]
Cahiers des Amériques Latines [France]
Cahiers du Monde Hispanique et Luso-Brésilien
 [France]
Cahiers Internationaux d'Histoire Economique et
 Sociale [Italy]
Canadian Dimension [Canada]
Canadian Geographic [Canada]
Canadian Geographical Journal (see Canadian
 Geographic) [Canada]
Canadian Historical Review [Canada]
Canadian Journal of Development Studies = Revue
 Canadienne d'Etudes du Développement
 [Canada]
Canadian Journal of History = Annales Canadiennes
 d'Histoire [Canada]
Canadian Journal of Political Science = Revue
 Canadienne de Science Politique [Canada]
Canadian Labour [Canada]
Canadian Review of Sociology and Anthropology =
 Revue Canadienne de Sociologie et
 d'Anthropologie [Canada]
Canadian Review of Studies in Nationalism = Revue
 Canadienne des Etudes sur le Nationalisme
 [Canada]
Caribbean Quarterly [Jamaica]
Caribbean Review
Casa de las Américas [Cuba]
Catholic Historical Review
Centennial Review
Center Magazine
Centerpoint
Československý Časopis Historický [Czechoslovakia]
Chronicles of Oklahoma
Church History
Civilisations [Belgium]
Civitas [Italy]
Civitas [Switzerland]
Colorado Quarterly
Commentary
Communautés: Archives de Sciences Sociales de la
 Coopération et du Développement [France]
Communautés: Archives Internationales de
 Sociologie de la Coopération et du
 Développement (see Communautés: Archives de
 Sciences Sociales de la Coopération et du
 Développement) [France]
Communist Viewpoint [Canada]
Comparative Political Studies
Comparative Politics
Comparative Studies in Society and History [Great
 Britain]
Comunità [Italy]
Comunità Internazionale [Italy]
Conflict
Contemporary Review [Great Britain]
Crisis
Critique [Great Britain]
Cuadernos Hispanoamericanos [Spain]
Cuban Studies
Cultures: Dialogue Between the Peoples of the
 World [France]
Cultures et Développement: Revue Internationale
 des Sciences du Développement [Belgium]
Current History

D

Défense Nationale [France]
Demografía y Economía [Mexico]
Desarrollo Economico [Argentina]
Development and Change [Netherlands]
Diogenes [Italy]
Diplomatic History
Dissent

E

Economic Development and Cultural Change
Economic Journal [Great Britain]

Ecrits de Paris [France]
Eesti NSV Teaduste Akadeemia Toimetised.
 Ühiskonnateadused [Union of Soviet Socialist
 Republic]
Einheit [German Democratic Republic]
Encounter [Great Britain]
Esprit [France]
Estudios Andinos [Peru]
Estudios Centro Americanos [El Salvador]
Estudios de Asia y Africa [Mexico]
Estudios de Derecho [Colombia]
Estudios de Historia Moderna y Contemporánea de
 México (IHE) [Mexico]
Estudios Internacionales [Chile]
Estudios Políticos [Mexico]
Estudios Sociales [Dominican Republic]
Estudios Sociales Centroamericanos [Costa Rica]
Ethnic and Racial Studies [Great Britain]
Ethnic Groups
Ethnohistory
Etudes [France]
Etudes Internationales [Canada]
Etudes Rurales [France]
Europa Archiv [German Federal Republic]
Explorations in Ethnic Studies

F

Far Eastern Affairs [Union of Soviet Socialist
 Republic]
Feminist Studies
Fides et Historia
Film and History
Folia Humanística [Spain]
Foreign Affairs
Foreign Policy
Foreign Service Journal
Foro Internacional [Mexico]
Frankfurter Hefte [German Federal Republic]
Freedom at Issue
Freedomways
Fuerzas Armadas de Venezuela (IHE) [Venezuela]

G

Gazette: International Journal for Mass
 Communication Studies [Netherlands]
Geographical Review
German Yearbook of International Law [German
 Federal Republic]
Government and Opposition [Great Britain]

H

Harvard Educational Review
Hispanic American Historical Review
Histoire [France]
Historia [Chile]
Historia Mexicana [Mexico]
Historia y Cultura [Peru]
Histórica [Peru]
Historical Methods
History of Education Quarterly
History of Political Economy
History Teacher
History Today [Great Britain]
Human Organization
Human Rights Quarterly
Humánitas [Mexico]
Humanities Association Review = Revue de
 l'Association des Humanités [Canada]

I

India Quarterly: Journal of International Affairs
 [India]
Indian Journal of Political Studies [India]
Indian Political Science Review [India]
Indian Review [India]
Inter-American Economic Affairs
Inter-American Review of Bibliography = Revista
 Interamericana de Bibliografía
Internasjonal Politikk [Norway]
International Affairs [Great Britain]
International Affairs [Union of Soviet Socialist
 Republic]
International Development Review
International Journal [Canada]
International Journal of Comparative Sociology
 [Canada]
International Journal of Contemporary Sociology

International Journal of Politics
International Journal of Women's Studies [Canada]
International Migration = Migrations
    Internationales = Migraciones Internacionales
    [Netherlands]
International Migration Review
International Organization
International Perspectives [Canada]
International Review (ceased pub 1975) [Great
    Britain]
International Review of Social History
    [Netherlands]
International Security
International Social Science Journal [France]
International Social Science Review
International Socialist Review
International Studies [India]
International Studies Notes
International Studies Quarterly
Investigación Económica [Mexico]
Islas [Cuba]
Istoriia SSSR [Union of Soviet Socialist Republic]

J

Jahrbuch für Geschichte [German Democratic
    Republic]
Jahrbuch für Geschichte von Staat, Wirtschaft und
    Gesellschaft Lateinamerikas [German Federal
    Republic]
Jahrbuch für Internationales Recht (see German
    Yearbook of International Law) [German
    Federal Republic]
Jahrbuch für Wirtschaftsgeschichte [German
    Democratic Republic]
Jamaica Journal [Jamaica]
Jerusalem Journal of International Relations [Israel]
Jewish Social Studies
Journal of American History
Journal of Arizona History
Journal of Belizean Affairs [Belize]
Journal of Black Studies
Journal of Caribbean History [Barbados]
Journal of Church and State
Journal of Common Market Studies [Great Britain]
Journal of Commonwealth and Comparative Politics
    [Great Britain]
Journal of Communication
Journal of Conflict Resolution
Journal of Contemporary History [Great Britain]
Journal of Developing Areas
Journal of Development Studies [Great Britain]
Journal of Economic History
Journal of Ethnic Studies
Journal of Imperial and Commonwealth History
    [Great Britain]
Journal of Interamerican Studies and World Affairs
Journal of International Affairs
Journal of Latin American Lore
Journal of Latin American Studies [Great Britain]
Journal of Negro Education
Journal of Negro History
Journal of Palestine Studies [Lebanon]
Journal of Peace Research [Norway]
Journal of Peasant Studies [Great Britain]
Journal of Political and Military Sociology
Journal of Political Economy
Journal of Politics
Journal of Popular Culture
Journal of Social and Political Studies (see Journal
    of Social, Political and Economic Studies)
Journal of Social, Political and Economic Studies
Journal of Strategic Studies [Great Britain]
Journal of the Afro-American Historical &
    Genealogical Society
Journal of the Hellenic Diaspora: Critical Thoughts
    on Greek and World Issues
Journal of the History of Ideas
Journal of the Royal United Services Institute for
    Defence Studies [Great Britain]
Journal of the Society of Archivists [Great Britain]
Journal of the West
Journal of World Trade Law [Switzerland]
Journalism History
Journalism Quarterly

K

Korea and World Affairs [South Korea]
Közgazdasági Szemle [Hungary]

L

Labor History
Land Economics

Lateinamerika [German Democratic Republic]
Latin American Perspectives
Latin American Research Review
Law & Society Review
Lock Haven Review (suspended pub 1974)
Lotería (IHE) [Panama]
Luso-Brazilian Review

M

Magazin Istoric [Romania]
Mankind
Marine Corps Gazette
Marine Rundschau [German Federal Republic]
Marxist Perspectives (ceased pub 1980)
Massachusetts Review
Meddelelser om Forskning i Arbejderbevaegelsens
    Historie (see Arbejder Historie) [Denmark]
Medjunarodni Problemi [Yugoslavia]
Memoria del Colegio Nacional [Mexico]
Mid-America
Midstream
Migraciones Internacionales (see International
    Migration = Migrations Internationales =
    Migraciones Internacionales) [Netherlands]
Migrations Internationales (see International
    Migration = Migrations Internationales =
    Migraciones Internacionales) [Netherlands]
Militärgeschichte [German Democratic Republic]
Military Affairs
Military Review
Millennium: Journal of International Studies [Great
    Britain]
Mirovaia Ekonomika i Mezhdunarodnye Otnosheniia
    [Union of Soviet Socialist Republic]
Monthly Review
Mouvement Social [France]
Movimento Operaio e Socialista [Italy]
Munger Africana Library Notes

N

Nationaløkonomisk Tidsskrift [Denmark]
Negro History Bulletin
New Mexico Historical Review
New Scholar
New World Review
New York University Journal of International Law
    and Politics
Nghien Cuu Lich Su [Vietnam]
North Dakota Quarterly
Nouvelle Revue des Deux Mondes (see Revue des
    Deux Mondes) [France]
Novaia i Noveishaia Istoriia [Union of Soviet
    Socialist Republic]
Nowe Drogi [Poland]

O

Orbis
Osteuropa [German Federal Republic]

P

Pacific Historian
Pacific Historical Review
Pacific Sociological Review (see Sociological
    Perspectives)
Pacific Viewpoint [New Zealand]
Pakistan Horizon [Pakistan]
Pan-African Journal [Kenya]
Parameters
Partisan Review
Párttörténeti Közlemények [Hungary]
Past and Present [Great Britain]
Patterns of Prejudice [Great Britain]
Peasant Studies
Peasant Studies Newsletter (see Peasant Studies)
Pensiero Politico [Italy]
Phylon
Plural Societies [Netherlands]
Policy Studies Journal
Polish Western Affairs [Poland]
Political Science Quarterly
Politico [Italy]
Politics [Australia]
Politics & Society
Politische Vierteljahresschrift [German Federal
    Republic]
Polity
Ponte [Italy]
Právněhistorické Studie [Czechoslovakia]
Present Tense
Problèmes d'Amérique Latine [France]
Problemi di Ulisse [Italy]

Problems of Communism
Proceedings of the Academy of Political Science
Proceedings of the South Carolina Historical
    Association
Progressive Labor
Prologue: the Journal of the National Archives
Przegląd Historyczny [Poland]
Przegląd Socjologiczny [Poland]
Public Policy

Q

Quaderni di Sociologia [Italy]
Quaderni Storici [Italy]
Quarterly Journal of Economics
Quarterly Review of Economics and Business
Queen's Quarterly [Canada]

R

Radical America
Radical History Review
Reason
Recherche Sociale [France]
Rekishigaku Kenkyū [Japan]
Relations Internationales [France]
Review of Politics
Review of Radical Political Economics
Reviews in American History
Revista Brasileira de Estudos Políticos [Brazil]
Revista Brasileira de Política Internacional (ceased
    pub 1979) [Brazil]
Revista Chilena de Historia del Derecho [Chile]
Revista Chilena de Historia y Geografía [Chile]
Revista de Ciência Política [Brazil]
Revista de Ciencias Sociales [Puerto Rico]
Revista de Estudios Histórico-Jurídicos [Chile]
Revista de Estudios Internacionales (supersedes
    Revista de Política Internacional) [Spain]
Revista de Estudios Políticos [Spain]
Revista de Filosofía de la Universidad de Costa Rica
    [Costa Rica]
Revista de História (suspended pub 1977) [Brazil]
Revista de Historia [Costa Rica]
Revista de Historia de América [Mexico]
Revista de Instituciones Europeas [Spain]
Revista de Istorie [Romania]
Revista de la Biblioteca Nacional "José Martí"
    (IHE) [Cuba]
Revista de la Biblioteca Nacional "José Martí"
    [Cuba]
Revista de la Facultad de Derecho de México
    [Mexico]
Revista de Marina (IHE) [Chile]
Revista de Política Internacional (superseded by
    Revista de Estudios Internacionales) [Spain]
Revista del Pensamiento Centroamericano
    [Nicaragua]
Revista do Instituto Histórico e Geográfico
    Brasileiro [Brazil]
Revista Española de Investigaciones Sociológicas
    [Spain]
Revista Española de la Opinión Pública [Spain]
Revista General de Marina [Spain]
Revista Interamericana (see Revista/Review
    Interamericana) [Puerto Rico]
Revista Interamericana de Bibliografía (see
    Inter-American Review of Bibliography =
    Revista Interamericana de Bibliografía)
Revista Mexicana de Ciencia Política (see Revista
    Mexicana de Ciencias Políticas y Sociales)
    [Mexico]
Revista Mexicana de Ciencias Políticas y Sociales
    [Mexico]
Revista Nacional de Cultura [Venezuela]
Revista/Review Interamericana [Puerto Rico]
Revue Canadienne de Science Politique (see
    Canadian Journal of Political Science = Revue
    Canadienne de Science Politique) [Canada]
Revue Canadienne de Sociologie et d'Anthropologie
    (see Canadian Review of Sociology and
    Anthropology = Revue Canadienne de
    Sociologie et d'Anthropologie) [Canada]
Revue Canadienne des Etudes sur le Nationalisme
    (see Canadian Review of Studies in Nationalism
    = Revue Canadienne des Etudes sur le
    Nationalisme) [Canada]
Revue Canadienne d'Etudes du Développement (see
    Canadian Journal of Development Studies =
    Revue Canadienne d'Etudes du Développement)
    [Canada]
Revue de l'Association des Humanités (see
    Humanities Association Review = Revue de
    l'Association des Humanités) [Canada]
Revue de l'Institut de Sociologie [Belgium]
Revue d'Economie Politique [France]

Revue des Deux Mondes [France]
Revue d'Histoire de la Deuxième Guerre Mondiale [France]
Revue d'Histoire Moderne et Contemporaine [France]
Revue Française de Science Politique [France]
Revue Française d'Histoire d'Outre-Mer [France]
Revue Historique des Armées [France]
Revue Roumaine d'Etudes Internationales [Romania]
Rivista di Studi Politici Internazionali [Italy]
Rivista Internazionale di Scienze Sociali [Italy]
Rivista Italiana di Scienza Politica [Italy]
Rivista Marittima [Italy]
Rivista Storica Italiana [Italy]
Rocky Mountain Social Science Journal (see Social Science Journal)
Round Table (ceased pub 1981-82) [Great Britain]

S

SAIS Review
Samtiden [Norway]
San José Studies
Santiago [Cuba]
Schweizer Monatshefte [Switzerland]
Science and Public Affairs (see Bulletin of the Atomic Scientists)
Science and Society
Secolas Annals
Shirin [Japan]
Signs: Journal of Women in Culture and Society
Smithsonian
Social and Economic Studies [Jamaica]
Social Forces
Social Policy
Social Problems
Social Research
Social Science (see International Social Science Review)
Social Science Journal
Social Science Quarterly
Social Science Research Council Items
Social Studies
Society
Sociological Analysis

Sociological Perspectives
Southern California Quarterly
Southern Economic Journal
Southern Exposure
Southern Folklore Quarterly
Southern Quarterly
Southwestern Historical Quarterly
Sovetskaia Etnografiia [Union of Soviet Socialist Republic]
Sovetskoe Gosudarstvo i Pravo [Union of Soviet Socialist Republic]
Soviet Studies in History
Spiegel Historiael [Netherlands]
Stimmen der Zeit [German Federal Republic]
Storia Contemporanea [Italy]
Studia Nauk Politycznych [Poland]
Studies in Comparative Communism
Studies in Comparative International Development
Studies in History and Society (suspended pub 1977)
Studies on the Developing Countries (ceased pub 1979) [Poland]
Survey [Great Britain]
Survival [Great Britain]
Svensk Tidskrift [Sweden]

T

Taamuli [Tanzania]
Terrorism
Texas Quarterly (ceased pub 1978)
Thought
Towson State Journal of International Affairs
Travaux & Mémoires de l'Institut des Hautes Etudes de l'Amérique Latine [France]
Trends in History

U

Ukrains'kyi Istorychnyi Zhurnal [Union of Soviet Socialist Republic]
Umoja: A Scholarly Journal of Black Studies
United States Naval Institute Proceedings
Universal Human Rights (see Human Rights Quarterly)
Universitas Humanistica [Colombia]
University of Toronto Quarterly [Canada]
Urban Affairs Quarterly

V

Veritas [Brazil]
Vestnik Leningradskogo Universiteta: Seriia Istorii, Iazyka i Literatury [Union of Soviet Socialist Republic]
Voenno-Istoricheskii Zhurnal [Union of Soviet Socialist Republic]
Voprosy Ekonomiki [Union of Soviet Socialist Republic]
Voprosy Istorii [Union of Soviet Socialist Republic]
Voprosy Istorii KPSS [Union of Soviet Socialist Republic]

W

Warship International
Washington Monthly
Wereld en Zending [Netherlands]
West Georgia College Studies in the Social Sciences
Western Historical Quarterly
Western Political Quarterly
Wiener Library Bulletin [Great Britain]
Wilson Quarterly
Working Papers for a New Society (see Working Papers Magazine)
Working Papers Magazine
World Affairs
World Marxist Review [Canada]
World Politics
World Survey [Great Britain]
World Today [Great Britain]
Worldview

Y

Youth and Society

Z

Z Pola Walki [Poland]
Zeitschrift für Geschichtswissenschaft [German Democratic Republic]

LIST OF ABSTRACTERS

A

Adams, E. J.
Adams, R. K.
Aldrich, R.
Alltmont, R. C.
Alvis, R.
Andrews, H. D.
Anstey, C.
Aoki, Y.
Ardia, D.
Athey, L. L.
Atkins, L. R.

B

Bailor, K. M.
Balmuth, D.
Barnard, J. D.
Barron, N.
Bauer, K. J.
Beck, P. J.
Beecher, L. N.
Belles, A. G.
Billigmeier, J. C.
Blum, G. P.
Blumberg, A.
Bobango, G. J.
Bolton, G. A.
Bonnycastle, S.
Boughton, G. J.
Broussard, J. H.
Brown, A.
Bruntjen, S.
Burkholder, M. A.
Bushnell, D.
Butchart, R.
Butcher, K.

C

Calkin, H. L.
Cameron, D. D.
Campbell, E. R.
Campbell, L. G.
Carr, S. P.
Casada, J. A.
Castillo, R. Griswold del
Chambers, J. M.
Chandler, B. J.
Clark, M. J.
Cleyet, G. P.
Cline, D. H.
Coleman, J. S.
Colenso, M. R.
Collins, D. N.
Conner, S. P.
Coutinho, J. V.
Cregier, D. M.
Curtis, G. H.

D

Davis, G. H.
Davis, T. B.

Dibert, D.
Dietz, J.
Dubay, R. W.
Durell, P. J.

E

Eads, O. W.
Eid, L. V.
Elison, W. W.
Elzy, M. I.
Eminhizer, E. E.
England, A. A.
English, J. C.
Estes, K. W.
Evans, A. J.
Evans, H. M.
Evans, J. L.

F

Farmerie, S. A.
Feingold, M.
Fitzgerald, C. B.
Forgus, S. P.
Fox, J. P.
Frank, W. C.
Franz, D. A.
Frederick, R. D.
Frenkley, N.
Frey, L. S.
Frey, M.
Fulton, R. T.

G

Gagnon, G. O.
Garfield, R.
Garland, A. N.
Garon, L.
Gassner, J. S.
Gilmont, K. E.
Glovins, G. A.
Gormly, M.
Grusin, J. R.

H

Hapak, J. T.
Harahan, J. P.
Harrington, J. F.
Hartigan, F. X.
Harvey, K. A.
Herritt, G.
Herstein, S. R.
Hetzron, R.
Hewlett, G. A.
Hidas, P. I.
Hinnebusch, P. D.
Hively, W. R.
Hobson, W. K.
Hoffman, A.
Hogg, M. K.

Holmes, L. E.
Holzinger, J.
Homan, G. D.
Hopkins, E. C.
Hough, C. M.
Howell, R.
Human, V. L.

I

Itō, S.

J

Jackson, S. G.
Jewsbury, G. F.
Jirran, R. J.
Johnson, B. D.
Johnson, E. S.
Jones, M. K.

K

Kalinowski, L.
Kascus, M. A.
Kawanami, H.
Keyser, E. L.
Khan, R. O.
Knafla, L. A.
Kommer, D. J.
Kubicek, R. V.
Kugler, R. F.

L

LaBue, B. J.
Lauber, J. M.
Law, D. G.
Ledbetter, B. D.
Lederer, N.
Lee, J. M.
Leedom, J. W.
Leonardis, M. de
Lewis, J. A.
Libbey, G. H.
Linkfield, T. P.
Lokken, R. N.
Long, J. W.

M

Mahood, H. R.
Makin, G.
Makin, L.
Maloney, L. M.
Marr, W. L.
Marti, D. B.
McCarthy, M. M.
McIntyre, W. D.
McLean, K. A.
McQuilkin, D. K.
Mendel, R. B.

Menicant, A.
Miller, H. J.
Miller, J. E.
Miller, K. E.
Moore, J.
Murdoch, D. H.
Myers, J. P. H.

N

Neville, G. L.
Neville, R. G.
Newhouse, N. A.
Nicholls, D. J.
Nielson, D. G.
Novitsky, A. W.

O

Ohl, J. K.
Ohrvall, C. W.
Olson, C. W.
Osur, A. M.

P

Palais, E. S.
Patzwald, G.-A.
Paul, J. F.
Perez, J.
Pergl, G. E.
Perkins, J. A.
Pfabe, J.
Pickens, D. K.
Pizzimenti, G.
Pollaczek, F.
Powell, J.
Powers, T. L.
Preece, C. A.
Pusateri, C. J.

R

Rahmes, R. D.
Raife, L. R.
Read, C. J.
Reed, J. B.
Reinfeld, B.
Richardson, T. P.
Riles, R.
Ring, D. F.
Rippy, M.
Ritter, R. V.
Rockwood, D. S.
Rodenburg, E.
Rodríguez, R. D.
Rosenblatt, N. A.
Ross, K. A.
Ruffo-Fiore, S.
Russell, L.

S

Samaraweera, V.
Sapper, N. G.
Sarna, J. D.

Sater, W. F.
Schoenberg, P. E.
Schoonover, T.
Scott, R.
Sevilla, S.
Shaw, F. J.
Smith, D. L.
Smith, L.
Snow, G. E.
Sobell, V.
Sobeslavsky, V.
Soff, H. G.
Spira, T.
Stevenson, D. R.
Stickney, E. P.
Strausberg, S. F.
Street, J. B.
Street, N. J.
Swiecicka-Ziemianek, M.

T

Talley, K. A.
Tate, M. L.
Taylor, P. R.
Taylorson, P. J.
Thacker, J. W.
Thomas, J.
Tomlinson, R. H.
Tomlinson-Brown, S.
Trauth, M. P.
Travis, P.
Tudor, F. P.
Tull, J.
Turk, E. L.

V

Valiulis, D. J.
Velicer, L. F.
Vexler, R. I.
Vivian, J. F.

W

Wagnleitner, R.
Walsh, J. M.
Ware, R. J.
Wasserstein, D.
Weltsch, R. E.
Wentworth, M. J.
Werlich, D. P.
White, J. L.
Wilson, M. T.
Wojcicka, H. Heitzman
Woodward, R. L.
Wrigley, W. D.
Wyk, L. Van

Y

Yeager, G. M.
Yerburgh, M. R.

Z

Ziewacz, L. E.

LIST OF ABBREVIATIONS

A.	Author-prepared Abstract
Acad.	Academy, Academie, Academia
Agric.	Agriculture, Agricultural
AIA	Abstracts in Anthropology
Akad.	Akademie
Am.	America, American
Ann.	Annals, Annales, Annual, Annali
Anthrop.	Anthropology, Anthropological
Arch.	Archives
Archaeol.	Archaeology, Archaeological
Art.	Article
Assoc.	Association, Associate
Biblio.	Bibliography, Bibliographical
Biog.	Biography, Biographical
Bol.	Boletim, Boletin
Bull.	Bulletin
c.	century (in index)
ca.	circa
Can.	Canada, Canadian, Canadien
Cent.	Century
Coll.	College
Com.	Committee
Comm.	Commission
Comp.	Compiler
DAI	Dissertation Abstracts International
Dept.	Department
Dir.	Director, Direktor
Econ.	Economy, Econom-.
Ed.	Editor, Edition
Educ.	Education, Educational
Geneal.	Genealogy, Genealogical, Genealogique
Grad.	Graduate
Hist.	History, Hist-.
IHE	Indice Historico Espanol
Illus.	Illustrated, Illustration
Inst.	Institute, Institut-.
Int.	International, Internacional, Internationaal, Internationaux, Internazionale
J.	Journal, Journal-prepared Abstract
Lib.	Library, Libraries
Mag.	Magazine
Mus.	Museum, Musee, Museo
Nac.	Nacional
Natl.	National, Nationale
Naz.	Nazionale
Phil.	Philosophy, Philosophical
Photo.	Photograph
Pol.	Politics, Political, Politique, Politico
Pr.	Press
Pres.	President
Pro.	Proceedings
Publ.	Publishing, Publication
Q.	Quarterly
Rev.	Review, Revue, Revista, Revised
Riv.	Rivista
Res.	Research
RSA	Romanian Scientific Abstracts
S.	Staff-prepared Abstract
Sci.	Science, Scientific
Secy.	Secretary
Soc.	Society, Societe, Sociedad, Societa
Sociol.	Sociology, Sociological
Tr.	Transactions
Transl.	Translator, Translation
U.	University, Universi-.
US	United States
Vol.	Volume
Y.	Yearbook

Abbreviations also apply to feminine and plural forms.
Abbreviations not noted above are based on *Webster's Third New International Dictionary*
and the *United States Government Printing Office Style Manual*.